The Manual to O...
Public Reco...

The Researcher's Tool to Online Resources
of Public Records and Public Information

By Hetherington & Sankey

Facts
ON DEMAND
PRESS

PO Box 27869, Tempe, AZ 85285
800.929.3811
www.brbpub.com

The Manual to Online Public Records

The Researcher's Tool to Online Resources of Public Records and Public Information
First Edition (*Replaces Public Records Online*)

©2008 By BRB Publications, Inc.
PO Box 27869 • Tempe, AZ 85285 • 800.929.3811
ISBN13: 1-978-1-889150-53-6
ISBN: 1-889150-53-3

Text written by: Cynthia Hetherington and Michael L. Sankey
Government Sites Complied by: BRB Publications, Inc. (Peter J. Weber, Annette Jackson, Michael L. Sankey)
Cover Design by: Robin Fox & Associates

Cataloging-in-Publication Data
(Provided by Quality Books, Inc.)

Hetherington, Cynthia.
        The manual to online public records : the
researcher's tool to online resources of public records
and public information / by Hetherington & Sankey. --
1st ed.
      p. cm.
      Includes index.
      "Replaces Public records online"--T.p. verso.
      ISBN-13: 978-1889150-53-6
      ISBN-10: 1-889150-53-3

      1. Electronic public records--United States--
Directories. 2. Public records--United States--
Directories. 3. Internet research.   I. Sankey,
Michael L., 1949- II. Title. III. Title: Online public
records. IV. Title: Public records online.

JK468.P76H43 2008   025.06'973
                         QBI08-600194

Table of Contents

5 ❖ State and Local Government Online Sources   105

51 state chapters with profiles of these online providers: major state agencies, state and local courts, assessors and recorders

6 ❖ Searching Federal Court Records   551

Federal Court Structure; How Federal Trial Courts are Organized; Electronic Access to Federal Court Records; Search the U.S./Party Case Index; PACER; Case Management/Electronic Case Files (CM/ECF); Other Search Methods; Federal Record Centers and the National Archives; Identifiers and Case Files for U.S. District and U.S. Bankruptcy Court Locations; Other Federal Courts

7 ❖ Public Record Database Vendors   573

Types of Public Record Vendors; Which Type of Vendor is Right for You?; 10 Questions to Ask a Public Record Vendor; Presentation of Database and Gateway Vendors

Quick-Find Index   594

Introduction

Today there are literally thousands of public record and public information sources accessible by anyone with a computer and web access. However, where are they and which sites are useful? For the online researcher, recognizing the advantages of these sources can be challenging. This book will assist you in how and where to search for public records and public information.

The first four chapters are especially helpful in leading you to many, many diverse and accurate sources of records. These chapters go well beyond a discussion of what is merely found online; they dissect many facets and techniques about searching for public records and public information.

Chapter 5 is the largest chapter. Presented state-by-state in an easy to use format, the chapter examines what is available online. Free online access and fee-based systems are denoted, with the type or category of records available. Each state section covers the following—

- State Public Record Agencies
- State Occupational Licensing and Regulatory Boards
- Courts
- Other Local or County Agencies (Recorders, Assessors, etc.)

Be sure to review the Online Access notes found at the beginning of each state's Courts and Recorder's Office sections. This is a good place to find out about statewide online systems.

Chapter 6 reviews how to access all the federal courts. Chapter 7 is devoted to record vendors who offer online access to their proprietary databases or gateways. The chapter analyzes how to spot the best vendors and determine the right vendor for your needs.

Regardless if you use public records for decision-making or on the job, or if you are a casual searcher – this book will help you and perhaps change the way you search for public records. Best of luck to you and your public record searching!

Cynthia Hetherington & Michael Sankey

August, 2008

The Fundamentals of Searching Public Records Online

The depth and scope of information that exists on people, businesses, and places is staggering. What used to be mostly paper and microfiche trails of data have turned into cyber trails of bytes managed by the government and by private companies. These trails, be they cyber or paper, reflect major events in people's lives – from birth to the first car and house, to death, wills, and probate. Add to this the new paths of the social networks and search engines that reflect an abundance of willingly shared personal information about people.

Actually, today's society treats public record information as a commodity. And public records are all on the Internet, right? Well..... not really, as you will learn.

What Information May be Found Online

The word "may" in the heading above is critical. Information found online about an individual or a company is not necessarily public, sometimes it is restricted. And the boundaries between public and private information are not well understood, and continually undergo intense scrutiny. The following are key concepts when discussing what data may be found online.

Public Record

Public records are records of incidents or actions filed or recorded with a government agency for the purpose of notifying others — the "public" — about the matter. The deed to your house recorded at the county recorder's office is a public record — it is a legal requirement that you record with the county recorder. Anyone requiring details about your property may review or copy the documents.

Public Information

Your telephone listing in the phone book is an example of public information; that is, you freely furnished the information to ease the flow of commercial and private communications.

Another example of how information becomes public is when people place information about themselves on social network sites such as myspace.com.

Personal Information

Any information about a person or business that the person or business might consider private and confidential in nature, such as your Social Security Number, DOB or address, is personal information. Such information will remain private to a limited extent unless it is disclosed to some outside entity that could make it public. Personal information may be found in either public records or in public information.

Accessibility Paradox

Adding to the mystique of online public records is the accessibility paradox. For example, in some states a specific category of records is severely restricted and therefore those records are not "public," while the very same category of records may be 100% open in other states. This is particularly true of criminal histories, vital records, and workers' compensation records.

Therefore, some of the records examined in this book have restrictions regarding access. And you will learn what is restricted in one jurisdiction can be open in another. The text in the box printed below is significant. As your public record searching takes you from state-to-state, this is the one important adage to keep in mind.

> Just because records are maintained in a certain way in your state or county, do not assume that any other county or state does things the same way.

Later chapters examine the many types of specific records that can be found online, what the records will reveal, and overall searching hints.

The rest of this chapter examines the key elements that guide a researcher on a quest to find public records online.

Where to Search for Public Records

Online access to public records comes in several varieties and packages, but the primary location resources are **government agencies** and **private company record vendors**. Online access can be an instant path to viewable or downloadable record data or the means to transmit record information along an information chain. The web is the primary online conduit, but there are a few dial systems (non-Internet) that still exist for access to certain subscription services. Also, there are many useful web pages maintained by the government and by private enterprise that provide valuable information about public records.

In order for record data to be computerized, the government agencies must convert their document files to electronic images. Many agencies that have converted to computerized storage will not necessarily place the complete record file on their online accessible systems; they are more apt to include only an index or summary data from these files.

Vendors provide records in a number of ways. Some make available their own proprietary database of public records online. These databases are created by buying records in bulk from specific government agencies. Some create their databases by sending personnel to a government office to make copies or to enter data into a laptop computer. Other vendors have created sophisticated gateways that enable customers to access data direct from database links of government agencies and other vendors.

Government Sources

The government is a huge producer of information. Much of this book is dedicated to examining where public records can be located, state-by-state and agency-by-agency. The issue with the government is that there is so much information and the cataloging system is so confusing, that it is sometimes easier to pay an online provider to dig up information and pass it through to you for a price.

Often the government will outsource online record access. Have you heard of the **National Information Consortium (NIC)**? You may be aware of its services but not realize how widespread this company's services are in the U.S. NIC is a provider of government web portals. NIC designs, manages, and markets eGovernment services on behalf of 21 states and a number of local governments. NIC does this without spending taxpayer dollars.

The state affiliates of the NIC offer services that range from managing the look-ups found at states' web pages to managing record access subscription accounts for MVRs, UCC filings, and court records. Examples of states with NIC affiliates include www.alabama.gov, www.kansas.gov, and www.idaho.gov. Of course, access to restricted records involves account approval from the managing state agency. Visit the NIC at www.nicus.com for a list of all affiliates and services.

Four Important Facts to Know About Searching Government Records

There are four important truths about searching public records online from government agencies—

1. Less than 50% of the available public records from the government can be found online.

2. Government sites can be free or fee-based. Generally, the fee-based sites are more robust.

3. Most free government public record websites contain no personal identifiers beyond the name.

4. Usually the searchable and viewable information found online is limited to name indexes and summary data rather than document images. Most access sites – especially the free access sites – permit the former, not the latter.

As long as you keep these four truths in mind, your public record searching will lead to better results.

For those on a budget or truly interested in getting to the source of federal information, start with the Government Printing Office located at http://catalog.gpo.gov. (See the screen on the next page.)

You can search by a publication name, author, keyword or subject. A search for "Public Records" as a Subject returned a number of matches. These are not necessarily online and waiting for you to click and grab, however many are. Actually this site will tell you which government depository library has a hard copy on the shelf or if it can be acquired through your local library.

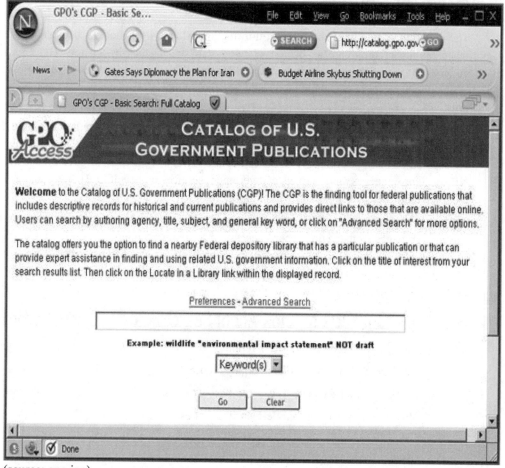

(source: gpo.jpg)

Also, for a terrific online tool to government records check out the U.S.A. Government search engine found at www. usa.gov.

There are over 100 different online functions that can be performed with the government, from opting out of marketing databases to locating zip codes. If you want to file a complaint against a government agency, or take a virtual White House tour, it is all available online through usa.gov.

When evaluating government sources, good advice is to be open and creative when considering which type of resource you are interested in researching.

The government spends billions of dollars every year in industry analysis, medical trials, land management studies, etcetera. Always consider a government document when conducting any form of research. If it can be studied, the government has a report on it! These reports are significantly cheaper (free!) compared to expensive market research reports.

When evaluating foreign government documents, consider the country of origin. China and Cuba, as communist nations which control their media, and will always demonstrate bias. Cultural norms in Asian and Middle Eastern countries guide writing and reporting styles. Canada is very open, almost as open as the United States in their corporate and government documents. Just remember to be observant of societal and cultural issues when researching outside of the U.S.

Using Public Record Vendors

Selecting the right record vendor for your particular search or case is a science. Before you sign up with every interesting online vendor that catches your eye, you need to narrow your search to the type of vendor suitable for your needs.

There are six definable and distinct main categories of public record professionals: distributors, gateways, search firms, local document retrievers, verification or screening firms and private investigation firms. Knowledge of how each these vendor categories operates and how they work with clients is invaluable.

Many specialized vendors are mentioned throughout this book. The topic of using and evaluating specialty vendor databases that are specifically oriented towards public records is discussed in Chapter 7.

Using Specialized Web Resources for Research

The public record searching guidelines and tips presented throughout this book will give you a solid knowledge foundation. But there are many more web pages at your disposal. The creative use of web resources is an art. Knowing where to find special topic web pages is important, but knowing **how to use these pages** to your advantage is more important. Using the web for any extensive research involves knowledge of search engines, directories, media site, social networking sites, and using effective search strategies.

Chapters 2 and 3 examine these topics in detail.

To learn more about overall web research fundamentals, we recommend books such as *Extreme Searcher's Internet Handbook* by Randolph Hock or *Find It Online* by Alan Schlein. For an excellent overview of how to use the Internet for legal and law-related research along with many useful links and guides, check out *The Virtual Chase* at www.virtualchase.com.

Using Links Lists and Consumer Gateway Sites

What happens when you type the words "public records" at Google? Your search result will be a huge list of web pages that are mostly *people finders* and *links lists*. These sites offer to do name searches for a fee or for free, or provide links to thousands of free government record databases.

If you are relying on a links list, consider one hosted by an association that understands the topic of interest. A few good sources are the Scout Project (scout.wisc.edu), which has been reviewing web sites for content since 1994.

Another review site is through the American Library Association, Machine Assisted Reference Section. www.ala.org/ala/rusa/rusaourassoc/rusasections/mars/mars.cfm

Consumer Gateways

Often the people-finder sites are called *consumer gateway sites,* since they are targeting the casual requester of public records. A casual requester is typically someone looking for a lost relative or classmate, or perhaps looking to find information about a neighbor or a person dating a relative. Some searchers may be "wannabe" private investigators.

Consumer sites can be quite useful if their limitations are kept in mind. The quick one-search of multiple free sites at once can be advantageous. Others offer access to specific, specialized searches such as a "reverse-phone directory."

Watch for These "Red Flags" at Consumer Gateways and Links List Sites

Some consumer sites are more helpful than others for someone who really is looking for a lost relative or classmate. But some of these sites are misleading or expensive. They often try to disguise themselves as sites used by professionals or they tout unrealistic features.

There are a few considerations to review before spending money on public record research at certain free links list sites. If I find a site using any of the marketing schemes listed below, a giant red flag pops up in my mind and I take a closer look—

Charging membership fees for the ability to access free sites or view free links lists

The most common type of site is charging a $29 to $35 fee for a one to five-year membership term. Some sites even offer an affiliate program to set up your own site in order to sell memberships to others. The "benefit" of membership is time savings of searching multiple free sites at once. But there are no magic or special databases used. The membership fee is paying for a sophisticated hit on a series of free search pages belonging to others.

Show endorsement by a phony or suspect trade association

Several of the suspect public records membership sites tout an endorsement from a national association of private investigators. Do a Google search on that association's name and read the results.

Promote non-FCRA compliant employment screening

Any public record professional will agree that you cannot purchase a "background check" on a new hire for $15 and be truly protected from a negligent hiring lawsuit or be in compliance with the Federal Fair Credit Reporting Act (FCRA). You may be able to do quick record search from a couple web pages or court repository, or from a supplementary database vendor, but that does not equate to due diligence or to a full background check.

Over exaggerate the number of free public record sites with links

If a people-searching site or free links list claims to access more than 40,000 "databases," then something may be misstated. There are not 40,000+ government agency web addresses in the U.S., each with a searchable database of free public records. The 40,000 number is calculated probably by duplicating the count of possible record types and jurisdictions within an existing database URL. For example, the docket index search for Iowa court records at www.judicial.state.ia.us includes criminal, civil, probate and traffic case data from all 99 Iowa counties. This is one database. But an over-exaggerator will count this one database as 396 databases (4 x 99) in the advertising text. Making the number count high will not fool a professional, but it can mislead the novice consumer.

The Difference Between a Name Search and a Document Request

One of the most enlightening concepts that casual requesters often discover is that "name search" will often find the location of a record or determine if a record exists, but will not uncover the record itself. There is a significant difference between searching an index to determine if a public record exists versus viewing an image or obtaining copies of documents in the record file. Many times the latter cannot be accomplished without first doing the former.

Depending on the type of public record, the reality is that many online record sites will not enable you to view an image of a document. This is especially true when searching court records or real estate recordings. However, these sites will let you know if records exist and may provide some identifiers if you are doing a name search.

Name Searching

Let us say you wish to determine if an individual has a criminal record or, say, if an individual has collateralized certain assets such as a real estate holding or ownership of equipment used in a business. The best way to perform this research is to do a "name search" – also known as an "alpha search" – of an index at the government agency that holds the records.

However, name searching is not always an easy task. An index may or may not contain the middle initial or the date of birth. Most indices no longer show the full or even a partial Social Security Number due to privacy concerns. Obviously, having this additional information – often referred to as "PI" which stands for "personal identifiers" – can be quite helpful as discussed below. Since many agencies withhold personal identifiers from appearing on the web, using an Internet site to perform a name search on such a site has lesser value and is often merely a supplemental search.

Other agencies, such as many of the county-based Supreme Courts in New York, refuse to allow the public to view an index online or in person AND refuse to perform a name search. For example, most New York courts direct searchers of criminal records to the New York State Office of Court Administration (OCA) for an online statewide criminal history search (CHRS) for a $55 fee.

Another problem when performing name searches is the correct spelling or variation of the name. There can be typos in the index and records could be filed under a variation of a first name (Ted vs. Theodore, Robert vs. Bob, Deborah vs. Debra vs. Debbie, etc.). Knowing how to maneuver through an agencies index, be it on-site or online, is quite important and worth investigating.

Requesting a Specific Document

When you know the "document number" or exact location of a record, it becomes much easier to view or obtain a copy. Some online sites provide this service, but most do not. If you are requesting a specific document in person or by mail, the government personnel are much more apt to help you compared to asking them to do a name search.

Using a government web page to search for a specific document is often easier when you have the document number or an identifier like the court docket number.

The Importance of Identifiers

Identifiers serve two different, though related purposes.

First, the identifiers of the subject must be used to analyze a public record for the purpose of determining if the record is about the subject. Perhaps the records are indexed by the last name and also by either the DOB or part of a SSN. If so, the searcher needs a DOB or SSN to search accurately.

Second, the identifiers act as an important safeguard for both the requesting party and the subject of the search. There is always the chance that the "Harold Johnson" on whom a given repository has a record is not the same "Harold Johnson" on whom a check has been requested. The possibility of a misidentification can be decreased substantially if other identifiers can match the individual to the record. Providing an identifier as simple as a middle initial is likely to identify the correct Harold Johnson.

The federal, state, and local agencies that maintain public record systems make substantial efforts to limit the disclosure of personal information such as Social Security Numbers, phone numbers, and addresses. The Social Security Number is no longer the key search tool identifier it was in the 1980s and early 1990s.

The lack of identifiers displayed when searching online is a real problem for employers or financial institutions who require a certain level of due diligence. The existence of any possible adverse information must be checked by a hands-on search to insure the proper identity of the subject. Even then the identifiers may be removed.

The government agencies that offer online access on a fee or subscription basis – usually to pre-approved requesters – are more apt to disclose personal identifiers such as the date of birth, than the free access sites. Very few give Social Security Numbers and those that do usually cloak or mask the first five digits. Some now even cloak the month and day of the birth and only release the year of birth. For example, most U.S. District Court and Bankruptcy Court PACER search systems give little (sometimes only the last four digits of SSN and no DOB) or no personal identifiers at all on search results, thus making a reliable "name search" nearly impossible.

What If the Index Doesn't Have Matching Identifiers?

You will often find that an online index of government agencies records does not contain a personal identifier. In that situation, one must search within in the record file itself or in associated paperwork.

For example, let us say you are searching for a record on Joe B. Cool with a DOB of 01/01/1985. And let us say the index gives you an index showing a possible record match of J Cool with no DOB, and another possible match with a Joseph Cool with a partial DOB match. The next step is to examine the two files. The content in the file may contain the matching personal identifiers you are looking for. If you are a professional and the highest form of accuracy is vital, then you may have times where a common name requires you to view dozens of files.

The Public Record Research Tips Book is a great resource for searching techniques and procedures you can use if you need to search for records on-site and you only have a name.

The Redaction Trend

Redaction is simply removing or hiding certain elements within a record itself or the record index. Almost daily news stories appear related to ongoing privacy debates and efforts to remove personal identifiers from public records.

In some cases, the anticipated cost of redacting records is forcing government agencies to instead block public access to the records. Yet at the same time many government officials understand the importance and benefits attached to the openness of public records. The balance of privacy interests versus public jeopardy goes beyond the purposes of this book. However, the key point here is to be aware of change and know that redactions can and will alter public record searching procedures.

Evaluate the Record Source

There are key questions that should be asked when you are determining the thoroughness and attributes of the record source, regardless if it's government or privately-held. Consider these questions—

- How far back are records kept and when are they updated?
- How are records indexed?
- What are the access procedures?
- Are there restrictions involved?
- Are record images available?

Finding the answers to these questions about data fundamentals is important when deciding if the online resource will match your needs. Let us examine each of these points.

Freshness of the Records

Knowing how "fresh" the information is – when it was last updated – is an important factor. Also it obviously beneficial to know the record retention period – how far back records are maintained.

Any answer except a clear, concise date is not going to be adequate. An index of records may have been updated last week at a courthouse or at a web page, but this data may reflect a 60-day delay or backlog. This update gap is extremely common with the state criminal record agencies like the State Police or Department of Public Safety who receive and hold criminal case information from the courts. Per a U.S. Department of Justice Study,[1] 27 states report they have a significant backlog (from 160 man-hours to 30,400 man-hours needed) for entering court data into the criminal history database. Similarly, many web vendors offering public record content do not indicate how up-to-date the content is.

---

[1] U.S. Department of Justice, Bureau of Justice Statistic's Survey of State Criminal History Information Systems, 2003 (released in 2006) found at www.ojp.usdoj.gov/bjs/abstract/sschis03.htm.

Ideally, when you search for or purchase items of information you should be provided access to a statement of accuracy without having to ask.

Record Indexing

As mentioned, many types of public records are searchable in an index. A record index serves as a pointer system to the location or file number where documents, such as recordings, case files, deeds, and articles of incorporation are kept. If you are searching an unfamiliar location, then the makeup of the index is one of first items you need to check. A public record index can be electronic, but also can exist on-site on card files, in books, on microfiche, etc. A record index can be organized in a variety of ways – by name, by year, by case or file number, or by name and year. Depending on the type of public record, an alpha index could be by plaintiff and/or defendant, by grantor and/or grantee, by address, etc.

If you are searching an index of court records, you are searching what is called the *docket*. A docket can be a list of cases on a court's calendar or a log containing the schedule and all the actions involved within a court case.

An important fact to take note of is that the primary search that government agencies provide is a search of the index. When someone tells you "I can view xxx county court records online," this person is most likely talking about an index summary of records and not about the records themselves.

Use of Disclaimers

Many government web sites offering online record access include a warning or disclosure stating that the data can have errors and/or should be used for informational purposes only. Such sites should be considered as supplemental or secondary sources only, especially if you are performing record searching that requires strict due diligence. For example, using a web source for a criminal record search, with such a disclaimer, usually indicates the search by itself will not comply with the federal Fair Credit Reporting Act regulating pre-employment screening.

About Record Fees and Charges

Remember that public records are records of incidents or transactions. It costs money (time, salaries, supplies, etc.) to record, store, and track these events. Although public records may be free of charge to view, they are not necessarily free of charge when obtaining file copies. Fees may be expected if government personnel must perform searches on-site.

The common charges found at government agencies – whether searching is performed online or on site – include **copy fees** (to make copies of documents), **search fees** (for clerical personnel to search for the record), **certification fees** (to certify a document as being accurate and coming from the particular agency), and **expedite fees** (to place you at the "front of the line").

Fees can and do vary widely from jurisdiction to jurisdiction for the same record type. Copy fees vary from $.10 to $10 per page, search fees range from under a dollar to as much as $55 search fee.

Government Subscription Accounts

The use of subscription accounts is more prevalent than many people may be aware. Also, many agencies, such as state motor vehicle agencies, only provide online record access to pre-approved, high-volume, ongoing accounts. Typically, this contractual access involves fees and a specified, minimum amount of usage. This is especially true for certain services provided by the NIC affiliates.

A growing trend is offering online access to information on a pay-as-you-go basis, usually with a credit card payment online. Some agencies will give you a glimpse of the index or docket, but will charge a fee for the record copy. Some allow the record to be printed on the spot, other times it is mailed.

Google is also getting involved in making public information more searchable on the web. Arizona, California, Utah, and Virginia have made their public databases more accessible to Google's crawler by using sitemaps to identify the structure of their sites. Visit http://blog.searchenginewatch.com/blog/070430-000946.

Note: BRB's Public Record Research System (PRRS) and *Sourcebook To Public Record Information* both indicate all the specific fees involved with all record access methods at more than 20,000 government agencies.

Keeping Track of Your Research

If you are searching for a specific public record or records from a government agency, then keeping track of your search results should not be difficult. But it may be wise to record the different aspects of the search such as cost, the period of time searched, and the record searching logic used. This is especially important if you are also hired to do the record retrieval. Creating a search form or perhaps a simple file on a spreadsheet program such as Microsoft's Excel is a good way to maintain a written progress report.

If your record searching entails extensive research at different locations or web pages, and the research branches off into many avenues, then it is imperative to take notes and record *where* you have researched and *what* you found.

Below are some ideas that may be quite useful when tracking your record searching techniques and results.

- Define your needs. What record are you searching for?
- Know the keywords or acronyms – MVR is a driving record, UCC is a uniform commercial code filing, etc.
- Define your search logic – time frame of search, name match only.
- Evaluate the sources – primary source vs. secondary, if data throughput dates indicated.
- Record the information found – if cannot be printed, then write results on paper or in a card file.

- Keep a log or an electronic folder. Record information you might need in case you what to find the source again.

Summary

Searching public records is not easy. Becoming an expert at public record searching is even harder. There are no shortcuts. If you hurry through your searches, eventually you are going to miss imperative information!

Hopefully this chapter has given you some highpoints on how to search and the chapters to follow will place you on the right road to becoming an expert.

The next two chapters explore how to use search engines, social networks, and media sites.

#### Chapter 2

Using Traditional Search Engines for Locating Public Information

The Internet has come a long way since the days of command line searching through services like Gopher, Veronica, Jughead and Archie. With billions of index-able web pages, search engines exist today as a viable search tools for locating public records and public information.

Online researchers rely on search engines to search web pages for specified keywords and return a list of the web pages where the keywords were found. You can find answers instantly, with zero effort. However, the simplicity in using these easy tools often takes away from the richer searches that can be conducted. Most users will plug in a word or phrase and hit the "Search" button, without any thought as to running a smarter search. Some will take advantage of adding quotes for phrases for common expressions, but most of us just type and go. Also missed is the other search tools created by these services, such as mapping, news, videos, etc.

(source: searchenginewatch.jpg)

Some of the earliest engines developed were Yahoo.com, Altavista.com, Google.com. To understand the history of these engines, as well as learn more about their functionality, how they rank pages, how to use these resources to their best ability and what else is on the horizon in the searcher's world, check out a few online resources such as searchenginewatch.com, Robert Berkman's blog Intelligent Agent ia-blog.com, and anything by Gary Price (Invisible Web guru) and Chris Sherman (founder of Searchenginewatch.com). Finally, Ran Hock's *The Extreme Searcher's Internet Handbook* is a handy resource for any new searcher.

This chapter examines the advanced search features of those search engines with the most robust and useful offerings for expert searching of public information.

Google.com

As the market share leader of free search tools on the Internet, Google certainly gets a good deal of use. However, it is probably one of the most under-whelmed search engines available. There is much more to searching Google than pushing words through and hitting "Search" or "I feel lucky."

There are certain advanced searches that can be performed in Google, if the searcher selects the advanced search feature, and takes advantage of the preferences setting.

Using Preferred Results

For example, one way to save a lot of time and not miss vital hits is to set the Number of Results from 10 (the default) to 100.

To do this, go to the first screen of Google.com, click on Preferences, which is the second link to the right of the search engine box, and then slide down to Number of Results. Here you see a choice to use the pull down menu which should have 10 showing in the box. Change that to 100 and click the Save Preferences button at the bottom of the page. Then every time you use Google.com on that page, it will give you 100 results per page.

Number of Results   Google's default (10 results) provides the fastest results.
Display [100 ▼] results per page.

(source: google_numbers.jpg)

Google Operators

There are several Google Operators that really smarten up a search and help get the user to the right link faster. Look in the first column in the table below for the bolded characters or operators that help define or narrow a search.

This Search	Finds Pages Containing...
cooking Italian	the words cooking and Italian
vegetarian **OR** vegan	information on vegetarian or vegan
"Can I get a witness"	the exact phrase Can I get a witness
Henry +8 Great Britain	information about Henry the Eighth (8), weeding out other kings of Great Britain
automobiles ~glossary	glossaries about automobiles, as well as dictionaries, lists of terms, terminology, etc.
salsa –dance	the word salsa but NOT the word dance (note the space before the hypen)
salsa-dancer	all forms of the term, whether spelled as a single word, a phrase, or hyphenated (note the lack of a space)
define:congo	definitions of the word congo from the web

Also available on Google are the common mathematical operators you would use on your computer. The following symbols between any two numbers will automatically perform a math function.

Symbol	Function
+	Addition
-	Subtraction
*	Multiplication
/	Division

Other *Advanced Google Operators* can be located through the Advanced Search Page, or performed right in the search box.

This Search	Example	Finds Pages Containing...
site:	site:virtuallibrarian.com	Searches only one website for expression, in this case virtuallibrarian.com
filetype:	filetype:doc	Find documents of the specified type, in this case MS Word documents.
link:	link:virtuallibrarian.com	Find linked pages, i.e., show pages that point to the URL.

Google operators can also be **combined**. Follow the example below:

site:hp.com filetype:pdf "5010 LaserJet" printer FAQ

This search is directed to the Hewlett Packard web site, looking for Adobe Acrobat PDF file of Frequently Asked Questions file regarding the 5010 LaserJet printer.

There are dozens more operators and search techniques to use. A great resource for search help for beginners to experts is www.googleguide.com.

Proximity Searching

When an **asterisk** "*" is used between words or expressions, Google offers a very rich proximity searching feature. Used between two expressions, proximity will return results that are within 15 words of each other.

For example, a search for "cynthia hetherington" investigator returned 755 matches in Google.

Whereas, the search "cynthia hetherington" * investigator resulted in 24 matches.

Hence, the expression "cynthia hetheington" did appear on the same web page as "investigator" 755 times, but it only occurred in close proximity to "investigator" 24 times out of the 755 matches.

Common Phrase Searching

For English language searches consider the common expressions people use in everyday language. With email, text messaging, and other basic device communications, writing has turned into an extension of speaking. People no longer think about what they are writing, as far as grammar is concerned, they tend to write like they speak. So shorthand and expressions stated are common. Below are common expressions used create phrase searching.

- I hate XXX (my job, my mom, my school, my employer)
- Better than XXX (<restaurant>, <product>, <any proper noun>)
- I love XXX (my job, my mom, my school, my employer)
- XXX was the nicest (<geography/location>, <company or person>)
- XXX was the worst
- XXX was off the charts
- XXX was off the hook
- XXX was off the map
- XXX was such a jerk/babe/<expletive>
- XXX was so hot/stupid/boring

An example search in Google.com for "Better than Disney" returned hits such as:

- Is Disney Land better than Disney World?
- Nick [Nickelodeon's children's network] is slightly better than Disney

Be inventive and try to consider how you would describe a similar topic, then run your searches in the same style using the quotes to contain the phrases.

Other Useful Google Tools

Beyond web searching, Google.com also offers Image Searching, News Searching, Books, Maps, Products, Translations, Documents, Calendars, etc. We will review how to use some of the more useful Google searches tools for record searching.

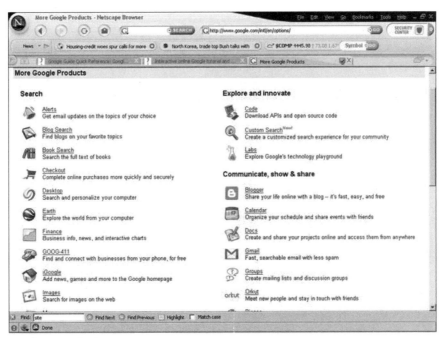

(source: google_more.jpg)

Google Alerts

This has to be one of the handiest tools that Google offers. Google Alerts sends emails automatically when there are new Google results for your submitted list of search terms. The results are culled from Google News, Web, Blogs, Video and Groups".[2]

The easiest way to get to the Alerts feature in Google.com is through the News link. Once there, you can set up your alert to email you as the event is found or once a day or once a month. Type in your search query – such as a proper name, expression or phrase search –then use the pull down menu to select what you want to track for your personalized alerts.

Source:
Google_alerts.jpg

---

2   See www.google.com/support/alerts/bin/static.py?page=faq.html&hl=en#q1

Google Images

Image searching in Google can offer a host of interesting results. Using the same type of search queries you can look up a personal name, company or idea. The Advanced Image Searching offers limiters by image type, such as black and white, color, drawing, and has a search feature for finding just faces and just news content. This is helpful to narrow down large result matches with the Faces Only feature. However the News Content feature is terrific considering the image search happens within media and press oriented web sites. Normally news and media searches are conducted on databases, such as LexisNexis or Factiva, where images have been stripped out of the stories. For more information, go to http://images.google.com/advanced_image_search

(source: google_images.jpg)

Google Maps Tool

This is a great tool that is quite useful beyond the well-known driving directions, and the *Where Is* feature. To become acquainted, search an area with familiarity to see the variety and tools that go beyond directions of East to West. For example, the *My Maps* tab offers a variety of features and tools that allow you to customize your own searches and really zero in on certain aspects of the geography.

The image on the next page shows how a search can be narrowed to show real estate listings, user contributed photos with Picasa Web Album or Panoramio, and places of interest. The distance measurement tool is handy when trying to establish the length between two points on the map, with various measurement results offered. For example, the distance between Minneapolis and St. Paul Minnesota is 8.73084 mi or 128.052 football fields, 13.1711 верста, 281.019 pools, etc.

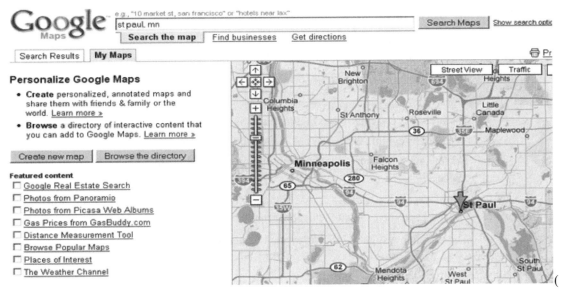

(source: google-1.gif)

Exalead.com

Exalead.com search engine offers a host of specialized searches, designed exclusively to be used on their site. Each service combined does not amount to the volume of web sites that Google.com is cataloging; however, the unique search algorithms and displayed results offer great results.

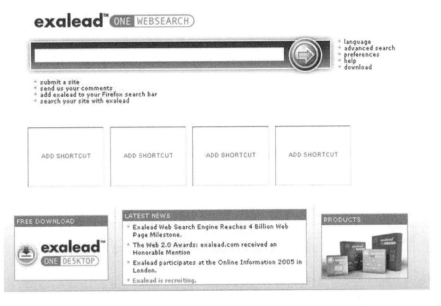

(source: exalead.jpg) - Exalead.com's special power is proximity searching.

Proximity Searching

When the word NEAR (note this is case sensitive) is used between words or expressions, proximity will return results which are within 15 words of each other, same as Google. However, you can narrow down the results with a /xx (xx=15 or less).

For example:

- A search for "Cynthia Hetherington" investigator returned 65 matches in Exalead.
- The search "cynthia hetherington" NEAR investigator resulted in 19 matches.
- Narrowing it further "cynthia hetherington" NEAR/5 investigator resulted in 13 matches.

Another useful expression is NEXT (use capital letters). Using NEXT forces the order of the expressions being searched so that they appear in the order you require.

- The search investigator NEXT "cynthia hetherington" resulted in 8 matches.

Other Worthy Search Engines

Other traditional search engines to check out for their unique features are—

- Alltheweb.com
- Altavista.com
- Ask.com
- Yahoo.com

Ebay.com

Ebay.com, and its partner, Paypal.com offer over a decades' worth of information on their users.

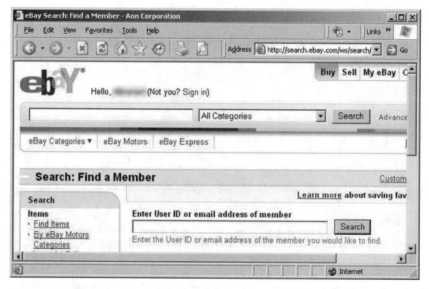

(source: ebay.jpg)

Using eBay

Here is how to search by a person's name, email address, or best of all, the first half of an email address, which is very likely also the person's username on Ebay.

- Go to "Advanced Search" from the homepage, upper right hand corner
- Choose "Find a Member" from the left hand column.
- Type in the first half of the person's personal email address. For example, for crazybird@gmail.com, type "crazybird"

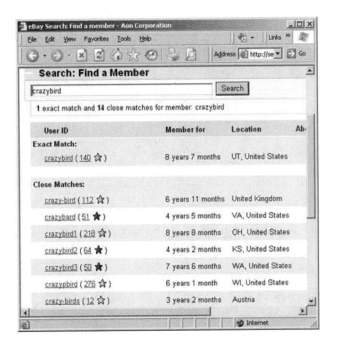

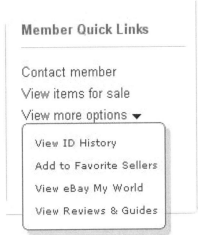

(source: ebay.jpg)

The results screen show one perfect match for crazybird in Utah. This person has held this account with eBay.com for over 8 years.

Note: Remember to take into account that this could be a mismatch, especially if the name is a common one like "baseballfan" or "nascarfanatic."

If you think you have a match to your person, visit the person's online profile on eBay and read EVERYTHING they have on their page. Insight can be developed by looking at the items bought and sold, and reviewing all comments made to and by person.

Once you gather the comments, click over to the *Feedback Profile* for the individual. Down the right hand side are a few selectable items under *Member Quick Links*. Look at *View ID History* to see if the member changed an ID in eBay in the past 10 years. You can also "Add to Favorite Sellers" to be alerted when the person places new items for sale on eBay.

Wayback Machine on Archive.org

The mission of Archive.org is "...to help preserve those artifacts and create an Internet library for researchers, historians, and scholars. The Archive collaborates with institutions including the Library of Congress and the Smithsonian."

Archive.org offers researchers and historians a view of a web site as captured by the Wayback Machine on a specific date. A web address is entered into the search parameter creating a results page. In the case of http://www.data2know.com, this web site has been continually archived since August 18, 2000 and as recently as August 18, 2007.

(source: archive.jpg)

From January 1, 1996 to August 18, 2007, the Wayback Machine recorded the web site http://www.data2know.com on the following dates.

Search Results for Jan 01, 1996 - Nov 19, 2007

99	2000	2001	2002	2003	2004	2005	2006	2007
ages	3 pages	13 pages	16 pages	23 pages	29 pages	17 pages	25 pages	16 pages
	Aug 18, 2000 *	Feb 03, 2001 *	Feb 07, 2002 *	Feb 01, 2003 *	Jan 28, 2004	Jan 22, 2005 *	Jan 05, 2006	Jan 02, 2007
	Nov 09, 2000 *	Mar 02, 2001	Mar 29, 2002 *	Feb 12, 2003	Feb 25, 2004	Feb 04, 2005 *	Jan 28, 2006	Jan 07, 2007
	Nov 17, 2000	Mar 03, 2001	May 23, 2002 *	Mar 30, 2003	Mar 27, 2004	Feb 05, 2005	Feb 01, 2006	Jan 12, 2007
		Mar 09, 2001	May 28, 2002	Apr 04, 2003	Apr 05, 2004	Mar 01, 2005	Feb 03, 2006 *	Jan 17, 2007
		Apr 01, 2001	Jun 02, 2002	Apr 16, 2003	Apr 11, 2004	Mar 03, 2005	Feb 05, 2006 *	Jan 22, 2007
		Apr 05, 2001 *	Jun 03, 2002	Apr 25, 2003	Apr 28, 2004	Mar 24, 2005 *	Feb 10, 2006	Jan 27, 2007
		Apr 07, 2001	Aug 02, 2002 *	May 24, 2003	Jun 04, 2004	Apr 01, 2005 *	Mar 03, 2006	Feb 03, 2007
		May 17, 2001 *	Sep 21, 2002	May 28, 2003	Jun 06, 2004	Apr 05, 2005	May 26, 2006	Feb 06, 2007
		Jun 23, 2001	Sep 24, 2002	Jun 02, 2003	Jun 07, 2004	May 07, 2005	Jun 10, 2006 *	Feb 16, 2007 *
		Sep 13, 2001 *	Sep 26, 2002	Jun 18, 2003	Jun 10, 2004	Jul 14, 2005	Jun 18, 2006 *	Apr 08, 2007 *
		Oct 20, 2001	Sep 27, 2002	Jun 20, 2003	Jun 11, 2004	Aug 18, 2005	Jul 08, 2006	Apr 09, 2007
		Nov 30, 2001 *	Nov 20, 2002 *	Jun 24, 2003	Jun 12, 2004	Oct 25, 2005	Jul 21, 2006	Jun 25, 2007
		Dec 05, 2001	Nov 22, 2002	Jul 22, 2003	Jun 14, 2004	Nov 07, 2005	Aug 04, 2006 *	Jun 29, 2007
			Nov 24, 2002	Jul 30, 2003	Jun 19, 2004	Nov 30, 2005	Aug 13, 2006 *	Jul 16, 2007
			Nov 27, 2002	Aug 04, 2003	Jun 24, 2004	Dec 01, 2005	Aug 20, 2006	Aug 10, 2007
			Dec 05, 2002	Aug 10, 2003	Jul 25, 2004	Dec 11, 2005	Aug 31, 2006	Aug 18, 2007
				Sep 20, 2003	Aug 04, 2004	Dec 19, 2005	Sep 02, 2006	
				Oct 03, 2003	Aug 18, 2004		Oct 04, 2006 *	

(source: archive.jpg)

The asterisks denote that a change occurred on the www.data2know.com web site. Hence from November 22, 2002 to February 7, 2003, there were no alterations of web site.

The correct date that the web site was captured is in the web address. Wayback Machine records their captures as follows:

http://web.archive.org/web/YYYYMMDDhhmmss/www.website.com/index.html

The phrase "YYYYMMDDhhmmss" is equal to the "year month date hour minute second"

Hence, in http://web.archive.org/web/20050403055101/www.data2know.com/index.html the code 20050403055101 equals the exact date and time of April 3, 2005 5:51:01 AM

Zoominfo.com

Another great source for free searching is www.zoominfo.com. Information is collated from web sites that the Zoominfo software *bots* – also known as intelligent agents – have captured and matched to a particular person or company. You can search by company, person or industry. This is truly one of the most useful specialist search engines on the Internet. You can locate an abundance of who's who straight from www.zoominfo.com. Keep in mind, though, that this information is being generated from other web sites and needs to be verified.

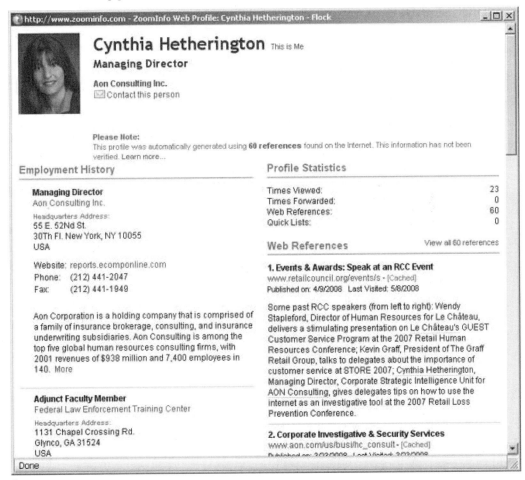

earching on Cynthia's name, Zoominfo.com produces what looks like a resume, with business experience, association connections, education credentials, and in some cases photos.

(source: zoominfo_1.jpg)

The information found in the left hand column is produced from the web matches Zoominfo agents found on the right hand side. These articles, web site matches, and directory listings are all assumed into the resume-like profile that you see above.

Keep in mind that when searching by a personal name there may be several matches in the results list. Be sure to look at each one because Zoominfo.com may not connect the dots between two profiles and will merely list the names separately. For example, Cynthia Hetherington has 12 separate line entries, including some listed as Cindy Hetherington. Look at each line item to insure that you do not miss any important, or even random, information for your subject.

One problem when using Zoominfo.com is when you are looking up a very common name, there will be thousands of entries. The best approach is to try to search a common name in the *advance search section* and narrow down by combining name and company name.

Guidestar.org

Private foundations, charities, non-profits, churches, hospitals, schools, or publicly supported organizations all are subject to special considerations regarding to federal taxes. These entities file different forms with the IRS and all must contribute detailed financial and member information, which can be a great asset for the online intelligence investigator.

Whether you are looking to reveal experts in the field, local interests to a region, or the financial participation of a particular foundation, these organizations can open a bevy of investigative leads. Finding out what organizations or affiliations a person belongs to can give you insight into the person's character. Categories can include religious, athletic, health, child focused, or specific-interest related. For example, there are two non-profit associations dedicated just to avocados.

Guidestar.org is a great starting point to find record data about non-profits. The information regarding officers and the financials in a non-profit organization is completely transparent in the Form 990, an annual reporting return that certain federally tax exempt organizations must file with the IRS. Form 990 provides information on the filing organization's mission, programs, and finances.

Below you can see Part 8 of a random Form 990 taken from GuideStar. The names are blocked out to protect the identities, but I can mention that they all have the same last name as the foundation itself. They appear to be siblings and children of the corporate owner. In other words, what better way to take care of your children than to appoint them as trustees of your own foundation!

Form 990-PF (2005)				Page 6
Part VIII **Information About Officers, Directors, Trustees, Foundation Managers, Highly Paid Employees, and Contractors**				
1 List all officers, directors, trustees, foundation managers and their compensation (see page 21 of the instructions).				
(a) Name and address	(b) Title, and average hours per week devoted to position	(c) Compensation (If not paid, enter -0-)	(d) Contributions to employee benefit plans and deferred compensation	(e) Expense account, other allowances
▓▓▓, Anchorage, AK ▓▓▓	Trustee 40	400,000		
▓▓▓, San Antonio, CA ▓▓▓	Trustee 40	400,000		
▓▓▓, Sausalito, CA ▓▓▓	Trustee 40	400,000		

(source: form990.jpg)

Other recommended sources for information about records and people associated with non-profits are—

- The Foundation Center at http://foundationcenter.org/
- The Taft Group at www.taftgroup.com/
- Practitioner Resources at www.practitionerresources.org/

Summary

What seems like a new phenomenon to many, web sites have opened doors for researchers to discover an online bevy of information on individuals' activities and antics. Although, I say "new" which the traditional web still looks, acts and feels like, it is almost 20 years old. With that type of age attributed to it, user histories have been stored for just as long. Hence eBay transactions from 1996 are still accessible; Google.com searches from its earliest days are stored in logs somewhere. Services like Zoominfo.com, and Archive.org, are preserving web sites long gone from their servers.

It takes imagination and creative searching, paired with the ability to know where these services are, what they cover, and how long they have been around to uncover valuable information.

With this history on the Worldwide Web, an individual's online activity can be lightly researched. Couple the online profile that is developed through these searches with any press releases and media found through online news channels, and a public records search, as outlined in the rest of this book, and you will have a robust profile.

Then the next generation, the Web 2.0 sites will be explored opening up a whole new resource of potential information. This side of the search is the "Public Information" mentioned in Chapter 1. Web 2.0's Social Networks is the best of the best for a researcher, as individuals post not only their preferences, likes and dislikes, hobbies, sports and interests, but they are diarists sharing their life story in a very public way. The next chapter will examine how once what was private and inane is now public and the new "reality."

#### Chapter 3

Researching Social Networks

Social networks are World Wide Web based interfaces which are used for communicating through text, video, sound and photos. The only things Social Networks do not provide (yet) are touch and smell!

The Quest for Public Exposure

Popular social networking sites known as Web Logs ("Blogs" for short), such as Myspace.com and Facebook.com, have opened up the web to individuals who want to participate on the Internet but do not have the technical know how, or time, money, etcetera to create a web site.

Social networks are a representation of Web 2.0 programming. Developers have created a way for end users, regardless of their ability, to tailor an environment to share stories through text, sound and pictures. What is more, the programming language is consistent throughout. Whereas traditional HTML web pages have too many inconsistencies between pages and there is a lack ease for tagging (indexing) these sites for easier search and retrieval.

In other words, Blogs allow for easier input, storage and are more searchable. A blog about Italian Cooking could be created for free in minutes. Once available, the author selects certain key words, known as tags, to draw traffic to their blog. These key words are updated as the blog grows, so specific restaurants can be named, recipes, points of interest, or whatever subject wants of focus by the author.

Other social network tools like Youtube.com or Flickr.com are video and photo sites that allow users to express themselves by uploading imagery and to share whatever they feel like with the world. These services also encourage tagging the photo or video in order to make it searchable. So photos of San Diego Zoo, would be tagged with 'San Diego' and 'zoo' thereby creating fast links for anyone looking for either topic.

In comparison, a web page is fully index-able, but there is nothing really guiding the reader to what the author wants attention to. Tags are focused and direct versus the hit or miss word match you get from full page indexing. This is not to say that blogs are not indexed by the full page. Google and other traditional search engines still scan and index the full pages of blogs. But specialized engines like Blogdigger.com and Technorati.com put the heavier emphasis, resulting in better search results, on the tags indicated by the author.

As an investigative source, this is a super benefit for those who are looking for individuals based on username, hobby or location, as will be explained site by site.

To summarize, social networks are using the latest in web development programming to make the Internet more accessible for those who were otherwise technically challenged. Anyone can get involved by creating an account for themselves in the form of a blog to communicate with the world or create an account with video service or photo service to share images and videos.

The rest of this chapter is devoted to analyzing all the major social networking services. We will examine what is possible, what they are offering, and how they can be used for locating information about the person who is posting or their topic.

Author TIP❖ A convenient trick that Cynthia recommends is to go to gmail.com, hotmail.com or yahoo.com and create an email account that you can use to register for the various social network sites. This will be referred to from this point as the "throw away email account" because you are able to move through the various sites and services without exposing your actual email account to spam, or unwanted to emails. In other words, when you are tired of it, throw it away.

Blog.com

Blog.com is just one of dozens of spaces to create your own web log, also known as a Blog.

As the following image portrays, a person can create a blog in 3 easy steps. The first is to signup, which in the case of blog.com is a simple name, address, email registration. Second, create the blog by giving a name and specifying what the topic will be. For example, Business Background Investigations is a blog about conducting due diligence on companies. The title of this blog is businessbackgroundinvestigations.blog.com. The initial setup only took minutes to specify the details about the name and the topic. The last step is to tailor an appearance by maneuvering through a selection of pre-established fonts, colors, backgrounds, and layouts. The entire process is point and click.

These blogs are not search engines in themselves, but instead offer searchable interfaces on their own sites. If they do not have a search engine within their own domain, than make sure to use Technorati.com and Icerocket.com to reach these services. Or you can try a trick with Google.com. Run a search as follows—

     site:blog.com <username, expression, persons name, whatever you are looking for>

The "site:domain.xxx" narrows down your search to just that particular domain.

Similar sites to blog.com include typepad.com, journalspace.com, xanga.com and livejournal.com. Also, a directory of free blog registry sites and tools can be found at diarist.net.

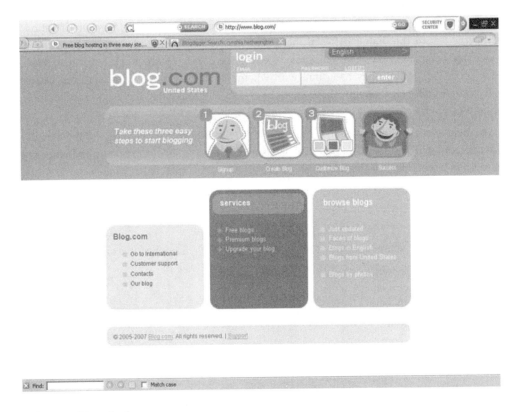

(source: blogs.jpg)

Myspace.com

Myspace.com is the most popular social networking site on the web. Began as a tool for local musicians to share songs, gig dates and information about themselves with their fans, it quickly took off as the go-to site for anyone who considers themselves hip. The largest portion of the subscriber base is teenagers and young adults. However, plenty of seniors, adults and professional service firms (hiring agencies) also are using Myspace.com

Use your *throw away* email address to create an account on Myspace.com. This will allow you to move smoothly through the various users' pages, viewing their photos and videos, as well as interacting with them as necessary.

Once logged in, utilize the search engine at the top of the page. Be sure to change the pull down menu on the right of the search box from **People** to **Myspace**, forcing the search to look within Myspace.com only.

Recommended searches are a person's name (yes, many do post their full name), the person's username, the town the person lives in, the school attended, or the employer's name. All of these items are generally self-reported within the users' profile. These profiles are extremely revealing. It is amazing how much information is disclosed including occupation, employer, sexual preference, marriage status, birthdays, and personal tastes in music, movies and hobbies.

Beyond what owner of the profile writes about themselves on their page, information can be discerned from the dialog between themselves and their friends (those people in the extended networks). For example, happy birthday messages are very common. One can learn much about the social life, where they hang out, with whom, and what crazy events occurred because these individuals talk pretty openly about themselves. Beyond looking at the users' profile, look as well at their friend's profiles for messages the posted to the friends by the users.

The next piece of information that is useful is the videos and pictures. Many details can be extracted just from looking at pictures. The surroundings, titles of the photos and other interesting facts can be found.

What can be discerned from the snapshot of this fellow's Myspace.com page is his full name, employer's name, where he lives, what he looks like. Looking deeper into his photos, there were references to bars in NY City that he appears to be visiting.

Other spaces that share this type of information and may be searched in a similar fashion are—

- Facebook.com
- Friendster.com
- Yahoo360.com
- Twitter.com
- Youtube.com

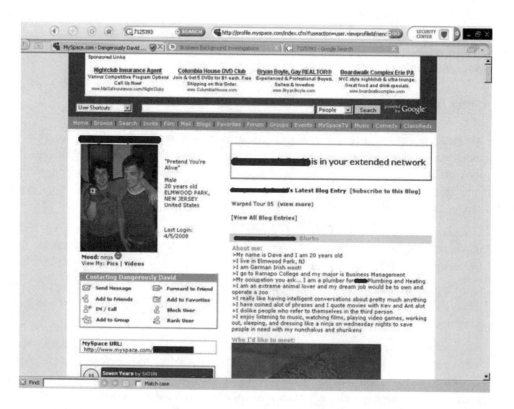

(source: Myspace.jpg)

Lococitato.com

Lococitato is an easy to use site that is an excellent resource to discover who a person's friends are and to whom the person is chatting with – providing the user has not made his network of friends and profile "private."

The best procedure tool to discern who these people are is to copy the address (URL) at the top of the Myspace.com page, and then visit Lococitato.com.

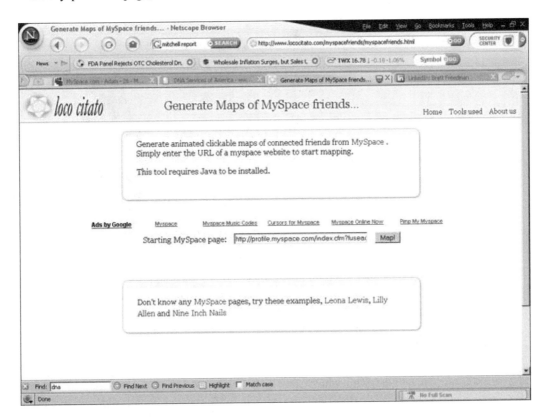

(source: lococitato.jpg)

Using the URL you have copied from the Myspace.com entry, go to the Myspace.com Visualizer and plug in the address to expand the network on. From here you can mouse over the buttons that pop up at the same time and you will see a quick snapshot of the person that is being connected, as in the example with Kristen Nicole on the next page.

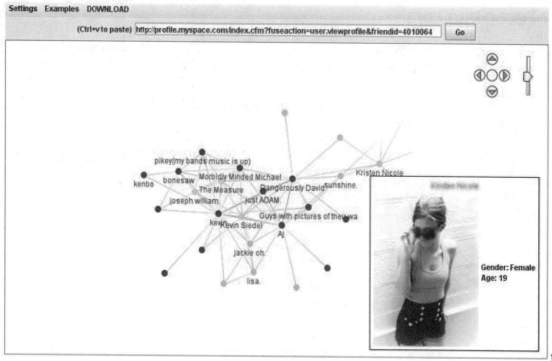

(source: lococitato.jpg)

The incredibly useful feature of this is that not only do you see who is connected to our subject, but who amongst them are also connected to each other. This helps establish groups of friends or colleagues. Often times you can discern who is in school together, who works together, or what cliques are rejoined through Myspace.com.

Yoname.com

If you are not familiar with which social networks your search subject may be involved, then check out Yoname.com. Here you can search by full name, email address, and even phone number.

Whichever term you select, your search will go against the following social network sites and will return whatever matches the name, email address or number you entered.

Warning – If you search by email address, that person will receive an email from Yoname.com stating someone was looking for them. It will not say who searched them, just that the search was conducted.

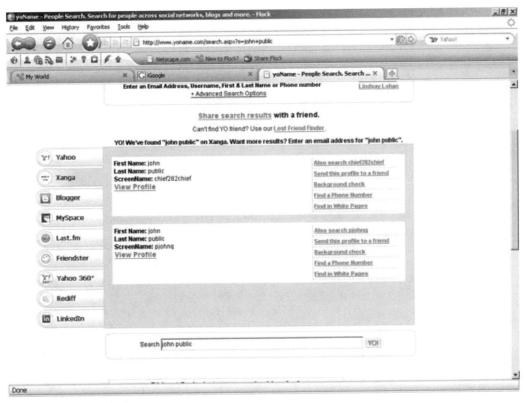

(source: yoname.jpg)

This is a sample of a search on the made up name of John Public. This search shows that yoname.com located results matching that name to Yahoo, Xanga, Blogger, Myspace and other similar social networks.

Linkedin.com

Linkedin.com is like Myspace.com but for adults. In reality, both adults and young people can register in either service. However, the focus of Linkedin.com is more concerned about professional networking than social networking.

There is an amazing amount of information is posted on these pages. The obvious data that jumps out includes the name, location, and work position. Also discoverable are ones' education, past employment, affiliations to associations, particular networking groups, and any posted recommendations.

Individuals can be quite revealing about themselves in Linkedin.com and they offer up probably too much personal information.

A popular social network tool very similar to Linkedin.com is Spoke.com.

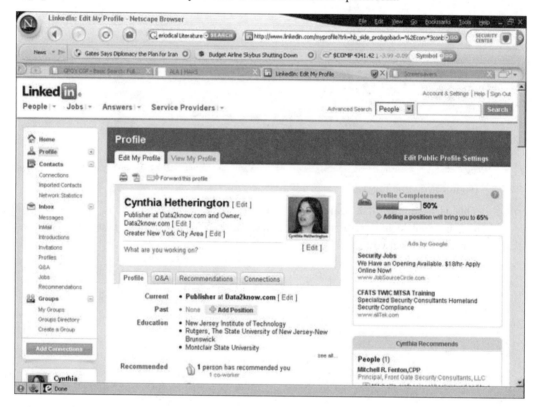

(souce: linkedin.jpg)

Technorati.com

(source: technorati.jpg)

Technorati.com is the "google" of blog search engines, meaning this is the market-share leader, at least for now. Technorati.com is the search engine for web sites like youtube.com, myspace.com, blog.com, xanga.com, and etcetera. The site covers almost 100 million blogs daily and offers a rich search engine that enables searches to efficiently narrow down a results list.

It is a must to search Technorati.com and Icerocket.com (following this) to obtain a thorough search through the web and Social Network world on a particular topic.

Using the Advanced Search option (shown on the next page), the search can be narrowed down to a particular blog, perhaps to search for the one or two times a topic was mentioned by a single blogger. Also, searching by tag (explained further in Icerocket.com), to sites that are linked to a particular blog, and by the usual phrase or single word search.

Advanced Search

You can search by Keyword, Website URL, or Tag. Fill out only the fields you need and leave the rest blank. If you only want to search blog posts, try search.technorati.com.

Keyword Search

Enter a word or a "phrase in quotes" to see all blog posts that contain your word or exact phrase.

Show posts that contain:

ALL of the words	
the EXACT phrase	
AT LEAST ONE of the words	
NONE of the words	

Search in:

- ⦿ All Blogs
- ◯ Blogs about
- ◯ This blog URL

[Search]

URL Search

Enter the URL of a website to see blogs that link to it and what they say.

Find posts that link to

[Search]

Tag Search

Enter a category like sports or books to see posts, photos, and links on that subject. Separate tags with "OR" to search multiple subjects.

Find posts tagged

(source: technorati.jpg)

Icerocket.com

Icerocket.com offers a unique array of tools that can be utilized for the blogger and the researcher. Backed by Mark Cuban, owner of the Dallas Mavericks and avid Blogger himself (see www.blogmaverick.com), this resource was created to track what people were searching for. Icerocket.com tracks focuses primarily on blog sites, using the meta-tagging to categorize and index the content within the blogs. In this way a search can be conducted by keyword which also captures any relevant matches found on a site, but will prioritize those matches that are marked as tagged searches.

For example, let us say a blog is written about places to eat in Seattle it names several Italian, Spanish, and French specific restaurants by design, such as—

Seattle Italian Restaurants

- La Trattatoria

Seattle Spanish Restaurants

- Papi's Cocina

The words will all be captured by the search bot and indexed. However if the writer tags or self indexes this post as Italian Restaurants, Spanish Restaurants, etc., it will move up in rank in our search results.

From the observer's perspective, one can watch the search terms being typed in by users to see what interests the average person and what they look for.

Top Searches

american idol angelina jolie apple autism barack obama battlestar galactica blogs brad pitt britney spears facebook chat google hillary clinton iphone john mccain love microsoft myspace news obama paris hilton spring the hills youtube

The real benefit to Icerocket.com is the search engine. Icerocket.com searches through blogs, image directories, and most importantly Myspace.com. Even though you can search directly in Myspace.com, using the Icerocket.com search engine tool for myspace.com searches often presents a more comfortable search environment, since it is a more traditional search.

Icerocket does allow you to narrow down your blog searches through the advanced search link or by using the search operators such as Title, Author and Tag to find blogs you are looking for.

Hence a search would look like, title: "public records" and the results would require that *public records* to show up in the title. The other examples are author: "Cynthia Hetherington" will return all mentions about Icerocket written by "Cynthia Hetherington" and tag:Yankees will return all posts tagged "Yankees." These advanced search features can be combined. For example search using *title: "Public Records" author: "Cynthia Hetherington"* to locate all blog posts by Cynthia Hetherington with Public Records in the title.

Flickr.com

Flickr.com, Photobucket.com, Kodak.com and similar online services, offer a great place to park your digital images to share with the world. These services are a great idea for families that live in different locations who want to share imagery of the kids or of events as they are happening. For example, if Grandma lives in Florida and the grandkids are in NY, the parents can send Grandma a link to Flickr.com after they celebrate a holiday.

However Grandma is not the only one looking at these photos and many of them are not of kids at holidays. You can find office workers at office parties taking snapshots of their cubes or office spaces, and sharing way too much on the business side of what happens internally. The photo sample to follow demonstrates the desktop of a busy right handed (mouse position) working gal (note the hand lotion on the shelf above desk), who is using Microsoft Outlook email, and working on some sort of office layout (plans on right side of desk).

The trick to searching in Flickr and others is to search by company name, personal name, username (if you know it) and also add phrases like "at work" or "at school" or "on the job." Just use your imagination.

(source: flickr.jpg)

Summary

In today's identity theft-aware environment, there are privacy advocates arguing for tighter controls on SSNs, personal identifiers, health and financial records and any other piece of information that can be used. The irony is while these advocates fight for discretion and privacy of an individual's personal information, that person is out "there" sharing even more than identifiers and addresses with the entire universe. Individuals, as we have seen through Web 2.0 and Social Networks, are living online. They rely on the web to relay their stories, carry their message, and carve out a bit of themselves virtually to anyone and everywhere who would login.

As researchers, it is to our advantage to take advantage of these self-exposing persons, and keep abreast of the latest Web 2.0 and beyond developments in order to keep informed. From this point forward, there can only be more service offerings on the web to take advantage of. So, good advice is to learn the resources outlined in this chapter and stay tuned to what is on the horizon.

#### Chapter 4

Online Resources Presented By Topic

This chapter presents key public record and public information topics in alphabetical order, from *Archives* to *Worker's Compensation*. The resources listed are a mix of searchable government sites and private company sites.

Note: Chapter 5 is a state-by-state look at over 10,000 web sites with online access. If you are looking for specific data found at the state, county /parish or local government levels, such as courts or recorder's offices, see Chapter 5.

Archives

The National Archives and Records Administration (NARA) is America's record keeper and serves as the archival arm of the federal government. NARA not only preserves documents and materials related to the U.S., but also ensures people can access the information.

The NARA web page at www.archives.gov has detailed information regarding documents, images, and how to research. To find all the 30 NARA locations and affiliated sites visit www.archives.gov/locations. Federal Record Centers (FRCs) are also part of NARA. These centers hold closed case files from Federal U.S. District Courts civil and criminal and Bankruptcy Courts. See Chapter 6 Searching Federal Court Records for information on how to obtain cases files.

The website for each state's archives is found in the next chapter.

Aviation Records

Accidents

The Federal National Transportation Safety Board (NTSB) maintains an aviation accident database with information from 1962 forward about civil aviation accidents and selected incidents within the U.S., its territories and possessions, and in international waters. Six different queries are available. Preliminary reports are posted within days; final reports may take months before posted. Some information prior to 1993 is sketchy. www.ntsb.gov

Aircraft, Airlines, Pilots

The main government information center regarding certification for pilots, airmen, airlines, aircraft, aircraft registration/ownership, and airports is the Federal Aviation Administration (FAA) at www.faa.gov.

Search Canadian aircraft information at www.tc.gc.ca/aviation/activepages/ccarcs/index.htm.

The International Civil Aviation Organization (www.icao.int) maintains aircraft registration standards for participating countries.

Leading private information resource centers for searching flights, pilot certifications, and regulatory overviews include:

- Landings at www.landings.com
- Jane's Information Group at www.janes.com
- Aviation Research Group at www.aviationresearch.com

Banks & Financial Institutions

The Office of the Comptroller of the Currency (OCC) maintains a variety of public information about the national banking system. Note: For Treasury Department sites, see the *Federal Agency Sanctions and Watch Lists* section later in this chapter.

Federal Deposit Insurance Corporation (FDIC)

The FDIC supervises the following entities and has the statutory authority to take enforcement actions against them—

- FDIC-insured state chartered banks that are not members of the Federal Reserve System
- FDIC-insured branches of foreign banks
- Officers, directors, employees, controlling shareholders, agents, and certain other categories of individuals (institution-affiliated parties) associated with such institutions

The FDIC Institution Directory is found at www2.fdic.gov/idasp/index.asp. To view **enforcement actions**, go to www.fdic.gov/bank/individual/enforcement/index.html.

Federal Reserve Board

The Federal Reserve supervises the following entities and has the statutory authority to take formal enforcement actions against them—

- State member banks
- Bank holding companies
- Non-bank subsidiaries of bank holding companies
- Edge and agreement corporations
- Branches and agencies of foreign banking organizations operating in the United States and their parent banks
- Officers, directors, employees, and certain other categories of individuals associated with the above banks, companies, and organizations (referred to as "institution-affiliated parties")

The National Information Center Institution Search web page at www.ffiec.gov/nicpubweb/nicweb/SearchForm.aspx allows you to search the Federal Reserve's database for an institution's current and non-current information by name and location. Also, you may search www.ffiec.gov/nicpubweb/nicweb/SearchForm.aspx?pS=2 for U.S. Branches and Agencies of Foreign Banking Organizations (FBOs).

Enforcement Actions

Generally, the Federal Reserve takes formal enforcement actions against the entities listed above for violations of laws, rules, or regulations, unsafe or unsound practices, breaches of fiduciary duty, and violations of final orders. Since August 1989, the Federal Reserve has made all final enforcement orders public. Search at www.federalreserve.gov/boarddocs/enforcement/search.cfm.

National Information Center

The National Information Center (NIC) is a central repository of overall data about banks and other institutions for which the Federal Reserve has a supervisory, regulatory, or research interest. The website provides access to detailed information about banking organizations. www.ffiec.gov/nicpubweb/nicweb/nichome.aspx

Office of the Comptroller of the Currency

The Office of the Comptroller of the Currency (OCC), a bureau of the U.S. Department of the Treasury, charters, regulates, and supervises all national banks and federally chartered branches and agencies of foreign banks that are not members of the Federal Reserve System. The OCC has the statutory authority to take action against Institution-Affiliated Parties (IAPs) including:

- Officers, directors, and employees,
- A bank's controlling stockholders, agents, and certain other individuals.

Information may be requested on formal enforcement actions against the above entities for violations of laws, rules or regulations, unsafe or unsound practices, violations of final orders, violations of conditions imposed in writing, and for IAP's breaches of fiduciary duty. Search **enforcement actions** at www.occ.treas.gov/enforcementactions/.

National Credit Union Administration

The National Credit Union Administration (NCUA) is the independent federal agency that charters and supervises federal credit unions. The web page www.ncua.gov offers plenty of research and data access.

Office of Thrift Supervision

The Office of Thrift Supervision regulates thrift associations. To find enforcement actions and orders, go to www.ots.treas.gov.

Business Entity Records

In the U.S., if a business is a public company (selling shares of ownership to the public, via the stock market) it must be registered with the Securities and Exchange Commission (SEC) or with a state securities regulator, or both. A registration discloses information on the management and financial condition of the entity, and describes how the proceeds of the offering will be used. The statement also is filed with the appropriate securities exchanges and state securities regulators.

In general, businesses that are not public companies are registered at the state level, usually with its Secretary of State. Fictitious names and trade names can be registered at either the local (county or city) or state level, depending on the state's specifications.

The types of business entities that have records available at the state level include:

- Corporations (including Foreign and Non-Pprofit)
- Partnerships (Limited, Limited Liability, and General)
- Limited Liability Companies
- Franchises
- Trade Names, Fictitious Names, Assumed Names

Searching Organization Records at State Agencies

As mentioned previously, businesses are organized and registered at the state level, usually with the Secretary of State. An initial search for a business entity's records usually starts there with a record index. An index "hit" will lead to a document file number or images of documents. Most states merge the indices of all their registered business entities (corporations, partnerships, LLCs, LLPs, etc.) and registered business names into one index. Usually this index is searchable online as well as at a public access terminal on-site.

> **Author TIP**❖ Corporations that are publicly traded or offer shares of ownership and are exempt from filing with the SEC must register with a state securities regulator. This is another source of public records information. See *Searching Publicly Owned (Traded) Companies* later in this chapter.

Information available from a registration file typically includes the date of registration, status, name and address of the registered agent and, sometimes, the names and addresses of officers, directors or principals. The registered agent is the person authorized to receive legal papers such as service of process. The registered agent can be a company attorney or a designated third party who specializes in representing business entities.

The registration file usually holds a myriad of other company documents. For example, a corporation registration file will typically include the articles of incorporation, annual reports, merger documents, name changes, and termination papers. Partnership and LLC filings may include similar documents with details such as how decisions are made, how profits are distributed, and names and addresses of all limited and general partners or owners. Finding this material is a good way to find the start of a paper trail and/or to find affiliates of the search subject.

All state agencies provide a business name check so that a new entity can make sure the name is not already used by an existing business entity. Doing a business name check is a good way to find where a business is located and leads to additional information about a business.

Checking to see if a company is currently incorporated is called a **status check.** If an entity's registration is current and there are no problems, a document known as a **Good Standing** may be purchased. If available, articles of incorporation or amendments to them as well as copies of annual reports also may provide useful information about an entity or business owner. Know that corporate records may not be a good source for a business address because most states allow corporations to use a registered agent as their address for service of process.

Web Access to Corporation & Business Entity Records

Every state provides a business search tool on the web to find information on state-registered business entities. Usually these look-ups are free and include all business entities types, including non-profits. You will find these URLs in the next chaper.

Before you begin searching these web pages, please consider the following useful tips.

Searching Tips

1. Most states have one central agency that oversees business entity records and filings, but there are several exceptions of note.

    Arizona – The Corporation Commission oversees corporation and LLC records. The Secretary of State oversees all partnerships including LPs and LLPs; as well as trademarks, servicemarks, and trade names.

    South Carolina – The Corporation Division oversees corporation, LP, LLP, LLC, trademark and servicemark records. The Department of Revenue oversees annual reports

    not have statutes requiring or permitting the registration or filing
    mes.

    ch is on-site or online, always familiarize yourself with the
    1 use. For example, knowing the answers to the questions below

)any name starts with the word *The*. Should you search for The
    .y or search by ABC Company, The ?

)any name starts with a number. Is the number alphabetized as a
    tings with numbers found at the front or the end of the index?

    y words that may indicate name changes, former entities, or related
    'or example, if a company is known as YESS Embroidery and
    1g, it would be worthwhile to search for YESS Embroidery, YESS
    1g, YESS Screenprinting and Embroidery, The YESS Company,
    :ertain if the use of an "&" in place of the word "And" will modify

- Know the capacity for error and forgiving of typos. If you can pull an alphabetical index list, make sure that screenprinting is not listed as screnprinting, or even screen printing, etc.

- Many large companies that do business in multiple states will incorporate in Delaware or Nevada.

3. Often, an investigation of a business entity entails public record searching on associated officers or company principals. Finding the names of these people within business records is certainly a good way to start. Searching for an individual's filings or other public records may lead to other associated business entities or assets. There are many other search avenues including occupational licensing databases, industry associations, and using the news media.

Searching Publicly Owned (Traded) Companies

There are two important facts to know about finding information about publicly traded companies:

1. Publicly traded companies operating in the U.S. are required by federal law to register with the Securities and Exchange Commission (SEC).

2. If a publicly traded company does not meet certain "thresholds," it submits filings with a state regulatory securities agency instead of the SEC.

Either the SEC or these state agencies monitor the registered companies for any irregularities or potential fraudulent behavior.

EDGAR and the SEC

Publicly traded companies must inform the public the complete truth about their businesses' financial data. EDGAR – the **E**lectronic **D**ata **G**athering **A**nalysis and **R**etrieval system – was established by the SEC as the means for companies to make required filings to the SEC by direct transmission. As of May 6, 1996, all non-exempt companies (see below), foreign and domestic, are required to file registration statements, periodic reports, and other forms electronically through EDGAR. Thus, EDGAR is an extensive repository of U.S. corporation information available online. Anyone can access and download this information for free.

Companies must file the following reports with the SEC:

- 10-K – an annual financial report that includes audited year-end financial statements.
- 10-Q – a quarterly, unaudited report.
- 8K – a report detailing significant or unscheduled corporate changes or events.
- Securities offering, trading registrations, and final prospectus.
- DEF-14 – a definitive proxy statement offering director names, their compensation and position.
- The list above is not all-inclusive. Other miscellaneous reports include items dealing with security holdings by institutions and insiders. Access to these documents provides a wealth of informative data about these companies.

EDGAR offers a guide on how to search publicly traded companies; go to www.sec.gov/investor/pubs/edgarguide.htm. The record searching site at EDGAR is www.sec.gov/edgar/searchedgar/webusers.htm.

Many private vendors offer access to EDGAR records along with some added features and searching flexibilities. Recommended sites include www.edgar-online.com, www.secinfo.com, www.edgarlive.com, and www.lexisnexis.com.

For more information about other SEC databases including enforcement actions, see the *Securities and Securities Dealers* section later in this chapter.

State Regulatory Agencies and Blue Sky Laws

Every state has securities laws—often referred to as **"Blue Sky Laws"** — designed to protect investors against fraud. These laws, which do vary from state to state, typically require companies making small offerings to register their offerings before they can be sold in a particular state.

Records of the filings by companies registering under Blue Sky Laws, as well as any records of legal actions, are held by designated state regulatory securities agencies. These records are open to the public and can be a great source of data when searching for assets, ownership records, or doing background investigations.

For links to all the state regulatory agencies visit the North American Securities Administrators Association web page at www.nasaa.org/QuickLinks/ContactYourRegulator.cfm. Another source is a vendor site at www.seclinks.com/id16.html.

Searching Franchise Records

Franchises are regulated by the Federal Trade Commission (FTC) and by state regulatory agencies. (See Blue Sky Laws above.) If the franchise involves a public offering, then records may also be in the SEC database.

A key public record document associated with a franchise is the Uniform Franchise Offering Circular (UFOC). Usually, this document may be obtained from a state agency or from a vendor, but not the FTC.

The International Franchise Association (IFA) is a great resource of basic information about member franchising and the members of this trade association. www.franchise.org.

Other Resources

There are many resources available to find general information about a publicly traded company. Every major stockbrokerage firm offers some free information on the web. Search engines Yahoo! and Google provide in-depth data on publicly traded companies. Also, check out The Motley Fool at www.fool.com and the *Investors Business Daily* at www.investors.com.

Business registrations, changes, and annual reports are available via each state's Secretary of State web page. The web links are presented in the next. Also, you can visit a site that offers free public record links such as - www.blackbookonline.info or www.brbpub.com.

Vendors provide company information. Several companies, including www.annualreports.com, tout access to annual reports. A Google search will uncover many more. Also, a number of commercial vendors with extensive proprietary databases are mentioned in Chapter 7.

Several sites of note with free or pay information, and other business related tools for searching public and private companies include–

- www.hoovers.com/free
- www.manta.com
- www.spoke.com

Searching Private Companies

Finding the ownership and records of private companies can be a difficult task. The entity may be registered at the state, but minimal public disclosure and required forms may be available. To the plus, there are a number of vendors who profile both public and private companies. Hoovers (www.hoovers.com) is perhaps the firm most widely known and used. Local Chambers of Commerce and Better Business Bureaus may be useful; to find their local offices go to www.worldchambers.com and www.bbb.org.

Other investigative resources are the business and credit report data that can be obtained from vendors such as Dun & Bradstreet (D&B), Experian, and SkyMinder.

Two websites to search ownership, and recommended by Cynthia Hetherington's *Business Background Investigations* book, are:

- https://solutions.dnb.com/wow/
- www.corporateaffiliations.com

One of the most powerful resources for searching industrial information, products and services is ThomasNet (www.thomasnet.com). From the home page you can also link to the Thomas Global Register then search worldwide industrial Information from more than 700,000 suppliers in 28 countries.

The rest of the *Business Entities* section is an excerpt taken from *Business Background Investigations*.

Searching Non-Profits and Foundations

Below are recommended organizations that are quite helpful for finding information on non-profits.

Capital Research Center (CRC) www.capitalresearch.org, established in 1984 to study non-profit organizations, provides a free database search of non-profits including associated activists and directors.

GuideStar is a non-profit entity that supplies detailed financial information about non-profits. It also offers free access to basic information on 1.5 million non-profits. Registration is required. Guidestar's fee-searching content includes searchable data from IRS Forms 990 and the IRS Business Master File, including comprehensive facts on employee compensation and grant activity. www.guidestar.org

The Foundation Center is a national organization that serves as an authoritative source of information on foundation and corporate giving. http://foundationcenter.org

The Taft Group publishes the *Corporate Giving Directory* that provides comprehensive profiles on America's major corporate foundations and corporate charitable-giving programs. Search The Taft Group indices by company name, location, recipient type, or officers and directors names. www.taftgroup.com

Enterprise Resources Database website provides fundraising tools with plenty of good information on how to find qualified prospects to donate money and help with fundraising. The site's search of qualifying potential donors is a quite useful as reference resource for finding personal and business assets and financial relationships. www.practitionerresources.org

More Searching Tips

Do not underestimate news stories, press releases, and a company's website. The "About Us" section may accurately offer company history and ownership information. However, it is best to verify any company-produced literature. Given that investigators always verify their leads, take a look to see what is on the website that offers clues. Visiting the website will give you a sense of what the company has to say.

When the question comes down to "who owns whom?" I recommend two valuable resources for finding the ultimate parent of a company—

1. The Directory of Corporate Affiliations   www.corporateaffiliations.com owned by LexisNexis.

    Per the web page... "Our database provides current, accurate corporate linkage information and company profiles on nearly 200,000 of the most prominent global public and private parent companies and their affiliates, subsidiaries and divisions—down to the seventh level of corporate linkage.

    "Not only does Corporate Affiliations publish corporate family trees, the database also contains over 700,000 corporate contacts, 110,000 board members, 150,000 brand names, and 140,000 competitors."

2. Who Owns Whom https://solutions.dnb.com/wow presented by Dun & Bradstreet.

    This international database covers the following industries since January 2006— "...manufacturing, retail trade , wholesale trade, agriculture, mining, construction, financial services, educational institutions, business services, professional services, also public, private and government-run companies."

Copyrights

In the U.S., the Copyright Act of 1976 and its major revisions enacted in 1978 and 1998, (www.loc.gov/copyright/title17/) govern the use of copyrighted works, including literary works; musical works including words; dramatic works including music; pantomimes and choreographic works; pictorial, graphic, and sculptural works; motion pictures and other audiovisual works; sound recordings; architectural work, but ***not*** titles, names, short phrases, and slogans; familiar symbols or designs; variations of typographic ornamentation, lettering, or coloring; mere listings of ingredients or contents; ideas; procedures; methods; systems; processes; concepts; principles; discoveries; devices; works of common property, nor containing no original authorship like calendars, rulers, and public lists or tables

Since 1978, copyright protection subsists from the time the work is created in fixed form and ordinarily given a term enduring for the author's life plus 70 years after. For works made for hire, and for anonymous and pseudonymous the duration of copyright is 95 years from publication or 120 years from creation, whichever is shorter. The copyright in the work of authorship immediately becomes the property of the author who created the work. Only the author or those deriving their rights through the author can rightfully claim copyright. In the case of works made for hire, the employer and not the employee is considered the author.

For further info see www.copyright.gov.

A free search the Library of Congress database is found at www.copyright.gov/rb.html

Search Canadian copyrights free at:

http://strategis.ic.gc.ca/app/cipo/copyrights/displaySearch.do?language=eng

A copyright availability search is one of many national and international IP, trademark and copyright services for a fee from Thomson Compumark at http://compumark.thomson.com/do/cache/off/pid/13.

Court Records

Court records are perhaps the most widely sought public record in the U.S., and researching court records can be very complicated because of the extensive diversity of the courts and their record keeping systems.

Courts exist at four levels: federal, state, county (or parish), and local municipalities. All four levels can be within the same county.

Each state has its own court system, created by statutes or constitution to enforce state civil and criminal laws. Sometimes the terms "state court" and "county court" can be a source of confusion because state trial courts are located at county courthouses. In this book we will refer to state courts as the courts belonging to the state court systems, and county courts as those administered by county authority. Local municipal courts can be managed by the local city, town or village government whose laws they enforce. Some lower level courts are called justice courts.

In Louisiana the word Parish is equivalent to what is a county in another state. Alaska is organized by Boroughs, and a few states have cities that are equivalent to counties. Rather than to continually restate these facts, we will assume the reader knows that if the text is speaking of state courts, these other courts are included.

Courts may have divisions – such as criminal and civil – that only hear specific case types. For instance there are courts that only hear appeals. Whether the case is filed in a state, municipal, or federal court, each case follows a similar process.

Note: Information on the individual federal, state, and local courts with online access are profiled in the next 2 chapters. More information about searching statewide criminal records is found in the Criminal Records section later in this chapter.

Before searching an online index of court records you should first familiarize yourself with basic court structures and procedures.

Understand How the State Courts Operate

An important first step in determining where a particular state court case is located is to know how the court system is structured in that particular state. The general structure of all state court systems has four tiers:

- Appellate courts
- Intermediate appellate courts
- General jurisdiction trial courts
- Limited jurisdiction trial courts

The two highest levels, appellate and intermediate appellate courts, only hear cases on appeal from the trial courts. "Opinions" of these appellate courts are of particular interest to attorneys seeking legal precedents for newer cases. However, opinions can be useful to record searchers because they summarize facts about the case that will not show on an index or docket.

General jurisdiction trial courts oversee a full range of civil and criminal litigation, usually handling felonies and higher dollar civil cases. The general jurisdiction court will often serve as the appellate court for cases appealed from limited jurisdiction courts and even from the local courts. Many court researchers refer to general jurisdiction courts as **upper courts**.

There are some courts — sometimes called special jurisdiction courts — that have general jurisdiction but are limited to one type of litigation. An example is the Court of Claims in New York which only processes liability cases against the state.

Limited jurisdiction trial courts come in several varieties. Many limited jurisdiction courts handle smaller civil claims (usually $10,000 or less), misdemeanors, and pretrial hearings for felonies. Localized municipal courts are also referred to as courts of limited jurisdiction. Many court researchers refer to limited jurisdiction courts as **lower courts**.

A number of states, Iowa for instance, have consolidated their general and limited court structure into one combined court system.

Watch for Divisions and Name Variations

Do not assume that the structure of the court system and the names used for courts in another state are anything like your own. Civil and criminal records may be handled by different divisions within a court or sometimes by completely different courts with different names. For example, in Tennessee the Chancery Court oversees civil cases but criminal cases are tried in Circuit Courts, except in districts with separate Criminal Courts as established by the state legislature. Also, in one state, the Circuit Court may be the highest trial court whereas in another it is a limited jurisdiction court. In New York, the Supreme Court is not very "supreme" and the downstate court structure varies from counties upstate.

About Municipal, Town, and Village Courts

These localized courts preside over misdemeanors, infractions, and city ordinance violations at the city, town or township level. Sometimes these courts may be known as justice courts. Notable is the state of New York where nearly 1,400 Town and Village Justice Courts handle misdemeanors, local ordinance violations, and traffic violations including DWIs.

In most states there is a distinction between state-supported courts and the local courts in terms of management and funding.

Types of Court Records Found Online

Below is a summary of the types of court cases and records found at the state or local level. Note that bankruptcies are not found on this list because bankruptcy cases are filed at the federal level.

- **Civil Actions** - For money damages usually greater than $5,000. Also, some states have designated dollar amount thresholds for upper or lower (limited) civil courts. Most civil litigation involves torts or contract.

- **Small Claims** - Actions for minor money damages, generally under $5,000, no juries involved.

- **Criminal Felonies** - Generally defined as crimes punishable by one year or more of jail time. There can be multiple levels or classes.

- **Criminal Misdemeanors** - Generally defined as minor infractions with a fine and less than one year of jail time. Misdemeanors also have multiple levels or classes.

- **Probate** - Estate matters, settling the estate of a deceased person, resolving claims and distributing the decedent's property.

- **Eviction Actions** - Landlord/tenant actions, can also known as an unlawful detainer, forcible detainer, summary possession, or repossession.

- **Domestic Relations** – Sometimes known as Family Law, with authority over family disputes, divorces, dissolutions, child support or custody cases.

- **Juvenile** – Authority over cases involving individuals under a specified age, usually 18 years but sometimes 21.

- **Traffic** – May also have authority over municipal ordinances.

- **Specialty Courts** – Water, equity in fiduciary questions, tort, contracts, tax, etc.

How Courts Maintain Records

Case Numbering

When a case is filed, a case number is assigned. Use of a case number is the primary indexing method in every court. Therefore, to search specific case records, you will need to know – or find – the applicable case number.

Be aware that case numbering procedures are not necessarily consistent throughout a state court system. One district may assign numbers by district while another may assign numbers by location (division) within the district, or by judge. Remember: case numbers appearing in legal text citations may not be adequate for searching unless they appear in the proper form for the particular court in which you are searching.

The Docket Sheet

Information from cover sheets and from documents filed as a case goes forward is recorded on the docket sheet. Thus the docket sheet is a running summary of a case history from initial filing to its current status. While docket sheets differ somewhat in format from court to court, the basic information contained on a docket sheet is consistent. All docket sheets contain:

- Name of court, including location (division) and the judge assigned;

- Case number and case name;

- Names of all plaintiffs and defendants/debtors;

- Names and addresses of attorneys for the plaintiff or debtor;

- Nature and cause (e.g., statute) of action.

File Storage and Computerization

Most courts enter the docket data into a computer system. Within a state or judicial district, the courts may be linked together via a single computer system.

But docket sheets from cases closed before the advent of computerization may not be in the computer system. And in some locations all docket information is non-computerized. Media formats include microfilm, microfiche, index cards, and paper that may even be hand-written.

As mentioned, case document images are not generally available online because courts are still experimenting and developing electronic filing and imaging. Generally, copies of case documents are only on-site.

Dispositions, Expungments, and Sealed Records

When a case is decided, a decision or disposition is rendered. (See the previous chapter for information about the importance of the disposition in a criminal case.) The disposition is entered onto the docket or index.

There are some cases where decisions were rendered, but the results are not recorded or the case file number is removed from the index. In certain situations, a judge can order the case file sealed or removed – expunged – from the public repository. Examples include if a defendant enters a diversion program (drug or family counseling), or a defendant makes restitution as part of a plea bargain; these cases may not be searchable. The only way to gain direct access to these types of case filings is through a subpoena. However, savvy researchers and investigators will sometimes search news media sources if need be.

Tips on Searching Online for Court Records

1. Online Searching is Generally Limited to Docket Sheets

Most courts that offer online access limit the search to the docket sheet data. But checking a courthouse's computer online docket index is the quickest way to find if case records exist online. Just be sure to check all name variations and spelling variations.

2. Learn the Index & Record Systems

Most civil courts index records by both plaintiffs and defendants, but some only index by the defendant name. A plaintiff search is useful, for example, to determine if someone is especially litigious.

3. Understand the Search Requirements

There is a strong tendency for courts to overstate their search requirements. For civil cases, the usual reasonable requirement is a defendant (or plaintiff) name – full name if it is a common name

– and the time frame to search – e.g., 1993-2002. For criminal cases, the court may require more identification, such as date of birth (DOB), to ascertain the correct individual.

4. Be Aware of Restricted Records

Courts have types of case records, such as juvenile and adoptions, which are not released without a court order. The presiding judge often makes a determination of whether a particular record type is available to the public. Some criminal court records include the arresting officer's report. In some locations this information is regarded as public record, while in other locations the police report may be sealed.

5. Watch for Multiple Courts as Same Location

When the general jurisdiction and limited jurisdiction courts are in the same building and use the same support staff, chances are the record databases are combined as well. But that does not necessarily mean you will receive a search of both databases and pay for one search unless you ask for it. Do not assume.

Look for the situation when a county wide database exists for outlying limited jurisdictional courts. Make sure you ask if you are receiving a search of all limited jurisdiction courts in the county or just the court you are speaking to.

The same holds true when using public access computer terminals. Ask what courts the index covers. In some states you can only view the case at the court, but other courts provide access to a statewide system!

6. Watch for Overlapping Jurisdictions

In some states, the general jurisdiction court and the limited jurisdiction court have overlapping dollar amounts for civil cases. That means a case could be filed in either court. Check both courts; never assume.

7. Using the State Court Administrator's Office

The state court administrator oversees the state court system and the web page is a good place to find opinions from supreme courts and appeals courts.

In some states, the state court administration office oversees a statewide online access system to court records. Some of these systems are commercial fee-based. Other systems offer free access, but are usually very limited by comparison. The *Summaries of State Court Systems* in the next chapter gives detailed information about how to access to these centralized (sometimes) index of trial court records.

Court Records - Native Americans

National Tribal Justice Resource Center

Per their web page, The National Tribal Justice Resource Center is "…the largest and most comprehensive site dedicated to tribal justice systems, personnel and tribal law. The Resource Center is the central national clearinghouse of information for Native American and Alaska Native tribal courts." The Resources tab on the web page gives access to Tribal Court Codes & Constitutions, Tribal Court Opinions from over 18 tribes, and a Tribal Court Directory to locate contact information for tribes and locate tribal courts, on the web.

The Center is located at 4410 Arapahoe Ave, #135, Boulder, CO 80303, 303-245-0786. www.tribalresourcecenter.org/

Tribal Court Clearinghouse

Sponsored by the Tribal Institute, the Tribal Court Clearinghouse is a comprehensive website established in June 1997 to serve as a resource for American Indian and Alaska Native Nations, American Indian and Alaska Native people, tribal justice systems, victim services providers, tribal service providers, and others involved in the improvement of justice in Indian country. *The General Guide to Criminal Jurisdiction in Indian Country* is an excellent and in-depth source; they have offices in Anchorage AK, West Hollywood CA, and St. Paul MN. www.tribal-institute.org/index.htm

Native Organizations and Federal Agencies

The Tribal Institute does a great job of listing and describing the many federal government agencies and native organizations involved with Native Americans. Go to http://tribal-institute.org/lists/fed_agen.htm.

Criminal Records

Criminal records are widely used in the U.S. Nearly everyone who has applied or been hired for a job, or has applied or been issued an accredited license related to an occupation, has probably been the subject of a criminal record search.

The information trail of a criminal record starts with a criminal case tried at one the 10,000+ county, town, and municipal courts, state trial courts, or federal courts. The county, local, and state courts usually forward record information to a centralized state repository controlled by a state law enforcement agency. The centralized state repositories and the federal courts forward records to the FBI. Also, a number of state court administrations maintain unified court systems that collect case record data, usually statewide.

Criminal records also exist in other repositories. Other criminal-related record sources are incarceration (prison) systems, sexual predator lists, federal government sanction and watch lists, and vendor databases. Each of these categories are described elsewhere in this book. See the section on *Court Records* and the state-by-state profiles in the next chapter for information on accessing criminal records from the courts.

This section examines searching criminal records at state repositories, at the state unified court sites, and at the so-called national databases offered by vendors.

Searching State Criminal Record Repositories

As mentioned, all states have a central repository of criminal records of those individuals who have been subject to that state's criminal justice system. The database is managed by a law enforcement agency, usually known as the State Police or Department of Public Safety. The information at the state repository is submitted by state, county, parish, and municipal courts as well as from local law enforcement. Information forwarded to the state includes notations of arrests and charges, sometimes the disposition, and a set of fingerprints.

There are two factors that must be taken into account when searching criminal records at the state law enforcement repositories:

- Access Restrictions
- Accuracy of Record Content

Restrictions to Access Factor

You do go to the state police headquarters URL to view the record index. A key point is once that in more than half the states when record from the court reaches the law enforcement agency that record is no longer public. Most law enforcement agencies impose a set of requirements for access and often a set of fingerprints must be submitted to do a record search. In fact, only 23 states release criminal records (name search) to the general public without consent of the subject. 18 states require a signed release from the subject and 9 states require submission of fingerprints

The Accuracy of the Records

There are four reasons why the completeness, consistency, and accuracy of state criminal record repositories are open to accuracy concerns—

- Level of Automation
- Level of Quality Control
- Timeliness of Receiving Arrest and Disposition Data
- Timeliness of Entering Arrest and Disposition Data into the Repository

So how widespread is the disposition problem? Consider these examples[1]—

- Only 30 states generate lists of arrests with no dispositions in order to give notice to criminal justice agencies and courts about obtaining missing dispositions.

- 12 states report they each have from 7,000 to 148,500 final court dispositions that cannot be linked to an arrest record.

- Only 21 states report they receive final felony trial court dispositions for 70% or more arrests within last five5 years.

Please don't misunderstand the message here – there are certainly good reasons for performing a search of a state repository record database. A statewide search covers a wider geographic range than a county search. And a state search is certainly less expensive than a separate search of each county. Many states do have strong database systems. But for proper due diligence for performing a criminal record search, using a state search AND a county search of criminal records AND even a search from a database vendor should be considered. This is extremely critical for employers making hiring decisions in states with legislative limitations on using criminal records without dispositions or using misdemeanor records.

---

[1] The statistics here are taken from BRB Publication's Public Record Research System and from the U.S. Department of Justice, Bureau of Justice Statistic's Survey of State Criminal History Information Systems, 2003 (released in 2006) found at www.ojp.usdoj.gov/bjs/abstract/sschis03.htm.

Searching the State Court Administrator's Records

In some states there is an alternative to searching the central state repository. Every state has a court administration that oversees the state's trial and appellate court system. In a surprising number of states – 28 – some or all of the state trial courts at the county (or parish) forward court records to the administrative office of the courts, often referred to as the AOC. The AOC then offers a searchable database, usually online, to the public. These sites are reviewed in the next chapter.

A Valuable Resource

A search from one of these court systems can be a particularly useful tool in those states that do not permit a state repository search – such as New York, North Carolina, or Utah.

Another value to using these record systems is there may be a higher likelihood that the disposition records are forwarded in a timely manner. Thus, the database may be very current.

State-by-State Variations

But there are many nuances to these searches. The value of an AOC court search varies by state. All counties may not be included. There may be no uniformity with respect to the length of time criminal activity is archived. For example, one county may have cases dating back for seven years, while another county may have only two years of history. The use or lack of identifiers as part of the search varies widely from state-to-state, but searches do not involve fingerprints.

When an AOC system is available, you need to know (1) the court structure in that state, (2) which particular courts are included in their online system, and (3) what types of cases are included.

For in-depth details about each state's court system including the AOC databases, see the Sourcebook to Public Record Information.

Searching Vendor Criminal Record Databases

The following article is copyrighted text appearing in Chapter 12 of *The Safe Hiring Manual*, written by Lester R. Rosen and published by Facts On Demand Press. Rosen has done an excellent job explaining how these databases are created and how they can be used. We sincerely thank him for giving his permission to reprint his text in this book.

Take Caution When Using Private Databases

By Lester R. Rosen

A new tool being touted to employers is a "national database search" of criminal records. A number of vendors advertise they have, or have access to, a "national database of criminal record information." These services typically talk about having over 160 million records from 38 or more states. When sexual offender data is added, these services claim even more states and records are covered. Unfortunately, this form of advertising can create an impression in an employer's mind that they are getting the real thing — access to the nation's criminal records. Nothing could be further from the truth.

These databases are compiled from a number of various state repositories, correctional, and county sources. There are a number of reasons why this database information may not be accurate or complete. It is critical to understand that these multi-state database searches represent a research tool only, and under no circumstances are they a substitute for a hands-on search at the county level.

There are values to using these databases, but there are also limitations.

Database Values

These database searches are of value because they cover a much larger geographical area than traditional county-level searches. By casting a much wider net, a researcher may pick up information that might be missed. The firms that sell database information can show test names of subjects that were "cleared" by a traditional county search, but criminal records were found in other counties through their searchable databases. In fact, it could be argued that failure to utilize such a database demonstrates a failure to exercise due diligence given the widespread coverage and low price.

Overall, the best use of these databases is as a secondary or supplemental research tool, or "lead generator" which tells a researcher where else to look.

Database Limitations

The compiled data typically comes from a mix of state repositories, correctional institutions, courts and any number of other counties agencies. The limitations of searching a private database are the inherent issues about completeness, name variations, timeliness, and legal compliance.

Completeness Issues

The various databases that vendors collect may not be the equivalent of a true all-encompassing multi-state database. First, the databases may not contain complete records from all jurisdictions — not all state court record systems contain updated records from all counties. Second, for reporting purposes, the records that are actually reported may be incomplete or lack sufficient detail about the offense or the subject. Third, some databases contain only felonies or contain only offenses where a state corrections unit is involved. Fourth, the database may not carry subsequent information or other matter that could render the results not reportable, or result in a state law violation concerning criminal records use.

The result is a crazy quilt patchwork of data from various sources, and lack of reliability. These databases can be more accurately described as "multi-jurisdictional databases."

Name and Date of Birth Issues

An electronic search of a vendor's database may not be able to recognize variations in a subject name, which a person may potentially notice if manually looking at the index. The applicant may have been arrested under a different first name or some variation of first and middle name. A female applicant may have a record under a previous name. Some database vendors have attempted to resolve this problem with a wild card first name search (i.e. instead of Robert, use Rob* so that any variations of ROB will come up). However, there are still too many different first and middle name variations. There is also the chance of name confusion for names where a combination of mother and father's name is used. In addition, some vendors require the use of date of birth in order to prevent too many records from being returned. Also, if an applicant uses a different date of birth it can cause errors.

Also, there are some states where a date of birth is not in the court records. Since databases match records by date of birth, search when no DOB exists is of little value since no "hits" will be reported. In those situations, it is necessary to run a search in just the state in question and then individually review each name match. That can be tedious, especially if a common name is being searched.2

Timeliness Issues

Records in a vendor's database may be stale to some extent. These records are normally updated monthly, at best. Even after a vendor receives new data, there can be lag time before the new data is downloaded into the vendor database. Generally the most current offenses are the ones less likely to come up in a database search.

Legal Compliance Issues

When there is a "hit" an employer must be concerned about legal compliance. If an employer uses a commercial database via the Internet, the employer must have an understanding of the proper use of criminal records in that state. If the employer acts on face value results without any additional due diligence research, potentially the applicant could sue the employer if the record was not about them.

If a screening firm locates a criminal hit, then the screening firm has an obligation under the FCRA Section 613 (a)(2) to send researchers to the court to pull the actual court records. This section requires that a background-screening firm must...maintain strict procedures designed to insure that whenever public record information, which is likely to have an adverse effect on a consumer's ability to obtain employment, is reported, it is complete and up-to-date. For purposes of this paragraph, items of public record relating to arrests, indictments, convictions, suits, tax liens, and outstanding judgments shall be considered up-to-date if the current public record status of the item at the time of the report is reported.

---

2 Technically, the issue comes down to how broad or how narrow the database provider sets the search parameters. If a database sets the search parameters on a narrow basis, so it only locates records based upon exact date of birth and last name, then the number of records located not related to the applicant would be reduced. In other words, there will be less "false positives." However, it can also lead to record being missed, either because of name variations or because some states do not provide date of birth in the records. That can lead to "false negatives." Conversely, if the parameters are set broadly to avoid missing relevant records, then there is a greater likelihood of finding criminal records relating to the applicant, but at the same time, there are likely to be a number of records that do not belong to the applicant. That can happen for example in a state where no date of birth is provide, and the database is run on a "name match only basis. The bottom-line: with use of databases, employers need to understand there is the possibility of both "false negatives" and "false positives," depending upon how the particular background firm runs the databases.

...FCRA section 613(a)(1) provides an alternative procedure. Instead of going to the courthouse, a CRA can notify the consumer that public record information is being reported by the consumer reporting, and give name and address of the requester. However, some states arguably do not permit this alternative procedure. This is a potential compliance issue for employers who operate in states that do not allow the "notification" procedure to be used instead of the "strict procedure" method of double-checking at the courthouse.

The best approach for an employer is to insist that a CRA always confirm the details of a database search by going to the courthouse to review the actual records.[3] [Additional information about the FCRA and databases is covered in Chapters 6 and 10 in *The Safe Hiring Manual*, not this book.]

Conclusion About Private Databases—

Just because a person's name appears in one of these databases it does not mean the subject is a criminal. On the other hand, if a person's name does not appear, this likewise should not be taken as conclusive the person is not a criminal. In other words, these databases can result in "false negatives" or "false positives;" and an over-reliance can cause one to develop a false sense of security.

Criminal record vendors and background firms should make clear, and employers need to understand, the exact nature and limitations of any database they access. These private database searches are ancillary and can be very useful, but proceed with caution. In other words, it cannot be assumed that a search of a proprietary criminal database by itself will show if a person is or is not a criminal, but these databases are outstanding secondary or supplemental tools with which to do a much wider search.

Environment

Many of the environmental public records held by the government rest at two locations: the **Environmental Protection Agency** and the **National Library of Medicine**. The content to follow looks at each agency and public records associated with health hazards. At the end of this section, be sure to check out **Scorecard**, a pollution information site.

Environmental Protection Agency (EPA)

The EPA's Environmental Facts Warehouse is a good starting place to search for environmental information. Go to www.epa.gov/enviro. Below are descriptions of some of the more useful search features.

EnviroMapper combines interactive maps and aerial photography to display various types of environmental information, including air releases, drinking water, toxic releases, hazardous wastes, water discharge permits, and Superfund sites. The site creates maps at the national, state, and county levels that can be linked to environmental text reports. Go to www.epa.gov/enviro/emef/.

---

[3] For a detailed discussion about the legal uses of a database, see an article co-written by Lester R. Rosen and national FCRA expert Carl Ernst titled *"National" Criminal History Databases* at www.brbpub.com/articles/CriminalHistoryDB.pdf

The EPA's Office of Enforcement and Compliance Assurance (OECA) works with EPA regional offices, state governments, tribal governments and other federal agencies on compliance with the nation's environmental laws. See www.epa.gov/compliance/index.html.

OECA offers online access to its database called Enforcement & Compliance History Online (ECHO). Search the database for inspection, violation, enforcement action, and penalty information about compliance and enforcement information on approximately 800,000 regulated facilities. ECHO can be found at www.epa-echo.gov/echo.

For a web search of cases and settlements go to http://cfpub.epa.gov/compliance/cases, additional information can be found at www.epa.gov/compliance/civil/index.html.

Federal law requires facilities in certain industries, which manufacture, process, or use significant amounts of toxic chemicals, to report annually on their releases of these chemicals to the EPA Toxics Release Inventory Program. Superfund sites are those throughout the United States and its territories which contain substances that are either designated as hazardous under the Comprehensive Environmental Response, Compensation and Liability Act (CERCLA), or identified as such under other laws. For information about the Superfund sites on the National Priorities List, email superfund.docket@epa.gov. Superfund sites are at http://cfpub.epa.gov/supercpad/cursites/srchsites.cfm. Search EPA Records of Decisions (ROD) at www.epa.gov/superfund/sites/rods.

National Library of Medicine (NLM)

Household Products Database

This resource indicates the chemical ingredients found in household products and who manufactures specific brands. The database contains information on over 7,000 products. Email tehip@teh.nlm.nih.gov or visit http://householdproducts.nlm.nih.gov.

TOXMAP

TOXMAP (http://toxmap.nlm.nih.gov) is a Geographic Information System (GIS) that uses maps of the U.S. to help users visually explore data from the EPA's Toxics Release Inventory (TRI) (www.epa.gov/tri/) and Superfund Programs. Maps can also show locations of Superfund sites on the National Priority List (NPL) at www.epa.gov/superfund/sites/npl, listing all chemical contaminants present at these sites. Users can search the system by chemical name, chemical name fragment, and/or location (such as city, state, or ZIP code). TOXMAP also overlays map data such as U.S. Census population information, income figures from the Bureau of Economic Analysis, and health data from the National Cancer Institute (www.cancer.gov) and the National Center for Health Statistics (www.cdc.gov/nchs).

TOXNET

TOXNET, the Toxicology Data Network, provides multiple databases on toxicology, hazardous chemicals, environmental health, and toxic releases. The free access at http://toxnet.nlm.nih.gov provides easy searching to a great many databases.

Tox Town

This interactive web page is a great source of non-technical descriptions of chemicals, assorted links to selected, authoritative chemical information, and lists everyday locations where one might find toxic chemicals. http://toxtown.nlm.nih.gov/

Scorecard

Scorecard is a very popular web resource for information about pollution problems and toxic chemicals. Per their web page, "Find out about the pollution problems in your community and learn who is responsible. See which geographic areas and companies have the worst pollution records. Visit www.scorecard.org.

Federal Agency Sanctions & Watch Lists

This section examines public record databases of individuals and companies that have sanctions, violations, enforcement actions, or warnings initiated against them by one of these federal government departments—

- Commerce Department
- Food & Drug Administration
- GSA – Government Services
- Human Health Care Services Department
- Justice Department
- Labor Department
- Occupational Safety & Health Administration
- State Department
- Treasury Department

Note: To find enforcement actions taken by the Federal Reserve, see the *Banks & Financial Institutions* Section. To find enforcement action involving stocks and securities see the *Securities and Securities Dealers* Section.

Commerce Department

The Bureau of Industry and Security (BIS), part of the U.S. Department of Commerce, provides the three lists described below that are relevant to import/export transactions. www.bis.doc.gov

Denied Persons List

The purpose of the Denied Persons List is to prevent the illegal export of dual-use items before they occur and to investigate and assist in the prosecution of violators of the Export Administration Regulations. www.bis.doc.gov/dpl/default.shtm

Unverified List

This is a list of parties whom BIS has been unable to verify in some manner in prior transactions. The Unverified List includes names and countries of foreign persons who in the past were parties to a transaction with respect to which BIS could not conduct a pre-license check ("PLC") or a post-shipment verification ("PSV") for reasons outside of the U.S. Government's control. www.bis.doc.gov/enforcement/unverifiedlist/unverified_parties.html

Entity List

The Entity List, available in PDF or ASCII text format, is a list of parties whose presence in a transaction can trigger a license requirement under the Export Administration Regulations. The original purpose of this list was to inform the public of entities whose activities imposed a risk of diverting exported and re-exported items into programs related to weapons of mass destruction. Now the list includes those with any license requirements imposed on the transaction by other provisions of the Export Administration Regulations. The list specifies the license requirements that apply to each listed party. www.bis.doc.gov/entities/default.htm

FDA – Food & Drug Administration

FDA regulates scientific studies that are designed to develop evidence to support the safety and effectiveness of investigational drugs (human and animal), biological products, and medical devices. Physicians and other qualified experts ("clinical investigators") who conduct these studies are required to comply with applicable statutes and regulations intended to ensure the integrity of clinical data on which product approvals are based and, for investigations involving human subjects, to help protect the rights, safety, and welfare of these subjects.

FDA Enforcement Report Index – Recalls, Market Withdrawals, and Safety Alerts

The FDA Enforcement Report, published weekly, contains information on actions taken in connection with agency regulatory activities. Activities include Recall and Field Correction, Injunctions, Seizures, Indictments, Prosecutions, and Dispositions. A record of all recalls (Class I, II, and III), including pre-1995, can be found at www.fda.gov/opacom/Enforce.html.

Visit www.fda.gov/opacom/7alerts.html for the most significant product actions of the last 60 days, based on the extent of distribution and the degree of health risk. These recalls on the list are mainly Class I, the most serious category.

Debarrment List

The FDA maintains a list of individuals and entities that are prohibited from introducing any type of food, drug, cosmetics or associated devices into interstate commerce. The list is found at www.fda.gov/ora/compliance_ref/debar/

Disqualified or Totally Restricted Clinical Investigator List

A disqualified or totally restricted clinical investigator is not eligible to receive investigational drugs, biologics, or devices. www.fda.gov/ora/compliance_ref/bimo/disqlist.htm

Partially Restricted Clinical Investigator List

All clinical investigators who have agreed to certain restrictions with respect to their conduct of clinical investigations are listed at www.fda.gov/ora/compliance_ref/bimo/restlist.htm

Search for all clinical investigators who previously agreed to certain restrictions, which have now been removed, at www.fda.gov/ora/compliance_ref/bimo/rest_removed.htm

GSA – Government Services

Excluded Party List

The Excluded Parties List System (EPLS) contains information on individuals and firms excluded by various Federal government agencies from receiving federal contracts or federally approved subcontracts and from certain types of federal financial and non-financial assistance and benefits. Note that individual agencies are responsible for their data. www.epls.gov

Human Health Services, Department of

Excluded Individuals/Entities (LEIE)

The LEIE maintained by the Office of Inspector General (OIG) for the Department of Human Health Services is a list of currently excluded parties for convictions for program-related fraud and patient abuse, licensing board actions, and default on Health Education Assistance Loans. The searchable database is found at http://exclusions.oig.hhs.gov/. The downloadable database is at http://oig.hhs.gov/fraud/exclusions/database.html.

Justice Department

There are a number of Divisions within the Justice Department that maintain news articles, stories, records lists, and most wanted lists that can be very useful for research and investigation purposes.

Bureau of Alcohol, Tobacco, Firearms and Explosives

Below are two online resources:

- Federal Firearms License Validator - https://www.atfonline.gov/fflezcheck
- Most Wanted List - www.atf.gov/wanted/index.htm

Bureau of Investigation (FBI)

The FBI's Most Wanted Site at www.fbi.gov/wanted.htm contains numerous lists to search, including kidnappings, missing persons, unknown bank robbers, and others. Department FOIA instructions are found at http://foia.fbi.gov/foia_instruc.htm. You can request online.

Drug Enforcement Administration (DEA)

Search DEA fugitives at www.usdoj.gov/dea/fugitives/fuglist.htm by Field Division, from a map showing by the states within each division. Major international fugitives and captured fugitives also found here.

Labor Department

Labor and Labor Unions

The Office of Labor-Management Standards (OLMS) in the U.S. Department of Labor is the Federal agency responsible for administering and enforcing most provisions of the Labor-Management Reporting and Disclosure Act of 1959, as amended (LMRDA). OLMS does not have jurisdiction over unions representing solely state, county, or municipal employees. OLMS responsibilities include:

- Public Disclosure of Reports

- Compliance Audits
- Investigations
- Education and Compliance Assistance

The OLMS Internet Public Disclosure Room web page enables users to view and print reports filed by unions, union officers and employees, employers, and labor relations consultants.

Visit www.dol.gov/esa/regs/compliance/olms/rrlo/lmrda.htm

Occupational Safety & Health Administration (OSHA)

The purpose of the Occupational Safety & Health Administration (OSHA) is to insure employee safety and health in the U.S. by setting and enforcing standards in the workplace. OSHA partners with the states for inspections and enforcements, along with education programs, technical assistance and consultation programs.

There are a number of searchable databases at OSHA (www.osha.gov). For example you can search by establishment name for information on over 3 million inspections conducted since 1972. Click on Establishment Search. The default option searches inspections for closed cases; however, a separate search may be made of open cases. Searches must be performed using no longer than a five-year date range. You can also search by the North American Industry Classification Code (NAIC) or the Standard Industrial Classification Code (SIC).

Another useful search is of the Accident Investigation database. This database contains abstracts dating back to 1984 and injury data dating back to 1972. Another available search is the OSHADocket. This is a rulemaking master file that includes the materials that are collected and reviewed in reaching decisions concerning the change or creation of an OSHA regulation.

State Department

ITAR Debarred List

A list compiled by the State Department of parties who are barred the International Traffic in Arms Regulations (ITAR) (22 CFR §127.7) from participating directly or indirectly in the export of defense articles, including technical data or in the furnishing of defense services for which a license or approval is required, is found at www.pmddtc.state.gov/debar059.htm

Nonproliferation Sanctions Lists

The State Department maintains lists of parties that have been sanctioned under various statutes and legal authority. **Seven separate lists** are found at www.state.gov/t/isn/c15231.htm

Treasury Department

Specifically Designated Nationals (SDN) List

The U.S. Department of the Treasury, Office of Foreign Assets Control (OFAC) publishes a list of individuals and companies owned or controlled by, or acting for or on behalf of, targeted foreign countries, terrorists, international narcotics traffickers, and those engaged in activities related to the proliferation of weapons of mass destruction. www.treas.gov/offices/enforcement/ofac/sdn/

Federal Contractor & Vendor Eligibility

An avenue of public record data sometimes overlooked is the licensing of individual and businesses to do business for the U.S. government.

Business Partner Network

The Business Partner Network is designed to be the single source for vendor data for the Federal Government. The web page at www.bpn.gov gives access to the CCR and OCRA (see below), as well as the Excluded Parties Listing System.

Central Contractor Registration (CCR)

The Central Contractor Registration (CCR) registers all companies and individuals that sell services and products to, or apply for assistance from, the federal government. The 450,000+ registrants at CRR are searchable online using a DUNS number, company name, or other criteria at https://www.bpn.gov/CCRSearch/Search.aspx.

Online Representations and Certifications Application (ORCA)

The ORCA system allows contractors to enter company data regarding certification needed on federal contracts. This is a publicly accessible database, but it does require the subject's DUNS number. Go to https://orca.bpn.gov.

Small Business Administration (SBA)

The SBA maintains a database of Dynamic Small Business (DSBS) that, while primarily self-certified, does indicate certifications relating to 8(a) Business Development, HUBZone or Small Disadvantaged Business status. Visit http://dsbs.sba.gov/dsbs/search/dsp_dsbs.cfm

To find woman-owned, veteran-owned, and service disabled veteran-owned specific profiles in this same SBA database, go to the Quick Market Search screen at http://dsbs.sba.gov/dsbs/search/dsp_quicksearch.cfm

Genealogy Resources

Perhaps the most well-known resource of genealogical information is the Church of Jesus Christ of Latter-day Saints (Mormon Church). The Church has been actively gathering and preserving genealogical records worldwide for over 100 years. One may access genealogy records on-site at churches across the nation and on foreign soil. The genealogy site is www.familysearch.org.

There are several other, huge genealogical sites that have collected public record information along with historical documents from various sources. Below are a few recommended sites and starting points for genealogy record searching, presented in alphabetical order.

- Ancestry Hunt www.ancestryhunt.com
- Cyndi's List www.cyndislist.com.

- Generations Network with three sites - www.ancestry.com, www.genealogy.com and www.myfamily.com.

- The National Genealogical Society in Arlington, VA www.ngsgenealogy.org.

- Rootsweb www.roostweb.com (Note: A good place to start is http://searches.rootsweb.com.)

GIS and Mapping

GIS is the acronym used for Geographic Information System. Commonly associated with maps, GIS data can be displayed in a variety of product types with many associated uses. GIS can link and layer data attributes to specific criteria, such as addresses to people or parcels to building.

GIS property details are then used by the assessing offices at the county or municipality level for taxation and real estate associated matters. Although they may appear intimidating, GIS mapping websites maintained by these government offices usually have a search mechanism for finding parcels, addresses, and sometimes, but not always, property owner names. A GIS website's search feature is not always displayed prominently, but many assessor sites have them.

For more information about GIS visit www.gis.com.

To find GIS searching sites, visit one of the many free public record link sites listed in the next chapter. A private site that does an excellent job of maintaining links is www.netronline.com.

Incarceration Records

Incarceration records are criminal-related records of inmates housed or formerly housed at jails and prisons. Since jails are usually found at the local level and hold a variety of inmates, *jail records* are often a mix of persons with misdemeanor sentences and persons being held until transport to a state of federal facility. Jails records are probably the least useful to professional record searchers. *Prisons records* refer to inmates held in state prisons and federal prisons. The details found in prison records vary widely by location and content.

A website devoted to information about prisons and corrections facilities is the Corrections Connection (www.corrections.com).

The Federal Bureau of Prisons offers an Inmate Locator and a Facility Locator at www.bop.gov. The Inmate Locator contains records on inmates incarcerated or released from 1982 to present.

State Prison Systems

Each state has a government agency that manages the corrections departments and prisons. These state agencies consider the inmate records to be public and will process information requests. Many states offer web pages with inmate locators or look-ups. The level of information available varies widely from state to state. All the searchable state sites are listed in the next chapter.

The web pages of several private companies are great resources to find links and searchable inmate locators to state prison systems. Check www.theinmatelocator.com and www.inmatesplus.com. Also most of the free public record links lists sites (such as www.searchsystems.net and www.brbpub.com) offer searching links.

VINElink is the online version of VINE (Victim Information and Notification Everyday), the National Victim Notification Network. This service allows crime victims to obtain timely and reliable information about criminal cases and the custody status of offenders 24 hours a day. Victims and other concerned citizens can also register to be notified by phone, email or TTY device when an offender's custody status changes. VINE provides a number of inmate locator links throughout the U.S. at https://www.vinelink.com/vinelink/initMap.do.

IRS Records

There are only a handful of records that may be accessed from the IRS, not all are public.

The Income Verification Express Service (IVES) program is used by mortgage lenders and others within the financial community to confirm the income of a borrower during the processing of a loan application. One may obtain a full return or just the income informational info (the W-2). The written consent of the taxpayer is required. Visit www.irs.gov/individuals/article/0,,id=161649,00.html.

A private company provides a similar service for employers. See TALX's W-2 Express at www.w2express.com.

Seized Property

Check what the IRS is auctioning at www.ustreas.gov/auctions/irs/.

Charitable Organizations

A Cumulative List of Organizations is a list of organizations eligible to receive tax-deductible charitable contributions. The IRS offers an online search at www.irs.gov/charities/article/0,,id=96136,00.html. The web page also has separate searching for revocations, deletions, and suspensions from the Cumulative List.

Liens

(See the section *Recorded Documents and Liens.*)

Media Resources

The media is an often overlooked resource for finding clues to public records and public record trails. Researching 24-hour news outlets, press releases, company announcements, trade journals and magazines is a good way to find many leads. Although many resources are online, a good starting point is often the local library. Below are some research sources and tips that should prove helpful.

News Journalism

Links to thousands of newspapers, radio and TV stations, magazines, and foreign outlets are found at two excellent web pages: www.editorandpublisher.com and www.newslink.org.

A couple of web pages specializing in magazine stories are http.findarticles.com and www.highbeam.com.

Investigative Reporters & Editors, Inc. is without a doubt the leading trade association for journalists. This organization promotes high standards while providing educational services to reporters, editors and others interested in investigative journalism. Visit the IRE web page at www.ire.org.

CNN provides a web page to obtain transcripts of broadcasts. Visit http://transcripts.cnn.com/TRANSCRIPTS/.

Back Issues in Print

The United States Book Exchange is a non-profit organization which supplies back issues of scholarly periodicals, trade journals, popular magazines and other serials to libraries worldwide. Visit them at www.usbe.com.

A good resource for a list of stores selling back issues of a magazine is presented at www.trussel.com/books/magdeal.htm.

Other Web Resources

Fee-Based Resources

One of the advantages of the fee-based resources is the length of time stories are kept available. Depending on the service, some vendors maintain comprehensive data dating back 40 years or more. The following entities are highly recommended by Cynthia Hetherington:

- Factiva (www.factiva.com)
- LexisNexis (www.nexis.com/research)
- EBSCO (www.ebsco.com)
- InfoTrac (www.infotrac.com)
- ProQuest (www.proquest.com)

Free Resources

Websites that offer free access to news stories usually allow searching by either topic or by location. Here are five sites excellent for investigations.

These sites are organized **by topic**.

- News Directory (www.newsdirectory.com) Drill down by topic; use this site to get free newspaper sources online.
- Google News (www.news.google.com) Offers current news (within 30 days) and is an excellent source for local news with approximately 4,500 news sources worldwide.

These sites are organized **by location**.

- NewsLibrary.com (www.newslibrary.com) Search by location and by available news on a specific topic.
- Newspapers.com (www.newspapers.com) Includes international locations.
- Thepaperboy (www.thepaperboy.com) Includes national and international locations.

Military Records

National Personnel Records Center (NPRC)

Military service records are kept by the National Personnel Records Center (NPRC) which is under the jurisdiction of the National Archives and Records Administration. www.archives.gov/veterans/military-service-records/

The type of information released to the general public is dependent upon the veteran's authorization. Also, the **key to searching military records** is form SF-180 (or a signed release). The **key military record** is the DD-214. Federal law [5 USC 552a(b)] requires that all requests for records and information be submitted in writing. Each request must be signed and dated.

Military Branches - Internet Sources

The Official Sites include—

www.army.mil	U.S. Army
www.af.mil	U.S. Air Force
www.navy.mil	U.S. Navy
www.usmc.mil	U.S. Marine Corps
www.arng.army.mil	Army National Guard
www.ang.af.mil	Air National Guard
www.uscg.mil/default.asp	U.S. Coast Guard

National Gravesite Locator

The Nationwide Gravesite Locator maintained by the U.S. Department of Veterans Affairs includes burial records from many sources. Go to http://gravelocator.cem.va.gov/j2ee/servlet/NGL_v1.

Missing Persons

A links list of missing persons compiled by state agencies is free at www.ancestorhunt.com/missing-persons.htm. View the FBI Kidnapping and Missing Persons Investigations web page free at www.fbi.gov/wanted/kidnap/kidmiss.htm. The privately operated Doe Network lists international missing persons and unidentified victims at www.doenetwork.org. Search the National Center for Missing Adults database at www.theyaremissed.org/ncma/index.php. Another private site – America's Most Wanted – features missing persons and missing children profiles at www.amw.com.

Where found, county sheriff websites often provide county missing persons web pages; these same sheriff websites may include most wanted lists, sexual predators, warrants, arrests, DUIs or other types of local pages as a public service.

Most Wanted Lists

Many federal agencies (and some international agencies) have a web page of a Most Wanted List with name searching capabilities. A web page with links to lists maintained by the FBI, U.S. Marshall, the Bureau of Alcohol, Tobacco, and Firearms (ATF), The Drug Enforcement Administration (DEA), and even the U.S. Postal Service is found at www.usa.gov/Citizen/Topics/MostWanted.shtml.

A quick way to find each state's Most Wanted Lists is at www.ancestorhunt.com/most-wanted-criminals-and-fugitives.htm.

Where found, County Sheriff websites often provide data on County Most Wanted individuals. These same sheriff websites may include missing persons, sexual predators, warrants, arrests, DUIs and other types of local pages as a public service. For those interested in these sites, www.searchsystems.net does a good job of collecting these URLs.

Motor Vehicle Records

Motor vehicle records are essential decision-making tools used by many industries and groups, particularly insurance companies, trucking firms, employers, lenders, and private investigators. In general, motor vehicle records can be made public only if personal information is not disclosed, depending on the type of record and the state involved.

The types of records characterized as motor vehicle records include—

- Driving history (also known as an MVR)
- Driver license status
- Accident report
- Traffic ticket
- Vehicle registration, status
- Vehicle title (ownership), title history, liens
- Vessel registration
- Vessel title, title history, liens
- VIN – Vehicle Identification Number

In general, the databases for each of these record types are maintained by state agencies, but in some jurisdictions a local agency is empowered to process record requests.

Three Critical Factors

Before we proceed with a review of motor vehicle record searching procedures, there are four important rules to consider when accessing this record data—

1. Each state maintains its own separate database(s) of licensed drivers, vehicle registrations, vehicle ownership, accident reports, and other associated records.

2. There is NO national, all inclusive database of motor vehicle records.

3. The federal Driver's Privacy Protection Act (DPPA) sets specific standards when personal information can be included on a record, dependent upon the purpose of the request. All states comply with DPPA.

State Similarities and Differences

Who is legally permitted to access driving or vehicle records? What degree of authority is needed to obtain a full record? What data is found on a record? What information is masked from the public's view? Will the records you request actually give you the information you seek?

Answers to these questions are all subject to individual state statutes, state administrative rules and regulations, and compliance with Federal laws. The manner in which states communicate internally or externally and their policies of reciprocity reflect the diversity that contributes to making each state unique.

The Affect of DPPA on Record Access

As mentioned, the Driver's Privacy Protection Act (DPPA) has an important influence on motor vehicle records. This is because DPPA mandates that states differentiate between permissible uses (14 are designated in DPPA) and uses by casual requesters. Thus the reason for the record request determines who may receive a record with personal information. Records with personal information are only given to those with a listed permissible use or with the written consent of the driver.

All states are in compliance with the DPPA standards. Note that these standards are only minimal and states can be more restrictive. Nearly half of the states sell "sanitized records" (personal information redacted) to casual requesters and some even offer access online. Some states refuse to disclose any certain personal information on their records to anyone.

A copy of DPPA can be found at http://uscode.house.gov/download/pls/18C123.txt.

Driving Records

The acronym MVR comes from the phrase "Motor Vehicle Record" or "Moving Violation Records." The majority of the time when the term MVR is used, it simply means a driving record.

> **Author TIP❖** If you talk to someone at a state motor vehicle department about records, be sure you are clear on what you want or mean. A state DMV official hearing the words motor vehicle record or MVR may think you are referring to a vehicle title or registration record, or perhaps a status record.

An MVR is a historical index of a driver's moving violation convictions, accidents, and license sanctions. Depending on the state's record reporting procedure, an MVR can show activity anywhere from 3 years to a lifetime. By far and away, the largest and primary users of MVRS are the insurance and trucking industries. Together they easily account for over 90% of all record requests.

Key Data Found On Driving Records

The information found on each state's record is somewhat standardized, but there are notable differences among states—

- License Status
- Traffic Violations and Accidents
- Withdrawals and Administrative Actions
- Personal Information about the Driver

Personal information found on an MVR may include the licensee's address, height, weight, date of birth. As a rule, Social Security Numbers and medical information are always redacted and never released to record requesters. As mentioned, the release of personal information on motor vehicle records is governed by the DPPA, based on if for a permissible use or if the consent of the subject is given.

However, the level of compliance with the Act is inconsistent from state-to-state; some states have stricter policies than the Act. Some states never release personal information and there are states that make available records either with or without personal information.

About Online Access

All states offer online access to driving records, but there are many caveats. To receive DPPA-compliant records, the requester must qualified, be pre-approved, and there may be a minimum monthly order level.

If the requester is not DPPA-Compliant, certain states offer record access, but records are sanitized.

Electronic access methods vary widely depending upon how orders are grouped or submitted, and by the media type. States provide interactive processing (results of a record request is shown immediately), electronic batch processing (usually by the web using File Transfer Protocol technology), or both.

The License Status Report

A status report – the top or header portion of a driving record – can sometimes be obtained as a separate record. The license status report generally indicates three important pieces of information:

- The type or class of license issued which in turn tells what types of vehicles (commercial, non-commercial, motorcycle) can be operated. Different commercial license classes regulate the size or weight of the vehicle licensed to be driven.
- Any special conditions placed on the license holder. These permissions and limitations are known as endorsements and restrictions. A typical restriction is a requirement to have

"corrective lenses" when driving. Another example is a CDL license may have an endorsement that regulates if hazardous material can be hauled.

- If the license is valid or under suspension or revocation.

A handful of states offer online status checks. Some are free and some are for a fee, as indicated in the state-by-state searching tips in the next chapter.

Accident or Crash Reports

Many states use the term "crash reports" and will bristle if you use the term "accident reports." Also, there are usually two types of accident records for each incident – the reports filed by the citizens involved and the reports prepared by the investigating officers. Copies of a citizen's accident report are not usually available to the public and are not reviewed herein. For the purposes of this publication, we will use the term accident reports and designate those records as reports prepared by the investigating officer.

There is no overall national database of historical accident information maintained by either a government agency or by private enterprise. A good rule of thumb is that accident records must be obtained from the agency that investigated the incident.

When records are maintained by the same agency that holds driving records, the DPPA guidelines are followed with regards to honoring record requests.

Typical information found on a state accident report includes drivers' addresses and license numbers as well as a description of the incident. Only a handful of states offer online access to accident reports.

Vehicle Records

Vehicle records available include ownership and titles, registration data, vehicle identification numbers (VINs), license plates, and liens placed on vehicles. Ownership and title records of vehicles can generally be ordered as either a current record or as a historical record showing all previous owners. Title data can indicate if a vehicle was at one time a junk vehicle or if the vehicle was once a subject of title washing (previously branded as a salvage or flood-damaged vehicle), or perhaps a government vehicle previously.

Usually the same state agency that administers driving records also administers vehicle records. In some states vehicle records are controlled by an entirely different state government department or division. Also, in some states the liens on vehicles are recorded at the county or at the Secretary of State's Office where UCCs are filed.

There are many similarities between accessing driving records and vehicle records, especially if records are administered by the same agency that handles driver records. Regardless of which agency oversees vehicle recordkeeping, record access is affected by DPPA as described for driving records. However, not every state offers online access. A few states offer status checks, as indicated in the next chapter.

The same description above holds true for vessel records if the vessels are administered by the same motor vehicle agency. When watercraft and watercraft records are governed by a different government agency, the access policies are usually not governed by DPPA. In these states certain records may be more open to access, but generally access is governed by administrative rules or even by statute.

Vehicle record data that includes personal identifiers is never sold for marketing purposes, per DPPA.

The VIN

VIN stands for "vehicle identification number." This number is internationally recognized as the way to identify an individual vehicle. When buying a used vehicle, many people and dealers check the history of a VIN with a private vendor to help make an informed decision about the quality and value of the vehicle. Vehicles have a metal plate stamped with unique VIN located somewhere on the dashboard or door, but the VIN may also be found attached to other locations on the vehicle.

A VIN consists of 17 characters (vehicles manufactured before 1981 may have fewer characters) in a highly coded but strict format structure. A code table that shows all the possible meanings for each position is a very extensive document, and it changes frequently. Web resources to decode a VIN include:

- www.autocheck.com
- www.cardetective.com
- www.carfax.com
- www.decodethis.com

Vessels Records

Vessels and watercraft that weigh more than five tons are registered with the U.S. Coast Guard, www.st.nmfs.noaa.gov/st1/CoastGuard/. Another handy location to search for larger vessels, or to search by lien or title, is the Coast Guard's National Vessel Documentation Center found at www.uscg.mil/hq/g-m/vdoc/poc.htm.

Smaller vessels, usually those for pleasure or sport, are registered through a state motor vehicle department or a state environmental agency such as a Fish & Game Department. Usually the same state agency that administers vehicle records also administers vessel records. In some states vessel records are controlled by an entirely different state government department or division.

The types of vessel records available from state agencies are very similar, with different terms used sometimes for the registration or plate type data. Not all states title watercraft, and those that do generally only require titles if over a certain length or motorized. Similar requirements may be imposed when registration is mandatory. Also, in some states the liens on vehicles are recorded at the county or at the Secretary of State's Office where UCCs are filed.

For in-depth, detailed information about each state's procedures regarding all types of motor vehicle records, see *The MVR Book*. [4]

---

[4] Published annually by BRB Publications, www.brbpub.com

Occupations & Licensing Boards

Professional occupational licensing, certifications, and registrations are generally a matter of public record, intended to protect the public from fraud and the unqualified. The Council on Licensure, Enforcement, and Regulation (CLEAR) is an organizational resource for entities or individuals involved in the licensing, non-voluntary certification or registration of hundreds of regulated occupations and professions. The set of definitions for occupational regulation that CLEAR provides is well stated:

> **"Registration** The least restrictive form of occupational regulation, usually taking the form of requiring individuals to file their names, addresses, and qualifications with a government agency before practicing the occupation. This may include posting a bond or filing a fee.
>
> **Certification** The state grants title protection to persons with certifications. Uncertified individuals may practice the same or similar job duties, but specialized titles are reserved only for individuals who have the related certification.
>
> **Licensure** The most restrictive form of professional and occupational regulation. Under licensure laws, it is illegal for a person to practice a profession without first meeting state standards."

Source: www.clearhq.org/

Types of Agencies Involved

With the above definition in mind, there are several, general types of agencies involved with the registration, licensing, or certification of credentials.

Private Entities

For many professions, the certification body is a private association that has set the licensing or certification standards. An example is the American Institute of Certified Public Accountants, which sets the standards for becoming a Certified Public Accountant (CPA).

Many other professional licenses are based on completion of the requirements of professional associations. In addition, there are many professional designations from such associations that are not recognized as official licenses by government. These designations are basic certifications in fields that are so specialized that they are not of interest to the states, but rather only to the professionals within an industry. For example, the initials "CFE" indicate an individual is a Certified Fraud Examiner and has met the minimum requirements for that title from the Association of Certified Fraud Examiners.

For other resources that may oversee credentialing, see the *Trade Associations* section later in this chapter

State Entities

A state agency can administer the registration, certification, and occupational licensing of an individual intending to offer specified products or services in the designated area. If registration alone is required, there may not be a certification status showing that the person has met minimum requirements. Using the CPA example above, the New York State Education Department, Office of the Professions, oversees the preparation, licensure, and practice of its CPAs.

Businesses may also fall under the administration of state entity, per statute. For example, a state may require business registration for an entity to do business or offer specified products or services in a designated area, such as registering a liquor license. Some business license agencies require testing or a background check. Others merely charge a fee after a cursory review of the application.

Often the state agencies are referred to as **licensing boards**. Sometimes many, many boards are under the direction of one specific branch of regulatory government. An example is health care related vocations. The BRB Publication's database of occupational licensing boards lists over 8,750 individual job titles or businesses that are administered for licensing, registration or certification by 1,976 different state entities. Some level of online searching exists for names and even enforcement actions on over 5,000 occupations or businesses.

Local Entities

Local government agencies at both the county and municipal levels require a myriad of business registrations and permits in order to do business (construction, signage, sell hot dogs on a street corner, etc.) within their borders. If you decide to check on local registrations and permits, call the offices at both the county — try the county recording office — and municipal level — try city hall — to find out what type of registrations may be required for the person or business you are checking out. Several of the free links lists sites will connect you to online searching sites if available.

CareerOneStop, a unique web resource for job seekers, provides information about finding certifications by occupation or industry, and licenses by occupation or agency. Agencies details are provided, but the site indicates that content is only updated every two years. Visit www.careeronestop.org

A number of private vendors also compile lists from these agencies and make them available online or on CD-ROM. We do not necessarily suggest these databases be used for credential searching because they may not be complete, may not be up-to-date, and may not contain all the information you can obtain directly from the licensing agency. However, these databases are extremely valuable as supplemental sources of background information on an individual or company that you may wish to do business with.

Patents

United States Patent and Trademark Office

Search the United States Patent and Trademark office (USPTO) databases for full-text patent information on U.S. patents granted since 1976 and full-page images since 1790 at www.uspto.gov/go/pats/. Patents issued from 1790 through 1975 are searchable only by patent number, issue date, and current US classifications. The USPTO's text-searchable patent database begins with patents granted since 1976.

Note that neither assignment changes nor address changes recorded at the USPTO are reflected in the patent full-text or the patent full-page images.

The Patent Application Information Retrieval (PAIR) system permits third parties to obtain information on published applications on issued patents, status of maintenance fee payments, and if a reissue application or reexamination request has been filed. PAIR can be accessed at http://portal.uspto.gov/external/portal/pair.

Other Patent Record Resources

The World Intellectual Property Organization (WIPO)

The World Intellectual Property Organization (WIPO) is a specialized agency of the United Nations dedicated to promoting the effective use and protection of intellectual property worldwide. WIPO offers an international patent search at www.wipo.int/pctdb/en/

Other Vendors of Note

There are a few reliable vendors who offer patent searching as alternatives to the USPTO, including in alphabetical order:

- www.freepatentsonline.com
- www.google.com/patents
- www.patentgenius.com
- http://scientific.thomson.com/products/dwpi (Derwent patent index)
- www.surfip.gov.sg/

Politics – Donations & Lobbyists

Political Action Committee – PAC

The purpose of a Political Action Committee (PAC) is to raise money in the support of political candidates. PACs usually represent businesses large or small, or special interest groups such as unions or the NRA, etc. PACs must register at the state or federal level, depending on the purpose of the PAC, and follow pre-set guidelines. Since PACs are a matter of public record, the registration information and donations are searchable by the public. Search locations follow.

Lobbyist

Lobbyists are individuals paid to communicate with public office holders in order to influence government decisions. As with PACs, lobbyists must be registered at the government level where they are trying to influence votes. The registration of lobbyists is a matter of public record.

Federal Agency Resources

Federal Election Commission (FEC)

The Federal Election Commission (FEC) administers and enforces the Federal Election Campaign Act (FECA), which is the statute that governs the financing of federal elections. To locate information about the political donations go to the Federal Election Commission's website at www.fec.gov. There are some excellent search tools under the Campaign Finance Reports and Data tab. Also, try the Search the Disclosure Database and Using FEC Public Records tabs.

Internal Revenue Service

The IRS monitors what can be deducted as donations to a PAC or by a PAC. At the web page http://forms.irs.gov/politicalOrgsSearch/search/basicSearch.jsp one can search for all electronic and paper submissions of Form 8871 Political Organization Notice of Section 527 Status, and Form 8872 Political Organization Report of Contributions and Expenditures. Also searchable from this site are the paper submissions of Form 990 Return of Organizations Exempt from Income Tax - the form filed by many public charities and other exempt organizations.

U.S. Senate Office of Public Records

Lobbyists must register with the Senate to disclose who hired them, how much they are paid, what issues or bills they are lobbying on, and the federal agencies they are contacting. Five criteria can be searched at once at http://sopr.senate.gov.

The Office of the Clerk for the U.S. House of Representatives maintains a web page at http://lobbyingdisclosure.house.gov that offers information about lobbying at the House, but the organization does not offer a searchable online database.

Agent for a Foreign Principal for Political Reasons

The Foreign Agents Registration Act (FARA) requires individuals acting as agents of foreign principals in a political or quasi-political capacity to make periodic public disclosure of their relationship with the foreign principal, as well as activities, receipts and disbursements in support of those activities. Search at www.usdoj.gov/criminal/fara/links/search.html.

State Political Donations and Lobbyist Registration Chart

The following table presents the searchable state sites for political donations and lobbyist registration.

AL	PAC resources are found at www.sos.alabama.gov/vb/election/pacsrch1.aspx. Download the current list as a PDF. The current list of lobbyists is at www.ethics.alalinc.net/news/lobbyist_list.pdf
AK	Search campaign and financial disclosures at https://webapp.state.ak.us/apoc/ Search for lobbyists at www.state.ak.us/apoc/lobcov.htm
AZ	Search lobbyists at www.azsos.gov/election/lobbyist. Search PACs at www.azsos.gov/cfs/CampaignFinanceSearch.htm
AR	A PAC and lobbyist search is at www.sos.arkansas.gov/elections/ce/index.php
CA	Find lobbyists at http://cal-access.ss.ca.gov/Lobbying/ Find PACs at http://cal-access.ss.ca.gov/Campaign/Committees/
CO	Click on Lobbyists at www.elections.colorado.gov/DDefault.aspx. Click on Campaign Finance Online Database at www.elections.colorado.gov/DDefault.aspx?tid=
CT	Search lobbyists at https://www.ctose.net/reportRequest/index.asp. Search PAC at www.ct.gov/seec/cwp/view.asp?a=2650&Q=329402&seecNav=|
DC	Search PAC and lobbyists at http://ocf.dc.gov/WebsiteReports/filetype.asp

DE	Search lobbyists at www.delawaregov.us/pic/index.cfm?ref=74391. For PAC, click on View Reports online at http://elections.delaware.gov/information/campaignfinance/campaignfinance.shtml
FL	Find lobbyists at www.leg.state.fl.us/lobbyist/ Find PACs at http://election.dos.state.fl.us/campfin/cfindb.shtml
GA	Data on lobbyists and campaign finance data is found at www.ethics.ga.gov/EthicsWeb/main.aspx
HI	Lobbyists data at www.state.hi.us/ethics/noindex/pubrec.htm. PACs at Campaign Spending Commission at http.hawaii.gov/campaign/NC/nc.htm
ID	Lobbyist data at www.idsos.state.id.us/elect/lobbyist/lobinfo.htm PAC data at www.idsos.state.id.us/eid/index.htm
IL	Lobbyist data is at www.cyberdriveillinois.com/departments/index/lobbyist/home.html PAC data is at www.elections.state.il.us/. Click on Campaign Disclosure
IN	Lobbyist data is at https://secure.in.gov/apps/ilrc/registration/browse PAC data is at www.indianacampaignfinance.com/INPublic/inSearch.aspx
IA	Lobbyist data is at www.legis.state.ia.us/Lobbyist.html. For PAC go to www.state.ia.us/government/iecdb/index.htm and click on campaigns.
KS	Lobbyist and PAC data at www.kansas.gov/ethics/
KY	Lobbyist data at http://klec.ky.gov/reports/employersagents.htm Search PACs at http://kref.ky.gov/
LA	Lobbyists and PACs at www.ethics.state.la.us/
ME	Lobbyists and PACs at www.mainecampaignfinance.com/public/home.asp
MD	Lobbyist at http://ethics.gov.state.md.us/listing.htm. Search PACs at www.elections.state.md.us/campaign_finance/index.html.
MA	Lobbyist data at www.sec.state.ma.us/lobbyist/LobbyistSearch/PublicSearch.asp?action=P PACs at www.mass.gov/ocpf/
MI	Lobbyists at http://miboecfr.nicusa.com/cgi-bin/cfr/lobby_srch.cgi PACs at www.michigan.gov/sos/0,1607,7-127-1633_8723---,00.html
MN	Lobbyists and PACs at www.cfboard.state.mn.us/
MS	Lobbyists at www.sos.state.ms.us/elections/Lobbying/Lobbyist_Dir.asp PACs at www.sos.state.ms.us/elections/CampFinc/
MO	Lobbyists at www.mec.mo.gov/Ethics/Lobbying/LobElecReports.aspx. Search PACs at www.mec.mo.gov/Ethics/CampaignFinance/CF_PublicSearch.aspx
MT	Lobbyists and PAC at http://politicalpractices.mt.gov/

NE	Lobbyists at www.unicam.state.ne.us/web/public/lobby PACs at http://nadc.nol.org/
NV	Lobbyists at www.leg.state.nv.us/lobbyistdb/index.cfm PACs at http://sos.state.nv.us/
NH	PACs and Lobbyists are found at www.sos.nh.gov/elections.htm
NJ	PACs and Lobbyists at www.elec.state.nj.us/PublicInformation/GAA_Annual.htm
NM	PACs and Lobbyists at www.sos.state.nm.us/Main/Ethics/EthicsHome.htm
NY	Lobbyists found at https://www.nytscol.org/lobby_tracker/search.pl. For PACs go to www.elections.state.ny.us and click on Campaign Finance tab.
NC	Lobbyists at www.secretary.state.nc.us/Lobbyists/LSearch.aspx. PACs at www.sboe.state.nc.us/
ND	Lobbyists at www.nd.gov/sos/lobbylegislate/lobbying/reg-mnu.html PACs at www.nd.gov/sos/campfinance/dis-report.html
OH	Lobbyist at www.jlec-olig.state.oh.us/AgentandEmployerLists.htm PACs at www.sos.state.oh.us/, click on Campaign Finance
OK	Lobbyists at www.state.ok.us/~ethics/lobbyist.html. For PACs, contact the Ethics Commission at 405-521-3451. Data not online.
OR	Lobbyists at www.oregon.gov/OGEC/public_records.shtml PACs at www.sos.state.or.us/elections/c&e/
PA	Lobbyists at www.palobbyingservices.state.pa.us/Act134/Public/RegistrationSearch.aspx PACs at www.dos.state.pa.us/campaignfinance/site/default.asp?bcelNav=|
RI	Lobbyists at www.sec.state.ri.us/resources_for/lobbyist.html PACs at www.elections.ri.gov/CampFinance/cfmain.htm
SC	For Lobbyists and PAC, visit www.ethics.sc.gov/
SD	Lobbyist at www.state.sd.us/applications/ST12ODRS/LobbyistViewlist.asp?cmd=resetall PACs at www.sdsos.gov/electionsvoteregistration/campaignfinance.shtm
TN	Lobbyists and PACs at www.state.tn.us/tref/
TX	Lobbyists and PACs at www.ethics.state.tx.us/
UT	Lobbyists and PACs at http://elections.utah.gov/
VT	Lobbyists and PACs at http://vermont-elections.org/soshome.htm
VA	Lobbyists at http://secure01.virginiainteractive.org/lobbyist/cgi-bin/search_lobbyist.cgi PACs at www.sbe.virginia.gov/cms/Campaign_Finance_Disclosure/Index.html
WA	Lobbyists and PACs at http://web.pdc.wa.gov/

WV	Lobbyists at www.wv.gov/Offsite.aspx?u=http://www.wvethicscommission.org
	PACs at www.wvsos.com/elections/cfreports/
WI	Lobbyists at http://ethics.state.wi.us/Scripts/2003Session/OELMenu.asp
	PACs at http://elections.state.wi.us/section.asp?linkid=325&locid=47
WY	Lobbyists at http://soswy.state.wy.us/election/lob-list.htm
	PACs at http://soswy.state.wy.us/election/pac.htm

Private Agencies of Note

Follow the Money

Per their web page www.followthemoney.org, the National Institute on Money in State Politics is "a nonpartisan 501(c)3 tax-exempt charitable organization dedicated to accurate, comprehensive and unbiased documentation and research on campaign finance at the state level."

Money Line

The Congressional Quarterly and *St. Petersburg Times* operate CQ MoneyLine, found at http://moneyline.cq.com/pml/home.do offers a number of free searches offered to find political campaign donors and lobbyists. There is even a search to find donors from one state who contribute to candidates in other states. PAC contributors are also searchable. This excellent web page also has many, many other database searches available on a subscription basis only.

Open Secrets – The Center for Responsive Politics

The Center for Responsive Politics is a non-partisan, non-profit research group based in Washington, D.C. that tracks money in politics and its effect on elections and public policy. The web page at www.opensecrets.org is extremely comprehensive and offers searching of the Center's database that tracks contributions.

Vote Smart

The Vote Smart site at www.vote-smart.org/index.htm tracks campaign contributions for more than 13,000 candidates and elected officials nationwide and includes voting records and evaluations by special interest groups.

Privacy Resources

Do Not Call – Opt Out Sites of Note

There are organizations that assist the public to remove their names and addresses from marketing list organizations, Below are several of the most effective—

- Center for Democracy and Technology
  http://opt-out.cdt.org/moreinfo/
- Do Not Call.com - www.donotcall.com
- National Do Not Call Registry - https://www.donotcall.gov

- Optout Prescreen.com - https://www.optoutprescreen.com/?rf=t
- Direct Marketing Association Opt Out https://www.dmachoice.org/MPS/

Privacy Rights Advocates

There are a number of organizations who represent the privacy interests of the consumer. Some of these groups are extremely one-sided in their approach to many issues. Other groups, while certainly advocating privacy rights, also demonstrate an understanding of the legitimacy of certain information requests from legitimate businesses with permissible use per statute vs. the purposes associated with data aggregators who cause harm by violating the privacy rights of unsuspecting individuals. The entities listed below are thought of very highly for their excellent programs to help individuals who have privacy concerns.

Privacy Rights Clearinghouse

We purposely placed this organization at the top of this list. Their web page supplies plenty of good information acknowledging the importance of balancing privacy with legitimate protection needs for the public good. The section called *Privacy Today* is excellent. www.privacyrights.org

World Privacy Forum

This is another top organization with plenty of informative data on the web page. They do a lot of work towards protecting medical information. www.worldprivacyforum.org

PrivacyExchange

This web page, a product of The Center for Social & Legal Research, is an excellent global information resource. www.privacyexchange.org

Recalls

There are several excellent resources that cover product recalls.

Six federal agencies with vastly different jurisdictions joined together to create www.recalls.gov. Searching is arranged by these topics: boats, consumer products, cosmetics, environment, food, medicine, and motor vehicle. Various search capabilities are offered. You can do a name search or use the tabs to find lists of recalls by product type.

Two of the more popular search sites found above are the vehicle recall site at www-odi.nhtsa.dot.gov/cars/problems/recalls/recallsearch.cfm and the FDA site of their recalls (Class I, II, and III), including pre-1995, at www.fda.gov/opacom/Enforce.html. Enfocrment actions and alerts are found at www.fda.gov/opacom/7alerts.html.

The U.S. Consumer Product Safety Commission is another great recall resource, go to www.cpsc.gov.

Another resource avenue to check are private companies or industries that monitor recalls on products associated with their businesses, for example Home Depot and *Consumer Reports* magazine. You can Google for these and others.

Real Estate Records

(See the next section.)

Recorded Documents and Liens

Recorded documents and liens notices are two of the most widely found categories of online public records. Documents are recorded for a number of reasons. Once properly recorded, they can show proof of ownership (deed to your house) or show when an asset is used as collateral for a loan (mortgage on your house). Finding recorded documents and lien notices is a necessity to making informed business-related decisions and these documents lead to a virtual treasure trove of data. Private investigators and attorneys research liens and recorded documents when doing an Asset Lien search. Since liens are part of an information trail in the public record, finding liens will lead to finding assets or to other liens which could lead to other assets.

The function of searching the many types of liens and recorded documents found in the U.S. public record is truly an art because—

- There are over 3,600 locations in the U.S. where one may file a lien notice or record a document.

- There are no standard rules or practices among these locations.

The 3,600+ locations where liens and recorded documents are found can be at any of three levels: local municipality, county or parish, or state agency. The jurisdictions maintain indexes to these recorded documents. Some government agencies maintain an overall index of all recorded documents and liens notices, while others maintain a series of separate indices within the same office. In other words, a researcher must know the particular index to search for a particular record. A good searcher knows to search ALL the indices.

The publicly recorded documents most often accessed are generally related to:

- Real Estate Transactions
- Uniform Commercial Code (UCC) Filings
- Other Liens

That does not imply that other records such as vital records, voter registration rolls, and fictitious names are inconsequential – far from it. Before examining each of the key documents types, let's look at some essential facts related to searching these documents.

The Difference Between Personal Property and Real Property

An important first distinction to know when searching recorded public records is the difference between personal property and real property. This is because documents related to real property generally are recorded in different locations from personal property records.

Personal property includes items such as bank accounts, vehicles, jewelry, computers, etc. It can be business collateral or 'consumer goods.' Often when personal property is given as collateral, the lender will secure the loan by filing a UCC financing statement on the asset.

Real property involves real estate related assets such as homes, apartment building, land, etc. A mortgage is an example of a recorded document that secures the associated loan to finance real property.

Types of Liens and Security Interests

Liens - With or Without Consent

A lien is a lawful claim or right against property or funds for payment of a debt or for services rendered. There are two types of liens that are recorded: those with consent (voluntary) or without consent (involuntary).

Examples of liens placed with the consent of an asset holder include mortgages, loans on car and vessels, and Uniform Commercial Code filings on business assets such as equipment or accounts receivable.

Examples of liens placed without the consent of an asset holder include federal and state tax liens, mechanic's liens, and liens filed on assets as the result of judgments issued by courts.

The Grantor-Grantee Index

Perhaps the most commonly used term to describe an index of recorded documents at a county/parish/city/town recorder's office is the Grantor-Granter Index.

The Grantor is the party that is a transferring title or some type of interest that involves a recording. The Grantee is the party that is the recipient of the title, interest or document. For example, if you purchase or re-finance real estate and borrow money from a bank, an instrument called a mortgage or deed of trust is generally involved. You, the borrower, are the Grantor since you giving a lien on the property to the bank. The bank is recorded as the Grantee since it is the recipient of the interest in the property as collateral for the loan. Sometimes the Grantor-Grantee Index is known as the Forward-Reverse or Direct-Indirect Index.

About Judgments

When a judgment is rendered in court, the winning party usually files and records a lien notice (called an abstract of judgment in many states) against real estate owned by the defendant or party against whom the judgment is given. Sometimes judgments can be used to garnish wages or can be placed on bank accounts.

Judgments can be searched at the local or county level usually in the same index as real estate records. Many times judgments are bought and sold as commodities. An Assignment of Judgment is the transfer of the title and interest in a judgment from one person to another person.

The Search Location Problem

Keeping variations in state laws and filing locations straight is a major challenge to the professional public record searching specialist. Where to search for recorded documents and property liens can be a perplexing puzzle. Just because a mailing address is Schenectady NY doesn't mean the property is located in Schenectady County. The property could be physically located in neighboring Albany County. The fact is over 8,000 of the 45,000 or so ZIP Codes cross county lines. Having access to an enhanced ZIP Code/place name/county locator product is a must. Finding involuntary liens—such as federal and state tax liens—and UCC filings can be even harder.

So, unless you know exactly where the real or personal property is located, and you are certain that everyone else who has filed or recorded liens also knows where to go, you may have a problem. You may have to search more than one county, town, city (or even state) to find the property or liens you need to know about. But knowing about the County Rule helps.

The County Rule by Carl R. Ernst

Author TIP❖ In most states, transactions are recorded at one designated recording office in the county where the property is located. But the key word in the last sentence is most. One of the most important searching tips to have in hand when searching for liens and recorded documents is the **County Rule.** The text to follow was written by Mr. Carl R. Ernst of Ernst Publishing.[5] We sincerely thank Mr. Ernst for allowing us to reproduce the article.

Where to search for recorded documents usually isn't a difficult problem to overcome in everyday practice. In most states, these transactions are recorded at one designated recording office in the county where the property is located.

We call this the "County Rule." It applies to types of public records such as real estate recordings, tax liens, Uniform Commercial Code (UCC) filings, vital records, and voter registration records. However, as with most government rules, there are a variety of exceptions which are summarized here.

The Exceptions

The five categories of exceptions to the County Rule (or Parish Rule, if searching in Louisiana) are listed below [Editor's Note: details for each state are listed in the State Profiles Section which follows.]—

1. Special Recording Districts (AK, HI)
2. Multiple Recording Offices (AL, AR, IA, KY, ME, MA, MS, TN)
3. Independent Cities (MD, MO, NV, VA)
4. Recording at the Municipal Level (CT, RI, VT)
5. Identical Names—Different Place (CT, IL, MA, NE, NH, PA, RI, VT, VA)

The Personal Property Problem and the Fifth Exception

The real estate recording system in the U.S. is self-auditing to the extent that you generally cannot record a document in the wrong recording office. However, many documents are rejected for recording because they are submitted to the wrong recording office. There are a number of reasons why this occurs, one of which is the overlap of filing locations for real estate and UCC.

Finding the right location of a related UCC filing is a different and much more difficult problem from finding a real estate recording. In the majority of states, the usual place to file a UCC financing statement is at the Secretary of States office—these are called central filing states. In the

---

[5] Ernst Publishing publishes two extensive industry manuals - *The UCC Filing Guide* and *The Real Estate Recording Guide.* Visit www.ernstpublishing.com for more information.

dual and local filing states, the place to file, in addition to the central filing office, is usually at the same office where your real estate documents are recorded. However, where there are identical place names referring to two different places, it becomes quite confusing, so hence, the fifth exemption.

Searching Real Estate Records

Every local entity (i.e. county, parish or town recorder of Deeds) records documents that transfer or encumber title. Many county, city, and parish government jurisdictions provide online access to indices of real estate records and recorded documents. Most sites are free if viewing an index, but an increasing number of government agencies will charge a fee to view or print an image or copy of a page within the file.

As with other types of public records, many investigators and researchers use these online resources as a pre-search or preliminary search, especially if dealing with an uncommon name.

Keep in mind there are a number of private companies who compile and maintain these records. Some offer free searching on the web as a way to drive users to their web pages. Some vendors offer bulk data for resale. Vendors are a very comprehensive resource to obtain electronic records.

There are a number of web pages that information on the property of specific homes (addresses). Check www.zillow.com and www.trulia.com. For interactive map information, check out http://nationalmap.gov.

Understanding the Index

The first step when performing a name search or a property search is to understand how the index works. About half of the recording offices in the U.S. use one index for all recorded documents, the rest use multiple indices. Each index may be organized on a yearly basis or a certain number of years, perhaps based on the media type. As you can imagine, it is important to know the fields that you can search by, and the variances or wild card terms the office provides. When searching online, there are some basic perimeters to examine. How does the site differentiate between a William or Bill, Debra or Deborah, etc.? Does each name require a separate search? Can you use Initials? What personal identifiers can you search by, i.e.: DOB, year in DOB, middle initial, sex?

William C. Asher, a licensed Texas private investigator and agency owner[6] provides the following tips—

- The search algorithms to use will vary quite a bit depending on the system. Start with a broad search, then narrow the search. Be careful not to be overly restrictive. Sometimes you must assume the system is weak or shot full of holes and you will have to look for work-arounds.

- Searching with variant names is important. For example, if the subject's name is Kermit T. Frog, also search using Kermit Frog, Kermie Frog, K.T. Frog, T.K. Frog, T. Frog, etc. In other words, search using all the variants. Other classic variant names include John vs. Jack, William vs. Bill vs. Wm, and Robert vs. Bob, among others.

---

[6] Mr. Asher is a writer and editor for multiple investigative journals, and is also active in federal legislative matters for the industry. He can be reached at washer@ticnet.com.

Types of Real Estate Recorded Documents Found Online

There many types of lien notices and recorded documents related to real estate files. Below are common names for documents that a public record researcher may find when searching real estate records. This list is certainly not all inclusive; there are many, many more. Also keep in mind that name variations will occur from state to state.

Deed of Trust or Mortgage of Deed of Trust Generally a mortgage that secures a debt, and names three parties - the borrower (trustor), the beneficiary (lender), and the trustee who holds title to real property under the terms of a deed of trust.

- **Bill of Sale** A Bill of Sale will be recorded to show the transfer of most any kind of personal property.

- **Assignment of Deed of Trust** A transfer or sale of a Deed of Trust from the current lender (beneficiary) to a new beneficiary.

- **Abstract of Judgment** A court issued money judgment to secure payment to the creditor, usually creates a general lien on real property of the judgment debtor.

- **Declaration of Homestead** A document recorded by either a homeowner or head of household on their primary residence to protect his home from forced sale in satisfaction of certain types of creditors' claims.

- **Mechanic's Lien** A document recorded to create a lien in favor of persons contributing labor, material, supplies, etc., to a work of improvement upon real property.

- **Notice of Default** A notice to show that the borrower under a mortgage or deed of trust is behind in payments.

- **Notice of Lis Pendens** A notice that litigation is pending in court which may affect the title of the real estate involved.

- **Notice of Trustee's Sale** This document is recorded to notify the public of pending the foreclosure sale by the trust for non-payment or non-performance of the conditions of the deed of trust.

- **Power of Attorney** This document delegates the authority of an entity to an agent (attorney-in-fact) to allow this agent to act behalf of the entity in a designated capacity.

- **Quitclaim Deed** A form of deed that conveys or releases any interest that the grantor may have acquired in real property. Many times this type of deed is issued without title insurance.

- **Reconveyance** The instrument releases the loan that was a lien against real property. Can also be called a satisfaction of the loan or a release of lien or a release of mortgage.

- **Satisfaction of Mortgage** Release of the loan that was a lien against real property. This document may also be called a release of mortgage.

- **Subordination Agreement** This document is recorded when a current lender agrees to makes their encumbrance deed of trust beneath or junior to another loan. These loans are sometimes called seconds.

- **Trustee Deed in Lieu of Foreclosure** Document indicates the transfer of real property from the defaulting borrower to the beneficiary (lender) in lieu of foreclosure.

- **Trustee's Deed** Deed given by the trustee when the real property is sold under the power of sale in a deed of trust in a foreclosure proceeding.

- **Writ or Notice of Levy** A document to notify a party served with writ of execution that specific property is being taken to satisfy a debt.

Real Estate Records and the County Rule

Remember the earlier section on the County Rule? The second, third and fourth County Rules are very important to observe when searching real estate records in the states listed below.

- **Multiple Recording Offices**. In these states, some counties have more than one recording office; AL, AR, IA, KY, LA, ME, MA, MS, and TN.

- **Independent Cities.** Four states (MD, MO, NV, VA) have independent cities that should be treated just as if they are counties. For example, St Louis City and St. Louis County are separate jurisdictions with separate sets of data.

- **Recording at the Municipal Level.** In CT, RI, and VT,) the recording jurisdiction is the town, not the county. The county clerk's office does not record documents.

Look at the Tax Assessor and Tax Collector Records

There is a county, parish, or local municipality official, usually called the Assessor, who is required by law to determine the value of all taxable property in a jurisdiction for property taxing purposes. This official publishes assessment reports and provides it to property owners with valuation notices. The official may also be known as the Auditor or Property Valuator. Records of unpaid property taxes can be found in the office of the treasurer or tax collector.

These government agencies frequently provide online access to their records. Usually tax assessment records are searchable by name or by legal description (plat number), and not necessarily by the address. These records are very public and very valuable.

The next chapter includes URLS to several thousand assessor type sites. There are also several good web pages that offer links lists to Tax Assessor offices. The site at www.pulawski.net is very easy to use, and indicates when pages are last updated. Another excellent site specializing in listing tax assessors and recorder offices with web pages offering record searching capabilities is http://publicrecords.netronline.com.

Uniform Commercial Code

Uniform Commercial Code (UCC) filings are to personal property what mortgages are to real estate property. UCCs indicate where personal property, usually business related, is placed as collateral. A UCC recording allows potential lenders to be notified that certain assets of a debtor are already pledged to secure a loan or lease. Therefore, examining UCC filings is an excellent way to find many types of assets, security interests, and financiers.

Delaware is the only state that does not offer online access to an index of UCC records, except through certain contracted firms. South Carolina offers access, but only to records filed prior to 10/27/2003. Most state UCC websites provide a free search of the index. A few will permit free access to images, but most states charge a fee to access the full records, which usually involves a subscription service and registration, login, and password.

A number of private companies compile their own proprietary database of UCC and tax lien records or offer real time gateway services. Vendors are a very comprehensive resource to obtain electronic records over multiple jurisdictions.

The next chapter gives the searchable web address for each state's central repository. Also, for specific links and updated information, visit the free public record searching sites found at www.brbpub.com.

Searching Tips

The place to file against individuals is the state where the person resides. Most UCC filings against businesses are found at the state where a business is organized, not where the collateral or chief executive offices are located. Therefore, you will need to know where a company is organized in order to know where to find recent UCC filings against it. However federal tax liens are still generally filed where the chief executive office is located.

The location to search UCC records changed dramatically in many states with the enactment of Revised Article 9 (see below).

Affect of Revised Article 9

A significant change in UCC filing that took effect in most states in July 2001 made significant changes about where to find UCC filings. Prior to that date UCC documents were recorded either at a centralized state agency or at a local recording office. At the time, there were over 4,200 locations in the U.S. that recorded UCCs. Revised Article 9 of the Code mandated effective July 2001 that all UCC documents were to be filed and recorded at a state level agency with the exception of certain real estate filings such as farm-related real estate (see Searching Real Estate Related UCC Collateral to follow).

Until June 30, 2001, liens on certain types of companies required dual filing (must file at BOTH locations) in some states, and records could be searched at BOTH locations. As of July 1, 2001, UCC filings other than those that go into real estate records were no longer filed at the local filing offices. According to the UCC Filing Guide (see www.ernstpublishing.com) now less than 3% of filings are done at the local level.

Although there are significant variations among state statutes, the state level is now the best starting place to uncover liens filed against an individual or business, but it is not the only place to search. Strict due diligence may require a local search also, depending on the state, how many years back you wish to search, and the type of collateral. The best technique is to check both locales of records.

General UCC Search Rules

As a result of Revised Article 9, the general rules for searching of UCC records are as follows:

- Except in former local filing states, a search at the state level is adequate to locate all legally valid UCC records on a subject.
- Credit due diligence searching requires use of flexible search logic provided either by the state agency or private database vendors.

- Mortgage record searches will include any real estate related UCC filings.

Searching Real Estate Related UCC Collateral

A specific purpose of lien statutes under both the UCC and real estate laws is to put a buyer or potential secured creditor on notice that someone has a prior security interest in real or personal property.

One problem is that certain types of property have the characteristics of both real and personal property. In those instances, it is necessary to have a way to provide lien notice to two different categories of interested parties: those who deal with the real estate aspect of the property and those who deal with the "personal" aspect of the property. The solution is addressed by UCC filings on real estate.

In general, the definition of real estate related UCC collateral is any property that in one form is attached to land, but that in another form is not attached. For the sake of simplicity, we can define the characteristics of two broad types of property that meet this definition:

1. Property that is initially attached to real property, but then is separated. Three specific types of collateral have this characteristic: minerals (including oil and gas), timber, and crops. These things are grown on or extracted from land. While they are on or in the ground they are thought of as real property, but once they are harvested or extracted they become personal property. Some states have a separate central filing system for crops.

2. Property that is initially personal property, but then is attached to land, is generally called fixtures. Equipment such as telephone systems or heavy industrial equipment permanently affixed to a building are examples of fixtures. It is important to realize that what is a fixture, like beauty, is in the eye of the beholder, since it is a somewhat vague definition.

UCC financing statements applicable to real estate related collateral must be filed where real estate and mortgage records are kept, which is generally at the county level — except in Connecticut, Rhode Island, and Vermont where the Town/City Clerk maintains these records.

Tax Liens

Tax liens are non-consensual liens placed by a government agency for non-payment of taxes. The federal government and every state have some sort of taxes, such as sales, income, withholding, unemployment, and/or personal property. When these taxes go unpaid, the appropriate state agency can file a lien on the real or personal property of the subject.

Tax liens filed against individuals are frequently maintained at separate locations from those liens filed against businesses. For example, many number of states require liens filed against businesses to be filed at a central state location (i.e., Secretary of State's office) and liens against individuals to be filed at the county level (i.e., Recorder, Registrar of Deeds, Clerk of Court, etc.).

Where to Search for Tax Liens

Normally, the state agency that maintains UCCs records also maintains the tax liens filed at the state level but this is not true in all states.

Liens on a company may not all be filed in the same location as those filed on individuals. A federal tax lien will not necessarily be filed (recorded) at the same location/jurisdiction as a state tax lien. Plus there can be different filing locations when these liens are filed against individuals versus filed against businesses. These variances are shown in the Recording Offices Summaries section later in this chapter. In general, state tax liens on personal property will be found where UCCs are filed and tax liens on real property will be found where real property deeds are recorded, with few exceptions.

Unsatisfied state and federal tax liens may be renewed if prescribed by individual state statutes. However, once satisfied, the time the record will remain in the repository before removal varies by jurisdiction. Many states will show a release of lien filing rather than deleting the original recording of the lien.

Other Types of Recorded Documents

There are numerous types of documents that can be recorded and are not related to real estate or personal property. Many of these documents are found at the same recording office that records real estate liens, and often times they appear in the same index. Mentioned below are several significant types.

Fictitious Names or Assumed Names

If a person operates a business not organized as a corporation, partnership, LLC, etc., under a name other his own, then it has a fictitious name. For example if Joe Cool is doing business as Costabunch General Store, that business name must be registered. Depending on the state, this registration can take place at municipal, county or state. A fictitious name is also known as a DBA – meaning Doing Business As.

Forcible Detainer

A Forcible Detainer is a landlord's lien against a tenant's property for unpaid rent or damages. Sometimes the document is filed to essentially 'give notice.' If the tenant does not comply within a designated time period, the landlord can forcibly move the tenant's belongings off the property, usually with the assistance of local law enforcement.

Searching for evidence of a Forcible Detainer is part of the tenant screening process (see the Tenant Screening section in the Searching A thru Z chapter).

Vital Records

Births, deaths, marriages, and divorces may be recorded at the local level or state level, with copies of the documents found at both the state and local agencies. See Vital Records section later in this chapter.

Wills

Many people record their Last Will and Testament at the local recorder's office. Some people confuse a probate court with this function. A probate court is not a recording office, but has records concerning decedents which include their will (if any) and a listing of assets.

Securities and Securities Dealers

There are a number of federal agencies who oversee the regulatory and compliance issues that deal with publicly traded securities or with security dealers. These agencies have the authority to investigate issues related to compliance or improprieties. Hence, these agencies are excellent resources to search for enforcement actions.

Perhaps the most well-know and informational federal agency, the Securities and Exchange Commission (SEC). Also, look in the State Agencies section.

SEC – Securities & Exchange Commission

The SEC oversees the participants in the securities world, including securities exchanges, securities brokers and dealers, investment advisors, and mutual funds.

EDGAR

EDGAR – the **E**lectronic **D**ata **G**athering **A**nalysis and **R**etrieval system – was established by the SEC as the means for companies to make required filings to the SEC by direct transmission. EDGAR provides an extensive online repository of U.S. corporation information available online. The record searching site at EDGAR is www.sec.gov/edgar/searchedgar/webusers.htm. EDGAR also offers a guide on how to search publicly traded companies, go to www.sec.gov/investor/pubs/edgarguide.htm.

A number of private vendors offer access to EDGAR records along with some added features and searching flexibilities. Recommended sites include www.edgar-online.com, www.secinfo.com, www.edgarlive.com, and www.lexisnexis.com.

Enforcement Actions

SEC-related enforcement actions are viewable online at www.sec.gov/divisions/enforce/enforceactions.shtml and include civil lawsuits brought by the Commission in Federal court, administrative proceedings as instituted and/or settled, opinions issued by Administrative Law Judges in contested administrative proceedings, and opinions on appeals issued by the Commission on appeal of Initial Decisions or disciplinary decisions issued by self-regulatory organizations (e.g., NYSE or NASD).

Litigation Actions

This web page, www.sec.gov/litigation.shtml, contains links to information on SEC enforcement actions, opinions issued by the Commission, briefs filed by SEC staff, trading suspensions, and notices concerning the creation of investors' claims funds in specific cases. Three links are mentioned below.

At www.sec.gov/litigation/litreleases.shtml there are informative press releases concerning **civil lawsuits** brought by the Commission in federal court. The list is in date order and not searchable by name.

At www.sec.gov/litigation/suspensions.shtml there are SEC **trading suspensions** with historical data to 1995, in date order.

At www.sec.gov/divisions/enforce/claims.htm are lists of **investors' claims funds**. The SEC enforcement cases are shown in which a Receiver, Disbursement Agent, or Claims Administrator has been appointed.

Financial Industry Regulatory Authority (FINRA)

Formerly the National Association of Securities Dealers (NASD), the Financial Industry Regulatory Authority (FINRA) is a resource to investigate brokers and brokerage firms. FINRA oversees over 5,000 brokerage firms, 172,000 branch offices, and more than 665,000 registered securities representatives. FINRA is probably the largest non-governmental regulator for all securities firms doing business in the U.S.

The website at www.finra.org allows name searching of an individual or a brokerage firm registered in FINRA. The user can download an eight-page Adobe Acrobat PDF file that outlines the subject's history, including employment. Brokerage firms also are searchable for any disciplinary actions taken against a company, or brokers who are involved with arbitration awards, disciplinary, and regulatory events. You can reach FINRA at 301-590-6500.

North American Securities Administrators Association (NASAA)

The North American Securities Administrators Association (NASAA) is devoted to investor protection. NASAA members license firms and their agents, investigate violations of state and provincial law, file enforcement actions when appropriate, and educate the public about investment fraud. NASAA members also participate in multi-state enforcement actions and information sharing.

The NASAA web page (www.nasaa.org/home/index.cfm) contains links to individual state, provincial, and territorial jurisdictions for securities laws, rules and regulations. Headquartered in Washington DC, NASAA can be reached at 202-737-0900.

Central Registration Depository (CRD)

The Central Registration Depository (CRD) is a collaborative effort of NASAA, FINRA, and the SEC. The CRD, a centralized filing system of licensed broker-dealers, was developed by state securities regulators, NASAA, FINRA, and the SEC. CRD reports are available through state regulatory authorities. A list is located at the NASAA web page.

National Futures Association (NFA)

The National Futures Association (NFA) is a self-regulatory organization to safeguard the U.S. futures.industry. NFA's web page permits name searching of individuals or firms. Results indicate any arbitration or regulatory action filed against any NFA listed individual or firm. Visit www.nfa.futures.org or call the Chicago headquarters at 312-781-1300.

Securities Class Action Clearinghouse

The Securities Class Action Clearinghouse provides detailed information relating to the prosecution, defense, and settlement of federal class action securities fraud litigation. The Clearinghouse maintains an index of than 21,500 complaints, briefs, filings, and other litigation-related materials. This content is maintained by the Stanford Law School and Cornerstone Research. Visit http://securities.stanford.edu.

State Security Agencies

Every state has its own securities laws – often referred to as **"Blue Sky Laws"** – that are designed to protect investors against fraud. The records of the filings by companies registering under the Blue Sky Laws, as well as any records of legal actions, are held by designated state regulatory securities agencies. The state agencies that oversee these records also, usually, license and hold records of brokerage firms, their brokers, and investment adviser representatives doing business there.

These records are open to the public although they are not generally found online. Rather than list each state's address and web page, we suggest the reader visit the North American Securities Administrators Association (see above) or the links found at www.seclinks.com/id16.html.

Sexual Predator Records

Sexual offenses include aggravated sexual assault, sexual assault, aggravated criminal sexual contact, endangering the welfare of a child by engaging in sexual conduct, kidnapping, and false imprisonment. Under Megan's Law, sex offenders are classified in one of three levels or "tiers" based on the severity of their crime as follows: Tier 3 (high); Tier 2 (moderate); and Tier 1 (low).

Sex offenders must notify authorities of their whereabouts. Also, there is a notification process when a registered sex offender moves into a community.

Usually, the state agency that oversees the criminal record repository also administrates a Sexual Offender Registry (SOR) and offers a free search of registered sexual offenders who are living within the particular state. . These state web pages are shown in the next chapter.

The National Sexual Offender Registry at www.nsopr.gov, coordinated by the Department of Justice, is a cooperative effort between the state agencies hosting public sexual offender registries and the federal government. The website has a national query to obtain information about sex offenders through a number of search options including name, Zip Code, county, and city or town. The site also has an excellent, detailed overview of each state's SOR policies and procedures.

Telephone and Communications

Area Codes - North American Numbering Plan (NANPA)

NANPA is an integrated telephone numbering plan serving the United States, its territories, and 18 other North American countries; Canada, Bermuda, Anguilla, Antigua & Barbuda, the Bahamas, Barbados, the British Virgin Islands, Cayman Islands, Dominica, Dominican Republic, Grenada, Jamaica, Montserrat, St. Kitts and Nevis, St. Lucia, St. Vincent and the Grenadines, Trinidad and Tobago, and Turks & Caicos.

NANPA holds overall responsibility for the administration of NANPA numbering resources, subject to directives from regulatory authorities in the countries that share participate in the NANP. www.nanpa.com/guide/guide.html

Key online searches include:

- Area code maps - Select a state and see area code boundaries.

- Central office code assignments - Find out what codes are assigned or available for assignment in each geographic area code

- Area code search - Get information about individual area codes, including dialing plans and pointers to planning letters with split/overlay information.

- Electronic mailing lists - Sign up to obtain the latest information on area code assignments and other areas of numbering interest.

Yellow and White Pages

www.yellowpages.com or www.superpages.com or www.addresses.com

Phone/People Finders

InfoSpace http://ypng.infospace.com/ lets you search by place and business type or name; results give address, phone, fax, and like results. www.411X411.com has a commercial appearance and will connect you to other finder services if you let it.

Phone List Services

Telephone number services such as www.infousa.com and Dun & Bradstreet's www.zapdata.com offer mailing-list services. Through various public records, news accounts, and telephone interviews, D&B has amassed a large amount of very specific contact information that can be purchased by the batch or in small doses. The lists are targeted for marketing purposes but investigators can use purchased lists to locate a target or subject by occupation, geography, or hobby.

Location & Service Provider Finders

There are several search service tools that provide the location and service provider for a telephone number. A good one is FoneFinder. Search by 7 digits of the telephone number or by city or ZIP Code at www.fonefinder.net/

Media Links

A great resource to find news media links is www.gebbieinc.com. Search for TV stations, radio stations, daily and weekly newspapers, magazines. You can search by magazine topic. Results give websites.

Trade Associations

Trade Associations and their websites provide a wealth of information. They are useful for not only industry knowledge, but also for finding members and entities with strong ties as vendors. Here is a short list of associations with strong ties to public records or public record searching. The list is presented in order of the acronym.

Acronym	Name	URL
AALL	American Assoc. of Law Librarians	www.aallnet.org/index.asp
AAMVA	Amererican Assocociation. of Motor Vehicle Administrators	www.aamva.org
AAPL	American Assoc. of Professional Landmen	www.landman.org
ABA	American Bar Association	www.abanet.org/home.html
ABA(2)	American Banking Association	www.aba.com/default.htm
ABFE	American Board of Forensic Examiners	www.acfei.com
ABI	American Bankruptcy Institute	www.abiworld.org
ABW	American Business Women	www.abwahq.org
ACA	Association of Collectors & Professionals	www.acainternational.org
ACFE	Association of Certified Fraud Examiners	www.acfe.com
AFIO	Association of Former Intelligence Officers	www.afio.com
AICPA	Assoc. of Certified Public Accountants	www.aicpa.org/index.htm
AIIP	Assoc. of Independent Information Professionals	www.aiip.org
AIPLA	Amer. Intellectual Property Law Association	www.aipla.org
ALA	American Library Association	www.ala.org
ALTA	American Land Title Association	www.alta.org
AMA	American Management Association	www.amanet.org/index.htm
APA(2)	American Psychological Association	www.apa.org
APG	Association of Professional Genealogists	www.apgen.org
ASIS	American Society for Industrial Security	www.asisonline.org
ASLET	American Soc. of Law Enforcement Trainers	www.aslet.org
ASSE	American Society of Safety Engineers	www.asse.org
ATA	American Truckers Association	www.trucking.org
ATLA	Association of Trial Lawyers of America	www.atlanet.org
CDIA	Consumer Data Industry Association	www.cdiaonline.org
CII	Council of Intl Investigators	www.cii2.org
DMA	Direct Marketing Association	www.the-dma.org
EAE	Environmental Assessment Association	www.iami.org
EMA	Employment Management Association	www.shrm.org/EMA
EPIC	Evidence Photographers Intl Council	www.epic-photo.org
FBINAA	FBI National Academy Association	www.fbinaa.org
IAAI	Intl Association of Arson Investigators	www.fire-investigators.org
IAHSS	Intl Assoc. of Healthcare Security & Safety	www.iahss.org
IALEIA	Intl Assoc. of Law Enforcement Intel. Analysts	www.ialeia.org
IASIR	Intl Assoc. of Security & Investigation Regulators	www.iasir.org
IIAA	Independent Insurance Agents of America	www.iiaba.net
INA	Intl Nanny Association	www.nanny.org
INOA	Intl Narcotics Officers Association	www.ineoa.org

Acronym	Name	URL
INTA	Intl Trademark Association	www.inta.org
ION	Investigative Open Network	www.ioninc.com
IREM	Institute of Real Estate Management	www.irem.org
LES	Licensing Executive Society	www.usa-canada.les.org
MBAA	Mortgage Bankers Association of America	www.mbaa.org
NAC	National Association of Counselors	http://nac.lincoln-grad.org
NACM	National Association of Credit Managers	www.nacm.org
NAFE	National Association of Female Executives	www.nafe.com
NAFI	National Association of Fire Investigators	www.nafi.org
NAHB	National Association of Home Builders	www.nahb.org
NAHRO	National Assoc. of Housing & Redevelopment Officials	www.nahro.org
NAIS	National Assoc. of Investigative Specialists	www.pimall.com/nais/
NALA	National Association of Legal Assistants	www.nala.org
NALFM	National Association of Law Firm Marketers	www.legalmarketing.org
NALI	National Association of Legal Investigators	www.nalionline.org
NALS	NALS... Association of Legal Professionals	www.nals.org
NALSC	National Assoc. of Legal Search Consultants	www.nalsc.org
NAMSS	National Association of Medical Staff Svcs	www.namss.org
NAPBS	Nat. Assoc. of Prof. Background Screeners	www.napbs.com
NAPIA	National Assoc. of Public Insurance Adjustors	www.napia.com
NAPPS	Nat. Assoc. of Professional Process Servers	www.napps.org
NAR	National Association of Realtors	www.realtor.com
NAREIT	Nat. Assoc. of Real Estate Investment Trusts	www.nareit.com/library/index.cfm
NARPM	Nat. Assoc. of Residential Property Mgrs	www.narpm.org
NASA	National Association of Screening Agencies	www.n-a-s-a.com
NAWBO	National Assoc. of Women Business Owners	www.nawbo.org
NBFAA	National Burglar & Fire Alarm Association	www.alarm.org/
NCISS	National Council of Investigation & Security Svcs	www.nciss.org
NCRA	National Court Reporters Association	www.verbatimreporters.com
NCRA	National Credit Reporting Association	www.ncrainc.org
NDIA	National Defender Investigator Association	www.ndia.net
NFIB	Nat. Federation of Independent Businesses	www.nfib.org
NFIP	National Flood Insurance Program	www.fema.gov/business/nfip/
NFPA	National Federation of Paralegal Association	www.paralegals.org
NGS	National Genealogical Society	www.ngsgenealogy.org
NHRA	National Human Resources Association	www.humanresources.org
NICB	National Insurance Crime Bureau	www.nicb.org
NLG	National Lawyers Guild	www.nlg.org
NPPRA	National Public Record Research Association	www.nprra.org
NSA	National Sheriffs' Association	www.sheriffs.org
PBUS	Professional Bail Agents of the United States	www.pbus.com
PIHRA	Profs in Human Resources Association	www.pihra.org
PRRN	Public Record Retriever Network	www.brbpub.com/prrn
REIPA	Real Estate Information Providers Assoc.	www.reipa.org

Acronym	Name	URL
SCIP	Society of Competitive Intelligence Professionals	www.scip.org
SFSA	Society of Former Special Agents of the FBI	www.socxfbi.org
SHRM	Society of Human Resources Management	www.shrm.org
SIIA	Software & Information Industry Association	www.siia.net
SILA	Society of Insurance License Administrators	www.sila.org
SLA	Special Libraries Association	www.sla.org
USFN	America's Mortgage Banking Attorneys	http://imis.usfn.org
W.A.D	World Association of Detectives	www.wad.net

Trademarks & Service Marks

United States Patent and Trademark Office

The U.S. Patent and Trademark Office (USPTO) reviews trademark applications for federal registration to determine if an applicant meets the requirements for federal registration. The USPTO does not decide who has the right to *use* a mark. Even without a registration, someone may still *use* any mark adopted to identify the source of your goods and/or services. Once a registration is issued, it is up to the owner of a mark to enforce their rights in the mark based on ownership of a federal registration.

Per the United States Patent and Trademark office (USPTO):

- A trademark is a word, phrase, symbol or design, or a combination of words, phrases, symbols or designs, that identifies and distinguishes the source of the goods of one party from those of others.

- A service mark is the same as a trademark, except that it identifies and distinguishes the source of a service rather than a product.

USPTO employees cannot conduct trademark searches for the public. However, the Electronic Business Center offers searching at www.uspto.gov/ebc/index_tm.html. There is no fee to search, but there are charges for certified copies.

Key Resources

An astounding list of international trademark resources is found at www.ggmark.com/#International_Trademark_Law

The Canadian version of Google, with most of the same features as the U.S. version, has trademark information. www.google.ca/

Unclaimed Funds

Unclaimed funds refers to money, stocks, bonds, dividends, utility deposits, vendor payments, gift certificates and insurance proceeds held by state or federal agencies who are looking for rightful owners. The Unclaimed Property Division is responsible for returning money, stocks, bonds, dividends, utility deposits, vendor payments, gift certificates and insurance proceeds of any type to the rightful owners.

Nearly every state provides a link to find unclaimed monies, and national links list are easily found on the web. The link to each state's search site is provided in the next chapter under the *Useful State Links* section.

A great resource is the National Association of Unclaimed Property Administrators (NAUPA), a non-profit organization affiliated with the National Association of State Treasurers. At www.unclaimed.org, one may do national searches or find a profile of the state agency responsible for holding unclaimed funds, including a link to the state's free web search page. Another important feature that NAUPA offers is its list of various U.S. government agencies that hold unclaimed assets. A recommended vendor is Missing Money at www.missingmoney.com.

Unions

Union Management and Reporting

The Office of Labor-Management Standards (OLMS) in the U.S. Department of Labor is the Federal agency responsible for administering and enforcing most provisions of the Labor-Management Reporting and Disclosure Act of 1959, representing employees in private industry, unions representing U.S. Postal Service employees and other Federal employee organizations. OLMS does not have jurisdiction over unions representing solely state, county, or municipal employees.

The OLMS Internet Public Disclosure Room web page enables one to search extensive public record information about unions. Go to www.dol.gov/esa/regs/compliance/olms/rrlo/lmrda.htm

Private Resources on Unions

Big Labor.com

Big Labor is sponsored by Union Communication Services Inc. And nearly every U.S.-based union with a website – national and local – can be found on the Big Labor list. www.biglabor.com

Unions.org

Unions.org manages a searchable database of union organizations across the U.S. Search by state to find a specific union or find a links list of existing unions in that state. www.unions.org

Job Tracker

Working America, an AFL-CIO affiliate, offers a unique search for companies who are "endangering their workers" or involved in cases with violations under the National Labor Relations Act. The database contains information on more than 60,000 companies nationwide. Search by ZIP Code, state or company name, or search by specific industry to see the detailed information. The Job Tracker database is at www.workingamerica.org/jobtracker.

Vessels and Boats

(See the section on *Motor Vehicle Records*.)

Vital Records

(Also see *Genealogy Resources* earlier in this chapter.)

Usually birth, death, marriage and divorce records can be searched at the local (county) level and/or at the state vital records office, which is usually part of a state health agency. If a certificate is needed, birth, death and marriage certificates are usually issued by the state; divorce certificates from the county or local entity.

Vital records are not necessarily public records. Some states place limitations, ranging from 50 to 100 years, before records are open. Therefore these "newer" records are not usually found online. In general, birth records are the most restrictive, death records the least restrictive, and marriage and divorce records somewhere in between. But the degree of restrictiveness may also depend on if a certified record is needed or if merely a computer printout will suffice.

There are several national vendors who specialize in providing vital records to clients, with a special emphasis on doing so on an expedited basis. Perhaps the most well-known one-stop shop is VitalChek Express Certificate Service at www.vitalchek.com. VitalChek has developed relationships with many of the state vital record agencies and is often promoted as the way to obtain records if you need to order by fax or online. Another vendor with similar services and direct ties to Ancestry (a vendor specialized in genealogy records) is Vitalrec.com found at http://vitalrec.com. This web page provides some excellent links and good basic searching information about each state.

Check out www.birthdatabase.net. Type in a name and approximate age and it will give a list of individuals with same name or a variant spelling, the DOBs, and the state of record location.

The web abounds with marriage record sources, most of which are genealogy based. Besides the sites mentioned above, try www.genealinks.com/register.htm.

Death Records & the Death Index of U.S. Social Security Admin

The Social Security Death Index (SSDI) contains the records of deceased persons who were assigned a SSN. Data is generated from the master death file of the U.S. Social Security Administration (SSA). The data is not searchable from a SSA site but a number of vendors purchase the data and make it available to the public. A good free search source of the SSDI is at a site maintained by Ancestry.com at http://ssdi.genealogy.rootsweb.com/cgi-bin/ssdi.cgi.

Also, there is a free search of 80,000,000+ retired-due-to-death Social Security Numbers or search by name at http://ssdi.rootsweb.com or search at www.ancestry.com/search/db.aspx?dbid=3693.

Obituaries

The database searches offered by Obituary Central at www.obitcentral.com includes not only obituaries, but also cemetery searches. The data gets stronger as you go further back in time. The site shows many resources and other links of interest. Also, search obituaries at www.ancestry.com/search/obit/.

The Nationwide Gravesite Locator

The Nationwide Gravesite Locator maintained by the U.S. Department of Veterans Affairs includes burial records from many sources. Go to http://gravelocator.cem.va.gov/j2ee/servlet/NGL_v1.

Voter Registration

Voting registration records are public record sources of addresses, voting history, and sometimes telephone numbers. Every state has a central election agency or commission, and all have a central repository of voter information collected from the local level agencies per federal mandate HAVA (Help America Vote Act of 2002, Public Law 107-252).[7]

The degree or level of accessibility to these records varies widely from state to state. Seventeen states and DC permit unrestricted access to voter registration rolls. These states generally permit the purchase of voter registration data on CD. Fees range from $2.50 (AR) to $500 (CO) for a statewide list. Thirty-three states place restrictions for record access at the state level. Generally, these states restrict access for only political or research purposes. Political purposes include purchase by political parties or candidates to solicit votes. However, all of these restrictive states permit the look-up of voter registration lists at the local level. The local level can be the county, the parish (LA), or at a municipal level.

As shown in the next chapter, 12 states offer an online search, ueasually of a voter's status. A number of public record vendors offer online access to their properitary database of voter records, but perhaps the best known vendor that specializes in voter registration records is Aristotle.com. Record data released generally includes name, address and telephone numbers, unless specifically blocked by the registrant. We believe all states and local agencies block the release of Social Security Numbers.

Weather

Historical facts on weather topics are sometimes critical in court cases. Below are several informative sites and resources that present weather information and a variety of calculators to assist planning.

- AccuWeather - www.accuweather.com
- CompuWeather - www.compuweather.com
- Forensic Meteorology Associates - www.forensic-weather.com
- Heat Index Chart - www.crh.noaa.gov/pub/heat.php

For official records of temperature go to—

- www.ncdc.noaa.gov
- www.compuweather.com
- www.weatherworksinc.com

---

[7] South Dakota is exempt from HAVA.

Workers' Compensation

Every state has an agency that administrates workers' compensation cases and records; there is no national database. Workers' compensation benefits are paid to people who have suffered an injury during the performance of their jobs. Workers' compensation records will contain the date of the incident, employer, insurance company, type of injury, body part injured, time lost, and if there is a job-related disability. Obviously, these records are useful in background investigations and fraud cases. However, most records are considered to be confidential or at least certain portions of each case file are. They're usually only released to parties involved in a case or by subpoena. Generally what is considered public record by some states is limited to determining if a subject has filed a claim, and decisions, awards or orders in disputed cases.

States that release at least a portion of workers' compensation files to the public are California, Florida, Illinois, Ohio, Oklahoma, and Wisconsin. In most other states, a signed release is necessary

Several state offer online access to some information. In Florida, access to the claims history database is provided online at www.fldfs.com/wc/databases.html, all personal information has been redacted. Case status for Illinois cases at shown at www.iwcc.il.gov. In Nebraska, workers' comp record requests may be made at www.nebraska.gov/WC/records.phtml. Unless specifically requested, responses will be limited to first and subsequent reports filed within the last five (5) years.

World Wide Web

Web Pages' "Public Records"

There is plenty of public information that can be found about a web page. A number of useful resources report who owns a URL and how to contact them, the webmaster, the software, and even if an address has been blacklisted.

Search for a URL at http://whois.domaintools.com to find physical details about a website including meta description, registry creation and expiration dates, server details, webmaster contact info, and its all-important basic WhoIs record of the registrant. At the URL above, click on 'wiki article about ~' and the www.aboutus.com site displays what the public sees as your main page opens and other public details about your site.

InterNIC (www.internic.net) provides public information and other useful information on popular web topics – viruses, IP address, website content, registries. InterNIC provides a simple WhoIs lookup. Another good IP search site is ARIN at www.arin.net/whois/index.html.

VeriSign provides a list of North American website registrars. Go to www.verisign.com/information-services/index.html and click on Find a Registrar.

See www.norid.no/domenenavnbaser/domreg.en.html for foreign registries.

Other Web Page Resources and Tools

- The Internet Corporation for Assigned Names and Numbers (ICANN) is a network of inter-related sites who manage the naming system for the millions of internet sites. From www.icann.net you may link to www.icann.org (operations), www.internic.net (instructions for names and registrations), www.iana.org (numbering), www.alac.icann.org (advisory), and www.gac.icann.org (government advising). There is also an ICANN chat forum.

- The WhoIs page at www.networksolutions.com/whois can conveniently tell you if a name is available or not and under what suffix, also lets you search for expired domain names.

- An excellent tool for analyzing a website is the NetSolutions' WhoIs search at www.networksolutions.com/whois/index.jsp. Results include who owns or registered a site, the IP address, a screen capture of the home page, traffic ranking, more.

- To find out if anyone is imitating your site to steal your customers use the Domain Search feature at http://domain-search.domaintools.com. This can also be used as an alerting tool that lets you know when someone uses registry terms too similar to your own.

- Use the Xenu web check tool for reports on URLs and broken links. Go to http://home.snafu.de/tilman/xenulink.html and download the free Xenu's Link Sleuth. You can check the status of a list of URLs by posted a list on the site and Xenu will generate a report.

- To find the IP address (e.g 200.100.100.80) you are using on your computer go to www.palserv.com/ipdisp.html or www.whatismyipaddress.com.

- To find information about an email address, check www.theultimates.com/email/.

- A "reverse" email address finder is at InfoSpace at www.infospace.com/home/white-pages/reverse-email.

- Historical web pages can be found at the WayBack Machine at www.archive.org/index.php. Another resource is GigaBlast at www.gigablast.com and Search Engine Showdown at www.searchengineshowdown.com

State and Local Government Online Sources

Individual state chapters have been compiled into an easy to use format that details what is available online. Fee-based systems and free online access systems are denoted with a specific ICON – **$$** or **Free** – next to the type or category of available records.

Within each state's section, these four sub-chapters or sections are presented in this order:

1. State Public Record Agencies

2. State Licensing and Regulatory Boards

3. County Courts

4. County Recorder & Assessor Offices

Be sure to review the Structure and Online Access notes found at the beginning of each state's Courts and Recorder's Office sections. This is a good place to find out about statewide online systems.

One last tip...remember that just because records are maintained in a certain way in your state or county do not assume that any other county or state does things the same way.

Alabama

Capital: Montgomery
            Montgomery County
Time Zone: CST
Population: 4,627,851
# of Counties: 67

Useful State Links

Website: www.alabama.gov
Governor: www.governor.state.al.us
Attorney General: www.ago.state.al.us
State Archives: www.archives.state.al.us
State Statutes and Codes: www.legislature.state.al.us/prefiled/prefiled.html
Legislative Bill Search: www.legislature.state.al.us
Unclaimed Funds: www.treasury.state.al.us/website/ucpd/ucpd_searchframe.html

Primary State Agencies

Criminal Records $$

Alabama Bureau of Investigation, Identification Unit - Record Checks,   http://dps.alabama.gov/ABI/cic.aspx   This agency recommends that searchers contact www.background.alabama.gov/. This is a subscription service with a $25 search fee and a $75 annual fee. Employers using a CRA must be registered first.

Sexual Offender Registry Free

Department of Public Safety, Sexual Offender Registry, http://community.dps.alabama.gov/ Sex offender data and a felony fugitives list are available online at the home page. Search by name, ZIP, city or county. Missing persons and felony fugitives are also shown.

Incarceration Records Free

Alabama Department of Corrections, Central Records Office, http://doc.state.al.us Information on current inmates only is available online at http://doc.state.al.us/inmatesearch.asp. Location, AIS number, physical identifiers, and projected release date are released. The database is updated weekly.

Corporation, LP, LLC, LLP, Trade Names, Trademarks/Servicemarks Free

Secretary of State, Corporations Division, www.sos.alabama.gov/ The website has free searches of corporate and UCC records. Search individual files for Active Names at http://arc-sos.state.al.us/CGI/SOSCRP01.MBR/INPUT. Also, search securities department administrative actions lists free at http://asc.state.al.us/Issued-Orders.htm.

Uniform Commercial Code, Federal & State Tax Liens Free

UCC Division - SOS, UCC Records, www.sos.state.al.us/vb/inquiry/inquiry.aspx?area=UCC The agency has UCC information available to search at www.sos.state.al.us/vb/inquiry/inquiry.aspx?area=UCC. There is no fee. You can search by debtor's name or file number. Farm UCC filings are no longer available thru online searches. Collateral information and /or image is not available to view online. Corporation data is available from this site as well. *Other Options:* Bulk sale by CD for $1,500 plus $300 a week for updates.

Driver Records $$

Department of Public Safety, Driver Records-License Division, http://dps.alabama.gov/DriverLicense/ Alabama.gov is designated the state's agent for online access of state driving records. A Subscriber Registration Agreement must be submitted. Both Alabama.gov and the Alabama DPS must approve all subscribers. There is a $75.00 annual administrative fee for new accounts and the search fee is $7.00 per record. The driver license number is needed to search. The system, open 24 hours daily, is Internet-based. Alabama.gov (Alabama Interactive) can be reached at 2 N. Jackson St, #301, Montgomery AL, 36104, (866) 353-3468.

Vital Records $$

Center for Health Statistics, Record Services Division, www.adph.org/vitalrecords/ Online ordering is available from the webpage through a service provider www.vitalchek.com. Check their sites for fees and turnaround times. *Other Options:* Index to death records are available on microfilm for $40.00 per roll. There are 6 rolls of records for 1908 through 1959. Microfilm rolls of marriage records are available for purchase at $40.00 each. There are 11 rolls available which includes index to records for 1936 to 1969. There is one microfilm roll of index for divorce records for 1950-59 available for $40.00.

Occupational Licensing Boards

Abortion/Reproductive Health Ctr..... www.adph.org/providers/
Accountant.. www.asbpa.alabama.gov/register/register.asp
Ambulatory Surgery Ctr .... www.adph.org/providers/
Anesthesiologist Assistant .... www.albme.org/Default.aspx?Page=LicenseeSearch
Architect .... www.boa.state.al.us/rostersearch/rostersearch.asp
Assisted Living Facility/Unit............. www.adph.org/providers/
Audiologist .... www.abespa.org/verify.htm
Bank .... www.bank.state.al.us/bank_search.aspx
Birthing Center .... www.adph.org/providers/
Certified Lead Firm .... www.adph.org/lead/Default.asp?id=1602
Check Casher...................................... www.bank.state.al.us/Search_All_Licences2.asp
Chiropractor....................................... https://www.alabamainteractive.org/asbce/VerificationEntryPoint.do
Clinical Nurse Specialist .... www.abn.state.al.us/Apps/Verification/Verification.aspx
Consumer Finance Company............. www.bank.state.al.us/Search_All_Licences2.asp
Contractor, General .... www.genconbd.state.al.us/DATABASE-SQL/roster.aspx
Cosmetologist www.aboc.state.al.us/Search1.htm
Counselor, Professional .... www.abec.state.al.us/PDFs/IndexofFinalOrders.pdf
Dietitian/Nutritionist.......................... www.boed.alabama.gov/license_search/search_form.aspx
Electrical Contractor.......................... www.aecb.state.al.us/Search/new_search.asp
Electrician, Journeyman .... www.aecb.state.al.us/Search/new_search.asp
Engineer/Engineer in Training .... www.bels.alabama.gov/LicenseeSearch/searchmenu.asp
Esthetician/Esthetician Apprentice www.aboc.state.al.us/Search1.htm
Esthetic'n Student/Inst'ct/Sch'l/Exam www.aboc.state.al.us/Search1.htm
Forester.. http://asbrf.alabama.gov/rosterofforesters.asp
Gas Fitter .... www.pgfb.state.al.us/Inquiry.aspx
Geologist .... www.algeobd.state.al.us/roster_search.asp
HazMat Service .... www.adem.state.al.us/LandDivision/Reports/reports.htm
Heating/Air Conditioning Contractor www.hvacboard.state.al.us/Lic_Search/searchform.asp
Home Builder .... www.hblb.state.al.us/Lic_Search/all-ind.asp
Home Health Agency .... www.adph.org/providers/
Home Medical Equip. Svcs. Provider www.homemed.state.al.us/search.htm
Hospital/or/Hospice .... www.adph.org/providers/
Insurance Adjuster/Agent .... www.aldoi.gov/SearchFor.aspx
Insurance Broker/Producer .... www.aldoi.gov/SearchFor.aspx
Insurance Corp./Co./Partnership........ www.aldoi.org/CompanySearch/
Interior Designer................................ www.idboard.alabama.gov/search/start.aspx
Interpreter .... www.albit.state.al.us/INTERPRETER_ROSTERS.htm
Landscape Architect .... www.abela.state.al.us/architects.html
Lender/Loan Source .... www.bank.state.al.us/Search_All_Licences2.asp
LPG-Liquefied Petrol. Gas Broker .... www.lpgb.state.al.us/Search.htm
Manicurist Salon/Sch'l/stud/instruct'r www.aboc.state.al.us/Search1.htm
Manicurist/Manicurist Appren./Exam www.aboc.state.al.us/Search1.htm
Marriage/Family Therapist .... www.mft.state.al.us/Search/search.asp
Massage Therapist .... www.almtbd.state.al.us/roster_search.asp
Medical Doctor................................... www.albme.org/Default.aspx?Page=LicenseeSearch
Medical Gas Piper .... www.pgfb.state.al.us/Inquiry.aspx
Mental Health Center .... www.adph.org/providers/
Midwife Nurse................................... www.abn.state.al.us/Apps/Verification/Verification.aspx
Mortgage Broker .... www.bank.state.al.us/Search_All_Licences2.asp
Notary Public..................................... www.sos.state.al.us/vb/inquiry/inquiry.aspx?area=Notaries%20Public
Nurse Anesthetist............................... www.abn.state.al.us/Apps/Verification/Verification.aspx

Nurse-LPN/RN .... www.abn.state.al.us/Apps/Verification/Verification.aspx
Nursing Disciplinary Action.............. www.abn.state.al.us/Apps/Verification/Verification.aspx
Nursing Home .... www.adph.org/providers/
Nursing Home Administrator .... www.alboenha.state.al.us/logon.html
Nutritionist .... www.boed.alabama.gov/license_search/search_form.aspx
Occupational Therapist/Asst............. www.asbot.state.al.us/search.htm
Optometrist...................................... http://optometry.alabama.gov/Search.aspx
Osteopathic Physician....................... www.albme.org/Default.aspx?Page=LicenseeSearch
Pawn Shop.. www.bank.state.al.us/Search_All_Licences2.asp
Pharmacist/Pharmacy Intern.............. https://www.cebroker.com/public/pb_index.asp?hIndexType=alabama
Physical Therapist/Therapist Asst ..... www.pt.state.al.us/License/searchform.asp
Physician .... www.albme.org/Default.aspx?Page=LicenseeSearch
Physician Assistant.......................... www.albme.org/Default.aspx?Page=LicenseeSearch
Physiological Lab, Clinical................ www.adph.org/providers/
Plumber .... www.pgfb.state.al.us/Inquiry.aspx
Podiatrist... www.podiatryboard.alabama.gov/current_licensees.html
Pre-Need Sales Agent....................... www.aldoi.gov/SearchFor.aspx
Public Account.-CPA-Non Licensee . www.asbpa.alabama.gov/register/register.asp
Real Estate Agent/Seller................... www.arello.com/
Real Estate Appraiser .... http://reab.state.al.us/appraisers/searchform.asp
Real Estate Broker........................... www.arello.com/
Registered Nurse Practitioner........... www.abn.state.al.us/Apps/Verification/Verification.aspx
Rehabilitation Center........................ www.adph.org/providers/
Renal Disease Terminal Treatm't Ctr www.adph.org/providers/
Rural Primary Care Hospital .... www.adph.org/providers/
School Superintendent...................... www.alsde.edu/html/super_listing.asp?menu=none&footer=general
Senior Volunteer, Medical................ www.albme.org/Default.aspx?Page=LicenseeSearch
Shampoo Assistant www.aboc.state.al.us/Search1.htm
Sleep Disorder Center....................... www.adph.org/providers/
Social Worker.................................. www.abswe.state.al.us/Lic_Search/search.asp
Social Worker, Private Practice .... www.abswe.state.al.us/Lic_Search/searchpip.asp
Soil Classifier .... www.swcc.state.al.us/Soil%20Roster&%20Forms.htm
Special Purpose License, Medical ..... www.albme.org/Default.aspx?Page=LicenseeSearch
Speech Pathologist/Audiologist......... www.abespa.org/verify.htm
Sports Agent.................................... www.sos.state.al.us/Downloads/dl1.aspx
Surgeon/or/ Surgeon's Assistant .... www.albme.org/Default.aspx?Page=LicenseeSearch
Surplus Line Broker .... www.aldoi.gov/SearchFor.aspx
Surveyor, Land .... www.bels.alabama.gov/LicenseeSearch/searchmenu.asp
Therapist, Marriage and Family .... www.mft.state.al.us/Search/search.asp
Transliterator .... www.albit.state.al.us/INTERPRETER_ROSTERS.htm
X-ray (Portable) Supplier .... www.adph.org/providers/

State and Local Courts

State Court Structure: Circuit Courts are the courts of general jurisdiction; District Courts have limited jurisdiction in civil matters. These courts are combined in all but eight larger counties. Barbour, Coffee, Jefferson, St. Clair, Talladega, and Tallapoosa Counties have two court locations within the county. Jefferson County (Birmingham), Madison (Huntsville), Marshall, and Tuscaloosa Counties have separate criminal divisions for Circuit Courts and/or District Courts. All counties have separate probate courts.

Statewide Court Online Access: Two sources of statewide online access exist; both are by subscription. There are significant differences between the two; one contains almost all court record types; the second contains only criminal data. The commercial online subscription services at www.alacourt.com draws its data from the State Judicial Information System (SJIS). This alacourt.com system is comprehensive and user friendly, includes civil, criminal, DR, traffic, warrants, and trial court dockets statewide. It also features multiple monthly payment plans. A record request form is found at http://helpdesk.alacourt.gov/requestform.asp that allows you to specify case data or search on a county basis.

The second subscription service is offered by Alabama Criminal Justice Information Center (ACJIC), the state agency responsible for information sharing among the state's criminal justice community. As such, ACJIC is the official repository for all state of Alabama criminal history records and it offeres an Alabama Background Check (ABC) to the public, tailored for background checkers. This is a subscription service with a $25 search fee and a $75 annual fee. Employers using a CRA must be registered first. See http://www.background.alabama.gov/

Also, State Supreme Court and Appellate decisions are available at www.judicial.state.al.us/.

❖ **Statewide Access Offered All Trial Courts — Read Above**

Below are Additional Sites ❖

Baldwin County

Probate Court `Free` Online access to the probate record index is free at www.deltacomputersystems.com/al/al05/probatea.html.

Mobile County

Probate Court `Free` Online access to the probate record index is free at http://probate.mobilecountyal.gov/.

Recorders, Assessors, and Other Sites of Note

Recording Office Organization: 67 counties, 71 recording offices. The recording officer is the Judge of Probate. Four counties have two recording offices- Barbour, Coffee, Jefferson, and St. Clair. Federal and state tax liens on personal property of businesses are filed with the Secretary of State. Other federal and state tax liens are filed with the County Judge of Probate.

Online Access Note: There is no statewide system but a increasing number of counties offer free online access to recorded documents and tax assessor data, and property info on GIS-mapping sites.

Autauga County *Property, Taxation Records* `Free` Access the GIS-property info database and Tax Office free at www.emapsplus.com/ALAutauga/maps/. Click on search by name.

Baldwin County *Real Estate, Deed, UCC Records* www.co.baldwin.al.us/PageView.asp?PageType=R&edit_id=1 `Free` Access to recordings, deeds, and UCCs is at the website, see the "Recording" box.
Property, Taxation Records `Free` Property tax data is at www.deltacomputersystems.com/AL/AL05/plinkquerya.html. Also, search property appraiser records at www.deltacomputersystems.com/AL/AL05/pappraisala.html.

Barbour County *Property, Taxation Records* `Free` Access the GIS-property info database and Tax Office free at www.emapsplus.com/ALBarbour/maps/. Click on search by name.

Bibb County *Property, Taxation Records* Access property and tax office data free at www.emapsplus.com/subscription/states/alabama/state.asp.

Blount County *Property, Taxation Records* `Free` Public records available from the Revenue Commissioner's Office at www.blountrevenue.com/Public_Records.htm includes property and assessment records.

Calhoun County *Property, Taxation Records* `Free` Access the GIS-property info database and Tax Office free at www.emapsplus.com/ALCalhoun/maps/. Click on search by name.

Chambers County *Real Estate, UCC Records* `$$` Access real estate and UCC data online by subscription for $65.00 monthly fee. Records are live and go back 5 years. For info, call 706-643-1010 or 334-864-4384.
Property, Taxation Records `Free` Access parcel data on the GIS-mapping site free at www.chamberscountymaps.com/. Must download Mapguide Viewer Software first. Password required for full data.

Chilton County *Property, Taxation Records* `Free` Access property and tax office data free at www.emapsplus.com/subscription/states/alabama/state.asp.

Clarke County *Property, Taxation Records* `Free` Access the GIS-property info database and Tax Office free at www.emapsplus.com/ALClarke/maps/. Click on search by name.

Coffee County *Real Estate, Deed, Lien, Mortgage, Personal Property Records* www.probateoffice.info `$$`
Subscription access to all Judge of Probate indexes available, call Michelle at 205-758-2000 x8112; $25.00 signup fee, view images at $.75 each or less, print images $.25 each. Data is same as appears on PAT.

Property, Taxation Records `Free` Access parcel data on GIS-property database at www.emapsplus.com/ALCoffee/maps/.

Colbert County *Property, Taxation Records* `Free` Access property tax records free at www.deltacomputersystems.com/search.html.

Coosa County *Property, Taxation Records* `Free` Access property and tax office data free at www.emapsplus.com/subscription/states/alabama/state.asp.

Cullman County *Real Estate, Deed, Lien, Mortgage Records* `$$` Subscription access to all Judge of Probate indexes available, call Michelle at 205-758-2000 x8112; $25.00 signup fee, view images at $.75 each or less, print images $.50 each. Data is same as appears on PAT.

Property, Taxation Records `Free` Access the GIS-property info database and Tax Office free at www.emapsplus.com/ALCullman/maps/. Click on search by name.

De Kalb County *Property, Taxation Records* `Free` Access the GIS-property info database and Tax Office free at www.emapsplus.com/ALDeKalb/maps/. Click on search by name.

Elmore County *Property, Taxation Records* `Free` Access the GIS-property info database and Tax Office free at www.emapsplus.com/ALElmore/maps/. Click on search by name.

Escambia County *Property, Taxation Records* `Free` Access to the county property appraisal data is free at www.deltacomputersystems.com/AL/AL30/INDEX.HTML . Also, access to the GIS-property information database and Tax Office is free at www.emapsplus.com/ALEscambia/maps/. Click on search by name.

Etowah County *Property, Taxation Records* `Free` Access to property data through a private company is free at www.deltacomputersystems.com/AL/AL31/pappraisala.html. Also, tax records are free at www.deltacomputersystems.com/AL/AL31/plinkquerya.html.

Fayette County *Property, Taxation Records* `Free` Access to property data is free at www.fayettealmaps.com; Use password "Ruby." You may have to download the map viewer. Also, access parcel data on the GIS-mapping site free at www.fayettealmaps.com/. Must download Mapguide Viewer Software first. Password required for full data.

Geneva County *Property, Taxation Records* `Free` Access the GIS-property info database and Tax Office free at www.emapsplus.com/ALGeneva/maps/. Click on search by name.

Henry County *Property, Taxation Records* `Free` Access tax data search database free at www.henrycountyrevenue.com/search.aspx. Also, access parcel data on the GIS-mapping site free at www.alabamagis.com/Henry/. Must download Mapguide Viewer Software first.

Houston County *Real Estate, Deed, Lien, Mortgage, Personal Property Records* `$$` Subscription access to all Judge of Probate indexes available, call Michelle at 205-758-2000 x8112; $25.00 signup fee, view images at $.75 each or less, print images $.15 each. Data is same as appears on PAT.

Jackson County *Property, Taxation Records* `Free` Access Rev Commission property tax lookup free at www.deltacomputersystems.com/AL/AL39/pappraisala.html. Also, search the property tax payment lookup free at www.jacksoncountyrevenue.com/search.aspx.

Jefferson County *Property, Taxation Records* `Free` Search tax assessor name list free at www.jeffcointouch.com/ecourthouse/ta-name-search.htm. Access the Tax Due Inquiry and Tax Sales list and Insolvents list free at http://tc.jeffcointouch.com/taxcollection/HTML/index.asp. Access equalization property records free at www.jeffcointouch.com/ecourthouse/boe-search-parcel-ID.htm but no name searching. Also, search tax collector data by name free at www.jeffcointouch.com/ecourthouse/tc-name-search.htm.

Lamar County *Property, Taxation Records* `Free` Access the GIS-property info database and Tax Office free at www.emapsplus.com/ALLamar/maps/. Click on search by name.

Lauderdale County *Property, Taxation Records* `Free` Access to property appraisal data is free at www.deltacomputersystems.com/AL/AL41/pappraisala.html.

Lawrence County *Property, Taxation Records* `Free` Access property data free at www.emapsplus.com/ALLawrence/maps/ including name searching.

Lee County *Property, Taxation Records* `Free` Access to property appraisal records is free at www.deltacomputersystems.com/AL/AL43/pappraisala.html. View property tax data free at www.deltacomputersystems.com/AL/AL41/plinkquerya.html. Also, access parcel data on the GIS-mapping site free at www.leecountymaps.com/. Must download Mapguide Viewer Software first. Password required for full data.

Limestone County *Real Estate, Deed, Lien, Mortgage, Personal Property Records* www.co.limestone.al.us `$$` Access to recording records by subscription to the PROMIS system; contact Michelle Wooley at Syscon at 205-758-2000 x8112. $25 signup. View images at $.75 each or less, print images $.25 each. Data is same as appears on PAT.

Property, Taxation Records **Free** Access the GIS-property information database and Tax Office free at www.emapsplus.com/ALlimestone/maps/. Click on search by name.

Macon County *Property, Taxation Records* **Free** Access property and tax office data free at www.emapsplus.com/subscription/states/alabama/state.asp.

Madison County *Real Estate, Deed, Lien, Judgment, Marriage, Military Discharge Records* www.co.madison.al.us/probate/home.shtml **Free** Access to the judge of probate's recording index is free at http://probate.co.madison.al.us/. Land records including images go back to 1971; marriage and military discharges back to 1976.
Property, Taxation Records **Free** Access the GIS-property info database and Tax Office free at www.emapsplus.com/ALMadison/maps/. Click on search by name.

Marion County *Property, Taxation Records* **Free** Access the county GIS-mapping and property information data for free at www.marioncountymaps.com/FrameSet.htm. Also, access parcel data on the GIS-mapping site free at www.marioncountymaps.com/. Must download Mapguide Viewer Software first.

Marshall County *Business License Records* www.mcit.us/ **Free** Search business license database free at www.mcit.us/businesslicenses/searchengine/. Search Town of Douglas licenses at www.mcit.us/businesslicenses/douglas/.
Property, Taxation Records **Free** Access property data free at www.marshallgis.org and click on Land Lookup.

Mobile County *Real Estate, Grantor/Grantee, Deed, Mortgage, UCC, Incorporation, Marriage, Estate Claim, Voter Registration Records* www.mobilecounty.org/probate/ **Free** Access real estate, grantor/grantee, deed records and more back to 2000 free at www.mobilecounty.org/probatecourt/recordssearch.htm. Also, search real and personal property, estate claims, and election results. Search marriages at http://records.mobile-county.net/Login.aspx?SessionExpired=I.
Property, Taxation Records **Free** Access real property and personal property tax records free at http://mobilerevenue.siteonestudio.com/TaxBill/search.asp. Also, City of Mobile property ownership data is free at http://maps.cityofmobile.org/webmapping.htm. Click on Property ownership information and choose to search by name.

Montgomery County *Property, Taxation Records* **Free** Access the GIS-property info database and Tax Office free at www.emapsplus.com/ALMontgomery/maps/.

Morgan County *Real Estate, Deed, Lien, Marriage, Probate, Judgment Records* www.morgancountyprobate.com **Free** Access the probate office recording index at www.morgancountyprobate.com/DesktopDefault.aspx?tabindex=4&tabid=8. Select to search by document type. Land records go back to 1999.
Property, Taxation Records **Free** Access GIS-property info data and Tax Office at www.emapsplus.com/ALMorgan/maps/. Click on search by name. Also, access property appraiser data free at www.deltacomputersystems.com/AL/AL52/pappraisala.html. Also, search Revenue Commissioner property tax payment search at https://secure.termnetinc.com/morgan/paymentType.jsp but no name searching.

Perry County *Property, Taxation Records* **Free** Access property and tax office data free at www.emapsplus.com/subscription/states/alabama/state.asp.

Pickens County *Property, Taxation Records* **Free** Access parcel data on the GIS-mapping site free at www.alabamagis.com/Pickens/. Must download Mapguide Viewer Software first.

Russell County *Property, Taxation Records* **Free** Access the GIS-property info database and Tax Office free at www.emapsplus.com/ALRussell/maps/. Click on search by name.

St. Clair County *Property, Taxation Records* **Free** Access to the GIS-property information database and Tax Office is free at www.emapsplus.com/ALstclair/maps/. Click on search by name. Also, access to property appraiser data is free at www.deltacomputersystems.com/AL/AL59/pappraisala.html. Also, access to county assessor data is free at www.deltacomputersystems.com/AL/AL59/plinkquerya.html.

Shelby County *Real Estate, Judgment, Deed, UCC, Notary, Fictitious Name, Marriage, Probate Records* www.shelbycountyalabama.com **Free** Access recording data free at www.shelbycountyalabama.com/probate/default.htm.
Property, Taxation Records **Free** Search property tax records free at www.shelbycountyalabama.com/prop_search.asp/

Talladega County *Property, Taxation Records* **Free** Access the GIS-property info database and Tax Office free at www.emapsplus.com/ALtalladega/maps/. Click on search by name.

Tallapoosa County *Property, Taxation Records* **Free** Access parcel data on the GIS-mapping site free at www.tallapoosacountymaps.com/. Must download Mapguide Viewer Software first. Password required for full data.

Tuscaloosa County *Real Estate, Grantor/Grantee, Deed, Lien, Judgment, UCC, Probate, Marriage, Mortgage, Plat Records* www.tuscco.com **Free** Access to the recorders database is free at www.tuscco.com/recordroom/. Also included are incorporations, bonds, discharges, exemptions. Probate court, miscellaneous.
Property, Taxation Records **Free** Access to property and assessor data is free at www.emapsplus.com/ALTuscaloosa/maps/. Click on owner search. Also, access tax sale and other records free at www.tuscco.com/recordroom/.

Walker County *Real Estate, Deed, Lien, Mortgage, Personal Property Records* www.walkercounty.com ▇▇
Access Probate office real estate/property records by subscription; $25.00 signup fee, view images at $.75 each or less, print images
$1 each. Data is same as appears on PAT. Call Michelle, 205-758-200 x8112 or email mwooley@syscomonline.com.
Property, Taxation Records **Free** Access parcel data on the GIS-mapping site free at www.walkercountymaps.com/. Must
download Mapguide Viewer Software first. Password required for full data.

Winston County *Property, Taxation Records* **Free** Access parcel data on the GIS-mapping site free at
www.alabamagis.com/winston/. Must download Mapguide Viewer Software first. Password required for full data.

Other Alabama Sites of Note:

Calhoun County - Sex Offenders List, Most Wanted www.calhouncountysheriff.org/ From Sept 1999 forward only.
Jefferson County - County Inmates http://sheriff.jccal.org
Jefferson County - Inmates, Offenders https://www.vinelink.com/vinelink/siteInfoAction.do?siteId=1960
Jefferson County - Most Wanted www.jeffcosheriff.org/most_wanted.php
Jefferson County - Unclaimed Property, Treasurer www.jeffcointouch.com/jeffcointouch/directory/dd35.html
Lee County - Sex Offenders www.icrimewatch.net/index.php?AgencyID=54018
Marshall County - Registered Sex Offenders www.alabamagis.org/sexoffenders/
Tuscaloosa County - Jail, Most Wanted, Missing Persons, Sex Offenders www.tcsoal.org

Alaska

Capital: Juneau
               Juneau Borough
Time Zone: AK (Alaska Standard Time)
Population: 683,478
# of Boroughs/Divisions: 23

Useful State Links

Website: www.state.ak.us
Governor: www.gov.state.ak.us
Attorney General- www.law.state.ak.us
State Archives: www.archives.state.ak.us
State Statutes and Codes: www.legis.state.ak.us/folhome.htm
Legislative Bill Search: www.legis.state.ak.us/basis/start.asp
Bill Monitoring: www.legis.state.ak.us/basis/btmf_login.asp?session=24
Unclaimed Funds: http://www.tax.alaska.gov/programs/programs/index.aspx?23050

Primary State Agencies

Sexual Offender Registry `Free`
Department of Public Safety, Statewide Services Div-SOCKR Unit, www.dps.state.ak.us/sorweb/Sorweb.aspx Name searching and geographic searching is available at the website. This is the primary search offered by the agency.

Corporation, LP, LLP, LLC, Fictitious/Assumed Names `Free`
Corporation Section, Department of Commerce, Community & Econ Dev, www.commerce.state.ak.us/occ/home.htm At the website, one can access status information on corps, LLCs, LLP, LP (all both foreign and domestic), registered and reserved names. Search by entity name, registered agent name, or by officer name. There is no fee. Also, search Dept of Commerce Securities Dept. Disciplinary actions at www.dced.state.ak.us/bsc/orders.htm. *Other Options:* The business license database can be downloaded from the web.

Uniform Commercial Code `Free`
UCC Central File Systems Office, State Recorder's Office, www.ucc.alaska.gov/ One can search by debtor or secured party name, date, document number or document type at www.ucc.alaska.gov/search.cfm. There is no fee. *Other Options:* CDs or FTPs of document images can be purchased from the State Recorder's Office (907-269-8878).

Driver Records `SS`
Division of Motor Vehicles, Driver's Records, www.state.ak.us/dmv/ Online access costs $10.00 per record. This is for pre-approved, ongoing requesters only. Inquiries may be made at any time, 24 hours a day. Batch inquiries may call back within thirty minutes for responses. Search by the first four letters of driver's name, license number and date of birth. Note this is not a web-based system.

Vital Records `SS`
Department of Health & Social Services, Bureau of Vital Statistics, www.hss.state.ak.us/dph/bvs/ Records may be ordered online via a state-designated vendor at www.vitalchek.com. There is a $5.50 service fee. Use of credit card required.

Occupational Licensing Boards

Acupuncturist www.commerce.state.ak.us/occ/search3.htm
Anesthetist, Dental, General/Permit .. www.commerce.state.ak.us/occ/search3.htm
Architect www.commerce.state.ak.us/occ/search3.htm
Athletic Event Promoter www.commerce.state.ak.us/occ/search3.htm
Athletic Trainer www.commerce.state.ak.us/occ/search3.htm

Attorney	www.alaskabar.org/index.cfm?id=4954
Audiologist/Hearing Aid Dealer	www.commerce.state.ak.us/occ/search3.htm
Bail Bondsman	www.commerce.state.ak.us/ins/apps/producersearch/InsLicStart.cfm
Bank	www.commerce.state.ak.us/bsc/pub/2007_Directory.pdf
Barber	www.commerce.state.ak.us/occ/search3.htm
Barber Shop Owner/School/Instruc.	www.commerce.state.ak.us/occ/search3.htm
Big Game Guide/Assist/Transporter	www.commerce.state.ak.us/occ/search3.htm
Boxer/Boxing Physician	www.commerce.state.ak.us/occ/search3.htm
Boxing/Wrestling Personnel	www.commerce.state.ak.us/occ/search3.htm
Child Care Provider/Home/Center	www.hss.state.ak.us/apps/dpa/SearchFacilities.aspx
Chiropractor	www.commerce.state.ak.us/occ/search3.htm
Collection Agency/Operator	www.commerce.state.ak.us/occ/search3.htm
Concert Promoter	www.commerce.state.ak.us/occ/search3.htm
Construction Contractor	www.commerce.state.ak.us/occ/search3.htm
Contractor, Residential	www.commerce.state.ak.us/occ/search3.htm
Contr'r, Civil/Elect./Mech./Mine/Petrol.	www.commerce.state.ak.us/occ/search3.htm
Cosmetologist/Hairdresser	www.commerce.state.ak.us/occ/search3.htm
Cosmetology Shop Owner/sch'l/instr	www.commerce.state.ak.us/occ/search3.htm
Counselor, Professional	www.dced.state.ak.us/occ/OccSearch/main.cfm
Defibrillator Technician	http://hss.state.ak.us/apps/EMSCert/portal.aspx
Dental Hygienist	www.commerce.state.ak.us/occ/search3.htm
Dentist/Dental Examiner	www.commerce.state.ak.us/occ/search3.htm
Dietitian/Nutritionist	www.dced.state.ak.us/occ/OccSearch/main.cfm
Drug Distributor/Drug Room	www.commerce.state.ak.us/occ/search3.htm
Electrical Administrator	www.commerce.state.ak.us/occ/search3.htm
Emergency Medical Technician	http://hss.state.ak.us/apps/EMSCert/portal.aspx
Employment Agency Operator	www.dced.state.ak.us/occ/search3.htm
Engineer	www.commerce.state.ak.us/occ/search3.htm
Esthetician	www.commerce.state.ak.us/occ/search3.htm
Funeral Director/Establishment	www.commerce.state.ak.us/occ/search3.htm
Geologist	www.commerce.state.ak.us/occ/search3.htm
Guide/Outfitter, Hunting	www.commerce.state.ak.us/occ/search3.htm
Hairdresser/Esthetician	www.commerce.state.ak.us/occ/search3.htm
Hearing Aid Dealer	www.commerce.state.ak.us/occ/search3.htm
Independent Adjuster	www.commerce.state.ak.us/ins/apps/producersearch/InsLicStart.cfm
Insurance Occupation	www.commerce.state.ak.us/ins/apps/producersearch/InsLicStart.cfm
Insurance Producer	www.commerce.state.ak.us/ins/apps/producersearch/InsLicStart.cfm
Landscape Architect	www.commerce.state.ak.us/occ/search3.htm
Lobbyist/Lobbyist Employer	www.state.ak.us/local/akpages/ADMIN/apoc/lobcov.htm
Marriage & Family Therapist	www.dced.state.ak.us/occ/OccSearch/main.cfm
Mechanical Administrator	www.commerce.state.ak.us/occ/search3.htm
Medical Doctor/Surgeon	www.commerce.state.ak.us/occ/search3.htm
Midwife	www.dced.state.ak.us/occ/OccSearch/main.cfm
Mortician/Embalmer	www.commerce.state.ak.us/occ/search3.htm
Naturopathic Physician	www.commerce.state.ak.us/occ/search3.htm
Notary Public	http://list.state.ak.us/guest/RemoteListSummary/AK_Notary
Nurse Anesthetist	www.commerce.state.ak.us/occ/search3.htm
Nurse-RN/LPN	www.commerce.state.ak.us/occ/search3.htm
Nurses' Aide	www.commerce.state.ak.us/occ/search3.htm
Nursing Home Administrator	www.commerce.state.ak.us/occ/search3.htm
Occupational Therapist/Assistant	www.commerce.state.ak.us/occ/search3.htm
Optician, Dispensing	www.commerce.state.ak.us/occ/search3.htm
Optometrist	www.commerce.state.ak.us/occ/search3.htm
Osteopathic Physician	www.commerce.state.ak.us/occ/search3.htm
Paramedic	www.commerce.state.ak.us/occ/search3.htm
Parenteral Sedation (Dental)	www.commerce.state.ak.us/occ/search3.htm
Pesticide Applicator	www.dec.state.ak.us/eh/pest/certified.htm

Pesticide Permit/ Pesticide Registr. ... www.dec.state.ak.us/eh/pest/permitholders.htm
Pharmacist/Pharmacist Intern www.commerce.state.ak.us/occ/search3.htm
Pharmacy/Pharmacy Technician........ www.commerce.state.ak.us/occ/search3.htm
Physical Therapist/Assistant............. www.commerce.state.ak.us/occ/search3.htm
Physician Assistant.......................... www.commerce.state.ak.us/occ/search3.htm
Pilot, Marine.................................. www.commerce.state.ak.us/occ/search3.htm
Podiatrist.. www.commerce.state.ak.us/occ/search3.htm
Process Server .... www.dps.state.ak.us/PermitsLicensing/images/CPSlist.pdf
Psychologist/Psycholog'l Assistant.... www.commerce.state.ak.us/occ/search3.htm
Public Accountant-CPA .... www.dced.state.ak.us/occ/OccSearch/main.cfm
Real Estate Agent/Broker/Assoc. www.commerce.state.ak.us/occ/search3.htm
Real Estate Appraiser www.commerce.state.ak.us/occ/search3.htm
Referee .... www.dced.state.ak.us/occ/OccSearch/main.cfm
Reinsurance Intermed'y Broker/Mgr. www.commerce.state.ak.us/ins/apps/producersearch/InsLicStart.cfm
School Administrator........................ www.eed.state.ak.us/TeacherCertification/CertSearchForm.cfm
School Special Service .... www.eed.state.ak.us/TeacherCertification/CertSearchForm.cfm
Security Guard................................. www.dps.state.ak.us/PermitsLicensing/SecurityGuards/index.asp
Social Worker.................................. www.dced.state.ak.us/occ/OccSearch/main.cfm
Social Worker, Clinical .... www.dced.state.ak.us/occ/OccSearch/main.cfm
Speech/Language Pathologist............ www.commerce.state.ak.us/occ/search3.htm
Surplus Line Broker .... www.commerce.state.ak.us/ins/apps/producersearch/InsLicStart.cfm
Surveyor, Land www.commerce.state.ak.us/occ/search3.htm
Tattoo Artist/Body Piercer................ www.commerce.state.ak.us/occ/search3.htm
Teacher .... www.eed.state.ak.us/TeacherCertification/CertSearchForm.cfm
Transporter, Game........................... www.commerce.state.ak.us/occ/search3.htm
Und'gr'd Storage Tank Workr/Contr. www.commerce.state.ak.us/occ/search3.htm
Vessel Agent................................... www.commerce.state.ak.us/occ/search3.htm
Veterinarian/Veterinary Technician .. www.dced.state.ak.us/occ/search3.htm
Viatical Settlement Broker .... www.commerce.state.ak.us/ins/apps/producersearch/InsLicStart.cfm
Wrestler .... www.dced.state.ak.us/occ/OccSearch/main.cfm

State and Local Courts

State Court Structure: Alaska has a unified, centrally administered, and totally state-funded judicial system with 4 Judicial Districts. Municipal governments do not maintain separate court systems. Alaska has 15 boroughs, not counties. 3 are unified home rule municipalities that are combination borough and city, and 12 boroughs. There are also 12 home rule cities which do not directly coincide with the 4 Judicial Districts. In other words, judicial boundaries cross borough boundaries.

The four levels of courts in the Alaska Court System are the Supreme Court, the Court of Appeals, the Superior Court, and the District Court. Magistrate Courts preside over certain District Court matters. The magistrate is a judicial officer of the District Court.

The Supreme Court and Court of Appeals are appellate courts, while Superior Courts and District Courts are trial courts. The Superior Court Probate is handled by Superior Courts.

The Superior Court is a trial court for both criminal and civil cases. The District Court hears cases that involve hear state misdemeanors and violations of city and borough ordinances, first appearances and preliminary hearings in felony cases, record vital statistics (in some areas of the state), civil cases valued up to $100,000, small claims cases ($10,000 maximum), cases involving children on an emergency basis, and domestic violence cases.

Statewide Court Online Access: You may do a name search of a partial statewide Alaska Trial Courts database index at www.courtrecords.alaska.gov/. There is an old and a new system since the Alaska Court System is migrating to a new electronic case information system called CourtView. Search results give case number, file date, disposition date, charge, and sentence. Note that the initial index gives the only the name used on the first pleading. The site at http://government.westlaw.com/akcases/ provides access to opinions of the Alaska Supreme Court and Alaska Court of Appeals.

> ❖ **Statewide Access Offered For All Trial Courts – Read Above** ❖

Note: No individual Alaska courts offer online access.

Recorders, Assessors, and Other Sites of Note

Recording Office Organization: The 23 Alaskan counties are called boroughs. However, real estate recording is done under a system that was established at the time of the Gold Rush (1893-1916) of 34 Recording Districts. Some of the Districts are identical in geography to boroughs such as the Aleutian Islands, but other boroughs and districts overlap. Therefore, you need to know which recording district any given town or city is located in. A helpful website is www.dnr.state.ak.us/recorders/findYourDistrict.htm

Online Access Note: Online access to the state recorder's office www.recorder.alaska.gov database from the Dept. of Natural Resources is free at www.dnr.state.ak.us/ssd/recoff/search.cfm. This includes property data, liens, deeds, bankruptcies, and more. Images go back to June, 2001; index to 2000. Also, a DNR "land records" database is searchable at http://plats.landrecords.info/.

> ❖ **Statewide Access Offered For All Districts – Read Above**
>
> **Below are Additional Sites** ❖

Anchorage District *Real Estate, Deed, UCC, Liens Records* www.recorder.alaska.gov `Free`
Recorded documents and other public records are free on the statewide system at http://recorder.alaska.gov/search.cfm.
Property, Taxation Records `Free` Access appraisal data free at http://propertytax.muni.org/propappraisal/public.html. Also, access Anchorage real estate property taxes data free at www.muni.org/services/departments/treasury/property/askViewer.cfm. Plat maps and surveys are free on the statewide system at http://recorder.alaska.gov/search.cfm.

Fairbanks District *Real Estate, Deed, UCC, Liens Records* www.co.fairbanks.ak.us `Free`
Recorded documents and other public records are free on the statewide system at http://recorder.alaska.gov/search.cfm.
Property, Taxation Records `Free` Access to the Fairbanks North Star Borough property database is free online at www.co.fairbanks.ak.us/property/. Plat maps and surveys are free on the statewide system at http://recorder.alaska.gov/search.cfm.

Homer District *Real Estate, Deed, UCC, Liens Records* `Free` Recorded documents and other public records are free on the statewide system at http://recorder.alaska.gov/search.cfm.
Property, Taxation Records `Free` Access borough tax assessor rolls free at www.borough.kenai.ak.us/assessingdept/Parcel_QUERY/SEARCH.HTM. Plat maps and surveys are free on the statewide system at http://recorder.alaska.gov/search.cfm.

Juneau District *Real Estate, Deed, UCC, Liens Records* www.juneau.org/cbj/index.php `Free`
Recorded documents and other public records are free on the statewide system at http://recorder.alaska.gov/search.cfm. Also, a statewide recording system and the UCC Central File is found at www.juneau.org/cbj/index.php
Property, Taxation Records `Free` Access to City of Juneau Property Records database is free online at www.juneau.org/assessordata/sqlassessor.php. Plat maps and surveys are free on the statewide system at http://recorder.alaska.gov/search.cfm.

Kenai District *Real Estate, Deed, UCC, Liens Records* www.recorder.alaska.com `Free`
Recorded documents and other public records are free on the statewide system at http://recorder.alaska.gov/search.cfm.
Property, Taxation Records `Free` Access to Kenai Peninsula Borough Assessing Dept. Public Information Search Page is free at www.borough.kenai.ak.us/assessingdept/Default.htm . Plat maps and surveys are free on the statewide system at http://recorder.alaska.gov/search.cfm.

Kodiak District *Real Estate, Deed, UCC, Liens Records* www.recorder.alaska.gov/info16.cfm `Free`
Recorded documents and other public records are free on the statewide system at http://recorder.alaska.gov/search.cfm.
Property, Taxation Records `Free` Search property assessor real property records free at www.kib.co.kodiak.ak.us. Click on "Real Property Records." Plat maps and surveys are free on the statewide system at http://recorder.alaska.gov/search.cfm.

Palmer District *Real Estate, Deed, UCC, Liens Records* `Free` Recorded documents and other public records are free on the statewide system at http://recorder.alaska.gov/search.cfm.
Property, Taxation Records `Free` Access borough property and property tax data free at www.matsugov.us:80/realpropertyquery/. Plat maps and surveys are free on the statewide system at http://recorder.alaska.gov/search.cfm.

Seldovia District *Real Estate, Deed, UCC, Liens Records* www.recorder.alaska.gov `Free`
Recorded documents and other public records are free on the statewide system at http://recorder.alaska.gov/search.cfm.
Property, Taxation Records `Free` Access borough tax assessor rolls is free at http://ak-kenai-property.governmax.com/propertymax/rover30.asp. Also, view Parcel Maps by pdf or tiff free at www.borough.kenai.ak.us/assessingdept/maps.htm. Parcel file downloads are also available. Plat maps and surveys are free on the statewide system at http://recorder.alaska.gov/search.cfm.

Seward District *Real Estate, Deed, UCC, Liens Records* www.recorder.alaska.gov `Free`
Recorded documents and other public records are free on the statewide system at http://recorder.alaska.gov/search.cfm.
Property, Taxation Records `Free` Access borough tax assessor rolls is free at www.borough.kenai.ak.us/assessingdept/Parcel_QUERY/SEARCH.HTM. Plat maps and surveys are free on the statewide system at http://recorder.alaska.gov/search.cfm.

Skagway District *Real Estate, Deed, UCC, Liens Records* `Free` Recorded documents and other public records are free on the statewide system at http://recorder.alaska.gov/search.cfm. Also, a statewide recording system and the UCC Central File is found at www.juneau.org/cbj/index.php
Property, Taxation Records `Free` A citywide assessor is free at www.juneau.org/cbj/index.php Plat maps and surveys are free on the statewide system at http://recorder.alaska.gov/search.cfm.

Talkeetna District *Real Estate, Deed, UCC, Liens Records* `Free` Recorded documents and other public records are free on the statewide system at http://recorder.alaska.gov/search.cfm.
Property, Taxation Records `Free` Access borough property and property tax data free at www.matsugov.us/myproperty/. Plat maps and surveys are free on the statewide system at http://recorder.alaska.gov/search.cfm.

Arizona

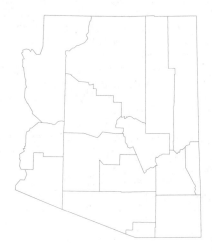

Capital: Phoenix
           Maricopa County
Time Zone: MST
Population: 6,338,755
# of Counties: 15

Useful State Links

Website: http://az.gov/webapp/portal/
Governor: www.governor.state.az.us
Attorney General: www.azag.gov
State Archives: www.lib.az.us/archives/
State Statutes and Codes: www.azleg.state.az.us/ArizonaRevisedStatutes.asp
Legislative Bill Search: www.azleg.state.az.us/Bills.asp
Bill Monitoring: http://alistrack.azleg.state.az.us/
Unclaimed Funds: www.azunclaimed.gov/

> **Editor's Tip:** Arizona, which is on Mountain Standard Time, does not observe Daylight Savings Time rules. Thus, from the first Sunday in April to the last Sunday in October, nearly all Arizona locations will have the same clock time as Pacific Daylight Time, the same time as in California.
> There are exceptions. Some Arizona Indian Reservation offices may observe Daylight Savings Time. Notable is the Navajo Nation Indian Reservation in northeastern Arizona. This does not include the Hopiland Indian Reservation, which is surrounded by the Navajos.

Primary State Agencies

Sexual Offender Registry   Free

Department of Public Safety, Sex Offender Compliance, http://az.gov/webapp/offender/main.do Searching of Level 2 and Level 3 offenders is available online at the website above. Search for an individual by name, or search by ZIP Code or address for known offenders. The site also lists, with pictures, absconders who are individuals whose whereabouts are unknown. *Other Options:* A download is available from the webpage for $25.00.

Incarceration Records   Free

Arizona Department of Corrections, Records Department, www.adc.state.az.us For online search, you must provide last name, first initial or ADC number. Any add'l identifiers are welcomed. Location, ADC number, physical Identifiers and sentencing information are released. Inmates admitted and released from 1972 to 1985 may not be searchable on the web. Also available is ADC Fugitives - an alphabetical Inmate Datasearch listing of Absconders and Escapees from ADC.

Corporation, LLC Records   Free

Corporation Commission, Corporation Records, www.azcc.gov/divisions/corporations/ STARPAS, functioning 24/7 is a resource for searching the index and viewing documents (without SSNs). Go to http://starpas.azcc.gov/scripts/cgiip.exe/WService=wsbroker1/main.p. Another site, http://edocket.azcc.gov/, gives access to the Corporation Commission's official dockets and rule-making proceedings, referred to herein as cases or dockets. Also, search Corp Commission's Securities Division Actions, Orders and Admin. Decisions pages at www.azcc.gov/divisions/securities/enforcement/. *Other Options:* To purchase the database, call 602-364-4433.

Partnerships, LP, LLP, Trademarks/Servicemarks, Trade Names `Free`

Secretary of State, Trademarks/Tradenames/Limited Partnership Division, www.azsos.gov/business_services/TNT/Default.htm The website links to three searchable databases. One searches for Registered Names, Trade Names, and Trademarks. Also available is the full Trade Name and Trademark index in data format. Anther lists the registered names in alpha order and states the type of records available. Another way to obtain this data is from http://starpas.azcc.gov/scripts/cgiip.exe/WService=wsbroker1/main.p. *Other Options:* Bulk purchase is available on microfiche.

Uniform Commercial Code, Federal & State Tax Liens `Free`

UCC Division, Secretary of State, www.azsos.gov/business_services/UCC/ The UCC record index can be searched for free at www.azsos.gov/scripts/ucc_search.dll. Searching can be done by debtor, secured party name, or file number. Images are available on records since 5/1994. SSNs have been redacted. Filings that exist before May 1994 have fiche locations at the bottom of the details page. *Other Options:* The agency offers six options of bulk database purchases. Requests must be in writing using their request form which can be downloaded from the web.

Sales Tax Registrations `Free`

Revenue Department, Transaction (Sales) Tax Licenses and Registration, www.revenue.state.az.us Search sales tax registrations by tax number online free at https://www.aztaxes.gov/default.aspx?target=LicenseVerification.

Driver Records `$$`

Motor Vehicle Division, Correspondence Unit, www.azdot.gov/mvd/index.asp Arizona's commercial online system is interactive and open 24 hours daily. Fee is $3.25 per record. This system is primarily for those requesters who qualify per DPPA. For more information call 602-712-7235. The state also permits licensed driver to view their own record. Fee is $3.00 and use of a credit card is required. Visit www.servicearizona.com. *Other Options:* Overnight cartridge ordering is available. Fee is $2.00 for 39 month record, $3.00 for 5 year record. Call 602-712-7235 for details.

Vehicle Ownership & Registration `$$`

Motor Vehicle Division - Director's Office, Record Services Section, www.azdot.gov/mvd/index.asp Online access is offered to permissible users. Fee is $3.00 per record. The system is open 24 hours a day, seven days a week. For more information, call 602-712-7235. The MVD also offers access for vehicle owners to view and print their own title and registration records. The fee is $3.00 per record and use of a credit card is required. Visit www.servicearizona.com. *Other Options:* Check the attorney general's stolen vehicle list free at http://theftaz.azag.gov.

Birth & Death Records `Free & $$`

Department of Health Services, Vital Records Section, www.azdhs.gov/vitalrcd/index.htm Records may be ordered online via www.vitalchek.com, a state-endorsed vendor. Images of birth certificates from 1887 to 1929 are available free online at http://genealogy.az.gov. Death certificates 1878-1953 are also available.

Occupational Licensing Boards

Accounting Firm, CPA/CP	www.azaccountancy.gov/scripts/BOAsearch.exe
Acupuncturist	www.azacuboard.az.gov/ASPSearch.htm
Acupuncturist Chiropractor	www.azchiroboard.com/ASPSearch.htm
Adoption Searcher	www.supreme.state.az.us/cip/directory.htm
Adult Care Home Manager	www.nciabd.state.az.us/managers.htm
Advance Fee Loan Broker	http://azdfi.gov/Lists/Lists.htm
Aerial Applicator, Pesticide	www.kellysolutions.com/az/Pilots/index.asp
Agricultural Grower/Seller/Permit	www.kellysolutions.com/az/RUPBuyers/index.asp
Agricultural Pest Control Advisor	www.kellysolutions.com/az/PCA/index.asp
Ambulance Service	www.azdhs.gov/bems/conmaps.htm
Ambulatory Surgical Ctr	www.azdhs.gov/als/index.htm
Applicator, Pesticide, Private/Com	www.kellysolutions.com/AZ/Applicators/index.asp
Architect	www.btr.state.az.us/listings/professional_registrant2.asp
Assayer	www.btr.state.az.us/listings/professional_registrant2.asp
Assisted Living Fac./Facility Mgr	www.azdhs.gov/als/search/index.htm
Attorney	www.azbar.org/LegalResources/findlawyer.cfm
Audiologist	www.azdhs.gov/als/search/index.htm
Bank, State Chartered	http://azdfi.gov/Lists/BA_List.HTML
Barber School/Instruction	www.boardofbarbers.az.gov/dir.htm
Barber/Barber Shop	www.boardofbarbers.az.gov/dir.htm
Behavi'l Health Emerg'y/Resi. Svcs	www.azdhs.gov/als/databases/
Behavioral Outpatient Clinic/Rehab	www.azdhs.gov/als/databases/

Bondsman (Insurance) .... www.id.state.az.us/
Charity .... www.azsos.gov/scripts/Charity_Search.dll
Charter School .... www.ade.az.gov/charterschools/search/
Child Care .... www.azdhs.gov/als/search/index.htm
Child Care Office, DES .... www.de.state.az.us/childcare/office.asp
Child Residential Home .... www.azdhs.gov/als/databases/providers_cc.pdf
Chiropractor .... www.azchiroboard.com/ASPSearch.htm
Citrus Broker www.azda.gov/CFV/CompaniesWithCurrentLicenses2.pdf
Clinic, Recovery Care/Rural Health .. www.azdhs.gov/als/index.htm
Collection Agency .... http://azdfi.gov/Lists/Lists.htm
Confidential Intermediary .... www.supreme.state.az.us/cip/directory.htm
Consumer Lender .... http://azdfi.gov/Lists/Lists.htm
Contractor .... www.azroc.gov/clsc/AZROCLicenseQuery
Cosmetology/Nail Tech. Salon/Sch'l www.cosmetology.state.az.us/licensing/SchoolList.htm
Counselor, Professional .... www.bbhe.state.az.us/verifications.htm
Court Reporter www.supreme.state.az.us/cr/pdf/3-20-08%20CR%20Directory.pdf
Credit Union, State Chartered .... http://azdfi.gov/Lists/CU_List.HTML
Cremationist/Crematory .... www.funeralbd.state.az.us/dir.htm
Day Care Establishment .... http://hsapps.azdhs.gov/ls/sod/SearchProv.aspx?type=CC
Debt Management Company .... http://azdfi.gov/Lists/Lists.htm
Defensive Driving Instructor www.supreme.state.az.us/drive/Certified%20Schools%20List.htm
Defensive Driving School www.supreme.state.az.us/drive/Certified%20Schools%20List.htm
Deferred Presentment Company .... http://azdfi.gov/Lists/DPC_List.HTML
Degree Program, Vocational .... http://azppse.state.az.us/directory.html
Detoxification Service .... www.azdhs.gov/als/databases/
Development'y Disab'd Group Home www.azdhs.gov/als/search/index.htm
Dispensing Naturopath .... www.npbomex.az.gov/directorysearch.asp
Drilling, Oil/Gas .... http://azogcc.az.gov/OGpermits.htm
Drug Mfg/Wholesaler .... https://az.gov/webapp/pharmacy/statuscodelookup/
Drug, Retail non-prescription .... https://az.gov/webapp/pharmacy/statuscodelookup/
Dry Well Registration .... www.azdeq.gov/databases/drywellsearch.html
Embalmer .... www.funeralbd.state.az.us/dir.htm
Emergency Response Division .... www.arra.state.az.us/
EMS ALS Base Hospital .... www.azdhs.gov/bems/basehosp.htm
Engineer .... www.btr.state.az.us/listings/professional_registrant2.asp
Escrow Agent .... http://azdfi.gov/Lists/Lists.htm
Family Day Care Home .... www.azdhs.gov/als/databases/providers_cc.pdf
Feed Dealer/Wholesaler .... www.kellysolutions.com/az/feeddealers/index.asp
Feed Distribution, Commercial .... www.kellysolutions.com/az/FeedDealers/index.asp
Fertilizer Dealer .... www.kellysolutions.com/az/fertdealers/index.asp
Fertilizer Distribution, Commercial ... www.kellysolutions.com/az/FertDealers/index.asp
Fertilizer Product .... www.kellysolutions.com/AZ/Fertilizer/fertilizerindex.asp
Fiduciary www.supreme.state.az.us/fiduc/pdf/01-10-08%20Fiduciary%20Directory.pdf
Food Establishment
    www.maricopa.gov/EnvSvc/envwebapp/business_search.aspx?as_page_title=Food%20Establishments%20Search&as_type=Food
Fruit Broker www.azda.gov/CFV/CompaniesWithCurrentLicenses2.pdf
Funeral Director/Establishment .... www.funeralbd.state.az.us/dir.htm
Funeral Pre-Need Trust Company ..... http://azdfi.gov/Lists/Lists.htm
Geologist .... www.btr.state.az.us/listings/professional_registrant2.asp
Group Home, Developm't Disabled .. www.azdhs.gov/als/search/index.htm
Group Home, Small .... www.azdhs.gov/als/search/index.htm
Headstart Facility .... http://hsapps.azdhs.gov/ls/sod/SearchProv.aspx?type=CC
Health Clinic .... www.azdhs.gov/als/search/index.htm
Hearing Aid Dispenser .... www.azdhs.gov/als/search/index.htm
Highway Engineer .... www.btr.state.az.us/listings/professional_registrant2.asp
Home Health Agency .... www.azdhs.gov/als/index.htm
Home Inspector .... www.btr.state.az.us/listings/professional_registrant2.asp

Homeopathic Physician .... www.azhomeopathbd.az.gov/phy_dir.htm
Hospital/or/Hospice .... www.azdhs.gov/als/index.htm
Hospital, Adv'd Life Support (EMS) . www.azdhs.gov/bems/basehosp.htm
Infirmary.. www.azdhs.gov/als/index.htm
Insurance Producer .... www.id.state.az.us/
Juvenile Group Home .... www.azdhs.gov/als/search/index.htm
Landscape Architect .... www.btr.state.az.us/listings/professional_registrant2.asp
Legal Document Preparer www.supreme.state.az.us/cld/pdf/3-20-08%20LDP%20Directory.pdf
Liquor Producer/Whlse...................... www.azliquor.gov/query/default.asp
Liquor Retail Co-Oper./Agent/Mgr. ... www.azliquor.gov/query/default.asp
Lobbyist.. www.azsos.gov/scripts/Lobbyist_Search.dll
Long Term Care Facility .... www.azdhs.gov/als/search/index.htm
Marriage & Family Therapist .... www.bbhe.state.az.us/verifications.htm
Massage Therapy School................... www.npbomex.az.gov/directories.asp
Medical Doctor, Intern/Resident........ www.azmd.gov/profile/getlicense.aspx
Medical Facility................................ www.azdhs.gov/als/search/index.htm
Mentally Retarded Care Facility........ www.azdhs.gov/als/search/index.htm
Midwife, Lay .... www.azdhs.gov/als/databases/index.htm
Money Transmitter .... http://azdfi.gov/Lists/Lists.htm
Mortgage Banker, Commercial .... http://azdfi.gov/Lists/BK_List.HTML
Mortgage Banker/Broker................... http://azdfi.gov/Lists/Lists.htm
Motor Vehicle Dealer/Sales Finance . http://azdfi.gov/Lists/MVD_List.HTML
Naturopathic Medical Asst. .... www.npbomex.az.gov/directories.asp
Naturopathic Physician..................... www.npbomex.az.gov/directorysearch.asp
Naturopathic School .... www.npbomex.az.gov/directories.asp
Neuro Rehab Center .... www.azdhs.gov/als/index.htm
Notary Public.................................... www.azsos.gov/scripts/Notary_Search.dll
Nuclear Medicine Technologist......... www.arra.state.az.us/
Nurse-LPN/RN .... https://www.azbn.gov/OnlineVerification.aspx
Nurses' Aide .... https://www.azbn.gov/OnlineVerification.aspx
Nursing Care Inst. Administrator....... www.nciabd.state.az.us/administrators.htm
Occupational Therapist/Assistant ...... www.occupationaltherapyboard.az.gov/ASPSearch.htm
On Site Worker/Superv'r .... www.btr.state.az.us/listings/professional_registrant2.asp
Optician/Optical Establishment .... www.do.az.gov/directory/default.asp
Optometrist....................................... www.optometry.az.gov/directory.asp
Osteopathic Physician/Surgeon .... www.azdo.gov/
Out-Patient Physical Therapy .... www.azdhs.gov/als/index.htm
Out-Patient Surgical Center.............. www.azdhs.gov/als/index.htm
Outpatient Treatment Clinic .... www.azdhs.gov/als/index.htm
P&C Man'g Agent, Life/Disability ... www.id.state.az.us/
Packer, Fruit/Vegetable www.azda.gov/CFV/CompaniesWithCurrentLicenses2.pdf
Pesticide Applicator/Supv./Advisor... www.sb.state.az.us/PCProfSearch.php
Pesticide Company .... www.sb.state.az.us/PCBusSearch.php
Pesticide Custom Applicator .... www.kellysolutions.com/az/CustomAppl/index.asp
Pesticide Distribution .... www.kellysolutions.com/az/Dealers/index.asp
Pesticide Registration .... www.kellysolutions.com/az/pesticideindex.htm
Pesticide Seller .... www.kellysolutions.com/az/Dealers/index.asp
Pharmacist .... https://az.gov/webapp/pharmacy/statuscodelookup/
Pharmacy Intern................................ https://az.gov/webapp/pharmacy/statuscodelookup/
Physical Therapist/Therapist Asst ..... www.ptboard.state.az.us/public/ptays/ptSearch.asp
Physician Assistant........................... www.azmd.gov/profile/getlicense.aspx
Physiotherapist .... www.azchiroboard.com/ASPSearch.htm
Plant Operator................................... www.azdeq.gov/databases/opcertsearch.html
Podiatrist.. www.podiatry.state.az.us/dir.htm
Political Action Committee .... www.azsos.gov/cfs/SuperPACList.aspx
Post-Secondary Educ. Institution....... http://azppse.state.az.us/directory.html
Post-Secondary Voc. Prog, Private.... http://azppse.state.az.us/directory.html

Premium Finance Company .... http://azdfi.gov/Lists/PF_List.HTML
Preschool .... http://hsapps.azdhs.gov/ls/sod/SearchProv.aspx?type=CC
Private Investigator............................ www.azdps.gov/license/Licensesecurityguard.asp
Process Server, Private www.supreme.state.az.us/cld/pdf/PPS%20Directory%203-6-08.pdf
Property Tax Agent .... www.appraisal.state.az.us/directory/Default.aspx
Psychologist....................................... www.psychboard.az.gov/directory.htm
Public Accountant-CPA .... www.azaccountancy.gov/scripts/BOAsearch.exe
Public Accounting Firm-CPA/PA ..... www.azaccountancy.gov/scripts/BOAsearch.exe
Radon Mitigation Specialist .... www.arra.state.az.us/
Real Estate Agent/Broker/Sales......... http://159.87.254.2/publicdatabase/SearchIndividuals.aspx?mode=2
Real Estate Appraiser .... www.appraisal.state.az.us/directory/Default.aspx
Real Estate School/Course................. http://159.87.254.2/publicdatabase/SearchSchools.aspx?mode=3
Recovery Center .... www.azdhs.gov/als/search/index.htm
Registered Medical Assistant .... www.azhomeopathbd.az.gov/asst_dir.htm
Rehabilitation Agency .... www.azdhs.gov/als/index.htm
Remediation Specialist .... www.btr.state.az.us/listings/professional_registrant2.asp
Renal Disease Facility .... www.azdhs.gov/als/index.htm
Respiratory Therapist .... https://az.gov/webapp/rce/respiratorycareexaminer/licensestatus/
Risk Management Producers .... www.id.state.az.us/
Sales Finance Company..................... http://azdfi.gov/Lists/SF_List.HTML
Sanitarian.. www.azdhs.gov/phs/oeh/rs/pdf/sanreg.pdf
Security Guard................................... www.azdps.gov/license/Licensesecurityguard.asp
Seed Dealer....................................... www.kellysolutions.com/az/SeedDealers/index.asp
Seed Labeler...................................... www.kellysolutions.com/az/SeedLabelers/index.asp
Social Worker.................................... www.bbhe.state.az.us/verifications.htm
Speech Pathology .... www.azdhs.gov/als/index.htm
Speech-Language Pathologist............ www.azdhs.gov/als/search/index.htm
Subdivision Public Report................. http://159.87.254.2/publicdatabase/SearchDevelopments.aspx?mode=2
Substance Abuse Counselor .... www.bbhe.state.az.us/verifications.htm
Surety .... www.id.state.az.us/
Surplus Line Broker .... www.id.state.az.us/
Surveyor, Land .... www.btr.state.az.us/listings/professional_registrant2.asp
Telemarketing Firm .... www.azsos.gov/scripts/TS_Search_engine.cgi
Travel Agent, Limited .... www.id.state.az.us/
Treatment Clinic................................ www.azdhs.gov/als/index.htm
Trust Company .... http://azdfi.gov/Lists/TC_List.HTML
Trust Div. of Chartered Financ'l Inst. http://azdfi.gov/Lists/Lists.htm
Veterinary Medicine/Surgery/Hosp... www.vetbd.state.az.us/directory/default.aspx
Veterinary Technician .... www.vetbd.state.az.us/directory/default.aspx
Waste Water Facility Operator .... www.azdeq.gov/databases/opcertsearch.html
Water Distribution System Operator . www.azdeq.gov/databases/opcertsearch.html
Well Drilling Firm............................ www.azwater.gov/dwr/content/Drillers/default.asp
X-ray Supplier .... www.arra.state.az.us/
X-ray, Portable .... www.azdhs.gov/als/index.htm

State and Local Courts

State Court Structure: Superior Court is the court of general jurisdiction. Justice Courts and Municipal Courts generally have separate jurisdiction over lessor case types. Estate cases are handled by Superior Court.

Statewide Court Online Access: The Public Access to Court Case Information is a valuable web service providing a resource for information about court cases from 153 out of 180 courts in Arizona. Courts not covered include certain parts of Pima, Yavapai, Mohave, and Maricopa counties. Information includes detailed case information (i.e., case type, charges, filing and disposition dates), the parties in the case (not including victims and witnesses), and the court mailing address and location. Go to: www.supreme.state.az.us/publicaccess/notification/default.asp.

Maricopa County Justice Court case histories available free at:
www.superiorcourt.maricopa.gov/docket/JusticeCourtCases/caseSearch.asp

Opinions from the Supreme Court and Court of Appeals are available from www.supreme.state.az.us/.

❖ **Statewide Access Offered Nearly All Trial Courts – Read Above**

Below are Additional Sites ❖

Apache County
Superior Court   www.co.apache.az.us/clerk   `Free`
Access monthly court calendar free at www.apacheclerk.net/calendar.htm

Maricopa County
Superior Court   www.superiorcourt.maricopa.gov   `Free`
Civil: Access to civil case dockets free at www.superiorcourt.maricopa.gov/docket/index.asp. Case file docket can be printed. Also, access to probate court dockets is at www.superiorcourt.maricopa.gov/docket/ProbateCourtCases/. Family court filings are at www.superiorcourt.maricopa.gov/docket/FamilyCourtCases/ *Criminal:* Access to criminal case dockets is free at www.superiorcourt.maricopa.gov/docket/CriminalCourtCases/.

Includes all Justice Courts in the County.

Pima County
Superior Court   www.cosc.co.pima.az.us   `Free`
Civil: Online access to superior court records is free at www.agave.cosc.pima.gov/PublicDocs/. *Criminal:* Online access to superior court criminal records may be available soon at www.agave.cosc.pima.gov/PublicDocs/.
Pima County includes Ajo Justice Court, Green Valley Justice Court, Pima County Consolidated Justice Court   www.jp.pima.gov/

Yavapai County
Superior Court   www.co.yavapai.az.us/supct.aspx   `Free`
*V*iew current warrants, sentencings and felony complaints at www.co.yavapai.az.us/VVJC.aspx.

Recorders, Assessors, and Other Sites of Note

Recording Office Organization: 15 counties, 16 recording offices (the Navajo Nation Recorder is the 16th office and covers northern parts of Apache and Navajo Counties). Recording officers are the County Recorders. Recordings are usually placed in a Grantor/Grantee index. Federal and state tax liens on personal property of businesses are filed with the Secretary of State. Federal and state tax liens on individuals are filed with the County Recorder.

Online Access Note: A number of county assessor offices offer online access. The Secretary of State offers online access to UCC records at www.sosaz.com/scripts/UCC_Search.dll.

Apache County   *Real Estate, Deed, Judgment, Lien Records*   www.co.apache.az.us/Recorder/   `Free`   Access to the recorder is free at www.thecountyrecorder.com/Search.aspx?CountyKey=5. Index goes back to 1985.
Property, Taxation Records   `Free`   Access assessor search page free at www.co.apache.az.us/parcelsearch/parcelsearch.aspx.

Cochise County   *Real Estate, Deed, Lien, Judgment, Mortgage Records*
www.co.cochise.az.us/recorders/Default.htm   `Free`   Access recorder's document search site free at www.thecountyrecorder.com.
Property, Taxation Records   `Free`   Access the treasurer's back tax list free at www.cochise.az.gov/cochise_treasurer.aspx?id=68&ekmensel=c580fa7b_148_0_68_4.

Coconino County   *Real Estate, Grantor/Grantee, Deed, Owner History, Plat, Map Records*
www.coconino.az.gov/recorder.aspx   `Free & $$`   Access the recorder system free at http://eaglerecorder.coconino.az.gov/recorder/web . Documents are $1.00 to print; online records go back to 1983; images back to 3/1999. For official or certified copies or inquiries on documents prior to 1983 please contact office at 1-800-793-6181.
Property, Taxation Records   `Free`   Search owner histories at www.coconino.az.gov/assessor/ASPublic/Search.aspx. Access property owner site for free at http://gis-map.coconino.az.gov/website/coconino/getgisdata.asp.

Gila County   *Real Estate, Grantor/Grantee, Deed, Lien Records*   www.gilacountyaz.gov   `Free & $$`   Access to the recorder's index are free at http://recorder.gilacountyaz.gov/recorder/web/. Search for free, but official copies are $1.00 per page. Records go back to 1985, images back to 1998.

Property, Taxation Records **Free** Search assessor property data free at www.co.gila.az.us/parcelsearch/parcelsearch.aspx

Graham County *Real Estate, Deed, Divorce, Judgment, Lien Records* www.graham.az.gov **Free** Access to
recorder records is at www.thecountyrecorder.com/Search.aspx?CountyKey=1; index goes back to 1984.
Property, Taxation Records **Free** Access the assessor database of property and assessments free at
http://72.165.8.78/parcelsearch/parcelsearch.aspx.

Greenlee County *Real Estate, Deed, Lien, Judgment, Vital Statistic Records*
www.co.greenlee.az.us/Recorder/RecorderHomePage.aspx **Free** Access to recorder records is free at
www.thecountyrecorder.com/Search.aspx?CountyKey=2. Index back to 1/1/1978.
Property, Taxation Records **Free** Search treasurer's tax lien sale list free at www.co.greenlee.az.us/treasurer/06sale.pdf.

La Paz County *Real Estate, Deed, Judgment, Lien Records* www.co.la-
paz.az.us/County_Departments/Dept_Recorder/recorder.htm **Free** Access to the recorder document index only back to 1986 is
free at www.thecountyrecorder.com/(jl14cu55x2riwz45rlfcieyq)/default.aspx.

Maricopa County *Real Estate, Deed, Mortgage, Lien, Plat, Death, Divorce Records* http://recorder.maricopa.gov
Free & $$ Access recordings by direct dial-up or the Internet. Dial-up access requires one-time $300 set-up fee plus $.06 per
minute. Dial-up hours are 8am-10pm, 8-5 Sat-Sun. Records date back to 1983. For add'l info, contact Linda Kinchloe, 602-506-3637.
Web access to Recorder's database is at http://recorder.maricopa.gov/recdocdata/. Index back to 1871, images to 9/91. Search data
back to 2002 free at the clerk's office.
Property, Taxation Records **Free** Assessor database is at www.maricopa.gov/assessor. Residential data available. Also,
perform tax appeal lookups at SBOE site at www.sboe.state.az.us/cgi-bin/name_lookup.pl. Search tresurers tax data free at
http://treasurer.maricopa.gov/parcels/.

Mohave County *Real Estate, Grantor/Grantee, Deed, Lien, Judgment, Death Records* www.co.mohave.az.us
Free Access the Recorder's System free at http://eagleweb.co.mohave.az.us/recorder/web/login.jsp. Registration-password
required; sign-up with IT Dept, x4357.
Property, Taxation Records **Free** Online access to the Assessor's property database is free at
http://legacy.co.mohave.az.us/depts/assessor/prop_info.asp. A sales history also available. Tax maps at
http://legacy.co.mohave.az.us/taxmaps/. Property sales history back to 2000 free at
http://legacy.co.mohave.az.us/1moweb/depts_files/assessor_files/saleshist.asp. Also, the treasurer's tax sale parcel search is at
http://legacy.co.mohave.az.us/depts/treas/tax_sale.asp.

Navajo County *Real Estate, Grantor/Grantee, Deed, UCC, Death Records* www.navajocountyaz.gov/ **Free**
Access to the recorder's database of land data, UCCs, Liens, and Grantor/Grantee indices is free at
www.thecountyrecorder.com/(gdzvqy55ijfb0h550lajpg55)/default.aspx. Documents go back to 1989; images to 1995.
Property, Taxation Records **Free** Access property assessor database free at www.navajocountyaz.gov/parcelsearch.aspx.
Also, the county GIS-mapping site allows manual parcel searching at http://navcogis.co.navajo.az.us/website/NavajoCountyGIS.htm.
Also, a Tax Lien Auction list is at found at www.navajocountyaz.gov/treasurer/

Navajo Nation *Real Estate, Grantor/Grantee, Deed, UCC, Death Records* www.navajobusiness.com/ **Free**
Access to the county recorder's database of land data, UCCs, Liens, and Grantor/Grantee indices is free at
www.thecountyrecorder.com/(gdzvqy55ijfb0h550lajpg55)/Introduction.aspx. Documents go back to 1989; images to 1995.
Property, Taxation Records **Free** Search the Navajo County assessor property tax data and also sales for free at
www.navajocountyaz.gov/parcelsearch.aspx. Also, the tax Lien Auction list is at
www.co.navajo.az.us/parcelsearch.aspx?Menu=ComParcelsTreasRoot. Also, the county GIS-mapping site allows manual parcel
searching at http://navcogis.co.navajo.az.us/website/NavajoCountyGIS.htm.

Pima County *Real Estate, Deed, Lien, Morgtage, Fictition Name* www.recorder.pima.gov **Free & $$** Access
recorder records index free at http://doc.recorder.pima.gov/search/search.html. Full image access is available as a subscription service
only. Also, a name/parcel/property tax lookup may be performed free on the SBOE site at www.sboe.state.az.us/cgi-
bin/name_lookup.pl.
Property, Taxation Records **Free** Records on the Pima County Tax Assessor database are free at
www.asr.co.pima.az.us/links/frm_AdvancedSearch_v2.aspx?search=Parcel. Also, search the property tax inquiry database at
www.to.co.pima.az.us/property_search.html. Also, search tax lien sale, bankrupties, and expiring liens free at
www.to.co.pima.az.us/tax_lien_sale.html. There is also a real estate property tax search at www.to.co.pima.az.us/tax_lien_sale.html
but no name searching.

Pinal County *Real Estate, Grantor/Grantee, Deed Records* http://co.pinal.az.us **Free** Access to the recorder's
index is free at http://co.pinal.az.us/Recorder/Search/.
Property, Taxation Records **Free** Search the assessor's property tax database free at
http://pinalcountyaz.gov/Departments/Assessor/Pages/ParcelInfoSearch.aspx. Also, access to the county treasurer's database of tax
liens, tax bills, and tax sales is free at http://co.pinal.az.us/treasurer. Click on appropriate "Tax Searches" button.

Santa Cruz County *Real Estate, Deed, Lien, Judgment, Marriage Records* www.co.santa-cruz.az.us `Free`
Access recording index free at www.thecountyrecorder.com/(zq1bs155v24ag545wiy24p55)/default.aspx. Index goes back to 1986.
Property, Taxation Records `Free` Access County Assessor data free at http://sccounty01.co.santa-cruz.ca.us/ASR/.

Yavapai County *Real Estate, Deed Records* www.co.yavapai.az.us `Free` Access to the recording office iCRIS
database is free at www.co.yavapai.az.us/Content.aspx?id=19122 Records from 1976 to present; images from 1976 to present.
Property, Taxation Records `Free` Assessor and land records on County GIS database are free at
http://mapserver.co.yavapai.az.us/interactive/map.asp. Data also at http://mapserver.co.yavapai.az.us/parcelinfo/map.asp. Also, the
board of supervisors tax sale list is at www.co.yavapai.az.us/Content.aspx?id=18198.

Yuma County *Property, Taxation Records* `Free` Access county property data free at
http://itax.co.yuma.az.us:8080/itax/taxSplash.jsp; registration required.

Other Arizona Sites of Note:

Cochise County - Inmates http://www.co.cochise.az.us/sheriff/Inmate_List/inmate%20list.pdf
Maricopa County - City of Phoenix - Accident Reports https://www.vectrareports.com/index.aspx No longer free;
registration required.
Maricopa County - County Inmates http://www.mcso.org/index.php?a=GetModule&mn=Mugshot
Mohave County - Most Wanted, Wanted Sex Offenders http://www.co.mohave.az.us/ContentPage.aspx?id=131&cid=83
Mohave County - Restaurant Health Inspections http://legacy.co.mohave.az.us/depts/health/eh_inspections_default.asp
Mohave County - Sex Offender http://www.ctaz.com/~mcso/page19.html
Pima County - Inmates http://www.pimasheriff.org/inmate/roster.html
Yavapai County - Inmates, Offenders http://www.co.yavapai.az.us/SOContent.aspx?id=19280

Arkansas

Capital: Little Rock
            Pulaski County
Time Zone: CST
Population: 2,834,797
# of Counties: 75

Useful State Links

Website: www.arkansas.gov
Governor: www.governor.arkansas.gov/
Attorney General: www.ag.state.ar.us
State Archives: www.ark-ives.com
State Statutes and Codes:
    www.arkleg.state.ar.us/NXT/gateway.dll?f=templates&fn=default.htm&vid=blr:code
Legislative Bill Search: www.arkleg.state.ar.us
Unclaimed Funds: www.state.ar.us/auditor/unclprop/

Primary State Agencies

Criminal Records $$

Arkansas State Police, Identification Bureau, www.asp.arkansas.gov Online access available to only employers or their agents, and professional licensing boards. A subscriber account with the Information Network of Arkansas (INA) is required, a $75 annual fee is imposed. The search fee is $22.00. Searches are conducted by name. Search results includes registered sex offenders. For more info on this online service, see https://www.ark.org/criminal/index.php. Accounts must maintain the signed release documents in-house for three years. Visit https://www.ark.org/ina/sub/bgcheck_agreement.php for an excellent overview of record release provisions.

Sexual Offender Registry Free

Arkansas Crime Information Center, Sexual Offender Registry, www.acic.org/Registration/index.htm Searching is available at www.acic.org/soff/index.php. Search by name or location (county). Includes Level 3 and Level 4 offenders. Also, registered sex offenders are indicated on the criminal record online system maintained by the State Police; however, this system is only available to employers and professional licensing boards.

Incarceration Records Free

Arkansas Department of Corrections, Records Supervisor, www.adc.arkansas.gov/ The online access at www.adc.arkansas.gov/inmate_info/index.html has many search criteria capabilities. *Other Options:* The inmate access web page offers a download of the inmate database. Fee includes an annual INA subscription of $75.00 plus $0.10 per record.

Corporation, Fictitious Name, LLC, Partnerships (LP, LLP LLLP, Foreign) Free

Secretary of State, Business & Commercial Service Division, www.sos.arkansas.gov/corps/ The Internet site permits free searching of corporation records. You can search by name, registered agent, or filing number. Also, search securities companies registered with the state at www.securities.arkansas.gov/starsqldb/asdsecifs/. *Other Options:* Bulk release of records is available for $.50 per page. Contact Records Dept. 501-682-3409 or visit website for details.

Trademarks/Servicemarks Free

Secretary of State, Trademarks Section, www.sos.arkansas.gov/corps/trademk/ Searching is available at no fee over the Internet site. Search by name, owner, city, or filing number. You can also search via email at corprequest@sosmail.state.ar.us. *Other Options:* Records can be provided in bulk for $.50 per page. Call 501-682-3409 or visit website for details.

Uniform Commercial Code, Federal Tax Liens $$

UCC Division - Commercial Srvs, Secretary of State, www.sos.arkansas.gov Subscribers of INA (Information Network of Arkansas) can search by file number or debtor name; subscription fees and search fees involved. See https://www.ark.org/sos/ucc/index.php for details. UCC Download is available via the Internet, but only to subscribers. Fee is $2,000.00 per month for weekly, bi-weekly or monthly downloads. Watch notifications are available for a $35.00 monthly fee. *Other Options:* A download of UCC data is available via the Internet, but only to subscribers. Fee is $2,000 per month for weekly, bi-weekly or monthly downloads.

Workers' Compensation Records $$

Workers Compensation Commission, Operations/Compliance, www.awcc.state.ar.us To perform an online claim search, one must be a subscriber to the Information Network of Arkansas (INA). Records are from May 1, 1997 forward. There is an annual $75 subscriber fee to INA. Each record request is $3.50; if more than 20 are ordered in one month, the fee is $2.50 each request over 20. For more information, visit www.awcc.state.ar.us/electron.html.

Driver Records $$

Department of Driver Services, Driving Records Division, www.accessarkansas.org/dfa/driver_services/ds_index.html Access is available through the Information Network of Arkansas (INA). The system offers both batch and interactive service. The system is only available to INA subscribers who have statutory rights to the data. The record fee is $8.50, or $11.50 for commercial drivers. Visit www.arkansas.gov/sub_services.php. The annual subscription fee is $75.00, other record services are available.

Vehicle Ownership & Registration $$

Office of Motor Vehicles, MV Title Records, www.accessarkansas.org/dfa/ Approved, DPPA compliant accounts may access records online by VIN, plate, or title number. The fee is $1.50. Name searches and certificated documents may be ordered. For further info, go to www.arkansas.gov/sub_services.php. *Other Options:* The bulk purchase of records, except for recall or statistical purposes, is prohibited.

Accident Reports Free & $$

Arkansas State Police, Crash Records Section, www.asp.state.ar.us/divisions/rs/rs_crash.html Limited information is available from the webpage for no charge (names involved), date, county but full record copy may be purchased for $12.00. Search by name, license number and/or date range. Once purchased, reports will be available for 30 days and may be repeatedly accessed with an Order ID. For further information regarding the contents of the report, please contact the Arkansas State Police at 501-618-8130. Credit card is required, unless requester is member of INA. Available records date back to 01/02/01.

Vital Records $$

Arkansas Department of Health, Division of Vital Records, www.healthyarkansas.com Orders can be placed via a state designated vendor. Go to www.vitalchek.com. Extra fees are involved.

Occupational Licensing Boards

Acupuncturist .... www.accessarkansas.org/asbce/acupuncture_roster.html
Aesthetician .... www.arkansas.gov/cos/search.php
Agriculture Educator .... http://arkedu.state.ar.us/teachers/accessing_licensure_info.html
Architect .... www.arkansas.gov/arch/search_ind.php
Asbestos-related Occupation .... www.adeq.state.ar.us/compsvs/webmaster/databases.htm
Athletic Trainer .... www.aratb.org/search.php
Attorney .... http://courts.arkansas.gov/attorneys/attorney_search.cfm
Auctioneer .... https://www.ark.org/auct_ds/app/index.html
Audiologist .... www.arkansas.gov/abespa_licv/app/enter.html
Bank .... www.sos.arkansas.gov/corps/search_all.php
Boiler Inspector/Installer/Repairer .... www.arkansas.gov/labor/online_services/online_services_p1.html
Boiler Operator .... www.arkansas.gov/labor/online_services/online_services_p1.html
Business Education Teacher .... http://arkedu.state.ar.us/teachers/accessing_licensure_info.html
Career Orientation Teacher .... http://arkedu.state.ar.us/teachers/accessing_licensure_info.html
Cemetery, Perpetual Care .... www.securities.arkansas.gov/starsqldb/asdcsifs/
Check Casher .... www.asbca.org/check_search/
Check Seller .... www.securities.arkansas.gov/starsqldb/asdcsifs/
Chemical, List 1, Wholesale Distr. .... www.ark.org/asbp/roster/index.php
Child Care Provider .... www.arkansas.gov/childcare/licensing/newweb.html
Chiropractor .... www.accessarkansas.org/asbce/search.html
Collection Agency-related .... www.asbca.org/collect_search/
Contractor .... www.accessarkansas.org/clb/search.html
Cosmetologist/Cosmetology Instr ...... www.arkansas.gov/cos/search.php
Counselor, Professional .... www.accessarkansas.org/abec/search.php
Court Reporter .... www.arkansas.gov/court_reporters/search/index.php

Dental Hygienist .... www.asbde.org/rdhroster/search.php
Dentist .... www.asbde.org/ddsroster/search.php
Drugs, Legend, Wholesale Distr. .... www.ark.org/asbp/roster/index.php
Electrical Contractor .... www.arkansas.gov/labor/online_services/online_services_p1.html
Electrician Journeyman/ Master .... www.arkansas.gov/labor/online_services/online_services_p1.html
Electrologist/Electrolysis Instructor .. www.arkansas.gov/cos/search.php
Embalmer/Embalmer Apprentice ...... www.arkansas.gov/fdemb/
Emergency Med. Tech.-Paramedic .... https://www.ark.org/dhhsems/index.php
Emergency Medical Technician .... https://www.ark.org/dhhsems/index.php
Engineer/Engineer in Training .... www.accessarkansas.org/pels/search.php
Fire Equipment Inspector/Repairer.... www.arfireprotection.org/roster/index.html
Fire Extinguisher Sprinkler Inspector www.arfireprotection.org/roster/index.html
Forester .... https://www.ark.org/foresters_rsearch/app/enter.html
Funeral Director/Apprentice .... www.arkansas.gov/fdemb/
Funeral Home/Crematory .... www.arkansas.gov/fdemb/
Geologist www.state.ar.us/agc/bordir2005.xls
Home Inspector .... www.ahib.org/
Insurance Agency .... http://insurance.arkansas.gov/is/Agency/agency.asp
Insurance Agency .... www.sos.arkansas.gov/corps/search_all.php
Insurance Company .... http://insurance.arkansas.gov/is/companysearch/cosearch.asp
Insurance Sales Agent .... http://insurance.arkansas.gov/is/agentsearch/agent.asp
Investment Advisor .... www.securities.arkansas.gov/starsqldb/asdsecifs/
Landscape Architect .... www.arkansas.gov/asbla/find_landscape_architect.html
Lobbyist... www.sosweb.state.ar.us/elections/elections_pdfs/lobby_lists/2005/2005list.pdf
Manicurist.. www.arkansas.gov/cos/search.php
Marriage & Family Therapist .... www.accessarkansas.org/abec/search.php
Medicaid Provider .... https://www.medicaid.state.ar.us/InternetSolution/
Medical Corporation........................ https://www.armedicalboard.org/licenseverf/
Medical Doctor/Surgeon.................. https://www.armedicalboard.org/licenseverf/
Midwife Nurse................................. www.arsbn.org/registry/index.html
Mortgage Loan Broker/Company ...... www.securities.arkansas.gov/starsqldb/asdcsifs/
Motor Vehicle Dealer/Distributor...... www.armvc.com/licensee_search/index.html
Motor Vehicle Mfg/Rep, New .... www.armvc.com/licensee_search/index.html
Notary Public................................... www.sos.arkansas.gov/corps/notary/index.php
NurseNurse Anesthetist .... www.arsbn.org/registry/index.html
Nursing Home Facility .... www.arhspa.org/agency_decisions.html
Occupational Therapist/Assistant ...... https://www.armedicalboard.org/licenseverf/
Optician .... www.ark.org/directory/detail2.cgi?ID-1050
Optometrist....................................... www.arbo.org/index.php?action=findanoptometrist
Osteopathic Physician....................... https://www.armedicalboard.org/licenseverf/
P & C Company .... http://insurance.arkansas.gov/pclh/pcweb.asp
Pharmacist/Pharmacy Technician ...... www.ark.org/asbp/roster/index.php
Pharmacy.. www.ark.org/asbp/roster/index.php
Physical Therapist .... www.arptb.org/ptroster/search.php
Physician Assistant........................... https://www.armedicalboard.org/licenseverf/
Political Action Committee .... www.sosweb.state.ar.us/elections/elections_pdfs/pac_lists/pac_list_02-03-05.pdf
Psychological Examiner .... www.arkansas.gov/abep/Licensees.htm
Psychologist...................................... www.arkansas.gov/abep/Licensees.htm
Public Accountant-CPA .... www.arkansas.gov/asbpa/
Real Estate Agent/Broker/Sales......... https://www.ark.org/arec_renewals/index.php/search/agent
Real Estate Appraiser .... www.arkansas.gov/alcb/search.php
Respiratory Care Practitioner .... https://www.armedicalboard.org/licenseverf/
School Principal/Admin/Super .... http://arkedu.state.ar.us/teachers/accessing_licensure_info.html
Securities Broker/Dealer/Agent......... www.securities.arkansas.gov/starsqldb/asdsecifs/
Securities Exemption......................... www.securities.arkansas.gov/starsqldb/asdsecifs/
Security Mutual Fund .... www.securities.arkansas.gov/starsqldb/asdsecifs/
Social Worker................................... www.accessarkansas.org/swlb/search/index.html

Solid Waste Facility Operator .... www.adeq.state.ar.us/compsvs/webmaster/databases.htm
Speech Pathologist .... www.arkansas.gov/abespa_licv/app/enter.html
Supplier of Legend Device/Med Gas. www.ark.org/asbp/roster/index.php
Supplier of Med Equipment .... www.ark.org/asbp/roster/index.php
Surveyor, Land .... www.accessarkansas.org/pels/search.php
Surveyor-in-Training .... www.accessarkansas.org/pels/search.php
Teacher .... http://arkedu.state.ar.us/teachers/accessing_licensure_info.html
Waste Water Plant Operator .... www.adeq.state.ar.us/water/wwl/wwlicdata_sql.asp

State and Local Courts

State Court Structure: Circuit Courts are the courts of general jurisdiction and are arranged in 28 circuits. Circuit Courts consist of five subject matter divisions: criminal, civil, probate, domestic relations, and juvenile. A Circuit Clerk handles the records and recordings, however some counties have a County Clerk that handles probate. District Courts, formerly known as Municipal Courts before passage of Amendment 80 to the Arkansas Constitution, exercise countywide jurisdiction over misdemeanor cases, preliminary felony cases, and civil cases in matters of less than $5,000, including small claims. The City Courts operate in smaller communities where District Courts do not exist and exercise citywide jurisdiction.

Statewide Court Online Access: Access to Supreme Court Opinions and Appellate Court dockets is at http://courts.state.ar.us/online/or.html where you will also find Court of Appeals dockets, corrected opinions, and parallel citations. An attorney search, court rules and administrative orders are also available. Online access to courts at the county level is not extensive.

Benton County
Circuit Court www.co.benton.ar.us `Free`
Search civil & criminal court docket information free at http://records.co.benton.ar.us:5061/

Miller County
Circuit Court `$$`
Civil: Online access to circuit court dockets by subscription through RecordsUSA.com. Credit card, username and password is required; choose either monthly or per-use plan. Visit the website for sign-up or call Lisa at 601-264-7701 for information. *Criminal:* Online access to criminal dockets is the same as civil.

Polk County
Circuit Court `$$`
Civil: Online access to circuit court dockets by subscription through RecordsUSA.com. Credit card, username and password is required; choose either monthly or per-use plan. Visit the website for sign-up or call Lisa at 601-264-7701 for information. *Criminal:* Online access to criminal dockets is the same as civil.

Pulaski County
Circuit Court `Free`
Civil: Access court records free at www.pulaskiclerk.com/Archives.html - civil back to 4/2005; Probate back to 1/2006; domestic back to 1/2007. *Criminal:* Access court records free at www.pulaskiclerk.com/Archives.html - criminal back to 4/2005.

Saline County
Circuit Court www.arkansas.gov/salinecourtrecords `Free & $$`
Civil: Court records index search is free at https://www.ark.org/grs/app/saline but records are $12 each or you may subscribe monthly. *Criminal:* Same.

Sebastian County
Fort Smith District Court www.districtcourtfortsmith.org `Free`
Civil: Access court records free at www.districtcourtfortsmith.org/ and click on Online Records Search. *Criminal:* same.

Sharp County
Circuit Court `$$`
Civil: Court has outsourced online access to probate and court orders to www.etitlesearch.com/. The data is mostly recorded documents, fees are involved.

Union County
Circuit Court $$
Civil: Online access to circuit court dockets by subscription through RecordsUSA.com. Credit card, username and password is required; choose either monthly or per-use plan. Visit the website for sign-up or call Lisa at 601-264-7701 for information. *Criminal:* Online access to criminal dockets is the same as civil.

Washington County
Circuit Court   www.co.washington.ar.us $$
Civil: Online case index at www.co.washington.ar.us/resolution/. Civil cases indexed from 1992 forward. This is a commercial system, fee is $50.00 per month prepaid. Search pre-1973 court indices free at www.co.washington.ar.us/ArchiveSearch/CourtRecordSearch.asp. *Criminal:* Online case index at www.co.washington.ar.us/resolution/. Criminal cases indexed from 1992 forward. This is a commercial system, fee is $50.00 per month prepaid. Pre-1933 criminal court indices free at www.co.washington.ar.us/ArchiveSearch/CourtRecordSearch.asp. Note that these cases are very old.

Recorders, Assessors, and Other Sites of Note

Recording Office Organization: 75 counties, 85 recording offices. The recording officer is the Clerk of Circuit Court who is Ex Officio Recorder. 10 counties have 2 recording offices - Arkansas, Carroll, Clay, Craighead, Franklin, Logan, Mississippi, Prairie, Sebastian, and Yell. Federal tax liens on personal property of businesses are filed with the Secretary of State. Other federal and all state tax liens are filed with the Circuit Clerk.

Online Access Note: Statewide access to UCC info is at https://www.ark.org/sos/ucc/index.php. There is no statewide access to assessor data; however, all counties cooperate with at least one commercial vendor. Registration and login is required to search assessor records for 39 counties at www.arcountydata.com. Signup fee is $200 plus $.10 per minute usage but 11 counties offers some free access. For signup or information call 479-631-8054 or visit at the web. Also, several counties are now on the new Citrix system - registration and logon is required to search assessor records on Citrix. Also, access property data free for 24 counties at www.actdatascout.com. Subscription for deeper info is $20 per month. 50% discount on add'l counties. Also, 36 counties are available at www.datascoutpro.com/ by various subscription plans up to $150 monthly for all.

Arkansas County *Property, Taxation Records* $$ Registration and logon required to search assessor records at www.arcountydata.com. See Online Access Note at beginning of section.

Ashley County *Property, Taxation Records*   Free   Access property data free at www.actdatascout.com; subscription for deeper info. See Online Access Note at beginning of section.

Baxter County *Real Estate, Deed Records* $$ Access recording office land data at www.etitlesearch.com; registration required, fee based on usage.
Property, Taxation Records $$ Registration and logon is required to search assessor records on Citrix system at www.arcountydata.com. See Online Access Note at beginning of section.

Benton County *Real Estate, Deed, Lien, Plat, Judgment, Medical Lien Records*   www.co.benton.ar.us $$
County recorder, medical liens, plats and circuit court data is free at www.benton.ar.us.landata.com/default.asp or phone 888-85-IMAGE. $49.95/$79.90 or monthly. Also, land records at http://etitlesearch.com; call 870-856-3055 for subscription info.
Property, Taxation Records   Free & $$ Search property and personal property tax data free at www.countyservice.net/bentax.asp. Search and pay taxes free at http://collector.co.benton.ar.us/searchpay.html#. Also, registration and logon required to search assessor records at www.arcountydata.com. See Online Access Note at beginning of section.

Boone County *Real Estate, Deed Records* $$ Land records are at http://etitlesearch.com. You can do a name search; choose from $45.00 monthly subscription or per click account.
Property, Taxation Records $$ Registration and logon required to search assessor records at www.arcountydata.com. See Online Access Note at beginning of section.

Bradley County *Property, Taxation Records* $$ Registration and logon required to search assessor records at www.arcountydata.com. See Online Access Note at beginning of section.

Calhoun County *Property, Taxation Records* $$ Registration and logon required to search assessor records at www.arcountydata.com. See Online Access Note at beginning of section.

Carroll County *Property, Taxation Records* `Free` Access property data free at www.actdatascout.com; subscription for deeper info. See Online Access Note at beginning of section. Also, with registration and logon you may search assessor records on Citrix system at www.arcountydata.com. See Online Access Note at beginning of section.

Chicot County *Property, Taxation Records* `SS` Registration and logon is required to search assessor records on Citrix system at www.arcountydata.com. See Online Access Note at beginning of section.

Clark County *Property, Taxation Records* `Free` Access property data free at www.actdatascout.com/default.aspx?ci=3. Subscription for deeper info. See Online Access Note at beginning of section.

Clay County (Eastern District) *Property, Taxation Records* `SS` Registration and logon is required to search assessor records on Citrix system at www.arcountydata.com. See Online Access Note at beginning of section.

Clay County (Western District) *Property, Taxation Records* `SS` Registration and logon required to search assessor records at www.arcountydata.com. See Online Access Note at beginning of section.

Cleburne County *Property, Taxation Records* `Free` Access property data free at www.actdatascout.com; subscription for deeper info. See Online Access Note at beginning of section.

Columbia County *Property, Taxation Records* `Free & SS` Registration and logon required to search assessor records at www.arcountydata.com. See Online Access Note at beginning of section. Also, search property and tax records free at www.countyofcolumbia.net/circuit-clerk/.

Conway County *Property, Taxation Records* `Free` Access property data free at www.actdatascout.com; subscription for deeper info. See Online Access Note at beginning of section.

Craighead County *Real Estate, Deed, Property Records* `SS` Access recording office land data at www.etitlesearch.com; registration required, fee based on usage.
Property, Taxation Records `Free & SS` Search property and personal property data free at www.countyservice.net/assess.asp?id=cratax. Also, with address you can search property tax records free at www.arcountydata.com/county.asp?county=Craighead. See Online Access Note at beginning of section.

Crawford County *Real Estate, Deed Records* www.crawford-county.org/circuit_clerk.htm `SS` Land records are at http://etitlesearch.com. You can do a name search; choose from $30.00 monthly subscription or per click account.
Property, Taxation Records `Free` Access property data free at www.actdatascout.com; subscription for deeper info. See Online Access Note at beginning of section.

Crittenden County *Property, Taxation Records* `SS` Registration and logon required to search assessor records at www.arcountydata.com. See Online Access Note at beginning of section.

Cross County *Property, Taxation Records* `Free` Access property data free at www.actdatascout.com; subscription for deeper info. See Online Access Note at beginning of section.

Dallas County *Property, Taxation Records* `SS` Registration and logon required to search assessor records at www.arcountydata.com. See Online Access Note at beginning of section.

Desha County *Property, Taxation Records* `SS` Registration and logon required to search assessor records at www.arcountydata.com. See Online Access Note at beginning of section.

Drew County *Property, Taxation Records* `SS` Search property data at www.actdatascout.com/default.aspx?ci=9. Subscription for deeper info. See Online Access Note at beginning of section.

Faulkner County *Property, Taxation Records* `SS` Registration and logon is required to search assessor tax and personal property tax records at www.arcountydata.com. Free search but fee for full data. See Online Access Note at beginning of section. Also, search property tax data free at https://www.ark.org/faulknercounty/index.php. At 2nd page you may search by name.

Franklin County (Ozark District) *Property, Taxation Records* `SS` Registration and logon required to search assessor records at www.arcountydata.com. See Online Access Note at beginning of section.

Fulton County *Property, Taxation Records* `SS` Registration and logon required to search assessor records at www.arcountydata.com. See Online Access Note at beginning of section.

Garland County *Property, Taxation Records* `Free` Access property data free at www.actdatascout.com; subscription for deeper info. See Online Access Note at beginning of section.

Grant County *Property, Taxation Records* `SS` Registration and logon required to search assessor records at www.arcountydata.com. See Online Access Note at beginning of section.

Greene County *Property, Taxation Records* `SS` Registration and logon required to search assessor records at www.arcountydata.com. See Online Access Note at beginning of section.

Hempstead County *Property, Taxation Records* `Free` Access property data free at www.actdatascout.com; subscription for deeper info. See Online Access Note at beginning of section.

Hot Spring County *Property, Taxation Records* `Free` Access property data free at www.actdatascout.com; subscription for deeper info. See Online Access Note at beginning of section.

Howard County *Property, Taxation Records* `SS` Registration and logon required to search assessor records at www.arcountydata.com. See Online Access Note at beginning of section.

Independence County *Real Estate, Deed Records* `SS` Land records are at http://etitlesearch.com. You can do a name search; choose from $200.00 monthly subscription or per click account.
Property, Taxation Records `Free` Access property data free at www.actdatascout.com; subscription for deeper info. See Online Access Note at beginning of section.

Izard County *Property, Taxation Records* `Free` Search free at www.arcountydata.com/county.asp?county=Izard but registration and logon is required to search full assessor records at www.arcountydata.com. See Online Access Note at beginning of section. Also, visit www.countyservice.net/assess.asp?id=izatax for free look-ups but address is required.

Jackson County *Property, Taxation Records* `Free` Access property data free at www.actdatascout.com; subscription for deeper info. See Online Access Note at beginning of section.

Jefferson County *Property, Taxation Records* `Free` Search property and personal property data free at www.countyservice.net. Also, ccess property data free at www.actdatascout.com; subscription for deeper info. See Online Access Note at beginning of section.

Johnson County *Property, Taxation Records* `SS` Registration and logon is required to search all participating counties on the Citrix system at www.arcountydata.com. See Online Access Note at beginning of section.

Lafayette County *Property, Taxation Records* `Free` Access property data free at www.actdatascout.com; subscription for deeper info. See Online Access Note at beginning of section.

Lawrence County *Property, Taxation Records* `Free` Access property data free at www.actdatascout.com; subscription for deeper info. See Online Access Note at beginning of section.

Lee County *Property, Taxation Records* `SS` Registration and logon required to search assessor records at www.arcountydata.com. See Online Access Note at beginning of section.

Lincoln County *Property, Taxation Records* `SS` Access property data free at www.actdatascout.com; subscription for deeper info. See Online Access Note at beginning of section.

Little River County *Property, Taxation Records* `Free` Access property data free at www.actdatascout.com. Subscription for deeper info is $20 per month.

Logan County *Property, Taxation Records* `Free & SS` Registration and logon is required to search assessor records on the Citrix system at www.arcountydata.com. Signup fee is $200 plus $.10 per minute usage. For signup or info, call 479-631-8054 or visit the website. Also, visit www.countyservice.net/assess.asp?id=logtax for free look-ups but address is required.

Lonoke County *Property, Taxation Records* `SS` Registration and logon required to search assessor records at www.arcountydata.com. See Online Access Note at beginning of section.

Madison County *Property, Taxation Records* `Free` Access property data free at www.actdatascout.com. Subscription for deeper info is $20 per month.

Marion County *Property, Taxation Records* `SS` Registration and logon is required to search assessor records on the Citrix system at www.arcountydata.com. See Online Access Note at beginning of section.

Miller County *Property, Taxation Records* `Free` Access property data free at www.actdatascout.com; subscription for deeper info. See Online Access Note at beginning of section.

Mississippi County (Osceola District) *Property, Taxation Records* `Free` Access to property assessment records is free at www.dsmone.com/missco/.

Monroe County *Property, Taxation Records* `SS` Access property data free at www.actdatascout.com; subscription for deeper info. See Online Access Note at beginning of section.

Montgomery County *Property, Taxation Records* `Free` Access property data free at www.actdatascout.com; subscription for deeper info. See Online Access Note at beginning of section.

Nevada County *Property, Taxation Records* `SS` Subscription access to property data available at www.actdatascout.com. See Online Access Note at beginning of section.

Newton County *Property, Taxation Records* SS Registration and logon required to search assessor records at www.arcountydata.com. See Online Access Note at beginning of section.

Ouachita County *Property, Taxation Records* Free Access property data free at www.actdatascout.com; subscription for deeper info. See Online Access Note at beginning of section.

Perry County *Property, Taxation Records* Free Access property data free at www.actdatascout.com; subscription for deeper info. See Online Access Note at beginning of section.

Phillips County *Real Estate, Deed Records* SS Access land records at http://etitlesearch.com. You can do a name search; choose from $25.00 monthly subscription or per-click account.

Pike County *Property, Taxation Records* SS Registration and logon required to search assessor records at www.arcountydata.com. See Online Access Note at beginning of section.

Poinsett County *Property, Taxation Records* SS Registration and logon required to search assessor records at www.arcountydata.com. See Online Access Note at beginning of section.

Polk County *Property, Taxation Records* Free Access property data free at www.actdatascout.com; subscription for deeper info. See Online Access Note at beginning of section.

Pope County *Real Estate, Deed, Lien Records* SS Access recording office land data and liens at www.etitlesearch.com; registration required, fee based on usage.
Property, Taxation Records Free Search assessor property data free at www.arcountydata.com/county.asp?county=Pope. See Online Access Note at beginning of section. Also, free access to assessor data is at www.countyservice.net/assess.asp?id=poptax but address is required.

Prairie County *Real Estate, Deed Records* SS Access recording office land data at www.etitlesearch.com; registration required, fee based on usage.
Property, Taxation Records SS Subscription access to property data available at www.actdatascout.com. See Online Access Note at beginning of section.

Pulaski County *Real Estate, Deed, Lien, Mortgage, Judgment, Plat, Voter Registration, Marriage Records*
www.co.pulaski.ar.us Free & SS At the main web page, Click on Online Services for the free search of voter registration, real estate, courts, marriages, minister credentials free at www.pulaskiclerk.com/SearchChoiceMain.html Also, access recording office land data at www.etitlesearch.com; registration required, fee based on usage.
Property, Taxation Records SS Registration and logon is required to search assessor and personal property records on the Citrix system at www.arcountydata.com. See Online Access Note at beginning of section. Data is no longer being updated as of 12/2005. Also, search current Personal Property - vehicles - free at http://vehicles.pulaskicountyassessor.net/webware/MotorVehicle/VehicleLogin.aspx.

Randolph County *Property, Taxation Records* Free Search property and personal property data free at www.countyservice.net. Also, access property data free at www.actdatascout.com; subscription for deeper info. See Online Access Note at beginning of section.

St. Francis County *Property, Taxation Records* Free & SS Search assessor data free at www.arcountydata.com/county.asp?county=St.%20Francis but Registration and logon is required to search full assessor records at www.arcountydata.com. See Online Access Note at beginning of section. Also, search assessor real estate and personal property records free at www.countyservice.net/stftax.asp but free search requires address.

Saline County *Property, Taxation Records* Free & SS Search assessor data free at www.arcountydata.com/county.asp?county=Saline but Registration and logon is required to search full assessor records. See Online Access Note at beginning of section. Also, search assessor records free at www.countyservice.net/assess.asp?id=saltax, free search requires address. Search tax collector records free at https://www.ark.org/salinecounty/index.php.

Scott County *Property, Taxation Records* SS Registration and logon is required to search assessor records on the Citrix system at www.arcountydata.com. See Online Access Note at beginning of section.

Searcy County *Property, Taxation Records* SS Access property data free at www.actdatascout.com; subscription for deeper info. See Online Access Note at beginning of section.

Sebastian County *Property, Taxation Records* Free & SS Registration and logon is required to search assessor records up to 1/2006 only is at www.arcountydata.com. For signup or info call 479-631-8054 or visit the website which is not updated. See Online Access Note at beginning of section. Also, search tax payment data free at https://www.ark.org/sebastiancounty/index.php. Also, access property data free at www.actdatascout.com; subscription for deeper info; see Online Access Note at beginning of section. Also, search property and personal property data free at www.countyservice.net.

Sevier County *Property, Taxation Records* Free Access property data free at www.actdatascout.com; subscription for deeper info. See Online Access Note at beginning of section.

Sharp County *Real Estate, Deed Records* $$ Access land records at http://etitlesearch.com. You can do a name search; choose from $25.00 monthly subscription or per-click account.
Property, Taxation Records $$ Registration and logon required to search assessor records at www.arcountydata.com. See Online Access Note at beginning of section.

Stone County *Property, Taxation Records* $$ Registration and logon is required to search assessor records on the Citrix system at www.arcountydata.com. See Online Access Note at beginning of section.

Union County *Property, Taxation Records* $$ Access property data free at www.actdatascout.com; subscription for deeper info. See Online Access Note at beginning of section.

Van Buren County *Real Estate, Deed Records* $$ Access land records at http://etitlesearch.com. You can do a name search; call 870-856-3055 for subscription info.
Property, Taxation Records Free & $$ Access assessor date free at www.arcountydata.com/county.asp?county=Van%20Buren but registration and logon is required to search full assessor records on the Citrix system. See Online Access Note at beginning of section. Also, search tax payments free at https://www.ark.org/vanburencounty/index.php and use name search to locate property owner

Washington County *Real Estate, Deed, Lien, UCC, Court, Vital Records* www.co.washington.ar.us $$
Search Clerk's index of real estate, liens, and UCCs (to '92) at www.co.washington.ar.us/resolution/. Username, password and $50.00 subscription required. Also, search court record archives at www.co.washington.ar.us/ArchiveSearch/CourtRecordSearch.asp. Also, access land records at http://etitlesearch.com. You can do a name search, fees involved, call 870-856-3055 for info. .
Property, Taxation Records Free Search property records free at www.co.washington.ar.us/PropertySearch/MapSearch.asp.

White County *Property, Taxation Records* Free & $$ Registration and logon required to search assessor records at www.arcountydata.com. See Online Access Note at beginning of section. Also, free access to assessor records at www.countyservice.net/assess.asp?id=whitax. Address required.

Woodruff County *Real Estate, Deed Records* $$ Access land records at http://etitlesearch.com. You can do a name search; choose from $25.00 monthly subscription or per-click account.
Property, Taxation Records $$ Access property data free at www.actdatascout.com; subscription for deeper info. See Online Access Note at beginning of section.

Other Arkansas Sites of Note:

Benton County - Inmates http://services.co.benton.ar.us/dcn/
Union County - Sheriff Most Wanted, Inmates, Warrants www.unioncountysheriff.net/news.php

California

Capital: Sacramento
             Sacramento County
Time Zone: PST
Population: 36,553,215
# of Counties: 58

Useful State Links

Website: www.ca.gov/
Governor: http://gov.ca.gov/
Attorney General: http://caag.state.ca.us
State Archives: www.sos.ca.gov/archives/archives.htm
State Statutes and Codes: www.leginfo.ca.gov/calaw.html
Legislative Bill Search: www.leginfo.ca.gov/bilinfo.html
Bill Monitoring: www.leginfo.ca.gov/cgi-bin/postquery?maison=$prfx&nro=$num&act=10
Unclaimed Funds: https://scoweb.sco.ca.gov

Primary State Agencies

Sexual Offender Registry `Free`

Department of Justice, Sexual Offender Program, www.meganslaw.ca.gov/ The web page offers online searching by a sex offender's specific name or by geographic location including ZIP Code, county or within a predetermined radius of a selected address, park, or school. This site will provide access to information on more than 63,000 persons required to register in California as sex offenders. One may search Specific home addresses are displayed on more than 33,500 offenders.

Corporation, LLC, LP, LLP `Free`

Secretary of State, Information Retrieval/Certification Unit, www.sos.ca.gov/business/business.htm The website at http://kepler.ss.ca.gov/list.html offers access to more than 2 million records including corporation, LLC, LP and LLP. Information available includes status, file number, date of filing and agent for service of process. The file is updated weekly. Also, search securities companies registered with the state at http://134.186.208.228/caleasi/pub/exsearch.htm.

Uniform Commercial Code, Federal & State Tax Liens `$$`

Business Programs Division, UCC Section, www.sos.ca.gov/business/ucc/ucc.htm See note above about the removal of SSNs. Site may be temporarily down. UCC Connect provides an online service at https://uccconnect.ss.ca.gov/acct/acct-login.asp to conduct a variety of inquiries and place orders for copies and debtor search certificates on records and submit UCC filings. Ongoing requesters can become subscribers. Fees are based on name inquires ($5.00) and images viewed ($1.00). The web page has a complete list of fees and excellent FAQ section. Click on the Help tab. *Other Options:* The database is available for purchase, daily updates are available for an additional fee on a yearly subscription basis. The web page has prices.

Sales Tax Registrations `Free`

Board of Equalization, Sales and Use Tax Department, www.boe.ca.gov The Internet site provides a permit verification service. Permit number is needed. System is open 5AM to midnight. *Other Options:* Lists, available for a fee, are sorted in a number of ways including CA Industry Code. For further information and fees, call the Technical Services Division at 916-445-5848

Driver Records `$$`

Department of Motor Vehicles, Information Services Branch, www.dmv.ca.gov The department offers online access, but a $10,000 one-time setup fee may be required. Entities who order from an online vendor must also be pre-approved and fees are involved. The fee is $2.00 per record. The system is available 24 hours, 7 days a week. For more information call 916-657-5582. *Other Options:* Employers may monitor their drivers in the Pull Notice Program. The DMV informs the organization when there is activity on enrolled drivers. Call 916-657-6346 for details.

Vehicle, Vessel Ownership & Registration ▊$$▊

Department of Motor Vehicle, Office of Information Services, www.dmv.ca.gov 24 hour online access is limited to certain Authorized Vendors. Requesters may not use data for direct marketing, solicitation, nor resell for those purposes. A bond is required and a $10,000 one-time permit fees is required. Then records are $2.00 ea. For more information, call the Electronic Access Administration Section at 916-657-5582. *Other Options:* California offers delivery of registration information on FTP VPN, magnetic tape, disk or paper within special parameters. Release of information is denied for commercial marketing purposes.

Birth & Death Records ▊Free & $$▊

State Department of Health Svcs, Office of Vital Records - MS 5103, www.dhs.ca.gov/chs/OVR/default.htm Records may be ordered from a state-designated vendor - www.vitalchek.com. Applicant must complete a Sworn Statement and a notarized Certificate of Acknowledgment in the presence of a Notary Public.

Occupational Licensing Boards

Acupuncturist .... www.acupuncture.ca.gov
Adoption Agency .... www.ccld.ca.gov/docs/ccld_search/ccld_search.aspx
Agricultural Engineer .... www.dca.ca.gov/pels/l_lookup.htm
Air Conditioning Contractor .... www2.cslb.ca.gov/CSLB_LIBRARY/Name+Request.asp
Alarm Firm/Employee/Mngr .... www.bsis.ca.gov/online_services/verify_license.shtml
Appraiser, Real Estate .... www.orea.ca.gov/html/lic_appraisers.asp
Apprentice Program, Skilled Labor ... www.dir.ca.gov/databases/das/aigstart.asp
Architect .... www.cab.ca.gov/consumers/license_verification.shtml
Asbestos Consultant/Surveillance ...... www.dir.ca.gov/databases/doshcaccsst/caccsst_query_1.html
Asbestos Contractor .... www.dir.ca.gov/databases/doshacru/acrusearch.html
Asbestos Trainer .... www.dir.ca.gov/databases/doshcaccsst/aheratp.asp
Asbestos Worker/Trainee .... www.dir.ca.gov/DOSH/ACRU/TP_AsbestosTrainingCertificates.html
Attorney .... http://members.calbar.ca.gov/search/member.aspx
Audiologist .... www.slpab.ca.gov/consumers/verify.shtml
Automobile Dealer/Repair .... www.smogcheck.ca.gov/stdPage.asp?Body=/Consumer/verify_a_license.htm
Bank Agencies/Branches, Foreign ..... www.dfi.ca.gov/licensees/otherstate/default.asp
Bank, Industrial, State-Chartered .... www.dfi.ca.gov/directory/regulate.asp
Bank, State-Chartered .... www.dfi.ca.gov/licensees/
Bar Association .... http://members.calbar.ca.gov/search/ba_search.aspx
Barber Instr't'r/School .... www2.dca.ca.gov/pls/wllpub/wllqryna$lcev2.startup?p_qte_code=FRM&p_qte_pgm_code=3300
Barber/Shop/Appren .... www2.dca.ca.gov/pls/wllpub/wllqryna$lcev2.startup?p_qte_code=IND&p_qte_pgm_code=3300
Baton Training Facility/Instructor ..... www.bsis.ca.gov/online_services/verify_license.shtml
Brake & Lamp Adjuster .... www.smogcheck.ca.gov/stdPage.asp?Body=/Consumer/verify_a_license.htm
Brake Station .... www.smogcheck.ca.gov/stdPage.asp?Body=/Consumer/verify_a_license.htm
Building Contr., General-Class B ...... www2.cslb.ca.gov/CSLB_LIBRARY/Name+Request.asp
Cabinet/Millwork Contractor .... www2.cslb.ca.gov/CSLB_LIBRARY/Name+Request.asp
Car Washing/Polishing .... www.dir.ca.gov/databases/dlselr/carwash.html
Care Facility for Chronically Ill .... www.ccld.ca.gov/docs/ccld_search/ccld_search.aspx
Care Facility, Children, Transitional . www.ccld.ca.gov/docs/ccld_search/ccld_search.aspx
Cemetery, Cemetery Broker/Seller .... www.cfb.ca.gov/consumer/lookup.shtml
Child Care Center .... www.ccld.ca.gov/docs/ccld_search/ccld_search.aspx
Chiropractic Corporation/Satellite ..... www.chiro.ca.gov/onlineservices/licsearch.html
Chiropractor .... www.chiro.ca.gov/onlineservices/licsearch.html
Clinic Pharmaceutical Permit .... www.pharmacy.ca.gov/online/verify_lic.shtml
Community Treatment Facility .... www.ccld.ca.gov/docs/ccld_search/ccld_search.aspx
Concrete Contractor/Company .... www2.cslb.ca.gov/CSLB_LIBRARY/Name+Request.asp
Conscious Sedation Permit .... www2.dca.ca.gov/pls/wllpub/wllquery$.startup
Construction Permit, Excav/Shoring . www.dir.ca.gov/dosh/PermitHolder/PermitHolder.asp
Continuing Education Provider .... www.bbs.ca.gov/quick_links/weblookup.shtml
Contractor, Business/Individual .... www.cslb.ca.gov
Cosmetician/Cosmetologist
            www2.dca.ca.gov/pls/wllpub/wllqryna$lcev2.startup?p_qte_code=IND&p_qte_pgm_code=3300

Cosmetology/Electrology Firm/Instr./School
www2.dca.ca.gov/pls/wllpub/wllqryna$lcev2.startup?p_qte_code=IND&p_qte_pgm_code=3300
Court Reporter/Shorthand Reporter
www2.dca.ca.gov/pls/wllpub/wllqryna$lcev2.startup?p_qte_code=CSR&p_qte_pgm_code=8100
CPA/CPA Firm.................................. www2.dca.ca.gov/pls/wllpub/wllquery$.startup
Crane Operator .... www.dir.ca.gov/databases/crane/cranesearch.html
Credit Union .... www.dfi.ca.gov/licensees/cu/default.asp
Cremated Remains Disposer............. www.cfb.ca.gov/consumer/lookup.shtml
Crematory.. www.cfb.ca.gov/consumer/lookup.shtml
Day Care, Adult/Child...................... www.ccld.ca.gov/docs/ccld_search/ccld_search.aspx
Dental Anesthesia Permit .... www2.dca.ca.gov/pls/wllpub/wllquery$.startup
Dental Assistant/or/Hygienist............ www.comda.ca.gov/licensestatus.html
Dentist/ Dental Registered Provider .. www2.dca.ca.gov/pls/wllpub/wllquery$.startup
Dentist Fictitious Name .... www2.dca.ca.gov/pls/wllpub/wllquery$.startup
Development Corporation .... www.dfi.ca.gov/directory/bidco.asp
Driving School/Instructor https://mv.dmv.ca.gov/olinq2/welcome.do
Drug Wholesaler/Drug Room............ www.pharmacy.ca.gov/online/verify_lic.shtml
Drywall Contractor .... www2.cslb.ca.gov/CSLB_LIBRARY/Name+Request.asp
Earthwork/Paving Contractor .... www2.cslb.ca.gov/CSLB_LIBRARY/Name+Request.asp
Electrical Contr. & Elec Sign Contr. . www2.cslb.ca.gov/CSLB_LIBRARY/Name+Request.asp
Electrologist..............www2.dca.ca.gov/pls/wllpub/wllqryna$lcev2.startup?p_qte_code=IND&p_qte_pgm_code=3300
Electronic & Appliance Repair.......... www.bear.ca.gov/consumer/look_up.shtml
Elevator Installation Contractor........ www2.cslb.ca.gov/CSLB_LIBRARY/Name+Request.asp
Embalmer/Embalmer Apprentice ...... www.cfb.ca.gov/consumer/lookup.shtml
Engineer (various disciplines) .... www.dca.ca.gov/pels/l_lookup.htm
Esthetician   www2.dca.ca.gov/pls/wllpub/wllqryna$lcev2.startup?p_qte_code=IND&p_qte_pgm_code=3300
Family Child Care Home................... www.ccld.ca.gov/docs/ccld_search/ccld_search.aspx
Farm Labor Contractor .... www.dir.ca.gov/databases/dlselr/Farmlic.html
Fencing Contractor .... www2.cslb.ca.gov/CSLB_LIBRARY/Name+Request.asp
Firearm Permit.................................. www.bsis.ca.gov/online_services/verify_license.shtml
Firearm Training Facility/Instr. .... www.bsis.ca.gov/online_services/verify_license.shtml
Flooring/Floor Covering Contractor.. www2.cslb.ca.gov/CSLB_LIBRARY/Name+Request.asp
Foster Family Agency .... www.ccld.ca.gov/docs/ccld_search/ccld_search.aspx
Funeral Director/Apprentice.............. www.cfb.ca.gov/consumer/lookup.shtml
Funerary Establish./Training Establ. . www.cfb.ca.gov/consumer/lookup.shtml
Garment Manufacturer .... www.dir.ca.gov/databases/dlselr/Garmreg.html
Geologist.................www2.dca.ca.gov/pls/wllpub/wllqryna$lcev2.startup?p_qte_code=GEO&p_qte_pgm_code=5100
Geophysicist.............www2.dca.ca.gov/pls/wllpub/wllqryna$lcev2.startup?p_qte_code=GEO&p_qte_pgm_code=5100
Glazier .... www2.cslb.ca.gov/CSLB_LIBRARY/Name+Request.asp
Group Home .... www.ccld.ca.gov/docs/ccld_search/ccld_search.aspx
Healing Art Supervisor..................... www.applications.dhs.ca.gov/rhbxray/
Hearing Aid Dispenser
www2.dca.ca.gov/pls/wllpub/wllqryna$lcev2.startup?p_qte_code=HA&p_qte_pgm_code=6700
Heating & Warm-Air Vent. Contr. .... www2.cslb.ca.gov/CSLB_LIBRARY/Name+Request.asp
Home Furnishings
www2.dca.ca.gov/pls/wllpub/wllqryna$lcev2.startup?p_qte_code=LIC&p_qte_pgm_code=5710
Horse Racing Entity/Occupation .... www.chrb.ca.gov/license_search.htm
Hospital Pharmaceutical Exemptee ... www.pharmacy.ca.gov/online/verify_lic.shtml
Hydrogeologist
www2.dca.ca.gov/pls/wllpub/wllqryna$lcev2.startup?p_qte_code=GEO&p_qte_pgm_code=5100
Hypodermic Needle & Syringe Dist.. www.pharmacy.ca.gov/online/verify_lic.shtml
Infant Center.................................... www.ccld.ca.gov/docs/ccld_search/ccld_search.aspx
Insulation/Acoustical Contractor .... www2.cslb.ca.gov/CSLB_LIBRARY/Name+Request.asp
Insurance Adjuster............................ www.insurance.ca.gov/0200-industry/0200-prod-licensing/0200-current-lic-info/
Insurance Agent/Broker/Producer ..... www.insurance.ca.gov/license-status/index.cfm
Insurance Company www.insurance.ca.gov/0200-industry/0070-check-license-status/index.cfm
Insurance(2) Agent/Broker www.insurance.ca.gov/0200-industry/0070-check-license-status/index.cfm

Investment Advisor ....http://search.dre.ca.gov/integrationaspcode/
Lamp Station ....www.smogcheck.ca.gov/stdPage.asp?Body=/Consumer/verify_a_license.htm
Land Surveyor-in-Training...............www.dca.ca.gov/pels/l_lookup.htm
Landscape Architect.........................www.latc.dca.ca.gov/licenseeinfo/search.htm
Landscaping Contractor....................www2.cslb.ca.gov/CSLB_LIBRARY/Name+Request.asp
Legal Specialist ....http://members.calbar.ca.gov/search/ls_search.aspx
Legal Specialization Provider...........http://members.calbar.ca.gov/search/cert.aspx
Lobbying Firm/Employer ....http://cal-access.ss.ca.gov/Lobbying/
Lobbyist..http://cal-access.ss.ca.gov/Lobbying/
Locksmith/Locksmith Company........www.bsis.ca.gov/online_services/verify_license.shtml
Mammographic Facility ....www.applications.dhs.ca.gov/rhbxray/
Manicurist   ... ... www2.dca.ca.gov/pls/wllpub/wllqryna$lcev2.startup?p_qte_code=IND&p_qte_pgm_code=3300
Marriage & Family Therapist ....www.bbs.ca.gov/quick_links/weblookup.shtml
Masonry Contractor...........................www2.cslb.ca.gov/CSLB_LIBRARY/Name+Request.asp
Medical Doctor, Enforcem't Docu't..www.medbd.ca.gov/lookup.html
Medical Doctor/Surgeon...................www.medbd.ca.gov/lookup.html
Medical Evaluator ....www.dir.ca.gov/databases/imc/imcstartnew.asp
Midwife, Midwife Nurse   www2.dca.ca.gov/pls/wllpub/wllqryna$lcev2.startup?p_qte_code=L
                        M&p_qte_pgm_code=6200qte_pgm_code=6200
Money Order Issuer...........................www.dfi.ca.gov/licensees/moneytransmitters/default.asp
Notary Education Vendors ....http://notaryeducation.sos.ca.gov/
Nuclear Medicine Technologist.........www.applications.dhs.ca.gov/rhbxray/
Nurse Regist'd
                        www2.dca.ca.gov/pls/wllpub/wllqryna$lcev2.startup?p_qte_code=RN&p_qte_pgm_code=7800qte_pgm_code=7800
Nursing Home Administrator ....www.applications.dhs.ca.gov/cvl/
Occupational Therapist/Therapist Assistant
                        www2.dca.ca.gov/pls/wllpub/wllqryna$lcev2.startup?p_qte_code=OT&p_qte_pgm_code=1475
Ornamental Metal Contractor ....www2.cslb.ca.gov/CSLB_LIBRARY/Name+Request.asp
Osteopath..www.opsc.org/displaycommon.cfm?an=1&subarticlenbr=9
Painting/Decorating Contractor ....www2.cslb.ca.gov/CSLB_LIBRARY/Name+Request.asp
Parking/Hi'way Improvement Contr. www2.cslb.ca.gov/CSLB_LIBRARY/Name+Request.asp
Patrol Operator, Private....................www.bsis.ca.gov/online_services/verify_license.shtml
Payment Instrument Issuer ....www.dfi.ca.gov/directory/pi.asp
Pesticide Applicator/Operator/Rep....www.pestboard.ca.gov/license.shtml
Pharmaceutical-related Business ....www.pharmacy.ca.gov/online/verify_lic.shtml
Pharmacist/Pharmacist Intern ....www.pharmacy.ca.gov/online/verify_lic.shtml
Pharmacy/Pharmacy Technician........www.pharmacy.ca.gov/online/verify_lic.shtml
Photogrammetrist ....www.dca.ca.gov/pels/l_lookup.htm
Physical Therapist/Assistant
                        www2.dca.ca.gov/pls/wllpub/wllqryna$lcev2.startup?p_qte_code=PT&p_qte_pgm_code=6800
Physician Assistant...........................www.pac.ca.gov/forms_pubs/online_services/license_lookup.shtml
Plastering Contractor ....www2.cslb.ca.gov/CSLB_LIBRARY/Name+Request.asp
Plumber ....www2.cslb.ca.gov/CSLB_LIBRARY/Name+Request.asp
Podiatrist...www.bpm.ca.gov/licensing/index.shtml
Premium Finance Company ....http://search.dre.ca.gov/integrationaspcode/
Private Investigator...........................www.bsis.ca.gov/online_services/verify_license.shtml
Psychiatric Technician......................www.bvnpt.ca.gov/License_Verification.asp
Psychological, and Assistant
                        www2.dca.ca.gov/pls/wllpub/wllqryna$lcev2.startup?p_qte_code=PSX&p_qte_pgm_code=7300
Psychologist, Educational..................www.bbs.ca.gov/quick_links/weblookup.shtml
Public Accountant-CPA ....www2.dca.ca.gov/pls/wllpub/wllquery$.startup
Public Works Trainer ....www.dir.ca.gov/databases/das/pwaddrstart.asp
Radioactive Material Licensee ....www.applications.dhs.ca.gov/rhbxray/
Radiologic Technologist....................www.applications.dhs.ca.gov/rhbxray/
Real Estate Agent/Seller....................http://search.dre.ca.gov/integrationaspcode/
Real Estate Appraiser ....www.orea.ca.gov/html/lic_appraisers.asp
Real Estate Broker/Corporation.........http://search.dre.ca.gov/integrationaspcode/

Refrigeration Contractor.....................www2.cslb.ca.gov/CSLB_LIBRARY/Name+Request.asp
Repossessor Agency/Mgr./Employee www.bsis.ca.gov/online_services/verify_license.shtml
Representative (Banking) Foreign.....www.dfi.ca.gov/licensees/otherstate/default.asp
Residential Care for Elderly/or/Adult www.ccld.ca.gov/docs/ccld_search/ccld_search.aspx
Respiratory Care Practitioner
                      www2.dca.ca.gov/pls/wllpub/wllqryna$lcev2.startup?p_qte_code=RCP&p_qte_pgm_code=7600
Roofing Contractor.............................www2.cslb.ca.gov/CSLB_LIBRARY/Name+Request.asp
Sanitation System Contractor ....www2.cslb.ca.gov/CSLB_LIBRARY/Name+Request.asp
Savings & Loan Association ....http://search.dre.ca.gov/integrationaspcode/
School Administrative Service ....www.ctc.ca.gov/credentials/default.html
Securities Broker/Dealer...................http://search.dre.ca.gov/integrationaspcode/
Security Guard....................................www.bsis.ca.gov/online_services/verify_license.shtml
Service Contract Seller, Appliance ....www.bear.ca.gov/consumer/look_up.shtml
Sheet Metal Contractor.....................www2.cslb.ca.gov/CSLB_LIBRARY/Name+Request.asp
Shelter, Temporary ....www.ccld.ca.gov/docs/ccld_search/ccld_search.aspx
Smog Check Station/Technician........www.smogcheck.ca.gov/stdPage.asp?Body=/Consumer/verify_a_license.htm
Social Rehabilitation Facility ....www.ccld.ca.gov/docs/ccld_search/ccld_search.aspx
Social Worker, Clinical ....www.bbs.ca.gov/quick_links/weblookup.shtml
Solar Energy Contractor ....www2.cslb.ca.gov/CSLB_LIBRARY/Name+Request.asp
Specialty Contractor-Class C............www2.cslb.ca.gov/CSLB_LIBRARY/Name+Request.asp
Speech Pathologist/Audiologist Asst. www.slpab.ca.gov/consumers/verify.shtml
Speech-Language Pathologist............www.slpab.ca.gov/consumers/verify.shtml
Steel Contractor................................www2.cslb.ca.gov/CSLB_LIBRARY/Name+Request.asp
Studio Teacher..................................www.dir.ca.gov/databases/dlselr/StudTch.html
Support Center, Adult........................www.ccld.ca.gov/docs/ccld_search/ccld_search.aspx
Surgical Clinic Pharm., Nonprofit .....www.pharmacy.ca.gov/online/verify_lic.shtml
Surplus Lines Brokers www.insurance.ca.gov/0100-consumers/0030-licensee-info/0030-lesli/
Surveyor, Land ....www.dca.ca.gov/pels/l_lookup.htm
Swimming Pool Contractor ....www2.cslb.ca.gov/CSLB_LIBRARY/Name+Request.asp
Talent Agency ....www.dir.ca.gov/databases/dlselr/Talag.html
Tax Education Provider.....................https://secure.ctec.org/provider/logon.asp
Tax Preparer ....http://ctec.org/verify.asp
Thrift & Loan Company ....http://search.dre.ca.gov/integrationaspcode/
Tile Contractor, Ceramic/Mosaic ......www2.cslb.ca.gov/CSLB_LIBRARY/Name+Request.asp
Trainer, Public Works........................www.dir.ca.gov/databases/das/pwaddrstart.asp
Travelers Checks Issuer....................www.dfi.ca.gov/licensees/moneytransmitters/default.asp
Trust Company ....www.dfi.ca.gov/licensees/trust/default.asp
Veterinarian/ Veterinary Premise ......www.vmb.ca.gov/consumers/licverif.shtml
Veteri'y Food/Animal Drug Retail'r . www.pharmacy.ca.gov/online/verify_lic.shtml
Veterinary Technician ....www.vmb.ca.gov/consumers/licverif.shtml
Viatical Settl'm'nt Insurer..........www.insurance.ca.gov/0100-consumers/0030-licensee-info/0040-viatical-settlements/
Vocational Nurse..............................www.bvnpt.ca.gov/License_Verification.asp
Water Well Driller.............................www2.cslb.ca.gov/CSLB_LIBRARY/Name+Request.asp
X-ray Technician/or/Machine Regis..www.applications.dhs.ca.gov/rhbxray/

State and Local Courts

State Court Structure: The Superior Court is the trial court in this state and handles all cases. However, in higher population counties, they are Limited Superior Courts. The reason is that between 1998 and 2000 the Superior Courts and Municipal Courts united within their respective counties. Some courts that were formerly Municipal Courts became Limited Jurisdiction Superior Courts. In some counties the Superior Courts and Municipal Courts were combined into one Superior Court. Civil cases under $25,000 is in a Limited Civil Court, over $25,000 is in Unlimited Civil Court, and if both covered in one court, then the court is a Combined Civil Court. It is important to note that Limited Courts may try minor felonies.

Statewide Court Online Access: The website at www.courtinfo.ca.gov offers access to all opinions from the Supreme Court and Appeals Courts from 1850 to present. Opinions not certified for publications are available for the last 60 days. This site also contains very useful information about the state court system, including opinions from the Supreme Court and Appeals Courts.

There is no statewide online computer access available. However, a number of counties have developed their own online access sytems and provide internet access at no fee. Los Angeles County has an extensive free and fee-based online system at www.lasuperiorcourt.org

Alameda County

All Superior Court Locations   www.alameda.courts.ca.gov/courts   `Free`
Civil: Online access to calendars, limited civil case summaries and complex litigations are free from Domain Web at the website. Search limited cases by number; litigations by case name or number. At the website, search "Find Your Court Date" to determine if a name has an upcoming court date. *Criminal:* At the website, search "Find Your Court Date" to see if a name has upcoming court date.

Butte County

All Superior Court Locations www.buttecourt.ca.gov   `Free`
Civil: Limited case index searching by name is free at www.buttecourt.ca.gov/online_index/cmssearch.cfm. There is also a calendar lookup at www.buttecourt.ca.gov/calendarlookup/cmscalendarlookup.cfm. *Criminal:* Limited case index searching by name is free online at www.buttecourt.ca.gov/online_index/cmssearch.cfm. There is also a calendar lookup, see above.

Contra Costa County

All Superior Court Locations   www.cc-courts.org   `Free`
Civil: Civil case, Probate, Family and Small Claims information is free at www.cc-courts.org/civilcms.htm. Also, lookup your court case info free at www.cc-courts.org/ and click on Case Info or Tell Me About My Case. *Criminal:* Lookup your court case info free at www.cc-courts.org/ and click on Case Info or Tell Me About My Case.

Fresno County

All Superior Court Locations   www.fresnosuperiorcourt.org   `Free`
Civil: Online access to civil, probate, family, small claims cases is free at www.fresnosuperiorcourt.org/case_info/.

Clovis Division - Superior Court   www.fresnosuperiorcourt.org   `Free`
Civil: Online access to civil, probate, family, small claims cases is free at www.fresnosuperiorcourt.org/case_info/.

Glenn County

Superior Court   www.glenncourt.ca.gov   `Free`
Civil: Search case index at www.glenncourt.ca.gov/online%5Findex/. *Criminal:* same.

Kern County

All Superior Court Locations   www.kern.courts.ca.gov   `Free`
Civil: Civil case info and calendars on special kiosk computers located at every court location and at website. *Criminal:* Access defendant database free at www.co.kern.ca.us/courts/crimcal/crim_index_def.asp; Results show year of birth only; old records being added. Current court calendars free at www.co.kern.ca.us/courts/crim_index_case_info_cal.asp. Access defendant hearings schedule at www.co.kern.ca.us/courts/crimcal/crim_hearing_srch.asp. Also, search sheriff inmate list at www.kern.courts.ca.gov/case-menu-main.asp. Click on "inmate search."

search county sheriff inmate list at www.co.kern.ca.us/courts/caseinfo_menu.asp. Click on "inmate search."

Los Angeles County

All Los Angeles Superior Court - Civil, Probate   www.lasuperiorcourt.org   `Free & $$`
Civil: For cases over $25,000 there is a fee-based lookup for case images at https://www.lasuperiorcourt.org/OnlineServices/CivilImages/index.asp. Search fee is $4.75, case document file is $7.50. There is a free case summary lookup for cases under $25,000 at https://www.lasuperiorcourt.org/OnlineServices/CivilImages/index.asp but lookup is by case number, not name.Throughput depends on the court lodation. Includes probate from 1/97.

All Los Angeles Superior Court Locations - Criminal   www.lasuperiorcourt.org   `$$`
Criminal: Felony and misdemeanor defendant records are online at www.lasuperiorcourt.org/OnlineServices/criminalindex/. Search fee is $4 to $4.75.

Marin County

Superior Court   www.co.marin.ca.us/courts   `Free`
Civil: Online access to the index is free at www.co.marin.ca.us/depts/MC/main/courtcal/name.cfm. *Criminal:* Online access to the criminal index is the same as civil.

Mendocino County

All Superior Court Loctaions   www.mendocino.courts.ca.gov   `Free`
Civil: Search index at www.mendocino.courts.ca.gov/caseindex.html. Online index may be up to 2 months behind. *Criminal:* same.

Monterey County

Superior Court - Salinas Division   www.monterey.courts.ca.gov   `Free`
Criminal: Access court data free at https://www.justicepartners.monterey.courts.ca.gov/Public/JPPublicIndex.aspx, Search calendars at https://www.justicepartners.monterey.courts.ca.gov/Public/JPPublicCalendarSearch.aspx.

King City Division - Consolidated Trial Court   www.monterey.courts.ca.gov   `Free`
Civil: Access court data free at https://www.justicepartners.monterey.courts.ca.gov/Public/JPPublicIndex.aspx, Search calendars at https://www.justicepartners.monterey.courts.ca.gov/Public/JPPublicCalendarSearch.aspx, *Criminal:* Access court data free at https://www.justicepartners.monterey.courts.ca.gov/Public/JPPublicIndex.aspx, Calendar search- same as civil, above.

Superior Court - Marina Division   www.monterey.courts.ca.gov   `Free`
Civil: Access court data free at https://www.justicepartners.monterey.courts.ca.gov/Public/JPPublicIndex.aspx.

Napa County

Superior Court - Civil   www.napa.courts.ca.gov   `Free & $$`
Civil: Access to tentative rulings is online free at www.napa.courts.ca.gov/Civil/civil_tentative.asp. These only go back about 1 week.

Superior Court - Criminal   www.napa.courts.ca.gov   `Free`
Criminal: Online access is at www.napa.courts.ca.gov. An AKA constitutes an additional or separate name search request.

Nevada County

All Superior Court Locations   http://court.co.nevada.ca.us/services/index.htm   `Free`
Civil: Access to case calendar is free at www.court.co.nevada.ca.us/cgi/dba/casecal/db.cgi. *Criminal:* Access to case calendar is free at www.court.co.nevada.ca.us/cgi/dba/casecal/db.cgi.

Orange County

All Superior Court Locations- Civil   www.occourts.org   `Free`
Access civil case index free at https://ocapps.occourts.org/CivilPub/Login.do. Civil, small claims, probate cases index for the county can be purchased on CD; index goes back to 12/31/01 or can be purchased on monthly basis. See www.occourts.org/caseinfo/ or email tthompson@occourts.org. Unlimited civil and family court calendars are online at www.occourts.org/calendars/.

All Superior Court Locations - Criminal Operations   www.occourts.org   `Free`
Online access to criminal and traffic and calendars are free at http://visionweb.occourts.org/Vision_Public/Index.do click on Cases. Search and results include DOB, also dispositions and dismissals. Index may go back to 1988. Also, felony record index for the county can be purchased on CD; index goes back to 12/31/01 or can be purchased on monthly basis. See www.occourts.org/caseinfo/ or email tthompson@occourts.org.

Orange County Probate Court   www.occourts.org/probate   `Free`   Search court calendars free at www.occourts.org/calendars/calendarsprob.asp; indices at www.occourts.org/caseinfo/.

Riverside County

All Superior Court Locations - Civil   www.riverside.courts.ca.gov/   `Free`
Civil: Access to civil records is free at www.riverside.courts.ca.gov/pubacc.htm. Online records date back to 1991 for Riverside, 1994 for Corona, 1996 forward for most remaining limited court cases. Also, civil indexes on CD-Rom; fee is $25.00 per month per dept. Civil index back to 1993; Complete name index history is $300 per dept.

All Superior Court Locations - Criminal   www.riverside.courts.ca.gov/   `Free`
Criminal: Access criminal records free at www.riverside.courts.ca.gov/pubacc.htm or logon as GUEST at http://75.28.114.12/OpenAccess/. Identifiers- month and year of birth. Online records go back to 1990, 1991-1993 for misd., 1998 for traffic.

Sacramento County

Superior Court   www.saccourt.com   `Free`
Civil: Access court records back to 1993 free at https://services.saccourt.com/indexsearchnew/. Includes civil, probate, small claims, unlawful detainer, family as well as criminal. *Criminal:* Access criminal records back to 1989 free at https://services.saccourt.com/indexsearchnew/.

Family Relations Courthouse   www.saccourt.com/geninfo/location/wrrfrc.asp   `Free`   Probate and domestic records available online free at https://services.saccourt.com/publicdms2/DefaultDMS.aspx.

San Bernardino County

All Superior Court Locations -   www.sbcounty.gov/courts   `Free`
Civil: Online access to civil cases is free at www.sbcounty.gov/courts/genInfo/openaccess.htm. Includes calendars. Online access to "Probate Notes" is free at www.co.san-bernardino.ca.us/courts/ Click on Probate. *Criminal:* Online access to criminal cases and traffic is free at www.sbcounty.gov/courts/genInfo/openaccess.htm. Includes calendars. Also, the daily criminal docket is free at the court main website.

San Diego County

All Superior Court Locations www.sdcourt.ca.gov **Free**
Searching of indexes, new filings, calendars and probate examiner notes is free at www.sdcourt.ca.gov/. Click on Online Services.

San Francisco County

Superior Court - Civil http://sfgov.org/site/courts_index.asp **Free**
Civil: Online access to the case management system is free at www.sftc.org but does not include family law, small claims, confidential or restricted cases. Access probate case data free at www.sftc.org.

Superior Court - Misdemeanor Division www.sfgov.org/site/courts_index.asp **Free**
Criminal: Online access to case management system is free at www.sftc.org.

San Joaquin County

All Superior Court Locations - Criminal www.stocktoncourt.org/courts **Free**
 Criminal: Access court calendars free at www.stocktoncourt.org/stkcrtwwwV5web/SCCalDayIndex.html.

All Superior Court Locations - Civil www.stocktoncourt.org/courts **Free**
Civil: Free access to civil case summaries, with name searching, at www.stocktoncourt.org/courts/caseinfo.htm. Also, access court calendars free at www.stocktoncourt.org/stkcrtwwwV5web/SCCalDayIndex.html.

San Mateo County

All Superior Court Locations www.sanmateocourt.org **Free**
Civil: Online access is free at www.sanmateocourt.org/director.php?filename=./includes/midx_open_access.html. *Criminal:* Search all county case records including criminal for free at www.sanmateocourt.org/midx/searchform4_tim.php. Also, search traffic citations at https://www.sanmateocourt.org/traffic/.

Superior Court - Southern Branch www.sanmateocourt.org **Free**
Civil: Online access is free at www.sanmateocourt.org/director.php?filename=./includes/midx_open_access.html. *Criminal:* Search all county case records including criminal for free at www.sanmateocourt.org/midx/searchform4_tim.php. Also, search traffic citations at https://www.sanmateocourt.org/traffic/.

Santa Barbara County

All Superior Court Locations www.sbcourts.org/index.asp **Free**
Civil: Search general civil index 1975 to present or limited civil back to 1977 free online at www.sbcourts.org/pubindex/. Daily calendars free at www.sbcourts.org/pubcal/. *Criminal:* A CD-Rom of monthly court indices from all divisions is $40.00.

Santa Clara County

Superior Court - Civil www.sccsuperiorcourt.org **Free**
Civil: Civil, Family, Probate, and Small Claims case records and court calendars are free online at www.sccaseinfo.org. CD-rom is also available, fee-$150.00.

Santa Cruz County

Superior Court - Civil www.santacruzcourt.org **Free**
Civil: Access civil records free at www.santacruzcourt.org/Case%20Info/index.htm. Access using case number or party name. Also, civil records online privately for fee from Westlaw.

Shasta County

Superior Court www.shastacourts.com **Free**
Civil: Access to civil division index free at www.shastacourts.com/indexes.php. *Criminal:* Access the criminal division index free at www.shastacourts.com/indexes/index_menu.php.

Siskiyou County

Superior Court www.siskiyou.courts.ca.gov **Free**
Civil: Access to county superior court records is free at www.siskiyou.courts.ca.gov/CaseHistory.asp. Includes traffic but not juvenile or confidential cases. *Criminal:* Online access to criminal records is available; see civil.

Solano County

Superior Court www.solanocourts.com/ **Free**
Civil: Online access to civil records is free at http://courtconnect.solanocourts.com/pls/bprod_cc/ck_public_qry_main.cp_main_idx. Also, civil tentative rulings and probate notes are free at www.solanocourts.com/civil_tent.htm. *Criminal:* Online access to criminal records is free at http://courtconnect.solanocourts.com/pls/bprod_cc/ck_public_qry_main.cp_main_idx.

Sonoma County

Superior Court - www.sonomasuperiorcourt.com/index.php **Free**
Search free case civil and criminal index directly at www.sonomasuperiorcourt.com/index.php by name or attorney; also calendars, cases recently filed, rulings. Online index does not provide register of actions, just case number and parties. Goes back 3 months.

Stanislaus County
Superior Court - www.stanct.org/ Free
Access the civil and crminla case indices free at www.stanct.org/Case_Index/index.html.

Tuolumne County
Superior Court - Criminal www.tuolumne.courts.ca.gov Free
Access criminal records by case number of DR# at www.tuolumne.courts.ca.gov; click on "Criminal Division."

Ventura County
Superior Court www.ventura.courts.ca.gov Free
Civil: Access to case information, calendars and dockets is free at www.ventura.courts.ca.gov/vent_frameset_puba.htm. Search by defendant or plaintiff name, case number, or date. Search probate at www.venturacogensoc.org/Probate.html. *Criminal:* Access to case information, calendars and dockets is free at www.ventura.courts.ca.gov/vent_frameset_puba.htm. DOB required for crim search.

Yolo County
Superior Court www.yolo.courts.ca.gov/ Free
Civil: Calendars are online free at www.yolocourts.com/calendar_daily.html. Search Probate Notes at www.yolocourts.com/probate_notes.html. *Criminal:* Access criminal and traffic records free at http://secure.yolo.courts.ca.gov:80/GetWeb/YoloCrimTrafStart.html but no name searching; search by case number or DL only. Also, calendars are free at www.yolocourts.com/calendar_daily.html.

Recorders, Assessors, and Other Sites of Note

Recording Office Organization: 58 counties, 58 recording offices. The recording officer is the County Recorder. Recordings are usually located in a Grantor/Grantee or General Index. Federal and state tax liens on personal property of businesses are filed with the Secretary of State. Other federal and state tax liens are filed with the County Recorder, and state tax liens on individuals can be found at both the Sec of State and county.

Online Access Note: A number of counties offer online access to assessor and real estate information. The assessor's system in Los Angeles County is a commercial subscription system.

Alameda County *Real Estate, Deed, Lien, Fictitious Name, Voter Status Records* www.acgov.org Free
Access the clerk-recorder's official public records and fictitious name databases for free at http://rechart1.co.alameda.ca.us/ Also, check voter registration status at www.acgov.org/rov/voter_reg_lookup.htm.
Property, Taxation Records Free Access to the Property Assessment database is free at www.acgov.org/MS/prop/index.aspx but no name searching. Also, property tax data is found at www.acgov.org/jsp_app/treasurer/tax_info/index.jsp.

Amador County *All Recorded Documents Records* www.co.amador.ca.us/depts/recorder/index.htm Free Access to the county's recorded documents is free at www.co.amador.ca.us/depts/recorder/criis.htm or www.criis.com/amador/recorded.htm.
Property, Taxation Records Free Access online property records at www.co.amador.ca.us/depts/assessor/inquery1.cfm. Also, tax sale data is at www.co.amador.ca.us/depts/treasurer/index.htm; search by year.

Butte County *Real Estate, Fictitious Business Name Records* http://clerk-recorder.buttecounty.net Free Access to the recorder's database of official documents is free at http://clerk-recorder.buttecounty.net/Riimsweb/Asp/ORInquiry.asp. Records go back to 1988. Marriages, births and deaths are no longer available.
Property, Taxation Records Free View property tax data free at http://ttc.buttecounty.net/Default.aspx?tabid=63 but no name searching. Also, access to tax sales lists is free through a private company at www.bid4assets.com.

Calaveras County *Property, Taxation Records* Free Access property data free at www.co.calaveras.ca.us/parcelsearch.asp. No name searching. Also, access the GIS Project of property data free at www.co.calaveras.ca.us/departments/gisproj.asp. Click on "The Parcel Information System." No name searching.

Contra Costa County *Real Estate, Deed, Lien, Judgment, Fictitious Business Names Records* www.co.contra-costa.ca.us/depart/elect/Rindex.html Free Recorder office records including marriage records back to 1992 are free at www.criis.com/contracosta/official.shtml. By order of governor, birth and death records have been removed from the internet. Fictitious Business names are at www.criis.com/contracosta/sfictitious.shtml.

El Dorado County *Real Estate, Deed, Lien, Mortgage, Vital Statistic, Fictitious Names Records* www.co.el-dorado.ca.us/countyclerk/ Free Access to the Recorder's index is free at http://main.co.el-dorado.ca.us/CGI/WWB012/WWM501/R. Records go back to 1850. Search business licenses free at http://main.co.el-dorado.ca.us/CGI/WWB012/WWM200/T?S=A. Search recorder's Official Records index free at http://main.co.el-dorado.ca.us/CGI/WWB012/WWM501/C. Search by date range, name or doc number. Search county non-confidential marriages and fictitious names for free at http://main.co.el-dorado.ca.us/CGI/WWB012/WWM500/C. Births and deaths have been removed.

Property, Taxation Records **Free**   Parcel, tax, and personal property information available free at http://main.co.el-dorado.ca.us/CGI/WWB012/WWM400/A.

Fresno County   *Real Estate, Deed, Lien, Mortgage, Birth, Death, Marriage Records*
www.co.fresno.ca.us/0420/recorders_web/index.htm   **Free**   Access to the recorder database is free at www.criis.com/fresno/srecord.shtml. Marriage records are at www.criis.com/fresno/smarriage.shtml. County Birth Records and death records have been removed from the internet.

Imperial County   *Real Estate, Grantor-Grantee, Deed, Lien, Marriage Records*
www.imperialcounty.net/Recorder/Default.htm   **Free**   Access the Recorder's Official records index free at http://implookup.imperialcounty.net/. Index goes back to 4/1/1986, but no images available. Fictitious business names are at www.imperialcounty.net/Recorder/FBN/Fbn_Page.htm.

Property, Taxation Records **Free**   A GIS-mapping site can assist you in finding parcel data free at www.geoviewerims.net/website/icpublic/viewer.htm but no name searching.

Kern County   *Real Estate, Deed, Fictitious Business Name Records*   http://recorder.co.kern.ca.us   **Free**
Search recorders database of deeds free at http://recorderonline.co.kern.ca.us/. Also, search county clerk's fictitious business name database free at www.co.kern.ca.us/ctyclerk/dba/default.asp. Search county recent sales data at http://kerndata.com.

Property, Taxation Records **Free**   Assessor database records available free at http://assessor.co.kern.ca.us/propertysearch/index.php. Search tax collector data at www.kcttc.co.kern.ca.us/payment/mainsearch.aspx.

Lake County   *Real Estate, Grantor/Grantee, Deed, Lien, Mortgage Records*   www.co.lake.ca.us   **Free**
Limited index display of official records can be accessed at http://acm.co.lake.ca.us/recorder/cms_recordssearch.asp.

Property, Taxation Records **Free**   Parcel records on the GIS Mapping site available by clicking on Lake County Base Maps free at http://gis.co.lake.ca.us/. No name searching.

Lassen County   *Real Estate, Deed Records*   www.lassencounty.org   **Free**   Access to the recorder database is free at
http://icris.lassencounty.org. Registration is required. Recorded documents go back to 7/1985.

Property, Taxation Records **Free**   Access to tax sales lists is free through a private company at www.bid4assets.com.

Los Angeles Registrar-Recorder/County Clerk   *Fictitious Business Names Records*
http://regrec.co.la.ca.us   **Free**   Search fictitious business names at http://regrec.co.la.ca.us/CLERK/FBN_Search.cfm.

Property, Taxation Records **Free & $$**   For assessments use the PDB Inquiry System dial-up svc. for $100 monthly plus $1.00 per inquiry, also $75 sign-up fee for 3-year dial-up with usage fee of $6.50 per hr or $.11 per minute. PDB registration at http://assessor.lacounty.gov/extranet/outsidesales/online.aspx. Tax info line- 213-974-3838. Also search property/assessor data (no name searching) free at http://assessormap.co.la.ca.us/mapping/viewer.asp.

Madera County   *Property, Taxation Records*   **Free**   Access parcel and ownership data free on the GIS-mapping site
free at www.madera-county.com/rma/parcelmap.html but no name searching.

Marin County   *Real Estate, Grantor/Grantee, Deed, Marriage Records*
www.co.marin.ca.us/depts/AR/main/index.cfm   **Free**   Search the county Grantor/Grantee index free at www.co.marin.ca.us/depts/AR/RiiMs/index.asp. Also, search the real estate sales lists by month and year by selecting the year. Also, search the marriage records by document index number at www.co.marin.ca.us/depts/AR/VitalStatistics/index.asp. Marriage records go back to 1948. Search business names by type at http://marinfo.marin.org/Bizmo/index.cfm.

Property, Taxation Records **Free**   Search the property tax database at www.co.marin.ca.us/depts/AR/COMPASS/index.asp but there is no name searching.

Merced County   *Real Estate, Grantor/Grantee, Deed Records*   www.co.merced.ca.us/recorder/   **Free**
Access to the recorder official records index PARIS system is free at www.recorder.merced.ca.us/.

Property, Taxation Records **Free**   Search parcel maps at www.co.merced.ca.us/CountyWeb/pages/parcelmap.aspx. Search by fee parcel number or assessment number at: www.co.merced.ca.us/assessor/assessmentinquiry.html

Modoc County   *Real Estate, Deed, Fictitious Business Name Records*   **Free**   Access to the county clerk recording
database soon to be free at www.criis.com/modoc/official.shtml. Fictitious business names may also be found.

Mono County   *Property, Taxation Records*   **Free**   Access property data free at http://gis.mono.ca.gov/IMS/PublicPV/
but no name searching.

Monterey County   *Real Estate, Grantor/Grantee, Deed, Lien Records*   www.co.monterey.ca.us./recorder/   **Free**
Access the county PARIS system including official records and fictitious business names free at http://65.249.61.8/. Official records go back to 1978.

Property, Taxation Records **Free**   Search assessment data free at www.co.monterey.ca.us/assessor/asmt-query.htm but no name searching. The county tax defaulted property list is at www.co.monterey.ca.us/taxcollector/Auction_Internet.htm.

Napa County *Real Estate, Grantor/Grantee, Deed, Judgment, Lien Records* www.co.napa.ca.us `Free & $$`
Access "Official Records" by subscription; fee- $3600 per year. Index goes back to May, 1986; images back to March, 1999. Also, search Official Records Inquiry site for real estate and Grantor/Grantee index back to 5/1986 free at www.co.napa.ca.us/orpublic/ORInquiry.asp.
Property, Taxation Records `Free` Search assessor's property tax payments free at www.co.napa.ca.us/commerce/propertypayments/ but no name searching. Also, search for property data by address for free at www.co.napa.ca.us/MyProperty/.

Nevada County *Real Estate, Deed, Judgment, Fictitious Name, Property Tax, GIS-mapping Records*
www.mynevadacounty.com/recorder/ `Free & $$` Access to the county clerk database of recordings and assumed names is free at www.criis.com/nevada/official.shtml. Also, subscription access to the recorders full database is $200 per month fee. Also,
Property, Taxation Records `Free` Search the GIS mapping site by address for property info for free at http://63.205.214.10:1711. Also, search property tax payment records at http://treas-tax.co.nevada.ca.us/searchtax.php; no name searching.

Orange County *Real Estate, Grantor/Grantee, Deed, Lien, Judgment, Fictitious Business Name Records*
www.ocrecorder.com `Free` Orange County Grantor/Grantee index is free online at http://cr.ocgov.com/grantorgrantee/index.asp. Also, search fictitious business names at http://cr.ocgov.com/fbn/index.asp.
Property, Taxation Records `Free` Search property tax records at http://tax.ocgov.com/tcweb/search_page.asp; no name searching. Also, search tax parcel data, aircraft, and vessels free at http://tax.ocgov.com/tcweb/search_page.asp but no name searching.

Placer County *Real Estate, Deed, Fictitious Name, Marriage Records* www.placer.ca.gov/Recorder.aspx `Free`
Recorder office index records are free at www.criis.com/placer/srecord_current.shtml. Marriage records are at www.criis.com/placer/smarriage.shtml. Search county Fictitious Business Names at www.criis.com/placer/sfictitious.shtml.
Property, Taxation Records `Free` Assessor's property assessment data free at www.placer.ca.gov/Departments/Assessor/Assessment%20Inquiry/Assessment%20Inquiry%20Iframe.aspx. Search GIS at http://lis.placer.ca.gov/gis.asp?s=1000&h2=545.

Riverside County *Real Estate, Grantor/Grantee, Deed, Lien, Judgment, Mortgage, Divorce, Fictitious Name*
Records http://riverside.asrclkrec.com `Free` Search Grantor/Grantee index and recorded data at www.enetwizard.com/shop/affiliates/11467_01/pre.asp. Also, access to county fictitious name database is free at http://riverside.asrclkrec.com/ACR/OSfbn.asp.
Property, Taxation Records `Free` Access property tax data free at http://pic.asrclkrec.com/Default.aspx but no name searching.

Sacramento County *Real Estate, Grantor/Grantee, Deed, Fictitious Names, Business License, Voter*
Registration Records www.ccr.saccounty.net `Free` Access Clerk-recorder Grantee/Grantor index back to 1965 for free at www.erosi.saccounty.net/Inputs.asp. Also, search registered voters by DOB at www.pollingplacelookup.saccounty.net/LookupPollingPlace_SearchByDOB.aspx. Search fictitious names at www.efbn.saccounty.net. Also, search City of West Sacramento business licenses at www.cityofwestsacramento.org/cityhall/departments/finance/buslic/blfind.cfm.
Property, Taxation Records `Free` Search property tax & parcels at www.eproptax.saccounty.net; no name searching. Also, find property data at http://assessorparcelviewer.saccounty.net/website/assessor/pv_blank.aspx?g=; no name searching.

San Bernardino County *Real Estate, Grantor/Grantee, Deed Records* www.co.san-bernardino.ca.us `Free`
Auditor/Controller Grantor/Grantee recording index back to 1980 is free at http://acrparis.co.san-bernardino.ca.us/cgi-bin/odsmnu1.html/input. Search fictitious business names at http://170.164.50.51/fbn/index.html.
Property, Taxation Records `Free` Records on the County Assessor database are free at www.mytaxcollector.com/trSearch.aspx. No name searching. Property can also be searched on PIMS system at https://nppublic.co.san-bernardino.ca.us/newpims/.

San Diego County *Real Estate, Grantor/Grantee, Deed, Property Sale, Fictitious Name Records*
http://arcc.co.san-diego.ca.us/arcc/default.aspx `Free` From the home page above or at http://arcc.co.san-diego.ca.us/services/grantorgrantee/search.aspx search for recorded documents and property sales. Search fictitious business names at https://arcc.co.san-diego.ca.us/services/fbn/search.aspx.
Property, Taxation Records `Free & $$` From the county home page above or at https://arcc.co.san-diego.ca.us/services/parcelmap/search.aspx search for assessor data on the parcel mapping site. Search for property sales data at http://arcc.co.san-diego.ca.us/services/propsales/propsales_search.aspx; no name searching. Assessor date also available in bulk, see https://arcc.co.san-diego.ca.us/subscription/login.aspx or call 619-685-2455.

San Francisco County *Real Estate, Deed, Real Estate, Lien, Judgment, Fictitious Business Name, Birth,*
Death Records www.sfgov.org `Free` Search recorders database free at www.criis.com/sanfrancisco/srecord.shtml. Fictitious business names are also searchable at http://services.sfgov.org/bns/start.asp. Limited vital statistic data is searchable at www.sfgenealogy.com/sf/, a privately operated site.

Property, Taxation Records Free Access the City Property Tax database free at https://services.sfgov.org/ptx/intro.asp. Click on begin. No name searching; address or block/lot number required.

San Joaquin County ***Property, Taxation Records*** Free Access property data on the GIS-mapping site free at www.sjmap.org/mapapps.asp; no name searching.

San Luis Obispo County ***Real Estate, Grantor/Grantee, Deed, Judgment, Lien, Mortgage, Divorce, Fictitious Business Name, Records*** www.slocounty.ca.gov/Page113.aspx Free Search the recorder database for free at http://services.sloclerkrecorder.org/officials/searchform.cfm.
Property, Taxation Records Free Access property information search free at www.slocounty.ca.gov/Assessor/Property_Information_Search.htm but no name searching. Also, parcel map records free at www.slocounty.ca.gov/Assessor/Parcel_Maps_Online.htm but name searching.

San Mateo County ***Real Estate, Grantor/Grantee, Deed, Property Tax, Fictitious Name Records*** www.smcare.org Free Access the recorder's grantor/grantee index free at www.smcare.org/records/recording/search_database.asp. Also, search fictitious business names at www.smcare.org/business/fictitious/default.asp.
Property, Taxation Records Free Records on county property tax data site is free at http://smctweb1.co.sanmateo.ca.us/index.html, view secured or unsecured.

Santa Barbara County ***Real Estate, Deed, Lien Records*** www.sbcrecorder.com Free Search the recorder's grantor/grantee index at www.sb-democracy.com/opis/ or http://sbcvote.com/opis/ or at www.sbcrecorder.com/opis/.
Property, Taxation Records Free Access to assessor online property info system (OPIS) in free at www.sbcrecorder.com/assessor/search.aspx but no name searching. Records go back 10 years. Full access requires registration. Subscribers may download data. Also, search property tax bills at http://taxes.co.santa-barbara.ca.us/propertytax.asp; click on View/Search Secured Property Tax Bills. No name searching.

Santa Clara County ***Real Estate, Grantor/Grantee, Deed, Fictitious Business Name, Birth Records*** www.clerkrecordersearch.org Free Access to the County Clerk-Recorder database is free at www.clerkrecordersearch.org/cgi-bin/odsmnu1.html/input. Search births 1905-1995 free at www.mariposaresearch.net/php/. Also, search fictitious business names for free at www.clerkrecordersearch.org/cgi-bin/FBNSearch.html/input. Also, search the tax collector database at http://payments.scctax.org/payment/jsp/startup.jsp. No name searching.
Property, Taxation Records Free Search assessment roll free a www.sccassessor.org/ari/home.do but no name searching.

Santa Cruz County ***Real Estate, Deed Records*** www.co.santa-cruz.ca.us/rcd/ Free Access to the recorder's official records is free at http://sccounty01.co.santa-cruz.ca.us/clerkrecorder/Asp/ORInquiry.asp. Online indexes go back to 1978.
Property, Taxation Records Free Access the assessor's parcel data free at http://sccounty01.co.santa-cruz.ca.us/ASR/. No name searching. Also, search for property data using the GIS map at http://gis.co.santa-cruz.ca.us.

Shasta County ***Vital Records Records*** www.co.shasta.ca.us Free A private site lists various birth, death, and marriage records of the county and more at http://myclouds.tripod.com/shasta/shastaco.html.
Property, Taxation Records Free Search assessor and recorded documents at www.co.shasta.ca.us/Departments/AssessorRecorder/PubInqDisclaimer.shtml Records on the City of Redding Parcel Search By Parcel Number Server are free at http://cor400.ci.redding.ca.us/nd/gow3lkap.ndm/input. CA state law has removed owner names.

Sierra County ***Property, Taxation Records*** Free Access to tax sales lists is free through a private company at www.bid4assets.com

Siskiyou County ***Real Estate, Deed, Lien, Fictitious Business Name Records*** Free Access to the Recorder records database is free at www.criis.com/siskiyou/srecord_current.shtml. Also, access to the fictitious names database is at www.criis.com/siskiyou/sfictitious.shtml.
Property, Taxation Records Free Access to tax sales lists is free through a private company at www.bid4assets.com.

Solano County ***Real Estate, Grantor/Grantee, Deed, Judgment, Lien Records*** www.solanocounty.com Free Access the recorder's and assessor's indexes free at http://recorderonline.solanocounty.com. Access recorded data free at http://recorderonline.solanocounty.com/cgi-bin/odsmnu1.html/input. Search inmates and offenders free on private site at https://www.vinelink.com/vinelink/siteInfoAction.do?siteId=5099.
Property, Taxation Records Free See the treasurer/tax collector search above for add't property data. Access the assessor's indexes free at http://recorderonline.solanocounty.com. Also, search the treasurer/tax collector/county clerk property tax database free at www.solanocounty.com/resources/scips/tax/situssearch.asp?navid=531. No name searching.

Sonoma County ***Real Estate, Deed, Lien, UCC, Voter Registration Records*** www.sonoma-county.org/recorder Free Access recorder index records free at http://deeds.sonoma-county.org/search.asp?cabinet=opr. No images on this system. Also, with address, ZIP, and DOB search voter registration records free at www.co.sonoma.ca.us/RegVoter/RegVoterLookup.htm
Property, Taxation Records Free Access assessor information free at www.sonoma-county.org/Assessor/.

Stanislaus County *Real Estate, Deed, Lien, Land, Fictitious Name Records* www.co.stanislaus.ca.us `Free`
Recorder office records index of recent records are free at www.criis.com/stanislaus/srecord_current.shtml. Birth, death and marriage records have been removed from the Internet. County Fictitious Business Name records are at www.criis.com/stanislaus/sfictitious.shtml.
Property, Taxation Records `Free` Access property assessment data free at www.co.stanislaus.ca.us/assessor/assessor-disclaimer2.shtm but no name searching. Fuller data for professional service companies is available by subscription.

Sutter County *Real Estate, Grantor/Grantee, Deed, Fictitious Name Records* www.suttercounty.org `Free`
Access the recorder database free at www.suttercounty.org/apps/recordsquery/clerk/. Records go back to 12/29/1994.
Property, Taxation Records `Free` Access assessment and property tax records free at www.suttercounty.org/doc/apps/recordsquery/recordsquery but no name searching.

Tehama County *Real Estate, Grantor/Grantee, Deed, Lien Records* www.co.tehama.ca.us `Free` Search recorder's official public records free at http://tehamapublic.countyrecords.com/
Property, Taxation Records `Free` Search property tax data on the county unsecured tax information lookup at www.co.tehama.ca.us/index.php?option=com_chronocontact&chronoformname=view_pay_taxes&Itemid=122.

Trinity County *Fictitious Business Name Records* www.trinitycounty.org/Departments/assessor-clerk-elect/clerkrecorder.htm `Free` Access to the Recorder's fictitious business names database is free at http://halfile.trinitycounty.org. For user name, enter "fbn"; leave password field empty.

Tulare County *Real Estate, Deed, Judgment, Lien, Vital Statistic, Fictitious Name Records* www.co.tulare.ca.us `Free & $$` Search the recorders database including births, marriages, deaths free at http://209.78.90.65/riimsweb/orinquiry.asp. A monthly subscription for full data and information services is $600.00.
Property, Taxation Records `Free` Search treasurer/tax collector property data free at www.co.tulare.ca.us/government/treasurertax/mytaxes/default.asp; no name searching.

Tuolumne County *Real Estate, Deed, Lien, Judgment Records* www.tuolumnecounty.ca.gov `Free` Access the recorder grantor/grantee index at https://www.records.co.tuolumne.ca.us/. Logon using 'web' for free access; turn off pop-up blocker.

Ventura County *Real Estate, Grantor/Grantee, Deed, Lien, Judgment, Fictitious Name Records*
http://recorder.countyofventura.org/venclrk.htm `Free` Access the county clerks database free at http://recorder.countyofventura.org/venclrk.htm.
Property, Taxation Records `Free` Search property tax data free at http://prop-tax.countyofventura.org/ but no name search.

Yolo County *Real Estate, Deed, Lien, Birth, Death, Fictitious Business Name, Marriage Records*
www.yolorecorder.org `Free` Access to recordings on the county clerk database are free at www.yolorecorder.org/recsearch and at www.criis.com/yolo/srecord_current.shtml. Marriage records are at www.criis.com/yolo/smarriage.shtml. County Fictitious Business Name at www.yolorecorder.org/recording/fictitious/lookup. Also look up fictitious names at www.criis.com/yolo/sfictitious.shtml.
Property, Taxation Records `Free` With an address, look up parcel numbers free at www.yolocounty.org/Index.aspx?page=344. Search for parcels free at www.yolocounty.org/index.aspx?page=587.

Yuba County *Real Estate, Deed, Judgment, Lien Records* www.co.yuba.ca.us/departments/clerk/ `Free` Access recorded document index free at www.co.yuba.ca.us/services/Land%20Records/. Online records go back to 1989.
Property, Taxation Records `Free` Access to property records is free at www.co.yuba.ca.us/services/Parcel%20Search/ but no name searching.

Other California Sites of Note:

Alameda County - Voter Registration Status www.acgov.org/rov/voter_reg_lookup.htm

Contra Costa County - Most Wanted www.cocosheriff.org/wanted/wanted.htm

El Dorado County - Judge's Tentative Rulings http://co.el-dorado.ca.us/superiorcourts/
For name searches, search text by division and by week.

Fresno County - Inmates www.fresnosheriff.org/InmateInfoCenter/Main.aspx

Kern County - Inmates www.kern.courts.ca.gov/case-menu-main.asp Click on "Inmate Search"

Kern County - Recent Sales http://kerndata.com Online parcel maps are also available to purchase.

Los Angeles County - Inmates http://app4.lasd.org/iic/ajis_search.cfm Sheriff Department site

Los Angeles County - Missing Persons www.lapdonline.org/get_involved/missing_persons/missing_persons_1.htm

Los Angeles County - Most Wanted www.lapdonline.org/get_involved/most_wanted/most_wanted_main.htm

Los Angeles County - Traffic Tickets www.lasuperiorcourt.org/traffic/index.asp?RT=CI Search by DL or ticket #

Marin County - Business Names http://marinfo.marin.org/Bizmo/index.cfm

Marin County - Sheriff Booking Log www.co.marin.ca.us/depts/SO/bklog/XMLProj/index.asp

Merced County - Missing Person, Most Wanted www.mercedsheriff.com

Monterey County - Most Wanted www.co.monterey.ca.us/sheriff/wanted.htm

Orange County - Sheriff Wanted Lists, Missing Persons, Blotter www.ocsd.org click on "Crime Bulletins."

Riverside County - Sheriff Most Wanted, Missing Person www.riversidesheriff.org/crime/

Sacramento County - City of West Sacramento - Business Licenses
www.cityofwestsacramento.org/cityhall/departments/finance/buslic/blfind.cfm

Sacramento County - DUI Most Wanted www.da.saccounty.net/DUIRecidivist/Wanted%20DUI%20Offenders.htm

Sacramento County - Restaurant Inspections www.emd.saccounty.net/eh/emdfoodprotect.htm

Sacramento County - Sex Offenders www.sacpd.org/sexoffender/

Sacramento County - Voter Registration www.pollingplacelookup.saccounty.net/LookupPollingPlace_SearchByDOB.aspx
DOB, address, and ZIP required to search.

Sacramento County - Wanted Suspects www.crimealert.org/wanted.cfm

San Benito County - Most Wanted www.sbcsheriff.org/wanted.html

San Bernardino County - Most Wanted www.sbcounty.gov/sheriff/PublicAffairs/Wanted_Persons/Wanted_Persons.asp

San Diego County - Sheriff (court) Restraining Orders www.sdsheriff.net/tro/tro.aspx

San Diego County - Sheriff (court) Warrants www.sdsheriff.net/waar/waar.aspx

San Francisco County - Sex Offenders www.sfgov.org/site/police_index.asp?id=24681

San Joaquin County - Court Calendars www.stocktoncourt.org/courts/caseinfo.htm

San Luis Obispo County - Most Wanted, Missing Person http://slosheriff.org/alerts.php

San Mateo County - Traffic Citations https://www.sanmateocourt.org/traffic/

Santa Barbara - Restaurant Inspection www.decadeonline.com/main.phtml?agency=SBC

Santa Barbara County - Most Wanted www.sbsheriff.org/mostwanted.html

Santa Clara County - City of San Jose - Sex Offenders www.sjpd.org/SexOffenders.cfm

Santa Cruz County - City of Santa Cruz - Business Licenses www.ci.santa-cruz.ca.us/bldb/index.html

Shasta County - Unofficial Births, Deaths, Marriages http://myclouds.tripod.com/shasta/shastaco.html
Not an official records site.

Sonoma County - Voter Registration www.co.sonoma.ca.us/RegVoter/RegVoterLookup.htm
DOB, address, and ZIP required to search.

Stanislaus County - Most Wanted, Missing Person www.stanislaussheriff.com/crimebulletin/

Tehama County - Inmates www.tehamaso.org/inmates/ICURRENT.HTM

Yolo County - Building Permits http://web-app2.yolocounty.org:80/WebPermit/PermitHistory/DateHistory.aspx

Yolo County - City of Davis - Business Licenses www.city.davis.ca.us/ed/business/

Yolo County - City of Davis - Police Log www.ci.davis.ca.us/police/log/ Goes back one week only.

Yolo County - Davis Cemetery District www2.dcn.org/orgs/cemetery

Colorado

Capital: Denver
           Denver County
Time Zone: MST
Population: 4,861,515
# of Counties: 64

Useful State Links

Website: www.colorado.gov
Governor: www.colorado.gov/governor
Attorney General: www.ago.state.co.us/index.cfm
State Archives: www.colorado.gov/dpa/doit/archives/
State Statutes and Codes: www.michie.com/colorado/lpext.dll?f=templates&fn=main-h.htm&cp=
Legislative Bill Search: www.leg.state.co.us/Clics/CLICS2008A/csl.nsf/MainBills?openFrameset
Unclaimed Funds: www.colorado.gov/treasury/gcp/

Primary State Agencies

Criminal Records `$$`

Bureau of Investigation, State Repository, Identification Unit, http://cbi.state.co.us There is an Internet access at https://www.cbirecordscheck.com/CBI_New/CBI_newIndex.asp. Requesters must use a credit card, an account does not need to be established. However, account holders may set up a batch system. The fee is $6.85 per record.

Sexual Offender Registry `Free`

Colorado Bureau of Investigation, SOR Unit, http://sor.state.co.us The website gives access to only certain high-risk registered sex offenders in the following categories: Sexually Violent Predator (SVP), Multiple Offenses, Failed to Register, and adult felony conviction.

Incarceration Records `Free`

Colorado Department of Corrections, Offender Records Customer Support, www.doc.state.co.us Search the Inmate Locater at https://exdoc.state.co.us/inmate_locator/offender_search_splash.php. This is not a historical search; only active offenders and parolees are listed. Also, one may email locator requests to pio@doc.state.co.us.

Corporation, LLC, LLLP, LLP, LP, Trademarks/Servicemarks, Fictitious/Assumed Name, Trade Name `Free`

Secretary of State, Business Division, www.sos.state.co.us The Sec. of State's Business Record Search page offers free searching of corporate names, trade names and associate information at www.sos.state.co.us/pubs/business/main.htm. Since 07/04, some e-filing documents are available. Click on Business Center. Also, search for charitable nonprofit members of CANPO - Colorado Association of Nonprofit Organizations - at www.coloradononprofits.org/member.cfm. Also, search securities dept. enforcement actions at www.dora.state.co.us/securities/enforcement.htm. *Other Options:* Various information is available as a one time order or via subscription. Transmittal can be through CDs, tapes or FTP.

Uniform Commercial Code, Federal Tax Liens `Free`

Secretary of State, UCC Division, www.sos.state.co.us There is free record searching of the index at this agency's website. Registration is required. See www.sos.state.co.us/pubs/business/search_records.htm. More extensive data is also available via subscription for ongoing business requesters. *Other Options:* Various information is available as a one time order or via subscription. Transmittal can be through CDs, tapes or FTP. The program may be delayed due to the redaction of SSNs.

Sales Tax Registrations `Free`

Revenue Department, Taxpayers Services Office, www.revenue.state.co.us/main/home.asp You can verify a sales tax license or exemption number at https://www.taxview.state.co.us/.

Driver Records $$

Division of Motor Vehicles, www.revenue.state.co.us/mv_dir/home.asp Colorado.gov, 600 17th Street, Ste. 2150 South, Denver, CO 80202 800-970-3468, www.colorado.gov. Colorado.gov is the entity designated by the state to provide online access to driving records to registered users. Both interactive and batch processing is offered. Requesters must be approved per state compliance requirements with DPPA. There is an annual $75.00 registration fee, records are $2.00 each. For more information call or visit the web page and click on "Registered Services Center." For questions about this service one may also call the MVD, contact Mary Tuttle at 303-205-5762. *Other Options:* A driver monitoring program offered by Colorado.gov is planned for the end of the third quarter in 2007.

Voter Registration Free

Department of State, Elections Department, www.elections.colorado.gov/DDefault.aspx Verify voter registration status at www.sos.state.co.us/Voter/voterHome.do;jsessionid=0000jamGh2eYmIJkKZog2OlQcip:11p1kuu1d. Search campaign finance information and registered lobbyists through links at the home page listed above. *Other Options:* The entire database is available on tape or CD-ROM. The cost is $500. No customization is available.

Vital Records Certificates Free & $$

Department of Public Health & Environment, Vital Records Section HSVR-A1, www.cdphe.state.co.us/certs/index.html Records can be ordered online from state designated vendors. Go to https://www.vitalchek.com/default.aspx. An index of older marriage records is found at www.cdphe.state.co.us/certs/genealogy.html. There is no fee.

Occupational Licensing Boards

Accident & Health Insurer................ http://cdilookup.asisvcs.com/CompanySearch.aspx
Acupuncturist .... https://www.doradls.state.co.us/alison.php
Addiction Counselor.......................... https://www.doradls.state.co.us/alison.php
Architect.. https://www.doradls.state.co.us/alison.php
Asbestos Abatement Contr'r .... www.cdphe.state.co.us/ap/asbestos/AsGenAbatCont.pdf
Asbestos Disposal Sites..................... www.cdphe.state.co.us/ap/asbestos/ASBESTOSDISPOSAL.pdf
Attorney.. www.coloradosupremecourt.com/Search/AttSearch.asp
Audiologist .... https://www.doradls.state.co.us/alison.php
Bail Bond Agent................................ http://cdilookup.asisvcs.com/IndividualSearch.aspx
Barber.. https://www.doradls.state.co.us/lic_database_req.php
Bus, Charter/Scenic/Children's .... www.dora.state.co.us/pls/real/puc_permit.search_form
Casualty Company............................. http://cdilookup.asisvcs.com/CompanySearch.aspx
CDL Third-party Testers .... www.revenue.state.co.us/mv_dir/wrap.asp?incl=drivingschoolslist
Charitable Organization..................... www.sos.state.co.us/ccsa/CcsaInquiryMain.do
Chiropractor...................................... https://www.doradls.state.co.us/alison.php
Collection Agency .... www.ago.state.co.us/CADC/CADCmain.cfm
Commercial Driving School.............. www.revenue.state.co.us/mv_dir/wrap.asp?incl=drivingschoolslist
Common Carrier/Contract Carrier ..... www.dora.state.co.us/pls/real/puc_permit.search_form
Contractor Registration...................... https://www.doradls.state.co.us/alison.php
Cosmetologist.................................... https://www.doradls.state.co.us/lic_database_req.php
Counselor, Professional..................... https://www.doradls.state.co.us/alison.php
Court Reporter................................... www.courts.state.co.us/district/19th/19reporters.htm
Credit Union .... www.dora.state.co.us/financial-services/homeregu.html
Dental Hygienist................................ https://www.doradls.state.co.us/lic_database_req.php
Dentist .... https://www.doradls.state.co.us/lic_database_req.php
Drug Company Mfg/Dist/Whlse........ https://www.doradls.state.co.us/alison.php
Electrical Contractor.......................... https://www.doradls.state.co.us/alison.php
Electrician Journeyman/Master .... https://www.doradls.state.co.us/alison.php
Engineer/Engineer Intern................... https://www.doradls.state.co.us/alison.php
Fundraising Consultant...................... www.sos.state.co.us/ccsa/PfcInquiryCriteria.do
HazMat Carrier.................................. www.dora.state.co.us/pls/real/puc_permit.search_form
Hearing Aid Dealer............................ https://www.doradls.state.co.us/alison.php
Household Goods/Property Carrier ... www.dora.state.co.us/pls/real/puc_permit.search_form
Insurance Agency/Agent .... http://cdilookup.asisvcs.com/IndividualSearch.aspx
Insurance Company .... http://cdilookup.asisvcs.com/CompanySearch.aspx
Land Surveyor/Land Surveyor Intern https://www.doradls.state.co.us/alison.php

Lead Abatement Worker/Supervisor . www.cdphe.state.co.us/ap/asbestos/AsGenAbatCont.pdf
Life Care Institution .... www.dora.state.co.us/financial-services/homeregu.html#life
Life Insurance Company .... http://cdilookup.asisvcs.com/CompanySearch.aspx
Limousine .... www.dora.state.co.us/pls/real/puc_permit.search_form
Lobbyist.. www.elections.colorado.gov/WWW/default/Lobbyists/prof_lobrpt.pdf
Lobbyist Volunteer www.elections.colorado.gov/WWW/default/Lobbyists/vol%20lobby%202005.pdf
Manicurist.. https://www.doradls.state.co.us/lic_database_req.php
Manufactured Housing-Related .... http://dola.colorado.gov/cdh/codes/index.htm
Marriage & Family Therapist .... https://www.doradls.state.co.us/alison.php
Medical Doctor................................. https://www.doradls.state.co.us/alison.php
Mental Health Psychotherap't, Unlic . https://www.doradls.state.co.us/alison.php
Midwife .... https://www.doradls.state.co.us/lic_database_req.php
Milk Shippers .... www.cdphe.state.co.us/cp/dairy/Othe_rlinks.html
Nurse .... https://www.doradls.state.co.us/alison.php
Nursery .... www.ag.state.co.us/dpi/nursery/nursery.html
Nurses' Aide .... https://www.doradls.state.co.us/alison.php
Nursing Home Administrator .... https://www.doradls.state.co.us/alison.php
Off-Road Charter............................. www.dora.state.co.us/pls/real/puc_permit.search_form
Optometrist...................................... https://www.doradls.state.co.us/alison.php
Outfitter .... https://www.doradls.state.co.us/alison.php
Pesticide Applicator......................... www.ag.state.co.us/dpi/pesticideapplicator/home.html
Pharmacist/Pharmacist Intern .... https://www.doradls.state.co.us/alison.php
Pharmacy... https://www.doradls.state.co.us/alison.php
Physical Therapist .... https://www.doradls.state.co.us/alison.php
Physician Assistant .... https://www.doradls.state.co.us/alison.php
Plumber Journeyman/Master/Resid'l . https://www.doradls.state.co.us/alison.php
Podiatrist... https://www.doradls.state.co.us/alison.php
Psychiatric Technician...................... https://www.doradls.state.co.us/alison.php
Psychologist..................................... https://www.doradls.state.co.us/alison.php
Public Accountant-CPA .... https://www.doradls.state.co.us/alison.php
Public Adjuster .... http://cdilookup.asisvcs.com/IndividualSearch.aspx
Real Estate Agent/Broker/Sales......... http://eservices.psiexams.com/crec/search.jsp
Real Estate Appraiser .... http://eservices.psiexams.com/crec/search.jsp
Reinsurance Intermediary Manager... http://cdilookup.asisvcs.com/IndividualSearch.aspx
Respiratory Therapist .... https://www.doradls.state.co.us/lic_database_req.php
River Outfitter .... https://www.doradls.state.co.us/alison.php
Savings & Loan Association .... www.dora.state.co.us/financial-services/homeregu.html
School Administrator/Principal .... https://forms.cde.state.co.us/pes/FirstLastSearch.jsp
School Special Service Associate ...... https://forms.cde.state.co.us/pes/FirstLastSearch.jsp
Securities Broker/Dealer................... www.finra.org/InvestorInformation/InvestorProtection/p005882
Ski Lift... https://www.doradls.state.co.us/lic_database_req.php
Social Work .... https://www.doradls.state.co.us/alison.php
Solicitor, Paid .... www.sos.state.co.us/
Stock Broker.................................... www.finra.org/InvestorInformation/InvestorProtection/p005882
Substitute Teacher .... https://forms.cde.state.co.us/pes/FirstLastSearch.jsp
Surplus Lines Seller......................... http://cdilookup.asisvcs.com/IndividualSearch.aspx
Teacher.. https://forms.cde.state.co.us/pes/FirstLastSearch.jsp
Towing Carrier .... www.dora.state.co.us/pls/real/puc_permit.search_form
Tramway.. https://www.doradls.state.co.us/lic_database_req.php
Travel Ticker Seller .... http://cdilookup.asisvcs.com/IndividualSearch.aspx
Veterinarian..................................... https://www.doradls.state.co.us/alison.php.
Vocational Education Teacher.......... https://forms.cde.state.co.us/pes/FirstLastSearch.jsp
Wireman, Residential .... https://www.doradls.state.co.us/alison.php

State and Local Courts

State Court Structure: The District and County Courts have overlapping jurisdiction over civil cases involving less than $15,000. Fortunately, District and County Courts are combined in most counties. Combined courts usually search both civil or criminal indexes for a single fee, except as indicated in the profiles. Co-located with seven district courts are divisions known as Water Courts. The Water Courts are located in Weld, Pueblo, Alamosa, Montrose, Garfield, Routt, and La Platta counties.

The Denver Court System differs from those in the rest of the state, in part because Denver is both a city and a county. The Denver County Court functions as a municipal and a county court, paid for entirely by Denver taxes, rather than by state taxes. The Denver County Court is not part of the state court system; the District Court is.

On November 15, 2001, Broomfield City & County came into existence, derived from parts of counties of Adams, Boulder, Jefferson, and Weld. A District and County Court (in 17th Judicial District) was established.

Colorado municipal courts only have jurisdiction over traffic, parking, and ordinance violations. Denver is the only county where the Probate Court and Juvenile Court is separate from the District Court.

Statewide Court Online Access: LexisNexis CourtLink was appointed to act as agent for the Colorado Judicial Department to act as the conduit for the ICON (Integrated Colorado Online Network) and provide access to vendors and to the general public. The vendors permit users to look at a name index - the Register of Actions - to court filings and appearance dates. **There is a fee.** The name search includes viewing all of the Registers of Actions related to that name. Images or copies of documents are not available from any of the commercial sites and may only be obtained by contacting the individual court where the documents were filed.

Opinions from the Court of Appeals are available from the website atwww.courts.state.co.us/.

❖ **Statewide Access Offered All Trial Courts — Read Above**

Below are Additional Sites ❖

Denver County

2nd District Court   www.courts.state.co.us/district/02nd/02dist.htm   `Free & $$`
Civil: Online access to civil records is at www.denvergov.org/apps/court/courtselect.asp and also https://litigator.lexisnexis.com/Courtlink/Login.aspx or www.courts.state.co.us/panda/publicaccess/ctrecords.htm. *Criminal:* Criminal case index at www.denvergov.org/apps/newcourt/court_select.asp. A subscription account is at www.courts.state.co.us/panda/publicaccess/ctrecords.htm.

County Court - Civil Division   www.courts.state.co.us/district/counties.htm   `Free & $$`
Civil: Online searching of Denver County Civil Division court cases is at www.denvergov.org/court/courtselect.asp. Search by name, business name, or case number.

County Court - Criminal Division   www.courts.state.co.us/district/02nd/02dist.htm   `Free & $$`
 Criminal: Criminal case index at www.denvergov.org/court/courtselect.asp. Criminal case index also at https://litigator.lexisnexis.com/Courtlink/Login.aspx or www.courts.state.co.us/panda/publicaccess/ctrecords.htm.

Probate Court www.denverprobatecourt.org   `Free`   Online access to selected opinions is available free at www.denverprobatecourt.org/selectedopinions.htm.

Recorders, Assessors, and Other Sites of Note

Recording Office Organization: 63 counties, 63 recording offices. The recording officer is the County Clerk and Recorder. November 15, 2001, Broomfield City and County came into existence, derived from portions of Adams, Boulder, Jefferson and Weld counties. To determine if an address is in Broomfield County, you may parcel search by address at the Broomfield County Assessor search site at www.co.broomfield.co.us/centralrecords/assessor.shtml or www.broomfield.org/maps/IMS.shtml.

Online Access Note: At least 17 Colorado counties offer free access to property assessor basic tax roll records and sometimes sales via www.qpublic.net/. For more data, there is a 3-level subscription service purchase plan.

At the state level, the Secretary of State offers web access to UCCs, and the Department of Revenue offers trade name searches. See the State Agencies section for details. Also, the state archives provides limited "inheritance tax" records for 14 Colorado counties at www.colorado.gov/dpa/doit/archives/inh_tax/index.html. Generally, these records extend forward only to the 1940s.

Adams County   *Real Estate, Deed, Lien, Marriage, Death, Judgment, Mortgage, UCC Records*
www.co.adams.co.us   **Free**   Search recorded documents free at www.co.adams.co.us/oncoreweb/.
Property, Taxation Records **Free**   Records from the Adams County Assessor database are free at http://co.adams.co.us/gis/quicksearch/.

Alamosa County   *Real Estate, Grantor/Grantee, Deed, Lien, Judgment, Marriage Records*
www.alamosacounty.org   **$$**   Access to recording data back to 1985 is by subscription to Image Silo; fee is $200.00 per month; for info and sign up, contact the Recording office.
Property, Taxation Records **Free**   Access property data free at www.qpublic.net/co/alamosa/search.html. Subscription required for full data. Also, search via www.alamosacounty.org/depts/Assessor/records.html

Arapahoe County   *Real Estate, Deed, Judgment, Lien Records*   www.co.arapahoe.co.us/Departments/CR/index.asp
Free   Access to the recorders database is free at www.co.arapahoe.co.us/Apps/LegalDocuments/default.aspx.
Property, Taxation Records **Free**   Centrally assessed tax data is available free at www.co.arapahoe.co.us/Apps/Tax/Default.aspx but no name searching. Search business personal property free at www.co.arapahoe.co.us/apps/PersProp/PersPropForm.asp. Search other tax/parcel data by category free at www.co.arapahoe.co.us/ and click on Online Tools. Search county foreclosures free at www.co.arapahoe.co.us/Apps/ForeClosure/index.aspx.

Archuleta County   *Real Estate, Deed, Lien Records*   http://archuletacounty.org   **$$**   Access to record data is by internet subscription, fee is $250 monthly. Call Recording office for further info and sign-up.
Property, Taxation Records **Free**   Search assessment property records at www.qpublic.net/co/archuleta/index.html for a fee for full data; a basic search is free. Also search index data free at http://64.234.218.210/cgi-bin/colorado_links.cgi?county=archuleta.

Baca County   *Real Estate, Deed, Lien, Vital Statistic, UCC, Judgment Records*   www.bacacounty.net   **Free**
Search recorded documents at www.thecountyrecorder.com/(vv5dpfytud3jdv55a5o3et45)/default.aspx. Online records go back to 1997. No name searching.

Bent County   *Real Estate, Deed, Lien, Judgment, Vital Statistic Records*   **$$**   Access to recorded data is available by subscription. Fee is $200 per month. To print documents, an add'l fee of $.25 per page applies. To sign-up, contact Patti Nickell; a sign up form will be faxed to you.tn046
Property, Taxation Records **Free**   Access assessor preoperty records free at www.qpublic.net/co/lasanimas/search.html. Search by parcel number, location, or owner name.

Boulder County   *Real Estate, Grantor/Grantee, Deed, Judgment, Lien, Voter Registration Records*
www.co.boulder.co.us/clerk   **Free & $$**   Recorder data is on the iCris system at http://icris.co.boulder.co.us/splash.jsp. To search free, login as public, password public. Also, search voter registration at www.co.boulder.co.us/clerk/elections/promptforname.html. Name and DOB required.
Property, Taxation Records **Free**   Search the assessor's property database for free at www.bouldercounty.org/assessor/disclaimer.htm. No name searching. Also, search property tax records at www.bouldercounty.org/treas/disclaim.htm. No name searching. Also, the county treasurer offers data electronically and on microfiche. Alpha index by owner name is $25.00 per set.

Broomfield County   *Voter Registration Records*   www.broomfield.org/centralrecords/clerk_and_recorder.shtml
Free   Verify voter registration records at www.broomfield.org/elections/voter_inquiry/. House number and registrant name both required.
Property, Taxation Records **Free**   Access to the property database portal is free at www.ci.broomfield.co.us/maps/IMS.shtml. Search by address or parcel ID only. Also, search property and tax assessment data free at https://info.ci.broomfield.co.us/Tax/Default.asp but no name searching. Also, you may download the GIS/Assessor 'Broomfield Parcels' database free at www.broomfield.org/maps/Data.shtml. Also, search tax sales list free at www.ci.broomfield.co.us/centralrecords/TaxSale.shtml.

Chaffee County   *Property, Taxation Records*   **Free**   Search assessor database free at http://annex.chaffeecounty.org/assessorsearch/searchhome.aspx.

Cheyenne County   *Real Estate, Grantor/Grantee, Deed, Lien, Mortgage, Judgment, Marriage Records*
www.co.cheyenne.co.us/countydepartments/clerkandrecorder.htm   **Free**   Access recorded documents online free at www.thecountyrecorder.com and choose Cheyenne, CO from the drop-down list.
Property, Taxation Records **Free**   Search the county property sales lists free at www.co.cheyenne.co.us/countydepartments/assessor.htm. Lookups at bottom of webpage.

Clear Creek County *Property, Taxation Records* `Free` Limited assessor information free at www.co.clear-creek.co.us/Depts/assess.htm.

Conejos County *Real Estate, Grantor/Grantee, Deed, Lien, Judgment, UCC Records* `$$` Access to recorder office index back to 1978 is by subscription, $100 per month. Call recorder for signup and info.
Property, Taxation Records `Free` Access data from the final tax roll free at http://qpublic.net/co/conejos/. There are also 3 levels of subscription service based on your needs.

Costilla County *Property, Taxation Records* `Free` Access assessor property data free at http://64.234.218.210/cgi-bin/colorado_links.cgi?county=costilla. Also, access data from the final tax roll free at http://qpublic.net/co/costilla/. There are also 3 levels of subscription service based on your need.

Crowley County *Property, Taxation Records* `Free` Access data from the final tax roll free at http://qpublic.net/co/crowley/. There are also 3 levels of subscription service based on your needs. Also, access property assessment data by subscription at http://64.234.218.210/cgi-bin/colorado.pl.

Custer County *Property, Taxation Records* `Free` Access assessor final tax roll data free at www.qpublic.net/co/custer/search.html. Full property data is available by subscription as well.

Delta County *Real Estate, Deed, Lien, Judgment, Death, Marriage, DOT Release Records* www.deltacounty.com `Free` Access recorder records free at http://clerk.deltacounty.com/Search.aspx.
Property, Taxation Records `Free` Access Assessor data on the GIS site for free at http://itax.deltacounty.com/assessor/web/
.

Denver County *Property, Taxation Records* `Free` Records on the Denver City and Denver County Assessor database are free at www.denvergov.org/realproperty.asp. With address, search business personal property at www.denvergov.org/apps/perspropertyapplication/persproperty.asp. Also, search real estate property tax data for free at www.denvergov.org/treasurypt/PropertyTax.asp. Address or parcel number required to search. Search foreclosures at www.denvergov.org/TabId/37910/TopicId/1313/default.aspx.

Dolores County *Property, Taxation Records* `Free & $$` Assessor information and free search at www.qpublic.net/co/dolores/index.html. Subscription and log-on required for legal information, go to http://64.234.218.210/cgi-bin/colorado.pl for new subscriber sign-up.

Douglas County *Real Estate, Grantor/Grantee, Deed, Judgment, Lien, Mortgage, UCC, Vital Statistic Records* www.douglas.co.us `Free` Access to recorders data is free at http://apps.douglas.co.us/apps/pubdocaccess/simpleSearch.do.
Property, Taxation Records `Free` Records on the county assessor database are free at www.douglas.co.us/assessor/. You may also download related list data from the site. Locate parcels free at http://publicstaging.douglas.co.us/website/default.htm.

Eagle County *Real Estate, Grantor/Grantee, Deed, Judgment, Lien, Vital Statistic, Will, UCC Records* www.eaglecounty.us `Free & $$` Search clerk and recorder data free at www.eaglecounty.us/cloe/search.cfm. Search index free, fee for images.
Property, Taxation Records `Free` Access the County Assessor and treasurer databases free at www.eaglecounty.us/patie/index_content.cfm. Search comps sales at www.eaglecounty.us/Assessor/saleslist.cfm.

Elbert County *Property, Taxation Records* `Free` Search Assessor data free at http://elbertco.tyler-esubmittal.com/assessor/web/ but no name searching; free registration required. Parcel and GIS-Map search free at http://projects.thetsrgroup.com/elbert/members/index.asp but no name searching.

El Paso County *Real Estate, Grantor-Grantee, Deed, Lien Judgment Records* http://car.elpasoco.com `Free` Search the grantor/grantee index at http://car2.elpasoco.com/rcdquery.asp. Search marriages back to 5/1/1991 on a separate lookup page. Also, search marriages 1/1985 to 5/1991 free on the OPR - Official Public Records - search page.
Property, Taxation Records `Free` Records on the county Assessor database are free at http://land.elpasoco.com.

Fremont County *Real Estate, Deed, Lien, Will, Mortgage, Death, Divorce, Marriage Records* www.fremontco.com/clerkandrecorder/index.shtml `Free` Search recorded documents free at www.fremontco.com/clerkandrecorder/aptitude/oncoreweb/Search.aspx.
Property, Taxation Records `Free` Access the assessors property and sales database free at http://qpublic.net/fremont/. There are also 3 levels of subscription service based on your needs.

Garfield County *Real Estate, Deed, Lien, Judgment, Mortgage, Divorce Records* www.garfield-county.com `Free` Access recording data free at www.garcoact.com/clerk/search.asp?.
Property, Taxation Records `Free` Search the assessor and treasurerproperty and tax data free at www.garcoact.com/assessor/search.asp. Also, you may search assessor sales data by subscription at www.garcoact.com/assessor/Login.asp. Fee is $300 per year or $35 per month. Also, access PDF parcel maps and property information free at www.garfield-county.com/Index.aspx?page=990.

Gilpin County *Marriage Records* www.co.gilpin.co.us `Free` Access to county marriage records from 1864 to 1944 is free at www.colorado.gov/dpa/doit/archives/marriage/gilpin_index.htm.
Property, Taxation Records `Free` Assessor data and research of property information at www.tylerworksasp.com/itax/taxSearch.jsp.

Grand County *Real Estate, Grantor/Grantee, Deed, Lien, Birth, Death, Marriage Records*
http://co.grand.co.us/Clerk/clerkand.htm `Free` Access to Clerk-Recorder index is free at http://co.grand.co.us/aptitude/oncoreweb/
Property, Taxation Records `Free` Access assessor data free at www2.co.grand.co.us/assessor_lookup/. Access the assessor database free at http://co.grand.co.us/Assessor/Download_Page.html.

Jefferson County *Real Estate, Grantor/Grantee, Deed, Judgment Records* https://cr-web.co.jefferson.co.us/
`Free` Search recorder's Grantor/Grantee index free at https://cr-web.co.jefferson.co.us. Index goes back to 1963; images to 1994.
Property, Taxation Records `Free` Records on the county Assessor database are free at www.co.jefferson.co.us/ats/splash.do. No name searching.

Kiowa County *Real Estate, Deed, Lien, Judgment, Marriage Records* `Free` Access to recording index is free from a 3rd party company at www.thecountyrecorder.com. Select Kiowa from the county list. Index goes back only to 2006.

Kit Carson County *Property, Taxation Records* `Free` Access data from the final tax roll free at http://qpublic.net/co/kitcarson/. There are also 3 levels of subscription service based on your needs.

Lake County *Property, Taxation Records* `Free` Access county assessor property data free at http://64.234.218.210/cgi-bin/colorado_links.cgi?county=lake or at http://qpublic.net/co/lake/index.html. Also, registration and password is required to search at www.coassessors.com; fee is $275.00 per year.

La Plata County *Property, Taxation Records* `Free & $$` Property information is available at http://itax.co.laplata.co.us/itax/taxSplash.jsp. Also Also, records on the county Real Estate Parcel Search Page are free at www.laplatainfo.com/search2.html. This is basic property data but for sales and tax data, there is a subscription service for $20.00 per month, credit cards accepted.

Larimer County *Real Estate, Deed, UCC, Lien, Judgment, Voter Registration Records* www.larimer.org `Free`
Search the county Public Record Databases for free at www.larimer.org/databases/index.htm. Search registered voter list free at www.co.larimer.co.us/depts/clerkr/elections/voter_inquiry.cfm.
Property, Taxation Records `Free` Search assessor and property data free at www.larimer.org/assessor/propertyExplorer/propertyexplorer.html. Download free FlashPlayer8. Also, search assessor and property data free at www.co.larimer.co.us/assessor/query/search.cfm. Search treasurer data free at www.larimer.org/treasurer/query/search.cfm but no name searching.

Las Animas County *Property, Taxation Records* `Free` Access data from the final tax roll free at http://qpublic.net/co/lasanimas/. There are also 3 levels of subscription service based on your needs.

Lincoln County *Property, Taxation Records* `Free & $$` Access data from the final tax roll free at http://qpublic.net/co/lincoln/. There are also 3 levels of subscription service based on your needs.

Logan County *Real Estate, Deed, Mortgage, Lien, Judgment, Birth, Death, Marriage, Will, UCC Records*
www.loganco.gov/ `Free & $$` Enter the recorder's database site free at https://64.187.69.141/recorder/web/ and click on Public Login button to search index, otherwise registration/username/password required to view and print images; subs are $300 per month.
Property, Taxation Records `Free` Access to assessor property data is free at http://logancountyco.gov/assessor/PropertySearch.aspx.

Mesa County *Real Estate, Grantor/Grantee, Deed, Judgment, Mortgage, Lien, UCC, Will, Parcel, GIS-mapping Records* www.mesacounty.us `Free` Search the recorder's Grantor/Grantee inde free at http://apps.mesacounty.us/oncore/Search.aspx. GIS-mapping and property data at http://gis.mesacounty.us/interactive.aspx.
Property, Taxation Records `Free` Records on the county Assessor database and sales are free at http://assessor.mesacounty.us/parsearch.aspx. Click on Assessor lookup and search by address or parcel number.

Mineral County *Property, Taxation Records* `Free` Access data from the final tax roll free at http://qpublic.net/co/mineral/. There are also 3 levels of subscription service based on your needs.

Moffat County *Property, Taxation Records* `Free` Access to assessor property data free at http://co.moffat.co.us/assessor/default.htm but may not be available at this time. Also, search the treasurer's tax database free at http://65.77.74.205/MoffatCounty/SearchSelect.aspx.

Montezuma County *Real Estate, Deed, Lien, Judgment, UCC, Marriage, Death, Divorce Records*
www.co.montezuma.co.us `Free` Access recorded records data back to 6/3/1996 free at http://eagleweb.co.montezuma.co.us/recorder/web/.

Property, Taxation Records `Free` Access county property tax data and property sales free at http://eagleweb.co.montezuma.co.us/assessor/web/ .

Montrose County *Property, Taxation Records* `Free` Access to Property Information Search System is free at www.co.montrose.co.us/assessor/index.cfm .

Morgan County *Real Estate, Grantor/Grantee, Deed, Lien, Judgment, Marriage Records*
www.co.morgan.co.us/index.html `Free & $$` Access the recorder's online index free or by subscription for images for $300 per year at www.co.morgan.co.us:8080/recorder/web/splash.jsp.
Property, Taxation Records `Free` Search the assessor database free at www.co.morgan.co.us/itax/TaxLogin.jsp. Username and password are both "Public".

Otero County *Real Estate, Deed, Lien Records* `$$` Access to recorded data is by subscription only. Fee is $200 per month but you may signup for a free 15-day trial. Contact the Clerk/Recorder office for more info and sign-up.
Property, Taxation Records `Free` Access property data free at www.oterocountyassessor.net.

Ouray County *Real Estate, Deed, Lien, Judgment, UCC, Marriage, Death Records* www.ouraycountyco.gov
`Free` Access the record data free at http://ouraycountyco.gov/recording/oncoreweb/Search.aspx.
Property, Taxation Records `Free` Access recorder data free at http://ouraycountyco.gov:8080/assessor/web/. With registration, you may also create and print reports for properties free of charge.

Park County *Divorce Records* www.parkco.org `Free` County divorce records from 1957 to 1974 are free at www.colorado.gov/dpa/doit/archives/divorce/1park.htm.
Property, Taxation Records `Free` Records on the county Assessor database are free at www.parkco.org/Search2.asp? including tax data, owner, address, building characteristics, legal and deed information.

Pitkin County *Real Estate, Grantor/Grantee, Deed, Lien, UCC, Mortgage, Judgment, Divorce, Probate Records*
www.aspenpitkin.com `Free` Search recorded documents free at www.pitkinclerk.org/oncoreweb/. Also, probate records from 1881 to 1953 are at www.colorado.gov/dpa/doit/archives/probate/pitkin_probate.htm. Divorce records 1931 to 1964 are at www.colorado.gov/dpa/doit/archives/divorce/1pitkin.htm.
Property, Taxation Records `Free` Records on the county Assessor database are free at www.pitkinassessor.org/Assessor/.

Pueblo County *Real Estate, Grantor/Grantee, Deed, Mortgage, Lien, Marriage, UCC, Judgment, Registered*
Voter Records www.co.pueblo.co.us/clerk/ `Free` Access clerk & recorder index of recorded docs at http://erecording.co.pueblo.co.us/recorder/web/ but no images. Also, access to voter registration data is free at www.co.pueblo.co.us/elections/votersrch.php.
Property, Taxation Records `Free` Access county assessor data free at http://assessor.co.pueblo.co.us.

Rio Blanco County *Property, Taxation Records* `Free` Access assessor property data free at www.co.rio-blanco.co.us/assessor/.

Rio Grande County *Property, Taxation Records* `Free` Access to the property assessor's data is free at www.qpublic.net/riogrande/. A property sale search is also available. For full data, there is 3 subscription levels.

Routt County *Real Estate, Deed, Judgment, Property Sale Records* www.co.routt.co.us `Free`
Search records free on the County Clerk & Recorder Reception Search database at www.co.routt.co.us/clerk.html.
Property, Taxation Records `Free` Records on the county Assessor/Treasurer Property Search database are free at www.co.routt.co.us/assessor.html. Also, a gis-mapping site has property data for free at http://maps.co.routt.co.us/website/parcels/index.asp. Search by name.

Saguache County *Real Estate, Deed, Lien, Death, Marriage Records* www.saguachecounty.net `Free`
Access Recorder database free at www.thecountyrecorder.com/(2taror55j1fchl45xgn5agjt)/Introduction.aspx. Index goes back to 1994; images back to 1994.
Property, Taxation Records `Free & $$` Search Assessor tax roll database free at www.qpublic.net/co/saguache/. Also 3 levels of subscription service based on your needs.

San Juan County *Real Estate, Deed, Lien, Judgment, Marriage Records* www.sanjuancountycolorado.us/ `Free`
Access to recording index is free from a 3rd party company at www.thecountyrecorder.com. Select San Juan from county list. Index goes back to 1997.
Property, Taxation Records `Free` Access data from the final tax roll free at www.qpublic.net/co/sanjuan/. There are also 3 levels of subscription service based on your needs.

San Miguel County *Real Estate, Deed, Lien, Mortgage, Judgment, Marriage Records* www.sanmiguelcounty.org
`Free` Access to recording index is free from a 3rd party company at www.thecountyrecorder.com. Choose San Miguel County from the county list. Index goes back to 1998.

Sedgwick County *Real Estate, Grantor/Grantee, Deed, Mortgage, Lien, Judgment, Marriage Records*
http://sedgwickcountygov.net/ Free & $$ Access recorder data free by logging in as a Public User at
http://204.9.250.63/sedgwick/web/.
Property, Taxation Records Free Access data from the final tax roll free at http://qpublic.net/co/sedgwick/. There are also 3
levels of subscription service based on your needs.

Summit County *Property, Taxation Records* Access to the GIS-mapping site property data is free at
www.co.summit.co.us/disclaimlive.htm.

Teller County *Real Estate, Grantor/Grantee, Deed Records* www.co.teller.co.us Free & $$
Access the county clerk real estate database free at http://data.co.teller.co.us/AsrData/wc.dll?Doc~GrantSearch. Records go back to
1978; fee for documents $.25 per page.
Property, Taxation Records Free Search the assessor database free at
http://data.co.teller.co.us/AsrData/wc.dll?AsrDataProc~OwnerNameSearch.

Washington County *Property, Taxation Records* Free Access data from the final tax roll free at
http://qpublic.net/co/washington/. There are also 3 levels of subscription service based on your needs.

Weld County *Property, Taxation Records* Free Access assessor data, property sales, ownership listings, transfers,
property cards free at www.co.weld.co.us/departments/assessor.html Search property data on the map server database free at
http://maps2.merrick.com/website/Weld/. Search treasurer's property database free at
www.co.weld.co.us/departments/treasurer/tax/index1.cfm.

Yuma County *Property, Taxation Records* Free Access data from the final tax roll free at
http://qpublic.net/co/yuma/. There are also 3 levels of subscription service based on your needs.

Other Colorado Sites of Note:

Arapahoe County - Permits www.co.arapahoe.co.us/Apps/CountyInfoOnWeb/default.aspx
Arapahoe County - Sex Offender www.co.arapahoe.co.us/Apps/SexOffender/Default.aspx
Boulder County - Most Wanted www.co.boulder.co.us/Sheriff/most_wanted/wanted.htm
Boulder County - Voter Registration www.co.boulder.co.us/clerk/elections/promptforname.html Click on "Check your Voter
Registration." Name and DOB is required to search.
Broomfield County - Voter Registration www.broomfield.org/elections/voter_inquiry/ Name and house number required.
Costilla County - Registered Contractors www.costilla-county.com/registeredcontractorlist.html
Denver County - Contracts www.denvergov.org/contracts/contrak.asp
Denver County - Prostitution Solicitation Request www.denvergov.org/johnstv/
Douglas County - Building Permits, Contractors https://apps.douglas.co.us/apps/building/contractorSearch.do
Eagle County - Most Wanted www.eaglecounty.us/sheriff/mostWanted.cfm
El Paso County - Area Contractors www.pprbd.org/contrnames.html
El Paso County - Sheriff Inmates http://shr2.elpasoco.com/inmates/inmates.aspx
Elbert County - Wills 1887-1966 www.colorado.gov/dpa/doit/archives/wills/1elbert.html
Larimer County - Most Wanted www.co.larimer.co.us/Sheriff/MostWanted/Wanted0.htm
Moffat County - Sex Offender www.moffatcountysheriff.com/sexoffenders.htm
Pitkin County - Inmates www.aspenpitkin.com/depts/28/inmates.cfm
San Miguel County - Inmates www.sanmiguelsheriff.com/index.cfm?fuseaction=standard&categoryId=5&subcategoryId=4
Weld County - Most Wanted, Sex Offender www.weldsheriff.com/

Connecticut

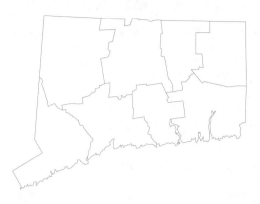

Capital: Hartford
             Hartford County
Time Zone: EST
Population: 3,502,309
# of Counties: 8

Useful State Links

Website: www.ct.gov
Governor: www.ct.gov/governorrell/site/default.asp
Attorney General: www.ct.gov/ag/site/default.asp
State Archives: www.cslib.org/archives/
State Statutes and Codes: www.cga.ct.gov/asp/menu/Statutes.asp
Legislative Bill Search: www.cga.ct.gov/asp/menu/Search.asp
Bill Tracking: www.cga.ct.gov/aspx/cgapublicbilltrack/cgapublicbilltrack.aspx
Unclaimed Funds: www.ctbiglist.com/

Primary State Agencies

Sexual Offender Registry `Free`

Department of Public Safety, Sex Offender Registry Unit,   www.ct.gov/dps/cwp/view.asp?a=2157&Q=294474&dpsNav=| The website has two searches: those convicted of a CT law, and those offenders who violated a law in a different state but are living or working in CT. Search by name or town, ZIP Code, or entire list. *Other Options:* Record data can be purchased in bulk.

Incarceration Records `Free`

Connecticut Department of Corrections, Public Information Office,   www.ct.gov/doc/site/default.asp   Current inmates may be searched at www.ctinmateinfo.state.ct.us/searchop.asp.

Corporation, LP, LLC, LLP, Statutory Trust, Trademarks/Servicemarks `Free`

Secretary of State, Commercial Recording Division,   www.sots.ct.gov/sots/site/default.asp   Click on the CONCORD option at the website for free access to corporation and UCC records. The system is open from 7AM to 11PM. You can search by business name, business ID or by filing number. The website also offers online filing. Go to www.concord-sots.ct.gov/CONCORD/index.jsp. Search securities division enforcement actions at www.ct.gov/dob/cwp/view.asp?a=2246&q=401762.

Uniform Commercial Code, Federal & State Tax Liens `Free`

UCC Division, Secretary of State,   www.concord-sots.ct.gov/CONCORD/index.jsp   An index search is offered at www.concord-sots.ct.gov/CONCORD/index.jsp. *Other Options:* Bulk lists and CDs are available for purchase, call 860-509-6165.

Driver Records `Free & $$`

Department of Motor Vehicles, Copy Records Unit,   www.ct.gov/dmv/site/default.asp   Electronic access is provided to approved businesses that enter into written contract. The contract requires a $37,500 prepayment deposit for the first 2,500 records. Fee is $15.00 per record. The address is part of the record. For more information, call 203-805-6093. Also, search disposed conviction and bond forfeitures at www.jud2.ct.gov/crdockets/SearchByDefDisp.aspx by Geographical Area court. Links include pending case lookup pages and docket/calendar lookup pages. *Other Options:* Batch requests are available for approved users, call 203-805-6093.

Occupational Licensing Boards

Accounting Firm...............................www.sboalicense.ct.gov/cpalookup/Default.aspx
Acupuncturist ....www.dph.state.ct.us/scripts/hlthprof.asp
Alcohol/Drug Counselor...................www.dph.state.ct.us/scripts/hlthprof.asp
Antenna Svcs Dealer/Technician.......https://www.ask-dcp.ct.gov/lookup/SearchCriteria.asp
Apple Product Mfg...........................https://www.ask-dcp.ct.gov/lookup/SearchCriteria.asp
Appraiser, MVPD/MVR...................www.ct-clic.com
Architect/Architectural Firm.............https://www.ask-dcp.ct.gov/lookup/SearchCriteria.asp
Asbesto-related Occupation...............www.dph.state.ct.us/scripts/hlthprof.asp
Association Manager........................https://www.ask-dcp.ct.gov/lookup/SearchCriteria.asp
Athletic Promoter............................https://www.ask-dcp.ct.gov/lookup/SearchCriteria.asp
Attorney/Attorney Firm....................http://civilinquiry.jud.ct.gov/GetAtty.asp
Audiologist......................................www.dph.state.ct.us/scripts/hlthprof.asp
Auto Glass Technician......................https://www.ask-dcp.ct.gov/lookup/SearchCriteria.asp
Auto Insurance Adjuster...................www.ct-clic.com
Bail Bond Agent..............................www.ct-clic.com
Bail Bondsman.................................www.ct.gov/dps/lib/dps/special_licensing_and_firearms/licensed_bondsman.pdf
Bail Enforcement Agent...................www.ct.gov/dps/lib/dps/special_licensing_and_firearms/licensed_bea.pdf
Bail Enforcement Instructor.............www.ct.gov/dps/lib/dps/special_licensing_and_firearms/bea_instructors.pdf
Bakery..https://www.ask-dcp.ct.gov/lookup/SearchCriteria.asp
Bank & Trust Company.............www.ct.gov/dob/cwp/view.asp?a=2239&Q=298138&dobNAV_GID=1659&dobNav=|
Barber...www.dph.state.ct.us/scripts/hlthprof.asp
Bazaar/Raffle Permit........................www.ct-clic.com/
Bedding Mfg/Renovation/Supplier....https://www.ask-dcp.ct.gov/lookup/SearchCriteria.asp
Beekeeper..www.ct.gov/caes/site/default.asp
Beverage/Water Bottler....................https://www.ask-dcp.ct.gov/lookup/SearchCriteria.asp
Bingo Registration...........................www.ct-clic.com/
Bottler, non-alcohol.........................https://www.ask-dcp.ct.gov/lookup/SearchCriteria.asp
Boxer/Boxing Professional...............https://www.ask-dcp.ct.gov/lookup/SearchCriteria.asp
Building Contractor.........................https://www.ask-dcp.ct.gov/lookup/SearchCriteria.asp
Casino/Casino Occupation................www.ct-clic.com/
Casualty Adjuster............................www.ct-clic.com
Caterer/Concessioner, Liquor...........https://www.ask-dcp.ct.gov/lookup/SearchCriteria.asp
Check Cashing Service.............www.ct.gov/dob/cwp/view.asp?a=2239&Q=298138&dobNAV_GID=1659&dobNav=|
Chiropractor....................................www.dph.state.ct.us/scripts/hlthprof.asp
Closing Out Sale..............................https://www.ask-dcp.ct.gov/lookup/SearchCriteria.asp
Collection Agency....................www.ct.gov/dob/cwp/view.asp?a=2239&Q=298138&dobNAV_GID=1659&dobNav=|
College/University............................www.ctdhe.org/database/default.htm
Contractor, Major/or/Mechanical......https://www.ask-dcp.ct.gov/lookup/SearchCriteria.asp
Controlled Substance Lab.................https://www.ask-dcp.ct.gov/lookup/SearchCriteria.asp
Cosmetologist..................................www.dph.state.ct.us/scripts/hlthprof.asp
Counselor, Professional....................www.dph.state.ct.us/scripts/hlthprof.asp
Credit Union/Debt Adjuster   www.ct.gov/dob/cwp/view.asp?a=2239&Q=298138&dobNAV_GID=1659&dobNav=|
Dental Anes./Sedation Permittee.......www.dph.state.ct.us/scripts/hlthprof.asp
Dentist/Dental Hygienist..................www.dph.state.ct.us/scripts/hlthprof.asp
Dessert Mfg, Frozen.........................https://www.ask-dcp.ct.gov/lookup/SearchCriteria.asp
Dietician/Nutritionist.......................www.dph.state.ct.us/scripts/hlthprof.asp
Dog Racing Owner/Trainer...............www.ct-clic.com/
Drug/Cosmetic Whlse/Mfg...............https://www.ask-dcp.ct.gov/lookup/SearchCriteria.asp
Druggist Liquor Permittee.................https://www.ask-dcp.ct.gov/lookup/SearchCriteria.asp
Electrical-related Occupation............https://www.ask-dcp.ct.gov/lookup/SearchCriteria.asp
Electrical Sign Installer....................https://www.ask-dcp.ct.gov/lookup/SearchCriteria.asp
Electrologist/Hypertricologist...........www.dph.state.ct.us/scripts/hlthprof.asp
Electronics Service Dealer/Tech........https://www.ask-dcp.ct.gov/lookup/SearchCriteria.asp
Elevator Inspector/Mechanic.............https://www.ask-dcp.ct.gov/lookup/SearchCriteria.asp

Embalmer .... www.dph.state.ct.us/scripts/hlthprof.asp
Emergency Med. Svc Professional .... www.dph.state.ct.us/scripts/hlthprof.asp
Engineer/or/Engineer-in-Training ..... https://www.ask-dcp.ct.gov/lookup/SearchCriteria.asp
Fire Protection Inspector/Contractor . https://www.ask-dcp.ct.gov/lookup/SearchCriteria.asp
Fire Sprinkler Technician .... https://www.ask-dcp.ct.gov/lookup/SearchCriteria.asp
Funeral Director/Home...................... www.dph.state.ct.us/scripts/hlthprof.asp
Gasoline Dealer, Retail...................... https://www.ask-dcp.ct.gov/lookup/SearchCriteria.asp
Glazier .... https://www.ask-dcp.ct.gov/lookup/SearchCriteria.asp
Hairdresser.. www.dph.state.ct.us/scripts/hlthprof.asp
Health Care Center Insurer .... www.ct-clic.com
Health Club.. https://www.ask-dcp.ct.gov/lookup/SearchCriteria.asp
Hearing Instrument Specialist........... www.dph.state.ct.us/scripts/hlthprof.asp
Heating/Pipe/Cooling Cont/Journey'nhttps://www.ask-dcp.ct.gov/lookup/SearchCriteria.asp
Home Heating Oil Seller .... https://www.ask-dcp.ct.gov/lookup/SearchCriteria.asp
Home Improvement Contr./Seller...... https://www.ask-dcp.ct.gov/lookup/SearchCriteria.asp
Home Inspector .... https://www.ask-dcp.ct.gov/lookup/SearchCriteria.asp
Homemaker Companion...................... https://www.ask-dcp.ct.gov/lookup/SearchCriteria.asp
Homeopathic Physician...................... www.dph.state.ct.us/scripts/hlthprof.asp
Honey Bee Registration..................... www.ct.gov/caes/site/default.asp
Hypertrichologist.............................. www.dph.state.ct.us/scripts/hlthprof.asp
Hypnotist .... https://www.ask-dcp.ct.gov/lookup/SearchCriteria.asp
Insurance Adjuster/Public Adjuster ... www.ct-clic.com
Insurance Agent, Fraternal................. www.ct-clic.com
Insurance Appraiser........................... www.ct-clic.com
Insurance Firm/Producer/Consultant . www.ct-clic.com
Interior Designer............................... https://www.ask-dcp.ct.gov/lookup/SearchCriteria.asp
Interstate Land Sales......................... https://www.ask-dcp.ct.gov/lookup/SearchCriteria.asp
Investment Advisor/Agent........ www.ct.gov/dob/cwp/view.asp?a=2239&Q=298138&dobNAV_GID=1659&dobNav=|
Juice Producer .... https://www.ask-dcp.ct.gov/lookup/SearchCriteria.asp
Land Sales, Interstate........................ https://www.ask-dcp.ct.gov/lookup/SearchCriteria.asp
Land Surveyor/Land Surveyor Firm.. https://www.ask-dcp.ct.gov/lookup/SearchCriteria.asp
Landscape Architect .... https://www.ask-dcp.ct.gov/lookup/SearchCriteria.asp
Lead Abatement Professional .... www.dph.state.ct.us/scripts/hlthprof.asp
Lead Consultant................................. www.dph.state.ct.us/scripts/hlthprof.asp
Legalized Gaming Occupation .... www.ct-clic.com/
Liquor License/Permittee .... https://www.ask-dcp.ct.gov/lookup/SearchCriteria.asp
Liquor Mfg/Dist/Whlse/Ship/Broker . https://www.ask-dcp.ct.gov/lookup/SearchCriteria.asp
Liquor Store...................................... https://www.ask-dcp.ct.gov/lookup/SearchCriteria.asp
Loan Company, Small...............www.ct.gov/dob/cwp/view.asp?a=2239&Q=298138&dobNAV_GID=1659&dobNav=|
Lottery/or/Lottery Sales Agent .... www.ct-clic.com/
Marriage & Family Therapist .... www.dph.state.ct.us/scripts/hlthprof.asp
Marshall, State................................... www.jud.ct.gov/faq/marshals.htm
Martial Arts Facility .... https://www.ask-dcp.ct.gov/lookup/SearchCriteria.asp
Massage Therapist .... www.dph.state.ct.us/scripts/hlthprof.asp
Mausoleum .... www.dph.state.ct.us/scripts/hlthprof.asp
Medical Doctor.................................. www.dph.state.ct.us/scripts/hlthprof.asp
Medical Response Technician .... www.dph.state.ct.us/scripts/hlthprof.asp
Midwife .... www.dph.state.ct.us/scripts/hlthprof.asp
Mobile Home Park/Seller.................. https://www.ask-dcp.ct.gov/lookup/SearchCriteria.asp
Money Forwarder..................... www.ct.gov/dob/cwp/view.asp?a=2239&Q=298138&dobNAV_GID=1659&dobNav=|
Money Order/Travel'rs Check Issuer www.ct.gov/dob/cwp/view.asp?a=2233&q=297862&dobNAV_GID=1663
Mortgage Broker/Lender..........www.ct.gov/dob/cwp/view.asp?a=2239&Q=298138&dobNAV_GID=1659&dobNav=|
Naturopathic Physician...................... www.dph.state.ct.us/scripts/hlthprof.asp
New Home Construction Contr. .... https://www.ask-dcp.ct.gov/lookup/SearchCriteria.asp
Nurse .... www.dph.state.ct.us/scripts/hlthprof.asp
Nurse, Advance Registered Practice.. www.dph.state.ct.us/scripts/hlthprof.asp
Nurse-LPN .... www.dph.state.ct.us/scripts/hlthprof.asp

Nursery Plant/or/Plant Dealer............ www.ct.gov/caes/site/default.asp
Nursing Home Administrator .... www.dph.state.ct.us/scripts/hlthprof.asp
Occupational Therapist/Assistant ...... www.dph.state.ct.us/scripts/hlthprof.asp
Off-Track Betting .... www.ct-clic.com/
Optical Shop .... www.dph.state.ct.us/scripts/hlthprof.asp
Optician .... www.dph.state.ct.us/scripts/hlthprof.asp
Optometrist .... www.dph.state.ct.us/scripts/hlthprof.asp
Osteopathic Physician....................... www.dph.state.ct.us/scripts/hlthprof.asp
Paramedic .... www.dph.state.ct.us/scripts/hlthprof.asp
Pesticide Applicator.......................... www.kellysolutions.com/CT/Applicators/index.htm
Pesticide-related Business .... www.kellysolutions.com/CT/Business/index.htm
Pharmacist/Pharmacist Intern .... https://www.ask-dcp.ct.gov/lookup/SearchCriteria.asp
Pharmacy/or/Pharmacy Technician ... https://www.ask-dcp.ct.gov/lookup/SearchCriteria.asp
Physical Therapist/Assistant............. www.dph.state.ct.us/scripts/hlthprof.asp
Physician/or/Physician Assistant ...... www.dph.state.ct.us/scripts/hlthprof.asp
Pipefitter .... https://www.ask-dcp.ct.gov/lookup/SearchCriteria.asp
Plumber .... https://www.ask-dcp.ct.gov/lookup/SearchCriteria.asp
Podiatrist... www.dph.state.ct.us/scripts/hlthprof.asp
Premium Finance Company .... www.ct-clic.com
Private Detective Co........www.ct.gov/dps/lib/dps/special_licensing_and_firearms/licensed_pi_security_companies.pdf
Private Investigator.........www.ct.gov/dps/lib/dps/special_licensing_and_firearms/licensed_pi_security_companies.pdf
Private Occupational School............. www.ctdhe.org/database/default.htm
Psychologist.................................... www.dph.state.ct.us/scripts/hlthprof.asp
Public Accountant-CPA .... www.sboalicense.ct.gov/cpalookup/Default.aspx
Public Service Technician .... https://www.ask-dcp.ct.gov/lookup/SearchCriteria.asp
Radiographer .... www.dph.state.ct.us/scripts/hlthprof.asp
Real Estate Agent/Broker/Seller........ https://www.ask-dcp.ct.gov/lookup/SearchCriteria.asp
Real Estate Appraiser .... https://www.ask-dcp.ct.gov/lookup/SearchCriteria.asp
Real Estate Educ. Provider .... https://www.ask-dcp.ct.gov/lookup/SearchCriteria.asp
Reinsurance Intermediary................. www.ct-clic.com
Rental Car Company .... www.ct-clic.com
Respiratory Care Practitioner .... www.dph.state.ct.us/scripts/hlthprof.asp
Risk Purchasing/Retention Group ..... www.ct-clic.com
Sales Finance Company............www.ct.gov/dob/cwp/view.asp?a=2239&Q=298138&dobNAV_GID=1659&dobNav=|
Sanitarian... www.dph.state.ct.us/scripts/hlthprof.asp
Sanitarian, Registered....................... www.dph.state.ct.us/scripts/hlthprof.asp
Savings & Loan Assoc Bank.....www.ct.gov/dob/cwp/view.asp?a=2239&Q=298138&dobNAV_GID=1659&dobNav=|
Savings Bank...........................www.ct.gov/dob/cwp/view.asp?a=2239&Q=298138&dobNAV_GID=1659&dobNav=|
School Principal/Superintendent .... www.csde.state.ct.us/public/csde/reports/SuperintendentContacts.asp
Securities Agent/Broker/Dealer......... www.finra.org/index.htm
Security Company, Priv...www.ct.gov/dps/lib/dps/special_licensing_and_firearms/licensed_pi_security_companies.pdf
Security Officer Instructor
                  www.ct.gov/dps/lib/dps/special_licensing_and_firearms/approved_cj_security_instructor_(public).pdf
Security Service..............www.ct.gov/dps/lib/dps/special_licensing_and_firearms/licensed_pi_security_companies.pdf
Sheet Metal Contr./Journeyman .... https://www.ask-dcp.ct.gov/lookup/SearchCriteria.asp
Shorthand Court Reporter.................. https://www.ask-dcp.ct.gov/lookup/SearchCriteria.asp
Social Worker................................... www.dph.state.ct.us/scripts/hlthprof.asp
Solar Energy Contr./Journeyman....... https://www.ask-dcp.ct.gov/lookup/SearchCriteria.asp
Speech Pathologist........................... www.dph.state.ct.us/scripts/hlthprof.asp
Sprinkler Layout Technician .... https://www.ask-dcp.ct.gov/lookup/SearchCriteria.asp
Student Athlete Agent .... https://www.ask-dcp.ct.gov/lookup/SearchCriteria.asp
Subsurface Sewer Installer/Cleaner ... www.dph.state.ct.us/scripts/hlthprof.asp
Surplus Lines Broker........................ www.ct-clic.com
Surveyor, Land .... https://www.ask-dcp.ct.gov/lookup/SearchCriteria.asp
Telecommunications Technician .... https://www.ask-dcp.ct.gov/lookup/SearchCriteria.asp
Television/Radio License .... https://www.ask-dcp.ct.gov/lookup/SearchCriteria.asp
Utilization Review Company .... www.ct-clic.com

Vehicle Dealer/or/Vehicle Repairer... www.ct.gov/dmv/cwp/view.asp?a=799&q=401814&dmvPNavCtr=|#48712
Vending Machine Operator .... https://www.ask-dcp.ct.gov/lookup/SearchCriteria.asp
Vendor, Itinerant................................ https://www.ask-dcp.ct.gov/lookup/SearchCriteria.asp
Veterinarian .... www.dph.state.ct.us/scripts/hlthprof.asp
Viatical Settlement Broker/Provider.. www.ct-clic.com
Water Bottler .... https://www.ask-dcp.ct.gov/lookup/SearchCriteria.asp
Weigher .... https://www.ask-dcp.ct.gov/lookup/SearchCriteria.asp
Weights/Measures Dl/Repair/Regul'r https://www.ask-dcp.ct.gov/lookup/SearchCriteria.asp
Well Driller...................................... https://www.ask-dcp.ct.gov/lookup/SearchCriteria.asp
Winery Farm..................................... https://www.ask-dcp.ct.gov/lookup/SearchCriteria.asp
Wrestler/Wrestling Manager .... https://www.ask-dcp.ct.gov/lookup/SearchCriteria.asp
Youth Camp .... www.dph.state.ct.us/BRS/Youth_camps/youthcamps.htm

State and Local Courts

State Court Structure: The Superior Court is the sole court of original jurisdiction for all causes of action, except for matters over which the Probate Courts have jurisdiction as provided by statute. The state is divided into 13 Judicial Districts, 20 Geographic Area Courts, and 13 Juvenile Districts. The Superior Court - comprised primarily of the Judicial District Courts and the Geographical Area Courts - has 5 divisions: Criminal, Civil, Family, Juvenile, and Administrative Appeals. When not combined, the Judicial District Courts handle felony and civil cases while the Geographic Area Courts handle misdemeanors, and most handle small claims. Divorce records are maintained by the Chief Clerk of the Judicial District Courts. Probate is handled by city Probate Courts and those courts not part of the state court system.

Statewide Court Online Access: The Judicial Branch offers web look-up to docket information for civil, family, criminal, motor vehicle, housing, and small claims cases at www.jud.ct.gov/jud2.htm. Case look-ups are segregated into four types- civil/family, criminal/motor vehicle, housing, and small claims. For civil/family and small claims cases statewide are available from one to 10 years after the disposition date, depending on location. Search statewide or by location. The criminal and motor vehicle case docket data is available on cases where a disposition or bond forfeiture occurred on or after 01/01/2000. To search statewide, leave the location field blank. For housing (landlord/tenant) cases, search by name, address, or docket number. Housing case records are only available from the Hartford, New Haven, New Britain, Bridgeport, Norwalk and Waterbury districts.

Opinions from the Supreme and Appellate courts are available at www.jud.state.ct.us/opinions.htm.

> ❖ **Statewide Access Offered For All Trial Courts – Read Above** ❖

Note: No individual Connecticut courts offer online access.

Recorders, Assessors, and Other Sites of Note

Recording Office Organization: 8 counties and 169 towns/cities. There is no county recording in Connecticut, all recording is at the town/city level. The recording officer is the Town/City Clerk. Be careful not to confuse searching in the following towns/cities as equivalent to a countywide search (since they have the same names): Fairfield, Hartford, Litchfield, New Haven, New London, Tolland, and Windham.

Online Access Note: A number of towns offer free access to assessor information. The State's Municipal Public Access Initiative has produced a website of Town and Municipality general information at www.munic.state.ct.us. Also, a private vendor has placed assessor records from a number of towns on the Internet. Visit http://data.visionappraisal.com.

Fairfield County

Bridgeport Town *Property, Taxation Records* <u>Free</u> Access assessor data free at www.ci.bridgeport.ct.us/newdepartments/tax_assessor/assessorspro.aspx.

Brookfield Town *Property, Taxation Records* `Free` Search the town assessor field cards at http://data.visionappraisal.com/BrookfieldCT/. Free registration for full data.

Danbury City *Real Estate, Deed, Lien, Water Information, Permit Records* www.ci.danbury.ct.us `Free` `& $$` Search land records free at http://tc.ci.danbury.ct.us/resolution/. An advanced search is also available. Also, search at www.ci.danbury.ct.us/Public_Documents/DanburyCT_WebDocs/publicaccess - Site may or may not allow you to logon anonymously for free. Indexes only, cannot view documents.
Property, Taxation Records `Free` Search the city assessor database at http://data.visionappraisal.com/DanburyCT/. Free registration for full data.

Easton Town *Property, Taxation Records* `Free & $$` Access property data free at www.prophecyone.us/index_prophecy.php?town=Easton. No name searching.

Fairfield Town *Property, Taxation Records* `Free` Search the town assessor database at http://data.visionappraisal.com/FairfieldCT/ . Free registration for full data.

Greenwich Town *Property, Taxation Records* `Free` Search current tax records free at www.greenwichct.org/ServicesOnline/services_online.asp#. You may also search real estate, personal property, and motor vehicles.

New Canaan Town *Property, Taxation Records* `Free` Access to property data is at http://data.visionappraisal.com/NewCanaanCT/. Free registration required.

New Fairfield Town *Property, Taxation Records* `Free` Access the assessor database free at http://data.visionappraisal.com/NewfairfieldCT/.

Newtown Town *Property, Taxation Records* `Free & $$` Access property data free at www.prophecyone.us/index_prophecy.php?town=Newtown. No name searching.

Norwalk City *Real Estate, Deed, Lien, Marriage, UCC Records* www.norwalkct.org `Free` Access to the town clerk's Official Records is free at www.norwalkct.org/TownClerk/landrecords/default.asp
Property, Taxation Records `Free` Access to Norwalk property records is free at www.norwalkct.org/norwalk/pckls.asp.

Stamford City *Trade Name, City Businesses Records* www.cityofstamford.org/ `Free` Search the city registry of trade names for free at www.cityofstamford.org/content/800/910.aspx.
Property, Taxation Records `Free` Access accessor tax data free at www.cityofstamford.org/apps/tax/default.htm. Also, search sales data by type for free at www.cityofstamford.org/content/25/52/131/144/152/2482.aspx

Stratford Town *Property, Taxation Records* `Free` Search town assessor database free after registration at http://data.visionappraisal.com/StratfordCT/.

Trumbull Town *Real Estate, Grantor/Grantee, Deed, Lien, UCC Judgment, Fictitious Name Records* www.trumbull-ct.gov `Free & $$` Search land records free at http://209.244.152.236/resolution/login.asp but registration and username required.
Property, Taxation Records `Free` Search the assessor database free after registration at http://data.visionappraisal.com/TrumbullCT.

Weston Town *Real Estate, Grantor/Grantee, Marriage, Death, Trade Name, UCC Records* www.weston-ct.com `Free` Access the Town Clerk's index records free at www.weston-ct.com/resolution/. For username and password use cott, cott.

Westport Town *Real Estate, Deed, Lien, Map, Death, Marriage, Civil Union, Trade Name, Burial Records* www.westportct.gov/ `Free` Search a variety of public record indexes only at http://publicrecords.westportct.gov/ including land records back to 1900, Civil unions back to 2005, deaths and marriages to 1949, maps/surveys to 1886, trade names to 1924, burials back to 2006.
Property, Taxation Records `Free` Search assessor data free at http://data.visionappraisal.com/WestportCT. Also, lookup assessment data on the town lookup site at www.westportct.gov/residents/assessments/default.htm. Also, search property data free on the GIS-mapping site at http://webmap.jws.com/website4/ccbviewer1.14.4/viewer_2.jsp.

Wilton Town *Property, Taxation Records* `Free` Search the town assessor database free at http://data.visionappraisal.com/WiltonCT/.

Hartford County

Avon Town *Real Estate, Grantor/Grantee, Deed, Mortgage, Lien, Judgment, Trade Name Records*
www.town.avon.ct.us/Public_Documents/AvonCT_Clerk/clerk `Free` Access land data and trade names free at
http://landrecords.town.avon.ct.us/.
Property, Taxation Records `Free` Access to property data is free at www.avonassessor.com/index.shtml.

Berlin Town *Real Estate, Deed, Maps Records* www.town.berlin.ct.us `Free` Access the recorders index
free at www.town.berlin.ct.us/resolution/.
Property, Taxation Records `Free` Search town assessor database at http://data.visionappraisal.com/BerlinCT/.
Free registration for full data.

Bloomfield Town *Property, Taxation Records* `Free` Access property data free at
www.prophecyone.us/index_prophecy.php?town=Bloomfield. No name searching.

Bristol City *Parcel, Maps Records* www.ci.bristol.ct.us `$$` Also, access to City of Bristol Zoning Map for
free at www.ci.bristol.ct.us/content/3326/3370/default.aspx.

Burlington Town *Property, Taxation Records* `Free` Search assessor database free after registration at
http://data.visionappraisal.com/BurlingtonCT.

Canton Town *Property, Taxation Records* `Free` Search of property address, search by owner name, or
search sales at www.cantonassessor.com.

East Granby Town *Property, Taxation Records* `Free` Access to property tax for free go to
www.eastgranby.net/index.php?option=com_content&task=view&id=2.

East Windsor Town *Property, Taxation Records* `Free & $$` Access property data free at
www.prophecyone.us/index_prophecy.php?town=East%20Windsor. No name searching.

Enfield Town *Real Estate, Deed Records* http://enfield-ct.gov/content/91/148/default.aspx `Free` Access
real estate records free at https://app7.enfield.org/.
Property, Taxation Records `Free` Access assessor's parcel data free at
https://app6.enfield.org/Find_a_Parcel.htm but no name searching. Also, search for parcel data free on the GIS-mapping
site at http://gis.cdm.com/enfieldct/map.htm. Use the Search For feature to search by name.

Farmington Town *Property, Taxation Records* `Free` Access property assessor data free at
www.farmington-ct.org/TownServices/Assessor//LandRecord.aspx.

Glastonbury Town *Real Estate, Deed, Lien, Mortgage, Judgment, Birth, Death Records*
www.glastonbury-ct.gov `Free` Access town clerks recorded document index free at
http://town.glasct.org/wb_or1/or_sch_1.asp.
Property, Taxation Records `Free` Access assessor data free after registration at
http://data.visionappraisal.com/GlastonburyCT/DEFAULT.asp. Search town assessment data free on the GIS Mapping site
at http://gis.glastonbury-ct.gov/ceo/.

Granby Town *Property, Taxation Records* `Free` Search the town assessor's database free at
http://data.visionappraisal.com/GranbyCT.

Hartford City *Property, Taxation Records* `Free` Search city assessor cata free at
http://assessor.hartford.gov/Default.asp?br=exp&vr=6.

Manchester Town *Property, Taxation Records* `Free` Search the town assessor database at
http://data.visionappraisal.com/ManchesterCT/. Also, click on TOMnet Public parcel viewer to search property free at
www.manchestergis.com/ but no name searching.

Marlborough Town *Property, Taxation Records* `Free` Search the assessor database free at
http://data.visionappraisal.com/MarlboroughCT. Free reggistration required.

New Britain Town *Property, Taxation Records* `Free` Search the city assessor database at
http://data.visionappraisal.com/NewbritainCT/. Free registration required.

Newington Town *Property, Taxation Records* `Free` Access to assessor property records is free at
http://newington.univers-clt.com.

Plainville Town *Property, Taxation Records* `Free` Access town assessor property data free at
http://plainville.univers-clt.com.

Rocky Hill Town *Land, Marriage, Death, Trade Name, Map Records* www.ci.rocky-hill.ct.us `Free`
Access to the Town Clerk's Index Search is free at www.ci.rocky-hill.ct.us/resolution/. Land records go back to 1973;
Marriages/Deaths to 1990; trade names to 1987; maps to 1982.

Simsbury Town *Property, Taxation Records* `Free & $$` Access property data free at
www.prophecyone.us/index_prophecy.php?town=Simsbury. Also, search pdf files of property sales by name and by
address free at www.simsbury-ct.gov/Public_Documents/Departments/SimsburyCT_Assessment/index.

Southington Town *Real Estate, Grantor/Grantee, Deed, Map/Survey, Voter Registration Records*
www.southington.org `Free & $$` Access to county land index back to 1926 at
http://townclerk.southington.org/resolution/ and also includes maps and surveys back to 1847. Access the voter registration
lookup free at http://registrars.southington.org/voterlist/voters.php.
Property, Taxation Records `Free` Access town assessor records free at
http://assessor.southington.org/Main/Home.aspx then click on Property Records.

Suffield Town *Property, Taxation Records* `Free` Search the town assessor's database at
http://data.visionappraisal.com/SuffieldCT. Free registration required.

West Hartford Town *Property, Taxation Records* `Free & $$` Access to the assessor property
recordson the GIS-mapping site is free, or by subscription for name searching. Details and sign-up are at
www.westhartford.org/whprs/, and option to free search. Also, lookup property tax data using address (no name searching)
free at www.westhartford.org/taxestimator/index.aspx.

Wethersfield Town *Property, Taxation Records* `Free` Access to property data is free after free
registration at http://data.visionappraisal.com/WethersfieldCT/.

Windsor Locks Town *Property, Taxation Records* `Free` Search the town assessor database free at
http://data.visionappraisal.com/WINDSORLOCKSCT/.

Windsor Town *Real Estate, Grantor/Grantee, Deed Records* www.townofwindsorct.com `Free`
Search the town clerk's land records index for free at www.townofwindsorct.com/records.htm. Index goes back to 1970.
Town services search page at www.townofwindsorct.com.
Property, Taxation Records `Free` Search the town GIS database at http://info.townofwindsorct.com/gis/.

Litchfield County

Bridgewater Town *Property, Taxation Records* `Free` Access assessor data free at
http://data.visionappraisal.com/BridgewaterCT/search.asp.

Canaan Town *Property, Taxation Records* `Free` Access assessor data free after free registration at
http://data.visionappraisal.com/CanaanCT/DEFAULT.asp.

Colebrook Town *Property, Taxation Records* `Free` Access assessor records free at
http://data.visionappraisal.com/ColebrookCT/.

Goshen Town *Property, Taxation Records* `Free` Search the town assessor database at
http://data.visionappraisal.com/goshenCT/. Free registration for full data.

Kent Town *Property, Taxation Records* `Free` Access to property assessor data is at
http://data.visionappraisal.com/KentCT/. Free registration required.

New Hartford Town *Real Estate, Grantor/Grantee, Deed, Lien, Judgment, Assumed Name Records*
www.town.new-hartford.ct.us `Free` Access real estate, assumed names records for free at
http://landrecords.town.new-hartford.ct.us/.
Property, Taxation Records `Free` Access to property data is at http://data.visionappraisal.com/NewhartfordCT/.
Free registration required.

New Milford Town *Property, Taxation Records* `Free` Search the town assessor database at
http://data.visionappraisal.com/NewMilfordCT/. Free registration required.

Roxbury Town *Property, Taxation Records* `Free` Access to property data is free after registration at
http://data.visionappraisal.com/RoxburyCT/.

Sharon Town *Property, Taxation Records* `Free` Access assessor data free after registration at
http://data.visionappraisal.com/SharonCT/.

Thomaston Town *Property, Taxation Records* `Free & $$` Search property data free at
www.prophecyone.us/index_prophecy.php?town=Thomaston but no name searching.

Torrington City *Property, Taxation Records* `Free` Access property data for free after registration at
http://data.visionappraisal.com/TorringtonCT/.

Town of Morris *Property, Taxation Records* `Free` Access assessor data free with registration at
http://data.visionappraisal.com/MorrisCT/DEFAULT.asp

Warren Town *Property, Taxation Records* `Free` Access assessor property data free after registration at
http://data.visionappraisal.com/warrenct/DEFAULT.asp

Watertown Town *Property, Taxation Records* `Free` Access property data free after registration at
http://data.visionappraisal.com/watertownct/.

Winchester Town *Property, Taxation Records* `Free` Access town property tax data after free
registration at http://data.visionappraisal.com/WinchesterCT/.

Middlesex County

Clinton Town *Property, Taxation Records* `Free` Search Assessor records at
http://data.visionappraisal.com/ClintonCT/.

Cromwell Town *Property, Taxation Records* `Free` Access assessor data free after free registration at
http://data.visionappraisal.com/CromwellCT/DEFAULT.asp Access property and GIS-mapping records free at
http://hosting.tighebond.com/cromwellct/main.htm.

Durham Town *Property, Taxation Records* `Free` Access the assessor's database at http://durham.univers-
clt.com. Also, Assessor maps access free at www.townofdurhamct.org/content/18701/18791/.

East Haddam Town *Property, Taxation Records* `Free` Access property data free at
http://easthaddam.org/property_value.htm.

East Hampton Town *Real Estate, Deed, Lien, Judgment, UCC Records* www.easthamptonct.org
`Free` Access to recorded land records and more to be available 2008.
Property, Taxation Records `Free` Access assessor database free at
www.rmsreval.com/login.asp?town=East%20Hampton after email registration. Data may be old.

Essex Town *Real Estate, Deed, Lien, Mortgage, Death, Trade Name Records*
www.essexct.gov/departments/townclerk.html `Free` Access land records back to 1982 free at
http://landrecords.essexct.gov/. Other records go back to 6/16/2004.
Property, Taxation Records `Free` Access to property data is free at http://data.visionappraisal.com/EssexCT/.

Haddam Town *Property, Taxation Records* `Free` Access the Assessor database free after email
registration at http://rmsreval.com/login.asp?town=Haddam. Data may be old.

Killingworth Town *Parcel, Tay Payment Records* `Free` Check town tax payments free at
www.mytaxbill.org/inet/revenue/revenueSearch.do.
Property, Taxation Records `Free` Access property data free at
www.prophecyone.us/index_prophecy.php?town=Killingworth. No name searching.

Middlefield Town *Property, Taxation Records* `Free` Search the town assessor database free at
http://data.visionappraisal.com/MiddlefieldCT/.

Middletown City *Property, Taxation Records* `Free` Access property data free at
http://host.appgeo.com/MiddletownCT/Default.aspx but no name searching.

New Haven County

Ansonia City *Property, Taxation Records* `Free` Access assessor property data free at
http://data.visionappraisal.com/AnsoniaCT/search.asp.

Branford Town *Real Estate, Deed, Trade Name Records* www.branford-ct.gov `Free` Access to town
clerk's recording records is free at http://deeds.branford-ct.gov/resolution/. Land records go back to 7/1/1994; maps and
trade names to 1/18/2005.
Property, Taxation Records `Free` Search the town assessor database at
http://data.visionappraisal.com/BranfordCT/. Free registration for full data.

Cheshire Town *Property, Taxation Records* `Free` Access property data free at
www.prophecyone.us/index_prophecy.php?town=Cheshire. No name searching.

East Haven Town *Property, Taxation Records* `Free & $$` Access property data free at www.prophecyone.us/index_prophecy.php?town=East%20Haven. No name searching.

Guilford Town *Property, Taxation Records* `Free & $$` Access property data by owner name, address, or legals free at www.prophecyone.us/index_prophecy.php?town=Guilford.

Hamden Town *Property, Taxation Records* `Free` Search the town assessor's database free at http://data.visionappraisal.com/hamdenct.

Madison City *Property, Taxation Records* `Free` Search the city assessor database at http://data.visionappraisal.com/MadisonCT/. Free registration required for full access. Also, access property data free at www.appraisalresource.com/Search.aspx?town=Madison.

Meriden City *Property, Taxation Records* `Free` Search by parcel ID or address for property assessor data at www.cityofmeriden.org. Click on Property Searches. Also, search property data free on a private site at www.appraisalresource.com/Search.aspx?town=Meriden but no searching. Also, access parcel data free at http://gis.ci.meriden.ct.us/website/default.asp.

Middlebury Town *Property, Taxation Records* `Free` Access assessor and property data free at http://data.visionappraisal.com/MiddleburyCT/DEFAULT.asp. Free registration required.

Milford City *Property, Taxation Records* `Free` Search the city assessor's database at http://data.visionappraisal.com/milfordct/.

Naugatuck Town *Property, Taxation Records* `Free` Search assessor database free at http://data.visionappraisal.com/NaugatuckCT/.

New Haven City *Property, Taxation Records* `Free` Search the city assessor database at http://data.visionappraisal.com/NewhavenCT/. Free registration required.

North Branford Town *Property, Taxation Records* `Free` Search assessor records at http://data.visionappraisal.com/NorthBranfordCT.

North Haven Town *Property, Taxation Records* `Free` Access property data free at http://north-haven.univers-clt.com.

Oxford Town *Property, Taxation Records* `Free & $$` Access property data free at www.prophecyone.us/index_prophecy.php?town=Oxford. No name searching.

Prospect Town *Property, Taxation Records* `Free & $$` Access property data free at www.prophecyone.us/index_prophecy.php?town=Prospect. No name searching.

Waterbury City *Real Estate, Grantor/Grantee, Deed, Lien, Mortgage Records* www.waterburyct.org `Free` Real Estate records and lien lists can be accessed at free www.waterburyct.org/content/609/648/652/default.aspx *Property, Taxation Records* `Free` Access to the assessor property data is free at www.totalvaluation.com/tvweb/mainsearch.aspx?city=waterbury.

West Haven City *Property, Taxation Records* `Free` Search the town assessor's database free at http://data.visionappraisal.com/Westhavenct/.

Wolcott Town *Property, Taxation Records* `Free & $$` Access property data free at www.prophecyone.us/index_prophecy.php?town=Wolcott. No name searching.

Woodbridge Town *Property, Taxation Records* `Free` Search the town assessor's database at http://data.visionappraisal.com/woodbridgeCT. Free registration required for full data. Assessor email: bquist@ci.woodbridge.ct.us

New London County

City of New London *Property, Taxation Records* `Free` Search the city assessor's database free at http://data.visionappraisal.com//NewLondonCT.

Colchester Town *Property, Taxation Records* `Free` Search the town assessor database at http://data.visionappraisal.com/ColchesterCT/. Free registration for full data.

East Lyme Town *Property, Taxation Records* `Free` Search the town assessor database free at http://data.visionappraisal.com/EastLymeCT/.

Groton Town *Property, Taxation Records* `Free` Access property data free at http://grotongis.town.groton.ct.us. Click on Interactive Mapping, then Property Viewer, then owner name. Records back to 1990. Search list of tax payments for 2005 free at www.town.groton.ct.us/taxes/listing.asp.

Ledyard Town *Property, Taxation Records* `Free` Search the assessor database at http://data.visionappraisal.com/LedyardCT. Free registration required.

Montville Town *Real Estate, Grantor/Grantee, Deed, Death, Marriage, Civil Union, Trade Name,* *Map Records* www.townofmontville.org `Free` Access to recorders databases are available free at http://66.212.195.75/resolution/. Land records go back to 1/1950; marriage and death back to 10/30/1870; trade names to 2/11/1938; civil unions back to 10/6/2005.
Property, Taxation Records `Free` Access assessor data free with registration at http://data.visionappraisal.com/MontvilleCT/DEFAULT.asp. Free registration required.

Norwich City *Real Estate, Deed Records* www.norwichct.org `$$` Also, access to the clerk's town land records is online by subscription. Index goes back to 1929 and images to 1997. Fee is $350.00 per year; sign-up online at www.norwichct.org/content/155/43/280/81/249.aspx or call 860-823-3734.
Property, Taxation Records `Free` Search the city assessor's database at http://data.visionappraisal.com/NorwichCT. Free registration required. Also, access to property data to be available soon at www.appraisalresource.com/OnlineDatabases.aspx.

Old Lyme Town *Property, Taxation Records* `Free` Search the town Assessor's database at http://data.visionappraisal.com/OLDLYMECT.

Preston Town *Property, Taxation Records* `Free` Access assessor data after free registration at http://data.visionappraisal.com/PrestonCT/DEFAULT.asp.

Stonington Town *Property, Taxation Records* `Free` Access Assessor property data free at http://data.visionappraisal.com/StoningtonCT/DEFAULT.asp. Access parcel and mapping data free at http://ceo.fando.com/stonington/.

Waterford Town *Property, Taxation Records* `Free & $$` Access property data free at www.prophecyone.us/index_prophecy.php?town=Waterford but no name searching.

Tolland County

Andover Town *Property, Taxation Records* `Free` Search town assessor database at http://data.visionappraisal.com/AndoverCT/. Free registration for full data.

Columbia Town *Property, Taxation Records* `Free` Access assessor data free with registration at http://data.visionappraisal.com/ColumbiaCT/DEFAULT.asp.

Coventry Town *Property, Taxation Records* `Free` Access assessor and property data free at http://ceo.fando.com/coventry/.

Ellington Town *Real Estate, Deed, Mortgage, Map Records* www.ellington-ct.gov `Free` Access land records (indexes only) back to 1963 free at http://landrecords.ellington-ct.gov/. Also, search maps and surveys back to 2005.
Property, Taxation Records `Free` Online access to assessor records at http://data.visionappraisal.com/EllingtonCT.

Hebron Town *Property, Taxation Records* `Free & $$` Access property data free at www.prophecyone.us/index_prophecy.php?town=Hebron. No name searching.

Mansfield Town *Parcel, GIS-Mapping Records* www.mansfieldct.org `Free` Access GIS-Mapping and parcels free at www.mainstreetmaps.com/CT/Mansfield/.
Property, Taxation Records `Free` Access property and GIS-Mapping free at www.mainstreetmaps.com/CT/Mansfield/.

Stafford Town *Real Estate, Deed, Lien Records* www.staffordct.org `Free` Access town clerk land records back to 1/03/1977 free at http://records.staffordct.org/Resolution/search_menu.asp but free registration is required.
Property, Taxation Records `Free` Access assessor property data free at http://stafford.univers-clt.com.

Tolland Town *Property, Taxation Records* `Free` Search town assessor database free at http://data.visionappraisal.com/TollandCT/.

Willington Town *Property, Taxation Records* `Free` Search virtual town hall for free.

Windham County

Ashford Town *Property, Taxation Records* `Free` Access to property assessment free after registration at
http://data.visionappraisal.com/AshfordCT/DEFAULT.asp

Brooklyn Town *Property, Taxation Records* `Free` Access assessor database records free at
www.rmsreval.com/login.asp?town=Brooklyn. Free email registration required. No name searching. Data may be old.

Canterbury Town *Property, Taxation Records* `Free` Access asessor property data free at
http://data.visionappraisal.com/CanterburyCT/DEFAULT.asp

Eastford *Property, Taxation Records* `Free` Access assessor data free after registration at
http://data.visionappraisal.com/EastfordCT/DEFAULT.asp.

Killingly Town *Property, Taxation Records* `Free` Access assessor records free at
www.killinglyct.gov/Pages/KillinglyCT_Assessor/index.

Plainfield Town *Property, Taxation Records* `Free` Search maps online for free at
www.plainfieldct.org/index_files/Page2267.htm and perform a property assessor search at http://plainfield.ias-clt.com/parcel.list.php.

Pomfret Town *Property, Taxation Records* `Free` Search town assessor database at
http://data.visionappraisal.com/PomfretCT/. Free registration required. Search for land data such as subdivisions, wetlands and zoning regulations at http://pomfretct.org.

Putnam Town *Property, Taxation Records* `Free` Access assessor property data free after registration at
http://data.visionappraisal.com/PutnamCT/.

Thompson Town *Property, Taxation Records* `Free` Search the town assessor database free at
http://data.visionappraisal.com/ThompsonCT/. Free registration required.

Windham Town *Property, Taxation Records* `Free` Access assessor valuation data free at
http://windham.univers-clt.com/.

Woodstock Town *Property, Taxation Records* `Free` Search the assessor database at
http://data.visionappraisal.com/WoodstockCT. Requires registration, but is free.

Delaware

Capital: Dover
              Kent County
Time Zone: EST
Population: 864,764
# of Counties: 3

Useful State Links

Website: http://delware.gov
Governor: www.state.de.us/governor/index.shtml
Attorney General: www.state.de.us/attgen
State Archives: http://archives.delaware.gov/
State Statutes and Codes: http://delcode.delaware.gov/
Legislative Bill Search: http://legis.delaware.gov/
Unclaimed Funds: http://revenue.delaware.gov/information/Escheat.shtml

Primary State Agencies

Sexual Offender Registry   `Free`

Delaware State Police, Sex Offender Central Registry, http://sexoffender.dsp.delaware.gov/ Statewide registry can be searched at the website. The site gives the ability to search by last name, Development, and city or Zip Code. Any combination of these fields may be used; however, a search cannot be performed if both a city and Zip Code are entered.

Corporation, LLC, LP, LLP, General Partnerships, Trademarks/Servicemarks   `Free`

Secretary of State, Corporation Records, www.corp.delaware.gov/ Check status on the web free for entity name, file number, incorporation/formation date, registered agent name, address, phone number and residency.

Driver Records   `$$`

Division of Motor Vehicles, Driver's License Unit, www.dmv.de.gov/ The Direct Access Program is provided 24 hours via the web. The fee is $15.00 per name. Searches are done by submitting the driver's license number. Requesters must be pre-approved, a signed contract application is required. Online searching is by single inquiry only; no batch request mode is offered. For more information about establishing an account, call Mr. Larry Bryant at 302-744-2596.

Vehicle Ownership & Registration   `$$`

Division of Motor Vehicles, Correspondence Section, www.dmv.de.gov/ The Direct Access Program is provided 24 hours via the web. The fee is $15.00 per name. Requesters must be pre-approved; a signed contract application is required. Online searching is by single inquiry only; no batch request mode is offered. For more information about establishing an account, call Mr. Larry Bryant at 302-744-2596. This program is strictly monitored and not available for non-permissible uses.

Vital Records   `$$`

Department of Health, Office of Vital Statistics, www.dhss.delaware.gov/dhss/dph/ss/vitalstats.html Access available for birth, death and marriage records at www.vitalchek.com, a state designated vendor.

Occupational Licensing Boards

Adult Entertainment https://dpronline.delaware.gov/mylicense%20weblookup/Search.aspx
Aesthetician https://dpronline.delaware.gov/mylicense%20weblookup/Search.aspx
Amateur Boxing-related https://dpronline.delaware.gov/mylicense%20weblookup/Search.aspx
Architect https://dpronline.delaware.gov/mylicense%20weblookup/Search.aspx
Athletic Agent/Trainer....................... https://dpronline.delaware.gov/mylicense%20weblookup/Search.aspx

Audiologist https://dpronline.delaware.gov/mylicense%20weblookup/Search.aspx
Barber https://dpronline.delaware.gov/mylicense%20weblookup/Search.aspx
Bodyworker https://dpronline.delaware.gov/mylicense%20weblookup/Search.aspx
Boxer/Boxing Professional https://dpronline.delaware.gov/mylicense%20weblookup/Search.aspx
Charitable Gaming Permittee https://dpronline.delaware.gov/mylicense%20weblookup/Search.aspx
Chiropractor..................................... https://dpronline.delaware.gov/mylicense%20weblookup/Search.aspx
Cosmetologist https://dpronline.delaware.gov/mylicense%20weblookup/Search.aspx
Counselor, Elem./Second'y School .... https://deeds.doe.k12.de.us/public/deeds_pc_findeducator.aspx
Counselor, Professional https://dpronline.delaware.gov/mylicense%20weblookup/Search.aspx
Deadly Weapons Dealer https://dpronline.delaware.gov/mylicense%20weblookup/Search.aspx
Dental Hygienist............................... https://dpronline.delaware.gov/mylicense%20weblookup/Search.aspx
Dentist https://dpronline.delaware.gov/mylicense%20weblookup/Search.aspx
Dietician/Nutritionist https://dpronline.delaware.gov/mylicense%20weblookup/Search.aspx
Electrical Inspector https://dpronline.delaware.gov/mylicense%20weblookup/Search.aspx
Electrician.. https://dpronline.delaware.gov/mylicense%20weblookup/Search.aspx
Electrologist..................................... https://dpronline.delaware.gov/mylicense%20weblookup/Search.aspx
Emergency Medical Tech/Paramedic https://dpronline.delaware.gov/mylicense%20weblookup/Search.aspx
Engineer .... www.dape.org/App/peRoster.asp
Engineering Firm.............................. www.dape.org/App/peRoster.asp
Funeral Director................................ https://dpronline.delaware.gov/mylicense%20weblookup/Search.aspx
Gaming Control https://dpronline.delaware.gov/mylicense%20weblookup/Search.aspx
Geologist https://dpronline.delaware.gov/mylicense%20weblookup/Search.aspx
Hearing Aid Dealer/Fitter https://dpronline.delaware.gov/mylicense%20weblookup/Search.aspx
Insurance-related Business .... https://sbs-de-public.naic.org/Lion-Web/jsp/sbsreports/AgentLookup.jsp
Landscape Architect https://dpronline.delaware.gov/mylicense%20weblookup/Search.aspx
Library/Media Specialist .... https://deeds.doe.k12.de.us/public/deeds_pc_findeducator.aspx
Liquid Waste Hauler......................... www.dnrec.state.de.us/water2000/Sections/GroundWat/GWDSLicenses.htm
Lobbyist.. www.delawaregov.us/pic/index.cfm?ref=74391
Massage https://dpronline.delaware.gov/mylicense%20weblookup/Search.aspx
Medical Doctor/Surgeon................... https://dpronline.delaware.gov/mylicense%20weblookup/Search.aspx
Medical Practice https://dpronline.delaware.gov/mylicense%20weblookup/Search.aspx
Mental Health Counselor.................. https://dpronline.delaware.gov/mylicense%20weblookup/Search.aspx
Midwife Nurse.................................. https://dpronline.delaware.gov/mylicense%20weblookup/Search.aspx
Nail Technician https://dpronline.delaware.gov/mylicense%20weblookup/Search.aspx
Nurse https://dpronline.delaware.gov/mylicense%20weblookup/Search.aspx
Nursing Home Administrator https://dpronline.delaware.gov/mylicense%20weblookup/Search.aspx
Nutritionist https://dpronline.delaware.gov/mylicense%20weblookup/Search.aspx
Occupational Therapist/Assistant https://dpronline.delaware.gov/mylicense%20weblookup/Search.aspx
Optometrist....................................... www.arbo.org/index.php?action=findanoptometrist
Osteopathic Physician....................... https://dpronline.delaware.gov/mylicense%20weblookup/Search.aspx
Pesticide Applicator.......................... www.kellysolutions.com/de/Applicators/index.htm
Pesticide Business .... www.kellysolutions.com/de/Business/index.htm
Pesticide Dealer .... www.kellysolutions.com/de/Dealers/index.htm
Pharmacist https://dpronline.delaware.gov/mylicense%20weblookup/Search.aspx
Pharmacy/Pharmacy-relat'd Business https://dpronline.delaware.gov/mylicense%20weblookup/Search.aspx
Physical Therapist/Assistant.............. https://dpronline.delaware.gov/mylicense%20weblookup/Search.aspx
Physician Assistant........................... https://dpronline.delaware.gov/mylicense%20weblookup/Search.aspx
Pilot, River https://dpronline.delaware.gov/mylicense%20weblookup/Search.aspx
Plumber https://dpronline.delaware.gov/mylicense%20weblookup/Search.aspx
Podiatrist... https://dpronline.delaware.gov/mylicense%20weblookup/Search.aspx
Psychologist/ Psycholog'l Assistant .. https://dpronline.delaware.gov/mylicense%20weblookup/Search.aspx
Public Accountant-CPA https://dpronline.delaware.gov/mylicense%20weblookup/Search.aspx
Real Estate Agent/Broker https://dpronline.delaware.gov/mylicense%20weblookup/Search.aspx
Real Estate Appraiser .... www.asc.gov/content/category1/appr_by_state.asp
Respiratory Care Practitioner https://dpronline.delaware.gov/mylicense%20weblookup/Search.aspx
School Admin. Supervisor/Asst......... https://deeds.doe.k12.de.us/public/deeds_pc_findeducator.aspx
School Counsel'r/Princip'l/Super'd't https://deeds.doe.k12.de.us/public/deeds_pc_findeducator.aspx

Social Worker	https://dpronline.delaware.gov/mylicense%20weblookup/Search.aspx
Speech Pathologist/Audiologist	https://dpronline.delaware.gov/mylicense%20weblookup/Search.aspx
Surplus Lines Broker	https://sbs-de-public.naic.org/Lion-Web/jsp/sbsreports/AgentLookup.jsp
Surveyor, Land	https://dpronline.delaware.gov/mylicense%20weblookup/Search.aspx
Teacher	https://deeds.doe.k12.de.us/public/deeds_pc_findeducator.aspx
Veterinarian	https://dpronline.delaware.gov/mylicense%20weblookup/Search.aspx

State and Local Courts

State Court Structure: The Superior Court has original jurisdiction over criminal and civil cases except equity cases.The Superior Court has exclusive jurisdiction over felonies and almost all drug offenses. The Court of Common Pleas has jurisdiction in civil cases where the amount in controversy, exclusive of interest, does not exceed $50,000. In criminal cases, the Court of Common Pleas handles all misdemeanors occurring in the state except certain drug-related offenses and traffic offenses. The Court of Chancery has jurisdiction to hear all matters relating to equity – litigation in this tribunal deals largely with corporate issues, trusts, estates, other fiduciary matters, disputes involving the purchase of land, and questions of title to real estate as well as commercial and contractual matters. The Justice of the Peace Court – the initial entry level into the court system for most citizens – has jurisdiction over civil cases in which the disputed amount is less than $15,000. In criminal cases, the Justice of the Peace Court hears certain misdemeanors and most motor vehicle cases (excluding felonies) and the Justices of the Peace may act as committing magistrates for all crimes. Alderman's Courts handle traffic matters.

Statewide Court Online Access: Chancery, Superior, Common Pleas, and Supreme Courts opinions and orders are available free online at http://courts.state.de.us/opinions. Supreme, Superior, and Common Pleas Courts calendars are available free at http://courts.delaware.gov/calendars. Chancery Courts and Supreme Courts filings are available from a vendor at www.virtualdocket.com. Registration and fees required.

Kent County

Chancery Court http://courts.delaware.gov/Courts/Court%20of%20Chancery/ $$
Civil: Access to civil records online is available by subscription through LexisNexis efiling company.

Sussex County

Chancery Court http://courts.delaware.gov/Courts/Court%20of%20Chancery/ $$
Civil: Access to civil records online is available by subscription through LexisNexis efiling company.

Recorders, Assessors, and Other Sites of Note

Recording Office Organization: Delaware has 3 counties and 3 recording offices. The recording officer is the County Recorder. Federal tax liens on personal property of businesses are filed with the Secretary of State. Other federal and all state tax liens on personal property are filed with the County Recorder.

Online Access Note: There is no statewide online system for county recorded documents.

Kent County Recorder of Deeds *Property, Land Record Records*
www.co.kent.de.us/Departments/RowOffices/Recorder/index.htm   Land/Deed Record Data also available by subscription at https://de.uslandrecords.com/delr/DelrApp/index.jsp; fee is $10.00 per 30 days.
Property, Taxation Records Free   Access county property data free at http://400.co.kent.de.us/PropInfo/PIName.HTM. Also locate parcels on the GIS-mapping site free at http://66.173.241.168/kent_co/ but no name searching and you must chose a 'hundred.'

New Castle County *Real Estate, Deed, Marriage, Corporation Records* www.ncc-deeds.com/recclkshr/default.asp
Free   Access to the Recorder of Deeds database is free at www.ncc-deeds.com/recclkshr/.
Property, Taxation Records Free   County property data is found at www.nccde.org/parcelview/. No name searching.

Sussex County *Property, Taxation Records* Free   Access tax info free at www.sussexcounty.net/e-gov/propertytaxes/propsearch.cfm or www.sussexcounty.net/e-service/propertytaxes/index.cfm?resource=search_page. Search parcels on GIS-mapping site free at http://map.sussexcountyde.gov/. Search current sheriff sale list free at www.sussexcountyde.gov/dept/sheriff/. Search county tax data free at www.sussexcountyde.gov/e-service/propertytaxes/index.cfm?resource=search_page.

District of Columbia

Time Zone: EST
Population: 588,292
# of Divisions/Counties: 1

Useful State Links

Website: www.dc.gov
Governor: http://dc.gov/mayor/index.shtm
State Statutes and Codes: http://government.westlaw.com/linkedslice/default.asp?SP=DCC-1000
Legislative Bill Search: www.dccouncil.us/lims/default.asp
Unclaimed Funds: http://cfo.washingtondc.gov/cfo/cwp/view,a,1326,q,590719,.asp

Primary State Agencies

Sexual Offender Registry `Free`

Metropolitan Police Department, Sex Offender Registry Unit, http://mpdc.dc.gov/mpdc/site/default.asp A list of Class A & B registered sex offenders is provided on the website. Under "Services" click on Sex Offender Registry.

Corporation, LP, LLC, Trade Name, Fictitious Name `Free`

Department of Consumer & Regulatory Affairs, Corporations Division, http://dcra.dc.gov/dcra/site/default.asp No online access to corporation or business entities filing records but the agency enables one to search for and reserve business names at http://mblr.dc.gov/corp/reservation/index.asp or simply search at http://mblr.dc.gov/corp/lookup/index.asp. *Other Options:* For information concerning lists and bulk file purchases, contact the Office of Information Services.

Uniform Commercial Code, Federal & State Tax Liens `Free & $$`

UCC Recorder, District of Columbia Recorder of Deeds, http://otr.cfo.dc.gov/otr/cwp/view,a,1330,q,594562.asp Search the index by name or document number at www.washington.dc.us.landata.com/. Registration is required. There are two commercial plans to purchase images. Note this for all recorded documents, not just UCC. A Subscriber pays $175 per month for unlimited views of images and $2.00 per document image downloaded. Accounts are also available for larger firms with multiple users. A registered "non-subscriber" pays no fee to view documents and $4.00 per document mage downloaded.

Driver Records `$$`

Department of Motor Vehicles, Driver Records Division, www.dmv.dc.gov/serv/dlicense.shtm Online requests are taken throughout the day and are available in batch the next morning after 8:15 am. There is no minimum order requirement. Fee is $13.00 per record; only the ten-year record is sold. Requesters are restricted to high volume, ongoing users. Each requester must be approved, sign a contract and pay a $100 annual fee. Billing is a "bank" system which draws from pre-paid account. For more information, call 202-727-5692.

Voter Registration `Free`

DC Board of Elections and Ethics, Voter Registration Records, www.dcboee.org One may check voter registration status at www.dcboee.org/voterreg/vic_step1.asp. Name, DOB and ZIP are required. *Other Options:* Records can be purchased on CD and on printed lists. A variety of data is available from party registration to voter history. Minimum fee is $50 plus $10 for a CD. Call at 202-727-2525 for details.

Birth Certificates `$$`

Department of Health, Vital Records Division, http://doh.dc.gov/doh/site/default.asp Orders may be placed online via a state designated vendor at www.vitalchek.com.

Death Records `Free & $$`

Department of Health, Vital Records Division, http://doh.dc.gov/doh/site/default.asp Orders may be placed online via a state designated vendor at www.vitalchek.com. Also, a Nationwide Gravesite Locator is located at http://gravelocator.cem.va.gov/j2ee/servlet/NGL_v1. Includes VA, national, state, military, veteran, DOI, and where grave is marked with a government grave marker.

Occupational Licensing Boards

Acupuncturist .... http://app.hpla.doh.dc.gov/weblookup/

Addiction Counselor.......................... http://app.hpla.doh.dc.gov/weblookup/

Alcohol Mfg/Vendor/Dis/Serv/Seller http://abra.dc.gov/abra/site/default.asp

Alcohol Susp'd/Revk'd License .... http://abra.dc.gov/abra/site/default.asp

Appraiser, Real Estate .... www.asc.gov/content/category1/appr_by_state.asp

Attorney... www.dcbar.org/find_a_member/index.cfm

Bank .... http://dbfi.dc.gov/dbfi/cwp/view,a,3,q,585840,dbfiNav,|31299|.asp

Barber .... www.asisvcs.com/indhome_fs.asp?CPCAT=1309STATEREG

Bingo Operation .... www.dclottery.com

Boxing Event/Professional .... www.asisvcs.com/indhome_fs.asp?CPCAT=BX09STATEREG

Card Tournament................................ www.dclottery.com

Check Casher..................................... http://app.dbfi.dc.gov/ifs/default.asp

Chiropractor....................................... http://app.hpla.doh.dc.gov/weblookup/

Cosmetologist.................................... www.asisvcs.com/indhome_fs.asp?CPCAT=2009STATEREG

Counselor, Professional .... http://app.hpla.doh.dc.gov/weblookup/

Dance Therapist................................. http://app.hpla.doh.dc.gov/weblookup/

Dentist/Dental Hygienist .... http://app.hpla.doh.dc.gov/weblookup/

Dietitian/Nutritionist......................... http://app.hpla.doh.dc.gov/weblookup/

Electrician.. www.asisvcs.com/indhome_fs.asp?CPCAT=3609STATEREG

Engineer .... www.asisvcs.com/indhome_fs.asp?CPCAT=EN09STATEREG

Funeral Director................................. www.asisvcs.com/indhome_fs.asp?CPCAT=FN09STATEREG

Gambling Party/Event .... www.dclottery.com

Insurance Broker/Agent..................... https://sbs-dc-public.naic.org/Lion-Web/jsp/sbsreports/AgentLookup.jsp

Insurance Company .... http://disb.dc.gov/disr/cwp/view,a,1300,q,581346,disrnav_gid,1644.asp

Investment Advisor www.finra.org/InvestorInformation/InvestorProtection/p005882

Lobbyist... http://ocf.dc.gov/WebsiteReports/repperiod_lob.asp

Lottery Retailer.................................. www.dclottery.com

Massage Therapist .... http://app.hpla.doh.dc.gov/weblookup/

Medical Doctor.................................. http://app.hpla.doh.dc.gov/weblookup/

Midwife Nurse................................... http://app.hpla.doh.dc.gov/weblookup/

Money Lender/Money Transmitter.... http://app.dbfi.dc.gov/ifs/default.asp

Mortgage Broker/Lender .... http://app.dbfi.dc.gov/ifs/default.asp

Naturopath... http://app.hpla.doh.dc.gov/weblookup/

Nurse Anesthetist............................... http://app.hpla.doh.dc.gov/weblookup/

Nurse, Clinical/or/LPN/RN .... http://app.hpla.doh.dc.gov/weblookup/

Nursing Home Administrator .... http://app.hpla.doh.dc.gov/weblookup/

Occupational Therapist...................... http://app.hpla.doh.dc.gov/weblookup/

Optometrist.. http://app.hpla.doh.dc.gov/weblookup/

Osteopath... http://app.hpla.doh.dc.gov/weblookup/

Pharmacist/Pharmacy .... http://app.hpla.doh.dc.gov/weblookup/

Physical Therapist .... http://app.hpla.doh.dc.gov/weblookup/

Physician Assistant............................ http://app.hpla.doh.dc.gov/weblookup/

Plumber .... www.asisvcs.com/indhome_fs.asp?CPCAT=4909STATEREG

Podiatrist.. http://app.hpla.doh.dc.gov/weblookup/

Political Campaign Contributor .... http://ocf.dc.gov/dsearch/dsearch.asp

Psychologist....................................... http://app.hpla.doh.dc.gov/weblookup/

Raffle... www.dclottery.com

Real Estate Agent/Broker/Seller https://www.asisvcs.com/services/licensing/Dcopla/LicRenewals/LrIndex.asp?CBCAT=0909BR

Real Estate Appraiser .... www.asc.gov/content/category1/appr_by_state.asp

Real Estate School.............http://dcra.dc.gov/dcra/cwp/view,a,1342,q,600757,dcraNav_GID,1697,dcraNav,|33466|.asp

Recreational Therapist....................... http://app.hpla.doh.dc.gov/weblookup/

Respiratory Care................................ http://app.hpla.doh.dc.gov/weblookup/

Sales Finance Company..................... http://app.dbfi.dc.gov/ifs/default.asp

Securities Agent/Broker/Dealer......... www.finra.org/InvestorInformation/InvestorProtection/p005882

Social Worker.....................................http://app.hpla.doh.dc.gov/weblookup/
Taxi Dispatch ....www.dctaxi.dc.gov/dctaxi/cwp/view.asp?a=1187&q=487917
Taxi Fleet/Company ....www.dctaxi.dc.gov/dctaxi/cwp/view.asp?a=1187&q=487910
Taxi Insurer ....www.dctaxi.dc.gov/dctaxi/cwp/view.asp?a=1187&q=487938

Courts

DC Court Structure: The Superior Court handles all local trial matters, including civil, criminal, family court, probate, tax, landlord-tenant, small claims, and traffic. Divisions include Civil, Criminal, Family, Domestic, and Probate. Eviction records are found at the Landlord & Tenant Branch.

District of Columbia
Superior Court - Civil   www.dccourts.gov/dccourts/superior/civil/index.jsp   **Free**
Access civil records free at https://www.dccourts.gov/pa/. Attorneys and legal professionals participating in the e-Filing Project must register for the CaseFileXpress eFile service either by logging onto www.lexisnexis.com/courtlink/online/ or calling 1-877-433-4533.

Superior Court - Small Claims Division and Landlord & Tenant Branch   **Free**
Access records free at https://www.dccourts.gov/pa/.

The Superior Court and Court of Appeals offer access to opinions at www.dccourts.gov/dccourts/index.jsp.

Recorders, Assessors, and Other Sites of Note

Recording Office Organization: Recording officer is the Recorder of Deeds. Financing statements are filed with the Recorder, including real estate related collateral. Federal tax liens on personal property of businesses are filed with the Secretary of State. Other federal and all state tax liens on personal property are filed with the Recorder. Note- a taxpayers who resides outside the U.S.A. is deemed to be a resident of D.C.

District of Columbia *Real Estate, Deed, Judgment, Lien, UCC Records* www.dc.gov   **Free & $$**   As
mentioned above, search the recorders database at www.washington.dc.us.landata.com. Registration is required; search index for free; $4.00 fee to view and copy. Subscribe for $175.00 per month or per use, and get docs for $2.00 per page. Records go back to 1973.
Property, Taxation Records   **Free**   Search the real property database at
https://www.taxpayerservicecenter.com/RP_Search.jsp?search_type=Assessment Search the real estate sales database at
https://www.taxpayerservicecenter.com/RP_Search.jsp?search_type=Sales. Search the tax sales list at
http://otr.cfo.dc.gov/otr/frames.asp?doc=/otr/lib/otr/532250601.pdf.

Florida

Capital: Tallahassee
            Leon County

Time Zone: EST

Florida's ten western-most counties are CST:
They are: Bay, Calhoun, Escambia, Gulf, Holmes,
Jackson, Okaloosa, Santa Rosa, Walton, Washington.

Population: 18,251,243

# of Counties: 67

Useful State Links

Website: www.myflorida.gov
Governor: www.myflorida.com/b_eog/owa/b_eog_www.html.main_page
Attorney General: http://myfloridalegal.com
State Archives: http://dlis.dos.state.fl.us/index.cfm
State Statutes and Codes: www.flsenate.gov/Statutes/index.cfm?submenu=-1&Tab=statutes
Legislative Bill Search: www.flsenate.gov/Welcome/index.cfm
Unclaimed Funds: www.fltreasurehunt.org/ControlServlet?ActionForm=GotoNewPublicSearch

Primary State Agencies

Criminal Records  Free & $$

Florida Department of Law Enforcement, User Services Bureau, www.fdle.state.fl.us Criminal history information may be ordered over the Department Program Internet site at https://www2.fdle.state.fl.us/cchinet/. The $23.00 fee applies. Juvenile records from 10/1994 forward are also available. Credit card ordering will return records to your screen or via email. Search state's wanted list at http://www3.fdle.state.fl.us/fdle/wpersons_search.asp.

Sexual Offender Registry Free

Florida Department of Law Enforcement, Offender Regsitration and Tracking Srvs, http://offender.fdle.state.fl.us/offender/homepage.do Search the registry from the web page. Searching can be done by name or by geographic area.

Incarceration Records Free

Florida Department of Corrections, Central Records Office, www.dc.state.fl.us Extensive search capabilities are offered at www.dc.state.fl.us/inmateinfo/inmateinfomenu.asp. Click on Inmate Population Information Search. *Other Options:* Bulk data may be purchased on a CD.

Corporation, LP, LLC, Trademarks/Servicemarks, Fictitious Names, Federal Tax Liens Free

Division of Corporations, Department of State, www.sunbiz.org The state's excellent Internet site gives detailed information on all corporate, trademark, limited liability company and limited partnerships; fictitious names; and lien records. Images of filed documents are available from 1996/7 to present. *Other Options:* This agency offers record purchases on microfiche sets and on CD disks.

Uniform Commercial Code Free

UCC Filings, FLORIDAUCC, Inc, www.floridaucc.com The Internet site allows access for no charge. Search by name or document number, for records 1997 to present. TIFF images of Florida UCC filings can be downloaded from the Internet for all filings from 1997 to present. Tax Liens are not included with UCC filing information. *Other Options:* Microfilm reels and CD's of images are available for bulk purchase requesters. Call for more information.

Workers' Compensation Records `Free`

Workers Compensation Division, Data Quality Section, www.fldfs.com/wc/ A myriad of information is available at www.fldfs.com/wc/databases.html. Access to the claims history database is provided, all personal information has been redacted.

Driver Records `Free & $$`

Division of Drivers Licenses, Bureau of Records, www.flhsmv.gov/ Record access online has been privatized through Network Providers. Requesters with 5,000 or more records per month are considered Network Providers. Requesters with less than 5,000 requests per month (called Individual Users) are directed to a Provider. Call 850-617-2014 to become a Provider. A list of providers is found at the website. The state fee is as stated above; Providers add a service fee, which varies by vendor. Online requests are processed on an interactive basis. Check the status of any Florida Driver License free at https://www6.hsmv.state.fl.us/dlcheck/dlchecking. Simply enter the driver license number. *Other Options:* This agency will process batch data via FTP or tape cartridge for approved users. Call 850-617-2634 for more details.

Vehicle Ownership & Registration `Free & $$`

Division of Motor Vehicles, Information Research Unit - MS73, www.flhsmv.gov/html/titlinf.html For a free vehicle status check enter the title # or VIN to check vehicle status at https://www6.hsmv.state.fl.us/rrdmvcheck/mvchecking. Florida has contracted to release detailed vehicle information through approved Network Providers. Accounts must first be approved by the state. For each record accessed, the charge is $.50 plus a transactional fee, and the subscriber fee. Users must work from an estimated 2 1/2 month pre-paid bank. New subscribers must complete an application with the Department, call 850-617-2634.

Occupational Licensing Boards

Acupuncturist http://ww2.doh.state.fl.us/irm00praes/praslist.asp
Air Ambulance .... www.doh.state.fl.us/demo/ems/Providers/Providers.html
Air Conditioning Contractor/Svc https://www.myfloridalicense.com/wl11.asp
Alcoholic Beverage Permit https://www.myfloridalicense.com/wl11.asp
Ambulance Service .... www.doh.state.fl.us/demo/ems/Providers/Providers.html
Architectural Firm/Individual https://www.myfloridalicense.com/wl11.asp
Athletic Agent https://www.myfloridalicense.com/wl11.asp
Athletic Trainer http://ww2.doh.state.fl.us/irm00praes/praslist.asp
Attorney .... www.floridabar.org/names.nsf/MESearch?OpenForm
Auctioneer/Auction Firm https://www.myfloridalicense.com/wl11.asp
Audiologist http://ww2.doh.state.fl.us/irm00praes/praslist.asp
Automobile Repossessor .... http://licgweb.doacs.state.fl.us/access/individual.html
Barber/Barber Assistant/Shop https://www.myfloridalicense.com/wl11.asp
Boxer https://www.myfloridalicense.com/wl11.asp
Building Code Administrator https://www.myfloridalicense.com/wl11.asp
Building Contractor/or/Inspector https://www.myfloridalicense.com/wl11.asp
Cemetery/Cem. Lot Salesperson .... https://apps.fldfs.com/fclicense/searchpage.aspx
Child Care Center .... www.dcf.state.fl.us/childcare/
Chiropractic-related Occupation http://ww2.doh.state.fl.us/irm00praes/praslist.asp
Chiropractor http://ww2.doh.state.fl.us/irm00praes/praslist.asp
Clinical Lab Personnel http://ww2.doh.state.fl.us/irm00praes/praslist.asp
Community Assoc. Manager https://www.myfloridalicense.com/wl11.asp
Company in Receivership .... www.fldfs.com/Receiver/receivership_list.asp
Construction Qualified Business https://www.myfloridalicense.com/wl11.asp
Continuing Edu. Provider, Medical ... http://ww2.doh.state.fl.us/irm00praes/praslist.asp
Contractor, General https://www.myfloridalicense.com/wl11.asp
Contractor, Residential https://www.myfloridalicense.com/wl11.asp
Cosmetologist, Nails/Salon https://www.myfloridalicense.com/wl11.asp
Crematory .... https://apps.fldfs.com/fclicense/searchpage.aspx
Day Care/Child Care/Nursery Sch'l ... www.dcf.state.fl.us/childcare/
Dentist/Dental Assistant http://ww2.doh.state.fl.us/irm00praes/praslist.asp
Dietician/Nutritionist http://ww2.doh.state.fl.us/irm00praes/praslist.asp
Doctor, Limited http://ww2.doh.state.fl.us/irm00praes/praslist.asp
Drywall/Gypsum Specialty Contr https://www.myfloridalicense.com/wl11.asp
Electrical Contractor https://www.myfloridalicense.com/wl11.asp
Electrologist/Electrologist Facility http://ww2.doh.state.fl.us/irm00praes/praslist.asp

Elevator Certificates of Operation https://www.myfloridalicense.com/wl11.asp
Embalmer .... https://apps.fldfs.com/fclicense/searchpage.aspx
Emergency Medical Technician .... www.doh.state.fl.us/demo/ems/Providers/Providers.html
Employee Leasing Company https://www.myfloridalicense.com/wl11.asp
Engineer .... www.fbpe.org/engineeringdirectory.asp
Engineering Firm .... www.fbpe.org/engineeringdirectory.asp
Finance Company, Consumer........... www.flofr.com/licensing/licensecheck.htm
Firearm Instructor/School/Agency .... https://licgweb.doacs.state.fl.us/account_maintenance/index.html
Firearms Instructor .... http://licgweb.doacs.state.fl.us/access/individual.html
Firearms License, Statewide.............. http://licgweb.doacs.state.fl.us/access/individual.html
Food Services Establishment............. https://www.myfloridalicense.com/wl11.asp
Fumigation Performance Special ID.. www.flaes.org/aes%2Dent/
Funeral Director/Funeral Home......... https://apps.fldfs.com/fclicense/searchpage.aspx
Gas Line Specialty Contractor........... https://www.myfloridalicense.com/wl11.asp
Geologist/Geology Firm https://www.myfloridalicense.com/wl11.asp
Hair Braider.................................... https://www.myfloridalicense.com/wl11.asp
Hearing Aid Specialist...................... http://ww2.doh.state.fl.us/irm00praes/praslist.asp
Home Improvement Financer .... www.flofr.com/licensing/licensecheck.htm
Hotel/Restaurant https://www.myfloridalicense.com/wl11.asp
In Home Family Day Care Center ..... www.dcf.state.fl.us/childcare/
Insect Sting Treatment Specialist ...... www.doh.state.fl.us/demo/ems/Providers/Providers.html
Installment Seller, Retail .... www.flofr.com/licensing/licensecheck.htm
Insurance Adjust/Agent/Title Agent.. www.fldfs.com/data/aar_alis1/
Insurance-related Company .... www.fldfs.com/Data/CompanySearch/index.asp
Interior Design Business/Individual .. https://www.myfloridalicense.com/wl11.asp
Investment Advisor .... www.flofr.com/licensing/licensecheck.htm
Kickboxer https://www.myfloridalicense.com/wl11.asp
Land Sale, Condominiums https://www.myfloridalicense.com/wl11.asp
Landscape Architecture Firm/Ind'v'l. https://www.myfloridalicense.com/wl11.asp
Landscape Maint./Pest Mgmt Co....... www.flaes.org/aes%2Dent/
Liquor Store.................................... https://www.myfloridalicense.com/wl11.asp
Lobbyist/Principal .... www.leg.state.fl.us/lobbyist/
Lodging Establishment https://www.myfloridalicense.com/wl11.asp
Marriage & Family Therapist http://ww2.doh.state.fl.us/irm00praes/praslist.asp
Massage Therapist/School/Facility.... http://ww2.doh.state.fl.us/irm00praes/praslist.asp
Mechanical Contractor https://www.myfloridalicense.com/wl11.asp
Medical Doctor................................ http://ww2.doh.state.fl.us/irm00praes/praslist.asp
Medical Faculty Member................... http://ww2.doh.state.fl.us/irm00praes/praslist.asp
Mental Health Counselor.................. http://ww2.doh.state.fl.us/irm00praes/praslist.asp
Midwife http://ww2.doh.state.fl.us/irm00praes/praslist.asp
Mobile Home................................... https://www.myfloridalicense.com/wl11.asp
Money Transmitter .... www.flofr.com/licensing/licensecheck.htm
Monument Dealer............................. https://apps.fldfs.com/fclicense/searchpage.aspx
Mortgage Broker .... www.flofr.com/licensing/licensecheck.htm
Mortgage Business School .... www.flofr.com/licensing/licensecheck.htm
Motel/Restaurant https://www.myfloridalicense.com/wl11.asp
Nail Specialist................................. https://www.myfloridalicense.com/wl11.asp
Naturopath/Naturopathic Physician ... http://ww2.doh.state.fl.us/irm00praes/praslist.asp
Notary Public.................................. http://notaries.dos.state.fl.us/not001.html
Nuclear Radiology Physicist.............. http://ww2.doh.state.fl.us/irm00praes/praslist.asp
Nurse, Practical http://ww2.doh.state.fl.us/irm00praes/praslist.asp
Nurse/Nursing Assistant................... http://ww2.doh.state.fl.us/irm00praes/praslist.asp
Nursing Home Administrator http://ww2.doh.state.fl.us/irm00praes/praslist.asp
Nutrition Counselor http://ww2.doh.state.fl.us/irm00praes/praslist.asp
Occupational Therapist...................... http://ww2.doh.state.fl.us/irm00praes/praslist.asp
Optician/Optician Apprentice http://ww2.doh.state.fl.us/irm00praes/praslist.asp
Optometrist..................................... http://ww2.doh.state.fl.us/irm00praes/praslist.asp

Orthotist/Prosthetist............................http://ww2.doh.state.fl.us/irm00praes/praslist.asp
Osteopathic Physician........................http://ww2.doh.state.fl.us/irm00praes/praslist.asp
Paramedic ....www.doh.state.fl.us/demo/ems/Providers/Providers.html
Pari-Mutuel Wagering https://www.myfloridalicense.com/wl11.asp
Pedorthist..http://ww2.doh.state.fl.us/irm00praes/praslist.asp
Pest Control Operator/Applicator www.flaes.org/aes%2Dent/
Pest Control, Structural......................www.flaes.org/aes%2Dent/
Pharmacist, Consulting......................http://ww2.doh.state.fl.us/irm00praes/praslist.asp
Pharmacist/Pharmacist Intern http://ww2.doh.state.fl.us/irm00praes/praslist.asp
PHPC Public Health Pest Control......www.flaes.org/aes%2Dent/
Physical Therapist/Assistant..............http://ww2.doh.state.fl.us/irm00praes/praslist.asp
Physician Assistant............................http://ww2.doh.state.fl.us/irm00praes/praslist.asp
Physicist, Medical.............................http://ww2.doh.state.fl.us/irm00praes/praslist.asp
Pilot, State/Deputy............................https://www.myfloridalicense.com/wl11.asp
Plumbing Contractor https://www.myfloridalicense.com/wl11.asp
Pollutant Storage System Contr.........https://www.myfloridalicense.com/wl11.asp
Polygraph Assn Member ....www.floridapolygraph.org/directory/
Polygraph Examiner ....www.floridapolygraph.org/directory/
Precision Tank Tester https://www.myfloridalicense.com/wl11.asp
Preneed Seller, Funeral......................https://apps.fldfs.com/fclicense/searchpage.aspx
Private Investigator/Agency ....http://licgweb.doacs.state.fl.us/access/individual.html
Psychologist/Ltd License Psycholog't http://ww2.doh.state.fl.us/irm00praes/praslist.asp
Public Accountant-CPA https://www.myfloridalicense.com/wl11.asp
Racing, Dog/Horse https://www.myfloridalicense.com/wl11.asp
Radiologic Physician http://ww2.doh.state.fl.us/irm00praes/praslist.asp
Radiologist http://ww2.doh.state.fl.us/irm00praes/praslist.asp
Real Estate Agent/Broker/Sales.........https://www.myfloridalicense.com/wl11.asp
Real Estate Appraiser https://www.myfloridalicense.com/wl11.asp
Recovery Agent School/Instrct./Mgr. http://licgweb.doacs.state.fl.us/access/agency.html
Recovery Agent/Agency/Intern ....http://licgweb.doacs.state.fl.us/access/agency.html
Respiratory Care Therapist/Provider . http://ww2.doh.state.fl.us/irm00praes/praslist.asp
Roofing Contractor https://www.myfloridalicense.com/wl11.asp
Sales Finance Company......................www.flofr.com/licensing/licensecheck.htm
School Psychologist...........................http://ww2.doh.state.fl.us/irm00praes/praslist.asp
Securities Agent/Broker Dealer/Sell.. www.flofr.com/licensing/licensecheck.htm
Securities Dealer................................www.flofr.com/licensing/licensecheck.htm
Securities Registration.......................www.flofr.com/licensing/licensecheck.htm
Security Officer School ....http://licgweb.doacs.state.fl.us/access/agency.html
Security Officer/Instructor.................http://licgweb.doacs.state.fl.us/access/individual.html
Sheet Metal Contractor......................https://www.myfloridalicense.com/wl11.asp
Social Worker, Clinical/Master http://ww2.doh.state.fl.us/irm00praes/praslist.asp
Solar Contractor https://www.myfloridalicense.com/wl11.asp
Solid Waste Facility Operator ....http://landfill.treeo.ufl.edu/Reports.aspx
Specialty Structure Contractor...........https://www.myfloridalicense.com/wl11.asp
Speech-Language Pathologist.............http://ww2.doh.state.fl.us/irm00praes/praslist.asp
Surveyor, Mapping https://www.myfloridalicense.com/wl11.asp
Swimming Pool/Spa Contr./Svc https://www.myfloridalicense.com/wl11.asp
Talent Agency https://www.myfloridalicense.com/wl11.asp
Teacher..www.fldoe.org/edcert/
Therapeutic Radiologic Physician http://ww2.doh.state.fl.us/irm00praes/praslist.asp
Tobacco Wholesale https://www.myfloridalicense.com/wl11.asp
Underground Utility Contractor https://www.myfloridalicense.com/wl11.asp
Veterinarian/Veterinary Establish't ...https://www.myfloridalicense.com/wl11.asp
Visiting Mental Health Faculty http://ww2.doh.state.fl.us/irm00praes/praslist.asp
X-ray, Pod, Assistant.........................http://ww2.doh.state.fl.us/irm00praes/praslist.asp
Yacht & Ship Broker/Salesman.........https://www.myfloridalicense.com/wl11.asp

State and Local Courts

State Court Structure: Circuit courts have general trial jurisdiction over matters not assigned by statute to the county courts and also hear appeals from county court cases. Thus, circuit courts are simultaneously the highest trial courts and the lowest appellate courts in Florida's judicial system.

The trial jurisdiction of Circuit Courts includes, among other matters, original jurisdiction over civil disputes involving more than $15,000; controversies involving the estates of decedents, minors, and persons adjudicated as incapacitated; cases relating to juveniles; criminal prosecutions for all felonies; tax disputes; actions to determine the title and boundaries of real property; suits for declaratory judgments that is, to determine the legal rights or responsibilities of parties under the terms of written instruments, laws, or regulations before a dispute arises and leads to litigation; and requests for injunctions to prevent persons or entities from acting in a manner that is asserted to be unlawful. The trial jurisdiction of County Courts is established by statute. The jurisdiction of county courts extends to civil disputes involving $15,000 or less.

Many counties have combined Circuit and County Courts. The Circuit Court is the court of general jurisdiction. The bulk of trial court decisions that are appealed are never heard by the Supreme Court. Rather, they are reviewed by three-judge panels of the District Courts of Appeal.

Statewide Court Online Access: Many courts offer online access to the public, usually through the Clerk of the Circuit Court. Fees are involved when ordering copies; save $1.50 per record by becoming a subscriber. Visit www.flcourts.org/gen_public/stratplan/privacy.shtml for the latest information regarding the electronic release of court records in Florida.

Search Supreme Court dockets online at http://jweb.flcourts.org/pls/docket/ds_docket_search.

Alachua County

Circuit & County Courts www.clerk-alachua-fl.org/Clerk/index.cfm `Free & $$`

Civil: Civil records can be searched www.clerk-alachua-fl.org/clerk/pubrec.html. Also, access an index of judgments & recorded documents at www.myfloridacounty.com. Fees involved to order copies; save $1.50 per record by becoming a subscriber. Also, search probate and other ancient records free at www.clerk-alachua-fl.org/archive/default.cfm. *Criminal:* Search traffic citations at http://assets.alachuacounty.us/ws/applications-asp/Traffic/.

Baker County

Circuit & County Courts - http://bakercountyfl.org/clerk `Free & $$`

Civil: Access an index of judgments, liens, recorded documents at www.myfloridacounty.com. Fees involved to order copies; save $1.50 per record by becoming a subscriber. *Criminal:* Access the circuit-wide criminal quick lookup at http://circuit8.org/golem/gencrim.html. Account and password is required; restricted usage. Call the court for details.

Bay County

Circuit Court - Civil www.baycoclerk.com `Free`

Civil: Also, search the court cases, including traffic and probate, for free at www.clerk.co.bay.fl.us/ovationweb/search.aspx. Also, access an index of judgments, liens, recorded documents at www.myfloridacounty.com. Fees involved to order copies; save $1.50 per record by becoming a subscriber.

Circuit Court - Criminal www.baycoclerk.com `Free`

Criminal: Search court cases free at www.clerk.co.bay.fl.us/ovationweb/search.aspx.

Circuit Court - Probate Division http://www.baycoclerk.com `Free` Search probate records free at www.clerk.co.bay.fl.us/ovationweb/search.aspx.

County Court - Civil www.baycoclerk.com `Free & $$`

Civil: Access an index of judgments, liens, recorded documents at www.myfloridacounty.com. Fees involved to order copies; save $1.50 per record by becoming a subscriber. Also, search the court cases, including traffic and probate, for free at www.clerk.co.bay.fl.us/ovationweb/search.aspx.

Bradford County

Circuit Court http://circuit8.org `Free & $$`

Civil: Access an index of judgments, liens, recorded documents at www.myfloridacounty.com. Fees involved to order copies; save $1.50 per record by becoming a subscriber. *Criminal:* Access to the circuit-wide criminal quick lookup is at http://circuit8.org/golem/gencrim.html. Account and password is required; restricted usage.

County Court www.bradford-co-fla.org `Free & $$`
Civil: Access an index of judgments, liens, recorded documents at www.myfloridacounty.com. Fees involved to order copies; save $1.50 per record by becoming a subscriber.

Brevard County

Circuit Court - www.brevardclerk.us `Free`
Access civl and criminal record index free at http://webinfo4.brevardclerk.us/facts/facts_search.cfm. Online records back to 1988 can be searched by name, case number or citation number.

County Court - Misdemeanor www.brevardclerk.us `Free`
Access records index free at http://webinfo4.brevardclerk.us/facts/facts_search.cfm. Online records back to 1989 can be searched by name, case number or citation number.

Broward County

Circuit & County Courts www.clerk-17th-flcourts.org/ `Free`
Civil: Basic information is free at www.browardclerk.org/bccoc2/default.asp. Search by name, case number or case type. A premium service with fees for full docket info is available. Direct email record requests to eclerk@browardclerk.org. *Criminal:* Basic information free at www.browardclerk.org/bccoc2/default.asp. Search by name. case number or case type. Also, there is a "Premium Access" for detailed case information; requires a fee, registration and password. Call 954-831-5654 for information or visit the website. Also, direct email record requests to eclerk@browardclerk.org.

Calhoun County

Circuit & County Court www.calhounclerk.com `Free & $$`
Civil: Access an index of judgments, liens, recorded documents at www.myfloridacounty.com. Fees involved to order copies; save $1.50 per record by becoming a subscriber.

Charlotte County

Circuit & County Courts - Civil Division http://co.charlotte.fl.us/clrkinfo/clerk_default.htm `Free`
Civil: Access civil court records free at
http://208.47.160.68/Magic94Scripts/mgrqispi94.dll?APPNAME=civ_casweb&PRGNAME=PUBSEARCHF. Also, online access to civil and probate records is by subscription, see the website. First payment is $186.00 ($150 refundable) plus a usage fee based on # of transactions. Allows copy printing. For info, call 941-637-4848. Also, access an index of judgments, liens, recorded documents at www.myfloridacounty.com fees for copies.

Circuit & County Courts - Criminal Division http://co.charlotte.fl.us/clrkinfo/clerk_default.htm `Free`
Criminal: Access index free at
https://www.co.charlotte.fl.us/scripts/mgrqispi.dll?appname=MPI%20Criminal&prgname=PUBSEARCHF. Name and birthdate required to search.

Citrus County

Circuit Court www.clerk.citrus.fl.us/home.jsp `Free & $$`
Civil: View court record index (no images) free at www.clerk.citrus.fl.us/home.jsp; Subscription system giving full identifiers also available. Also there is an index of judgments, liens, recorded documents at www.myfloridacounty.com. Fees involved to order copies; save $1.50 per record by becoming a subscriber. *Criminal:* View court record index (no images) free at www.clerk.citrus.fl.us/home.jsp; Subscription system giving full address and DOB identifiers also available.

County Court www.clerk.citrus.fl.us/home.jsp `Free & $$`
Civil: View court record index (no images) free at www.clerk.citrus.fl.us/home.jsp; Subscription system with identifiers also available. Access an index of judgments, liens, recorded documents at www.myfloridacounty.com/services/official records_intro.shtml; Fees involved to order copies; save $1.50 per record by becoming a subscriber. *Criminal:* same.

Clay County

Circuit Court http://clerk.co.clay.fl.us `Free`
Civil: Clerk of the circuit court provides free access to records at http://clerk.co.clay.fl.us/asp/pub_pi_queryname.asp. Access an index of judgments, liens, recorded documents at www.myfloridacounty.com. Fees involved to order copies; save $1.50 per record by becoming a subscriber. *Criminal:* Access to criminal records is free at http://clerk.co.clay.fl.us/asp/cr_pi_queryname.asp.

County Court http://clayclerk.com/default.html `Free & $$`
Civil: Access civil records free at http://clerk.co.clay.fl.us/asp/pub_pi_queryname.asp. Online records go back to 1992. *Criminal:* Access criminal records free at http://clerk.co.clay.fl.us/asp/cr_pi_queryname.asp.

Collier County

Circuit Court www.clerk.collier.fl.us `Free`
Civil: Online access is free at www.clerk.collier.fl.us/PLB/default.htm. Records include probate, traffic and domestic. Access an index of judgments, liens, recorded documents at www.myfloridacounty.com. Fees involved to order copies; save $1.50 per record by becoming a subscriber. *Criminal:* Criminal records access is free at www.collierclerk.com/.

County Court   www.clerk.collier.fl.us   `Free`
Civil: Online access is free at www.clerk.collier.fl.us/PLB/default.htm. Records include probate, traffic and domestic. *Criminal:* Criminal records access is free at www.collierclerk.com/.

Columbia County

Circuit & County Courts   http://www2.myfloridacounty.com/wps/wcm/connect/columbiaclerk   `Free`
Civil: Access to County Clerk of Circuit Court records is at https://www2.myfloridacounty.com/ccm/?county=12 *Criminal:* Same.

Dade County

Circuit & County Courts - Civil   www.miami-dadeclerk.com/dadecoc/   `Free & $$`
Civil: Clerk of Court's online services- choose between Standard (free) and Premier fee-based services. Subscribers to the Premier service may access 3 advanced options: Civil/Family/Probate, Public Records, Traffic. Fees based on # of units purchased; minimum $5.00 in advance. Also, though limited, search felony, misdemeanor, civil and county ordinance violations free at www.miami-dadeclerk.com/cjis/default.asp. Search Civil/Family/Probate free at www.miami-dadeclerk.com/dadecoc/.

Circuit & County Courts - Criminal   www.miami-dadeclerk.com/dadecoc/   `Free & $$`
 Criminal: Free and Premier fee-based online services available. Though limited, search felony, misdemeanor, civil and county ordinance violations free at www.miami-dadeclerk.com/cjis/search1.asp. Subscribers to the Clerk's Premier Services may Access advanced options in 3 of the Clerk's internet-based systems: Civil/Family/Probate, Public Records, Traffic. Fee is $.25 per search, in advance. Also, search traffic cases free at www.miami-dadeclerk.com/spirit/publicsearch/defnamesearch.asp.

De Soto County

Circuit & County Courts   www.desotoclerk.com   `Free & $$`
Civil: Free access to civil, marriage/divorce, small claims, traffic/parking, Muni ordinances, domestic relations, name changes, foreclosures at www.desotoclerk.com. Also, access an index of judgments, liens, recorded documents at www.myfloridacounty.com. Fees involved to order copies; save $1.50 per record by becoming a subscriber. *Criminal:* Access to records at www.myfloridacounty.com. Fees involved to order copies.

Dixie County

Circuit & County Courts   http://www2.myfloridacounty.com/wps/wcm/connect/dixieclerk   `Free`
Civil: Access to County Clerk of Circuit Court records is at https://www2.myfloridacounty.com/ccm/?county=12 *Criminal:* Online access is the same as civil, see above.

Duval County

Circuit & County Courts - Civil Division   www.duvalclerk.com/ccWebsite/   `Free & $$`
Civil: Two sources are available. First, access court records free at https://showcase.duvalclerk.com/Login.aspx?ReturnUrl=%2fDefault.aspx. Access an index of judgments, liens, recorded documents at www.myfloridacounty.com. Fees involved to order copies; save $1.50 per record by becoming a subscriber.

Circuit & County Courts - Criminal Division   www.duvalclerk.com   `Free`
Criminal: Access court records free at https://showcase.duvalclerk.com/Login.aspx?ReturnUrl=%2fDefault.aspx.

Escambia County

Circuit & County Courts - Civil Division   www.escambiaclerk.com/   `Free`
Civil: Online access to county clerk records is free at the web page. Search by name, citation, or case number. Small claims, traffic, and marriage data also available. Access an index of judgments, liens, recorded documents at www.myfloridacounty.com. Fees involved to order copies; save $1.50 per record by becoming a subscriber.

Circuit & County Courts - Criminal Division   www.escambiaclerk.com/   `Free`
 Criminal: Online access to criminal records is free at web page. Search by name, citation, or case number.

Franklin County

Circuit & County Courts   www.franklinclerk.com
Civil: Access an index of judgments and recorded documents at www.myfloridacounty.com. Fees involved to order copies; save $1.50 per record by becoming a subscriber. *Criminal:* Access criminal records by subscription at https://www.myfloridacounty.com/subscription/. Fees are involved.

Gadsden County

Circuit & County Courts - Civil Division   www.clerk.co.gadsden.fl.us   `Free`
Civil: Access to the index of civil court judgments, etc. is free from the County Clerk at www.clerk.co.gadsden.fl.us. Direct email civil record requests to clerkofcourt@clerk.co.gadsden.fl.us. Also, access an index of judgments, liens, recorded documents at www.myfloridacounty.com. Fees involved to order copies; save $1.50 per record by becoming a subscriber.

Gilchrist County

Circuit & County Courts   http://gilchrist.fl.us/   `Free`

Civil: Search judgments and liens online at http://records.gilchrist.fl.us/oncoreweb/. Access to County Clerk of Circuit Court records is at https://www2.myfloridacounty.com/ccm/?county=21 *Criminal:* Access to County Clerk of Circuit Court records is at https://www2.myfloridacounty.com/ccm/?county=12.

Glades County
Circuit & County Courts   http://gladesclerk.com   `Free & $$`
Civil: Access an index of judgments only available at www.myfloridacounty.com. Fees involved to order copies; save $1.50 per record by becoming a subscriber.

Hamilton County
Circuit & County Courts   `Free & $$`
Civil: Access an index of judgments, liens, recorded documents at www.myfloridacounty.com. Fees involved to order copies; save $1.50 per record by becoming a subscriber.

Hardee County
Circuit & County Courts   www.hardeeclerk.com/   `Free`
Civil: Access an index of judgments, liens, recorded documents at www.myfloridacounty.com. Fees involved to order copies; save $1.50 per record by becoming a subscriber.

Hendry County
Circuit & County Courts   www.hendryclerk.org/   `Free`
Civil: Access an index of judgments, liens, recorded documents at www.myfloridacounty.com. Fees involved to order copies; save $1.50 per record by becoming a subscriber.

Hernando County
Circuit & County Courts   www.clerk.co.hernando.fl.us   `Free`
Civil: Online access to court records is free at www.clerk.co.hernando.fl.us/SearchType.asp. Online records may go as far back as 1/1983. Your browser must be JavaScript enables (MS Explorer 4.0 or above). Access an index of judgments, liens, recorded documents at www.myfloridacounty.com. Fees involved to order copies; save $1.50 per record by becoming a subscriber. *Criminal:* Same.

Highlands County
Circuit & County Courts   www.hcclerk.org   `Free & $$`
Civil: Access to county clerk civil and probate records is free at http://courts.hcclerk.org/iquery/ back to 1991. Also includes small claims, probate, and tax deeds. Access an index of judgments, liens, recorded documents at www.myfloridacounty.com. Fees involved to order copies; save $1.50 per record by becoming a subscriber. *Criminal:* Access a subscription for court records go to http://courts.hcclerk.org/iquery/.

Hillsborough County
Circuit & County Courts   www.hillsclerk.com/publicweb/home.aspx   `Free`
Civil: Online access to records at http://publicrecord.hillsclerk.com/. Search the Court Progress Dockets free at http://publicrecord.hillsclerk.com/courtdisclaimer.html. A subscription service is also available for records; visit the home page for details and fees. Also, access an index of judgments, liens, recorded documents at www.myfloridacounty.com. Fees involved to order copies; save $1.50 per record by becoming a subscriber. *Criminal:* Online access to Criminal Court Progress Dockets Search is same as civil.

Holmes County
Circuit & County Courts   www.holmesclerk.com/   `Free`
Civil: Access to County Clerk of Circuit Court records is at https://www2.myfloridacounty.com/ccm/?county=30 *Criminal:* Online access to criminal is the same as civil, see above.

Indian River County
Circuit & County Courts   www.clerk.indian-river.org   `Free & $$`
Civil: Online access to county recordings index is free at www.clerk.indian-river.org/recordssearch/ori.asp. Records go back to 1983. Full access to court records is via the clerk's subscription service. Fee is $25.00 per month, with onetime $100 setup fee. For information about free and fee access, call Gary at 772-567-8000 x1216. *Criminal:* Same.

Jackson County
Circuit & County Courts   www.jacksonclerk.com   `Free`
Civil: Access an index of judgments, liens, recorded documents at www.myfloridacounty.com. Fees involved to order copies; save $1.50 per record by becoming a subscriber.

Jefferson County
Circuit & County Courts   www.jeffersonclerk.com   `Free`
Civil: Access to County Clerk of Circuit Court records is at https://www2.myfloridacounty.com/ccm/?county=33 *Criminal:* Same.

Lafayette County

Circuit & County Courts   www.lafayetteclerk.com   `Free & $$`

Civil: Access an index of judgments, liens, recorded documents at www.myfloridacounty.com. Fees involved to order copies; save $1.50 per record by becoming a subscriber.

Lake County

Circuit & County Courts   www.lakecountyclerk.org/default1.asp   `Free`

Civil: Online access to Clerk of Court records is free at www.lakecountyclerk.org/services.asp?subject=Online_Court_Records. County civil records go back to 1985; Circuit records go back to 9/84. Also, previous 2-weeks civil records and divorces on a private site at http://extra.orlandosentinel.com/publicrecords/search.asp. *Criminal:* Online access is the same as civil, see above.

Lee County

Circuit & County Courts   www.leeclerk.org   `Free`

Civil: Access records free at www.leeclerk.org/court_inquiry_disclaimer.htm. Online records go back to 1988. Includes traffic, felony, misdemeanor, civil, small claims and probate. Access an index of judgments, liens, recorded documents at www.leeclerk.org or www.myfloridacounty.com. Search free but fees involved to order certified copies; save the per-record copy fee by becoming a subscriber; sub fee is $25.00 per month. *Criminal:* Same.

Leon County

Circuit & County Courts   www.clerk.leon.fl.us   `Free & $$`

Civil: Also, you may search cases and "High Profile Cases" (re: Election 2000) at www.clerk.leon.fl.us under "Search Court Databases." Registration required. Access an index of judgments, liens, recorded documents at www.myfloridacounty.com. Fees involved to order copies; save $1.50 per record by becoming a subscriber. *Criminal:* Online access for high profile cases only.

Liberty County

Circuit & County Courts   www.libertyclerk.com   `Free`

Civil: Access an index of judgments, liens, and civil court-related documents at www.myfloridacounty.com. Fees involved to order copies; save $1.50 per record by becoming a subscriber.

Madison County

Circuit & County Courts   `Free & $$`

Civil: Access an index of judgments, liens, recorded documents at www.myfloridacounty.com. Fees involved to order copies; save $1.50 per record by becoming a subscriber.

Manatee County

Circuit & County Courts   www.manateeclerk.com   `Free`

Civil: Access court records at Circuit clerk's office free at www.manateeclerk.com/mpa/cvweb.asp but images before 3/1/2004 are not available. Also, you may direct email record requests to lori.tolksdorf@manateeclerk.com. Access an index of judgments, liens, recorded documents at www.myfloridacounty.com. Fees involved to order copies; save $1.50 per record by becoming a subscriber. *Criminal:* Same.

Marion County

Circuit & County Courts   www.marioncountyclerk.org   `Free`

Civil: Online access to county clerk records is free at www.marioncountyclerk.org/. Click on Case Search found on left side under Courts. Access an index of judgments, liens, recorded documents at www.myfloridacounty.com. Fees involved to order copies; save $1.50 per record by becoming a subscriber. *Criminal:* Online access fro criminal same as civil.

Martin County

Circuit & County Courts   http://clerk-web.martin.fl.us/ClerkWeb   `Free`

Civil: Search all court records free at http://clerk-web.martin.fl.us/ClerkWeb/ccis_disclaimer.htm. Also includes small claims, recordings, other document types. Search online by name or SSN. *Criminal:* Search all court records free at http://clerk-web.martin.fl.us/ClerkWeb/ccis_disclaimer.htm. Search online by name or SSN.

Monroe County

Circuit & County Courts   www.monroe.fl.us.landata.com/default.asp

Civil: Online access to civil cases is free at www.clerk-of-the-court.com/searchCivilCases.asp. Subscription is required for viewing full document library. *Criminal:* Online access to criminal records is free at www.clerk-of-the-court.com/searchCriminalCases.asp. Includes traffic cases online. Subscription is required for viewing full document library.

Nassau County

Circuit & County Courts   www.nassauclerk.com   `Free`

Civil: Search civil cases free at www.nassauclerk.org/clerk/pubcocoa.html. Access an index of judgments, sentences, county commitments, uniform state commitments, disposition notices and nolle prosequi only at www.myfloridacounty.com. Fees involved to order copies; save $1.50 per record by becoming a subscriber. *Criminal:* Search criminal and traffic cases free at www.nassauclerk.org/clerk/pubcocoa.html.

Okaloosa County
Circuit & County Courts www.clerkofcourts.cc **Free**
Civil: Civil records are free at www.clerkofcourts.cc/court/courtsearch.htm. Records go back to 1/83. Search civil index by defendant or plaintiff, date, or file type. Also, access an index of judgments, liens, recorded documents back to 1/1983 at www.myfloridacounty.com. Fees involved to order copies; save $1.50 per record by becoming a subscriber. *Criminal:* County clerk has criminal records some back to 1980s free on the Internet at www.clerkofcourts.cc/court/courtsearch.htm.

Okeechobee County
Circuit & County Courts www.clerk.co.okeechobee.fl.us/ **Free & $$**
Civil: Index of judgments and recorded documents can be searched at http://204.215.37.218/wb_or1/. Also, access to County Clerk of Circuit Court records is at https://www2.myfloridacounty.com/ccm/?county=47 *Criminal:* Same.

Orange County
Circuit & County Courts http://myorangeclerk.com/ **Free**
Civil: The free myclerk Case Inquiry System is at http://myorangeclerk.com/criminal/iclerk_disclaimer.shtml. Civil and Probate records available. Also, previous 2-weeks civil records on a private site at http://extra.orlandosentinel.com/publicrecords/search.asp. This court also accepts email requests at hr@orange-clerk.org. *Criminal:* Access criminal records free on the myclerk Case Inquiry System at http://myorangeclerk.com/criminal/iclerk_disclaimer.shtml.

County Courts - http://orangeclerk.ocfl.net **Free**
Civil: The free myclerk Case Inquiry System is at http://myorangeclerk.com/criminal/iclerk_disclaimer.shtml. Civil and Probate records available. Also, previous 2-weeks civil records on a private site at http://extra.orlandosentinel.com/publicrecords/search.asp. *Criminal:* Access criminal records free on the myclerk Case Inquiry System at http://myorangeclerk.com/criminal/iclerk_disclaimer.shtml.

Osceola County
Circuit Court - Civil www.ninja9.org **Free & $$**
Civil: Online access to court records on the Clerk of Circuit Court database are free at www.osceolaclerkcourt.org/genrlmnu.htm. Also, access an index of judgments, liens, recorded documents at www.myfloridacounty.com. Fees involved to order copies; save $1.50 per record by becoming a subscriber. Also, previous 2-weeks civil records on a private site at http://extra.orlandosentinel.com/publicrecords/search.asp.

County Court - Civil www.osceolaclerk.com **Free**
Civil: Online access to court records on the Clerk of Circuit Court database are free at www.osceolaclerkcourt.org.

Circuit & County Courts - Criminal Division www.osceolaclerk.com **Free**
Criminal: Online access to criminal records is free at www.osceolaclerkcourt.org/search.htm. Includes party index and case summary searching. Search inmates at www.osceola.org/index.cfm?lsFuses=inmates.

Palm Beach County
Circuit Court - Civil Division www.pbcountyclerk.com **Free**
Civil: Access to the countywide online remote system is free. Civil index goes back to '88. Records also include probate, traffic and domestic. Contact June Reese at 561-355-1556 for information. Also, civil records are free at http://courtcon.co.palm-beach.fl.us/pls/jiwp/ck_public_qry_main.cp_main_idx. Records include criminal and traffic.

County Court - Civil Division www.pbcountyclerk.com **$$**
Civil: Access to the countywide remote online system requires $145 setup and $65 per month fees. Civil index goes back to '88. Records also incPlude probate, traffic and domestic. Contact June Reese at 561-355-1556 for information. Also, civil records are free at http://courtcon.co.palm-beach.fl.us/pls/jiwp/ck_public_qry_main.cp_main_idx.

Circuit & County Courts - Criminal Division www.pbcountyclerk.com **Free**
Criminal: Access to the countywide criminal online system is available at http://courtcon.co.palm-beach.fl.us/pls/jiwp/ck_public_qry_main.cp_main_idx. Records also include civil, probate, traffic and domestic.

Circuit Court - Probate Division http://www.pbcountyclerk.com **Free** Access to the countywide court online system is available at http://courtcon.co.palm-beach.fl.us/pls/jiwp/ck_public_qry_main.cp_main_idx.

Pasco County
Circuit & County Courts - Civil Division www.pascoclerk.com/ **Free & $$**
Civil: From the home page, click on "search court records." A fee online access to Clerk of Court records via the Internet is $80.00 per month plus a one-time charge of $35. Probate records also available. Call 3P52-521-4563 for more information.

Circuit & County Courts - Criminal Division www.jud6.org **Free**
Criminal: From the home page, click on "search court records." This is a free search. Also, access to County Clerk of Circuit Court records is at https://www2.myfloridacounty.com/ccm/?county=51.

Pinellas County

Circuit & County Courts - Civil Division   www.jud6.org   `Free`
Civil: Access to the countywide civil system requires $60 fee plus $5.00 a month & $.05 per screen over 100. Index back to 1972. Includes probate & traffic records. Contact Sue Maskeny-727-464-3779. Also, access clerk's criminal & other data free as a non-subscriber at https://pubtitles.co.pinellas.fl.us/login/loginx.jsp. You're on the clock, may be booted. Also, access index of judgments and recorded docs at www.myfloridacounty.com. Fees to order copies; subscribers save $1.50 per record.

County Court - Criminal Division   www.jud6.org   `$$`
Criminal: Access to the countywide criminal online system requires $60 fee plus $5.00 a month and $.05 per screen over 100. Criminal index goes back to 1972. Contact Sue Maskeny at 727-464-3779 for information. Also, you can access the clerk's criminal and other data as a free non-subscriber at https://pubtitles.co.pinellas.fl.us/login/loginx.jsp. However, you are on the clock and may be booted if you overuse the system.

Polk County

Circuit & County Courts - Felony Division   www.polk-county.net/clerk/clerk.html   `Free`
Criminal: Access to County Clerk of Circuit Court records is free at www.polkcountyclerk.net/. Criminal index goes back to 1991; Records may also be accessed at https://www2.myfloridacounty.com/ccm/?county=53.

Circuit Court - Civil Division   www.polkcountyclerk.net/   `Free & $$`
Civil: Free online access to dockets at www.polkcountyclerk.net/RecordsSearch/disclaimer.aspx. A subscription account for attorneys only for complete database access requires $150 setup fee, but there is no monthly fees. Call 863-534-7575 for more information. Also, access to County Clerk of Circuit Court records is at https://www2.myfloridacounty.com/ccm/?county=53.

County Court - Civil Division   www.polkcountyclerk.net   `Free`
Civil: Case index information back to 1983 is free from the County Clerk's website at www.polkcountyclerk.net. Also, access to County Clerk of Circuit Court records is at https://www2.myfloridacounty.com/ccm/?county=53.

Circuit & County Courts - Misdemeanor Division   www.polkcountyclerk.net   `Free`
Criminal: Access to County Clerk of Circuit Court records is at https://www2.myfloridacounty.com/ccm/?county=53.

Putnam County

Circuit & County Courts - Civil Division   www.putnam-fl.com   `$$`
Civil: Access to the countywide remote online system requires $400 setup fee and $40. monthly charge plus $.05 per minute over 20 hours. Civil records go back to 1984. System includes criminal and real property records. Contact Putnam County IT Dept at 386-329-0390 to register. Also, access an index of judgments, liens, recorded documents at www.myfloridacounty.com. Fees involved to order copies; save $1.50 per record by becoming a subscriber.

Circuit & County Courts - Criminal Division   www.putnam-fl.com   `$$`
Criminal: Access to the countywide criminal online system requires $400 setup fee and $40. monthly charge plus $.05 per minute over 20 hours. Criminal records go back to 1972. System includes civil and real property records. Contact 386-329-0390 to register. Also, you may direct email criminal record requests to putn.clerk@co.putnam.fl.us.

Santa Rosa County

Circuit & County Courts - Civil Division   www.santarosaclerk.com   `Free`
Civil: Access an index of judgments, liens, and court records free at http://www2.myfloridacounty.com/ccm/?county=57. Also, access to County Clerk of Circuit Court records is at https://www2.myfloridacounty.com/ccm/?county=57.

Circuit & County Courts - Criminal Division   www.santarosaclerk.com   `Free`
Criminal: Access an index of judgments, liens, and court records free at http://oncoreweb.srccol.com/oncoreweb4101/Search.aspx Also, access to County Clerk of Circuit Court records is at http://www2.myfloridacounty.com/ccm/?county=57.

Sarasota County

Circuit & County Courts - Civil   www.sarasotaclerk.com   `Free`
Civil: Civil and DV case dockets from the Clerk of Circuit Court database are free at www.clerk.co.sarasota.fl.us/srqapp/civilinq.asp. Probate court dockets are at www.clerk.co.sarasota.fl.us/srqapp/probinq.asp. Also see the clerk's judgment/official document search for images back 10 years. Also, access an index of judgments, liens, recorded documents at www.myfloridacounty.com. Fees involved to order copies; save $1.50 per record by becoming a subscriber.

Circuit & County Courts - Criminal   www.sarasotaclerk.com   `Free`
Criminal: Criminal and traffic case dockets from the Clerk of the Circuit Court database are free online at http://clerk.co.sarasota.fl.us/cvdisclaim.htm. Civil, probate and domestic dockets are also available.

Seminole County

Circuit & County Courts - Civil Division   www.seminoleclerk.org   `Free`
Civil: Access to judgment and probate records is free at http://officialrecords.seminoleclerk.org/.

Circuit & County Courts - Criminal Division   www.seminoleclerk.org   `Free`
Civil: Access civil dockets free at www.seminoleclerk.org click on Civil Docket Search. *Criminal:* Access criminal dockets free at www.seminoleclerk.org click on Criminal Dockets Search.

St. Johns County
Circuit & County Courts - Civil Division   www.co.st-johns.fl.us   `Free`
Civil: Also, access the county Clerk of Circuit Court recording data free at http://doris.clk.co.st-johns.fl.us/oncoreweb/Search.aspx. Access an index of judgments, liens, recorded documents at www.myfloridacounty.com. Fees involved to order copies; save $1.50 per record by becoming a subscriber at $25.00 per month.

Circuit & County Courts - Criminal Division   www.co.st-johns.fl.us   `$$`
Criminal: Access to the countywide criminal online system requires $200 setup fee plus a monthly fee of $50. Searching is by name or case number. Call Mark Dearing at 904-819-3611 for more information. (Not setting up new accounts at this time).

St. Lucie County
Circuit & County Courts - Civil Division   www.slcclerkofcourt.com/circuitcivil/circuitcivil.htm   `Free`
Civil: Online access to civil records at http://public.slcclerkofcourt.com. Case tracking and bond record tracking are available. Access an index of judgments, liens, recorded documents at www.myfloridacounty.com. Fees involved to order copies; save $1.50 per record by becoming a subscriber.

Circuit & County Courts - Criminal Division   www.slcclerkofcourt.com/felony/felony.htm   `Free`
Criminal: Online access to bonds, traffic and misdemeanor records is free at http://public.slcclerkofcourt.com. Online records go back to 7/6/1992. Felony records only available to government agencies.

Sumter County
Circuit & County Courts - Civil Division   www.sumterclerk.com/public/   `Free`
Civil: Access an index of civil, probate and domestic relationship records at https://www2.myfloridacounty.com/ccm/?county=60.F.

Circuit & County Courts - Criminal Division   www.sumterclerk.com/public/   `Free`
Criminal: Access an index of felony, criminal traffic and misdemeanor records at https://www2.myfloridacounty.com/ccm/?county=60.

Suwannee County
Circuit & County Courts   www.suwclerk.org/mambo/   `Free`
Civil: Access to County Clerk of Circuit Court records is at https://www2.myfloridacounty.com/ccm/?county=61. Also court records on recording index free at http://67.141.186.38/oncoreweb/. *Criminal:* Same

Taylor County
Circuit & County Courts   http://www2.myfloridacounty.com/wps/wcm/connect/taylorclerk   `Free`
Civil: Access an index of judgments, liens, recorded documents at www.myfloridacounty.com. Fees involved to order copies; save $1.50 per record by becoming a subscriber.

Union County
Circuit & County Courts   http://circuit8.org   `$$`
Civil: Access an index of judgments, liens, recorded documents at www.myfloridacounty.com. Fees involved to order copies; save $1.50 per record by becoming a subscriber. *Criminal:* Access the circuit-wide criminal quick lookup at http://circuit8.org/golem/gencrim.html. Account and password is required; restricted usage.

Volusia County
Circuit & County Courts - Civil Division   www.clerk.org   `Free`
Civil: Online access is now available free at www.clerk.org/cm/publicrecords/publicrecords.jsp. Also, access an index of judgments, liens, recorded documents at www.myfloridacounty.com with fees for copies. Also, previous 2-weeks civil records on a private site at http://extra.orlandosentinel.com/publicrecords/search.asp.

Circuit & County Courts - Criminal Division   www.clerk.org   `Free`
Criminal: Access to the countywide Clerk of Circuit Ct court records is free at www.clerk.org/cm/publicrecords/publicrecords.jsp. Access to the Clerk of Circuit Courts database of Citation Violations and 24-hour Arrest Reports is free at www.clerk.org/index.html.

Wakulla County
Circuit & County Courts   www.wakullaclerk.com   `Free`
Civil: Access to County Clerk of Circuit Court records is at https://www2.myfloridacounty.com/ccm/?county=65 *Criminal:* Same.

Walton County
Circuit & County Courts   http://clerkofcourts.co.walton.fl.us   `Free`
Civil: Access final judgments or orders on closed cases at http://clerkofcourts.co.walton.fl.us/ORSearch/. Also, access to County Clerk of Circuit Court records is at https://www2.myfloridacounty.com/ccm/?county=66. *Criminal:* Access felony judgments of guilt only at

http://clerkofcourts.co.walton.fl.us/ORSearch/. Also, access to County Clerk of Circuit Court records is at https://www2.myfloridacounty.com/ccm/?county=66.

Washington County

Circuit & County Courts www.washingtonclerk.com `Free & $$`

Civil: Access an index of judgments, liens, recorded documents at www.myfloridacounty.com. Fees involved to order copies; save $1.50 per record by becoming a subscriber.

Recorders, Assessors, and Other Sites of Note

Recording Office Organization: 67 counties, 67 recording offices. The recording officer is the Clerk of the Circuit Court. All transactions are recorded in the "Official Record," a grantor/grantee index. Some counties will search by type of transaction while others will return everything on the index. Federal tax liens on personal property of businesses are filed with the Secretary of State. All other federal and state tax liens on personal property are filed with the county Clerk of Circuit Court. Usually tax liens on personal property are filed in the same index with UCC financing statements and real estate transactions.

Online Access Note: There are numerous county agencies that provide online access to records, but the statewide system MyFlorida.com predominates. My Florida offers free access to the over 60 counties Circuit Clerks of Court recorded document indexes, including real estate records liens, judgments, marriages, and deaths at www.myfloridacounty.com/services/officialrecords_intro.shtml. Fees involved to order copies; save $1.50 per record by becoming a subscriber. Subscription fee is $120.00 per year plus monthly transaction fees for copies.

Alachua County *Real Estate, Deed, Lien, Judgment, Vital Statistic Records* `Free & $$` Access Clerk's recording database free at alachuaclerk.org. Index goes back to 1971; images to 1990. Also, search county property by various methods free at www.acpafl.org. Search ancient records -pre-1940 plats, pre-1970 marriages, deeds, transcriptions, more- free at www.clerk-alachua-fl.org/archive/default.cfm but may be temporarily unavailable. Access index of recordings at www.myfloridacounty.com.
Property, Taxation Records `Free` Search Appraiser's Property pages free at www.acpafl.org. Tax Deed Sales search and GIS search also here. Property also at www.emapsplus.com/FLAlachua/maps/. Sales data free at www.acpafl.org/salessearch.asp. Tax deed sales- www.alachuacounty.us/government/clerk/taxdeed/. Tax rolls-http://alachuataxcollector.governmax.com/collectmax/collect30.asp.

Baker County *Real Estate, Deed, Lien Records* www.bakercountyfl.org/clerk/ `$$` Access recorded documents at www.mywashingtoncounty.com, see note above.
Property, Taxation Records `Free` Search assessor data free at www.emapsplus.com/FLBaker/maps/. Also, search appraiser data free at www.bakerpa.com/index_disclaimer.asp. Also, name search the Tax Collector database free at http://70.84.137.66/~baker/search.html. Also, create sales reports free at www.bakerpa.com/GIS/Search_F.asp?SalesReport.

Bay County *Real Estate, Deed, Lien, Judgment, Death, Marriage, Plat Records* www.baycoclerk.com `Free & $$` Access to the Clerk of the Circuit Court Recordings database is free at www.baycoclerk.com/index.cfm. Records go back to 1/1987. Search court judgments and probate free at www.clerk.co.bay.fl.us/ovationweb/search.aspx. Also, Access recorded documents at www.mywashingtoncounty.com, see note above.
Property, Taxation Records `Free` Search property appraiser data free at www.qpublic.net/bay/ or at www.qpublic.net/bay/search1.html. Also, Search the tax collector data at http://bctc.elementaldata.com/disclaimer.asp.

Bradford County *Real Estate, Deed, Lien, Judgment, Marriage, Court Records* www.bradford-co-fla.org `$$` Access recorded documents at www.mywashingtoncounty.com, see note above.
Property, Taxation Records `Free` Search the property appraiser database at www.bradfordappraiser.com/Search_F.asp. Also, search assessor data free at www.emapsplus.com/FLBradford/maps/.

Brevard County *Real Estate, Deed, Lien, Marriage, Mortgage Records* http://199.241.8.125/ `Free & $$` Access clerk's tax lien (1981-95), land records (1995-) & indexed records 1981-9/30/1995 at http://cfweb2.brevardclerk.us/ORM/if_orm_choice.cfm. Registration/password required for full data; application fee- $5.00. Free access to marriage records also. For all records, visit http://199.241.8.125/index.cfm?FuseAction=OfficialRecords.Home. Also, the clerk offers a public system at http://webfyi.clerk.co.brevard.fl.us/netfyi/instruct.html that includes plats, traffic, courts, and more.
Property, Taxation Records `Free` Access property tax and personal property records free at http://brevardpropertyappraiser.com/asp/disclaimer.asp. Access parcels and property/GIS free at www.emapsplus.com/FLBrevard/maps/. Property Sales & tax records at http://brevardpropertyappraiser.com/asp/disclaimer.asp. Also, tax deed sale lists free at http://199.241.8.125/index.cfm?FuseAction=TaxDeedAuctions.TaxDeedSales.

Broward County *Real Estate, Deed, Lien, Mortgage Records* www.broward.org/records `Free` Access to the county records Public Search database 1978-present is free at http://205.166.161.12/oncoreV2/.

Property, Taxation Records `Free` Access assessor and property/GIS free at www.emapsplus.com/FLBroward/maps/. Also, access property appraisal data free at www.bcpa.net/search.asp. Also, search property tax data for free at http://bcegov.co.broward.fl.us/revenue/nameform.asp.

Calhoun County *Real Estate, Deed, Lien, Judgment Records*
http://www2.myfloridacounty.com/wps/wcm/connect/calhounclerk `$$` Access recorded documents at www.mywashingtoncounty.com, see note above.
Property, Taxation Records `Free` Search assessor's data free at calhouncountytaxcollector.com/Disclaimer.aspx, or go to http://calhounpa.net and click on "Search Records."

Charlotte County *Real Estate, Deed, Lien, Marriage, Mortgage Records* www.co.charlotte.fl.us `Free & $$`
Search recorded data and marriages free at http://208.47.160.77/or/Search.aspx. Access index of recorded documents at www.myfloridacounty.com. Fees involved to order copies; subscribers save $1.50 per record.
Property, Taxation Records `Free` Property records are free at www.ccappraiser.com/record.asp. Search Assessor and property/GIS free at www.emapsplus.com/FLCharlotte/maps/. Sales records are on the tax collector database free at www.cctaxcol.com/record.asp?.

Citrus County *Real Estate, Deed, Lien, Marriage, Probate, Military Discharge, Tax Deed Sale Records*
www.clerk.citrus.fl.us `Free & $$` Access to the Clerk of Circuit Court recording records is free at http://search.clerk.citrus.fl.us/. Also, download land sales data free at www.pa.citrus.fl.us/sales_download.html. Access recorded documents index at www.myfloridacounty.com. Fees involved to order copies; save $1.50 per record by becoming a subscriber. View tax deed sales at www.clerk.citrus.fl.us/home.jsp?section=8&item=88.
Property, Taxation Records `Free` Search property appraiser and personal property records free at www.pa.citrus.fl.us/ccpaask.html. Also, download land sales data free at www.pa.citrus.fl.us/sales_download.html. Search property and other related-tax records free at https://www.citrus.county-taxes.com/tcb/app/main/home.

Clay County *Real Estate, Deed, Lien, Mortgage Records* www.clayclerk.com `Free & $$` County Clerk of
Circuit Court allows free access to recording records at http://clerk.co.clay.fl.us/oncoreweb42/. Records go back to 1993. Also, Access recorded documents at www.mywashingtoncounty.com, see note above.
Property, Taxation Records `Free` Access property appraiser records free at www.ccpao.com/search1.html; tangible property at http://64.148.133.165/tpp/srchasmt.asp. Also, search assessor data free at www.emapsplus.com/FLClay/maps/. Search treasurer RE & tangible personal property at www.claycountytax.com/Tax_Searchr/porr.html. Tax search free at www.claycountytax.com/Tax_Searchr/taxsearch.cgi.

Collier County *Real Estate, Deed, Lien, UCC, Vital Statistic Records* www.collierclerk.com/ `Free & $$`
Access court, lien, real estate, UCCs and vital records free at www.clerk.collier.fl.us/PLB/default.htm. Lending agency data available. Also, access recorded document index at www.myfloridacounty.com. Fees involved to order copies; save $1.50 per record by becoming a subscriber.
Property, Taxation Records `Free` Access Property Appraiser data free at www.collierappraiser.com/Search.asp. Also property assessor/GIS free at www.emapsplus.com/FLCollier/maps/. Search property tax roll at www.colliertax.com/search/. Tax deeds sales data is free at www.clerk.collier.fl.us/OfficialRecords/Tax_Deeds/Tax%20Deeds.htm.

Columbia County *Real Estate, Deed, Lien Records*
http://www2.myfloridacounty.com/wps/wcm/connect/columbiaclerk `Free & $$` Access Clerk of Circuit Courts recording database index free at www.columbiaclerk.com. Click on Order Official Records. Search by name, book/page, file number of document type. This is a www.myfloridacounty.com website; fees are involved to order copies; save $1.50 per record by becoming a subscriber.
Property, Taxation Records `Free` Search property appraiser records free at http://columbia.floridapa.com/GIS/Search_F.asp. Also, search property assessor data free at www.emapsplus.com/FLColumbia/maps/. Search property/GIS free at www.emapsplus.com/FLColumbia/maps/. Also, search the tax rolls and occupational licenses for free at www.columbiataxcollector.com/collectmax/collect30.asp

Dade County *Real Estate, Deed, Lien, Judgment, Marriage Records* www.miami-dadeclerk.com/dadecoc/ `Free`
Access records and index free at http://miamidade.gov/wps/portal. Recorded docs at www.miami-dadeclerk.com/public-records/.
Property, Taxation Records `Free` Access assessor data free at www.miamidade.gov/pa/property_search.asp. Also, lookup property tax free at www.miamidade.gov/proptax/home.asp. Search assessor property and GIS site free at www.emapsplus.com/FLDade/maps/. Tax collector records free at www.co.miami-dade.fl.us/proptax/.

De Soto County *Real Estate, Deed, Lien, Mortgage Records* www.desotoclerk.com `$$` Access recorded
documents at www.mywashingtoncounty.com, see note above.
Property, Taxation Records `Free` Access the property appraiser data free at http://qpublic.net/desoto/search.html. Also, search property assessor/GIS free at www.emapsplus.com/FLdesoto/maps/.

Dixie County *Real Estate, Deed, Lien, Mortgage Records* `$$` Access recorded documents at
www.mywashingtoncounty.com, see note above.

Property, Taxation Records **Free** Access assessor's property data free at http://dixiefl.patriotproperties.com/default.asp.

Duval County *Real Estate, Grantor/Grantee, Deed, Lien, Judgment, Vital Statistic Records*
www.duvalclerk.com/ccWebsite/ **Free & $$** Access Clerk of Circuit Court and City of Jacksonville Official Records grantor/grantee index free at www.duvalclerk.com/oncoreweb/. Access an index of recorded documents at www.myfloridacounty.com. Fees involved to order copies.
Property, Taxation Records **Free** Search Property Appraiser records free at http://apps.coj.net/pao_propertySearch/Basic/Search.aspx. Search personal property records free at http://apps.coj.net/PAO/tppf/. Search parcel data free at http://maps.coj.net/jaxgis/ click on Duval Maps. Also, access Property Assessor/GIS data free at www.emapsplus.com/Flduval/maps/. Search tax collector real estate, personal property data free and Oc licensing at http://fl-duval-taxcollector.governmax.com/collectmax/collect30.asp.

Escambia County *Real Estate, Grantor/Grantee, Deed, Lien, Vital Statistic Records* www.clerk.co.escambia.fl.us
Free & $$ Access to the Clerk of Court Public Records database is free at www.clerk.co.escambia.fl.us/public_records.html. This includes grantor/grantee index and marriage, traffic, court records, tax sales. Access an index of recorded documents at www.myfloridacounty.com. Fees involved to order copies; save $1.50 per record by becoming subscriber.
Property, Taxation Records **Free** Search the property appraiser records and sales, condos and subdivisions free at www.escpa.org/Search.asp. Find tax sale info at http://ectc.co.escambia.fl.us/Pageview.asp?edit_id=103. Also, access the tax collector's Property Tax database free at http://escambiataxcollector.governmaxa.com/collectmax/collect30.asp.

Flagler County *Real Estate, Deed, Lien, Probate, Judgment, Marriage, Death, Military Discharge, Property Sale Records* www.flaglerclerk.com **Free & $$** Search recording records free at www.flaglerclerk.com/oncoreweb/Search.aspx. Also, name search the tax collector tax records site free at http://fl-flagler-taxcollector.governmax.com/collectmax/collect30.asp. Check property sales at www.qpublic.net/flagler/flaglersearch.html. The state recorders' meta-search site is free at www.myflaglercounty.com. Click on Official Records. Also, Access recorded documents at www.mywashingtoncounty.com, see note above.
Property, Taxation Records **Free** Search appraiser property data free at www.qpublic.net/flagler/search.html or http://flaglerpa.com. Also, search Property Assessor/GIS free at www.emapsplus.com/FLflagler/maps/.

Franklin County *Real Estate, Deed, Lien Records* http://www2.myfloridacounty.com/wps/wcm/connect/franklinclerk
$$ Access recorded documents at www.mywashingtoncounty.com, see note above.
Property, Taxation Records **Free** Property record search is free at http://qpublic.net/franklin/.

Gadsden County *Real Estate, Deed, Lien, Judgment, Vital Statistic Records* www.clerk.co.gadsden.fl.us **Free**
Access official records index free at http://69.21.116.234/chronicleweb/. Index records go back to 1990. Provides index numbers only.
Property, Taxation Records **Free** Access to the property appraiser database is free at www.qpublic.net/gadsden/search.html. Search property sales at www.qpublic.net/gadsden/gadsdensearch.html. No name searching. Also, search tax collector records at www.gadsdentaxcollector.com/collectmax/collect30.asp

Gilchrist County *Real Estate, Deed, Lien, Judgment, Marriage, Death Records* http://gilchrist.fl.us/ **Free &**
$$ Access is free to recorded documents generally and some courts records at records.gilchrist.fl.us. Images available for deeds, mortgages, and some other document types. Access an index of recorded documents at http://mygilchristcounty.com or www.myfloridacounty.com. Fees involved to order copies; save $1.50 per record by becoming a subscriber.
Property, Taxation Records **Free** Access to the property appraiser database is free at www.qpublic.net/gilchrist/search.html. Also, property sales searches are at www.gcpaonline.net; click on Search.

Glades County *Real Estate, Deed, Lien Records* http://www2.myfloridacounty.com/wps/wcm/connect/gladesclerk
Free & $$ Access an index of recorded documents at www.myfloridacounty.com. View docs back to 1/1990 without ordering. Fees involved to order copies; save $1.50 per record by becoming a subscriber.
Property, Taxation Records **Free** Search Property Assessor/GIS free at www.emapsplus.com/FLglades/maps/. Also, sales searches are at www.gcpaonline.net; click on Search.

Gulf County *Real Estate, Deed, Judgment, Marriage, Death Records*
http://www2.myfloridacounty.com/wps/wcm/connect/gulfclerk **$$** Access recorded documents at www.mywashingtoncounty.com, see note above.
Property, Taxation Records **Free** Access to the property appraiser database is free at www.gulfpa.com

Hamilton County *Real Estate, Deed, Lien Records* www.hamiltoncountyflorida.com/cd_clerk.aspx **$$** Access recorded documents at www.mywashingtoncounty.com, see note above.
Property, Taxation Records **Free** Access to the property appraiser database is free at www.hamiltoncountytaxcollector.

Hardee County *Real Estate, Deed, Lien, Judgment Records* www.hardeeclerk.com **$$** Access recorded documents at www.mywashingtoncounty.com, see note above.

Property, Taxation Records Free Access to the property appraiser data is free at www.hardeecounty.net/cfaps/appraiser/propform.cfm. Search assessor data on the GIS site free at www.emapsplus.com/Flhardee/maps/.

Hendry County *Real Estate, Deed, Lien Records* www.hendryclerk.org Free & $$ Access an index of recorded documents at www.myfloridacounty.com. Also, access Official Records Data free at www.hendryclerk.org/officialrecords.htm - has images from 12/30/1988 - Book 450 Page 1 to latest available. Web records updated daily.
Property, Taxation Records Free Access the property appraiser database at www.hendryprop.com/GIS/Search_F.asp. Also, search Property Assessor/GIS free at www.emapsplus.com/FLhendry/maps/.

Hernando County *Real Estate, Deed, Lien, Marriage, Judgment Records* www.clerk.co.hernando.fl.us Free & $$
Access to the clerk's Official Records database is now free at www.clerk.co.hernando.fl.us/disclaimer.asp. Your browser must be JavaScript enabled. Includes recordings, marriages, and court records. Also, access recorded document index at www.myfloridacounty.com. Fees involved to order copies.
Property, Taxation Records Free Search 2 levels of the Public Inquiry System Property Appraiser Real Estate database - Easy Search and Real Time Search - free at www.co.hernando.fl.us/pa/propsearch.htm. Search by owner, address, or parcel key.

Highlands County *Real Estate, Deed, Lien Records* www.hcclerk.org Free & $$ Online access to the recorders' meta-search site is at www.myflorida.com. Click on Official Records. Free search; fee for documents. Also, online access to official records -deeds, mortgages, judgments, etc - from the county recording database is free at www.hcclerk.org/SearchOfficialRecords.aspx. Records go back to 1983.
Property, Taxation Records Free Search Property Assessor/GIS free at www.emapsplus.com/FLhighlands/maps/. Also, property appraiser records are free at www.appraiser.co.highlands.fl.us/search.html; tangible personal property records available. Also, search tax deed sales by date free at www.hcclerk.org/TaxDeedsSales.aspx. Also, county tax collector database free at https://www.highlands.county-taxes.com/tcb/app/re/accounts. Also, search Property/GIS free at www.emapsplus.com/FLhighlands/maps/.

Hillsborough County *Real Estate, Deed, Lien, Judgment, Mortgage Records* www.hillsclerk.com Free & $$
The clerk's recordings index can be searched free at http://publicrecord.hillsclerk.com. Images of official records from 1990 to present. Also, access recorded document index at www.myfloridacounty.com; fees involved to order copies; subscribers save $1.50 per record. Call 813-276-8100 x4444 for info.
Property, Taxation Records Free Search property appraiser records free at www.hcpafl.org/www/search/index.shtml. Receive owner data, legal, sales, value summaries. Also, search for similar tax data free on the tax collector site at www.hillstax.org/taxapp/property_information.asp. Search property on GIS site at http://propmap3.hcpafl.org/main.asp?cmd=ZOOMFOLIO&folio=.

Holmes County *Real Estate, Deed, Lien Records* http://www2.myfloridacounty.com/wps/wcm/connect/holmesclerk
$$ Access recorded documents at www.mywashingtoncounty.com, see note above.
Property, Taxation Records Free Access property appraiser data free including property, sales and sales lists free at http://qpublic.net/holmes.

Indian River County *Real Estate, Deed, Lien, Mortgage Records* www.clerk.indian-river.org Free & $$
Access to Clerk's recording indices are free at www.clerk.indian-river.org/recordssearch/ori.asp. Records go back to 1983. Full real estate, lien and court and vital records from the Clerk of the Circuit Court is at their fee site; subscriptions start at $25.00 per month, increasing with amount of access. For info about free and fee access, call 772-567-8000 x216.
Property, Taxation Records Free Appraiser records free at www.ircpa.org. Also, search Property Assessor/GIS free at www.emapsplus.com/FLindianriver/maps/.

Jackson County *Real Estate, Lien, Deed, Marriage, Probate Records*
http://www2.myfloridacounty.com/wps/wcm/connect/jacksonclerk Free & $$ Access recorded documents at www.mywashingtoncounty.com, see note above. Images will go back to 5/1990.
Property, Taxation Records Free Search property tax data free at www.jacksoncountytaxcollector.com/SearchSelect.aspx.

Jefferson County *Property, Real Estate, Lien, UCC, Marriage Records* http://jeffersonclerk.com Free & $$
Access recorded documents at www.mywashingtoncounty.com, see note above. Also, access the Clerk of Circuit Court recordings database free at www.myjeffersoncounty.com.
Property, Taxation Records Free Access Property Appraiser data free at http://qpublic.net/jefferson/search.html. Sales searches are also available. Search assessor parcel map at http://archie.co.jefferson.co.us/website/aspin/disclaimer.htm. Also, search property records free at www.co.jefferson.co.us/ats/splash.do. Also, search the tax collector database free at www.jeffersoncountytaxcollector.com/SearchSelect.aspx.

Lafayette County *Real Estate, Deed, Lien Records* http://www2.myfloridacounty.com/wps/wcm/connect/lafayetteclerk
Free & $$ Access recorded documents at www.mywashingtoncounty.com, see note above.
Property, Taxation Records Free Search appraiser's property data free at www.lafayettepa.com/GIS/Search_F.asp. Also, search property sales free at www.lafayettepa.com/GIS/Search_F.asp?SalesReport.

Lake County *Real Estate, Deed, Lien, Marriage Records* www.lakecountyclerk.org `Free & $$` Access to the new county clerk official records database is free at www.lakecountyclerk.org/services.asp?subject=Online_Official_Records. Records go as far back as 1957. Includes court records. Also, marriage records back to 11/2000 are at www.lakecountyclerk.org/departments.asp?subject=Marriage_Licenses. Also, access to state recorders' meta-search site is free at www.myfloridacounty.com. Click on Official records.

Property, Taxation Records `Free` Search the County Property Assessor parcel and tax data also property sales free at www.lakecopropappr.com/. Also, search property on the tax collector site free at http://laketaxcollector.governmax.com/collectmax/collect30.asp.

Lee County *Real Estate, Deed, Lien, Judgment, Mortgage Records* www.leeclerk.org `Free & $$` Ssearch the recorders index free at www.leeclerk.org/OR/Search.aspx or other indexes (subject to change) at www.leeclerk.org/SearchOfficialRecords.htm. Also, obtain certified copies at the Clerk's office or order certified copies online and search other Florida Counties' Official Records at www.myfloridacounty.com and click on Order Official Records.

Property, Taxation Records `Free` Search tangible business property at www.leepa.org/Tangible/Business%20Search.htm. The online property info inquiry is at www.leepa.org/Queries/SearchCriteria.htm. A generic tax search page for tax rolls, certificates, mobiles, vessels, vehicles is free at www.leetc.com/search_criteria.asp.Search property assessor/GIS free at www.emapsplus.com/FLlee/maps/.

Leon County *Real Estate, Deed, Lien, Mortgage, Marriage Records* www.clerk.leon.fl.us `Free & $$` Real Estate, lien, and foreclosure records from the County Clerk are free at www.clerk.leon.fl.us. Lending agency data is also available. Also, access to full document images requires user name and password, plus $100 per month. Marriages are at http://cvweb.clerk.leon.fl.us/index_marriage.html. Also, access recorded documents index at www.myfloridacounty.com. Fees involved to order copies.

Property, Taxation Records `Free` Search Property Appraiser database records free at www.co.leon.fl.us/propappr/search.cfm. Search tax collector rolls at http://dta.co.leon.fl.us/tax/default.asp.

Levy County *Real Estate, Deed, Lien Records* www.levyclerk.com `Free & $$` Access the Clerk of Circuit Court recording database free at http://oncore.levyclerk.com/oncoreweb/Search.aspx. Search by name, book/page, file number or document type. Access recorded documents at www.mywashingtoncounty.com, see note above. Also, search county warrants list for free at www.levyso.com.

Property, Taxation Records `Free` Access to the property appraiser data is free at www.qpublic.net/levy/search.html. Also, search tax collector data free at www.levytaxcollector.com/collectmax/collect30.asp.

Liberty County *Real Estate, Deed, Lien Records* http://www2.myfloridacounty.com/wps/wcm/connect/libertyclerk `$$` Access recorded documents at www.mywashingtoncounty.com, see note above.

Property, Taxation Records `Free` Access assessor property records free at www.qpublic.net/liberty.

Madison County *Real Estate, Deed, Lien Records* http://www2.myfloridacounty.com/wps/wcm/connect/madisonclerk `Free & $$` Access recorded documents at www.mywashingtoncounty.com, see note above. Official Records indexes are for past 10 years.

Property, Taxation Records `Free` Access property assessor and sale data free at www.madisonpa.com/GIS/Search_F.asp.

Manatee County *Real Estate, Deed, Lien, Judgment, Death, Marriage, Condominium Records* www.manateeclerk.com `Free` Several sources exist. Search and view real estate and recordings records free from the Clerk of Circuit Court and Comptroller's database at www.manateeclerk.com.

Property, Taxation Records `Free` Search Property Assessor/GIS data free at www.emapsplus.com/FLmanatee/maps/. Also, access index of recorded docs at www.myfloridacounty.com. Fees involved to order copies. Property Appraiser records free at www.manateepao.com/Search/GenericSearch.aspx. Tax deed sales at www.clerkofcourts.com/Sales/TaxDeeds/taxdeed.pdf. Also, property tax records are at www.taxcollector.com/dataaccess/design/1owner.asp. Search foreclosure sales at www.manateeclerk.com.

Marion County *Real Estate, Deed, Lien, Judgment, Death, Marriage Records* www.marioncountyclerk.org `Free & $$` Search recorder records free at http://216.255.240.38/wb_or1/or_sch_1.asp. Also, Access recorded documents at www.mywashingtoncounty.com, see note above.

Property, Taxation Records `Free` Access property appraiser data free at www.propappr.marion.fl.us/MCPASCH.HTML. Search county tax rolls free at https://www.mariontax.com/itm.asp. Also, access property data via the GIS mapping site at www.marioncountyfl.org/IS251/GISWEB/gis_home.htm. Click on County Interactive map, then the red question mark.

Martin County *Real Estate, Deed, Lien, Mortgage Records* http://clerk-web.martin.fl.us/ClerkWeb/ `Free & $$` Access to the clerk of the circuit court recordings database are free at http://216.255.240.38/wb_or1/or_sch_1.asp. Also, online access to the state recorders' metasearch site is free at www.myfloridacounty.com. Fees apply for images.

Property, Taxation Records `Free` Records on the county property appraiser database are free at http://paoweb.martin.fl.us. Choose from "Real Property Searches." Personal property searches are also available. County tax collector data files are free at http://taxcol.martin.fl.us/ITM/. Also, search Property Assessor/GIS free at www.emapsplus.com/FLmartin/maps/.

Monroe County *Real Estate, Deed, Lien, Mortgage Records* www.clerk-of-the-court.com/ `Free` Access to the clerk of circuit courts database is free at www.clerk-of-the-court.com.
Property, Taxation Records `Free` Access to property appraiser data is free on the GIS-mapping site at www.mcpafl.org/datacenter/mapdisc.asp? Also, search property tax, tax deed sales, and occupational licenses free at www.monroetaxcollector.com.

Nassau County *Real Estate, Deed, Lien, Marriage, Will, Divorce Records* www.nassauclerk.com `Free & $$`
Access recorders database free at www.nassauclerk.com/clerk/publicrecords/oncoreweb/Search.aspx. Access recorded documents at www.mywashingtoncounty.com, see note above.
Property, Taxation Records `Free` Access property data free at www.nassauflpa.com/. Search Property Assessor/GIS free at www.emapsplus.com/FLnassau/maps/.

Okaloosa County *Real Estate, Deed, Lien, Vital Statistic, Mortgage Records* www.clerkofcourts.cc `Free & $$`
Several databases are available. Access to Okaloosa County online system requires a monthly usage fee of $100. No addresses listed. Lending agency, traffic and domestic records are free. For info, contact Don Howard at 850-689-5000 x3361. Access clerk's land and official records for free at http://officialrecords.clerkofcourts.cc/; includes marriage, civil, traffic records. Also, online access to the state recorders' meta-search site is free at www.myfloridacounty.com.
Property, Taxation Records `Free` Access property appraiser records and sales lists free at www.okaloosapa.com. With user ID and password you may access tax collector data at http://okaloosa.governmax.com/collectmax/search_collect.asp?. Registration required.

Okeechobee County *Real Estate, Deed, Lien, Judgment, Mortgage, Tax Deed Records*
www.clerk.co.okeechobee.fl.us `Free & $$` Search the statewide recording database via www.myfloridacounty.com. There is a fee to order. Also, search the Clerk of Courts Tax Deed data free at http://204.215.37.218/wb_or1/or_sch_1.asp.
Property, Taxation Records `Free` Search assessor data on the GIS site at okeechobeepa.com/GIS/Search_F.asp?GIS. Also, search property on the private GIS site at www.emapsplus.com/FLOkeechobee/maps/.

Orange County *Real Estate, Deed, Lien, Vital Statistic Records* www.occompt.com `Free` Real Estate, Lien, and Marriage records on the county Comptroller database are free at http://officialrecords.occompt.com/wb_or1/or_sch_1.asp. Lending Agency data available.
Property, Taxation Records `Free` Access appraiser records free at www.ocpafl.org/disclaimer.html; click on Record Searches; includes personal property and resi. sales records. Search tax collector site free www.octaxcol.com includes tax sales. Search Property on the GIS site at www.emapsplus.com/FLorange/maps/.

Osceola County *Real Estate, Deed, Lien Records* www.osceolaclerk.com `Free & $$` Search recorded documents at www.myfloridacounty.com. Fees involved to order copies; save $1.50 per record by becoming a subscriber. Also, recording/land records at www.osceolaclerk.com. Click on On-Line Records Search, then Recording Records.
Property, Taxation Records `$$` Subscription required for property appraiser records at www.osceolataxcollector.com/. Also, with registration & password, access Occ. licenses and tax collector data at www.osceolataxcollector.com. Also, search Property Assessor/GIS free at www.emapsplus.com/FLosceola/maps/.

Palm Beach County *Real Estate, Deed, Lien, Judgment, Vital Statistic Records* www.pbcountyclerk.com `Free & $$` Access clerk's recording database free at www.pbcountyclerk.com/records_home.html. Records go back to 1968; images back to 1968; includes marriage records 1979 to present. Also, search property/GIS free at www.emapsplus.com/FLpalmbeach/maps/. Also, access an index of recorded documents at www.myfloridacounty.com with fees involved to order copies.
Property, Taxation Records `Free` Access property appraiser records at www.co.palm-beach.fl.us/papa/aspx/GeneralSearch/GeneralSearch.aspx. Rearch real estate, property tax, personal property data at www.pbcgov.com/tax/i&p_property.shtml. Also, search property/GIS free at www.emapsplus.com/FLpalmbeach/maps/. Search tax deeds at www.pbcountyclerk.com/dt_web2/or_sch_1.asp.

Pasco County *Real Estate, Deed, Lien, Vital Statistic Records* www.pascoclerk.com `Free & $$` Several sources available. Access to real estate, liens, marriage records requires $25 annual fee plus a $50 deposit. Billing rate is $.05 per minute, $.03 evenings. For info, call 352-521-4529. Also, free access to indexes and copies at www.pascoclerk.com. Click on "records." Access an index of recorded documents at www.myfloridacounty.com. Fees involved to order copies.
Property, Taxation Records `Free` Access property appraiser data and sales data and maps free at http://appraiser.pascogov.com. Search tax records and occupational licenses at http://taxcollector.pascogov.com/search/prclsearch.asp.

Pinellas County *Real Estate, Deed, Lien, Judgment Records* http://pinellasclerk.org `Free & $$` Access recorded document index at www.myfloridacounty.com. Fees involved to order copies.
Property, Taxation Records `Free` Assessor property records are free at www.pcpao.org. Also, search tax collector data free at www.visualgov.com/pinellascounty/. Tax deed sales lists are at www.pinellasclerk.org/tributeweb2/.

Polk County *Real Estate, Deed, Lien, Vital Statistic Records* www.polkcountyclerk.net `Free & $$` Search the county clerk database at www.polkcountyclerk.net/RecordsSearch/disclaimer.aspx for free court records, deeds, mortgages, plats, marriages, resolutions. For copies of documents, call 863-534-4524; fee is $1.00 per page.

Property, Taxation Records `Free`   Access appraiser property tax, personal property, and sales data free at www.polkpa.org/CamaDisplay.aspx.

Putnam County *Real Estate, Deed, Lien, Mortgage Records* http://www1.putnam-fl.com/live/clkmain.asp `$$`
Access to the county clerk database requires a $400 setup fee and monthly charge of $40 plus $.05 per minute over 20 hours. Includes civil court records and real property records back to 10/1983. For info, call 904-329-0353. Also, Access recorded documents at www.mywashingtoncounty.com, see note above.

Property, Taxation Records `Free`   Search property assessor data free on GIS site at www.emapsplus.com/FLPutnam/maps/. Also, search the online tax rolls at www.putnam-fl.com/app/disclaimer.htm. No name searching. Also, search the treasurer's tax rolls and occupational licensing at www.putnam-fl.com/txc/onlineinquiry.htm.

St. Johns County *Real Estate, Deed, Lien, Probate, UCC, Judgment Records* www.co.st-johns.fl.us `Free &`
`$$`   Access to the county Clerk of Circuit Court recording database is free at http://doris.clk.co.st-johns.fl.us/oncoreweb/Search.aspx. Search by name, parcel ID, instrument type. Includes civil and probate records, UCCs. Access recorded documents at www.mywashingtoncounty.com, see note above.

Property, Taxation Records `Free`   Access county property appraiser database free at www.sjcpa.us/Disclaimer%20for%20as400.htm. Also, search Property/GIS free at www.emapsplus.com/FLstjohns/maps/.

St. Lucie County *Real Estate, Deed, Lien, Marriage, Mortgage, Fictitious Name Records*
www.slcclerkofcourt.com/ `Free & $$`   Access clerk of circuit courts database of recordings free at http://public.slcclerkofcourt.com. Business searching is also available for a small fee. Access an index of recorded documents at www.myfloridacounty.com. Fees involved to order copies.

Property, Taxation Records `Free`   Access property appraiser records free at www.paslc.org. Click on "Real estate" or "Personal property" for search options. Also, search 3 tax rolls- Real Estate, Tangibles, business- for free at https://www.stlucie.county-taxes.com/tcb/app/main/home. Also, earch assessor property data free at www.emapsplus.com/FLStLucie/maps/.

Santa Rosa County *Real Estate, Deed, Lien, Marriage, Death, Judgment Records*
http://www2.myfloridacounty.com/wps/wcm/connect/santarosaclerk `Free & $$`   Access to the Clerk's index of recorded documents is at http://oncoreweb.srccol.com/oncoreweb/. Or, go to www.myflorida.com where you may search the index free; fees involved to order copies or view images.

Property, Taxation Records `Free`   Access the appraiser property records free at www.srcpa.org/property.html or at the main Property Appraiser page at www.srcpa.org click on "Record Search." Also, search the real estate tax collector data for free at http://santarosataxcollector.governmax.com/collectmax/collect30.asp; occupational licenses at http://santarosataxcollector.governmax.com/collectmax/search_collect.asp?l_nm=occlic_bus_name&sid.

Sarasota County *Real Estate, Deed, Lien, Vital Statistic, Marriage, Probate Records* www.sarasotaclerk.com
`Free & $$`   Access Clerk of Circuit Court recordings database free at www.sarasotaclerk.com. Includes civil, criminal, and traffic court indexes. Also search indexes at www.sarasotaclerk.com. Search marriage licenses; probate also. Also, zccess index of recorded documents at www.myfloridacounty.com. Fees involved to order copies.

Property, Taxation Records `Free`   Access property appraiser data free at www.sarasotaproperty.net/scpa_record_search.asp; includes subdivision/condominium sales. Also, search tax collector and occ licenses at http://sarasotataxcollector.governmax.com/collectmax/collect30.asp. Search property assessor/GIS data free at www.emapsplus.com/FLsarasota/maps/.

Seminole County *Real Estate, Deed, Lien, Marriage, Divorce Records* www.seminoleclerk.org `Free`
Access the county clerk of circuit court's recordings database free at http://officialrecords.seminoleclerk.org/.

Property, Taxation Records `Free`   Property appraisal tax records free at www.scpafl.org/scpaweb05/index.jsp also a map search. Access property and real estate tax data free at http://seminoletax.org/Tax/TaxSearch.shtml. Also, GIS free at www.emapsplus.com/FLseminole/maps/. Search tax collector personal property and real estate records free at http://seminoletax.org.

Sumter County *Real Estate, Deed, Lien, Mortgage Records* www.sumterclerk.com `$$`
Access recorded documents at www.mywashingtoncounty.com, see note above.

Property, Taxation Records `Free`   Access property assessor data free at http://qpublic.net/sumter/search1.html. Also, search tax collector and occupational licenses for free at http://fl-sumter-taxcollector.governmax.com/collectmax/agency/fl-sumter-taxcollector/homepage_v5_6.asp? Also, tax deed, foreclosures and other sales lists are available in pdf format.

Suwannee County *Real Estate, Deed, Lien, UCC, Mortgage, Marriage, Death Records* www.suwclerk.org
`Free & $$`   Access of the county clerk of circuit database index is free at www.suwclerk.org. This directs you to the statewide database; search index free; subscription required for documents. Also, document index for variety of recordings free at http://67.141.186.38/oncoreweb/Search.aspx.

Property, Taxation Records `Free`   Search property assessor data free at http://suwanneepa.com/GIS/Search_F.asp. Also, search on the GIS-mapping site at www.emapsplus.com/FLSuwannee/maps/. Also, search the tax collector database free at www.suwanneecountytax.com/collectmax/collect30.asp also register to view tax deed sale records.

Taylor County   *Real Estate, Deed, Lien, Judgment, Voter Registration Records*
http://www2.myfloridacounty.com/wps/wcm/connect/taylorclerk   Free & $$ Access recorded documents at www.mywashingtoncounty.com, see note above. Also, check voter registration for names free at www.voterfocus.com/vfvoters.php?county=taylor.
Property, Taxation Records   Free   Access the property and GIS search site free at http://gis.taylorcountygov.com/taylormap/Default.aspx. Also search tax collector tax roll data free at http://fl-taylor-taxcollector.governmax.com/collectmax/collect30.asp.

Union County   *Real Estate, Deed, Lien, Mortgage Records*   www.myfloridacounty.com   Free & $$
Access recorded documents at www.mywashingtoncounty.com, see note above.
Property, Taxation Records   Free   Access assessor's records free at www.qpublic.net/union/search.html. Check tax records free at http://unioncountytaxcollector.com; click on "Tax Record Search" to search by name, parcel number, or address. Search property sales free at http://union.floridapa.com/GIS/Search_F.asp?SalesReport. Also, search the GIS-mapping site for assessor property data free at http://union.floridapa.com/GIS/Search_F.asp?GIS or at www.emapsplus.com/FLUnion/maps/.

Volusia County   *Real Estate, Deed, Lien, Vital Statistic, Mortgage Records*   www.clerk.org/index.html   Free & $$
Recording data is free at www.clerk.org. Click on Search Public Records. Recorder indices go back to 1990. Arrest ledger, tax deed sales and citations also at this website. County also offers full real estate, lien, court and vital records on a commercial site; set up is $100 with $25 monthly. For info, contact clerk. Also, access index of recorded documents at www.myfloridacounty.com. Fees involved to order copies; save $1.50 per record by becoming a subscriber.
Property, Taxation Records   Free   Access property search free at http://webserver.vcgov.org/vc_search.html. Also search property assessor/GIS free at www.emapsplus.com/FLVolusia/maps/.

Wakulla County   *Real Estate, Lien, Deed, Death, Marriage, UCC, Judgment Records*   www.wakullaclerk.com
Free & $$ Access an index of recorded documents at www.wakullaclerk.com/oncoreweb/. Also, the Clerk's office has plat images online free at www.wakullaclerk.com/plats.asp Also, access index of recorded documents at www.myfloridacounty.com. Fees involved to order copies; save $1.50 per record by becoming a subscriber.
Property, Taxation Records   Free   Access assessor property data free at www.qpublic.net/wakulla/search1.html. Access clerk of court's foreclosure monthly lists and Tax Deed Sales free at www.wakullaclerk.com/index.asp. Click on Link in Quick Links Section. Search tax collector data free at www.wakullacountytaxcollector.com/SearchSelect.aspx

Walton County   *Real Estate, Grantor/Grantee, Deed, Lien, Vital Statistic Records*
http://clerkofcourts.co.walton.fl.us   Free   Records back to 1/1976 on the County Clerk database are free at http://clerkofcourts.co.walton.fl.us/ORSearch/.
Property, Taxation Records   Free   Property appraiser records are free at www.qpublic.net/walton/search1.html. Also, search tax collector data free at http://fl-walton-taxcollector.governmaxa.com/collectmax/collect30.asp.

Washington County   *Real Estate, Deed, Lien, Judgment Records*
http://www2.myfloridacounty.com/wps/wcm/connect/washingtonclerk/ $$ Access recorded documents at www.mywashingtoncounty.com, see note above. Also, tax deed and foreclosures lists in pdf format can be downloaded from the clerk's website.
Property, Taxation Records   Free   Search the property appraiser sales and tax records for free at www.qpublic.net/washington/index-pa-search.html. Also, search the tax collector records for free at www.qpublic.net/wctc/index-tc-search.html.

Other Florida Sites of Note:

Alachua County - Traffic Citations http://assets.alachuacounty.us/ws/applications-asp/Traffic/

Brevard County - Most Wanted, Arrests www.sheriff.co.brevard.fl.us

Broward County - Occupational Licenses http://bcegov2.broward.org/olsearch/olsearch.asp

Broward County - Sheriff, Most Wanted, Missing Person, Arrests, Sex Offenders www.sheriff.org

Charlotte County - Arrests, Most Wanted, Sex Offender www.ccso.org/localcrime/crimedatabase.cfm

Citrus County - Sex Offender www.sheriffcitrus.org/sexoffenders.aspx

Clay County - Most Wanted, Sex Offender http://claysheriff.com

Collier County - Occupational Licenses www.colliertax.com/search/ols.php

Collier County - Wanted/Missing Persons www.colliersheriff.org/

De Soto County - Most Wanted www.desotosheriff.com/most_wanted

Duval County - Inmates http://inmatesearch.jaxsheriff.org/

Duval County - Occupational Licenses http://fl-duval-taxcollector.governmax.com/COLLECTMAX/COLLECT30.ASP

Escambia County - Inmates http://66.210.33.206/oiscript/oiget.asp

Hardee County - Most Wanted, Missing, Arrests, Warrants, Inmates www.hardeeso.com

Hernando County - Arrests, Most Wanted, Civil Papers Filed On www.hcso.hernando.fl.us

Hillsborough County - Warrants, Inmates, Repo/Impounds www.hcso.tampa.fl.us/Page_Headers/online.htm

Indian River County - Inmates, Sheriff's Criminal History www.ircsheriff.org/programs.cfm

Lee County - Occupational Licenses
www.leetc.com/search_criteria.asp?searchtype=OCCLIC&c=home&r=1&page_id=searchcriteria

Leon County - Contractor Licensees www.leonpermits.org/contractors/

Leon County - Inmates, Most Wanted, Sex Offender http://lcso.leonfl.org/

Marion County - Sheriff's Jail Inmates http://jail.marionso.com/search.asp

Miami-Dade County - See Dade County see Dade County

Monroe County - Arrests, Inmates, Warrants www.keysso.net

Monroe County - Warrants www2.keysso.net/WebWarrants/WebWarrantsA.htm

Orange County - Contractor Licenses www.orangecountyfl.net/ebuilding/ContractorSearch/ContractorSearch.asp

Osceola County - Inmates www.osceola.org/index.cfm?lsFuses=inmates

Palm Beach County - Occupational Licenses www.pbcgov.com/tax/services_business_request.shtml
    Is now subscription site; $120 yearly fee.

Palm Beach County - Sheriff Bookings, Wanted Fugitives, Sexual Predators www.pbso.org

Pasco County - Contractors, Construction Permits http://opal.pascocountyfl.net

Pasco County - Most Wanted, Sexual Predators http://pascosheriff.com

Pinellas County - Most Wanted www.co.pinellas.fl.us/sheriff/csprofiles.htm

Polk County - Warrants, Most Wanted www.polksheriff.org/wanted/

Putnam County - Sheriff Warrants, Jail Log, Most Wanted www.pcso.us

Santa Rosa - Occupational Licenses
    http://santarosataxcollector.governmax.com/collectmax/search_collect.asp?l_nm=occlic_bus_name&sid

Sarasota County - Arrest Cards www.sarasotasheriff.org/arrests.asp Daily records go back 30 days.

Seminole County - Felon, Offenders, Sex Offenders www.seminolesheriff.org/en-us/ Search under "Criminal Information" on righthand side of website.

St. Johns County - Most Wanted, Sexual Offender www.sjso.org/

Suwannee County - Most Wanted, Inmates www.suwanneesheriff.com

Volusia County - Citations, 24-hr Arrest Report www.clerk.org/index.html Click on Public Records then "Arrest downloads" at left menu. Ditto for Citations; Citation data goes back to 1990. You must enter your name to access.

Volusia County - Civil Suits, Real Estate, Bldg Permits, Divorce, Marriage
    http://extra.orlandosentinel.com/publicrecords/search.asp Records only go back 2 weeks on this private website.

Volusia County - Inmates http://volusia.org/corrections/search_page.htm.

Georgia

Capital: Atlanta
                 Fulton County
Time Zone: EST
Population: 8,829,383
# of Counties: 159

Useful State Links

Website: www.georgia.gov
Governor: www.ganet.org/governor/
Attorney General: www.law.state.ga.us
State Archives: http://sos.georgia.gov/archives/
State Statutes and Codes: http://www.lexis-nexis.com/hottopics/gacode/default.asp
Legislative Bill Search: www.legis.state.ga.us
Bill Monitoring: www.gatrack.com
Unclaimed Funds: https://www.etax.dor.ga.gov/unclaimedproperty/main.aspx

Primary State Agencies

Sexual Offender Registry   Free

Georgia Bureau of Investigations, GCIC - Sexual Offender Registry, http://services.georgia.gov/gbi/gbisor/disclaim.html Records may be searched at http://services.georgia.gov/gbi/gbisor/disclaim.html. Earliest records go back to 07/01/96. Close to 80% of registered offenders have photographs on the web site. Searches may be conducted for sex offenders, absconders, and predators.

Incarceration Records   Free

Georgia Department of Corrections, Inmate Records Office - 6th Fl, East Tower, www.dcor.state.ga.us The website has an extensive array of search capabilities.

Corporation, LP, LLP, LLC, Not-for-Profits   Free & $$

Sec of State - Corporation Division, Record Searches, http://sos.georgia.gov/corporations/ Records are available from the corporation database on the Internet site above. The corporate database can be searched by entity name or registered agent for no fee. Document Image and certificates are available for a $10.00 fee at www.ganet.org/services/corp/corpsearch.shtml or at https://corp.sos.state.ga.us/corp/soskb/login.asp. Other services include name reservation, filing procedures, downloading of forms/applications. Also, search securities companies registered with the state at www.sos.ga.gov/sbr_weblookup_prod/.

Trademarks/Servicemarks   Free

Secretary of State, Trademark Division, www.georgiatrademarks.org/ A record database is searchable from the web. Search by registration #, mark name, description, connection, owner, or classification.

Uniform Commercial Code   Free & $$

Superior Court Clerks' Cooperative Authority, www.gsccca.org/Projects/aboutucc.asp Free name searching is available at the website. Also search by secured party, tax payer ID, date, or file number. There is a monthly charge of $9.95 and a $.25 fee per image for unlimited access to images. Certified searches are $10.00. Billing is monthly. The system is open 24 hours daily. The website also includes real estate indexes and images, lien index, and notary index. *Other Options:* The entire UCC Central Index System can be purchased on a daily, weekly, biweekly basis. For more information, contact the Director's office.

Driver Records $$

Department of Driver Services, Driver's Services Section, www.dds.ga.gov Through the coordinated efforts of the GA Department of Motor Vehicle Safety and the Georgia Technology Authority, driving records are now available via the Internet for "certified users, including insurance, employers, and car rental companies. The fees are $5.00 for a three-year record and $7.00 for a seven-year record. For further information, visit https://online.dds.ga.gov/onlineservices/MVRInfo.aspx.

Vehicle Ownership & Registration $$

Department of Revenue, Motor Vehicle Division, http://motor.etax.dor.ga.gov/ Online subscription access available to Georgia dealers only; registration is required.

Voter Registration Free

Secretary of State - Elections Division, 1104 West Tower, http://sos.georgia.gov/elections/ Name and DOB needed to search unofficial registration information at http://sos.georgia.gov/cgi-bin/Locator.asp. The results will provide address and district-precinct information, no SSNs released. *Other Options:* CDs, Internet files, disks, and paper lists are available for purchase for non-commercial purposes. Look at the website for pricing.

Birth & Death Certificates $$

Department of Human Resources, Vital Records Unit, http://health.state.ga.us/programs/vitalrecords/index.asp Records may be ordered online through an approved vendor - www.vitalchek.com. A credit card fee applies. *Other Options:* The death index is available for the years 1919-1998 on microfiche for $50.00.

Occupational Licensing Boards

Acupuncturist	http://services.georgia.gov/dch/mebs/jsp/index.jsp
Air Conditioning Contractor	https://secure.sos.state.ga.us/myverification/
Architect	https://secure.sos.state.ga.us/myverification/
Athletic Agent/Athletic Trainer	https://secure.sos.state.ga.us/myverification/
Attorney	www.gabar.org/directories/member_directory_search/
Auctioneer/Auction Dealer	https://secure.sos.state.ga.us/myverification/
Audiologist	https://secure.sos.state.ga.us/myverification/
Barber/Barber Shop	https://secure.sos.state.ga.us/myverification/
Cemetery	https://secure.sos.state.ga.us/SBR_Weblookup_Prod/Search.aspx
Charity	https://secure.sos.state.ga.us/SBR_Weblookup_Prod/Search.aspx
Chiropractor	https://secure.sos.state.ga.us/myverification/
Cosmetologist/Cosmetology Shop	https://secure.sos.state.ga.us/myverification/
Counselor	https://secure.sos.state.ga.us/myverification/
Credit Union	https://dbfweb.dbf.state.ga.us/WebCUData.html
Dentist/or/ Dental Hygienist	https://secure.sos.state.ga.us/myverification/
Detox Specialist	http://services.georgia.gov/dch/mebs/jsp/index.jsp
Dietitian	https://secure.sos.state.ga.us/myverification/
Drug Whlse/Retail/Mfg (Hospital)	https://secure.sos.state.ga.us/myverification/
Electrical Contractor	https://secure.sos.state.ga.us/myverification/
Embalmer	https://secure.sos.state.ga.us/myverification/
Engineer	https://secure.sos.state.ga.us/myverification/
Esthetician	https://secure.sos.state.ga.us/myverification/
Family Therapist	https://secure.sos.state.ga.us/myverification/
Financial Statement (Ethics Dept.)	www.ethics.ga.gov/EthicsWeb/lobbyists/lobbyist.aspx
Forester	https://secure.sos.state.ga.us/myverification/
Funeral Director/Apprentice/Estab't	https://secure.sos.state.ga.us/myverification/
Geologist	https://secure.sos.state.ga.us/myverification/
Hearing Aid Dealer/Dispenser	https://secure.sos.state.ga.us/myverification/
Insurance Adjuster	www.gainsurance.org/INSURANCE/AgencyStatus.aspx
Insurance Agent/Counselor	www.gainsurance.org/INSURANCE/AgentStatus.aspx
Insurance Company	www.gainsurance.org/INSURANCE/SearchCompanies.aspx
Interior Designer	https://secure.sos.state.ga.us/myverification/
Landscape Architect	https://secure.sos.state.ga.us/myverification/
Liquor Control/Liquor Retailer	www.ganet.org/alcohol/
Lobbyist/Lobbyist Organization	www.ethics.ga.gov/EthicsWeb/lobbyists/lobbyist.aspx
Low Voltage Contractor	https://secure.sos.state.ga.us/myverification/
Manicurist/Nail Care	https://secure.sos.state.ga.us/myverification/
Marriage Counselor	https://secure.sos.state.ga.us/myverification/
Medical Doctor	http://services.georgia.gov/dch/mebs/jsp/index.jsp
Notary Public	www.gsccca.org/search/notary/search.asp
Nuclear Pharmacist	https://secure.sos.state.ga.us/myverification/

Nurse-LPN-RN .... https://secure.sos.state.ga.us/myverification/
Nursing Home Administrator .... https://secure.sos.state.ga.us/myverification/
Occupational Therapist/Assistant ...... https://secure.sos.state.ga.us/myverification/
Optician, Dispensing .... https://secure.sos.state.ga.us/myverification/
Optometrist .... https://secure.sos.state.ga.us/myverification/
Osteopathic Physician .... http://services.georgia.gov/dch/mebs/jsp/index.jsp
Perfusionist .... http://services.georgia.gov/dch/mebs/jsp/index.jsp
Pesticide Applic't'r/Contr./Employee www.kellysolutions.com/ga/Applicators/index.htm
Pharmacist .... https://secure.sos.state.ga.us/myverification/
Pharmacy School, Clinic Researcher . https://secure.sos.state.ga.us/myverification/
Physical Therapist/Therapist Asst ..... https://secure.sos.state.ga.us/myverification/
Physician Assistant .... http://services.georgia.gov/dch/mebs/jsp/index.jsp
Plumber Journeyman/Contractor .... https://secure.sos.state.ga.us/myverification/
Podiatrist .... https://secure.sos.state.ga.us/myverification/Search.aspx
Poison Pharmacist .... https://secure.sos.state.ga.us/myverification/
Private Detective .... https://secure.sos.state.ga.us/myverification/
Psychologist .... https://secure.sos.state.ga.us/myverification/
Public Accountant-CPA .... https://secure.sos.state.ga.us/myverification/
Public Adjuster .... www.gainsurance.org/INSURANCE/AgentStatus.aspx
Real Estate Agent/Seller/Broker .... www.grec.state.ga.us/clsweb/realestate.aspx
Real Estate Appraiser .... www.grec.state.ga.us/clsweb/appraiser.aspx
Real Estate Community Assn. Mgr. .. www.grec.state.ga.us
Real Estate Firm .... www.grec.state.ga.us/clsweb/company.aspx
Rebuilder (Motor Vehicle) .... https://secure.sos.state.ga.us/myverification/
Respiratory Care Practitioner .... http://services.georgia.gov/dch/mebs/jsp/index.jsp
Salvage Pool Operator/Yard Dealer .. https://secure.sos.state.ga.us/myverification/
School Librarian .... https://secure.sos.state.ga.us/myverification/
Security Guard/Agency .... https://secure.sos.state.ga.us/myverification/
Social Worker .... https://secure.sos.state.ga.us/myverification/
Speech-Language Pathologist .... https://secure.sos.state.ga.us/myverification/
Surplus Line Broker .... www.gainsurance.org/INSURANCE/AgentStatus.aspx
Surveyor, Land .... https://secure.sos.state.ga.us/myverification/
Teacher .... https://www.gapsc.com/certification/look_up.asp
Used Car Dealer .... https://secure.sos.state.ga.us/myverification/
Used Car Parts Dist. .... https://secure.sos.state.ga.us/myverification/
Utility Contractor .... https://secure.sos.state.ga.us/myverification/
Veterinarian/Veterinary Technician .. https://secure.sos.state.ga.us/myverification/
Waste Water System Oper'r/Analyst . https://secure.sos.state.ga.us/myverification/
Water Distribution System Operator . https://secure.sos.state.ga.us/myverification/
Water Laboratory Operator .... https://secure.sos.state.ga.us/myverification/

State and Local Courts

State Court Structure: The Georgia court system has five classes of trial-level courts: the Magistrate, Probate, Juvenile, State, and Superior courts. In addition, there are approximately 350 municipal courts operating locally. The Superior Court, arranged in 49 circuits, is the court of general jurisdiction. The Superior Court will also assume the role of a State Court if the county does not have one. State courts exercise limited jurisdiction within one county. These judges hear misdemeanors including traffic violations, issue search and arrest warrants, hold preliminary hearings in criminal cases and try civil matters not reserved exclusively for the Superior Courts.

Magistrate Courts also issue arrest warrants and set bond on all felonies. Magistrate Courts also have jurisdiction for bad checks, arrest warrants, preliminary hearings, and county ordinance violations. The Magistrate Court has jurisdiction over civil actions under $15,000, also one type of misdemeanor related to passing bad checks. Two counties (Bibb and Richmond) have Civil/Magistrate courts with varied civil limits.

Probate Courts can, in certain cases, issue search and arrest warrants, and hear miscellaneous misdemeanors.

Statewide Court Online Access: Search the dockets of the Court of Appeals at www.gaappeals.us/. Search dockets of the Supreme Court at www.gasupreme.us/computer_docket.php. Make online purchases of certificates of admission and good standing ($3.00), Supreme Court opinions ($5.00), and certified copies of Supreme Court opinions ($8.00) using Paypal. Go to www.gasupreme.us/purchase_online.php.

A limited number of county courts offer online access to court records, but there is no statewide online access available statewide.

Bartow County

Probate Court www.bartowga.org/probate **Free** Search citations free at https://www.ncourt.com/courtpayment/Lookup.aspx?Juris=GABartow.

Bibb County

Superior Court www.co.bibb.ga.us/ **Free**
Civil: Court calendars online at www.co.bibb.ga.us/CalendarDirectory/CalendarDirectory.asp. *Criminal:* Superior court calendars at www.co.bibb.ga.us/CalendarDirectory/CalendarDirectory.asp.

State Court www.co.bibb.ga.us **Free**
Civil: Search civil court calendars online at www.co.bibb.ga.us/StateCourtClerk/Civil/Default.htm. Website will have access to full court record indexes in the future.

Chatham County

Superior Court www.chathamcourts.org/chatcourts.html **Free**
Civil: Search county court civil records at www.chathamcounty.org/jims/. *Criminal:* Search county court criminal records at www.chathamcounty.org/jims/.

State Court www.statecourt.org **Free**
Civil: Search county civil dockets and records free at www.chathamcounty.org/jims/. Search by name or case number. *Criminal:* Search county criminal dockets and records free at www.chathamcounty.org/jims/.

Magistrate Court www.chathamcourts.org/chatcourts.html **Free** Search dockets online at www.chathamcounty.org/jims/.

Clayton County

Superior Court www.co.clayton.ga.us/superior_court/clerk_of_courts/ **Free**
Civil: Online access is the same as criminal, see below. *Criminal:* Search records free at http://weba.co.clayton.ga.us:8006/index.shtml. Court calendars at www.co.clayton.ga.us/courtcalendars/index.htm. Searches and records also available on the statewide system.

State Court www.co.clayton.ga.us/state_court/clerk_of_courts/ **Free**
Criminal: Can search criminal database by name or case at http://weba.co.clayton.ga.us:8006/index.shtml.

Magistrate Court www.co.clayton.ga.us/courts.htm **Free** Online access free at http://weba.co.clayton.ga.us:8006/index.shtml.

Cobb County

Superior Court www.cobbsuperiorcourtclerk.com **Free**
Civil: Civil indexes and images of Clerk of Superior Court are free at www.cobbsuperiorcourtclerk.org/courts/Civil.htm. Search by name, type or case number. Data updated Fridays. Images go back thru 2004. *Criminal:* Criminal indexes and images of Clerk of Superior Court are free at www.cobbsuperiorcourtclerk.org/courts/Criminal.htm. Search by name, type or case number. Data updated Fridays but indexing can be nearly a month behind.

Coweta County

Superior Court **Free**
Criminal: Access court records free online at http://sccweb.coweta.ga.us/cmwebsearchppp/.

State Court www.coweta.ga.us/Resources/stateclk.html **Free**
Civil: Current court calendar is available at the website; make court record searches free at www.courtinnovations.net/webcasemanagement/ and login as CowetaView and password coweta. *Criminal:* Current court calendar is available at the website; public record searches are to be online at the website later in 2007.

De Kalb County

Superior Court www.co.dekalb.ga.us/superior/index.htm **Free**
Civil and Criminal: Online access is free at www.ojs.dekalbga.org. Jail and inmate records are also available.

State Court www.dekalbstatecourt.net **Free**
Civil: Online access is free at www.ojs.dekalbga.org. Also, current court calendars free at www.dekalbstatecourt.net. *Criminal:* Online access free at www.ojs.dekalbga.org. Jail and inmate records available. Also, current court calendars free at www.dekalbstatecourt.net.

Magistrate Court   http://dekalbstatecourt.net   **Free**
Civil: Online access is free at www.ojs.dekalbga.org.

Dougherty County

Superior & State Court   www.albany.ga.us/court_system/court_system.htm   **Free**
Civil: Access pre-2003 civil and criminal court docket data free at www.albany.ga.us/court_system/court_clerk.htm The same system permits access to probate, tax, deeds, death certificate records, and older civil/criminal records. *Criminal:* Same.

Magistrate Court   www.doughertycourt.com   **Free**
Civil: Online access to court records is through the county clerk's system at www.albany.ga.us/court_system/court_clerk.htm Records are pre-7/2002.

Probate Court   **Free**   Search the probate court index free at www.albany.ga.us/court_system/court_clerk.htm.

Echols County

Magistrate & Probate Court   **Free**   Name search for citations free at
https://www.ncourt.com/courtpayment/Lookup.aspx?Juris=GAEchols.

Fulton County

Superior Court - Civil   www.fcclk.org   **Free**
Civil: Access Clerk of Superior Court Judicial civil records free at www.fcclkjudicialsearch.org/CivilSearch/civfrmd.htm. Search by either party name, case number, and date range. Search includes status, attorney. Also a Hearing Search free at www.fcclkjudicialsearch.org/CVHearSearch/cvhearfrmd.htm.

Gwinnett County

Superior & State Court   www.gwinnettcourts.com/#home/   **Free**
Civil: Online access to court case party index is free at www.gwinnettcourts.com/home.asp#partycasesearch/. Search by name or case number. *Criminal:* Same.

Magistrate Court   www.gwinnettcourts.com/#home   **Free**
Civil: Online access to court case party index is free at www.gwinnettcourts.com/home.asp#partycasesearch/.

Probate Court and Magistrate Court   www.gwinnettcourts.com/#home/   **Free**   Search cases and calendars countywide free.

Harris County

Superior Court   **Free & $$**
Civil: Access court records by subscription; for information and signup contact Lisa Culpeper at 706-628-4944. *Criminal:* same.

Jones County

Probate Court   **Free**   Search for tickets free at https://www.ncourt.com/courtpayment/Lookup.aspx?Juris=GAJones.

Muscogee County

Superior & State Court   www.muscogeecourts.com   **Free**
Civil: Dockets and current calendars are free at www.muscogeecourts.com. Also, a court case management system is available by subscription; username and password required. *Criminal:* Online access to criminal is the same as civil; see above.

Richmond County

Superior Court   www.augustaga.gov/departments/clerk%5Fsup/   **Free**
Civil: Access court dockets free at www.augustaga.gov/WebDocket/ for records 2001 forward. *Criminal:* Access court dockets free at www.augustaga.gov/WebDocket/ for records 2001 forward.

State Court   www.augustaga.gov   **Free**
Civil: Name search civil dockets free at www.augustaga.gov/WebDocket/. *Criminal:* Search state warrants free at www.augustaga.gov/WebDocket/.

Telfair County

Probate Court   http://telfaircounty.georgia.gov   **Free**   Search the courts citations database free at
https://www.ncourt.com/courtpayment/Lookup.aspx?Juris=GATelfair.

Recorders, Assessors, and Other Sites of Note

Recording Office Organization: 159 counties, 159 recording offices. The recording officer is the Clerk of Superior Court. All transactions are recorded in a "General Execution Docket." All tax liens on personal property are filed with the county Clerk of Superior Court in a "General Execution Docket" (grantor/grantee) or "Lien Index."

Online Access Note: The Georgia Superior Court Clerk's Cooperative Authority (GSCCCA) at www.gsccca.org/search offers free access to a number of state indices. The Real Estate Index contains property transactions from ALL counties since January 1, 1999. The Lien Index includes liens filed on real and personal property. Throughput varies, but is generally from January 10, 2002. The UCC Index contains financing statement data from all counties since January, 1995 and can be searched by name, taxpayer ID, file date and file number. Additionally, the actual image of the corresponding UCC statement can be downloaded for a fee. Visit the GSCCCA website for details.

❖ **Statewide Access Offered For All Districts – Read Above**

Below are Additional Sites With Major Coverage ❖

Basic assessor and property records in these Georgia Counties are available free via http://www.gaassessors.com/ and/or http://qpublic.net/ga/ - Appling, Atkinson, Bacon, Baker, Baldwin, Banks, Barrow, Bartow, Ben Hill, Berrien, Bibb, Bleckley, Brantley, Brooks, Bryan, Bulloch, Burke, Butts, Calhoun, Camden, Candler, Carroll, Catoosa, Charlton, Chatham, Chattahoochee, Chattooga, Cherokee, Clarke, Clay, Clayton, Clinch, Cobb, Coffee, Colquitt, Columbia, Cook, Coweta, Crawford, Crisp, Dade, Dawson, Decatur, DeKalb, Dodge, Dooly, Dougherty, Douglas, Early, Echols, Effingham, Elbert, Emanuel, Evans, Fannin, Fayette, Floyd, Forsyth, Franklin, Fulton, Gilmer, Glascock, Glynn, Gordon, Grady, Greene, Gwinnett, Habersham, Hall, Hancock, Haralson, Harris, Hart, Heard, Henry, Houston, Irwin, Jackson, Jasper, Jeff Davis, Jefferson, Jenkins, Johnson, Jones, Lamar, Lanier, Laurens, Lee, Liberty, Lincoln, Long, Lowndes, Lumpkin, Macon, Madison, Marion, McDuffie, McIntosh, Meriwether, Miller, Mitchell, Monroe, Montgomery, Morgan, Murray, Muscogee, Newton, Oconee, Oglethorpe, Paulding, Peach, Pickens, Pierce, Pike, Polk, Pulaski, Putnam, Quitman, Rabun, Randolph, Richmond, Rockdale, Schley, Screven, Seminole, Spalding, Stephens, Stewart, Sumter, Talbot, Taliaferro, Tattnall, Taylor, Telfair, Terrell, Thomas, Tift, Toombs, Towns, Treutlen, Troup, Turner, Twiggs, Union, Upson, Walker, Walton, Ware, Warren, Washington, Wayne, Webster, Wheeler, White, Whitfield, Wilcox, Wilkes, Wilkinson, and Worth.

You may subscribe at http://qpublic.net/ga/ for full assessor, property data for these Georgia Counties - Baker, Ben Hill, Brantley, Brooks, Camden, Colquitt, Gordon, Hancock, Irwin, Jenkins, Macon, Marion, McDuffie, Montgomery, Morgan, Pulaski, Quitman, Randolph, Seminole, Taliaferro, Taylor, Towns, Treutlen, Turner, Webster, Wilcox, Worth.

Baldwin County www.baldwincountyga.com *Property, Taxation Records* `Free` Property searching available free at http://baldwinta.com/

Banks County *Property, Taxation Records* `Free` Access assessor property data free on the GIS-mapping site search page at www.bankscountymaps.com/reports/searchmenu.cfm.

Bartow County *Property, Taxation Records* `Free` Access property data free on the GIS-mapping site search page at www.bartowcountymaps.com/reports/searchmenu.cfm.

Bibb County *RE Deed, UCC, Lien, Notary, Plat Records* www.co.bibb.ga.us/ `Free` See www.gsccca.org for Deed, Lien and UCC indexes. Also, search land, financing statements and liens on the Superior Court clerk search page for free at http://68.109.200.17/resolution.
Property, Taxation Records `Free` Free property records search at www.co.bibb.ga.us/TaxAssessors/index1.html Also, search for property ownership for free at www.co.bibb.ga.us/engineering/property/search.htm. Also, search property info at www.co.bibb.ga.us/gisonline/advancedsearch.asp and Ad Valorem tax statements at www.co.bibb.ga.us/TaxBills/Searchpage.asp.

Brooks County *Property, Taxation Records* `Free` Poperty records searching available free at http://gaassessors.com/loadpage.php?refurl=http://qpublic.net/ga/brooks

Candler County *Property, Taxation Records* **Free** Access property records free at www.candlertax.org/.

Chatham County www.chathamcourts.org *Property, Taxation Records* **Free** Search the assessor database free at www.chathamcounty.org/prc.html.

Chattahoochee County *Property, Taxation Records* **Free** Access property data on the GIS-mapping site free at http://webmap.jws.com/chattahoochee/.

Cherokee County *Real Estate, Grantor/Grantee, Deed, Lien, UCC, Plat Records* www.cherokeega.com **Free** See www.gsccca.org for Deed, Lien and UCC indexes. Also, access recording records free at http://deeds.cherokeega.com/Search.aspx.
Property, Taxation Records **Free** Free property records search from the Tax Assessor's Database at http://gaassessors.com/loadpage.php?refurl=www.cherokeega.com/ccweb/departments/assessor/

Clarke County http://athensclarke.allclerks.us *Property, Taxation Records* **Free** View property data for free at https://athens-clarke.ga.ezgov.com/ezproperty/review_search.jsp but no name searching.

Clayton County www.co.clayton.ga.us/ *Property, Taxation Records* **Free** Search tax assessor records for free at www.qpublic.net/clayton/search.html. Also, search property card index free at http://weba.co.clayton.ga.us:8003/indextax.shtml.

Cobb County *Real Estate, Grantor/Grantee, Deed, Lien UCC Records* www.cobbsuperiorcourtclerk.org/index.htm **Free** Property records on the County Superior Court Clerk website are free at www.cobbsuperiorcourtclerk.org/home.asp. Search by name, address, land description, instrument type, or book & page; includes court records. Also, see www.gsccca.org for online access to Deed, Plat and UCC indexes.
Property, Taxation Records **Free** Free property records search at http://gaassessors.com/loadpage.php?refurl=www.cobbcounty.org. Also, search for parcel data on the GIS-mapping site free at http://gis.cobbcountyga.gov/. Click on Launch Online Mapping; no name searching. Also, search Tax Commissioner property tax records for free at www.cobbtax.org/Search/GenericSearch.aspx.

Columbia County *Property, Taxation Records* **Free** Search parcel data free on the mapping site at http://68.216.79.105/columbia/default.htm and click on parcel search.

Coweta County *Property, Taxation Records* **Free** Access to property records at www.cowetatax.com/.

Crawford County *Property, Taxation Records* **Free** GIS-mapping system free at www.crawfordcountymaps.com.

Dade County *RE Deed, UCC, Lien, Notary, Plat Records* www.dadegaclerkofcourt.com **Free** See www.gsccca.org for Deed, Lien and UCC indexes. Attorney access to clerk records is available at www.dadeclerkofcourt.com. Calendars are also available.

Dawson County www.dawsoncounty.org *Property, Taxation Records* **Free** Search the assessor property data and sales for free at www.qpublic.net/ga/dawson/search1.html. Also, access property data for free at www.dawsontaxassessors.org/.

De Kalb County *Property, Taxation Records* **Free** Search tax commissioner property tax data for free at https://dklbweb.dekalbga.org/taxcommissioner/search.asp. No name searching.

Dougherty County *Real Estate, Tax, Court, Deed, Mortgage, UCC, Death, Divorce, Trade Name Records* www.albany.ga.us/court_system/court_clerk.htm **Free** Access to the clerk of courts Dept. of Deeds public menu is at www.albany.ga.us/court_system/court_clerk.htm. Click on "Real Estate." Also, see www.gsccca.org for online access to Deed and UCC indexes.
Property, Taxation Records **Free** Search the tax records system and sales lists free at www.qpublic.net/ga/dougherty/.

Douglas County *Property, Taxation Records* **Free** Access property data and gis-mapping free at http://douglas.binarybus.com/.

Effingham County www.effinghamcounty.org/ *Property, Taxation Records* **Free** Access assessor and parcel records free at www.effinghamcounty.org/pages/egis.html. Also, search assessment and property records free at www.qpublic.net/ga/effingham/search.html

Fayette County www.admin.co.fayette.ga.us *Property, Taxation Records* **Free** Records on the County Assessor database are free on the GIS-mapping site at www.fayettecountymaps.com.

Floyd County *Property, Taxation Records* **Free** Access property data via the GIS-mapping site free at http://gis.romega.us/app/. Now has name searching.

Forsyth County *RE Deed, Lien, UCC, Notary, Hospital Lien, Plat, Old Land, Trade Name Records* www.forsythco.com **Free** See www.gsccca.org for free access to Deeds, Liens and UCCs; see online note at beginning of section. Also, search land records, liens, plats, and trade names free at http://resolution.forsythco.com/.
Property, Taxation Records **Free** Search the county assessor data free at www.qpublic.net/ga/forsyth/search1.html.

Franklin County www.franklincountyga.com/ *Property, Taxation Records* `Free` Access assessor property and sales data free at http://qpublic.net/ga/franklin/search1.html. Also, access properrty tax data free at https://franklincounty.paytaxes.net/customer/enhanced_property_tax_search.php.

Fulton County www.fcclk.org *Property, Taxation Records* `Free` Search assessor property data free at www.fultonassessor.org click on Property Search, but no name searching. Search tax commissioner's delinquent property pdf lists by district at https://www.fultoncountytaxes.org/fultoniwr/Delinquent_Properties.htm. Also, search for property tax bills at https://www.fultoncountytaxes.org/fultoniwr/11_depts_property_taxes.asp but no name searching.

Glascock County *Property, Taxation Records* `Free` Access assessor parcel data free on the Central Savannah River Area GIS site at www.csrardc.org/viewer.htm. Click on Search and choose Glascock.

Glynn County *Property, Taxation Records* `Free & $$` Access the county assessor property tax records free on the GIS mapping site at http://glynn.binarybus.com. Click on Launch Free Standard Viewer. A subscription service also available with deeper data. Also, search appraisal office tax data free at http://glynn.binarybus.com/tapc/.

Gordon County www.gordoncounty.org/ *Property, Taxation Records* `Free` Access property data free at http://gordon.binarybus.com/lookup/. Also, search proerpty tas payment database free at https://gordon.paytaxes.net//customer/enhanced_property_tax_search.php

Gwinnett County *RE Deed, UCC, Lien, Notary, Plat Records* www.gwinnettcourts.com `Free` See www.gsccca.org for free access; see online note at beginning of section. Also, search for civil court judgments at www.gwinnettcourts.com/home.asp#home/.
Property, Taxation Records `Free` Access property, property tax, GIS-mapping, treasurer, assessor data and more free at https://ssl.gwinnetttaxcommissioner.com/Property/Property.aspx. Also search property data and online payments free at https://ssl.gwinnetttaxcommissioner.com/Property/Search.aspx.

Habersham County www.co.habersham.ga.us *Property, Taxation Records* `Free` Search property/GIS data free at www.emapsplus.com/GAHabersham/maps/. Click on Owner to name search.

Hall County www.hallcounty.org *Property, Taxation Records* `Free` Access property data free on the GIS site at http://gispublic.hallcounty.org. Click on quick search, then select name search.

Henry County www.co.henry.ga.us *Property, Taxation Records* `Free` Search property tax data free at www.co.henry.ga.us/MapsZonesDistricts/index_2.htm.

Houston County *RE Deed, UCC, Lien, Notary, Plat Records* www.houstoncountyga.com/index.htm `Free` See www.gsccca.org for free access to Deeds back to 1999, Liens back to 2004, and UCCs back to 1995, plats back to 2004. Also, the clerks recording indices of plats, land records, liens is free at http://67.32.12.213/resolution/. Pre-1998 real estate and pre-1994 financing statements are also available.
Property, Taxation Records `Free` Access to the assessor Mapguide database is free at www.assessors.houstoncountyga.org. Download the Autodesk MapGuide viewer. Also, access assessor property data free at http://qpublic.net/ga/houston/search1.html.

Jasper County *Property, Taxation Records* `Free` Access Property Records free at www.jaspercountyboa.org/ click on Search Records.

Jefferson County *Property, Taxation Records* `Free` Access assessor property and sales data free at http://qpublic.net/ga/jefferson/search1.html. Also, access assessor parcel data free on the Central Savannah River Area GIS site at www.csrardc.org/viewer.htm. Click on Search and choose Jefferson.

Liberty County www.libertyco.com *Property, Taxation Records* `Free` Search the assessor data free at http://ww2.libertycountyga.com:8088/EGSV2Liberty/RPSearch.do

Lincoln County *Property, Taxation Records* `Free` Search assessor property records and sales free at http://qpublic.net/ga/lincoln/. Also, access assessor parcel data free on the Central Savannah River Area GIS site at www.csrardc.org/viewer.htm. Click on Search and choose Lincoln.

Lowndes County *Property, Taxation Records* `Free` Search site at http://qpublic.net/ga/lowndes/ converted to a fee-based service but free public search is still available. Other search abilities, data, maps available to subscribers; 1 user - $20/mo or $200/yr, fees increase for multiple users. Credit card required.

McDuffie County www.thomson-mcduffie.com *Property, Taxation Records* `Free` Access assessor parcel data free on the Central Savannah River Area GIS site at www.csrardc.org/viewer.htm. Click on Search and choose McDuffie.

McIntosh County *Real Estate, Deed, UCC, Lien Records* www.gsccca.org `Free & $$` Call 800-304-5175 to subscribe to UCCs and Deed indexes online service. Deeds go back to 2000. Also, see note at beginning of section- www.gsccca.org for online access to Deed, Lien and UCC indexes.
Property, Taxation Records `Free` Access property data free at www.mcintoshtaxassessor.com and click on Search Records.

Madison County www.madisoncountyGA.us *Property, Taxation Records* `Free` Access assessor property data free at www.qpublic.net/ga/madison/search1.html. Also, search tax bill data free at https://madison.paytaxes.net/customer/enhanced_property_tax_search.php.

Muscogee County *RE Deed, UCC, Lien, Notary, Plat Records* www.columbusga.org/ `Free` See www.gsccca.org for Deed, Lien and UCC indexes. Also, search the clerk's index free at http://clerk-web.columbusga.org/oncoreweb/Search.aspx.
Property, Taxation Records `Free` Access assessor property recrods free by searching free at http://ccga1.columbusga.org/PropertyInformation.nsf//

Newton County *Property, Taxation Records* `Free` Search assessor and property data free at http://newton.binarybus.com/lookup/.

Oconee County *Property, Taxation Records* `Free` Search assessor's information online at http://qpublic.net/ga/oconee/index.html, access GIS Map information at www.oconeecounty.com

Peach County www.peachcounty.net/ *Property, Taxation Records* `$$` Subscribe to the GIS-mapping site for property data at www.peachcountymaps.com. For registration and password, contact the Tax Office at 478-825-5924.

Pickens County *Property, Taxation Records* `Free` Access assessor property records free at http://qpublic.net/ga/pickens/search1.html. Also, access records on the mapping site free at www.tscmaps.com/mg/ga/pickens/index.asp.

Rabun County *Property, Taxation Records* `Free` Rabun County property records found at http://rabun.binarybus.com/lookup/. Search by owner name, address, or parcel number.

Richmond County www.augustaga.gov/ *Property, Taxation Records* `Free` Access GIS Maps at http://augustaga.gov/departments/gis/home.asp. Access Real Estate Property Search System at http://mapweb.augustaga.gov/augusta/. Search parcels by owner name, address, subdivision, and parcel number.

Taliaferro County *Property, Taxation Records* `Free` Access Property Records at http://gaassessors.com/loadpage.php?refurl=http://qpublic.net/ga/taliaferro. Access assessor parcel data free on the Central Savannah River Area GIS site at www.csrardc.org/viewer.htm. Click on Search and choose Taliaferro.

Tift County *Property, Taxation Records* `Free` Access property on MapGuide viewer at www.tiftcountymaps.com/.

Troup County *Property, Taxation Records* `Free` Troup County property records at http://hosted.3xatlanta.com/sites/troup/TCPropertyRecords.nsf.

Twiggs County *Property, Taxation Records* `Free` Map site at www.twiggscountymaps.com/ site requires the use of Autodesk's Mapguide Viewer, must download the installation program (MGControl6.5sp1.exe).

Walker County *Property, Taxation Records* `Free` Access property data on the GIS-mapping site free at www.georgiagis.com/walker/activexframeset.cfm.

Warren County *Property, Taxation Records* `Free` Access assessor property records free at http://qpublic.net/ga/warren/search1.html. Also, access assessor parcel data free on the Central Savannah River Area GIS site at www.csrardc.org/viewer.htm. Click on Search then County then choose Warren.

White County *Property, Taxation Records* `Free` Search assessor's webpage free at www.whitecounty.net/assessors_office/assessor.htm. Search of property records by parcel number, map number, owner first or last name, address.

Whitfield County www.whitfieldcountyga.com/ *Property, Taxation Records* `Free & $$` Access to property tax data is available free at www.whitfieldcountyga.com/GIS/Public/searchassessor.asp. A subscription service is also available for professions requiring full property data.

Other Georgia Sites of Note:
Bibb County - Business License www.co.bibb.ga.us/MBOTax/MBOSearch.asp
Bibb County - Inmates www.co.bibb.ga.us/BSOInmatesOnline/BSOSearchPage.asp
Chatham County - Fines, Tickets, Restitutions www.chathamcounty.org/jims/fines/default.asp
Columbia County - Sex Offender www.columbiacountyga.gov/index.aspx?page=2391
Fulton County - Inmates www.fultonsheriff.org Click on Inmate Information.
Jones County - Traffic Citations https://www.ncourt.com/courtpayment/Lookup.aspx?Juris=GAJones
Richmond County, City of Augusta - Gravesite www.augustaga.gov/departments/trees_landscaping/graveside_default.asp
Rockdale County (Conyers) - Accident Reports www.govhost.com/conyers-ga/default.asp Click on "click here" in E-Services, then "Accident reports" under "Police." 12/01/00 through the present.

Hawaii

Capital: Honolulu
         Honolulu County
Time Zone: HT
Population: 1,262,840
# of Counties: 4

Useful State Links

Website: http://hawaii.gov/portal/
Governor: www.hawaii.gov/gov/
Attorney General: www.hawaii.gov/ag/
State Archives: www.hawaii.gov/dags/divisions/archives_division
State Statutes and Codes: www.capitol.hawaii.gov/site1/hrs/default.asp
Legislative Bill Search: www.capitol.hawaii.gov/site1/docs/docs.asp?press1=docs
Unclaimed Funds: http://pahoehoe.ehawaii.gov/lilo/app

Primary State Agencies

Criminal Records   Free & $$

Hawaii Criminal Justice Data Center, Criminal Record Request, http://hawaii.gov/ag/hcjdc/ Online access is available view eCrim at http://ecrim.ehawaii.gov/ahewa/. There is no fee to view the results of your search; the option is available to purchase a certified copy of the record for $13.00. Registration is required. Questions are directed to 808-587-4220.

Sexual Offender Registry   Free

Hawaii Criminal Justice Data Center, Sexual Offender Registry, http://sexoffenders.hawaii.gov/index.html Search at http://sexoffenders.ehawaii.gov/sexoff/search.jsp?. Search by name, street or ZIP Code.

Corporation, LP, LLC, LLP, Trade Name, Assumed Name, Trademarks, Servicemarks   Free

Business Registration Division, http://hawaii.gov/dcca/areas/breg Online access to business names is available at http://hawaii.gov/dcca/areas/breg/online/. There are no fees, the system is open 24 hours. For assistance during business hours, call 808-586-2727. Tax license searching is available free at http://pahoehoe.ehawaii.gov/tls/app. Search by name, ID number of DBA name. *Other Options:* Bulk data can be purchased online through ehawaiigov.com. Visit the website or call 808-587-4220 for more information.

Uniform Commercial Code, Tax Liens, Real Estate Recordings   Free

UCC Division, Bureau of Conveyances, http://hawaii.gov/dlnr.boc Search the indices from 1976 forward at home page or from http://bocweb.dlnrbc.hawaii.gov/boc/. Search by grantor, grantee, business name. Includes real estate recordings.

Driver Records   Free & $$

Traffic Violations Bureau, Abstract Section, www.courts.state.hi.us/index.jsp Online ordering by DPPA complaint requesters is available from the state-designated entity - Hawaii Information Consortium (HIC). The record fee is $9.00 per record plus a $75.00 annual subscription fee is required. Record requests are accepted via FTP. Results, if clear, are returned via FTP. Results with hits on convictions on the record are returned on paper. Visit their website at www.ehawaii.gov/dakine/docs/subscription.html or call HIC at 808-587-4220 for more information. Name checks of traffic court records may be ordered from the court. *Other Options:* HIC offers other means to obtain records. Please call the number listed above for more information.

Birth & Marriage Certificates $$

State Department of Health, Vital Records Section, http://hawaii.gov/health/vital-records/ Requests may also be placed for birth and marriage certificates on a limited basis through https://www.ehawaii.gov/doh/vitrec/exe/vitrec.cgi. There is a surcharge of $1.50 fee for requests made through the Internet, use of a credit card is required.

Occupational Licensing Boards

Acupuncturist	http://pvl.ehawaii.gov/pvlsearch/app
Architect	http://pvl.ehawaii.gov/pvlsearch/app
Attorney	www.hsba.org/lawyerstatus.aspx
Auction	http://pvl.ehawaii.gov/pvlsearch/app
Bank/Bank Agenciy/Office	www.hawaii.gov/dcca/areas/dfi/regulate/regulate/
Barber/Barber Apprentice.Shop	http://pvl.ehawaii.gov/pvlsearch/app
Beauty Instructor	http://pvl.ehawaii.gov/pvlsearch/app
Beauty Operator/School/Shop	http://pvl.ehawaii.gov/pvlsearch/app
Boxer	http://pvl.ehawaii.gov/pvlsearch/app
Cemetery	http://pvl.ehawaii.gov/pvlsearch/app
Certified Public Accountant-CPA	http://pvl.ehawaii.gov/pvlsearch/app
Chiropractor	http://pvl.ehawaii.gov/pvlsearch/app
Collection Agency	http://pvl.ehawaii.gov/pvlsearch/app
Condominium Hotel Operator	http://pahoehoe.ehawaii.gov/ils/app
Condominium Managing Agent	http://pahoehoe.ehawaii.gov/ils/app
Contractor	http://pvl.ehawaii.gov/pvlsearch/app
Credit Union	www.hawaii.gov/dcca/areas/dfi/regulate/regulate/
Dentist/or/Dental Hygienist	http://pvl.ehawaii.gov/pvlsearch/app
Elected Officials Financ'l Disclosure	www.state.hi.us/ethics/noindex/pubrec.htm
Electrician	http://pvl.ehawaii.gov/pvlsearch/app
Electrologist	http://pvl.ehawaii.gov/pvlsearch/app
Emergency Medical Personnel	http://pvl.ehawaii.gov/pvlsearch/app
Employment Agency	http://pvl.ehawaii.gov/pvlsearch/app
Engineer	http://pvl.ehawaii.gov/pvlsearch/app
Escrow Company	www.hawaii.gov/dcca/areas/dfi/regulate/regulate/
Financial Services Loan Company	www.hawaii.gov/dcca/areas/dfi/regulate/regulate/
Guard/Agency	http://pvl.ehawaii.gov/pvlsearch/app
Hearing Aid Dealer/Fitter	http://pvl.ehawaii.gov/pvlsearch/app
Insurance Adjuster	http://pahoehoe.ehawaii.gov/ils/app
Insurance Agent/Producer/Solicitor	http://pahoehoe.ehawaii.gov/ils/app
Lobbyist	www.state.hi.us/ethics/noindex/pubrec.htm
Marriage & Family Therapist	http://pvl.ehawaii.gov/pvlsearch/app
Massage Therapist/Establishment	http://pvl.ehawaii.gov/pvlsearch/app
Mechanic	http://pvl.ehawaii.gov/pvlsearch/app
Medical Doctor	http://pvl.ehawaii.gov/pvlsearch/app
Mortgage Broker/Solicitor	http://pvl.ehawaii.gov/pvlsearch/app
Motor Vehicle Dealer/Broker/Seller	http://pvl.ehawaii.gov/pvlsearch/app
Motor Vehicle Repair Dealer	http://pvl.ehawaii.gov/pvlsearch/app
Naturopathic Physician	http://pvl.ehawaii.gov/pvlsearch/app
Nurse	http://pvl.ehawaii.gov/pvlsearch/app
Nursing Home Administrator	http://pvl.ehawaii.gov/pvlsearch/app
Occupational Therapist	http://pvl.ehawaii.gov/pvlsearch/app
Optician, Dispensing	http://pvl.ehawaii.gov/pvlsearch/app
Optometrist	http://pvl.ehawaii.gov/pvlsearch/app
Osteopathic Physician	http://pvl.ehawaii.gov/pvlsearch/app
Pest Control Field Rep./Operator	http://pvl.ehawaii.gov/pvlsearch/app
Pesticide Dealer	http://hawaii.gov/hdoa/pi/pest/RUPD2008LIST.pdf
Pesticide Product	http://hawaii.gov/hdoa/pi/pest/liclist_alpha.pdf
Pharmacist/Pharmacy	http://pvl.ehawaii.gov/pvlsearch/app

Physical Therapist .... http://pvl.ehawaii.gov/pvlsearch/app
Physician Assistant .... http://pvl.ehawaii.gov/pvlsearch/app
Pilot, Port.. http://pvl.ehawaii.gov/pvlsearch/app
Plumber .... http://pvl.ehawaii.gov/pvlsearch/app
Podiatrist... http://pvl.ehawaii.gov/pvlsearch/app
Private Detective/Investigative Agcy http://pvl.ehawaii.gov/pvlsearch/app
Psychologist....................................... http://pvl.ehawaii.gov/pvlsearch/app
Public Accountant - PA .... http://pvl.ehawaii.gov/pvlsearch/app
Real Estate Agent/Broker/Sales......... http://pahoehoe.ehawaii.gov/ils/app
Real Estate Appraiser .... http://pvl.ehawaii.gov/pvlsearch/app
Savings & Loan Association/Bank .... www.hawaii.gov/dcca/areas/dfi/regulate/regulate/
Social Worker.................................... http://pvl.ehawaii.gov/pvlsearch/app
Speech Pathologist/Audiologist......... http://pvl.ehawaii.gov/pvlsearch/app
Tattoo Artist .... http://hawaii.gov/health/environmental/sanitation/tattoo.html
Timeshare.. http://pvl.ehawaii.gov/pvlsearch/app
Travel Agency .... http://pvl.ehawaii.gov/pvlsearch/app
Trust Company .... www.hawaii.gov/dcca/areas/dfi/regulate/regulate/
Veterinarian...................................... http://pvl.ehawaii.gov/pvlsearch/app

State and Local Courts

State Court Structure: Hawaii's trial level is comprised of Circuit Courts (includes Family Courts) and District Courts. These trial courts function in four judicial circuits: First (Oahu), Second (Maui-Molokai-Lanai), Third (Hawaii County), and Fifth (Kauai-Niihau). The Fourth Circuit was merged with the Third in 1943.

Circuit Courts are general jurisdiction and handle all jury trials, felony cases, and civil cases over $20,000, also probate and guardianship. There is con-current jurisdiction with District Courts in civil non-jury cases that specify amounts between $10,000-$25,000. The District Court handles criminal cases punishable by a fine and/or less than one year imprisonment and some civil cases up to $25,000, also landlord/tenant, traffic and DUI cases. The Family Court Division rules in all legal matters involving children, such as delinquency, waiver, status offenses, abuse and neglect, termination of parental rights, adoption, guardianships and detention. Also hears traditional domestic-relations cases, including divorce, nonsupport, paternity, uniform child custody jurisdiction cases and miscellaneous custody matters.

Statewide Court Online Access: Free online access to all Circuit Court and Family Court records, and civil records from the District Courts is available at www.courts.state.hi.us/index.jsp, click on "Search Court Records" tab. Also search the traffic case index here. Search by name or case number. These records are not considered "official" for FCRA compliant searches. Most courts have access back to mid 1980s. Opinions from the Appellate Court are available also. Click on "Opinions."

> ❖ **Statewide Access Offered For All Trial Courts – Read Above** ❖

Note: No individual Hawaii courts offer online access.

Recorders, Assessors, and Other Sites of Note

Recording Office Organization: All UCC financing statements, tax liens, and real estate documents are filed centrally with the Bureau of Conveyances located in Honolulu. Details below.

Bureau of Conveyances *Real Estate, Grantor-Grantee, Deed, Lien, Conveyance Records*
www.hawaii.gov/dlnr/bc `Free & $$`   Indices to all documents recorded in the Bureau of Conveyances from 1976 to current are at http://bocweb.dlnrbc.hawaii.gov/boc/. Certified copies of documents may also be ordered.
Property, Taxation Records `Free`   Property records from the Hawaii County property assessor database are free at www.hawaiipropertytax.com. Also, search Honolulu real estate records at www.honolulupropertytax.com. No name searching. Maui Assessor Property records are free at www.mauipropertytax.com.

Idaho

Capital: Boise
           Ada County
Time Zone: MST

Idaho's ten northwestern-most counties are PST:
They are: Benewah, Bonner, Boundary, Clearwater,
Idaho, Kootenai, Latah, Lewis, Nez Perce, Shoshone.

Population: 1,499,402
# of Counties: 44

Useful State Links

Website: www.idaho.gov/
Governor: http://gov.idaho.gov
Attorney General: www2.state.id.us/ag/
State Archives: www.idahohistory.net/library_archives.html
State Statutes and Codes: www.legislature.idaho.gov/statutesrules.htm
Legislative Bill Search: www3.state.id.us/legislat/legtrack.html
Unclaimed Funds: http://tax.idaho.gov/ucp_search_idaho.htm

Primary State Agencies

Sexual Offender Registry `Free`

State Repository, Central Sexual Offender Registry, www.isp.state.id.us Access from the web page is available to the public. Inquires can be made by name, address, or by county or ZIP Code. Mapping is also available.

Incarceration Records `Free`

Idaho Department of Corrections, Records Bureau, www.idoc.idaho.gov/ This database search at https://www.accessidaho.org/public/corr/offender/search.html provides information about offenders currently under Idaho Department of Correction jurisdiction: those incarcerated, on probation, or on parole. Names of individuals who have served time and satisfied their sentence will appear - their convictions will not.

Corporation, LP, LLP, LLC, Trademarks/Servicemarks, Assumed Name `Free`

Secretary of State, Corporation Division, www.sos.idaho.gov/corp/corindex.htm Business Entity Searches at www.accessidaho.org/public/sos/corp/search.html?SearchFormstep=crit. This is a free Internet service open 24 hours daily. Includes not-for-profit entities. Trademarks may be searched at www.accessidaho.org/public/sos/trademark/search.html. *Other Options:* There are a variety of formats and media available for bulk purchase requesters. Requesters can subscribers to a monthly CD update.

Uniform Commercial Code, Federal & State Tax Liens `Free & $$`

UCC Division, Secretary of State, www.sos.idaho.gov/ucc/uccindex.htm There is a free limited search at https://www.accessidaho.org/secure/sos/liens/search.html. We recommend professional searchers to subscribe to the extensive commercial service at this site. The fee is $3.00 per name searched with a $95.00 annual subscription fee. *Other Options:* A summary data file on current filing is available on CD.

Sales Tax Registrations `Free`

Revenue Operations Division, Records Management, www.tax.idaho.gov/ Email requests are accepted at rmcmichael@tax.id.gov.

Death Records `Free & $$`

Vital Records, www.healthandwelfare.idaho.gov/site/3335/default.aspx The agency has made the death index of records from 1911 - 1956 available at http://abish.byui.edu/specialCollections/fhc/Death/searchForm.cfm. There is no fee. For newer records, no online access available, but requests can be made online via a vendor www.vitalchek.com.

Driver Records $$

Idaho Transportation Department, Driver's Services, www.itd.idaho.gov/dmv/ Idaho offers online access (CICS) to the driver license files through its portal provider, Access Idaho. Fee is $6.00. Idaho drivers can also order their own record from this site, fee is $6.24. For more information about a subscriber account, call 208-332-0102 or visit www.accessidaho.org. There is a free DL status check at https://www.accessidaho.org/secure/itd/reinstatement/index.html. Be aware that Access Idaho refers to driving records as 'Driver License Records' and refers to records related to vehicle title or registration as MVRs. *Other Options:* Idaho offers bulk retrieval of basic drivers license information with a signed contract. For information, call 208-334-8602.

Vehicle Ownership & Registration, Vessel Ownership $$

Idaho Transportation Department, Vehicle Services, www.itd.idaho.gov/dmv/vehicleservices/vs.htm Idaho offers online and batch access to registration and title files through its portal provider Access Idaho. Records are $5.50 ($6.00 effective 5/1/08) each or $3.50 for a lien search for subscribers. For more information, call 208-332-0102 or visit www.accessidaho.org. There is a $95 annual subscription fee. Interestingly, be aware that Access Idaho refers to these as records MVRs; they do not mean driving records. *Other Options:* Idaho offers bulk retrieval of registration, ownership, and vehicle information with a signed contract. For more information, call 208-334-8601.

Death Records Free & $$

Vital Records, www.healthandwelfare.idaho.gov/site/3335/default.aspx The agency has made the death index of records from 1911 - 1956 available at http://abish.byui.edu/specialCollections/fhc/Death/searchForm.cfm. There is no fee. For newer records, no online access available, but requests can be made online via a vendor www.vitalchek.com.

Occupational Licensing Boards

Acupuncturist	https://secure.ibol.idaho.gov/eIBOLPublic/LPRBrowser.aspx
Applicator, Pesticide, Private/Com.	www.agri.state.id.us/Categories/Pesticides/licensing/licenseLookUp.php
Appraiser, General/Resid'l/Trainee.	https://secure.ibol.idaho.gov/eIBOLPublic/LPRBrowser.aspx
Architect	https://secure.ibol.idaho.gov/eIBOLPublic/LPRBrowser.aspx
Assignees (Lender)	http://finance.idaho.gov/CreditCodeLicence.aspx
Athlete Agent	https://secure.ibol.idaho.gov/eIBOLPublic/LPRBrowser.aspx
Athletic Trainer	www.accessidaho.org/public/bomed/license/search.html
Attorney	http://www2.state.id.us/isb/gen/menu.htm#Mem
Audiologist	https://secure.ibol.idaho.gov/eIBOLPublic/LPRBrowser.aspx
Backflow Assembly Tester	https://secure.ibol.idaho.gov/eIBOLPublic/LPRBrowser.aspx
Bank	http://finance.idaho.gov/CreditCodeLicence.aspx
Barber-related Occupation	https://secure.ibol.idaho.gov/eIBOLPublic/LPRBrowser.aspx
Chemigator	www.agri.state.id.us/Categories/Pesticides/licensing/licenseLookUp.php
Chiropractor	https://secure.ibol.idaho.gov/eIBOLPublic/LPRBrowser.aspx
Clinical Nurse Specialist	http://www2.state.id.us/ibn/licenseesearch.htm
Collection Agency/Collector	http://finance.idaho.gov/CollectionAgencyLicence.aspx
Construction Mgr, Public Works	https://www.dbs.idaho.gov/edbspublic/lprbrowser.aspx
Consumer Loan Co. & Credit Seller	http://finance.idaho.gov/CreditCodeLicence.aspx
Contracting Business/Registered	https://secure.ibol.idaho.gov/eIBOLPublic/LPRBrowser.aspx
Contractor, Public Works	https://www.dbs.idaho.gov/edbspublic/lprbrowser.aspx
Cosmetics Dealer, Retail	https://secure.ibol.idaho.gov/eIBOLPublic/LPRBrowser.aspx
Cosmetology-related Occupation	https://secure.ibol.idaho.gov/eIBOLPublic/LPRBrowser.aspx
Counselor, Clinical/Professional	https://secure.ibol.idaho.gov/eIBOLPublic/LPRBrowser.aspx
Counselor, Debt/Credit	http://finance.idaho.gov/CollectionAgencyLicence.aspx
Credit Seller	http://finance.idaho.gov/CreditCodeLicence.aspx
Credit Union	http://finance.idaho.gov/CreditCodeLicence.aspx
Crematory	https://secure.ibol.idaho.gov/eIBOLPublic/LPRBrowser.aspx
Dental Assistant/ Dental Hygienist	http://www2.state.id.us/isbd/search.cfm
Dental Specialists	http://www2.state.id.us/isbd/search.cfm
Dentist	http://www2.state.id.us/isbd/search.cfm
Denturist/ Denturist Intern/Establ'mt	https://secure.ibol.idaho.gov/eIBOLPublic/LPRBrowser.aspx
Dietitian	www.accessidaho.org/public/bomed/license/search.html
Drinking Water Professionals	https://secure.ibol.idaho.gov/eIBOLPublic/LPRBrowser.aspx
Elections & Campaign Disclosure	www.idsos.state.id.us/notary/npindex.htm
Electrical-related Occupation	https://www.dbs.idaho.gov/edbspublic/lprbrowser.aspx

Electrolysis, Electrolysis Instructor ... https://secure.ibol.idaho.gov/eIBOLPublic/LPRBrowser.aspx
Engineer .... www.ipels.idaho.gov/rostdown.htm
Escrow Licensee .... http://finance.idaho.gov/EscrowLicense.aspx
Esthetician, Esthetician Instructor ..... https://secure.ibol.idaho.gov/eIBOLPublic/LPRBrowser.aspx
Finance Company .... http://finance.idaho.gov/CreditCodeLicence.aspx
Fire Sprinkler System Contractor ...... www.doi.idaho.gov/sfm/SprinklerContractorList.aspx
Funeral Director/Dir. Trainee .... https://secure.ibol.idaho.gov/eIBOLPublic/LPRBrowser.aspx
Funeral Establishment .... https://secure.ibol.idaho.gov/eIBOLPublic/LPRBrowser.aspx
Geologist http://www2.state.id.us/ibpg/search.htm
Glamour Photography Studio .... https://secure.ibol.idaho.gov/eIBOLPublic/LPRBrowser.aspx
Guide .... www.oglb.idaho.gov/ofdirectory.htm
Hearing Aid Fitter/Dealer .... https://secure.ibol.idaho.gov/eIBOLPublic/LPRBrowser.aspx
HVAC Contractor/Journeyman .... https://www.dbs.idaho.gov/edbspublic/lprbrowser.aspx
Insurance Producer .... www.doi.idaho.gov/Insurance/search.aspx
Insurance Surplus Lines Broker .... www.doi.idaho.gov/Insurance/search.aspx
Insurer, Domestic/Mutual/Foreign ..... www.doi.idaho.gov/Insurance/search.aspx
Investment Advisor .... http://finance.idaho.gov/SecuritiesLicense.aspx
Landscape Architect .... https://secure.ibol.idaho.gov/eIBOLPublic/LPRBrowser.aspx
Lobbyist .... www.idsos.state.id.us/elect/lobbyist/lobinfo.htm
LPG Dealer/Facility .... https://secure.ibol.idaho.gov/eIBOLPublic/LPRBrowser.aspx
Manufact'd Homes- Housing Related https://www.dbs.idaho.gov/edbspublic/lprbrowser.aspx
Manufactured Commercial Building . https://www.dbs.idaho.gov/edbspublic/lprbrowser.aspx
Marriage & Family Counselor .... https://secure.ibol.idaho.gov/eIBOLPublic/LPRBrowser.aspx
Medical Doctor .... www.accessidaho.org/public/bomed/license/search.html
Medical Resident .... www.accessidaho.org/public/bomed/license/search.html
Medical, Temporary .... www.accessidaho.org/public/bomed/license/search.html
Midwife Nurse http://www2.state.id.us/ibn/licenseesearch.htm
Money Transmitter .... http://finance.idaho.gov/MoneytransmittersLicence.aspx
Mortgage Broker/Banker/Firm .... http://finance.idaho.gov/MortgageLicense.aspx
Mortgage Loan Originator .... http://finance.idaho.gov/LoLicense.aspx
Mortician/Mortician Resi.Trainee ..... https://secure.ibol.idaho.gov/eIBOLPublic/LPRBrowser.aspx
Nail Technician/Instructor .... https://secure.ibol.idaho.gov/eIBOLPublic/LPRBrowser.aspx
Naturopath .... https://secure.ibol.idaho.gov/eIBOLPublic/LPRBrowser.aspx
Notary Public .... www.idsos.state.id.us/notary/npindex.htm
Nurse Anesthetist http://www2.state.id.us/ibn/licenseesearch.htm
Nurse-LPN/RN http://www2.state.id.us/ibn/licenseesearch.htm
Nursing Home Administrator .... https://secure.ibol.idaho.gov/eIBOLPublic/LPRBrowser.aspx
Occupational Therapist/Assistant ...... www.accessidaho.org/public/bomed/license/search.html
Optometrist .... https://secure.ibol.idaho.gov/eIBOLPublic/LPRBrowser.aspx
Osteopathic Physician .... www.accessidaho.org/public/bomed/license/search.html
Outfitter .... www.oglb.idaho.gov/ofdirectory.htm
Payday Lender .... http://finance.idaho.gov/CreditCodeLicence.aspx
Pest Control Consultant .... www.agri.state.id.us/Categories/Pesticides/licensing/licenseLookUp.php
Pesticide Appl'r/Oper'r/Dealer/Mfg ... www.agri.state.id.us/Categories/Pesticides/licensing/licenseLookUp.php
Physical Therapist/Assistant .... www.accessidaho.org/public/bomed/license/search.html
Physician Assistant .... www.accessidaho.org/public/bomed/license/search.html
Plumbin-related Occupation .... https://www.dbs.idaho.gov/edbspublic/lprbrowser.aspx
Podiatrist .... https://secure.ibol.idaho.gov/eIBOLPublic/LPRBrowser.aspx
Polysomnography Technologist .... www.accessidaho.org/public/bomed/license/search.html
Psychologist/Psych-service extend'r . https://secure.ibol.idaho.gov/eIBOLPublic/LPRBrowser.aspx
Public Accountant-CPA/LPA/Firm ... http://isba.idaho.gov/htm/databasesearch.htm
Real Estate Agent/Broker/Company .. www.irec.idaho.gov/licensee-search.html
Real Estate Appraiser .... https://secure.ibol.idaho.gov/eIBOLPublic/LPRBrowser.aspx
Residential Care Administrator .... https://secure.ibol.idaho.gov/eIBOLPublic/LPRBrowser.aspx
Respiratory Therapist .... www.accessidaho.org/public/bomed/license/search.html
Savings & Loan Association .... http://finance.idaho.gov/CreditCodeLicence.aspx
Securities Broker/Seller/Issuer .... http://finance.idaho.gov/SecuritiesLicense.aspx

Shorthand Reporter............................http://www2.state.id.us/csr/csr_searchform.cfm
Social Worker....................................https://secure.ibol.idaho.gov/eIBOLPublic/LPRBrowser.aspx
Speech/Language Pathologist............https://secure.ibol.idaho.gov/eIBOLPublic/LPRBrowser.aspx
Surveyor, Land ....www.ipels.idaho.gov/rostdown.htm
Temporary Medical ....www.accessidaho.org/public/bomed/license/search.html
Title Loan Lender.............................http://finance.idaho.gov/CreditCodeLicence.aspx
Trust Company ....http://finance.idaho.gov/CreditCodeLicence.aspx
Utility Regulator...............................www.puc.idaho.gov
Waste Water Professionals ....https://secure.ibol.idaho.gov/eIBOLPublic/LPRBrowser.aspx
Water Collection/Dist. Operator........https://secure.ibol.idaho.gov/eIBOLPublic/LPRBrowser.aspx
Water Rights Examiner ....www.idwr.idaho.gov/water/rights/examiners.htm
Water Treatment Operator.................https://secure.ibol.idaho.gov/eIBOLPublic/LPRBrowser.aspx

State and Local Courts

State Court Structure: The District judges hear felony criminal cases and civil actions if the amount involved is more than $10,000, and appeals of decisions of the Magistrate Division. The Magistrate Division hears probate matters, divorce proceedings, juvenile proceedings, initial felony proceedings through the preliminary hearing, criminal misdemeanors, infractions, civil cases when the amount in dispute does not exceed $10,000. Magistrates also hear Small Claims cases, established for disputes of $4,000 or less. 42 of the 44 counties have combined the courts.

Statewide Court Online Access: The statewide computer system at www.idcourts.us offers free online access to court records back to at least 1995, from the state Supreme Court Data Repository. Online results include identifiers year of birth and middle initial. All courts provide public access terminals onsite. Also, appellate and supreme court opinions are available at www.isc.idaho.gov/opinions/.

> ❖ **Statewide Access Offered For All Trial Courts – Read Above.** ❖

Note: No individual Idaho courts offer online access.

Recorders, Assessors, and Other Sites of Note

Recording Office Organization: 44 counties, 44 recording offices. The recording officer is the County Recorder. Many counties utilize a grantor/grantee index containing all transactions recorded with them. Until July 1, 1998, state tax liens were filed at the local county recorder. Now they are filed with the Secretary of State who has all active case files. Federal tax liens on personal property of businesses are filed with the Secretary of State. Other federal tax liens are filed with the county recorder.

Online Access Note: Few counties offer web access.

Ada County *Property, Taxation Records* Free Search the property assessor database for property data for free at www.adacountyassessor.org. Click on "Online Property Information System". No name searching.

Canyon County *Property, Taxation Records* $$ Access to the Assessor and Treasurer's databases requires $35 registration/setup fee and 150 yearly fee. For subscription info, email clane@canyoncounty.org or call 208-454-7401 or visit the website.

Kootenai County *Property, Taxation Records* Free Access assessor data free on the mapping site at www.kcgov.us/departments/mapping/mapSearch/. Login as Guest to search without registration.

Lewis County *Property, Taxation Records* Free Access property and assessor data on the PATS system free at https://fortress.wa.gov/lewisco/home/PATS/ but no name searching.

Madison County *Property, Taxation Records* Free Limited assessor information available at www.co.madison.id.us/modules/smartsection/category.php?categoryid=1

Payette County *Real Estate, Deed, Grantor/Grantee, Deed Records* www.payettecounty.org Free Access to recorded documents is free at www.payettecounty.org/clerk/imagesilo.html. Username is "public" and password is "look."

Illinois

Capital: Springfield
        Sangamon County
Time Zone: CST
Population: 12,852,548
# of Counties: 102

Useful State Links

Website: www.illinois.gov
Governor: www.illinois.gov/gov
Attorney General: www.ag.state.il.us
State Archives: www.sos.state.il.us/departments/archives/archives.html
State Statutes and Codes: www.ilga.gov/legislation/ilcs/ilcs.asp
Legislative Bill Search: www.ilga.gov/legislation/default.asp
Unclaimed Funds: www.cashdash.net

Primary State Agencies

Criminal Records $$

IL State Police Bureau of Identification, Civil Processing Unit, www.isp.state.il.us/crimhistory/crimhistoryhome.cfm Online access costs $10.00 per name or $16.00 if fingerprints submitted electronically. Upon signing an interagency agreement with ISP and establishing an escrow account, users can submit inquiries by email. Responses are sent back in 24 to 48 hours by either email or fax. Visit www.isp.state.il.us/services/convictioninquiries.cfm to enroll.

Sexual Offender Registry   Free

Illinois State Police, SOR Unit, www.isp.state.il.us/sor/ The website provides an online listing of sex offenders required to register in the State of Illinois. The database is updated daily and allows searching by name, city, county, and ZIP Code.

Incarceration Records   Free

Illinois Department of Corrections, www.idoc.state.il.us Click on Inmate Search at the website or at www.idoc.state.il.us/subsections/search/default.asp. *Other Options:* A CD of data since 1982 may be purchased for $45. Send request to FOIA Officer at address above.

Corporation, LP, LLP, LLLP, RLLP, LLC, Trade Names, Assumed Name   Free & $$

Department of Business Services, Corporate Department, www.ilsos.net The website gives free access to corporate and LLC records at www.ilsos.gov/corporatellc/. A commercial access program is also available. Fees vary. Potential users must submit in writing the purpose of the request. Submit your request to become involved in this program to the Director's Office. Search the database of LP, LLP, LLLP, and RLLP at www.ilsos.gov/lprpsearch. *Other Options:* List or bulk file purchases are available. Contact the Director's office for details.

Uniform Commercial Code, Federal Tax Liens   Free

Secretary of State, UCC Division, www.cyberdriveillinois.com Searching is offered at www.ilsos.gov/UCC/. *Other Options:* The entire database can be purchased and for $2500 with weekly updates at $200 per week. A CD update service is available for $250 per month.

Workers' Compensation Records   Free

IL Workers' Compensation Commission, www.iwcc.il.gov Case information status for active cases only is available at the webpage. Click on the IIC box on the right side of the screen.

Driver Records $$

Abstract Information Unit, Drivers Services Department, www.sos.state.il.us A program for high volume, approved users may be available. Records are $12.00 each. Call 217-785-3094 for further information. *Other Options:* Overnight cartridge batch processing may be available to high volume users (there is a 200 request minimum per day). Call 217-785-3094 for more information.

Accident Reports (Crash Reports) $$

Illinois State Police, Patrol Records Unit, www.isp.state.il.us Records can be requested and paid for online via E-Pay at the webpage. Visit www.isp.state.il.us/traffic/crashreports.cfm. The fee is $6.00 per report.

Birth and Death Records $$

IL Department of Public Health, Division of Vital Records, www.idph.state.il.us/vitalrecords/index.htm Records may requested from www.vitalchek.com, a state-endorsed vendor. Also, detailed instructions are at the website. Records are processed within 3-5 days.

Marriage Certificates, Divorce Records Free & $$

Department of Public Health, Division of Vital Records, www.idph.state.il.us/vitalrecords/index.htm There is a free online search of a statewide Marriage Index for 1763-1900 found at the Illinois State Archives website at www.cyberdriveillinois.com/departments/archives/marriage.html.

Occupational Licensing Boards

Acupuncturist	https://www.idfpr.com/dpr/licenselookup/default.asp
Alarm Contractor	https://www.idfpr.com/dpr/licenselookup/default.asp
Alcohol Abuse Counselor	www.iaodapca.org
Amusement Attraction/Ride	www.state.il.us/agency/idol/Listings/Carnlist.htm
Architect	https://www.idfpr.com/dpr/licenselookup/default.asp
Armed Security Agency/Agent	https://www.idfpr.com/dpr/licenselookup/default.asp
Asbestos Contractor	www.idph.state.il.us/
Athletic Trainer	https://www.idfpr.com/dpr/licenselookup/default.asp
Attorney	www.iardc.org/lawyersearch.asp
Auctioneer	https://www.idfpr.com/DPR/licenselookup/default.asp
Audiologist	https://www.idfpr.com/dpr/licenselookup/default.asp
Bank	www.obrelookupclear.state.il.us/default.asp
Barber	https://www.idfpr.com/dpr/licenselookup/default.asp
Bilingual Teacher, Transitional	https://secqa1.isbe.net/otis/
Bull Ride	www.state.il.us/agency/idol/Listings/Carnlist.htm
Bungee Jump	www.state.il.us/agency/idol/Listings/Carnlist.htm
Carnival	www.state.il.us/agency/idol/Listings/Carnlist.htm
Check Seller/Distributor	www.obrelookupclear.state.il.us/default.asp
Chiropractor	https://www.idfpr.com/dpr/licenselookup/default.asp
Classr'm Training Course, Basic	https://www.idfpr.com/dpr/licenselookup/default.asp
Collection Agency	https://www.idfpr.com/dpr/licenselookup/default.asp
Controlled Substance Registrant	https://www.idfpr.com/dpr/licenselookup/default.asp
Cosmetologist	https://www.idfpr.com/dpr/licenselookup/default.asp
Counselor/Clinical Prof Counselor	https://www.idfpr.com/dpr/licenselookup/default.asp
CPA- Public Accountant	https://www.idfpr.com/dpr/licenselookup/default.asp
Dentist/Dental Hygienist	https://www.idfpr.com/dpr/licenselookup/default.asp
Design Firm	https://www.idfpr.com/dpr/licenselookup/default.asp
Dietitian/Nutrition Counselor	https://www.idfpr.com/dpr/licenselookup/default.asp
Doctor/Physician	https://www.idfpr.com/dpr/licenselookup/default.asp
Drug Distributor, Wholesale	https://www.idfpr.com/dpr/licenselookup/default.asp
Early Childhood Teacher	https://secqa1.isbe.net/otis/
Engineer, Structural	https://www.idfpr.com/dpr/licenselookup/default.asp
Engineer/Engineer Intern	https://www.idfpr.com/dpr/licenselookup/default.asp
Environmental Health Practitioner	https://www.idfpr.com/dpr/licenselookup/default.asp
Esthetician	https://www.idfpr.com/dpr/licenselookup/default.asp
Euthanasia Tech	https://www.idfpr.com/dpr/licenselookup/default.asp
Firearms Trainer	https://www.idfpr.com/dpr/licenselookup/default.asp
Funeral Director/Embalmer	https://www.idfpr.com/dpr/licenselookup/default.asp

Gambling Addiction Counselor .... www.iaodapca.org
Geologist .... https://www.idfpr.com/dpr/licenselookup/default.asp
Go-kart track .... www.state.il.us/agency/idol/Listings/Carnlist.htm
Home Health Aide (CNAs-ASHHA) www.idph.state.il.us/nar/home.htm
Home Inspector .... www.obrelookupclear.state.il.us/defaultRE.asp
Home Medical Equip Provider .... https://www.idfpr.com/dpr/licenselookup/default.asp
Insurance Producer http://neonwebh.cmcf.state.il.us:8080/ins/imsfor
Interior Designer .... https://www.idfpr.com/dpr/licenselookup/default.asp
Landscape Architect .... https://www.idfpr.com/dpr/licenselookup/default.asp
Lead Contractor .... http://app.idph.state.il.us/Envhealth/Lead/LeadProfessionalListing.asp
Lead Risk Assessor/Insp./Supr. .... http://app.idph.state.il.us/Envhealth/Lead/LeadProfessionalListing.asp
Lead Training Provider .... http://app.idph.state.il.us/Envhealth/lead/LeadProfessionalListing.asp
Liquor License, Retail/Dist./Mfg. .... http://www2.state.il.us/lcc/license_search.asp
Lobbyist .... www.cyberdriveillinois.com/departments/index/lobbyist/home.html
Locksmith .... https://www.idfpr.com/dpr/licenselookup/default.asp
Long Term Care Insurance Firm http://neonwebh.cmcf.state.il.us:8080/ins/imsfor
Marriage & Family Therapist .... https://www.idfpr.com/dpr/licenselookup/default.asp
Massage Therapist .... https://www.idfpr.com/dpr/licenselookup/default.asp
Medical Corporation .... https://www.idfpr.com/dpr/licenselookup/default.asp
Medical Doctor .... https://www.idfpr.com/dpr/licenselookup/default.asp
Mental Health Counselor .... www.iaodapca.org
Mortgage Banker/Broker .... www.obrelookupclear.state.il.us/default.asp
Nail Technician .... https://www.idfpr.com/dpr/licenselookup/default.asp
Naprapath .... https://www.idfpr.com/dpr/licenselookup/default.asp
Notary Public .... www.cyberdriveillinois.com/departments/index/notary/home.html
Nuclear Medicine Technologist .... https://www.state.il.us/iema/dns.asp
Nurse, LPN, RN, APN .... https://www.idfpr.com/dpr/licenselookup/default.asp
Nurses' Aide .... www.idph.state.il.us/nar/home.htm
Nursing Home .... https://www.idfpr.com/dpr/licenselookup/default.asp
Nursing Home Administrator .... https://www.idfpr.com/DPR/licenselookup/default.asp
Occupational Therapist/or/Aide .... https://www.idfpr.com/dpr/licenselookup/default.asp
Optometrist .... https://www.idfpr.com/dpr/licenselookup/default.asp
Orthotist .... https://www.idfpr.com/dpr/licenselookup/default.asp
Osteopathic Physician .... https://www.idfpr.com/dpr/licenselookup/default.asp
Pawnbroker .... www.obrelookupclear.state.il.us/default.asp
Pedorthist .... https://www.idfpr.com/dpr/licenselookup/default.asp
Perfusionist .... https://www.idfpr.com/dpr/licenselookup/default.asp
Pest Control Technician/Business ..... www.idph.state.il.us/
Pesticide Applicator .... www.idph.state.il.us/
Pharmacist/Pharmacy .... https://www.idfpr.com/dpr/licenselookup/default.asp
Physical Therapist/or/Aide .... https://www.idfpr.com/dpr/licenselookup/default.asp
Physician Assistant .... https://www.idfpr.com/dpr/licenselookup/default.asp
Podiatrist .... https://www.idfpr.com/dpr/licenselookup/default.asp
Polygraph/Deception Detect.Exam'r . https://www.idfpr.com/dpr/licenselookup/default.asp
Private Detective .... https://www.idfpr.com/dpr/licenselookup/default.asp
Private Security Contractor .... https://www.idfpr.com/dpr/licenselookup/default.asp
Psychologist .... https://www.idfpr.com/dpr/licenselookup/default.asp
Psychology Business .... https://www.idfpr.com/dpr/licenselookup/default.asp
Public Accountant-CPA .... https://www.idfpr.com/dpr/licenselookup/default.asp
Radiation Therapist .... https://www.state.il.us/iema/dns.asp
Radon Measurement Specialist .... https://www.state.il.us/iema/radon/RadonCounty_Frames.asp
Real Estate Agent/Broker/Seller .... www.obrelookupclear.state.il.us/defaultRE.asp
Real Estate Appraiser .... www.obrelookupclear.state.il.us/defaultRE.asp
Rehabilitation Aide .... https://www.idfpr.com/dpr/licenselookup/default.asp
Respiratory Care Practitioner .... https://www.idfpr.com/dpr/licenselookup/default.asp
Roofer/Roofing Contractor .... https://www.idfpr.com/dpr/licenselookup/default.asp
Savings & Loan Association/Bank .... www.obrelookupclear.state.il.us/default.asp

Securities Salesperson/Dealer............ www.finra.org/index.htm
Security Guard Firm/Agency/Force... https://www.idfpr.com/dpr/licenselookup/default.asp
Sewage System Contractor............... www.idph.state.il.us/
Shorthand Reporter.......................... https://www.idfpr.com/dpr/licenselookup/default.asp
Ski Lift, Tram.................................. www.state.il.us/agency/idol/Listings/Carnlist.htm
Social Worker.................................. https://www.idfpr.com/dpr/licenselookup/default.asp
Special Teacher https://secqa1.isbe.net/otis/
Speech-Language Pathologist............ https://www.idfpr.com/dpr/licenselookup/default.asp
Stock Broker.................................... www.finra.org/index.htm
Substance Abuse Counselor .... www.iaodapca.org
Substitute Teacher https://secqa1.isbe.net/otis/
Suppliers... www.igb.state.il.us/Pending/ILSUPPUBweb.pdf
Surgical Technician .... https://www.idfpr.com/dpr/licenselookup/default.asp
Surveyor, Land .... https://www.idfpr.com/dpr/licenselookup/default.asp
Teacher.. https://secqa1.isbe.net/otis/
Timber Buyer www.dnr.state.il.us/law3/timber.htm
Timeshare.. https://www.idfpr.com/dpr/licenselookup/default.asp
Timeshare/Land Sales....................... www.obrelookupclear.state.il.us/defaultRE.asp
Training Facilities............................ www.ptb.state.il.us/allfacilities.asp
Veterinarian..................................... https://www.idfpr.com/dpr/licenselookup/default.asp
Water Well & Pump Install Contr. .... www.idph.state.il.us/

State and Local Courts

State Court Structure: Illinois is divided into 22 judicial circuits; 3 are single county: Cook, Du Page (18th Circuit) and Will (12th Circuit). The other 19 circuits consist of 2 or more contiguous counties. There are two kinds of judges in the circuit court: circuit judges and associate judges. Circuit judges, elected for six years, can hear any kind of case. The Circuit Court of Cook County is the largest unified court system in the world. Its 2,300-person staff handles approximately 2.4 million cases each year. The civil part of the various Circuit Courts in Cook County is divided as follows– under $30,000 are "civil cases" and over $30,000 are "civil law division cases." Probate is handled by the Circuit Court in all counties.

Statewide Court Online Access: While there is no statewide public online system available, other than Appellate Court and Supreme Court opinions from the website. A number of Illinois Circuit Courts offer online access, many through a vendor at www.judici.com.

Adams County

Circuit Court   www.co.adams.il.us   **Free**
Civil: Online access to 8th Circuit Clerk of Court records is free at www.judici.com/courts/cases/case_search.jsp?court=IL001025J. Search by name, case or docket number back to 1987. Direct email search requests to rfrese@co.adams.il.us. *Criminal:* Same. The county inmate list and warrant list is at the home page.

Bond County

Circuit Court   www.bondcountyil.com/circuitclerk   **Free & $$**
Civil: Online access is same as criminal, see below. *Criminal:* Online access is free at www.judici.com/courts/cases/index.jsp?court=IL003015J. Premium/fee service is also available.

Boone County

Circuit Court   www.boonecountyil.org   **Free & $$**
Civil: Search cases free online at www.judici.com/courts/cases/case_search.jsp?court=IL004015J. Also, a premium fee service is available. *Criminal:* Online access is the same as civil.

Bureau County

Circuit Court   www.bccirclk.gov   **Free**
Civil: Online access to Judicial Circuit records is free at http://75.149.91.99/bureau/caseinfo.htm. Index includes dates, defendants, record sheets and dispositions and goes back to 8/1988. *Criminal:* Same.

Carroll County

Circuit Court   www.15thjudicialcircuit.com   **Free & $$**

Civil: Access is free to civil, small claims, probate and traffic records at www.judici.com/courts/index.jsp?court=IL008015J. Records go back to 1988. A premium fee service is also available. *Criminal:* Criminal records access is free at www.judici.com/courts/index.jsp?court=IL008015J. Records go back to 1988.

Champaign County
Circuit Court   www.cccircuitclerk.com   `Free`
Civil: Access to the circuit clerk's case query online system called PASS is now free at https://secure.jtsmith.com/clerk/clerk.asp. Online case records go back to '92. *Criminal:* Same.

Clark County
Circuit Court   `Free & $$`
Civil: Access court index and records free at www.judici.com/courts/cases/case_search.jsp?court=IL012015J. *Criminal:* Access to criminal records online is same as civil, see above.

Clay County
Circuit Court   `Free & $$`
Civil: Search cases free online at www.judici.com/courts/cases/case_search.jsp?court=IL013015J. Also, a premium fee service is available. *Criminal:* Online access to criminal same as civil, see above.

Clinton County
Circuit Court   `Free & $$`
Civil: Search cases free online at www.judici.com/courts/cases/index.jsp?court=IL014015J. Also, a premium fee service is available. *Criminal:* Online access to criminal same as civil, see above.

Coles County
Circuit Court   www.judici.com/courts/index.jsp?court=IL015025J
Civil: Access civil, small claims, probate and traffic records for free at www.judici.com/courts/index.jsp?court=IL015025J, to 1989. A premium fee service is also available. *Criminal:* Criminal records access is free at www.judici.com/courts/index.jsp?court=IL015025J.

Cook County
All Circuit Courts – Civil   www.cookcountyclerkofcourt.org   `Free & $$`
Civil: Search full case dockets free at www.cookcountyclerkofcourt.org/terms/full_docket_search/index.htm. Limited case snapshots are also online at www.cookcountyclerkofcourt.org/Terms/terms.htm. Search by name, number, or date. Data includes up to 3 parties, attorneys, case type, filing date, the amount of damages sought, division/district, and most current court date. Also, search the new BETA site free at http://198.173.15.31/V2/COUNTY/.

Crawford County
Circuit Court   `Free & $$`
Civil: Access is free to civil, small claims, probate and traffic records at www.judici.com/courts/cases/index.jsp?court=IL017015J. Premium fee service also available. *Criminal:* Criminal records access is free at www.judici.com/courts/cases/index.jsp?court=IL017015J.

De Kalb County
Circuit Court   www.co.kane.il.us/judicial   `$$`
Civil: Online access to civil court records is the same as criminal, see below. *Criminal:* Online access to court records is via a internet subscription system. Fee is $20 per month or $240 per year for this county or $300 for Will, Madison, Sangamon, Winnebago, Kane, Kendall, DeKalb courts. Visit www.clericusmagnus.com or call 866-511-2892.

De Witt County
Circuit Court   `Free & $$`
Civil: Access court index and records free at www.judici.com/courts/cases/case_search.jsp?court=IL020015J. *Criminal:* Access to criminal court records online is same as civil, see above.

Edwards County
Circuit Court
Civil: Access is free to civil, small claims, probate and traffic records at www.judici.com/courts/cases/index.jsp?court=IL024015J. A premium fee service also available. *Criminal:* Criminal records access is free at www.judici.com/courts/cases/index.jsp?court=IL024015J.

Effingham County
Circuit Court
Civil: Access is free to civil, small claims, probate and traffic records at www.judici.com/courts/cases/index.jsp?court=IL025015J. A premium fee service also available. *Criminal:* Criminal records access is free at www.judici.com/courts/cases/index.jsp?court=IL025015J.

Fayette County

Circuit Court   Free & $$

Civil: Access court index and records free at www.judici.com/courts/cases/case_search.jsp?court=IL026015J. *Criminal:* Access to criminal records is same as civil, see above.

Ford County

Circuit Court   Free & $$

Civil: Search cases free online at www.judici.com/courts/cases/index.jsp?court=IL027015J. Also, a premium fee service is available. *Criminal:* Online access to criminal is same as civil, see above.

Franklin County   Free & $$

Circuit Court

Civil: Access is free to civil, small claims, probate and traffic records at www.judici.com/courts/cases/index.jsp?court=IL028015J. A premium fee service also available. *Criminal:* Criminal records access is free at www.judici.com/courts/cases/index.jsp?court=IL028015J.

Hamilton County   Free & $$

Circuit Court   Free & $$

Civil: Access is free to civil, small claims, probate and traffic records at www.judici.com/courts/cases/index.jsp?court=IL033015J. Premium fee service also available. *Criminal:* Criminal records access is free at www.judici.com/courts/cases/index.jsp?court=IL033025J.

Henry County   Free & $$

Circuit Court   www.henrycty.com/codepartments/CircuitClerk/index.html

Civil: Access is free to civil, small claims, probate and traffic records at www.judici.com/courts/index.jsp?court=IL037015J. A premium fee service also available. *Criminal:* Criminal records access is free at www.judici.com/courts/index.jsp?court=IL037015J.

Iroquois County   Free & $$

Circuit Court   www.judici.com/courts/index.jsp?court=IL038025J

Civil: Search cases free online at www.judici.com/courts/cases/index.jsp?court=IL038025J. A premium fee service is also available. *Criminal:* Access criminal records free at www.judici.com/courts/cases/index.jsp?court=IL038025J.

Jackson County

Circuit Court   www.circuitclerk.co.jackson.il.us/index-2.html   Free & $$

Civil: Access civil, small claims, and traffic records free at the home page or at www.judici.com/search/search.html?court=IL039015J. Also, premium service with full info is available $77 per 6-months. *Criminal:* Criminal records access is free from home page. Click on "Case information." Also, premiums service subscription with full info is available $77 per 6-months, see www.judici.com/search/search.html?court=IL039015J.

Jefferson County

Circuit Court   Free & $$

Civil: Access to 2nd Circuit Clerk of Court records is free at www.judici.com/courts/index.jsp?court=IL041025J. *Criminal:* Same

Jersey County

Circuit Court   www.jerseycounty-il.us   Free

Civil: Court records may be accessed free at www.jerseycounty-il.us by clicking on Court Record Search. *Criminal:* Same

Jo Daviess County   Free & $$

Circuit Court   www.jodaviess.org/index.asp?Type=B_BASIC&SEC=%7B0363DEF2-42F1-4DE5-A8A5-5C01B81E8655%7D

Civil: Access is free to civil, small claims, probate and traffic records at www.judici.com/courts/index.jsp?court=IL043015J. A premium fee service also available. *Criminal:* Online access to criminal records is free at www.judici.com/courts/index.jsp?court=IL043015J.

Kane County

Circuit Court   www.cic.co.kane.il.us $$

Civil: Online access to civil court records is the same as criminal, see below. *Criminal:* Online access to court records is via subscription system. $59 setup fee plus $20 per month or $240 per year for this county or $300 for Will, Madison, Sangamon, Winnebago, Kane, Kendall, DeKalb courts. Visit www.clericusmagnus.com or call 866-511-2892.

Kendall County

Circuit Court $$

Civil: Online access to civil court records is the same as criminal, see below *Criminal:* Online access to court records is via subscription system. $59 setup fee plus $20 per month or $240 per year for this county or $300 for Will, Madison, Sangamon, Winnebago, Kane, Kendall, DeKalb courts. Visit www.clericusmagnus.com or call 866-511-2892.

La Salle County
Circuit Court - Civil Division   www.lasallecounty.com $$
Civil: Online access to Judicial Circuit records requires a $200 setup fee (waived for not-for-profits) and $.10 per minute usage fee. Call Clerk's office at 815-434-8671 for details.

Circuit Court - Criminal Division   www.lasallecounty.com $$
Criminal: Online access to Judicial Circuit records requires a $200 setup fee (waived for not-for-profits) and $.10 per minute usage fee. Call the Clerk's office at 815-434-8671 for details.

Lawrence County   Free & $$
Circuit Court
Civil: Access is free to civil, small claims, probate and traffic records at www.judici.com/courts/cases/index.jsp?court=IL051015J. Premium fee service also available. *Criminal:* Criminal records access is free at www.judici.com/courts/cases/index.jsp?court=IL051015J.

Lee County   Free & $$
Circuit Court
Civil: Access is free to civil, small claims, probate and traffic records at www.judici.com/courts/index.jsp?court=IL052025J. A premium fee service also available. *Criminal:* Criminal records access is free at www.judici.com/courts/index.jsp?court=IL052025J.

Livingston County
Circuit Court   Free
Civil: Probate along with divorce, traffic, miscellaneous remedy cases, law, all in separate indexes at this same address. Search probate index 1837-1958 at www.cyberdriveillinois.com/departments/archives/pontiac.html.

Logan County   Free & $$
Circuit Court   www.co.logan.il.us/circuit_clerk/
Civil: Online access to civil, small claims, probate and traffic records is free at www.judici.com/courts/cases/index.jsp?court=IL054025J. A premium fee service is also available. *Criminal:* Criminal records access is free at www.judici.com/courts/cases/index.jsp?court=IL054025J.

Macon County
Circuit Court   www.court.co.macon.il.us   Free
Civil: Access to court records is free at www.court.co.macon.il.us/Templates/SearchCaseInfo.htm. Search docket information back to 04/96. Includes traffic, probate, family, small claims. *Criminal:* Access to court records is free online at www.court.co.macon.il.us/Templates/SearchCaseInfo.htm. Search docket information back to 04/96.

Macoupin County
Circuit Court   Free & $$
Civil: Access court index and records free at www.judici.com/courts/cases/case_search.jsp?court=IL059015J. *Criminal:* Access to criminal records online is same as civil, see above.

Madison County   Free & $$
Circuit Court   www.co.madison.il.us   *Civil:* Online access to court records is via subscription system. $59 setup fee plus $20 per month or $240 per year for this county or $300 for Will, Madison, Sangamon, Winnebago, Kane, Kendall, DeKalb courts. Visit www.clericusmagnus.com or call 866-511-2892. *Criminal:* Online access is the same as civil, see above.

Marion County   Free & $$
Circuit Court
Civil: Online access to civil, small claims, probate and traffic records is free at www.judici.com/courts/cases/index.jsp?court=IL061015J. A premium fee service is also available. *Criminal:* Criminal records access is free at www.judici.com/courts/cases/index.jsp?court=IL061015J.

McHenry County   Free & $$
Circuit Court   www.mchenrycircuitclerk.org   *Civil:* Access to civil, traffic and domestic records is the same as criminal, see below. *Criminal:* Access to records on the remote online system requires $750 license fee and $53.50 password card fee, plus $50 per month. Records date back to 1990 with civil, criminal, probate, traffic, and domestic records. For more info, call 815-334-4193.

McLean County
Circuit Court   www.mcleancountyil.gov   Free
Criminal: Free public access at www.mcleancountyil.gov/circuitclerk/PA_main.htm. System has traffic as well as criminal index.

Mercer County   Free & $$
Circuit Court   www.mercercountyil.org
Civil: Access is free to civil, small claims, probate and traffic records at www.judici.com/courts/index.jsp?court=IL066015J. Premium fee service also available. *Criminal:* Criminal records access is free at www.judici.com/courts/index.jsp?court=IL066015J.

Montgomery County

Circuit Court   www.montgomeryco.com/circlerk.htm   `Free & $$`

Civil: Search cases free online at www.judici.Bcom/courts/cases/case_search.jsp?court=IL068015J. Also, a premium fee service is available. *Criminal:* Online access to criminal same as civil, see above.

Morgan County

Circuit Court   www.morgancounty-il.com   `Free & $$`

Civil: Access court index and records free at www.judici.com/courts/cases/case_search.jsp?court=IL069015J. *Criminal:* Access to criminal court records online is same as civil, see above.

Moultrie County

Circuit Court   www.circuit-clerk.moultrie.il.us   `Free & $$`

Civil: Access court index and records free at www.judici.com/courts/cases/case_search.jsp?court=IL070015J. *Criminal:* Access to criminal court records online is same as civil, see above.

Ogle County

Circuit Court   www.oglecounty.org/marty/circuitclerk.html   `Free & $$`

Civil: Access is free to civil, small claims, probate and traffic records at www.judici.com/courts/cases/index.jsp?court=IL071015J. Premium fee service also available. *Criminal:* Criminal records access is free at www.judici.com/courts/cases/index.jsp?court=IL071015J.

Pike County

Circuit Court   `Free & $$`

Civil: Access is free to civil, small claims, probate and traffic records at www.judici.com/courts/cases/index.jsp?court=IL075015J. Premium fee service also available. *Criminal:* Criminal records access is free at www.judici.com/courts/cases/index.jsp?court=IL075015J.

Richland County

Circuit Court   `Free & $$`

Civil: Access is free to civil, small claims, probate and traffic records at www.judici.com/courts/cases/index.jsp?court=IL080015J. Premium fee service also available. *Criminal:* Criminal records access is free at www.judici.com/courts/cases/index.jsp?court=IL080015J.

Rock Island County

Circuit Court   www.co.rock-island.il.us/CoClk.aspx?id=547   `Free & $$`

Civil: Full access to court records on the remote online system requires $300 setup fee plus a $1.00 per minute for access. Civil, criminal, probate, traffic, and domestic records can be accessed by name or case number. Also, access to civil, small claims, probate and traffic records is free at www.judici.com/courts/cases/index.jsp?court=IL081025J. *Criminal:* Same - there are two methods.

Sangamon County

Circuit Court   www.sangamoncountycircuitclerk.org   `$$`

Civil: Online access to civil records is the same as criminal, see below. *Criminal:* Online access to court records is via subscription system. $20 per month or $240 per year for this county or $300 for Will, Madison, Sangamon, Winnebago, Kane, Kendall, DeKalb courts. Visit www.clericusmagnus.com or call 866-511-2892.

Shelby County

Circuit Court   `Free & $$`

Civil: Access is free to civil, small claims, probate and traffic records at www.judici.com/courts/cases/index.jsp?court=IL087025J. Premium fee service also available. *Criminal:* Criminal records access is free at www.judici.com/courts/cases/index.jsp?court=IL087025J.

Stephenson County

Circuit Court   `Free & $$`

Civil: Access is free to civil, small claims, probate and traffic records at www.judici.com/courts/cases/index.jsp?court=IL089015J. Premium fee service also available. *Criminal:* Criminal records access is free at www.judici.com/courts/cases/index.jsp?court=IL089015J.

Union County

Circuit Court   `Free & $$`

Civil: Access is free to civil, small claims, probate and traffic records at www.judici.com/courts/cases/index.jsp?court=IL091015J. Premium fee service also available. *Criminal:* Criminal records access is free at www.judici.com/courts/cases/index.jsp?court=IL091015J.

Vermilion County

Circuit Court   www.co.vermilion.il.us   `Free & $$`

Civil: Search the index at www.judici.com/courts/cases/case_search.jsp?court=IL092015J. Records are current to 1989. Premium svc also. *Criminal:* Search the index at www.judici.com/courts/cases/case_search.jsp?court=IL092015J. Records are current to 1989.

Wabash County

Circuit Court　　Free & $$

Civil: Access is free to civil, small claims, probate and traffic records at www.judici.com/courts/cases/index.jsp?court=IL093015J. Premium fee service also available. *Criminal:* Criminal records access is free at www.judici.com/courts/cases/index.jsp?court=IL093015J.

Washington County

Circuit Court　　Free & $$

Civil: Access is free to civil, small claims, probate and traffic records at www.judici.com/courts/index.jsp?court=IL095015J. Premium fee service also available. *Criminal:* Criminal records access is free at www.judici.com/courts/index.jsp?court=IL095015J.

Wayne County

Circuit Court　www.illinoissecondcircuit.info/county_wayne.html　　Free & $$

Civil: Access is free to civil, small claims, probate and traffic records at www.judici.com/courts/cases/index.jsp?court=IL093015J. Premium fee service also available. *Criminal:* Criminal records access is free at www.judici.com/courts/cases/index.jsp?court=IL093015J.

White County

Circuit Court　　Free & $$

Civil: Access is free to civil, small claims, probate and traffic records at www.judici.com/courts/cases/index.jsp?court=IL097015J. Premium fee service also available. *Criminal:* Criminal records access is free at www.judici.com/courts/cases/index.jsp?court=IL097015J.

Whiteside County

Circuit Court　　Free & $$

Civil: Access is free to civil, small claims, probate and traffic records at www.judici.com/courts/cases/case_search.jsp?court=IL098015J. Premium fee service also available. *Criminal:* Access to criminal records is the same as civil.

Will County

Circuit Court　www.willcountycircuitcourt.com　　$$

Civil: Online access to civil court records is the same as criminal, see below. *Criminal:* Online access to court records is via subscription system. $59 setup fee plus $20 per month or $240 per year for this county or $300 for Will, Madison, Sangamon, Winnebago, Kane, Kendall, DeKalb courts. Visit www.clericusmagnus.com or call 866-511-2892.

Williamson County

Circuit Court　www.state.il.us/court/CircuitCourt/default.asp　　Free & $$

Civil: Search cases free online at www.judici.com/courts/cases/case_search.jsp?court=IL100025J. Also, a premium fee service is available. Also, court calendars available free at http://williamsoncountycourthouse.com/p/calendars.php. *Criminal:* Online access to criminal same as civil, see above.

Winnebago County

Circuit Court　www.cc.co.winnebago.il.us　　$$

Civil: Online access to civil court records is the same as criminal, see below. *Criminal:* Online access to court records is via subscription system. Visit www.clericusmagnus.com or call 866-319-4303.

Woodford County

Circuit Court　　Free

Civil: Online access to civil cases same as criminal, see below. *Criminal:* Online access to criminal cases free at www.judici.com/courts/cases/case_search.jsp?court=IL102015J. Premium fee subscription services also available.

Recorders, Assessors, and Other Sites of Note

Recording Office Organization:　102 counties, 102 recording offices. The recording officer is the County Recorder, but some counties prefer the name Recorder of Deeds. Many counties utilize a grantor/grantee index containing all transactions. Cook County had separate offices for real estate recording and UCC filing until they combined offices June 30, 2001. Since that date only UCC extension, amendments or terminations can be filed on exisiting UCCs, with exception of UCCs on real estate related collateral whch are still filed here.

Online Access Note:　A number of counties offer online access, participating with vendors. There is no statewide system.

Adams County *Property, Taxation Records* **Free** Access property data free at www.emapsplus.com/ILAdams/maps/ including name searching.

Boone County *Property, Taxation Records* **Free & $$** Property assessments and tax info is free at www.boonecountyil.org/assessor/assessor.htm. Also, access to property data is free at www.helpillinois.net/boone/public.htm but no name searching Access land data on commercial site - PropertyMax - at http://booneilpropertymax.governmaxa.com/propertymax/rover30.asp. Subscription packages from $20.00 per month.

Bureau County *Real Estate, Deed, Lien Records* **$$** The recorder's office has a subscription service with web access to land records and lien documents; Montly $50.00 fee; Images go back to 10/1992, index to 8/1986. call recorder for details. Also, access recording office data by subscription on either the Laredo system using subscription and fees or the Tapestry System using credit card, www.landrecords.net; $3.99 search; $.50 per image.

Cass County *Property, Taxation Records* **$$** Search assessor property data for a fee on the GIS system at http://beacon.schneidercorp.com/. Registration and username required.

Champaign County *Real Estate, Deed, Lien Records* www.co.champaign.il.us/recorder/recorder.htm **$$** Recorder land data by subscription on either the Laredo system using subscription and fees or the Tapestry System using credit card, http://tapestry.fidlar.com; $3.99 search; $.50 per image. Index goes back to 5/1975; images to 1/1987.
Property, Taxation Records **Free** Search property tax records free at www.co.champaign.il.us/ccao/Assessors.htm. Also, search the treasurer's real estate property tax database free at www.co.champaign.il.us/taxlookup but no name searching.

Christian County *Real Estate, Deed, Lien, UCC Records* **$$** Recorder land data by subscription on either the Laredo system using subscription and fees or the Tapestry System using credit card, http://tapestry.fidlar.com; $3.99 search; $.50 per image. Index and images go back to 1/1990.

Clinton County *Real Estate, Deed, Lien Records* www.clintonco.org **$$** Recorder land data by subscription on either the Laredo system using subscription and fees or the Tapestry System using credit card, http://tapestry.fidlar.com; $3.99 search; $.50 per image. Index back to 1988; images to 1992.

Coles County *Real Estate, Deed, Lien, UCC Records* www.co.coles.il.us/CoClerk/index.htm **Free & $$** Record index from the recorder's database back to 1978 is free at www.landaccess.com/proi/county.jsp?county=ilcoles; Fees apply to see images and make copies.
Property, Taxation Records **Free** Access property tax data free at www.fikeandfike.com/propertytax/coles/Inquiry2.aspx.

Cook County Recorder *Real Estate, Grantor/Grantee, Deed, Mortgage Records* www.ccrd.info **Free & $$** Search Grantor/Grantee index and locate property data at www.ccrd.info. Fee for documents. Search DIMS database of recordings since 10/1985; registration and fees apply. Includes Treasurer's Current Year Tax System APIN and DuPage recorder. Sign-up info is at www.ccrd.info/CCRD/il031/index.jsp. Also, you may purchase the real estate transfer list; $100 per year on disk or $50 if you pick-up at agency.
Property, Taxation Records **Free** Online search and retrieval of parcel data with GIS pictures of residential and nonresidential properties as well as prior and current assessment values are available. Also, search assessor data at www.cookcountyassessor.com/ccao/online.html but no name searching.

De Kalb County *Real Estate, Deed, Lien Records* www.dekalbcounty.org **$$** The De Kalb County online system requires a $350 subscription fee, with a per minute charge of $.25, $.50 if printing. Records date back to 1980. Lending agency data is available. For further info, contact recorder office.
Property, Taxation Records **Free** Search property assessor data free at www.dekalbcounty.org/GIS/TASDisclaimer.html Also, GIS mapping search page available through the county website. Also, you may subscribe, fees involved, to the Treasurer's PIN - Parcel Info Network - at http://dcggisweb.co.de-kalb.il.us/taxquery/welcome.asp.

De Witt County *Property, Taxation Records* **Free** Access parcel data free at http://helpillinois.net/dewitt/treasurer.htm. Click on Real Estate Tax Inquiry.

Du Page County *Real Estate, Deed, Lien Records* www.dupageco.org/recorder/ **$$** For access to Du Page County database one must lease a live interface telephone line from a carrier to establish a connection. There is a fee of $.05 per transaction. Records date back to 1977. For info, contact Fred Kieltcka at 630-682-7030. Internet access is available via the recorder website; click on Online Documents. Fees per document, username and password required.
Property, Taxation Records **Free** Search Wayne Township property records at www.waynetownshipassessor.com/disclaimer.html. Search Bloomingdale Township property records at www.bloomingdaletownshipassessor.com/Assessor/Search.asp. Search Wheatland Township at www.wheatlandtownship.com/sd/wlt/AssessorDB/Search.aspx. Search Addison Township records at www.addisontownship.com/SD/addison/assessordb/search.aspx?ID=2. No name searching in any of these towns.

Effingham County *Property, Taxation Records* **Free** Access to tax parcel data is free or by subscription to the GIS site at www.co.effingham.il.us/GIS.html.

Fulton County *Real Estate, Deed, Lien Records* www.fultonco.org `$$` Recorder land data by subscription on either the Laredo system using subscription and fees or the Tapestry System using credit card, http://tapestry.fidlar.com; $3.99 search; $.50 per image. Index goes back to 6/1985; images to 6/1999.

Henry County *Property, Taxation Records* `Free` Access to the assessor property database is free at www.henrycty.com/assessor/search.asp. Access the treasurer's tax payment data free at www.henrycty.com/treasurer/search.asp. Search county foreclosure list free at www.foreclosure.com/search.html?rsp=6252&st=IL&cno=073.

Jackson County *Grantor/Grantee, Real Estate. Judgments, Assumed Name Records* www.co.jackson.il.us `$$` Access to records at www.landrecords.net for a fee of $5.95 per search and $.50 per page for copy.

Kane County *Real Estate, Deed, Lien, Tract, Plat Records* www.co.kane.il.us `Free` Access recorders real estate records free at www.kanecountyrecorder.net/lrs/Source/Home.aspx.
Property, Taxation Records `Free` Search the treasurer's property tax info free at www.co.kane.il.us/treasurer/. Search by parcel number only; no name searching.

Kendall County *Property, Taxation Records* `Free` Search property data free at www.co.kendall.il.us/propertyservices.htm. Search tax data by name or parcel number.

Knox County *Real Estate, Deed, Lien, Mortgage, Judgment Records* `$$` Recording office data by subscription on either the Laredo system using subscription and fees or the Tapestry System using credit card, www.landrecords.net; $3.99 search; $.50 per image. Index goes back to 1986; images to 5/1/1996.

Lake County *Real Estate, Grantor/Grantee, Deed, Lien, Mortgage, Judgment, Lis Penden Records* www.co.lake.il.us/recorder/ `$$` Access to county recorded documents is by subscription; fee is $150 per quarter, per user. Index and images go back to 1980; older records being added. for info and signup, call 847-377-2069.
Property, Taxation Records `Free` Search the tax assessor's database at www.co.lake.il.us/assessor/assessments/default.asp. No name searching. Also, search property by address or legal description for free on the GIS-mapping site at http://gis2.co.lake.il.us/maps/.

La Salle County *Real Estate, Grantor/Grantee, Deed, Lien, Judgment, UCC, Mortgage, Birth, Death, Marriage Records* www.lasallecounty.org `Free & $$` Search the recorded data back to 1992 free at www.lasallecounty.org/np/recorder/index.htm and click on Online Document Search. Registration is suggested. Fees for images, plats, and deeper info.
Property, Taxation Records `Free` Last 2 years assessment data (Parcel number required) and treasurer parcel data (name search okay) can be accessed free at www.lasallecounty.org/contents3.htm. Also, 1999-2000 Assessor/property records online at www.lasallecounty.org/cidnet/asrpfull.htm. Registration and password required; $200.00 per year fee, plus per minute charges. For info, phone 815-434-8233.

Livingston County *Property, Taxation Records* `Free` Free parcel search at www.livingston.illinoisassessors.com/basic-search.php?nz=a2, no name searching. Advanced property searches available at www.livingston.illinoisassessors.com/search.php?mode=search but registration required. Call assessor's office for subscription information.

Logan County *Property, Taxation Records* `Free` Search the tax assessor database at http://loganilpropertymax.governmaxa.com/propertymax/rover30.asp Also, access property data free at http://taxsearch.co.logan.il.us/TaxInquiry.

McHenry County *Real Estate, Deed, Lien Records* www.co.mchenry.il.us/Common/CountyDpt/Recorder/default.asp `$$` Access recorder land data by subscription on either the Laredo system using subscription and fees or the Tapestry System using credit card, http://tapestry.fidlar.com; $3.99 search; $.50 per image. Index and images go back to 9/1972
Property, Taxation Records `Free` Records on the County Treasurer Inquiry site are free at www.co.mchenry.il.us/common/countyDpt/treas/default.asp. The sheriff's foreclosure list is free at www.co.mchenry.il.us.

McLean County *Real Estate, Deed, UCC, Lien, Assumed Name, Elected Official Records* www.mcleancountyil.gov/recorder `Free` Access to recorder official records and UCCs is free at www.mcleancountyil.gov/resolution/. Also, access county parcel and mobile home lots free at www.mcleancountyil.gov/tax/; no name searching. Also, search the assumed named list at www.mcleancountyil.gov/CountyClerk/CountyClerkAssumedNamesMain.asp. Search election officials by precinct at the website.
Property, Taxation Records `Free` Access Township of Normal assessor database free at www.normaltownship.org/assessor/parcelsearch.php. No name searching. Access City of Bloomington assessor database free at www.assessor-blm.com/propertydatabase.htm. No name searching; parcel number or address required.

Macon County *Real Estate, Deed, Lien, Judgment, UCC Records* www.maconcounty-il.gov `Free` Search recorded data free at http://64.107.106.116/.

Madison County *Real Estate, Deed, Lien Records* www.co.madison.il.us $$ Recorder land data by subscription on either the Laredo system using subscription and fees or the Tapestry System using credit card, http://tapestry.fidlar.com; $3.99 search; $.50 per image. Index goes back to 1/1985; images to 1/1996.
Property, Taxation Records Free Free parcel data at http://gisweb.co.madison.il.us/parceldata/ Search by name, address or parcel number.

Marshall County *Property, Taxation Records* $$ Access to assessor property records is by subscription; $20 per month, minimum of 3 months. Contact the Assessor office for signup- 309-246-2350.

Monroe County *Real Estate, Deed, Lien Records* $$ Recorder land data by subscription on either the Laredo system using subscription and fees or Tapestry System using credit card, http://tapestry.fidlar.com; $3.99 search; $.50 per image. Index goes back to 1/1984; images to 6/1/2002.

Morgan County *Real Estate, Deed Records* $$ Access recording office land data at www.etitlesearch.com; registration required, fee based on usage.

Ogle County *Real Estate, Deed, UCC Records* Free & $$ Access to recorder data is available for subscription at https://www.illandrecords.com/illr/il141/index.jsp. Also, the index of recorded documents may be accessed from https://www.landaccess.com.
Property, Taxation Records $$ Search assessor property data for a fee on the GIS system at http://beacon.schneidercorp.com/ but registration and username required for a name search.

Peoria County *Real Estate, Deed Records* www.co.peoria.il.us Free & $$ The recorder's office has a subscription service with web access to land records and other official documents; call recorder for details.

Perry County *Real Estate, Deed Records* www.perrycountyil.org Free
Searching is planned at www.perrycountyil.org.

Randolph County *Real Estate, Deed, Lien Records* www.randolphco.org $$ Recorder land data by subscription on either the Laredo system using subscription and fees or the Tapestry System using credit card, http://tapestry.fidlar.com; $3.99 search; $.50 per image. Images back to 5/3/1993; index to 1989.

Rock Island County *Real Estate, Deed, Lien, Subdivision Records* www.rockislandcounty.org/Rec.aspx?id=123 $$ Recorder land data by subscription on either the Laredo system using subscription and fees or the Tapestry System using credit card, http://tapestry.fidlar.com; $3.99 search; $.50 per image. Index goes back to 1982, images 1992; subdivisions back to 8/21/1995. Also, for the application for certified copy of vital records go to http://ricoclerk.revealed.net/.
Property, Taxation Records Free Access to property tax searches at www.rockislandcounty.org/Index.aspx?id=6374. Moline Town assessor records are free at www.molinetownship.com/OnlineSearch/Search.asp. No name searching.

St. Clair County *Real Estate, Grantor/Grantee, Deed, Lien, Judgment Records* www.stclaircountyrecorder.com Free & $$ Access to the recorder records is free at https://www.stclaircountyrecorder.com/app/static. Three search methods are available. Copy fee online is $3.50 per page.
Property, Taxation Records Free
Access parcel data free at http://www.co.st-clair.il.us/Departments/Assessor+Department/parcel.htm.

Sangamon County *Real Estate, Deed, Lien Records* www.co.sangamon.il.us $$ Recorder land data by subscription on either the Laredo system using subscription and fees or the Tapestry System using credit card, http://tapestry.fidlar.com; $3.99 search; $.50 per image. Images goes back to 1992; index to 1970.
Property, Taxation Records Free View the status of property tax payments or property assessments at http://tax.co.sangamon.il.us/SangamonCountyWeb/index.jsp

Vermilion County *Real Estate, Deed. Lien, UCC Records* www.vercounty.org/recorder.htm $$ Access real estate records at https://www.illandrecords.com/illr/il183/index.jsp. There is a $5.00 fee per doc found and $5.00 fee to view it, or you may subscribe for $1000 per month. Also, recorder land data by subscription on either the Laredo system (subscription & fees) or the Tapestry System (use credit card) at http://tapestry.fidlar.com; $3.99 search; $.50 per image. Index and images go back to 7/1/1987.
Property, Taxation Records Free Access property data free on the gis-mapping site at www.vcgis.org/. Find information on subscribing to the county's property tax database at www.vercounty.org/TechServ/taxinquiry.pdf.

Wayne County *Property, Taxation Records* Free & $$ Records on the Wayne Township Assessor Office database are free at www.waynetownshipassessor.com/OPID.html. Also, you may subscribe to the advanced search feature for a fee. Access includes legal, assessment, sales history, buildings and other data.

Whiteside County *Property, Taxation Records* $$ Search assessor property data for a fee on the GIS system at http://beacon.schneidercorp.com/?site=WhitesideCountyIL. Obtain form for map request at www.whiteside.org/download/Assessor/MAP_REQUEST_FORM.pdf.

Will County   *Real Estate, Deed, Lien, Mortgage, Voter Registration, Corporation, UCC, Judgment Records*
www.willcountyrecorder.com   `Free & $$`   Access to the Recorder's real estate and lien records back to 1973 free at www.willcountyrecorder.com; fees apply for full data and to print copies. Access to voter registration data is free at https://www.willcountydata.com/voterstatus/Voter_lookup_input.htm.

Property, Taxation Records   `Free`   Access to property/parcel number for free go to www.willcountysoa.com/disclaimer.aspx.

Winnebago County   *Real Estate, Deed Records*   www.co.winnebago.il.us   `Free & $$`   Access county property and court data by subscription at www.co.winnebago.il.us; registration and $10.00 per month fee required. Also, access county land and UCC records at https://www.illandrecords.com/illr/il201/index.jsp but must pay per use or subscribe.

Property, Taxation Records   `Free`   Access parcel and assessment data free at http://cis.co.winnebago.il.us/property/sofa/c-sofa_inqIndex.asp. Registration and password required to access fuller data. Search property data at http://cis.co.winnebago.il.us/property/treas/Treas_inqLOGIN.asp. Get userID and password from treasurer office. Also, access property data via the GIS-mapping site free at http://ims.wingis.org/ParcelSearch.asp. Also, search Rockford Township assessment data free at www.rockfordtownshipassessor.net/propertysearch.asp

Other Illinois Sites of Note:
Adams County - Inmate and Warrant Lists   www.co.adams.il.us
Cook County - (Chicago City) - Sex Offender   http://12.17.79.4
Cook County - Heirs (Treasurer)   www.cookcountytreasurer.com/inheritance.aspx?ntopicid=238
Cook County - Inmates, Wanted Sex Offenders   www.cookcountysheriff.org
Du Page County - Most Wanted, Deadbeat Parents, Sex Offenders   www.co.dupage.il.us/sheriff/
Henry County - Most Wanted, Fugitive, Sex Offender   www.henrycty.com/sheriff/index.html
McLean County - Immigration   www.mcleancountyil.gov/CircuitClerk/imgrecs/imgrecs.html
McLean County - Restaurant Inspections   www.mcleancountyil.gov/health/InspectionScores.asp
Ogle County - Sexual Offender, Most Wanted   www.oglecountysheriff.org
Peoria County - Sheriff's Warrants   www.co.peoria.il.us/sheriff.php?dept=sheriff&page=warrants
White County - Most Wanted   www.whitecounty-il.gov/sheriff/topTenWarrants.asp

Indiana

Capital: Indianapolis
      Marion County
Time Zone: EST

> 11 western Indiana counties are CST and observe DST. They are: Gibson, Jasper, Laporte, Lake, Newton, Porter, Posey, Spencer, Starke, Vanderburgh, Warrick. The remainder are EST and do not observe DST except for Clark, Dearborn, Floyd, Harrison, Ohio.

Population: 6,345,289
# of Counties: 92

Useful State Links

Website: www.in.gov/
Governor: www.in.gov/gov/
Attorney General: www.in.gov/attorneygeneral
State Archives: www.in.gov/icpr/archives/
State Statutes and Codes: www.in.gov/legislative/ic/code/
Legislative Bill Search: www.in.gov/apps/lsa/session/billwatch/billinfo
Bill Monitoring: www.in.gov/apps/lsa/session/billwatch/
Unclaimed Funds: https://www.indianaunclaimed.com/apps/ag/ucp/index.html

Primary State Agencies

Criminal Records `Free & $$`

Indiana State Police, Criminal History Records, www.IN.gov/isp/ A Limited Criminal History with only felonies and class A misdemeanor arrests is available at www.in.gov/ai/appfiles/isp-lch//. Using a credit card, the search fee is $16.32. Subscribers to accessIndiana can obtain records for $15.00 per search or for no charge if statutorily exempt, or $7.00 with a government exemption. Response of No Records Found is an official search result. The state Attorney General's Office has a searchable web page of companies that have violated consumer laws. Visit http://atgindsha01.atg.in.gov/cpd/enforcement/search.aspx.

Sexual Offender Registry `Free`

Sex and Violent Offender Directory Manager, Indiana Government Center South, E334, www.insor.org/insasoweb/ The website has a searching capabilities by name and city or county at www.insor.org/insasoweb/.

Incarceration Records `Free`

Indiana Department of Correction, IGCS, Supervisor of Records, Room E-334, www.in.gov/idoc/ At the website, click on Offender Locator or visit www.in.gov/apps/indcorrection/ofs/. Also, a private company provides statewide offender and inmate searching free at https://www.vinelink.com/vinelink/siteInfoAction.do?siteId=15000.

Corporation, LP, LLC, LLP, Fictitious/Assumed Name `Free`

Corporation Division, Secretary of State, www.in.gov/sos/ You can conduct Business Entity Name Searches, Name Availability Checks and acquire official Certificates of Existence or Authorization at www.in.gov/sos/business/corporations.html. The site also gives access to UCC records. Frequent users of Business Services Online should subscribe to accessIndiana at www.ai.org/ai/business/. Also, search securities companies registered with the state at www.in.gov/apps/sos/securities/sos_securities. *Other Options:* Monthly lists of all new businesses are available online, as are bulk data and specialized searches. Look for Special Business Entity Search Orders at the website.

Trademarks/Servicemarks `Free`

Secretary of State, Trademark Division, www.in.gov/sos/business/trademarks.html Visit www.in.gov/apps/sos/trademarks/. This database contains information regarding the status of all trademarks on file with the state of Indiana. Access is free. Results allow one to view application, certificate or the mark.

Uniform Commercial Code Free & $$

UCC Division, Secretary of State, www.in.gov/sos/business/ucc.html You may browse lien records at https://secure.in.gov/sos/bus_service/online_ucc/browse/default.asp. There is no charge. An official search may be performed for $4.08. If requester is subscriber to AccessIndiana then fee to obtain record is $3.00. Filing services are also available to subscribers. Bulk downloads and special orders are available online.

Workers' Compensation Records Free

Workers Compensation Board, www.in.gov/wcb/ Search disputed claims at http://wcbnec03.wcb.state.in.us/search.asp.

Driver Records $$

BMV-Driving Records, 100 N Senate Ave, www.IN.gov/bmv/ IN.gov is the state owned interactive information and communication system which provides batch and interactive access to driving records. There is an annual $50.00 fee. Online access costs $7.50 per record. For more information, call 317-233-2010 or go to www.in.gov/subscriber_center.htm.

Vehicle, Vessel Ownership & Registration $$

Bureau of Motor Vehicles, Records, www.in.gov/bmv/ AccessIndiana at 317-233-2010 is the state appointed vendor. Visit www.in.gov for more information. Search the Indiana Bureau of Motor Vehicles database for title and lien information by VIN number, title number, or social security number. Salvage titles included. The fee is $5.00 per record plus an annual fee of $50.00.

Accident Reports $$

Holt, Sheets - Crash Records Section, 100 N Senate, www.buycrash.com/Public/CommunitySearch.aspx Records may be downloaded online as a PDF file, after fee payment. *Other Options:* For information about bulk file purchasing, contact the Data Section at 317-233-5133.

Birth and Death Certificates $$

State Department of Health, Vital Records Office, www.in.gov/isdh/index.html Records may be ordered online via the website, but the requester ofr a birth record must still fax a photo copy of an ID before the record request is processed. Also, records may requested from www.vitalchek.com, a state-endorsed vendor.

Occupational Licensing Boards

Acupuncturist	https://extranet.in.gov/WebLookup/Search.aspx
Alcohol Bev. Dist./Retail'r/Employee	www.in.gov/ai/appfiles/atc-license-lookup/
Alcoholic Beverage Dealer/Mfg	www.in.gov/ai/appfiles/atc-license-lookup/
Appraiser, Resi/General/Trainee	https://extranet.in.gov/WebLookup/Search.aspx
Architect	https://extranet.in.gov/WebLookup/Search.aspx
Athletic Trainer	https://extranet.in.gov/WebLookup/Search.aspx
Attorney	http://hats.courts.state.in.us/rollatty/roa1_inp.jsp
Auctioneer	https://extranet.in.gov/WebLookup/Search.aspx
Audiologist	https://extranet.in.gov/WebLookup/Search.aspx
Bank & Trust Company	http://extranet.dfi.in.gov/dfidb/deplist.aspx
Barber/Barber Instructor	https://extranet.in.gov/WebLookup/Search.aspx
Boxer	https://extranet.in.gov/WebLookup/Search.aspx
Boxing Occupation	https://extranet.in.gov/WebLookup/Search.aspx
Check Casher	http://extranet.dfi.in.gov/dfidb/nondeplist.aspx
Child Care Center/Home/Provider	https://secure.in.gov/apps/fssa/carefinder/index.html
Chiropractor	https://extranet.in.gov/WebLookup/Search.aspx
Clinical Nurse Specialist	https://extranet.in.gov/WebLookup/Search.aspx
Collection Agency	www.in.gov/apps/sos/securities/sos_securities
Cosmetologist	https://extranet.in.gov/WebLookup/Search.aspx
CPA-Public Accountant	https://extranet.in.gov/WebLookup/Search.aspx
Credit Union	http://extranet.dfi.in.gov/dfidb/deplist.aspx
Dental Anesthetist/ Dental Hygienist	https://extranet.in.gov/WebLookup/Search.aspx
Dentist	https://extranet.in.gov/WebLookup/Search.aspx
Dietitian	https://extranet.in.gov/WebLookup/Search.aspx
Electrologist	https://extranet.in.gov/WebLookup/Search.aspx
Embalmer	https://extranet.in.gov/WebLookup/Search.aspx
Emergency Medical Technician	www.in.gov/dhs/3880.htm
EMS Providers	www.in.gov/dhs/3880.htm
Engineer	https://extranet.in.gov/WebLookup/Search.aspx

Engineering Intern .... https://extranet.in.gov/WebLookup/Search.aspx
Environmental Health Specialist .... https://extranet.in.gov/WebLookup/Search.aspx
Esthetician .... https://extranet.in.gov/WebLookup/Search.aspx
Funeral/Cemetery Director .... https://extranet.in.gov/WebLookup/Search.aspx
Hazardous Waste Facility/Handler .... http://extranet.in.gov/mylicense/
Health Services Administrator .... https://extranet.in.gov/WebLookup/Search.aspx
Hearing Aid Dealer .... https://extranet.in.gov/WebLookup/Search.aspx
Hypnotist .... https://extranet.in.gov/WebLookup/Search.aspx
Industrial Authority, State .... http://extranet.dfi.in.gov/dfidb/deplist.aspx
Insurance Agent/Consultant   https://www.sircon.com/ComplianceExpress/Inquiry/consumerInquiry.do?nonSscrb=Y
Investment Advisor .... www.in.gov/apps/sos/securities/sos_securities
Landscape Architect .... https://extranet.in.gov/WebLookup/Search.aspx
Lender, Small .... http://extranet.dfi.in.gov/dfidb/nondeplist.aspx
Loan Broker .... www.in.gov/apps/sos/securities/sos_securities
Lobbyist, Executive Branch .... https://secure.in.gov/apps/idoa/lobbyist/registration/search.aspx
Lobbyist, Legislative .... www.in.gov/ilrc/data/index.html
Lottery Retailer .... www.in.gov/hoosierlottery/games/retailerlocator.asp
Manicurist .... https://extranet.in.gov/WebLookup/Search.aspx
Marriage & Family Therapist .... https://extranet.in.gov/WebLookup/Search.aspx
Medical Doctor .... https://extranet.in.gov/WebLookup/Search.aspx
Medical Residency Permit .... https://extranet.in.gov/WebLookup/Search.aspx
Mental Health Counselor .... https://extranet.in.gov/WebLookup/Search.aspx
Midwife Nurse .... https://extranet.in.gov/WebLookup/Search.aspx
Money Transmitter .... http://extranet.dfi.in.gov/dfidb/nondeplist.aspx
Notary Public .... www.ai.org/serv/sos_notary
Nurse .... https://extranet.in.gov/WebLookup/Search.aspx
Nurse Midwife .... https://extranet.in.gov/WebLookup/Search.aspx
Nursing Home Administrator .... https://extranet.in.gov/WebLookup/Search.aspx
Occupational Therapist .... https://extranet.in.gov/WebLookup/Search.aspx
Occupational Therapy Assistant .... https://extranet.in.gov/WebLookup/Search.aspx
Optometrist .... https://extranet.in.gov/WebLookup/Search.aspx
Optometrist Drug Certification .... https://extranet.in.gov/WebLookup/Search.aspx
Osteopathic Physician .... https://extranet.in.gov/WebLookup/Search.aspx
Pawnbroker .... http://extranet.dfi.in.gov/dfidb/nondeplist.aspx
Pesticide Applic'rTech//Consultant ... www.isco.purdue.edu/pesticide/index_pest1.html
Pharmacist/Pharmacist Intern .... https://extranet.in.gov/WebLookup/Search.aspx
Pharmacy Technician .... https://extranet.in.gov/WebLookup/Search.aspx
Physical Therapist/Therapist Asst ..... https://extranet.in.gov/WebLookup/Search.aspx
Physician .... https://extranet.in.gov/WebLookup/Search.aspx
Physician Assistant .... https://extranet.in.gov/WebLookup/Search.aspx
PI Company Employee .... https://extranet.in.gov/WebLookup/Search.aspx
Placement Officer, School .... http://mustang.doe.state.in.us/TEACH/teach_inq.cfm
Plumber .... https://extranet.in.gov/WebLookup/Search.aspx
Plumbing Contractor .... https://extranet.in.gov/WebLookup/Search.aspx
Podiatrist .... https://extranet.in.gov/WebLookup/Search.aspx
Polygraph Examiner .... www.indianapolygraphassociation.com/members.asp
Private Detective .... https://extranet.in.gov/WebLookup/Search.aspx
Psychologist .... https://extranet.in.gov/WebLookup/Search.aspx
Public Accountant .... https://extranet.in.gov/WebLookup/Search.aspx
Real Estate Agent/Broker/Seller .... https://extranet.in.gov/WebLookup/Search.aspx
Real Estate Appraiser .... https://extranet.in.gov/WebLookup/Search.aspx
Rental Purchase Lender .... http://extranet.dfi.in.gov/dfidb/nondeplist.aspx
Respiratory Care Practitioner .... https://extranet.in.gov/WebLookup/Search.aspx
Savings & Loan .... http://extranet.dfi.in.gov/dfidb/deplist.aspx
School Administr'r/Principal/Director http://mustang.doe.state.in.us/TEACH/teach_inq.cfm
School Counselor/Nurse .... http://mustang.doe.state.in.us/TEACH/teach_inq.cfm
Securities Broker/Dealer .... www.in.gov/apps/sos/securities/sos_securities

Shampoo Operator .... https://extranet.in.gov/WebLookup/Search.aspx
Social Worker .... https://extranet.in.gov/WebLookup/Search.aspx
Solid Waste Facility .... http://extranet.in.gov/mylicense/
Speech Pathologist .... https://extranet.in.gov/WebLookup/Search.aspx
Surveyor, Land .... https://extranet.in.gov/WebLookup/Search.aspx
Teacher .... http://mustang.doe.state.in.us/TEACH/teach_inq.cfm
Trust Company .... http://extranet.dfi.in.gov/dfidb/deplist.aspx
Veterinarian .... https://extranet.in.gov/WebLookup/Search.aspx
Veterinary Tech .... https://extranet.in.gov/WebLookup/Search.aspx
Waste Tire Processor/Transporter ..... http://extranet.in.gov/mylicense/
Waste Water Treatm't Plant Operat'r. http://extranet.in.gov/mylicense/
Yard Waste Composting Facility .... http://extranet.in.gov/mylicense/

State and Local Courts

State Court Structure: Trial courts include Circuit Courts, Superior Courts, County Courts, and local City or Town Courts. Though these courts have different names, the four trial courts are actually more alike than they are different. Trial courts have different names primarily due to accidents of legislative history and local custom, not true differences in the nature or purpose of the courts. The cases these courts hear can vary tremendously from county to county. Indiana has 92 counties, and 88 of these counties comprise their own circuit, with their own Circuit Court. The remaining four small counties (Ohio, Dearborn, Jefferson, and Switzerland Counties) have been combined to form two circuits with two counties in each circuit. In counties without Superior or County Courts, the Circuit Courts in addition to all other cases, also handle small claims cases for civil disputes involving less than $6,000 and minor offenses, such as misdemeanors, ordinance violations, and Class D felonies. County Courts are gradually being restructured into divisions of the Superior Courts. Note that Small Claims cases in Marion County are heard at the township and records are maintained at that level.

Statewide Court Online Access: Implementation of an online record search system available for the public, called Odyssey, began with all Monroe County Courts and the Marion County Washington Township Small Claims Court in December 2007. An additional 9 counties are planned to be integrated into the system by early 2009. Visit http://mycase.in.gov/default.aspx.

Also, a vendor is working closely with many counties to provide electroinc access. An expanding limited free search of open case index is available at www.doxpop.com/prod/welcome.jsp. Full access to case records requires registration and subscription, $25.00 per month minimum. Although not statewide, this is an expaning service that is alos adding recording office data.

The judiciary home page at www.in.gov/judiciary gives free access to an index of docket information for Supreme, Appeals, and Tax Court cases.

The following county courts permit access to records www.doxpop as described above.

Throughput dates will vary.

Allen County - Circuit & Superior Court
Bartholomew County - Circuit & Superior Court
Brown County - Circuit Court
Clay County Circuit & Superior Court
Clinton County Circuit & Superior Court
Daviess County Circuit & Superior Court
Decatur County Circuit & Superior Court
Dubois County Circuit & Superior Court
Fayette County Circuit & Superior Court
Fountain County Circuit Court
Fulton County Circuit Court/Superior Court
Gibson County Circuit & Superior Court
Grant County Circuit & Superior Court
Hamilton County Circuit & Superior Court

Hancock County Circuit & Superior Court
Henry County Circuit & Superior Courts I & II
Howard County Circuit & Superior Court
Jay County Circuit & Superior Court
Johnson County Circuit & Superior Court
Kosciusko County Circuit & Superior Court
La Porte County Circuit & Superior Court
LaGrange County Circuit & Superior Court
Madison County Circuit, Superior & County Court
Marshall County Circuit & Superior Court 1 & 2
Miami County Circuit & Superior Court
Montgomery County Circuit & Superior Court
Morgan County Circuit & Superior Court
Perry County Circuit Court
Pike County Circuit Court
Putnam County Circuit & Superior Court
Randolph County Circuit & Superior Court
Ripley County Circuit Court
Spencer County Circuit Court
Sullivan County Circuit & Superior Court
Wabash County Circuit & Superior Court
Warrick County Circuit & Superior Court
Wayne County Circuit & Superior Court
White County Circuit & Superior Court
Whitley County Circuit & Superior Court

Below are other county online access sytems available:

Delaware County Circuit Court www.dcclerk.org A limited free search of open cases is available. Index from Muncie City court also available online.

Elkhart County

Elkhart Superior Courts 1, 2, 5, 6 www.in.gov/judiciary/elkhart/
Civil: Online subscription service at https://www.doxpop.com. Fees involved. Records date from 1/92. A limited free search of open cases is available. *Criminal:* Same.

Goshen Circuit & Superior Courts 3, 4 www.elkhartcountyindiana.com/administrative/clerk.html **Free & $$**
Civil: Online subscription service at https://www.doxpop.com. Fees involved; $39.00 per month. Records date from 01/92. A limited free search of open cases is available. *Criminal:* Same.

Floyd County

Circuit, Superior & County Court **Free**
Civil: Online access is the same as criminal, see below. *Criminal:* Access to court records is free at www.floydcounty.in.gov/court_rec_menu.asp. Name search or view calendars or case summaries.

Hendricks County

Circuit & Superior Court www.co.hendricks.in.us/ **Free**
Civil: Will only do mail request if out of state. Online docket found at www.nasaview.com/Hendricks/index.jsp Records available to 1992. *Criminal:* Search docket online at www.nasaview.com/Hendricks/index.jsp. Records go back to 1992.

Lake County

Circuit & Superior Court www.lakecountyin.org/index.jsp **Free & $$**
Civil: Online searching for docket records available at https://www.lakecountyin.org/portal/media-type/html/user/anon/page/online-docket. Search free but $.25 per page copy fee with $1.00 minimum. *Criminal:* Online search of docket records at https://www.lakecountyin.org/portal/media-type/html/user/anon/page/online-docket. Search free but $.25 page copy fee; $1.00 min.

Marion County

Circuit & Superior Court www.indygov.org/eGov/County/Clerk/home.htm
Civil: Search names online for free at www.civicnet.net. There is a $7.50 charge assessed to view each Case Summary. Online records go back to 1991. Also, search Washington Township civil, family, and probate dockets free at http://mycase.in.gov/default.aspx. *Criminal:* Access to online criminal records at https://www.civicnet.net/criminal/ requires a subscription or you may search at rate of

$4.50 per name and pay with credit card. Criminal records go back to 1988. Also, search Washington Township criminal dockets and citations free at http://mycase.in.gov/default.aspx.

Monroe County

Circuit Court   www.co.monroe.in.us   **Free**
Civil: Online access by free service at http://mycase.in.gov/default.aspx. Includes civil, fmaily, probate dockets. *Criminal:* Online access by free service at http://mycase.in.gov/default.aspx. Includes criminal and citations.

Noble County

Circuit, Superior I & Superior II Court   www.nobleco.org/   **Free**
Civil: Access court records free at http://noble.nasaview.com:8080/Noble/index.jsp. *Criminal:* Same.

Starke County

Circuit Court   www.in-map.net/counties/STARKE/government/index.htm   **Free & $$**
Civil: Online subscription service at https://www.doxpop.com. Fees involved. Records date back to 9/2005 A limited free search of open cases is available. *Criminal:* Same.

Tippecanoe County

Circuit, Superior & County Court   www.tippecanoe.in.gov   **Free**
Civil: Online access to court records through CourtView are free at www.county.tippecanoe.in.us/court/pa.urd/pamw6500-display. *Criminal:* Same.

Vigo County

Circuit Court   www.vigocounty.org/courts/   **Free & $$**
Civil: Online subscription service at https://www.doxpop.com. Fees involved. Records date from 04/96. A limited free search of open cases is available. *Criminal:* Same.

Wells County

Circuit & Superior Court   www.wellscounty.org/superiorcourt.htm   **Free & $$**
Civil: Online subscription service to **Bluffton city courts** at https://www.doxpop.com. Fees involved. A limited free search of open cases is available. Online index goes back to 1/2000. *Criminal:* Online access to Blufton city criminal records is the same as civil.

Recorders, Assessors, and Other Sites of Note

Recording Office Organization: 92 counties, 92 recording offices. The recording officer is the County Recorder but see the office of the Circuit Clerk for state tax liens on personal property. Many counties utilize a "Miscellaneous Index" for tax and other liens. All federal tax liens on personal property are filed with the County Recorder. State tax liens on personal property are filed with Circuit Clerk in a different office than the Recorder.

Online Access Note: A growing number of agencies offer online access. Perhaps the most notable is the subscription service offered by Marion County at www.civicnet.net.

Adams County   *Property, Taxation Records*   **Free**   Access to property tax and GIS-mapping site free at www.adams-county.com/gis.html

Allen County   *Real Estate, Deed, Lien Records*   www.allencountyrecorder.us/   **$$**   Access real estate recording data back to 1/1979 free at http://inallen.fidlar.com/websearch/. Also, access recording office data by subscription on either the Laredo system using subscription and fees or the Tapestry System using credit card, http://tapestry.fidlar.com
Property, Taxation Records   **Free**   Access property database card data free at www.co.allen.in.us/CustomApps/PropCard/address_search.php.

Bartholomew County   *Property, Taxation Records*   **Free**   Access to county Public Access Geographic Information System is free at http://gis.bartholomewco.com/pagis/login.aspx; you must have an email for free registration and login.

Blackford County   *Property, Taxation Records*   **Free & $$**   Access property data at http://beacon.schneidercorp.com/. Registration, username and password required.

Boone County   *Property, Taxation Records*   **Free**   Search for property data free on the GIS-mapping site at http://boonecounty.in.gov/Default.aspx?tabid=57. At map, click on 'Search for' at bottom left and choose 'parcels' to search by name.

Clark County   *Property, Taxation Records*   **Free**   Online access to property records is available at http://in10.plexisgroup.com/ecama/index.cfm.

Clinton County *Property, Taxation Records* `$$` Search assessor property data for a fee on the GIS system at http://beacon.schneidercorp.com/. Registration and username required.

Daviess County *Property, Taxation Records* `Free` Online access to property records is available at http://in14.plexisgroup.com/ecama/index.cfm.

Dearborn County *Property, Taxation Records* `Free` Access to free property search go to http://in-dearborn-assessor.governmaxa.com/propertymax/rover30.asp.

Decatur County *Property, Taxation Records* `$$` Access county property data for a fee at http://beacon.schneidercorp.com/ with registration and password.

Dubois County *Real Estate, Deed, LLien, Judgment Records* `Free & $$` Online access to recorded records available via Doxpop.com subscription service. Index goes back to 4/1994, images to 12/1999.
Property, Taxation Records `Free` Access property search information free at www.duboiscountyassessor.com/propertymax/rover30.asp.

Elkhart County *Real Estate, Deed, Lien Records* www.elkhartcountyindiana.com `$$` Access Elkhart County records for an annual fee of $50. plus a minimum of $20. per month of use. The minimum fee allows for 2 hours access, and add'l use is billed at $10 per hour. Lending agency data is available. For info, call at 574-535-6777.
Property, Taxation Records `Free` Search parcel data for free at www.macoggis.com and includes Michiana area which is St Joseph and Elkhart Counties.

Fayette County *Property, Taxation Records* `Free` Access assessor property record cards and tax records free at www.co.fayette.in.us/auditor.htm. Also access property data free at http://in-fayette-assessor.governmaxa.com.

Floyd County *Real Estate, Deed Records* www.floydcounty.in.gov `Free` Computerized versions of microfiche cards to be on the internet; call clerk at 812-948-5430 for update information.

Fountain County *Property, Taxation Records* `Free` Access the assessor property tax and property sales data free at http://in-fountain-assessor.governmax.com/propertymax/rover30.asp?sid=735BBA9CF58B460191BF753F01FFCECF.

Franklin County *Real Estate, Deed, Lien, Judgment Records* www.franklincounty.in.gov `$$`
Online access to recorded records available via Doxpop.com subscription service. Index and images go back to 2002.
Property, Taxation Records `Free & $$` Free search online at http://in-franklin-assessor.governmaxa.com/propertymax/rover30.asp. Search by name, address, parcel number. Access to the GIS web map for free at http://thinkopengis.franklin.in.wthengineering.com/. To name search, click on Parcel.

Gibson County *Property, Taxation Records* `Free` Access assessor property data free at http://in-gibson-assessor.governmaxa.com. Click on "Start your search." Also, search for property assessor parcel data at http://beacon.schneidercorp.com/ but registration and password required.

Grant County *Real Estate, Deed, UCC, Mortgage, Voter Registration Records* www.grantcounty.net `Free`
Access to recorder data is free at http://recorder.grant.in.uinquire.us/. Click on "Recorder Information." Also, voter registration is at http://voters.grant.in.uinquire.us/nxweb.exe; registration, login, and password required.
Property, Taxation Records `Free` Access to assessor property data is free at www.xsoftin.com/grant/parcelsearch.aspx. Tax data is free at http://auditor.grant.in.uinquire.us/. Click on "Tax Information."

Hamilton County *Real Estate, Deed, Tax Lien, Judgment Records* `$$` Index of recorded documents is available from 01/87 and scanned images from 02/96 available for subscribers at https://www.doxpop.com/prod/recorder/.
Property, Taxation Records `Free` Access property and tax information at www.co.hamilton.in.us/apps/reports/defaulttax2.asp but no name searching. View county maps at www.co.hamilton.in.us/gis/start.html. Search the auditor database free at www.hamiltoncountyauditor.org/realestate/

Hancock County *Property, Taxation Records* `Free` Access to the assessor property data is free on the gis-mapping site at http://beacon.schneidercorp.com/?site=HancockCountyIN. Click on Search to search by name. Also, sales disclosure data is free at www.hancockcoingov.org/assessor/sales_disclosure_search.asp. Also, search City of Greenfield property data free at http://beacon.schneidercorp.com/.

Hendricks County *Property, Taxation Records* `Free` Search the assessor's property data free at www.co.hendricks.in.us/DWLookup/Disclaimer.asp. Access to county property data on the GIS mapping site is free at http://in32.plexisgroup.com/map/index.html. Click on "Query" to select query by owner name. Also, search the GIS mapping for Town of Plainfield data free at http://beacon.schneidercorp.com.

Henry County *Property, Taxation Records* `Free` Access property assessment lookup free at www.henryco.net/cm/node/8. Also, search the property tax payment site free at https://www.paytrustsolutions.com/paytrust/SelectTransactionType.do?action=view&transactionTypeId=168.

Howard County *Property, Taxation Records* `Free` Search assessor property data free on the GIS system at http://beacon.schneidercorp.com/ with registration and username required.

Huntington County *Property, Taxation Records* `Free` Access to the assessor property data is free on the gis-mapping site at http://gis.huntington.in.us/.

Jay County *Property, Taxation Records* `Free` Access to GIS-mapping property data is free at http://in38.plexisgroup.com/map/index.cfm and click on Query to name search.

Jennings County *Property, Taxation Records* `Free` Access to the assessor property data is free on the gis-mapping site at http://thinkopengis.jennings.in.wthtechnology.com/.

Johnson County *Property, Taxation Records* `Free` Access to the assessor GIS database of property and sales data is free at http://beacon.schneidercorp.com/.

Kosciusko County *Property, Taxation Records* `Free` Access to property records on the searchable GIS mapping site is free at http://kcgov.com/application/gis/viewer.htm. Click on "Search" to find name search mode.

LaGrange County *Property, Taxation Records* `Free` Access assessor's data and search free at http://in-lagrange-assessor.governmax.com/propertymax/rover30.asp.

Lake County *Property, Taxation Records* `Free` Access property tax data online at http://in-lake-assessor.governmaxa.com/propertymax/rover30.asp. Search free as Guest, but no name searching. Subscription service allows name searching; sub fee is $19.95 per month.

La Porte County *Real Estate, Deed, Lien Records* www.laportecounty.org/ `SS` Recorder land data by subscription on either the Laredo system using subscription and fees or the Tapestry System using credit card, http://tapestry.fidlar.com; $3.99 search; $1.00 per image. Index back to 1978; images to 1978.

Marion County *Real Estate, Lien, Deed, UCC, Property Tax Records*
www.indygov.org/eGov/County/Recorder/home.htm `SS` Access to Marion County online records requires a $200 set up fee, plus an escrow balance of at least $100 must be maintained. add'l charges are $.25 per minute, $.05 display charge for 1st page; $.05 each add'l page. Records date back to 1964; images from 1964. Federal tax liens and UCC data available. For info, contact Mike Kerner at 317-327-4587 or visit www.civicnet.net. Also, access recording office land data at www.etitlesearch.com; registration required, fee based on usage.
Property, Taxation Records `Free` Property tax information is free at http://cms.indygov.org/MyAssessedValue/. Also, search City of Beech Grove property data at http://beacon.schneidercorp.com/ with registration required.

Marshall County *Property, Taxation Records* `Free` Search property data free at www.beacon.schneidercorp.com/.

Monroe County *Property, Taxation Records* `Free` Access to GIS/Maps information for free go to http://in53.plexisgroup.com/

Newton County *Property, Taxation Records* `Free` Access assessor's property database free at http://in56.plexisgroup.com/ecama/propsearch.cfm.

Noble County *Property, Taxation Records* `Free` Access the property ownership roster in pdf format for free at www.nobleco.org/GIS/Land_Ownership_Roster.pdf.

Ohio County *Property, Taxation Records* `Free` Access property data free at http://in-ohio-assessor.governmaxa.com/propertymax/rover30.asp. Click on property search, then search by owner, address or parcel number.

Porter County *Real Estate, Deed, Lien Records* www.porterco.org `SS` Recorder land data by subscription on either the Laredo system using subscription and fees or the Tapestry System using credit card, http://tapestry.fidlar.com; $3.99 search; $1.00 per image. Index goes back to 1991; images to 1975. The county offers an enhanced access subscription system for county property data and court information for $50.00 per month for 40 hours; contract and info available at www.porterco.org/enhanced_access.html.
Property, Taxation Records `Free` Access to property assessment data and sales is free at http://in64.plexisgroup.com/ecama/. Also search property tax information for free at www.porterco.org/taxes.html.

St. Joseph County *Real Estate, Deed, Lien Records* www.stjosephcountyindiana.com `SS`
Recorder land data by subscription on either the Laredo system using subscription and fees or the Tapestry System using credit card, http://tapestry.fidlar.com; $5.95 search; $1.00 per image. Index back to 12/1992; images back to 1992.
Property, Taxation Records `Free` Search parcel data for free at www.macoggis.com and includes Michiana area which is St Joseph and Elkhart Counties.

Shelby County *Real Estate, Deed, Tax Lien, Judgment Records* `SS` Online access to recorded records available via Doxpop.com subscription service. Index and images go back to 5/1998.

Steuben County *Property, Taxation Records* `Free` Access property data free on the GIS mapping site at www.co.steuben.in.us/ Also, access parcel and subdivision data free on the GIS mapping site at http://beacon.schneidercorp.com/?site=SteubenCountyIN.

Tippecanoe County *Property, Taxation Records* `$$` A subscription fee of $10 per month plus a one-time set-up fee of $50 allows full access to both the tax database and the assessment database. Click on Access Property Tax & Assessment Records. Also, access to the county GIS-mapping site free at http://gis.tippecanoe.in.gov/public/.

Tipton County *Property, Taxation Records* `Free` Search assessor property data free on the GIS system at the Tipton county site or http://beacon.schneidercorp.com/.

Union County *Property, Taxation Records* Assessor records not yet available online.

Vanderburgh County *Property, Taxation Records* `Free` Access assessor property database free at www.vanderburghassessor.org/.

Vigo County *Real Estate, Deed, Tax Lien, Judgment Records* www.vigocounty.org/recorder/ `$$` Online access to recorded records available via Doxpop.com subscription service. Index goes back to 11/1996, images to 1/2001. Also images can be purchased at doxpop.com at $1.00 per image back to 2001.
Property, Taxation Records `Free` Search Vigo County property data by parcel, name or address at www.vigocounty.org/assessor/ by clicking on Search Vigo County Property information. Also, search property data for a fee at http://beacon.schneidercorp.com/ with registration and password; includes City of Terra Haute.

Wabash County *Property, Taxation Records* `Free` Access property data free from the Property List at http://assessor.wabash.in.datapitstop.us. Click on Property Information.

Warrick County *Property, Taxation Records* `Free` Access property data free at www.emapsplus.com/ILAdams/maps/ including name searching. Assessor's property tax data free at www.warrickcounty.gov/warrickassessor/. GIS Map information available at http://thinkopengis.warrick.in.wthengineering.com/start

Wayne County *Real Estate, Deed, Lien, Mortgage, Assumed Name, Marriage Records* http://co.wayne.in.us/recorder/ `Free & $$` Access recorded document indexes through a private company at www.doxpop.com. Subscriptions start at $25.00 monthly; add'l $1.00 or less fee to purchase a full-size document. Index goes back to 1/1994; images to 4/2000. Also, marriage records being added irregularly to the website at www.co.wayne.in.us/marriage/retrieve.cgi. Records are from 1811 forward.
Property, Taxation Records `Free` Access county property records free at http://prc.co.wayne.in.us but this site is dated 2004. Also, search current property tax records free at the gis-mapping site at www.gis.co.wayne.in.us/. Free registration required. Also, search plat records free at the gis-mapping site at www.gis.co.wayne.in.us/. Also, access sheriff tax sale list free at www.co.wayne.in.us/legals/sales.html.

Wells County *Property, Taxation Records* `Free` Access assessor records free on the GIS-mapping site at www.wellscountygis.org/application/gis/disclaimer.htm. At the map page, click on Search to search by name.

White County *Real Estate, Deed, Lien Records* `$$` Recorder land data by subscription on either the Laredo system using subscription and fees or the Tapestry System using credit card, http://tapestry.fidlar.com; $3.99 search; $1.00 per image. Index and images go back to 1980.
Property, Taxation Records `Free` Property and tax data is available at www.wcgconline.net/

Whitley County *Property, Taxation Records* `Free` Search assessor property data free on the GIS system at http://beacon.schneidercorp.com/.

Other Indiana Sites of Note:

Boone County - Sheriff Sale http://boonecounty.in.gov/Default.aspx?tabid=280
Grant County - Sex Offender http://sheriff.grant.in.uinquire.us/ Click on "Sex Offenders"
St Joseph County - Most Wanted www.skyenet.net/cstoppers/mostwanted/mostwant.html
Wayne County - Sheriff Sale, Sex Offenders www.co.wayne.in.us

Iowa

Capital: Des Moines
Polk County
Time Zone: CST
Population: 2,988,046
# of Counties: 99

Useful State Links

Website: www.iowa.gov/
Governor: www.governor.iowa.gov
Attorney General: www.state.ia.us/government/ag
State Archives: www.iowahistory.org
Legislative Bill Search: http://www.legis.state.ia.us
Bill Monitoring:
    https://coolice.legis.state.ia.us/secure/default.asp?Category=BillWatch&Service=BWSignIn
Unclaimed Funds: http://greatiowatreasurehunt.com/dsp_search.cfm

Primary State Agencies

Sexual Offender Registry

Division of Criminal Investigations, SOR Unit -, www.iowasexoffender.com/ The website permits name searching, enables a requester to be notified on the movement of an offender, and provides a map of registrants.

Incarceration Records   Free

Iowa Department of Corrections, 510 E 12th Street, www.doc.state.ia.us At the agency website, click on Offender Information for an inmate search. Also, coming online in 2008 is county and state inmate searching free on a private site at https://www.vinelink.com/vinelink/siteInfoAction.do?siteId=16000.

Corporation, LLC, LP, LLP, Fictitious Name, Trademarks/Servicemarks   Free

Secretary of State - Business Services Div, 321 E 12th Street, www.sos.state.ia.us For free searching, go to www.sos.state.ia.us/corp/corp_search.asp. *Other Options:* This agency will sell the records in database format. Call the number listed above and ask for Karen Ubaldo for more information.

Uniform Commercial Code, Federal Tax Liens   Free

UCC Division - Sec of State, 321 E 12th Street, www.sos.state.ia.us Visit www.sos.state.ia.us/Search/UCC/search.aspx?ucc. This search uses the filing office standard search logic for UCC or federal tax liens. It allows one to print a certified lien search report. By default the search reveals all liens that have not reached their lapse date. UCC searches have the option to include liens that have lapsed within the past year. An additional, alternative search is at www.sos.state.ia.us/Search/UCCAlternative/search.aspx. This is helpful in finding names that are similar too but not exactly the same as the name searched.

Driver Records $$

Department of Transportation, Driver Service Records Section, www.dot.state.ia.us/mvd/ The state requires that all ongoing requesters/users access records via IowaAccess. The fee is $8.50 per record, the service is interactive or batch. Requesters must be approved and open an account. The records contain personal information, so requesters must comply with DPPA. For more information, contact IowaAccess at 515-323-3468 or 866-492-3468. *Other Options:* Per DPPA provisions, the state will sell the header file on a per computer minute basis. Also, a driver license/suspension/revocation file is available via FTP. Call 512-244-1052 for details.

Vehicle Ownership & Registration   Free

Department of Transportation, Office of Vehicle Services, www.dot.state.ia.us/mvd/ Online access is available to those who qualify per DPPA including dealers, Iowa licensed investigators and security companies. There is no fee. All accounts must register and be pre-approved per DPPA. Write to the Office of Motor Vehicle, explaining purpose/use of records. *Other Options:* Iowa makes the entire vehicle file or selected data available for purchase. Weekly updates are also available for those purchasers. Requesters subject to DPPA requirements. For more information, call 515-237-3110.

Occupational Licensing Boards

Acupuncturist	http://medicalboard.iowa.gov/FindADoc.html
Adoption Investigator	www.dhs.iowa.gov/Partners/Partners_Providers/FindAProvider/LicensingAdoptFC.html
Anesthesiologist	http://medicalboard.iowa.gov/FindADoc.html
Architect	www.state.ia.us/government/com/prof/home.html
Asbestos-related Occupation	http://www2.iwd.state.ia.us/LaborServices/LabrAsbs.nsf
Athletic Trainer	https://eservices.iowa.gov/licensediniowa/index.php?pgname=pubsearch
Attorney	https://www.iacourtcommissions.org/icc/SearchLawyer.do
Audiologist	https://eservices.iowa.gov/licensediniowa/index.php?pgname=pubsearch
Bank	www.idob.state.ia.us
Barber	https://eservices.iowa.gov/licensediniowa/index.php?pgname=pubsearch
Chiropractor	https://eservices.iowa.gov/licensediniowa/index.php?pgname=pubsearch
Cosmetologist	https://eservices.iowa.gov/licensediniowa/index.php?pgname=pubsearch
Cosmetol'y Salon/School/Instruct	https://eservices.iowa.gov/licensediniowa/index.php?pgname=pubsearch
Crematory	https://eservices.iowa.gov/licensediniowa/index.php?pgname=pubsearch
Debt Management Company	www.idob.state.ia.us/license/lic_default.htm
Delayed Deposit Service Business	www.idob.state.ia.us/license/lic_default.htm
Dietitian	https://eservices.iowa.gov/licensediniowa/index.php?pgname=pubsearch
Doctor	http://medicalboard.iowa.gov/FindADoc.html
Electrologist	https://eservices.iowa.gov/licensediniowa/index.php?pgname=pubsearch
Emergency Med. Tech. - Paramedic	www.idph.state.ia.us/ems/report_get_provider_list.asp
EMS Bureau Staff	www.idph.state.ia.us/ems/report_get_provider_list.asp
EMS Provider/EMS Service	www.idph.state.ia.us/ems/report_get_provider_list.asp
Engineer	www.state.ia.us/government/com/prof/home.html
Esthetician	https://eservices.iowa.gov/licensediniowa/index.php?pgname=pubsearch
Excursion Gambling Boat	www.iowa.gov/irgc/
Finance Company	www.idob.state.ia.us/license/lic_default.htm
First Response Paramedic	www.idph.state.ia.us/ems/report_get_provider_list.asp
Funeral Director/Home	https://eservices.iowa.gov/licensediniowa/index.php?pgname=pubsearch
Hearing Aid Dispenser/Dealer	https://eservices.iowa.gov/licensediniowa/index.php?pgname=pubsearch
Insurance Agency/Firm	www.iid.state.ia.us/agent_company_search/find_insuranceco.asp
Insurance Producer	https://sbs-ia-public.naic.org/Lion-Web/jsp/sbsreports/AgentLookup.jsp
Landscape Architect	www.state.ia.us/government/com/prof/home.html
Lobbyist	http://coolice.legis.state.ia.us/Cool-ICE/default.asp?Category=Matt&Service=Lobby
Manicurist	https://eservices.iowa.gov/licensediniowa/index.php?pgname=pubsearch
Marriage & Family Therapist	https://eservices.iowa.gov/licensediniowa/index.php?pgname=pubsearch
Massage Therapist	https://eservices.iowa.gov/licensediniowa/index.php?pgname=pubsearch
Medical Doctor	http://medicalboard.iowa.gov/FindADoc.html
Mental Health Counselor	https://eservices.iowa.gov/licensediniowa/index.php?pgname=pubsearch
Money Transmitter	www.idob.state.ia.us/license/lic_default.htm
Mortgage Banker/Broker	www.idob.state.ia.us/license/lic_default.htm
Mortgage Loan Service	www.idob.state.ia.us/license/lic_default.htm
Mortuary Science	https://eservices.iowa.gov/licensediniowa/index.php?pgname=pubsearch
Nail Technologist	https://eservices.iowa.gov/licensediniowa/index.php?pgname=pubsearch
Notary Public	www.sos.state.ia.us/search/notary/notary_search.asp
Nurse	www.state.ia.us/nursing/index.html
Nursing Home Administrator	https://eservices.iowa.gov/licensediniowa/index.php?pgname=pubsearch
Occupational Therapist/Assistant	https://eservices.iowa.gov/licensediniowa/index.php?pgname=pubsearch
Optometrist	https://eservices.iowa.gov/licensediniowa/index.php?pgname=pubsearch
Orthopedic Doctor	http://medicalboard.iowa.gov/FindADoc.html
Osteopathic Physician	http://medicalboard.iowa.gov/FindADoc.html
Pari-Mutuel Race Track Enclosure	www.iowa.gov/irgc/

Pediatrician..http://medicalboard.iowa.gov/FindADoc.html
Pesticide Commercial Applicator......www.kellysolutions.com/ia/Business/index.asp
Pesticide Commercial Certification...www.kellysolutions.com/ia/Applicators/index.asp
Pesticide Dealer.................................www.kellysolutions.com/ia/Dealers/index.asp
Pesticide Private Applicator.............www.kellysolutions.com/ia/Applicators/index.asp
Physical Therapist/Assistant.............https://eservices.iowa.gov/licensediniowa/index.php?pgname=pubsearch
Physician Assistant..........................https://eservices.iowa.gov/licensediniowa/index.php?pgname=pubsearch
Podiatrist...https://eservices.iowa.gov/licensediniowa/index.php?pgname=pubsearch
Psychiatrist.....................................http://medicalboard.iowa.gov/FindADoc.html
Psychologist....................................https://eservices.iowa.gov/licensediniowa/index.php?pgname=pubsearch
Real Estate Agent/Broker/Sales.........www.state.ia.us/government/com/prof/home.html
Real Estate Appraiser.......................https://eservices.iowa.gov/licensediniowa/index.php?pgname=pubsearch
Respiratory Therapist.......................https://eservices.iowa.gov/licensediniowa/index.php?pgname=pubsearch
School Coach....................................www.boee.iowa.gov/search_warn.html
School Principal/Superintendent.......www.boee.iowa.gov/search_warn.html
Shorthand Reporter..........................https://www.iacourtcommissions.org/icc/SearchCsr.do
Social Worker..................................https://eservices.iowa.gov/licensediniowa/index.php?pgname=pubsearch
Speech Pathologist/Audiologist.........https://eservices.iowa.gov/licensediniowa/index.php?pgname=pubsearch
Surveyor, Land................................www.state.ia.us/government/com/prof/home.html
Tattoo Artist...................................https://eservices.iowa.gov/licensediniowa/index.php?pgname=pubsearch
Teacher..www.boee.iowa.gov/search_warn.html

State and Local Courts

State Court Structure: The District Court is the court of general jurisdiction. Vital records were moved from the courts to the County Recorder's office in each county.

Statewide Court Online Access: From the home page www.judicial.state.ia.us one may access Supreme Court and Appellate Court opinions. District criminal, civil, probate, and traffic information is available from all 99 Iowa counties at www.iowacourts.state.ia.us/ESAWebApp/SelectFrame. Name searches are available on either a statewide or specific county basis. Names of juveniles who are 10 to 17 will only appear for completed cases with a guilty verdict. There is no fee for basic information. A $25.00 per month pay system is offered for more detailed requests. While this is an excellent site with much information, there is one important consideration to keep in mind– although records are updated daily, the historical records offered are not from the same starting date on a county-by-county basis.

> ❖ **Statewide Access Offered For All Trial Courts – Read Above** ❖

Note: No individual Iowa courts offer online access.

Recorders, Assessors, and Other Sites of Note

Recording Office Organization: All 99 counties, 100 recording offices. Lee County has two recording offices. The recording officer is the County Recorder. Many counties utilize a grantor/grantee index containing all transactions recorded with them. Federal tax liens on personal property of businesses are filed with the Secretary of State. Other federal and all state tax liens on personal property are filed with the County Recorder.

Online Access Note: Land records **for all counties** are available on the state system at http://iowalandrecords.org after you register. This County Land Record Information System offers free searching and pdf images of deeds, liens, even UCCs and judgments, though this service may begin charging at any time. There is also features for monitoring for new documents and saving documents.

A links list for assessor records for many counties plus cities of Ames, Cedar Rapids, Davenport, Dubuque, Iowa City, and Souix City is at www.iowaassessors.com. A statewide Property Tax lookup and payment page is at www.iowatreasurers.org/iscta/access/home.do. First, select county then follow prompts to the search page where you can first look-up the name, then parcel information.

> ### ❖ Statewide Access Offered For Land Records From All Counties (Read Above). Listed Below are Additional Sites. ❖

Adair County *Property, Taxation Records* `Free` Access to the assessor database of property and sales data is free at www.adair.iowaassessors.com.

Allamakee County *Property, Taxation Records* `Free` Search assessor property data free on the GIS system at http://beacon.schneidercorp.com/.

Audubon County *Property, Taxation Records* `$$` Search assessor property data for a fee on the GIS system at http://beacon.schneidercorp.com/. Registration and username required.

Benton County *Property, Taxation Records* `Free` Search assessor property data free on the GIS system at http://beacon.schneidercorp.com/.

Black Hawk County *Property, Taxation Records* `Free` Access to the assessor database of property and sales data is free at www.co.black-hawk.ia.us/depts/bhentry.htm but no name searching. Also, search the tax delinquencies list free, manually at www.co.black-hawk.ia.us/depts/treasurer.html.

Boone County *Property, Taxation Records* `Free` Access to the assessor GIS database of property and sales data is free at http://beacon.schneidercorp.com/.

Bremer County *Property, Taxation Records* `Free` Search assessor property records at http://bremer.iowaassessors.com but no name searching.

Buchanan County *Property, Taxation Records* `Free` Access county property data free at http://buchanan.iowaassessors.com/ but no name searching. Includes property sales.

Buena Vista County *Property, Taxation Records* `Free` Search the property assessor and Ag sales databases for free at www.co.buena-vista.ia.us/assessors/. No name searching.

Butler County *Property, Taxation Records* `Free` Search county property data free at http://butler.iowaassessors.com/ but no name searching.

Calhoun County *Property, Taxation Records* `Free` Access to the assessor database of property and sales data is free at www.calhoun.iowaassessors.com. Access to the treasurers property database is free; see Online Access note at beginning of section.

Carroll County *Property, Taxation Records* `Free` Access to the assessor database of property and sales data is free at www.co.carroll.ia.us/Assessor/property_records.htm.

Cedar County *Property, Taxation Records* `Free` Search county property and sales data free at http://cedar.iowaassessors.com/ but no name searching.

Cerro Gordo County *Real Estate, Deed, Lien Records* www.co.cerro-gordo.ia.us `Free & $$` Access to recorded documents at www.co.cerro-gordo.ia.us/document_search/docindex_search.cfm. Also, with registration you search county land records on the statewide site at www.iowalandrecords.org/.
Property, Taxation Records `Free` Access to the County and Mason City property records is free at www.co.cerro-gordo.ia.us/property_search/property_search.cfm.

Chickasaw County *Property, Taxation Records* `Free` Search assessor property data free on the GIS system at http://beacon.schneidercorp.com/ but name searching requires you to have an account.

Clarke County *Property, Taxation Records* `Free` Search parcels free on the GIS-mapping site at www.clarkecoiagis.com/clarke/.

Clay County *Real Estate, Deed, Mortgage Records* www.co.clay.ia.us `Free` Access recorded doc index free at http://65.240.48.156/rindex.html.
Property, Taxation Records `Free` Search assessments, parcels, and sales free at http://clay.iowaassessors.com. also, search tax sale certificates free at http://65.240.48.156/tindex.html. Also, search land and tax database free at http://65.240.48.156/index.html.

Clayton County *Property, Taxation Records* Free Search county property records free at http://clayton.iowaassessors.com/.

Clinton County *Real Estate, Deed Records* www.clintoncountyiowa.com/recorder/default.asp Free
At http://iowalandrecords.org/portal/clris/SwitchToCountiesTab, an index of recorded land records and their images are available from 1/1997.
Property, Taxation Records Free Access to the assessor database of property and sales data is free at www.qpublic.net/clinton/search1.html.

Crawford County http://crawfordcounty.org *Property, Taxation Records* Free & $$ Search county property records free at http://crawford.iowaassessors.com but no name searching or sales info until you subscribe.

Dallas County *Property, Taxation Records* Free Access to the assessor database of property and sales data is free at www.dallas.iowaassessors.com.

Davis County *Property, Taxation Records* Free Access to the assessor GIS database of property and sales data is free at http://beacon.schneidercorp.com/.

Delaware County *Property, Taxation Records* $$ Search assessor property data for a fee on the GIS system at http://beacon.schneidercorp.com/. Registration and username required.

Des Moines County *Property, Taxation Records* Free Access to the assessor database of property and sales data is free at www.dmcgis.com/.

Dickinson County *Real Estate, Grantor/Grantee, Deed Records* www.co.dickinson.ia.us/ $$
Access to recorder's records for a fee go to www.iowalandrecords.org
Property, Taxation Records Free Access to the assessor database of property and sales data is free at http://dickinson.iowaassessors.com.

Dubuque County *Real Estate, Deed, Lien, Judgment, Corporation Records* www.dubuquecounty.org Free
Access recorder general, tax lien, and corporations indexes free at www.dbqco.org/resolution/. General index goes back to 1988; tax liens to 10/19/2005, corporations to 1/1972. Also, at http://iowalandrecords.org/portal/clris/SwitchToCountiesTab, view index of recorded land records from 1/2004, images from 1/2004.
Property, Taxation Records Free Access the assessor database of property and sales data free at http://beacon.schneidercorp.com but no name searching.

Emmet County *Property, Taxation Records* Free Access the assessor GIS database of property and sales data free at http://beacon.schneidercorp.com/.

Fayette County *Property, Taxation Records* Free Access to the assessor GIS database of property and sales data is free at http://beacon.schneidercorp.com/.

Floyd County *Property, Taxation Records* Free Search assessor property data free on the GIS system at http://beacon.schneidercorp.com/ but name searching; requires registration and password. Also, access property and sales data is free at www.floydcoia.org/features/gis.asp.

Greene County *Property, Taxation Records* Free Access to the assessor database of property and sales data is free at http://greene.iowaassessors.com.

Grundy County *Property, Taxation Records* Free Access to the assessor GIS database of property and sales data is free at http://beacon.schneidercorp.com/ but registration and fee required to name search.

Guthrie County *Property, Taxation Records* Free Access to the assessor database of property and sales data is free at www.guthrie.iowaassessors.com.

Hamilton County *Property, Taxation Records* Free Search assessor property records and residential and commercial sales free at http://hamilton.iowaassessors.com.

Hardin County *Property, Taxation Records* $$ Search City of Iowa Falls assessor property data for a fee on the GIS system at http://beacon.schneidercorp.com/. Registration and username required.

Harrison County *Property, Taxation Records* Free Access to the assessor database of property and sales data and maps is free at http://maps.harrisoncountyia.org. Also, search assessor property data free on the GIS system at http://beacon.schneidercorp.com/.

Henry County *Property, Taxation Records* Free Assessor records for free on the GIS system at http://beacon.schneidercorp.com/.

Humboldt County *Property, Taxation Records* Free Assessor property records and sales free at www.humboldt.iowaassessors.com.

Iowa County *Real Estate, Grantor/Grantee, Deed Records* www.co.iowa.ia.us Free Access real estate indexing free at http://65.240.48.153/index.html. Also, at http://iowalandrecords.org/portal/clris/SwitchToCountiesTab, view an index of recorded land records back to 1/2004, images back to 1/2004.
Property, Taxation Records Free Access to the assessor database of property and sales data is free at http://iowa.iowaassessors.com.

Jackson County *Property, Taxation Records* SS Search assessor property data for a fee on the GIS system at http://beacon.schneidercorp.com/. Registration and username required.

Jasper County *Property, Taxation Records* Free Access to the assessor database of property and sales data is free at http://jasper.iowaassessors.com/

Jefferson County *Real Estate, Grantor/Grantee, Deed, Lien Records* Free With registration and username, access land records free on private site at www.iowalandrecords.org. Online records from 1/1/2004 to present only.
Property, Taxation Records Free Access to the assessor database of property and sales data is free at http://jefferson.iowaassessors.com but no name searching.

Johnson County *Real Estate, Deed, Lien, Mortgage, Corporation Records* www.johnson-county.com/recorder/
Free Access the recorders data free at http://www2.johnson-county.com/resolution/. Images and indexes go back to 11/1993, Book 670. At http://iowalandrecords.org/portal/clris/SwitchToCountiesTab, view index of recorded land records from 2004, images from 2/27/2004.
Property, Taxation Records Free Access to the assessor database of property and sales data is free at http://beacon.schneidercorp.com/?site=JohnsonCountyIA but no name searching. Also, access to Iowa City assessor and property data is free at http://iowacity.iowaassessors.com.

Keokuk County *Property, Taxation Records* Free Access to the assessor GIS database of property and sales data is free at http://beacon.schneidercorp.com/.

Kossuth County *Property, Taxation Records* Free Access to the assessor database of property and sales data is free at www.co.kossuth.ia.us/assessor/assessor.htm.

Lee County (Northern District) *Property, Taxation Records* Free Access to the assessor database of property and sales data is free at http://lee.iowaassessors.com.

Lee County (Southern District) *Property, Taxation Records* Free Access to the assessor database of property and sales data is free at http://lee.iowaassessors.com.

Linn County *Property, Taxation Records* Free Access to the assessor database of property data is free at www.linn.iowaassessors.com/search.php. Also, access to City of Cedar Rapids property data is free at www.cedar-rapids.org/assessor/pmc/. No name searching.

Louisa County *Property, Taxation Records* Free Access the assessor database of property and sales data is free at http://beacon.schneidercorp.com/?site=LouisaCountyIA.

Lucas County *Real Estate, Deed Records* Free At http://iowalandrecords.org/portal/clris/SwitchToCountiesTab, view an index of recorded land records from 1/2004, images from 1/2004.

Lyon County *Property, Taxation Records* Free Access to the assessor database of property and sales data is free at http://lyon.iowaassessors.com/.

Madison County *Real Estate, Grantor/Grantee, Deed, Property Tax Sale Records* www.madisoncoia.us Free At http://iowalandrecords.org/portal/clris/SwitchToCountiesTab, view an index of recorded land records from 1/1999, images from 1/1999. Access the Recorders Indexing Query and tax sales at http://65.240.48.155/rindex.html.
Property, Taxation Records Free Access to the assessor database of property and sales data is free at http://madison.iowaassessors.com.

Mahaska County *Property, Taxation Records* Free Access to the assessor GIS database of property and sales data is free at http://beacon.schneidercorp.com/.

Marion County *Property, Taxation Records* Free Access to the assessor GIS database of property and sales data is free at http://beacon.schneidercorp.com/.

Marshall County *Real Estate, Deed, Lien, UCC Records* www.marshallcountyrecorder.com Free
Access the recorders land & UCC indexes free at http://ntcott.co.marshall.ia.us/ResolutionPublic/. Records go back to 1983, images only 1980-82. Also, search on statewide land records site- http://iowalandrecords.org/portal/clris/SwitchToCountiesTab.
Property, Taxation Records Free Access to the assessor property record card system and sales data is free at www.co.marshall.ia.us/departments/assessor/disclaimer_html.

Mills County *Property, Taxation Records* `Free` Access to the assessor database of property and tax sales data is free at http://65.240.48.154/index.html.

Mitchell County *Real Estate, Deed, Lien, UCC Records* `Free` At http://iowalandrecords.org/portal/clris/SwitchToCountiesTab, view an index of recorded land records from 1/2000, images from 3/09/2004.

Monona County *Property, Taxation Records* `Free` Access to the assessor GIS database of property and sales data is free at http://beacon.schneidercorp.com/.

Monroe County *Real Estate, Deed Records* `Free` At http://iowalandrecords.org/portal/clris/SwitchToCountiesTab, view an index of recorded land records from 1/2004, images from 1/2004.

Montgomery County *Property, Taxation Records* `Free` Access to the assessor GIS database of property and sales data is free at http://beacon.schneidercorp.com/ but no name searching.

Muscatine County *Property, Taxation Records* `Free` Search area property and sales data free at http://beacon.schneidercorp.com/, registration required to name search.

Plymouth County *Property, Taxation Records* `Free` Access the assessor database of property and sales data free at http://plymouth.iowaassessors.com.

Polk County *Property, Taxation Records* `Free` Access to the Polk County assessor database is free at www.assess.co.polk.ia.us/web/basic/search.html. Search by property or by sales. Also, download residential, commercial, or agricultural data free at www.assess.co.polk.ia.us/web/basic/exports.html.

Pottawattamie County *Property, Taxation Records* `Free` Records on the County Courthouse/Council Bluffs property database and sales are free at www.pottco.org and click on real estate. Search by owner name, address, or parcel number. Records since 7/1/89, images since 10/20/2002. Also, search the sheriff foreclosure sale data at http://pottcounty.com/html/Sheriff_Foreclosure.php.

Poweshiek County *Property, Taxation Records* `Free` Access to the assessor database of property and sales data is free at http://poweshiek.iowaassessors.com.

Ringgold County *Property, Taxation Records* `Free` Property sales data cards available free at /www.iowa-assessors.org:8080/cgi/wiki.pl?Sales_Property_Cards.

Sac County *Property, Taxation Records* `$$` Assessor's property records online for a small fee; contact the Auditors Office at 712-662-7310 or visit www.saccounty.org/features/gis.asp. Also, search property data after registration on the GIS system at http://beacon.schneidercorp.com/ and registration and a fee applies.

Scott County *Real Estate, Deed, Lien, UCC, Trade Name Records* www.scottcountyiowa.com `Free` At http://iowalandrecords.org/portal/clris/SwitchToCountiesTab, view an index of recorded land records from 1/1989 to current. Also see www.scottcountyiowa.com/recorder/records.php for recorder records; includes land, lien, plats, incorporations, trade names, and UCCs back to 1/1989.
Property, Taxation Records `Free` Access to assessor property records is free at www.scottcountyiowa.com/query.php. Also, sheriff sales lists free at www.scottcountyiowa.com/sheriff/sales.php.

Shelby County *Real Estate, Deed, Lien, UCC, Judgment Records* www.shco.org `Free & $$` At http://iowalandrecords.org/portal/clris/SwitchToCountiesTab, view an index of recorded land records from 1/2000, images from 1/2000. Also, access recording office land data at www.etitlesearch.com; registration required, fee based on usage.
Property, Taxation Records `Free` Access to the assessor GIS database of property and sales data is free at http://beacon.schneidercorp.com/ but no name searching.

Sioux County *Property, Taxation Records* `Free & $$` Access property data information free at http://gis.siouxcounty.org/gisweb/assessmenthome.asp. Also, search the treasurer's property tax records online by subscription; for info please contact Micah Van Maanen at 712-737-6818, http://siouxcounty.org/treasurer.htm.

Story County *Property, Taxation Records* `Free` Records on the county assessor database are free at www.storyassessor.org/pmc/ but no name searching. Also, City of Ames property assessor data is free at www.amesassessor.org/pmc/ but no name searching.

Tama County *Property, Taxation Records* `Free` Access to the assessor database of property and sales data is free at http://tama.iowaassessors.com.

Van Buren County *Property, Taxation Records* `Free` Search parcel data information free at http://vanburen.iowaassessors.com/search.php?mode=search&showdis=true. Advanced search by document type available at http://vanburen.iowaassessors.com/search.php?mode=advsearch&showdis=true.

Wapello County *Property, Taxation Records* `Free` Search assessor property and sales data free at http://wapello.iowaassessors.com/.

Warren County *Property, Taxation Records* `Free & $$` Access to property sales data is free at http://beacon.schneidercorp.com/.

Washington County *Property, Taxation Records* `Free` Access to the assessor database of property and sales data is free at http://washington.iowaassessors.com.

Webster County *Property, Taxation Records* `Free` Access to the assessor database of property and sales data is free at http://webster.iowaassessors.com but no name searching. Also, property data is free at www.webstercountyia.org

Winnebago County *Property, Taxation Records* `Free` Property data may be searched free at the GIS map site www.winnebago.ia.promap.com. Also, access to the assessor GIS database of property and sales data is free at http://beacon.schneidercorp.com/.

Winneshiek County *Property, Taxation Records* `Free` Access to the assessor database of property and sales data is free at http://beacon.schneidercorp.com/?site=WinneshiekCountyIA.

Woodbury County *Property, Taxation Records* `Free` Access to the assessor GIS database of property and sales data is free at http://beacon.schneidercorp.com/ but no name searching. Name search county property free at www.woodburyiowa.com/treasurertaxdata/. Also, search tax sale properties free at www.woodburyiowa.com/departments/treasurer/taxsale.asp. Also, search property free at http://sidwellmaps.com/website/siouxcity/php/index.php but no name searching.

Wright County *Property, Taxation Records* `Free` Search assessor property and sales data free at www.wright.iowaassessors.com.

Other Iowa Sites of Note:

Buena Vista - Accident/Incident Reports www.bvsheriff.com/accident-incident/index.html
Buena Vista - Jail Inmates www.bvsheriff.com/jailroster/index.html
Calhoun County - Deaths www.rootsweb.ancestry.com/~usgenweb/ia/calhoun/deaths.html
Cass County - Sheriff's Warrants www.sheriffcass.com/warrants.html
Fayette County - Most Wanted www.fayettecountysheriff.com/mostwanted.htm
Polk County - Inmates www.polkcountyiowa.gov/InmatesOnTheWeb/main.aspx
Scott County - Most Wanted www.scottcountyiowa.com/sheriff/mostwanted.php
Scott County - Restaurant Inspections www.scottcountyiowa.com/health/food.php
Scott County - Sheriff Sale Lists www.scottcountyiowa.com/sheriff/sales.php
Story County - City of Ames - Accident Reports http://beacon.schneidercorp.com/ Search by location.
Story County - City of Ames - Traffic Accidents http://beacon.schneidercorp.com/
Tama County - Sex Offenders www.tamacounty.org/sheriff.html

Kansas

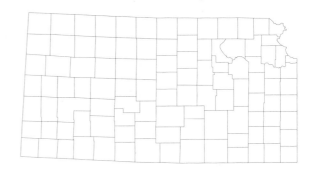

Capital: Topeka
Shawnee County

Time Zone: CST

Kansas' five western-most counties are MST:
They are: Greeley, Hamilton, Kearny, Sherman, Wallace.

Population: 2,775,997

# of Counties: 105

Useful State Links

Website: www.accesskansas.org
Governor: www.ksgovernor.org
Attorney General: www.ksag.org/home/
State Archives: www.kshs.org
State Statutes and Codes: www.kslegislature.org/legsrv-statutes/index.do
Legislative Bill Search: www.kslegislature.org/legsrv-legisportal/bills.do
Bill Monitoring: https://www.accesskansas.org/lobbyist/demo.html
Unclaimed Funds: www.kansascash.com/prodweb/up/disclaimer_page.php

Primary State Agencies

Criminal Records Free & $$

Kansas Bureau of Investigation, Criminal Records Division, www.accesskansas.org/kbi/ Anyone may obtain non-certified criminal records online at www.accesskansas.org/kbi/criminalhistory/. The system is also available for premium subscribers of accessKansas. The fee is $17.50 per record; credit cards accepted online. The system is unavailable between the hours of midnight and 4 AM daily. A Kansas "Most Wanted" list is available at www.accesskansas.org/kbi/mw.htm.

Sexual Offender Registry Free

Kansas Bureau of Investigation, Offender Registration, www.kansas.gov/kbi/ro.shtml Searching is available at the website. All open registrants are searchable. The information contained in a registration entry was provided by the registrant. Neither the Kansas Bureau of Investigation (KBI) nor the sheriff's office can guarantee the accuracy of this information.

Incarceration Records Free

Kansas Department of Corrections, Public Information Officer, www.dc.state.ks.us/ Web access to the database known as KASPER gives information on offenders who are: currently incarcerated; under post-incarceration supervision; and, who have been discharged from a sentence. The database does not have information available about inmates sent to Kansas under the provisions of the interstate compact agreement. Go to www.dc.state.ks.us/kasper. Also, view the escapee list at www.dc.state.ks.us/kasper/index.htm. *Other Options:* Bulk lists are available on CD for $.01 per record.

Corporation, LP, LLC Free

Secretary of State, Memorial Hall, 1st Floor, www.kssos.org/business/business.html Free entity searching is available at www.accesskansas.org/srv-corporations/index.do. Search by company name or organizational number. There is no fee to search records, but must be a subscriber to order copies of letters or certificates of good standings.

Trademarks/Servicemarks Free

Secretary of State, Trademarks/Servicemarks Division, www.kssos.org Free searching by a variety of ways (keyword, owner, trademark, etc.) at www.kssos.org/business/trademark/trademark_search.aspx. *Other Options:* For bulk file purchase call Ann at 785-296-6271.

Uniform Commercial Code, Federal & State Tax Liens $$

Secretary of State - UCC Searches, Memorial Hall, 1st Fl, www.kssos.org/business/business_ucc.html Online service is provided by accessKansas at www.kansas.gov. The system is open 24 hours daily. A subscription is required with a modest annual fee. UCC records are $10.00 per record. This is the same online system used for corporation records. For more information, call at 800-4-KANSAS or go to www.kansas.gov and review online services. *Other Options:* Records in a bulk or database format is available from accessKansas.com.

Driver Records, Accident Reports $$

Department of Revenue, Driver Control Bureau, www.ksrevenue.org/vehicle.htm Kansas has contracted with the Kansas.gov (800-452-6727) to service all electronic media requests of driver license histories at www.kansas.gov/subscribers/. The fee per record is $6.00 for batch requests or $6.50 for immediate inquiry. There is an initial $75 subscription fee and an annual $60 fee. Billing is monthly. I not paid via EFT, a 3% surcharge is added. The system is open 24 hours a day, 7 days a week. Batch requests are available at 7:30 am (if ordered by 10 pm the previous day).

Vehicle Ownership & Registration $$

Division of Vehicles, Title and Registration Bureau, www.ksrevenue.org/vehicle.htm Online batch inquires are $6.00 per record; online interactive requests are $6.50 per record. Visit www.kansas.gov for a complete description of accessKansas (800-452-6727), the state authorized vendor. There is an initial $75 subscription fee and an annual $60 fee to access records from Kansas.Gov.

Vital Records $$

Kansas Department of Health & Environment, Office of Vital Statistics, www.kdheks.gov/vital/ Records may be ordered online via a state designated vendor VitalChek at www.vitalchek.com.

Occupational Licensing Boards

Adult Care Home Administrator	www.kdhehealthlicense.org
Alcohol/Drug Counselor	www.ksbsrb.org/verification.html
Architect	www.accesskansas.org/roster-search/index.html
Athletic Trainer	www.ksbha.org
Audiologist	www.kdhehealthlicense.org
Body Piercer	www.accesskansas.org/kboc/LicenseeDatabase.htm
Certified Public Accountant-CPA	www.da.ks.gov/boa/searchforindividual.aspx
Charity Organization	www.kscharitycheck.org
Chiropractor	www.ksbha.org
Clinical Psychotherapist	www.ksbsrb.org/verification.html
Cosmetology-related Occupation	www.accesskansas.org/kboc/LicenseeDatabase.htm
Cosmetology-related School	www.accesskansas.org/kboc/SchoolListing.htm
Counselor, Professional	www.ksbsrb.org/verification.html
CPA Firm	www.da.ks.gov/boa/SearchforFirms.aspx
Crematories	www.kansas.gov/ksbma/listings.html
Dental Hygienist	www.accesskansas.org/srv-dental-verification/start.do
Dentist	www.accesskansas.org/srv-dental-verification/start.do
Dietitian	www.kdhehealthlicense.org
Electrologist	www.accesskansas.org/kboc/LicenseeDatabase.htm
Embalmer	www.kansas.gov/ksbma/listings.html
Engineer	www.accesskansas.org/roster-search/index.html
Esthetician	www.accesskansas.org/kboc/LicenseeDatabase.htm
Funeral Director/Assis't Financ'l Dir.	www.kansas.gov/ksbma/listings.html
Funeral Establishments	www.kansas.gov/ksbma/listings.html
Geologist	www.accesskansas.org/roster-search/index.html
Home Health Aide	www.ksnurseaidregistry.org
Insurance Agent	http://towerii.ksinsurance.org/agent/agent.jsp?pagnam=agentsearch
Insurance Company	http://towerii.ksinsurance.org/agent/agency.jsp?pagnam=agencysearch
Landscape Architect	www.accesskansas.org/roster-search/index.html
Lobbyist	www.kssos.org/elections/elections_lobbyists.html
Marriage & Family Therapist	www.ksbsrb.org/verification.html
Medical Doctor	www.ksbha.org
Medical School	https://www.lcme.org/privatelcme/
Medication Aide	www.ksnurseaidregistry.org

Nail Technician .... www.accesskansas.org/kboc/LicenseeDatabase.htm
Nurse .... https://www.accesskansas.org/app/nursing/verification/
Nurses' Aide .... www.ksnurseaidregistry.org
Occupational Therapist/Assistant ...... www.ksbha.org
Optometrist .... www.kssbeo.com/license.htm
Osteopathic Physician .... www.ksbha.org
Permanent Cosmetic Technician .... www.accesskansas.org/kboc/LicenseeDatabase.htm
Pharmacist .... https://www.accesskansas.org/pharmacy_verification/index.html
Physical Therapist/Assistant .... www.ksbha.org
Physician Assistant .... www.ksbha.org
Podiatrist .... www.ksbha.org
Private Investigator .... https://www.accesskansas.org/ssrv-kbi-pi-verify/index.do
Psychologist .... www.ksbsrb.org/verification.html
Radiologic Technologist .... www.ksbha.org
Real Estate Agent/Seller/Broker .... https://www.accesskansas.org/ssrv-krec-verification/index.do
Real Estate Appraiser .... www.kansas.gov/kreab
Respiratory Therapist/Student .... www.ksbha.org
Social Worker .... www.ksbsrb.org/verification.html
Speech/Language Pathologist .... www.kdhehealthlicense.org
Surveyor, Land .... www.accesskansas.org/roster-search/index.html
Tanning Facility .... www.accesskansas.org/kboc/LicenseeDatabase.htm
Tattoo Artist .... www.accesskansas.org/kboc/LicenseeDatabase.htm
Teacher .... https://online.ksde.org/teal/cert_search.aspx
Veterinarian .... www.accesskansas.org/veterinary/listing.html

State and Local Courts

State Court Structure: The District Court is the court of general jurisdiction. There are 110 courts in 31 districts in 105 counties. If an individual in Municipal Court wants a jury trial, the request must be filed de novo in a District Court.

Statewide Court Online Access: Commercial online access for civil and criminal records is available for District Court Records in all counties. Access is web-based at www.accesskansas.org. An initial $95.00 subscription is required, access fees are involved, usually $1.00 per record. The system also provides state criminal records and motor vehicle records among other records. For additional information or a registration packet, telephone 800-4-KANSAS (800-452-6727) or visit the web page.

The Kansas Appellate Courts offer free online access to case information at www.kscourts.org. Published opinions from the Appellate Courts and Supreme Court are also available.

❖ **Statewide Access Offered All Trial Courts – Read Above**

Below are Additional Sites ❖

Allen County
District Court   www.31stjudicialdistrict.org   `Free`
Civil: Court calendars, limited action hearing results, and service results appear online. *Criminal:* same.

Anderson County
District Court   www.kscourts.org/dstcts/4anco.htm   `Free & $$`
Civil: Access is web-based at www.kansas.gov/subscribers/. A $95.00 annual subscription is required plus usage fee as little as $1.00 per search. Records go back to 11/01/01. Also, current court calendars are free online at www.franklincoks.org/4thdistrict.htm. Also, access to probate court records is free at www.kscourts.org/dstcts/4anprrec.htm. *Criminal:* Online access to criminal index and calendars is the same as civil.

Coffey County

District Court   www.kscourts.org/dstcts/4coco.htm   `Free & $$`

Civil: Current court calendars are free online at www.franklincoks.org/4thdistrict/coffeybydate.html. Probate and marriage records are accessible at this website. Also, access is web-based at www.kansas.gov/subscribers/. Access is web-based at www.kansas.gov/subscribers/. A $95.00 subscription is required plus access fee as little as $1.00 per search. *Criminal:* Online access to subscription service and the court calendar is the same as civil.

Franklin County

District Court   www.kscourts.org/dstcts/4frco.htm   `Free & $$`

Civil: Index online through Kansas.gov; see www.kansas.gov/subscribers/ for information. A $95.00 subscription required plus usage fee as little as $1.00 per search. Also, current court calendars are free at www.franklincoks.org/4thdistrict/franklinbydate.html. Also, access to probate court records is free at www.kscourts.org/dstcts/4frprrec.htm. *Criminal:* Online access to criminal docket and calendars is the same as civil.

Gove County

District Court   www.23rdjudicial.org   `Free & $$`

Civil: Access is web-based at www.kansas.gov/subscribers/. A $95.00 annual subscription is required plus usage fee as little as $1.00 per search. Case filings from previous week available online. Case filings from previous week available online at the county site. *Criminal:* Same. Case filings from previous week available online. Criminal records available at www.accesskansas.org/kbi/criminalhistory/ for a fee.

Johnson County

District Court   http://rta.jocogov.org   `Free & $$`

Civil: Search Johnson County District Court records available free at www.jococourts.org with index back to 1980. Access is web-based at www.kansas.gov/subscribers/. A $95.00 annual subscription is required plus usage fee as little as $1.00 per search. *Criminal:* Access to criminal records online is same as civil.

Osage County

District Court   www.kscourts.org/dstcts/4osco.htm   `Free & $$`

Civil: Current court calendars are free online at www.franklincoks.org/4thdistrict/osagebydate.html. Also, access to old probate court and marriage records is free at www.kscourts.org/dstcts/4osprrec.htm. Access is web-based at www.kansas.gov/subscribers/. A $95.00 subscription is required plus usage fee as little as $1.00 per search. The system has 6 county District Courts, state criminal records, MVRs, and others. *Criminal:* Same.

Shawnee County

District Court   www.shawneecourt.org   `Free`

 See www.shawneecourt.org/doe/index.html. Also, online access to court record images is free at www.shawneecourt.org/img_temp.htm. Also find "viewing restricted" domestic documents here. Also, daily dockets lists free at www.shawneecourt.org/docket/. *Criminal:* Online access to criminal records and dockets is the same as civil.

Recorders, Assessors, and Other Sites of Note

Recording Office Organization: 105 counties, 105 recording offices. The recording officer is the Register of Deeds. Many counties utilize a "Miscellaneous Index" for tax and other liens, separate from real estate records. Federal tax liens on personal property of businesses are filed with the Secretary of State. Other federal tax liens and all state tax liens on personal property are filed with the county Register of Deeds.

Online Access Note: A number of counties allow online access to recorder records; there is no statewide system.

Atchison County   *Property, Taxation Records*   `Free`   Search the property and tax database free at www.atchisoncountyks.org/Appraisal.asp. Not regularly updated.

Barton County   *Property, Taxation Records*   `Free`   Access to the County Property value list by address and name is at www.bartoncounty.org/propvals.pdf.

Bourbon County   *Real Estate, Deed, Lien Records*   http://bourboncountyks.org   `Free & $$`   Access recordings on the Deeds Management System subscription service at http://bourboncountyks.org/dms_online_search.htm. User name and password required; contact Register of Deeds to register.

Property, Taxation Records `Free & $$` Access to property data index is free at www.bourbon.kansasgov.com/parcel/. Subscription is required for full data. These is also a separate subscription level for appraisers. Contact Appraiser's office at 620-223-3800 x34. Also, search property tax information free at www.bourboncountyks.org/tax_search.htm. Also, search property tax data at www.bourbon.kansasgov.com/tax/ or subscribe for full data; contact the Treasurer's office.

Brown County *Real Estate, Deed, Other County Data Records* www.brown.kansasgov.com `$$`
Access to recorded docs and tax records and CAMA online is currently under development; see www.brown.kansasgov.com/MV2Base.asp?VarCN=513. Contact office at 785-742-3741 8AM-5PM or email scarter@brcoks.org. It will be subscription for $250.00 per yr.

Property, Taxation Records `Free & $$` Search assessment data free or by subscription at www.brown.kansasgov.com/parcel/.

Butler County *Real Estate, Grantor/Grantee, Deed, Lien Records*
www.bucoks.com/depts/regdeeds/register_of_deeds.htm `Free` An index of recorded real estate records from 1993 forward is available at www.bucoks.com/depts/regdeeds/disclaimer.htm.

Property, Taxation Records `Free` Access the appraiser's Real Estate Market Values data free at www.bucoks.com/depts/appr/values/values.htm. No name searching. Also search tax and property data free at www.bucoks.com/depts/regdeeds/disclaimer.htm.

Cloud County *Property, Taxation Records* `Free` Search property tax information free at
www.cloud.kansasgov.com/Tax/. Parcel searches free at www.cloudcountyks.org/Parcel/

Coffey County *Marriage Records* www.coffeycountyks.org `Free` Access to marriage records is by alpha search up
to 1/18/2001 for free at www.kscourts.org/dstcts/4osmarec.htm.

Cowley County *Property, Taxation Records* `Free` Search property data free at
www.cowleycounty.org/parcel/V2RunLev2.asp?submit1=OK.

Crawford County *Real Estate, Deed, Lien Records* `$$` Recorder land data by subscription on either the Laredo
system using subscription and fees or the Tapestry System using credit card, http://tapestry.fidlar.com; $3.99 search; $1.00 per image. Index goes back to 1991; images to 8/1/99.

Dickinson County *Property, Taxation Records* `Free` Access to county property tax data is free at
www.dickinson.kansasgov.com/disclaimerlev2.asp.

Douglas County *Real Estate, Deed, Lien, Court, Voter Registration Records* www.douglas-county.com `Free &`
`$$` Register of Deeds data by subscription; for info and signup call IT Dept at 785-832-5183/5299. Yearly sub is $360 plus $60 setup fee and may include courts. Check voter registration names at www.douglas-county.com/clerk/regvoters.asp.

Property, Taxation Records `Free` Two sites provide free access to assessor records. Find County Property Appraiser records at www.douglas-county.com/value/disclaimer.asp. Property valuations also free at http://old.hometown.lawrence.com/valuation/valuation.cgi. Also, view parcel property on GIS free at www.douglas-county.com/egovt/mapviewer.asp but no name searching.

Ellis County *Property, Taxation Records* `Free` Access to assessor property data is available free at
www.ellisco.net/index.asp?page=app_search.

Finney County *Property, Taxation Records* `Free` GIS-Map searching available free at
www.finneycounty.net/publicaccess.htm.

Ford County *Property, Taxation Records* `Free` Property information including parcels and taxes are available at
www.fordcounty.net/

Franklin County *Marriage Records* www.franklincoks.org `Free` Access to county marriage records is by alpha
search for free at www.kscourts.org/dstcts/4frmarec.htm.

Geary County *Real Estate, Deed Records* www.geary.kansasgov.com/MV2Base.asp?VarCN=171 `$$`
County offers a fee system to access recorded document index and images. Index goes back to 1992, images back to 1/2001, using the DMS On-line Access Module. Webpage has limited info about registering; call the office for an information packet.

Harvey County *Property, Taxation Records* `Free & $$` Access property tax records from the appraiser and
treasurer free at www.harvey.kansasgov.com/parcel/DisclaimerLev2.asp. Also, with registration and password you may access deeper property data at www.harvey.kansasgov.com/parcel/v2loginreg.asp.

Jefferson County *Property, Taxation Records* `Free` Access parcel data free at
http://appraiser.jfcountyks.com/parcel/disclaimerlev2.asp. Registration and login required for full data.

Johnson County *Property, Taxation Records* `Free` Search records on the Land Records database free at
http://land.jocogov.org/landsearch.aspx. No name searching.

Leavenworth County *Real Estate, Deed, Lien Records* www.leavenworthcounty.org $$ Recorder land data by subscription on either the Laredo system using subscription and fees or the Tapestry System using credit card, http://tapestry.fidlar.com; $3.99 search; $1.00 per image.
Property, Taxation Records Free Free search of county parcel data at www.leavenworthcounty.org/cama/disclaimerlev1.asp.

Linn County *Property, Taxation Records* Free Request treasurer's Tax foreclosure sale information at www.linncountyks.com/html/taxsalehome.html. County Maps available at www.linncountyks.com/html/maps.htm.

Lyon County *Property, Taxation Records* Free Access parcel data free at www.lyoncounty.org/parcel/ or register for full data with the Appraiser's office. Also, check tax sale notices free at www.lyoncounty.org/Tax_Sale_Notices.htm.

McPherson County *Real Estate, Recoding, Deed Records* www.mcphersoncountyks.us $$ Access recording office land data at www.etitlesearch.com; registration required, fee based on usage.
Property, Taxation Records Free Search property data free at www.mcphersoncountyks.us/Appraisal.asp.

Marion County *Property, Taxation Records* Free Access property tax records free at www.marion.kansasgov.com/Tax/TaxSearch.asp.

Marshall County *Property, Taxation Records* Free Access property data free at www.marshall.kansasgov.com/Parcel/.

Miami County *Real Estate, Deed, Lien Records* www.miamicountyks.org $$ Recorder land data by subscription on either the Laredo system using subscription and fees or the Tapestry System using credit card, http://tapestry.fidlar.com; $3.99 search; $1.00 per image. Index goes back to 1994; some deed images go back to 10/1932, mortgages to 11/1993.
Property, Taxation Records $$ Access property data and cemetery data free at http://beacon.schneidercorp.com/?site=MiamiCountyKS. Registration, username and password required.

Nemaha County *Property, Taxation Records* Free Access property data free or by registering for full subscription access at www.nemaha.kansasgov.com/parcel/. Click on 'Parcel Search Level One' for free access and name search. Subscription service for full data is $200 per year.

Osage County *Property, Taxation Records* Free Online access to property appraiser is free at www.osageco.org/MV2Base.asp?VarCN=34. There are two levels- public and registered user. The latter can see sales as well as property data.

Osborne County *Property, Taxation Records* Free Access to property appraisal land data is free at www.osbornecounty.org. Search field is at bottom right of page. CAMA Records found at www.osbornecounty.org. Tax Sale data at www.osbornecounty.org; click on Tax Foreclosure Sale.

Ottawa County *Property, Taxation Records* Free Search property data at www.ottawacounty.org on the lower right hand of webpage.

Pawnee County *Property, Taxation Records* Free Access the public parcel search site free at www.pawneecountykansas.com/.

Pottawatomie County *Property, Taxation Records* Free Access county parcel search free at www.pottawatomie.kansasgov.com/parcel/V2RunLev1.asp?submit1=OK. For fuller data, obtain username and password from Appraiser's Office. Also search GIS maps free at www.pottcounty.org/Website/PottCoMaps/viewer.htm.

Reno County *Property, Taxation Records* Free Parcel Information, Election Results, Tax Information, Tax Sale information free at www.renogov.org/.

Riley County *Real Estate, Deed, Lien, UCC Records* www.rileycountyks.gov $$ Access to recorder office land data is by subscription; Fee is $100 per year plus $.50 per page printed. Records go back to 1850. Registration through the Recorder's Office
Property, Taxation Records Free Access to online appraisal data for free go to www.rileycountyks.gov/index.asp?NID=84

Russell County *Property, Taxation Records* Free Access assessor property data free at www.russell.kansasgov.com/parcel/.

Saline County *Property, Taxation Records* Free & $$ Access property data free at www.saline.org/parcel/ and click on Parcel Search Public.

Scott County *Property, Taxation Records* Free Access parcel data free at www.scott.kansasgov.com/parcel/v2loginreg.asp. Registration and password required for full data.

Sedgwick County *Real Estate, Deed, Lien, Property Sale, Marriage, Probate Records* www.sedgwickcounty.org/deeds/ Free & $$ Access to the exhaustive County online system (all departments) require a $225 set up fee, $49 monthly fee and a per transaction fee of $.09. For info on this and county record access generally, call 316-660-9860.

Also, access recorder deeds free at https://rod.sedgwickcounty.org. Also, access marriage, courts, probate records with subscription at www.accesskansas.org.

Property, Taxation Records **Free** Search property appraisal/tax data at www.sedgwickcounty.org/realpropertyinfo/realproperty.html. Also, access property appraisal and tax data free at https://ssc.sedgwickcounty.org/taxwebapp/searchlinks.aspx but no name searching.

Shawnee County ***Property, Taxation Records*** **Free** Access the residential property list free at www.co.shawnee.ks.us/AP/R_prop/Disclaimer.shtm; commercial at www.co.shawnee.ks.us/ap/C_prop/Disclaimer.shtm. Also search the county mapping site for parcel owner and map data at http://maps.kansasgis.org/sn_co/ims.cfm.

Smith County ***Property, Taxation Records*** **Free** Search parcel data free at www.smithcoks.com/parcel/.

Sumner County ***Property, Taxation Records*** **Free** Access to the Parcel Search is free or by registration for username and password from assessor, at www.co.sumner.ks.us/parcel%20lookup/. Perform a level one tax search free at http://search.co.sumner.ks.us/tax/. Register with treasurer to access more data.

Thomas County ***Property, Taxation Records*** **Free** Access the parcel search database with subscription, login and password at www.thomas.kansasgov.com/parcel/ or click on Disclaimer for free search.

Wabaunsee County ***Property, Taxation Records*** **Free** Access to the assessor parcel search data is at www.wabaunsee.kansasgov.com/Parcel/V2RunLev1.asp?submit1=OK; registration is asked for for full data, but you may search basic data for free. To subscribe, phone 785-765-3508. Also, access the treasurer's property tax data free at www.wabaunsee.kansasgov.com/MV2Base.asp?VarCN=22.

Woodson County ***Property, Taxation Records*** **Free** Access property data free or by registering for full subscription access at www.woodson.kansasgov.com/parcel/. Click on 'Parcel Search Level One' for free access and name search. Subscription service for full data is $200 per year.

Wyandotte County ***Real Estate, Deed, Lien, Judgment, Property, Treasurer, Tax Claim Property Records*** **$$** County records are online; property tax records are on dial-up. The Register has online subscription services named Laredo and Tapestry; index goes back to 1975 (1983 missing), images to 1991. Tapestry accepts credit card searches $3.99 a search, $.50 per image. Also, Judgments and Liens are available by subscription at www.accesskansas.org.

Property, Taxation Records **$$** The property dial-up services requires a $20 set up fee, $5 monthly minimum and $.05 each transaction. Lending agency info also available. Contact Louise Sachen 913-573-2885 for signup. Also, records from the County Treasurer Tax database are free at https://www.accesskansas.org/wyandotte-propertytax/index.html. Name search for personal property only; property searches require street number/name.

Other Kansas Sites of Note:

Ellis County - Sheriff Sales, Most Wanted www.ellisco.net/index.asp?DocumentID=230
Miami County - Birth Index http://skyways.lib.ks.us/genweb/miami/birth/ Somewhat limited, more genealogy oriented
Nemaha County - Surnames (Genealogical) http://skyways.lib.ks.us/genweb/nemaha/.
Sedgwick County - Most Wanted, Unnamed Suspect www.co.sedgwick.ks.us/sheriff/
Shawnee County - Most Wanted, Warrants www.co.shawnee.ks.us/SH/

Kentucky

Capital: Frankfort
　　　　Franklin County

Time Zone: EST

　　Kentucky's forty western-most counties are CST.
　　CST counties are– Adair, Allen, Ballard, Barren, Breckinridge, Butler, Caldwell, Calloway, Carlisle, Christian, Clinton,
　　Crittenden, Cumberland, Daviess, Edmonson, Fulton, Graves, Grayson, Hancock, Hart, Henderson, Hickman, Hopkins,
　　Livingstone, Logan, Marshall, McCracken, McLean, Metcalfe, Monroe, Muhlenberg, Ohio,Russell, Simpson, Todd, Trigg,
　　Union, Warren, Wayne, and Webster.

Population: 4,241,474
# of Counties: 120

Useful State Links

Website: www.kentucky.gov/
Governor: http://governor.ky.gov
Attorney General: http://ag.ky.gov
State Archives: www.kdla.ky.gov/index.htm
State Statutes and Codes: http://lrc.ky.gov/statrev/frontpg.htm
Legislative Bill Search: www.lrc.ky.gov/record_search.htm
Unclaimed Funds: http://up.treasury.ky.gov/

Primary State Agencies

Sexual Offender Registry　Free

Kentucky State Police, Criminal Identification and Records Branch, http://kspsor.state.ky.us Access is available via the website.
Search by Last Name, City, ZIP, or County.

Incarceration Records　Free

Kentucky Department of Corrections, Offender Information Services, www.corrections.ky.gov The website
http://apps.corrections.ky.gov/KOOL/ioffsrch.asp provides current inmate information on the Kentucky Online Offender Lookup
(KOOL) system as a service to the public. It can take as long as 120 days for the data to be current. *Other Options:* The IT
Department has the database on CD available for $50.00; call 502-564-4360.

Corporation, LP, Assumed Name, LLC Records　Free

Secretary of State, Corporate Records - Records, http://sos.ky.gov/business/ The web page has several distinct searches available.
Search business filings and records and also business organizations. Also search by registered agent or officer name. Also, search
securities companies registered with the state at http://fi.ky.gov/scr/ifs/old/sec/default.asp. *Other Options:* Monthly lists of new
corporations are available at www.sos.ky.gov/business/bulkdata/.

Trademarks/Servicemarks　Free

Secretary of State, Trademarks Section,　http://sos.ky.gov/business/trademarks/　Free, searchable database at
http://apps.sos.ky.gov/business/trademarks/.

Uniform Commercial Code　Free

UCC Branch, Secretary of State, http://sos.ky.gov/business/ucc/ UCC record searching is offered free of charge at the website or see
http://sos.ky.gov/business/ucc/online/. Search by debtor name or file number. SSNs are withheld from the online system. *Other
Options:* Monthly or weekly lists of new UCC filing are available at www.sos.ky.gov/business/bulkdata/.

Driver Records `$$`

Division of Driver Licensing, KY Transportation Cabinet, http://drlic.kytc.ky.gov/ There are 2 systems. Permissible use requesters who need personal information can order by batch, minimum order is 150 requests per batch. Input received by 3 PM will be available the next morning. Fee is $5.00 per record and billing is monthly. Call for details to subscribe. Records without personal info can be obtained at http://dhr.ky.gov/DHRWeb/. The same $5.00 fee applies and up to 50 records can be ordered and received immediately.

Voter Registration `Free`

State Board of Elections, http://elect.ky.gov/registrationinfo/ The agency offers a voter information status search at https://cdcbp.ky.gov/VICWeb/index.jsp. First name, last name and DOB are required. *Other Options:* Data is available on CD-Rom, labels or lists for eligible persons, pursuant to state statutes

GED Certificates `$$`

Kentucky Adult Education, GED Program, http://kyae.ky.gov/students/ged.htm Requests for transcripts ($5.00) may be submitted online at https://ged.ky.gov. Requests are accepted from agency, but a signed released must be submitted.

Vital Records `Free & $$`

Department for Public Health, Vital Statistics, http://chfs.ky.gov/dph/vital/ In cooperation with the University of Kentucky, there is a searchable death index at http://ukcc.uky.edu/vitalrec/. This is for non-commercial use only. Death records are from 1911 through 1992. The index for marriage and divorce records runs from 1973 through 1993.Also, there is a free genealogy site at http://vitals.rootsweb.ancestry.com/ky/death/search.cgi. Death Indexes from 1911-2000 are available. Search by surname, given name, place of death, residence, or year. Records may be ordered online via a state designated vendor at www.vitalchek.com.

Occupational Licensing Boards

Addiction Psychiatrist MD	http://web1.ky.gov/gensearch/
Alcohol/Drug Counselor	https://web1.ky.gov/OnPPub/Verification.aspx
Anesthesiologist	http://web1.ky.gov/gensearch/
Architect	http://kybera.com/roster.shtml
Art Therapist	https://web1.ky.gov/OnPPub/Verification.aspx
Athlete Agent	https://web1.ky.gov/OnPPub/Verification.aspx
Athletic Trainer, Medical	http://web1.ky.gov/gensearch/
Attorney	www.kybar.org/Default.aspx?tabid=26
Auctioneer, Livestock, Ltd.	http://web1.ky.gov/gensearch/LicenseSearch.aspx?AGY=3
Auctioneer, Tobacco, Ltd.	http://web1.ky.gov/gensearch/LicenseSearch.aspx?AGY=3
Auctioneer/Auctioneer Apprentice	http://web1.ky.gov/gensearch/LicenseSearch.aspx?AGY=3
Audiologist	https://web1.ky.gov/OnPPub/Verification.aspx
Bank	www.kfi.ky.gov/search.htm
Broker/Dealer Agent, Securities	www.kfi.ky.gov/search.htm
Check Casher/Check Seller	www.kfi.ky.gov/search.htm
Chiropractor	http://web1.ky.gov/gensearch/LicenseSearch.aspx?AGY=22
Cosmetologist	www.hnslicense.net
Counselor, Pastoral/Professional	https://web1.ky.gov/OnPPub/Verification.aspx
CPA	http://web1.ky.gov/GenSearch/LicenseSearch.aspx?AGY=7
CPA Company	http://web1.ky.gov/GenSearch/LicenseSearch.aspx?AGY=6
Credit Union	www.kfi.ky.gov/search.htm
Dental Hygienist	http://web1.ky.gov/gensearch/LicenseSearch.aspx?AGY=11
Dental Laboratory	http://web1.ky.gov/gensearch/LicenseSearch.aspx?AGY=13
Dentist	http://web1.ky.gov/gensearch/LicenseSearch.aspx?AGY=9
Dialysis Technician	https://secure.kentucky.gov/kbn/bulkvalidation/basic.aspx
Dietitian/Nutritionist	https://web1.ky.gov/OnPPub/Verification.aspx
EDP Servicer	www.kfi.ky.gov/search.htm
Electrical Contractor/Inspector	https://hbc.ky.gov/licensing/electrical/license_lookup.asp
Engineer/Land Surveyor Firm	http://apps.kyboels.ky.gov/SearchableRoster.aspx
Esthetician	www.hnslicense.net
Geologist	https://web1.ky.gov/OnPPub/Verification.aspx
Hearing Instrument Specialist	https://web1.ky.gov/OnPPub/Verification.aspx
Home Health Aid	https://secure.kentucky.gov/kbn/bulkvalidation/basic.aspx
Insurance Agent	www.doi.state.ky.us/kentucky/search/agent/
Insurance CE Provider	www.doi.state.ky.us/kentucky/search/provider/

Insurance Company/Insurer .... www.doi.state.ky.us/kentucky/search/company/
Interior Designer .... www.kybera.com/idlist.shtml
Investment Advisor/Rep/Firm .... www.kfi.ky.gov/search.htm
Legislative Employer of Lobbyists .... http://klec.ky.gov/reports/employersagents.htm
Liquor License .... http://kentucky.gov/abc/licenseLookup/
Loan Company, Comm./Industrial .... www.kfi.ky.gov/search.htm
Lobbyist .... http://klec.ky.gov/reports/employersagents.htm
Malt Beverage Distributor .... http://kentucky.gov/abc/licenseLookup/
Marriage & Family Therapist https://web1.ky.gov/OnPPub/Verification.aspx
Medical Doctor/Surgeon http://web1.ky.gov/gensearch/
Medical Specialist MD http://web1.ky.gov/gensearch/
Midwife Nurse .... https://secure.kentucky.gov/kbn/bulkvalidation/basic.aspx
Mortgage Broker/Loan Company ...... www.kfi.ky.gov/search.htm
Nail Technician .... www.hnslicense.net
Notary Public .... http://apps.sos.ky.gov/adminservices/notaries/
Nurse Anesthetist .... https://secure.kentucky.gov/kbn/bulkvalidation/basic.aspx
Nurse-RN/LPN/Specialist/Permit ...... https://secure.kentucky.gov/kbn/bulkvalidation/basic.aspx
Nurses Aide .... https://secure.kentucky.gov/kbn/bulkvalidation/basic.aspx
Nursing Home Administrator https://web1.ky.gov/OnPPub/Verification.aspx
Occupational Therapist/Assistant https://web1.ky.gov/OnPPub/Verification.aspx
Ophthalmic Dispenser https://web1.ky.gov/OnPPub/Verification.aspx
Optician/Apprentice https://web1.ky.gov/OnPPub/Verification.aspx
Optometrist .... http://web1.ky.gov/gensearch/LicenseSearch.aspx?AGY=8
Osteopathic Physician http://web1.ky.gov/gensearch/
Physical Therapist/Therapist Assist ... http://web1.ky.gov/gensearch/
Physician Assistant http://web1.ky.gov/gensearch/
Plumber .... https://hbc.ky.gov/licensing/electrical/license_lookup.asp
Podiatrist .... http://web1.ky.gov/gensearch/LicenseSearch.aspx?AGY=24
Private Investigator https://web1.ky.gov/OnPPub/Verification.aspx
Proprietary Education School https://web1.ky.gov/OnPPub/Verification.aspx
Psychiatrist MD http://web1.ky.gov/gensearch/
Psychologist https://web1.ky.gov/OnPPub/Verification.aspx
Public Accountant Company .... http://web1.ky.gov/GenSearch/LicenseSearch.aspx?AGY=6
Public Accountant-CPA .... http://web1.ky.gov/GenSearch/LicenseSearch.aspx?AGY=7
Real Estate Agent/Broker/Sales .... http://weba.state.ky.us/realestate/LicenseeLookUp.asp
Real Estate Appraiser .... www.kreab.ky.gov/
Real Estate Brokerage/Firm .... http://weba.state.ky.us/realestate/FirmLookUp.asp
Retired LPN .... http://kbn.ky.gov/onlinesrvs/retired.htm
Savings & Loan .... www.kfi.ky.gov/search.htm
School-related Occupation .... www.kyepsb.net
Securities Broker/Dealer/Agent .... www.kfi.ky.gov/search.htm
Sexual Assault Nurse Examiner .... https://secure.kentucky.gov/kbn/bulkvalidation/basic.aspx
Social Worker https://web1.ky.gov/OnPPub/Verification.aspx
Speech-Language Pathologist https://web1.ky.gov/OnPPub/Verification.aspx
Surveyor, Land .... http://apps.kyboels.ky.gov/SearchableRoster.aspx
Teacher .... www.kyepsb.net
Trust Company .... www.kfi.ky.gov/search.htm
Veterinarian https://web1.ky.gov/OnPPub/Verification.aspx

State and Local Courts

State Court Structure: The Circuit Court is the court of general jurisdiction and the District Court is the limited jurisdiction court. Most of Kentucky's counties combined the courts into one location and records are co-mingled. Circuit Courts have jurisdiction over cases involving capital offenses and felonies, divorces, adoptions, terminations of parental rights, land dispute title problems, and contested probates of will. Juvenile matters, city and county ordinances, misdemeanors, traffic offenses, uncontested probate of wills, felony preliminary hearings, and civil cases involving $4,000 or less are heard in District Court. 90% of all Kentuckians involved in court proceedings appear in District Court.

Statewide Court Online Access: There is a free access to limited criminal record info at http://apps.kycourts.net/CourtRecords/. Also, you may search daily court calendars by county for free at http://apps.kycourts.net/dockets. KY Bar attorneys may register to use the KCOJ court records data at http://apps.kycourts.net/courtrecordsKBA/, this is a commerial system. No courts offer direct online access to record images. Also, you may search online opinons and case informaion for the Supreme Court and Court of Appeals at http://courts.ky.gov/research/.

> ❖ **Statewide Access Offered All Trial Courts – Read Above**
>
> **Below are Additional Sites ❖**

Caldwell County
Circuit & District Court   www.sangamoncountycircuitclerk.org   **Free**
Civil: Search parties and case number index only free at http://apps.kycourts.net/CourtRecords/. Also, online access by subscription available at www.janojustice.com/products/magnus_dot_com/cm.htm. Email sales@janojustice.com for information, fees and set-up. *Criminal:* Same.

Recorders, Assessors, and Other Sites of Note

Recording Office Organization: 120 counties, 122 recording offices. The recording officer is the County Clerk. Kenton County has two recording offices. All federal and state tax liens on personal property are filed with the County Clerk, often in an "Encumbrance Book."

Online Access Note: A number of counties offer free access to assessor or real estate records. Several other counties offer commercial systems.

Allen County   *Property, Taxation Records*   **Free**   General property valuation information available at www.allenpva.ky.gov.

Boone County   *Real Estate, Deed, Lien, UCC, Marriage Records*   www.boonecountyky.org/   **$$**   Access the county clerk database through eCCLIX, a fee-based service; $200.00 sign-up and $65.00 monthly. Records go back to 1989; images to 1998. For info, see the website or call 502-266-9445.
Property, Taxation Records   **Free**   Assessor property data is available at www.boonepva.org/

Boyd County   *Real Estate, Deed, Lien Records*   **$$**   Access to the County Clerk online records requires a $10 monthly usage fee but this is only available to local attorneys; records date back to 1/1979. Lending agency data is available. For info, contact Doris Stephen Hollan-Clerk or Kathy Fisher at 606-739-5116.
Property, Taxation Records   **Free**   Access to property tax index is free at www.pvdnetwork.com/PVDNet.asp?SiteID=102.

Boyle County   *Property, Taxation Records*   **Free & $$**   Access to property tax index is free at www.pvdnetwork.com/PVDNet.asp?SiteID=106. A subscription required for full data; $100 for 120 documents, and up to 1200 docs for $750 per year.

Breckinridge County   *Real Estate, Deed, Lien, Mortgage Records*   **$$**   Access to land index back to 1996 and images to 8/20/2007 by subscription at www.titlesearcher.com/countyInfo.php?cnum=S99.

Caldwell County   *Real Estate, Deed, Lien, Marriage, UCC Records*   **Free**   Register to receive free username and password to search recording indexes free at http://216.135.47.158/search/.

Calloway County   *Property, Taxation Records*   **Free**   Access to property data is free at www.ccpva.org/searchdb/default.htm.

Campbell County   *Property, Taxation Records*   **$$**   Search county clerk and PVA records at www.campbellcountykyrecords.org. Login and password are required. Subscription fees vary from $5.00 hourly, $25 daily, $100 monthly, $1200 yearly; $200 setup fee applies to monthly or yearly. Also, access to the Property Valuation Administrator assessment search at www.campbellcountykypva.org/ Search by any or all: owner name, parcel ID, street name, street number, property type, district, sale date, sale price, deed book, deed page.

Christian County *Real Estate, Deed, Marriage, Tax Lien, UCC, Will Records* `$$` Access recorded docs bu subscription; usename and password required. Contact Betty via county clerk's office, request must be in writing. $75 set-up and $50 monthly fee. Marriage index back to 1973, Wills back to 8/2002, mortgage index 1940-1984, mortgage and land recording index and images back to 1987.

Property, Taxation Records `$$` Access property tax data by subscription at http://christianpva.com/wps-html/TaxRoll/; fees starts as low as $50 for 60 records.

Clark County *Property, Taxation Records* `$$` Online access by subscription, call office for info and signup.

Crittenden County *Property, Taxation Records* `$$` Access to data is available by subscription, fees start at 120 hits for $100. per 12 months; see www.crittendenpva.com/wps-html/TaxRoll/.

Estill County *Property, Taxation Records* No public use computer terminal. Office will search.

Fayette County *Property, Taxation Records* `Free` Search property index free at www.fayettepva.com/Main/Home.aspx. No name searching. Subscription fees have been dropped, tax roll/property search info is now free.

Franklin County *Property, Taxation Records* `Free & $$` Access to property index is free at www.franklincountypva.com/. A subscription is required for full data; $150 per 6 months or $250 per year.

Garrard County *Property, Taxation Records* `Free` Access county property assessment data index free at www.pvdnetwork.com/pvdnet.asp?siteid=121. For full data, a subscription is required; yearly or 120 documents for $100.00.

Grant County *Property, Taxation Records* `Free` Access property index free at www.pvdnetwork.com/PVDNet.asp?SiteID=113. Subscription required for full data, 120 documents for $100 up to 500 for $250.

Hancock County *Property, Taxation Records* `Free` View Delinquent tax list free at www.hancockky.us/Government/DelTaxBill.htm.

Hardin County *Real Estate, Deed, Mortgage, Marriage, Will, Assumed Name Records* www.hccoky.org `Free` Access the Clerk's permanent and temporary records search page free at www.hccoky.org/search.asp. Deeds go back to 1978; mortgages to 1974; most other records all available.

Property, Taxation Records `Free` Search County Parcels at www.hardincountypva.com/parcelsearch.asp. Property maps available at www.hardincountypva.com/propertymaps.asp. Form for requests for reproduction of public records found at www.hardincountypva.com/pdfs/repreq.pdf

Henderson County *Property, Taxation Records* `Free` Access county property assessment index free at www.pvdnetwork.com/pvdnet.asp?siteid=104. For full data, a subscription is required; yearly for $275 or $25 per month.

Henry County *Property, Taxation Records* `Free` Access property assessment index free at www.henrypva.com/Default.aspx?tabid=674. A subscription is required for full data; 120 documents for $120 yearly or unlimited docs for $250 yearly.

Hopkins County *Property, Taxation Records* `Free` Access property assessment index free at www.pvdnetwork.com/PVDNet.asp?SiteID=119. A subscription is required for full data; 120 documents for $120 yearly or unlimited docs for $250 yearly.

Jefferson County *Real Estate, Grantor/Grantee, Deed, Lien, Will, Voter Registration Records* www.jeffersoncountyclerk.org `Free` Access county land records free at www.landrecords.jcc.ky.gov; 8AM-midnight. Images go back to 6/1992. Check voter registration by name free at https://cdcbp.ky.gov/VICWeb/index.jsp.

Property, Taxation Records `Free` Access to the county property valuation administrator's assessment roll is free at www.pvalouky.org. Click on 'Assessment Roll.' No name searching. There is also a subscription service, call 502-574-6380 for info and signup.

Kenton County (1st District) *Real Estate, Deed, Lien, Mortgage Records* www.kcor.org `Free & $$` Access the county clerks official data or the Property Valuation database at www.kcor.org. To search the summarized guest access, click "Property Data" and click "Guest Access" and "PVA Real Estate". Records go back to 5/15/1991. For full, professional property data you may subscribe; fee for clerk only- $75.00; PVA only $50.00; PVA plus clerk official records- $100 per month. $5.00 per hour and 12-hr for $25 accounts also available.

Kenton County (2nd District) *Property, Taxation Records* `Free & $$` Access the county Property Valuation database at www.kcor.org. Search for free by using "Guest Access." For full, professional property data you may subscribe; fee for username and password is $50. per month, or use hourly account. Also, access the property valuation site for a fee at www.kentonpva.com/ or call 859-392-1750.

Laurel County *Property, Taxation Records* `Free` Access property records free at www.pvdnetwork.com/107/splash.asp

Lawrence County *Property, Taxation Records* Free & $$ Access the property index free at www.pvdnetwork.com/PVDNet.asp?SiteID=108. A subscription is required for full data; 120 documents for $120 yearly up to 1200 docs for $750.

Lyon County *Deed, Mortgage, Deed, Lien, UCC, Marriage, Will, Plat, Delinquent Tax Records* http://68/222/251/95search Free & $$ Access county recorded dockets and images free at http://68.222.251.95/search/. Password and user ID is "public."

McCracken County *Property, Taxation Records* $$ Acesss to tax roll data available after subscription, username and password at www.pva.paducah.com/taxroll/records.html.

Marshall County *Property, Taxation Records* $$ Access to PVA property data requires registration, username and password at http://marshallpva.ky.gov/PVA/. Subscription fees appply. For info call 270-527-4728 or email marshallpva@ky.gov.

Meade County *Real Estate, Deed, Lien, Judgment, Marriage, Will Records* $$ Access to recorder office records is by internet subscription; fee is $50 monthly; signup through recorder office, contact Katrina. Index back to 1828, images to late 1960's. No images of wills.

Montgomery County *Property, Taxation Records* $$ Access to PVA property data requires registration, username and password at www.montgomerypva.com/. Subscription fees appply.

Ohio County *Property, Taxation Records* Free Access the property index free at www.pvdnetwork.com/PVDNet.asp?SiteID=103. A subscription is required for full data; 120 documents for $120 yearly up to 1200 docs for $750.

Oldham County *Real Estate, Lien, UCC, Marriage Records* http://oldhamcounty.state.ky.us $$ Access to the database is through eCCLIX database, a fee-based service; $200.00 sign-up & $65.00 monthly. Real estate records and marriages go back to 1980. UCC images to 2/97. For info, see http://oldhamcounty.state.ky.us/ecclix.stm or call 502-266-9445.
Property, Taxation Records Free & $$ Access property index free at www.pvdnetwork.com/PVDNet.asp?SiteID=111. Subscription required for full data; 150 documents for $150 or unlimited access for $500 yearly.

Owen County *Real Estate, Deed, Lien, Mortgage Records* www.owencounty.ky.gov/clerk/ $$ Access to index back to 1986 and images back to 4/8/2208 by subscription at www.titlesearcher.com/countyInfo.php?cnum=T66.

Pendleton County *Property, Taxation Records* Free & $$ Access property index free at www.pvdnetwork.com/PVDNet.asp?SiteID=120. Subscription and payment arrangement is required to view full data; 120 docs for $100. Also, may set up account for $20 and pay $1.00 per record; they are flexible.

Pulaski County *Property, Taxation Records* Free Access to property index is free at www.pulaskipva.com/PVAWebsite/. Subscription required for full data; 100 records a month for $25 up to 5000 a year for $600.

Rowan County *Property, Taxation Records* $$ Access to county tax rolls requires registration and password; fees apply, see www.rowanpva.com/wps-html/TaxRoll/. 120 records over 12 months is $100, up to 1200 records for $750.

Scott County *Property, Taxation Records* Free & $$ Access property data after resitration, username and password at http://scpva.com/resources.html

Shelby County *Real Estate, Deed Records* www.shelbycountyclerk.com $$ Access is via the eCCLIX subscription system at www.shelbycountyclerk.com/ecclix.stm. Images go back to 1998; index to 1995. Sign-up fee is $100 plus $65 per month for unlimited access. For more info, phone 502-266-9445.
Property, Taxation Records Free & $$ Access to property index is free at www.pvdnetwork.com/PVDNet.asp?SiteID=112. A subscription is required for full data; 120 records for $100 or unlimited access for $250 yearly.

Warren County *Real Estate, Deed, Lien, UCC, Marriage, Mortgage, Plat, Will Records* http://warrencounty.state.ky.us $$ Access the county clerk database through eCCLIX, a fee-based service; $200.00 sign-up and $65.00 monthly. Records go back to 1989; images to 1998. For info, see the website or call 502-266-9445.
Property, Taxation Records Free & $$ Property data avaiable at https://warrenpva.ky.gov/TelicPVWI/Inq.dll/SearchInput. Use 'guest' as username and 'password' for password for free access

Wayne County *Property, Taxation Records* Free Access to property tax information for free go to www.waynepva.ky.gov/

Woodford County *Property, Taxation Records* Free Access to property index is free at www.pvdnetwork.com/PVDNet.asp?SiteID=118. A subscription is required for full data; 120 records for $100 or unlimited access for $250 yearly.

Louisiana

Capital: Baton Rouge
         East Baton Rouge Parish
Time Zone: CST
Population: 4,293,204
# of Parishes: 64

Useful State Links

Website: www.louisiana.gov
Governor: www.gov.louisiana.gov/
Attorney General: http://ag.louisiana.gov/
State Archives: www.sos.louisiana.gov/tabid/53/Default.aspx
State Statutes and Codes: www.legis.state.la.us/searchlegis.htm
Legislative Bill Search: www.legis.state.la.us
Unclaimed Funds: www.treasury.state.la.us/ucpm/index.htm

Primary State Agencies

Sexual Offender Registry `Free`

State Police, Sex Offender and Child Predator Registry, http://lasocpr1.lsp.org Search by name, ZIP Code, or view the entire list at the website. Also search by city, school area or parish. Also, email requests are accepted, use SOCPR@dps.state.la.us.

Incarceration Records `Free`

Department of Public Safety and Corrections, PO Box 94304, www.corrections.state.la.us Access is limited to schedules for upcoming Parole Board hearings, as well as decisions from previous Parole Board hearings. Go to www.corrections.state.la.us/Offices/paroleboard/paroledockets.htm. View the system's fugitive, escapee, and absconder lists free at www.doc.louisiana.gov/Fugitives_Escapees_Absconders/escapees.htm.

Corporation, LP, LLP, LLC, Trademarks/Servicemarks `Free & $$`

Commercial Division, Corporation Department, www.sos.louisiana.gov/ There are 2 ways to go: free on the Internet or pay. To view limited information on the website, go to "Commercial Division, Corporations Section," then "Search Corporations Database." The pay system is $360 per year for unlimited access. The system is open from 6:30 am to 11pm. For more information, call Carolyn Vogelaar at 225-925-4792. Also, a 2006 list of securities companies (and other firms in CAPCO) registered with the state is at www.ofi.state.la.us/capcolst.pdf. *Other Options:* This agency offers corporation, LLC, partnership, and trademark information on tape cartridges. For more info, call 225-925-4792.

Uniform Commercial Code `$$`

Secretary of State, UCC Records, www.sos.louisiana.gov/tabid/99/Default.aspx An annual $400 fee gives unlimited access to UCC filing information at Direct Access. This dial-up service is open from 6:30 AM to 11 PM daily. Most any software communications program can be configured to work. For further information, visit www.sos.louisiana.gov/tabid/130/Default.aspx or call the number above or 225-925-4701.

Driver Records `$$`

Dept of Public Safety and Corrections, Office of Motor Vehicles, www.expresslane.org There are two methods. The commercial requester, interactive mode is available from 7 AM to 9:30 PM daily. There is a minimum order requirement of 2,000 requests per month. A bond or large deposit is required. Fee is $6.00 per record. For more information, call 225-925-6335. The 2nd method is for individuals to order their own record from the Internet site at www.expresslane.org. The fee is $17.00 and requires a credit card. *Other Options:* Tape ordering is available for batch delivery.

Birth Certificates, Death Records `$$`

Vital Records Registry, Office of Public Health, www.dhh.louisiana.gov/offices/page.asp?id=252&detail=6489 Orders can be placed online at www.vitalchek.com, a state-approved vendor.

Occupational Licensing Boards

Acupuncturist .... www.lsbme.louisiana.gov/apps/verifications/lookup.aspx
Addiction Counselor........................... www.la-adra.org/database.asp
Alcoholic Beverage Vendor .... www.atc.rev.state.la.us/licenselookup.html
Architect/Architectural Firm .... www.lastbdarchs.com/roster.htm
Athletic Trainer .... www.lsbme.louisiana.gov/apps/verifications/lookup.aspx
Auctioneer/Auction Firm................... www.lalb.org/database.asp
Auto Buyer (In & Out of State) .... www.lrumvc.louisiana.gov/search/search.htm
Auto Parts Dealer/Dismantler........... www.lrumvc.louisiana.gov/search/search.htm
Bank .... www.ofi.state.la.us
Bond For Deed Agency .... www.ofi.state.la.us
Cemetery .... www.lcb.state.la.us/search.html
Check Casher..................................... www.ofi.state.la.us
Chemical Engineer .... www.lapels.com/indiv_search.asp
Child Residential Care....................... www.dss.state.la.us/departments/os/child_care_facilities_by_parish.html
Chiropractor...................................... www.lachiropracticboard.com/lic-drs.htm
Clinical Lab Personnel...................... www.lsbme.louisiana.gov/apps/verifications/lookup.aspx
Clinical Supervisor .... www.labswe.org/databases.htm
Collection Agency .... www.ofi.state.la.us
Construction Project, +$50000 .... www.lslbc.louisiana.gov/findcontractor_type.htm
Consumer Credit Grantor .... www.ofi.state.la.us
Contractor.. www.lslbc.louisiana.gov/findcontractor.asp
Contractor, General/Subcontractor .... www.lslbc.louisiana.gov/findcontractor_type.htm
Counselor, Professional (LPC) .... www.lpcboard.org/lpc_alpha_list.htm
Credit Repair Agency .... www.ofi.state.la.us
Credit Union .... www.ofi.state.la.us
Day Care Facility.............................. www.dss.state.la.us/departments/os/child_care_facilities_by_parish.html
Dentist/Dental Hygienist .... www.lsbd.org/DentistSearch.aspx
Dietitian.. www.lbedn.org/licensee_database.asp
Drug Distributor, Wholesale.............. www.lsbwdd.org
Electrical Engineer .... www.lapels.com/indiv_search.asp
Emergency Shelter............................. www.dss.state.la.us/departments/os/child_care_facilities_by_parish.html
Engineer/Engineer Intern.................. www.lapels.com/indiv_search.asp
Engineering Firm............................... www.lapels.com/firm_search.asp
Environmental Engineer .... www.lapels.com/indiv_search.asp
Exercise Physiologist, Clinical .... www.lsbme.louisiana.gov/apps/verifications/lookup.aspx
Foster Care/Adoption Care................ www.dss.state.la.us/departments/os/child_care_facilities_by_parish.html
Home Improvem't Cont'r +$75,000 .. www.lslbc.louisiana.gov/findcontractor_type.htm
Insurance Agent/Broker/Producer ..... www.ldi.state.la.us/search_forms/searchforms.htm
Interior Designer................................ http://lsbid.org/licensees.asp
Land Surveyor/Surveyor Intern/Firm www.lapels.com/indiv_search.asp
Lender.. www.ofi.state.la.us
Lobbyist... www.ethics.state.la.us/Lobs.pdf
Marriage and Family Therapist .... www.lpcboard.org/lpc_alpha_list.htm
Medical Doctor................................. www.lsbme.louisiana.gov/apps/verifications/lookup.aspx
Midwife .... www.lsbme.louisiana.gov/apps/verifications/lookup.aspx
Mold Remediation .... www.lslbc.louisiana.gov/findcontractor_type.htm
Mortgage Lender/Broker, Residential www.ofi.state.la.us/newrml.htm
Motor Vehicle-related Occupations... www.lrumvc.louisiana.gov/search/search.htm
Notary Public.................................... www.sos.louisiana.gov/tabid/502/Default.aspx
Notification Filer www.ofi.state.la.us/Notification%20Licensees.htm

Nuclear Engineer .... www.lapels.com/indiv_search.asp
Nuclear Medicine Technologist .... www.lsrtbe.org/search.cfm
Nurse, RN .... https://www.lsbn.state.la.us/services/service.asp?s=1&sid=8
Nurse-LPN .... www.lsbpne.com/license_verification.htm
Nurses' Aide .... www.labenfa.com
Nursing Home Administrator .... www.labenfa.com
Nutritionist .... www.lbedn.org/licensee_database.asp
Occupational Therapist/Technologist www.lsbme.louisiana.gov/apps/verifications/lookup.aspx
Optometrist .... www.arbo.org/index.php?action=findanoptometrist
Osteopathic Physician .... www.lsbme.louisiana.gov/apps/verifications/lookup.aspx
Pawnbroker .... www.ofi.state.la.us/newpawn.htm
Payday Lender .... www.ofi.state.la.us/
Pharmacist/Pharmacy/Pharm Tech .... www.labp.com/pbs.html
Physical Therapist/Therapist Asst ..... www.laptboard.org
Physician Assistant .... www.lsbme.louisiana.gov/apps/verifications/lookup.aspx
Podiatrist .... www.lsbme.louisiana.gov/apps/verifications/lookup.aspx
Prevention Specialist (Social Work) .. www.la-adra.org/database.asp
Private Investigator/PI Company .... www.lsbpie.com
Psychologist .... www.onesimuswebs.com/lsbep_db.asp
Radiation Therapy Technologist .... www.lsrtbe.org/search.cfm
Radiographer/Radiologic Techn'gist . www.lsrtbe.org/search.cfm
Radiologic Technologist, Private .... www.lsbme.louisiana.gov/apps/verifications/lookup.aspx
Real Estate Agent/Broker/Sales .... www.lrec.state.la.us/sblist/csblistmain.asp
Real Estate Appraiser .... www.lreasbc.state.la.us/dbfiles/appraiserinfo.htm
Residential Construction +$50,000 .... www.lslbc.louisiana.gov/findcontractor_type.htm
Respiratory Therapist/Therapy Tech. http://mt.gov/dli/rcp/
Savings & Loan .... www.ofi.state.la.us/newcus.htm
Social Worker .... www.labswe.org/databases.htm
Solicitor .... www.ldi.state.la.us/search_forms/searchforms.htm
Speech Pathologist/Audiologist .... www.lbespa.org/lbespa_db.asp
Substance Abuse Counselor .... www.la-adra.org/database.asp
Thrift & Loan Company .... www.ofi.state.la.us/newthrift.htm
Vocational Rehabilitation Counselor. www.lrcboard.org/licensee_database.asp

State and Local Courts

State Court Structure: The trial court of general jurisdiction in Louisiana is the District Court. A District Court Clerk in each Parish holds all the records for that Parish. Each Parish has its own clerk and courthouse. City Courts are courts of record and generally exercise concurrent jurisdiction with the District Court in civil cases where the amount in controversy does not exceed $15,000. In criminal matters, City Courts generally have jurisdiction over ordinance violations and misdemeanor violations of state law. City judges also handle a large number of traffic cases. Parish Courts exercise jurisdiction in civil cases worth up to $10,000 and criminal cases punishable by fines of $1,000 or less, or imprisonment of six months or less. Cases are appealable from the Parish Courts directly to the courts of appeal. A municipality may have a Mayor's Court; the mayor may hold trials, but nothing over $30.00, and there are no records.

Statewide Court Online Access: Search opinions from the state Supreme Court at www.lasc.org/opinion_search.asp. Online records go back to 1995. There is no statewide system open to the public for trial court dockets, but a number of parishes offer online access.

Assumption Parish

23rd District Court   www.assumptionclerk.com/   Free

Civil: After registration yuu may earch civil court records and probate records back to 4/16/2005 at http://97.89.251.18/resolution/ or call 985-369-6653 for info or signup. *Criminal:* After registration you may login to search criminal records at http://97.89.251.18/qGov/Verdict/Criminal/Index.aspx or call 985-369-6653 for info or signup. Registration is free.

Bienville Parish

2nd District Court   www.bienvilleparish.org/clerk $$

Civil: An online subscription service to record images is available. Contact the Clerk of Court for details and pricing. *Criminal:* same.

Bossier Parish

26th District Court   www.bossierclerk.com   Free & $$

Civil: Access to the Parish Clerk of Court online records requires $50 setup fee and a $35 monthly flat fee, see www.bossierparishassessor.org/cgi-bin/pro_search.pl Civil, criminal, probate (1982 forward), traffic and domestic index information is by name or case number. Call 318-965-2336 for more information. *Criminal:* Same.

Caddo Parish

1st District Court   www.caddoclerk.com   Free & $$

Civil: Online access to civil records back to 1994 and name index back to 1984 is through county internet service. Registration and $100 set-up fee and $30 monthly usage fee is required. Marriage and recording information is also available. Online images $.25 each to print. For information and sign-up, call 318-226-6523. *Criminal:* Same. Online criminal name index goes back to '80; minutes to '84. Current calendar is also available.

Calcasieu Parish

14th District Court   www.calclerkofcourt.com   Free

Civil: Online access to civil records is the same as criminal, see below. *Criminal:* Online access to court record indices is free at http://207.191.42.34/resolution/. Registration and password required. Full documents requires $100.00 per month subscription.

De Soto Parish

11th District Court   www.desotoparishclerk.org/ $$

Civil: Access index via a web-based subscription service. Search indexes only for $50.00 per month, search index, view, & print image is $100.00 per month, plus a one-time setup fee of $150.00. Contact Jessica or Valerie at 318-872-3110 to set-up an account. *Criminal:* Same.

East Baton Rouge Parish

19th District Court   www.ebrclerkofcourt.org $$

Civil: Online access to the clerk's database is by subscription. Civil record indexes go back to '88; case tracking of civil and probate back to 1991. Setup fee is $100.00 plus $15.00 per month plus per-minute usage charges. Call MIS Dept at 225-389-5295 for info or visit the website. *Criminal:* Same. Criminal case tracking goes back to 8/1990.

Baton Rouge City Court   www.brgov.com/dept/citycourt/   Free

Civil: Access city court's database including attorneys and warrants free at from the web page. *Criminal:* Access city court's criminal dockets database and warrants free at http://brgov.com/dept.citycourt.

East Feliciana Parish

20th District Court   www.eastfelicianaclerk.org/court.html $$

Civil: Online subscription service is available. $400.00 per quarter permits access to viewable documents; $250 per quarter permits access in indices. This database also includes recordings, conveyances, mortgages, and marriage records.

Iberville Parish

18th District Court $$

Civil: Access to civil records online by subscription, contact clerk for details.

Jefferson Parish $$

24th District Court   www.jpclerkofcourt.us

Civil: Online access is through dial-up service; initiation fee is $100, plus $50.00 monthly and $.25 per minute usage. Includes recordings, marriage index, and assessor rolls. For further information and sign-up, call 504-364-2908 or visit the website and click on "Jeffnet." *Criminal:* Online access is via a dial-up service, see civil.

Lafayette Parish

15th District Court   www.lafayetteparishclerk.com $$

Civil: Access to the remote online system requires $100 setup fee plus $65 per month. Civil index goes back to 1986. For more information, call Derek Comeaux at 337-291-6433 or visit www.lafayetteparishclerk.com/onlineIndex.cfm. *Criminal:* Online access to criminal index is the same as civil. May not be available, yet.

Livingston Parish

21st District Court   www.livclerk.org $$

Civil: Online access is available to local attorneys only, with registration, call 225-686-2216 x1107. $50.00 per year fee for online access. *Criminal:* same.

Orleans Parish

Civil District Court   www.orleanscdc.com/ $$
Civil: CDC Remote provides access to civil cases from 1985 and First City Court cases as well as parish mortgage and conveyance indexes. The fee is $500 per year. Call 504-592-9264 for more information.

New Orleans City Court   www.orleanscdc.com/ $$
Civil: CDC Remote provides access to First City Court cases from 1988 as well as civil cases, parish mortgage and conveyance indexes. The fee is $250 or $300 per year. Call 504-592-9264 for more information.

Sabine Parish

11th District Court   www.sabineparishclerk.com/   **Free**
Civil: Access civil court records free at www.sabineparishclerk.com and follow links to search page. Site may be temporarily down. *Criminal:* Access criminal records online- same as civil, see above.

St. Bernard Parish

34th District Court   www.stbclerk.com   **Free**
Civil: Search Civil suits back to 1/1989 free at www.stbclerk.com/modules.php?name=system&file=records. *Criminal:* Search criminal index back to 1/1989 free at www.stbclerk.com/modules.php?name=system&file=records.

St. Landry Parish

27th District Court   www.stlandry.org $$
Civil: Online subscription access program to civil cases is available. The fee is $50.00 per month. Includes civil court records back to 1997, also land indexes and images. Contact the court or visit the web page for details.

St. Martin Parish

16th District Court   www.stmartinparishclerkofcourt.com   **Free**
Civil: Court indices to be available at www.stmartinparishclerkofcourt.com.

St. Tammany Parish

22nd District Court   www.sttammanyclerk.org/main/index.asp $$
Civil: Internet access to civil records is from the Clerk of Court. $50 initial setup fee, $50.00 per month and $.20 to print a page. For information, call Kristie Howell at 985-809-8787. A non-Internet dial-up service is also available; $100 setup and $.20 per minute. Civil index goes back to 1992; images to 1995. Search index free at https://www.sttammanyclerk.org/liveapp/default.asp. *Criminal:* Internet access to criminal records is the same as civil. Dialup criminal indices go back to 1988.

Tangipahoa Parish

21st District Court   www.tangiclerk.org   **Free**
Civil: Online access to Parish notaries index records is $25.00 set-up fee (name only-no history). Index back to 1974. Visit www.tangiclerk.org/OnlineServices/onlineservices.asp for information or call Andi Matheu: 985-748-4146. *Criminal:* .

Webster Parish

26th District Court   www.websterclerk.org/ $$
Civil: Access court records by subscription; fee is $50.00 setup fee plus $35.00 per month for index searches and images. Civil index goes back to 4/16/1992; images back to 2005. Sub includes criminal, probate, civil, traffic, also marriages and conveyances. Login, signup or find more information at www.websterclerk.org/records.html. *Criminal:* Access to criminal index and images is included in the general subscription service described in the civil section, above. The criminal subecription index goes back to 11/28/1992; images go back to early 2007.

Recorders, Assessors, and Other Sites of Note

Recording Office Organization: 64 parishes, 64 recording offices. One parish – St. Martin – has two non-contiguous segments. In Orleans Parish, deeds are recorded in a different office from mortgages. All federal and state tax liens are filed with the Clerk of Court. Parishes usually file tax liens on personal property in the same index. However, tax liens are not kept on the same statewide database as UCCs.

Online Access Note: A number of parishes offer online access to recorded documents. Most are commercial fee systems but newer systems are allowing for free index searching, then a fee for images, usually $1.00 each. A statewide system (excluding Jefferson Davis, Orleans, Sabine, St. Tammany, Terrebonne, Winn) at www.latax.state.la.us/TaxRoll_ParishSelect.asp offers free access to assessor parish tax roll data.

> ❖ **Statewide Access of Tax Rolls Offered For All Districts – Read Above. Listed Below are Additional Sites** ❖

Assumption Parish *Mortgage, Probate, Civil, UCC, Marriage, Civil Court Records* www.assumptionclerk.com
$$ Online access is by subscription at http://68.191.90.65/resolution/. Civil/Probate goes back to 4/2005. UCCs to 3/1990; marriages back to 9/18/1996; mortgages to 1/8/1981. User ID and password required.

Avoyelles Parish *Real Estate, Land, Deeds, Conveyance, Mortgage, Oil & Gas, Plat Records*
www.avoyellesclerk.com/ **$$** Access to land record at www.avoyellesclerk.com/Default.aspx?tabid=110. Application fee is $50.00 and a monthly service fee of $125.00. Contact the Clerk's Office for application at 318-253-7523.

Bienville Parish *Property, Taxation Records* **Free** Access to property tax index to be available free at
www.bienvilleparish.org, click on Tax Assessor. A fee may apply to access full data, and registration may be required. Also, search tax roll data on statewide website, www.latax.state.la.us.

Bossier Parish *Real Estate, Deed, Marriage, Civil Court Records* www.bossierclerk.com **$$** Access to the
clerk's WebView System is by subscription; one-time signup fee is $50 plus $35 per month, plus small fee per image printed. Monthly billing. Mortgages go back to 1984, marriages to 1843, courts back to 1980s; see http://209.209.204.34/WebInquiry.
Property, Taxation Records **Free** Free public address search available at www.bossierparishassessor.org/cgi-bin/pro_search.pl. Access to full data requires username and login ID, signup online; fee amounts to less than $1.00 per day. For more information, call 318-221-8718. Also, tax roll data on statewide website, www.latax.state.la.us.

Caddo Parish *Real Estate, Deed, Lien, Marriage, Mortgage Records* www.caddoclerk.com **Free & $$**
Access to the Parish online records requires a $100 set up fee plus $30 monthly fee; $.25 per image. Mortgages and indirect conveyances index dates back to 1981; direct conveyances date back to 1914. Lending agency data is available. Mortgage images back to 1/1995. Also, access marriage licenses free back to 1937; use username "muser" and password "caddo." Signup and info at www.caddoclerk.com/remote.htm or call 318-226-6523.
Property, Taxation Records **Free & $$** Search assessor property free at www.caddoassessor.org/cgi-bin/pub_search.pl; no name searching for free; Annual sub for full data-$1.00 per day.

Calcasieu Parish *Real Estate, Deed, Mortgage, Marriage, Court, UCC Records* www.calclerkofcourt.com **Free**
& $$ Online access to court record indices is free at www.calclerkofcourt.com. Registration and password required. Full documents requires $100.00 per month subscription.

De Soto Parish *Real Estate, Deed, Judgment, Lien, Mortgage Records* www.desotoparishclerk.org **$$**
Access Clerk of Court records index by subscription at www.desotoparishclerk.org/online.html; set-up fee is $150.00 plus either $50 per month for index only searching or $100 per month for index, doc viewing, and images.

East Baton Rouge Parish *Real Estate, Deed, Lien, Marriage, Probate, Court, Judgment, Map Data Index*
Records www.ebrclerkofcourt.org **$$** Access to online records requires a $100 set up fee with a $5 monthly fee and $.33 per minute of use. Four years worth of data is kept active on the system. Lending agency data is available. For info, contact Wendy Gibbs at 225-398-5295.

East Feliciana Parish *Real Estate, Lien, Mortgage, Marriage, Civil Court Records* www.eastfelicianaclerk.org/
Free & $$ Access to online records requires a subscription, $100 set up fee with a $50 monthly usage fee for indices or $100.00 per month for indices plus images, in quarterly advances. Conveyances go back to 1962, mortgages to 1981; viewable back to 6/18/1982. Marriages go back to 1987, viewable free to 1995, and miscellaneous index goes back to 1984. For info, contact clerk's office at 225-683-5145 or visit www.eastfelicianaclerk.org.

Iberia Parish *Real Estate, Conveyance, Deed, Mortgage, Lien, Marriage, Divorce, Civil/Criminal Court,*
Probate Records www.iberiaclerk.com **Free & $$** Access to the Parish online records requires a $100.00 monthly usage fee. Lending agency data is available. For info, contact Mike Thibodeaux at 337-365-7282. Registration is also required for the Clerk's index search at www.iberiaclerk.com/resolution/default.asp which includes civil, conveyances, criminal, marriages back to 2000, mortgages back to 1959, and probate back thru 2000.

Iberville Parish *Real Estate, Deed Records* www.ibervilleparish.com **Free** Office is in the process of implementing
an online system; records are to be accessible free on the Internet; call clerk office for detail, 225-687-5160.

Jackson Parish *Real Estate, Grantor/Grantee, Deed, Mortgage, Lien, Judgment, Marriage Records*
www.jacksonparishclerk.org **$$** Access to the clerk's WebView Online Records system is available by subscription; $50 installation and account setup fee plus $50.00 per month usage fee; Sub form at http://72.149.195.202/Webinquiry_Jackson/(s2uty0ioozzflf45tewwkeb5)/subscribe.aspx.
Property, Taxation Records **Free** Search tax roll data on statewide website, www.latax.state.la.us/TaxRoll_ParishSelect.asp.

Jefferson Parish *Real Estate, Deed, Marriage, Civil Court Records* www.jpclerkofcourt.us `$$`

Access to the clerk's JeffNet database is by subscription; set-up fee is $100.00 plus $50.00 monthly and $.50 per image printed. Mortgage and conveyance images go back to 1971 and changing; index to 1967. Marriage and property records go back to 1992. For info, visit https://ssl.jpclerkofcourt.us/JeffnetSetup/default.asp. Also, search inmates and offenders on a private site at https://www.vinelink.com/vinelink/siteInfoAction.do?siteId=19002

Property, Taxation Records `Free` Search the assessor property rolls free at www.jpassessor.com. Call Donna Richoux at 504-364-2900 for fee info. Also, Search tax roll data on statewide website, www.latax.state.la.us/TaxRoll_ParishSelect.asp.

Lafayette Parish *Real Estate, Deed, Mortgage, Lien, UCC Records* www.lafayetteparishclerk.com `$$`

Access to Parish online records requires a $100 set up fee plus $15 per month and $.50 per minute. Conveyances date back to 1936; mortgages to 1948; other records to 1986. Lending agency data is available. For info, contact Derek Comeaux at 337-291-6433. Tax and UCC lien data is for this parish only.

Property, Taxation Records `Free` Search tax roll data on statewide website, www.latax.state.la.us/TaxRoll_ParishSelect.asp. Also, assessor property data is free at www.lafayetteassessor.com/search.html but no name searching.

Lincoln Parish *Property, Taxation Records* `Free` Access property assessor data at

http://assessor.lincolnparish.org/WebTaxRoll/UserLogin.aspx with free registration. Also, search by owner name for parcel and property data free on the GIS-mapping site at http://gis.lincolnparish.org. Also, tax roll data on statewide website, see www.latax.state.la.us.

Livingston Parish *Real Estate, Deed, Lien, Judgment, UCC, Plat Records* https://www.livclerk.org `Free & $$`

Access the clerk's search pages at www.livclerk.org/combined/Disclaimer.aspx after free registration. User name and password required to search; $1.00 per page fee for images. $50.00 yearly fee for an account. For assistance, call Vanessa Barnett at 225-686-2216 x1107 or 225-505-8200 cell.

Natchitoches Parish *Real Estate, Deed, Marriage, Divorce, Judgment, Wills/Probate, Assumed Name*

Records www.npclerkofcourt.org/ `$$` With username and password to WebView you can search and access marriage and property records back to 1976. Direct subscription inquires to Linda Cockrell at 318-352-8152.

Property, Taxation Records `Free` Access assessor property data free at www.natchitochesassessor.org/SearchProperty.aspx. Also, search tax roll data on statewide website, www.latax.state.la.us.

Orleans Parish, Conveyances *Real Estate, Deed, Mortgage, Lien, Birth, Death Records*

www.orleanscdc.com `$$` Access the Parish online records requires a $300 yearly subscription fee, prorated. Records date back to 1989. Access includes real estate, liens, civil, 1st city court records. For info/signup, phone 504-592-9264. Conveyances back to 1989, mortgages to 9/21/97.

Property, Taxation Records `Free` Access City of New Orleans property data free at www.cityofno.com/pg-137-1.aspx. Access City property data free at https://secure.cityofno.com/portal.aspx?portal=1&load=~/Services/Assessor/PropertyDatabase/PropertySearch.ascx. Also, tax roll data on statewide website, www.latax.state.la.us.

Ouachita Parish *Property, Taxation Records* `Free & $$` Access to assessor property data is free at

www.ouachitaparishassessor.com/online_property_search.htm. A subscription is required to view full details, legal description, etc.; fee is determined by number of logins.

Sabine Parish *Real Estate, Deed Records* Access to recorded docs is to be available soon.

St. Bernard Parish *Real Estate, Conveyance, Mortgage, Chattel, Bond, Marriage, Partnership, Civil/Criminal*

Court Records www.stbclerk.com `Free` Search clerk's court and recording records indexes free at www.stbclerk.com/modules.php?name=system&file=records. Mortgages back to 1974, marriages to 4/1938, conveyances and partnerships back to 1974, courts and chattel back to 1/1989, Misc. and bonds and partnerships back to 1974.

St. John the Baptist Parish *Property, Taxation Records* `Free` Access property data free at

www.stjohnassessor.org/PropertySearch.aspx.

St. Landry Parish *Real Estate, Deed, Mortgage, Conveyance Records* www.stlandry.org/index.htm `$$`

Access to recorder office land records is by subscription; fee is $35-50 per month. Data includes mortgages and conveyances, also perhaps court records. For registration and password contact Ms Lisa at Clerk of Court office, extension 103.

St. Martin Parish *Property, Taxation Records* `Free` Access parish assessor property records free at

www.stmartinassessor.org/propsrch_disclaim.html.

St. Mary Parish *Property, Taxation Records* `Free` Search tax roll data on statewide website,

www.latax.state.la.us/TaxRoll_ParishSelect.asp.

St. Tammany Parish *Real Estate, Deed, Mortgage, Lien, Marriage, Court, Traffic, Map Records*

www.sttammanyclerk.org `Free & $$` Full access to clerk's Premium Service requires a $50 per month plus $50.00 start-up fee, plus $.20 per printed page. Records date back to 1961; viewable images on conveyances back to 1980. For info, contact Eli Wilson or

Kristie Howell at 985-809-8787. A dialup service is also available; $100 setup and $.10 per minute. Free public access to indices is also at https://www.sttammanyclerk.org/liveapp/main/main.asp. Free access includes marriages, maps, land/mortgage, traffic and court cases.

Property, Taxation Records **Free** Search assessor and property value database free at www.stassessor.org/assessor.php.

Tangipahoa Parish *Real Estate, Lien, Civil, Marriage, Mortgage Records* www.tangiclerk.org **SS**

Access to Parish online records requires registration and a trial membership. Print documents for $1.00 each. One time setup fee is $25.00. Record dates vary though most indexes go back before 1990. Lending agency data is available. For info, contact Alison Carona at 985-748-4146. Bulk prints also available. Also, access the mapping feature that includes assessor basic property data.

Property, Taxation Records **SS** The county offers a subscription service which includes a mapping service with assessor property information.

Terrebonne Parish *Property, Taxation Records* **Free** Access to free tax roll information go to
www.tpcg.org/Tax_Roll/TaxRoll_Main.asp

Union Parish *Property, Taxation Records* **Free** Access property index free at
www.unionparishassessor.com/online_property_search.htm but for full data registration and fees based on usage are required.

West Baton Rouge Parish *Property, Taxation Records* **Free** Access property data via the GIS mapping site for
free at www.geoportalmaps.com/atlas/wbr/viewer.htm. Click on Search Parcels by owner name. Also, search the View Your Assessment database free at www.wbrassessor.org/Library/Library.asp.

Other Louisiana Sites of Note:
Orleans Parish - Death (pre-1950), Birth (pre-1900) www.rootsweb.ancestry.com/~usgenweb/la/orleans.htm
    Unofficial records. Also includes unofficial, limited marriage lists.
Orleans Parish - New Orleans Notarial Archives, Land, Vendor/Vendee http://nonaweb.notarialarchives.org/
Orleans Parish - Property, Recovery-related data www.cityofno.com/pg-137-1.aspx
Ouachita Parish - Sex Offender http://watchsystems.com/la/ouachita/
Ouachita Parish - Sheriff Sale www.opso.net/sale.html
Plaquemines Parish - Sexual Offender www.lasocpr.lsp.org/Static/Search.htm

Maine

Capital: Augusta
            Kennebec County
Time Zone: EST
Population: 1,317,207
# of Counties: 16

Useful State Links

Website: www.maine.gov/
Governor: www.maine.gov/governor/baldacci/index.shtml
Attorney General: www.maine.gov/ag/
State Archives: http://www.maine.gov/sos/arc/
State Statutes and Codes: http://janus.state.me.us/legis/statutes/
Legislative Bill Search: http://janus.state.me.us/legis/LawMakerWeb/search.asp
Unclaimed Funds: www.maine.gov/treasurer/unclaimed_property/

Primary State Agencies

Criminal Records `$$`

Maine State Police, State Bureau of Identification, http://www10.informe.org/PCR/ One may request a record search from the web. Results are usually returned via e-mail in 2 hours. Fee is $25.00, unless requester is an in-state subscriber to InforME, then fee is $15.00 per record. There is a $75.00 annual fee to be a subscriber.

Sexual Offender Registry `Free`

State Bureau of Investigation, Sex Offender Registry, http://sor.informe.org/sor/ Search at the web page. Information is only provided for those individuals that are required to register pursuant to Title 34-A MRSA, Chapter 15. Records date to 01/01/82 and forward. The date of the last address verification is indicated next to the registrant's address.

Incarceration Records `Free`

Maine Department of Corrections, Inmate Records, www.maine.gov/corrections/ One may also do a search by sending an email to Corrections.Webdesk@maine.gov. Include your full name, address, and reasons for the search. Public information is provided. There is no direct online access available at this time (check website for updated information).

Corporation, LP, LLP, LLC, Trademarks/Servicemarks, Assumed Name `Free & $$`

Secretary of State, Reports & Information Division, www.maine.gov/sos/cec/corp/ A free search of basic information about the entity including address, corporate ID, agent, and status is found at https://icrs.informe.org/nei-sos-icrs/ICRS. A commercial subscriber account also gives extensive information and ability to download files. Also, search securities Division Enforcement Actions and Consent Agreements free at www.maine.gov/pfr/securities/enforcement.shtml. *Other Options:* Bulk data purchase is available, a list of available databases for sale if found at the web. Monthly lists of new entities filed with this office are also available. Call 207-624-7752.

Uniform Commercial Code, Federal & State Tax Liens `Free & $$`

Secretary of State, UCC Records Section, www.maine.gov/sos/cec/ucc/index.html There is a free search of the index to search only the debtor name or name variations at www.maine.gov/sos/cec/corp/debtor_index.shtml. For search and purchase of official UCC documents and fees visit https://www10.informe.org/ucc/search/begin.shtml. If no record found, the fee is still incurred. *Other Options:* Farm products - buyers reports, secured party available in bulk.

Driver Records `$$`

BMV - Driver License Services, 101 Hospital Street, www.maine.gov/sos/bmv/ Access is through InforME via the Internet. There are two access systems. Casual requesters can obtain records that have personal information cloaked. There is a subscription service for approved requesters, records contain personal information. There is a subscription service for approved requesters, records contain personal information as records are released per DPPA. The fee for either system is $7.00 per request for a 3-year record and $12.00

for a 10-year record. There is a $75.00 annual fee for the subscription service. A myriad of other state government records are available. Visit www.informe.org/bmv/drc/ or call 207-621-2600. *Other Options:* The state offers "Driver Cross Check" - a program for employers, to provide notification when activity occurs on a specific record.

Vehicle Ownership & Registration $$

Department of Motor Vehicles, Registration Section, www.maine.gov/sos/bmv/ Maine offers online access to title and registration records via InforME. Fee is $5.00 per record. Search title records by VIN or title number. Search registration records by name and DOB, or by plate number. Records are available as interactive online or FTP with a subscription account. There are many other services available with the subscription. There is a $75.00 annual fee. Contact InforME at info@informe.org or visit the web page.

Accident Reports $$

Maine State Police, Traffic Division, www.informe.org/mcrs/ Records from 01/2003 forward may be ordered from www.informe.org/mcrs/ for $10.00 per record. If you do not have a subscription to InforME, then a credit card must be used. Resulting reports is either returned by mail, or emailed in a PDF format. You can search by name, date of birth, crash location, crash date, or investigating agency (police department). These reports may include officer narratives. *Other Options:* Subscribers may purchase monthly database updates or use the "Crash Tracker" notification program for no charge.

GED Certificates Free

Dept of Education, GED Office, www.maine.gov/education/aded/dev/ged/transcript.htm Email requests can be made by sending email to: lisa.perry@maine.gov

Death Records Free

Department of Health and Human Services, Office of Vital Records, www.maine.gov/dhhs/vitalrecords.htm Search death records for 1960 thru 1997 from the web page at http://portalx.bisoex.state.me.us/pls/archives_mhsf/archdev.death_archive.search_form. Also, a free genealogy site at http://vitals.rootsweb.ancestry.com/me/death/search.cgi has Death Indexes from 1960-1997. Search by surname, given name, place or year. *Other Options:* Bulk file purchases are available, with the exclusion of restricted data.

Marriage Certificates Free

Department of Health and Human Services, Office of Vital Records, www.maine.gov/dhhs/vitalrecords.htm Records are available at the web page from 1892- thru 1996. *Other Options:* Bulk file purchasing is available, with restricted data excluded.

Occupational Licensing Boards

Acupuncturist	http://pfr.informe.org/ALMSOnline/ALMSQuery/Welcome.aspx
Aesthetician	http://pfr.informe.org/ALMSOnline/ALMSQuery/Welcome.aspx
Alcohol/Drug Abuse Counselor	http://pfr.informe.org/ALMSOnline/ALMSQuery/Welcome.aspx
Alcoholic Beverage Distributor	www.maine.gov/dps/liqr/active_licenses.htm
Animal Medical Technician	http://pfr.informe.org/ALMSOnline/ALMSQuery/Welcome.aspx
Appraiser, Resi. Real Estate	http://pfr.informe.org/ALMSOnline/ALMSQuery/Welcome.aspx
Architect	http://pfr.informe.org/ALMSOnline/ALMSQuery/Welcome.aspx
Assisted Living Facility	https://portalxw.bisoex.state.me.us/dhhs-apps/assisted/certificate.asp
Athletic Trainer	http://pfr.informe.org/ALMSOnline/ALMSQuery/Welcome.aspx
Auctioneer	http://pfr.informe.org/ALMSOnline/ALMSQuery/Welcome.aspx
Barber	http://pfr.informe.org/ALMSOnline/ALMSQuery/Welcome.aspx
Boiler	http://pfr.informe.org/ALMSOnline/ALMSQuery/Welcome.aspx
Boxer	http://pfr.informe.org/ALMSOnline/ALMSQuery/Welcome.aspx
Charitable Solicitation	http://pfr.informe.org/ALMSOnline/ALMSQuery/Welcome.aspx
Chiropractor	http://pfr.informe.org/ALMSOnline/ALMSQuery/Welcome.aspx
Cosmetologist	http://pfr.informe.org/ALMSOnline/ALMSQuery/Welcome.aspx
Counselor	http://pfr.informe.org/ALMSOnline/ALMSQuery/Welcome.aspx
Dental Radiographer	http://pfr.informe.org/ALMSOnline/ALMSQuery/SearchIndividual.aspx?c=1
Dentist/Denturist/ Dental Hygienist	http://pfr.informe.org/ALMSOnline/ALMSQuery/SearchIndividual.aspx?c=1
Dietitian	http://pfr.informe.org/ALMSOnline/ALMSQuery/Welcome.aspx
Electrician	http://pfr.informe.org/ALMSOnline/ALMSQuery/Welcome.aspx
Elevator/Tramway	http://pfr.informe.org/ALMSOnline/ALMSQuery/Welcome.aspx
Employee Leasing Company	http://pfr.informe.org/ALMSOnline/ALMSQuery/Welcome.aspx
Engineer/ Engineer Intern	https://www.maine.gov/professionalengineers/database.shtml
Forester	http://pfr.informe.org/ALMSOnline/ALMSQuery/Welcome.aspx
Fund Raiser	http://pfr.informe.org/ALMSOnline/ALMSQuery/Welcome.aspx
Funeral Service	http://pfr.informe.org/ALMSOnline/ALMSQuery/Welcome.aspx

Geologist .... http://pfr.informe.org/ALMSOnline/ALMSQuery/Welcome.aspx
Hearing Aid Dealer/Fitter.................. http://pfr.informe.org/ALMSOnline/ALMSQuery/Welcome.aspx
HMO .... www.maine.gov/pfr/insurance/
Home Health Agency   http://pfr.informe.org/almsonline/almsquery/welcome.aspx?AspxAutoDetectCookieSupport=1
Hospice   ... ...   http://pfr.informe.org/almsonline/almsquery/welcome.aspx?AspxAutoDetectCookieSupport=1
Hospital   ... ...   http://pfr.informe.org/almsonline/almsquery/welcome.aspx?AspxAutoDetectCookieSupport=1
Insurance Adjuster........................... http://pfr0.informe.org/almsquery/LicLookup.aspx
Insurance Advisor/Consultant .... http://pfr.informe.org/ALMSOnline/ALMSQuery/Welcome.aspx
Insurance Agent/Agency/Company ... http://pfr.informe.org/ALMSOnline/ALMSQuery/Welcome.aspx
Insurance Producer http://pfr0.informe.org/almsquery/LicLookup.aspx
Interior Designer............................... http://pfr.informe.org/ALMSOnline/ALMSQuery/Welcome.aspx
Interpreter.. http://pfr.informe.org/ALMSOnline/ALMSQuery/Welcome.aspx
Investment Advisor/Representative ... http://pfr.informe.org/ALMSOnline/ALMSQuery/Welcome.aspx
Kickboxer.. http://pfr.informe.org/ALMSOnline/ALMSQuery/Welcome.aspx
Landscape Architect .... http://pfr.informe.org/ALMSOnline/ALMSQuery/Welcome.aspx
Liquor License, On & Off Premise.... www.maine.gov/dps/liqr/active_licenses.htm
Liquor Store/Wholesaler.................... www.maine.gov/dps/liqr/active_agency_liquor_stores.htm
Lobbyist... www.mainecampaignfinance.com/public/entity_list.asp?TYPE=LOB
Lottery Retailer................................ www.mainelottery.com/cgi/findAgent.pl
Manicurist.. http://pfr.informe.org/ALMSOnline/ALMSQuery/Welcome.aspx
Manufactured Housing .... http://pfr.informe.org/ALMSOnline/ALMSQuery/Welcome.aspx
Marriage & Family Therapist .... http://pfr.informe.org/ALMSOnline/ALMSQuery/Welcome.aspx
Massage Therapist............................ http://pfr.informe.org/ALMSOnline/ALMSQuery/Welcome.aspx
Medical Doctor................................. www.docboard.org/me/licensure/dw_verification.html
Naturopathic Physician...................... http://pfr.informe.org/ALMSOnline/ALMSQuery/Welcome.aspx
Notary Public................................... www.maine.gov/online/notary/search/
Nurse .... https://portalx.bisoex.state.me.us/pls/msbn_nlv/bnxdev.license_search.main_page
Nursing Home   ... ...   http://pfr.informe.org/almsonline/almsquery/welcome.aspx?AspxAutoDetectCookieSupport=1
Nursing Home Administrator .... http://pfr.informe.org/ALMSOnline/ALMSQuery/Welcome.aspx
Occupational Therapist...................... http://pfr.informe.org/ALMSOnline/ALMSQuery/Welcome.aspx
Oil & Solid Fuel Profes'l/Company .. http://pfr.informe.org/ALMSOnline/ALMSQuery/Welcome.aspx
Optometrist...................................... http://pfr.informe.org/ALMSOnline/ALMSQuery/Welcome.aspx
Osteopathic Physician/Physic'n Asst. www.docboard.org/me-osteo/df/index.htm
Osteopathic Resident/Intern.............. www.docboard.org/me-osteo/df/index.htm
Pastoral Counselor............................ http://pfr.informe.org/ALMSOnline/ALMSQuery/Welcome.aspx
Pesticide Applicator/Dealer .... www.maine.gov/agriculture/pesticides/cert/index.htm
Pharmacist.. http://pfr.informe.org/ALMSOnline/ALMSQuery/Welcome.aspx
Physical Therapist .... http://pfr.informe.org/ALMSOnline/ALMSQuery/Welcome.aspx
Physician Assistant............................ www.docboard.org/me/licensure/dw_verification.html
Pilot .... http://pfr.informe.org/ALMSOnline/ALMSQuery/Welcome.aspx
Plumber .... http://pfr.informe.org/ALMSOnline/ALMSQuery/Welcome.aspx
Podiatrist.. http://pfr.informe.org/ALMSOnline/ALMSQuery/Welcome.aspx
Preferred Provider Organization........ www.maine.gov/pfr/insurance/
Psychologist..................................... http://pfr.informe.org/ALMSOnline/ALMSQuery/Welcome.aspx
Public Accountant-CPA .... http://pfr.informe.org/ALMSOnline/ALMSQuery/Welcome.aspx
Radiologic Technician....................... http://pfr.informe.org/ALMSOnline/ALMSQuery/Welcome.aspx
Real Estate Appraiser/Broker .... http://pfr.informe.org/ALMSOnline/ALMSQuery/Welcome.aspx
Reinsurance Intermediary.................. http://pfr0.informe.org/almsquery/LicLookup.aspx
Re-insurer, Approved .... http://pfr.informe.org/ALMSOnline/ALMSQuery/Welcome.aspx
Respiratory Care Therapist................ http://pfr.informe.org/ALMSOnline/ALMSQuery/Welcome.aspx
RN, Advanced Practice/Professional . https://portalx.bisoex.state.me.us/pls/msbn_nlv/bnxdev.license_search.main_page
Securities Broker-Dealer/Agent......... http://pfr.informe.org/ALMSOnline/ALMSQuery/Welcome.aspx
Social Worker................................... http://pfr.informe.org/ALMSOnline/ALMSQuery/Welcome.aspx
Soil Scientist.................................... http://pfr.informe.org/ALMSOnline/ALMSQuery/Welcome.aspx
Speech Pathologist/Audiologist......... http://pfr.informe.org/ALMSOnline/ALMSQuery/Welcome.aspx
Substance Abuse Counselor .... http://pfr.informe.org/ALMSOnline/ALMSQuery/Welcome.aspx
Surplus Lines Company.................... http://pfr.informe.org/ALMSOnline/ALMSQuery/Welcome.aspx

Surveyor, Land .... http://pfr.informe.org/ALMSOnline/ALMSQuery/Welcome.aspx
Third Party Administrator http://pfr0.informe.org/almsquery/LicLookup.aspx
Utilization Review Entity .... www.maine.gov/pfr/insurance/
Vendor, Itinerant/Transient............... http://pfr.informe.org/ALMSOnline/ALMSQuery/Welcome.aspx
Veterinarian/Veterinary Technician .. http://pfr.informe.org/ALMSOnline/ALMSQuery/Welcome.aspx
Wrestler .... http://pfr.informe.org/ALMSOnline/ALMSQuery/Welcome.aspx

State and Local Courts

State Court Structure: A Superior Court – the court of general jurisdiction – is located in each of Maine's
sixteen counties, except for Aroostook County which has two Superior Courts. Both Superior and District Courts
handle misdemeanor and felony cases, with jury trials being held in Superior Court only. The District Court hears
both civil and criminal and always sits without a jury.

Within the District Court is the Family Division, which hears all divorce and family matters, including child
support and paternity cases. The District Court also hears child protection cases, and serves as Maine's juvenile
court. Actions for protection from abuse or harassment, mental health, small claims cases, and money judgments
are filed in the District Court. Traffic violations are processed primarily through a centralized Violations Bureau,
part of the District Court system. Prior to year 2001, District Courts accepted civil cases involving claims less
than $30,000. Now, District Courts have jurisdiction concurrent with that of the Superior Court for all civil
actions, except cases vested in the Superior Court by statute.

Probate Courts are part of the county court system, not the state system. Although the Probate Court may be
housed with other state courts, it is on a different phone system and calls may not be transferred.

Statewide Court Online Access: The website at www.courts.state.me.us provides access to Maine
Supreme Court opinions and administrative orders, but not all documents are available online. Also, the website
offers access to trial court schedules by region and case type. Some county level courts are online through a
private vendor. Search probate records free at https://www.maineprobate.net/index.html. Docs are $2.00 each if
not registered; $1.00 each if you subscribe.

Kennebec County

Probate Court   http://www.datamaine.com/probate   `Free & $$`   Search dockets back to 1995 online at
www.datamaine.com/probate/docket.html. Also, search probate records free at https://www.maineprobate.net/index.html. $2 fee for
docs, $1 if registered.

Penobscot County

Millinocket District Court - North 13   `Free`
Civil: Record searches found at www.maine.gov/portal/online_services/ *Criminal:* Search records at
www.maine.gov/portal/online_services/.

Recorders, Assessors, and Other Sites of Note

Recording Office Organization: 16 counties, 18 recording offices. The recording officer is the County
Register of Deeds. Counties maintain a general index of all transactions recorded. Aroostock and Oxford
Counties each have 2 recording offices. There are no county assessors; each town and city has its own.

Online Access Note: There is no statewide system, however a number of counties offer access. Some
counties outsource via vendors. Where known, local jusrisdictions with web access to assessment records are
indicated in the county profile.

Androscoggin County *Real Estate, Deed, Lien Records*   http://androscoggindeeds.com   `Free & $$`
Access the Registry index by subscription for a $300.00 annual fee plus $1.25 per page/image printed. Indexes go back to 1976. For
info and sign-up, contact Registry of Deeds at 207-782-0191. Search for free at http://androscoggindeeds.com/ALIS/WW400R.PGM.
Index goes back to 1/1976 but images cannot be printed.
Property, Taxation Records   `Free`   Town of Lisbon assessor data is free at
www.mygovnow.com/lisbto/Invision/assessing/index.htm. No name searching. Also City of Auburn tax assessor data is free at

www.auburnmaine.org/html/webgis.htm. Also, access Sabattus Town assessor data free at
http://data.visionappraisal.com/SabattusME/DEFAULT.asp.

Aroostook County (Northern District) *Real Estate, Deed, Lien, Judgment Records*

www.aroostook.me.us/deeds.html `$$`   Remote access via a commercial online system has been replaced by a subscription
internet-based system. Data on the internet system includes deeds, mortgages, liens, judgment, and land recording generally. Records
go back to 1985. Subscription fee is $100 for North District, $100 for South. For more info and signup, see
www.aroostookdeedsnorth.com then click on Access Information button on left side of page.

Aroostook County (Southern District) *Real Estate, Deed, Lien, Judgment Records*

www.aroostook.me.us/indexhome.html `$$`   Remote access via a commercial online system has been replaced by a subscription
internet-based system. Data on the internet system includes deeds, mortgages, liens, judgment, and land recording generally. Records
go back to 1985. Subscription fee is $100 for South District, $150 for both North and South. For more info and signup, see
www.aroostookdeedsnorth.com then click on Access Information button on left side of page.

Cumberland County *Real Estate, Deed, Lien, Judgment Records* www.mainelandrecords.com `$$`
Search Register of Deeds fee site at https://www.mainelandrecords.com. $3.00 fee per doc, or register and pay monthly fee.
Property, Taxation Records `Free`   Cape Elizabeth data free- www.capeelizabeth.com/taxdata.html. Gray Town assessor
data- www.mygovnow.com/grayto/Invision/assessing/index.htm. Portland assessor- www.portlandassessor.com. Scarborough-
www.scarborough.me.us/townhall/assessing/search.html. Falmouth assessor & GIS- http://gis.cdm.com/FalmouthMaineGIS/l.
Cumberland, Raymond, Freeport, Gorham, Harpswell, Standish, S. Portland, Westbrook, Windham, Yarmouth town assessors at
www.visionappraisal.com/databases/maine/index.htm

Franklin County *Real Estate, Deed, Lien, Judgment, Divorce, UCC Records* www.franklincountydeedsme.com
`Free & $$`   Access to recorders data index is free at www.franklincountydeedsme.com. Land index goes back to 1984; images go
back to part of 1993 (in process). For full access and to print documents, registration and fees are required.

Hancock County *Real Estate, Deed, Lien, UCC Records* www.co.hancock.me.us/ `Free & $$`
Access to the county registry of deeds database at www.registryofdeeds.com requires registration. Viewing of index back to 1790 is
free, but $1.50 per page to print document. For info see website or call 888-833-3979. Also, City of Ellsworth real estate data is free at
www.ci.ellsworth.me.us/realestatedb.html.
Property, Taxation Records `Free`   Access to Bar Harbor property data is free at
http://data.visionappraisal.com/BarHarborME/. Free registration required. Access Mount Desert assessor-
http://data.visionappraisal.com/MountDesertME/. Also, access Ellsworth property data free at
www.mygovnow.com/ellsci/Invision/assessing/index.htm or download from www.cityofellsworthme.org/reweb.txt

Kennebec County *Real Estate, Deed Records* www.kennebeccounty.org `Free & $$`   Register free and search
recorder index free at www.kennebec.me.us.landata.com. Fee for images by subscription or pay-per-view.
Property, Taxation Records `Free`   Access Winslow Town Property database free at www.winslowmaine.org/assessing.html.
Records on the Town of Waterville Assessor's database are free at http://data.visionappraisal.com/WatervilleME/. For full data, user
ID is required; registration is free. Also, search City of Augusta assessor database at http://data.visionappraisal.com/AugustaME/. Free
registration for full data. Also, search Winthrop Town data free at http://data.visionappraisal.com/WinthropME/DEFAULT.asp.

Knox County *Real Estate, Grantor/Grantee, Deed, Mortgage, Lien, Judgment, UCC Records*
www.knoxcounty.midcoast.com `Free & $$`   Search property records at mainelandrecords.com. Indexes are available from 1966
to present. Document images are available from 1966 to present; fees for images. $3.00 fee per doc, or register and pay monthly fee.
Property, Taxation Records `Free`   Search Camden, Rockland, Rockport, and South Thomaston town assessors data at
www.visionappraisal.com/databases/maine/index.htm.

Lincoln County *Real Estate, Deed Records* www.lincolncomeregofdeeds.com `Free & $$`
Search Register of Deeds indices and images back to 1954 for free at www.lincolncomeregofdeeds.com. Click on Free Access at left.
Images for a fee go back to 1/1993.
Property, Taxation Records `Free`
Search Town of Boothbay property data free at http://data.visionappraisal.com/BoothbayME/.

Oxford County *Real Estate, Grantor/Grantee, Deed, Mortgage, Lien, Judgment Records*
www.oxfordcounty.org/registry_of_deeds.htm `Free & $$`   Search recording records for the Eastern portion of the county at
https://www.mainelandrecords.com/melr/MelrApp/index.jsp. $3.00 fee per doc, or register and pay monthly fee.

Penobscot County *Real Estate, Deed Records* www.penobscotdeeds.com `Free & $$`   Search the Register of
Deeds index back to 1967 and images back to 1976 for free at www.penobscotdeeds.com. A fee is charged for copies and you may
not download with registering.
Property, Taxation Records `Free`   Search the City of Old Town real estate database for free at www.old-
town.me.us/assessor/rev.asp.

Piscataquis County *Real Estate, Grantor/Grantee, Deed, Mortgage, Lien, Judgment Records* Free & $$
Search free on Register of Deeds site at https://www.mainelandrecords.com. $3.00 fee per doc, or register and pay monthly fee plus $.50 per name search and $.25 per doc.

Sagadahoc County *Real Estate, Grantor/Grantee, Deed Records* www.sagadahocdeedsme.com $$ Register of Deeds records are online for a $300.00 per year fee plus $.50 per page to view or copy. Records go back to 1964 on Grantor/Grantee index. Images go back to 03/80. For info and registration, call Register of Deeds.
Property, Taxation Records Free Search records on the City of Bath Assessor database free at http://assessdb.cityofbath.com.

Somerset County *Real Estate, Grantor/Grantee, Deed, Mortgage, Lien, Judgment Records* Free & $$
Access real estate records free at https://www.mainelandrecords.com/melr_me005/MelrApp/index.jsp Subscription required for full data and images. Records goes back to 1956. $3.00 fee per doc, or register and pay monthly fee.

Waldo County *Real Estate, Grantor/Grantee, Deed, Mortgage, Lien, Judgment Records* $$ Access real estate records by subscription at https://www.mainelandrecords.com/melr/MelrApp/index.jsp. Index back to 1985, images back to 1985. $3.00 fee per doc, or register and pay monthly fee.

York County *Real Estate, Deed Records* www.york.me.us.landata.com/ Free & $$ Search Register of Deeds records at www.york.me.us.landata.com. Register then search basic index free; get doc copies either by sub @ $1.50 per pg or non-sub @$2.25 per page.
Property, Taxation Records Free Search Kennebunk Town data free at www.kennebunkmaine.us/index.asp; click on Dept then Assessor. Data as pdf or as spreadsheet. Also, Berwick, Cornish, Eliot, Kennebunkport, Kittery, Ogunquit, Old Orchard Beach, Saco, Wells, and York Town assessors data is free at www.visionappraisal.com/databases/maine/index.htm. Free registration required.

Maryland

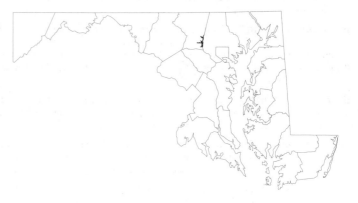

Capital: Annapolis
　　　　 Anne Arundel County
Time Zone: EST
Population: 5,618,344
# of Counties: 23

Useful State Links

Website: www.maryland.gov
Governor: www.gov.state.md.us
Attorney General: www.oag.state.md.us
State Archives: www.msa.md.gov/
State Statutes and Codes: http://mlis.state.md.us/#stat
Legislative Bill Search: http://mlis.state.md.us/#gena
Unclaimed Funds: https://interactive.marylandtaxes.com/unclaim/default.asp

Primary State Agencies

Sexual Offender Registry Free

Criminal Justice Information System, PO Box 32708, www.socem.info/ Online access is free at www.socem.info/. Search by name or ZIP Code. An interactive map is also available. *Other Options:* A printout is available of partial or complete SOR. Request must be in writing,

Incarceration Records Free

Dept of Public Safety and Correctional Services, Maryland Division of Corrections, www.dpscs.state.md.us Search inmates online at www1.dpscs.state.md.us/inmate/. The Locator may not list some short sentenced inmates who, although committed to the Commissioner of Correction, are in fact housed at Division of Pretrial and Detention Services facilities. Also, a private company offers free web access at https://www.vinelink.com/vinelink/siteInfoAction.do?siteId=21999 including state, DOC, and a few county jails.

Corporation, LP, LLP, LLC, Fictitious Name, Trade Name Free & $$

Department of Assessments and Taxation, Charter Corporation Division, www.dat.state.md.us Search for corporate name and trade name records for free at the main website (see above); also includes real estate statewide (cannot search by name) and UCC records. A Certificate of Good Standing is available online at http://sdatcert1.resiusa.org/certificate/ for the $20.00 fee. *Other Options:* This agency will release information in a bulk output format through a contactor. Obtain prices, formats, production schedules, etc. from Specprint, Inc. Contact Mr. Joe Jenkins of Specprint, Inc. at 410- 561-9600.

Trademarks/Servicemarks Free

Secretary of State, Trademarks Division, www.marylandsos.gov Online searching is available at the Internet site. Search can be by keyword in the description field, the service or product, the owner, the classification, or the mark name or keyword in the mark name. Site offers application forms to register, renew, or assign trade and service marks, and general info about registration. Click on "Trade & Service Marks" or search at www.sos.state.md.us/Registrations/Trademarks/TMSearch.htm. *Other Options:* A computer printout of all marks registered, renewed or assigned within a 3 month period is available for $.05 per trademark.

Uniform Commercial Code Free

UCC Division-Taxpayer's Services, Department of Assessments & Taxation, http://sdatcert3.resiusa.org/ucc-charter/ The Internet site above or http://sdatcert3.resiusa.org/ucc-charter/ offers free access to UCC index information. Also, there is a related site offering access to real property data for the whole state at www.dat.state.md.us/. *Other Options:* The agency has available for sale copies of public release master data files including corporation, real estate, and UCC. In addition, they can produce customized files on paper or disk. Visit the website for more information.

Sales Tax Registrations `Free`

Taxpayer Services, Revenue Administration Division, www.comp.state.md.us Using the web, one can determine if a MD sales tax account number is valid.

Workers' Compensation Records `Free & $$`

Workers' Compensation Commission, www.wcc.state.md.us Free access is provided and there is a more in-depth service available for a fee. The free Public Information is found at www.wcc.state.md.us/WFMS/public_inquiry.html. The free access is at Request for online hook-up must be in writing on letterhead. There is no search fee, but programming fees must be paid in advance. The system is open 24 hours a day to only in-state accounts. Write to the Commission at address above, care of Information Technology Division, or at 410-864-5170. *Other Options:* This agency will sell its entire database depending on the use of the purchaser. Intended use must be validated and approved. Contact the commission for further information.

Driver Records `$$`

MVA, Driver Records Unit, Rm 145, www.mva.state.md.us Under the Direct Access Record System (DARS), participants access driver and vehicle record information via an Internet connection. The system is open 24/6 to qualified and bonded individuals and businesses. Fee is $9.00 per record. Inquiries are processed interactive and require using either the driver's license number, name and date of birth, VIN or tag number. A batch system (VORS) is also available using FTP or tape cartridge. *Other Options:* Drivers may view their own record online at https://secure.marylandmva.com/emvaservices/VRR/dept.asp after obtaining a PIN. Also, under the License Monitoring System (LMS), transfers of record data to employers can occur via FTP.

Vehicle Ownership & Registration `$$`

Department of Motor Vehicles, Vehicle Registration Division, www.mva.state.md.us The state offers vehicle and ownership data over the same online network (DARS) utilized for driving record searches. Fee is $9.00 per record. Access by VIN, tag # or full name. The network is available six days a week, twenty-four hours a day to qualified bonded accounts. Email MVRSdatarequests@mdot.state.md.us for information on setting up an account.

Vital Records `$$`

Department of Health, Division of Vital Records, www.dhmh.state.md.us Records may be ordered over the web at www.vitalchek.com. Use of credit card is required.

Occupational Licensing Boards

Architect	www.dllr.state.md.us/pq/
Architectural Partnership/Corp	www.dllr.state.md.us/pq/
Attorney	www.courts.state.md.us/cpf/attylist.html
Barber	www.dllr.state.md.us/pq/
Business, Any Licensed	www.blis.state.md.us/
Charity	www.sos.state.md.us/charity/charityhome.htm
Collection Agency	https://www.dllr.state.md.us/cgi-bin/fin_reg_el/rel2/PQ_Application.cgi?calling_app=Query::PQ_main
Condominium/Timeshare	www.sos.state.md.us/Registrations/condo_TS.htm
Contractor	https://www.dllr.state.md.us/cgi-bin/ElectronicLicensing/OP_search/PQ_search.cgi?calling_app=HIC::HIC_qselect
Cosmetologist	www.dllr.state.md.us/pq/
CPA-Public Accountant	www.dllr.state.md.us/pq/
Election	www.sos.state.md.us/ElectionsInfo.htm
Electrician, Master	www.dllr.state.md.us/pq/
Electrologist	http://209.60.234.65/mdbon_weblookup/
Engineer, Examining/Professional	www.dllr.state.md.us/pq/
Extradition/Requisition	www.sos.state.md.us/Services/Extradit.htm
Finfishing, Commercial	www.mass.gov/dfwele/dmf/
Forester	www.dllr.state.md.us/pq/
Fund Raising Counsel	www.sos.state.md.us/charity/RegisterProfSol.htm
Fur Buyer	www.mass.gov/dfwele/dfw/
Gem Dealer	www.dllr.state.md.us/pq/
Grain Dealer	www.mda.state.md.us/pdf/grainbrochure2005.pdf
Home Improvement Contractor	www.dllr.state.md.us/pq/
Home Improv't Seller	https://www.dllr.state.md.us/cgi-bin/ElectronicLicensing/OP_search/PQ_search.cgi?calling_app=HIC::HIC_qselect
Home Inspector	www.dllr.state.md.us/pq/
HVACR Contractor	www.dllr.state.md.us/pq/

Interior Designer..............................www.dllr.state.md.us/pq/

Land Surveyor ....www.dllr.state.md.us/pq/

Landscape Architect ....www.dllr.state.md.us/pq/

Lead Inspectors/Contr. www.mde.state.md.us/Programs/LandPrograms/LeadCoordination/homeOwners/search/contractor.asp

Limousine Driver..............................www.psc.state.md.us/psc/

Lobbyist/Lobbyist Employer.............http://ethics.gov.state.md.us/listing.htm

Lobstering...www.mass.gov/dfwele/dmf/

Medical Doctor.................................www.mbp.state.md.us/

Mortgage Broker   https://www.dllr.state.md.us/cgi-bin/fin_reg_el/rel2/PQ_Application.cgi?calling_app=Query::PQ_main

Notary Public....................................www.sos.state.md.us/Notary/NotarySearch.htm

Nurse-RN/LPN/Assistant ....http://209.60.234.65/mdbon_weblookup/

Nursery, Plant   www.mda.state.md.us/plants-pests/plant_protection_weed_mgmt/nurseries_plant_dealers/

Nursing Occupation...........................http://209.60.234.65/mdbon_weblookup/

Optometrist.......................................www.arbo.org/index.php?action=findanoptometrist

Pardon/Commutation.........................www.sos.state.md.us/Services/Pardons.htm

Pawnbroker.......................................www.dllr.state.md.us/pq/

Pesticide-related Occupation ....www.mda.state.md.us/plants-pests/pesticide_regulation/pesticide_db.php

Pharmacist ....www.mdbop.org/verifications/index.htm

Plant Broker/Dealer   www.mda.state.md.us/plants-pests/plant_protection_weed_mgmt/nurseries_plant_dealers/

Plumber ....www.dllr.state.md.us/pq/

Polygraph Examiner ....www.mpapolygraph.org/examiners.htm

Precious Metal & Gem Dealer...........www.dllr.state.md.us/pq/

Public Accountant-CPA ....www.dllr.state.md.us/pq/

Radiation Therapy Technician...........www.mbp.state.md.us/

Real Estate Agent/Broker   https://www.dllr.state.md.us/cgi-bin/ElectronicLicensing/RE/certification/RECertification1.cgi

Real Estate Appraiser ....www.dllr.state.md.us/pq/

Respiratory Care Practitioner ....www.mbp.state.md.us/

Seafood Dealer ....www.mass.gov/dfwele/dmf/

Shellfishing, Commercial ....www.mass.gov/dfwele/dmf/

Solicitor, Professional.......................www.sos.state.md.us/charity/RegisterProfSol.htm#ps

Special Police/Railroad Police...........www.sos.state.md.us/Services/Police.htm

Subcontractor   https://www.dllr.state.md.us/cgi-bin/ElectronicLicensing/OP_search/PQ_search.cgi?calling_app=HIC::HIC_qselect

Taxi Driver ....www.psc.state.md.us/psc/

Taxicab..www.psc.state.md.us/psc/

Taxidermist.......................................www.mass.gov/dfwele/dfw/

Trapping ....www.mass.gov/dfwele/dfw/

State and Local Courts

State Court Structure: Circuit Court is the highest court of record. There is a Circuit Court with an elected clerk in each county of Maryland and Baltimore City.

The jurisdiction of the District Court includes all landlord/tenant cases, replevin actions, motor vehicle violations, misdemeanors and certain felonies. In civil cases the District Court has exclusive jurisdiction in claims for amounts up to $5,000, and concurrent jurisdiction with the circuit courts in claims for amounts above $5,000 but less than $25,000, and some District Courts' limits were raised to $30,000 in late 2007. The jurisdiction of the court in criminal cases is concurrent with the Circuit Court for offenses in which the penalty may be confinement for three years or more or a fine of $2,500 or more; or offenses which are felonies. The Circuit Court handles probate in only Montgomery and Harford counties. In other counties, probate is handled by the Register of Wills and is a county, not a court, function.

Statewide Court Online Access: The Appellate opinions are available from www.courts.state.md.us/opinions.html. There is a free seach of dockets from all the the trial courts at http://casesearch.courts.state.md.us/inquiry/inquiry-index.jsp. **The search includes all district courts and circuit courts.** Records are updated daily, but note that case information from Montgomery and Prince George's counties are always lagging one day behind. All case information may be searched by party name or case number.

Bulk subscription data of civil record information can be requested for a fee using a form found at www.courts.state.md.us/district/forms/acct/dca107.pdf. Plans are underway for subscribing parties to access statewide Case Search bulk data and data extracts through a standards-based interface in XML format. Also, there is an attorney Calendar Service that displays information related to an Attorney's trial and hearing schedule such as case number, attorney name, trial or hearing date, defendant name, time, room, etc.

❖ Statewide Access Offered For All Trial Courts – Read Above ❖

Note: No individual Maryland courts offer online access.

Recorders, Assessors, and Other Sites of Note

Recording Office Organization: 23 counties and one independent city; 24 recording offices. The recording officer is the Clerk of the Circuit Court. Baltimore City has a recording office separate from the County of Baltimore. Watch for ZIP Codes that include both the city and the county. All tax liens are filed with the county Clerk of Circuit Court.

Online Access Note: Search statewide property records data free at http://sdatcert3.resiusa.org/rp_rewrite/. There is no name searching. Also, the Maryland State Dept. of Planning offers MDPropertyview with property maps/parcels and assessments on the web or CD-rom. Registration required; visit http://www.mdp.state.md.us/tax_mos.htm or call 410-767-4614 or 410-767-4474. There is no name searching. Also, the state launched an experimental Digital Image Retrieval System for Land Record Indices at www.mdlandrec.net/msa/stagser/s1700/s1741/cfm/index.cfm.

The Maryland Judiciary, the 24 elected Maryland Court Clerks, and Maryland State Archives have joined in partnership to provide up-to-date access to all verified land record instruments in Maryland. This service is currently being provided free to all those interested in testing the system. Users are encouraged to provide feedback and inform the Maryland State Archives of any problems encountered.

Also, vendors provide online access in several places. County tax records are at www.taxrecords.com. Land survey, condominium, and survey plats are available free by county at www.plats.net. Use username "Plato" and password "plato#". No name searching.

❖ Statewide Access Offered For All Districts – Read Above.

Below are Additional Maryland Sites. ❖

Charles County *Property, Taxation Records*   Free   Access to property tax data is free at www.charlescounty.org/treas/taxes/acctinquiry/selection.jsp. Also, tax sale list search free at www.charlescounty.org/treas/taxes/taxsale/selection.jsp.

Dorchester County *Property, Taxation Records*   Free   Access to free property tax information, go to http://ww2.paragon-csi.com/dorchester-MD/. Must have property ID, address or map, grid, and parcel codes to look at them

Montgomery County *Property, Taxation Records*   Free   Access to the assessor's property tax account database is free at https://www.montgomerycountymd.gov/apps/tax/index.asp.

Prince George's County *Real Property, Deed, Land Survey/Plat Records*   www.co.pg.md.us   Free & $$
Land records online from www.mdlandrec.net/msa/stagser/s1700/s1741/cfm/index.cfm, and www.plats.net (use username "Plato" and password "plato#") and MDPropertyview at www.mdp.state.md.us/data/mdview.htm.
Property, Taxation Records   Free   Search real property data free at http://sdatcert3.resiusa.org/rp_rewrite. No name searching. See Clerk of Circuit Court recording office for online property search options. Also, search the Treasurer's property tax inquiry system at http://tax-acct-info.goprincegeorgescounty.com/PropertyTaxes/TaxInquiry.aspx.

Massachusetts

Capital: Boston
　　　　Suffolk County
Time Zone: EST
Population: 6,449,755
# of Counties: 14

Useful State Links

Website: www.mass.gov/gov
Governor: http://mass.gov/gov
Attorney General: www.ago.state.ma.us
State Archives: www.sec.state.ma.us/arc/
State Statutes and Codes: www.mass.gov/legis/laws/mgl/index.htm
Legislative Bill Search: www.mass.gov/legis/ltsform.htm
Unclaimed Funds: http://abpweb.tre.state.ma.us/abp/frmNewSrch.aspx

Primary State Agencies

Criminal Records $$

Criminal History Systems Board, CORI, www.mass.gov/chsb/ Certified agencies may order $15.00 records online. However this is limited to only true employers. Consumer Reporting Agencies that represent employers are not currently permitted to use the online system, but plans are underway to permit access.

Sexual Offender Registry Free

Sex Offender Registry Board, www.mass.gov/sorb/ Search free from links found at home page. Pursuant to M.G.L. C. 6, §§ 178C - 178P, individuals who appear on the web page have been designated a Level 3 Sex Offender by the Sex Offender Registry Board.

Incarceration Records Free

Massachusetts Executive Office of Public Safety, Department Of Corrections, www.mass.gov/doc/ No searching online is offered by this agency; however this agency promotes a private company offers free web access to DOC offenders at https://www.vinelink.com/vinelink/siteInfoAction.do?siteId=20000.

Corporation, Trademarks/Servicemarks, LLP, LP, LLC Free

Secretary of the Commonwealth, Corporation Division, www.sec.state.ma.us/cor/coridx.htm There is a free Internet lookup from the website. This site also provides UCC information. *Other Options:* Bulk sale on CD is available.

Uniform Commercial Code, State Tax Liens Free

UCC Division, Secretary of the Commonwealth, www.sec.state.ma.us/cor/corpweb/corucc/uccmain.htm There is free access to record index from http://corp.sec.state.ma.us/uccfiling/uccSearch/Default.aspx. Search by name, organization or file number. *Other Options:* Microfiche may be purchased.

Driver Records-Registry $$

Registry of Motor Vehicles, Driver Control Unit, www.mass.gov/rmv/ Access is only available for the insurance industry. Fee is $6.00 per record. Call the above number for further details.

Driver Records-Insurance $$

Merit Rating Board, Attn: Detailed Driving History Records, www.mass.gov/mrb An online service is available to authorized insurance companies and agents to view driving records maintained by the MRB. This service is available through the RMV Uninsured Motorist System at www.mass.gov/rmv/ums/. A FTP site is used for file transfer between the MRB and insurers. The MRB transfers SDIP driving history record information to insurers. The information is used to adjust automobile insurance rates. Per statute, this method is not available to the general public.

Vehicle Ownership & Registration `Free`

Registry of Motor Vehicles, Document Control, www.mass.gov/rmv/ Searching is limited to Massachusetts based insurance companies and agents for the purpose of issuing or renewing insurance. This system is not open to the public. There is no fee, but line charges will be incurred.

Vital Records `$$`

Registry of Vital Records and Statistics, www.mass.gov/dph/bhsre/rvr/vrcopies.htm Orders can be placed via a state designated vendor. Go to www.vitalchek.com. Extra fees are involved.

Occupational Licensing Boards

Adjuster, Fire Loss	www.mass.gov/doi/Producer/Producer_list.html
Adoption Center	www.eec.state.ma.us/adoptSearchResult.aspx?city=&zipcode=&type=ADOPT
Aesthetician	http://license.reg.state.ma.us/pubLic/licque.asp?color=red&Board=HD
Alarm Installer, Burglar/Fire	http://license.reg.state.ma.us/pubLic/licque.asp?color=red&Board=EL
Ambulance Service	http://db.state.ma.us/dph/amb/amb_search.asp
Amusement Device Inspector	www.mass.gov/dps/inspectors.htm
Appraiser, MVR Damage	www.mass.gov/doi/Producer/Producer_list.html
Architect	http://license.reg.state.ma.us/pubLic/licque.asp?color=red&Board=AR
Asbestos/Lead Abatement Vocation	www.mass.gov/?pageID=elwdsubtopic&L=4&L0=Home&L1=Workers+and+Unions&L2=Licensing+and+Certification&L3=Asbestos+Program&sid=Elwd
Athletic Trainer	http://license.reg.state.ma.us/pubLic/licque.asp?color=red&Board=AH
Attorney	http://massbbo.org/bbolookup.php
Audiologist	http://license.reg.state.ma.us/pubLic/licque.asp?color=red&Board=SP
Auto Repair Shop	www.aib.org/BDYSHOP/bdshind.htm
Automobile Sales Financer	www.mass.gov/Eoca/docs/dob/mvlist.xls
Bank & Savings Institution	http://db.state.ma.us/dob/in-choose.asp
Bank, Cooperative	http://db.state.ma.us/dob/in-choose.asp
Barber/Barber Shop	http://license.reg.state.ma.us/pubLic/licque.asp?color=red&Board=BR
Boiler Engineer	www.mass.gov/dps/LIC_SRCH.HTM
Boilers/Pressure Vessel Inspector	www.mass.gov/dps/LIC_SRCH.HTM
Brokerage Firm	www.finra.org/InvestorInformation/InvestorProtection/p005882
Building Inspector/Local Inspector	www.mass.gov/bbrs/inf_cert_build_officials.pdf
Building Producer	www.mass.gov/bbrs/mfg98.pdf
Check Casher	www.mass.gov/Eoca/docs/dob/cclist.xls
Check Casher/Seller	http://db.state.ma.us/dob/licenseelist.asp
Chiropractor	http://license.reg.state.ma.us/pubLic/licque.asp?color=red&Board=CH
Collection Agency	http://db.state.ma.us/dob/licenseelist.asp
Concrete Technician	www.mass.gov/?pageID=eopsterminal&L=3&L0=Home&L1=Public+Safety+Agencies&L2=Massachusetts+Department+of+Public+Safety&sid=Eeops&b=terminalcontent&f=dps_license_lookup&csid=Eeops
Construction Supervisor	www.mass.gov/bbrs/cslsearch.htm
Construction Supervisor, Resid'l	www.mass.gov/bbrs/programs.htm
Consumer Credit Grantor	http://db.state.ma.us/dob/licenseelist.asp
Contractor, Home Improvement	www.mass.gov/bbrs/Hicsearch.htm
Cosmetolog'st/Manicur't/Aesthetic'n	http://license.reg.state.ma.us/pubLic/licque.asp?color=red&Board=HD
Credit Union	http://db.state.ma.us/dob/in-choose.asp
Day Care Center	www.eec.state.ma.us/oo_licensing.aspx
Debt Collector	www.mass.gov/Eoca/docs/dob/dclist.xls
Dentist/Dental Hygienist	http://license.reg.state.ma.us/pubLic/licque.asp?color=red&Board=DN
Electrician	http://license.reg.state.ma.us/pubLic/licque.asp?color=red&Board=EL
Electrologist	http://license.reg.state.ma.us/pubLic/licque.asp?color=red&Board=ET
Embalmer	http://license.reg.state.ma.us/pubLic/licque.asp?color=red&Board=EM
Emergency Medical Technician	http://db.state.ma.us/dph/emtcert/cert_search.asp
EMS Training Institution	www.mass.gov/dph/oems/emt/institutes.htm
Engineer	http://license.reg.state.ma.us/pubLic/licque.asp?color=red&Board=EN
Engineers/Fireman School	www.mass.gov/dps/schools.htm

Family Child Care Provider.............. www.eec.state.ma.us/childCareSearchResult.aspx?city=&zipcode=&type=FCC
Fire Sprinkler Contractor/Fitter .... www.mass.gov/dps/LIC_SRCH.HTM
Fireman, 1st/2nd Class .... www.mass.gov/dps/LIC_SRCH.HTM
Foreign Transmittal Agency .... http://db.state.ma.us/dob/licenseelist.asp
Foster Care Provider......................... www.eec.state.ma.us/fosterSearchResult.aspx?city=&zipcode=&type=FOSTER
Funeral Director................................ http://license.reg.state.ma.us/pubLic/licque.asp?color=red&Board=EM
Gas Fitter .... http://license.reg.state.ma.us/pubLic/licque.asp?color=red&Board=PL
Health Insurer .... www.mass.gov/doi/Companies/companies_lists.html
Health Profession, Allied.................. http://license.reg.state.ma.us/pubLic/licque.asp?color=red&Board=AH
HMO .... www.mass.gov/doi/Consumer/CSS_health_HMO_Licensed.HTML
Hoisting Machinery Operator .... www.mass.gov/dps/LIC_SRCH.HTM
Home Improvement Contractor .... www.mass.gov/bbrs/Hicsearch.htm
Home Improvement Supervisor
       www.mass.gov/?pageID=eopsterminal&L=3&L0=Home&L1=Public+Safety+Agencies&L2=Mass
       achusetts+Department+of+Public+Safety&sid=Eeops&b=terminalcontent&f=dps_license_lookup&csid=Eeops
Home Inspector .... http://license.reg.state.ma.us/pubLic/hi_biz/v_list_hi.asp
Inspection Agency, 3rd Party .... www.mass.gov/bbrs/MFB.htm
Insurance Advisor/Adjuster/Broker... www.mass.gov/doi/Producer/Producer_list.html
Insurance Premium Financer .... http://db.state.ma.us/dob/licenseelist.asp
Insurance, Domestic/Foreign Firm .... www.mass.gov/doi/Companies/companies_lists.html
Investment Advisor www.finra.org/InvestorInformation/InvestorProtection/p005882
Land Surveyor .... http://license.reg.state.ma.us/pubLic/licque.asp?color=red&Board=EN
Landscape Architect .... http://license.reg.state.ma.us/pubLic/licque.asp?color=red&Board=LA
Loan Company/Loan Servicer .... www.mass.gov/Eoca/docs/dob/lslist.xls
Lobbyist/Lobbyist Employer............. www.sec.state.ma.us/lobbyist/LobbyistSearch/PublicSearch.asp?action=P
Lumber Producer, Native .... www.mass.gov/bbrs/lumber.pdf
Mammography Radiologic Tech'g't . http://db.state.ma.us/dph/Radtechs/
Manufactured Building Producer....... www.mass.gov/bbrs/MFB.htm
Marriage & Family Therap'st http://license.reg.state.ma.us/pubLic/licque.asp?query=personal&color=red&board=MH
Medical Doctor.................................. http://profiles.massmedboard.org/MA-Physician-Profile-Find-Doctor.asp
Mental Health Counselor   http://license.reg.state.ma.us/pubLic/licque.asp?query=personal&color=red&board=MH
Mortgage Broker .... www.mass.gov/Eoca/docs/dob/mblist.xls
Mortgage Broker/Lender .... www.mass.gov/Eoca/docs/dob/mclist.xls
Mortgage Lender .... www.mass.gov/Eoca/docs/dob/mllist.xls
Motor Vehicle Sales Financer .... http://db.state.ma.us/dob/licenseelist.asp
Notary Public..................................... www.mass.gov/legal/notaries.html
Nuclear Plant Engineer/Oper'tor .... www.mass.gov/dps/LIC_SRCH.HTM
Nurse, LPN/RN/Midwife................... http://license.reg.state.ma.us/pubLic/licque.asp?color=red&Board=RN
Nursing Home Admin/Health Ofc ..... http://license.reg.state.ma.us/public/licque.asp?color=blue
Nursing Home Psychologist/Provider http://license.reg.state.ma.us/public/licque.asp?color=blue
Occupational Therapist/Assistant ...... http://license.reg.state.ma.us/pubLic/licque.asp?color=red&Board=AH
Oil Burner Technician/Contr. .... www.mass.gov/dps/LIC_SRCH.HTM
Optician   ... ...   http://license.reg.state.ma.us/pubLic/licque.asp?query=personal&color=red&board=DO
Optician, Dispensing .... http://license.reg.state.ma.us/pubLic/licque.asp?color=red&Board=DO
Optometrist.. http://license.reg.state.ma.us/pubLic/licque.asp?color=red&Board=OP
P&C Insurance Agency .... www.mass.gov/doi/Producer/Producer_list.html
Perfusionist....................................... http://license.reg.state.ma.us/pubLic/licque.asp?color=red&Board=PF
Pharmacist .... http://license.reg.state.ma.us/pubLic/licque.asp?color=red&Board=PH
Physical Therapist/Assistant.............. http://license.reg.state.ma.us/pubLic/licque.asp?color=red&Board=AH
Physician Assistant
   www.mass.gov/?pageID=eohhs2subtopic&L=5&L0=Home&L1=Provider&L2=Certification%2c+Licensure%2c+
   and+Registration&L3=Occupational+and+Professional&L4=Physician+Assistants&sid=Eeohhs2
Pipefitter... www.mass.gov/dps/LIC_SRCH.HTM
Pipefitter School .... www.mass.gov/dps/schools.htm
Plumber .... http://license.reg.state.ma.us/pubLic/licque.asp?color=red&Board=PL
Podiatrist... http://license.reg.state.ma.us/pubLic/licque.asp?color=red&Board=PD
Polygraph Examiner www.polygraphplace.com/docs/c-15-s-Massachusetts-examiners.html

Psychologist, Educational   http://license.reg.state.ma.us/pubLic/licque.asp?query=personal&color=red&board=MH
Public Accountant-CPA .... http://license.reg.state.ma.us/pubLic/licque.asp?color=red&Board=PA
Radiation Therapy/Radiologic Tech .. http://db.state.ma.us/dph/Radtechs/
Radio & TV Repair Technician .... http://license.reg.state.ma.us/pubLic/licque.asp?color=red&Board=TV
Radiographer/Radiologic Techn'g'st. http://db.state.ma.us/dph/Radtechs/
Real Estate Agent/Broker/Sales .... http://license.reg.state.ma.us/pubLic/licque.asp?color=red&Board=RE
Real Estate Appraiser .... http://license.reg.state.ma.us/pubLic/licque.asp?color=red&Board=RA
Refrigeration Technician School .... www.mass.gov/dps/schools.htm
Refrigeration Technician/Contr. .... www.mass.gov/dps/LIC_SRCH.HTM
Rehabilitation Therapist   http://license.reg.state.ma.us/pubLic/licque.asp?query=personal&color=red&board=MH
Residential Care, Youth .... www.eec.state.ma.us/oo_adop_res.aspx
Respiratory Care Therapist .... http://license.reg.state.ma.us/pubLic/licque.asp?color=red&Board=RC
Retail Installment Financer .... http://db.state.ma.us/dob/licenseelist.asp
Sales Finance Company .... www.mass.gov/Eoca/docs/dob/mvlist.xls
Sanitarian .... http://license.reg.state.ma.us/pubLic/licque.asp?color=red&Board=SA
School Bus .... http://db.state.ma.us/dpu/qorders/frmTransportation.asp
Securities Agent/Broker/Dealer www.finra.org/InvestorInformation/InvestorProtection/p005882
Social Worker .... http://license.reg.state.ma.us/pubLic/licque.asp?color=red&Board=SW
Speech-Language Pathologist .... http://license.reg.state.ma.us/pubLic/licque.asp?color=red&Board=SP
Sprinkler Fitting School .... www.mass.gov/dps/schools.htm
Surplus Lines Broker .... www.mass.gov/doi/Producer/Producer_list.html
Trauma Center .... www.facs.org/trauma/verified.html
Trust Company .... http://db.state.ma.us/dob/in-choose.asp
Veterinarian .... http://license.reg.state.ma.us/pubLic/licque.asp?color=red&Board=VT
Water Supply Facility Operator .... http://license.reg.state.ma.us/pubLic/licque.asp?color=red&Board=DW

State and Local Courts

State Court Structure: The various court sections are called "Departments." While Superior Courts and District Courts have concurrent jurisdiction in civil cases, the practice is to assign cases less than $25,000 to the District Court and those over $25,000 to Superior Court. In addition to misdemeanors, District Courts and Boston Municipal Courts have jurisdiction over certain minor felonies. Eviction cases may be filed at a county District Court or at the regional "Housing Court." A case may be moved from a District Court to a Housing Court, but never the reverse. Housing Courts also hear misdemeanor "Code Violation" cases and prelims for these. There are five Housing Court Regions - Boston (Suffolk County), Worcester (County), Southeast (Plymouth and Bristol Counties), Northeast (Essex County), and Western (Berkshire, Franklin, Hampden and Hampshire Counties). The Southeast Housing Court has three branches - Brockton, Fall River, and New Bedford.

There are 15 Probate and Family Court locations in Massachusetts - one per county plus two in Bristol.

Statewide Court Online Access: Opinions from the Supreme Court and Appellate Courts can be found at http://massreports.com. Online access to records on the statewide Trial Courts Information Center website with both criminal and civil superior court cases is available BUT to attorneys and law firms ONLY at www.ma-trialcourts.org/tcic/welcome.jsp. Access is free but BBO number is a requisite. Middlesex, Suffolk, Worcester indices go back to 1990s; other counties go back to active cases as of 2000-2001. The system plan is to have all courts online by early 2009. For more information, contact Peter Nylin by email at nylin_p@jud.state.ma.us or Victoria Palmarcci at victoria.palmacci@jud.state.ma.us.

> ❖ **Statewide Access Offered For All Trial Courts to Limited Parties –**
> **Read Above** ❖

Note: No individual Massachusetts courts offer online access.

Recorders, Assessors, and Other Sites of Note

Recording Office Organization: 14 counties, 21 recording offices. Berkshire and Bristol counties each have three recording offices. Essex, Middlesex, and Worcester counties each have two recording offices. Cities/towns bearing the same name as a county are Barnstable, Essex, Franklin, Hampden, Nantucket, Norfolk, Plymouth, and Worcester. Federal tax liens on personal property are filed with the U.S. District Court in Boston as well as with the towns/cities. State tax liens on personal property are filed with the Town/City Clerk or the Tax Collector. All tax liens against real estate are filed with the county Register of Deeds.

Online Access Note: A large number of towns and several counties offer online access to assessor records via the internet for no charge. Also, a private vendor has placed assessor records from a number of towns online at www.visionappraisal.com/databases/mass/index.htm

> **Editor's Tip:** Towns and cities that offer online access are listed under their county location.

Barnstable County *Real Estate, Deed, Lien Records* www.bcrd.co.barnstable.ma.us `Free & $$`
Access to County records is free at http://199.232.150.242/ALIS/WW400R.PGM. Search for free, but to print requires a $50 annual fee. Records date back to 1940. Lending agency data is available.

> **Barnstable Town** *Property, Taxation Records* `Free` Access town assessor records free at www.town.barnstable.ma.us/vsapps20/propertylookup08/default.aspx. Email questions or comments to webadm@town.barnstable.ma.us or call the Assessing Dept. at 508-862-4022.

> **Bourne Town** *Property, Taxation Records* `Free` Access to property taxes free go to www.townofbourne.com/

> **Brewster Town** *Property, Taxation Records* `Free` Access to assessors' property data at www.town.brewster.ma.us/content/category/9/71/97/. Requires free registration, username and password.

> **Chatham Town** *Property, Taxation Records* `Free` Free access to assessor database at http://data.visionappraisal.com/ChathamMA/.

> **Dennis Town** *Property, Taxation Records* `Free` Access to assessor property records is free at http://townofdennis.bonsailogic.com/.

> **Eastham Town** *Property, Taxation Records* `Free` Assessor's online database of property card data is free with registration at www.assessedvalues.com/index.zhtml?jurcode=86. Signup online or contact the Assessor's Office 508-240-5900 x215.

> **Falmouth Town** *Property, Taxation Records* `Free` Access property data free at http://falmouth.patriotproperties.com/default.asp.

> **Mashpee Town** *Property, Taxation Records* `Free` Search Town of Mashpee Assessor database free at www.assessedvalues.com/index.zhtml?jurcode=172,

> **Orleans Town** *Property, Taxation Records* `Free` Search current assessment data free at www.town.orleans.ma.us/~orleans/cgi-bin/webdata_ass.pl?cgifunction=user,

> **Provincetown Town** *Property, Taxation Records* `Free` Records on the Provincetown Assessor database including sales are free at www.provincetown-ma.gov/assessor.html.

> **Wellfleet Town** *Property, Taxation Records* `Free` Access to property assessment records for free at www.assessedvalues.com/index.zhtml?jurcode=318

> **Yarmouth Town** *Property, Taxation Records* `Free` Records on the Assessor's database are free at http://data.visionappraisal.com/yarmouthma. Free registration for full data. Non-registered users can access a limited data.

Berkshire County *Real Estate, Judgment, Deed, Lien, Judgment, Will Records* www.berkshiresouthdeeds.com
`Free` Access to Southern District Recorder's records is free at www.masslandrecords.com/malr/controller; records date back to 1971. Searchable indices include recorded land, plans, registered land. Lending agency data available. Also, search Register of Deeds Records for all Berkshire districts free at www.masslandrecords.com. Click on appropriate Division on map.

> **Alford Town** *Property, Taxation Records* `Free` Access assessor rolls and property sales free at http://csc-ma.us/AlfordPubAcc/jsp/Home.jsp.

Becket Town *Property, Taxation Records* `Free` Access to parcel information and maps for free go to www.townofbecket.org/Public_Documents/BecketMA_BComm/assessorboard

Egremont Town *Property, Taxation Records* `Free` Access assessor rolls and property sales free at http://csc-ma.us/PropertyContent/jsp/Home.jsp?Page=1. Select Egremont Town.

Great Barrington Town *Property, Taxation Records* `Free` Access assessor rolls and property salesfree at http://csc-ma.us/PropertyContent/jsp/Home.jsp?Page=1.

Hinsdale Town *Property, Taxation Records* `Free` Access assessor rolls and property sales free at http://csc-ma.us/PropertyContent/jsp/Home.jsp?Page=1.

Lee Town *Property, Taxation Records* `Free` Access assessor rolls and property sales free at http://csc-ma.us/PropertyContent/jsp/Home.jsp?Page=1.

Lenox Town *Property, Taxation Records* `Free` Access and search assessor's data free at www.assessedvalues.com/search.zhtml?jurcode=152.

Otis Town *Property, Taxation Records* `Free` Search town assessor database at http://data.visionappraisal.com/OtisMA/. Free registration and username required.

Richmond Town *Property, Taxation Records* `Free` Access assessor rolls and property sales free at http://csc-ma.us/PropertyContent/jsp/Home.jsp?Page=1.

Sheffield Town *Property, Taxation Records* `Free` Access assessor rolls and property sales free at http://csc-ma.us/PropertyContent/jsp/Home.jsp?Page=1.

Windsor Town *Property, Taxation Records* `Free` Access assessor rolls and property sales free at http://csc-ma.us/PropertyContent/jsp/Home.jsp?Page=1.

Bristol County *Real Estate, Deed, Lien, Judgment, Death Records* www.fallriverdeeds.com `Free & $$`
Access to County records requires a $100 set up fee and $.50 per minute of use. All three districts are on this system; the record dates vary by district. Lending agency data is available. For info, contact Sherrilynn at 508-993-2605 x17. Real Estate searches found at www.newbedforddeeds.com/mason/main/search/.

Attleboro City *Property, Taxation Records* `Free` Property data available free at www.cityofattleboro.us/assessor/ .

Berkley Town *Property, Taxation Records* `Free` Access assessor rolls and property sales free at http://csc-ma.us/PropertyContent/jsp/Home.jsp?Page=1. Click on Berkley Town.

Dartmouth Town *Property, Taxation Records* `Free` Search the town assessor database at http://data.visionappraisal.com/DartmouthMA/. Free registration for full data.

Dighton Town *Property, Taxation Records* `Free` Access assessor rolls and property sales free at http://csc-ma.us/PropertyContent/jsp/Home.jsp?Page=1.

Easton Town *Vital Records Records* www.easton.ma.us `Free` Access to Family Vital Records from 1725-1843 for free at www.easton.ma.us/Directory/townclerk/TownClerkFS.htm

Fall River City *Property, Taxation Records* `Free` Access property data free at http://fallriver.patriotproperties.com/default.asp.

Freetown Town *Property, Taxation Records* `Free` Access property data free at http://assessedvalues.com/search.zhtml?jurcode=102.

Mansfield Town *Property, Taxation Records* `Free` Search town assessor database at http://data.visionappraisal.com/MansfieldMA/. Free registration for full data.

New Bedford City *Property, Taxation Records* `Free` Access to the assessor property database is free at www.newbedford-ma.gov/Assessors/RealProperty/RealpropertyLookup.html.

North Attleborough Town *Property, Taxation Records* `Free` Search the town assessor database at http://data.visionappraisal.com/NorthAttleboroMA/. Free registration for full data.

Raynham Town *Property, Taxation Records* `Free` Access the Online Property Viewer free at http://host.appgeo.com/raynham/. Also, access to property data to be available free on a private site at www.appraisalresource.com/OnlineDatabases.aspx.

Seekonk Town *Property, Taxation Records* `Free` Access assessor rolls and property sales free at http://csc-ma.us/PropertyContent/jsp/Home.jsp?Page=1.

Somerset Town *Property, Taxation Records* Free Access assessor rolls and property sales free at http://csc-ma.us/PropertyContent/jsp/Home.jsp?Page=1. Select Somerset Town.

Swansea Town *Property, Taxation Records* Free Access tassessor rolls and property sales free at http://csc-ma.us/PropertyContent/jsp/Home.jsp?Page=1. Select Swansea Town.

Taunton City *Property, Taxation Records* Free Access assessor data free at http://data.visionappraisal.com/TauntonMA/.

Dukes County *Real Estate, Deed, Lien, Judgment Records* http://dukescounty.org Free Access to Registry of Deeds data is free at www.masslandrecords.com. Select Dukes County on map.
Property, Taxation Records Free Access Assessor's database free at http://data.visionappraisal.com/EdgartownMA/DEFAULT.asp

Edgartown Town *Property, Taxation Records* Free Search the Town assessor's database at http://data.visionappraisal.com/EdgartownMA. Free registration for full data.

Oak Bluffs Town *Property, Taxation Records* Free Search the town assessor database at http://data.visionappraisal.com/OakBluffsMA/. Free registration for full data.

Tisbury Town *Property, Taxation Records* Free Search the town assessor database at http://data.visionappraisal.com/TisburyMA/. Free registration for full data.

West Tisbury Town *Property, Taxation Records* Free Access assessor data at http://data.visionappraisal.com/WestTisburyMA/. Free registration for full data.

Essex County (Northern District) *Real Estate, Grantor/Grantee, Deed, Lien Records*
www.lawrencedeeds.com Free Search the recorder database for free at http://72.72.82.242/alis/ww400r . Also see Andover Town and Essex County Southern District.

Essex County (Southern District) *Real Estate, Grantor/Grantee, Deed, Lien Records* www.salemdeeds.com
Free Records on the Essex County South Registry of Deeds database are free at www.salemdeeds.com/goget.asp. Click on "Deeds online". Images start 1/1992; records back to 1/1984. Search by grantee/grantor, town & date, street, or book & page. Search the recorder database for free at www.lawrencedeeds.com/dsSearch.asp. Also see Andover Town and Essex County Northern District.

Amesbury Town *Property, Taxation Records* Free Search the town assessor data at http://data.visionappraisal.com/AmesburyMA/. Free registration for full data.

Andover Town *Property, Taxation Records* Free Property tax records on the Assessor's database are free at http://andoverma.gov/assessors/values.php.

Beverly City *Property, Taxation Records* Free Access city property data free at http://beverly.patriotproperties.com/default.asp.

Boxford Town *Property, Taxation Records* Free Tax roll data on statewide website, see www.latax.state.la.us/TaxRoll_ParishSelect.asp.

Danvers Town *Property, Taxation Records* Free Access property data free at http://danvers.patriotproperties.com/default.asp.

Georgetown Town *Property, Taxation Records* Free Free access to assessor database at http://data.visionappraisal.com/GeorgetownMA. Registration required.

Haverhill City *Property, Taxation Records* Free Access property data free at http://haverhill.patriotproperties.com/default.asp.

Ipswich Town *Property, Taxation Records* Free Access property data free at http://ipswich.patriotproperties.com/default.asp.

Lynn City *Property, Taxation Records* Free Access property data free at http://lynn.patriotproperties.com/default.asp.

Lynnfield Town *Property, Taxation Records* Free Access property data free at http://lynnfield.patriotproperties.com/default.asp.

Manchester-by-the-Sea Town *Property, Taxation Records* Free Search the property assessment data at http://manchester.patriotproperties.com/default.asp.

Marblehead Town *Property, Taxation Records* Free Access property data free at http://marblehead.patriotproperties.com/default.asp?br=exp&vr=6.

Methuen City *Property, Taxation Records* `Free` Search the property assessment data free at http://host229.ci.methuen.ma.us.

Nahant Town *Property, Taxation Records* `Free` Access property data free at http://nahant.patriotproperties.com/default.asp.

Newbury Town *Property, Taxation Records* `Free` Access property tax data free at http://newbury.patriotproperties.com/default.asp.

Newburyport City *Property, Taxation Records* `Free` Search the city assessor database at http://data.visionappraisal.com/NewBURYPORTMA/. Free registration for full data.

North Andover Town *Property, Taxation Records* `Free` Access assessor rolls and property sales free at http://csc-ma.us/PropertyContent/jsp/Home.jsp?Page=1.

Peabody City *Property, Taxation Records* `Free` Access property data free at http://host.appgeo.com/PeabodyMA/

Rowley Town *Property, Taxation Records* `Free` Search the town assessor data at http://data.visionappraisal.com/RowleyMA/. Free registration for full data.

Salem City *Property, Taxation Records* `Free` Search property data by location or parcel ID for free at www.salem.com/Pages/SalemMA_WebDocs/maps but no name searching. Also, access property data free at http://salem.patriotproperties.com/default.asp. No name searching.

Salisbury Town *Property, Taxation Records* `Free` Access property data free at http://salisbury.patriotproperties.com/default.asp.

Saugus Town *Property, Taxation Records* `Free` Access assessor rolls and property sales free at http://csc-ma.us/PropertyContent/jsp/Home.jsp?Page=1.

Swampscott Town *Property, Taxation Records* `Free` Access property data free at http://swampscott.patriotproperties.com/default.asp.

Franklin County *Real Estate, Deed, Lien, Judgment Records* http://franklindeeds.com, or www.masslandrecords.com `Free` Access to Registry of Deeds data is free at www.masslandrecords.com. Select Franklin County on map.

Bernardston Town *Property, Taxation Records* `Free` Access assessor rolls and property sales free at http://csc-ma.us/PropertyContent/jsp/Home.jsp?Page=1. Select Bernardston Town.

Charlemont Town *Property, Taxation Records* `Free` Access assessor rolls and property sales free at http://csc-ma.us/PropertyContent/jsp/Home.jsp?Page=1.

Deerfield Town *Property, Taxation Records* `Free` Access property data free at http://deerfield.patriotproperties.com/default.asp.

Franklin Town *Property, Taxation Records* `Free` Access property data free at http://franklin.patriotproperties.com/default.asp.

Greenfield Town *Property, Taxation Records* `Free` Access the property search database free at http://75.147.40.237/Assessors/Permitsearch.asp.

Heath Town *Property, Taxation Records* `Free` Access assessor rolls and property sales free at http://csc-ma.us/PropertyContent/jsp/Home.jsp?Page=1. Select Heath Town.

Monroe Town *Property, Taxation Records* `Free` Access assessor rolls and property sales free at http://csc-ma.us/PropertyContent/jsp/Home.jsp?Page=1.

Montague Town *Property, Taxation Records* `Free` Access property and assessment data free at http://montague.patriotproperties.com/default.asp?br=exp&vr=6.

Hampden County *Real Estate, Deed, Lien Records* http://registryofdeeds.co.hampden.ma.us `Free & $$` Access to the county index of land records is free or via subscription at http://204.213.242.147/alis/ww400r.pgm. Images can be viewed free, but cannot be printed unless you subscribe. Access to images via dial-up or web requires a $100 annual fee and $.50 per minute of use. Records go back to 1962. Lending agency info is available. Searchable indexes are bankruptcy (from PACER), unregistered land site, and registered land site. For info, contact Mary Caron at 413-755-1722 x121.

Agawam Town *Property, Taxation Records* `Free` Access Property Assessment Data free at http://agawam.patriotproperties.com/default.asp.

Blandford Town *Property, Taxation Records* `Free` Access property data free at www.townofblandford.org/search.aspx#Results.

Chester Town *Property, Taxation Records* `Free` Access assessor rolls and property sales free at http://csc-ma.us/PropertyContent/jsp/Home.jsp?Page=1. Select Chester Town.

Holland Town *Property, Taxation Records* `Free` Access assessor data free at http://data.visionappraisal.com/HollandMA/search.asp.

Longmeadow Town *Property, Taxation Records* `Free` Access to tax records is at http://data.visionappraisal.com/LONGMEADOWMA/. Free registration for full data.

Southwick Town *Property, Taxation Records* `Free` Search the town assessor database at http://data.visionappraisal.com/SouthwickMA/. Free registration for full data.

Springfield City *Tax Lien Records* www.springfieldcityhall.com/COS/ `Free` Search city properties/owners with tax liens free at www.springfieldcityhall.com/finance/index.php?id=tax-liens *Property, Taxation Records* `Free` Access to city assessor property valuations is free at www.springfieldcityhall.com/finance/assr-search.0.html. Also, search the city GIS-mapping site for property data at http://www2.springfieldcityhall.com/gis/ but no name searching.

Tolland Town *Property, Taxation Records* `Free` Access property data in pdf format free at www.tolland-ma.gov/Public_Documents/TollandMA_Assessor/property_lookup. Also, access assessor rolls and property sales free at http://csc-ma.us/PropertyContent/jsp/Home.jsp?Page=1.

West Springfield Town *Property, Taxation Records* `Free` Search the town assessor database at http://data.visionappraisal.com/WestSpringfieldMA/. Free registration for full data.

Westfield City *Property, Taxation Records* `Free` Assessor records can be found free for Westfield City at http://data.visionappraisal.com/WestfieldMA/.

Hampshire County *Real Estate, Deed, Lien, Judgment, Will Records* `Free & $$` Access to property records is available; records date back to 9/2/1983. Lending agency data is available. For info, contact Marianne Foster at 413-584-3637. Also, Registry of Deeds records are searchable at www.masslandrecords.com. Click on Hampshire on map. Images go back to 1873.

Amherst Town *Property, Taxation Records* `Free` Search the town assessor data at http://data.visionappraisal.com/AmherstMA/. Free registration for full data. Also, the town has a GIS-mapping site but it is not currently available on the internet to the public, see http://gis.amherstma.gov.

Belchertown Town *Property, Taxation Records* `Free` Access property data free at http://belchertown.patriotproperties.com/default.asp.

Easthampton City *Property, Taxation Records* `Free` Access assessor data free with registration at http://data.visionappraisal.com/EasthamptonMA/DEFAULT.asp.

Northampton City *Property, Taxation Records* `Free` Access to property evaluation information for free go to www.northamptonassessor.us/

Southampton Town *Property, Taxation Records* `Free` Access assessor property data in spreadsheet format free at www.town.southampton.ma.us/dbcc/files/SOUTHAMPTON%20FY2008%20ASSESSED%20VALUES.xls

Westhampton Town *Property, Taxation Records* `Free` Access assessor rolls and property sales free at http://csc-ma.us/PropertyContent/jsp/Home.jsp?Page=1.

Middlesex County *Real Estate, Deed, Lien, Judgment, UCC, Will Records* www.lowelldeeds.com `Free` Access Register of Deeds data free at www.masslandrecords.com. Click on North or South Middlesex on map.

Arlington Town *Property, Taxation Records* `Free` Search the town assessor database free at http://arlserver.town.arlington.ma.us/Property/.

Ashby Town *Property, Taxation Records* `Free` Access assessor rolls and property sales free at http://csc-ma.us/PropertyContent/jsp/Home.jsp?Page=1. Click on Ashby Town. Also, access to parcel maps for free at www.ci.ashby.ma.us/assessors/maplink.html

Ashland Town *Property, Taxation Records* `Free` Access assessor rolls and property sales free at http://csc-ma.us/PropertyContent/jsp/Home.jsp?Page=1.

Ayer Town *Property, Taxation Records* `Free` Access assessor rolls and property sales free at http://csc-ma.us/PropertyContent/jsp/Home.jsp?Page=1. Click on Ayer Town.

Bedford Town *Property, Taxation Records* `Free` Access assessor rolls and property sales free at http://csc-ma.us/PropertyContent/jsp/Home.jsp?Page=1.

Belmont Town *Property, Taxation Records* `Free` Access to the town assessor data is free at http://24.61.156.140/Belmont/.

Billerica Town *Property, Taxation Records* `Free` Access property data free at http://billerica.patriotproperties.com/default.asp. No name searching.

Burlington Town *Property, Taxation Records* `Free` Access property data free at http://burlington.patriotproperties.com/default.asp.

Cambridge City *Property, Taxation Records* `Free` Search city assessor database at www.cambridgema.gov/fiscalaffairs/PropertySearch.cfm. Does not require a username and password, simply click on link.

Chelmsford Town *Property, Taxation Records* `Free` Search town assessor database at http://data.visionappraisal.com/ChelmsfordMA/. Free registration for full data.

Concord Town *Property, Taxation Records* `Free` Alpha search residential and commercial assessments at www.concordnet.org/assessor/.

Dracut Town *Property, Taxation Records* `Free` Search the town assessor database at http://data.visionappraisal.com/DracutMA/.

Framingham Town *Property, Taxation Records* `Free` Access assessor rolls and property sales free at http://csc-ma.us/PropertyContent/jsp/Home.jsp?Page=1.

Groton Town *Property, Taxation Records* `Free` Access the property search site for free at http://host.appgeo.com/grotonma/.

Holliston Town *Property, Taxation Records* `Free` Access assessor rolls and property sales free at http://csc-ma.us/PropertyContent/jsp/Home.jsp?Page=1. Select Holliston Town.

Hopkinton Town *Property, Taxation Records* `Free` Access Board of Assessors maps free at www.hopkinton.org/gov/assessor/listing.htm; no name searching. View pdf pages of current assessment reports free at www.hopkinton.org/gov/assessor/pdf/08-appraisal-report.pdf.

Hudson Town *Property, Taxation Records* `Free` Access assessor records free at http://data.visionappraisal.com/HudsonMA/DEFAULT.asp.

Lexington Town *Property, Taxation Records* `Free` Access assessor data free at http://data.visionappraisal.com/LexingtonMA/.

Lowell City *Property, Taxation Records* `Free` Access property assessment data free at www.lowellma.gov/services/gis/.

Marlborough City *Property, Taxation Records* `Free` Search the city assessor data at http://data.visionappraisal.com/MarlboroughMA/. Free registration for full data.

Maynard Town *Property, Taxation Records* `Free` Access assessor rolls and property sales free at http://csc-ma.us/PropertyContent/jsp/Home.jsp?Page=1.

Medford City *Property, Taxation Records* `Free` Search the city assessor database at http://data.visionappraisal.com/MedfordMA/. Free registration for full data.

Melrose City *Property, Taxation Records* `Free` Access property data free at http://melrose.patriotproperties.com/default.asp.

Natick Town *Property, Taxation Records* `Free` Search town assessments free at www.natickma.org/assess/assessinfo.asp. Includes name searches.

Newton City *Property, Taxation Records* `Free` Records on the City of Newton 2003 assessment database are free at www.ci.newton.ma.us/assessors2003/Search.asp. Data represents market value as of January of current year.

North Reading Town *Property, Taxation Records* `Free` Access assessor rolls and property sales free at http://csc-ma.us/NreadingPubAcc/jsp/Home.jsp?Page=1 but no name searching.

Reading Town *Property, Taxation Records* `Free` Records on the Town of Reading Assessor database are free at www.ziplink.net/~reading1/assessor.htm but no name searching.

Shirley Town *Property, Taxation Records* `Free` Access property data free at http://shirley.patriotproperties.com/default.asp.

Somerville City *Property, Taxation Records* `Free` Search the city assessor database at http://data.visionappraisal.com/SomervilleMA/. Free registration for full data.

Sudbury Town *Property, Taxation Records* `Free` Access to the property valuations list for current year is free at www.town.sudbury.ma.us/services/department_home.asp?dept=Assessors. No name search on address index list.

Tewksbury Town *Property, Taxation Records* `Free` Search lists of yearly tax assessments free at www.tewksbury.info/assessor/FY2006Assessments.html. Also, address search recent property sales list free at www.tewksbury.net/assessor/sales.html; link to the pdf list is at the bottom of page.

Wakefield Town *Property, Taxation Records* `Free` Access property data free at http://wakefield.patriotproperties.com/default.asp.

Waltham City *Property, Taxation Records* `Free` Access property data free at http://waltham.patriotproperties.com/default.asp.

Watertown Town *Property, Taxation Records* `Free` Access property data free at http://watertown.patriotproperties.com/default.asp.

Wayland Town *Property, Taxation Records* `Free` Access assessor property records free at http://data.visionappraisal.com/WAYLANDMA/DEFAULT.asp.

Westford Town *Vital Record, Voter Registration Records* www.westfordma.gov `Free` Check voter registration verification free at http://data.westfordma.gov/voter/.
Property, Taxation Records `Free` Access the town online offerings - property, GIS-mapping - free at www.westfordma.gov/pages/onlineservices/gis.

Weston Town *Property, Taxation Records* `Free` Access to property data is free at www.mapsonline.net/westonma/ but no name searching.

Winchester Town *Property, Taxation Records* `Free` Access property data free at http://winchester.patriotproperties.com/default.asp.

Woburn City *Property, Taxation Records* `Free` Search the city assessor data at http://data.visionappraisal.com/WoburnMA/. Free registration for full data.

Nantucket County *Real Estate, Deed, Lien, Mortgage Records* `Free` Access land records for free at masslandrecords.com; click Nantucket under "Select a County."

Nantucket Town *Property, Taxation Records* `Free` Access property data free at http://data.visionappraisal.com/nantucketma/DEFAULT.asp.

Norfolk County *Real Estate, Deed, Lien, Judgment Records* www.norfolkdeeds.org `Free & $$`
Access to county online records is on two levels, both accessible via http://research.norfolkdeeds.org/ALIS/WW400R.PGM. You may search images and indices free, however, to print requires a subscription; $100 per year plus $1.00 per page. Land records go back to 1956; images to 1993. Land court records go back to 9/1984, with images back to 1901.

Bellingham Town *Property, Taxation Records* `Free` Access property data free at http://bellingham.patriotproperties.com/default.asp.

Braintree Town *Property, Taxation Records* `Free` Access property data free at http://braintree.patriotproperties.com/default.asp.

Brookline Town *Property, Taxation Records* `Free` Records on the Town of Brookline Assessors database are free at www.townofbrooklinemass.com/Assessors1/propertylookup.asp

Canton Town *Property, Taxation Records* `Free` Access assessed value data at www.town.canton.ma.us/assessors/assessors.htm. No name searching; search by address only.

Dedham Town *Property, Taxation Records* `Free` Property records on the Assessor's database are free at http://data.visionappraisal.com/dedhamma/. Does not require a username & password, simply click on link. Also, search the GIS mapping site for owner and property data free at http://host.appgeo.com/dedham_gis/.

Dover Town *Property, Taxation Records* `Free` Access to the assessor property values data is free at www.doverma.org/assessorsproposedvaluesnew.php. You must open individual tables to search by name.

Holbrook Town *Property, Taxation Records* `Free` Access property data free at http://holbrook.patriotproperties.com/default.asp.

Medfield Town *Property, Taxation Records* `Free` Access town property data free at http://medfield.patriotproperties.com/default.asp?br=exp&vr=6.

Needham Town *Property, Taxation Records* `Free` Access assessor rolls and property sales free at http://csc-ma.us/PropertyContent/jsp/Home.jsp?Page=1. Select Needham Town.

Norfolk Town *Property, Taxation Records* Free Access to town property data is free at http://host.appgeo.com/NorfolkMA/ but no name searching.

Quincy City *Property, Taxation Records* Free Access assessor property data free at http://data.visionappraisal.com/QuincyMA/DEFAULt.asp. No name searching. Also a sales look-up.

Walpole Town *Property, Taxation Records* Free Search the town assessor database at http://data.visionappraisal.com/WalpoleMA/. Free registration for full data.

Wellesley Town *Property, Taxation Records* Free Property tax records on the Assessor's database are free at wellesleyma.virtualtownhall.net/Pages/WellesleyMA_Assessor/index. Click on Fiscal Year Accessed Values.

Westwood Town *Property, Taxation Records* Free Search the town assessor data at http://data.visionappraisal.com/WestwoodMA/ but no searching.

Weymouth Town *Property, Taxation Records* Free Access to property data is free at www.weymouth.ma.us/propview/.

Plymouth County *Real Estate, Deed, Lien, Judgment Records* www.plymouthdeeds.org/ Free & $$
Access to Titleview requires a usage charge of $30.00 per month, plus $1.00 per image page, but guests may do index searches for free, but no image printing. Indices date back to 1955. Access is by dial-up or internet. For info call 508-830-9283. A fax back service is $3 plus $1 per page in county, $5. plus $1 per page, outside.

Abington Town *Property, Taxation Records* Free Search town assessor database at http://data.visionappraisal.com/AbingtonMA/. Also, search revaluation data free at http://abingtonmass.com/reval.html.

Bridgewater Town *Property, Taxation Records* Free Access property data free on the GIS-mapping site at www.bridgewaterma.org/gisviewer/Index.cfm. No name searching.

Brockton City *Property, Taxation Records* Free Tax roll data on statewide website, see www.latax.state.la.us/TaxRoll_ParishSelect.asp.

Duxbury Town *Property, Taxation Records* Free Access assessor rolls and property sales free at http://csc-ma.us/PropertyContent/jsp/Home.jsp?Page=1.

Hanson Town *Property, Taxation Records* Free Access property records free on the GIS-mapping site at http://gis.virtualtownhall.net/hanson/index.htm; no name searching.

Hingham Town *Property, Taxation Records* Free Search the assessor rolls and property sales free at http://csc-ma.us/HinghamPubAcc/jsp/Home.jsp?. Click on "New Search" or "Sales."

Lakeville Town *Property, Taxation Records* Free Access assessor data free at http://data.visionappraisal.com/LakevilleMA/DEFAULT.asp.

Marion Town *Property, Taxation Records* Free Search town assessor data at http://data.visionappraisal.com/MarionMA/. Free registration for full data.

Marshfield Town *Property, Taxation Records* Free Search town assessor database at http://marshfield.patriotproperties.com.

Mattapoisett Town *Property, Taxation Records* Free Access property data and sales free at http://data.visionappraisal.com/MattapoisettMA/DEFAULT.asp.

Middleborough Town *Property, Taxation Records* Free Search town assessor database at http://data.visionappraisal.com/MiddleboroMA/.

Norwell Town *Property, Taxation Records* Free Access assessor property data free at http://data.visionappraisal.com/NorwellMA/.

Pembroke Town *Property, Taxation Records* Free Access assessor data free at http://pembroke.patriotproperties.com/default.asp?br=exp&vr=6.

Plymouth Town *Property, Taxation Records* Free Access property data free at http://plymouth.patriotproperties.com/default.asp.

Rockland Town *Property, Taxation Records* Free Access to property data to be available free on a private site at www.appraisalresource.com/OnlineDatabases.aspx.

Scituate Town *Property, Taxation Records* Free Search the Assessor property data for free at www.town.scituate.ma.us/assessor/index.html. Click on "Town of Scituate Property Assessment Data as of..."

Wareham Town *Property, Taxation Records* `Free` Search town assessor database at http://data.visionappraisal.com/WarehamMA/. Free registration for full data. Also, access to GIS-mapping information for free at http://gis.virtualtownhall.net/wareham_new/index.asp

Suffolk County *Real Estate, Deed, Lien, Judgment Records* www.suffolkdeeds.com `Free` Records on the County Registry of Deeds database are free at www.suffolkdeeds.com/search/default.asp. Search by name, corporation, and grantor/grantee. Recorded land records begin 1979; Registered land, 1983. Also search deeds via www.masslandrecords.com/malr/controller. Also, Registry of Deeds data is free at www.masslandrecords.com; click on Suffolk on the map.
Property, Taxation Records `Free` Search Boston assessor property records free at www.cityofboston.gov/assessing/search/. City property taxes also available, but no name searching.

Boston City *Property, Taxation Records* `Free` Records on the City of Boston Assessor database are free at www.cityofboston.gov/assessing/search/. Also, property tax bill and payment is searchable by parcel number for free at www.cityofboston.gov/assessing/paysearch.asp.

Chelsea City *Property, Taxation Records* `Free` Search the city assessor database at http://data.visionappraisal.com/ChelseaMA/. Free registration for full data.

Revere City *Property, Taxation Records* `Free` Access property data free at http://revere.patriotproperties.com/default.asp. Free registration for full data.

Worcester County (Northern District) *Real Estate, Deed, Lien, Land Court Records*
www.fitchburgdeeds.com `Free & $$` Access to Registry of Deeds is free at www.fitchburgdeeds.com. Scroll down left column then click 'Click here to access…' Small fee to copy or certify documents. Land index back to 1973; images to 1868. Also, county recorded land images from 1731 to 1974 are free at www.worcesterdeeds.com/worcester/dsbppagelist.asp; book and page number required. Also search recorded docs free at www.masslandrecords.com/malr/controller.

Worcester County (Worcester District) *Real Estate, Grantor/Grantee, Deed, Lien, Judgment, Will Records* www.worcesterdeeds.com `Free` Access to the Register of Deeds database is free at www.masslandrecords.com. Click on South Worcester on map.

Blackstone Town *Property, Taxation Records* `Free` Access property data free at http://data.visionappraisal.com/BlackstoneMA/.

Bolton Town *Property, Taxation Records* `Free` Access tassessor rolls and property sales free at http://csc-ma.us/PropertyContent/jsp/Home.jsp?Page=1.

Brookfield Town *Property, Taxation Records* `Free` Access assessor rolls and property sales free at http://csc-ma.us/PropertyContent/jsp/Home.jsp?Page=1. Select Brookfield Town.

Charlton Town *Property, Taxation Records* `Free` Access property data free at http://charlton.patriotproperties.com/default.asp.

Douglas Town *Property, Taxation Records* `Free` Access to assessor property data is free at www.mapsonline.net/douglasma/.

Dudley Town *Property, Taxation Records* `Free` Search the town assessor database at http://data.visionappraisal.com/DudleyMA/. Free registration for full data.

East Brookfield Town *Property, Taxation Records* `Free` Access assessor rolls and property sales free at http://csc-ma.us/PropertyContent/jsp/Home.jsp?Page=1. Select East Brookfield Town.

Fitchburg City *Property, Taxation Records* `Free` Access city property data free at http://216.129.143.192:56789/home/webpro/.

Gardner City *Property, Taxation Records* `Free` Search the city assessor data at http://data.visionappraisal.com/GardnerMA/. Free registration for full data.

Grafton Town *Property, Taxation Records* `Free` Access to property data is free at http://csc-ma.us/GraftonPubAcc/jsp/Home.jsp?Page=1; also at http://csc-ma.us/PropertyContent/jsp/Home.jsp?Page=1.

Hardwick Town *Property, Taxation Records* `Free` Access assessor rolls and property sales free at http://csc-ma.us/PropertyContent/jsp/Home.jsp?Page=1. Select Harwick Town.

Harvard Town *Property, Taxation Records* `Free` Search town assessor database at http://data.visionappraisal.com/HARVARDMA/. Free registration for full data.

Holden Town *Property, Taxation Records* `Free` Search the Town assessor's database free at http://data.visionappraisal.com/HOLDENMA. Free registration for full data.

Hopedale Town *Property, Taxation Records* `Free` Access town assessment data free at
http://hopedale.patriotproperties.com/default.asp?br=exp&vr=6.

Lancaster Town *Property, Taxation Records* `Free` Access assessor rolls and property sales free at
http://csc-ma.us/PropertyContent/jsp/Home.jsp?Page=1. Select Lancaster Town.

Leicester Town *Property, Taxation Records* `Free` Access property data free at
http://leicester.patriotproperties.com/default.asp.

Leominster City *Property, Taxation Records* `Free` Search the assessor's database at
http://data.visionappraisal.com/leominsterma. Free registration for full data.

Lunenburg Town *Property, Taxation Records* `Free` Access assessor rolls and property sales free at
http://csc-ma.us/PropertyContent/jsp/Home.jsp?Page=1.

Milford Town *Property, Taxation Records* `Free` Access property data free at
http://milford.patriotproperties.com/default.asp.

Millbury Town *Property, Taxation Records* `Free` Access to the town tax assessor info is free at
http://data.visionappraisal.com/MillburyMA/.

New Braintree Town *Property, Taxation Records* `Free` Access assessor rolls and property sales free at
http://csc-ma.us/PropertyContent/jsp/Home.jsp?Page=1.

North Brookfield Town *Property, Taxation Records* `Free` Access assessor rolls and property sales
free at http://csc-ma.us/PropertyContent/jsp/Home.jsp?Page=1. Select North Brookfield Town.

Northborough Town *Property, Taxation Records* `Free` Access assessor rolls and property sales free at
http://csc-ma.us/PropertyContent/jsp/Home.jsp?Page=1.

Oakham Town *Property, Taxation Records* `Free` Access assessor rolls and property sales free at
http://csc-ma.us/PropertyContent/jsp/Home.jsp?Page=1. Select Oakham Town.

Oxford Town *Property, Taxation Records* `Free` Search the property assessments by street name for free at
https://security.town.oxford.ma.us/WebUserInterface/.

Paxton Town *Property, Taxation Records* `Free` Search town assessor database at
http://data.visionappraisal.com/PaxtonMA/.

Royalston Town *Property, Taxation Records* `Free` Access assessor rolls and property sales free at
http://csc-ma.us/PropertyContent/jsp/Home.jsp?Page=1. Select Royalston Town.

Rutland Town *Property, Taxation Records* `Free` Access to Rutland town assessor records is free at
http://data.visionappraisal.com/RutlandMA/.

Southborough Town *Property, Taxation Records* `Free` Access assessor rolls and property sales free
at http://csc-ma.us/SouthboroughPubAcc/jsp/Home.jsp?Page=1. No name searching.

Southbridge Town *Property, Taxation Records* `Free` Access assessor data free with registration at
http://data.visionappraisal.com/SouthbridgeMA/DEFAULT.asp.

Sturbridge Town *Property, Taxation Records* `Free` Access assessor property data free with registration
at http://data.visionappraisal.com/SturbridgeMA/DEFAULT.asp.

Templeton Town *Property, Taxation Records* `Free` Access assessor data at
http://data.visionappraisal.com/TempletonMA/. Free registration for full data.

Upton Town *Property, Taxation Records* `Free` Access property ownership data free at
www.appraisalresource.com/Search.aspx?town=Upton.

Uxbridge Town *Property, Taxation Records* `Free` Access to assessor rolls and property sales is free at
http://csc-ma.us/PropertyContent/jsp/Home.jsp?Page=1. Search maps by owner's name or address at
www.mapsonline.net/uxbridgema/.

West Brookfield Town *Property, Taxation Records* `Free` Access assessor rolls and property sales free
at http://csc-ma.us/PropertyContent/jsp/Home.jsp?Page=1.

Westborough Town *Property, Taxation Records* `Free` Access property data free at
http://westborough.patriotproperties.com/default.asp.

Worcester City *Property, Taxation Records* `Free` Online access to the City Assessor Valuation Search
database is free at www.ci.worcester.ma.us/aso/value_search.htm.

Michigan

Capital: Lansing
            Ingham County
Time Zone: EST
> Four NW Michigan counties are in the CST:
> They are: Dickinson, Gogebic, Iron, Menominee.

Population: 10,071,822
# of Counties: 83

Useful State Links

Website: www.michigan.gov
Governor: www.michigan.gov/gov
Attorney General: www.michigan.gov/ag
State Archives: www.michigan.gov/hal/0,1607,7-160-17445_19273_19313---,00.html
State Statutes and Codes: www.legislature.mi.gov
Legislative Bill Search: www.legislature.mi.gov
Unclaimed Funds: www.michigan.gov/treasury/0,1607,7-121-1748_1876_1912-7924--,00.html

Primary State Agencies

Criminal Records $$

Michigan State Police, Criminal History Section, Criminal Justice Information Center, www.michigan.gov/msp Online access is available at http://apps.michigan.gov/ICHAT/Home.aspx. Results are available in seconds; fee is $10.00 per name. Call 517-322-1377. This is a non-fingerprint search. You are also allowed up to three variations on one name search. Use of a MasterCard or VISA is required. This is the only method available for a non-fingerprint search.

Sexual Offender Registry Free

Michigan State Police, SOR Section, www.mipsor.state.mi.us One may search the registry at the website, there is no charge.

Incarceration Records Free

Michigan Department of Corrections, Central Records Office, www.michigan.gov/corrections The online access found at www.state.mi.us/mdoc/asp/otis2.html has many search criteria capabilities. There is also a DOC Most Wanted list at www.state.mi.us/mdoc/MostWanted/MostWanted.asp. *Other Options:* Bulk sales of database information is available.

Corporation, LLC, LP, LLP, Assumed Name Free

Department of Labor & Economic Growth, Bureau of Commercial Services - Corp Div, http://michigan.gov/corporations At the website, search by company name or file number for records of domestic corporations, limited liability companies, and limited partnerships and of foreign corporations, and limited partnerships qualified to transact business in the state. *Other Options:* The database is for sale by contract.

Trademarks/Servicemarks Free

Dept of labor & Economic Growth, Commercial Srvs - Trademarks & Service Marks, www.michigan.gov/dleg/0,1607,7-154-35299_35413_35431---,00.html Free searching is available at www.dleg.state.mi.us/bcsc/forms/corp/mark/markcom.pdf. This is a search of a PDF file of their system.

Uniform Commercial Code, Federal & State Tax Liens Free & $$

MI Department of State, UCC Section, www.michigan.gov/sosucc From the website, click on Login or Register. Conducting a Debtor Name Quick Search is free. No login is needed. Documents may be ordered for a fee. Registration is required. A credit card is necessary unless the requester has an established billing account. *Other Options:* A monthly subscription service is available for the bulk purchase of UCC filings on microfilm. The fee is $50 or actual cost, whichever is greater. Call 517-322-1144 for additional information.

Workers' Compensation Records `Free`

Department of Labor & Economic Dev., Workers' Compensation Agency, www.michigan.gov/wca Go to the website and follow the links to see if an employer has coverage. The site does not allow searching by employee name.

Driver Records `$$`

Department of State, Record Lookup Unit, www.michigan.gov/sos Online ordering is available on an interactive basis. The system is open 7 days a week. Ordering is by DL or name and DOB. An account must be established and billing is monthly. Access is also available from the Internet. Fee is $7.00 per record. A $25,000 surety bond is required. Also, the agency offers an activity notification service for employers who register their drivers. For more information on either program, call 517-322-6281. *Other Options:* The state offers the license file for bulk purchase. Customized runs are $64 per thousand records; complete database can be purchased for $16 per thousand. A $25,000 surety bond is required. Call 517-322-1042.

Vehicle, Vessel Ownership & Registration `Free & $$`

Department of State, Record Lookup Unit, www.michigan.gov/sos Online searching via the Internet is single inquiry and requires a VIN or plate number (no name searches). An account is required with a $25,000 surety bond. Fee is $7.00 per record. For more information, call 517-322-6281. The program is called Direct Access and details are found on the web. A unique service offered is the Repeat Offender Inquiry. This web search function allows dealers and others to learn if a vehicle purchaser is ineligible for license plates and subject to registration denial under Michigan's Repeat Offender Law. Search results state if the purchaser is eligible, not eligible, or if not on file. The web site is https://services.sos.state.mi.us/RepeatOffender/Inquiry.aspx. *Other Options:* Michigan offers bulk retrieval from the VIN and plate database. A written request letter, stating purpose, must be submitted and approved. A $25,000 surety bond is required upon approval. Please call 517-322-1042.

Accident Reports `$$`

Department of State Police, Criminal Justice Information Center, www.michigan.gov/msp/0,1607,7-123-1589_1878_15889---,00.html Records may be requested from the Traffic Crash Purchasing System at https://mdotwas1.mdot.state.mi.us/TCPS/login/welcome.jsp. The fee is $10.00, a credit cards may be used unless billing arrangements are made. Records are available going back 10 years. For specific questions email CrashPurchaseTCPS@michigan.gov.

GED Certificates `Free`

MI Department of Labor & Econ Growth, Adult Education - GED Testing, www.michigan.gov/adulteducation Will accept e-mail requests with a scanned signature.

Vital Records `$$`

Department of Health, Vital Records Requests, www.michigan.gov/mdch Records can be ordered from the web site, credit card is required. Processing time is 2 weeks.

Occupational Licensing Boards

Adoption Svc/Child Placing Agency. www.michigan.gov/dhs/0,1607,7-124-5455_27716_27721---,00.html
Adult Foster Care/Homes for Aged ... www.dleg.state.mi.us/brs_afc/sr_afc.asp
Airport Manager .... www.michigan.gov/documents/Mgr_List_147366_7.pdf
Alarm System Service https://www2.dleg.state.mi.us/colaLicVerify/
Ambulance Attendant .... www.cis.state.mi.us/free/default.asp
Amusement Ride .... http://cis.state.mi.us/verify.htm
Appraiser, Real Estate/Gen./Resi'l ..... http://cis.state.mi.us/verify.htm
Aquaculture Operation .... www.michigan.gov/documents/mda/mda_aquaculture_192478_7.pdf
Architect .... http://cis.state.mi.us/verify.htm
Asbestos Accreditation, Individ'l .... www.dleg.state.mi.us/asbestos_program/sr_individual.asp
Asbestos Contractor.......................... www.dleg.state.mi.us/asbestos_program/sr_contractor.asp
Asbestos Training Provider .... www.dleg.state.mi.us/asbestos_program/sr_tcp.asp
Assessor... www.michigan.gov/documents/CertificationLevel_3022_7.pdf
Atmosphere Storage Operator .... www.michigan.gov/mda/0,1607,7-125-1569_16993_19105-46661--,00.html
Attorney, State Bar .... www.michbar.org/memberdirectory/
Auto Dealer/Mech'/Repair Facility .... www.michigan.gov/sos/0,1607,7-127-1631_8849-51047--,00.html
Bank & Trust Company..................... www.michigan.gov/cis/1,1607,7-154--22352--,00.html
Barber/Barber Shop/School .... http://cis.state.mi.us/verify.htm
Boxing/Wrestling Occupation .... http://cis.state.mi.us/verify.htm
Builder, Residential .... http://cis.state.mi.us/verify.htm
Camp, Child/Adult Foster Care .... www.michigan.gov/dhs/0,1607,7-124-5455_27716_27723---,00.html
Carnival .... http://cis.state.mi.us/verify.htm
Casino Interest Personnel/Firm.......... http://miboecfr.nicusa.com/cgi-bin/cfr/casino_srch.cgi

Cemetery .... http://cis.state.mi.us/verify.htm
Check Seller .... www.michigan.gov/cis/0,1607,7-154-10555_13251_13257---,00.html
Child Care Family/Group/Center....... www.michigan.gov/dhs/0,1607,7-124-5455_27716_27718---,00.html
Child Care Institution .... www.michigan.gov/dhs/0,1607,7-124-5455_27716_27719---,00.html
Child Facility, Court Operated .... www.michigan.gov/dhs/0,1607,7-124-5455_27716_27722---,00.html
Child Foster Care Family Home........ www.dleg.state.mi.us/brs_cwl/sr_cf.asp
Chiropractor...................................... www.cis.state.mi.us/free/default.asp
Collection Manager .... http://cis.state.mi.us/verify.htm
Community Planner........................... http://cis.state.mi.us/verify.htm
Community Planner (Mfg. Home)..... https://www2.dleg.state.mi.us/colaLicVerify/
Consumer Financial Service .... www.michigan.gov/cis/0,1607,7-154-10555_13251_13257---,00.html
Contractor, Residential .... http://cis.state.mi.us/verify.htm
Cosmetologist................................... http://cis.state.mi.us/verify.htm
Cosmetology Shop/School .... http://cis.state.mi.us/verify.htm
Counselor .... www.cis.state.mi.us/free/default.asp
Credit Card Issuer............................. www.michigan.gov/cis/0,1607,7-154-10555_13251_13257---,00.html
Credit Union www.michigan.gov/cis/1,1607,7-154--22352--,00.html
Debt Management Firm..................... www.michigan.gov/documents/cis_ofis_debtlist_25540_7.pdf
Dental Hygienist............................... www.cis.state.mi.us/free/default.asp
Dentist/Dental Assistant .... www.cis.state.mi.us/free/default.asp
Election Campaign Finance Com'tee http://miboecfr.nicusa.com/cgi-bin/cfr/mi_com.cgi
Election Candidate Committee .... http://miboecfr.nicusa.com/cgi-bin/cfr/can_search.cgi
Emergency Medical Personnel .... www.cis.state.mi.us/free/default.asp
Employment Agency, fee only .... http://cis.state.mi.us/verify.htm
EMT Advanced/Specialist/Instruc'r .. www.cis.state.mi.us/free/default.asp
Engineer .... http://cis.state.mi.us/verify.htm
Flight School   ... ... www.michigan.gov/documents/AERO_Flight_Schools_Aug_2005_134972_7.pdf
Forester.. http://cis.state.mi.us/verify.htm
Funeral Home/Salesperson .... http://cis.state.mi.us/verify.htm
Funeral, Prepaid Contract Regis. .... http://cis.state.mi.us/verify.htm
Grain Dealer/Truckers .... www.mda.state.mi.us/prodag/GrainDealers/dealers.html
Health Facility/Laboratory................ www.cis.state.mi.us/free/default.asp
Hearing Aid Dealer........................... http://cis.state.mi.us/verify.htm
HMO .... www.michigan.gov/cis/0,1607,7-154-10555_13251_13262---,00.html
Insurance Adjuster............................ www.michigan.gov/cis/0,1607,7-154-10555_13251_13262---,00.html
Insurance Agent/counsel/solic/admin.www.michigan.gov/cis/0,1607,7-154-10555_13251_13262---,00.html
Insurance Counselor .... www.cis.state.mi.us/fis/ind_srch/ins_agnt/insurance_agent_criteria.asp
Insurance Solicitor........................... www.cis.state.mi.us/fis/ind_srch/ins_agnt/insurance_agent_criteria.asp
Insurance-related Entity.................... www.michigan.gov/cis/0,1607,7-154-10555_13251_13262---,00.html
Investment Adviser........................... http://adviserinfo.sec.gov/IAPD/Content/Search/iapd_OrgSearch.aspx
Landscape Architect .... http://cis.state.mi.us/verify.htm
Liquor Dist./Whlse./Mfg./License https://www2.dleg.state.mi.us/MWPR/
Liquor Licensing Director https://www2.dleg.state.mi.us/MWPR/
Living Care Facility.......................... www.michigan.gov/documents/cis_ofis_lclist_25541_7.pdf
Lobbyist/Lobbyist Agent.................. http://miboecfr.nicusa.com/cgi-bin/cfr/lobby_srch.cgi
Long Term Care Company .... www.michigan.gov/cis/0,1607,7-154-10555_13251_13262---,00.html
Mammography Facility .... www.cis.state.mi.us/free/default.asp
Marriage & Family Therapist .... www.cis.state.mi.us/free/default.asp
Medical Doctor................................. www.cis.state.mi.us/free/default.asp
Medical First Responder................... www.cis.state.mi.us/free/default.asp
Mortgage Licensee .... www.michigan.gov/cis/0,1607,7-154-10555_13251_13257---,00.html
Mortuary Science.............................. http://cis.state.mi.us/verify.htm
Motor Vehicle Loan Seller/Financer . www.michigan.gov/cis/0,1607,7-154-10555_13251_13257---,00.html
Nurse/Nurses' Aide........................... www.cis.state.mi.us/free/default.asp
Nursery Dealer/Grower .... www.mda.state.mi.us/industry/Nursery/license/index.html
Nursing Home .... www.cis.state.mi.us/bhs_car/sr_car.asp
Nursing Home Administrator .... www.cis.state.mi.us/free/default.asp

Ocularist .... http://cis.state.mi.us/verify.htm
Optometrist .... www.cis.state.mi.us/free/default.asp
Osteopathic Physician .... www.cis.state.mi.us/free/default.asp
Paramedic .... www.cis.state.mi.us/free/default.asp
Personnel Agency https://www2.dleg.state.mi.us/colaLicVerify/
Pesticide Application Business .... www.mda.state.mi.us/pest/
Pharmacist .... www.cis.state.mi.us/free/default.asp
Physical Therapist .... www.cis.state.mi.us/free/default.asp
Physician Assistant .... www.cis.state.mi.us/free/default.asp
Podiatrist .... www.cis.state.mi.us/free/default.asp
Political Action Committee .... http://miboecfr.nicusa.com/cgi-bin/cfr/pac_search.cgi
Political Party Committee .... http://miboecfr.nicusa.com/cgi-bin/cfr/mi_com.cgi?com_type=PPY
Polygraph Examiner .... http://cis.state.mi.us/verify.htm
Potato Dealer .... www.michigan.gov/mda/0,1607,7-125-1566_1733_2321-11149--,00.html
Private Investigator/Detective https://www2.dleg.state.mi.us/colaLicVerify/
Priv Security/Secur'y arrest author'y .. https://www2.dleg.state.mi.us/colaLicVerify/
Psychologist .... www.cis.state.mi.us/free/default.asp
Public Accountant-CPA .... http://cis.state.mi.us/verify.htm
Real Estate Agent/Broker/Seller .... http://cis.state.mi.us/verify.htm
Regulatory Loan Licensee .... www.michigan.gov/cis/0,1607,7-154-10555_13251_13257---,00.html
Sanitarian .... www.cis.state.mi.us/free/default.asp
Savings Bank www.michigan.gov/cis/1,1607,7-154--22352--,00.html
Securities Agent/Broker/Dealer .... www.finra.org/index.htm
Security Agency/Guard https://www2.dleg.state.mi.us/colaLicVerify/
Security Alarm Installer https://www2.dleg.state.mi.us/colaLicVerify/
Social Worker .... www.cis.state.mi.us/free/default.asp
Surety Company .... www.michigan.gov/cis/0,1607,7-154-10555_13251_13262---,00.html
Surplus Line Broker .... www.michigan.gov/cis/0,1607,7-154-10555_13251_13262---,00.html
Surveyor, Professional .... http://cis.state.mi.us/verify.htm
Teacher .... https://mdoe.state.mi.us/teachercert/
Third-Party Administrator .... www.michigan.gov/cis/0,1607,7-154-10555_13251_13262---,00.html
Veterinarian/Veterinary Technician .. www.cis.state.mi.us/free/default.asp
Weights & Measures Person/Agency www.mda.state.mi.us/industry/lab/service/index.html

State and Local Courts

State Court Structure: The Circuit Court is the court of general jurisdiction. District Courts and Municipal Courts have jurisdiction over certain minor felonies and handle all preliminary hearings. There is a Court of Claims in Lansing that is a function of the 30th Circuit Court with jurisdiction over claims against the state of Michigan. The Family Division of the Circuit Court was created in 1998. Domestic relations actions and juvenile cases, including criminal and abuse/neglect, formerly adjudicated in the Probate Court, were transferred to the Family Division of the Circuit Court. Mental health and estate cases continue to be handled by Probate Courts.

Several counties (Barry, Berrien, Iron, Isabella, Lake, and Washtenaw) and the 46th Circuit Court are participating in a "Demonstration" pilot project designed to streamline court services and consolidate case management. These courts may refer to themselves as County Trial Courts.

Statewide Court Online Access: There is a wide range of online computerization of the judicial system from "none" to "fairly complete," but there is no statewide court records network. Some Michigan courts provide public access terminals in clerk's offices, and some courts are developing off-site electronic filing and searching capability. A few offer remote online to the public. Subscribe to email updates of appellate opinions at http://courtofappeals.mijud.net/resources/subscribe.htm. There is no fee.

Antrim County
13th Circuit Court   www.antrimcounty.org/circuitcourt.asp   `Free`
Civil: Access to a record index is at http://online.co.grand-traverse.mi.us/iprod/clerk/cccivil.html . *Criminal:* Access to criminal record index is found at http://online.co.grand-traverse.mi.us/iprod/clerk/cccriminal.html.

Bay County

74th District Court   www.baycountycourts.com   **Free**
Civil: Access court case files free at http://68.22.255.190/c74/c74_cases.php. *Criminal:* same.

Probate Court   **Free**   Access the county courts' calendar of scheduled cases for free at www.baycountycourts.com/bcc/home.nsf/public/court_calendar.htm.

Crawford County

46th Circuit Court   www.Circuit46.org   **Free**
Civil: Online access to court case records (closed cases for 90 days only) is free at http://66.129.39.149/c46_Cases.php. *Criminal:* Same.

46th Circuit Trial Court - District Division   www.Circuit46.org   **Free**
Civil: Online access to limited index of court records is free at http://66.129.39.149/c46_Cases.php. *Criminal:* Same. There are limitations, this system is not meant to be used for background checks; it is supplemental only.

Probate Court   http://www.Circuit46.org   **Free**   Search cases by name free at http://66.129.39.149/c46_Cases.php.

Eaton County

56th Circuit Court   www.eatoncountycourts.org/courts.html   **Free**
Civil: Recent day divorce decrees at www.eatoncounty.org/Departments/Circuit_Court_Clerk/COUNTY_SERVICES.htm. *Criminal:* Last 12-13 months of criminal case dispositions listed at www.eatoncounty.org/Departments/Circuit_Court_Clerk/COUNTY_SERVICES.htm.

Genesee County

7th Circuit Court   www.co.genesee.mi.us   **Free**
Civil: Online access to court records is free at www.co.genesee.mi.us/clerk/#; click on "Circuit Court Records." *Criminal:* Same.

67th District Court   www.co.genesee.mi.us/districtcourt/   **Free**
Civil: Search by name or case number at www.co.genesee.mi.us/districtcourt/recordschk.htm. *Criminal:* Search by name or case number at www.co.genesee.mi.us/districtcourt/recordschk.htm. Also includes traffic.

Probate Court   http://www.co.genesee.mi.us/probate/index.htm   **Free**   Access records free at www.co.genesee.mi.us/probate/index.htm -click on Probate Court Records,

Grand Traverse County

13th Circuit Court   www.co.grand-traverse.mi.us   **Free**
Civil: Search civil records free at http://online.co.grand-traverse.mi.us/iprod/clerk/cccivil.html . 1981 through 1985 contain only index information. 1986 to present include case information and register of actions. Database updated nightly. *Criminal:* Access to a record index is found at http://online.co.grand-traverse.mi.us/iprod/clerk/cccriminal.html.

Jackson County

4th Circuit Court   www.co.jackson.mi.us/CCinfo.asp   **Free**
Civil: Access court records free at http://69.222.215.225/c12/c12_cases.php. *Criminal:* same.

12th District Court   www.d12.com   **Free**
Civil: Access court records free at http://69.222.215.225/c12/c12_cases.php. *Criminal:* same.

Probate Court   http://www.co.jackson.mi.us/CCinfo.asp   **Free**   Access probate court records free at http://69.222.215.225/c12/c12_cases.php.

Kalkaska County

46th Circuit Court   www.Circuit46.org   **Free**
Civil: Online access to court case records (open or closed cases for 90 days only) is free at http://66.129.39.149/c46_Cases.php. *Criminal:* Same.

46th Circuit Trial Court - District Court   www.Circuit46.org   **Free**
Civil: Online access to limited index of court records is free at http://66.129.39.149/c46_Cases.php. *Criminal:* Same. There are limitations, this system is not meant to be used for background checks, it is supplemental only.

Circuit Trial Court - Probate Division   http://www.Circuit46.org   **Free**   Search cases by name free at http://66.129.39.149/c46_Cases.php.

Kent County

17th Circuit Court   www.accesskent.com/CourtsAndLawEnforcement   **Free & $$**
Civil: Search for $6.00 per name at https://www.accesskent.com/CourtNameSearch/. DOB not required but credit card is for record found. Also, search hearings schedule free at https://www.accesskent.com/CCHearing/ *Criminal:* Search for $6.00 per name at

https://www.accesskent.com/CourtNameSearch/. DOB and credit card required for results. Also, search for accident reports at $3.00 per name at https://www.accesskent.com/AccidentReports/.

61st District Court - Grand Rapids www.grcourt.org/ `Free`
Civil: Search online at https://www.grcourt.org/CourtPayments/ *Criminal:* Search at https://www.grcourt.org/CourtPayments/.

Leelanau County
13th Circuit Court `Free`
Civil: Access to a record index is at http://online.co.grand-traverse.mi.us/iprod/clerk/cccivil.html . Family court records also included. Search by name or case number. *Criminal:* Access to a record index is found at http://online.co.grand-traverse.mi.us/prod/clerk/cccriminal.html. Search by name or case number to 1981.

Livingston County
44th Circuit Court www.co.livingston.mi.us `Free & $$`
Civil: Access civil records online free or by subscription at https://www.livingstonlive.org/CourtRecordValidation/. *Criminal:* Access criminal records back to 1997 free or by subscription at https://www.livingstonlive.org/CourtRecordValidation/ but a DOB is required to search on the free access.

53 A District Court http://co.livingston.mi.us/DistrictCourt `Free`
Civil: Access civil records after registration or by subscription at https://www.livingstonlive.org/CourtRecordValidation/. *Criminal:* Access criminal records back to 1997 after registration or by subscription at https://www.livingstonlive.org/CourtRecordValidation/ but a DOB is required to search on the free access.

53 B District Court http://co.livingston.mi.us/DistrictCourt/brighton.htm `Free`
Civil: Access civil records after registration or by subscription at https://www.livingstonlive.org/CourtRecordValidation/. *Criminal:* Access criminal records back to 1997 after registration or by subscription at https://www.livingstonlive.org/CourtRecordValidation/ but a DOB is required to search on the free access.

Macomb County
16th Circuit Court www.macombcountymi.gov/clerksoffice/ `Free`
Civil: Civil online access is the same as criminal, see below. Online records include divorces. *Criminal:* Access Circuit Court index for free at http://209.131.29.171/pa/ or http://maxweb01.macombcountymi.gov/pa/. Fee to copy and view docket entries.

38th District Court - Eastpointe www.judgeredmond.com `Free`
Civil: Access case name look-ups free at https://secure.courts.michigan.gov/jis/ *Criminal:* Access case name look-ups at https://secure.courts.michigan.gov/jis/.

Oakland County
6th Circuit Court www.oakgov.com/courts/ `Free & $$`
Civil: Access scanned court records free at www.oakgov.com/clerkrod/courtexplorer/index.html. An enhanced access fee starting at $2.50 is charged for viewing. *Criminal:* Online criminal access is the same as civil see above.

Otsego County
46th Circuit Court www.Circuit46.org `Free`
Civil: Access to court case records (closed cases for 90 days only) is free at http://66.129.39.149/c46_Cases.php. *Criminal:* Same.

46th Circuit Trial Court - District Court www.circuit46.org `Free`
Civil: Online access to limited index of court records is free at http://66.129.39.149/c46_Cases.php. *Criminal:* Access to online criminal records is the same as civil. There are limitations, this system is not meant to be used for background checks, it is supplemental only.

Probate Court http://www.Circuit46.org `Free` Online access to limited index of court records is free at http://66.129.39.149/c46_Cases.php.

Saginaw County
10th Circuit Court www.saginawcounty.com/clerk/court/index.html `Free`
Civil: Search civil records online free at www.saginawcounty.com/clerk/circuit_civil_records.html. Calendars may be searched at www.saginawcounty.com/clerk/docket/index.html. *Criminal:* Search criminal records online free at www.saginawcounty.com/clerk/circuit_criminal_records.html.

St. Clair County
31st Circuit Court www.stclaircounty.org/Offices/courts `Free`
Civil: A index of records can be viewed at www.stclaircounty.org/Offices/courts/circuit/records.asp. *Criminal:* Records index can be viewed at www.stclaircounty.org/Offices/courts/circuit/records.asp.

72nd District Court www.stclaircounty.org/offices/courts/ `Free`
Civil: Access court case index free at www.stclaircounty.org/DCS/search.aspx. *Criminal:* same.

Washtenaw County

22nd Circuit Court www.washtenawtrialcourt.org `Free`
Civil: Only signed orders back 30 days are free online at http://washtenawtrialcourt.org/signed_orders; search by judge. *Criminal:* same.

14A1 District Court www.14adistrictcourt.org `Free`
Civil: Only dockets and calendars are searchable online at www.14adistrictcourt.org/cases. *Criminal:* same.

14A2 District Court www.14adistrictcourt.org `Free`
Civil: Only dockets and calendars are searchable online at www.14adistrictcourt.org/cases. *Criminal:* same.

14A3 District Court www.14adistrictcourt.org `Free`
Civil: Only dockets and calendars are searchable online at www.14adistrictcourt.org/cases. *Criminal:* same.

15th District Court - Civil Division www.15thdistrictcourt.org `Free`
Civil: Access court records free at https://secure.courts.michigan.gov/jis/.

15th District Court - Criminal Division www.15thdistrictcourt.org `Free`
 Criminal: Access court records free at https://secure.courts.michigan.gov/jis/. Online results include address. Online records of open case records back to 8/6/2006 available, with searches for case numbers available on closed cases.

Wayne County

Probate Court http://www.waynecounty.com/courts/probate/ `Free` Search probate records at http://public.wcpc.us/pa/pa.urd/pamw6500.display. summary, party, event, docket, disposition, costs available; records go back to 80s.

Recorders, Assessors, and Other Sites of Note

Recording Office Organization: 83 counties, 83 recording offices. The recording officer is the County Register of Deeds. Federal and state tax liens on personal property of businesses are filed with the Secretary of State. Other federal and state tax liens are filed with the Register of Deeds.

Online Access Note: There is no statewide online access but a number of counties, including Wayne, offer free access to Assessor and Register of Deeds records.

Allegan County *Property, Taxation Records* `Free` Search index by name or address at https://is.bsasoftware.com/bsa.is/SelectUnit.aspx. The site includes Cities of Otsego, Plainwell, Douglas, and Saugatuck Township. Search tax index or foreclosures by name or address at www.allegancounty.org/Government/TR/TaxSearch.asp?pt= or https://is.bsasoftware.com/bsa.is/. The latter site includes Cities of Otsego, Plainwell, Wayland, Douglas, and Saugatuck Township.

Alpena County *Property, Taxation Records* `Free` Search the assessor property tax data free at www.alpena.mi.govern.com/parcelquery.php.

Antrim County *Property, Taxation Records* `Free` Search parcel data information free at www.antrimcounty.org/parcelsearch.asp.

Barry County *Real Estate, Deed, Lien, Mortgage, Judgment, Vital Record Records* www.barrycounty.org `Free`
Access recorded images back to 4/1993 free at www.barrycounty.org/online-services/register-of-deeds-image-search/. Pre 1993 images being added. Search Vital Records data free at http://internal.barrycounty.org/clerkweb/
Property, Taxation Records `Free` Access to county parcel data is free at www.barrycounty.org/online-services/parcel-search/. County property Index is from 12/95 to 12/2005; assessment rolls should not be used for a title search or legal description. Also, access county property data free on the tax parcel lookup at http://barryco.readyhosting.com/ParcelMaps.htm.

Bay County *Real Estate, Deed, Lien Records* www.co.bay.mi.us `Free` Access the register's land records data, click on Internet Land Records Search at the bottom of www.co.bay.mi.us/bay/home.nsf/Public/Bay_County_Register_Of_Deeds.htm. Log-in as Guest. Index goes back to 1985; no images.
Property, Taxation Records `Free` Access county property tax data for free at http://ptq.baycounty-mi.gov/. Also, access tax data for City of Essexville and Hampton Township at https://is.bsasoftware.com/bsa.is/SelectUnit.aspx.

Benzie County *Real Estate, Deed, Lien, Parcel Records* www.benzieco.net/dept_register_of_deeds.htm `$$`
Recorder land data by subscription on either the Laredo system using subscription and fees or the Tapestry System using credit card, http://tapestry.fidlar.com; $3.99 search; $.50 per image. Index goes back to 1982, images to 7/1998.
Property, Taxation Records `Free` Access land and property tax data free for Almira Township at https://is.bsasoftware.com/bsa.is/SelectUnit.aspx.

Berrien County *Property, Taxation Records* Free Access to City of Niles property data is free with registration at https://is.bsasoftware.com/bsa.is/SelectUnit.aspx.

Branch County *Real Estate, Deed, Lien, Vital Statistic, Business Name Records* www.co.branch.mi.us $$
Recorder land data by subscription on either the Laredo system using subscription and fees or the Tapestry System using credit card, https://www.landrecords.net; $5.95 search; $.50 per image. Index and images go back to 1/1/1997. Currently, search the county vital records (death records only) free at www.co.branch.mi.us/deathsearch.taf. Search business names and DBAs at www.co.branch.mi.us/dbasearch.taf.
Property, Taxation Records Free Access City of Coldwater and Township of Coldwater property tax and special assessments free after registration at https://is.bsasoftware.com/bsa.is/SelectUnit.aspx.

Calhoun County *Real Estate, Grantor/Grantee, Deed, Lien, Parcel, Special Assessment Records*
http://co.calhoun.mi.us Free Access the recorder's Land Records Index free back to 1/3/1980 at http://rod.co.calhoun.mi.us/indexsearch.html.
Property, Taxation Records Free Access to data for Cities of Albion, Battle Creek, Marshall, Springfield and Townships of Marshall, Newton, and Sheridan is free with registration at https://is.bsasoftware.com/bsa.is/SelectUnit.aspx.

Cass County *Property, Taxation Records* Free Access county property tax records free at www.cass.mi.govern.com/parcelquery.php.

Charlevoix County *Real Estate, Deed Records* www.charlevoixcounty.org Free Register of Deeds records free back to 1/2005 only at http://12.150.40.69/rodweb/
Property, Taxation Records Free Access the assessor's basic property data or property tax payment free at www.charlevoixcounty.org/. Also, access to county and Township of Evangeline tax data is free with registration at https://is.bsasoftware.com/bsa.is/SelectUnit.aspx. Index search is free but registration is required to view and print documents for $2.00 each.

Cheboygan County *Property, Taxation Records* Free Access to assessor property index is free at www.cheboygancounty.net/equal/property.php.

Clinton County *Real Estate, Deed, Judgment, Lien, Fictitious Business Name Records* www.clinton-county.org/rod/register_of_deeds.htm Free Register to search free on the recorders database at www.clinton-county.org/rod/index_search.htm. Username and password is required. Also, search fictitious business names free at www.clinton-county.org/clerk/dba_search.asp.
Property, Taxation Records Free Access DeWitt, Eagle, Victor, and Watertown tax data, utility bills, and assessments free with registration at https://is.bsasoftware.com/bsa.is/SelectUnit.aspx. Property data available at http://maps.clinton-county.org/ClintonCountyCX/Disclaimer.htm, no name searching. Property tax data by subscription at www.clinton-county.org/treasurer/delq_tax_search.htm, $20 processing fee plus $.25 per parcel.

Dickinson County *Property, Taxation Records* Free Access City of Iron Mountain land and property tax data free with registration at https://is.bsasoftware.com/bsa.is/SelectUnit.aspx. County plans to have Register of Deeds records online in 2007.

Eaton County *Marriage License, New Business Records* www.eatoncounty.org/County_Clerk/CountyClerk.htm Free Access marriage license filings free at http://207.74.121.30/VitalStats/Marriage.aspx. Search new business filings free at http://207.74.121.30/VitalStats/NewBus.aspx.
Property, Taxation Records Free & $$ Search access property and tax data for Cities of Charlotte, Eaton Rapids, Grand Ledge, and Townships of Carmel and Delta for free at https://is.bsasoftware.com/bsa.is/SelectUnit.aspx. Images are $2.00 each. Includes access to delinquent tax data. Free registration and password required to access parcel data on the GIS-mapping site at http://207.74.121.41/imsweb/. For delinquent tax data, see Assessor listing for Eaton County.

Emmet County *Real Estate, Deed, Lien Records* www.co.emmet.mi.us/deeds/ Free Access recorder land records at www.co.emmet.mi.us:8080/icris/Login.jsp; registration, logon and password required to view full data; full access to all images back to 1982 is $1,000.00 per month. Also, search marriages, deaths, and assumed names free at www.co.emmet.mi.us/clerk/.
Property, Taxation Records Free Access assessor property records free at www.co.emmet.mi.us/equalization/propsrcheq.htm. Use username "general" and password "general." Also, access county property tax, land, animal licenses, and delinquent taxes free with registration at https://is.bsasoftware.com/bsa.is/SelectUnit.aspx.

Genesee County *Real Estate, Deed, Marriage, Death Records* www.co.genesee.mi.us Free Access to Register of Deeds database is free at www.co.genesee.mi.us/rod/. But to view documents back to 10/2000, there is a fee, and user ID and password required. Also, online access to the county clerk's marriage (back to 1963) and death (back to 1930) indexes are free at www.co.genesee.mi.us/vitalrec.
Property, Taxation Records Free Search property index at www.co.genesee.mi.us/cgi-bin/gweb.exe?mode=7800&sessionname=gentax&command=connect. Also, access property data for the county and for Cities of Burton, Linden and townships of Fenton, Davison, Grand Blanc, and Vienna free with registration at https://is.bsasoftware.com/bsa.is/SelectUnit.aspx.

Gladwin County *Property, Taxation Records* `Free` Access City of Gladwin property data free with registration at https://is.bsasoftware.com/bsa.is/SelectUnit.aspx.

Grand Traverse County *Real Estate, Deed, Tax Lien, Judgment, Assumed Name, Construction Permit, Marriage, Death Records* www.co.grand-traverse.mi.us `Free & $$` Except for document images, Recorder's document index search back to 1986 is free at www.co.grand-traverse.mi.us/services/online_records.htm. Images require fee; pay by credit card. Deaths go back to 1867; marriages to 1853. Also, access death and marriage indices free at www.tcnet.org/gtcounty/index.html or via the county online svcs page. Also, recording data by sub on Laredo system or Tapestry credit card system at http://tapestry.fidlar.com; $3.99 search; $.50 per image back to 1986. Also, access tax & special assessments free at https://is.bsasoftware.com/bsa.is/.
Property, Taxation Records `Free` Access property tax and special assessments free at https://is.bsasoftware.com/bsa.is/SelectUnit.aspx.

Hillsdale County *Real Estate, Deed, Judgment, Lien, UCC Records* www.co.hillsdale.mi.us `Free & $$` Access to the recorder's index is free but images available only by sub. Records go back to 9/1984 and more being added. Fee is $300.00 for recorder, or $50.00 for just the assessor's equalization records. Copies included. Call recorder for signup. Also, access to recorders index is free via a private firm at http://counties.recordfusion.com/countyweb/login.jsp?countyname=Hillsdale. Search free as Guest; registration and fees for full data. Fees to view images.
Property, Taxation Records `Free` Search parcels free at www.hillsdalecounty.info/parcelsearch.asp but no name searching. Also, access City of Hillsdale tax records free with registration at https://is.bsasoftware.com/bsa.is/SelectUnit.aspx. Map searching is available at www.gis.hillsdale.us. See County Register of Deeds section for subscription info for county assessment data.

Houghton County *Real Estate, Deed, Lien, Mortgage, UCC, Vital Records Records* www.houghtoncounty.net/directory-hcdeeds.shtml `Free` Site may be temporarily down. Access recording index free at http://fidlar.houghtoncounty.net/Search/CriteriaPage.aspx. Some death and divorce records may be on this index.

Ingham County *Real Estate, Grantor/Grantee, Deed, Marriage, Fictitious Name Records* www.ingham.org/rd/rodindex.htm `Free` Access the Register of Deeds database indexes back to 1956 - after free registration at https://qdocs.ingham.org/recorder/web/login.jsp?submit=Enter+Eagle+Web. Also, marriage applicants can be searched by the week for free at www.ingham.org/CL/Vital_Records/Marriage_Weekly_Lists.htm. Search fictitious names and campaign finance filings free at www.ingham.org/cl/Business_Filings/DBA_Lists.htm.
Property, Taxation Records `Free` Access land, tax, utility records and more free with registration for Cities of East Lansing, Lansing, Leslie, Mason and townships of Aurelius, Lansing, Vevay, and Village of Stockbridge at https://is.bsasoftware.com/bsa.is/.

Ionia County *Real Estate, Deed, Judgment, Lien, Will, Death Records* www.ioniacounty.org `Free & $$` Access recorder records free at http://66.39.252.38/cland2/landweb.dll. Login as "guest" for free name search.
Property, Taxation Records `Free` Access county property data free at www.ioniacounty.org/taxweb/viewparcels.asp. Also, access City of Belding and Ionia City and Lyons Town land and property records free with registration at https://is.bsasoftware.com/bsa.is/SelectUnit.aspx. Use www.ioniacounty.org under the heading "online parcel information" to search tax records online.

Iosco County *Property, Taxation Records* `Free` 3 jurisdictions are available free at https://is.bsasoftware.com/bsa.is/SelectUnit.aspx - City of East Tawas, and Oscoda, Plainfield, and Baldwin Townships.

Isabella County *Real Estate, Grantor/Grantee, Deed, Lien, Mortgage, UCC Records* www.isabellacounty.org `Free` Access recorder land data back to 1940 on ACS at https://mi.uslandrecords.com/milr/MilrApp/index.jsp.
Property, Taxation Records `Free` Access to City of Mt Pleasant property and tax data is free with registration at https://is.bsasoftware.com/bsa.is/SelectUnit.aspx.

Jackson County *Real Estate, Grantor/Grantee, Deed, Lien, Foreclosed Property Sale Records* www.co.jackson.mi.us/rod/ `Free` Search recorded documents at http://70.227.252.194/icris/documentSearch.jsp.
Property, Taxation Records `Free` Access property, tax and land data for the county and City of Jackson and townships of Columbia & Rives for free with registration at https://is.bsasoftware.com/bsa.is/SelectUnit.aspx. Search Columbia utility bills as well.

Kalamazoo County *Property, Taxation Records* `Free` Access property assessor data free at www.kalcounty.com/equalization/parcel_search.php. Also, access property, land, and tax data for Cities of Kalamazoo, Parchment, Portage and the townships of Alamo, Brady, Comstock, Kalamazoo, Oshtemo, Pavilion, Ross, Schoolcraft, and Wakeshma for free with registration at https://is.bsasoftware.com/bsa.is/SelectUnit.aspx. Search the treasurer's delinquent taxes free at https://is.bsasoftware.com/bsa.is/default.aspx.

Kent County *Real Estate, Deed, Lien, Vital Records, Fictitious Names Records* www.accesskent.com/YourGovernment/RegisterofDeeds/deeds_index.htm `Free & $$` Access Kent deeds index free at https://www.accesskent.com/deeds/. Fee for document $2.00 per page plus a $.50 convenience fee. Search and purchase accident reports $3.00 at https://www.accesskent.com/AccidentReports/. Order vital statistic records $7 at https://www.accesskent.com/servlet/VitalRec. Search fictitious business names free at https://www.accesskent.com/BusinessNames/.
Property, Taxation Records `Free` Search county parcel data free at https://www.accesskent.com/Property/. With username, password & credit card, view records for $1. or subscribe for $75. per year; call 616-632-6516. Also, search Grand Rapids property at

www.ci.grand-rapids.mi.us/22. Walker City assessor and more- https://is.bsasoftware.com/bsa.is/SelectUnit.aspx free registration. Search Ada, Bowne, Caledonia, Courtland, Grand Rapids, Lowell, Vergennes assessments- www.addorio.com/netparcel.htm.

Lapeer County   *Real Estate, Deed, Lien, Judgment Records*   www.county.lapeer.org/deeds/   `Free & $$`
Access recorder data free by name by clicking on "Guest Login" at http://207.72.70.14/scripts/landweb.dll. Registration and fees required for full search. Pop-up blocker must be off. Indexed images may go back to 1946.
Property, Taxation Records   `Free`   Access property, land and tax data for Cittes of Lapeer and Imlay, and townships of Almont, Imlay, Mayfield free with registration at https://is.bsasoftware.com/bsa.is/. Also has special assessment records for Lapeer.

Leelanau County   *Real Estate, Deed, Lien,Mortgage, Judgment Records*   www.leelanau.cc   `Free & $$`   Access
the recorders database of indexes free at www.leelanau.cc/RODSearch.asp. Records go back past 1/1991 to 1980 but may be subject to errors and omissions. Subscription service for full data and images; $1.25 per page or $200 per month unlimited.
Property, Taxation Records   `Free`   Access assessor property data free at www.leelanau.cc/PropertySearch.asp.

Lenawee County   *Real Estate, Deed, Will, Lien Records*   www.lenawee.mi.us/register_of_deeds/index.html   `$$`
Access to recording records available by subscription, $700 per month, $50. per hour, but nre contracts are not being taken. Some other type of online access is planned for the future.
Property, Taxation Records   `Free`   Search assessing/property data free at http://lenawee.zenacomp.com. Also, access to City of Tecumseh data including animal licensing is free with registration at https://is.bsasoftware.com/bsa.is/.

Livingston County   *Real Estate, Deed, Lien, Death Records*   www.co.livingston.mi.us/RegisterofDeeds/   `$$`
Web access to county records is available to occasional users; a dedicated line is available for professionals for $1200 fee. Annual fee for occasional use- $400, plus $.000043 per second. Records date back to 1984. Lending agency data is available. For info, contact IT Dept at 517-548-3230. Also, search the county death indices to 1948 for free at www.livgenmi.com/deathlisting.htm.
Property, Taxation Records   `Free`   Access property, tax, and other civil data for Cities of Brighton, Howell, and Townships of Brighton, Handy, Hartland, Putnam free with registration at https://is.bsasoftware.com/bsa.is/SelectUnit.aspx. Includes Village of Fowler property tax data. Also, access property data at https://www.livingstonlive.org/Property/noLogin.do.

Macomb County   *Real Estate, Deed, Business Registration, Death Records*
http://macombcountymi.gov/clerksoffice/index.asp   `Free & $$`   Property records database found at www.landaccess.com/index.jsp?content=register. Free registration for password and user name. Subscription by month or purchase on pay-per-view basis. Search business registrations free at https://macombvitals.macombcountymi.gov/dba.php. Death records at https://macombvitals.macombcountymi.gov/death.php by name or date. Also, county recorder images from a private source at www.courthousedirect.com; fees/registration required.
Property, Taxation Records   `Free`   13 cities' and towns' property, tax, and certain other civil records are free with registration at https://is.bsasoftware.com/bsa.is/.

Manistee County   *Property, Taxation Records*   `Free`   Access property records free at www.liaa.org/manisteeparcels/propertysearch.asp.

Marquette County   *Real Estate, Deed, Lien Records*   www.co.marquette.mi.us/register.htm   `$$`
Recorder land data by subscription on either the Laredo system using subscription and fees or the Tapestry System using credit card, http://tapestry.fidlar.com; $3.99 search; $.50 per image. Index and images go back to 1988.
Property, Taxation Records   `Free`   Access City of Marquette only property, tax, and building records free with registration at https://is.bsasoftware.com/bsa.is/SelectUnit.aspx.

Mason County   *Real Estate, Deed, Lien Records*   www.masoncounty.net/   `Free & $$`   3 options available to search
county register database: free- www.masoncounty.net/content.aspx?Page=Online%20Services&departmentID=10 (to be available soon). Other methods require subscription on either the Laredo system using subscription and fees or the Tapestry System using credit card, www.landrecords.net. Data goes back to 10/1994.
Property, Taxation Records   `Free`   Access county property data at www.liaa.org/masonparcels/propertysearch.asp. Access to City of Ludington parcels and tax data is free with registration at https://is.bsasoftware.com/bsa.is/SelectUnit.aspx. Ditto for Hamlin Township property, and ditto for Pere Marquette Township property and utility bills.

Mecosta County   *Property, Taxation Records*   `Free`   Access county property, land, and tax data index free with
registration at https://is.bsasoftware.com/bsa.is/SelectUnit.aspx. May charge fees to view images. Data includes City of Big Rapids and Animal License, Special Assessments, Delinquent Taxes.

Menominee County   *Real Estate, Deed Records*   www.menomineecounty.com/   `Free & $$`   Access to land
records is free at www.menomineecounty.com/online_services/category_general/ then click on '...County Land Records. Search is free - use "Guest Login." Document images may be ordered by fax for $1.50 each or mail for $1.00 each. Subs available for full data.
Property, Taxation Records   `Free`   Access property tax and land data for City of Menominee asnd Township of Menominee free with registration at https://is.bsasoftware.com/bsa.is/SelectUnit.aspx.

Midland County   *Real Estate, Deed, Lien, Judgment, Vital Records Records*   www.co.midland.mi.us   `Free & $$`
Access the county register's land records search system free at http://64.7.165.88/landweb.dll and login as Guest. Subscription required for full data; call for signup and usage fees.

Property, Taxation Records `Free` Access the county and City of Midland property data free with registration at https://is.bsasoftware.com/bsa.is/SelectUnit.aspx. County access via www.co.midland.mi.us also includes delinquent tax and animal license data.

Monroe County *Real Estate, Deed, Lien, Fictitious Name Records* www.co.monroe.mi.us/monroe/default.aspx

`Free & $$` Recorder land data by subscription on either the Laredo system using subscription and fees or the Tapestry System using credit card, http://tapestry.fidlar.com; $5.95 search; $.50 per image printed. Index goes back to 2/15/91, images to 1980. Access fictitious business names free at https://www.co.monroe.mi.us/egov/searchdbanames.aspx.

Property, Taxation Records `Free` Access assessment database land index free at https://www.co.monroe.mi.us/egov/landrecords/. Printing of images requires credit card payment. Also, access county tax bill and delinquent tax data for free with registration at https://is.bsasoftware.com/bsa.is/. This also offers access to City of Monroe Property, tax, and utility bill data.

Montcalm County *Real Estate, Deed, Lien Records* www.montcalm.org `Free & $$` Access to recorders index is

free via a private firm at http://counties.recordfusion.com/countyweb/login.jsp?countyname=Montcalm. Search free as Guest; registration and fees for full data. Fee to view images.

Property, Taxation Records `Free` Assessor property tax data is free at www.montcalm.org/taxweb/viewparcels.asp. Also, search tax roll and tax sale data free at www.co.whatcom.wa.us/treasurer/index.jsp. Access to Cities of Greenville property, tax, and land data is free with registration at https://is.bsasoftware.com/bsa.is/SelectUnit.aspx.

Muskegon County *Real Estate, Grantor/Grantee, Deed, Mortgage, Lien, Death Records*

www.co.muskegon.mi.us/deeds/ `Free & $$` Login as Great, password Muskegon, to search recorder land records free at http://216.157.207.54:8080/icris/splash.jsp. Registration and fees apply in access images. Access the county genealogical death index system for free at www.co.muskegon.mi.us/clerk/websearch.cfm. Records 1867-1965.

Property, Taxation Records `Free` Access to the city of Norton Shores tax data is free with registration at https://is.bsasoftware.com/bsa.is/. Also at this site you may access City of Roosevelt property and tax data.

Newaygo County *Real Estate, Deed, Lien, Judgment Records* www.countyofnewaygo.com `Free & $$`

Access the county land records search system free at http://rod.countyofnewaygo.com/landweb.dll. Login as Guest. Subscription required for full access, $500 monthly plus $1 per page.

Property, Taxation Records `Free` Search property data free on the GIS-mapping site at http://gis.countyofnewaygo.com/MapViews/Public%5FV2/Newaygo/viewer.htm but no name searching. A subscription version offering various options is available, call 231-689-7281 or see Also, access City of Fremont land/property data free with registration at https://is.bsasoftware.com/bsa.is/SelectUnit.aspx.

Oakland County *Real Estate, Deed, Lien, Mortgage, Assumed Name Records* www.oakgov.com/clerkrod/

`Free & $$` Access to Oakland recorded land data is by subscription at www.landaccess.com/, available $40.00 monthly (lowest fee) or $5.00 per search plus $1.00 per doc view. Search fictitious/assumed names for free at www.oakgov.com/crts0003/main.

Property, Taxation Records `Free & $$` Access to Oakland property data is by subscription, available monthly or per use. For info or sign-up, visit www.oakgov.com (click on "Access Oakland") or call Information Services at 248-858-0861. Search Rochester Hills tax assessor data at http://64.7.183.246/Services/TaxandAssessing/SearchOverview.asp. No name searching. Also access 8 municipalities land, property tax records and more free at https://is.bsasoftware.com/bsa.is/SelectUnit.aspx.

Oceana County *Real Estate, Deed Records* www.oceana.mi.us/ `Free` Access the record index back to 1/2002 free

at http://mi-oceana-recorder.governmaxa.com/recordmax/record40.asp. No images currently available.

Property, Taxation Records `Free` Access property tax and land records for Hart Township for free with registration at https://is.bsasoftware.com/bsa.is/SelectUnit.aspx. Also, access property data at http://mi-oceana-equalization.governmax. com/collectmax/collect30.asp. All Townships are included in the database except Hart - (64-007) and Benona - (64-011).

Ogemaw County *Property, Taxation Records* `Free` Access assessor equalization data free at

http://ogemaw.mi.govern.com/parcelquery.php. Also, access property data free at http://ogemawgis.com/parcelquery/website/.

Otsego County *Real Estate, Deed, Property Records* `Free` Access recorder data free at

http://66.84.47.80/otsearch.htm. Includes assessment data.

Property, Taxation Records `Free` Search assessment data on the Equalization Dept search site at http://66.84.47.80/otsearch.htm. Also, access property data at http://maps.otsegocountymi.gov/.

Ottawa County *Real Estate, Deed,Lien, Mortgage, Judgment Records* www.co.ottawa.mi.us `Free & $$`

Search recorded index and property data free at https://www.miottawa.org/Property/noLogin.do but a fee applies to view docs, purchase by subscription or with credit card. Also, access recorder records by subscription at https://www.landaccess.com/ottawa/sub.jsp?county=miottawa. Fee- $80.00 per month plus $1.00 per page to view and print; maximum $10.00 per doc. Credit card search only.

Property, Taxation Records `Free` Holland City land and tax data free at https://is.bsasoftware.com/bsa.is/SelectUnit.aspx. Also, access property and tax records for 8 municipalities free with registration as well. Includes some building and assessment data. Also, free online mapping service with parcel ID at www.gis.co.ottawa.mi.us/ottawa/. No name searching. 2nd interactive mapping site free/fee at http://miottawa.org/CoGov/Depts/GIS/mapping.htm.

Presque Isle County *Property, Taxation Records* `Free` Search property tax data free at
www.presqueisle.mi.govern.com/parcelquery.php.

Roscommon County *Real Estate, Deed, Lien, Lien, Mortgage Records* `Free`
Access land recorded index free at https://mi.uslandrecords.com/milr/controller. Select Roscommon.

Saginaw County *Real Estate, Grantor/Grantee, Deed, Assumed Business Name, Marriage, Death, Election*
Records www.saginawcounty.com `Free & $$` Search the Register of Deeds index at
www.saginawcounty.com/ROD/Simple.htm. Images are $1.00 to print, plus a $5.00 convenience fee if credit card used. Access
county clerks assumed names, marriages, death free at www.saginawcounty.com/clerk/search/index.html. Vital statistic records go
back to 1995.
Property, Taxation Records `Free` Search equalization board tax records at www.saginawcounty.com/equ/prop_info.htm.
Also, a general property and sales search on the GIS site is free at www.sagagis.org/search/.

St. Clair County *Real Estate, Deed, Lien, Marriage Records* www.stclaircounty.org/Offices/register_of_deeds/
`Free` Access register's data free at https://publicdeeds.stclaircounty.org:444/. Click on OPR. Online records go back to 5/1984.
Property, Taxation Records `Free` Search tax equalization data free at
www.stclaircounty.org/offices/equalization/search.aspx. Also, land data may be available at
http://gis.stclaircounty.org/landmanagement on the map site. Also, access land and property tax data for Cities of Algonac, Marysville,
St Clair also Townships of Clay, Cottleville, East China, and Ira for free with registration at
https://is.bsasoftware.com/bsa.is/SelectUnit.aspx.

St. Joseph County *Property, Taxation Records* `Free` Search assessor records for free at
www.stjosephcountymi.org/taxsearch/default.asp. Also, property tax and delinquent tax data and City of Sturgis land data for free
with registration at https://is.bsasoftware.com/bsa.is/SelectUnit.aspx.

Sanilac County *Property, Taxation Records* `Free & $$` Access parcel information by subscription at
www.sanilaccounty.net/subinfo.asp. Fee is $204 per year. Also, access county land and property tax records free with registration at
https://is.bsasoftware.com/bsa.is/. Access Argyle Township and Moore Township property records for free there also.

Shiawassee County *Property, Taxation Records* `Free` Access land and property tax data for Cities of Laingsburg
and Perry, and Caledonia Township for free with registration at https://is.bsasoftware.com/bsa.is/SelectUnit.aspx. Also at this site is
property tax data for Venice Township.

Tuscola County *Real Estate, Grantor/Grantee, Deed, Lien, Mortgage, Judgment, UCC Records*
www.tuscolacounty.org `Free` Access the recorder's index free at www.landaccess.com/sites/mi/tuscola/index.php.

Van Buren County *Property, Taxation Records* `Free` Access City/Township of South Haven property tax, land,
and special assessment data for free with registration at https://is.bsasoftware.com/bsa.is/SelectUnit.aspx. Also includes property
records for Townships of Antwerp and Paw Paw.

Washtenaw County *Real Estate, Deed, Lien, Judgment, Vital Records, Business Name Records*
www.ewashtenaw.org/government/clerk_register `Free & $$` Access a menu of searchable databases at
www.ewashtenaw.org/online. $1.00 fee for real estate images from Register of Deeds search page; click on Deeds Document Search.
Property, Taxation Records `Free` Search land and property tax data and more for Cities of Ann Arbor, Chelsea, Milan,
Saline, Ypsilanti, and townships of Ann Arbor, Augusta, Bridgewater, Dexter, Lodi, Pittsfield, Superior, Webster, York, Ypsilanti and
Village of Dexter for free with registration at https://is.bsasoftware.com/bsa.is/SelectUnit.aspx. Also, for Property/Parcel Lookup for
free go to http://secure.ewashtenaw.org/ecommerce/property/pStart.do

Wayne County *Real Estate, Deed, Judgment, Lien, Assumed Name Records* www.waynecounty.com/register/
`Free & $$` Search county recorder land records database for free back to '86 at www.waynecountylandrecords.com. A full data
on-demand svc and a business svc available for a fee, call 313-967-6857 for info/sign-up or see www.waynecountylandrecords.com/.
Search assumed names at www.waynecounty.com/clerk/AssumedNames/.
Property, Taxation Records `Free` Property and tax data and more for 16 municipalities free at
https://is.bsasoftware.com/bsa.is/SelectUnit.aspx. Search delinquent tax list at www.waynecounty.com/pta/Disclaimer.asp. Dearborn
property data free at www.dearbornfordcenter.com/dbnassessor/. No name searching. Also, City of Livona property data is free at
www.ci.livonia.mi.us/. No name searching. Also, search Wyandotte City tax billings free at
http://click2gov.wyan.org/Click2GovTX/Index.jsp?selection=Owner.

Wexford County *Property, Taxation Records* `Free` Access the land parcel and Assessment roll site free at
www.liaa.info/wexford/propertysearch.asp.

Other Michigan Sites of Note:
~8 counties - Ingham, Jackson, Kalamazoo, Livingston, Muskegon, Ottawa, Washtenaw, Wayne -Restaurant Reports
www.swordsolutions.com/inspections/pgeSearchRest.asp?Hit=DirectSearch&LastCty=34

Minnesota

Capital: St. Paul
          Ramsey County
Time Zone: CST
Population: 5,100,958
# of Counties: 87

Useful State Links

Website: www.state.mn.us
Governor: www.governor.state.mn.us
Attorney General: www.ag.state.mn.us
State Archives: www.mnhs.org/index.htm
State Statutes and Codes: https://www.revisor.leg.state.mn.us/pubs/
Legislative Bill Search: www.leg.state.mn.us/leg/legis.asp
Bill Monitoring: www.house.leg.state.mn.us/leg/billsublogin.asp
Unclaimed Funds: www.state.mn.us/portal/mn/jsp/content.do?id=-536881373&agency=Commerce

Primary State Agencies

Criminal Records   `Free`

Bureau of Criminal Apprehension, CJIS - Criminal History Access Unit,   www.bca.state.mn.us/CJIS/Documents/cjis-intro.html
Access to the public criminal history record (15 year, no consent) is available free at https://cch.state.mn.us/SearchOffenders.aspx.
Other Options: A public database is available on CD-ROM. Monthly updates can be purchased. Data is in ASCII format and is raw
data. Fee is $40.00

Sexual Offender Registry   `Free`

Bureau of Criminal Apprehension, Minnesota Predatory Offender Program,   https://por.state.mn.us/ Offenders and non-compliant
offender if 16 or older may be searched at https://por.state.mn.us/OffenderSearch.aspx. Risk level 3 search available at DOC site
www.doc.state.mn.us/level3/Search.asp.

Incarceration Records   `Free`

Minnesota Department of Corrections, Records Management Unit,   www.corr.state.mn.us Search at the web to retrieve public
information about adult offenders who have been committed to the Commissioner of Corrections, and who are still under our
jurisdiction (i.e. in prison, or released from prison and still under supervision). Search by name, with or without DOB, or by OID
number at http://info.doc.state.mn.us/publicviewer/main.asp. Also, there is a separate search for Level 3 offender/predatory
information. Also, a private company offers free web access at https://www.vinelink.com/vinelink/siteInfoAction.do?siteId=24002
including state, DOC, and most county jail systems.

Corporation, LLC, LP, Assumed Name, Trademarks/Servicemarks   `Free & $$`

Business Services, Secretary of State,   www.sos.state.mn.us/home/index.asp Go to www.sos.state.mn.us/home/index.asp?page=6.
This Internet site permits free look-ups of business names and corporation files. Also, a commercial program called Direct Access is
available 24 hours. There is an annual subscription fee of $75.00. Record copies or certificates may be ordered for an additional
$10.00 fee using Express Service. *Other Options:* Information can be purchased in bulk format. Call for more information.

Uniform Commercial Code, Federal & State Tax Liens   `Free & $$`

UCC Division, Secretary of State,   www.sos.state.mn.us/home/index.asp?page=89 There is a free look-up by filing number available
from the website. A fee is charged for a name search. A comprehensive commercial program called Direct Access is available 24
hours. There is an annual subscription fee of $75.00 per year, plus $5.00 per debtor name. Call 651-296-2803 for more information.
Other Options: This agency will provide information in bulk form on paper, CD or disk. Call 651-296-2803 or 877-551-6767 for more
information.

Sales Tax Registrations `Free`

Minnesota Revenue Dept, Sale and Use Tax, www.taxes.state.mn.us Email requests are accepted at business.registration@state.mn.us.

Driver Records `Free & $$`

Driver & Vehicle Services, Records Section, www.mndriveinfo.org Online access costs $1.25 per record. Online inquiries can be processed either as interactive or as batch files (overnight) 24 hours a day, 7 days a week. Requesters operate from a "bank." Records are accessed by either DL number or full name and DOB. Call Data Services at 651-297-5352 for more information. A free view of a DL status report is found at the home page above. The DL# is needed, no personal information is released. *Other Options:* Minnesota will sell its entire database of driving record information with monthly updates per DPPA guidelines. Customized request sorts are available. Fees vary by type with programming and computer time and are quite reasonable.

Vehicle Ownership & Registration `Free & $$`

Driver & Vehicle Services, Vehicle Record Requests, www.dps.state.mn.us/dvs/index.html Online access costs $5.00 per record. There is an additional monthly charge for dial-in access. The system, the same as described for driving record requests, is open 24/7. Search by name, plate, VIN or title number. Lien holder information is included. Users, who must qualify per DPPA, will receive address information. Call Records & Management Information 651-297-5352 for more information. Also, to obtain a renewal status report on a plate go to https://dutchelm.dps.state.mn.us/dvsinfo/mainframepublic.asp. Need the plate number and the last four digits of the VIN.

Birth and Death Certificates `Free`

Minnesota Department of Health, Vital Records, www.health.state.mn.us Limited online access available. You may search the Birth Certificates Index free from 1900 to 1934 at http://people.mnhs.org/bci/Search.cfm?bhcp=1. The State Historical Society offers a free Death Certificate Search at http://people.mnhs.org/dci/Search.cfm?bhcp=1. Records are from 1906 to 1996. *Other Options:* Bulk lists and files of information, if public record, are available on paper and in electronic format. Call Cheri Denardo at 651-201-5970 for details.

Occupational Licensing Boards

Abstractor/Abstractor Company
    www.state.mn.us/mn/externalDocs/Commerce/Abstractors_Enforcement_Actions_040208010433_Abstractors00-06.htm
Acupuncturist .... www.docboard.org/mn/df/mndf.htm
Adjuster .... www.commerce.state.mn.us/LicenseLookupMain.html
Alcohol/Drug Counselor................... www.health.state.mn.us/divs/hpsc/hop/adc/index.html
Ambulance Svc/Personnel................. www.emsrb.state.mn.us/cert.asp?p=s
Appraiser .... www.commerce.state.mn.us/LicenseLookupMain.html
Architect... www.aelslagid.state.mn.us/roster.html
Athletic Trainer .... www.docboard.org/mn/df/mndf.htm
Attorney.. www.courts.state.mn.us/mars/default.aspx
Barber ... ... https://www.hlb.state.mn.us/mnbce/glsuiteweb/clients/mnboc/public/License_Verifications.aspx
Barber Instructor/School https://www.hlb.state.mn.us/mnbce/glsuiteweb/clients/mnboc/public/License_Verifications.aspx
Bingo Operation .... www.gcb.state.mn.us/
Boiler Inspector .... www.doli.state.mn.us/stateinspectors.html
Bondsman (Insurance)....................... www.commerce.state.mn.us/LicenseLookupMain.html
Building Contractor, Residen'l.......... www.commerce.state.mn.us/LicenseLookupMain.html
Campground Membership Agent....... www.commerce.state.mn.us/LicenseLookupMain.html
Chiropractor....................................... https://www.hlb.state.mn.us/chi/publicaccess/search.asp
Collection Agency .... www.commerce.state.mn.us/LicenseLookupMain.html
Consumer Credit/Payday Lender....... www.commerce.state.mn.us/LicenseLookupMain.html
Contract'r/Remodeler, Resid'l........... www.commerce.state.mn.us/LicenseLookupMain.html
Controlled Substance........................ https://www.hlb.state.mn.us/mnbop/glsuiteweb/homeframe.aspx
Cosmelot't Inst/Sch https://www.hlb.state.mn.us/mnbce/glsuiteweb/clients/mnboc/public/License_Verifications.aspx
Cosmetologist/ School/Shop.............. www.commerce.state.mn.us/LicenseLookupMain.html
CPA.. www.boa.state.mn.us/Licensees/LicenseeList.aspx
CPA Firm .... www.boa.state.mn.us/Licensees/FirmList.aspx
Credit Union...................................... www.commerce.state.mn.us/LicenseLookupMain.html
Crematory.. www.health.state.mn.us/divs/hpsc/mortsci/mortsciselect.cfm
Currency Exchange .... www.commerce.state.mn.us/LicenseLookupMain.html
Debt Collector/Prorate Company....... www.commerce.state.mn.us/LicenseLookupMain.html

Dentist/Dental Asst/Dental Hygienist https://www.hlb.state.mn.us/mnbod/glsuiteweb/homeframe.aspx
Dietitian .... www.dieteticsnutritionboard.state.mn.us/Default.aspx?tabid=1001
Drug Mfg./Whlse./Dist. .... https://www.hlb.state.mn.us/mnbop/glsuiteweb/homeframe.aspx
Electrical Contractor .... www.electricity.state.mn.us/E_contrs/Elec_cty/LicensedElectricalContractors.pdf
Electrical Inspector .... www.electricity.state.mn.us/pdf/ElectricalInspectorDirectory.pdf
Electrical Techn. System Contractor . www.electricity.state.mn.us/pdf/LicensedTechnologySystemsContractors.pdf
Elevator Contractor .... www.electricity.state.mn.us/pdf/LicensedElevatorContractors.pdf
Emergency Medical Technician .... www.emsrb.state.mn.us/cert.asp?p=s
EMS Examiner .... www.emsrb.state.mn.us/examiner.asp?p=s
Engineer .... www.aelslagid.state.mn.us/roster.html
Esthetician .... www.commerce.state.mn.us/LicenseLookupMain.html
Funeral Director/Establishment .... www.health.state.mn.us/divs/hpsc/mortsci/mortsciselect.cfm
Gambling Equipment Dist./Mfg .... www.gcb.state.mn.us/
Gambling, Lawful Organization .... www.gcb.state.mn.us/
Geologist .... www.aelslagid.state.mn.us/roster.html
Grain Licensing http://www2.mda.state.mn.us/webapp/lis/default.jsp
High Pressure Inspector .... www.doli.state.mn.us/stateinspectors.html
Insurance Agency/Agent/Salesman ... www.commerce.state.mn.us/LicenseLookupMain.html
Interior Designer .... www.aelslagid.state.mn.us/roster.html
Landscape Architect .... www.aelslagid.state.mn.us/roster.html
Lawyer, Discipline .... www.courts.state.mn.us/lprb/SearchLawyer.aspx
Lender, Small .... www.commerce.state.mn.us/LicenseLookupMain.html
Liquor On-sale Retail .... www.dps.state.mn.us/age/?118,23
Liquor Store, On-sale Retail/Munic... www.dps.state.mn.us/age/?118,23
Livestock Dealer/Market/Weigher http://www2.mda.state.mn.us/webapp/lis/default.jsp
Loan Company .... www.commerce.state.mn.us/LicenseLookupMain.html
Lobbyist .... www.cfboard.state.mn.us/lob_lists.html
Lottery Retailer .... www.lottery.state.mn.us/retailer/lookup.html
Managing General Agent .... www.commerce.state.mn.us/LicenseLookupMain.html
Manicurist .... www.commerce.state.mn.us/LicenseLookupMain.html
Medical Doctor .... www.docboard.org/mn/df/mndf.htm
Medical Gas Mfg./Whlse./Dist. .... https://www.hlb.state.mn.us/mnbop/glsuiteweb/homeframe.aspx
Medical Professional Firm .... www.docboard.org/mn/df/mndf.htm
Midwife .... www.docboard.org/mn/df/mndf.htm
Mortgage Originator/Svc, Resid'l ...... https://www.egov.state.mn.us/Commerce/license_lookup.do?action=lookupForm
Mortician .... www.health.state.mn.us/divs/hpsc/mortsci/mortsciselect.cfm
Motor Vehicle Financer .... www.commerce.state.mn.us/LicenseLookupMain.html
Notary Public .... www.commerce.state.mn.us/LicenseLookupMain.html
Nurse-LPN or RN ... ...   https://www.hlb.state.mn.us/mbn/Portal/DesktopDefault.aspx?tabindex=0&tabid=41
Nursing Home Administrator .... www.benha.state.mn.us/beta/Default.aspx?tabid=782
Nutritionist .... www.dieteticsnutritionboard.state.mn.us/Default.aspx?tabid=1001
Occupational Therapist .... www.health.state.mn.us/divs/hpsc/hop/otp/licprac.html
Optometrist .... www.optometryboard.state.mn.us/Default.aspx?tabid=799
Pesticide Applicator .... www.mda.state.mn.us/licensing/online/default.htm
Pharmaceutical Technician .... https://www.hlb.state.mn.us/mnbop/glsuiteweb/homeframe.aspx
Pharmacist/Pharmacy .... https://www.hlb.state.mn.us/mnbop/glsuiteweb/homeframe.aspx
Physician Assistant .... www.docboard.org/mn/df/mndf.htm
Podiatrist .... https://www.hlb.state.mn.us/sblmonline/public/default.aspx
Political Action Committee .... www.cfboard.state.mn.us/campfin/pcfatoz.html
Political Candidate .... www.cfboard.state.mn.us/cand_lists.html
Preceptor .... https://www.hlb.state.mn.us/mnbop/glsuiteweb/homeframe.aspx
Real Estate Agent/Broker/Dealer .... www.commerce.state.mn.us/LicenseLookupMain.html
Re-Insurance Intermediary .... www.commerce.state.mn.us/LicenseLookupMain.html
Respiratory Care Practitioner .... www.docboard.org/mn/df/mndf.htm
Securities Sales/Investment Advisor . www.commerce.state.mn.us/LicenseLookupMain.html
Social Worker   https://www.hlb.state.mn.us/BOSW/Online/DesktopModules/ServiceForm.aspx?svid=21&mid=164
Soil Scientist .... www.aelslagid.state.mn.us/roster.html

Surgeon...www.docboard.org/mn/df/mndf.htm
Surveyor, Land ....www.aelslagid.state.mn.us/roster.html
Teacher http://education.state.mn.us/mde/Teacher_Support/Educator_Licensing/View_an_Individual_Educators_License/index.html
Telemedicine ....www.docboard.org/mn/df/mndf.htm
Thrift/Industrial Loan Company........www.commerce.state.mn.us/LicenseLookupMain.html
Undergr'nd Storage Tank Contr./Svr. www.pca.state.mn.us/cleanup/ust.html#certification
Veterinarian......................................www.vetmed.state.mn.us/Default.aspx?tabid=801

State and Local Courts

State Court Structure: There are 97 District Courts (some counties gave divisional courts) comprising 10 judicial districts. The limit for small claims is $7500 unless the case involves a consumer credit transaction then the limit is $4000.

Statewide Court Online Access: Minnesota offers the Trial Court Public Access (MPA) at http://pa.courts.state.mn.us/default.aspx. Search statewide or by county. Records available include criminal, civil, family, and probate. Searches can be performed using a case number or by name. Calenders can be looked-up by district at www.mncourts.gov/default.aspx?page=512.

But there are a number of caveats - certain publicly-accessible case records cannot be viewed online.

Electronic copies of public documents filed by parties also cannot be viewed online at this time. Name searches for criminal case records will not return pre-conviction criminal records. A statewide case inquiry may exclude district courts that have not yet converted to the system. Also, the public access terminals found at the courthouses do not use this system. For example, party street address and name searches on criminal pre-conviction case records are publicly accessible and available at the courthouse, but not online. The federal Violence Against Women Act (VAWA) also prevents the state from displaying harassment and domestic abuse case records online, but these are available at the courthouse. Comment fields for all case types are not available online but are available at the courthouse. Online users are not notified when such public data is restricted from online viewing.

The bottom line is the public access terminals found at courthouses are still the most accurate searching locations. In Judicial Districts (arranged by number and often covering several counties) many court's public access terminals contain court records for that entire district. The online system is supplemental at best.

The state provides free access to Appellate and Supreme Court opinions at www.mncourts.gov/default.aspx?page=1650. An approved bail bond agent list search is also free.

❖ **Statewide Access Offered For All Trial Courts – Read Above** ❖

Note: No individual Minnesota courts offer online access.

Recorders, Assessors, and Other Sites of Note

Recording Office Organization: 87 counties, 87 recording offices. The recording officer is the County Recorder. Federal and state tax liens on personal property of businesses are filed with the Secretary of State. Other federal and state tax liens are filed with the County Recorder.

Online Access Note: There is no statewide system but a number of counties offer web access to assessor data and recorded deeds.

Aitkin County *Property, Taxation Records* Free Access property data free at http://gisweb.co.aitkin.mn.us/wf2_aitkinpublic/Default.aspx. Click on Search to search by name.

Anoka County *Real Estate, Deed Records* www.co.anoka.mn.us SS Access to the County online records requires an annual fee of $35 and a $25 monthly fee and $.25 per transaction. Records date back to 1995. Lending agency data is available. For info, contact Pam LeBlanc at 763-323-5424. There is also a dial-up property information system at 763-323-5400.

Property, Taxation Records `Free` Access property data at https://prtinfo.co.anoka.mn.us. No name searching.

Becker County *Property, Taxation Records* `Free` Access to the assessor property data is free at http://gis-server.co.becker.mn.us/website/beckerpublic/. Also, search plat images free at www.co.becker.mn.us/dept/recorder/plats_online.aspx.

Beltrami County *Real Estate, Deed, Lien Records* www.co.beltrami.mn.us `$$` Recorder land data by subscription on either the Laredo system using subscription and fees or the Tapestry System using credit card, see http://tapestry.fidlar.com; $3.99 search; $.50 per image. Index goes back to 1985, images to 2002.

Benton County *Plats/Tract Records* www.co.benton.mn.us `Free` Access to plats/tract available for free at www.co.benton.mn.us/Recorder/plats.asp
Property, Taxation Records `Free` Free search of Auditor property tax data at http://65.77.74.200/bentoncounty/parcelsearch.aspx but no name searching.

Blue Earth County *Property, Taxation Records* `Free` Access to the property data search database is free at www.co.blue-earth.mn.us/tax/. Also, you may search at www.blueearth.minnesotaassessors.com. No name searching at either site, but a subscription service is available at the latter.

Brown County *Real Estate, Grantor/Grantee, Deed, Tract Records* www.co.brown.mn.us `Free` Real Estate, Grantor/Grantee Index and Tract index to be available 10/2008.
Property, Taxation Records `Free` Search property maps for assessment data free at www.co.brown.mn.us/brown_mn/gismain.htm. No name search.

Carlton County *Real Estate, Deed, Lien Records* www.co.carlton.mn.us `$$` Access recorder land records via the Laredo/Tapestry subscription web system. Fees start at $50 per month; $.35 to print an image. Index goes back to 1989, images to 2003 with earlier being added. Also a per search service; pay with credit card.

Carver County *Real Estate, Grantor/Grantee, Deed, Lien Records* www.co.carver.mn.us `Free` Access to recorder land records free at http://landshark.co.carver.mn.us/ with registration required.
Property, Taxation Records `Free` Access property and tax roll data free at https://www.co.carver.mn.us/carvercountyrecap/ParcelSearch.aspx but no name searching. Also search the GIS-mapping site free at http://gis.co.carver.mn.us/website/gishome/disclaimer_parcel_search.html but no name searching.

Cass County *Real Estate, Deed, Lien Records* www.co.cass.mn.us `$$` Real estate data available by subscription on either the Laredo system using sub and fees or the Tapestry System using credit card, http://tapestry.fidlar.com; $3.99 search; $.50 per image. Index goes back to 4/1/87; images to 5/5/1965.
Property, Taxation Records `Free` Access property data at www.co.cass.mn.us/cassmnpublicreports/taxsearch/search.aspx but no name searching. View GIS-mapping data free at www.co.cass.mn.us/website/cass/viewer.asp?theValue=cassparcel&Cmd=INIT. No name searching.

Chippewa County *Real Estate, Deed, Lien Records* www.co.chippewa.mn.us/ `$$` Recorder land data by subscription on either the Laredo system using subscription and fees or the Tapestry System using credit card, http://tapestry.fidlar.com; $3.99 search; $.50 per image. Index goes back to 1991; images to 1998.
Property, Taxation Records `Free` Access property tax records free at www.co.chippewa.mn.us/taxdisclaim.htm but no name searching.

Chisago County *Real Estate, Grantor/Grantee, Deed Records* www.co.chisago.mn.us `Free & $$` Access to the recorder's real property data back to 1988 is by subscription with LandShark, see http://24.56.144.170/LandShark/login.jsp.
Property, Taxation Records `Free` Search the treasurer's search site at http://24.56.144.168/chisagocountyrecap. Also, access parcel data at the GIS-mapping site after discalimer at http://24.56.144.170/wf2_chisagopublic/Default.aspx but no name searching.

Clay County *Real Estate, Deed, Lien, Plat, Corner Certificate Records* www.co.clay.mn.us `$$` Access recorder land data by subscription on either the Laredo system using sub and fees or the Tapestry System using credit card, http://tapestry.fidlar.com; $5.95 search; $.50 per image. Index goes back to 1987; images to 1976. Plats and corner certificates online free at www.co.clay.mn.us/depts/recorder/laredo/rerrol.htm.
Property, Taxation Records `Free` Search property tax data free at www.tax.co.clay.mn.us/claycountymn/ but not name searching. Also, search property data free on the GIS mapping site at www.maps.co.clay.mn.us/map/Clay/disclaimer.htm but no name searching.

Clearwater County *Property, Taxation Records* `Free` Search property records free at taxinfo.co.clearwater.mn.us by address or parcel number. Also, access free online maps at www.co.clearwater.mn.us/website/clearwaterpublic/main.php.

Cook County *Real Estate, Deed, Lien Records* www.co.cook.mn.us `$$` Recorder land data by subscription on either the Laredo system using fees or the Tapestry System using credit card, http://tapestry.fidlar.com; $3.99 search; $.50 per image. Abstracts go back to 1987, Torrens to 1974.
Property, Taxation Records `Free` Access Cook County Maps free at www.co.cook.mn.us/maps/maps.html.

Cottonwood County *Real Estate, Deed, Lien Records* www.co.cottonwood.mn.us/countyrecorder.html $$
Recorder land data by subscription on either the Laredo system using subscription and fees or the Tapestry System using credit card, http://tapestry.fidlar.com; $3.99 search; $.50 per image. Index and images go back to 9/12/2000.

Crow Wing County *Real Estate, Deed, Lien Records* www.co.crow-wing.mn.us $$ Access to recorder data is available by subscription, $50.00 per month and $.25 per image. Email the County Recorder at kathyl@co.crow-wing.mn.us for info and signup, or visit http://erecord.co.crow-wing.mn.us/LandShark/
Property, Taxation Records Free Access assesor data free at www.taxdata.co.crow-wing.mn.us/taxdata/ but no name searching. Access county plat maps for free at www.co.crow-wing.mn.us/surveyor/crow_wing_county_plat_maps.html.

Dakota County *Property, Taxation Records* Free Real Estate Inquiry records database is free at http://gis.co.dakota.mn.us/scripts/esrimap.dll?Name=webq1&Cmd=Map&. Includes address, estimated value, taxes, last sale price, building details.

Dodge County *Property, Taxation Records* Free access to property tax records is free at http://secure.co.dodge.mn.us/dodgeCounty/.

Douglas County *Property, Taxation Records* Free Look-up assessor property tax data free at http://morris.state.mn.us/tax/.

Faribault County *Real Estate, Deed, Lien Records* $$ Recorder land data by subscription on either the Laredo system using subscription and fees or the Tapestry System using credit card, http://tapestry.fidlar.com; $3.99 search; $.50 per image. Index back to 1995; images to 9/15/03.

Freeborn County *Property, Taxation Records* Free Online access to property records is available at http://qpublic.net/mn/freeborn/.

Goodhue County *Real Estate, Deed, Lien Records* www.co.goodhue.mn.us $$ Access to recorder's land records is by subscription through LandShark at http://156.99.35.20/LandShark/login.jsp. Fees $50.00 monthly. Username, and password required.
Property, Taxation Records Free Access property and sales data free at www.co.goodhue.mn.us/goodhuecountyrecap/ but no name searching. Search property data free on the GIS-mapping site at http://goodhuecounty.plansightgis.com/launch.htm but no name searching. There is also a forfeited land list at www.co.goodhue.mn.us/departments/auditortreasurer/ForfeitedLandList.aspx.

Grant County *Property, Taxation Records* Free Look-up assessor property tax data free at http://morris.state.mn.us/tax/ or also, search current property tax free at http://206.145.187.205/tax/disclaimer.asp?cid=26 but no name searching.

Hennepin County *Real Estate, Deed, Lien Records* www.co.hennepin.mn.us $$ Access to Hennepin County online records requires a $35 annual fee with a charge of $5 per hour from 7AM-7PM, or $4.15 per hour at other times. Records date back to 1988. Only lending agency data is available. An Automated phone system is also available; 612-348-3011.
Property, Taxation Records Free Search parcel property tax records on county Property Information Search database free at http://www16.co.hennepin.mn.us/pins/.

Houston County *Property, Taxation Records* Free & $$ Online access to property records is available at http://beacon.schneidercorp.com/.

Hubbard County *Real Estate, Deed, Lien Records* www.co.hubbard.mn.us/Recorder.htm $$ Recorder land data by subscription on either the Laredo system using subscription and fees or the Tapestry System using credit card, http://tapestry.fidlar.com; $3.99 search; $.50 per image. Index and images go back to 6/1992.
Property, Taxation Records Free Access property tax data free at www.co.hubbard.mn.us/wf2_hubbardpublic/Default.aspx.

Isanti County *Property, Taxation Records* Free Search assessor property and tax data free at http://65.77.74.200/IsantiCounty/parcelsearch.aspx. Access monthly sales sheets by Town for free at www.co.isanti.mn.us/depart.htm#assess. Access property data free on the GIS-mapping site at http://204.73.107.41/isanti7/index.htm. No name searching.

Itasca County *Real Estate, Deed, Lien Records* www.co.itasca.mn.us $$ Access recorder land data by sub on either the Laredo system using subscription and fees or the Tapestry System using credit card, http://tapestry.fidlar.com; $3.99 search; $.50 per image. Index goes back to 4/87; images to 10/15/93.
Property, Taxation Records Free Access property and parcel data free from a private company at www.parcelinfo.com/parcels/.

Kanabec County *Property, Taxation Records* Free Online access to property records is available at www.qpublic.net/mn/kanabec/.

Kandiyohi County *Real Estate, Deed, Lien Records* www.co.kandiyohi.mn.us `$$` Access recorder land data by subscription on either the Laredo system using subscription w/ fees or the Tapestry System using credit card, https://www.landrecords.net; $3.99 search; $.50 per image. Index back to 3/1987; images to 1/1998.
Property, Taxation Records `Free` Look-up assessor property tax data free at http://morris.state.mn.us/tax/.

Koochiching County *Real Estate, Deed, Lien Records* www.co.koochiching.mn.us `$$` Access recorder land data by subscription on either the Laredo system using sub and fees or the Tapestry System using credit card, http://tapestry.fidlar.com; $3.99 search; $.50 per image. Index goes back to 1980, images to 3//2000.
Property, Taxation Records `Free` Access to property and parcel data is free from a private company at www.parcelinfo.com.

Lake County *Real Estate, Deed, Lien, Mortgage, Misc. Records* www.co.lake.mn.us `$$` Recorder land data by subscription on either the Laredo system using subscription and fees or the Tapestry System using credit card, http://tapestry.fidlar.com; $3.99 search; $.50 per image. Links available through county website. Index goes back to 1996; images to 1997.
Property, Taxation Records `Free` Access property data free at www.parcelinfo.com; click on Lake County Users Click Here. Also can access via the county website www.co.lake.mn.us/.

Le Sueur County *Real Estate, Deed Records* www.co.le-sueur.mn.us/Recorder.html `$$` Access to recorder's land records is by subscription through LandShark at http://156.99.35.20/LandShark/login.jsp. Fees of $50.00 installation, $2.00 per doc viewed, username, and password required.

Lincoln County *Real Estate, Deed, Lien Records* www.mncounties3.org/lincoln/ `$$` Recorder land data by subscription on either the Laredo system using subscription and fees or the Tapestry System using credit card, http://tapestry.fidlar.com; $3.99 search; $.50 per image. Index and images go back 1/1997.

Lyon County *Real Estate, Deed, Lien Records* www.lyonco.org `$$` Recorder land data by subscription on either the Laredo system using subscription and fees or the Tapestry System using credit card, http://tapestry.fidlar.com; $3.99 search; $.50 per image. Index back to 1987; images to 1998.
Property, Taxation Records `Free` Look-up assessor property tax data free at http://morris.state.mn.us/tax/.

McLeod County *Real Estate, Deed Records* www.co.mcleod.mn.us/recorder `$$` Access recorder data by subscription at http://landshark.co.mcleod.mn.us/eddie/. Set-up $50 plus $50.00 per month, plus $2.00 per image.
Property, Taxation Records `Free` Access to property records and tax information for free go to www.co.mcleod.mn.us/. Check property taxes and delinquent taxes online at www.co.mcleod.mn.us. Click on the link to the right of the county logo in the middle of the page. Info goes back to 1993.

Marshall County *Property, Taxation Records* `Free` Look-up assessor property tax data free at http://morris.state.mn.us/tax/.

Martin County *Real Estate, Deed, Lien Records* www.co.martin.mn.us `$$` Recorder land data by subscription on either the Laredo system using sub and fees or the Tapestry System using credit card, http://tapestry.fidlar.com; $5.95 search; $.50 per image. Index and images go back to 1982.
Property, Taxation Records `Free & $$` Online access to property records is available at http://beacon.schneidercorp.com/.

Meeker County *Property, Taxation Records* `Free` Look-up assessor property tax data free at http://morris.state.mn.us/tax/.

Mille Lacs County *Property, Taxation Records* `Free` Look-up assessor property tax data free at http://morris.state.mn.us/tax/.

Morrison County *Real Estate, Deed, Lien Records* www.co.morrison.mn.us `$$` Access is via a subscription dial-up service; $50 setup plus $50 monthly charged annually, and $25 de-activation fee if you quit. Info and Signup with Bunny at 320-632-0145.
Property, Taxation Records `Free` Search for property data on a GIS-mapping site free at http://beacon.schneidercorp.com/. Search delinquent taxes list free at www.co.morrison.mn.us/category.aspx?Id=2B87D349-BED5-40F5-9E73-705EDC6A8880.

Mower County *Real Estate, Grantor/Grantee, Deed, Lien Records* www.co.mower.mn.us/Recorder01.htm `$$` Access recorder land data for fee on either the Laredo system using subscription and fees or the Tapestry System using credit card, http://tapestry.fidlar.com; $3.99 search; $.50 per image. Index back to 1988; images to 8/1999.
Property, Taxation Records `Free` Search property assessor data free at www.mower.minnesotaassessors.com. No name searching for free, but a sub service is available which does.

Nobles County *Property, Taxation Records* `Free` Look-up assessor property tax data free at http://morris.state.mn.us/tax/.

Norman County *Property, Taxation Records* `Free` Look-up assessor property tax data free at http://morris.state.mn.us/tax/.

Olmsted County *Property, Taxation Records* `Free` Property records and GIS-map data is available free at https://webapp.co.olmsted.mn.us/propertytax/Site/Default.aspx

Otter Tail County *Real Estate, Deed Records* www.co.otter-tail.mn.us `$$` Access recorder office real estate data by a LandShark subscription at www.co.otter-tail.mn.us/LandShark/login.jsp. User name and login required. Call recorder office for details and sign-up
Property, Taxation Records `Free` Search property tax data at www.co.otter-tail.mn.us/taxes/. Parcel searching or map searching only.

Pope County *Real Estate, Deed, Lien Records* www.mncounties3.org/pope/ `$$` Recorder land data by subscription on either the Laredo system using subscription and fees or the Tapestry System using credit card, http://tapestry.fidlar.com; $3.99 search; $.50 per image. Index and images goes back to 11/1987.
Property, Taxation Records `Free` Look-up assessor property tax data free at http://morris.state.mn.us/tax/disclaimer.asp?cid=61. Also, access to county property/parcel data is free at http://morris.state.mn.us/tax/.

Ramsey County *Real Estate, Deed Records* www.co.ramsey.mn.us/prr/recorder/index.htm `$$` This agency's extensive search product including recorded documents is available by subscription; see http://rrinfo.co.ramsey.mn.us/public/Document/index.pasp.
Property, Taxation Records `Free` Search the property assessment rolls free at http://rrinfo.co.ramsey.mn.us/public/characteristic/index.pasp but no name searching.

Redwood County *Property, Taxation Records* `Free` Look-up assessor property tax data free at http://morris.state.mn.us/tax/.

Renville County *Property, Taxation Records* `Free` Look-up assessor property tax data free at http://morris.state.mn.us/tax/.

Rice County *Property, Taxation Records* `Free & $$` Search assessor property data free on the GIS system at http://beacon.schneidercorp.com/ but no name searching. Search parcel data and residential/commercial sales data free at www.rice.minnesotaassessors.com. No name searching for free but a sub service is also available with name searching.

Rock County *Real Estate, Deed, Lien Records* www.co.rock.mn.us `$$` Access Recorder land data by subscription on either the Laredo system using subscription and fees or the Tapestry System using credit card, http://tapestry.fidlar.com; $3.99 search; $.50 per image. Index and images goes back to 10/1992.
Property, Taxation Records `Free` Look-up assessor property tax data free at http://morris.state.mn.us/tax/.

Roseau County *Property, Taxation Records* `Free & $$` Online access to property records is available at http://136.234.18.34/website/roseau/login.php. For access, please contact Trish Harren at trish.harren@co.roseau.mn.us or at (218) 463-4248.

St. Louis County *Property, Taxation Records* `Free & $$` Access auditor tax records for tax professionals database by subscription. Fee is $100 monthly. For info or sign-up, contact Pam Palen at 218-726-2380 or email to palenp@co.st-louis.mn.us or visit www.co.st-louis.mn.us/auditorsoffice/subscription.pdf. Also, search auditor info for free at www.co.st-louis.mn.us/auditor/parcelinfo/. Also, search the City of Duluth property assessor data free at www.ci.duluth.mn.us/city/assessor/index.htm.

Scott County *Property, Taxation Records* `Free` Search assessor and a variety of other property data free at http://www2.co.scott.mn.us/stellent/idcplg/records/pxs?IdcService=SC_PROPERTYTAX_HOME but no name searching. Search the county property databases free by link at www.co.scott.mn.us/wps/portal/ScottCounty/. There is also a free online document subscription service and GIS mapping.

Sherburne County *Property, Taxation Records* `Free & $$` Property records from the county tax assessor database are free at http://beacon.schneidercorp.com/?site=SherburneCountyMN. However, to perform a name search, you must subscribe; fee is $25.00 setup and $300.00 per year. Also, search plats free at www.co.sherburne.mn.us/pubworks/Plat/plat_search.asp.

Stearns County *Property, Taxation Records* `Free` Records from the county tax assessor database are free at http://secure.co.stearns.mn.us/. No name searching.

Steele County *Real Estate, Deed, Lien Records* www.co.steele.mn.us `$$` Access recorder land data by subscription on either the Laredo system using sub and fees or the Tapestry System using credit card, http://tapestry.fidlar.com; $3.99 search; $.50 per image. Index goes back to 4/1991; images to 11/13/93.
Property, Taxation Records `Free` Search parcel data free at www.co.steele.mn.us/auditor/auditor.html.

Stevens County *Property, Taxation Records* `Free` Look-up assessor property tax data free at http://morris.state.mn.us/tax/.

Swift County *Property, Taxation Records* Free Access parcel data by address, ID, or book/page for free at http://morris.state.mn.us/tax/.

Todd County *Property, Taxation Records* Free Access property data on the GIS-mapping site free at www.co.todd.mn.us/TODDCOUNTY/propertyinfo0003.asp but no name or address searching. Also, look-up assessor property tax data free at http://morris.state.mn.us/tax/. Search buildings at www.co.todd.mn.us/TODDCOUNTY/propertyinfo0012.asp. Also, access to county property/parcel data is free at http://morris.state.mn.us/tax/.

Wabasha County *Property, Taxation Records* Free Access property information free at www.co.wabasha.mn.us/index.php?option=com_wrapper&Itemid=108.

Wadena County *Property, Taxation Records* Free Search tax parcels free at www.co.wadena.mn.us/website/wadenapublic/main.php but no name searching.

Waseca County *Real Estate, Deed, Mortgage. Records* www.co.waseca.mn.us/recorder.htm $$ With registration, username and password you may access recording data on LandShark system at http://landshark.co.waseca.mn.us/LandShark/login.jsp. Fee is $50.00 per month, plus copy fee for images.

Washington County *Real Estate, Deed, Lien, Mortgage, Plat, Tract Records* www.co.washington.mn.us $$ Access to county tract records requires a $50.00 set up fee and $30.00 monthly fee; abstract images go back to 7/1994; Torrens images to 10/1989; tracts to 1984. UCC and Torrens cert. data is not on this system.
Property, Taxation Records Free Access to property tax records is free at http://www2.co.washington.mn.us/opip/; no name searching - property ID or address required.

Wright County *Real Estate, Grantor/Grantee, Deed, Lien Records* www.co.wright.mn.us Free Access to Land Title database is free at www.co.wright.mn.us/department/recorder/landtitle/index.htm.
Property, Taxation Records Free Search the property tax database for free at www.co.wright.mn.us/department/audtreas/proptax/default.asp.

Yellow Medicine County *Property, Taxation Records* Free Look-up assessor property tax data free at http://morris.state.mn.us/tax/.

Other Minnesota Sites of Note:

Cass County - Warrants, Most Wanted www.co.cass.mn.us/sheriff/sheriff_home.html
Clay County - Jail www.info.co.clay.mn.us/DailyLockup/LockUp.pdf Daily County lock-up list in pdf format.
Cook County - Maps www.co.cook.mn.us/maps/maps.html
Goodhue County - Sheriff Inmates, Warrants www.co.goodhue.mn.us/departments/sheriff/jailrostersearch.aspx

Mississippi

Capital: Jackson
                Hinds County
Time Zone: CST
Population: 2,918,785
# of Counties: 82

Useful State Links

Website: www.mississippi.gov
Governor: www.governor.state.ms.us
Attorney General: www.ago.state.ms.us
State Archives: www.mdah.state.ms.us
State Statutes and Codes: www.sos.state.ms.us/ed_pubs/mscode/
Legislative Bill Search: http://billstatus.ls.state.ms.us/
Unclaimed Funds: www.treasury.state.ms.us/Unclaimed/

Primary State Agencies

Sexual Offender Registry   `Free`

DPS- MS Bureau of Investigations, Sexual Offender Registry, www.sor.mdps.state.ms.us The state Sex Offender Registry can be accessed at the website. Search by last name, city, county, or ZIP Code.

Incarceration Records   `Free`

Mississippi Department of Corrections, Records Department, www.mdoc.state.ms.us Search online by name only from the website. Click on Inmate Search. Also, search the Parole Board records (click on Parole Board and follow instructions).

Corporation, LP, LLP, LLC, Trademarks/Servicemarks   `Free`

Secretary of State, Business Services, www.sos.state.ms.us/busserv/index.asp A variety of online search services are available at www.sos.state.ms.us/busserv/corp/soskb/csearch.asp. There is no fee to view records, including officers and registered agents. A Good Standing can be ordered. You can download images for no charge. Also, search securities companies, charities, fundraisers, and pre-needs registered with the state at www.sos.state.ms.us/regenf/ifs/. *Other Options:* The Data Division offers bulk release of information on an annual subscription basis ($1500). Monthly subscription to list of new corporations and new qualifications is $25.00.

Uniform Commercial Code, Federal & State Tax Liens   `Free`

Secretary of State, Business Services - UCC, www.sos.state.ms.us/busserv/ucc/ucc.asp Free searching for UCC debtors is at www.sos.state.ms.us/busserv/ucc/soskb/SearchStandardRA9.asp. *Other Options:* monthly list of farm liens is available for purchase.

Workers' Compensation Records   `Free`

Workers Compensation Commission, www.mwcc.state.ms.us The First Report of Injury and other documents are available via the web. There is no fee, but users must register.

Driver Records   `$$`

Department of Public Safety, Driver Services, www.dps.state.ms.us/dps/dps.nsf/main?OpenForm Both interactive and batch delivery is offer for high volume users only. Billing is monthly. Hook-up is through the Advantis System, fees apply. Lookup is by name only; not by driver license number. Fee is $11.00 per record. For more information, call the Director's office. Another service is available. Drivers may view their own record online at https://www.ms.gov/hp/drivers/license/motorVehicleReportBegin.do. The MVR shows the current status of the license and the moving violations on record. Use of credit card required. *Other Options:* Overnight batch delivery by tape is available.

Vehicle Ownership & Registration   `$$`

Mississippi State Tax Commission, Registration Department, www.mstc.state.ms.us/mvl/main.htm Internet access to vehicle records is available to approved, DPPA compliant entities. Accounts must pay an annual $100 registration fee, record search fees are the same as listed above. Access is via the web. *Other Options:* Mississippi offers some standardized files as well as some customization for bulk requesters of VIN and registration information. For more information, contact MLVB at the address listed above.

Vital Records $$

State Department of Health, Vital Statistics & Records, www.msdh.state.ms.us/phs/index.htm Orders for birth, death and marriage records can be placed via a state designated vendor. Go to www.vitalchek.com.Fees are involved.

Occupational Licensing Boards

Architect	www.archbd.state.ms.us/main_find_licensee.html
Attorney/Attorney Firm	www.msbar.org/lawyerdirectory.php
Camp, Youth	www.msdh.state.ms.us/msdhsite/index.cfm/30,332,183,html
Charity	www.sos.state.ms.us/regenf/charities/charannrpt/index.asp
Child Care/Residential Facility	www.msdh.state.ms.us/msdhsite/index.cfm/30,332,183,html
Chiropractor	www.msbce.ms.gov/msbce/msbce.nsf/Search?OpenForm
Contractor, Commercial-Residential	www.msboc.us/search.cfm
Counselor, Professional	www.lpc.state.ms.us/html/search.html
CPA-Certified Public Accountant	www.msbpa.state.ms.us/licsearch.html
Dentist/or/Dental Hygienist	www.msbde.state.ms.us/msbde/msbdesearch.nsf/WebStart?OpenFOrm
Dental Radiologist	www.msbde.state.ms.us/msbde/msbdesearch.nsf/WebStart?OpenFOrm
Domestic Insurance Company	www.doi.state.ms.us/pdf/domesticlist.pdf
Engineer	http://dsitspe01.its.state.ms.us/pepls/EngSurveyors.nsf
Fund Raiser	www.sos.state.ms.us/regenf/charities/charannrpt/index.asp
Funeral Pre-Need Contractor	www.sos.state.ms.us
Geologist	www.msbrpg.state.ms.us/rpg.htm
HMO	www.doi.state.ms.us/pdf/hmolist.pdf
Home Inspector	http://appserver.mrec.ms.gov/findlicensee.asp
Insurance Agent/Solic./Adviser/Firm	www.doi.state.ms.us/licapp/
Investment Advisor	www.sos.state.ms.us
Landscape Architect	www.archbd.state.ms.us/main_find_licensee.html
Lobbyist	www.sos.state.ms.us/elections/Lobbying/Lobbyist_Dir.asp
Long Term Care Insurance Firm	www.doi.state.ms.us/pdf/ltclist.pdf
Medical Doctor	www.msbml.state.ms.us
Notary Public	www.sos.state.ms.us/busserv/notaries/notaries.asp
Nurse-LPN-RN	https://www.ms.gov/msbn/inquiry_disclaimer.do
Nursing Home Administrator	www.bnha.state.ms.us/msbnha/roster.nsf/webpage/bnha_1?editDocument
Optometrist	www.msbo.ms.gov/msbo/OptoRoster.nsf/webpage/Opto_1?editdocument
Osteopathic Physician	www.msbml.state.ms.us
Pharmacy/Pharmacist/Intern/Techn	www.mbp.state.ms.us/mbop/PharmRoster.nsf/webpage/Pharm_1?editdocument
Podiatrist	www.msbml.state.ms.us
Psychologist	www.psychologyboard.state.ms.us/msbp/msbp.nsf/Search?OpenForm
Real Estate Agent/Seller/Broker	http://appserver.mrec.ms.gov/findlicensee.asp
Real Estate Appraiser	http://appserver.mrec.ms.gov/findappraiser.asp
Securities Agent/Broker/Dealer	www.sos.state.ms.us
Security Offering	www.sos.state.ms.us
Surplus Lines Insurer	www.doi.state.ms.us/licapp/downloadlist.aspx
Surveyor, Land	http://dsitspe01.its.state.ms.us/pepls/EngSurveyors.nsf

State and Local Courts

State Court Structure: The court of general jurisdiction is the Circuit Court with 70 courts in 22 districts. Justice Courts were first created in 1984, replacing Justice of the Peace Courts. Prior to 1984, records were kept separately by each Justice of the Peace, so the location of such records today is often unknown. Jasper County added a 2nd Justice Court in 5/2008, located in City of Paulding. In MS, Probate matters are handled by the Chancery Courts, as are property matters.

Statewide Court Online Access: A statewide online computer system is in use internally for court personnel. The website at www.mssc.state.ms.us offers searching of the MS Supreme Court and Court of Appeals Decisions and dockets.

Adams County
Circuit & County Court   **$$**
Civil: The Circuit Court Case and Judgment Roll Information is $25/monthly or $275/yearly. A user account must be created and subscription purchased to use this service at www.deltacomputersystems.com/MS/MS01/ *Criminal:* The Circuit Court Case and Judgment Roll Information will be $25/monthly or $275/yearly. A user account must be created and subscription purchased to use this service at www.deltacomputersystems.com/MS/MS01/.

De Soto County
Circuit & County Court   www.desotoms.com   **Free**
Civil: Search docket information, records and judgments free at www.desotoms.info/. *Criminal:* Search docket info and records free at www.desotoms.info/.

Harrison County
Circuit Court - 1st District   **Free**
Civil: Access to Judicial District judgments are free at http://co.harrison.ms.us/departments/circlerk/rolls/. Search current court dockets free at http://co.harrison.ms.us/dockets/. *Criminal:* Search current court dockets free at http://co.harrison.ms.us/dockets/.

Circuit Court - 2nd District   **Free**
Civil: Access to Judicial District judgments are free at http://co.harrison.ms.us/departments/circlerk/rolls/. Search current court dockets free at http://co.harrison.ms.us/dockets/. *Criminal:* Search current court dockets free at http://co.harrison.ms.us/dockets/.

Justice Courts District 1 & 2   http://co.harrison.ms.us/departments/justice/cntdst1.asp   **Free**   Search Justice court tickets free at http://co.harrison.ms.us/departments/justice/tickets/index.asp.

Biloxi and Gulfport Chancery Courts   http://co.harrison.ms.us/departments/chanclerk/court.asp   **Free**   Search Chancery Court dockets for free at http://co.harrison.ms.us/dockets/.

Jackson County
Circuit Court   www.co.jackson.ms.us/DS/CircuitCourt.html   **Free**
Civil: Access to only Circuit Court monthly dockets is free at www.co.jackson.ms.us/DS/CircuitDockets.html. *Criminal:* Online access to criminal dockets only is the same as civil.

Chancery Court   http://www.co.jackson.ms.us/DS/ChanceryCourts.html   **Free**   Access Chancery Court monthly dockets free at www.co.jackson.ms.us/DS/ChanceryDockets.html.

Madison County
Chancery Court   http://www.madison-co.com/court_systems/chancery_court/index.php   **Free**   Search chancery cases free at www.madison-co.com/elected_offices/chancery_clerk/court_house_search/case_file_inquiry.php, also docket descriptions www.madison-co.com/elected_offices/chancery_clerk/court_house_search/search_docket_descriptions.php.

Marion County
Chancery Court   **Free**   Court records and calendars online at www.deltacomputersystems.com/MS/MS46/INDEX.html.

Pearl River County
Chancery Court   **Free**   Search court cases free at www.deltacomputersystems.com/search.html and click on Pearl River.

Recorders, Assessors, and Other Sites of Note

Recording Office Organization: 82 counties, 92 recording offices. The recording officers are Chancery Clerk, and Clerk of Circuit Court for state tax liens. Ten counties have two separate recording offices - Bolivar, Carroll, Chickasaw, Harrison, Hinds, Jasper, Jones, Panola, Tallahatchie, and Yalobusha. Federal tax liens on personal property of businesses are filed with the Secretary of State. Federal tax liens on personal property of individuals are filed with the county Chancery Clerk. State tax liens on personal property are filed with the county Clerk of Circuit Court. State tax liens on real property are filed with the Chancery Clerk.

Online Access Note: A limited number of counties offer online access to records; there is no statewide system except for the Secretary of State's UCC access, and the State Tax Commission Property Tax Landrolls by County at www.mstc.state.ms.us/taxareas/property/countylr07.htm.

Adams County *Judgment, Circuit Court, Voter Registration Records* `$$` Access judgments, voter registration, circuit courts (go back to 1997, scanned 12/02 to present) for a fee go to www.deltacomputersystems.com/search.html.

Alcorn County *Property, Taxation Records* `Free` Access is free at www.deltacomputersystems.com/MS/MS02/index.html

Clay County *Property, Taxation Records* `Free` Search records free at www.mstc.state.ms.us/taxareas/property/countylr07.htm

Covington County *Property, Taxation Records* `Free` Land rolls available at www.mstc.state.ms.us/taxareas/property/countylrs.htm.

De Soto County *Real Estate, Grantor/Grantee, Deed, Voter Registration, Foreclosure, Subdivision, Marriage Records* www.desotoms.info `Free` Access to Chancery Clerk grantor/grantee index is available at www.desotoms.info; click on "Chancery Clerk." For voter registration data, click on Circuit Clerk and then Voter Registration tab. Also available, county board and planning commission minutes. For courts and marriages, click on Circuit Clerk.
Property, Taxation Records `Free` Access to assessor property data and tax collector data is free at www.desotoms.info. Click on "Tax Assessor." GIS-mapping site is also available.

Forrest County *Property, Taxation Records* `Free` Access property tax or appraisal records free at www.deltacomputersystems.com/search.html.

George County *Property, Taxation Records* `Free` Access to the property tax records is free at www.deltacomputersystems.com/MS/MS20/plinkquerym.html.

Grenada County *Property, Taxation Records* `Free` Search assessor real property and tax sale free at www.tscmaps.com/mg/ms/grenada/index.asp but no name searching.

Hancock County *Property, Taxation Records* `Free` Access property data free through the GIS-mapping site owner search page free at www.geoportalmaps.com/atlas/hancock/asp/owner.asp. Search parcel data generally on the mapping site free at www.geoportalmaps.com/atlas/hancock/viewer.htm.

Harrison County *Real Estate, Grantor/Grantee, Deed, UCC, Voter Registration, Marriage, Judgment Records* http://co.harrison.ms.us `Free` Access all records through the county portal at http://co.harrison.ms.us. Also, search chancery clerk Deed & Record index back 20 years. Also, search voter registration and marriage licenses. Also, search circuit court judgment rolls at http://co.harrison.ms.us/departments/circlerk/rolls/.
Property, Taxation Records `Free` Access property tax data free at www.deltacomputersystems.com/MS/MS24DELTA/DATALINK.html or http://co.harrison.ms.us/departments/chanclerk/proplink.asp.

Hinds County *Real Estate, Grantor/Grantee, Deed, Judgment Records* www.co.hinds.ms.us `Free` Access to the county clerk database index is free at www.co.hinds.ms.us/pgs/apps/gindex.asp. Chose to search general index, land roll, judgments, acreage, subdivision, condominiums.
Property, Taxation Records `Free` Access tax roll, property, and other assessor-related data free at www.co.hinds.ms.us/pgs/apps/gindex.asp or www.co.hinds.ms.us/pgs/apps/landroll_query.asp.

Lafayette County *Property, Taxation Records* `Free` Access to property data is free at www.deltacomputersystems.com/ms/ms36/plinkquerym.html

Lamar County *Property, Taxation Records* `Free` Access to property data is free at www.deltacomputersystems.com/MS/MS37/INDEX.html

Lauderdale County *Property, Taxation Records* `Free` Access property data free at www.deltacomputersystems.com/MS/MS38/INDEX.html.

Lawrence County *Property, Taxation Records* `Free` Search appraisal, Real Property Tax, and tax sales lists free at www.tscmaps.com/mg/ms/lawrence/index.asp.

Lee County *Property, Tax Records* `Free` Access land at www.deltacomputersystems.com/MS/MS41/INDEX.html.

Leflore County *Property, Taxation Records* `Free` Access real property data for free at http://cdms.datasysmgt.com/dsmh/WWREALH1.

Lincoln County *Real Estate, Grantor/Grantee, Deed Records* `Free` Access to county deed records is free at www.deltacomputersystems.com/MS/MS43/drlinkquerym.html.

Lowndes County *Property, Taxation Records* `Free` Access property assessor data free at www.lowndesassessor.com/mappage.asp.

Madison County *Real Estate, Deed, Mortgage, Federal Lien, Plat, Covenant Records* www.madison-co.com/elected_offices/chancery_clerk/ **Free** Access the Chancery clerks recorded land records free at www.madison-co.com/elected_offices/chancery_clerk/. Other databases available. Also, search at www.madison-co.com/online_services/index.php for Federal Lien, Chancery Ct, Plat, Covenant, and more.
Property, Taxation Records **Free** Access Land Roll data free at www.madison-co.com/elected_offices/tax_assessor/real_property_search.php. Also, search personal property tax data free at www.madison-co.com/elected_offices/tax_assessor/personal-property-tax-roll.php. Also, search parcels/property on the GIS-mapping site free at www.tscmaps.com/mg/ms/madison/mappage.asp?county=43

Marion County *Real Estate, Deed, Probate, Judgment, Redemption Records* **Free** Access county records free at www.deltacomputersystems.com/MS/MS46/INDEX.HTML. Says it is a subscription service, but searching is free. Recorder index goes back to 5/1997; no images.
Property, Taxation Records **Free** Access property data free at www.deltacomputersystems.com/MS/MS46/pappraisalm.html Also, access property tax data free at www.deltacomputersystems.com/MS/MS46/PLINKQUERYM.HTML.

Marshall County *Property, Taxation Records* **Free** Access to property tax records is free at www.deltacomputersystems.com/MS/MS47/INDEX.html.

Monroe County *Property, Taxation Records* **Free** Access property records free on the mapping site at www.tscmaps.com/mg/ms/monroe/index.asp.

Neshoba County *Property, Taxation Records* **Free** Access to property data is free at www.deltacomputersystems.com/MS/MS50/index.html.

Oktibbeha County *Real Estate, Deed, Lien Records* www.oktibbehachanceryclerk.com **$$** Search county information at www.oktibbehachanceryclerk.com/online-search/index.php. An account with username and password is required to login; call Larry Bellipani at 601-583-7373.
Property, Taxation Records **Free** Online access to property records, appraisals, tax sale lists free at www.tscmaps.com/mg/ms/oktibbeha/index.asp

Pearl River County *Property, Taxation Records* **Free** Access to property data is free at www.pearlrivercounty.net/tax/index.htm

Pike County *Real Estate, Grantor/Grantee, Deed Records* www.co.pike.ms.us **Free** Access to county Deeds & Records is free at www.co.pike.ms.us/drlinkquery.html.
Property, Taxation Records **Free** Search property assessor and tax records free at www.co.pike.ms.us/plinkquery.html.

Rankin County *Property, Taxation Records* **Free** Records on the county Land Roll database are free at www.rankincounty.org/TA/LandRollDB.asp.

Scott County *Property, Taxation Records* **Free** Online access to property tax records is available on the state site at www.mstc.state.ms.us/taxareas/property/main.htm.

Stone County *Property, Taxation Records* **Free** Access property tax records free at www.deltacomputersystems.com/search.html.

Tate County *Property, Taxation Records* **Free** Access real property data for free at http://cdms.datasysmgt.com/dsmh/WWREALH1.

Union County *Property, Taxation Records* **Free** Access property tax records free at www.deltacomputersystems.com/MS/MS73/INDEX.HTML.

Warren County *Property, Taxation Records* **Free** Access is free at www.deltacomputersystems.com/MS/MS75/INDEX.html.

Washington County *Property, Taxation Records* **Free** Access is free at www.deltacomputersystems.com/MS/MS76/INDEX.html.

Winston County *Property, Taxation Records* **Free** Access real property data for free at http://cdms.datasysmgt.com/dsmh/WWREALH1.

Other Mississippi Sites of Note:
Harrison County - Voter Registration http://co.harrison.ms.us/departments/circlerk/voter/

Missouri

Capital: Jefferson City
           Cole County
Time Zone: CST
Population: 5,878,415
# of Counties: 114

Useful State Links

Website: www.state.mo.us
Governor: www.mo.gov/mo/govoffices.htm
Attorney General: http://ago.mo.gov/
State Archives: www.sos.mo.gov/archives/Default.asp
State Statutes and Codes: www.moga.state.mo.us/STATUTES/STATUTES.HTM
Legislative Bill Search: www.house.mo.gov/billcentral.aspx
Unclaimed Funds: www.treasurer.mo.gov/mainUCP.asp

Primary State Agencies

Sexual Offender Registry `Free`

Missouri State Highway Patrol, Sexual Offender Registry, www.mshp.dps.mo.gov/CJ38/search.jsp The name index can be searched at the website, by name, county or ZIP Code. The web page also gives links lists to the county sheriffs that have online access. *Other Options:* Look at bottom of disclaimer page for access to Excel spreadsheet.

Incarceration Records `Free`

Missouri Department of Corrections, Probation and Parole, www.doc.missouri.gov No Internet searching is available from this agency. However, you may email a single request to probation&parole@doc.mo.gov or constituentservices@doc.mo.gov. Spell the full name correctly. An email response will be provided to you, usually within 24 hours of receipt during regular business hours. This only provides general search information and policy information. Department does not provide search data to companies conducting background checks.

Corporation, LLC, LP, LLP, Fictitious Name, Trademarks/Servicemarks `Free`

Secretary of State, Corporation Services, www.sos.mo.gov/business/corporations/ Search free online at https://www.sos.mo.gov/BusinessEntity/soskb/csearch.asp. The corporate name, the agent name or the charter number is required to search. The site will indicate the currency of the data. Many business entity type searches are available.

Uniform Commercial Code `Free`

UCC Division, Attn: Records, www.sos.mo.gov/ucc/ Free searching for debtor names is available on the Internet at www.sos.mo.gov/ucc/soskb/searchstandardRA9.asp. Search by name or file number. Images are no longer available. For an electronic copy of the image of the UCC filing, send an e-mail to UCCMail@sos.mo.gov. The e-mail must contain the File #, name, and address of the filing. *Other Options:* The agency will release information for bulk purchase, call for procedures and pricing.

Workers' Compensation Records `Free`

Labor & Industrial Relations Department, Workers Compensation Division, www.dolir.mo.gov/wc/index.htm Online access is available to claimants using a pre-assigned PIN.

Driver Records `$$`

Department of Revenue, Motor Vehicle Bureau, http://dor.mo.gov/mvdl/drivers/ Online access of Information Exchange costs $1.25 per record plus network charges that will vary for $.05 to $1.00 per record. Online inquiries can be put in Missouri's "mailbox" any time of the day. These inquiries are then picked up at 2 AM the following morning, and the resulting MVR's are sent back to each customer's "mailbox" approx. 2 hours later. Record requests may also be emailed to dlrecords@dor.mo.gov. Include credit card information for processing. Note: This system may undergo extensive changes in the late Spring of 2008, including a fee increase. *Other Options:* The entire license file can be purchased, with updates. Call 573-751-0299 for more information.

Vehicle, Vessel Ownership & Registration $$

Department of Revenue, Motor Vehicle Bureau, http://dor.mo.gov/ Online record searches are available to registered entities who have a DPPA security access code issued by the Department. The fee is $1.25 per record and is automatically withdrawn through the requestor's ACH account. Access is via the Internet. Visit the web page for more information. *Other Options:* Missouri has an extensive range of records and information available on magnetic tape, labels or paper. Besides offering license, vehicle, title, dealer, and marine records, specific public report data is also available.

Accident Reports Free

Missouri State Highway Patrol, Traffic Division, www.mshp.dps.missouri.gov/MSHPWeb/PatrolDivisions/TFD/index.html Information on accidents investigated by the Highway Patrol for the most recent 29 days only are found at www.mshp.dps.mo.gov/HP68/search.jsp. *Other Options:* Some crash reconstruction reports may be available via CD, depending on date of crash. CD includes photos and other attachments.

Birth and Death Certificates Free & $$

Department of Health & Senior Srvs, Bureau of Vital Records, www.dhss.mo.gov Orders may be placed online at www.vitalchek.com. Birth records prior to 1910 and death records 50 years and older can be searched at www.sos.mo.gov/archives/resources/birthdeath/.

Occupational Licensing Boards

Acupuncturist .... http://pr.mo.gov/licensee-search.asp
Anesthesia Permit, Dental .... http://pr.mo.gov/licensee-search.asp
Animal Technician .... http://pr.mo.gov/licensee-search.asp
Ankle Specialist................................. http://pr.mo.gov/licensee-search.asp
Announcer, Athletic Event/Ring........ http://pr.mo.gov/licensee-search.asp
Architect.. http://pr.mo.gov/licensee-search.asp
Athletic Trainer .... http://pr.mo.gov/licensee-search.asp
Attorney... http://members.mobar.org/members/LawyerSearch/GSSearch.aspx
Audiologist .... http://pr.mo.gov/licensee-search.asp
Audiologist/Speech Path'gist, Clin'l.. http://pr.mo.gov/licensee-search.asp
Barber Instructor/School.................... http://pr.mo.gov/licensee-search.asp
Barber/Barber Shop .... http://pr.mo.gov/licensee-search.asp
Beauty Shop .... http://pr.mo.gov/licensee-search.asp
Body Piercing/Branding Estab. .... http://pr.mo.gov/licensee-search.asp
Boxer/Boxing Professional................ http://pr.mo.gov/licensee-search.asp
Brander... http://pr.mo.gov/licensee-search.asp
Cemetery .... http://pr.mo.gov/licensee-search.asp
Chiropractor....................................... http://pr.mo.gov/licensee-search.asp
Cosmetology-related Occupation ...... http://pr.mo.gov/licensee-search.asp
Counselor, Professional/Trainee........ http://pr.mo.gov/licensee-search.asp
Dentist/Dental Hygienist .... http://pr.mo.gov/licensee-search.asp
Drug Distributor .... http://pr.mo.gov/licensee-search.asp
DSGA Permit/Site Certificate............ http://pr.mo.gov/licensee-search.asp
ECS Permit/Site Certificate .... http://pr.mo.gov/licensee-search.asp
Embalmer .... http://pr.mo.gov/licensee-search.asp
Engineer .... http://pr.mo.gov/licensee-search.asp
Esthetician .... http://pr.mo.gov/licensee-search.asp
Funeral Director/Establishm't/Seller . http://pr.mo.gov/licensee-search.asp
General Anesthesia Permit .... http://pr.mo.gov/licensee-search.asp
Geologist .... http://pr.mo.gov/licensee-search.asp
Hairdresser... http://pr.mo.gov/licensee-search.asp
Hearing Instrument Specialist............ http://pr.mo.gov/licensee-search.asp
Insurance Agent/Broker..................... www.insurance.mo.gov/industry/producer/agtstatus.htm
Insurance Consultant, Chiropractic.... http://pr.mo.gov/licensee-search.asp
Interior Designer................................ http://pr.mo.gov/licensee-search.asp
Interpreter for the Deaf...................... http://pr.mo.gov/licensee-search.asp
Landscape Architect .... http://pr.mo.gov/licensee-search.asp
Lobbyist Report.................................. www.mec.mo.gov/Ethics/Lobbying/LobElecReports.aspx

Manicurist...http://pr.mo.gov/licensee-search.asp
Marital & Family Therapist..............http://pr.mo.gov/licensee-search.asp
Martial Artist/Martial Art Occ..........http://pr.mo.gov/licensee-search.asp
Massage Therapist...........................http://pr.mo.gov/licensee-search.asp
Medical Doctor.................................http://pr.mo.gov/licensee-search.asp
Notary Public...................................www.sos.mo.gov/Notary/NotarySearch/NotarySearch.aspx
Nurse/or/ Nurse Midwife..................http://pr.mo.gov/licensee-search.asp
Nursing Home Administrator ....www.dhss.mo.gov/BNHA/
Nursing School ....http://pr.mo.gov/licensee-search.asp
Occupation'l Therapist/Therap't Asst http://pr.mo.gov/licensee-search.asp
Optometrist......................................http://pr.mo.gov/licensee-search.asp
Osteopathic Physician.......................http://pr.mo.gov/licensee-search.asp
Parentaral Conscious Sedation ....http://pr.mo.gov/licensee-search.asp
PCS Permit/Site Certificate ....http://pr.mo.gov/licensee-search.asp
Perfusionist.....................................http://pr.mo.gov/licensee-search.asp
Pesticide Applicator/Tech/Dealer......www.kellysolutions.com/MO/
Pharmacist/Pharmacy Intern/Techn...http://pr.mo.gov/licensee-search.asp
Physical Therapist/ Therapist Assist..http://pr.mo.gov/licensee-search.asp
Physician Assistant...........................http://pr.mo.gov/licensee-search.asp
Physician, Athletic Event ....http://pr.mo.gov/licensee-search.asp
Podiatrist...http://pr.mo.gov/licensee-search.asp
Pre-Need Provider/Seller, Funeral.....http://pr.mo.gov/licensee-search.asp
Psychologist.....................................http://pr.mo.gov/licensee-search.asp
Public Accountant CPA/Partnership..http://pr.mo.gov/licensee-search.asp
Real Estate-related Occupation..........http://pr.mo.gov/licensee-search.asp
Real Estate Appraiser ....http://pr.mo.gov/licensee-search.asp
Respiratory Care Practitioner ....http://pr.mo.gov/licensee-search.asp
School Nurse ....http://pr.mo.gov/licensee-search.asp
Social Worker...................................http://pr.mo.gov/licensee-search.asp
Speech Language Pathologist ....http://pr.mo.gov/licensee-search.asp
Statewide/Legis. Candidate Com'tee. www.mec.mo.gov/Ethics/CampaignFinance/CF_PublicSearch.aspx?Candidate
Surveyor, Land ....http://pr.mo.gov/licensee-search.asp
Tattoo Artist/Establishment...............http://pr.mo.gov/licensee-search.asp
Teacher...https://k12apps.dese.mo.gov/webapps/tcertsearch/tc_search1.asp
Timekeeper, Athletic Event...............http://pr.mo.gov/licensee-search.asp
Veterinarian/Vet Tech/Vet Facility ...http://pr.mo.gov/licensee-search.asp
Wrestler/Wrestling Professional........http://pr.mo.gov/licensee-search.asp

State and Local Courts

State Court Structure: The Circuit Court is the court of general jurisdiction. There are 45 circuits comprised of 115 county Circuit Courts and one independent City Court. There are also Associate Circuit Courts with limited jurisdiction. A growing trend is to form Combined Courts (23 consolidated in 2005/2006). Municipal Courts only have jurisdiction over traffic and ordinance violations.

Statewide Court Online Access: Available at www.courts.mo.gov/casenet/cases/searchCases.do is Missouri Casenet, an online system for access to docket data. The system includes all Circuit Courts, City of St. Louis, the Eastern, Western, and Southern Appellate Courts, the Supreme Court, and Fine Collection Center. Some counties only offer probate case data. Cases can be searched case number, filing date, or litigant name from 6AM-1AM M-F. Also, search Supreme Court and Appellate Court opinions at the home page.

❖ **Statewide Access Offered All Trial Courts — Read Above**

On Next Page are Additional Sites ❖

St. Louis County

Circuit Court of St. Louis County - Civil   www.stlouisco.com/circuitcourt   **Free**
Civil: Search civil index free at www.stlouisco.com/CourtCaseSearch/index.aspx?TabId=ac or at
www.courts.mo.gov/casenet/base/welcome.do.

Associate Circuit - Civil Division   www.stlouisco.com/circuitcourt   **Free**
Civil: Search civil index free at www.stlouisco.com/CourtCaseSearch/index.aspx?TabId=ac. Also, search small claims index free at
www.stlouisco.com/CourtCaseSearch/index.aspx?TabId=sc. Search probate index free at
www.stlouisco.com/CourtCaseSearch/frmProbateSearch.aspx?TabId=pr. Also search probate records back to July 6, 2004 free on the
state online court record system at www.courts.mo.gov/casenet/base/welcome.do.

Circuit Court of St. Louis County - Criminal   www.stlouisco.com/circuitcourt   **Free**
Criminal: Participates in the free state online court record system at www.courts.mo.gov/casenet/base/welcome.do. Online records go
back to 1986.

St. Louis City

Circuit Courts - Civil   www.courts.mo.gov/hosted/circuit22/   **Free**
Civil: Online access to civil records is free at www.courts.mo.gov/casenet/base/welcome.do Remote access is also through MoBar Net
and is open only to attorneys. Call 314-535-1950 for information. Also, probate records are free online at
www.courts.mo.gov/casenet/base/welcome.do. Online probate records go back to 1/1990.

City of St Louis Circuit Court - Criminal   www.courts.mo.gov/hosted/circuit22/   **Free**
Criminal: Participates in the free state online court record system at www.courts.mo.gov/casenet/base/welcome.do.

Recorders, Assessors, and Other Sites of Note

Recording Office Organization: 114 counties and one independent city; 115 recording offices. The
recording officer is the Recorder of Deeds. City of St. Louis has its own recording office. Watch for ZIP Codes
that may be City of St. Louis or County of St. Louis. All federal and state tax liens are filed with the county
Recorder of Deeds. Tax liens are usually indexed together.

Online Access Note: A limited number of counties offer online access to records; there is no statewide system
except for the Secretary of State's UCC access.

Audrain County   *Property, Taxation Records*   **$$**   Search assessor property data for a fee on the GIS system at
http://beacon.schneidercorp.com. Registration and username required. At the default website, choose Missouri then Audrain County,
then register.

Boone County   *Real Estate, Lien, Marriage, UCC Records*   www.showmeboone.com/RECORDER/   **Free**
Access to the recorder database is free at www.showmeboone.com/recorder.
Property, Taxation Records   **Free**   Assessor data of real and personal property is free at www.showmeboone.com/assessor/.
Free registration and password required.

Buchanan County   *Real Estate, Deed, Lien, UCC, Marriage, Divorce, Judgment, Will, Military Discharge*
Records   www.co.buchanan.mo.us   **Free**   Access the recorder database free at http://67.98.136.123/or_wb1/default.asp.
Property, Taxation Records   **Free**   Search the GIS-mapping site for property data free at www.buchanancomogis.com but no
name searching.

Cape Girardeau County   *Real Estate, Deed, Lien Records*   **$$**   Recorder land data by subscription on either the
Laredo system using subscription and fees or the Tapestry System using credit card, http://tapestry.fidlar.com; $5.99 search; $.50 per
image. Index goes back to 1/1989; images to 1995.

Cass County   *Real Estate, Deed, Lien Records*   www.casscounty.com/cassfr.htm   **Free & $$**   Access to the
recorders official records database at http://207.14.218.122/or_wb1/ requires a username/password; inquire through Recorder's office.
Property, Taxation Records   **Free**   Username and password required from assessor (phone- 816-380-8179) to access assessor
property data at www.cass.mo.promap.com. Also, search for property tax records free at
https://mylocalgov.com/casscountymo/pubbizinq21.asp?countyname2=cass. Look up tax bills free at
https://mylocalgov.com/casscountymo/pubbizinq9.asp?countyname2=cass.

Christian County   *Real Estate, Deed, Marriage, Tax Lien Records*   www.christiancountymo.gov   **Free & $$**
Access the recording office records free at http://landrecords.christiancountymo.gov. Real estate, marriage, and UCC records go back
to 10/1994; tax liens to 1/3/2000. Username and password is Public.

Property, Taxation Records **Free** Search tax payment lookup at www.christiancountycollector.com/christian-payment.php.

Clay County *Real Estate, Deed, RE UCCs, Marriage, Military Discharge Records*
http://recorder.claycogov.com/pages/index.asp **Free** Access to the recorder's database is free at http://recorder.claycogov.com/pages/online_access.asp. Overall index goes back to 7/1986; images back to 1986. Real estate only UCCs back to 1986. No images for marriages, discharges, just data.

Property, Taxation Records **Free** Access assessor property records free at http://gisweb.claycogov.com/realEstate/realEstate.jsp but no name searching. Also, access real estate records from Collector's Office free at https://collector.claycogov.com. Also, search county property manually on the GIS-mapping site free at http://gisweb.claycogov.com/gis/viewer.htm.

Cole County *Property, Taxation Records* **Free & $$** Access property and other mapping data free at www.midmogis.org/InteractiveMapIndex.html. There is a add'l GIS-mapping site with data, but subscription is required at www.midmogis.org/website/colecounty/

De Kalb County *Property, Taxation Records* **$$** Search assessor property data for a fee on the GIS system at http://beacon.schneidercorp.com/. Registration and username required.

Franklin County *Real Estate, Deed, Lien Records* www.franklinmo.org. **$$** Recorder land data by subscription on either the Laredo system using subscription and fees or the Tapestry System using credit card, http://tapestry.fidlar.com; $3.99 search; $.50 per image. Index and images go back to 1/1983.

Greene County *Real Estate, Recoding, Deed, Lien, UCC Records* www.greenecountymo.org **Free** Search the recorder database for free at www.greenecountymo.org/recorder/realsearch.php. Search UCCs and tax liens at www.greenecountymo.org/recorder/ucctaxsearch.php.

Property, Taxation Records **Free** Search assessors data free at www.greenecountyassessor.org/OwnerSearch.asp.

Howell County *Real Estate, Deed, Lien Records* **$$** Access recorder land data by subscription on either the Laredo system using subscription and fees or Tapestry System using credit card, http://tapestry.fidlar.com; $3.99 search; $.50 per image. Index goes back to 1991; images to 1/1998.

Jackson County (Kansas City) *Real Estate, Grantor/Grantee, Deed, Lien, Marriage, Judgment, UCC Records* www.jacksongov.org **Free & $$** Search the recorder Grantor/Grantee database for free at http://records.co.jackson.mo.us/search.asp?cabinet=opr. Also, access recording office land data at www.etitlesearch.com; registration required, fee based on usage. Also, search Kansas City land data free at http://kivaweb.kcmo.org/kivanet/2/land/lo okup/index.cfm?fa=dslladdr. Search the marriage records free at http://records.co.jackson.mo.us/search.asp?cabinet=marriage. Search the UCC database at http://records.co.jackson.mo.us/search.asp?cabinet=ucc.

Property, Taxation Records **Free** Search property tax data free at www.jacksongov.org/TaxSrch/.

Jefferson County *Real Estate, Deed Records* www.jeffcomo.org **$$** Access recording office land data at www.etitlesearch.com; registration required, fee based on usage; call 870-856-3055 for info. Also, recorder land data by subscription on either the Laredo system using subscription and fees or the Tapestry System using credit card, http://tapestry.fidlar.com; $3.99 search; $.50 per image. Index goes back to 1/1985; images to 6/17/2002.

Property, Taxation Records **Free** Search assessor property data for free at www.jcao.org/.

Laclede County *Real Estate, Grantor/Grantee, Deed, Marriage, Tax Lien, Plat, Survey Records*
http://lacledecountymissouri.org/recorder/ **Free & $$** Access to recorders documents indexes is free at http://69.68.214.114/search.php but registration and fees for images.

Lincoln County *Real Estate, Deed, Tax Lien, UCC Records* www.lincoln.mo.us.landata.com **Free & $$** Access recording real estate and UCC records after registering at www.lincoln.mo.us.landata.com. Click on New To This Site to register. Index search is free; there is a fee to purchase documents; credit cards accepted. Real estate records index goes back to 1/1/1988; Tax liens back to 10/1/2001.

Property, Taxation Records **Free** For free parcel searches go to www.lincolncomogis.com/lincoln/. Click on Parcel Search.

Miller County *Property, Taxation Records* **$$** Property data is on CD-rom; fees vary. Call Assessor office to order.

Mississippi County *Real Estate, Deed Records* **Free & $$** Access land records at http://etitlesearch.com. You can do a name search; choose from $200.00 monthly subscription or per click account.

New Madrid County *Real Estate, Deed Records* **$$** Land records may be available at http://etitlesearch.com. You can do a name search; choose from $200.00 monthly subscription or per click account.

Newton County *Real Estate, Deed, Mortgage, UCC, Lien, Vital Statistic Records* www.ncrecorder.org **Free**
Search the index free back to 1994 at www.ncrecorder.org/searchaccess.htm.

Pemiscot County *Real Estate, Deed Records* **$$** Access land records at http://etitlesearch.com. You can do a name search; choose from $200.00 monthly subscription or per click account.

Perry County *Real Estate, Deed, Lien Records* $$ Recorder land data by subscription on either the Laredo system using subscription and fees or the Tapestry System using credit card, http://tapestry.fidlar.com; $5.95 search; $.50 per image. Index goes back to 1989; images to 12/99.

Pettis County *Real Estate, Deed, Lien Records* www.pettiscomo.com $$ Recorder land data by subscription on either the Laredo system using subscription and fees or the Tapestry System using credit card, http://tapestry.fidlar.com; $3.99 search; $.50 per image. Index and images go back to 7/1/93.
Property, Taxation Records $$ Search assessor property data for a fee on the GIS system at http://beacon.schneidercorp.com/ with registration and username required.

Platte County *Real Estate, Lien, UCC, Marriage Records* www.co.platte.mo.us/county_off_rec.html Free To access recorder's indexes online, complete the online deed form and a password will be issued; No fee at this time.
Property, Taxation Records Free Assessor data available free at http://maps.co.platte.mo.us/. Also, access the Collector's tax payments data free at www.plattecountycollector.com/platte-payment.php but parcel ID or account number required.

Putnam County *Property, Taxation Records* Free Free parcel search at http://putnam.missouriassessors.com/search.php?mode=search.

Ray County *Property, Taxation Records* Free Free assessor parcel search at http://ray.missouriassessors.com/search.php?mode=search.

St. Charles County *Property, Taxation Records* Free Access recorder records free at http://scharles.landrecordsonline.com/. Search index free; images -$1.00 per page. Also, search property assessment data free at http://assessor.sccmo.org/assessor/index.php?option=com_assessordb&Itemid=49. No name searching.

St. Francois County *Real Estate, Deed, Lien Records* www.sfcgov.org $$ Recorder land data by subscription on the Tapestry System using credit card, http://tapestry.fidlar.com; $3.99 search; $.50 per image. Index goes to 1994; images to 2005.
Property, Taxation Records Free Access property assessor data free at www.sfcassessor.org/parcel_search.html.

St. Louis County *Property, Taxation Records* Free Access county property data free at http://revenue.stlouisco.com/ias/. Search personal property tax data free at http://revenue.stlouisco.com/Collection/ppInfo/.

St. Louis City *Real Estate, Deed, Lien Records* $$ Recorder land data by subscription on either the Laredo system using subscription and fees or the Tapestry System using credit card, http://tapestry.fidlar.com; $3.99 search; $.50 per image. Index goes back to 1/1881. Images are only available with a Laredo subscription, or via the recorder office.
Property, Taxation Records Free Mapping site available free at www.co.st-louis.mo.us/plan/gis/. Search personal property by account number, address, or name at http://revenue.stlouisco.com/Collection/ppInfo/

Saline County *Real Estate, Grantor/Grantee, Deed, Lien Records* $$ Recorder land data by subscription on either the Laredo system using subscription and fees or the Tapestry System using credit card, http://tapestry.fidlar.com; $3.99 search; $.50 per image. Index goes back to 1992; images to 1996.

Scott County *Real Estate, Deed Records* Access recording office land data at www.etitlesearch.com; registration required, fee based on usage.

Stone County *Real Estate, Grantor/Grantee, Deed, UCC, Subdivision, Condominium Records* www.stoneco-mo.us Free Access to recorder data is free through land access.com at www.landaccess.com/sites/mo/stone/index.php?mostone
Property, Taxation Records Free Access property data from the GIS interactive map at www.stoneco-mo.us/disclaim.htm. Download the MapGuide viewer first.

Taney County *Real Estate, Deed, Lien Records* www.co.taney.mo.us $$ Recorder land data by subscription on either the Laredo system using subscription and fees or the Tapestry System using credit card, http://tapestry.fidlar.com; $3.99 search; $.50 per image. Index and images go back to 7/1/1994.
Property, Taxation Records Free Search assessor property data free on the GIS system at http://beacon.schneidercorp.com.

Warren County *Real Estate, Deed, Lien Records* $$ Recorder land data by subscription on either the Laredo system using subscription and fees or the Tapestry System using credit card, http://tapestry.fidlar.com; $3.99 search; $.50 per image.

Webster County *Real Estate, Deed, Lien, UCC Records* $$ Access to recorded data is by subscription; $200.00 per month. Get info and register through the recorder's office.

Other Missouri Sites of Note:
Cass County - Most Wanted, Sex Offender www.cassmosheriff.org
Clay County - Sex Offender, Most Wanted www.claycogov.com/county/offices/sheriff/
Greene County - Sex Offender www.greenecountymo.org/Soffend/
Jackson County - Sex Offenders www.jacksongov.org/JCSOR/

Montana

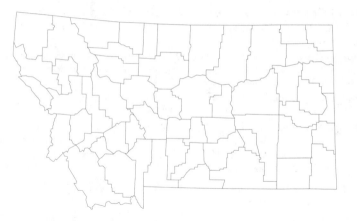

Capital: Helena
         Lewis and Clark County
Time Zone: MST
Population: 957,862
# of Counties: 56

Useful State Links

Website: http://mt.gov/
Governor: http://mt.gov/gov2/default.asp
Attorney General: www.doj.mt.gov/department/attorneygeneral.asp
State Archives: www.montanahistoricalsociety.org
State Statutes and Codes: http://data.opi.mt.gov/bills/mca_toc/index.htm
Legislative Bill Search: http://leg.mt.gov/css/research/laws.asp
Unclaimed Funds: http://mt.gov/revenue/programsandservices/unclaimedproperty.asp

Primary State Agencies

Criminal Records $$

Department of Justice, Criminal Records,   http://doj.mt.gov/   Access is available for "public users" or "registered users" at https://app.mt.gov/choprs/. Fee is $11.00 per record. Registered users must pay a $75 annual fee and have access to other data. Search using the name and DOB. The SSN is helpful but not required. Results include up to 4 aliases, dispositions, detentions, sentences, and correctional status.

Sexual Offender Registry   Free & $$

Department of Justice, Sexual and Violent Offender Registry,   http://doj.mt.gov/svor/search.asp   The state sexual offender list is available at the website. You can search for this information by name, by city or county, or by ZIP Code Also, the entire database may be purchased as a download for $300.00.

Incarceration Records   Free

Montana Department of Corrections, Directors Office, www.cor.state.mt.us Search current or former inmates on the ConWeb system at http://app.mt.gov/conweb/. Search by ID# or name. *Other Options:* Entire offender database is available for purchase for $100.00; call Discovering Montana, 406-449-3468. Academic or social researchers can acquire the same database for no charge.

Corporation, LLC, LP, Fictitious Name, Trademarks/Servicemarks   Free & $$n

Business Services Bureau, Secretary of State,   http://sos.mt.gov/bsb/index.asp   Visit http://app.mt.gov/bes/ for free searches of MT business entities. Certified copies may be ordered online for $10.00 using a credit card. There is a commercial service for finding registered principles. Go to http://app.mt.gov/registered/. *Other Options:* Lists of the new corporations per month are available.

Uniform Commercial Code, Federal Tax Liens $$

Business Services Division, Secretary of State, Rm 260, http://sos.mt.gov/BSB/UCC.asp With registration and $75.00 annual fee you may search UCCs at http://app.mt.gov/uccs/. Registration also lets you search other MT databases. A web-based subscription service provides information about all active liens filed with the office. To use the service you need to establish an account with Discovering Montana for a fee of $25 per month. Contact Discovering Montana at 101 N Rodney #3, Helena MT 59601, or call 866-449-3468, or visit their website at http://mt.gov/default.asp. *Other Options:* The agency offers farm bill filings lists on a monthly basis for $5.00 per category on paper or microfiche. A CD-Rom for all Farm Products is available for $20.00.

Driver Records $$

Motor Vehicle Division, Driver's Services, www.doj.mt.gov/driving/default.asp There are two methods offered, one for Public User requests and a subscription service. The fee is $7.25. The Public Access results do not offer address information. For registered subscribers, an agreement must be signed and there is an annual $75.00 registration fee. Batch access is available. Services online also include a License Status Conviction Activity batch or monitoring search, at a reduced price. For more about online services visit https://app.mt.gov/dojdrs/ or call 406-449-3468.

Vehicle, Vessel Ownership & Registration `Free & $$`

Department of Justice, Title and Registration Bureau, http://doj.mt.gov/driving/vehicletitleregistration.asp Both "Public User" and Registered User" interfaces are offered at https://app.mt.gov/dojvs. The Registered User system is for ongoing registered accounts approved by the Motor Vehicle Division. Depending on the level of authority granted, the following is available: Vehicle Information, License Plate Information, Vehicle Owner Information, Lien History, Title History and Registration Information. The fee is $2.00 per search. There is an annual $75.00 registration fee for 10 users. The "Public User" system is designed for Montana citizens or users with an occasional need to know the ownership history of a pre-owned car. Sensitive information, such as the SSN or home address is not released. A $5.00 fee applies and a credit card must be used. *Other Options:* Bulk or batch ordering of registration information is available on tape, disk, or paper. The user must fill out a specific form, which gives the user the capability of customization. For further information, contact the Registrar at address above.

Voter Registration `$$`

Secretary of State, Elections Bureau, http://sos.mt.gov/ELB/index.asp Access voter registration records at http://app.mt.gov/voterfile/select_criteria.html. Records can be purchased for non-commercial use only. *Other Options:* This agency database or customized portions can be purchased on disk or CD-ROM. Fee to purchase database is $1,000 or $5,000 for subscription with updates. For more information, contact Lisa Kimmet.

Birth and Death Certificates `$$`

Montana Department of Health, Vital Records, http://vhsp.dphhs.mt.gov/certificates/ordercertificates.shtml Orders can be placed via a state designated vendor. Go to www.vitalchek.com. Extra fees are involved.

Occupational Licensing Boards

Acupuncturist	http://app.mt.gov/lookup/
Adoption Agency	www.dphhs.mt.gov/cfsd/adoption/privateadoptionagencies.shtml
Alarm Response Runner	http://app.mt.gov/lookup/
Architect	http://app.mt.gov/lookup/
Athletic Event/Event Timekeeper	http://app.mt.gov/lookup/
Audiologist	http://mt.gov/dli/slp/
Barber/Barber Shop/Barber Instruct	http://app.mt.gov/lookup/
Boxer/Boxing Professional	http://app.mt.gov/lookup/
Cemetery, Privately Owned	http://app.mt.gov/lookup/
Chemical Dependency Counselor	http://app.mt.gov/lookup/
Child Care Provider	http://oraweb.hhs.state.mt.us:9999/ccrd/plsql/ccrd_provider.startup
Chiropractor	http://app.mt.gov/lookup/
Clinical Nurse Specialist	http://app.mt.gov/lookup/
Clinical Social Worker	http://app.mt.gov/lookup/
Construction Blaster	http://app.mt.gov/lookup/
Cosmetologist/Cosmet'y Instr./Sch'l	http://app.mt.gov/lookup/
CP Installer/Designer	http://deq.mt.gov/UST/licensees.asp
Crematory/Crematory Oper./Tech.	http://app.mt.gov/lookup/
Day Care Center	http://oraweb.hhs.state.mt.us:9999/ccrd/plsql/ccrd_provider.startup
Dentist/Dental Assist/Hygienist	http://app.mt.gov/lookup/
Denturist	http://app.mt.gov/lookup/
Drug Registration, Dangerous	http://app.mt.gov/lookup/
Drug Wholesaler	http://app.mt.gov/lookup/
Electrician	http://app.mt.gov/lookup/
Electrologist	http://app.mt.gov/lookup/
Emergency Medical Technician	http://app.mt.gov/lookup/
Engineer	http://app.mt.gov/lookup/
Esthetician	http://app.mt.gov/lookup/
Firearms Instructor	http://app.mt.gov/lookup/
Funeral Director	http://app.mt.gov/lookup/
Guide	http://app.mt.gov/lookup/
Hearing Aid Dispenser	http://app.mt.gov/lookup/
Insurance Adjuster/Producer	http://sao.mt.gov/insurance/findagent.asp

Land Surveyor .... http://app.mt.gov/lookup/
Landscape Architect .... http://app.mt.gov/lookup/
Living Trust Seller............................ www.sao.mt.gov
Lobbying Principal/Lobbyist .... http://app.mt.gov/cgi-bin/camptrack/lobbysearch/lobbySearch.cgi
Manicurist... http://app.mt.gov/lookup/
Medical Doctor.................................. http://app.mt.gov/lookup/
Midwife Nurse/Direct Entry/Appren . http://app.mt.gov/lookup/
Monitoring Well Installer .... http://deq.mt.gov/UST/licensees.asp
Mortuary/Mortician .... http://app.mt.gov/lookup/
Multi-level Marketing Company .... www.sao.mt.gov
Naturopathic Physician...................... http://app.mt.gov/lookup/
Nurse Anesthetist............................... http://app.mt.gov/lookup/
Nurse-RN/LPN/Practitioner .... http://app.mt.gov/lookup/
Nutritionist .... http://app.mt.gov/lookup/
Occupational Therapist...................... http://mt.gov/dli/otp/
Optometrist.. http://app.mt.gov/lookup/
Osteopathic Physician........................ http://app.mt.gov/lookup/
Outfitter, Hunting/Fishing .... http://app.mt.gov/lookup/
Pharmacist .... http://app.mt.gov/lookup/
Physical Therapist .... http://app.mt.gov/lookup/
Physician Assistant............................ http://app.mt.gov/lookup/
Plumber .... http://app.mt.gov/lookup/
Podiatrist.. http://app.mt.gov/lookup/
Private Investigator/Trainee............... http://app.mt.gov/lookup/
Private Placement Offering................ www.sao.mt.gov
Private Security Guard....................... http://app.mt.gov/lookup/
Process Server .... http://app.mt.gov/lookup/
Property Manager .... http://mt.gov/dli/rre/
Proprietary Security Organization ..... http://app.mt.gov/lookup/
Psychologist....................................... http://app.mt.gov/lookup/
Public Accountant .... http://mt.gov/dli/pac/
Radiologic Technologist.................... http://mt.gov/dli/rts/
Real Estate Agent/Broker/Sales......... http://mt.gov/dli/rre/
Real Estate Appraiser .... http://mt.gov/dli/rea/
Referee .... http://app.mt.gov/lookup/
Resident Manager.............................. http://app.mt.gov/lookup/
Respiratory Care Practitioner .... http://mt.gov/dli/rcp/
School Guidance Couns'r/Psychol't... http://data.opi.state.mt.us/edcredentials/index.asp
School Principal/Superintendent .... http://data.opi.state.mt.us/edcredentials/index.asp
Securities Broker/Salesperson .... www.sao.mt.gov
Security Alarm Installer..................... http://app.mt.gov/lookup/
Security Company/Organization .... http://app.mt.gov/lookup/
Social Worker, LSW .... http://app.mt.gov/lookup/
Speech Pathologist............................. http://mt.gov/dli/slp/
Surveyor, Land .... http://app.mt.gov/lookup/
Teacher.. http://data.opi.state.mt.us/edcredentials/index.asp
Telephone, Customer-Owned, Coin .. www.sao.mt.gov
Timeshare Broker/Salesperson .... http://mt.gov/dli/rre/
Underground Tank Related................. http://deq.mt.gov/UST/licensees.asp
Variable Annuities Seller................... www.sao.mt.gov
Veterinarian .... http://app.mt.gov/lookup/
Wrestler .... http://app.mt.gov/lookup/
X-ray Technician .... http://mt.gov/dli/rts/

State and Local Courts

State Court Structure: The District Courts have no maximum amount for civil judgment cases. Most District Courts handle civil cases over $7,000 but there are exceptions that handle a civil minimum as low as $5,000. Limited Jurisdiction Courts, which are also known as Justice Courts or City Courts or Municipal Courts handle real property rights cases up to $7,000. The Small Claims limit is $3000. Some Justice Courts and City Courts have consolidated.

Statewide Court Online Access: Supreme Court opinions, orders, and recently filed briefs may be found at http://searchcourts.mt.gov. There is no statewide access to docket information from the trial courts.

Note: No individual Montana courts offer online access.

Recorders, Assessors, and Other Sites of Note

Recording Office Organization: 57 counties, 56 recording offices. Yellowstone National Park is considered a county but is not included as a filing location. The recording officer is the County Clerk and Recorder, and Clerk of District Court for state tax liens. Federal tax liens on personal property of businesses are filed with the Secretary of State. Other federal tax liens are filed with the county Clerk and Recorder.

Online Access Note: Search for a for a Montana property owner by name and county on the Montana Cadastral Mapping Project GIS mapping database at http://gis.mt.gov. This works for all counties.

Cascade County *Real Estate, Deed Records* www.co.cascade.mt.us `SS` Recording office land data to be available at a later date at www.etitlesearch.com; registration and fees required.

Dawson County *Real Estate, Deed Records* www.dawsoncountymontana.org `SS` Recording office land data to be available at a later date at www.etitlesearch.com; registration and fees required.

Deer Lodge County *Real Estate, Deed Records* `SS` Recording office land data to be available at a later date at www.etitlesearch.com; registration and fees required.

Fergus County *Real Estate, Deed Records* www.co.fergus.mt.us `SS` Recording office land data to be available at a later date at www.etitlesearch.com; registration and fees required.

Flathead County *Real Estate, Grantor/Grantee, Deed, Mortgage, Lien, Judgment Records* www.co.flathead.mt.us `SS` Access recorded lard records by subscribing to the idoc system at www.co.flathead.mt.us/idoc/. Annual fee is $180.00; contact the Clerk and Recorder's office for info and signup, or visit the web.

Gallatin County *Real Estate, Deed Records* www.gallatin.mt.gov `SS` Recording office land data to be available at a later date at www.etitlesearch.com; registration and fees required.
Property, Taxation Records `Free` Statewide cadastral mapping site found at http://gis.mt.gov/. Links to parcel search and property maps. Search parcel by GEO code, owner, or subdivision. also search property data free at http://webapps.gallatin.mt.gov/webtax/ Also, search property data on the GIS-mapping site free at http://webapps.gallatin.mt.gov/mappers/ (but no name searching).

Granite County *Recorded Documents* `SS` Recording office land data to be available at a later date at www.etitlesearch.com; registration and fees required.

Judith Basin County *Real Estate, Deed Records* `SS` Recording office land data to be available at a later date at www.etitlesearch.com; registration and fees required.

Lake County *Real Estate, Deed, Map, Survey Records* www.lakecounty-mt.org `Free` Real estate doc images, COS's, maps, and surveys can be downloaded free from the ftp site at ftp://lakecounty-mt.org. Folders by type and month.
Property, Taxation Records `Free` Access the Web Tax System at www.lakecounty-mt.org but password is required. Statewide cadastral mapping site found at http://gis.mt.gov/. Links to parcel search and property maps. Search parcel by GEO code, owner, or subdivision. Also, search treasurer's tax payment list after registration at www.lakecounty-mt.org/scripts/xworks.exe.

Lewis and Clark County *Real Estate, Grantor/Grantee, Deed, Lien Records* www.co.lewis-clark.mt.us `Free & $$` Search Grantor/Grantee index and recorder records free at http://records.co.lewis-clark.mt.us/icris/splash.jsp. Registration, logon and password required. This new automation includes document imaging via subscription online service. Records go back to 4/2001.

Property, Taxation Records `Free` Search property tax data free at http://webtax.csa-inc.net/lewisandclarkmt/. Statewide cadastral mapping site found at http://gis.mt.gov/. Links to parcel search and property maps. Search parcel by GEO code, owner, or subdivision.

Missoula County *Real Estate, Deed Records* www.co.missoula.mt.us `SS`
Recording office land data to be available at a later date at www.etitlesearch.com; registration and fees required.

Property, Taxation Records `Free` Access the county property data system free at www.co.missoula.mt.us/owner. Property search by Address, Tax ID, Geocode, Map. Records search by Tax ID, Geocode, Book/Page. No name searching.

Musselshell County *Property, Taxation Records* `Free` Statewide cadastral mapping site found at
http://gis.mt.gov/. Links to parcel search and property maps. Search parcel by GEO code, owner, or subdivision.

Park County *Real Estate, Grantor/Grantee, Deed, Lien Records* www.parkcounty.org/ `SS` Access to document
searches at www.parkcounty.org/idoc/. The computer document indexing begins from January 1, 1989. Users are required to sign a user contract & pay a yearly user's fee payable on a prorated schedule and payable on January 1 each year.

Ravalli County *Property, Real Estate, Deed, Property Records* www.ravallicounty.mt.gov/clerkrecorder/default.htm
`SS` Access property tax and recorded document info at www.ravallicounty.mt.gov/clerkrecorder/access.htm. Signed Access Authorization Memo with the County required; must pay the annual fee, either $120 yearly for companies of 5 or less, or $400 for large companies. Call IT office for info and sign-up at 406-375-6700.

Property, Taxation Records `Free & SS` Name search on the statewide Cadastral database free at http://gis.mt.gov (incomplete revenue tax records). Access property tax and recorded document info at www.ravallicounty.mt.gov/clerkrecorder/access.htm. Signed Access Authorization Memo with the County required; must pay the annual fee. Call IT office for info and sign-up at 406-375-6700.

Yellowstone County *Real Estate, Grantor/Grantee, Deed, Lien, Mortgage Records*
www.co.yellowstone.mt.us/clerk `Free & SS` Access the county clerk & recorder document searches free at https://secure.co.yellowstone.mt.us/clerk/. Click on Free Service Search or you may register and login for full data for a fee.

Property, Taxation Records `Free` Access tax assessor records free at www.co.yellowstone.mt.us/gis.

Nebraska

Capital: Lincoln
          Lancaster County

Time Zone: CST

Nebraska's nineteen western-most counties are MST. They are: Arthur,
Banner, Box Butte, Chase, Cherry, Cheyenne, Dawes, Deuel, Dundy, Garden,
Grant, Hooker, Keith, Kimball, Morrill, Perkins, Scotts Bluff, Sheridan, Sioux.

Population: 1,774,571

# of Counties: 93

Useful State Links

Website: www.nebraska.gov/
Governor: http://www.gov.state.ne.us/
Attorney General: www.ago.state.ne.us
State Archives: www.nebraskahistory.org
State Statutes and Codes: http://uniweb.legislature.ne.gov/QS/laws.html
Legislative Bill Search: www.unicam.state.ne.us/web/public/home
Bill Monitoring: www.nebraska.gov/billtracker/
Unclaimed Funds: www.treasurer.state.ne.us/up/index.asp

Primary State Agencies

Sexual Offender Registry `Free`

Nebraska State Patrol, Sexual Offender Registry, www.nsp.state.ne.us/sor/ A Level 3 sexual offender registry search is available at the website. The records may be searched by either ZIP Code, last name, city, or county. Search or review the entire list of names.

Incarceration Records `Free`

Nebraska Department of Correctional Services, Central Records Office, www.corrections.state.ne.us Click on Inmate Records at the website for a search of inmates incarcerated after 1977.

Corporation, LLC, LP, Trade Names, Trademarks/Servicemarks `Free & $$`

Secretary of State, Corporation Division, www.sos.state.ne.us/business/corp_serv/ There are two levels of service. The free lookup at https://www.nebraska.gov/sos/corp/corpsearch.cgi?nav=search provides general information to obtain information on the status of corporations and other business entities registered in this state. The state has designated Nebraska.gov (800-747-8177) to facilitate online retrieval of records. This access to records requires fees and the lookup can be accessed from the same webpage. Also, search securities companies registered with the state at www.ndbf.org/searches/securities.shtml. *Other Options:* Nebraska.gov has the capability of offering database purchases.

Uniform Commercial Code, Federal & State Tax Liens `$$`

UCC Division, Secretary of State, Rm 1301, www.sos.state.ne.us/business/ucc/ Access is outsourced to Nebraska.gov To set an account, go to www.nebraska.gov/subscribe.phtml. The system is available 24 hours daily. There is an annual $50.00 fee in addition to charges to view records. Call 800-747-8177 for more information. *Other Options:* Check with Nebrask@ Online for bulk purchase programs.

Workers' Compensation Records `$$`

Workers' Compensation Court, www.wcc.ne.gov This is for requesting records, not viewing online. Record requests may be made at https://www.nebraska.gov/WC/records.phtml. Unless specifically requested, responses will be limited to first and subsequent reports filed within the last five (5) years. First reports will include the original report of injury and the current status of the report if updated information has been filed. Same fee schedule above applies.

Driver Records `$$`

Department of Motor Vehicles, Driver & Vehicle Records Division, www.dmv.state.ne.us Nebraska outsources all electronic record requests to Nebraska.gov at www.nebraska.gov/subscriber or call 402-471-7810 The system is interactive and open 24 hours a day, 7 days a week. Fee is $3.00 per record. There is an annual fee of $50.00 and a $.12 per minute connect fee or no connect fee if through the Internet. *Other Options:* Bulk requesters must be authorized by state officials. Purpose of the request and subsequent usage are reviewed. For information, call 402-471-3885.

Vehicle, Vessel Ownership & Registration `$$`

Department of Motor Vehicles, Driver & Vehicle Records Division, www.dmv.state.ne.us Electronic access is through Nebraska.gov at www.nebraska.gov/subscribe.phtml. There is a start-up fee addition to the $1.00 per record fee. The system is open 24 hours a day, 7 days a week. Call 800-747-8177 for more information. *Other Options:* Bulk requesters must be authorized by state officials. Purpose of the request and subsequent usage are reviewed. For more information, call 402-471-3885.

Vital Records `$$`

Health & Human Services System, Vital Statistics Section, www.hhs.state.ne.us/VitalRecords/ Records may be ordered online the web page. For Internet requests, fax to 402-471-8230 the indicating name(s) on the record(s) requested and the Internet confirmation number.

Occupational Licensing Boards

Abstracting Company .... www.abe.state.ne.us/local/company_search.phtml
Abstractor .... www.abe.state.ne.us/local/license_search.phtml
Adult Day Care .... www.hhs.state.ne.us/crl/rosters.htm
Air Cond/Heat'g Cont'r (Lincoln) ...... www.lincoln.ne.gov/main/s_record.htm
Alcohol/Drug Tester .... www.nebraska.gov/LISSearch/search.cgi
Animal Technician .... www.nebraska.gov/LISSearch/search.cgi
Architect .... www.ea.state.ne.us/search/search.php
Asbestos-related Occupation .... www.nebraska.gov/LISSearch/search.cgi
Assisted Living Facility .... www.hhs.state.ne.us/crl/rosters.htm
Athletic Trainer .... www.nebraska.gov/LISSearch/search.cgi
Attorney .... www.nebar.com/publicinfo/lawyersearch.asp
Audiologist .... www.nebraska.gov/LISSearch/search.cgi
Bank .... www.ndbf.org/searches/fisearch.shtml
Barber School .... www.barbers.state.ne.us/
Boxer www.athcomm.state.ne.us/content/pdf/LICOFF2004.pdf
Check Sales .... www.ndbf.org/searches/fisearch.shtml
Child Care Center .... www.hhs.state.ne.us/crl/rosters.htm
Child Caring/Placing Agency .... www.hhs.state.ne.us/crl/rosters.htm
Chiropractor .... www.nebraska.gov/LISSearch/search.cgi
Collection Agency .... www.sos.state.ne.us/licensing/collection/pdf/col_agn.pdf
Contractor, Building (Lincoln) .... www.lincoln.ne.gov/main/s_record.htm
Cosmetology-related Occupation ...... www.nebraska.gov/LISSearch/search.cgi
Cosmetology Salon/School .... www.nebraska.gov/LISSearch/search.cgi
Credit Union .... www.ndbf.org/searches/fisearch.shtml
Debt Management Agency .... www.sos.state.ne.us/business/pdf/debt_list.pdf
Delayed Deposit Service .... www.ndbf.org/searches/fisearch.shtml
Dental Anesthesia Permit .... www.nebraska.gov/LISSearch/search.cgi
Dentist/Dental Hygienist .... www.nebraska.gov/LISSearch/search.cgi
Developmentally Disabled Center ..... www.hhs.state.ne.us/crl/rosters.htm
Drug Distributor/Whlser/Facility .... www.hhs.state.ne.us/crl/rosters.htm
Electrologist .... www.nebraska.gov/LISSearch/search.cgi
Electrology Facility .... www.nebraska.gov/LISSearch/search.cgi
Embalmer .... www.nebraska.gov/LISSearch/search.cgi
Emergency Medical Care Facility ..... www.nebraska.gov/LISSearch/search.cgi
Engineer .... www.ea.state.ne.us/search/search.php
Esthetician .... www.nebraska.gov/LISSearch/search.cgi
Esthetician Establishment .... www.nebraska.gov/LISSearch/search.cgi
Fire Protection Cont'r (Lincoln) .... www.lincoln.ne.gov/main/s_record.htm

Fund Transmission .... www.ndbf.org/searches/fisearch.shtml
Funeral Director/Establishment .... www.nebraska.gov/LISSearch/search.cgi
Geologist .... www.geology.state.ne.us/pdf/roster.pdf
Health Clinic...................................... www.nebraska.gov/LISSearch/search.cgi
Hearing Aid Dispenser/Fitter............. www.nebraska.gov/LISSearch/search.cgi
Home Health Agency .... www.hhs.state.ne.us/crl/rosters.htm
Hospice.. www.hhs.state.ne.us/crl/rosters.htm
Hospital .... www.nlc.state.ne.us/docs/pilot/pubs/h.html
Insurance Agency/Agent/Broker .... www.doi.ne.gov/appointments/search/index.cgi
Insurance Company/Prod./Consult't.. www.doi.ne.gov/appointments/search/index.cgi
Intermediate Care Facility (Retarded)www.hhs.state.ne.us/crl/rosters.htm
Investigator, Plainclothes................... www.sos.state.ne.us/licensing/private_eye/pdf/PDA%20Apr2008.pdf
Investment Advisor/Advisor Rep. ..... www.ndbf.org/searches/fisearch.shtml
Labor/Delivery Service/Clinic........... www.hhs.state.ne.us/crl/rosters.htm
Laboratory .... www.hhs.state.ne.us/crl/rosters.htm
Landscape Architect .... www.landarch.state.ne.us/registrants.pdf
Liquor Retailers/ Whlse/Shipper .... www.lcc.ne.gov/license_search/licsearch.cgi
Lobbyist... www.unicam.state.ne.us/web/public/lobby
Local Anesthesia Certification .... www.nebraska.gov/LISSearch/search.cgi
Long Term Care Center .... www.hhs.state.ne.us/crl/rosters.htm
Marriage & Family Therapist .... www.nebraska.gov/LISSearch/search.cgi
Massage Establish't/Therapy School . www.nebraska.gov/LISSearch/search.cgi
Medical Doctor.................................. www.nebraska.gov/LISSearch/search.cgi
Mental Health Center .... www.nebraska.gov/LISSearch/search.cgi
Mentally Retarded Care Service .... www.hhs.state.ne.us/crl/rosters.htm
Nail Technologist .... www.nebraska.gov/LISSearch/search.cgi
Nurse .... www.nebraska.gov/LISSearch/search.cgi
Nursing Home/Home Administrator . www.nebraska.gov/LISSearch/search.cgi
Nutrition Therapy, Medical .... www.nebraska.gov/LISSearch/search.cgi
Occupational Therapist...................... www.nebraska.gov/LISSearch/search.cgi
Optometrist.. www.nebraska.gov/LISSearch/search.cgi
Osteopathic Physician........................ www.nebraska.gov/LISSearch/search.cgi
Pesticide Applicator/Dealer............... www.kellysolutions.com/ne/
Pharmacist/Pharmacy .... www.nebraska.gov/LISSearch/search.cgi
Physical Therapist .... www.nebraska.gov/LISSearch/search.cgi
Physician .... www.nebraska.gov/LISSearch/search.cgi
Physician Assistant............................ www.nebraska.gov/LISSearch/search.cgi
Plumber (Lincoln) .... www.lincoln.ne.gov/main/s_record.htm
Podiatrist... www.nebraska.gov/LISSearch/search.cgi
Polygraph Examiner .... www.sos.state.ne.us/licensing/poly_menu.html
Preschool .... www.hhs.state.ne.us/crl/rosters.htm
Private Detective .... www.sos.state.ne.us/licensing/private_eye/pdf/PD%20Apr2008.pdf
Private Detective Agency .... www.sos.state.ne.us/licensing/private_eye/pdf/PDA%20Apr2008.pdf
Psychologist...................................... www.nebraska.gov/LISSearch/search.cgi
Public Accountant-CPA .... www.nbpa.ne.gov/search/index.phtml
Radiographer .... www.nebraska.gov/LISSearch/search.cgi
Real Estate Agent/Seller/Broker........ www.nrec.state.ne.us/licinfodb/index.cgi
Real Estate Appraiser .... www.appraiser.ne.gov/appraiser_listing.html
Rehabilitation Agency .... www.hhs.state.ne.us/crl/rosters.htm
Respiratory Care Practitioner .... www.nebraska.gov/LISSearch/search.cgi
Respite Care Service.......................... www.hhs.state.ne.us/crl/rosters.htm
Sales Finance Company..................... www.ndbf.org/searches/fisearch.shtml
Saving & Loan................................... www.ndbf.org/searches/fisearch.shtml
Securities Agent/Broker/Dealer......... www.ndbf.org/searches/fisearch.shtml
Social Worker.................................... www.nebraska.gov/LISSearch/search.cgi
Speech-Language Pathologist............ www.nebraska.gov/LISSearch/search.cgi
Substance Abuse Treatment Center ... www.nlc.state.ne.us/docs/pilot/pubs/h.html

Surplus Lines Seller............................www.doi.ne.gov/appointments/search/index.cgi
Surveyor, Land ....www.sso.state.ne.us/bels/lsalpha.html
Swimming Pool Operator ....www.nebraska.gov/LISSearch/search.cgi
Trust Company ....www.ndbf.org/searches/fisearch.shtml
Veterinarian/Vet Technician..............www.nebraska.gov/LISSearch/search.cgi
Voice Stress Examiner/Analyzer.......www.sos.state.ne.us/licensing/poly_menu.html
Water Operator ....www.nebraska.gov/LISSearch/search.cgi
X-ray Unit Portable ....www.nebraska.gov/LISSearch/search.cgi

State and Local Courts

State Court Structure: The District courts have original jurisdiction in all felony cases, equity cases, domestic relations cases, and civil cases where the amount in controversy involves more than $51,000. District Courts also have appellate jurisdiction in certain matters arising out of County Courts. Prior to the current level, historically the state raised the County Court limit on civil matters from $15,000 to $45,000 Sept. 1, 2001. County Courts have original jurisdiction in probate matters, violations of city or village ordinances, juvenile court matters without a separate juvenile court, adoptions, preliminary hearings in felony cases, and eminent domain proceedings. The county courts have concurrent jurisdiction in civil matters when the amount in controversy is $51,000 or less, criminal matters classified as misdemeanors or infractions, some domestic relations matters, and paternity actions.Nearly all misdemeanor cases are tried in the County Courts.

County Courts have juvenile jurisdiction in all but 3 counties. Douglas, Lancaster, and Sarpy counties have separate Juvenile Courts.

Statewide Court Online Access: An online access subscription service is available for Nebraska District Courts and County courts, except Douglas County District Court. Case details, all party listings, payments, and actions taken for criminal, civil, probate, juvenile, and traffic is available. Users must be registered with Nebraska.gov; there is a start-up fee. The fee is $.60 per record or a flat rate of $300.00 per month. Also, for $15.00 fee per search, you may access the JUSTICE Court Case system statewide at https://www.nebraska.gov/justicecc/ccname.cgi. Go to www.nebraska.gov/faqs/justice or call 402-471-7810 for more info and info on how far back records go per county. Supreme Court opinions are available from http://court.nol.org/opinions.

❖ **Statewide (Except One County) Access Offered – Read Above.** ❖

Douglas County

District Court www.co.douglas.ne.us `$$`
Civil: Access to the Internet system at www.dotcomm.org/cpan/index.htm requires registration and password. Call CPAN at 402-444-6374 for more information. System can be searched by name or case number. *Criminal:* Access to the Internet system at www.dotcomm.org/cpan/index.htm requires registration and password. Call CPAN at 402-444-6374 for more information. System can be searched by name or case number.

County Court Civil www.co.douglas.ne.us `$$`
Civil: Access at www.dotcomm.org/cpan/ requires registration and password. Call CPAN at 402-444-7117 for more info.

County Court Criminal www.co.douglas.ne.us `$$`
Criminal: Access at www.dotcomm.org/cpan/ requires registration and password. Call CPAN at 402-444-7117 for more info.

Recorders, Assessors, and Other Sites of Note

Recording Office Organization: 93 counties, 109 recording offices. The recording officers are County Clerk (UCCs and some state tax liens) and Register of Deeds (real estate and most tax liens). Most counties have a combined Clerk/Register office that is designated as "County Clerk" for our purposes. Still, in combined offices, the Register of Deeds is frequently a different person from the County Clerk. Sixteen counties have separate offices for real estate recording and UCC filing - Adams, Cass, Dakota, Dawson, Dodge, Douglas, Gage, Hall, Lancaster, Lincoln, Madison, Otoe, Platte, Sarpy, Saunders, and Scotts Bluff. Most federal and state tax liens are filed with the County Register of Deeds. Some state tax liens on personal property are filed with the County Clerk. Some federal tax liens on individuals are filed at the Sec. of State's office.

Online Access Note: Access real estate or personal property data for free for over 50 counties at www.nebraskataxesonline.us/. All are profiled below.

Adams County Register of Deeds *Property, Taxation Records* `Free`
Access real estate or personal property data free at www.nebraskataxesonline.us/taxcollpage1.aspx?county=Adams.

Boone County *Property, Taxation Records* `Free` Access real estate or personal property data free at
www.nebraskataxesonline.us.

Box Butte County *Property, Taxation Records* `Free` Access real estate or personal property data free at
www.nebraskataxesonline.us/taxcollpage1.aspx?county=BoxB.

Butler County *Property, Taxation Records* `Free` Search assessor property data on the GIS site free at
http://butler.gisworkshop.com/ButlerIMS/.

Cass County Register of Deeds *Property, Taxation Records* `Free`
Access GIS and Assessor data free at www.gis-srv.cassne.org/CassIMSPublic/index.html. Also, access property data free at
www.nebraskataxesonline.us/taxcollpage1.aspx?county=Cass.

Chase County *Property, Taxation Records* `Free` Access real estate or personal property data free at
www.nebraskataxesonline.us/taxcollpage1.aspx?county=Chase.

Colfax County *Property, Taxation Records* `Free` Access real estate or personal property data free at
www.nebraskataxesonline.us.

Cuming County *Property, Taxation Records* `Free` Access real estate or personal property data free at
www.nebraskataxesonline.us/taxcollpage1.aspx?county=Cuming.

Dakota County Register of Deeds *Property, Taxation Records* `Free`
Access assessor records free at http://dakota.pat.gisworkshop.com/.

Dawes County *Property, Taxation Records* `Free` Access real estate or personal property data free at
www.nebraskataxesonline.us/taxcollpage1.aspx?county=Dawes.

Dawson County Register of Deeds *Property, Taxation Records* `Free`
Access property or personal property data free at www.nebraskataxesonline.us.

Dodge County Register of Deeds *Real Estate, Deed, Mortgage Records* www.registerofdeeds.com
`Free & $$` Access to Register of Deeds mortgages database site is under development. Registration will be required. Also,
search legal descriptions lists free at www.registerofdeeds.com/Legal%20Index.htm.
Property, Taxation Records `Free` Access assessor records free at http://dodge.pat.gisworkshop.com/.

Douglas County Clerk *Property, Taxation Records* `Free` Records on the county Assessor Property Information
Search database are free at www.dcassessor.org/disclaimer.html and also Search property tax online payments database free at
http://webapps.dotcomm.org:8080/TreasTax/ but no name searching.

Douglas County Register of Deeds *Marriage Records* www.co.douglas.ne.us `Free`
Search the clerk/comptroller marriage database free at www.co.douglas.ne.us/dept/Clerk/marriagelicense.htm.
Property, Taxation Records `Free` Assessor to the county assessor property valuation lookup is free at
http://douglasne.mapping-online.com/DouglasCoNe/static/valuation.jsp. Also search the treasurer's property tax data free at
http://webapps.dotcomm.org:8080/TreasTax/ but no name searching.

Dundy County *Property, Taxation Records* `Free` Access real estate or personal property data free at
www.nebraskataxesonline.us/taxcollpage1.aspx?county=Dundy.

Frontier County *Property, Taxation Records* `Free & $$` Access to basic property assessor data is available free at
http://frontier.gisworkshop.com. A subscription is required for full data including sales, photos, history, buildings for $200 per year.
Also, access real estate or personal property data free at www.nebraskataxesonline.us/taxcollpage1.aspx?county=Frontier.

Gage County Register of Deeds *Property, Taxation Records* `Free` Access real estate or personal property
data free at www.nebraskataxesonline.us/taxcollpage1.aspx?county=Gage. Also, access property data via the county Assessor GIS
service free at http://gage.gisworkshop.com/GageIMS/.

Garfield County *Property, Taxation Records* `Free` Access parcel records free at
http://garfield.pat.gisworkshop.com/.

Greeley County *Property, Taxation Records* `Free` Access real estate or personal property data free at
www.nebraskataxesonline.us/taxcollpage1.aspx?county=Greeley also access parcel records free at
http://greeley.pat.gisworkshop.com/.

Hall County Clerk *Real Estate, Grantor/Grantee, Deed Records* www.hcgi.org `Free`
Access register of deeds real estate data free at http://deeds.hallcountyne.gov/fSearch.aspx.

Hall County Register of Deeds *Real Estate, Grantor/Grantee, Deed, Lien, Judgment Records* www.hcgi.org
`Free` Access to the county Register of Deeds Document Search is free at http://deeds.hallcountyne.gov.
Property, Taxation Records `Free` Access property data free at http://gis.grand-island.com/mapsifter/landinfofront/. Also,
access parcel records free at www.taxsifter.hallcountyne.gov/.

Hamilton County *Property, Taxation Records* `Free` Access real estate or personal property data free at
www.nebraskataxesonline.us. Also, access parcel records free at http://hamilton.gisworkshop.com/.

Harlan County *Property, Taxation Records* `Free` Access parcel records free at http://harlan.pat.gisworkshop.com/.

Hitchcock County *Property, Taxation Records* `Free` Access real estate or personal property data free at
www.nebraskataxesonline.us and also access parcel records free at http://hitchcock.pat.gisworkshop.com/.

Jefferson County *Property, Taxation Records* `Free` Access real estate or personal property data free at
www.nebraskataxesonline.us/taxcollpage1.aspx?county=Jefferso.

Johnson County *Property, Taxation Records* `Free` Access property data free at
http://johnsonne.taxsifter.com/taxsifter. Also, access parcel or personal property data free at
www.nebraskataxesonline.us/taxcollpage1.aspx?county=Johnson.

Kearney County *Property, Taxation Records* `Free` Access property data and parcel records free at
http://kearney.gisworkshop.com/KearneyIMS or at http://kearney.gisworkshop.com/

Keith County *Property, Taxation Records* `Free` Access real estate or personal property data free at
www.nebraskataxesonline.us/taxcollpage1.aspx?county=Keith and also access parcel records free at
http://keith.pat.gisworkshop.com/.

Kimball County *Property, Taxation Records* `Free` Access real estate or personal property data free at
www.nebraskataxesonline.us/taxcollpage1.aspx?county=Kimball.

Lancaster County Clerk *Marriage, Building Permit Records* http://interlinc.ci.lincoln.ne.us `Free`
Search Lincoln Document Management records site free at www.lincoln.ne.gov/asp/city/clerk/docman.asp. See also Register of
Deeds. Search county marriages at www.lincoln.ne.gov/cnty/clerk/marrsrch.htm; building permits-
www.lincoln.ne.gov/city/build/bldgsrv/permits.htm.
Property, Taxation Records `Free` Access parcel records at http://orion.lancaster.ne.gov/Appraisal/PublicAccess/. Also,
search treasurer' property info at www.lincoln.ne.gov/cnty/treas/property.htm.

Lancaster County Register of Deeds *Real Estate, Deed, Grantor/Grantee, Lien, Judgment Records*
www.mynevadacounty.com/recorder `Free` Search register of deeds Grantor/Grantee index free at
http://deeds.lincoln.ne.gov/recorder/web/login.jsp. Use Public Login or you may register. See also County Clerk for other databases
online.

Lincoln County Register of Deeds *Property, Taxation Records* `Free` Access real estate or personal
property data free at www.nebraskataxesonline.us/taxcollpage1.aspx?county=Lincoln.

Madison County Clerk *Property, Taxation Records* `Free` Access county taxes online free at
www.nebraskataxesonline.us/taxcollpage1.aspx?county=Madison.

Madison County Register of Deeds *Property, Taxation Records* `Free` Access real estate or personal
property data free at www.nebraskataxesonline.us and also access assessor records free at http://madison.gisworkshop.com/.

Nance County *Property, Taxation Records* `Free` Access tax data free at www.nebraskataxesonline.us/

Nemaha County *Property, Taxation Records* `Free` Access real estate or personal property data free at
www.nebraskataxesonline.us/taxcollpage1.aspx?county=Nemaha.

Otoe County Register of Deeds *Property, Taxation Records* `Free` Access real estate or personal property
data free at www.nebraskataxesonline.us/taxcollpage1.aspx?county=Otoe.

Pawnee County *Property, Taxation Records* `Free` Access real estate or personal property data free at
www.nebraskataxesonline.us/taxcollpage1.aspx?county=Pawnee.

Perkins County *Property, Taxation Records* `Free` Access to property searches for free go to
www.perkins.gisworkshop.com/

Phelps County *Property, Taxation Records* `Free` Access real estate or personal property data free at www.nebraskataxesonline.us/taxcollpage1.aspx?county=Phelps. Also, search property records free on the GIS mapping site at www.phelps.gisworkshop.com.

Platte County Register of Deeds *Property, Taxation Records* `Free` Access the assessor index, including a name search at http://platte.gisworkshop.com/PlatteIMS/. Access real estate or personal property data free at www.nebraskataxesonline.us/taxcollpage1.aspx?county=Platte.

Polk County *Property, Taxation Records* `Free` Search property and mapping free at http://polk.gisworkshop.com/. Access the treasurer county tax record search free at http://polktreasurer.gisworkshop.com/.

Red Willow County *Property, Taxation Records* `Free` Search auditor's county property data on the gis-mapping site free at http://redwillow.gisworkshop.com.

Saline County *Property, Taxation Records* `Free` Access property data free at www.saline.gisworkshop.com. Also, access real estate or personal property data free at www.nebraskataxesonline.us/taxcollpage1.aspx?county=Saline.

Sarpy County Register of Deeds *Real Estate, Grantor/Grantee, Deed, Lien Records* www.sarpy.com `Free` Search the historical grantor/grantee index 1857-1990 free at www.sarpy.com/rodggi.
Property, Taxation Records `Free & $$` A simple property search is available free at www.sarpy.com/assessor/property-search.htm but no name searching. A premium subscription service built based on your needs is available starting at $240 per year and goes higher; see contract at www.sarpy.com/oldterra/SarpyContract.pdf. Also, register to accept tax sales lists at www.sarpy.com/taxsale/.

Saunders County Register of Deeds *Property, Taxation Records* `Free` Access assessment data on the GIS-mappinng site free at www.saunders.pat.gisworkshop.com/. Also, access real estate or personal property data free at www.nebraskataxesonline.us/taxcollpage1.aspx?county=Saunders.

Scotts Bluff County Clerk *Real Estate, Deed, Lien Records* www.scottsbluffcounty.org/deeds/deeds.htm `Free` View and download recorded documents free after registration; instructions at www.scottsbluffcounty.org/deeds/deeds.htm or from jbauer@scottsbluffcounty.org. Login page at www.scottsbluffcounty.org/deedsonline/.
Property, Taxation Records `Free` Search the TaxSifter Parcel Search database for property data free at http://scottsbluffne.taxsifter.com/taxsifter/T-Parcelsearch.asp. Also, access real estate or personal property data free at www.nebraskataxesonline.us/taxcollpage1.aspx?county=Scotts.

Seward County *Property, Taxation Records* `Free` Access real estate or personal property data free at www.nebraskataxesonline.us. Also, search parcel records free at http://seward.gisworkshop.com/.

Sherman County *Property, Taxation Records* `Free` Access parcel records free at http://sherman.pat.gisworkshop.com/.

Stanton County *Property, Taxation Records* `Free` Access real estate or personal property data free at www.nebraskataxesonline.us/taxcollpage1.aspx?county=Stanton.

Thayer County *Property, Taxation Records* `Free` Access real estate or personal property data free at www.nebraskataxesonline.us/taxcollpage1.aspx?county=Thayer.

Wayne County *Property, Taxation Records* `Free` Access real estate or personal property data free at www.nebraskataxesonline.us/taxcollpage1.aspx?county=Wayne. Search the sheriff's sales list free at http://county.waynene.org/County_Offices/Sheriff/.

Webster County *Property, Taxation Records* `Free` Access real estate or personal property data free at www.nebraskataxesonline.us/taxcollpage1.aspx?county=Webster.

York County *Property, Taxation Records* `Free` Access parcel records free at http://yorkne.taxsifter.com/taxsifter/t-parcelsearch.asp but no name searching.

Other Nebraska Sites of Note:
Clay County - Sheriff's Warrants www.claycounty.ne.gov/content/warrant_list.htm
Dawson County - Sheriff Warrants and Fugitives www.dawsoncountyne.net/sheriff/
Hall County - Inmates, Warrants, Most Wanted, Accident Reports www.hcgi.org Click on How Do I Locate...
Lancaster County - City of Lincoln - Accident Reports www.lincoln.ne.gov/city/police/stats/acc.htm View city accidents since 1-1-2000 by a case number OR a specific date, OR list them by a person's exact last and first name. You may view accidents from 1999 only by a case number or exact name.
Lancaster County - City of Lincoln - Parking Ticket Look-up www.lincoln.ne.gov/city/finance/treas/tickets.htm
Wayne County - Sheriff Sales, Warrants http://county.waynene.org/County_Offices/Sheriff/

Nevada

Capital: Carson City
            Carson City County
Time Zone: PST
Population: 2,565,382
# of Counties: 17

Useful State Links

Website: www.nv.gov
Governor: http://gov.state.nv.us
Attorney General: http://ag.state.nv.us
State Archives: http://dmla.clan.lib.nv.us/docs/nsla
State Statutes and Codes: www.leg.state.nv.us/NRS/
Legislative Bill Search: www.leg.state.nv.us
Bill Monitoring: https://www.leg.state.nv.us/74th/Subscriber/
Unclaimed Funds: https://nevadatreasurer.gov/index.html

Primary State Agencies

Sexual Offender Registry `Free`

Records and Identification Bureau, Sex Offender Registry, www.nvsexoffenders.gov Information available on the website is extensive, including aliases, photograph (where available), injury and conviction information, and latest registered address. Information is provided for sex offenders with a risk assessment score of a TIER Level 3 or TIER Level 2. Search by name, ZIP Code, or even license plate number.

Incarceration Records `Free`

Nevada Department of Corrections, Attn: Records, www.doc.nv.gov There are two ways to access information at the web page. The first is by clicking on Online Inmate Search or www.doc.nv.gov/notis/search.php. This will allow you to look up information about a particular individual. If you prefer, you may click on Download Information to obtain text files of all the information available via the Inmate Search. This system contains information about current inmates and those discharged in the past 18 months.

Corporation, LP, LLP, LLC `Free`

Secretary of State, Records, www.secretaryofstate.biz/ Online access is offered on the Internet site for no charge. You can search by corporate name, resident agent, corporate officers, or by file number.

Trademarks/Servicemarks `Free`

Secretary of State, Corporate Expedite Office, http://secretaryofstate.biz/business/trademarks/faq.asp Search marks at https://esos.state.nv.us/SOSServices/AnonymousAccess/CorpSearch/CorpSearch.aspx. While this may look like a business entity search, it will bring up marks. Look on the document number; SM is servicemark; TM is trademark.

Uniform Commercial Code, Federal & State Tax Liens `Free & $$`

UCC Division, Secretary of State, www.sos.state.nv.us/business/ucc/faq.asp After registration, searching is available at https://esos.state.nv.us/NVUCC/user/login.asp. To receive documents the fee is $20.00, an order form may be downloaded. A full commercial system is also available. *Other Options:* Bulk purchase services are available. Got to https://esos.state.nv.us/sosservices/ and click on fee schedule.

Driver Records `$$`

Department of Motor Vehicles, Records Section, www.dmvnv.com/ The state has an FTP type online system available for high volume users. All files received by 5:30 PM are processed and returned at 6:30 PM. Fee is $7.00 per record. Call 775-684-4702 for details. Only three year histories are available online. A person may order his or her own record at online. Go to https://dmvapp.state.nv.us/OL_DH/Drvr_Usr_Info.aspx. The fee is $7.00.

Birth and Death Certificates $$

Nevada Department of Health, Office of Vital Statistics, www.health.nv.gov/ Expedited service is available from state designated vendor at www.vitalchek.com.

Occupational Licensing Boards

Advanced Nurse Practitioner .... www.nursingboard.state.nv.us/Verification/formLicense.html
Ambulatory Surgery Ctr (Pharm) http://nvbop.glsuite.us/renewal/glsweb/homeframe3.aspx
Animal Technician .... https://www.nvvetboard.us/renewal/glsweb/homeframe.aspx
Architect .... http://nsbaidrd.state.nv.us/directory.htm
Attorney .... www.nvbar.org/findalawyer.asp
Audiologist .... http://speech_pathology.state.nv.us/LicenseVerification.htm
Auditor, Accountancy .... www.nvaccountancy.com/search.fx
Auto/Vehicle-related ... ...   https://dmvapp.state.nv.us/DMV/OBL/Business_Reports/Pages/BusinessLicenses.aspx
Bank .... http://fid.state.nv.us/New_LicenseeMenu.htm
Body Shop   ... ...   https://dmvapp.state.nv.us/DMV/OBL/Business_Reports/Pages/BusinessLicenses.aspx
Boxing Gym .... http://boxing.nv.gov/New_Gyms.htm
Building Mover .... www.nvcontractorsboard.com
Carpentry Contractor .... www.nvcontractorsboard.com
Check Casher .... http://fid.state.nv.us/New_LicenseeMenu.htm
Chiropractor .... http://chirobd.nv.gov/query_licensee2.asp
Collection Agency .... http://fid.state.nv.us/New_LicenseeMenu.htm
Concrete Contractor .... www.nvcontractorsboard.com
Contractor, General .... www.nvcontractorsboard.com
Credit Union .... http://fid.state.nv.us/New_LicenseeMenu.htm
Debt Adjuster .... http://fid.state.nv.us/New_LicenseeMenu.htm
Deferred Deposit Company .... http://fid.state.nv.us/New_LicenseeMenu.htm
Denied/Unsuitable Gaming Person .... http://gaming.nv.gov/unsuitable.htm
Dental Hygienist .... www.nvdentalboard.nv.gov/Vertification.htm
Dentist .... www.nvdentalboard.nv.gov/Vertification.htm
Doctor .... http://medboard.nv.gov/default.asp
Doctor, Disciplinary Action .... http://medboard.nv.gov/Disciplinary%20Actions/disciplinary_list.htm
Driving School   ... ...   https://dmvapp.state.nv.us/DMV/OBL/Business_Reports/Pages/BusinessLicenses.aspx
Drug Wholesaler/Dist./Mfg. http://nvbop.glsuite.us/renewal/glsweb/homeframe3.aspx
DUI School ... ...   https://dmvapp.state.nv.us/DMV/OBL/Business_Reports/Pages/BusinessLicenses.aspx
Electrical Contractor .... www.nvcontractorsboard.com
Elevator/Conveyor .... www.nvcontractorsboard.com
Emergency Medical Service Nurse .... www.nursingboard.state.nv.us/Verification/formLicense.html
Engineer .... http://boe.state.nv.us/ROST_HOME.HTM
Engineering, General .... www.nvcontractorsboard.com
Euthanasia Technician .... https://www.nvvetboard.us/Renewal/glsweb/homeframe.aspx
Euthanasia Technician (Animal) http://nvbop.glsuite.us/renewal/glsweb/homeframe3.aspx
Fencing .... www.nvcontractorsboard.com
Financial Advisor/Investm't Advis'r . www.sos.state.nv.us/securities/
Fire Protection Contractor .... www.nvcontractorsboard.com
Fishing Guide .... www.ndow.org/law/licensed/
Floor/Tile/Carpet Layer .... www.nvcontractorsboard.com
Fur Dealer .... www.ndow.org/law/licensed/
Garage, Registered   https://dmvapp.state.nv.us/DMV/OBL/Business_Reports/Pages/BusinessLicenses.aspx
Gas Fitter .... www.nvcontractorsboard.com
GCB Most-Wanted & Banned List .... http://gaming.nv.gov/unsuitable.htm
Glazier Contractor .... www.nvcontractorsboard.com
Guard Dog Handler .... http://nevadapilb.glsuite.us/
Heating & Air Conditioning Mech'c . www.nvcontractorsboard.com
Hospital Pharmacy, Institutional http://nvbop.glsuite.us/renewal/glsweb/homeframe3.aspx
Installment Loan Company .... http://fid.state.nv.us/New_LicenseeMenu.htm

Insulation Installer Contractor .... www.nvcontractorsboard.com
Interior Designer............................... http://nsbaidrd.state.nv.us/directory.htm
Investment Advisor .... www.sos.state.nv.us/securities/
Landscape Architect .... http://nsbla.state.nv.us/Licensed.htm
Landscape Contractor .... www.nvcontractorsboard.com
Lobbyist.. www.leg.state.nv.us/lobbyistdb/index.cfm
Mason .... www.nvcontractorsboard.com
Medical Device, Equipment or Gas ... http://nvbop.glsuite.us/renewal/glsweb/homeframe3.aspx
Medical Doctor .... http://medboard.nv.gov/default.asp
Money Transmitter Agent .... http://fid.state.nv.us/New_LicenseeMenu.htm
Money Transmitter Company .... http://fid.state.nv.us/New_LicenseeMenu.htm
Narcotic Treatment Center http://nvbop.glsuite.us/renewal/glsweb/homeframe3.aspx
Nurse Aide, CAN .... www.nursingboard.state.nv.us/Verification/formLicense.html
Nurse Anesthetist.............................. www.nursingboard.state.nv.us/Verification/formLicense.html
Nurse, Adv'd Practitioner (Pharm) http://nvbop.glsuite.us/renewal/glsweb/homeframe3.aspx
Nurse, Adverse Action Report........... www.nursingboard.state.nv.us/dactions/
Nurse, RN/LPN/Advanced Practice .. www.nursingboard.state.nv.us/Verification/formLicense.html
Occupational Therapist/Assistant ...... www.nvot.org/index.php?click=search
Optometrist....................................... http://optometry.nv.gov/Qry-LicenseeInfoForm1.asp
Oriental Medical Doctor (OMD) .... www.oriental.nv.gov/qry-licensees_name.asp
Osteopathic Physician........................ http://nvboo.glsuite.us/glsuiteweb/homeframe.aspx
Osteopathic Physician Assistant .... http://nvboo.glsuite.us/glsuiteweb/homeframe.aspx
Painter.. www.nvcontractorsboard.com
Painter/Paper Hanger........................ www.nvcontractorsboard.com
Patrol Company/Man, Private .... http://nevadapilb.glsuite.us/
Pharmacist/Pharmaceutical Tech http://nvbop.glsuite.us/renewal/glsweb/homeframe3.aspx
Pharmacy/Pharmacy Practitioner....... http://nvbop.glsuite.us/renewal/glsweb/homeframe3.aspx
Physical Therapist/Therapist Asst ..... http://ptboard.nv.gov/PT-verif-index.htm
Physician Assistant .... http://medboard.nv.gov/default.asp
Physician Assistant (Pharm).............. http://nvbop.glsuite.us/renewal/glsweb/homeframe3.aspx
Plaster/Lather................................... www.nvcontractorsboard.com
Plasterer/Drywall Installer................ www.nvcontractorsboard.com
Playground Builder........................... www.nvcontractorsboard.com
Plumber .... www.nvcontractorsboard.com
Podiatrist.. http://podiatry.state.nv.us/qry-Licenses.asp
Polygraph Examiner .... http://nevadapilb.glsuite.us/
Prison Pharmacy............................... http://nvbop.glsuite.us/renewal/glsweb/homeframe3.aspx
Private Investigator........................... http://nevadapilb.glsuite.us/
Process Server .... http://nevadapilb.glsuite.us/
Public Accountant-CPA .... www.nvaccountancy.com/search.fx
Pump Installer................................... www.nvcontractorsboard.com
Referee/Judge/Timekeeper .... http://boxing.nv.gov/New_ROfficInsp.htm
Refractory/Firebrick Contractor .... www.nvcontractorsboard.com
Repossessor .... http://nevadapilb.glsuite.us/
Residential Designer......................... http://nsbaidrd.state.nv.us/directory.htm
Respiratory Care Practitioner .... http://medboard.nv.gov/default.asp
Roofer.. www.nvcontractorsboard.com
Savings & Loan .... http://fid.state.nv.us/New_LicenseeMenu.htm
Scientific Collector........................... www.ndow.org/law/licensed/
Securities Broker/Dealer................... www.sos.state.nv.us/securities/
Sewerage Contractor .... www.nvcontractorsboard.com
Sheet Metal Fabricator...................... www.nvcontractorsboard.com
Siding Installer .... www.nvcontractorsboard.com
Sign Erector..................................... www.nvcontractorsboard.com
Social Worker................................... www.socwork.nv.gov/
Solar Contractor .... www.nvcontractorsboard.com
Speech Pathologist............................ http://speech_pathology.state.nv.us/LicenseVerification.htm

Steel Contractor .... www.nvcontractorsboard.com
Surveyor, Land .... http://boe.state.nv.us/pls.htm
Tank Installer, Pressure/Storage .... www.nvcontractorsboard.com
Taxicab Authority.............................. www.taxi.state.nv.us
Thrift Company .... http://fid.state.nv.us/New_LicenseeMenu.htm
Traffic Safety School ... https://dmvapp.state.nv.us/DMV/OBL/Business_Reports/Pages/BusinessLicenses.aspx
Transporter, Vehicle   ... https://dmvapp.state.nv.us/DMV/OBL/Business_Reports/Pages/BusinessLicenses.aspx
Trust Company .... http://fid.state.nv.us/New_LicenseeMenu.htm
Vehicle Broker/Dealer   https://dmvapp.state.nv.us/DMV/OBL/Business_Reports/Pages/BusinessLicenses.aspx
Veterinarian...................................... https://www.nvvetboard.us/Renewal/glsweb/homeframe.aspx
Veterinary Facility............................ https://www.nvvetboard.us/Renewal/glsweb/homeframe.aspx
Water Well Driller............................ http://water.nv.gov/Engineering/wd/wd_queries.cfm
Well Driller...................................... www.nvcontractorsboard.com
Well Driller/Monitor .... http://water.nv.gov/Engineering/wd/wd_queries.cfm
Wrecker ... ...   https://dmvapp.state.nv.us/DMV/OBL/Business_Reports/Pages/BusinessLicenses.aspx
Wrecker/Demolisher.......................... www.nvcontractorsboard.com

State and Local Courts

State Court Structure: 17 District Courts are the courts of general jurisdiction and are within 9 judicial
districts. Their minimum civil limit raised from $7,500 to $10,000 on Jan 1, 2005. The Justice Courts are named
for the township of jurisdiction. Due to their small populations, some townships no longer have Justice Courts.
The Justice Courts handle misdemeanor crime and traffic matters, small claims disputes, evictions, and other civil
matters less than $10,000. The Justices of the Peace also preside over felony and gross misdemeanor
arraignments and conduct preliminary hearings to determine if sufficient evidence exists to hold criminals for
trial at District Court. Probate is handled by the District Courts.

Statewide Court Online Access: Only Clark and Washoe counties offer online access to the public. A
statewide court automation system is being implemented. The Supreme Court website found at
www.nvsupremecourt.us/index.php gives access to opinions.

Clark County

8th Judicial District Court   www.co.clark.nv.us/district_court/courthome.htm   **Free**
Civil: Records from the court are free online at http://courtgate.coca.co.clark.nv.us:8490. Search by case number or party name.
Probate also available. *Criminal:* Same.

Goodsprings Township Jean Justice Court   www.lasvegascourts.org/   **Free**
Civil: Court cases and calendars may be available free at
www.accessclarkcounty.com/depts/clark_county/pages/justicecourt_index.aspx. *Criminal:* same.

Washoe County

2nd Judicial District Court   www.washoecourts.com   **Free**
Civil: CourtConnect online access is at the website. Case data in CourtConnect only limited to cases filed after 1/2000. Calendars also
free at website. *Criminal:* same.

Recorders, Assessors, and Other Sites of Note

Recording Office Organization: 16 counties and one independent city; 17 recording offices. The recording
officer is the County Recorder. Carson City has a separate filing office. Federal tax liens on personal property of
businesses are filed with the Secretary of State. Federal tax liens on personal property of individuals are filed
with the County Recorder. Although not called state tax liens, employment withholding judgments have the same
effect and are filed with the County Recorder.

Online Access Note: A number of counties have searchable databases online. A private company, GoverNet,
offers online access to Assessor, Treasurer, Recorder and other county databases for Churchill, Clark, Esmeralda,
and Pershing. Registration is required; sliding monthly and per-hit fees apply. See
http://nv.gov/On_Line_Services.htm or call 208-522-1225.

Carson City   *Real Estate, Deed, Marriage, Vital Statistic Records*   www.carson-city.nv.us/   `Free`
Most all recordings are indexed online at www.carson-city.nv.us/Index.aspx?page=155 but no images. Use the pull-down menu.
Property, Taxation Records   `Free`   Access assessor data of parcels and secured property free at
http://207.228.41.46/jwalk/assessorcached.html. Access secured property data free at http://207.228.41.46/jwalk/taxcollcached.html.
Find Carson city parcel maps searchable by parcel number at www.carson-city.nv.us/Index.aspx?page=59

Churchill County   *Real Estate, Grantor/Grantee, Deed, Judgment, UCC, Lien Records*
www.churchillcounty.org/recorder/   `Free`   Access recorder records at www.churchillcounty.org/recorder/. Documents 2005 and
forward can be viewed, all maps can be viewed.
Property, Taxation Records   `Free`   Access assessor property records free at www.churchillcounty.org/assessor/.

Clark County   *Real Estate, Deed, Lien, UCC, Marriage, Fictitious Name, Business License, Voter Registration Records*   www.accessclarkcounty.com/recorder   `Free`   Recorder's real estate, UCC and vital records free at
www.accessclarkcounty.com/recorder but no images. UCCs go back to 1986; liens to '84. Search county fictitious names at
http://sandgate.co.clark.nv.us:8498/clarkcounty/clerk/clerkSearch.html. Marriages- http://redrock.co.clark.nv.us/RecSearch. Biz
license- http://sandgate.co.clark.nv.us/businessLicense/businessSearch/blindex.asp. Voter Reg.-
www.accessclarkcounty.com/depts/election.
Property, Taxation Records   `Free`   Property records, assessor maps, manufactured housing, road documents, and business
personal property on the county Assessor database are free at www.accessclarkcounty.com/depts/assessor/pages/Disclaim.aspx.
Property-GIS at http://gisgate.co.clark.nv.us.

Douglas County   *Real Estate, Deed, Mortgage, Lien, Judgment, Voter Registration, Building Permit Records*
www.douglascountynv.gov/sites/recorder/   `Free`   Access recorded documents index back thru 1983 free at
www.douglascountynv.gov/sites/recorder/database/default.asp (iindex only, images not available online). Also, search voter rolls free
at http://cltr.co.douglas.nv.us/elections/vripri-general.cfm with birthdate required. Also, search building permits free at
www.douglascountynv.gov/sites/cd-building/index.cfml.
Property, Taxation Records   `Free`   Property records on the Assessor's database are free at
http://assessor.co.douglas.nv.us/database/default.asp. Also, download maps at http://assessor.co.douglas.nv.us/database/newma
ps/index.asp. Also, the clerk/treasurer property tax database is free at http://cltr.co.douglas.nv.us/database/default.asp.

Elko County   *Real Estate, Deed, Marriage Records*   www.elkocountynv.net   `Free`   Access to the recorder database
including marriages is free at www.elkocountynv.net/recorder.htm. Recording records go back to 1984. Most documents back to 2000
are viewable and/or printable.
Property, Taxation Records   `Free`   Access to the assessor database including personal property is free at
www.elkocountynv.net/assessor.htm.

Esmeralda County   *Property, Taxation Records*   `Free`   Access the assessment roll free at
www.accessesmeralda.com/Assessor.htm. Click on Assessment Roll.

Eureka County   *Real Estate, Deed, Lien, Judgment, Vital Statistic Records*   www.co.eureka.nv.us   `Free`   Access
to the recorders index is free at http://eurekacounty.net:1403/cgi-bin/diw200.
Property, Taxation Records   `Free`   Search the assessor property data at http://eurekacounty.net:1401/cgi-bin/asw100. Search
the treasurer's secured property tax roll at http://eurekacounty.net:1401/cgi-bin/tcw100.

Humboldt County   *Property, Taxation Records*   `Free`   Online access at www.humboldtcountynv.org:1401/cgi-
bin/asw100. Treasurers secured tax inquiry at www.humboldtcountynv.org:1401/cgi-bin/tcw100.

Lander County   *Property, Taxation Records*   `Free`   Access real property tax, personal property, and sales free at
www.landercounty.org:1401/cgi-bin/asw100.

Lyon County   *Real Estate, Deed, UCC, Map Records*   www.lyon-county.org/index.asp   `Free`   Access recorder
records free at www.lyon-county.org/index.asp?nid=110; images go back to 1/2006.   *Property, Taxation Records*   `Free`
Search assessor data at www.lyon-county.org/index.asp?nid=55 and click on On-Line Data.

Nye County   *Property, Taxation Records*   `Free`   Search property assessor data free at http://asdb.co.nye.nv.us:1401/cgi-
bin/asw100. Access secured tax data sheets free at www.nyecounty.net/.

Storey County   *Property, Taxation Records*   `Free`   Search assessor's assessment roll free at
www.storeycounty.org/assessor/search_new.asp.

Washoe County   *Real Estate, Grantor/Grantee, Deed, Voter Registration Records*   www.co.washoe.nv.us/recorder
`Free & $$`   Access grantor/grantee index free at www.co.washoe.nv.us/recorder/icris.washoecounty.us; a $1.00 per page fee for
documents. Search voter registration roll at www.co.washoe.nv.us/voters/regsearch.php~color=grey&text_version=.
Property, Taxation Records   `Free`   Access property tax data at www.co.washoe.nv.us/assessor/cama/search.php. Download
property sales 2003-2005 data free at www.co.washoe.nv.us/assessor/SalesRpt.htm. Also, search aircraft, business property, mobile
home data free at www.co.washoe.nv.us/assessor/index.htm.

New Hampshire

Capital: Concord
           MerrimackCounty
Time Zone: EST
Population: 1,315,828
# of Counties: 10

Useful State Links

Website: www.nh.gov/
Governor: www.nh.gov/governor/
Attorney General: http://doj.nh.gov
State Archives: www.sos.nh.gov/archives/
State Statutes and Codes: http://gencourt.state.nh.us/rsa/html/indexes/default.html
Legislative Bill Search: http://gencourt.state.nh.us/index/
Unclaimed Funds: www.state.nh.us/treasury/Divisions/AP/APsearch2.htm

Primary State Agencies

Sexual Offender Registry   `Free`

State Police Headquarters, Special Investigations Unit-SOR, www.egov.nh.gov/nsor/ For web access, click on the Offenders Against Children link. This list only contains certain information about registered offenders who have committed certain criminal offenses against children. The list also contains outstanding arrest warrants for any sexual offender or offender against children who did not register.

Incarceration Records   `Free`

New Hampshire Department of Corrections, Offender Records Office, www.nh.gov/nhdoc/ An inmate locator is available on their web page. The inmate locator displays the offender's current controlling sentence and does not show concurrent sentences also being served or consecutive sentences that have yet to be served.

Corporation, LP, LLP, LLC, Trademarks/Servicemarks, Trade Names   `Free`

Secretary of State, Corporation Division, www.sos.nh.gov/corporate/ A free business name lookup is available at the website. Results include a wealth of information including registered agent. Documents filed after 12/2004 and some older documents have been imaged and are also available in the entity's Filed Documents. *Other Options:* Monthly lists of corporations, LLCs, or trade names are $50 per month or $500 for last 12 months. . A list of all non-profits on file is available for $250.00.

Uniform Commercial Code, Federal & State Tax Liens   `$$`

UCC Division, Secretary of State, www.sos.nh.gov/ucc/index.html Visit https://www.sos.nh.gov/uccegov/ for commercial online access to records. Accounts may be established using either automated clearing house (ACH) debit account or credit card. The fee is $27.00 per debtor name on a pay as you go basis, or for a $5,000 subscription fee receive unlimited online searches for one full year. Users can apply for an ACH (Automated Clearing House) account to be used as a payment option for filings or search.

Driver Records   `$$`

Department of Motor Vehicles, Driving Records, www.nh.gov/safety/divisions/dmv/ Online access and FTP (file transfer protocol) is offered for approved commercial accounts. Searches are by license number or by name and DOB. Fee is $8.00 per record. For more information, call the Director's Office and ask for Kirsten Provost.

Vital Records   `$$`

Department of State, Bureau of Vital Records, www.sos.nh.gov/vitalrecords/index.html Records may be ordered online from www.vitalchek.com.

Occupational Licensing Boards

Architect	www.state.nh.us/jtboard/arlist.htm
Bank	www.nh.gov/banking/banking.html
Bank Holding Company	www.nh.gov/banking/banking.html
Bank, Cooperative	www.nh.gov/banking/banking.html
Banking Service Unit	www.nh.gov/banking/banking.html
Cash Dispenser Machine, Non-bank	www.nh.gov/banking/machines.html
Credit Union	www.nh.gov/banking/banking.html
Debt Adjuster	www.nh.gov/banking/consumer.html
Drug Wholesaler/Manufacturer	www.nh.gov/pharmacy/database2.html
Forester	www.nh.gov/jtboard/forlist.htm
Liquor Keg Shipper, Direct	www.nh.gov/liquor/direct_shippers.shtml
Liquor Product	www.nh.gov/liquor/pllicen.shtml
Liquor Store	www.nh.gov/liquor/stores.shtml
Lobbyist	www.sos.nh.gov/lobbyist%20information.htm
Marital Mediator	www.nh.gov/marital/mediators.htm
Marriage & Family Therapist	http://nhlicenses.nh.gov/WebLookUp/
Mental Health Counselor, Clinical	http://nhlicenses.nh.gov/WebLookUp/
Midwife	www.acnm.org/find.cfm
Mortgage Banker/Broker/Servicer	www.nh.gov/banking/consumer.html
Motor Vehicle Financer/Retailer	www.nh.gov/banking/consumer.html
Nurse, LPN/Practical/Advanced	www.nhlicenses.nh.gov/WebLookUp/
Nursing Assistant	www.nhlicenses.nh.gov/WebLookUp/
Optometrist	www.arbo.org/index.php?action=findanoptometrist
Pastoral Psychotherapist	http://nhlicenses.nh.gov/WebLookUp/
Pharmacist/Pharmacy/Pharm Tech	www.nh.gov/pharmacy/database2.html
Physician/Physician Assistant	http://pierce.state.nh.us/MedicineBoard/licensecode.asp
Psychologist	http://nhlicenses.nh.gov/WebLookUp/
Public Health Clinic	www.nh.gov/pharmacy/database2.html
Real Estate Appraiser	www.asc.gov
Real Estate Broker/Firm/Agent/Seller	www.nhlicenses.nh.gov/WebLookUp/
Savings Bank	www.nh.gov/banking/banking.html
Small Loan Lender	www.nh.gov/banking/consumer.html
Social Worker, Clinical	http://nhlicenses.nh.gov/WebLookUp/
Surveyor, Land	www.nh.gov/jtboard/lsis.htm
Trust Company	www.nh.gov/banking/banking.html

State and Local Courts

State Court Structure: The Superior Court is the court of General Jurisdiction and has jurisdiction over a wide variety of cases, including criminal, domestic relations, and civil cases (if over $1,500), and provides the only forum in this state for trial by jury. Felony cases include Class A misdemeanors. The District Court cases involve families, juveniles, small claims ($5,000), landlord tenant matters, minor crimes and violations and civil cases in which the disputed amount does not exceed $25,000. The Superior Court and the District Court share jurisdiction over domestic violence cases. In Grafton and Rockingham Counties, the Family Division Pilot Project has jurisdiction over divorce, custody/support and domestic violence cases.

Filing a civil case in the monetary "overlap area" between the Superior Court minimum and the District Court maximum is at the discretion of the filer. Older Municipal Courts have all been closed, the caseload and records were absorbed by the nearest District Court.

Statewide Court Online Access: While there is no statewide access available for trial court records,the home page has useful information including opinions and directives from the Supreme Court, Superior Courts, and District Courts; search at www.courts.state.nh.us/search/index.htm.

Note: No individual New Hampshire courts offer online access.

Recorders, Assessors, and Other Sites of Note

Recording Office Organization: New Hampshire has 10 recording offices. There are 233 cities/town which previously handled the filing of UCCs. The recording officers are Register of Deeds (for real estate only) and Town/City Clerk (for UCCs). Be careful to distinguish the following names that are identical for both a town/city and a county - Grafton, Hillsborough, Merrimack, Strafford, and Sullivan. The following unincorporated towns do not have a Town Clerk, so all liens are located at the corresponding county: Cambridge (Coos), Dicksville (Coos), Green's Grant (Coos), Hale's Location (Carroll), Millsfield (Coos), and Wentworth's Location (Coos). New Hampshire is in the Eastern Time Zone (EST). Real estate transactions are recorded at the county level, and property taxes are handled at the town/city level. Federal and state tax liens on personal property of businesses are filed with the Secretary of State. Other federal and state tax liens on personal property are filed with the Town/City Clerk. Federal and state tax liens on real property are filed with the county Register of Deeds.

Online Access Note: The New Hampshire Counties Registry of Deeds website at www.nhdeeds.com allows free searching of real estate related records for Belknap, Cheshire, Coos, Hillsborough, Rockingham, Strafford and Sullivan counties. Also, a private vendor has placed assessor records from a number of towns on the internet, visit www.visionappraisal.com/databases/. An additional vendor offers Property Card data for 75+ NH Towns, see www.avitarofneinc.com. Fees apply.

Belknap County *Real Estate, Grantor/Grantee, Deed, Mortgage, Lien Records* www.nhdeeds.com Access to county register of deeds data is free at www.nhdeeds.com/belk/web/BeDisclaimer.html. Online records go back to 1765. To establish an account for copies of documents from the internet, go to www.nhdeeds.com/belk/web/BeSearchWeb.html.

Alton Town *Property, Taxation Records* `Free` Search the assessor database at http://data.visionappraisal.com/AltonNH/.

Belmont Town *Property, Taxation Records* `Free` Access to property assessor data is at http://data.visionappraisal.com/BelmontNH/.

Gilford Town *Property, Taxation Records* `Free` Access assessor and other town online documents free at www.gilfordnh.org/Public_Documents/GilfordNH_BBoard/Document%20Index. Click on Alpha with Addresses.

Laconia City *Property, Taxation Records* `Free` Records on the town assessor database are online at http://data.visionappraisal.com/LaconiaNH. Free registration is required for full access.

Meredith Town *Property, Taxation Records* `Free` Access to Belknap County Registry of Deeds records is at www.nhdeeds.com. Also, search town assessor database free at http://data.visionappraisal.com/MeredithNH/.

New Hampton Town *Property, Taxation Records* `Free` Access assessment lists free at www.new-hampton.nh.us and click on Assessment Lists and choose to view by owner.

Sanbornton Town *Property, Taxation Records* `Free` Access to assessor property data is at http://data.visionappraisal.com/SanborntonNH/. Free registration for full data.

Tilton Town *Property, Taxation Records* `Free` Search the assessor database at http://data.visionappraisal.com/TiltonNH/, there is no charge. For UCCs go to www.sos.nh.gov/ucc/index.html

Carroll County

Albany Town *Property, Taxation Records* `$$` Access assessor property card data by subscription at www.avitarofneinc.com or call 603-798-4419. Annual subscription fee is $150 per Town.

Effingham Town *Property, Taxation Records* `$$` Access assessor property card data by subscription at www.avitarofneinc.com or call 603-798-4419. Annual subscription fee is $150 per Town.

Hart's Location Town *Property, Taxation Records* The town is intending on posting property data on the internet in the future.

Jackson Town *Property, Taxation Records* `$$` Access assessor property card data by subscription at www.avitarofneinc.com or call 603-798-4419. Annual subscription fee is $150 per Town.

Madison Town *Property, Taxation Records* `$$` Access assessor property card data by subscription at www.avitarofneinc.com or call 603-798-4419. Annual subscription fee is $150 per Town.

Moultonborough Town *Property, Taxation Records* `Free` Search town assessor database at http://data.visionappraisal.com/MoultonboroughNH/. Free registration for full data.

Sandwich Town *Property, Taxation Records* `Free & $$` Access assessor property card data formerly by subscription at www.avitarofneinc.com or call 603-798-4419.

Tuftonboro Town *Property, Taxation Records* `$$` Access assessor property card data by subscription at www.avitarofneinc.com or call 603-798-4419. Annual subscription fee is $150 per Town.

Wakefield Town *Property, Taxation Records* `$$` Access assessor property card data by subscription at www.avitarofneinc.com or call 603-798-4419. Annual subscription fee is $150 per Town.

Wolfeboro Town *Property, Taxation Records* `Free` Access to assessor property data is at http://data.visionappraisal.com/wolfeboroNH/. Free registration for full data. Also Also, access assessor property card data back to 11/07 by subscription at www.avitarofneinc.com or call 603-798-4419. Annual subscription fee is $150 per Town, but free index searching.

Cheshire County *Real Estate, Deed, Mortgage, Lien Records* http://nhdeeds.com `Free` Access to county register of deeds data is free at www.nhdeeds.com/chsr/web/ChDisclaimer.html . Online records go back to 1980.

Dublin Town *Property, Taxation Records* `$$` Access assessor property card data by subscription at www.avitarofneinc.com or call 603-798-4419. Annual subscription fee is $150 per Town.

Fitzwilliam Town *Property, Taxation Records* `Free` Search the assessor database at http://data.visionappraisal.com/FitzwilliamNH. Registration required, but search is free. Also search free after registration at www.avitarofneinc.com/listoftowns.asp.

Gilsum Town *Property, Taxation Records* `$$` Access assessor property card data by subscription at www.avitarofneinc.com or call 603-798-4419. Annual subscription fee is $150 per Town.

Harrisville Town *Property, Taxation Records* `$$` Access assessor property card data by subscription at www.avitarofneinc.com or call 603-798-4419. Annual subscription fee is $150 per Town.

Jaffrey Town *Property, Taxation Records* `Free` Search town assessor database at http://data.visionappraisal.com/JaffreyNH/.

Keene City *Property, Taxation Records* `Free` Online access to property values at www.ci.keene.nh.us/onlineservices/index.htm.

Rindge Town *Property, Taxation Records* `Free` Search town assessor database at http://data.visionappraisal.com/RindgeNH/.

Roxbury Town *Property, Taxation Records* `$$` Access assessor property card data by subscription at www.avitarofneinc.com or call 603-798-4419. Annual subscription fee is $150 per Town.

Sullivan Town *Property, Taxation Records* `$$` Access assessor property card data by subscription at www.avitarofneinc.com or call 603-798-4419. Annual subscription fee is $150 per Town.

Surry Town *Property, Taxation Records* `$$` Access assessor property card data by subscription at www.avitarofneinc.com or call 603-798-4419. Annual subscription fee is $150 per Town.

Swanzey Town *Property, Taxation Records* `Free` Access assessor data at http://data.visionappraisal.com/SwanzeyNH/. Free registration for full data.

Walpole Town *Property, Taxation Records* `$$` Access assessor property card data by subscription at www.avitarofneinc.com or call 603-798-4419. Annual subscription fee is $150 per Town.

Westmoreland Town *Property, Taxation Records* `$$` Access assessor property card data by subscription at www.avitarofneinc.com or call 603-798-4419. Annual subscription fee is $150 per Town.

Winchester Town *Property, Taxation Records* `$$` Access assessor property card data by subscription at www.avitarofneinc.com or call 603-798-4419. Annual subscription fee is $150 per Town.

Coos County *Real Estate, Deed, Mortgage, Lien Records* www.nhdeeds.com/coos/web/start.htm `Free & $$` Access to county register of deeds data is free at www.nhdeeds.com/coos/web/start.htm. Subscription required to print images.

Berlin City *Property, Taxation Records* `Free` Access assessor property card data by subscription at www.avitarofneinc.com or call 603-798-4419. Annual subscription fee is $150 per Town. Free information and searching available at www.mapsonline.net/berlinnh/

Colebrook Town *Property, Taxation Records* `$$` Access assessor property card data by subscription at www.avitarofneinc.com or call 603-798-4419. Annual subscription fee is $150 per Town.

Columbia Town *Property, Taxation Records* `SS` Access assessor property card data by subscription at www.avitarofneinc.com or call 603-798-4419. Annual subscription fee is $150 per Town.

Dummer Town *Property, Taxation Records* `SS` Access assessor property card data by subscription at www.avitarofneinc.com or call 603-798-4419. Annual subscription fee is $150 per Town.

Milan Town *Property, Taxation Records* `SS` Access assessor property card data by subscription at www.avitarofneinc.com or call 603-798-4419. Annual subscription fee is $150 per Town.

Pittsburg Town *Property, Taxation Records* `SS` Access assessor property card data by subscription at www.avitarofneinc.com or call 603-798-4419. Annual subscription fee is $150 per Town.

Stark Town *Property, Taxation Records* `SS` Access assessor property card data by subscription at www.avitarofneinc.com or call 603-798-4419. Annual subscription fee is $150 per Town.

Stewartstown Town *Property, Taxation Records* `SS` Access assessor property card data by subscription at www.avitarofneinc.com or call 603-798-4419. Annual subscription fee is $150 per Town.

Grafton County *Real Estate, Deed, Lien, Mortgage Records* `Free & SS` Access to county register of deeds data is free at www.nhdeeds.com/gftn/web/GfHome.html. A subscription is required to print images. Access to the County dial-up service requires a $100 set up fee and $40 per month access fee. Two years of data are kept on system; prior years on CD. Lending agency data is available. A fax-back service is in-state only. For info, call 603-787-6921.

Alexandria Town *Property, Taxation Records* `SS` Access assessor property card data by subscription at www.avitarofneinc.com or call 603-798-4419. Annual subscription fee is $150 per Town.

Bridgewater Town *Property, Taxation Records* `Free` Search town assessor database free at http://data.visionappraisal.com/BridgewaterNH/.

Canaan Town *Property, Taxation Records* `SS` Access assessor property card data by subscription at www.avitarofneinc.com or call 603-798-4419. Annual subscription fee is $150 per Town. Yearly assessor data available at www.townofcanaannh.us/stories/storyReader$45

Dorchester Town *Property, Taxation Records* `SS` Access assessor property card data by subscription at www.avitarofneinc.com or call 603-798-4419. Annual subscription fee is $150 per Town.

Ellsworth Town *Property, Taxation Records* `SS` Access assessor property card data by subscription at www.avitarofneinc.com or call 603-798-4419. Annual subscription fee is $150 per Town.

Enfield Town *Property, Taxation Records* `Free` Assessor data is free at www.visionappraisal.com/databases/nh.

Franconia Town *Property, Taxation Records* `SS` Access assessor property card data by subscription at www.avitarofneinc.com or call 603-798-4419. Annual subscription fee is $150 per Town.

Groton Town *Property, Taxation Records* `SS` Access assessor property card data by subscription at www.avitarofneinc.com or call 603-798-4419. Annual subscription fee is $150 per Town.

Hanover Town *Property, Taxation Records* `Free` Access current assessment data free by owner name or locations at www.hanovernh.org/assessing. Click on Current Assessment Information.

Hebron Town *Property, Taxation Records* `SS` Access assessor property card data by subscription at www.avitarofneinc.com or call 603-798-4419. Annual subscription fee is $150 per Town.

Holderness Town *Property, Taxation Records* `Free` Property assessment data at www.holderness-nh.gov/Public_Documents/HoldernessNH_Assessor/assessments

Lebanon City *Property, Taxation Records* `Free` Records from the city assessor database are free at http://data.visionappraisal.com/LEBANONNH/. Free registration is required to view full data. Search interactive GIS maps free at http://ims.lebcity.com/website/lebgis/default.htm.

Littleton Town *Property, Taxation Records* `Free` Search town assessor database at http://data.visionappraisal.com/LittletonNH/.

Lyman Town *Property, Taxation Records* `SS` Access assessor property card data by subscription at www.avitarofneinc.com or call 603-798-4419. Annual subscription fee is $150 per Town.

Orford Town *Property, Taxation Records* `SS` Access assessor property card data by subscription at www.avitarofneinc.com or call 603-798-4419. Annual subscription fee is $150 per Town.

Thornton Town *Property, Taxation Records* `SS` Access assessor property card data by subscription at www.avitarofneinc.com or call 603-798-4419. Annual subscription fee is $150 per Town.

Hillsborough County *Real Estate, Grantor/Grantee, Deed, Mortgage, Lien Records* `Free` Access to county register of deeds data is free at www.nhdeeds.com/hils/web/HiDisclaimer.html. Online records go back to 1966.

Amherst Town *Property, Taxation Records* `Free` Records on the town assessor database are free at http://data.visionappraisal.com/AmherstNH/. Registration is required to view full data.

Antrim Town *Property, Taxation Records* `Free` Name search the map page free at www.mapsonline.net/antrimnh/.

Bedford Town *Property, Taxation Records* `Free` Access assessor data at http://data.visionappraisal.com/BedfordNH/DEFAULT.asp. Free registration for full data.

Deering Town *Property, Taxation Records* `SS` Access assessor property card data by subscription at www.avitarofneinc.com or call 603-798-4419. Annual subscription fee is $150 per Town.

Francestown Town *Property, Taxation Records* `SS` Access assessor property card data by subscription at www.avitarofneinc.com or call 603-798-4419. Annual subscription fee is $150 per Town.

Greenfield Town *Property, Taxation Records* `SS` Access assessor property card data by subscription at www.avitarofneinc.com or call 603-798-4419. Annual subscription fee is $150 per Town.

Greenville Town *Property, Taxation Records* `SS` Access assessor property card data by subscription at www.avitarofneinc.com or call 603-798-4419. Annual subscription fee is $150 per Town.

Hillsborough Town *Property, Taxation Records* `SS` Access assessor data by subscription from private company at www.avitarofneinc.com/online.html. Subscription starts at $50.00 per year, $150 per year professional; may be bundled with other towns on system, but search is free. Limited property data may be made available on the town website occasionally.

Hollis Town *Property, Taxation Records* `Free` Access assessor data free at http://data.visionappraisal.com/HollisNH/.

Hudson Town *Property, Taxation Records* `Free` Access property data free at http://hudsonnh.patriotproperties.com.

Litchfield Town *Property, Taxation Records* `SS` Access assessor property card data by subscription at www.avitarofneinc.com or call 603-798-4419. Annual subscription fee is $150 per Town.

Manchester City *Property, Taxation Records* `Free` Search Property valuations lists manually for free at www.manchesternh.gov/CityGov/Asr/RevalInfo.html. Also, search Tax Collector accounts free at http://216.204.202.85/Click2GovTX/entry.html but no name searching. Also, search city assessor database free at http://data.visionappraisal.com/ManchesterNH/.

Milford Town *Property, Taxation Records* `Free` Search town assessor database free at http://data.visionappraisal.com/MilfordNH/.

Nashua City *Property, Taxation Records* `Free` Search the City Assessor database of property, GIS-mapping, sales hsitories for free at www.ci.nashua.nh.us/CityGovernment/Departments/Assessing/tabid/440/Default.aspx

New Boston Town *Property, Taxation Records* `Free` Access assessor property card data by subscription at www.avitarofneinc.com or call 603-798-4419. Annual subscription fee is $150 per Town. This data is accessible through the town website for free.

New Ipswich Town *Property, Taxation Records* `SS` Access assessor property card data by subscription at www.avitarofneinc.com or call 603-798-4419. Annual subscription fee is $150 per Town.

Pelham Town *Property, Taxation Records* `Free` Search town assessor database at http://data.visionappraisal.com/PelhamNH/. Free registration for full data.

Sharon Town *Property, Taxation Records* `SS` Access assessor property card data by subscription at www.avitarofneinc.com or call 603-798-4419. Annual subscription fee is $150 per Town.

Temple Town *Property, Taxation Records* `SS` Access assessor property card data by subscription at www.avitarofneinc.com or call 603-798-4419. Annual subscription fee is $150 per Town.

Windsor Town *Property, Taxation Records* `SS` Access assessor property card data by subscription at www.avitarofneinc.com or call 603-798-4419. Annual subscription fee is $150 per Town.

Merrimack County *Real Estate, Grantor/Grantee, Deed Records* www.merrimackcounty.nh.us.landata.com `Free` Access records on the county Registry of Deeds index for free after registration; images require subscription at www.merrimackcounty.nh.us.landata.com. Indexes are 1920-present, document images, 1945-present.

Andover Town *Property, Taxation Records* `$$` Access assessor property card data by subscription at www.avitarofneinc.com or call 603-798-4419. Annual subscription fee is $150 per Town.

Boscawen Town *Real Estate, Grantor/Grantee, Deed Records* `Free & $$` Access records on the county Registry of Deeds index for free after registration; images require subscription at www.merrimackcounty.nh.us.landata.com.
Property, Taxation Records `$$` Access assessor property card data by subscription at www.avitarofneinc.com or call 603-798-4419. Annual subscription fee is $150 for 1st Town, $50.00 for each add'l town, or $500 for all 70+ Towns.

Bow Town *Property, Taxation Records* `Free` Records on the town assessor database are free at http://data.visionappraisal.com/BowNH/. Registration is required to view full data. Property searching available free at www.mapsonline.net/bownh/

Bradford Town *Property, Taxation Records* `$$` Access assessor property card data by subscription at www.avitarofneinc.com or call 603-798-4419. Annual subscription fee is $150 per Town.

Canterbury Town *Property, Taxation Records* `$$` Access assessor property card data by subscription at www.avitarofneinc.com or call 603-798-4419. Annual subscription fee is $150 per Town.

Chichester Town *Property, Taxation Records* `$$` Access assessor property card data by subscription at www.avitarofneinc.com or call 603-798-4419. Annual subscription fee is $150 per Town.

Concord City *Property, Taxation Records* `Free` Records on the city assessor database are free at http://data.visionappraisal.com/ConcordNH/. Registration is required to view full data.

Dunbarton Town *Property, Taxation Records* `Free` Search town assessor database at http://data.visionappraisal.com/DunbartonNH/.

Epsom Town *Property, Taxation Records* `$$` Access assessor property card data by subscription at www.avitarofneinc.com or call 603-798-4419. Annual subscription fee is $150 per Town.

Henniker Town *Property, Taxation Records* `Free` Search the assessor database free at http://data.visionappraisal.com/HennikerNH/.

Loudon Town *Property, Taxation Records* `$$` Access assessor property card data by subscription at www.avitarofneinc.com or call 603-798-4419. Annual subscription fee is $150 per Town.

Merrimack Town *Property, Taxation Records* `Free` Access assessor properrty data free at http://merrimacknh.patriotproperties.com/default.asp.

New London Town *Property, Taxation Records* `Free` Search the town assessor database at http://data.visionappraisal.com/NEWLONDONNH/.

Newbury Town *Property, Taxation Records* `Free` Access to property assessor data is at http://data.visionappraisal.com/NorthHamptonNH/. Free registration required.

Northfield Town *Property, Taxation Records* `$$` Access assessor property card data by subscription at www.avitarofneinc.com or call 603-798-4419. Annual subscription fee is $150 per Town.

Pembroke Town *Property, Taxation Records* `Free` Access assessor data free at http://data.visionappraisal.com/PembrokeNH/.

Rockingham County *Real Estate, Grantor/Grantee, Deed, Lien Records* www.nhdeeds.com/rock/web/start.htm `Free` Access to the register of deeds database is free at www.nhdeeds.com/rock/web/start.htm. Index goes back to 1980; search by book and page numbers.

Atkinson Town *Real Estate Transfer, Building Permit Records* www.town-atkinsonnh.com `Free` Search the last 3 months of real estate transfers and 4 months of building permits for free at www.town-atkinsonnh.com.
Property, Taxation Records `Free` Access town property values for free at www.town-atkinsonnh.com/values.htm. Also, access assessor property card data by subscription at www.avitarofneinc.com or call 603-798-4419. Annual subscription fee is $150 for 1st Town, $50.00 for each add'l town, or $500 for all 70+ Towns.

Auburn Town *Property, Taxation Records* `$$` Access assessor property card data by subscription at www.avitarofneinc.com or call 603-798-4419. Annual subscription fee is $150 per Town.

Candia Town *Property, Taxation Records* `Free` Access assessor data at http://data.visionappraisal.com/CandiaNH/. Free registration for full data.

Chester Town *Property, Taxation Records* `Free` Search town assessor database free at http://data.visionappraisal.com/ChesterNH.

Deerfield Town *Property, Taxation Records* `Free` Access assessor property card data by subscription at www.avitarofneinc.com or call 603-798-4419. Annual subscription fee is $150 per Town, but search is free.

Derry Town *Property, Taxation Records* `Free` Access Derry Town assessor database free at http://data.visionappraisal.com/DerryNH/.

East Kingston Town *Property, Taxation Records* `$$` Access assessor property card data by subscription at www.avitarofneinc.com or call 603-798-4419. Annual subscription fee is $150 per Town.

Epping Town *Property, Taxation Records* `Free` Search the assessor database at http://data.visionappraisal.com/EppingNH/.

Exeter Town *Property, Taxation Records* `Free` Access assessor property data free at http://data.visionappraisal.com/ExeterNH/search.asp.

Fremont Town *Property, Taxation Records* `Free` Search town assessor database at http://data.visionappraisal.com/FremontNH/.

Greenland Town *Property, Taxation Records* `Free` Access is via a private company at http://data.visionappraisal.com/GreenlandNH/. Free registration is required to view full data.

Hampton Town *Property, Taxation Records* `Free` Access town property assessor database free at www.town.hampton.nh.us/assessing/Assessing_database.html.

Londonderry Town *Property, Taxation Records* `Free` Access property data free at http://londonderrynh.patriotproperties.com/default.asp.

New Castle Town *Property, Taxation Records* `$$` Access assessor property card data by subscription at www.avitarofneinc.com or call 603-798-4419. Annual subscription fee is $150 per Town.

Newmarket Town *Property, Taxation Records* `Free` Access is free via a private company at http://data.visionappraisal.com/NewmarketNH/DEFAULT.asp.

Newton Town *Property, Taxation Records* `$$` Access assessor property card data by subscription at www.avitarofneinc.com or call 603-798-4419. Annual subscription fee is $150 per Town.

North Hampton Town *Property, Taxation Records* `Free` Access to property assessor data is at http://data.visionappraisal.com/NorthHamptonNH/.

Northwood Town *Property, Taxation Records* `$$` Access assessor property card data by subscription at www.avitarofneinc.com or call 603-798-4419. Annual subscription fee is $150 per Town.

Nottingham Town *Property, Taxation Records* `$$` Access assessor property card data by subscription at www.avitarofneinc.com or call 603-798-4419. Annual subscription fee is $150 per Town.

Plaistow Town *Property, Taxation Records* `Free` Property owner list free at www.plaistow.com/Pages/PlaistowNH_Assessor/index and click on Current Year Property Owner List. Also, mapping and property interface is being developed; check www.plaistow.com/Pages/PlaistowNH_WebDocs/maps

Portsmouth City *Property, Taxation Records* `Free` Search the Portsmouth Assessed Property Values database free at www.portsmouthnh.com/realestate//

Raymond Town *Property, Taxation Records* `Free` Search the town assessor database at http://data.visionappraisal.com/RaymondNH. Free registration required to view full data.

Rye Town *Property, Taxation Records* `Free` Access is via a private company at http://data.visionappraisal.com/RyeNH. Free registration is required to view full data.

Salem Town *Property, Taxation Records* `Free` Records from the town database are free at http://data.visionappraisal.com/SalemNH/. Free registration for full data.

Stratham Town *Property, Taxation Records* `$$` Access assessor property card data by subscription at www.avitarofneinc.com or call 603-798-4419. Annual subscription fee is $150 per Town.

Windham Town *Property, Taxation Records* `Free` Access lists of parcels and sales data free at http://windhamnewhampshire.com/depts/assess(3).htm.

Strafford County *Real Estate, Grantor/Grantee, Deed, Mortgage, Lien Records*
www.co.strafford.nh.us/registry_of_deeds.htm `Free` Access to county register of deeds data is free at www.nhdeeds.com/stfd/web/agree3.htm. Online records go back to 1970.

Barrington Town *Property, Taxation Records* `Free` Search by address, owner name, parcel number, parcel ID, or distance for property data free at www.mapsonline.net/barringtonnh/

Durham Town *Property, Taxation Records* `Free` Assessor data is free at http://data.visionappraisal.com/DurhamNH/.

Lee Town *Property, Taxation Records* `$$` Access assessor property card data by subscription at www.avitarofneinc.com or call 603-798-4419. Annual subscription fee is $150 for 1st Town, $50.00 for each add'l town, or $500 for all 70+ Towns.

Madbury Town *Property, Taxation Records* `$$` Assessor property card data by subscription at www.avitarofneinc.com or call 603-798-4419. Annual subscription fee is $150 for 1st Town, $50.00 for each add'l town, or $500 for all 70+ Towns.

Middleton Town *Property, Taxation Records* `$$` Access assessor property card data by subscription at www.avitarofneinc.com or call 603-798-4419. Annual subscription fee is $150 for 1st Town, $50.00 for each add'l town, or $500 for all 70+ Towns.

Milton Town *Property, Taxation Records* `$$` Access assessor property card data by subscription at www.avitarofneinc.com or call 603-798-4419. Annual subscription fee is $150 for 1st Town, $50.00 for each add'l town, or $500 for all 70+ Towns.

New Durham Town *Property, Taxation Records* `Free` Acess assessor data free at http://data.visionappraisal.com/NewDurhamNH/.

Rochester City *Property, Taxation Records* `Free` Access property data free at http://rochesternh.patriotproperties.com/default.asp.

Rollinsford Town *Property, Taxation Records* `$$` Access assessor property card data by subscription at www.avitarofneinc.com or call 603-798-4419. Annual subscription fee is $150 for 1st Town, $50.00 for each add'l town, or $500 for all 70+ Towns.

Strafford Town *Property, Taxation Records* `Free` Search property data free at http://data.visionappraisal.com/StraffordNH/search.asp.

Sullivan County *Real Estate, Grantor/Grantee, Deed, Lien Records* `Free` Access to the county Register of Deeds database is free at www.nhdeeds.com/slvn/web/agree7.htm.

Acworth Town *Property, Taxation Records* `Free` Access assessor property data free at http://data.visionappraisal.com/AcworthNH/DEFAULT.asp.

Charlestown Town *Property, Taxation Records* `Free` Search town assessor database free at http://data.visionappraisal.com/CharlestownNH.

Grantham Town *Property, Taxation Records* `Free` Access property data free on the MapsOnline site at www.mapsonline.net/granthamnh/. Also, search town assessor database free at http://data.visionappraisal.com/GranthamNH/.

Lempster Town *Property, Taxation Records* `$$` Access assessor property card data by subscription at www.avitarofneinc.com or call 603-798-4419. Annual subscription fee is $150 per Town.

Newport Town *Property, Taxation Records* `Free` Access assessor property card data by subscription at www.avitarofneinc.com or call 603-798-4419. Annual subscription fee is $150 per Town, but search is free.

Springfield Town *Property, Taxation Records* `$$` Access assessor property card data by subscription at www.avitarofneinc.com or call 603-798-4419. Annual subscription fee is $150 per Town.

Washington Town *Property, Taxation Records* `$$` Access assessor property card data by subscription at www.avitarofneinc.com or call 603-798-4419. Annual subscription fee is $150 per Town.

Other New Hampshire Sites of Note:

Rockingham County - Most Wanted www.rockso.org/wanted.htm Sheriff's small list.

New Jersey

Capital: Trenton
         Mercer County
Time Zone: EST
Population: 8,685,920
# of Counties: 21

Useful State Links

Website: www.state.nj.us
Governor: www.state.nj.us/governor
Attorney General: www.state.nj.us/lps
State Archives: www.state.nj.us/state/darm/index.html
State Statutes and Codes: http://lis.njleg.state.nj.us/cgi-bin/om_isapi.dll?clientID=37640657
Legislative Bill Search: www.njleg.state.nj.us
Bill Monitoring: www.njleg.state.nj.us/bills/BillsSubscriptionLogin.asp
Unclaimed Funds: www.state.nj.us/treasury/taxation/index.html?missingmoney.htm~mainFrame

Primary State Agencies

Sexual Offender Registry `Free`

Division of State Police, Sexual Offender Registry, www.njsp.org Data can be searched online at the website. Click on NJ Sex Offender Registry. There are a variety of searches available including geographic, individual, advanced, and fugitives,

Incarceration Records `Free`

New Jersey Department of Corrections, Central Reception & Assignment Facility,   www.state.nj.us/corrections/index.shtml Extensive search capabilities are offered from the website; click on "Offender Search" or visit https://www6.state.nj.us/DOC_Inmate/inmatefinder?i=I. Offenders on Work Release, Furlough, or in a Halfway House are not necessarily reflected as such in their profile. Also, search offenders and inmates on a private site free at https://www.vinelink.com/vinelink/siteInfoAction.do?siteId=29017.

Corporation, LLC, LP, LLP, Fictitious Name `Free`

Division of Revenue, Records Unit, www.state.nj.us/treasury/revenue/certcomm.htm Business entities may be searched at https://accessnet.state.nj.us/home.asp. Records are available from the New Jersey Business Gateway Service (NJBGS) website at www.state.nj.us/njbgs/. There is no fee to browse the site to locate a name; however fees are involved for copies or status reports. There is also a business list search function at www.state.nj.us/treasury/revenue/searchfile.htm. Also, search securities agency enforcement actions at www.njsecurities.gov/bosdisc.htm.

Trademarks/Servicemarks `Free`

Department of Treasury, Trademark Division, www.state.nj.us/treasury/revenue/regmark.htm Search the trademark database at https://accessnet.state.nj.us/home.asp.

Uniform Commercial Code `Free & $$`

UCC Section, Certification and Status Unit, www.state.nj.us/njbgs/
Go to https://www.state.nj.us/treasury/revenue/dcr/filing/ucc_lead.htm search the UCC index. Go to https://accessnet.state.nj.us/home.asp to find a business entity, UCC debtor, or other business name without accruing a service charge with the Division of Revenue. However, if you wish to receive status reports or other information services, you need to pay the applicable statutory fee.

Workers' Compensation Records `$$`

Labor Department, Division of Workers Compensation, www.nj.gov/labor/wc/wcindex.html COURTS on-line is a secure Internet website that provides authorized subscribers access to the Division's database. Possible subscribers include: Insurance Carrier/Law Firms; Court Reporting Firms; and WC Forensic Experts (Physicians).

Driver Records $$

Motor Vehicle Commission, Driver History Abstract Unit, www.state.nj.us/mvc/ The commercial access system is called CAIR. Fee is $10.00 per record. Access is limited to approved vendors entities per DPPA. For more information, visit www.state.nj.us/mvc/Licenses/CustomerAbstract.htm or call 609-292-4572. NJ drivers may order their own record online at www.state.nj.us/mvc/Licenses/DriverHistory.htm. A user ID number must be obtained first. The fee is $10.00 per record.

Vehicle, Vessel Ownership & Registration $$

Motor Vehicle Commission, Office of Communictaion, www.state.nj.us/mvc/Vehicle/index.htm Limited online access is available for approved commercial, public and non-profit organizations. Fees are $4.00 per request for registration and title records, and $8.00 for ownership history. Call 609-292-4572 or visit the web for further details.

GED Certificates $$

GED Testing Program, Dept. of Education - Bureau Adult Ed. & Literacy, www.state.nj.us/education/students/ged/ Electronic transcript capability provided for the $5.00 fee, but only for record holder.

Occupational Licensing Boards

Acupuncturist	www.state.nj.us/cgi-bin/consumeraffairs/search/searchentry.pl?searchprofession=3251
Alcohol/Drug Counselor	www.state.nj.us/cgi-bin/consumeraffairs/search/searchentry.pl?searchprofession=3703
Appraiser, General/Resi	www.state.nj.us/cgi-bin/consumeraffairs/search/searchentry.pl?searchprofession=4202
Architect	www.state.nj.us/cgi-bin/consumeraffairs/search/searchentry.pl?searchprofession=210
Athletic Trainer	www.state.nj.us/cgi-bin/consumeraffairs/search/searchentry.pl
Audiologist	www.state.nj.us/cgi-bin/consumeraffairs/search/searchentry.pl?searchprofession=4101
Barber	www.state.nj.us/lps/ca/nonmedical/coshair.htm
Barber Shop	www.state.nj.us/lps/ca/nonmedical/coshair.htm
Beautician	www.state.nj.us/lps/ca/nonmedical/coshair.htm
Candidate Report	www.elec.state.nj.us/publicinformation.htm
Cemetery/Cemetery Salesperson	www.state.nj.us/cgi-bin/consumeraffairs/search/searchentry.pl?searchprofession=4701
Certificate of Authorization	www.state.nj.us/cgi-bin/consumeraffairs/search/searchentry.pl?searchprofession=210
Charity	www.njconsumeraffairs.gov/charity/chardir.htm
Check Casher/Seller	https://www6.state.nj.us/DOBI_LicSearch/Jsp/bnkSearch.jsp
Chiropractor	www.state.nj.us/cgi-bin/consumeraffairs/search/searchentry.pl?searchprofession=3801
Contributor, Political	www.elec.state.nj.us/publicinformation.htm
Cosmetologist/Hairstylist	www.state.nj.us/lps/ca/nonmedical/coshair.htm
Cosmetology/Manicurist Shop	www.state.nj.us/lps/ca/nonmedical/coshair.htm
Counselor, Professional	www.state.nj.us/cgi-bin/consumeraffairs/search/searchentry.pl
Court Reporter	www.state.nj.us/cgi-bin/consumeraffairs/search/searchentry.pl?searchprofession=3000
CPA/Public Accountant	www.state.nj.us/cgi-bin/consumeraffairs/search/searchentry.pl?searchprofession=2000
Dentist/Dental Assist/Hygienist	www.state.nj.us/cgi-bin/consumeraffairs/search/searchentry.pl
Electrical Contractor	www.state.nj.us/cgi-bin/consumeraffairs/search/searchentry.pl?searchprofession=3400
Embalmer	www.state.nj.us/cgi-bin/consumeraffairs/search/searchentry.pl?searchprofession=2
Emergency Medical Svc Provider	www.state.nj.us/health/ems/documents/providers.pdf
Engineer	www.njconsumeraffairs.com/nonmedical/pels.htm
Engineer/Survey Company	www.njconsumeraffairs.com/nonmedical/pels.htm
Funeral Home	www.state.nj.us/cgi-bin/consumeraffairs/search/searchentry.pl
Funeral Practitioner	www.state.nj.us/cgi-bin/consumeraffairs/search/searchentry.pl?searchprofession=2
Hearing Aid Dispenser/Fitter	www.state.nj.us/cgi-bin/consumeraffairs/search/searchentry.pl?searchprofession=2253
Home Health Aide	www.state.nj.us/lps/ca/medical/nursing.htm
Home Repair Contractor/Seller	www.state.nj.us/cgi-bin/consumeraffairs/search/searchentry.pl?searchprofession=1301
Insurance Agent	https://www6.state.nj.us/DOBI_LicSearch/Jsp/index.jsp
Insurance Public Adjuster	https://www6.state.nj.us/DOBI_LicSearch/Jsp/index.jsp
Interior Design	www.state.nj.us/cgi-bin/consumeraffairs/search/searchentry.pl?searchprofession=210
Lab Director, Bio-Analytical	www.state.nj.us/cgi-bin/consumeraffairs/search/searchentry.pl?searchprofession=2505
Landfill	www.nj.gov/dep/dshw/
Landscape Architect	www.state.nj.us/cgi-bin/consumeraffairs/search/searchentry.pl?searchprofession=210
Lender, Consumer	https://www6.state.nj.us/DOBI_LicSearch/Jsp/index.jsp
Lobbyist	www.elec.state.nj.us/PublicInformation/GAA_Annual.htm
Manicurist/Manicurist Shop	www.state.nj.us/lps/ca/nonmedical/coshair.htm

Marriage & Family Counselor   www.state.nj.us/cgi-bin/consumeraffairs/search/searchentry.pl?searchprofession=3703
Medical Doctor ... ...   www.state.nj.us/cgi-bin/consumeraffairs/search/searchentry.pl?searchprofession=2501
Midwife ... ...   www.state.nj.us/cgi-bin/consumeraffairs/search/searchentry.pl?searchprofession=2510
Mortgage (2nd) Lender.....................https://www6.state.nj.us/DOBI_LicSearch/Jsp/index.jsp
Mortician ... ...   www.state.nj.us/cgi-bin/consumeraffairs/search/searchentry.pl?searchprofession=2
Nuclear Medicine Tech   http://datamine2.state.nj.us/DEP_OPRA/OpraMain/categories?category=Radiologic%20Technologists
Nurse-LPN/RN/Advanced Practice ... www.state.nj.us/lps/ca/medical/nursing.htm
Nursing Home Administrator ....http://nj.gov/health/healthfacilities/ltclicensure.shtml
Occupational Therapist ... ...   www.state.nj.us/cgi-bin/consumeraffairs/search/searchentry.pl?searchprofession=4601
Occupational Therapy Asst   www.state.nj.us/cgi-bin/consumeraffairs/search/searchentry.pl?searchprofession=4603
Ophthalmic Dispenser ....www.state.nj.us/cgi-bin/consumeraffairs/search/searchentry.pl
Optician/Ophthalmic Tech   www.state.nj.us/cgi-bin/consumeraffairs/search/searchentry.pl?searchprofession=3102
Optometrist.....................................www.state.nj.us/cgi-bin/consumeraffairs/search/searchentry.pl
Orthopedist/Orthotist/Prosthetist ....www.state.nj.us/cgi-bin/consumeraffairs/search/searchentry.pl
Pharmacist ... ...   www.state.nj.us/cgi-bin/consumeraffairs/search/searchentry.pl?searchprofession=2801
Physical Therapist/Assistant   www.state.nj.us/cgi-bin/consumeraffairs/search/searchentry.pl?searchprofession=4001
Physician ... ...   www.state.nj.us/cgi-bin/consumeraffairs/search/searchentry.pl?searchprofession=2501
Physician Assistant...........................www.state.nj.us/cgi-bin/consumeraffairs/search/searchentry.pl
Planner, Professional ... ...   www.state.nj.us/cgi-bin/consumeraffairs/search/searchentry.pl?searchprofession=3300
Plumber/Master Plumber   www.state.nj.us/cgi-bin/consumeraffairs/search/searchentry.pl?searchprofession=3601
Podiatrist ... ...   www.state.nj.us/cgi-bin/consumeraffairs/search/searchentry.pl?searchprofession=2507
Psychologist ... ...   www.state.nj.us/cgi-bin/consumeraffairs/search/searchentry.pl?searchprofession=3
Radiation Techn'g't   http://datamine2.state.nj.us/DEP_OPRA/OpraMain/categories?category=Radiologic%20Technologists
Radon Tester.....................................www.nj.gov/dep/rpp/radon/CERTMES2.HTM
Real Estate Agent/Broker/Seller........https://www6.state.nj.us/DOBI_LicSearch/Jsp/recSearch.jsp
Real Estate Appraiser/Appren   www.state.nj.us/cgi-bin/consumeraffairs/search/searchentry.pl?searchprofession=4202
Real Estate School/ Instructor ....www.state.nj.us/cgi-bin/dobi/urs/schlist.pl
Recycle Coordinator/Facility.............www.nj.gov/dep/dshw/
Respiratory Therapist ....www.state.nj.us/cgi-bin/consumeraffairs/search/searchentry.pl
Skin Care Specialist/Shop ....www.state.nj.us/lps/ca/nonmedical/coshair.htm
Social Worker ... ...   www.state.nj.us/cgi-bin/consumeraffairs/search/searchentry.pl?searchprofession=4401
Speech-Language Pathologist   www.state.nj.us/cgi-bin/consumeraffairs/search/searchentry.pl?searchprofession=4101
Surveyor, Land ....www.njconsumeraffairs.com/nonmedical/pels.htm
Tree Expert.....................................www.state.nj.us/dep/parksandforests/forest/community/cte.html
Veterinarian ... ...   www.state.nj.us/cgi-bin/consumeraffairs/search/searchentry.pl?searchprofession=2901
Viatical Settlement Broker ....https://www6.state.nj.us/DOBI_LicSearch/Jsp/index.jsp
Waste Company ....www.nj.gov/dep/dshw/
X-Ray Equipment   http://datamine2.state.nj.us/DEP_OPRA/OpraMain/categories?category=Radiologic%20Technologists

State and Local Courts

State Court Structure: Each Superior Court has 2 divisions; one for Civil and one for Criminal. Search requests should be addressed separately to each division.

Civil cases in which the amount in controversy exceeds $15,000 are heard in the Civil Division of Superior Court. Cases in which the amounts in controversy are between $3,000 and $15,000 are heard in the Special Civil Part of the Civil Division. Those in which the amounts in controversy are less than $3,000 also are heard in the Special Civil Part and are known as Small Claims cases. Probate is handled by Surrogates.

Statewide Court Online Access: The Judiciary's civil motion calendar and schedule is searchable at www.judiciary.state.nj.us/calendars.htm. The database includes all Superior Court Motion calendars for the Civil Division (Law-Civil Part, Special CivilPart and Chancery-General Equity), and proceeding information for a six-week period (two weeks prior to the current date and four weeks following the current date). Another useful website giving decisions is maintained by the Rutgers Law School at http://lawlibrary.rutgers.edu/search.shtml. Supreme and Appellate case data is found at www.judiciary.state.nj.us/opinions/index.htm.

Restricted online access to all civil records is available through the ACMS, AMIS, and FACTS systems. The fee is $1.00 per minute of use. For more information, contact the Superior Court Clerk's Office, Electronic Access

Program. Write to 25 Market St, CN971, Trenton NJ 08625, or fax 609-292-6564, or call 609-292-4987. Ask for the Inquiry System Guidebook containing hardware and software requirements and an enrollment form.

Note: No individual New Jersey courts offer online access.

Recorders, Assessors, and Other Sites of Note

Recording Office Organization: 21 counties, 21 recording offices. The recording officer title varies depending upon the county, either the Register of Deeds or the County Clerk. The Clerk of Circuit Court records the equivalent of some state's tax liens. All federal tax liens are filed with the County Clerk/Register of Deeds and are indexed separately from all other liens. State tax liens comprise two categories - certificates of debt are filed with the Clerk of Superior Court (some, called docketed judgments are filed specifically with the Trenton court), and warrants of execution are filed with the County Clerk/Register of Deeds.

Online Access Note: A statewide database of property tax records can be accessed at http://taxrecords.com. The site is operated by a private company; register for the free or the fee services at http://imac.taxrecords.com/login/signup.html?url=www.taxrecords.com.

You may also search property data for New Jersey counties free at http://tax1.co.monmouth.nj.us/cgi-bin/prc6.cgi?menu=index&ms_user=glou&passwd=. This is a backdoor URL for a free search; it may close.

Atlantic County *Real Estate, Deed Records* www.atlanticcountyclerk.org `Free` Access to public record index for free go to www.atlanticcountyclerk.org/deeds.htm
Property, Taxation Records `Free` Access property data free at http://tax1.co.monmouth.nj.us/cgi-bin/prc6.cgi?menu=index&ms_user=glou&passwd=. This is a backdoor and may be closed. Also, see online notes in state summary.

Bergen County *Property, Taxation Records* `Free` Access property data free at http://tax1.co.monmouth.nj.us/cgi-bin/prc6.cgi?menu=index&ms_user=glou&passwd=. This is a backdoor and may be closed. Also, see online notes in state summary.

Burlington County *Property, Taxation Records* `Free` Access property data free at http://tax1.co.monmouth.nj.us/cgi-bin/prc6.cgi?menu=index&ms_user=glou&passwd=. This is a backdoor and may be closed. Att http://tax1.co.monmouth.nj.us use username "monm" and password "data" then select county. Also, see online notes in state summary.

Camden County *Property, Taxation Records* `Free` Access property data free at http://tax1.co.monmouth.nj.us/cgi-bin/prc6.cgi?menu=index&ms_user=glou&passwd=. This is a backdoor and may be closed. Also, see online notes in state summary.

Cape May County *Real Estate, Deed, Lien Records* www.capemaycountygov.net `Free & $$` Property records for Cape May county are free to view online at http://209.204.84.120/ALIS/WW400R.PGM. To print, registration and login is required. $1.00 per page copy and/or $10.00 certification fees apply to documents. Online documents go back to 1996, images to 2000. For assistance, telephone 609-465-1010. Also, see online notes in state summary at beginning of section.
Property, Taxation Records `Free` Access property data free at http://tax1.co.monmouth.nj.us/cgi-bin/prc6.cgi?menu=index&ms_user=glou&passwd=. Also, see online notes in state summary.

Cumberland County *Property, Taxation Records* `Free` Access property data free at http://tax1.co.monmouth.nj.us/cgi-bin/prc6.cgi?menu=index&ms_user=glou&passwd=. This is a backdoor and may be closed. Also, see online notes in state summary.

Essex County *Property, Taxation Records* `Free` Access property data free at http://tax1.co.monmouth.nj.us/cgi-bin/prc6.cgi?menu=index&ms_user=glou&passwd=. This is a backdoor and may be closed. Also, see online notes in state summary.

Gloucester County *Real Estate, Deed, Lien, UCC, Mortgage, Trade Name Records* www.co.gloucester.nj.us `Free` Access recording office land records free at https://www.landaccess.com/sites/nj/gloucester/. For more recording sources, see online notes in state summary at beginning of section. A variety of online services at www.co.gloucester.nj.us/OnlineSrv/onlinesrv.cfm.
Property, Taxation Records `Free` Access property data free at http://tax1.co.monmouth.nj.us/cgi-bin/prc6.cgi?menu=index&ms_user=glou&passwd=. This is a backdoor and may be closed. Also, see online notes in state summary.

Hudson County *Property, Taxation Records* `Free` Access property data free at http://tax1.co.monmouth.nj.us/cgi-bin/prc6.cgi?menu=index&ms_user=glou&passwd=. Also, see online notes in state summary.

Hunterdon County *Property, Taxation Records* `Free` Access property data free at http://tax1.co.monmouth.nj.us/cgi-bin/prc6.cgi?menu=index&ms_user=glou&passwd=. This is a backdoor and may be closed. Also, see online notes in state summary.

Mercer County *Property, Taxation Records* Free Access property data free at http://tax1.co.monmouth.nj.us/cgi-bin/prc6.cgi?menu=index&ms_user=glou&passwd=. This is a backdoor and may be closed. Also, see online notes in state summary.

Middlesex County *Real Estate, Deed, Lien, Mortgage Records* www.co.middlesex.nj.us/countyclerk/ $$ Access to the county public access system requires registration and password at www.co.middlesex.nj.us/countyclerk/. There is a sign up fee plus $.25 per page, call Bob Receine at 732-745-3769 for more details. Also, see notes in summary at beginning of section. *Property, Taxation Records* Free Access property data free at http://tax1.co.monmouth.nj.us/cgi-bin/prc6.cgi?menu=index&ms_user=glou&passwd=. This is a backdoor and may be closed. Also, see online notes in state summary.

Monmouth County *Real Estate, Grantor/Grantee, Deed, Mortgage Records* www.co.monmouth.nj.us/countyclerk/ Free & $$ Access county clerk deed and mortgage data free at http://oprs.co.monmouth.nj.us/Oprs/clerk/ClerkHome.aspx?op=basic. Records go back to 10/1996. Also, go to www.njcountyrecording.com/NJCR/Counties.aspx for NJ Electronic Recordation. Also, see online notes in state summary at beginning of section. Access the recorder index via www.landex.com/webstore/jsp/cart/DocumentSearch.jsp. Full access to Recorder of Deeds is by subscription at www.landex.com/remote/. Index goes back to 1930; images to 10/1996. *Property, Taxation Records* Free Search Tax list by owner free at http://oprs.co.monmouth.nj.us/Oprs/taxboard/tbindex.aspx?idx=own or Taxation Board free at http://oprs.co.monmouth.nj.us/Oprs/taxboard/HeadFrame.aspx?idx=mod. Access property data free at http://tax1.co.monmouth.nj.us/cgi-bin/prc6.cgi?menu=index&ms_user=glou&passwd=. Also search GIS Taxview free at http://oprs.co.monmouth.nj.us/Oprs/Clerk/Gis.aspx.

Morris County *Real Estate, Deed, Lien, Judgment, Will Records* www.morriscountyclerk.com/ Free Access the county clerk's access site free at http://mcclerkweb.co.morris.nj.us/or_wb1/or_sch_1.asp. *Property, Taxation Records* Free Access property data free at http://tax1.co.monmouth.nj.us/cgi-bin/prc6.cgi?menu=index&ms_user=glou&passwd=. Also, search assessor/treasurer property tax data free at http://mcweb1.co.morris.nj.us/TaxBoard/SearchTR.jsp. Also, see online notes in state summary.

Ocean County *Real Estate, Deed, Lien, Mortgage, UCC Records* www.oceancountyclerk.com Free Land records on the County Clerk database are free at www.oceancountyclerk.com/search.htm. Search by parties, document or instrument type, or township. Also, see online notes at beginning of section. *Property, Taxation Records* Free County tax records available from a private company at http://imac.taxrecords.com/login/signup.html?url=ww1.taxrecords.com. Free index search, but fees for deeper info. Search by name, address, or property description. Also, access property data free at http://tax1.co.monmouth.nj.us/cgi-bin/prc6.cgi?menu=index&ms_user=glou&passwd=. This is a backdoor and may be closed. Also, see online notes in state summary.

Passaic County *Real Estate, Deed, Mortgage Records* www.passaiccountyNJ.org Free & $$ Access the county clerk index at www.landex.com/webstore/jsp/cart/DocumentSearch.jsp. Full access is by subscription at www.landex.com/remote/. Index goes back to 8/1998, images to 12/2000. *Property, Taxation Records* Free Access property data free at http://tax1.co.monmouth.nj.us/cgi-bin/prc6.cgi?menu=index&ms_user=glou&passwd=. This is a backdoor and may be closed. Also, see online notes in state summary.

Salem County *Property, Taxation Records* Free Access property data free at http://tax1.co.monmouth.nj.us/cgi-bin/prc6.cgi?menu=index&ms_user=glou&passwd=. This is a backdoor and may be closed. Also, see online notes in state summary.

Somerset County *Real Estate, Deed, Lien, Judgment Records* www.co.somerset.nj.us Free Access to the County Clerk's recordings database is free at http://204.8.192.169/search.asp?cabinet=opr. Free index goes back to 1/93; images back to 6/11/01. Also, see online notes in state summary at beginning of section. *Property, Taxation Records* Free Access property data free at http://tax1.co.monmouth.nj.us/cgi-bin/prc6.cgi?menu=index&ms_user=glou&passwd=. This is a backdoor and may be closed. Also, see online notes in state summary.

Sussex County *Real Estate, Deed, Lien, Judgment, Miscellaneous Records* www.sussexcountyclerk.com Free Access recorder records back to 1/1964 free at http://sussex.landrecordsonline.com/. Also, see online at beginning of section. *Property, Taxation Records* Free Access property data free at http://tax1.co.monmouth.nj.us/cgi-bin/prc6.cgi?menu=index&ms_user=glou&passwd=. This is a backdoor and may be closed. Also, see online notes in state summary.

Union County *Real Estate, Grantoor/Grantee, Deed, Lien, Mortgage, UCC Records* http://clerk.ucnj.org Free Search recorded real estate related documents at http://clerk.ucnj.org/UCPA/DocIndex. *Property, Taxation Records* Free Access property data free at http://tax1.co.monmouth.nj.us/cgi-bin/prc6.cgi?menu=index&ms_user=glou&passwd=. This is a backdoor and may be closed. Also, see online notes in state summary.

Warren County *Property, Taxation Records* Free Access property data free at http://tax1.co.monmouth.nj.us/cgi-bin/prc6.cgi?menu=index&ms_user=glou&passwd=. This is a backdoor and may be closed. Also, see online notes in state summary.

New Mexico

Capital: Santa Fe
            Santa Fe County
Time Zone: MST
Population: 1,969,915
# of Counties: 33

Useful State Links

Website: www.newmexico.gov/
Governor: www.governor.state.nm.us
Attorney General: www.nmag.gov/
State Archives: www.nmcpr.state.nm.us
State Statutes and Codes: www.conwaygreene.com/NewMexico.htm
Legislative Bill Search: http://legis.state.nm.us/lcs/BillFinder.asp
Bill Monitoring: http://legis.state.nm.us:8080/billwatcher/
Unclaimed Funds: https://ec3.state.nm.us/ucp/SearchUCP.htm

Primary State Agencies

Sexual Offender Registry Free

Department of Public Safety, Records Bureau, www.nmsexoffender.dps.state.nm.us The website offers a variety of search methods including by name, county, city, and ZIP Code. The site also offers a complete state list, also an absconder list.

Incarceration Records Free

New Mexico Corrections Department, Central Records Unit, http://corrections.state.nm.us To search at the website, you must first click on Offender Information, then on Offender Search.

Corporation, LLC Records Free

New Mexico Public Regulation Commission, Corporations Bureau, www.nmprc.state.nm.us/cb.htm There is no charge to view records at the Internet site, www.nmprc.state.nm.us/cii.htm. Records can be searched by company name or by director name. *Other Options:* Agency makes database available on electronic format- on 3480 tape cartridge. Fee is $3,600, monthly updates for $600.

Uniform Commercial Code Free

UCC Division, Secretary of State, http://secure.sos.state.nm.us/ucc/default.asp The website permits searching and provides a form to use to order copies of filings. *Other Options:* Microfilm and images (from 7/99) on disk may be purchased.

Birth and Death Records Free & $$

Department of Health, Bureau of Vital Records, www.health.state.nm.us Expedited records can be ordered at www.vitalchek.com, a state designated vendor. A free lookup is of death records at www.usgwarchives.org/nm/nmdi.htm. Records date from 1899 to 1949.

Driver Records Free & $$

Motor Vehicle Division, Driver Services Bureau, www.tax.state.nm.us/mvd/ Visit www.nmcourts.gov/dwi.html for a free DUI Offender History search. This is not an official record and may not contain all court records. A 2nd DUI search option is www.dwiresourcecenter.org/datacenter/statedata.shtml. Records are available, for authorized users, from the state's designated vendors - Oso Grande (505-343-7639) www.osogrande.com and Samba (888-94-samba) www.samba.biz. In general, subscription fees are $1.49 to $3.50 depending on the type of record ordered, plus possible network or access fees. The systems are open 24 hours a day, batch requesters must wait 24 hours.

Vehicle, Vessel Ownership & Registration $$

Motor Vehicle Division, Vehicle Services Bureau, www.tax.state.nm.us/mvd/ Records are available, for authorized users, from either of the state's designated vendors. Oso Grande offers XML interface as well as interactive searching. Call them at 505-343-7639.

SAMBA offers interactive and operates a title and registration program for car dealers and banks. Call SAMBA at 505-797-2622 x3. Authorization to work with either vendor must first come from the state agency. *Other Options:* Bulk requests for vehicle or ownership information must be approved by the Director's office. Once a sale is made, further resale is prohibited.

Occupational Licensing Boards

Acupuncturist	www.rld.state.nm.us/Acupuncture/LicenseeSearch.asp
Alcohol Server	www.rld.state.nm.us/agd/search.html
Announcer, Athletic Event/Ring	www.rld.state.nm.us/Athletic_Commission/LicenseeSearch.asp
Architect	www.nmbea.org/People/Aroster.htm
Armored Car Company	www.rld.state.nm.us/b&c/pipolygraph/licensee_search.asp
Art Therapist	www.rld.state.nm.us/counseling/LicenseeSearch.asp
Athletic Promoter/Matchmaker	www.rld.state.nm.us/Athletic_Commission/LicenseeSearch.asp
Athletic Trainer	www.rld.state.nm.us/Athletic_Trainers/LicenseeSearch.asp
Attorney	www.nmbar.org/findattorney/attorneyfinder.aspx
Audiologist	www.rld.state.nm.us/b&c/speech/licensee_search.asp
Bank	www.rld.state.nm.us/fid/search.html
Barber/Barber Shop/School	www.rld.state.nm.us/Barber_Cosmo/LicenseeSearch.asp
Booking Agent	www.rld.state.nm.us/Athletic_Commission/LicenseeSearch.asp
Boxing-related Occupation	www.rld.state.nm.us/Athletic_Commission/LicenseeSearch.asp
Cemetery, Endow'd/Perpet'l Care	www.rld.state.nm.us/fid/search.html
Certified Court Reporter	www.imagehost.net/ccrboard/courtreporterslist.html
Chiropractor	www.rld.state.nm.us/Chiropractic/LicenseeSearch.asp
Clinical Nurse Specialist	www.bon.state.nm.us/lookup.html
Collection Agency/Manager	www.rld.state.nm.us/fid/search.html
Consumer Credit Grantor/Loaner	www.rld.state.nm.us/fid/search.html
Contractor	http://public.psiexams.com/index_login.jsp
Cosmetology-related Occupation	www.rld.state.nm.us/Barber_Cosmo/LicenseeSearch.asp
Counseling/Therapy Practice	www.rld.state.nm.us/counseling/LicenseeSearch.asp
Credit Union	www.rld.state.nm.us/fid/search.html
Crematory	www.rld.state.nm.us/b&c/thanato/Licensee%20Search/licensee_search_index.asp
Dentist/Dental Assistant/Hygienist	www.rld.state.nm.us/Dental/LicenseeSearch.asp
Dietitian/Nutritionist	www.rld.state.nm.us/b&c/Nutrition/licensee_search.asp
Direct Disposer (Funerary)	www.rld.state.nm.us/b&c/thanato/Licensee%20Search/licensee_search_index.asp
Dispens'g Physician Cont'd Subst.	http://rld.state.nm.us/b&c/pharmacy/Licensee%20Search/licensee-lookup.htm
Electrologist	www.rld.state.nm.us/Barber_Cosmo/LicenseeSearch.asp
Electrophysician	www.rld.state.nm.us/Barber_Cosmo/LicenseeSearch.asp
Engineer	www.state.nm.us/PEPSBoard/PEPSBoard.jsp
Escrow Company	www.rld.state.nm.us/fid/search.html
Esthetician	www.rld.state.nm.us/Barber_Cosmo/LicenseeSearch.asp
FSI (Funerary-related Occupations)	www.rld.state.nm.us/b&c/thanato/Licensee%20Search/licensee_search_index.asp
Hearing Aid Specialist	www.rld.state.nm.us/b&c/speech/licensee_search.asp
Hemodialysis Technician	www.bon.state.nm.us/lookup.html
Interior Designer	www.rld.state.nm.us/b&c/Interior/licensee_search.asp
Journeyman Contractor	http://public.psiexams.com/index_login.jsp
Landscape Architect	www.rld.state.nm.us/Landscape/LicenseeSearch.asp
Loan Company, Small	www.rld.state.nm.us/fid/search.html
Lobbying Org/Lobbyist	http://ethics.sos.state.nm.us/LOBBY/LOB.htm
LPG Gas License	http://public.psiexams.com/index_login.jsp
Manicurist	www.rld.state.nm.us/Barber_Cosmo/LicenseeSearch.asp
Marriage & Family Therapist	www.rld.state.nm.us/counseling/LicenseeSearch.asp
Martial Arts Contest	www.rld.state.nm.us/Athletic_Commission/LicenseeSearch.asp
Massage Therapist/Instr./Practition'r	www.rld.state.nm.us/Massage/LicenseeSearch.asp
Massage Therapy School	www.rld.state.nm.us/massage/schools.html
Medical Doctor	www.docboard.org/nm/
Medical Researcher/ Facility/Whlse	http://rld.state.nm.us/b&c/pharmacy/Licensee%20Search/licensee-lookup.htm
Medication Aide	www.bon.state.nm.us/lookup.html

Mental Health Counselor .... www.rld.state.nm.us/counseling/LicenseeSearch.asp
Midwife .... www.health.state.nm.us/midwife-roster.html
Money Order Agent/Firm/Exempts ... www.rld.state.nm.us/fid/search.html
Mortgage Firm/Loan Broker/Branch . www.rld.state.nm.us/fid/search.html
Motor Vehicle Sales Financier .... www.rld.state.nm.us/fid/search.html
Nuclear Medicine Technologist .... www.nmenv.state.nm.us/nmrcb/radtech.html
Nurse Anesthetist .... www.bon.state.nm.us/lookup.html
Nurse-LPN, RN, Practitioner .... www.bon.state.nm.us/lookup.html
Nursing Home Administrator .... www.rld.state.nm.us/NursingHomeAdministrators/LicenseeSearch.asp
Occupational Therapist/Assistant ...... www.rld.state.nm.us/b&c/ptb/licensee_search.asp
Optometrist .... www.rld.state.nm.us/b&c/optometry/licensee_search.asp
Oriental Medicine Doctor .... www.rld.state.nm.us/Acupuncture/LicenseeSearch.asp
Osteopathic Physician/Phy Asst .... www.rld.state.nm.us/b&c/osteo/licensee_search.asp
Patrol Operator, Private .... www.rld.state.nm.us/b&c/pipolygraph/licensee_search.asp
Pharmacist .... www.rld.state.nm.us/Pharmacy/index.html
Pharmacy, Non-Residential .... www.rld.state.nm.us/Pharmacy/index.html
Physical Therapist/Assistant .... www.rld.state.nm.us/b&c/ptb/licensee_search.asp
Physician Assistant .... www.docboard.org/nm/
Podiatrist .... www.rld.state.nm.us/b&c/Podiatry/licensee_search.asp
Polygraph Examiner .... www.rld.state.nm.us/b&c/pipolygraph/licensee_search.asp
Private Investigator .... www.rld.state.nm.us/b&c/pipolygraph/licensee_search.asp
Psychologist/Psychologist Associate . www.rld.state.nm.us/b&c/psychology/licensee_search.asp
Public Accountant-CPA .... www.rld.state.nm.us/accountancy/search.html
Radiation Therapy Technologist .... www.nmenv.state.nm.us/nmrcb/radtech.html
Radiologic Technologist .... www.nmenv.state.nm.us/nmrcb/NM_Radtech_Registrations.xls
Real Estate Agent/Salesperson .... www.rld.state.nm.us/Real_Estate_Commission/licenseesearch.html
Real Estate Appraiser .... www.rld.state.nm.us/b&c/reappraisers/licensee_search.asp
Real Estate Broker .... www.rld.state.nm.us/Real_Estate_Commission/licenseesearch.html
Referee .... www.rld.state.nm.us/Athletic_Commission/LicenseeSearch.asp
Respiratory Care Therapist .... www.rld.state.nm.us/b&c/rcb/licensee_search.asp
Savings & Loan .... www.rld.state.nm.us/fid/search.html
Security Guard/Firm/Guard Dog .... www.rld.state.nm.us/b&c/pipolygraph/licensee_search.asp
Social Worker .... www.rld.state.nm.us/b&c/socialwk/licensee_search.asp
Speech-Language Pathologist .... www.rld.state.nm.us/b&c/speech/licensee_search.asp
Substance Abuse Counselor/Intern .... www.rld.state.nm.us/counseling/LicenseeSearch.asp
Surveyor, Land .... www.state.nm.us/PEPSBoard/PEPSBoard.jsp
Trust Company .... www.rld.state.nm.us/fid/search.html
Veterinarian/Vet Tech/Facility .... www.newmexicoveterinaryboard.us/
Wrestler .... www.rld.state.nm.us/Athletic_Commission/LicenseeSearch.asp

State and Local Courts

State Court Structure: The 30 District Courts in 13 districts are the courts of general jurisdiction. The Magistrate Courts handle civil cases up to $10,000, and are referred to as Small Claims. The Bernalillo Metropolitan Court has jurisdiction in cases up to $10,000. Municipal Courts handle petty misdemeanors, DWI/DUI, traffic violations, and other municipal ordinance violations.

County Clerks handle "informal" (uncontested) probate cases, and the District Courts handle "formal" (contested) probate cases.

Statewide Court Online Access: The judicial home page at www.nmcourts.com offers free access to District Courts and Magistrate Courts case information (except Bernalillo Metropolitan Court, see below). In general, records are available from June, 1997 forward. The site also offers a DWI Offender History tool for researching an individual's DWI history. Search by name. A commercial online service is available for the Metropolitan Court of Bernalillo County. There is a $35.00 set up fee, a connect time fee based on usage. The system is available 24 hours daily. Call 505-345-6555 for more information.

Supreme Court opinions may be researched at www.supremecourt.nm.org.

> ❖ **Statewide Access Offered All District Courts – Read Previous Page. Below are Additional Sites** ❖

Bernalillo County

2nd Judicial District Court   www.seconddistrictcourt.com   `Free`
Civil: Online access is free at www.nmcourts.com Most data goes back to 6/1985. *Criminal:* Online access to criminal records is free at www.nmcourts.com. Most data goes back to 6/1979.

Metropolitan Court   www.metrocourt.state.nm.us   `Free`
Civil: Access Metropolitan court civil records online at www.metrocourt.state.nm.us. *Criminal:* Search Metro Court criminal case records free at www.metrocourt.state.nm.us.

Cibola County - Sandoval County - Valencia County

13th Judicial District Court   www.13districtcourt.com   `Free`
Civil: Access to court records from 1997 forward is free at www.nmcourts.com. Also, view all civil jury verdicts in the 13th Judicial District Court free back to 1995 at www.13districtcourt.com/verdict/jury_verdict_intro.php. *Criminal:* Online access to criminal records is free at www.nmcourts.com.

Recorders, Assessors, and Other Sites of Note

Recording Office Organization: 33 counties, 33 recording offices. The recording officer is the County Clerk. Most New Mexico counties maintain both a grantor/grantee index and a miscellaneous index. All federal and state tax liens are filed with the County Clerk.

Online Access Note: A handful of counties offer online access but there is no statewide system.

Bernalillo County *Real Estate, Deed, Lien, Judgment, Death, Marriage, UCC Records*   `Free & $$`
www.bernco.gov   Search recorders data and Grantor/Grantee index free at www.bernco.gov/live/departments.asp?dept=2315 . Free registration but small charge for copies of images.
Property, Taxation Records   `Free`   Search assessor records at
www.bernco.gov/property/default.asp?qpaction=search_form&type=situs.

Dona Ana County *Property, Taxation Records*   `Free & $$`   Access county real property index free at
www.donaanacounty.org/clerk/docs/. Index search free; Login and password is required to view documents; contact the office of the assessor for an access agreement. Access property data free on the GIS-mapping site at http://gis.co.dona-ana.nm.us/advparcels/viewer.htm. No name searching. Use the black circle with the 'I' in it to show parcel data.

Lincoln County *Property, Taxation Records*   `Free`   Access to the assessor property records is free at
www.lincolncountynm.net/ACCESS[1].htm. Registration, software, username and password is required. Follow prompts at website.

Los Alamos County *Real Estate, Deed, Lien Records*   `Free & $$`   Access to recorded data at
http://counties.recordfusion.com/countyweb/login.jsp?countyname=LosAlamos username/password required or logon free at Guest.

Otero County *Property, Taxation Records*   `Free`   Search the treasurer's tax data inquiry site free at
http://ocwebserver2.co.otero.nm.us:81/webtaxinq/default.asp?action=taxdatainq.

Sandoval County *Property, Taxation Records*   `Free`   Access assessor property data free at
www.sandovalcounty.com/images/assessor/disclaimer.htm

San Juan County *Property, Taxation Records*   `Free`   Access to county property tax data is free at
www.sjcassessor.net/search.asp

Santa Fe County *Real Estate, Grantor/Grantee, Deed Records*   www.santafecounty.org/   `$$`   Access to recorder's grantor/grantee index available by subscription on the the WEBXtender Document Imaging System; call Melanie at 505-986-6375. $30.00 setup fee and $25.00 monthly and $7.00 per hour usage fee.
Property, Taxation Records   `Free & $$`   Access to county property data is at
www.santafecounty.org/find/appraisal_tax_information.php but registration and account number may be required. Also, for appraisal and tax information for free go to www.santafecounty.org/assessor/appraisal_tax_information.php

New York

Capital: Albany
                 AlbanyCounty
Time Zone: EST
Population: 19,297,729
# of Counties: 62

Useful State Links

Website: www.ny.gov
Governor: www.ny.gov/governor/
Attorney General: www.oag.state.ny.us
State Archives: www.nysarchives.org/gindex.shtml
State Statutes and Codes:
     http://public.leginfo.state.ny.us/menugetf.cgi?COMMONQUERY=LAWS
Legislative Bill Search: http://public.leginfo.state.ny.us/menuf.cgi
Unclaimed Funds: www.osc.state.ny.us/ouf/

Primary State Agencies

Sexual Offender Registry `Free`

Division of Criminal Justice Srvs, Sexual Offender Registry, www.criminaljustice.state.ny.us/nsor/index.htm   The sex offender registry Level 3 can be searched at the website. Requesters are required to register.

Incarceration Records `Free`

New York Department of Correctional Services, Building 2 - Central Files, www.docs.state.ny.us Computerized inmate information is available from the Inmate Lookup at http://nysdocslookup.docs.state.ny.us/kinqw00 or follow "inmate lookup" link at main site. Records go back to early 1970s. To acquire inmate DIN number, you may call 518-457-5000. The site is open, in general, from Mon. thru Sat. 2:00 a.m.-11:00 p.m. & Sun. 4:00 a.m. thru 11:00 p.m. which has state DOC data but not data from all counties.

Corporation, LP, LLC, LLP `Free & $$`

Division of Corporations, Department of State, www.dos.state.ny.us A commercial account can be set up for direct access. Fee is $.75 per transaction through a draw down account. There is an extensive amount of information available including historical information. Also, the Division's corporate and business entity database may be accessed via the Internet without charge. The direct link is http://appsext8.dos.state.ny.us/corp_public/CORPSEARCH.ENTITY_SEARCH_ENTRY. The web has not-for-profit corporations, limited partnerships, limited liability companies and limited liability partnerships as well. *Other Options:* You may submit an email search request to corporations@dos.state.ny.us.

Uniform Commercial Code, Federal & State Tax Liens `Free`

Department of State, UCC Unit - Records, www.dos.state.ny.us/corp/ucc.html   Free access is available at http://appsext8.dos.state.ny.us/pls/ucc_public/web_search.main_frame. Search financing statements and federal tax lien notices by debtor name, or secured party name, or by filing number and date. Document images are no longer provided until further notice. There are two other searchable databases from this site, the State Child Support Enforcement Warrant Notice System and the State Tax Warrant Notice System. *Other Options:* This agency offers its database for sale on microfilm.

Driver Records `$$`

Department of Motor Vehicles, MV-15 Processing, www.nydmv.state.ny.us NY has implemented a "Dial-In Display" system which enables customers to obtain data online 24 hours a day. An application and pre-paid escrow account are required. The fee is $7.00 per record. For more information, visit www.nysdmv.com/dialin.htm. Drivers may use the Dial-in Search Account to request their own DMV records at www.nydmv.state.ny.us/driverabstract/default.html; however, records are returned by mail. *Other Options:* This agency offers a program to employers whereby the agency will notify the employers when a change posts to an employee's record. To find out about the "LENS" program, visit www.nysdmv.com/lens.htm.

Vehicle, Vessel Ownership & Registration `Free & $$`

Department of Motor Vehicles, MV-15 processing, www.nydmv.state.ny.us/reg.htm New York offers plate, VIN and ownership data through the same network discussed in the Driving Records Section. The system is interactive and open 24 hours a day. The fee is $7.00 per record. All accounts must be approved, requesters must follow DPPA guidelines. Call 518-474-4293 or visit www.nysdmv.com/dialin.htm for more information. A free title/lien status check is offered at www.nydmv.state.ny.us/titlestat/default.html. The VIN is needed, this is not a name search. *Other Options:* Vehicle owners and drivers may order their own title abstract by phone at 518-473-5595.

Vital Records `$$`

Vital Records Section, Certification Unit, www.health.state.ny.us/vital_records/ Online ordering is available via an approved third party vendor, go to www.vitalchek.com.

Occupational Licensing Boards

Accountant, CPA/Public....................www.op.nysed.gov/opsearches.htm#nme
Acupuncturist/Acupuncture Assis't ...www.op.nysed.gov/opsearches.htm#nme
Addiction Counselor/Treatm't Ctr.....www.oasas.state.ny.us/credentialingVerification/verification/home.cfm
Adult Care Medical Facility ....www.health.state.ny.us/facilities/adult_care/
Adult Care Suspended List ....www.health.state.ny.us/facilities/adult_care/memorandum.htm
Alarm Installer..................................http://appsext8.dos.state.ny.us/lcns_public/chk_load
Alcohol Abuse Provider ....www.oasas.state.ny.us/credentialingVerification/verification/home.cfm
Alcohol/Substance Abuse Counselor.www.oasas.state.ny.us/credentialingVerification/verification/home.cfm
Apartment Info Vendor/Agent...........http://appsext8.dos.state.ny.us/lcns_public/chk_load
Apartment Sharing Manager..............http://appsext8.dos.state.ny.us/lcns_public/chk_load
Appearance Enhancement Firm.........http://appsext8.dos.state.ny.us/lcns_public/chk_load
Appearance Enhancement Prof..........http://appsext8.dos.state.ny.us/lcns_public/chk_load
Architect...www.op.nysed.gov/opsearches.htm#nme
Armored Car/Car Carrier...................http://appsext8.dos.state.ny.us/lcns_public/chk_load
Athlete Agent ....http://appsext8.dos.state.ny.us/lcns_public/chk_load
Athletic Trainer ....www.op.nysed.gov/opsearches.htm#nme
Attorney..www.nycourts.gov/attorneys/registration/index.shtml
Audiologist.......................................www.op.nysed.gov/opsearches.htm#nme
Backflow Prev't'n Device Tester........www.health.state.ny.us/environmental/water/drinking/cross/cross.htm
Bail Enforcement Agent ....http://appsext8.dos.state.ny.us/lcns_public/chk_load
Bank Branch, Foreign........................www.banking.state.ny.us/sifbranc.htm
Bank Rep. Office, Foreign.................www.banking.state.ny.us/silicrepo.htm
Bank, Domestic ....www.banking.state.ny.us/sibank.htm
Bank, Foreign ....www.banking.state.ny.us/sifagen.htm
Banker, Private ....www.banking.state.ny.us/siprivat.htm
Banking Regulatory Action ....www.banking.state.ny.us/ea.htm
Barber/Barber Shop ....http://appsext8.dos.state.ny.us/lcns_public/chk_load
Bedding Manufacturing.....................http://appsext8.dos.state.ny.us/lcns_public/chk_load
Boat Launch Site ....www.nysparks.com/boating/resource.asp
Budget Planner, Banking-related.......www.banking.state.ny.us/sibudget.htm
Casino Employee...............................www.racing.state.ny.us/racing/licsrch/searchlicense.php
Charitable Gaming............................www.racing.state.ny.us/racing/licsrch/searchlicense.php
Check Casher....................................www.banking.state.ny.us/sicheckc.htm
Chemical Dependence Operation ......www.oasas.state.ny.us/credentialingVerification/verification/home.cfm
Chiropractor......................................www.op.nysed.gov/opsearches.htm#nme
Cigarette/Tobacco-related Occupat'n http://www7.nystax.gov/CGTX/cgtxHome
Cosmetologist...................................http://appsext8.dos.state.ny.us/lcns_public/chk_load
Credit Union.....................................www.banking.state.ny.us/sicredit.htm
Day Care, Farm Worker (ABCD)......www.agmkt.state.ny.us/programs/childdev.html
DEC Permit Application....................www.dec.state.ny.us/cfmx/extapps/envapps/index.cfm?view=wizard
Dental Hygienist...............................www.op.nysed.gov/opsearches.htm#nme

Dentist/Dental Assistant .... www.op.nysed.gov/opsearches.htm#nme
Dietitian .... www.op.nysed.gov/opsearches.htm#nme
Dispatch Facility- Alarm/Sec./Fire .... http://appsext8.dos.state.ny.us/lcns_public/chk_load
Dog License .... www.agmkt.state.ny.us/AI/doglic.html
Emergency Medical Technician .... www.health.state.ny.us/nysdoh/ems/charta.htm
Engineer .... www.op.nysed.gov/opsearches.htm#nme
Environmental Permit .... www.dec.state.ny.us/cfmx/extapps/envapps/index.cfm?view=wizard
Esthetics Specialist .... http://appsext8.dos.state.ny.us/lcns_public/chk_load
Farm Products Dealer .... www.agmkt.state.ny.us/AP/LicFarmProdDealersList.asp
Foreign Banking Agency .... www.banking.state.ny.us/sifagen.htm
Greenhouse .... www.agmkt.state.ny.us/PI/PlantGrower.asp
Guard/Patrol Agency/Guard Dog ...... http://appsext8.dos.state.ny.us/lcns_public/chk_load
Hair Styling, Natural .... http://appsext8.dos.state.ny.us/lcns_public/chk_load
Hearing Aid Dealer .... http://appsext8.dos.state.ny.us/lcns_public/chk_load
HMO (Insurance) www.ins.state.ny.us/tocol4.htm
Holding Company .... www.banking.state.ny.us/siholdmu.htm
Hospital .... www.health.state.ny.us/nysdoh/hospital/index.htm
Insurance Company www.ins.state.ny.us/tocol4.htm
Interior Designer .... www.op.nysed.gov/opsearches.htm#nme
Investment Company Article XII ...... www.banking.state.ny.us/siinvest.htm
Kosher Food .... www.agmkt.state.ny.us/kosher/search.aspx
Landscape Architect .... www.op.nysed.gov/opsearches.htm#nme
Lender, Licensed .... www.banking.state.ny.us/silicend.htm
Lobbyist/Client/Public Corporation ... www.nyintegrity.org/public/lobby_data.html
Mammography Facility .... www.accessdata.fda.gov/scripts/cdrh/cfdocs/cfMQSA/mqsa.cfm
Massage Therapist .... www.op.nysed.gov/opsearches.htm#nme
Medicaid Long-Term Care Service ... www.health.state.ny.us/health_care/managed_care/mltc/mltcplans.htm
Medical Doctor .... www.op.nysed.gov/opsearches.htm#nme
Medical Examiner, Independent .... www.wcb.state.ny.us/content/main/hcpp/ListofAuthIME.jsp
Mentally Retarded Facility/Service ... www.omr.state.ny.us/ws/servlets/WsAdminServlet
Midwife .... www.op.nysed.gov/opsearches.htm#nme
Minority/Woman-owned Business http://205.232.252.35/
Money Transmitter .... www.banking.state.ny.us/simoneyt.htm
Mortgage Banker .... www.banking.state.ny.us/simbanke.htm
Mortgage Broker .... www.banking.state.ny.us/simbroke.htm
Nail Technologist .... http://appsext8.dos.state.ny.us/lcns_public/chk_load
Notary Public .... http://appsext8.dos.state.ny.us/lcns_public/chk_load
Nurse-LPN/RPN .... www.op.nysed.gov/opsearches.htm#nme
Nursery, Plant .... www.agmkt.state.ny.us/PI/PlantGrower.asp
Nurses' Aide .... https://nynar.chauncey.com/registry/public/
Nursing Home .... www.health.state.ny.us/facilities/nursing/
Nursing Home Administrator .... www.health.state.ny.us/professionals/nursing_home_administrator/
Nutritionist .... www.op.nysed.gov/opsearches.htm#nme
Occupational Therapist/Assistant ...... www.op.nysed.gov/opsearches.htm#nme
Off-Track Betting .... www.racing.state.ny.us/racing/licsrch/searchlicense.php
Ophthalmic Dispenser .... www.op.nysed.gov/opsearches.htm#nme
Optometrist .... www.op.nysed.gov/opsearches.htm#nme
Out-of-state Bank Rep Ofc. .... www.banking.state.ny.us/sioosrep.htm
Pesticide Business .... www.dec.ny.gov/docs/materials_minerals_pdf/busweb.pdf
Pesticide/Commercial Applicator ...... www.dec.ny.gov/docs/materials_minerals_pdf/appweb.pdf
Pet Dealer .... www.agmkt.state.ny.us/petdealer/petdealerextract.asp
Pharmacist .... www.op.nysed.gov/opsearches.htm#nme
Physical Therapist/Assistant .... www.op.nysed.gov/opsearches.htm#nme
Physician/Physician Assistant .... www.op.nysed.gov/opsearches.htm#nme
Plant Dealer .... www.agmkt.state.ny.us/PI/PlantDealer.asp
Podiatrist .... www.op.nysed.gov/opsearches.htm#nme
Premium Finance Company .... www.banking.state.ny.us/sipremfi.htm

Private Investigator............................http://appsext8.dos.state.ny.us/lcns_public/chk_load
Psychologist.......................................www.op.nysed.gov/opsearches.htm#nme
Public Accountant-CPA ....www.op.nysed.gov/opsearches.htm#nme
Racing Occupation ....www.racing.state.ny.us/racing/licsrch/searchlicense.php
Radiologic Technologist....................www.health.state.ny.us/professionals/doctors/radiological/
Radiologic Technology School..........www.health.state.ny.us/professionals/doctors/radiological/schlist2.htm
Radon Testing Lab ....www.wadsworth.org/labcert/elap/radon.html
Real Estate Agent/Broker/Office.......http://appsext8.dos.state.ny.us/lcns_public/id_search_frm
Real Estate Appraiser ....http://appsext8.dos.state.ny.us/lcns_public/chk_load
Respiratory Therapist/Therapy Tech. www.op.nysed.gov/opsearches.htm#nme
Safe Deposit Company ....www.banking.state.ny.us/sisafede.htm
Sales Finance Company.....................www.banking.state.ny.us/sisalesf.htm
Savings & Loan ....www.banking.state.ny.us/sisavloa.htm
Savings Bank.....................................www.banking.state.ny.us/sisaving.htm
School, Non-Degree Proprietary........www.highered.nysed.gov/bpss/directory_main_page.htm
Security & Fire Alarm Installer ....http://appsext8.dos.state.ny.us/lcns_public/chk_load
Security Guard...................................http://appsext8.dos.state.ny.us/lcns_public/chk_load
Social Worker....................................www.op.nysed.gov/opsearches.htm#nme
Speech Pathologist/Audiologist.........www.op.nysed.gov/opsearches.htm#nme
State Telecommunication Contractor www.ogs.state.ny.us/purchase/telecomContracts.asp
Substance Abuse Provider ....www.oasas.state.ny.us/credentialingVerification/verification/home.cfm
Summer Camp for Mental Retarded.. www.omr.state.ny.us//hp_camp_directory.jsp
Surveyor, Land ....www.op.nysed.gov/opsearches.htm#nme
Teacher ... http://eservices.nysed.gov/teach/certhelp/CpPersonSearchExternal.jsp?trgAction=INQUIRY
Telemarketer Business.......................http://appsext8.dos.state.ny.us/lcns_public/chk_load
Trust Company ....www.banking.state.ny.us/sibank.htm
Uniform Procedures Act Permit ....www.dec.state.ny.us/cfmx/extapps/envapps/index.cfm?view=wizard
Upholster & Bedding Industry...........http://appsext8.dos.state.ny.us/lcns_public/chk_load
Vendor, New York City.....................http://slnx-prd-web.nyc.gov/cfb/cfbSearch.nyc?method=search
Veteran Home-Skill'd Nursing Home www.nysvets.org/
Veterinarian/Veterinary Technician .. www.op.nysed.gov/opsearches.htm#nme
Water Processing Facility, Bulk ....www.health.state.ny.us/environmental/water/drinking/bulk_bottle/bulkwter.htm
Water Supply Permit ....www.dec.state.ny.us/cfmx/extapps/envapps/index.cfm?view=wizard
Water Treatment Plant Operator........www.health.state.ny.us/environmental/water/drinking/operate/operate.htm
Waxing Establishm't/Operator/Tech . http://appsext8.dos.state.ny.us/lcns_public/chk_load
Workers Comp Appr'v'd Provid'r ......www.wcb.state.ny.us/hps/HPSearch.jsp

State and Local Courts

State Court Structure: The "Supreme and County Courts" are the highest trial courts in the state, equivalent to Circuit or District Courts in other states. New York's Supreme and County Courts may be administered together or separately. When separate, there is a clerk for each. Supreme and/or County Courts are not appeals courts. Supreme Courts handle civil cases – usually civil cases over $25,000 – but there are many exceptions. County Courts handle felony cases and, in many counties, these County Courts also handle misdemeanors.

City Courts handle misdemeanors and lower-value civil cases, small claims, and eviction cases. Not all counties have City Courts, thus cases there fall to the Supreme and County Courts respectively, or, in a many counties, to the small Town and Village Courts, which can number in the dozens within a county.

Probate is handled by Surrogate Courts. Surrogate Courts may also hear Domestic Relations cases in some counties.

Statewide Court Online Access: The OCA offers online access to "approved requesters" for criminal records. Requesters receive information back via email. Call the OCA for details on how to set up an account. 212-428-2700. www.courts.state.ny.us

Visit https://iapps.courts.state.ny.us/caseTrac/jsp/ecourt.htm. This site provides access to a number of records, including WebCrims to criminal case dockets with future appearance dates in 13 counties, open landlord tenant cases from NYC, and open family court cases from all 62 counties. Also from here access or monitor Supreme

Court and Family Court case information on open cases for all 62 New York counties. Appellate decisions are available at www.nycourts.gov/ctapps/latdec.htm.

Supreme Court opinions may be researched at www.supremecourt.nm.org.

> ❖ **Statewide Access Offered All Trial Courts — Read Above.**
>
> **Below are Additional Sites. ❖**

Bronx County

Supreme Court - Civil Division www.courts.state.ny.us/courts/12jd/ `Free`
Civil: Access to current/pending WebCivil Supreme Court civil cases is at http://iapps.courts.state.ny.us/webcivil/FCASMain. Also, access docket data free on the law case search at www.bronxcountyclerkinfo.com/law/UI/Admin/login.aspx and signin as guest.

Supreme Court - Criminal Division www.courts.state.ny.us/courts/12jd/ `Free`
Criminal: Subscribe or login as guest to search eCourts WebCrims future appearances system at http://iapps.courts.state.ny.us/webcrim_attorney/Login. Also, register and access docket data free on the law case search at www.bronxcountyclerkinfo.com/law/UI/Admin/login.aspx and signin as guest.

Broome County

County Clerk www.gobcclerk.com `Free`
Civil: Access to current/pending WebCivil Supreme Court civil cases is at http://iapps.courts.state.ny.us/webcivil/FCASMain. Also, search clerk's court and judgment indexes free at www.gobcclerk.com/cgi/Official_Search_Types.html/input; records go back to 1987. Also, access to civil (judgment) records are available; for registration information on the county clerk online system, call Renny at 607-778-2377. *Criminal:* Online access to criminal record index available; for online date and registration information on the county clerk online system, call Danielle at 607-778-2377. Also, search index for criminal actions include in civil actions 1987 to present free at www.gobcclerk.com/cgi/Official_Search_Types.html/input.

Supreme & County Court `Free & $$`
Civil: Historical records are not online, but access to current/pending Supreme Court civil cases is at http://iapps.courts.state.ny.us/webcivil/FCASMain. *Criminal:* Online access is via the state OCA statewide system.

Cortland County

County Clerk www.cortland-co.org/cc/index.htm `Free`
Civil: Online access at the home page gives judgments and other county clerk records. Login using "public" as user name and password. A subscription service is also available Also, access to current/pending WebCivil Supreme Court civil cases is at http://iapps.courts.state.ny.us/webcivil/FCASMain.

Dutchess County

County Clerk www.dutchessny.gov/dcclerk.htm `Free`
Civil: Access to current/pending WebCivil Supreme Court civil cases is at http://iapps.courts.state.ny.us/webcivil/FCASMain. Also, access to civil, criminal and recording office records is to be available by subscription from the county. Fee will be $35.00 monthly; civil records back to 1986 and criminal back to 1987. Contact Andee Fountain (845-486-2397) for additional information. *Criminal:* Online access is the same as civil; subscriber or login as guest to search eCourts WebCrims future appearances system at http://iapps.courts.state.ny.us/webcrim_attorney/Login.

Erie County

County Clerk www.erie.gov/depts/government/clerk/civil_criminal.phtml `Free`
Civil: Online access to the county clerk's database of civil matters is free at http://ecclerk.erie.gov. Records go back to 01/93. Also, access to current/pending Supreme Court civil cases is at https://iapps.courts.state.ny.us/caseTrac/jsp/ecourt.htm. *Criminal:* Subscribe or login as guest to search eCourts WebCrims future appearances system at http://iapps.courts.state.ny.us/webcrim_attorney/Login.

Monroe County

County Clerk www.clerk.co.monroe.ny.us `Free`
Civil: Online access to felony, civil, and divorce records free online at www.clerk.co.monroe.ny.us. Records go back to 6/1993, and earlier film images are being added. Call 585-428-5151 for username, password, or more information. Also, access to current/pending WebCivil Supreme Court civil cases is at http://iapps.courts.state.ny.us/webcivil/FCASMain. *Criminal:* Same.

Supreme & County Court www.clerk.co.monroe.ny.us `Free`
Civil: Online access to felony, civil, and divorce records free online at www.clerk.co.monroe.ny.us. Records go back to 6/1993, and earlier film images are being added. Call 585-428-5151 for username, password, or more information. Also, access to current Supreme court cases and some closed cases is at http://iapps.courts.state.ny.us/webcivil/FCASMain. *Criminal:* Same.

New York County

Supreme Court - Civil Division   www.nycourts.gov/supctmanh   **Free**

Civil: Search the Sup. Ct Online records CCIS (back to 1986) or CCOP (back to 1972) free at http://iapps.courts.state.ny.us/iscroll/index.jsp. Click Advanced Search. $39.90 monthly sub; $19.95 base rate to purchase case file copy. Also, access to current/pending Supreme Court civil cases is at http://iapps.courts.state.ny.us/webcivil/FCASMain. Opinions/decisions free at www.nycourts.gov/supctmanh/Decisions_Online.htm.

Supreme Court - Criminal Division   **Free**

Criminal: Subscribe or login as guest to search eCourts WebCrims future appearances system at http://iapps.courts.state.ny.us/webcrim_attorney/Login.

Civil Court of the City of New York   www.courts.state.ny.us/courts/1jd/index.shtml   **Free**

Civil: Court decisions at http://decisions.courts.state.ny.us/search/query3.asp .

Oneida County

County Clerk   **Free**

Civil: Access to current/pending WebCivil Supreme Court civil cases is at http://iapps.courts.state.ny.us/webcivil/FCASMain.

Surrogate's Court   **Free**   Access to limited (some, not all) 5th District Surrogate's Court records is free after registration at http://surrogate5th.courts.state.ny.us/public/.

Onondaga County

County Clerk   **Free**

Civil: Access to current/pending WebCivil Supreme Court civil cases is at http://iapps.courts.state.ny.us/webcivil/FCASMain.

Surrogate's Court   http://surrogate5th.courts.state.ny.us/public/   **Free**   Access to limited (some, not all) 5th District Surrogate's Court records is free after registration at http://surrogate5th.courts.state.ny.us/public/.

Rockland County

County Clerk   www.rocklandcountyclerk.com   **Free**

Civil: Online access to county clerk index is free at www.rocklandcountyclerk.com/court_records.html. Online includes civil judgments, real estate records, tax warrants. Call 845-638-5221 for info. Also, access to current Supreme court cases is at https://iapps.courts.state.ny.us/caseTrac/jsp/ecourt.htm. *Criminal:* Online access to county clerk INDEX is free at www.rocklandcountyclerk.com/court_records.html. Index includes criminal records back to 1982. Free registration required. Also, subscribe or login as guest to search eCourts WebCrims system at http://iapps.courts.state.ny.us/webcrim_attorney/Login. Also, access calendar of current Supreme court cases at https://iapps.courts.state.ny.us/caseTrac/jsp/ecourt.htm.

Supreme & County Court   **Free & $$**

Civil: Historical records are not online, but access to current/pending Supreme Court civil cases is at http://iapps.courts.state.ny.us/webcivil/FCASMain. *Criminal:* Online access is via the state OCA statewide system. Also, subscribe or login as guest to search eCourts WebCrims future appearances system at http://iapps.courts.state.ny.us/webcrim_attorney/Login.

Westchester County

County Clerk   www.westchesterclerk.com   **Free**

Civil: Access civil cases on the county clerk database search site back to 2002 at http://ccpv.westchesterclerk.com. Search is free, but registration and fees for images. Data includes liens, judgments, tax warrants, foreclosures, divorces. Also, access current/pending WebCivil Supreme Court civil cases is at http://iapps.courts.state.ny.us/webcivil/FCASMain. *Criminal:* Access criminal records on the county clerk database search site back to 2002 at http://ccpv.westchesterclerk.com. Search is free, but registration and fees for images. Also, subscribe or login as guest to search eCourts WebCrims future appearances system at http://iapps.courts.state.ny.us/webcrim_attorney/Login.

Recorders, Assessors, and Other Sites of Note

Recording Office Organization: 62 counties, 62 recording offices. Recording officer is the County Clerk except in the counties of Bronx, Kings, New York, and Queens where the recording officer is the New York City Register. Federal tax liens on personal property of businesses are filed with the Secretary of State. Other federal tax liens are filed with the County Clerk. State tax liens are filed with the County Clerk and placed on a master list - called state tax warrants - available at the Secretary of State's office. Federal tax liens are usually indexed with UCC records. State tax liens are usually indexed with other miscellaneous liens and judgments.

Online Access Note: Many counties and towns offer free internet access to assessor records. The New York City Register offers free access to all borough's real estate records (also including Staten Island) at http://nyc.gov/html/dof/html/home/home.shtml. Search by address or legal description. A private company offers property assessment data for many New York Counties online at www.accuriz.com/index.htm.

Albany County *Real Estate, Deed, Mortgage Records* www.albanycounty.com/clerk `Free`
Access deeds and mortgages free at https://access.albanycounty.com/clerk/deedsandmortgages/.
Property, Taxation Records `Free` A private company offers property assessment data online at
www.accuriz.com/index.htm. Also search Town of Guilderland property data free at https://www.taxlookup.net.

Bronx Borough *Real Estate, Deed, Lien, Judgment, UCC, Mortgage, Property, Assumed Name Records*
`Free & $$` Recording data from City Register is free at http://a836-acris.nyc.gov/scripts/docsearch.dll/index. Also, for deeper
financial data back 10 years, subscribe to the NYC Dept of Finance dial-up system; fee-$250 monthly and $5.00 per item.
Iinfo/signup- call Richard Reskin 718-935-6523. NYC's Dept of Finance offers daily downloads for borough-wide transactions of
UCCs, Fed lien, deeds, real estate at http://nyc.gov/html/dof/html/home/home.shtml. Assumed names, court dockets at-
www.bronxcountyclerksoffice.com/dynamic/user/create_profile.jsp, free registration required.
Property, Taxation Records `Free` NYC's Dept of Finance Property Assessment Rolls are free at
http://nyc.gov/html/dof/html/home/home.shtml. No name searching. Also, a private company offers property assessment data online at
www.uspdr.com/consumer/ownersearch.asp.

Broome County *Real Estate, Deed, Mortgage, Real Estate, Lien, Judgment, Court Index Records*
www.gobcclerk.com `Free` Search the clerk's indexes free at www.gobcclerk.com/cgi/Official_Search_Types.html/input. Online
miscellaneous and lien records go back to 1989, deeds & mortgages go back to 1963, court records (civil and criminal) from 1985 to
present. *Property, Taxation Records* `Free & $$` A private company offers property assessment data online at
www.accuriz.com/index.htm. Also search City of Binghampton and Towns of Chenango, Conklin, Dickinson, Fenton, Kirkwood,
Maine, Union, Vestal, and Windsor property tax data free at https://www.taxlookup.net. City allows name searching; Town does not.

Cattaraugus County *Property, Taxation Records* `Free` Search for property info on the interactive map at
www.cattco.org/real_property/parcel_disclaimer.asp. To name search, select to search without the map. Also, a private company
offers property assessment data at www.accuriz.com/index.htm. Also, records on the City of Olean assessor database are free at
www.cattco.org/real_property/ .

Cayuga County *Real Estate, Deed, Mortgage Records* www.co.cayuga.ny.us/clerk `$$`
Search mortgages & deeds at www.landaccess.com/proi/county.jsp?county=nycayuga. Subscription fee is $440 per year or $40 per
month, $5.00 per image,plus a one time usage fee, credit cards accepted. Index goes back to 1972; images back to 1980.
Property, Taxation Records `Free & $$` Search tax data, rolls, current sales, tax maps, final assessments free at
www.cayugacounty.us/realproperty/index.htm County-wide real estate/parcel/property data required registration and password at
http://12.177.200.161/imate/. Search property sales lists free at http://co.cayuga.ny.us/realproperty/sales/index.html.

Chautauqua County *Property, Taxation Records* `Free` Access property data free on the GIS-mapping site at
www.chautauquagis.com. On the map page, click on Locate Parcel to search by name, address, etc.

Chemung County *Property, Taxation Records* `$$` A private company offers property assessment data online at
www.accuriz.com/index.htm. Also, search the treasurer's property tax data by year at http://24.97.218.8:81/42BB0001/rps.html.

Chenango County *Property, Taxation Records* `$$` A private company offers property assessment data online at
www.accuriz.com/index.htm.

Cortland County *Real Estate, Deed, Mortgage, Judgment, UCC, Lien, Fictitious Business Name Records*
www.cortland-co.org/cc `Free & $$` Online access at http://72.43.24.100/cortland/login.aspx gives judgments and other county
clerk records. Login using "public" as user name and password. A subscription service is also available
Property, Taxation Records `$$` A private company offers property assessment data online at www.accuriz.com/index.htm.
Also, property data is available by $40 per month subscription at www.cortland-co.org/rpts/Imagemate.htm.

Delaware County *Property, Taxation Records* `$$` A private company offers property assessment data online at
www.accuriz.com/index.htm.

Dutchess County *Real Estate, Deed, Judgment Records* www.dutchessny.gov `Free` Subscription access to
court records and recorder land data is to be available from the county in 2008. For information and registration, call Andee 845-486-
2397. *Property, Taxation Records* `Free` Search the county tax roll at http://geoaccess.co.dutchess.ny.us/parcelaccess/.
Search the Town of East Fishkill property tax roll data free at https://www.taxlookup.net.

Erie County *Real Estate, Deed, Mortgage, UCC, Judgment Records* http://ecclerk.erie.gov `Free & $$`
Access to the county clerk's database index and images is at http://ecclerk.erie.gov:9080/prod_public_view/login.jsp. Login as Guest.
View index free. $5.00 fee to view full documents; a $250 initial escrow account required.
Property, Taxation Records `Free & $$` Parcel data is free at http://erie-gis.co.erie.ny.us/website/erie_help/help.htm. To
name search, click on Internet Mapping System, then "Locate property." Also, a private company offers property assessments at
www.accuriz.com/index.htm. Also, a private company that sells county tax claim property, view list free at
www.xspand.com/investors/realestate_sale/index.aspx

Essex County *Property, Taxation Records* `Free` Parcel data available free at www.co.essex.ny.us/realproperty.asp. Also, a private company offers property assessment data online at www.accuriz.com/index.htm. Also, assessor and property data available free at www.co.essex.ny.us/realproperty.asp.

Fulton County *Real Estate, Deed, UCC Records* `Free` Search recorder documents free at www.landaccess.com/sites/oh/disclaimer.php?county=ohfulton. *Property, Taxation Records* `Free` Search county auditor data and sales free at http://66.194.132.76/.

Genesee County *Property, Taxation Records* `$$` A private company offers property assessment data online at www.accuriz.com/index.htm.

Greene County *Property, Taxation Records* `Free` Access to the Web Map for free go to http://gis.greenegovernment.com/giswebmap/.

Hamilton County *Property, Taxation Records* `$$` A private company offers property assessment data online at www.accuriz.com/index.htm.

Herkimer County *Property, Taxation Records* `Free` A private company offers property assessment data online at www.accuriz.com/index.htm. Also, search City of Little Falls property data free at https://www.taxlookup.net.

Jefferson County *Property, Taxation Records* `$$` A private company offers property assessment data online at www.accuriz.com/index.htm. Also property assessment data offered online at www.co.jefferson.ny.us/rpstoweb.nsf/$$search.

Kings County *Real Estate, Deed, Lien, Judgment, UCC, Mortgage Records* `Free & $$` Recording data from the City Register free at http://a836-acris.nyc.gov/scripts/docsearch.dll/index. Also, for deeper financial data back 10 years, subscribe to the NYC Dept of Finance dial-up system; fee-$250 monthly and $5.00 per item. For info/signup, call Richard Reskin 718-935-6523. *Property, Taxation Records* `Free` Property assessment rolls from NYC's Dept. of Finance are free at http://nyc.gov/html/dof/html/home/home.shtml. No name searching. Also, a private company offers property assessment data online at www.accuriz.com/index.htm.

Lewis County *Property, Taxation Records* `$$` A private company offers property assessment data online at www.accuriz.com/index.htm.

Livingston County *Real Estate, Deed Records* www.co.livingston.state.ny.us/clerk.htm `Free & $$` Access to recorded data at hhttp://counties2.recordfusion.com/countyweb/login.jsp?countyname=Livingston. Username/password required or logon free at Guest.

Madison County *Property, Taxation Records* `Free & $$` A private company offers property assessment data online at www.accuriz.com/index.htm. County tax information is found at www.madisoncounty.org/rpts/PROPERTYTAXINFO.htm. Search by town or village name.

Monroe County *Real Estate, Deed, Lien, Judgment, UCC Records* www.monroecounty.gov/clerk-index.php `Free & $$` Access the county clerk database at www.clerk.co.monroe.ny.us. Includes mortgages, deeds, court records; free registration. Land records back to 1984. Liens, judgments, UCCs back to 5/1989. *Property, Taxation Records* `Free` Search the County Real Property Portal at www.monroecounty.gov/apps/propertyapp.php. Also, a private company offers property assessment data online at www.accuriz.com/index.htm. Also search Town of Penfield property data free at https://www.taxlookup.net.

Montgomery County *Property, Taxation Records* `$$` A private company offers property assessment data online at www.accuriz.com/index.htm. Also, access property data via the GIS-mapping site free at www.co.montgomery.ny.us/mpv/frameset.asp? To name search, click on Search For Parcels. May be temporary.

Nassau County *Property, Taxation Records* `Free & $$` Access to the county assessor tax data for free at www.nassaucountyny.gov/mynassauproperty/main.jsp. No name searching. Also, access to property reports is through a private company at www.courthousedirect.com. Fee for data.

New York County *Real Estate, Deed, Lien, Judgment, UCC, Mortgage Records* `Free & $$` Recording data from the City Register are free at http://a836-acris.nyc.gov/scripts/docsearch.dll/index. Also, for deeper financial data back 10 years, subscribe to the NYC Dept of Finance dial-up system; fee-$250 monthly and $5.00 per item. For info/signup, call Rich 718-935-6523. *Property, Taxation Records* `Free & $$` Assessment roll searches are free at http://nycserv.nyc.gov/nycproperty/nynav/jsp/selectbbl.jsp; no name searching. Also, search assessments free at www.accuriz.com/index.htm. Also, a private company sells county tax claim property, view list free at www.xspand.com/investors/realestate_sale/index.aspx

Niagara County *Real Estate, Deed, Mortgage, Lien, Judgment Records* http://niagaracounty.com/ `$$` A private company offers access to recorder documents at http://www2.landaccess.com/cgibin/homepage?County=8003. Username and password required; register online. *Property, Taxation Records* `Free` Search Town of Wilson property data free at https://www.taxlookup.net but no name searching.

Oneida County *Property, Taxation Records* `$$` A private company offers property assessment data online at www.accuriz.com/index.htm.

Onondaga County *Property, Taxation Records* `Free` Search for property data free on the GIS-mapping page at www.maphost.com/syracuse%2Donondaga/main.asp. Click on "Query" and then "Find Tax Parcels." Access county property data free at www.ongov.net/Realproptax/taxinformation.html, includes access to City of Syracuse property data. Also, search Town of Tully tax roll free at www.taxlookup.net/tully/search_method.php.

Ontario County *Property, Taxation Records* `Free` A private company offers property assessment data online at www.accuriz.com/index.htm. Also, City of Canandaigua property, assessment, and sales lists in pdf format available free at www.canandaiguanewyork.gov/index.asp?Type=B_BASIC&SEC={27669D54-CE6F-4445-9CED-0861BE56EFA0}

Orange County *Property, Taxation Records* `Free` Real Property Tax Assessment Information is available free at http://propertydata.orangecountygov.com/imate/search.aspx. Registration and fees apply for fuller data.

Orleans County *Property, Taxation Records* `$$` A private company offers property assessment data online at www.accuriz.com/index.htm.

Oswego County *Real Estate, Deed Records* www.oswegocounty.com/clerk/index.html `$$` Access county clerk records 1963 to present at http://72.43.24.100/. Username and password required. You may email sales@InfoQuickSolutions.com for a free trial account or for info, or call Info Quick Solutions at 800-320-2617.
Property, Taxation Records `Free` Access tax roll data for Towns of Sandy Creek, Schroeppel, and Scriba free at www.taxlookup.net/#Oswego

Otsego County *Property, Taxation Records* `Free & $$` Search the county real property lookup free at www.otsegocounty.com/public/v4lookup.aspx. A private company offers property assessment data online at www.accuriz.com/index.htm. Search for property info on the GIS mapping site free at http://map.otsegocounty.com/Freeance/Client/PublicAccess1/index.html?appconfig=ParcelQuery.

Putnam County *Real Estate, Deed, UCC, Lien Records* www.putnamcountyny.com `$$` Recorder records are accessible by subscription through a private online service at www.landaccess.com. Registration is required; pay per use or monthly plans available.

Queens Borough *Real Estate, Deed, Lien, Judgment, UCC, Mortgage Records* www.queensbp.org/
`Free & $$` Recording data from the City Register are free at http://a836-acris.nyc.gov/scripts/docsearch.dll/index. Also, for deeper financial data back 10 years, subscribe to the NYC Dept of Finance dial-up system; fee-$250 monthly and $5.00 per item. For info/signup, call Richard Reskin 718-935-6523.
Property, Taxation Records `Free` Property assessment rolls from NYC's Dept. of Finance are free at http://nyc.gov/html/dof/html/home/home.shtml. No name searching.

Rensselaer County *Real Estate, Deed, Lien Records* www.rensco.com/departments_countyclerk.asp `$$`
Search real estate deeds and liens at www.nylandrecords.com. Click on Rennselaer. Registration required. Commercial users can subscribe for $25.00 per month and $.25 per search; Personal users can purchase documents for $5.00 each, no monthly fee.

Richmond County *Real Estate, Deed, Lien, Judgment, UCC, Mortgage Records* www.statenislandusa.com/
`Free & $$` Recording data from the City Register are free at http://a836-acris.nyc.gov/scripts/docsearch.dll/index. Also, for deeper financial data back 10 years, subscribe to the NYC Dept of Finance dial-up system; fee-$250 monthly and $5.00 per item. For info/signup, call Richard Reskin 718-935-6523.
Property, Taxation Records `Free` Property assessment rolls from NYC's Dept. of Finance are free at http://nycserv.nyc.gov/nycproperty/nynav/jsp/selectbbl.jsp. No name searching.

Rockland County *Real Estate, Deed, Lien, Judgment, Court Records* www.rocklandcountyclerk.com `Free`
Access is the county clerk's records index is free at www.rocklandcountyclerk.com/court_records.html. Includes criminal records back to 1982, civil judgments, real estate records, tax warrants. View images back to 6/96, and more are being added. Call Paul Pipearto at 845-638-5221 for more info.
Property, Taxation Records `$$` A private company offers property assessment data online at www.accuriz.com/index.htm.

St. Lawrence County *Real Estate, Deed, Lien, Mortgage, Plat Records* www.co.st-lawrence.ny.us/CoTOC2.htm
`$$` Access recording office land data at https://www.nylandrecords.com/nylr/index.htm; select St Lawrence County. Pay per access fee- $5.00 fee per doc viewed. Monthly users charged $0.25 per search, $.25 per doc view and $40.00 per month subscription fee.
Property, Taxation Records `Free` County assessor rolls available at www.co.st-lawrence.ny.us/Real_Property/SLCRP.htm.
Search Towns of Brasher, Canton, Clare, Clifton, Colton, DeKalb, Depeyster, Edwards, Fine, Fowler, Gouverneur, Hammond, Hermon, Hopkinton, Lawrence, Lisbon, Louisville, Macomb, Madrid, Massena, Morristown, Norfolk, Oswegatchie, Parishville, Piercefield, Pierrepont, Pitcairn, Potsdam, Rossie, Russell, Stockholm, Waddington property data free at https://www.taxlookup.net. 14 Villages also available.

Saratoga County *Property, Taxation Records* `$$` A private company offers property assessment data online at www.accuriz.com/index.htm.

Schenectady County *Real Estate, Deed, Mortgage, Lien, UCC Records* www.schenectadycountyclerk.com `Free & $$` Access county land records back to 1996 free at http://landrecords.schenectadycounty.com. Also, access the county clerk court and land indexes via www.landex.com/webstore/jsp/cart/DocumentSearch.jsp. Full access to records is by subscription at www.landex.com/remote/. The land records index goes back to 1984; courts indexes back to 1988. Images go back to 12/1999.

Schoharie County *Property, Taxation Records* `Free` A private company offers property assessment data online at www.accuriz.com/index.htm. Also, search property tax data free at www.schohariecounty-ny.gov/remote/RPSSearchMgr?menuItem=New.

Schuyler County *Property, Taxation Records* `$$` A private company offers property assessment data online at www.accuriz.com/index.htm.

Seneca County *Property, Taxation Records* `$$` A private company offers property assessment data online at www.accuriz.com/index.htm.

Steuben County *Property, Taxation Records* `Free` Search Town of Erwin Real Property Assessment Roll free online at www.erwinny.org/ertxsrch.htm.

Suffolk County *Real Estate, Grantor/Grantee, Deed, Mortgage, Lien, Judgment,Corporation, Business Name Records* www.suffolkcountyny.gov `Free` Access county land records, business names, and limited civil court records free at www.co.suffolk.ny.us/scco/web/. Land records is index only. Search the county corporation database free at www.co.suffolk.ny.us/Clerk/Corp/search.aspx.
Property, Taxation Records `Free` County GIS-mapping site will have property data available at http://gis.co.suffolk.ny.us/.

Sullivan County *Property, Taxation Records* `Free & $$` A private company offers property assessment data online at www.accuriz.com/index.htm. Also search Towns of Bethel, Callicoon, Cocheeton, Delaware, Fallsburg, Fremont, Forestburgh, Highland, Liberty, Lumberland, Mamakating, Neversink, Rockland, Thompson and Tusten property data free at https://www.taxlookup.net. Also includes Villages of Bloomingburg and Liberty.

Tioga County *Property, Taxation Records* `Free` Search Town of Owego property data free at https://www.taxlookup.net.

Tompkins County *Property, Taxation Records* `$$` Access to property records on ImageMate system at www.tompkins-co.org/assessment/online.html has 2 levels: basic free and a registration/password fee-based full system. Free version has no name searching. Fee service is $20 monthly or $200 per year. For info or registration for the latter, email assessment@tompkins-co.org. Also, a private company offers property assessment data online at www.uspdr.com/consumer/ownersearch.asp.

Ulster County *Real Estate, Deed, Lien, Mortgage, Voter Registration Records* www.co.ulster.ny.us `$$` Access to county online records requires a $33.33 (under 25 transactions) or $44.55 monthly fee; 12 month agreement required. Land Records date back to 1984. Includes county court records back to 7/1987. Lending agency data available. For info, contact Valerie Harris at 845-334-5367.
Property, Taxation Records `$$` A private company offers property assessment data at www.accuriz.com/index.htm.

Warren County *Property, Taxation Records* `$$` A private company offers property assessment data online at www.accuriz.com/index.htm.

Wayne County *Property, Taxation Records* `Free` Access tax property data free at www.co.wayne.ny.us/TaxSearch/. Also, search the real property tax data free at www.co.wayne.ny.us/RPT-TaxSearch/default.aspx

Westchester County *Real Estate, Deed, Land, Fictitious Name, Judgment, Lien, UCC Records* www.westchesterclerk.com/sections.asp?mu_step=001 `Free & $$` Access to the clerk's land record database is free at http://ccpv.westchesterclerk.com/WCCLogin.asp. There is also an advanced search that features images; registration is required. Data also includes corporations, foreclosures, divorces, civil courts.
Property, Taxation Records `Free` Access Sleepy Hollow Village tax roll data free at www.taxlookup.net/ and click on Westchester County; no name searching.

Wyoming County *Real Estate, Deed, Lien, Judgment Records* www.wyomingco.net `Free & $$` Recorder index is accessible free through a private online service at http://www2.landaccess.com/cgibin/homepage?County=8008. This is a subscription service, fees and registration may be required.
Property, Taxation Records `$$` A private company offers property assessment data online at www.accuriz.com/index.htm.

Yates County *Property, Taxation Records* `$$` A private company offers property assessment data online at www.accuriz.com/index.htm.

North Carolina

Capital: Raleigh
            Wake County
Time Zone: EST
Population: 8,451,221
# of Counties: 100

Useful State Links

Website: www.ncgov.com
Governor: www.governor.state.nc.us
Attorney General: www.ncdoj.com/default.jsp
State Archives: www.ah.dcr.state.nc.us
State Statutes and Codes: www.ncleg.net/gascripts/Statutes/Statutes.asp
Legislative Bill Search: www.ncleg.net
Unclaimed Funds: https://www.treasurer.state.nc.us/dsthome/AdminServices/UnclaimedProperty

Primary State Agencies

Sexual Offender Registry `Free`

State Bureau of Investigation, Criminal Information & Ident Sect - SOR Unit, http://ncfindoffender.com/disclaimer.aspx Search Level 3 records at the website. Search by name or geographic region. *Other Options:* Agency can provide data on CD-Rom.

Incarceration Records `Free`

North Carolina Department of Corrections, Combined Records, www.doc.state.nc.us The web access allows searching by name or ID number for public information on inmates, probationers, or parolees since 1973. Go to http://webapps6.doc.state.nc.us/apps/offender/menu1.

Corporation, LP, LLC, Trademarks/Servicemarks `Free`

Secretary of State, Corporations Division, www.sosnc.com The website offers a free search of status, corporate documents, and search by registered agent. The trademark database is not available online. *Other Options:* This agency makes database information available for purchase via an FTP site. Contact Bonnie Elek at 919-807-2196 for details.

Uniform Commercial Code, Federal Tax Liens `Free`

UCC Division, Secretary of State, www.secretary.state.nc.us/UCC/ Free access is available at www.secretary.state.nc.us/ucc/. Click on "UCC research" or "Tax Liens." Search by ID number or debtor name. *Other Options:* The UCC or tax lien database can be purchased on either a weekly or monthly basis via an FTP site. For more information, call 919-807-2196.

Sales Tax Registrations `Free`

Revenue Department, Sales & Use Tax Division, www.dor.state.nc.us Verify if an account is valid at https://dorprod.ncdor.state.nc.us/salesdatabase/. Delinquent debtors are shown on the web at www.dor.state.nc.us/collect/delinquent.html.

Workers' Compensation Records `Free`

NC Industrial Commission, Worker's Comp Records, www.comp.state.nc.us Extensive information about employers and insurers may be searched online at www.comp.state.nc.us/iwcnss/. This site also gives access to court decisions involving worker's comp.

Driver Records `$$`

Division of Motor Vehicles, Driver License Records, www.ncdot.org/dmv/driver_services/ To qualify for online availability, a client must be an insurance agent or insurance company support organization. The mode is interactive and is open from 7 AM to 10 PM. The DL# and name are needed when ordering. Records are $8.00 each. A minimum $500 security deposit is required. Call 919-861-3062 for details. *Other Options:* Magnetic tape for high volume batch users is available. Requests must be pre-paid.

Voter Registration [Free]

State Board of Elections, www.sboe.state.nc.us Online access to voter registration records is available free at www.sboe.state.nc.us/votersearch/seimsvot.htm. A DOB is needed for best results. *Other Options:* Most records are sold in CD format, FTP or sent via email. The maximum fee is $25.00. Request forms are available at the webpage. This is the most prompt access to records, other than in person.

Vital Records [$$]

Center for Health Statistics, Vital Records Branch, http://vitalrecords.dhhs.state.nc.us/vr/index.html Online ordering is available using a credit card via a state-designated vendor at www.vitalchek.com. Total fee is $55.45 and includes use of credit card and express delivery.

Occupational Licensing Boards

Amusement Device .... www.nclabor.com/elevator/elevator.htm
Anesthetist Nurse.............................. https://www.ncbon.com/License/form1.asp
Architect .... www.memberbase.com/ncbarch/public/lic/searchdb.asp
Architectural Firm .... www.memberbase.com/ncbarch/public/firms/searchdb.asp
Athletic Trainer .... www.ncbate.org/Licenses.pdf
Attorney .... www.ncbar.com/discipline/
Auction Company............................ www.ncalb.org/search.cfm
Auctioneer Disciplinary Action......... www.ncalb.org/discActions.cfm
Auctioneer/Auctioneer Apprentice.... www.ncalb.org/search.cfm
Bank .... https://www.nccob.org/Online/brts/BanksAndTrusts.aspx
Bank Branch .... https://www.nccob.org/Online/brts/BankBranchSearch.aspx
Barber Inspector/Instructor............... www.ncbarbers.com/
Beauty Shop/Salon   https://www.member-base.net/NCCOSMORenew/login.aspx?ReturnUrl=/nccosmorenew/Welcome.aspx
Bodywork Therapist .... www.bmbt.org/MTSEARCH.ASP
Boiler/Pressure Vessel Inspector .... www.nclabor.com/boiler/boiler.htm
Building Inspector .... www.ncdoi.com/OSFM/Engineering/COQB/engineering_coqb_inspectors.asp
Cemetery   ... ...   http://www2.nccommerce.com/servicenter/blio/redbook/Licenselist.asp?DivID=42
Cemetery Salesperson   ... ...   http://www2.nccommerce.com/servicenter/blio/redbook/Licenselist.asp?DivID=42
Charitable/Sponsor Organization....... www.secretary.state.nc.us/csl/Search.aspx
Check Casher.................................... https://www.nccob.org/Online/CCS/CompanyListing.aspx
Chiropractor..................................... http://ncchiroboard.com/
Clinical Nurse Specialist https://www.ncbon.com/License/form1.asp
Clinical Social Worker .... www.ncswboard.org/
Consumer Financer........................... https://www.nccob.org/online/CFS/CFSCompanyListing.aspx
Contractor, General .... www.nclbgc.org/lic_fr.html
Cosmetologist Instruct/Appentice/Practit'r/Disciplinary Actions
        https://www.member-base.net/NCCOSMORenew/login.aspx?ReturnUrl=/nccosmorenew/Welcome.aspx
Counselor, Professional.................... www.ncblpc.org/verify.php
Crematory.. www.ncbfs.org/dir_crematoriesdb.htm
Dental Hygienist.............................. www.ncdentalboard.org/ncdbe_search.asp
Dentist .... www.ncdentalboard.org/ncdbe_search.asp
DME-Rx Device............................... www.ncbop.org/ncbop_verification.htm
Electrical Contractor/Inspector.......... http://lookup.ncbeec.org/
Electrologist.................................... www.ncbee.com/electrologist_search.php
Electrology Instructor....................... www.ncbee.com/approved_schools.php
Elevator Inspector............................ www.nclabor.com/elevator/elevator.htm
Embalmer .... www.ncbfs.org/dir_licenseedb.htm
Engineer .... https://www.membersbase.com/ncbels-vs/public/searchdb.asp
Engineering/Surveying Firm .... https://www.membersbase.com/ncbels-vs/public/searchdb.asp
Esthetician Instruc./Appren/Practition'r
        https://www.member-base.net/NCCOSMORenew/login.aspx?ReturnUrl=/nccosmorenew/Welcome.aspx
Family Therapist.............................. www.nclmft.org/index.cfm?fuseaction=licenseVerify.home
Fire Sprinkler Contractor/Inspect ...... www.nclicensing.org/OnlineReg.htm
Forester... www.ncbrf.org/list.htm

Fund Raiser Consultant/Solicitor .... www.secretary.state.nc.us/csl/Search.aspx
Funeral Chapel .... www.ncbfs.org/dir_chapeldb.htm
Funeral Director/Service................... www.ncbfs.org/dir_licenseedb.htm
Funeral Home.................................. www.ncbfs.org/dir_funeralhomedb.htm
Funeral Trainee................................ www.ncbfs.org/dir_traineesdb.htm
Geologist .... www.ncblg.org/licensees.html
Hearing Aid Dispenser/Fitter............ http://pop.nchalb.org/queryname.aspx
Heating Contractor .... www.nclicensing.org/OnlineReg.htm
HMO .... http://infoportal.ncdoi.net/cmp_lookup.jsp
Home Inspector .... www.ncdoi.com/OSFM/Engineering/hilb/engineering_hilb_directories.asp
Insurance Agent............................... http://infoportal.ncdoi.net/agent_lookup.jsp
Insurance Company .... http://infoportal.ncdoi.net/cmp_lookup.jsp
Insurer, Life/Health .... http://infoportal.ncdoi.net/filelookup.jsp?divtype=3
Insurer, Property/Casualty .... http://infoportal.ncdoi.net/filelookup.jsp?divtype=2
Landscape Architect .... www.ncbola.org/licensees.htm
Lobbyist... www.secretary.state.nc.us/lobbyists/directory.aspx
Manicurist Instruct/Appren/Practitioner
            https://www.member-base.net/NCCOSMORenew/login.aspx?ReturnUrl=/nccosmorenew/Welcome.aspx
Manuf'd Housing Retail/Mfg/Contr... www.ncdoi.com/osfm/manufacturedbuilding/licensees/mainmenu.asp
Manuf'd Housing Seller/Qualifier...... www.ncdoi.com/osfm/manufacturedbuilding/licensees/mainmenu.asp
Marriage & Family Therapist .... www.nclmft.org/index.cfm?fuseaction=licenseVerify.home
Massage Therapist .... www.bmbt.org/MTSEARCH.ASP
Medical Doctor/Physician .... www.ncmedboard.org/
Midwife Nurse................................. https://www.ncbon.com/License/form1.asp
Money Transmitter .... https://www.nccob.org/Online/MTS/MTSCompanyListing.aspx
Nurse Practitioner............................ www.ncmedboard.org/
Nurse Practitioner............................ https://www.ncbon.com/License/form1.asp
Nurse-LPN https://www.ncbon.com/License/form1.asp
Nursing Home Administrator .... www.ncbenha.org/searchdb.asp
Occupation Therapist/Therapy Asst .. www.ncbot.org/
Optometrist...................................... www.ncoptometry.org/verify.aspx
Osteopathic Physician....................... www.ncmedboard.org/
Pesticide Appl./Dealer/Consultant..... www.ncagr.com/SPCAP/pesticides/license.htm
Pharmacist/Pharmacy Technician...... www.ncbop.org/ncbop_verification.htm
Pharmacy/Physician Pharmacy.......... www.ncbop.org/ncbop_verification.htm
Physical Therapist/Therapist Assist... www.ncptboard.org/login.aspx?ReturnUrl=%2ftransfer.aspx
Physician Assistant........................... www.ncmedboard.org/
Plumber .... www.nclicensing.org/OnlineReg.htm
Podiatrist... www.ncbpe.org/search.php
Psychologist/ Psychological Assoc.... www.ncpsychologyboard.org/search.htm
Public Accountant-CPA .... www.nccpaboard.gov/Clients/NCBOA/Public/Static/search_the_database.htm
RAL... https://www.nccob.org/online/RALS/RALSCompanyListing.aspx
Real Estate Agent/Broker/Dealer....... www.memberbase.com/ncrec-new/licdb/indv/searchdb.asp
Real Estate Firm .... www.memberbase.com/ncrec-new/licdb/firms-new/searchdb.asp
Sanitarian... www.rsboard.com/rsweb/directory/directory.htm
Social Worker.................................. www.ncswboard.org/
Soil Scientist.................................... www.ncblss.org/director.html
Speech Pathologist/Audiologist......... www.ncboeslpa.org/BOE.htm
Surveyor, Land .... https://www.membersbase.com/ncbels-vs/public/searchdb.asp
Therapist, Bodywork-Massage .... www.bmbt.org/MTSEARCH.ASP
Trust Company .... https://www.nccob.org/Online/BRTS/TrustLicensees.aspx

State and Local Courts

State Court Structure: The Superior Court is the court of general jurisdiction; the District Court is limited jurisdiction. The counties combine the courts, thus searching is done through one court, not two, within the county. Small Claims Court is part of the District Court Division and handles civil cases where a plaintiff requests assignment to a magistrate and the amount in controversy is $5000 or less (raised up from $4000 in Summer, 2005). The principal relief sought in Small Claims Court is money, the recovery of specific personal property, or summary ejectment (eviction).

Statewide Court Online Access: The state AOC has public access for approved requesters on its Virtual Private Network. Charges are based on screens viewed rather than a specific fee per name. A lesser valued product known as the Criminal Extract is available, but does not have the depth and quality of data as the Virtual Private Network. Call 919-716-5088 for details on these programs. Also, search the District and Superior Court Query system for current criminal defendants free at http://www1.aoc.state.nc.us/www/calendars/CriminalQuery.html. There are also querys for Impaired Driving, Citations, and Current Civil and Criminal Calendars. Appellate and Supreme Court opinions are at www.aoc.state.nc.us/www/public/html/opinions.htm.

All counties: Search civil and criminal court calendars at www1.aoc.state.nc.us/www/calendars.html. No individual North Carolina courts offer online access.

Recorders, Assessors, and Other Sites of Note

Recording Office Organization: 100 counties, 100 recording offices. The recording officer is the Register of Deeds but for tax liens it is the Clerk of Superior Court. Federal tax liens on personal property of businesses are filed with the Secretary of State. Other federal and all state tax liens are filed with the county Clerk of Superior Court. Oddly, even tax liens on real property are also filed with the Clerk of Superior Court, not with the Register of Deeds.

Online Access Note: A growing number of counties offer free access to assessor and real estate records.

Alamance County *Real Estate, Deed, Lien, Birth, Death, Marriage, UCC Records* www.alamance-nc.com
Free Access the recorded document database free at http://deeds.alamance-nc.com/. Vitals go back to 1984, UCCs back to 2001, real estate back to 1973.
Property, Taxation Records **Free** Property tax and parcel data available free at www.alamance-nc.com/Alamance-NC/Online+Services/Real+Estate+Tax+System.htm but site is temporarily down. Also, search the GIS-mapping site for free parcel data at www.alamance-nc.com/alamancegis/.

Alexander County *Real Estate, Deed, Lien Records* www.alexandercountync.gov/index/index.asp **Free**
Access recorder land records free at www.alexanderrod.com/view/disclaimer.html. Also, real property index and records available through 09/07/2007 (Book 512) for free at www.alexandercountync.gov/index/online_services.php
Property, Taxation Records **Free** Access parcel data free on the GIS/mapping site at http://maps.co.alexander.nc.us/gomaps/index.cfm Also, real property index and records available through 09/07/2007 (Book 512) for free at www.alexandercountync.gov/index/online_services.php

Alleghany County *Real Estate, Grantor/Grantee, Deed Records* www.alleghanycounty-nc.gov **Free**
Access to the Register of Deeds database is free at http://24.172.15.58/Opening.asp. All Deed images are online back thru 1859 to current. Real property indexes available 1/1/1989 to current.
Property, Taxation Records **Free** Search for property data on a GIS mapping site at http://arcims.webgis.net/nc/Alleghany/default.asp. To name search click on Quick Search.

Anson County *Property, Taxation Records* **Free** Search the county Online Tax Inquiry System free at www.co.anson.nc.us/pubcgi/taxinq. Tax collections search at www.co.anson.nc.us/pubcgi/colinq/.

Ashe County *Real Estate, Grantor/Grantee, Deed Records* www.ashencrod.org **Free** Access to the register of deeds real estate data is free at www.ashencrod.org/Opening.asp. Full index goes back to 1/1995; images to 1/1934.
Property, Taxation Records **Free** Access to records on the county Tax Parcel Information System is free at http://ashegis.ashecountygov.com/webgis/.

Avery County *Real Estate, Grantor/Grantee, Deed Records* www.averyrod.com **Free**
Search the recorders database free at www.averyrod.com/view/disclaimer.html.
Property, Taxation Records **Free** Access to property data is free on the GIS mapping site at http://arcims.webgis.net/nc/avery/. To name search click Quick Search.

Bertie County *Real Estate, Deed, Lien Records* www.co.bertie.nc.us/Directory/departments/rod/rod.html Free
Access real property data back to 10/2001 free at http://bertie.gsaweb.com/web1.html
Property, Taxation Records Free Access property records through gis-mapping system free at
www.co.bertie.nc.us/website/bertiegisweb/viewer.htm.

Bladen County *Real Estate, Grantor/Grantee, Deed, Lien, Mortgage Records* www.bladeninfo.org Free
Access unofficial register of deeds site at www.withersravenel.com/deeds/; search comprehensive index or direct images.
Property, Taxation Records Free & $$ Search the GIS-mapping site for property info free at
http://bladenrod.withersravenel.com/. Login as Guest and leave password blank.

Brunswick County *Real Estate, Deed, Mortgage Records* http://rod.brunsco.net Free Access to the recorder
database is free at http://rod.brunsco.net. Free registration, logon and password are required. Records are updated on the 10th, 20th,
and 30th of the month.
Property, Taxation Records Free Search the tax administration data for free at www.brunsconctax.org/.

Buncombe County *Real Estate, Deed, Mortgage, Fictitious Name, Marriage, Death Records*
www.buncombecounty.org Free Access to county Register of Deeds records is free at
http://registerofdeeds.buncombecounty.org/resolution/login.asp. Free registration is required; includes marriages, deaths, fictitious
names, deeds.
Property, Taxation Records Free County assessor tax records are free at www.buncombetax.org/lookup/. Also, GIS
property search searching available at www.buncombecounty.org/governing/depts/GIS/disclaimer.htm. Also, search tax property sales
free at www.buncombecounty.org/governing/citizens/prop4Sale.htm.

Burke County *Property, Taxation Records* Free Access to property data is free on the GIS mapping site at
http://arcims.webgis.net/nc/Burke/default.asp. To name search click on Quick Search.

Cabarrus County *Real Estate, Grantor/Grantee, Deed, Lien, UCC Records* www.cabarrusncrod.org Free
Access to the recorder records is free at www.cabarrusncrod.org by two methods: full system or image-only system. Land records go
back to 1983; images to 1983.
Property, Taxation Records Free Search property data on the ClaRIS system free at
www.co.cabarrus.nc.us/ClarisPC/Main.aspx. Also, search tax appraisal cards by name free at
http://onlineservices.cabarruscounty.us/Tax/TaxAppraisalCard/. Also, search tax bill scroll for free at
www.co.cabarrus.nc.us/Tax/scrollsearch.html. Also, search land records of all kinds including GIS free on the ClaRIS system at
www.co.cabarrus.nc.us/ClarisPC/Main.aspx.

Caldwell County *Real Estate, Deed, Birth, Death, Marriage, Notary, Business Name Records*
www.caldwellrod.org/ Free Access register of deeds recording data with images back to 1930 free at
http://rod.co.caldwell.nc.us/resolution/. Choose advanced or simple search; online registration is required.
Property, Taxation Records Free Property data is available free on the GIS map server site at http://maps.co.caldwell.nc.us.
Click on "Start Spatial-data Explorer" then find query field at bottom of next page.

Camden County *Real Estate, Grantor/Grantee, Deed, Lien, Mortgage Records* Free
Access recorders data free at www.camdenrod.com/view/disclaimer.html.
Property, Taxation Records Free Search property records on the gis-mapping system free at
www.camdencountync.gov/services/GIS.htm.

Carteret County *Real Estate, Grantor/Grantee, Deed, Lien, Assumed Name Records* www.co.carteret.nc.us
Free Access to Register of Deeds database for free at www.co.carteret.nc.us/. These records are book 641 to present.
Property, Taxation Records Free Search tax parcel cards free at http://tax.carteretcountygov.org.

Caswell County *Real Estate, Grantor/Grantee, Deed, Lien, Birth, Death, Marriage, Military Discharge*
Records www.caswellrod.net/ Free Search recorded deeds at www.caswellrod.net/ and click Search Online. Images are
shown.
Property, Taxation Records Free Access to property data is free on the GIS mapping site at
http://arcims.webgis.net/nc/caswell/. To name search click on Quick Search.

Catawba County *Real Estate, Grantor/Grantee, Deed, Mortgage Records* www.catawbacountync.gov Free
Also, search Register of Deeds records free at www.catawbarod.org/Opening.asp. Land index goes back to 1993; images to
12/27/1979.
Property, Taxation Records Free Search the Catawba County GIS Map Server database free at
www.gis.catawba.nc.us/website/Parcel/parcel_main.asp. Search property tax bill data free at
http://taxbill.catawbacountync.gov/ptsweb/main/billing/default.aspx. Also, access real estate reports at
www.gis.catawba.nc.us/nomap/parcel_search.asp.

Chatham County *Real Estate, Deed, Mortgage, UCC Records* www.chathamncrod.org/Opening.asp Free
Access land records free at www.chathamncrod.org/welcome.asp. Land Index Data back to 1771; UCC data goes back to 2008.

Property, Taxation Records **Free**   Access property data and tax records free at http://ustaxdata.com/nc/chatham/Search.cfm.

Cherokee County *Real Estate, Deed, Lien Records* www.cherokeencrod.org/ **Free**   Access to land records and imaging for free go to www.cherokeencrod.org/. Images go back to 5/28/1999, index back to 1993.

Property, Taxation Records **Free**   Access to property data is free on the GIS mapping site at http://65.14.20.19/viewer.htm. Click on TaxWeb Online.

Chowan County *Real Estate, Deed Records* www.chowancounty-nc.gov **Free**   Access county property data free at http://208.27.112.94/paas/. You may also build customized data downloads.

Property, Taxation Records **Free**   Access property tax records free at http://208.27.112.94/paas/. Double click on Parcels. Search property data on the GIS-mapping site free at http://www2.undersys.com/choweb/chowan.html and click on Property Search.

Clay County *Real Estate, Deed Records* **$$**   Access to property and deeds indexes and images is via a private company at www.titlesearcher.com. Fee/registration required. Deeds go back to 1/1999; indices back to 1/1/94; images to 8/22/2003.

Cleveland County *Real Estate, Grantor/Grantee, Deed Records* www.clevelandrod.com **Free**   Access to o register of deeds grantor/grantee index and property data is free at http://cleveland.parker-lowe.net/view/softlic.html.

Property, Taxation Records **Free**   Access property records free on the GIS-mapping site at http://quicksearch.webgis.net/search.php?site=nc_cleveland_co.

Columbus County *Real Estate, Deed, Assumed Name, Corporation, UCC Records* **Free**   Access to the Recorder's database is free at www.columbusdeeds.com/

Property, Taxation Records **Free**   Access property tax data free at http://webtax.columbusco.org/viewer.htm.

Craven County *Real Estate, Grantor/Grantee, Deed, Boat, Birth, Death, Marriage, UCC, Corporation Records* www.co.craven.nc.us **Free**   Access to deeds on the county Public Inquiry System is free at http://206.107.97.91/ with many other databases available. Or, simply search register of deeds data free at www.co.craven.nc.us/departments/reg/regwwwdisclaimer.cfm.

Property, Taxation Records **Free**   Access to assessor and property data is free at http://gismaps.cravencounty.com/maps/map.asp. Access the tax database including foreclosures, mobiles, boats, parcel, appraisal and also deeds free at http://206.107.97.91/

Cumberland County *Real Estate, Deed, UCC Records* www.ccrod.org **Free**   Search two systems free at www.ccrodinternet.org. The land records index and images go back to 1978; images go back to 1/21/1972; UCCs are from 1995 to 6/29/2001.

Property, Taxation Records **Free**   Assessor real estate search is free at http://mainfr.co.cumberland.nc.us/. Also, search property data free on the GIS mapping site at http://152.31.99.8/. Click on Search on the Parcel Viewer.

Currituck County *Real Estate, Deed, Notary Records* www.co.currituck.nc.us/registerofdeeds/registerofdeeds.aspx **Free**   Access to land recorded documents and notaries is free at https://currituckeoc.com/resolution/.

Property, Taxation Records **Free**   Search property, sales, assessor data and more free at www.co.currituck.nc.us/Tax.cfm. Also, name search for parcel ownership data free on the GIS-mapping site at www.co.currituck.nc.us/Interactive-Online-MappingDup2.cfm.

Dare County *Real Estate, Grantor/Grantee, Deed, Marriage, UCC Records* www.co.dare.nc.us **Free**   Certain recording office records are free at www.co.dare.nc.us/index.htm. Real estate from 1976 forward, UCC from 1989 forward, and marriage from 1990 forward. Additionally, tax files can be downloaded from this site. Also, a land transfer search is free at www.darenc.com/public/LT/LTsearch.asp.

Property, Taxation Records **Free**   County assessor records free at www.co.dare.nc.us/public/TaxInquiry.htm. Search propert data on the GIS-mapping site free at www.darenc.com/public/gis.htm but no name searching.

Davidson County *Real Estate, Deed, Lien, Mortgage, Judgment, UCC, Assumed Name Records* www.co.davidson.nc.us/home.asp **Free & $$**   Access recorders database free at http://davidsoncorod.org/. Registration for full subscription data also available.

Property, Taxation Records **Free**   Records on the county Tax Dept database are free at www.co.davidson.nc.us/taxnet/. Search for property info on the GIS mapping site for free at http://arcims2.webgis.net/davidson/default.asp. To name search click on Quick Search.

Davie County *Property, Taxation Records* **Free**   Access to county property data on the GIS-mapping site is free at http://maps.co.davie.nc.us/website/mapviewer/GISviewerhome.htm.

Duplin County *Real Property, Deed, Mortgage, Marriage, Death, Notary, Military Discharge Records* http://rod.duplincounty.org **Free**   Access to the Register's multiple databases is free at http://rod.duplincounty.org. Vital stats and discharges are index only.

Property, Taxation Records **Free**   Access assessment data on real estate and personal property free at http://duplintax.duplincounty.org/

Durham County *Real Estate, Deed, Judgment, Voter Registration Records* www.durhamcountync.gov/index.html
Free   Access the Register of Deeds database free at http://rodweb.co.durham.nc.us/. Also, search voter registration free at www.durhamcountync.gov/departments/elec/votersearch/index.cfm.
Property, Taxation Records Free   Search property records and tax bills free at www.durhamcountync.gov/departments/txad/Tax_Record_Searches.html. Search property records from the GIS mapping site free at http://gisweb2.ci.durham.nc.us/sdx/imap_launch.html. Click on "Go Maps" to search.

Edgecombe County *Real Estate, Deed, Lien, UCC Records* www.edgecombecountync.gov Free
Access the recorder's database free at http://71.0.29.40/resolution/. RE index goes back to 1973, financing statements 1993 to 2005.
Property, Taxation Records Free   Access to county property data is free at http://207.4.48.133/paas/default.htm.

Forsyth County *Real Estate, Deed, Lien, Voter Registration Records* www.co.forsyth.nc.us/ROD/ $$
Access to property and deeds indexes and images is via a private company at www.titlesearcher.com. Fee/registration required; monthly and per day access available. Deeds and indices go back to 1849; images to 1973. Search voter registration records free at www.sboe.state.nc.us/votersearch/seimsvot.htm.
Property, Taxation Records Free   Access assessor records on Geo-Data free- www.co.forsyth.nc.us/Tax/geodata.aspx. Click "Launch Geo-Data Explorer." Search tax bills free- www.co.forsyth.nc.us/Tax/taxbilllookup/regular.aspx? Tax Admin tax bill svc free at www.co.forsyth.nc.us/tax/taxbill.aspx. View tax sale and auction lists at www.forsyth.cc/Tax/fcl_info.aspx. Also, assessment data for City of Winston-Salem available free at www.cwsonline.org/assessments/.

Franklin County *Real Estate, Grantor/Grantee, Deed, Line, UCC Records* www.co.franklin.nc.us Free
Access to recording records index free at http://deeds.co.franklin.nc.us/resolution/. Consolidated real estate back to 1995, UCCs 1990 to 6/30/2001, Pre-1995 maps. Fee for deeper data.
Property, Taxation Records Free   Access to tax data on the county spatial data explorer database is free at www.co.franklin.nc.us/ROK/mapviewer/viewer.htm or at parcel search page at http://maps.roktech.net/Franklin/map/Index.cfm.

Gaston County *Real Estate, Deed, Lien, Corporation, Assumed Name, UCC Records*
www.co.gaston.nc.us/registerofdeeds Free & $$ Access to recorded documents is free at http://207.235.60.108/resolution/ - registration and username are required.
Property, Taxation Records Free   Access property data and tax records free at http://egov1.co.gaston.nc.us/website/ParcelDataSite/WelcomePage.html. Click on Search.

Gates County *Real Estate, Grantor/Grantee, Deed Records* www.gatesrod.com Free
Real property records available free at www.gatesrod.com/view/disclaimer.html.

Graham County *Real Estate, Deed, Mortgage Records* http://deeds.grahamncrod.com Free   Access the consolidated real property database back to 1/1995 free at http://deeds.grahamncrod.com/. Also search pre-1995 real estate 7/1/1978 to 12/31/1994.

Granville County *Real Estate, Deed, Lien Records* www.granvillecountydeeds.org/resolution/ Free
Access recorders index free at www.granvillecountydeeds.org/resolution/. Registration, username and password required.
Property, Taxation Records $$ Access to assessor property data is available for a one-time $250 fee, call Tax Assessor office a 919-693-4181 or visit www.granvillegis.org.

Guilford County *Real Estate, Deed, Lien, UCC Records* www.guilforddeeds.com Free   Access to county databases is free at http://gcms0004.co.guilford.nc.us/services/index.php. Vital statistic records have been removed from http://66.162.203.229/vital/guilfordVitalSearch.php.
Property, Taxation Records Free   Search for property data free on the GIS-mapping site at http://gisweb02.co.guilford.nc.us/guilford/default.htm. Also, name search tax data free at www.co.guilford.nc.us/Novation/taxpub.html. Add'l data may be available at www.co.guilford.nc.us/services/index.php.

Halifax County *Real Estate, Deed, Lien, UCC, Map Records* www.halifaxnc.com Free   Access to the Register's land records is at http://65.254.204.43/resolution/. Real Estate in two indexes back to 1976; UCCs from 1996 to 8/31/2001; maps are pre-1995.
Property, Taxation Records Free   Search assessor property tax records free at http://gis.halifaxnc.com/Main/Home.aspx.

Harnett County *Real Estate, Grantor/Grantee, Vital Statistic, UCC Records* http://rod.harnett.org Free
County real estate and property tax data is free at http://rod.harnett.org. Search Births, Deaths, Marriages, UCCs and official public records.
Property, Taxation Records Free   Access property tax records free at http://tax.harnett.org/pws10/main/billing/default.aspx.

Haywood County *Real Estate, Deed Records* http://rodweb.haywoodnc.net/ Free   Records on the Register of Deeds database are free at http://haywood.bisonline.com/sites/haywooddeeds/deedsearch/disclaimer.php. Real estate records go back to 1986. Also, search for deeds for free at http://rodweb.haywoodnc.net/
Property, Taxation Records Free   Access property tax records and GIS mapping free at http://public.haywoodnc.net/. Also, search for property data on the GIS-mapping site for free at www.undersys.com/cweb/haywood.html.

Henderson County *Property, Taxation Records* `Free` Look-up tax bills free at www.hendersoncountync.org/ca/redirect.html. Access the GIS mapping system free at http://hendersoncountync.org/gis/. Also, search property data free at www.hendersoncountync.org/ca/realpropertydata.html.

Hertford County *Real Estate, Deed Records* www.co.hertford.nc.us/rod.asp `Free` Access recorded land data free at www.hertfordrod.com/index.html; click on Documents & Indexes.

Hoke County *Real Estate, Deed, Lien Records* www.hokencrod.org `Free` Access recorder data for free at www.hokencrod.org/Opening.asp. Land records index goes back to 7/1992; images back to 12/1994.
Property, Taxation Records `Free` Access property data on GIS mapping site free at http://gis.hokecounty.org/connectgis/hoke/welcome.htm.

Hyde County *Real Estate, Grantor/Grantee, Deed Records* www.hyderod.com `Free` Access to the Register of Deeds real property records is free at www.hyderod.com/view/disclaimer.html.

Iredell County *Real Estate, Deed, Vital Statistic, Pre-2001 UCC Records* www.co.iredell.nc.us `Free & $$` Access recorder records at www.co.iredell.nc.us/resolution/. Registration required.
Property, Taxation Records `Free` Search property appraisal cards free at www.co.iredell.nc.us/apprcard/. Also, search property data free on the GI-mapping site at www.co.iredell.nc.us/Gismaps.asp. Once on the map page, click on the binoculars to text search.

Jackson County *Real Estate, Deed, UCC Records* www.jacksonnc.org `Free` Access datat at http://deeds.jacksonnc.org/resolution/. Includes 2 real estate indexes back to 10/1991; Plats back to 1969; UCCs from 1992 to 2/2003.
Property, Taxation Records `Free` Search assessor and property data free at http://maps.jacksonnc.org/gomaps/map/Index.cfm. This is a new site being tested and data is incomplete. Property cards to be available.

Johnston County *Real Estate, Deed, UCC Records* www.johnstonnc.com `Free` Access to Register's indexes is free at http://johnstonnc.com/deedsearch. Land records go back to 1972; UCCs back to 7/1997.
Property, Taxation Records `Free` Access property records free at www.johnstonnc.com/mainpage.cfm?category_level_id=497&content_id=1127.

Jones County *Real Estate, Grantor/Grantee, Deed Records* www.jonesrod.com `Free`
Access recorded documents index at www.jonesrod.com/view/disclaimer.html.

Lee County *Real Estate, Grantor/Grantee, Deed, Mortgage Records* www.leecountync.gov/ `Free`
Access Register of Deeds index and images free at www.leencrod.org/Opening.asp. Land record index goes back to 1985; images to 1908-1984, and all plat images.
Property, Taxation Records `Free` Access sales data and maps free at www.leecountync.gov/departments/StrategicServices/default.html.

Lenoir County *Real Estate, Deed, UCC Records* www.co.lenoir.nc.us `Free` Access land records index back to 1995 at http://cottweb.co.lenoir.nc.us/resolution/ and financing statements 1976-1995. Older real estate 1976-1994 also available.
Property, Taxation Records `Free` Access property records free at www.co.lenoir.nc.us/docs/disclaim.htm#. Click on Search.

Lincoln County *Real Estate, Deed, Lien, Mapping, UCC, Comparable Sale Records* www.lincolncounty.org
`Free` Access tax, property, and recording data for free at www.lincolncounty.org/County/faq.htm. Enable browser for Java. Grantor/Grantee indices go back to 1993. Images go back to Book 186. Search either of the 2 databases. There is also a comparable properties search utility.
Property, Taxation Records `Free` Access tax and property data for free at www.lincolncounty.org/County/faq.htm. Enable browser for Java. Also, access to the county GIS Land System is free at http://207.4.172.206/website/lcproperty2/viewer.htm. At the website, under Data Tools, click on Search.

McDowell County *Real Estate, Deed Records* `$$` Access to property and deeds indexes and images is via a private company at www.titlesearcher.com. Fee/registration required; see state introduction. Records go back to 1/1971.

Macon County *Real Estate, Deed, UCC, Map Records* www.maconnc.org `Free` Access deed images back to book 6 free and selected other recording types free at www.maconncdeeds.com/sites/maconncdeeds.com/files/deedsearch/. Also, download property and map data free at http://216.119.24.38/website/macgis/download.htm.
Property, Taxation Records `Free` Access property tax records free at http://216.119.24.38/pubaccess/macon.htm. Lookup Land records free at http://216.119.24.38/website/macgis/dbaccess/.

Madison County *Real Estate, Grantor/Grantee, Deed Records* www.madisonrod.com `Free`
Access real property records free at www.madisonrod.com/view/disclaimer.html.

Mecklenburg County *Real Estate, Grantor/Grantee, Deed, Judgment, Lien, Mortgage, UCC, Vital Statistic Records* http://meckrod.manatron.com/ Free Access to birth, death, marriage, recordings, judgments, liens, and grantor/grantee indices are free at http://meckrod.manatron.com/localization/menu.aspr.
Property, Taxation Records Free Access to the assessors records for real estate, personal property, and tax bills are free at www.charmeck.org/Departments/LUESA/Property+Assessment+and+Land+Records/home.htm . Also, a real estate lookup at http://meckcama.co.mecklenburg.nc.us/relookup/. Search property ownership and data free on the GIS site at http://polaris.mecklenburgcountync.gov/website/redesign/viewer.htm.

Mitchell County *Real Estate, Granter/Grantee, Deed Records* www.mitchellrod.com Free & $$
Search records free at www.mitchellrod.com/view/disclaimer.html.

Montgomery County *Real Estate, Grantor/Grantee, Deed, Lien Records* www.montgomeryrod.net/ Free
Access to recorders real estate data is free at www.montgomeryrod.net/.
Property, Taxation Records Free Search property records free on the GIS mapping site at http://arcims.webgis.net/nc/montgomery.

Moore County *Real Estate, Grantor/Grantee, Deed, Lien, Birth, Death, UCC Records*
http://rod.moorecountync.gov Free Find a menu of search choices for recordings, land records at http://rod.moorecountync.gov
Property, Taxation Records Free Access property and tax data free at www.moorecountync.gov/main/page.asp?rec=/pages/Taxapp/index.asp

Nash County *Real Estate, Grantor/Grantee, Deed, UCC Records* www.deeds.co.nash.nc.us Free
Search real estate and UCCs free back to 1970 free at www.deeds.co.nash.nc.us/resolution.

New Hanover County *Real Estate, Grantor/Grantee, Deed, UCC, Marriage, Military Discharge, Birth, Death, Plat, Condo Records* www.nhcgov.com Free & $$ Access to the Register of Deeds database is free at http://srvrodweb.nhcgov.com. Subscription svc also available.
Property, Taxation Records Free Access to the real estate tax database is free at http://etax.nhcgov.com/Search/Disclaimer2.aspx?. Also, access property data on the GIS-mappings site at www.nhcgov.com/AgnAndDpt/INFO/GIS/Pages/GISMaps.aspx .

Onslow County *Real Estate, Birth, Death, Marriage, UCC, Parcel, GIS-mapping Records* www.co.onslow.nc.us/
Free Access recorder office index data free at http://deeds.onslowcountync.gov. Real estate goes back to 1995, births 1980-2001, deaths 1983-2003, marriages 1962-1/2004, UCCs 1977-1994, conveyances 1977-1994.
Property, Taxation Records Free Access to property data is free at http://maps.onslowcountync.gov/. Enter the site and name search using the advanced search in the Parcel Query box.

Orange County *Property, Taxation Records* Access to property records on the GIS mapping site is free at http://gis.co.orange.nc.us/gisdisclaimer.htm.

Pamlico County *Real Estate, Grantor/Grantee, Deed Records* www.pamlicorod.com Free
Access records for grantor/grantee and real property free at www.pamlicorod.com/view/disclaimer.html. Images go back to 1997.
Property, Taxation Records Free Search the GIS-mapping site for property data free at http://www2.undersys.com/pamweb/pamlicomain.html. Tax data to be available at www.pamlicorod.com/taxindex.html soon.

Pasquotank County *Real Estate, Grantor/Grantee, Deed Records*
www.co.pasquotank.nc.us/departments/rod/default.htm Free Access recorder data free at http://pasquotankrod.com/view/softlic.html. Click on "I Agree."
Property, Taxation Records Free Search assessor database at http://207.4.214.118/gis/taxsearch.cfm.

Pender County *Real Estate, Grantor/Grantee, Deed Records* www.pender-county.com/Departments/rod/ Free
Access recorder data free with registration at http://pender-rod.inttek.net/.
Property, Taxation Records Free GIS land records are available at www.pender-county.com/disclaimer.php but no name searching.

Perquimans County *Real Estate, Deed, Lien Records* www.perquimansrod.com Free
Access to county real property records is free at www.perquimansrod.com/view/disclaimer.html.
Property, Taxation Records Free Access property assessor, tax, property card and GIS data free at http://mapping.perquimanscountync.gov/perquimans.

Person County *Real Estate, Grantor/Grantee, Deed Records* www.personrod.net Free
Access to county real estate records is free at http://12.174.150.120/personnc/disclaimer.asp. Index goes back to 1/1/1995.

Pitt County *Real Estate, Deed, Lien, UCC Records* www.co.pitt.nc.us/depts/ Free Access recorder land data back to 1969 and UCCs from 1992 to 2001 free at http://regdeeds.pittcountync.gov/resolution/.

Property, Taxation Records `Free`   Online access to property records is available at http://gis.pittcountync.gov/website/opis/. Also, view overdue tax accounts at http://tax.pittcountync.gov/ptsweb/main/billing/default.aspx.

Polk County   *Real Estate, Grantor/Grantee, Deed Records*   www.polkrod.com   `Free`
Access the recorder land records free at www.polkrod.com/view/disclaimer.html.

Randolph County   *Real Estate, Deed, Plat Records*   www.randrod.com   `Free & $$`   Real Estate records and plat
access at www.randrod.com/officialrecords.html after registration; index goes back to 1/1986, images to 4/1990. Registration required.
Property, Taxation Records `Free`   Access to the county GIS database is free at www.co.randolph.nc.us/gis.htm. In the "Search functions" on the map page, click on "parcel owner." Access property owners/property data, liens, and foreclosure lists free at www.co.randolph.nc.us/tax/default.htm.

Richmond County   *Real Estate, Deed, Plat Records*   `Free & $$`   With registration, username and password you
may access Register of Deeds land records at http://216.27.81.170/login.asp. For login, use account ID "richmondnc" and password "richmondnc001". Also, access to County property records is via a subscription service; registration and fees are required. For info and signup, call 334-344-3333.
Property, Taxation Records `Free`   Access property data on the GIS-mapping site at www.richmondnc.org/rc%5Fims/. Click on black dot with "i" to identify parcels or click on search to name search.

Robeson County   *Real Estate, Grantor/Grantee, Deed, Lien Records*   http://rod.co.robeson.nc.us   `Free & $$`
Access to recorder data is free at http://rod.co.robeson.nc.us/search.php. Also, access to property and deeds indexes and images is via a private company at www.titlesearcher.com. Fee/registration required. Deeds and images go back to 1/12/1974; Indices back to 2/2/1974.
Property, Taxation Records `Free`   Access assessor property records free at www.ustaxdata.com/nc/robeson/robesonsearch.cfm. Also, search parcels, sales, and subdivisions free at the GIS-mapping site at www.gis.co.robeson.nc.us/ConnectGISWeb/

Rockingham County   *Real Estate, Grantor/Grantee, Deed, Judgment Records*   www.co.rockingham.nc.us/
`Free`   Access to Register of Deeds database is free at http://rod.co.rockingham.nc.us/oncoreweb/Search.aspx. Land indexes 1996 to present; recorded images 1984 to present; plats 1907 to present.
Property, Taxation Records `Free`   Access to Tax Admin. property data (1996 forward) also tax bills are free at www.ustaxdata.com/nc/rockingham/RockinghamSearch.cfm. Also, search property data free at the GIS site at http://arcims.webgis.net/nc/rockingham/default.asp. To name search, click on Quick Search. Also, online access to the tax sales property is at www.co.rockingham.nc.us/forecl.htm.

Rowan County   *Real Estate, Deed, UCC Records*   www.co.rowan.nc.us   `Free`   Access to the Register of Deeds land
records database is free after registration at www.co.rowan.nc.us. Records go back to 1975; financing statements back to 1993; deed images back to 1975.
Property, Taxation Records `Free`   Access to the county GIS mapping site is free at http://arcims2.webgis.net/nc/Rowan/default.asp. To name search click on Quick Search. Also, there is a tax inquiry quick search at www.co.rowan.nc.us/taxinq/name/default.asp. More tax and property data may be available at http://extranet.rowancountync.gov/wc/java/publictax.html.

Rutherford County   *Real Estate, Deed, Birth, Death, Marriage, UCC, Notary Records*
www.rutherfordcountync.gov   `Free`   Access property data free at www.rutherfordcountync.gov/dept/register_of_deeds/Main.php. UCCs 1995 to 2001; RE goes back to 1974; births 1991 to 2006; Deaths and marriages back t0 1994/1995.

Sampson County   *Real Estate, Grantor/Grantee, Deed Records*   www.sampsonrod.org   `Free`
Access to county Register of Deeds land data is free at www.sampsonrod.org/Opening.asp. Index goes back to 1988.

Scotland County   *Real Estate, Grantor/Grantee, Deed, Lien, UCC Records*   www.scotlandcounty.org   `Free`
Access to ROD real estate records and also financing statements from 1999 to 2/2004 are available free at http://rod.scotlandcounty.org/resolution/. Also, search the tax payments page free at www.scotlandcountytaxes.com.
Property, Taxation Records `Free`   Search property data free on the GIS site at http://65.254.200.14/ConnectGIS/Laurinburg/. Includes City of Laurinburg.

Stanly County   *Real Estate, Grantor/Grantee, Deed, Mortgage, Plat Records*   www.co.stanly.nc.us   `Free`
Access the Register of Deeds index back to 1841 at http://216.27.81.170/login.asp?password=stqn342&accountid=stanlyhome. Search deeds, plats by address or number free at www.stanlygis.net/website/public/DeedPlatSearch.htm.
Property, Taxation Records `Free`   Access property data on the GIS search free at www.stanlygis.net/website/quicksearch/quicksearch.aspx.

Stokes County   *Real Estate, Grantor/Grantee, Deed, UCC Records*   www.stokescorod.org   `Free`
Access to the Register of Deeds Remote Access site is free at www.stokescorod.org/Opening.asp. Land records go back to 1993, images to 2/1924; UCCs back to 1994.

Property, Taxation Records `Free` Access to property info on the GIS mapping site is free at http://arcims2.webgis.net/stokes/default.asp. To name search click on Quick Search.

Surry County *Real Estate, Deed, Plat, UCC Records* www.co.surry.nc.us `Free` Access recording index free at www.co.surry.nc.us/Departments/RegisterOfDeeds/RecordSearch.htm. Real property index goes back to 1/1995; financing statements 1989-6/30/2001; plats are 1/1980 to 12/21/1994.

Property, Taxation Records `Free` Access property data free at http://arcims.webgis.net/nc/surry/default.asp. Click on Quick search. Tax maps also located at this site.

Swain County *Real Estate, Grantor/Grantee, Deed Records* www.swaincounty.org/ `Free & $$` Access to recorder land data is free at www.swaincorod.org. There is a full system and an image only system. Land Record Indexing data goes back to 1/1995; images back to 8/1979.

Transylvania County *Real Estate, Deed Records* www.transylvaniacounty.org `Free & $$` Access real estate records at www.titlesearcher.com. Registration and username required. Images are viewable back to 12/30/2003; deeds and indices back to 1/3/1973.

Property, Taxation Records `Free` Access full or partial property data free on the GIS site at http://arcims.webgis.net/nc/transylvania/default.asp.

Tyrrell County *Real Estate, Grantor/Grantee, Deed Records* www.tyrrellrod.com `Free` Access to Register of Deeds real estate records is free at www.tyrrellrod.com/view/disclaimer.html. Index goes back to 1997; images are from Book 137 forward.

Union County *Real Estate, Grantor/Grantee, Deed Records* www.unionconcrod.org `Free` Access to recorder land records is free at www.unionconcrod.org/Opening.asp; index go back to 6-15-2003; images to 6/3/2000.

Wake County *Real Estate, Deed, Lien, Judgment, Voter Registration Records* http://web.co.wake.nc.us/rdeeds/ `Free` Records from the County are available through the portal website at www.wakegov.com/tax/default.htm. Also, online access to the Register of Deeds database is free at http://rodweb01.co.wake.nc.us/books/genext/genextsearch.asp. Records go back to 1900. Registered voters data can be found at http://msweb03.co.wake.nc.us/bordelec/Waves/WavesOptions.asp.

Property, Taxation Records `Free` Free real estate property and tax bill search is at http://services.wakegov.com/realestate/search.asp. Also, access to Town of Cary property info on the map site for free at http://209.42.194.57/CaryMap/ViewMap.aspx?ItemID=11&PortalID=1. Also, download individual town property data free at www.wakegov.com/tax/downloads/default.htm.

Washington County *Real Estate, Grantor/Grantee, Deed, Lien, Corporation Records* www.washingtonrod.com/ `Free` Access to recorder land records is available free at www.washingtonrod.com/view/disclaimer.html. You may choose to search all books.

Property, Taxation Records `Free` Search assessor property record cards free at http://taxweb.washconc.org.

Watauga County *Real Estate, Grantor/Grantee, Deed, UCC Records* www.wataugacounty.org/deeds/index.html `Free` Access to register of deeds database is free at www.wataugacounty.org/deeds/disclaimer.shtml.

Property, Taxation Records `Free` Access to county tax search data is free at www.wataugacounty.org/tax/search_tax.shtml. Also, search Town of Blowing Rock property info at http://arcims2.webgis.net/nc/blowingrock/ .

Wayne County *Real Estate, Grantor/Grantee, Deed, UCC Records* www.waynegov.com `Free` Access to the registers CRP, financing statement, and real estate databases is free at www.waynegov.com/departments/rod/disclaimer.asp. Real Estate includes records from 1969-1994; beginning 1995 all real estate records are indexed under CRP.

Property, Taxation Records `Free` Access property records free at www.waynegov.com/departments/tax/taxinquiry.asp. Only available 8AM-5PM.

Wilkes County *Property, Taxation Records* `Free` Access to property data is free on the GIS-mapping site at www.undersys.com/wilkesweb/wilkes.html.

Wilson County *Real Estate, Deed Records* www.wilson-co.com/rod.html `Free & $$` Access the Register of Deeds search site at www.wilson-co.com/wcjav_begin.html. If using property search function, username or password required; deeds section does not.

Property, Taxation Records `Free` Records on Geo-link property tax database are free at www.wilson-co.com/intro.html.

Yadkin County *Real Estate, Grantor/Grantee, Deed, Lien Records* www.yadkincountync.gov/content/view/19/327/ `Free` Access recorder's land records free at www.yadkincorod.org/welcome.asp. Index goes back to 1/1/1993. Land Record Imaging Data back to Volume 0210 8/24/1978 through Volume 0790 page 76 6/20/2006. Search either full system or imaging system.

Property, Taxation Records `Free` Search property tax date free at www.ustaxdata.com/nc/yadkin/.

Yancey County *Real Estate, Grantor/Grantee, Deed, Lien Records* www.yanceyrod.com `Free` Access to recording office records is free at www.yanceyrod.com/view/disclaimer.html.

North Dakota

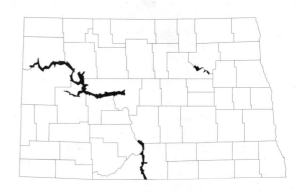

Capital: Bismarck
             Burleigh County

Time Zone: The southwestern area of North Dakota
(west and south of the Missouri River) is in Mountain
Time Zone. The remainder of the state is in
the Central Time Zone.

Population: 639,715

# of Counties: 53

Useful State Links

Website: www.nd.gov/
Governor: www.governor.state.nd.us
Attorney General: www.ag.state.nd.us
State Archives: www.nd.gov/hist/sal.htm
State Statutes and Codes: www.legis.nd.gov/information/statutes/cent-code.html
Legislative Bill Search: www.legis.nd.gov/assembly/59-2005/leginfo/bill-inquiry/index.html
Unclaimed Funds: www.land.nd.gov/abp/abphome.htm

Primary State Agencies

Sexual Offender Registry Free

Bureau of Criminal Investigation, SOR Unit, www.sexoffender.nd.gov/ Access is available from the website. Information on all offenders with a registration requirement (including moderate and low risk offenders) can be downloaded at: Printable List of All Offenders at www.sexoffender.nd.gov/PublicListing.aspx.

Corporation, LLC, LP, LLP, Trademarks/Servicemarks, Fictitious Name Free

Secretary of State, Business Information/Registration, www.nd.gov/sos/businessserv/ The Secretary of State's registered business database may be viewed at the Internet for no charge. Documents are not available online. Records include corporations, limited liability companies, limited partnerships, limited liability partnerships, limited liability limited partnerships, partnership fictitious names, trade names, trademarks, and real estate investment trusts. The database includes all active records and records inactivated within past twelve months. Access by the first few words of a business name, a significant word in a business name, or by the record ID number assigned. If questions, email sosbir@nd.gov. Also, search securities industry professionals database free at www.ndsecurities.com/links/industry-professionals.asp. *Other Options:* This agency provides a database purchase program. Cost is $35.00 per database and processing fees vary for type of media.

Uniform Commercial Code, Federal & State Tax Liens $$

UCC Division, Secretary of State, www.nd.gov/sos/businessserv/centralindex/index.html Access to the Central Indexing System provides both filing and online searching. There is an annual subscription $150 fee and a one-time $50.00 registration fee. The UCC-11 search fee (normally $7.00) applies, but documents will not be certified. Searches include UCC-11 information listing and farm product searches. *Other Options:* The agency offers bulk access on IBM cartridge or paper copy. Call for details.

Sales Tax Registrations Free

Office of State Tax Commissioner, Sales & Special Taxes Division, www.nd.gov/tax/salesanduse/ A permit number may be verified online at www.nd.gov/tax/salesanduse/permitinquiry/. System indicates valid permit registered to company name.

Driver Records $$

Department of Transportation, Driver License & Traffic Safety Division, www.dot.nd.gov/public/public.htm There are two systems. Ongoing, approved commercial accounts may request records with personal information via a commercial system. There is a minimum of 100 requests per month. For more information, call 701-328-4790. Also, at https://secure.apps.state.nd.us/dot/dlts/dlos/welcome.htm one may view and print a limited record. The fee is $3.00 per record and a use of a credit card is required. The limited record does not include total points or convictions more than three years old, violations less than three points, or any crash information. No documents will be sent via mail. *Other Options:* Magnetic tape ordering is available for high volume users.

Vessel Ownership & Registration `Free`

North Dakota Game & Fish Department, Boat Registration Records, http://gf.nd.gov There is a free public inquiry system at the web page. Click on "Register a Boat" then Find Watercraft Registration or visit https://secure.apps.state.nd.us/gnf/onlineservices/lic/public/online/main.htm. Form this site one amy also search watercraftsafety cards, lottery hunting permit applications and hunter safety listings. *Other Options:* A printed list is available of all registered vessels.

GED Certificates `Free`

Department of Public Instruction, GED Testing - CKEN-11, www.dpi.state.nd.us/adulted/index.shtm One may request records via email at JMarcellais@state.nd.us. There is no fee, unless a transcript is ordered.

Vital Records `$$`

ND Department of Health, Vital Records, http://ndhealth.gov/vital/ Birth, death (if over one year old) and marriage records may be ordered online from the Internet site or from vitalchek.com. Records are not returned online.

Occupational Licensing Boards

Alcoholic Beverage Control	www.ag.nd.gov/Licensing/Beverage/Beverage.htm
Amusement Device, Coin-Op	www.ag.nd.gov/Licensing/Amusement/Amusement.htm
Architect	www.ndsba.net/?id=221&page=Active+License+Query
Asbestos Contractor	www.health.state.nd.us/AQ/IAQ/ASB/Asbestos%20Contractor%20List.pdf
Attorney	www.court.state.nd.us/court/lawyers/index/frameset.htm
Auctioneer /Auction Clerk	www.psc.state.nd.us/jurisdiction/auctioneers-entities.html
Bank, Commercial	www.nd.gov/dfi/regulate/reg/regulated.asp
Broker, Corporate	www.nd.gov/ndins/producer/details.asp?ID=303
Charitable Solicitation	www.nd.gov/sos/forms/pdf/charorg.pdf
Coal Mine, Surface	www.psc.state.nd.us/jurisdiction/reclamation.html
Collection Agency	www.nd.gov/dfi/regulate/reg/regulated.asp
Consumer Finance Company	www.nd.gov/dfi/regulate/reg/regulated.asp
Contractor/General Contractor	https://secure.apps.state.nd.us/sc/busnsrch/busnSearch.htm
Counselor, Professional	www.ndbce.org/licensing.shtml
Credit Union	www.nd.gov/dfi/regulate/reg/regulated.asp
Debt Collector	www.nd.gov/dfi/regulate/reg/regulated.asp
Deferred Presentment Provider	www.nd.gov/dfi/regulate/reg/regulated.asp
Drug Mfg./Wholesaler	www.nodakpharmacy.com
Electrical Contractor	www.ndseb.com/findcontractor.asp
Fireworks, Wholesale	www.ag.nd.gov/Licensing/Fireworks/Fireworks.htm
Funeral Home	http://ndfda.org/index.htm
Gaming	www.ag.nd.gov/Gaming/Gaming.htm
Gaming Distributor	www.ag.nd.gov/Licensing/LicenseHolders/LicGADist.pdf
Gaming Manufacturer	www.ag.nd.gov/Licensing/LicenseHolders/LicGAMan.pdf
Grain Buyer/Warehouse/Elevator	www.psc.state.nd.us/jurisdiction/grain-entities.html
Home Inspector	www.nd.gov/sos/forms/pdf/home-inspectors.pdf
Insurance Agency/Agent/Broker	www.nd.gov/ndins/producer/details.asp?ID=303
Investment Advisor	www.ndsecurities.com/links/industry-professionals.asp
Livestock Agent	www.agdepartment.com/Programs/Livestock/Agents.html
Livestock Auction Market	www.agdepartment.com/Programs/Livestock/markets.html
Livestock Dealer	www.agdepartment.com/Programs/Livestock/Dealers.html
Lobbyist	www.nd.gov/sos/lobbylegislate/lobbying/reg-mnu.html
Medical Doctor	www.ndbomex.com/SearchPage.asp
Medication Assistant	https://www.ndbon.org/verify_renew/verify_default.asp
Money Broker Firm	www.nd.gov/dfi/regulate/reg/regulated.asp
Nurse-LPN/RN/ Nurse Assistant	https://www.ndbon.org/verify_renew/verify_default.asp
Optometrist	www.ndsbopt.org/directory.asp
Osteopathic Physician	www.ndbomex.com/SearchPage.asp
Pharmacist	www.nodakpharmacy.com

Pharmacy/PharmTechnician/Intern ... www.nodakpharmacy.com
Physical Therapist/Assistant .... https://secure.ndbpt.org/www/verify.asp
Physician Assistant .... www.ndbomex.com/SearchPage.asp
Polygraph Examiner .... www.ag.nd.gov/Licensing/Polygraph/Polygraph.htm
Private Investigator/Agency .... www.nd.gov/pisb/holders.html
Public Accountant-CPA/Firm............ www.nd.gov/ndsba/database/sbasearch.asp
Sale of Check.................................... www.nd.gov/dfi/regulate/reg/regulated.asp
Securities Agent/Dealer.................... www.ndsecurities.com/links/industry-professionals.asp
Security Provider/Company............... www.nd.gov/pisb/holders.html
Social Worker.................................. http://secure.ebigpicture.com/ndbswe/live/public.asp
Soil Classifier .... www.soilsci.ndsu.nodak.edu/soilclassifiers/roster.htm
Speech-Lang. Patholog't/Audiologist http://governor.state.nd.us/boards/bcpublicsearch.asp?searchtype=member
Telecommunications Company .... www.psc.state.nd.us/jurisdiction/telecom.html
Telecommunications Personnel .... www.psc.state.nd.us/jurisdiction/telecom.html
Tobacco, Retail/Wholesale .... www.ag.nd.gov/Licensing/Tobacco/Tobacco.htm
Transient Merchant........................... www.ag.nd.gov/Licensing/Transient/TransientMerchant.htm
Trust Company .... www.nd.gov/dfi/regulate/reg/regulated.asp
Water Well Driller............................ www.health.state.nd.us/wq/gw/wells.htm
Water Well Pump & Pitless Unit....... www.health.state.nd.us/wq/gw/wells.htm
Weighing Device Tester.................... www.psc.state.nd.us/jurisdiction/weights-list.html
Well Contractor, Monitoring .... www.health.state.nd.us/wq/gw/wells.htm

State and Local Courts

State Court Structure: The District Courts are general jurisdiction over criminal, civil, and juvenile matters. Municipal courts in North Dakota have jurisdiction of all violations of municipal ordinances, with some exceptions. At one time there were County Courts, but these courts merged with the District Courts statewide in 1995. These older County Court records are held by the 53 District Court Clerks in the seven judicial districts.

Statewide Court Online Access: Access district court criminal index on the state system at www.ndcourts.gov/publicsearch/contactsearch.aspx. This includes 9 municipal courts as well. Each counties index only goes back to their month of computerization. Also, you may now search North Dakota Supreme Court dockets and opinions at www.ndcourts.com. Search by docket number, party name, or anything else that may appear in the text. Records are from 1982 forward. Email notification of new opinions is also available.

❖ **Statewide Access Offered All Trial Courts – Read Above**

Below are Additional Sites ❖

Cass County
East Central Judicial District Court   `Free`
Search probate records from the 1870s to 1944 online at www.lib.ndsu.nodak.edu/ndirs/databases/probate.php. There is no fee.

Nelson County
Northeast Central Judicial District Court   `Free`
Civil: Will accept email record requests at rstevens@pioneer.state.nd.us. *Criminal:* Court will accept email record requests at rstevens@pioneer.state.nd.us.

Recorders, Assessors, and Other Sites of Note

Recording Office Organization: 53 counties, 53 recording offices. The recording officer is the County Recorder. Federal tax liens on personal property of businesses are filed with the Secretary of State. Other federal and all state tax liens are filed with the County Recorder. All counties will perform tax lien searches. Some counties automatically include business federal tax liens as part of a UCC search because they appear on the statewide database. However, be careful - federal tax liens on individuals may only be in the county lien books, and not on the statewide system.

Online Access Note: The North Dakota Recorders Information Network (NDRIN) is a electronic central repository representing a number of North Dakota counties – 37 currently, with more being added - and offering internet access to records, indices, and images. There is a $100 set-up fee a $25 monthly usage fee, and a $1.00 charge per image printed. Register or request information via the website at www.ndrin.com

Barnes County *Real Estate, Deed Records* www.co.barnes.nd.us `$$` Subscription access the recorder's land records via NDRIN's central repository at www.ndrin.com. See section introduction.
Property, Taxation Records `Free` Tax lien sale list free at www.co.barnes.nd.us/dept/aud/. Link at bottom of page.

Benson County *Real Estate, Deed Records* `$$` Subscription access the recorder's land records via NDRIN's central repository at www.ndrin.com. Registration and monthly fee applies. See section introduction.

Bowman County *Real Estate, Deed Records* `$$` Subscription access the recorder's land records via NDRIN's central repository at www.ndrin.com. Registration and monthly fee applies. See section introduction.

Burleigh County *Real Estate, Deed Records* `$$` Subscription access the recorder's land records via NDRIN's central repository at www.ndrin.com. Registration and monthly fee applies. See section introduction.
Property, Taxation Records `Free` Access to treasurer and auditor property data is free at www.co.burleigh.nd.us/property-information/. No name searching.

Cass County *Real Estate, Deed Records* `$$` Subscription access the recorder's land records via NDRIN's central repository at www.ndrin.com. Registration and monthly fee applies. See section introduction.
Property, Taxation Records `Free` Access the treasurer's property tax data free at https://cass.nd.ezgov.com/ezproperty/review_search.jsp but no name searching. Also, search parcel and property data free at the GIS-mapping site at http://gis.ci.fargo.nd.us/website/cassnd/search.asp but no name searching.

Cavalier County *Real Estate, Deed Records* `$$` Subscription access the recorder's land records via NDRIN's central repository at www.ndrin.com. Registration and monthly fee applies. See section introduction.

Dunn County *Real Estate, Deed Records* `$$` Subscription access the recorder's land records via NDRIN's central repository at www.ndrin.com. Registration and monthly fee applies. See section introduction.

Foster County *Real Estate, Deed Records* `$$` Subscription access the recorder's land records via NDRIN's central repository at www.ndrin.com. Registration and monthly fee applies. See section introduction.

Golden Valley County *Real Estate, Deed Records* `$$` Subscription access the recorder's land records via NDRIN's central repository at www.ndrin.com. Registration and monthly fee applies. See section introduction.

Grand Forks County *Real Estate, Grantor/Grantee, Deed, Death, Judgment, Lien Records* www.co.grand-forks.nd.us/homepage.htm `Free` Access county property data free at www.co.grand-forks.nd.us/search.htm. Also, access the recorder's Grantor/Grantee database free at www.co.grand-forks.nd.us/recorders%20search.htm.

Griggs County *Real Estate, Deed Records* `$$` Access the recorder's land records by subscription via NDRIN's central repository at www.ndrin.com. See section introduction.

Kidder County *Real Estate, Deed Records* `$$` Subscription access the recorder's land records via NDRIN's central repository at www.ndrin.com. Registration and monthly fee applies. See section introduction.

La Moure County *Real Estate, Deed Records* http://lamoco.drtel.net/countyrecorder.html `$$` Subscription access the recorder's land records via NDRIN's central repository at www.ndrin.com. Registration and monthly fee applies. See section introduction.

McHenry County *Real Estate, Deed Records* `$$` Subscription access the recorder's land records via NDRIN's central repository at www.ndrin.com. Registration and monthly fee applies. See section introduction.

McIntosh County *Real Estate, Deed Records* `$$` Subscription access the recorder's land records via NDRIN's central repository at www.ndrin.com. Registration and monthly fee applies. See section introduction.

McKenzie County *Real Estate, Deed Records* www.4eyes.net/McKenzieCounty/Default.aspx `$$` Access the recorder's land records 5/1998 to present by subscription via NDRIN's central repository at www.ndrin.com. See section introduction.

McLean County *Real Estate, Deed Records* www.visitmcleancounty.com `$$` Subscription access the recorder's land records via NDRIN's central repository at www.ndrin.com. Registration and monthly fee applies. See section introduction.

Mercer County *Real Estate, Deed Records* `$$` Subscription access the recorder's land records via NDRIN's central repository at www.ndrin.com. Registration and monthly fee applies. See section introduction.

Morton County *Real Estate, Deed Records* `$$` Subscription access the recorder's land records via NDRIN's central repository at www.ndrin.com. Registration and monthly fee applies. See section introduction.

Nelson County *Real Estate, Deed Records* www.nelsonco.org `$$` Subscription access the recorder's land records via NDRIN's central repository at www.ndrin.com. Registration and monthly fee applies. See section introduction.

Pembina County *Real Estate, Deed Records* www.pembinacountynd.gov `$$` Subscription access the recorder's land records via NDRIN's central repository at www.ndrin.com. Registration and monthly fee applies. See section introduction.

Pierce County *Real Estate, Deed Records* `$$` Subscription access the recorder's land records via NDRIN's central repository at www.ndrin.com. Registration and monthly fee applies. See section introduction.

Ramsey County *Real Estate, Deed Records* www.co.ramsey.nd.us `$$` Subscription access the recorder's land records via NDRIN's central repository at www.ndrin.com. Registration and monthly fee applies. See section introduction.

Ransom County *Real Estate, Deed Records* www.ndaco.org `$$` Subscription access the recorder's land records via NDRIN's central repository at www.ndrin.com. Registration and monthly fee applies. See section introduction.

Richland County *Real Estate, Deed Records* `$$` Subscription access the recorder's land records via NDRIN's central repository at www.ndrin.com. Registration and monthly fee applies. See section introduction.

Rolette County *Real Estate, Deed Records* www.rolettecounty.com `$$` Subscription access the recorder's land records via NDRIN's central repository at www.ndrin.com. Registration and monthly fee applies. See section introduction.

Sargent County *Real Estate, Deed Records* `$$` Subscription access the recorder's land records via NDRIN's central repository at www.ndrin.com. Registration and monthly fee applies. See section introduction.

Slope County *Real Estate, Deed Records* `$$` Subscription access the recorder's land records via NDRIN's central repository at www.ndrin.com. Registration and monthly fee applies. See section introduction.

Stark County *Real Estate, Deed Records* http://mylocalgov.com/starkcountynd/index.asp `$$` Subscription access the recorder's land records via NDRIN's central repository at www.ndrin.com. Registration and monthly fee applies. See section introduction.

Steele County *Real Estate, Deed Records* `$$` Subscription access the recorder's land records via NDRIN's central repository at www.ndrin.com. Registration and monthly fee applies. See section introduction.

Stutsman County *Real Estate, Deed Records* www.co.stutsman.nd.us `$$` Subscription access the recorder's land records via NDRIN's central repository at www.ndrin.com. Registration and monthly fee applies. See section introduction.

Towner County *Real Estate, Deed Records* `$$` Subscription access the recorder's land records via NDRIN's central repository at www.ndrin.com. Registration and monthly fee applies. See section introduction.

Walsh County *Real Estate, Deed Records* www.co.walsh.nd.us `$$` Subscription access the recorder's land records via NDRIN's central repository at www.ndrin.com. Registration and monthly fee applies. See section introduction.

Ward County *Real Estate, Deed Records* www.co.ward.nd.us/recorder/ `$$` Subscription access the recorder's land records via NDRIN's central repository at www.ndrin.com. Registration and monthly fee applies. See section introduction.

Wells County *Real Estate, Deed Records* http://mylocalgov.com/wellscountynd `$$` Subscription access the recorder's land records via NDRIN's central repository at www.ndrin.com. Registration and monthly fee applies. See section introduction.

Williams County *Real Estate, Deed Records* www.williamsnd.com `$$` Also, subscription access to the recorder's land records via NDRIN's Central Repository available at www.ndrin.com. See section introduction.
Property, Taxation Records `Free` Access to county tax data is free at www.williamsnd.com/tax/search/. Also, access to property tax records for free at www.williamsnd.com/Tax.aspx.

Ohio

Capital: Columbus
             Franklin County
Time Zone: EST
Population: 11,466,917
# of Counties: 88

Useful State Links

Website: www.ohio.gov
Governor: http://governor.ohio.gov
Attorney General: www.ag.state.oh.us
State Archives: www.ohiohistory.org/ar_tools.html
State Revised Code: http://codes.ohio.gov/orc
Legislative Bill Search: www.legislature.state.oh.us/search.cfm
Unclaimed Funds: www.unclaimedfundstreasurehunt.ohio.gov

Primary State Agencies

Criminal Records $$

Ohio Bureau of Investigation, Civilian Background Section, www.ag.state.oh.us/business/fingerprint/index.asp Civilian Background Checks (WebCheck) is a web-based system for all in-state record requests. Results are NOT returned via the Internet. Agencies can send fingerprint images and other data via the Internet using a single digit fingerprint scanner and a driver's license magnetic strip reader. Hardware costs are involved.

Sexual Offender Registry Free

Ohio Bureau of Investigation, Sexual Offender Registry, www.esorn.ag.state.oh.us/Secured/p1.aspx Search online eSORN at www.esorn.ag.state.oh.us/Secured/p21_2.aspx. Users can search by offender name, zip code, county and / or school district. The site is linked to all 88 of Ohio's sheriff's offices.

Incarceration Records Free

Ohio Department of Rehabilitation and Correction, Bureau of Records Management, www.drc.state.oh.us From the website, in the Select a Destination box, select Offender Search or see www.drc.state.oh.us/OffenderSearch/Search.aspx. You can search by name or inmate number. The Offender Search includes all offenders currently incarcerated or under some type of Department supervision (parole, post-release control, or transitional control). Also, search a private company site for offender and inmates for free at https://www.vinelink.com/vinelink/siteInfoAction.do?siteId=36001. also has most county inmate lists, but not all.

Corporation, LLC, LP, LLP, Fictitious/Assumed Name, Trademarks/Servicemarks
 Free & $$

Secretary of State, Corporate Records Access, www.sos.state.oh.us/SOS/businessServices.aspx The agency provides free Internet searching for business and corporation records form the home page. A Good Standing can be ordered. Validation is available for $5.00. Also, search securities exemption filings (ERNIE) free at www.securities.state.oh.us/secu_apps/offering/default.aspx. Search securities enforcement orders by year at www.securities.state.oh.us/FinalOrders/Orders.aspx. *Other Options:* This agency makes the database available for purchase, call for details.

Uniform Commercial Code Free

UCC Records, Secretary of State, www.sos.state.oh.us/SOS/Uniform%20Commercial%20Code.aspx The Internet site offers free online access to records. Search by debtor, secured party, or financing statement number. *Other Options:* The complete database is available on electronic media with weekly updates. Call for current pricing.

Workers' Compensation Records `Free`

Bureau of Workers Compensation, Customer Contact Center - Records Mgr, www.ohiobwc.com Injured workers, injured worker designees, representatives and managed care organizations (MCOs) can view a list of all claims associated with a given SSN, but are limited to viewing only the claims with which they are associated. Employers, their representatives or designees, and managed care organizations can view a list of all claims associated to their BWC policy number. Medical providers can view all claims associated with any given SSN. Access is through the website listed above. *Other Options:* Bulk data is released to approved accounts; however, the legal department must approve requesters. The agency has general information available on a website.

Driver Records `Free & $$`

Department of Public Safety, Bureau of Motor Vehicles, www.ohiobmv.com The Online Abstract System by FTP is suggested for requesters who order 100 or more motor vehicle reports per day in batch mode. The DL# or SSN and name are needed when ordering. Fee is $2.00 per record. For more information, call Fiscal Svrs at 614-752-2091. Also, Ohio drivers may view an unofficial copy of their record at https://www.dps.state.oh.us/netsys/netdb/ENGLISH/MMENU.asp. There is no fee.

Vehicle Ownership & Registration `Free & $$`

Bureau of Motor Vehicles, Motor Vehicle Title Records, www.ohiobmv.com Ohio offers online access through AAMVAnet. All requesters must comply with a contractual agreement prior to release of data, which complies with DPPA regulations. Fee is $2.00 per record. Call 614-752-7598 for more information. The website offers free access to title records for vehicles and watercraft. No personal information is released. Search by title number or ID. Also search at https://www.dps.state.oh.us/atps/. *Other Options:* Bulk records are available for purchase, per DPPA guidelines.

Accident Reports `$$`

Department of Public Safety, OSHP Central Records, 1st Fl, http://statepatrol.ohio.gov/crash.htm Crash reports purchased online will be sent to your e-mail account the same day. Crash photographs purchased online will be sent in the mail. Online crash reports are available for crashes that 5 years to present. The webpage to search is http://crsweb.dps.state.oh.us/crashreports/index.asp. Reports must be purchased for $4.00 using a credit card.

Vessel Ownership & Registration `Free`

DNR-Division of Watercraft, Titles and Registration, www.dnr.state.oh.us/Watercraft/tabid/2062/Default.aspx A free title inquiry is available at www.dps.state.oh.us/atps/. Note this is through another agency, but people are directed to this site from the DNR site. The title information available from this web page is obtained from Ohio county title offices. Records are from 1993 forward.

Birth and Death Records `Free & $$`

Ohio Department of Health, Bureau of Vital Statistics, www.odh.ohio.gov The Ohio Historical Society Death Certificate Index Searchable Database at http://ohsweb.ohiohistory.org/death// permits searching by name, county, index. Data is available from 1913 to 1944 only. Both birth and death records can be ordered from a state-designated vendor – www.vitalcheck.com.

Occupational Licensing Boards

Accounting Firm	http://acc.ohio.gov/lookup.htm
Acupuncturist	https://license.ohio.gov/lookup/default.asp
Anesthesiologist Assistant	https://license.ohio.gov/lookup/default.asp
Architect	https://license.ohio.gov/lookup/
Athlete Agent	www.aco.ohio.gov/pdf/RegAthAg.pdf
Athletic Trainer	https://license.ohio.gov/lookup/default.asp
Attorney, State	www.sconet.state.oh.us/atty_reg/Public_AttorneyInformation.asp
Audiologist/Audiologist Aide	https://license.ohio.gov/lookup/default.asp
Backflow Prev. Assembly Insp	www.com.state.oh.us/dic/plans/scripts/bkfloqy.htm
Bank	http://elicense2-lookup.com.ohio.gov/
Barber-related Occupation	https://license.ohio.gov/lookup/default.asp?division=87
Boiler Contractor	www.com.state.oh.us/dic/scripts/boilerctrqy.htm
Boiler Inspector	https://www.comapps.ohio.gov/dic/dico_apps/boil/boiler_contractors/Default.aspx
Boiler Operator	www.com.ohio.gov/OnlineServices.aspx
Boxer/Boxing Professional	www.aco.ohio.gov/pdf/Boxers.pdf
Cemetery	https://www.com.state.oh.us/real/elicense.aspx
Check Cashing/Lending Service	http://elicense2-lookup.com.ohio.gov/
Child Care Type A or B House	www.odjfs.state.oh.us/cdc/query.asp
Child Day Care Facility	www.odjfs.state.oh.us/cdc/query.asp
Chiropractor	https://license.ohio.gov/lookup/default.asp?division=90
Clinical Nurse Specialist	www.nursing.ohio.gov/verification.stm
Coil Cleaner (Liquor/Beverage)	www.liquorcontrol.ohio.gov/coilalpha.txt

Consumer Finance Company............. http://elicense2-lookup.com.ohio.gov/
Contractor.. www.com.state.oh.us/dic/lics/elicense.aspx
Cosmetic Therapist............................ https://license.ohio.gov/lookup/default.asp
Cosmetology-related Occupation ...... https://license.ohio.gov/lookup/default.asp
Day Camp, Children's........................ www.odjfs.state.oh.us/cdc/query.asp
Dental Assistant Radiologist.............. https://license.ohio.gov/lookup/default.asp?division=95
Dentist/or/ Dental Hygienist.............. https://license.ohio.gov/lookup/default.asp?division=95
Dialysis Technician .... www.nursing.ohio.gov/verification.stm
Dietitian.. https://license.ohio.gov/lookup/default.asp?division=85
Drug Wholesaler/Distributor .... http://pharmacy.ohio.gov/license.htm
Electrical Safety Inspector................. www.com.state.oh.us/dic/default.htm
Electrician... www.com.state.oh.us/dic/lics/elicense.aspx
Elevator Inspection .... https://www.comapps.ohio.gov/dic/dico_apps/elev/elev_lookup/Default.aspx
Emergency Medical Tech. Instr......... https://www.dps.state.oh.us/ems/cert.asp
Emergency Medical Technician .... https://www.dps.state.oh.us/ems/cert.asp
Engineer .... https://license.ohio.gov/lookup/default.asp?division=100
Engineering/Surveying Company...... https://license.ohio.gov/lookup/default.asp?division=100
Esthetician/Managing Esthetician...... https://license.ohio.gov/lookup/default.asp
Fire Protection System Designer .... www.com.state.oh.us/dic/default.htm
Firefighter/Firefighter Instructor........ https://www.dps.state.oh.us/ems/cert.asp
Foreign Real Estate Property .... https://www.com.state.oh.us/real/elicense.aspx
Heating/Refrigeration (HVAC) .... www.com.state.oh.us/dic/lics/elicense.aspx
Hydronic-related Occupation............. www.com.state.oh.us/dic/lics/elicense.aspx
Insurance Agent................................. www.ohioinsurance.gov/ConsumServ/ocs/agentloc.asp
Landscape Architect .... https://license.ohio.gov/lookup/
Legislative Agent/Agent Employer ... www.jlec-olig.state.oh.us/olig2/search_form.aspx
Liquor Distributor.............................. www.liquorcontrol.ohio.gov/safekeep.txt
Liquor License/Store .... www.liquorcontrol.ohio.gov/phone.txt
Liquor License Cancellation.............. www.liquorcontrol.ohio.gov/canceled.txt
Liquor Permit www.liquorcontrol.ohio.gov/liquor5.htm
Lobbyist List..................................... www.jlec-olig.state.oh.us/AgentandEmployerLists.htm
Lobbyist/Lobbyist Employer .... www.jlec-olig.state.oh.us/olig2/search_form.aspx
Manicuring/Esthetician Instructor ..... https://license.ohio.gov/lookup/default.asp
Manicurist/Managing Manicurist ...... https://license.ohio.gov/lookup/default.asp
Massage Therapist............................. https://license.ohio.gov/lookup/default.asp
Mechanotherapist .... https://license.ohio.gov/lookup/default.asp
Medical Doctor.................................. https://license.ohio.gov/lookup/default.asp
Midwife Nurse................................... www.nursing.ohio.gov/verification.stm
Milk Processor/Producer/Plant .... www.ohioagriculture.gov/oda3/_Apps/Admn_License/Default.aspx
Mortgage Broker http://elicense2-lookup.com.ohio.gov/
Naprapath .... https://license.ohio.gov/lookup/default.asp
Notary Public.................................... www.sos.state.oh.us/SOS/Notary/Search.aspx
Nurse Anesthetist............................... www.nursing.ohio.gov/verification.stm
Nurse-RN/LPN/Practitioner .... www.nursing.ohio.gov/verification.stm
Occupational Therapist/Assistant ...... https://license.ohio.gov/lookup/default.asp
Ocularist/Ocularist Apprentice .... https://license.ohio.gov/lookup/default.asp
Optical Dispenser .... https://license.ohio.gov/lookup/default.asp
Optician/Optician Apprentice............ https://license.ohio.gov/lookup/default.asp
Optometrist.. https://license.ohio.gov/lookup/default.asp?division=91
Osteopathic Physician........................ https://license.ohio.gov/lookup/default.asp
Pawnbroker.. http://elicense2-lookup.com.ohio.gov/
Pesticide-related Occupation/Firm .... www.ohioagriculture.gov/pubs/divs/plnt/plnt-licensing.stm
Pharmacist .... http://pharmacy.ohio.gov/license.htm
Pharmacy/Pharmacy Dispensary .... http://pharmacy.ohio.gov/license.htm
Physical Therapist/Assistant.............. https://license.ohio.gov/lookup/default.asp
Physician Assistant .... https://license.ohio.gov/lookup/default.asp
Plumber .... www.com.state.oh.us/dic/lics/elicense.aspx

Plumbing Inspector............................https://www.com.state.oh.us/dic/plans/scripts/plumbqy.htm
Podiatrist...https://license.ohio.gov/lookup/default.asp
Precious Metals Dealer.....................http://elicense2-lookup.com.ohio.gov/
Premium Finance Company http://elicense2-lookup.com.ohio.gov/
Prescriptive Authority.......................www.nursing.ohio.gov/verification.stm
Pressure Piping Inspector ....www.com.ohio.gov/dico/
Psychologist......................................https://license.ohio.gov/lookup/default.asp?division=83
Public Accountant-CPA ....http://acc.ohio.gov/lookup.htm
Real Estate Agent/Seller/Broker........https://www.com.state.oh.us/real/elicense.aspx
Real Estate Appraiser ....https://www.com.state.oh.us/real/elicense.aspx
Respiratory Therapist/Student ....https://license.ohio.gov/lookup/default.asp
Savings & Loan Association http://elicense2-lookup.com.ohio.gov/
Savings Bank.....................................http://elicense2-lookup.com.ohio.gov/
School Psychologist...........................https://license.ohio.gov/lookup/default.asp?division=83
Securities Filing................................www.securities.state.oh.us/secu_apps/offering/disclaimer.aspx
Speech Pathologist/Audiologist.........https://license.ohio.gov/lookup/default.asp
Sprinkler Equipment Inspector ....www.com.ohio.gov/dico/
Sprinkler Inspector ....www.com.ohio.gov/OnlineServices.aspx
Steam Engineer..................................www.com.state.oh.us/dic/scripts/boilerctrqy.htm
Storage Tank Corrective Action ....https://www.com.state.oh.us/sfm/bustr/CorrectiveActions.htm
Surveyor, Land ....https://license.ohio.gov/lookup/default.asp?division=100
Underground Storage Tank.................https://www.com.state.oh.us/sfm/bustr/PublicInquiry.htm
Underground Tank Inspector..............https://www.com.state.oh.us/sfm/bustr/PDFs/Data/WEBInspectorList
Underground Tank Installer................https://www.com.state.oh.us/sfm/bustr/PDFs/Data/WEBInstallerList
Underground Tank Instructor ....https://www.com.state.oh.us/sfm/bustr/PDFs/TrainerApprovedlist.xls
Veterinarian/Veterinary Tech ....https://license.ohio.gov/lookup/default.asp?division=88

State and Local Courts

State Court Structure: The Court of Common Pleas is the general jurisdiction court and County/Municipal Courts have limited jurisdiction. Ohio Common Pleas Courts may name their own minimum threshold civil actions. Although most courts elect to use $15,000 as a standard minimum, some use $3,000 and some $10,000. In effect, these Common Pleas courts may take any civil cases. However, civil maximum limits for Ohio's County Courts and Municipal Courts remains the same – $15,000. County and Municipal Courts handle virtually the same subject matter with some minor operational differences.

Probate Courts are now divisions of the Court of Common Pleas, they were separate at one time.

Statewide Court Online Access: There is no statewide computer system for trial court dockets but a number of counties and municipal courts offer online access. Appellate and Supreme Court opinions may be researched from the Supreme Court website at www.supremecourtofohio.gov.

Allen County
Common Pleas Court   www.allencountyohio.com/cle.php   **Free**
Civil: Access civil records including judgment liens free at http://65.17.134.12/pa/pa.urd/pamw6500.display. *Criminal:* Online access is free at http://65.17.134.12/pa/pa.urd/pamw6500.display. Records go back to 12/1/1988.

Lima Municipal Court   www.limamunicipalcourt.org   **Free**
Civil: Search index information at www.limamunicipalcourt.org, click on Case Inquiry. Direct email search requests to limamuni@wcoil.com *Criminal:* same.

Ashland County
Common Pleas Court   www.ashlandcounty.org/clerkofcourts   **Free**
Civil: Access records at www.ashlandcountycpcourt.org. Computerized court records go back to 6/7/1995. *Criminal:* same.

Ashtabula County
Common Pleas Court   http://courts.co.ashtabula.oh.us/pa.htm   **Free**
Civil: Access to index is free at http://courts.co.ashtabula.oh.us/pa.htm. *Criminal:* same.

County Court Eastern Division   http://courts.co.ashtabula.oh.us/pa.htm   **Free**
Civil: Access to records are free at http://courts.co.ashtabula.oh.us/pa.htm. *Criminal:* same.

County Court Western Division   www.co.ashtabula.oh.us   **Free**
Civil: Access records free at http://courts.co.ashtabula.oh.us/pa.htm. *Criminal:* same.

Ashtabula Municipal Court   www.ashtabulamunicipalcourt.com/   **Free**
Civil: Online access to civil court cases are free at www.ashtabulamunicourt.com/searchcivildocket.asp. *Criminal:* Online access to court cases, including traffic, are free at www.ashtabulamunicipalcourt.com/searchdocket.asp.

Athens County

Common Pleas Court   www.athenscountycpcourt.org/   **Free**
Civil: Online access to CP court records are free at http://coc.athenscountygovernment.com/pa/ *Criminal:* Same.

Athens Municipal Court   www.athensmunicipalcourt.com   **Free**
Civil: Search by name or case number at http://docket.webxsol.com/athens/index.html . Records available from 1992. *Criminal:* same.

Auglaize County

Common Pleas Court   www.auglaizecounty.org/Common_Pleas_Court/index.htm   **Free & $$**
Civil: Access civil records back to 2/2000 free at www.auglaizecounty.org/pa/. *Criminal:* Access criminal records back to 2/2000 free at www.auglaizecounty.org/pa/.

Auglaize County Municipal Court   www.auglaizecounty.org/Municipal_Court/Index.htm   **Free**
Civil: Access civil and small claims court records back to 4/1/1994 free at www.auglaizecounty.org/pa/. *Criminal:* Access criminal and traffic records back to 10/1/1993 free at www.auglaizecounty.org/pa/.

Brown County

Common Pleas Court   www.browncountyclerkofcourts.org   **Free**
Civil: Search court records free at www.browncountyclerkofcourts.org/Search/. *Criminal:* same.

County Municipal Court   www.browncountycourt.org   **Free**
Civil: Access to records are free at www.browncountycourt.org/search.html. *Criminal:* same.

Butler County

Common Pleas Court   www.butlercountyclerk.org   **Free**
Civil: Online access to County Clerk of Courts records are free at www.butlercountyclerk.org/pa/pa.urd/pamw6500-display. Search by name, dates, or case number and type. Online access to Probate Court records is free are http://66.117.197.22/index.cfm?page=courtRecords Search the Estate or Guardianship databases. *Criminal:* Same.

County Court Area #1   **Free**
Civil: Access to dockets is coming soon and free at www.butlercountyohio.org/areacourts/. *Criminal:* same.

County Court Area #2   **Free**
Civil: Access to dockets is coming soon and free at www.butlercountyohio.org/areacourts/. *Criminal:* same.

County Court Area #3   www.butlercountyohio.org/areacourts/   **Free**
Civil: Access to dockets is coming soon and free at www.butlercountyohio.org/areacourts/. *Criminal:* same.

Fairfield Municipal Court   www.fairfield-city.org/court/index.cfm   **Free**
Civil: Search records online back to 1988 free at www.fairfield-city.org/court/records.cfm. *Criminal:* same.

Hamilton Municipal Court   www.hamiltonmunicipalcourt.org   **Free**
Civil: Search record access free at http://hamiltonmunicipalcourt.org/connect/court/. *Criminal:* Search records free at http://hamiltonmunicipalcourt.org/connect/court/.

Champaign County

Champaign County Municipal Court   www.champaigncountymunicipalcourt.com   **Free**
Civil: Access court records back to 1992 free at www.champaigncountymunicipalcourt.com/Docket.aspx includes civil, criminal and traffic. *Criminal:* Same

Clark County

Common Pleas Court   www.clarkcountyohio.gov/courts/index.htm   **Free**
Civil: Online access to clerk's records is free at http://64.56.107.134:80/pa/. *Criminal:* Online access to clerk's records are free at http://64.56.107.134:80/pa/. The Sheriff's most wanted list is found at www.clarkcountysheriff.com.

Clark County Municipal Court   www.clerkofcourts.municipal.co.clark.oh.us/   **Free**
Civil: Online access to case information is free at www.clerkofcourts.municipal.co.clark.oh.us/. Images available back to 4/15/06. Name searching on "New Cases;" other types require a case number. Online records go back to 3/90. *Criminal:* Access to criminal records is the same as civil.

Clermont County

Common Pleas Court   www.clermontclerk.org/Case_Access.htm   **Free**
Civil: Online access to civil records is the same as criminal, see following. *Criminal:* Online access to court records is free at www.clermontclerk.org/Case_Access.htm. Online records go back to 1/1987. Includes later Municipal Court records.

Clermont County Municipal Court   www.clermontclerk.org   **Free**
Civil: Online access to court records is the same as criminal, see following. *Criminal:* Online access to court records is free at www.clermontclerk.org/Case_Access.htm. Online records go back to 5/1/1996.

Clinton County

Clinton County Municipal Court   www.clintonmunicourt.org   **Free**
Civil: Search court records online at www.clintonmunicourt.org/search.html. *Criminal:* same.

Columbiana County

Common Pleas Court   www.ccclerk.org   **Free**
Civil: Access all county court index and docket records free at www.ccclerk.org/case_access.htm. Includes probate. *Criminal:* Access all county court index and docket records free at www.ccclerk.org/case_access.htm.

Municipal Court   www.ccclerk.org/the_courts.htm   **Free**
Civil: Access all county court index and docket records free at www.ccclerk.org/case_access.htm. *Criminal:* same.

East Liverpool Municipal Court   www.eastliverpool.com/court.html   **Free**
Civil: Access all county court index and docket records free at www.ccclerk.org/case_access.htm. *Criminal:* same.

Coshocton County

Coshocton Municipal Court   www.coshoctonmunicipalcourt.com   **Free**
Civil: Online access to civil records is at the website. Search by name, case number, attorney, date. *Criminal:* Same. Search by name, attorney, citation or case number.

Crawford County

Common Pleas Court   www.crawford-co.org/Clerk/default.html   **Free**
Civil: Online access to Common Pleas court records is free at www.crawford-co.org/Clerk/default.html and click on "Internet Inquiry." *Criminal:* Online access to criminal cases is the same as civil.

Cuyahoga County

Common Pleas Court - General Division   http://cp.cuyahogacounty.us/internet/index.aspx   **Free**
Civil: Online access to Common Please civil courts; click on Civil Case Dockets at http://cpdocket.cp.cuyahogacounty.us/TOS.aspx. Access or Probate is at http://probate.cuyahogacounty.us/pa/. *Criminal:* Online access to criminal records dockets is free at http://cpdocket.cp.cuyahogacounty.us/TOS.aspx.

Bedford Municipal Court   www.bedfordmuni.org/   **Free**
Civil: Access index to court records at www.bedfordmuni.org/ Click on Case Information. *Criminal:* Access index to court records at www.bedfordmuni.org/ Click on Case Information.

Berea Municipal Court   www.bereamunicourt.org/   **Free**
Civil: Search docket information at www.bereamunicourt.org/info.asp?pageId=5 . *Criminal:* Search docket info at www.bereamunicourt.org/info.asp?pageId=5.

Cleveland Heights Municipal Court   www.clevelandheightscourt.com   **Free**
Civil: Search Muni civil (to $15,000) or misdemeanor docket records on the website. Search by name or case number. *Criminal:* Same.

Euclid Municipal Court   www.ci.euclid.oh.us/citydepartments/court.cfm   **Free**
Civil: Docket index and daily docket lists of civil cases available at www.ci.euclid.oh.us/citydepartments/court.cfm and click on Case Information. *Criminal:* Docket index and daily docket lists of misdemeanor and traffic cases are available at www.ci.euclid.oh.us/citydepartments/court.cfm and click on Case Information.

Garfield Heights Municipal Court   www.ghmc.org   **Free**
Civil: Online access is limited to dockets; search by name, date or case number at http://docket.ghmc.org. *Criminal:* same.

Lakewood Municipal Court   www.lakewoodcourtoh.com   **Free**
Civil: View weekly dockets only at www.lakewoodcourtoh.com/CourtDockets.htm. *Criminal:* Search weekly dockets only at www.lakewoodcourtoh.com/CourtDockets.htm.

Lyndhurst Municipal Court   www.lyndhurstmunicipalcourt.org   **Free**
Civil: Access court records free at www.lyndhurstmunicipalcourt.org/ but may be temporarily down. *Criminal:* same.

Rocky River Municipal Court   www.rrcourt.net   `Free`
Civil: Public access to record index at https://rrcourt.net/pa/pa.urd/pamw6500.display. *Criminal:* Access record index free at https://rrcourt.net/pa/pa.urd/pamw6500.display.

Shaker Heights Municipal Court   www.shakerheightscourt.org/home/   `Free`
Civil: Search case records and dockets at www.shakerheightscourt.org/home/. *Criminal:* same.

Delaware County

Common Pleas Court   www.delawarecountyclerk.org   `Free`
Civil: Access to court records is free at www.delawarecountyclerk.org. Probate court index from 1852 to 1920 is free at www.midohio.net/dchsdcgs/probate.html. *Criminal:* Access to court records is free at www.delawarecountyclerk.org. Search the sheriff's county database of sex offenders, deadbeat parents, and most wanted list for free at www.delawarecountysheriff.com.

Delaware Municipal Court   www.municipalcourt.org   `Free`
Civil: Municipal courts records are at www.municipalcourt.org:81/connection/court/lookup.xsp?in=cv. *Criminal:* Misdemeanor and traffic case records are free at www.municipalcourt.org:81/connection/court/lookup.xsp?in=ct. Also, search the court's DUI list at www.municipalcourt.org/main_dui.asp.

Erie County

Sandusky Municipal Court   www.sanduskymunicipalcourt.org/   `Free`
Civil: Access Muni court records free at www.sanduskymunicipalcourt.org/search.shtml. *Criminal:* same.

Vermilion Municipal Court   www.vermilionmunicipalcourt.org   `Free`
Civil: Online access to Municipal court records at the website. *Criminal:* Same.

Vermilion Municipal Court   www.vermilionmunicipalcourt.org   `Free`
Civil: Online access to Municipal court records at www.vermilionmunicipalcourt.org/search.html. *Criminal:* Online access to municipal court records is at www.vermilionmunicipalcourt.org/search.html.

Fairfield County

Common Pleas Court   www.fairfieldcountyclerk.com   `Free`
Civil: Online access to County Clerk's court records database is free at www.fairfieldcountyclerk.com/Search/. *Criminal:* same.

Fairfield County Municipal Court   www.fairfieldcountymunicipalcourt.org   `Free`
Civil: Search cases online at www.fairfieldcountymunicipalcourt.org/connection/court/. *Criminal:* same.

Fayette County

Common Pleas Court   www.fayette-co-oh.com/Commplea/index.html   `Free`
Civil: Search docket information free at http://cp.onlinedockets.com/fayettecp/case_dockets/search.aspx . *Criminal:* Search docket info free at http://cp.onlinedockets.com/fayettecp/case_dockets/search.aspx.

Municipal Court   http://216.29.108.131/   `Free`
Civil: Search record index free at http://216.29.108.131/search.shtml. *Criminal:* same.

Franklin County

Common Pleas Court   www.franklincountyohio.gov/clerk/   `Free`
Civil: Access records 3AM-11PM at http://fcdcfcjs.co.franklin.oh.us/CaseInformationOnline/ and includes domestic relations cases. *Criminal:* Access records 3AM-11PM at http://fcdcfcjs.co.franklin.oh.us/CaseInformationOnline/.

Franklin County Municipal Court - Civil Division   www.fcmcclerk.com   `Free`
Civil: Records from the Clerk of Court Courtview database free online at www.fcmcclerk.com/pa/pa.php. Search by name or case number.

Franklin County Municipal Court - Criminal Division   www.fcmcclerk.com   `Free`
Criminal: Criminal and traffic records from the Clerk of Court Courtview database free online at www.fcmcclerk.com/pa/pa.php. Search by name, dates, ticket, address or case numbers.

Probate Court   `Free`   Search probate online at www.co.franklin.oh.us/probate/ProbateSearch.html.

Fulton County

Common Pleas Court   www.fultoncountyoh.com/
Civil: Access an index of civil case records at http://mail.fultoncountyoh.com/pa/. *Criminal:* Access the criminal record index at http://mail.fultoncountyoh.com/pa/. Search by name and case type.

County Court Eastern District   www.fultoncountyoh.com/   `Free`
Civil: Access court records back to 1995 free at http://mail.fultoncountyoh.com/pa/pa.urd/pamw6500.display. *Criminal:* same.

County Court Western District   `Free`
Civil: Access court records back to 1995 free at http://mail.fultoncountyoh.com/pa/pa.urd/pamw6500.display. *Criminal:* same.

Geauga County

Common Pleas Court   www.co.geauga.oh.us   `Free`
Civil: Online access is free from the Clerk of Courts at www.co.geauga.oh.us/departments/clerk_of_courts/Docket2/Courtintro.asp. Online records go back to 1990. Includes domestic cases. *Criminal:* Online access is same as civil.

Chardon Municipal Court   www.co.geauga.oh.us/departments/muni_court.htm   `Free`
Civil: Search court records free at www.auditor.co.geauga.oh.us/pa/. *Criminal:* same.

Greene County

Common Pleas Court   www.co.greene.oh.us/COC/clerk.htm   `Free`
Civil: Online access to clerk of court records is free at www.co.greene.oh.us/pa/pa.htm. Search by name or case number. Also, search probate cases free at www.co.greene.oh.us/Probate/search/case_search.asp. *Criminal:* same.

Fairborn Municipal Court   http://ci.fairborn.oh.us/court.htm   `Free`
Civil: Website offers free online access to civil, misdemeanor and traffic records, or search at http://70.62.41.228/connection/court/ *Criminal:* Same.

Xenia Municipal Court   www.ci.xenia.oh.us/index.php?page=municipal-court   `Free`
Civil: Online access to Municipal Court records free at www.ci.xenia.oh.us/index.php?page=public-access. *Criminal:* Access to criminal records is the same as civil.

Guernsey County

Common Pleas Court   http://66.219.161.39/pa/   `Free`
Civil: Access case index data free at http://74.218.3.68/pa/, *Criminal:* Access case index data free at http://74.218.3.68/pa/.

Cambridge Municipal Court   www.cambridgeoh.org/court.htm   `Free`
Civil: Access Muni Court records free at http://webconnect03.civicacmi.com/cambridge/court/. An agency login also available; registration required. *Criminal:* Access criminal and traffic index online- same as civil above.

Hamilton County

Common Pleas Court   www.courtclerk.org   `Free`
Civil: Records from the court clerk are free at the website or www.courtclerk.org/queries.aps. Online civil index goes back to 1991. Also, search probate records free at www.probatect.org/case_search/casesearch.asp. *Criminal:* Same. Online criminal index goes back to 1986.

Hamilton County Municipal Court - Civil   www.courtclerk.org   `Free`
Civil: Records from the court clerk are free at the website or www.courtclerk.org/queries.aps.

Hancock County

Common Pleas Court   www.co.hancock.oh.us/commonpleas   `Free`
Civil: Search records online back to 1985 at http://pa.co.hancock.oh.us/. *Criminal:* same.

Findlay Municipal Court   www.ci.findlay.oh.us/municourt/   `Free`
Civil: Online access from www.ci.findlay.oh.us/municourt/searchcivildocket.asp?pageId=71. *Criminal:* Same.

Highland County

Hillsboro County Municipal Court   www.hillsboroohio.net   `Free`
Civil: Online access is same as criminal, see below. *Criminal:* Online access is free at http://24.123.13.34/.

Hocking County

Common Pleas Court   www.co.hocking.oh.us/clerk/index.htm   `Free`
Civil: Access the court case index free at www.court.co.hocking.oh.us/cgi-bin/db2www.pgm/cpq.mbr/main. *Criminal:* same.

Hocking County Municipal Court   www.hockingcountymunicipalcourt.com   `Free`
Civil: Access civil records free at www.hockingcountymunicipalcourt.com/search.shtml. Shows case number, docket entry, charge, case type. *Criminal:* Access criminal records free at www.hockingcountymunicipalcourt.com/search.shtml. Shows case number, docket entry, charge, case type.

Huron County

Common Pleas Court   www.huroncountyclerk.com   `Free`
Civil: Search court dockets and public records free at the website www.huroncountyclerk.com/html/case_search.html Civil results on internet do not include DOB. *Criminal:* same .

Norwalk Municipal Court   www.norwalkmunicourt.com   `Free`
Civil: Access records free at www.norwalkmunicourt.com/search.htm. *Criminal:* same.

Jackson County

Jackson County Municipal Court   www.jacksoncountymunicipalcourt.com/   `Free`
Civil: Search record index free at www.jacksoncountymunicipalcourt.com/Search/. *Criminal:* Search the record index at www.jacksoncountymunicipalcourt.com/Search/.

Jefferson County

Common Pleas Court   www.jeffersoncountyoh.com/cgi-bin/template.pl?countycourts.html   `Free`
Civil: Access court index free at www.jeffersoncountyoh.com/cgi-bin/template.pl?/courts/searchCP.html. *Criminal:* Online access to criminal is same as civil, see above.

County Court #1   www.jeffersoncountyoh.com/cgi-bin/template.pl?countycourts.html   `Free`
Civil: Search court records free at www.jeffersoncountyoh.com/cgi-bin/template.pl?/courts/search.html. *Criminal:* Online access to criminal is same as civil, see above.

County Court #2   www.jeffersoncountyoh.com/cgi-bin/template.pl?countycourts.html   `Free`
Civil: Search court records free at www.jeffersoncountyoh.com/cgi-bin/template.pl?/courts/search.html. *Criminal:* Online access to criminal is same as civil, see above.

County Court #3   www.jeffersoncountyoh.com/cgi-bin/template.pl?countycourts.html   `Free`
Civil: Search court records free at www.jeffersoncountyoh.com/cgi-bin/template.pl?/courts/search.html. *Criminal:* Online access to criminal is same as civil, see above.

Knox County

Common Pleas Court   www.knoxcountyclerk.org/   `Free`
Civil: Search court index, dockets, calendars free online at www.knoxcountycpcourt.org/. Search by name or case number. *Criminal:* Same.

Mount Vernon Municipal Court   www.mountvernonmunicipalcourt.org   `Free`
Civil: Access to the clerk's civil records are free at www.mountvernonmunicipalcourt.org/cmiflash/court/home.html. *Criminal:* Access to the clerk's criminal and traffic records are free at www.mountvernonmunicipalcourt.org/cmiflash/court/home.html,.

Lake County

Common Pleas Court   www.lakecountyohio.org   `Free`
Civil: Online access to court records, dockets, and quick index, including probate records, is free at https://phoenix.lakecountyohio.gov/pa/. *Criminal:* Same.

Mentor Municipal Court   www.mentormunicipalcourt.org/   `Free`
Civil: Record searches at www.mentormunicipalcourt.org/search.shtml *Criminal:* Search records at www.mentormunicipalcourt.org/search.shtml.

Painesville Municipal Court   www.pmcourt.com   `Free`
Civil: Free online access to index at www.pmcourt.com/search.shtml. *Criminal:* same.

Lawrence County

Common Pleas Court   www.lawrencecountyclkofcrt.org   `Free`
Civil: Online access to civil records is free at the website. *Criminal:* Online access to criminal records is free at www.lawrencecountyclkofcrt.org.

Lawrence County Municipal Court   www.lawcomunicourt.com/   `Free`
Civil: Click on "Record Search" at the web page for a search of the record index. *Criminal:* same.

Licking County

Common Pleas Court   www.lcounty.com/clerkofcourts/   `Free`
Civil: County clerk's office offers free Internet access to current records at www.lcounty.com/pa/pa.urd/pamw6500.display. *Criminal:* County clerk's office offers free Internet access to current records at www.lcounty.com/pa/pa.urd/pamw6500.display.

Licking County Municipal Court   www.lcmunicipalcourt.com   `Free`
Civil: Online access to Municipal Court records free at http://67.141.197.6/connection/court/. Results include addresses. *Criminal:* Same.

Lorain County

Common Pleas Court   www.loraincounty.com/clerk   `Free`
Civil: Website offers free access to indices and dockets for civil and domestic relationship cases. Access probate records at www.loraincounty.com/probate/search.shtml. *Criminal:* Same.

Avon Lake Municipal Court   www.avonlakecourt.com/   `Free`
Civil: Search docket index by name at www.avonlakecourt.com/Search/. *Criminal:* same.

Elyria Municipal Court www.elyriamunicourt.org `Free`
Civil: Search at the Internet site, also you can request information by email to civil@elyriamunicourt.org. *Criminal:* Search misdemeanor and traffic records at the website, also send email requests to crtr@elyriamunicourt.org.

Lorain Municipal Court www.lorainmunicourt.org `Free`
Civil: Access municipal court records free at www.lorainmunicourt.org/search.shtml. Search by name, date, case number, driver license number or attorney. *Criminal:* Same.

Oberlin Municipal Court www.oberlinmunicipalcourt.org `Free`
Civil: Access case information free online at www.oberlinmunicipalcourt.org/public.htm. *Criminal:* same.

Lucas County

Common Pleas Court www.co.lucas.oh.us/default.asp?RequestedAlias=clerk `Free`
Civil: Online access to clerk of courts dockets is free at http://apps.co.lucas.oh.us/OnlineDockets/. Online records go back to 9/1997. Search probate records at www.lucas-co-probate-ct.org/. *Criminal:* Online access to clerk of courts dockets is free at http://apps.co.lucas.oh.us/OnlineDockets/. Online record go back to 9/1997. Search sex offenders at www.lucascountysheriff.org/sheriff/disclaimer.asp.

Maumee Municipal Court www.maumee.org/municipal/default.htm `Free`
Civil: Online access to web court system database is free at www.maumee.org/municipal/caseinfo.htm. Online includes civil, criminal, traffic. *Criminal:* Same.

Oregon Municipal Court www.ci.oregon.oh.us/ctydpt/court/court.htm `Free`
Civil: Direct email civil search requests to court@ci.oregon.oh.us. Search court cases and schedules free at http://72.241.59.130/connection/court/. *Criminal:* Search court cases and schedules free at http://72.241.59.130/connection/court/.

Sylvania Municipal Court www.sylvaniacourt.com `Free`
Civil: Online access free at http://72.240.45.101/. *Criminal:* same.

Toledo Municipal Court www.tmc-clerk.com `Free`
Civil: Daily dockets are online at www.tmc-clerk.com/case/default.asp. Direct email requests to tmc-clerk@noris.org *Criminal:* Daily dockets are online at www.tmc-clerk.com/case/default.asp. Direct email requests to tmc-clerk@noris.org.

Madison County

Common Pleas Court www.co.madison.oh.us/10206.html `Free`
Civil: Search probate records (but no civil records) at http://12.32.69.179/Search/.

Madison County Municipal Court www.co.madison.oh.us/10227.html `Free`
Civil: Access civil case record free at www.madisonmunict.com/search.shtml. Shows case number, docket entry, charge, case type. *Criminal:* Access criminal case record free at www.madisonmunict.com/search.shtml. Shows case number, docket entry, charge, case type.

Mahoning County

Common Pleas Court www.mahoningcountyoh.gov/tabid/810/default.aspx `Free`
Civil: For online access, see criminal section. *Criminal:* Access integrated justice system cases back to 1995 free at http://courts.mahoningcountyoh.gov/. Attorney searching also available.

County Court #2 www.mahoningcountyoh.gov/tabid/810/default.aspx `Free`
Civil: For online access, see criminal section. *Criminal:* Access integrated justice system cases back to 1995 free at http://courts.mahoningcountyoh.gov/. Attorney searching also available.

County Court #3 www.mahoningcountyoh.gov/tabid/810/default.aspx `Free`
Civil: For online access, see criminal section *Criminal:* Access integrated justice system cases back to 1995 free at http://courts.mahoningcountyoh.gov/. Attorney searching also available.

County Court #4 www.mahoningcountyoh.gov/tabid/810/default.aspx `Free`
Civil: For online access, see criminal section. *Criminal:* Access integrated justice system cases back to 1995 free at http://courts.mahoningcountyoh.gov/. Attorney searching also available.

County Court #5 www.mahoningcountyoh.gov/tabid/810/default.aspx `Free`
Civil: For online access, see criminal section. *Criminal:* Access integrated justice system cases back to 1995 free at http://courts.mahoningcountyoh.gov/. Attorney searching also available.

Struthers Municipal Court www.cityofstruthers.com/city_gov/court.htm `Free`
Civil: Access court records at http://74.219.105.102/searchMC.shtml - records go back to 1996. *Criminal:* same.

Youngstown Municipal Court - Criminal Records www.youngstownmuniclerk.com/ `Free`
Criminal: Access integrated justice system cases back to 1995 free at http://courts.mahoningcountyoh.gov/. Attorney searching also available.

Marion County

Common Pleas Court   http://mcoprx.co.marion.oh.us/
Civil: Access online by the end of 2008. *Criminal:* same.

Marion Municipal Court   www.marionmunicipalcourt.org   **Free**
 Criminal: Online case searching to be available at the website.

Medina County

Common Pleas Court   www.medinacommonpleas.com   **Free**
Civil: Online access is the same as criminal, see below. *Criminal:* Search court documents, motion dockets, sexual predator judgments and court notices at the web page.

Medina Municipal Court   www.medinamunicipalcourt.org   **Free**
Civil: Access the online Civil Case Lookup free at http://206.183.7.90/connection/court/index.xsp. *Criminal:* Access the online Criminal and Traffic Case Lookup free at http://206.183.7.90/connection/court/index.xsp.

Wadsworth Municipal Court   www.wadsworthmunicipalcourt.com/main.htm   **Free**
Civil: Access civil case lookups and case queries free at www.wadsworthmunicipalcourt.com/index.php?folder=1&page=45.
Criminal: Online access to criminal case and traffic lookups and case queries is the same as civil, see above.

Meigs County

Meigs County Municipal Court   **Free**
Civil: Access civil records free at http://docket.webxsol.com/meigs/index.html. *Criminal:* samel.

Miami County

Miami County Municipal Court   www.co.miami.oh.us/muni/index.htm   **Free**
Civil: Online access to records is free at www.co.miami.oh.us/pa/index.htm. *Criminal:* same.

Montgomery County

Common Pleas Court   www.clerk.co.montgomery.oh.us   **Free**
Civil: Online access to the Courts countywide PRO system is free at www.clerk.co.montgomery.oh.us/legal/records.cfm. Access probate court-related records free at www.mcohio.org/revize/montgomery/government/probate/prodcfm/casesearchx.cfm. *Criminal:* Same.

County Court - Area 1   www.clerk.co.montgomery.oh.us   **Free**
Civil: Search countywide records online at www.clerk.co.montgomery.oh.us/. *Criminal:* Same.

County Court - Area 2   www.mcohio.org/revize/montgomery/government/clerkofcourts/index.html   **Free**
Civil: Search countywide records online at www.clerk.co.montgomery.oh.us/. *Criminal:* Same.

Dayton Municipal Court - Civil Division   www.daytonmunicipalcourt.org   **Free**
Civil: Online access to Municipal court records free at www.daytonmunicipalcourt.org/scripts/rgw.dll/Docket; includes traffic and criminal.

Dayton Municipal Court - Criminal Division   www.daytonmunicipalcourt.org   **Free**
Criminal: Online access to municipal court records is free at www.daytonmunicipalcourt.org/scripts/rgw.dll/Docket; includes traffic and civil.

Kettering Municipal Court   www.ketteringmunicipalcourt.com   **Free**
Civil: Access case lookups and calendars free at http://caselookup.ketteringmunicipalcourt.com/connection/court/. *Criminal:* Online access same as civil, see above.

Miamisburg Municipal Court   www.miamisburgcourts.com   **Free**
Civil: Access case lookup options and case schedules for free at http://64.56.106.117/connection/court/. *Criminal:* same.

Vandalia Municipal Court   www.vandaliacourt.com   **Free**
Civil: Search records, including traffic, at http://docket.vandaliacourt.com/. *Criminal:* same.

Dayton Municipal Court - Traffic Division   www.daytonmunicipalcourt.org   **Free**
Criminal: Online access to municipal court records is free at www.daytonmunicipalcourt.org/scripts/rgw.dll/Docket; includes traffic, felony, and civil.

Muskingum County

Common Pleas Court   http://cpc.muskingumcounty.org/   **Free**
Civil: Online access to court records is available at http://clerkofcourts.muskingumcounty.org/PA/. Records indexed back to 1994.
Criminal: Online access to criminal index is same as civil, above.

County Court   www.muskingumcountycourt.org   **Free**
Civil: Access to county court records is free at www.muskingumcountycourt.org/sear.html. *Criminal:* same.

Zanesville Municipal Court   www.coz.org/municipal_court.cfm   `Free`
Civil: Online access free at http://74.219.84.227/searchMC.shtml *Criminal:* Online access is free at http://74.219.84.227/searchMC.shtml and includes traffic and civil searching.

Ottawa County

Common Pleas Court   www.ottawacocpcourt.com   `Free`
Civil: Record search and dockets free at http://65.209.149.134/search.shtml. *Criminal:* same.

Ottawa County Municipal Court   www.ottawacountymunicipalcourt.com   `Free`
Civil: Search record index is at www.ottawacountymunicipalcourt.com/search.html. Includes small claims. *Criminal:* Search records at www.ottawacountymunicipalcourt.com/search.html. Includes traffic.

Paulding County

County Court   www.pauldingcountycourt.com   `Free`
Civil: Access to civil records is free at www.pauldingcountycourt.com/Search/index.shtml. *Criminal:* Access to criminal records is free at www.pauldingcountycourt.com/Search/index.shtml.

Perry County

Perry County Court   www.perrycountycourt.com   `Free`
Civil: Access court records 24 hours after entry for free at www.perrycountycourt.com/Search/. *Criminal:* Online access to criminal records is same as civil.

Pickaway County

Common Pleas Court   www.pickawaycountycpcourt.org   `Free`
Civil: Search docket information at www.pickawaycountycpcourt.org. *Criminal:* Search docket info at www.pickawaycountycpcourt.org.

Circleville Municipal Court   www.circlevillecourt.com   `Free`
Civil: Search online at www.circlevillecourt.com/AccessCourtRecords.asp. *Criminal:* Search at www.circlevillecourt.com/AccessCourtRecords.asp.

Portage County

Common Pleas Court   www.co.portage.oh.us/index.html   `Free`
Civil: For online records from 1992 forward, go to www.co.portage.oh.us/courtsearch.htm. *Criminal:* For records from 1992 forward, go to www.co.portage.oh.us/courtsearch.htm. Direct questions about online access to Kathy Postlethwait at 330-297-3648.

Portage County Municipal Court - Ravenna   www.co.portage.oh.us   `Free`
Civil: Search records back to 1992 free at http://67.39.103.41/courtsearch.htm. *Criminal:* Search records back to 1992 free at http://67.39.103.41/courtsearch.htm. Direct questions about online access to Cindy W. at 330-297-5654.

Portage Municipal Court - Kent Branch   www.co.portage.oh.us   `Free`
Civil: Online records from 1992 forward at www.co.portage.oh.us/. *Criminal:* Records from 1992 forward at www.co.portage.oh.us/. Direct questions about online access to Robyn Godfrey at 330-296-2530.

Preble County

Common Pleas Court   `Free`
Civil: Access to court records and calendars free at www.preblecountyohio.net/. *Criminal:* same.

Eaton Municipal Court   www.eatonmunicipalcourt.com   `Free`
Civil: Search by name or case number free at www.eatonmunicipalcourt.com/docket/index.html. Records back to 1989. *Criminal:* Search by name or case number free at www.eatonmunicipalcourt.com/docket/index.html. Computerized records begin in 1992 for online civil, criminal and traffic cases.

Putnam County

Common Pleas Court   www.putnamcountycourtsohio.com/   `Free`
Civil: Online access is free at www.putnamcountycourtsohio.com/. *Criminal:* same.

Putnam County Court   `Free`
Civil: Online access is free at www.putnamcountycourtsohio.com/. *Criminal:* same.

Richland County

Common Pleas Court   www.richlandcountyoh.us/coc.htm   `Free`
Civil: Access to civil records is at www.richlandcountyoh.us/courtv.htm. *Criminal:* Access to criminal dockets at www.richlandcountyoh.us/courtv.htm.

Mansfield Municipal Court   www.ci.mansfield.oh.us/   `Free`
Civil: Online access at http://docket.webxsol.com/mansfield/index.html for records from 1992 forward. *Criminal:* same.

Ross County

Common Pleas Court   www.co.ross.oh.us   `Free`
Civil: Search records back to 11/89 at the website. *Criminal:* same.

Chillicothe Municipal Court   www.chillicothemunicipalcourt.org   `Free`
Civil: Search docket information at http://216.201.21.130/Search/. *Criminal:* Search docket info at http://216.201.21.130/Search/.

Sandusky County

Common Pleas Court   `Free`
Criminal: Access misdemeanor traffic and criminal data free at www.sandusky-county.org/Clerk/Clerk_of_Courts/sccoc/search.php.

County Court #1   www.sandusky-county.org   `Free`
Criminal: Access misdemeanor traffic and criminal data free at www.sandusky-county.org/Clerk/Clerk_of_Courts/sccoc/search.php.

County Court #2   www.sandusky-county.org   `Free`
Criminal: Access misdemeanor traffic and criminal data free at www.sandusky-county.org/Clerk/Clerk_of_Courts/sccoc/search.php.

Fremont Municipal Court   `Free`
 Criminal: Access misdemeanor traffic and criminal data free at www.sandusky-county.org/Clerk/Clerk_of_Courts/sccoc/search.php.

Scioto County

Common Pleas Court   www.sciotocountycpcourt.org   `Free`
Civil: Online access to civil records back to 1/1986 is free at www.sciotocountycpcourt.org/search.htm. Search by court calendar, quick index, general index or docket sheet. *Criminal:* Same.

Portsmouth Municipal Court   www.pmcourt.org   `Free`
Civil: Access is free at www.pmcourt.org/disc.html. *Criminal:* Access criminal records online free at www.pmcourt.org/disc.html.

Seneca County

Common Pleas Court   www.senecaco.org/clerk/default.html   `Free`
Civil: Search dockets online at www.senecaco.org/clerk/default.html. Click on Internet Inquiry. *Criminal:* same.

Tiffin Municipal Court   `Free`
Civil: Access records free at www.tiffinmunicipalcourt.org/search.shtml. *Criminal:* same.

Stark County

Common Pleas Court - Civil Division   www.starkclerk.org   `Free`
Civil: Online access to the county online case docket database is free at www.starkcourt.org/docket/index.html. Search by name or case number.

Common Pleas Court - Criminal Division   www.starkclerk.org   `Free`
Criminal: Online access to county case docket database is free at www.starkcourt.org/docket/index.html. Search by name, case number.

Alliance Municipal Court   www.alliancecourt.org/   `Free`
Civil: Search the Online Case Docket of the Alliance Court at www.starkcountycjis.org/cjis2/docket/main.html *Criminal:* Search the Online Case Docket of the Alliance Court at www.starkcountycjis.org/cjis2/docket/main.html includes traffic and misdemeanor records.

Canton Municipal Court   www.cantoncourt.org   `Free`
Civil: Search docket information at www.cantoncourt.org/docket.html. *Criminal:* Search docket info at www.cantoncourt.org/docket.html. Includes traffic.

Massillon Municipal Court   www.massilloncourt.org   `Free`
Civil: Search the Online Case Docket of the Massillon Court at www.massilloncourt.org. *Criminal:* Search the Online Case Docket of the Massillon Court at the website, includes traffic and misdemeanor records. Traffic can be reached at 330-830-1732.

Summit County

Common Pleas Court   www.cpclerk.co.summit.oh.us   `Free`
Civil: Access to county clerk of courts records is free at www.cpclerk.co.summit.oh.us. Click on "Case Search." Access to probate records at http://summitohioprobate.com/pa/pa.urd/pamw6500*display. *Criminal:* same .

Akron Municipal Court   http://courts.ci.akron.oh.us   `Free`
Civil: Online access to court records is free at http://courts.ci.akron.oh.us/disclaimer.htm. *Criminal:* same.

Barberton Municipal Court   www.cityofbarberton.com/clerkofcourts   `Free`
Civil: Online records for Barberton, Green, Norton, Franklin, Clinton, Copley and Coventry are free at http://24.123.45.19/. *Criminal:* same.

Cuyahoga Falls Municipal Court www.cfmunicourt.com `Free`
Civil: Court docket information is free at the website. *Criminal:* same.

Trumbull County

Common Pleas Court www.clerk.co.trumbull.oh.us `Free`
Civil: Online access to court records is free at www.clerk.co.trumbull.oh.us/search/search.htm. Records go back to May, 1996. Online access to probate court records is free at www.trumbullprobate.org/paccessfront.htm. *Criminal:* Same.

Girard Municipal Court `Free`
Civil: Access available with username and password at www.girardmunicipalcourt.com -contact clerk of court. *Criminal:* same.

Newton Falls Municipal Court www.newtonfallscourt.com `Free`
Civil: Search record index free at www.newtonfallscourt.com/Search/. *Criminal:* same.

Tuscarawas County

Common Pleas Court www.co.tuscarawas.oh.us `Free`
Civil: Search dockets online at www.co.tuscarawas.oh.us/ClerkofCourts/DocketSearch.htm. *Criminal:* Search dockets online at www.co.tuscarawas.oh.us/ClerkofCourts/DocketSearch.htm.

County Court www.tusccourtsouthern.com/ `Free`
Civil: Search records free at http://64.5.189.247/. Warrants are also available on the court website. *Criminal:* same.

Union County

Common Pleas Court www.co.union.oh.us/ `Free`
Civil: Online access to the court clerk's public records and index is free at http://www3.co.union.oh.us/clerkofcourts/. Records go back to 1/1990, older records added as accessed. Images go back to 1/2002. *Criminal:* Online access to court clerk's public record and index is free at http://www3.co.union.oh.us/clerkofcourts/. Records go back to 1/1990, older records added as accessed. Images go back to 1/2002.

Warren County

Common Pleas Court www.co.warren.oh.us/clerkofcourt/ `Free`
Civil: Access to court records is free at www.co.warren.oh.us/clerkofcourt/search/index.htm. Index goes back to 1980. *Criminal:* same.

County Court www.co.warren.oh.us/countycourt/ `Free`
Civil: Search court records on the Courtview system free at http://countycourt.co.warren.oh.us/pa/. Online records go back to 1990; no DOBs on civil results. *Criminal:* Search court records on the Courtview system free at http://countycourt.co.warren.oh.us/pa/. Online records go back to 1990.

Mason Municipal Court www.masonmunicipalcourt.org `Free`
Civil: Online access to court records is free at http://courtconnect.masonmunicipalcourt.org/connection/court/. *Criminal:* same.

Washington County

Marietta Municipal Court www.mariettacourt.com `Free`
Civil: Online access to from 1992 of court dockets is free at www.mariettacourt.com. *Criminal:* Same.

Wayne County

Common Pleas Court www.wayneohio.org/index.html `Free`
Civil: Online access same as criminal, see below. *Criminal:* Online access free at www.wayneohio.org/public_access.php; probate index included.

Wayne County Municipal Court Clerk www.wayneohio.org/clerkofcourts/municipal.html `Free`
Civil: Online access is same as criminal, see below. *Criminal:* Online access free at www.wayneohio.org/public_access.php.

Williams County

Bryan Municipal Court www.bryanmunicipalcourt.com `Free`
Civil: Muni Ct data available free at www.bryanmunicipalcourt.com/search_courtrecords.asp. *Criminal:* same.

Wood County

Common Pleas Court `Free`
Civil: Access court index free at https://pub.clerkofcourt.co.wood.oh.us/pa/. *Criminal:* same.

Bowling Green Municipal Court www.bgcourt.org `Free`
Civil: Access is free to civil records at http://bgcourtweb.bgohio.org/connection/court/. *Criminal:* Free access to criminal and traffic records from http://bgcourtweb.bgohio.org/connection/court/.

Perrysburg Municipal Court www.perrysburgcourt.com `Free`
Civil: Online access to court records is free at www.perrysburgcourt.com/disc.html. *Criminal:* same.

Wyandot County

Common Pleas Court   www.co.wyandot.oh.us/clerk/index.html   `Free`
Civil: Click on "Common Pleas Inquiry" form web page to view record index. *Criminal:* Click on "Common Pleas Inquiry" at web page to view record index.

Recorders, Assessors, and Other Sites of Note

Recording Office Organization: 88 counties, 88 recording offices. The recording officer is the County Recorder. State tax liens are managed by the Clerk of Common Pleas Court. Federal tax liens are filed in the "Official Records" of each county. All federal tax liens are filed with the County Recorder where the property is located. All state tax liens are filed with the Clerk of Common Pleas Court.

Online Access Note: A growing number of Ohio counties offer internet access to assessor/real estate data, usually free.

Adams County   *Property, Taxation Records*   `Free`   Access the treasurer and auditor property tax data free at http://adamspropertymax.governmaxa.com/propertymax/rover30.asp.

Allen County   *Real Estate, Deed, Mortgage, Lien Records*   www.co.allen.oh.us/rec.php   `Free`   Access recorder index and images free after registration, username and password at http://recorder.allencountyohio.com/ext/logon.asp. Contact the clerk office for sign-up or get user agreement info at www.co.allen.oh.us/rec.php.
Property, Taxation Records   `Free`   Access to the auditor property data is free at http://oh-allen-auditor.governmaxa.com/propertymax/rover30.asp.

Ashland County   *Property, Taxation Records*   `Free`   Access property records and sales on the Auditor's database free at www.ashlandcoauditor.org/propertymax/rover30.asp.

Ashtabula County   *Real Estate, Deed Records*   www.co.ashtabula.oh.us   `Free`   Search real estate data back to 1/1984 at www.landaccess.com.   *Property, Taxation Records*   `Free`   Property records on the county Auditor's database are free at www.ashtabulacountyauditor.org/propertymax/rover30.asp.

Athens County   *Real Estate, Deed, UCC, Lien, Mortgage Records*   www.athenscountygovernment.com   `Free`   Access to county land and UCC records is free at www.landaccess.com. Records go back to 1/1981.
Property, Taxation Records   `Free`   Search the GIS mapping site by name at http://132.235.241.200/website/athens_v1/viewer.htm.

Auglaize County   *Real Estate, Deed, Lien, UCC Records*   `Free`   Search recorder data free at www.landaccess.com/sites/oh/disclaimer.php?county=auglaize. Records from 1/11950 forward.
Property, Taxation Records   `Free`   Look-up assessor property tax data free at www.auglaizeauditor.ddti.net/.

Belmont County   *Real Estate, Deed, Mortgage Records*   www.belmontcountyohio.org   `Free`   Access to recorder deed data is free at www.landaccess.com/sites/oh/disclaimer.php?county=belmont.
Property, Taxation Records   `Free`   Online access to property records free at www.belmontcountyohio.org/auditor.htm. Also, search auditor records at http://belmontpropertymax.governmaxa.com/propertymax/rover30.asp.

Brown County   *Real Estate, Deed, UCC Records*   `Free`   Access to recordings is free at www.landaccess.com/sites/oh/disclaimer.php?county=brown.
Property, Taxation Records   `Free`   Visit www.browncountygis.com/PUBLIC-MAP/PUBLICMAP.HTM for parcel information and maps.

Butler County   *Real Estate, Deed, UCC, Probate, Voter Registration, Vendor Records*   http://66.117.197.5/recorder/
`Free & $$`   Access county land and UCC records free at www.landaccess.com. Records go back to 1/1987. Also, www.butlercountyohio.org/recorder/index.cfm?page=regLand_search offers access to recorded documents free; no images available. Login as Guest. Also, county voter records are at www.butlercountyelections.org/index.cfm?page=voterSearch. Also, search county vendors lists free at www.butlercountyauditor.org/index.cfm?page=vl_search.   *Property, Taxation Records*   `Free`   Search auditor property records free at http://propertysearch.butlercountyohio.org/butler/Main/Home.aspx. Search tax bills/payments by name free at https://epay.butlercountyohio.org/payment/portal.exe. The sheriff's tax sale list is at www.butlersheriff.org.

Carroll County   *Real Estate, Deed Records*   www.carrollcountyohio.us/recorder.html   `Free`   Free access to recorded documents back to 1/1990 at www.landaccess.com.
Property, Taxation Records   `Free`   Access to the Auditor's property data is free at http://carrollpropertymax.governmaxa.com/propertymax/rover30.asp.

Champaign County *Property, Taxation Records* `Free` Online access to property records is free at http://champaignoh.ddti.net/.

Clark County *Real Estate, Deed, UCC Records* www.co.clark.oh.us/ `Free` Access to county land and UCC records is free at www.landaccess.com. Records go back to 1/1988.

Clermont County *Real Estate, Deed, UCC, Property, Sex Offender, Child Support Records* http://recorder.co.clermont.oh.us `Free` Access to the recorder's property, deed, and UCC records at www.landaccess.com. *Property, Taxation Records* `Free` Records from the auditor's county property database are free at www.clermontauditorrealestate.org.

Clinton County *Property, Taxation Records* `Free` Access the Auditor's property database including weekly sales for free at http://clintonoh.ddti.net/PropertySearch/Home.aspx. Access deed references alphabetically by name at www.clintoncountyohgis.org/DeedReferences.htm.

Columbiana County *Real Estate, Deed, UCC Records* www.columbianacounty.org `Free` Access the recorder index of official records back to 1993 and financing statements back to 3/1995 free at www.ccclerk.org/resolution/default.asp. *Property, Taxation Records* `Free` Access property records and tax sale land on the Auditor's database free at www.columbianacntyauditor.org/propertymax/rover30.asp.

Coshocton County *Real Estate, Deed, UCC Records* www.co.coshocton.oh.us `Free` Access to county land and UCC records is free at www.landaccess.com. Records go back to 1/1980. Registration required. *Property, Taxation Records* `Free` Search property tax records for free at www.coshcoauditor.org; click on "Property Search."

Crawford County *Property, Taxation Records* `Free` Access the auditor database free at www.crawford-co.org/auditor/default.html. Access to GIS-mapping for free at http://gis.crawford-co.org/giswebsite/viewer.htm.

Cuyahoga County *Real Estate, Deed, Lien, Probate, Marriage, Death Records* http://recorder.cuyahogacounty.us `Free` Access the Recorders database free at http://recorder.cuyahogacounty.us/Searchs/GeneralSearchs.aspx; includes land documents from 1810-2006. Also, search 22 categories of Probate records including marriages free at http://probate.cuyahogacounty.us/pa/. *Property, Taxation Records* `Free` Search the auditor property tax database free at http://auditor.cuyahogacounty.us/repi/default.asp. Access vendors list at https://auditor.cuyahogacounty.us/genservices/vendorList_report.asp. Also, a private company sells county tax claim property, view list free at www.xspand.com/investors/realestate_sale/index.aspx

Darke County *Property, Taxation Records* `Free` Property and property tax records on the Darke County database are free at http://darkepropertymax.governmax.com/propertymax/rover30.asp?.

Defiance County *Property, Taxation Records* `Free` Access auditor real estate data free at http://66.194.132.17/. Also search weekly property sales.

Delaware County *Real Estate, Deed, UCC Records* www.co.delaware.oh.us `Free` Access to the Recorder's data plus UCCs is free at www.landaccess.com. *Property, Taxation Records* `Free` Access to auditor's property and sales data is free at www.delawarecountyauditor.org/propertymax/rover30.asp?.

Erie County *Real Estate, Deed Records* www.erie-county-ohio.net `Free` Access recorded documents free at www.co-erie-oh-us-recorder.com. Click on Document Search. *Property, Taxation Records* `Free` Access the auditor property database including weekly sales for free at www.erie.iviewtaxmaps.com/PropertySearch/Home.aspx

Fairfield County *Real Estate, Deed, UCC Records* www.co.fairfield.oh.us `Free` Access to county land and UCC records is free at www.landaccess.com. Records go back to 08/96. Also, access to the sheriff's real estate sale list at www.sheriff.fairfield.oh.us/. *Property, Taxation Records* `Free` Access to the Auditor's property and sales database is free at http://realestate.co.fairfield.oh.us/. Also, access to the sheriff's real estate sale list at www.sheriff.fairfield.oh.us/.

Fayette County *Real Estate, Deed, Lien Records* www.fayette-co-oh.com `Free` Access to recorders index database is free at www.landaccess.com. Images go back to 5/20/02. *Property, Taxation Records* `Free` Access the auditor's database for property data at http://fayettepropertymax.governmax.com/propertymax/rover30.asp.

Franklin County *Real Estate, Deed, Marriage Records* www.co.franklin.oh.us/recorder/ `Free` Access to the recorded data is free at www.co.franklin.oh.us/recorder/documents.html. Free registration required. Search marriage licenses back to 1995 at www.co.franklin.oh.us/recorder/. Other county/municipal databases are free at www.co.franklin.oh.us.

Property, Taxation Records Free & $$ Auditor's property data is at http://franklin.governmaxa.com/propertymax/rover30.asp. Access auditor's GIS-data site with property lookup, history, and more free at http://209.51.193.83/.

Fulton County *Real Estate, Deed, UCC Records* www.fultoncountyoh.com Free Access to property, deed, and UCC records is to be free at www.landaccess.com/sites/oh/disclaimer.php?county=ohfulton.
Property, Taxation Records Free Search auditor property data free at http://66.194.132.76/.

Gallia County *Property, Taxation Records* Free Property records on the county auditor real estate database are free at http://galliaauditor.ddti.net. Click on "attributes" for property data; click on "sales" to search by real estate attributes.

Geauga County *Property, Taxation Records* Free Search the Auditor's property database at www.co.geauga.oh.us/. Search the sheriff's tax sale lists for free at www.sheriff.geauga.oh.us.

Greene County *Real Estate, Grantor/Grantee, Deed, Mortgage, Marriage, Probate Records* www.co.greene.oh.us/recorder.htm Free Access to the recorders data is free at www.co.greene.oh.us/recorder/documentSearch.asp. Also, search marriages free at www.co.greene.oh.us/Probate/search/marriageLic.asp. Search probate cases at www.co.greene.oh.us/Probate/search/case_search.asp.
Property, Taxation Records Free Assessor data free at www.co.greene.oh.us/website/gcMaps/. Also, records on the county Internet Map Server are free at www.co.greene.oh.us/gismapserver.htm. Data includes owner, address, valuation, taxes, sales data, and parcel ID number.

Guernsey County *Marriage, Birth, Probate, Will Records* Free Access to court-related records free at http://74.218.3.68/pa/.

Hamilton County *Real Estate, Deed, Lien, Mortgage, UCC, Marriage, Military Discharge, Partnership, Subdivision Records* http://recordersoffice.hamilton-co.org Free Access to recorder land records is free at http://recordersoffice.hamilton-co.org/hcro-pdi/index.jsp. Search the marriage license database at www.probatect.org/case_search/mlsearch.asp. Also, search probate records back to 1/2000 at www.probatect.org/case_search/casesearch.asp.
Property, Taxation Records Free Access to the auditor's tax records database is free at www.hamiltoncountyauditor.org/realestate/.

Hancock County *Real Estate, Deed, UCC Records* http://co.hancock.oh.us/recorder/recorder.htm Free Access to recorder records is free at www.landaccess.com. Index goes back to 1986; images to 12/19/2000.
Property, Taxation Records Free Search the auditor's property database free at http://hancock.iviewauditor.com. No name searching.

Hardin County *Property, Taxation Records* Free Access property records from the auditor's database free at www.co.hardin.oh.us. Click on "Real Estate Internet Inquiry." Also, search property data on the GIS-mapping site at http://hcgis.com. Use QuickSearch.

Henry County *Real Estate, Deed, Lien Records* www.henrycountyohio.com Free Access recorder data free at www.landaccess.com/sites/oh/disclaimer.php?county=ohhenry.
Property, Taxation Records Free Access and search property data free at www.co.henry.oh.us/. Click on "Real Estate Internet Inquiry." Also, search sheriff sales list for free at www.henrycountysheriff.com.

Highland County *Real Estate, Deed, UCC Records* Free Access to recorders database is free at www.landaccess.com/sites/oh/disclaimer.php?county=highland.
Property, Taxation Records Free Access and search property data free at http://highlandpropertymax.governmaxa.com. Click on "start your search" to begin. Search auditor's tax and sales data for free at www.co.highland.oh.us/. The sheriff's sales lists are free at www.highlandcoso.com/rso.htm.

Hocking County *Property, Taxation Records* Free Access to the auditor's real estate data and dog tag ownership is free at www.co.hocking.oh.us/auditor/default.html.

Holmes County *Property, Taxation Records* Free Access the auditor's property data and sales free at www.holmescountyauditor.org.

Huron County *Real Estate, Deed, Lien, UCC Records* www.huroncountyrecorder.org Free Search the recorder's land records free at www.huroncountyrecorder.org.
Property, Taxation Records Free Access to the auditor data and property sales is free at www.huroncountyauditor.org.

Jackson County *Property, Taxation Records* Free Access property and sales data free at www.jacksoncountyauditor.org/Disclaimer.aspx.

Jefferson County *Voter Registration Records* Free Search voter names free at www.voterfind.com/public/ohjefferson/pages/vtrlookup.asp

Property, Taxation Records **Free** Access to the county auditor property data is free at http://public.jeffersoncountyoh.com/realtax/. Also, download real estate data from the auditor's database free at http://public.jeffersoncountyoh.com/tax/realdown.htm. Access the sheriff, treasurer, and auditor foreclosure sales lists free at www.jeffersoncountyoh.com/cgi-bin/template.pl?sheriff/sheriff.html.

Knox County *Real Estate, Deed, UCC, Plat, Map Records* www.recorder.co.knox.oh.us **Free**
Access index records free at www.recorder.co.knox.oh.us/Resolution/default.asp.
Property, Taxation Records **Free** Online access to property records is available at http://www.knoxcountyauditor.org/.

Lake County *Real Estate, Deed, Lien, UCC Records* www.lakecountyrecorder.org/recorders/ **Free** Access the
Recorder's Document Index free at http://www2.lakecountyohio.org/RecordersNewSearch/Search.aspx. Records go back to 1986. UCCs are index only. Images of documents not available.
Property, Taxation Records **Free** Access to the treasurer and auditor's real estate databases is free at www.lake.iviewauditor.com.

Lawrence County *Real Estate, Deed, Lien, Mortgage Records* www.lawrencecountyohiorecorder.org **Free**
Access to the recorders database is free at www.lawrencecountyohiorecorder.org/record_search.htm. Deeds go back to 1982; mortgages to 1988; liens back to 1981.
Property, Taxation Records **Free** Search the auditor's data free at www.lawrencecountyauditor.org.

Licking County *Real Estate, Deed, Lien Records* www.lcounty.com/rec/ **Free** Access to the recorders database is
free at www.lcounty.com/recordings/. Records with images go back to 1984.
Property, Taxation Records **Free** Access the Assessor's county property database free at www.lcounty.com/itrac/feedback.php .

Logan County *Real Estate, Deed, Lien, Delinquent Property, Jail Inmate, Sex Offender Records*
www.co.logan.oh.us/recorder/index.html **Free** Access to the recorders database is free at http://www3.co.logan.oh.us/recordmax401/record40.asp. Click on "Document Search." Treasurer's delinquent property tax lists free at www.co.logan.oh.us/Treasurer/Delinquent_Real.htm
Property, Taxation Records **Free** Records on the County Auditor's database are free at http://lcaweb.co.logan.oh.us/aweb/. Also, search the sheriff's sales lists at www.co.logan.oh.us/sheriff/sales.htm.

Lorain County *Real Estate, Deed, Lien Records* http://loraincounty.com/recorder **Free** Access the county Indexed
Records database at http://162.39.12.36/qGov/Main/Index.aspx. Free registration is required or login as Guest.
Property, Taxation Records **Free** Access property records and sales on the County Auditor's database for free at http://oh-lorain-auditor.governmaxa.com/propertymax/rover30.asp. Search sheriff sales lists for free at www.loraincountysheriff.com.

Lucas County *Real Estate, Deed Records* www.co.lucas.oh.us/ **Free** Access to recorder real estate records is free
with registration at www.co.lucas.oh.us/Recordings/.
Property, Taxation Records **Free** Property records on the County Auditor's Real Estate Information System (AREIS) database are free at www.co.lucas.oh.us/real_estate/AREISmain/areismain.asp.

Madison County *Real Estate, Deed, UCC Records* www.co.madison.oh.us **Free** Access recorder's office records
free at www.co.madison.oh.us/436/41301.html or www.landaccess.com/sites/oh/disclaimer.php?county=madison. Records go back to 5/1994.
Property, Taxation Records **Free** Access records on the County Auditor's database free at www.co.madison.oh.us/373/24285.html. Also, access to the sheriff's sale list is at www.madisonsheriff.org.

Mahoning County *Real Estate, Deed, UCC, Lien, Judgment Records* www.mahoningcountyoh.gov/MahoningWeb
Free Access to recorder's property, deed, and UCC records is to be free at www.co.madison.oh.us/436/41301.html. Records go back to 1985.
Property, Taxation Records **Free** Property tax records on the Auditor's database are free at http://ohmahoningpropertymax.governmaxa.com/propertymax/rover30.asp. Also, access property data free on the GIS site at http://gis.mahoningcountyoh.gov/gis/asp.htm.

Marion County *Real Estate, Grantor/Grantee, Deed, Lien, Plat, UCC, Partnership Records* www.co.marion.oh.us
Free Access the recorders index after registration at http://recorder.co.marion.oh.us/resolution/. Official records go back to 1983; UCCs to 1990; plats back to 1820.
Property, Taxation Records **Free** Access to the county auditor real estate database is free at www.co.marion.oh.us/auditor/index1.htm. Click on "Real Estate Internet Inquiry." Also, access the sheriff sales list free at www.co.marion.oh.us/sheriffsales/public_view.asp.

Medina County *Real Estate, Deed, Mortgage Records* www.recorder.co.medina.oh.us **Free** Access to indexes
1983 to present on the recorder database is free at www.recorder.co.medina.oh.us/fcquery.htm. ***Property, Taxation Records***
Free Access property records, dog tags, and unclaimed funds on the Medina County Auditor database free at www.medinacountyauditor.org/allsearches.htm. The sheriff's county tax sale list is at www.medinacountyauditor.org/shersale/.

Mercer County *Real Estate, Deed, Lien, Mortgage, Judgment, UCC Records* www.mercercountyohio.org/recorder/
`Free` Accesss recorder data free at http://www2.mercercountyohio.org/oncoreweb42/
Property, Taxation Records `Free` Access property records on County Auditor Real Estate database free at www.mercercountyohio.org/auditor/ParcelSearch/.

Miami County *Property, Taxation Records* `Free` Access auditor data free at www.miamicountyauditor.org.

Monroe County *Property, Taxation Records* `SS` A commercial subscription program is available from the Auditor's office at http://monroecountyauditor.org. Call first to register, 740-472-0873; $15 fee per month fee applies.

Montgomery County *Real Estate, Deed, Lien, Probate, Estate, Marriage, Trade Name, Vendor License Records* www.mcrecorder.org `Free` Access to the recorders data is free at www.mcrecorder.org/search_selection.cfm. Search Probate-related records free at www.mcohio.org/revize/montgomery/government/probate/prodcfm/casesearchx.cfm
Property, Taxation Records `Free` Search auditor's property data and GIS-data free at www.mcrealestate.org/Main/Home.aspx. Property tax records on the county treasurer tax information database are free at www.mctreas.org. Also, search auditor's trade name and vendor license free at www.mcauditor.org/VEN_list.cfm?letter=D. Also, search sheriff sales at www.co.montgomery.oh.us/Sheriff/.

Morgan County *Property, Taxation Records* `Free` Access the auditor property data free at http://morgancountyauditor.org. Use Quick search or Attribute Search. Also, search the Engineer website for tax map property data free at www.morganoengineer.com. Click on Tax Maps.

Morrow County *Property, Taxation Records* `Free` Access to the county auditor database is free at http://co.morrow.oh.us/PropertySearch/. Includes property sales data.

Muskingum County *Real Estate, Deed, Line, UCC, Plat Records*
http://recorder.muskingumcounty.org/recorder1024.htm `Free` Access the recorders database free at http://landrecords.muskingumcounty.org/. Official records go back to 1977. Also, the sheriff's site provides sale lists and sex offender data at www.ohiomuskingsheriff.org.
Property, Taxation Records `Free` Records on the county auditor database are free at www.muskingumcountyauditor.org/PropertySearch/Home.aspx. Parcel data and GIS-mapping free at www.muskingumcountyauditor.org/PropertySearch/Home.aspx. Also, the sheriff's site provides sale lists at www.ohiomuskingsheriff.org.

Ottawa County *Property, Taxation Records* `Free` Access to the auditor's property database including sales is free at www.ottawacountyauditor.org/PropertySearch/Home.aspx.

Paulding County *Real Estate, Deed, Lien, UCC Records* `Free` Access recorder data free at www.landaccess.com/sites/oh/disclaimer.php?county=paulding.

Pickaway County *Real Estate, Deed, UCC Records* `Free` Also, search the recorder database free at www.landaccess.com/sites/oh/disclaimer.php?county=pickaway.
Property, Taxation Records `Free` Access to the county auditor property data is free at http://pickaway.iviewauditor.com/PropertySearch/.

Pike County *Real Estate, Deed, Lien, UCC Records* www.ohiorecorders.com/pike.html `Free`
Access to the recorder's database is free at www.landaccess.com/sites/oh/disclaimer.php?county=pike.
Property, Taxation Records `Free` Access auditor databases free at www.pike-co.org/ including assessments, parcels, sales, personal property, dog tags, GIS-mapping. Search sheriff sales lists at www.pikecosheriff.com/

Portage County *Property, Taxation Records* `Free` Access to the auditor's property records and sales is free at http://portagepropertymax.governmaxa.com/propertymax/rover30.asp. Access to the sheriff's property sales list is free at www.co.portage.oh.us.

Preble County *Property, Taxation Records* `Free` Property records on the County Auditor's database are free at www.preblecountyauditor.org/iView.asp.

Richland County *Real Estate, Deed Records* www.richlandcountyauditor.org `Free` Access county land records free at www.landaccess.com. Records go back to 4/1989.
Property, Taxation Records `Free` Property records from the County Auditor database are free at www.richlandcountyauditor.org/Main/home.aspx. Also, search the sheriff sales lists for free at www.sheriffrichlandcounty.com.

Ross County *Real Estate, Deed, UCC Records* www.co.ross.oh.us `Free` Access to county land, recording and UCC records is free at www.landaccess.com. Index goes back to 1/1974.
Property, Taxation Records `Free` Access to the auditor's property and sales data is free at www.co.ross.oh.us/Auditor/PropertySearch/Home.aspx.

Sandusky County *Property, Taxation Records* `Free` Access to county auditor and treasurer property data is free at http://ohsanduskypropertymax.governmaxa.com/propertymax/rover30.asp. Click on "Property Search" and choose to search by name.

Scioto County *Property, Taxation Records* `Free` Access to the auditor's property data is free at www.sciotocountyauditor.org/propertymax/rover30.asp; click on Property Search.

Seneca County *Real Estate, Deed Records* www.landaccess.com `Free` Recorder RE data is accessible at www.landaccess.com.

Shelby County *Property, Taxation Records* `Free` Access sheriff's sale list free at www.shelbycountysheriff.com

Stark County *Real Estate, Deed, Mortgage, Lien, UCC Records* www.co.stark.oh.us/internet/HOME.DisplayPage?v_page=recorder `Free` Access the recorder's database free after registration at http://app.recorder.co.stark.oh.us/Recorder_Disclaimer.htm. Chose simple, advanced or instrument search. *Property, Taxation Records* `Free` Search auditor's property data free at http://66.194.132.64/AccuGlobe/iView.asp. Also, a weekly delinquent taxpayers list is at www.starktaxes.com/list.cgi. Access to sheriff sales lists are at www.sheriff.co.stark.oh.us/RealEstate.htm.

Summit County *Property, Taxation Records* `Free` Access tax map data from the county fiscal officer for free at http://scids.summitoh.net/gis/; choose Interactive Online Tax Map Application, then Parcel search. Also property appraisal, images and tax data are on this site. Also, search property tax bill and appraisal records free at http://megatron.summitoh.net/summit/html/webintg.html. Also, search sheriff tax sale list free at www.co.summit.oh.us/sheriff.

Trumbull County *Real Estate, Deed, Mortgage, Lien Records* www.tcrecorder.co.trumbull.oh.us `Free` Access the recorder's database free at http://69.68.42.167:13131/. *Property, Taxation Records* `Free` Search auditor property tax data free at http://69.68.42.167:7036/propertysearch/ureca_asp/index.htm. Also, search the Sheriff sales list free at www.tclegalnews.com/subscribe/ssa.php

Tuscarawas County *Property, Taxation Records* `Free` County real estate records are free at www.co.tuscarawas.oh.us/tusca208/LandRover.asp. The auditor's delinquent tax list is updated in September.

Union County *Real Estate, Deed, Lien, Mortgage, Judgment, UCC Records* www.co.union.oh.us/Recorder/recorder.html `Free` Search recorded documents at www.co.union.oh.us/GD/Templates/Pages/UC/UCCrumbTrail.aspx?page=70. *Property, Taxation Records* `Free` Access to the Auditors tax assessment/property records database and the appraiser property information database is free at http://www3.co.union.oh.us/PSEngine/. Also search for property data via the GIS mapping site at http://www3.co.union.oh.us/website/pub_webgis/viewer.htm. Also, search the treasurers' list of delinquent taxpayers at http://www2.co.union.oh.us/Treasurer/Default.aspx.

Van Wert County *Real Estate, Deed, UCC Records* www.vanwertcounty.org/recorder/ `Free` Access to county land and UCC records is free at www.landaccess.com. Index go back to 1/1994, copies of document back to May, 1995; earlier records being added. *Property, Taxation Records* `Free` Online access to property records free at www.co.vanwert.oh.us/.

Warren County *Real Estate, Deed, Lien, Sex Offender, Sheriff Sale Records* www.co.warren.oh.us/recorder `Free` Access Recorders records free back to 1979 at www.co.warren.oh.us/recorder. *Property, Taxation Records* `Free` Access to the auditor Property Search database is free at www.co.warren.oh.us/auditor/property_search/index.htm. Also, search sheriff sales records free at www.wcsooh.org/sheriff/search/shfentry.htm.

Washington County *Real Estate, Deed, UCC Records* `Free` Access to records is free at www.landaccess.com/sites/oh/disclaimer.php?county=washington. *Property, Taxation Records* `Free` Access to the county auditor's property search database is free at www.washingtoncountyauditor.org/propertymax/rover30.asp.

Wayne County *Property, Taxation Records* `Free` Access to the auditor's property and sales data is free at www.waynecountyauditor.org. The late taxpayer list appears on the treasurer's website at www.co.wayne.oh.us/LateTaxpayers.aspx.

Williams County *Real Estate, Deed, Lien, UCC Records* www.co.williams.oh.us `Free` Search recorder records free at www.landaccess.com/sites/oh/disclaimer.php?county=williams. *Property, Taxation Records* `Free` Access to the auditor's property data and sales is free at http://williamsoh.ddti.net/.

Wood County *Property, Taxation Records* `Free` Access to the auditor's property data is free at http://auditor.co.wood.oh.us/. No name searching. Also, search the treasurer's tax data for free at http://woodtaxcollector.governmax.com/collectmax/collect30.asp?

Wyandot County *Property, Taxation Records* `Free` Access to the Auditor's real estate database is free at www.co.wyandot.oh.us/auditor/default.html. Click on "Real Estate Internet Inquiry." Also may search dog tags.

Other Ohio Sites of Note:

Allen County - Cemetery, War Casualty, Deaths   www.delphos-ohio.com/cemeteri.htm

Athens County - Inmates   http://xw.textdata.com:81/cgi/progcgi.exe?program=search

Butler County - Registered Vendors   www.butlercountyauditor.org/index.cfm?page=vl_search

Butler County - Tax Sales, Sex Offender   www.butlersheriff.org

Butler County - Voter Registration   www.butlercountyelections.org/index.cfm?page=voterSearch

Clark County - Obituaries   http://guardian.ccpl.lib.oh.us/obits/

Clark County - Sheriff Tax Sales, Sexual Offender, Most Wanted   www.clarkcountysheriff.com

Clermont County - Child Support Lists   www.clermontsupportskids.org

Clermont County - Dog License   www.clermontauditor.org/default.php?section=dogSearch

Clermont County - Sex Offenders   www.clermontsheriff.org/registered_sex_offenders.htm

Coshocton County - Sex Offender   www.coshoctonsheriff.com/sexualpred.cfm

Cuyahoga County - Cemetery   www.geocities.com/micheledanielle/cemetery.html

Cuyahoga County - Licensed Vendors   https://auditor.cuyahogacounty.us/genservices/vendorList_report.asp

Delaware County - Cemeteries   http://delcohist.tripod.com/burials.htm

Delaware County - Dog Tags   https://secure.co.delaware.oh.us/dogtagrenew.htm

Delaware County - DUI Offenders   www.municipalcourt.org/main_dui.asp

Fairfield County - Inmates   http://xw.textdata.com:81/cgi/progcgi.exe?program=search3

Franklin County - City of Columbus - Accident Reports   www.columbuspolice.org/public/   Accident reports dated prior to 2000 are not available on this site.

Gallia County - Sex Offender, Inmate, Most Wanted   www.galliasheriff.org

Geauga County - Sheriff's Sale, Most Wanted, Sex Offender   www.sheriff.geauga.oh.us

Greene County - Sheriff Sales, Sex Offender   www.co.greene.oh.us/sheriff/

Guernsey County - Sex Offenders   www.guernseysheriff.com/geninfo/sexualoffenderinfo.html

Hamilton County - Mental Health Probate Ct Index   www.probatect.org/case_search/mh-case_input.asp

Hamilton County - Sheriff Sales, Most Wanted, Sex Offender, Missing Persons   www.hcso.org

Hancock County - Sex Offender   www.hancocksheriff.org/sheriff2_009.htm

Henry County - Sheriff Sales, Sex Offender   www.henrycountysheriff.com

Highland County - Sex Offender, Sheriff Sales   www.highlandcoso.com

Hocking County - Inmates   http://xw.textdata.com:81/cgi/progcgi.exe?program=search3

Jackson County - Inmates   http://xw.textdata.com:81/cgi/progcgi.exe?program=search3

Jefferson County - Registered Voter   www.voterfind.com/public/ohjefferson/pages/vtrlookup.asp

Lake County - Warrants, Sex Offenders   www.lakecountyohio.org/sheriff/index.htm

Lawrence County - Death   www.lawrencecountyohio.com/deaths/index/   Private site; search by index years.

Licking County - Cemeteries   www.rootsweb.ancestry.com/~cemetery/ohio/licking.htm

Marion County - Sheriff Sales List   www.co.marion.oh.us/sheriffsales/public_view.asp

Marions County - Tax Auction   www.marioncountyohioauctions.com/app/

Montgomery County - Sheriff Sales, Missing Persons, Sex Offenders   www.co.montgomery.oh.us/Sheriff/

Montgomery County - Trade Name, Vendor License   www.mcauditor.org/VEN_list.cfm?letter=D

Morgan County - Inmates   http://xw.textdata.com:81/cgi/progcgi.exe?program=search3

Muskingum County - Sheriff's Sale, Sexual Offender   www.ohiomuskingumsheriff.org

Ottawa County - Cemetery   www.rootsweb.ancestry.com/~cemetery/ohio/ottawa.htm

Perry County - Inmates   http://xw.textdata.com:81/cgi/progcgi.exe?program=search3

Pike County - Inmates   http://xw.textdata.com:81/cgi/progcgi.exe?program=search3

Pike County - Sheriff Sale, Sex Offender   www.pikecosheriff.com/

Richland County - Sheriff Sales, Sex Offender   www.sheriffrichlandcounty.com

Sandusky County - Jail Inmates   www.textdata.com:81/cgi/progcgi.exe?program=search&fid=oh072

Shelby County - Sheriff Sales, Sex Offender   http://shelbycountysheriff.com/disclaimer.asp

Stark County - Sheriff's Sales, Sex Offenders   www.sheriff.co.stark.oh.us

Summit County - Sex Offenders, Most Wanted, Sheriff Sales   www.co.summit.oh.us/sheriff/

Trumbull County - Probate's Unclaimed Funds   www.trumbullprobate.org/UnclaimedFunds.htm

Tuscarawas County - County Court Warrants, Most Wanted   www.tusccourtsouthern.com/main.html

Vinton County - Inmates   http://xw.textdata.com:81/cgi/progcgi.exe?program=search3

Wood County - Obituaries   http://wcdpl.lib.oh.us/databases/obitsearch.asp

Oklahoma

Capital: Oklahoma City
            Oklahoma County
Time Zone: CST
Population: 3,617,316
# of Counties: 77

Useful State Links

Website: www.ok.gov/
Governor: www.governor.state.ok.us
Attorney General: www.oag.state.ok.us
State Archives: www.odl.state.ok.us
State Statutes and Codes: www.lsb.state.ok.us
Legislative Bill Search: www.lsb.state.ok.us
Bill Monitoring: http://www.gov.ok.gov/billtrack/index.php
Unclaimed Funds: https://www.ok.gov/unclaimed/index.php

Primary State Agencies

Sexual Offender Registry `Free`

Oklahoma Department of Corrections, Sex Offender Registry, http://docapp8.doc.state.ok.us/servlet/page?_pageid=422&_dad=portal30&_schema=PORTAL30&id=1 Searching is available from the website. There are a number of search options. A parole status search is available at http://gov.ok.gov/parole/parole_lookup.php. *Other Options:* Database and bulk purchases can be requested from the IT department. Call for pricing and media.

Incarceration Records `Free`

Oklahoma Department of Corrections, Offender Records, www.doc.state.ok.us At the main website, click on Offender Information or visit www.doc.state.ok.us/offenders/offenders.htm. The online system is not available between 3:15 AM to 3:20 AM Monday through Friday, and 3:15 AM to 7:00 AM Saturdays for system maintenance.

Corporation, LLC, LP, LLP, Trade Name, Fictitious Name, Trademark `Free & $$`

Secretary of State, Business Records Department, www.sos.state.ok.us Visit SOONERAccess at https://www.sooneraccess.state.ok.us/home/home-default.asp for free searches on business entities, including registered agents and Trademarks. Customers may also order and receive status certificates as well as certified and plain copies. Fees vary, see the web page for details. There is a list of domestic LLCs. Also, search securities brokers/investment advisors at www.securities.ok.gov/_private/DB_Query/IA_Query/IA_Search_Form.asp. Also securities firms at www.securities.ok.gov/_private/DB_Query/Licensing/IA_Search_FOI.asp.

Uniform Commercial Code `Free`

UCC Central Filing Office, Oklahoma County Clerk, http://countyclerk.oklahomacounty.org/UCC.html Records of all UCC financing statements may be viewed free at http://countyclerk.oklahomacounty.org/UCC-SearchSite.html. Search by debtor or secured party. The site gives a strong disclaimer, their may be significant lag time between the date of filing and the date the record is posted on this site. Neither certified searches nor record requests are accepted at the web page. *Other Options:* The entire database is available on microfilm or computer tapes. The initial history is $500 with $50 per update. Images are available for $.04 per image.

Sales Tax Registrations `Free`

Taxpayer Assistance, Sales Tax Registration Records, www.tax.ok.gov/bustax.html A free tax permit look-up service is provided at www.oktax.onenet.net/permitlookup/. *Other Options:* Current sales tax permit holders are permitted to purchase the sales tax database on microfiche or disk. Monthly updates are available. Call for fees.

Driver Records $$

MVR Desk, Records Management Division, www.dps.state.ok.us/dls/default.htm Online access is available for qualified, approved users through www.ok.gov/. Both a batch mode and interactive processes are offered. The $12.50 fee includes a $2.50 service fee. You will not find information about this program on the web since it is not for the general public. For further information, call 800-955-3468.

Voter Registration Free

State Election Board, Voter Records, www.elections.state.ok.us/ Record requests may be emailed to info@elections.ok.gov *Other Options:* A statewide database can be purchased on CD for a fee of $150. Large counties are available on CD for $50-75, and smaller counties or precincts or district or school district are available on disk for $10-35.

Occupational Licensing Boards

Accounting Firm.................................www.ok.gov/oab/search.php
Alarm Firm/Employee   www.ok.gov/health/documents/20080307_OklaLicAlarmAndLocksmithIndustryIndiv_A-Z.pdf
Architect/Architectural Firm ....https://www.ok.gov/architects/licensee_search.php
Athletic Trainer/Appren.   www.okmedicalboard.org/display.php?content=md_search_advanced:md_search_advanced
Attorney...www.oklahomafindalawyer.com/FindALawyer
Audiologist www.obespa.state.ok.us/License%20Data.htm
Bank ....www.state.ok.us/~osbd
Barber Schools   www.ok.gov/health/documents/OKLAHOMA%20LICENSED%20BARBER%20SCHOOLS_9%2011%2007.pdf
Beauty School...................................www.state.ok.us/~cosmo/schools.html
Chiropractor......................................www.ok.gov/chiropracticboard/Disciplined_Chiropractors/index.html
Counselor LPC/MLFT/LBP www.ok.gov/health/documents/LICENSEE%20SEARCH%20-%20LPC.doc
Credit Services Organization............www.okdocc.state.ok.us/ROSTERS/rosters.php
Credit Union.....................................www.state.ok.us/~osbd
Dental Laboratory.............................www.dentist.state.ok.us/lists/index.htm
Dentist/Dental Assistant/Hygienist....www.dentist.state.ok.us/lists/index.htm
Dietitian/Prov'l Dietitian   www.okmedicalboard.org/display.php?content=md_search_advanced:md_search_advanced
Electrologist   ... ...   www.okmedicalboard.org/display.php?content=md_search_advanced:md_search_advanced
Engineer ....www.pels.state.ok.us/roster/index.html
Health Spa ....www.okdocc.state.ok.us/ROSTERS/rosters.php
Home Inspector ....www.health.state.ok.us/program/ol/homeinspectorlist.pdf
Insurance Agent/Repr.   https://www.sircon.com/ComplianceExpress/Inquiry/consumerInquiry.do?nonSscrb=Y
Landscape Architect ....https://www.ok.gov/architects/licensee_search.php
Lobbyist...www.state.ok.us/~ethics/lobbyist.html
LPG-Liq. Petrol. Dealer/Mfg./Mgr....www.oklpgas.org/search/index.php
Medical Doctor   ...   www.okmedicalboard.org/display.php?content=md_search_advanced:md_search_advanced
Money Order Agent...........................www.state.ok.us/~osbd/
Money Order Company ....www.state.ok.us/~osbd/
Mortgage Broker ....www.okdocc.state.ok.us/ROSTERS/rosters.php
Notary Public....................................https://www.sooneraccess.state.ok.us/notary/notary_search-menu.asp
Nurse Anesthetist, Cert. Register'd....https://www.ok.gov/nursing/verify/index.php
Nurse Midwife..................................https://www.ok.gov/nursing/verify/index.php
Nurse -RN/LPN/all types..................https://www.ok.gov/nursing/verify/index.php
Occ Therapist/Assistant   www.okmedicalboard.org/display.php?content=md_search_advanced:md_search_advanced
Optometrist.......................................www.arbo.org/index.php?action=findanoptometrist
Orthotist/Prosthetist   www.okmedicalboard.org/display.php?content=md_search_advanced:md_search_advanced
Osteopathic Physician.......................www.docboard.org/ok/df/oksearch.htm
Pawnbroker.......................................www.okdocc.state.ok.us/ROSTERS/rosters.php
Pedorthist   www.okmedicalboard.org/display.php?content=md_search_advanced:md_search_advanced
Perfusionist   www.okmedicalboard.org/display.php?content=md_search_advanced:md_search_advanced
Pesticide Applicator/Regis./Dealer....http://kellysolutions.com/ok/
Pharmacist/Pharmacy Intern/Tech.....www.ok.gov/OSBP/License_Verification/index.html
Pharmacy..www.ok.gov/OSBP/License_Verification/index.html
Physical Therapist/Asst   www.okmedicalboard.org/display.php?content=md_search_advanced:md_search_advanced

Physician Assistant ... www.okmedicalboard.org/display.php?content=md_search_advanced:md_search_advanced
Podiatrist ... www.okmedicalboard.org/display.php?content=md_search_advanced:md_search_advanced
Precious Metals & Gem Dealer .... www.okdocc.state.ok.us/ROSTERS/rosters.php
Private Investigator Person/Agency... www.opia.com/find_a_pi/default.asp
Prosthetist ... www.okmedicalboard.org/display.php?content=md_search_advanced:md_search_advanced
Psychologist....................................... https://www.ok.gov/OSBEP/_app/search/index.php
Public Accountant-CPA .... www.ok.gov/oab/search.php
Real Estate Agent/Broker/Seller/Firmwww.orec.ok.gov/licensee_lookup/lookup.php
Registrants Performing Audits/GAS . www.ok.gov/oab/search.php
Rent to Own Dealer .... www.okdocc.state.ok.us/ROSTERS/rosters.php
Respiratory Care Practit'r www.okmedicalboard.org/display.php?content=md_search_advanced:md_search_advanced
Savings & Loan Association .... www.state.ok.us/~osbd/
Social Worker.................................... www.osblsw.state.ok.us/licensee_search.php
Speech Pathologist............................ www.obespa.state.ok.us/License%20Data.htm
Surveyor, Land .... www.pels.state.ok.us/roster/index.html
Trust Company .... www.state.ok.us/~osbd/

State and Local Courts

State Court Structure: There are 82 District Courts in 26 judicial districts. Cities with populations in excess of 200,000 (Oklahoma City and Tulsa) have criminal Municipal Courts of Record. Cities with less than 200,000 do not have such courts.

Statewide Court Online Access: Free Internet access to docket information is available for District Courts in 13 counties and all Appellate courts at www.oscn.net. Both civil and criminal docket information is available for the counties invoved. Also, search the Oklahoma Supreme Court Network from the website.

Case information is available in bulk form for downloading to computer. For information, call the Administrative Director of Courts, 405-521-2450.

Also, the Oklahoma District Court Records free website at www.odcr.com offers searching for over 60 District Courts. More counties are being added as they are readied. The hope is to eventually feature all Oklahoma District Courts. Please note few counties in this system do not go back seven years.

Adair County

15th Judicial District Court   **Free**
Civil: Online access to court dockets is free at www.oscn.net/applications/oscn/casesearch.asp. Not all cases prior to 1/2006 will appear online, only cases with docs filed after 1/2006 will appear online. *Criminal:* Online access to court dockets is free at www.oscn.net/applications/oscn/casesearch.asp.

Alfalfa County

4th Judicial District Court   **Free**
Civil: Free court records from 8/1998 to present online at www.odcr.com; updated monthly. *Criminal:* same.

Atoka County

25th Judicial District Court   **Free**
Civil: Free court records from 1/1998 to present online at www.odcr.com; updated monthly. *Criminal:* same.

Beaver County

1st Judicial District Court   **Free**
Civil: Free court records from 6/1/1997 to present online at www.odcr.com; updated monthly. *Criminal:* same.

Beckham County

2nd Judicial District Court   www.odcr.com   **Free**
Civil: Free court records from 1/2000 to present online at www.odcr.com; updated daily. *Criminal:* same.

Blaine County

4th Judicial District Court   www.odcr.com/   **Free**
Civil: Search court records free from 8/1998 to present at www.odcr.com; updated daily. *Criminal:* Free court records from 8/1998 to present online at www.odcr.com; updated daily.

Bryan County
19th Judicial District Court   Free
Civil: Search court records free from 7/1/1994 to present online at www.odcr.com; updated daily. *Criminal:* Free court records from 7/1/1994 to present online at www.odcr.com; updated daily.

Caddo County
6th Judicial District Court   Free
Civil: Free court records from 1/1997 to present online at www.odcr.com; updated monthly. *Criminal:* same.

Canadian County
26th Judicial District Court   Free
Civil: Online access to court dockets is free at www.oscn.net/applications/oscn/casesearch.asp. Dockets go back to 3/1993. *Criminal:* Online access to criminal dockets is same as civil.

Carter County
20th Judicial District Court   www.brightok.net/cartercounty/courtclerk.html   Free
Civil: Free court records from 1/1997 to present online at www.odcr.com; updated monthly. *Criminal:* same.

Cherokee County
15th Judicial District Court   Free
Civil: Free court records from 1/1997 to present online at www.odcr.com; updated daily. *Criminal:* same.

Choctaw County
17th Judicial District Court   Free
Civil: Free court records from 8/2002 to present online at www.odcr.com; updated daily. *Criminal:* same.

Cleveland County
21st Judicial District Court - Civil Branch   Free
Civil: Online access to court dockets is free at www.oscn.net/applications/oscn/casesearch.asp. Dockets go back to 1/1989.

21st Judicial District Court - Criminal   Free
Criminal: Online access to court dockets is free at www.oscn.net/applications/oscn/casesearch.asp. Dockets go back to 1/1999.

Coal County
25th Judicial District Court   www.oscn.net/applications/oscn/start.asp?viewType=COUNTYINFO&county=COAL   Free
Civil: Free court records from 6/1999 to present online at www.odcr.com; updated daily. *Criminal:* same.

Comanche County
5th Judicial District Court   www.oscn.net   Free
Civil: Online access to court dockets is free at www.oscn.net/applications/oscn/casesearch.asp. Dockets go back to 8/1988. *Criminal:* same.

Cotton County
5th Judicial District Court   Free
Civil: Free court records from 1/1997 to present online at www.odcr.com; updated daily. *Criminal:* same.

Craig County
12th Judicial District Court   www.odcr.com   Free
Civil: Free court records from 4/1/1997 to present online at www.odcr.com; updated daily. *Criminal:* same.

Creek County
24th Judicial District Court - Sapulpa   Free
Civil: Free court records from 3/1998 to present online at www.odcr.com; updated daily. *Criminal:* same.

24th Judicial District Court - Bristow   Free
Civil: Free court records from 10/25/1999 to present online at www.odcr.com; updated daily. *Criminal:* Court records from 10/25/1999 to present free at www.odcr.com; updated daily.

24th Judicial District Court - Drumright   Free
Civil: Free court records from 11/15/2004 to present online at www.odcr.com; updated daily. *Criminal:* Court records from 11/15/2004 to present free at www.odcr.com; updated daily.

Custer County
2nd Judicial District Court   Free
Civil: Free court records from 8/1/2001 to present online at www.odcr.com; updated daily. *Criminal:* same.

Delaware County

13th Judicial District Court   **Free**

Civil: Free court records from 6/1/1991 to present online at www.odcr.com; updated daily. *Criminal:* same.

Dewey County

4th Judicial District Court   **Free**

Civil: Search online 3/1988 to present free on the statewide system at www.odcr.com. Updated daily. *Criminal:* Search 3/1988 to present free on the statewide system at www.odcr.com. Updated daily.

Ellis County

2nd Judicial District Court   **Free**

Civil: Online access to court dockets is free at www.oscn.net/applications/oscn/casesearch.asp. *Criminal:* same.

Garfield County

4th Judicial District Court   **Free**

Civil: Online access to court dockets is free at www.oscn.net/applications/oscn/casesearch.asp. Dockets go back to 3/1989 *Criminal:* Online access to criminal dockets is same as civil.

Garvin County

21st Judicial District Court   **Free**

Civil: Access court records from 6/1/1995 to present free at www.odcr.com; updated daily. *Criminal:* same.

Greer County

3rd Judicial District Court   **Free**

Civil: Free court records from 8/2002 to present online at www.odcr.com; updated daily. *Criminal:* same.

Harmon County

3rd Judicial District Court   **Free**

Civil: Free court records from 1/2003 to present online at www.odcr.com; updated daily. *Criminal:* same.

Harper County

1st Judicial District Court   **Free**

Civil: Access to court dockets is reportedly free at www.oscn.net/applications/oscn/casesearch.asp. Also, free court records from 1/2000 to present online at www.odcr.com; updated daily. *Criminal:* same.

Haskell County

16th Judicial District Court   **Free**

Civil: Free court records from 11/1/1997 to present online at www.odcr.com; updated daily. *Criminal:* Access to the state Dist. Ct. records site is free at www.odcr.com.

Hughes County

22nd Judicial District Court   **Free**

Civil: Free court records from 12/1998 to present online at www.odcr.com; updated daily. *Criminal:* same.

Jackson County

3rd Judicial District Court   www.jacksoncountyok.com/court.htm   **Free**

Civil: Free court records from 7/1997 to present online at www.odcr.com; updated daily. *Criminal:* same.

Jefferson County

5th Judicial District Court   **Free**

Civil: Free court records from 1/1998 to present online at www.odcr.com; updated monthly. *Criminal:* same.

Kay County

8th Judicial District Court   www.courthouse.kay.ok.us/home.html   **Free**

Civil: Free court records from 5/1/1995 to present online at www.odcr.com; updated daily. Blackwell and Ponca City online goes back to 1/1997. *Criminal:* same.

Kingfisher County

4th Judicial District Court   **Free**

Civil: Free court records from 10/1/1997 to present online at www.odcr.com; updated daily. *Criminal:* same.

Kiowa County

3rd Judicial District Court   **Free**

Civil: Free court records from 1/1996 to present online at www.odcr.com; updated daily. *Criminal:* same.

Latimer County

16th Judicial District Court   Free

Civil: Free court records from 11/1999 to present online at www.odcr.com; updated 2:00 PM each day (view only). *Criminal:* same.

Le Flore County

16th Judicial District Court   Free

Civil: Free court records from 7/1/1997 to present online at www.odcr.com; updated daily. *Criminal:* same.

Lincoln County

23rd Judicial District Court   Free

Civil: Free court records from 7/1/1994 to present online at www.odcr.com; updated daily. *Criminal:* same.

Logan County

9th Judicial District Court   www.oscn.net   Free

Civil: Search court dockets free at www.oscn.net/applications/oscn/casesearch.asp. *Criminal:* same.

Love County

20th Judicial District Court   Free

Civil: Free court records from 4/1997 to present online at www.odcr.com; updated daily. *Criminal:* same.

Major County

4th Judicial District Court   Free

Civil: Free court records from 1/1/1998 to present online at www.odcr.com; updated monthly. *Criminal:* same.

Marshall County

20th Judicial District Court   Free

Civil: Free court records from 1/1/1998 to present online at www.odcr.com; updated daily. *Criminal:* same.

Mayes County

12th Judicial District Court   Free

Civil: Free court records from 7/1/1998 to present online at www.odcr.com; updated daily. *Criminal:* Free court records from 1/1/1998 to present online at www.odcr.com; updated daily.

McClain County

21st Judicial District Court   Free

Civil: Free court records from 1/1997 to present online at www.odcr.com; updated daily. *Criminal:* same.

McCurtain County

17th Judicial District Court   Free

Civil: Free court records from 6/1/1998 to present online at www.odcr.com; updated daily. *Criminal:* same.

McIntosh County

18th Judicial District Court   Free

Civil: Free court records from 5/1/1996 to present online at www.odcr.com; updated monthly. *Criminal:* same.

Murray County

20th Judicial District Court   Free

Civil: Free court records from 1/1/1998 to present online at www.odcr.com; updated monthly. *Criminal:* same.

Muskogee County

15th Judicial District Court   Free

Civil: Free court records from 1/3/2003 to present online at www.odcr.com; updated daily. *Criminal:* same.

Noble County

8th Judicial District Court   Free

Civil: Free court records from 1/1997 to present online at www.odcr.com; updated daily. *Criminal:* same.

Nowata County

11th Judicial District Court   Free

Civil: Free court records from 7/1/1998 to present online at www.odcr.com; updated monthly. *Criminal:* same.

Okfuskee County

24th Judicial District Court   Free

Civil: Free court records from 1/1997 to present online at www.odcr.com; updated daily. *Criminal:* Free court records from 1/1997 to present online at www.odcr.com; updated monthly.

Oklahoma County

District Court   Free

Civil: Online access to court dockets is free at www.oscn.net/applications/oscn/casesearch.asp. Civil dockets go back to 12/1984. *Criminal:* Online access to criminal dockets is same as civil. Criminal dockets go back to 9/1988. The sheriff's current inmates and warrants list is free at www.oklahomacounty.org/cosheriff/.

Okmulgee County

24th Judicial District Court - Henryetta Branch   Free

Civil: Free court records from 1/1998 to present online at www.odcr.com; updated monthly. *Criminal:* same.

24th Judicial District Court - Okmulgee Branch   Free

Civil: Free court records from 1/1998 to present online at www.odcr.com; updated monthly. *Criminal:* same.

Osage County

10th Judicial District Court www.odcr.com   Free

Civil: Free court records from 1/1996 to present online at www.odcr.com; updated daily. *Criminal:* same.

Ottawa County

13th Judicial District Court www.odcr.com   Free

Civil: Free court records from 9/1/1997 to present online at www.odcr.com; updated daily. *Criminal:* same.

Pawnee County

14th Judicial District Court   Free

Civil: Free court records from 1/1997 to present online at www.odcr.com; updated daily. *Criminal:* same.

Payne County

9th Judicial District Court   Free

Civil: Online access to court dockets is free at www.oscn.net/applications/oscn/casesearch.asp. Dockets go back to 1/1994. *Criminal:* Online access to criminal dockets is same as civil.

Pittsburg County

18th Judicial District Court   Free

Civil: Free court records from 7/1/1997 to present online at www.odcr.com; updated monthly. *Criminal:* same.

Pontotoc County

22nd Judicial District Court   Free

Civil: Free court records from 1/1997 to present online at www.odcr.com; updated monthly. *Criminal:* same.

Pottawatomie County

23rd Judicial District Court   Free

Civil: Free court records from 7/1/1997 to present online at www.odcr.com; updated daily. *Criminal:* same.

Pushmataha County

17th Judicial District Court   Free

Civil: Online access to court dockets is free at www.oscn.net/applications/oscn/casesearch.asp. *Criminal:* same.

Roger Mills County

2nd Judicial District Court   Free

Civil: Online access to court dockets is free at www.oscn.net/applications/oscn/casesearch.asp. *Criminal:* same.

Rogers County

12th Judicial District Court www.oscn.net   Free

Civil: Online access to court dockets is free at www.oscn.net/applications/oscn/casesearch.asp. Dockets go back to 7/1997. *Criminal:* Online access to criminal dockets is the same as civil.

Seminole County

22nd Judicial District Court - Wewoka Branch   Free

Civil: Free court records from 1/1995 to present online at www.odcr.com; updated daily. *Criminal:* same.

Sequoyah County

15th Judicial District Court   Free

Civil: Free court records from 7/1/1997 to present online at www.odcr.com; updated daily. *Criminal:* same.

Stephens County

5th Judicial District Court   Free

Civil: Free court records from 1/1996 to present online at www.odcr.com; updated monthly. *Criminal:* same.

Texas County

1st Judicial District Court www.odcr.com/ `Free`
Civil: Free court records from 1/15/1995 to present online at www.odcr.com; updated daily. *Criminal:* same.

Tillman County

3rd Judicial District Court `Free`
Civil: Free court records from 1/1998 to present online at www.odcr.com; updated daily. *Criminal:* same.

Tulsa County

14th Judicial District Court `Free`
Civil: Online access to court dockets is free at www.oscn.net/applications/oscn/casesearch.asp. Civil dockets go back to 10/1984.
Criminal: Online access to criminal dockets is same as civil. Criminal dockets go back to 1/1988.

Wagoner County

15th Judicial District Court www.odcr.com `Free`
Civil: Free court records from 1/1990 to present online at www.odcr.com; updated daily. *Criminal:* Access to criminal records same as civil.

Washington County

11th Judicial District Court `Free`
Civil: Free court records from 1/1999 to present online at www.odcr.com; updated daily. *Criminal:* same.

Washita County

2nd Judicial District Court `Free`
Civil: Free court records from 10/1/1997 to present online at www.odcr.com; updated daily. *Criminal:* Free court records from 10/1/1997 to present online at www.odcr.com; updated daily. Online results also show address.

Woods County

4th Judicial District Court `Free`
Civil: Free court records from 7/2002 to present online at www.odcr.com; updated monthly. *Criminal:* same.

Woodward County

4th Judicial District Court `Free`
Civil: Access court records from 2/1/1997 to present free at www.odcr.com; updated daily. *Criminal:* same.

Recorders, Assessors, and Other Sites of Note

Recording Office Organization: 77 counties, 77 recording offices. The recording officer is the County Clerk. Federal tax liens on personal property of businesses are filed with the County Clerk of Oklahoma County, which is the central filing office for the state. Other federal and all state tax liens are filed with the County Clerk. Usually state and federal tax liens on personal property are filed in separate indexes, state liens on businesses or individuals usually in the real estate index.

Online Access Note: Very little is available online directly from the counties. A private company provides subscription access to assessor indices and property images for all but 1 Oklahoma county; see http://oklahoma.usassessor.com/ or call 800-535-6467 or email tracy@okassessor.com for information. Generally, all records are within 90 days of current. Sub packages: $30 per county or 10 counties $150 or $250 for entire state, except for Osage County which is separate and not on the OKAssessors.com system. Data is also available on CD-rom. Plat Maps also available.

Another second private company offers almost all Oklahoma counties assessment data on CD-rom, also plats and land maps; fees vary by county, see https://secure.vlsmaps.com/ecom_vls/store.php. Also a limited free search is offered for all counties except Texas and Roger Mills at www.pvplus.com/freeaccess/free_login.aspx. Advanced search data is available by subscription.

Good news for researchers is www.okcountytreasurers.com/ links to over half of Oklahoma's treasurer offices that offer free online access to parcel and property tax data.

Adair County *Property, Taxation Records* `Free`   After registration you may search assessment data free temporarily at www.pvplus.com/freeaccess/free_login.aspx.

Atoka County *Property, Taxation Records* `$$` Access to property data is available by subscription at http://oklahoma.usassessor.com.

Beaver County *Property, Taxation Records* `Free & $$` Access to property data is available by subscription at http://oklahoma.usassessor.com. Also, access treasurer property records free at http://beaver.okcountytreasurers.com/.

Beckham County *Real Estate, Grantor/Grantee, Deed, Lien, Judgment, Fictitious Name Records* `Free`
Recording records available free online at http://okcountyrecords.com/search.php?County=005.
Property, Taxation Records `Free` Access treasurer property data free at http://beckham.okcountytreasurers.com/.

Blaine County *Real Estate, Grantor/Grantee, Deed, Lien, Judgment, Fictitious Name Records*
http://blainecountyok.com `Free` Recording records available free at http://okcountyrecords.com/search.php.

Bryan County *Property, Taxation Records* `Free` Access treasurer property data free at http://bryan.okcountytreasurers.com/.

Caddo County *Property, Taxation Records* `Free` Access treasurer property data free at http://caddo.okcountytreasurers.com/.

Canadian County *Real Estate, Grantor/Grantee, Deed, Lien, Judgment Records* www.canadiancounty.org
`Free` Access to recorders database is free http://search.cogov.net/okcana/.
Property, Taxation Records `Free & $$` Subscriber-based access to Assessor records and free access to property records is available at http://canadian.oklahoma.usassessor.com/. Also, access treasurer property data free at www.canadiancountytreasurer.org/.

Carter County *All recorded documents Records* www.brightok.net/chickasaw/ardmore/county/coclerk.html `Free`
Recorded records available free at http://okcountyrecords.com/search.php.
Property, Taxation Records `Free` Search the county assessor database for free at www.cartercountyassessor.org/disclaim.htm. Also, access treasurer property data free at www.cartercountytreasurer.org/cws/c5launch.dll?730634AE/TI.html.

Cherokee County *Real Estate, Grantor/Grantee, Deed, Lien, Judgment, Fictitious Name Records* `Free`
Recording records available free at http://okcountyrecords.com/search.php.

Choctaw County *Property, Taxation Records* `Free` See notes at beginning of section. With registration you may search assessment data free temporarily at www.pvplus.com/freeaccess/free_login.aspx.

Cleveland County *Real Estate, Deed, Lien, Judgment, UCC, Fictitious Name Records*
http://search.cogov.net/okclev/ `Free` Access to the Clerk Index is free at http://search.cogov.net/okclev/default.asp or www.clevelandcountyclerk.net. Includes access to various liens, Real Estate, UCCs.
Property, Taxation Records `Free` Access to property records is free at www.clevelandcountyassessor.us/. Also, access treasurer property data free at www.clevelandcountytreasurer.com/collectmax/collect30.asp.

Comanche County *Property, Taxation Records* `Free` Access treasurer property data free at http://comanchecountyok.org/cws/c5launch.dll?7266640F/TI.html.

Craig County *Real Estate, Grantor/Grantee, Deed, Lien, Judgment, Fictitious Name Records* `Free`
Recording records available free at http://okcountyrecords.com/search.php.
Property, Taxation Records `Free` Access treasurer property data free at http://craig.okcountytreasurers.com/.

Creek County *Property, Taxation Records* `Free & $$` Access to access property records is by subscription from OK Assessors.com, 800-535-6467; weekly and monthly plans available. See note about OKassessors.com at beginning of section. Also, access treasurer property data free at www.creekcountyok.org/cws/c5launch.dll?351C2089/TI.html.

Custer County *Real Estate, Grantor/Grantee, Deed, Lien, Judgment, Fictitious Name Records* `Free`
Recording records available free at http://okcountyrecords.com/search.php.
Property, Taxation Records `Free` Access treasurer property data free at www.custercountyok.org/cws/c5launch.dll?7FA42785/TI.html.

Delaware County *Real Estate, Grantor/Grantee, Deed, Lien, Judgment, Fictitious Name Records*
www.delawareclerk.org `Free & $$` Access land records index free at http://okcountyrecords.com/search.php?County=021. Subscription required for images; $10.00 per month.

Dewey County *Property, Taxation Records* `Free` Access to assessor data may be available at www.pvplus.com/freeaccess/free_login.aspx. Registration required. Subscription and fees for full access.

Garfield County *Property, Taxation Records* `Free` Access treasurer property data free at www.gctreasurer.org/cws/c5launch.dll?36EE4151/TI.html.

Garvin County *Real Estate, Grantor/Grantee, Deed, Lien, Judgment, Fictitious Name Records* `Free`
Recording records available free at http://okcountyrecords.com/search.php.
Property, Taxation Records `Free` Access treasurer property data free at http://garvin.okcountytreasurers.com/.

Grady County *Real Estate, Grantor/Grantee, Deed, Lien, Judgment, Fictitious Name Records*
www.gradycountyok.com/ `Free` Recording records available free at http://okcountyrecords.com/search.php.
Property, Taxation Records `Free` Access treasurer property data free at http://grady.okcountytreasurers.com/

Grant County *Property, Taxation Records* `Free & $$` Assessor and property data available by subscription at
http://grant.oklahoma.usassessor.com/. Access treasurer property data free at http://grant.okcountytreasurers.com/.

Greer County *Property, Taxation Records* `Free` Access treasurer property data free at
http://greer.okcountytreasurers.com/.

Harmon County *Property, Taxation Records* `Free` Access treasurer property data free at
http://harmon.okcountytreasurers.com/.

Harper County *Property, Taxation Records* `Free` Access a trial version of treasurer data free at
http://harper.okcountytreasurers.com/.

Haskell County *Property, Taxation Records* `$$` Access to property data is available by subscription at
http://oklahoma.usassessor.com.

Jackson County *Property, Taxation Records* `Free` Access to parcel, treasurer and property tax data free at
http://jackson.okcountytreasurers.com/.

Jefferson County *Property, Taxation Records* `Free & $$` Access assessor property data by subscription at
http://jefferson.oklahoma.usassessor.com/. Plats and maps also available. Also,access treasurer property data free at
http://jefferson.okcountytreasurers.com/.

Johnston County *Real Estate, Grantor/Grantee, Deed, Lien, Judgment, Fictitious Name Records* `Free`
Records available free at http://okcountyrecords.com/search.php?County=035.
Property, Taxation Records Access treasurer property data free at http://johnston.okcountytreasurers.com/.

Kay County *Real Estate, Grantor/Grantee, Deed, Lien, Judgment, Fictitious Name Records* `Free` Recording
records available free at http://okcountyrecords.com/search.php.
Property, Taxation Records `Free & $$` The assessor office has a subscription service with property data; fee is $10.00 per
month with new data being added. A basic index search is to be available. Call 580-362-2565 for details and to request a signup form.
Access the treasurer tax lookup page free at www.kaycounty.org/Creek1.htm or
www.gctreasurer.org/cws/c5launch.dll?36EE4151/TI.html.

Kingfisher County *Real Estate, Grantor/Grantee, Deed, Lien, Judgment, Fictitious Name Records* `Free`
Recording records available free at http://okcountyrecords.com/search.php.

Latimer County *Property, Taxation Records* `Free` Access treasurer property data free at
http://latimer.okcountytreasurers.com/.

Le Flore County *Real Estate, Grantor/Grantee, Deed, Lien, Judgment, Fictitious Name Records*
www.okcountyrecords.com `Free & $$` Access land records index free at http://okcountyrecords.com/search.php. Subscription
required for images; $1.00 per copy printed, money has to be credited to account first.
Property, Taxation Records `Free & $$` A subscription is required to access assessment data at
http://leflore.oklahoma.usassessor.com/. $30.00 per month. For more info contact Tracy Leniger or Heather Brown at 405-379-5280,
or signup online. Also, access treasurer property data free at http://leflore.okcountytreasurers.com/.

Lincoln County *Property, Taxation Records* `Free` Access treasurer property data free at
www.lctreasurer.org/cws/c5launch.dll?D090212/TI.html.

Logan County *Real Estate, Grantor/Grantee, Deed, Lien, Judgment, Fictitious Name, Divorce Records*
www.logancounty-ok.org `Free` Assess recorded data free at http://okcountyrecords.com/search.php. Images available from 1994
to current. Can not print, call office to request copies.
Property, Taxation Records `Free` Access treasurer property data free at
http://68.99.64.40/cws/c5launch.dll?5025099C/TI.html.

Love County *Real Estate, Grantor/Grantee, Deed, Lien, Judgment, Fictitious Name Records* `Free`
Recording records available free at http://okcountyrecords.com/search.php.
Property, Taxation Records `Free` Access treasurer property data free at http://love.okcountytreasurers.com/.

McClain County *Property, Taxation Records* `Free & $$` Access to access property records is by subscription from OK Assessors.com, 800-535-6467; weekly and monthly plans available. See note about OKassessors.com at beginning of section. Also, search the tax roll inquiry site free at www.mcclaincounty.org:8080/32BE00E3/TI.html.

McCurtain County *Real Estate, Grantor/Grantee, Deed, Lien, Judgment, Fictitious Name Records* `Free`
Records available free at http://okcountyrecords.com/search.php?County=045.
Property, Taxation Records `Free` Access treasurer property data free at http://mccurtain.okcountytreasurers.com/.

McIntosh County *Property, Taxation Records* `$$` Access to property data is by subscription at http://mcintosh.oklahoma.usassessor.com/.

Major County *Real Estate, Grantor/Grantee, Deed, Lien, Judgment, Fictitious Name Records* `Free`
Recording records available free at http://okcountyrecords.com/search.php.

Marshall County *Real Estate, Grantor/Grantee, Deed, Lien, Judgment, Fictitious Name Records* `Free`
Recording records available free at http://okcountyrecords.com/search.php.
Property, Taxation Records `Free & $$` Access to access property records is by subscription from OK Assessors.com, 800-535-6467; weekly and monthly plans available. See note about OKassessors.com at beginning of section. Access treasurer property data free at http://marshall.okcountytreasurers.com/.

Mayes County *Property, Taxation Records* `Free` Access treasurer property data free at http://69.152.83.134/cws/c5launch.dll?64375756/TI.html.

Murray County *Property, Taxation Records* `Free` With registration you may search assessment data free temporarily at www.pvplus.com/freeaccess/free_login.aspx.

Muskogee County *Real Estate, Grantor/Grantee, Deed, Lien, Judgment, Fictitious Name Records* `Free`
Recording records available free at http://okcountyrecords.com/search.php.
Property, Taxation Records `Free` Access treasurer property data free at www.muskogeetreasurer.org/cws/c5launch.dll?230A09BB/TI.html.

Noble County *Real Estate, Grantor/Grantee, Deed, Lien, Judgment, Fictitious Name Records* `Free`
Recording records available free at http://okcountyrecords.com/search.php.
Property, Taxation Records `Free` Access treasurer property data free at http://noble.okcountytreasurers.com/.

Oklahoma County *Real Estate, Grantor/Grantee, Deed, UCC Records* www.oklahomacounty.org `Free` Real estate, UCC, grantor/grantee records on the county clerk database are free at www.oklahomacounty.org/coclerk. Images, index and printing available.
Property, Taxation Records `Free` Assessor and property data on county assessor database is free at www.oklahomacounty.org/assessor/disclaim.htm. Also, search the treasurer's property info at www.oklahomacounty.org/treasurer/PublicAccessSearch.htm.

Okmulgee County *Property, Taxation Records* `Free` Access is free for basic info from a private company at www.pvplus.com/freeaccess/register.aspx but free registration is required.

Osage County *Real Estate, Grantor/Grantee, Deed, Lien, Judgment, Fictitious Name Records* `Free`
Recording records available free at http://okcountyrecords.com/search.php.

Ottawa County *Real Estate, Grantor/Grantee, Deed, Lien, Judgment, Fictitious Name Records* `Free`
Recording records available free at http://okcountyrecords.com/search.php.
Property, Taxation Records `Free & $$` Access to property data is through a subscription with a private company, visit www.pvplus.com. Fee is $10.00 per month per county. Also, access treasurer property data free at http://ottawa.okcountytreasurers.com/.

Pawnee County *Property, Taxation Records* `Free` Access treasurer property data free at http://pawnee.okcountytreasurers.com/.

Payne County *Real Estate, Grantor/Grantee, Deed, Lien, Judgment, Fictitious Name Records*
www.okcountyrecords.com `Free` Access land records index free at http://okcountyrecords.com/search.php. Index and details only; no images available.
Property, Taxation Records `Free` Access treasurer property data free at http://paynecountytreasurer.org:8080/4AD40E0/TI.html.

Pittsburg County *Real Estate, Grantor/Grantee, Deed, Lien, Judgment, Fictitious Name Records* `Free`
Recording records available free at http://okcountyrecords.com/search.php.
Property, Taxation Records `$$` Access to access property records is by subscription from OK Assessors.com, 800-535-6467; weekly and monthly plans available. See note about OKassessors.com at beginning of section.

Pontotoc County *Real Estate, Deed, UCC, Judgment, Lien, Military Records* www.pontotoccountyclerk.org
`Free & $$` Access recorder's index free at http://okcountyrecords.com/search.php?county=062. Access to the clerk's recorded records requires registration and subscription. To register, contact the county clerk.
Property, Taxation Records `Free` Access treasurer property data free at http://pontotoc.okcountytreasurers.com/.

Pottawatomie County *Real Estate, Deed, Tract, UCC Records* `Free` Access property data and UCCs free at www.landaccess.com/sites/ok/pottawatomie/index.php.
Property, Taxation Records `Free` Access assessment and property data by subscription at http://pottawatomie.oklahoma.usassessor.com/.

Rogers County *Real Estate, Grantor/Grantee, Deed, Lien, Judgment, Fictitious Name Records*
www.rogerscounty.org `Free & $$` Recording records available free at http://okcountyrecords.com/search.php. Also, access land records at http://etitlesearch.com; for registration and subscription, call 870-856-3055.
Property, Taxation Records `Free` Access to the assessor database is free at www.rogerscounty.org/search.html. Also, search the treasurers tax roll database free at www.rogerscounty.org/treasurer/search.html.

Stephens County *Real Estate, Grantor/Grantee, Deed, Lien, Judgment, Fictitious Name Records* `Free & $$`
Access land records index free at http://okcountyrecords.com/search.php. Subscription required for images; $10.00 per month.
Property, Taxation Records `Free` Access treasurer property data free at http://stephens.okcountytreasurers.com/.

Tillman County *Property, Taxation Records* `Free` Access treasurer property data free at http://tillman.okcountytreasurers.com/.

Tulsa County *Real Estate, Deed, Property Records* www.tulsacounty.org `Free & $$` Access to Tulsa County's Land Records System requires an approved user agreement, username and password, see http://lrmis.tulsacounty.org. Monthly access fee is $30.00 and $1.00 per doc printed. Records go back to 1979. For info or signup, contact Dorise at 918-596-5206 or LRMIShelp@tulsacounty.org.
Property, Taxation Records `$$` Access to Tulsa County's Land Records System requires an agreement, username and password, and fees, see hhttps://lrmis.tulsacounty.org/.

Wagoner County *Real Estate, Grantor/Grantee, Deed, Lien, Judgment Records* www.wagonercountyclerk.com
`Free & $$` Access recorders official records free at www.edoctecinc.com/. There may be a 2 week to 1 month lag time. Also, access to land records for free go to www.wagonercountyclerk.com/wagoner_land_records.htm.
Property, Taxation Records `Free` Access treasurer property data free at www.wagonertreasurer.org:8080/31DC0BAA/TI.html.

Washington County *Real Estate, Deed, Mortgage, Lien Records* www.countycourthouse.org `Free`
Access to the recorders database is free at www.countycourthouse.org/countyclerk/disclaimer.htm.
Property, Taxation Records `Free` Access treasurer property tax and parcel date free at http://ok-washington-treasurer.governmax.com/collectmax/collect30.asp

Washita County *Property, Taxation Records* `$$` Access to property data is by subscription from a private company, registration and login required, see http://washita.oklahoma.usassessor.com/Shared/base/Subscriber/Subscribe.php.

Woods County *Property, Taxation Records* `Free` Access treasurer property data free at http://woods.okcountytreasurers.com/.

Woodward County *Real Estate, Grantor/Grantee, Deed, Lien, Judgment, Fictitious Name Records* `Free`
Recording records available free at http://okcountyrecords.com/search.php.

Oregon

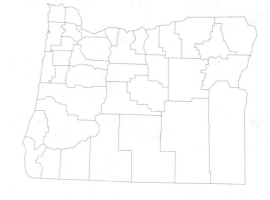

Capital: Salem
              Marion County
Time Zone: PST
Population: 3,747,455
# of Counties: 36

Useful State Links

Website: www.oregon.gov
Governor: www.governor.state.or.us
Attorney General: www.doj.state.or.us
State Archives: http://arcweb.sos.state.or.us
State Statutes and Codes: www.leg.state.or.us/ors/home.htm
Legislative Bill Search: www.leg.state.or.us/bills_laws/
Unclaimed Funds: http://mscfprod2.iservices.state.or.us/dsl/unclaimed_property/search.cfm

Primary State Agencies

Criminal Records $$

Oregon State Police, Unit 11, Identification Services Section, http://egov.oregon.gov/OSP/ID/ A web based site is available for requesting and receiving criminal records. Website is ONLY for high-volume requesters who must be pre-approved. Results are posted as "No Record" or "In Process" ("In Process" means a record will be mailed in 14 days). Use the "open records" link to get into the proper site. Fee is $10.00 per record. Call 503-373-1808 x230 to receive the application, or visit the website.

Sexual Offender Registry Free

Oregon State Police, SOR Unit, http://egov.oregon.gov/OSP/SOR/index.shtml Visit http://sexoffenders.oregon.gov/ for online searching of sex offenders who have been designated as Predatory. A mapping function is also offered. *Other Options:* Lists by city or zip can usually be requested for no fee, a statewide list be purchased for $85.00.

Incarceration Records Free

Oregon Department of Corrections, Offender Information & Sentence Computation, www.doc.state.or.us No online offender searching is available from this agency; there is a "Corrections Most Wanted" list in the pull down menu box. The agency web page mentions a private company offering free web access at https://www.vinelink.com/vinelink/siteInfoAction.do?siteId=38000; includes state, DOC, and most county jails. Also, use imate.info@doc.state.or.us to request by email. *Other Options:* Bulk sale of information is available. Contact ISSD.

Corporation, LP, LLC, Trademarks/Servicemarks, Fictitious/Assumed Name Free

Corporation Division, Public Service Building, www.filinginoregon.com There is free access at the website for business registry information. Search by name or business registry number. Displays active and inactive records. *Other Options:* New business lists on email or CDs of the database are available for $50.00 per month or week. Call 503-986-2343 for more information.

Uniform Commercial Code, Federal & State Tax Liens Free

UCC Division, Attn: Records, www.filinginoregon.com/ucc/index.htm Search the web page for information on UCC secured transactions, as well as Farm Product notices, IRS Tax Liens, Agricultural searches Liens, Agricultural Produce Liens, Grain Producer's Liens, Revenue Warrants and Employment Warrants. You can search by debtor name or by lien number. You can also download forms from here. *Other Options:* UCC database extracts ($200) are offered, this is full extratc, not an update service. UCC images are available in bulk for $200 per week. New filings can be purchased weekly or monthly on CD, can give by type of lien for $15.00 per week.

Vital Records `Free & $$`

Department of Human Services, Vital Records, http://oregon.gov/DHS/ph/chs/order/index.shtml Order records online at www.vitalchek.com, a state designated vendor. Death records from 1903-1930 are available at www.heritagetrailpress.com/Death_Index/

Workers' Compensation Records `Free`

Department of Consumer & Business Srvs, Workers Compensation Division, www.cbs.state.or.us/external/wcd/ Search of employers with coverage or that have coverage ending soon is found at www.oregonwcd.org/compliance/ecu/empcoverage.html. Claimant names not listed, companies with 10 or fewer employees not listed. Search by claims number or by employer's claim number at http://www4.cbs.state.or.us/ex/imd/reports/rpt/index.cfm?ProgID=CE8039. *Other Options:* State is allowed to deliver data in other forms to parties that qualify under ORS 192.502(19).

Driver Records `$$`

Driver and Motor Vehicle Services, Record Services, www.oregondmv.com The Oregon DMV offers a Real-Time Driving Record Service (RADR) that allows qualified customers to access Oregon driving records via a real time connection through AAMVAnet. Records are $.50 each, including employment, non-employment, and court records. However, a onetime set-up fee of $4,500 is required. Qualified Requestors must meet technical requirements, sign an agreement, and establish a Record Inquiry Account. For more information, contact the Records Policy Unit at 503-945-8905 or 503-945-8906. *Other Options:* The agency offers an automated "flag program" that informs customers of activity on a name list, for approved account holders only. Call the Automated Reporting Service at 503-945-5427 for more information.

Vehicle Ownership & Registration `$$`

Driver and Motor Vehicle Services, Record Services Unit, www.oregondmv.com Online ordering form option of records is available, but only for approved account holders. The fillable form may be downloaded from the web page. Records are returned by fax or mail, per requester's instructions. Fes range from $4.00 to $22.50 depedning on type of record needed. *Other Options:* Bulk lists available on cartridge to qualified accounts. Call 503-945-8906 for more information.

GED Certificates `Free`

Dept of Community Colleges/ Workforce Development, Oregon GED Program, www.oregon.gov/CCWD/GED/index.shtml For records from 2002 forward, online access is available with the access code provided by the testing center.

Occupational Licensing Boards

Acupuncturist	www.bme.state.or.us/search.html
Animal Euthanasia Tech./Facility	http://ovmeb.oregonlookups.com
Animal Feed (Livestock)	http://egov.oregon.gov/ODA/license.shtml
Animal Food Processor	http://egov.oregon.gov/ODA/license.shtml
Architect/Architectural Firm	http://new.orbae.com/index.php?option=com_obae
Athletic Trainer	https://elite.hlo.state.or.us/elitepublic/LPRBrowser.aspx
Attorney	www.osbar.org/members/start.asp
Audiologist	http://bspa.oregonlookups.com
Auditor, Municipal	http://boahost.com/egovlicsearch.lasso
Bakery	http://egov.oregon.gov/ODA/license.shtml
Barber	https://elite.hlo.state.or.us/elitepublic
Body Piercer	https://elite.hlo.state.or.us/elitepublic
Brand (Livestock)	http://egov.oregon.gov/ODA/license.shtml
Brand Inspector	http://egov.oregon.gov/ODA/license.shtml
Chiropractor/Chiropractic Assistant	http://obce.alcsoftware.com/liclookup.php
Christmas Tree Grower	www.oregon.gov/ODA/PLANT/NURSERY/index.shtml
Construction Contractor/Subcontr.	https://ccbed.ccb.state.or.us/ccb_frames/consumer_info/
Cosmetologist	https://elite.hlo.state.or.us/elitepublic
Counselor, Professional	www.oblpct.state.or.us/OBLPCT/type.shtml
Dairy Establishment	http://egov.oregon.gov/ODA/license.shtml
Dentist/ Dental Hygienist	http://obd.oregonlookups.com/
Denturist/ Denture Technologist	https://elite.hlo.state.or.us/elitepublic/LPRBrowser.aspx
Diagnostic Radiologic Technologist	http://obrt.oregonlookups.com/
Dietitian	http://bld.oregonlookups.com/
Direct Entry Midwife	https://elite.hlo.state.or.us/elitepublic/LPRBrowser.aspx
Dog Racing Occupation	http://licenseinfo.oregon.gov/
Drug Manufacturer/Wholesaler	http://my.oregon.gov/pharmacy_search/searchResults-submit.do

Drug Outlet, Over-the-Counter	http://my.oregon.gov/pharmacy_search/searchResults-submit.do
Egg Handler/Breaker	http://egov.oregon.gov/ODA/license.shtml
Electrologist	https://elite.hlo.state.or.us/elitepublic
Electrology Instructor/School	https://elite.hlo.state.or.us/elitepublic
Engineer	www.osbeels.org
Environmental Health Specialist	https://elite.hlo.state.or.us/elitepublic/LPRBrowser.aspx
Escrow Agent/Agency	http://outside.rea.state.or.us/weblookup/
Facial Technician/Technologist	https://elite.hlo.state.or.us/elitepublic
Farm Labor Contractor	http://licenseinfo.oregon.gov/
Fertilizer/Mineral/Lime Registrant	http://oda.state.or.us/dbs/licenses/search.lasso?&division=pest
Florist	www.oregon.gov/ODA/PLANT/NURSERY/index.shtml
Food-related Facility	http://egov.oregon.gov/ODA/license.shtml
Forest Labor Contractor	http://licenseinfo.oregon.gov/
Frozen Desert-related Industry	http://egov.oregon.gov/ODA/license.shtml
Geologist/Geologist Engineering	www.open.org/~osbge/registrants.htm
Greenhouse/herbaceous plant	www.oregon.gov/ODA/PLANT/NURSERY/index.shtml
Hair Salon	https://elite.hlo.state.or.us/elitepublic
Hair Stylist	https://elite.hlo.state.or.us/elitepublic
Hearing Aid Dealer/Dispenser	http://elite.hlo.state.or.us/elitepublic/
Hearing Aid Specialist	https://elite.hlo.state.or.us/elitepublic/LPRBrowser.aspx
Home Inspector	https://ccbed.ccb.state.or.us/ccb_frames/consumer_info/
Horse Racing Occupation	http://licenseinfo.oregon.gov/
Insurance Agent/Adjuster/Consultant	http://www4.cbs.state.or.us/ex/ins/inslic/agent/
Insurance Agency	www.cbs.state.or.us/external/imd/database/inslic/agency_main.htm
Insurance Company	www.cbs.state.or.us/external/imd/database/inslic/comp_main.htm
Landscape Architect	www.oregon.gov/LANDARCH/registrants.shtml
Landscaper	www.oregon.gov/ODA/PLANT/NURSERY/index.shtml
Livestock-Related Business	http://egov.oregon.gov/ODA/license.shtml
Lobbyist	www.oregon.gov/OGEC/public_records.shtml
Manicurist/Nail Technician	https://elite.hlo.state.or.us/elitepublic
Marriage & Family Therapist	www.oblpct.state.or.us/OBLPCT/type.shtml
Massage Therapist	www.oregonmassage.org/liclookup.php
Measuring Device	http://oda.state.or.us/dbs/search.lasso#msd
Medical Doctor/Surgeon	www.bme.state.or.us/search.html
Milk Hauler/Milk Stabilizer/Handler	http://egov.oregon.gov/ODA/license.shtml
Motor Fuel Quality	http://oda.state.or.us/dbs/search.lasso#msd
Nail Technician	https://elite.hlo.state.or.us/elitepublic
Naturopathic Physician	www.obne.state.or.us/OBNE/FindADoctor.shtml
Non-Alcoholic Beverage Plant	http://egov.oregon.gov/ODA/license.shtml
Notary Public	www.filinginoregon.com/notary/
Nurse	www.osbn.state.or.us/search/searchResults-submit.do
Nursery Dealer	www.oregon.gov/ODA/PLANT/NURSERY/index.shtml
Nursery Stock/Native Plant Collector	www.oregon.gov/ODA/PLANT/NURSERY/index.shtml
Nursing Assistant	www.osbn.state.or.us/search/searchResults-submit.do
Nursing Home Administrator	http://nhabd.oregonlookups.com
Occupational Therapist/or/Assistant	http://otlb.oregonlookups.com
Optometrist	www.oregonobo.org/doctorinfo.htm
Oral Pathology Endorsement	https://elite.hlo.state.or.us/elitepublic/LPRBrowser.aspx
Oregon Product	http://egov.oregon.gov/ODA/license.shtml
Osteopathic Physician/Surgeon	www.bme.state.or.us/search.html
Permanent Color Technician	https://elite.hlo.state.or.us/elitepublic
Pesticide-related Occupation	http://oda.state.or.us/dbs/licenses/search.lasso?&division=pest
Pesticide Product	http://oda.state.or.us/dbs/licenses/search.lasso?&division=pest
Pharmacy/Pharmacist	http://my.oregon.gov/pharmacy_search/searchResults-submit.do
Physical Therapist/Assistant	http://ptlb.oregonlookups.com/
Physician/Physician Assistant	www.bme.state.or.us/search.html
Podiatrist	www.bme.state.or.us/search.html

Political Candidate Statement............ www.gspc.state.or.us/GSPC/public_records.shtml
Polygraph Examiner .... www.oregon.gov/DPSST/SC/Polygraph.shtml
Property Manager .... http://outside.rea.state.or.us/weblookup/
Psychologist..................................... http://obpe.alcsoftware.com/liclookup.php
Psychologist Associate .... http://obpe.alcsoftware.com/liclookup.php
Public Accountant-CPA/Firm............ http://boahost.com/egovlicsearch.lasso
Pump Installation Contr., Limited ..... www.cbs.state.or.us/bcd/licensing.html
Radiologic Technologist Ltd Permit.. http://obrt.oregonlookups.com/
Radiologic Therapy Technologist...... http://obrt.oregonlookups.com/
Real Estate Agent/Seller/Broker........ http://outside.rea.state.or.us/weblookup/
Real Estate Appraiser   ...   http://oregonaclb.org/index.php?option=com_content&task=view&id=20&Itemid=112
Refrigerated Plant............................. http://egov.oregon.gov/ODA/license.shtml
Respiratory Care Practitioner .... https://elite.hlo.state.or.us/elitepublic/LPRBrowser.aspx
Respiratory Therapist .... https://elite.hlo.state.or.us/elitepublic/LPRBrowser.aspx
Sanitarian... http://elite.hlo.state.or.us/elitepublic/
Shellfish-related Industry .... http://egov.oregon.gov/ODA/license.shtml
Sign Contractor, Limited .... www.cbs.state.or.us/bcd/licensing.html
Slaughterhouse .... http://egov.oregon.gov/ODA/license.shtml
Social Worker, Clinical .... http://bcsw.oregonlookups.com/
Speech Language Pathologist............ http://bspa.oregonlookups.com
Surveyor, Land .... www.osbeels.org
Tattoo Artist .... https://elite.hlo.state.or.us/elitepublic/LPRBrowser.aspx
Therapeutic Radiologic Technologist http://obrt.oregonlookups.com/
Transaction Verification .... http://oda.state.or.us/dbs/search.lasso#msd
Veterinarian..................................... http://ovmeb.oregonlookups.com
Veterinary Clinic/Product, Livestock http://egov.oregon.gov/ODA/license.shtml
Veterinary Technician .... http://ovmeb.oregonlookups.com
Waste Water System Operator........... www.deq.state.or.us/wq/OpCert/opcert.htm
Water Rights Examiner .... www.osbeels.org
Weighing Device .... http://oda.state.or.us/dbs/search.lasso#msd

State and Local Courts

State Court Structure: Oregon has two types of state trial courts, the Circuit Courts, which are general jurisdiction courts, and the Oregon Tax Court, whose jurisdiction is limited to cases involving taxes. Probate is handled by the Circuit Court except in six counties (Gilliam, Grant, Harney, Malheur, Sherman, and Wheeler) where Probate in handled by County Courts. There are over 100 Municipal Courts and 35 Justice Courts that oversee minor misdemeanor, traffic, and ordinance cases.

Statewide Court Online Access: Online computer access is available through the Oregon Judicial Information Network (OJIN) which includes cases filed in the Oregon state courts. There is a one-time setup fee of $295.00 plus usage fees of $10-13.00 per hour, plus $10 per month per user. The database contains criminal, civil, small claims, tax, domestic, usually probate when not at the county court, and some but not all juvenile records. However, it does not contain any records from municipal or county courts. **Searching is done by county, there is no statewide search available.** For further information visit www.ojd.state.or.us/ojin, or call 800-858-9658 or 503-986-5588.

Appellate opinions are found at www.publications.ojd.state.or.us.

❖ **Statewide Access Offered For All Trial Courts — Read Above** ❖

Recorders, Assessors, and Other Sites of Note

Recording Office Organization: 36 counties, 36 recording offices. The recording officer is the County Clerk. All federal and state tax liens on personal property are filed with the Secretary of State. Other federal and state tax liens are filed with the County Clerk. Government agencies file 'warrants' that represent liens for unpaid taxes and other state fees. Certain warrants are filed with the Sec. of State such as those related to income tax and hazardous waste and are included in a UCC search. Other warrants are filed at the county level, such as those relating to employment taxes.

Online Access Note: A number of counties offer internet access to assessor records. From a statewide perspective, the ORMAP Tax Viewing System at www.ormap.com/disclaimer.cfm provides maps for free, and searching by county, then by address. Though there is no name searching and maps are pdfs arranged in folders (and you may zoom in to a map location), this is a step toward owner identification.

Baker County *Property, Taxation Records* `Free` Access to the assessor property database is free at www.bakercounty.org/Assessor/Assessor_Search.html. Access maps via the statewide mapping site free at www.ormap.com/maps/index.cfm.

Benton County *Property, Taxation Records* `Free & $$` Assessor has a number of searches at www.co.benton.or.us/assess/prop_search.php. Also, see note at beginning of section. County is developing a GIS Internet site for viewing property data at www.co.benton.or.us/maps/bentonmaps.php. A fee may apply to purchase of maps, etc.

Clackamas County *Property, Taxation Records* `Free` Parcel records and GIS-Map on the County Metromap database are free at www.metro-region.org/article.cfm?articleid=1055. No name searching. Also, see note at beginning of section.

Clatsop County *Property, Taxation Records* `Free` Access property data free at http://maps.co.clatsop.or.us/applications/WebMap/Source/login.asp; click on Agree then click on Search on map page. Other online access available via private companies.

Columbia County *Property, Taxation Records* `Free` Access maps via the statewide mapping site free at www.ormap.com/maps/index.cfm.

Coos County *Property, Taxation Records* `Free` Access to the assessor property and sales data is free at http://assessor.cooscotax.com. You may name search to lookup account numbers. Also see note at beginning of section.

Crook County *Property, Taxation Records* `Free` Access property data free on the GIS-mapping site at http://gis.co.crook.or.us/DisclaimerPublic/tabid/74/Default.aspx but no name searching. Also see note at beginning of section.

Curry County *Property, Taxation Records* `Free` Access the GIS-mapping site free at www.co.curry.or.us/GIS/WebCoverfix.html but no name searching. You may also choose to search pdf maps. Also, see note at beginning of section.

Deschutes County *Real Estate, Deed, Mortgage, Lien Records* http://recordings.co.deschutes.or.us `Free`
Search real estate, deeds, mortgages, liens on the clerk's recording system web inquiry for free at http://recordings.co.deschutes.or.us. Free registration for username and password required. Index goes back to 1985; images back to 1999.
Property, Taxation Records `Free` View records on the Assessor Inquiry System site at www.co.deschutes.or.us/dial.cfm. There is also business property searching. Access property tax map records on the Lava system free at http://lava.deschutes.org/gisapps/index.cfm but no name searching. Various land/ownership records at www.co.deschutes.or.us/dial.cfm; appraisal details, sales data, transaction-account histories, land use, and lot numbers for no fee. Also a business property search button. Also, see note at beginning of section.

Douglas County *Property, Taxation Records* `Free` Access to the assessor property data and sales is free at www.co.douglas.or.us/puboaa/cgi/oaasearch.pl. Access to property sales is free at www.co.douglas.or.us/puboaa/ressales.asp. Also see note at beginning of section.

Gilliam County *Property, Taxation Records* `Free` Access maps via the statewide mapping site free at www.ormap.com/maps/index.cfm.

Grant County *Property, Taxation Records* `Free` Access maps via the statewide mapping site free at www.ormap.com/maps/index.cfm.

Harney County *Property, Taxation Records* `Free` Access maps via the statewide mapping site free at www.ormap.com/maps/index.cfm.

Hood River County *Property, Taxation Records* `Free` Access maps via the statewide mapping site free at www.ormap.com/maps/index.cfm.

Jackson County *Property, Taxation Records* `Free` Access property via the Map Book Viewer free at www.smartmap.org/MapBookViewer/Search.asp but no name searching. Also see note at beginning of section.

Jefferson County *Property, Taxation Records* `Free` Access assessor property and tax data free at http://159.121.192.44/AandTWebQuery/. Access maps via the statewide mapping site free at www.ormap.com/maps/index.cfm.

Josephine County *Real Estate, Deed, Lien, Judgment Records* `$$` Access to recording office index and documents is by subscription; fee is $25 per month, minimum 3 months. Contact Art at the recording office for signup, username and password.
Property, Taxation Records `Free` Access property via the Map Book Viewer free at www.smartmap.org/MapBookViewer/Search.asp but no name searching. Also, search property data on the LION system free at http://68.185.2.151/website/pumaweb/ but no name searching. Also see note at beginning of section.

Klamath County *Property, Taxation Records* `Free & $$` Assessors property data available by subscription at www.co.klamath.or.us:8008/. Call 541-883-5142 for info and sign-up. Search tax property sales annual list free at www.co.klamath.or.us/PropertySales/index.html. Also see note at beginning of section.

Lake County *Property, Taxation Records* `Free` Access maps via the statewide mapping site free at www.ormap.com/maps/index.cfm.

Lane County *Real Estate, Deed Records* `$$` Access recorded land data on the Reg. Land Information Database RLID by subscription. Visit www.rlid.org or call Eric at 541-682-4338 for info/signup. Initiation fee is $200; monthly access fee is $80.00.
Property, Taxation Records `Free & $$` Access property and sales data on the Reg. Land Information Database RLID by subscription. Visit www.rlid.org or call Eric at 541-682-4338 for info/signup. Initiation fee is $200; monthly access fee is $80.00. Property records on the County Tax Map site are free at www.co.lane.or.us/TaxStatement/Search.aspx. No name searching. Also see note at beginning of section for add'l access.

Lincoln County *Property, Taxation Records* `Free` Access limited property info via the County Map Site free at www.co.lincoln.or.us/assessor/maps.html but no name searching. Download the free viewer and search by Township. Map pdfs also available. Also see note at beginning of section.

Linn County *Property, Taxation Records* `Free` Tax assessor rolls and sales may be viewed at www.co.linn.or.us/assessorshomep/assessor.htm. Also, search property via the ELLA Maps site free at www.co.linn.or.us/webmap/. On the map page, click on Search to search by addresses, but no name searching. Also see note at beginning of section.

Malheur County *Property, Taxation Records* `Free` Search assessment data free at http://assessor.malheurco.org/. Access maps via the statewide mapping site free at www.ormap.com/maps/index.cfm.

Marion County *Property, Taxation Records* `Free & $$` Access assessor property data via the GIS-mapping pages at www.co.marion.or.us/IT/GIS/gisdata.htm. Fee is $82.50; other GIS property-related packages available. Search free on the Mapper page at http://apps.co.marion.or.us/mcim/mcimdis.aspx but no name searching.

Morrow County *Property, Taxation Records* `Free` Access maps via the statewide mapping site free at www.ormap.com/maps/index.cfm.

Multnomah County *Property, Taxation Records* `Free & $$` Search assessor maps free at http://gis.co.multnomah.or.us/mcormap/. Records on the County Metromap database are free at http://metromap.metro-region.org/. No name searching. The GIS-mapping site is very similar at http://gis.co.multnomah.or.us/sail/. Also, search property info at http://multcoproptax.com/ or on the Catbird subscription site; fee is $150 setup plus a monthly fee equaling $.25 per page viewed. For info/signup, call 503-988-3345.

Polk County *Property, Taxation Records* `Free` Access property data free at http://apps.co.polk.or.us/webmap/source/login.asp and click on Agree and Accept, then click on Search on left hand side, then choose Tax Lots. Search by name, address, etc. Also, search for assessor maps for free at www.co.polk.or.us/Assessor/MapSearch.htm but no name searching. Also see note at beginning of section.

Sherman County *Property, Taxation Records* `Free` Access maps via the statewide mapping site free at www.ormap.com/maps/index.cfm.

Tillamook County *Real Estate, Deed, Lien, Judgment Records* www.co.tillamook.or.us/gov/clerk/default.htm
`Free` Access to recorded document index free at www.co.tillamook.or.us/gov/clerk/recinq/Login.asp; use username "public" and password "inquiry." Viewing document images is not available online.
Property, Taxation Records `Free` Assessment and taxation records on the County Property database are free at www.co.tillamook.or.us/Documents/Search/query.asp. Search by property ID number or by name in the general query. Also, search for property info on the GIS-mapping service site at www.co.tillamook.or.us/gov/gis/parcelmaps.htm. Also see note at beginning of section.

Umatilla County *Property, Taxation Records* `Free` Access maps via the statewide mapping site free at www.ormap.com/maps/index.cfm.

Union County *Property, Taxation Records* `Free` Access property tax data free at www.union-county.org/assessor_search.html.

Wallowa County *Property, Taxation Records* `Free` Access maps via the statewide mapping site free at www.ormap.com/maps/index.cfm.

Wasco County *Property, Taxation Records* `$$` The GIS-mapping services offers custom designed and also pre-packaged property data products, including the assessor data CD-rom for $300. View product line at www.co.wasco.or.us/gis/GISPrices2002.html. Other online access through private companies.

Washington County *Property, Taxation Records* `Free` Records on County GIS Intermap database are free at www.co.washington.or.us/deptmts/lut/gis/intermap/map_land.htm but no name searching. Also see note at beginning of section.

Yamhill County *Property, Taxation Records* `Free` Search assessor property data free at www.co.yamhill.or.us/taxinfo/PropSearch.aspx. No name searching. Also, access maps via the statewide mapping site free at www.ormap.com/maps/index.cfm. Limited property data from the county surveyor is free at www.co.yamhill.or.us/surveyor/; no name searching.

Other Oregon Sites of Note:

Benton County - Most Wanted www.co.benton.or.us/sheriff/corrections/bccc/Absconders/
Jefferson County - Sheriff Warrants, Inmates www.co.jefferson.or.us/Default.aspx?alias=www.co.jefferson.or.us/sheriff
Klamath County - High Risk Sex Offenders www.co.klamath.or.us/CommunityCorrections/sex_offender.htm
Marion County - Sex Offenders Registry, Inmates www.co.marion.or.us/so/ With pictures.
Multnomah County - Inmates, Bookings www.mcso.us/PAID/Default.aspx
Multnomah County - Restaurant Inspections www2.co.multnomah.or.us/Health/mchealthinspect/
Umatilla County - Jail roster www.co.umatilla.or.us/deptwebs/jail/inmates/ICURRENT.HTM
Yamhill County - Sheriff's Inmates, Most Wanted www.co.yamhill.or.us/sheriff/index.asp

Pennsylvania

Capital: Harrisburg
          Dauphin County
Time Zone: EST
Population: 12,432,792
# of Counties: 67

Useful State Links

Website: www.pa.gov
Governor: www.governor.state.pa.us
Attorney General: www.attorneygeneral.gov
State Archives: www.phmc.state.pa.us
State Statutes and Codes: http://members.aol.com/StatutesPA/Index.html
Legislative Bill Search: www.legis.state.pa.us/cfdocs/legis/home/session.cfm
Unclaimed Funds: www.patreasury.org/search.htm

Primary State Agencies

Criminal Records

State Police, Central Repository -164, www.psp.state.pa.us/psp/site/default.asp Record checks are available for approved agencies through the Internet on the Pennsylvania Access to Criminal Histories (PATCH). Ongoing requesters may become registered users. This is a commercial system, the same $10.00 fee per name applies. PATCH accepts Visa, Discover, MasterCard, AmEx cards. Go to https://epatch.state.pa.us/Home.jsp or call 717-705-1768 to register. Up to 10 records may be requested at one session.

Sexual Offender Registry Free

State Police Burau of Records and Ident., Megan's Law Unit, www.pameganslaw.state.pa.us Limited information on all registered sex offenders can be viewed online from the webpage. Complete address information is listed for all active offenders. Upon opening the offender's record, you are provided tabs to click on access details such as alias, address, offense, vehicle, and physical characteristics information.

Incarceration Records Free

Pennsylvania Department of Corrections, Bureau of Inmate Services, www.cor.state.pa.us At the website, click on Inmate Locator for information about each inmate currently under the jurisdiction of the Department of Corrections, or visit www.cor.state.pa.us/inmatelocatorweb/. The site indicates where an inmate is housed, race, date of birth, marital status and other items. The Inmate Locator does not contain information on inmates not currently residing in a state correctional institution. Also, search the SAVIN list (victim notifications) for free at a private company site at https://www.vinelink.com/vinelink/siteInfoAction.do?siteId=39000. Not a DOC list; it's PDIA (AG ofc) and PCCD (Crime Commission) data.

Corporation, LP, LLC, LLP, Trademarks/Servicemarks, Fictitious Name Free

Corporation Bureau, Department of State, www.dos.state.pa.us/corps/site/default.asp There is free general searching by entity name or number from the website. Searching by name provides a list of entities whose name starts with the search name entered. Users can click on any one entity in the list displayed to get more detailed information regarding that entity. Also, search securities department enforcement actions database at https://www.secure.psc.state.pa.us/releases/Members/index.cfm. *Other Options:* The entire database of Image data is available for purchase. There is a $5,000 start fee and an annual fee of $12,000. Contact Web Services.

Uniform Commercial Code Free

UCC Division, Department of State, www.dos.state.pa.us/DOS/site/default.asp
https://www.corporations.state.pa.us/ucc/soskb/SearchStandardRA9.asp allows a search of UCC-1 financing statements filed with the Corporation Bureau by debtor name or financing statement number; a list of financing statements is displayed. The site also allows a

search of financing statement records filed with the Corporation Bureau by financing statement number. *Other Options:* Daily computer tapes and copies of microfilm are available. Call the number above for details.

Driver Records $$

Department of Transportation, Driver Record Services, www.dmv.state.pa.us The online system is available to high volume requesters for three or ten-year records. Fee is $5.00 per record. The driver's license number and first two letters of the last name are required. Call 717-705-1051 for more information about establishing an account. The resale of records by vendors to other vendors is strictly forbidden. PA licensed drivers may order their own record from the web page using a credit card. *Other Options:* Magnetic tape processing is available for batch requesters. There is a 500 record minimum order per day.

Occupational Licensing Boards

Acupuncturist .... www.licensepa.state.pa.us/
Amphetamine Program...................... www.licensepa.state.pa.us/
Anesthesia Permit, Dental .... www.licensepa.state.pa.us/
Animal Health Technician................ www.licensepa.state.pa.us/
Appraiser, Residential .... www.licensepa.state.pa.us/
Appraiser/Broker .... www.licensepa.state.pa.us/
Architect.. www.licensepa.state.pa.us/
Architectural Firm .... www.licensepa.state.pa.us/
Athletic Agent/Athletic Trainer......... www.licensepa.state.pa.us/
Attorney.. http://padisciplinaryboard.org/attsearchdc.php
Attorney, Disciplined .... http://padisciplinaryboard.org/attsearchdcd.php
Auction Company/House .... www.licensepa.state.pa.us/
Auctioneer .... www.licensepa.state.pa.us/
Audiologist .... www.licensepa.state.pa.us/
Bank .... www.banking.state.pa.us/Banking/Banking/InstListQuery.asp
Barber-related Occupation................. www.licensepa.state.pa.us/
Boxer .... www.dos.state.pa.us/sac/cwp/view.asp?a=1090&q=436810&sacNav=|
Builder/Owner, Real Estate .... www.licensepa.state.pa.us/
Campaign Finance Report .... www.campaignfinance.state.pa.us/
Campground Membership Seller .... www.licensepa.state.pa.us/
Cemetery Broker/Seller/Regis. .... www.licensepa.state.pa.us/
Check Casher..................................... www.banking.state.pa.us/Banking/Banking/InstListQuery.asp
Chiropractor...................................... www.licensepa.state.pa.us/
Consumer Discount Company........... www.banking.state.pa.us/Banking/Banking/InstListQuery.asp
Continuing Edu. Provider, Financial . www.banking.state.pa.us/Banking/Banking/InstListQuery.asp
Cosmetology-related Occupation ...... www.licensepa.state.pa.us/
Counselor, Professional..................... www.licensepa.state.pa.us/
Credit Services Loan Broker .... www.banking.state.pa.us/Banking/Banking/InstListQuery.asp
Credit Union..................................... www.banking.state.pa.us/Banking/Banking/InstListQuery.asp
Debt Collector .... www.banking.state.pa.us/Banking/Banking/InstListQuery.asp
Dental Assistant, Expanded Function www.licensepa.state.pa.us/
Dentist/or/Dental Hygienist............... www.licensepa.state.pa.us/
Dietitian/Nutritionist LDN................. www.licensepa.state.pa.us/
Emergency Medical Technician https://app1.health.state.pa.us/emsportal/
Engineer .... www.licensepa.state.pa.us/
Evaluator, Appraisal .... www.licensepa.state.pa.us/
Financial Holding Company.............. www.banking.state.pa.us/Banking/Banking/InstListQuery.asp
Funeral Director/Superv'r/Establ'mt . www.licensepa.state.pa.us/
Funeral Establishment .... www.licensepa.state.pa.us/
Geologist .... www.licensepa.state.pa.us/
Hearing Aid Fitter/Fitter Apprentice . www.licensepa.state.pa.us/
Hearing Examiner.............................. www.licensepa.state.pa.us/
Installment Loan Seller..................... www.banking.state.pa.us/Banking/Banking/InstListQuery.asp
Insurance Agent/Company http://164.156.71.30/producer/ilist1.asp
Laboratory, Medical .... www.dsf.health.state.pa.us/health/lib/health/labs/clia_certificate.pdf

Landscape Architect .... www.licensepa.state.pa.us/
Loan Correspondent .... www.banking.state.pa.us/Banking/Banking/InstListQuery.asp
Lobbyist/Lobbying Firm................... www.palobbyingservices.state.pa.us/Act134/Public/RegistrationSearch.aspx
Manicurist.. www.licensepa.state.pa.us/
Marriage & Family Therapist .... www.licensepa.state.pa.us/
Medical Doctor................................. www.licensepa.state.pa.us/
Midwife .... www.licensepa.state.pa.us/
Money Transmitter .... www.banking.state.pa.us/Banking/Banking/InstListQuery.asp
Mortgage Banker/Broker/Lender....... www.banking.state.pa.us/Banking/Banking/InstListQuery.asp
Nuclear Medicine Technologist......... www.licensepa.state.pa.us/
Nurse .... www.licensepa.state.pa.us/
Nurses Aide .... www.asisvcs.com/services/registry/search_fs.asp?CPCat=0639NURSE
Nursing Home http://app2.health.state.pa.us/commonpoc/nhLocatorie.asp
Nursing Home Administrator .... www.licensepa.state.pa.us/
Occupational Therapist/Assistant ...... www.licensepa.state.pa.us/
Optometrist....................................... www.licensepa.state.pa.us/
Osteopathic-related Occupation......... www.licensepa.state.pa.us/
Pawnbroker....................................... www.banking.state.pa.us/Banking/Banking/InstListQuery.asp
Pesticide Applicator/Technician   https://www.paplants.state.pa.us/PesticideApplicator/ApplicatorExternalSearch.aspx
Pharmacist/Pharmacy .... www.licensepa.state.pa.us/
Physical Therapist/Assistant............. www.licensepa.state.pa.us/
Physician Assistant........................... www.licensepa.state.pa.us/
Pilot, Navigational........................... www.licensepa.state.pa.us/
Podiatrist.. www.licensepa.state.pa.us/
Political Committee/Contributor........ www.campaignfinance.state.pa.us/
Political Finance Statement www.palobbyingservices.state.pa.us/Act134/Public/RegistrationSearch.aspx
Psychologist...................................... www.licensepa.state.pa.us/
Public Accountant-CPA/Corp./Partn. www.licensepa.state.pa.us/
Public Adjuster/ Solicitor http://164.156.71.30/producer/ilist1.asp
Radiation Therapy Technician........... www.licensepa.state.pa.us/
Radiologic Auxiliary, Chiropractic.... www.licensepa.state.pa.us/
Radiologic Technologist.................... www.licensepa.state.pa.us/
Real Estate Agent/Broker/Seller........ www.licensepa.state.pa.us/
Real Estate Appraiser .... www.licensepa.state.pa.us/
Rental Listing Referral Agent............ www.licensepa.state.pa.us/
Repossessor .... www.banking.state.pa.us/Banking/Banking/InstListQuery.asp
Respiratory Care Practitioner .... www.licensepa.state.pa.us/
Sales Finance Company.................... www.banking.state.pa.us/Banking/Banking/InstListQuery.asp
Savings Association.......................... www.banking.state.pa.us/Banking/Banking/InstListQuery.asp
Social Worker................................... www.licensepa.state.pa.us/
Speech-Language Pathologist............ www.licensepa.state.pa.us/
Surplus Lines Broker http://164.156.71.30/producer/ilist1.asp
Surveyor, Land .... www.licensepa.state.pa.us/
Table Funder, Wholesale .... www.banking.state.pa.us/Banking/Banking/InstListQuery.asp
Teacher .... https://www.tcs.ed.state.pa.us/
Therapist, Drugless........................... www.licensepa.state.pa.us/
Thrift Holding Company .... www.banking.state.pa.us/Banking/Banking/InstListQuery.asp
Timeshare Salesperson .... www.licensepa.state.pa.us/
Title Insurance................................. http://164.156.71.30/producer/ilist1.asp
Trust Company .... www.banking.state.pa.us/Banking/Banking/InstListQuery.asp
Used Vehicle Lot.............................. www.licensepa.state.pa.us/
Vehicle Auction................................ www.licensepa.state.pa.us/
Vehicle Dealer/Manuf't'r/Dist./Seller. www.licensepa.state.pa.us/
Veterinarian/Veterinary Techn'c'n ..... www.licensepa.state.pa.us/

State and Local Courts

State Court Structure: The Courts of Common Pleas are the general trial courts, with jurisdiction over both civil and criminal matters and appellate jurisdiction over matters disposed of by the special courts. The civil records clerk of the Court of Common Pleas is called the Prothonotary. The Superior Court is a Couryt of Appeals. Probate is handled by the Register of Wills.

Small claims cases are, usually, handled by the District Justice Courts. These courts, which are designated as "special courts," also handle civil cases up to $8,000. However, all small claims and civil actions are recorded through the Prothonotary Section of the Court of Common Pleas, which then holds the records. It is not necessary to check with each Magisterial District Court, but rather to check with the Prothonotary for the county.

Statewide Court Online Access: The web page at http://ujsportal.pacourts.us/ offers access to a variety of the Judiciary's Electronic Services (E-Services) such as Web Docket Sheets, DA Link, Superior Court's Web Docketing Statements, etc. Web Docket provides public access to view and print case docket sheets from the criminal cases of the Courts of Common Pleas and from the Appellate Courts. Search by docket number, name or organization.

The Infocon County Access System provides a commercial direct dial-up access to court record information for at least 25 counties. There is a $25.00 base set-up fee plus a minimum $25.00 per month based on a $1.10 fee per minute. For Information, call Infocon at 814-472-6066 or visit www.infoconcountyaccess.com.

❖ **Statewide Access Offered All Trial Courts – Read Above**

Below are Additional Sites ❖

Allegheny County
Court of Common Pleas - Civil www.alleghenycourts.us `Free`
Civil: Access opinions free at www.alleghenycourts.us/search/default.asp?source=opinions_civil.

Armstrong County
Court of Common Pleas - Civil www.co.armstrong.pa.us/ `$$`
Civil: Online access is by subscription from private company-Infocon at www.infoconcountyaccess.com, 814-472-6066. See note in court summary section.

Register of Wills www.co.armstrong.pa.us/registerindex.htm
Civil: Online access available by subscription from private company-Infocon.

Bedford County
Court of Common Pleas - Criminal/Civil/Probate `Free & $$`
Online access is by subscription from private company-Infocon at www.infoconcountyaccess.com, 814-472-6066. See note in court summary section.

Berks County
Court of Common Pleas - Civil www.co.berks.pa.us/courts/site/default.asp `$$`
Civil: The Prothonotary has a remote system to access dockets from 2002 forward. Subscription fee is $300 per year. For information, call 610-478-6967.

Blair County
Court of Common Pleas - Criminal/Civil/Probate `Free & $$`
Online access is by subscription from private company-Infocon at www.infoconcountyaccess.com, 814-472-6066. See note in court summary section.

Bucks County
Court of Common Pleas – Civil/Probate www.buckscounty.org/courts `Free`
Civil: For a limited time, access is free at http://4.43.65.248/autoform.asp?app=cvr. Register of Wills is also included. Domestic and family court dockets are free at http://4.43.65.248/autoform.asp?app=fcr.

Butler County

Court of Common Pleas - Civil www.co.butler.pa.us **$$**
Civil: Online access is by subscription from a private company - Infocon at www.infoconcountyaccess.com, 814-472-6066. See note in court summary section.

Register of Wills **Free** search free at http://66.117.197.22/index.cfm?page=home. Click on "lookup" type at bottom of webpage

Cambria County

Court of Common Pleas - Civil www.co.cambria.pa.us/cambria/site/default.asp **$$**
Civil: Access to civil index is available by subscription at Infocon.com; Signup online or get details at 814-472-6066.

Carbon County

Court of Common Pleas – Civil/Crimonal/Probate www.carboncourts.com **Free**
Civil: Online access to the clerk of courts docket records is free at www.carboncourts.com/pubacc.htm. Registration required.

Chester County

Court of Common Pleas - Civil http://dsf.chesco.org **Free**
Civil: Internet access to county records including court records requires a sign-up and credit card payment. Application fee: $50. There is a $10.00 per month minimum (no charge for no activity); and $.10 each transaction beyond 100. Sign-up and/or logon at http://epin.chesco.org/. Also, a court case list is free at http://dsf.chesco.org/courts/site/default.asp; click on "Miscellaneous List." .

Register of Wills **$$** Internet access to probate records requires a sign-up and payment. Sign-up and/or logon at http://epin.chesco.org.

Clarion County

Court of Common Pleas – Civil/Criminal/Register of Wills www.co.clarion.pa.us/ **$$**
Civil: Online access is by subscription from private company-Infocon at www.infoconcountyaccess.com, 814-472-6066. See note in court summary section.

Clearfield County

Register of Wills & Clerk of Orphans Court **$$** Search records 1990 to present by name at www.landex.com; registration and fees required.

Clinton County

Court of Common Pleas - Criminal/Civil www.clintoncountypa.com/courts.htm **$$**
Civil: See note at beginning of section. *Criminal:* Internet access to court records is by subscription from a private company-Infocon at www.ic-access.com, 814-472-6066. See note at beginning of section.

Cumberland County

Court of Common Pleas - Criminal www.ccpa.net/index.asp?nid=1129 **Free**
Criminal: Search dockets online free at http://ujsportal.pacourts.us/WebDocketSheets/WebDocketSheets.aspx back to 1994. Also, you may also search at www.ccpa.net/index.asp?NID=2743 and select Criminal Records and Documents. First acquire username and password from Clerk of Courts Office. Selected opinions free at http://records.ccpa.net/weblink_judges/Browse.aspx?dbid=3.

Dauphin County

Court of Common Pleas - Civil www.dauphincounty.org/court-departments/ **Free**
Civil: Access civil cases back to 11/21, suits (1992-10/31/2001) and judgments back to 1983 free at www.dauphinc.org/onlineservices/public/header.asp.

Delaware County

Court of Common Pleas - Criminal/Civil www.co.delaware.pa.us **Free**
Civil: Online access to court civil records free (may begin charging at any time) at /www2.co.delaware.pa.us/pa/default.htm. For more information, call 610-891-4370. Search online by document type, document number, etc. *Criminal:* Search dockets online free at http://ujsportal.pacourts.us/WebDocketSheets/WebDocketSheets.aspx back to 1974.

Erie County

Court of Common Pleas - Civil www.eriecountygov.org/ **$$**
Civil: Online access is by subscription from private company-Infocon at www.infoconcountyaccess.com, 814-472-6066. See note in court summary section.

Fayette County

Court of Common Pleas - Civil **$$**
Civil: Internet access to court records is by subscription from a private company-Infocon at www.ic-access.com, 814-472-6066. See note at beginning of section.

Franklin County
Court of Common Pleas - Civil   `$$`
Civil: Access index by subscription from private company-Infocon at www.infoconcountyaccess.com, 814-472-6066. See note at beginning of section.

Huntingdon County
Court of Common Pleas - Criminal/Civil   `$$`
Civil: Online access is by subscription from private company-Infocon at www.infoconcountyaccess.com, 814-472-6066. See note in court summary section. *Criminal:* Internet access to court records is by subscription from a private company-Infocon at www.ic-access.com, 814-472-6066.

Lancaster County
Court of Common Pleas - Civil   www.co.lancaster.pa.us/courts/site/default.asp   `Free`
Civil: Access to the Prothonotary's civil court records is free at www.co.lancaster.pa.us/scripts/bannerweb.dll. Also, historical court case schedules are free at www.co.lancaster.pa.us, click on "Court Schedules" Includes Register, Treasurer, and other courthouse record data. Results include addresses. Call Kathy Harris at 717-299-8252 for info.

Register of Wills   http://www.co.lancaster.pa.us   `Free`   Access probate back to 1933 and marriage records back to 1948 free at http://paperless.co.lancaster.pa.us/viewerportal/.

Lawrence County
Court of Common Pleas - Criminal/Civil   www.co.lawrence.pa.us   `$$`
Online access is by subscription from private company-Infocon at www.infoconcountyaccess.com, 814-472-6066. See note in court summary section.

Register of Wills   http://www.co.lawrence.pa.us/rr/index.html   `Free & $$`   Record access may also be free or subscription at www.lawrencecountyrecordspa.us/countyweb/login.jsp?countyname=Lawrence.

Lehigh County
Court of Common Pleas - Civil   www.lccpa.org   `$$`
Civil: Access to the county online system requires $300.00 annual usage fee. Search by name or case number. Call Lehigh Cty Fiscal Office at 610-782-3112 for more information.

Mercer County
Court of Common Pleas - Civil   www.mcc.co.mercer.pa.us   `$$`
Civil: Online access is by subscription from private company-Infocon at www.infoconcountyaccess.com, 814-472-6066. See note in court summary section.

Mifflin County
Court of Common Pleas - Criminal/Civil   www.co.mifflin.pa.us/mifflin/site/default.asp   `Free`
Civil: Court calendar available at the website. Internet access to court records is by subscription from a private company-Infocon at www.ic-access.com, 814-472-6066. See note at beginning of section. *Criminal:* Court calendar at the website. Internet access to court records is by subscription from a private company-Infocon at www.ic-access.com, 814-472-6066. See note at beginning of section. Also, search dockets online free at http://ujsportal.pacourts.us/WebDocketSheets/WebDocketSheets.aspx back to 1986.

Monroe County
Register of Wills   `$$`   Access wills records online at www.landex.com/remote/. Fee is $.20 per minute and $.50 per fax page. Wills go back to 11/1836.

Montgomery County
Court of Common Pleas - Civil   http://prothy.montcopa.org/prothy/site/default.asp   `Free`
Civil: Court and other records are free at http://webapp.montcopa.org/PSI/Viewer/Search.aspx?c=CaseSearch&panel=CaseNumber. This includes active and purged civil cases, also active probate cases, also calendars.

Register of Wills   http://www.courts.montcopa.org/courts/site/default.asp   `Free`   Search active cases at www.montcopa.org/registerofwillsorphanscourt/rwocviewer/. Email registerofwillsorphanscourt@mail.montcopa.org. If you provide a name, they will search docket books and computer for a file number.

Montour County
Court of Common Pleas - Criminal/Civil   www.montourco.org   `$$`
Civil: Online access is by subscription from private company-Infocon at www.infoconcountyaccess.com, 814-472-6066. See note in court summary section. *Criminal:* Internet access to court records is by subscription from a private company-Infocon at www.ic-access.com, 814-472-6066. See note at beginning of section.

Northampton County
Court of Common Pleas - Criminal   www.nccpa.org   `Free`
Search calendars and schedules for free online at www.nccpa.org/schedule.html. Opinions to be available soon.

Philadelphia County

Court of Common Pleas - Civil   http://courts.phila.gov   **Free**
Civil: Access to 1st Judicial District Civil Trial records is free at http://fjdwebserver.phila.gov. Free registration required. Search by name, judgment and docket info. Also search civil free at http://fjd.phila.gov. There is also a civil docket and judgment name search at http://fjdweb2.phila.gov/fjd1/repl1/zk_fjd_public_qry_00.zp_main_idx.html.

Municipal Court - Civil   http://fjd.phila.gov   **Free**
Civil: Access muni court dockets online free at hhttp://fjdclaims.phila.gov/phmuni/cms/search2.do .

Register of Wills   **Free**   Search Orphan's Court records free at http://fjdweb2.phila.gov/fjd/zk_fjd_public_qry_11.zp_orphans_idx. Site may be temporarily down.

Pike County

Court of Common Pleas   www.pikepa.org   **$$**
Civil: Online access is by subscription from private company-Infocon at www.infoconcountyaccess.com, 814-472-6066. See note in court summary section. *Criminal:* Internet access to court records is by subscription from a private company-Infocon at www.ic-access.com, 814-472-6066. See note at beginning of section.

Potter County

Court of Common Pleas   **Free & $$**
Civil: Online access is by subscription from private company-Infocon at www.infoconcountyaccess.com, 814-472-6066. See note in court summary section.

Schuylkill County

Court of Common Pleas - Civil   www.co.schuylkill.pa.us   **Free**
Civil: Access civil court records and judgments free at www.co.schuylkill.pa.us/info/Civil/Inquiry/Search.csp.

Susquehanna County

Court of Common Pleas – Civil   **$$**
Online access is by subscription from private company-Infocon at www.infoconcountyaccess.com, 814-472-6066. See note in court summary section.

Union County

Register of Wills   http://www.unionco.org   **Free**   Search wills online at www.courthouseonline.com/WillsSearch.asp?State=PA&County=Union&Abbrev=Un&Office=RW

Washington County

Court of Common Pleas - Civil   www.co.washington.pa.us   **Free & $$**
Civil: Access to prothonotary civil records including also orphans court is by subscription; enroll form at www.co.washington.pa.us/downloadpage.aspx?menuDept=28. Also, records available on Common Pleas Ct database at www.co.washington.pa.us/wccourtdocuments/code/login.asp. Registration, username, and password required.

Court of Common Pleas - Criminal   www.co.washington.pa.us   **Free**
Criminal: Search dockets online free at http://ujsportal.pacourts.us/WebDocketSheets/WebDocketSheets.aspx back to 1987. Also, records available on Common Pleas Ct database at www.co.washington.pa.us/wccourtdocuments/code/login.asp. Registration, username, and password required.

Register of Wills   http://www.co.washington.pa.us/maindepartment.aspx?menuDept=30   **Free & $$**   Wills available on Common Pleas Ct database at www.co.washington.pa.us/wccourtdocuments/code/login.asp. Registration, username, and password required.

Wayne County

Court of Common Pleas - Criminal   **Free**
Criminal: Search dockets online free at http://ujsportal.pacourts.us/WebDocketSheets/WebDocketSheets.aspx back to 1995.

Westmoreland County

Court of Common Pleas - Civil, Register of Wills   www.co.westmoreland.pa.us   **Free & $$**
Civil: Access civil court dockets back to 1985 free at http://westmorelandweb400.us:8088/EGSPublicAccess.htm. Also, search Register of Wills and marriages free back to 1986. Access to full remote online system has $100 setup (no set-up if accessed via Internet) plus $20 monthly minimum. System includes civil, criminal, Prothonotary indexes and recorder data. For info, call 724-830-3874, or click on "e-services" at website.

York County

Register of Wills   **$$**   Online access to wills is available through a private company at http://www.landex.com/remote/. Fee is $.20 per minute and $.50 per fax page. Images and wills go back to 2/1999.

Recorders, Assessors, and Other Sites of Note

Recording Office Organization: 67 counties, 67 recording offices and 134 UCC filing offices. Each county has two different recording offices. One is the Prothonotary - Pennsylvania's term for "clerk" - who accepted UCC and tax lien filings until July 1, 2001. The other is the Recorder of Deeds who maintains real estate records. All federal and state tax liens on personal property and on real property are filed with the Prothonotary. Usually, tax liens on personal property are filed in the judgment index of the Prothonotary.

Online Access Note: A number of counties provide web access to assessor data. Also, the Infocon County Access System provides internet and direct dial-up access to recorded record information for over twenty Pennsylvania counties; for information call Infocon at 814-472-6066 or visit www.infoconcountyaccess.com

Allegheny County Prothonotary *Civil, Judgment, UCC, Tax Lien Records*
http://prothonotary.county.allegheny.pa.us ▊Free & $$▊ Access to Prothonotary pre-1995 indices is free at http://prothonotary.county.allegheny.pa.us/allegheny/welcome.htm. Registration is required for the complete prothonotary system. Credit card purchasing available. UCC records are pre-7-1-2001. Online access to the certified values database is free at the website. Also, there is a free case search.

Allegheny County Recorder *Real Estate, Deed, Mortgage Records* www.county.allegheny.pa.us ▊Free & $$▊
Access Recorder's Index free at https://www.recorder.county.allegheny.pa.us/palr/pa003/index.jsp. Index goes back to 1986; images to 2001. Fee for doc is $1.00 per page, max fee 10 pages; Commercial draw down account copy fee is $.50 per page.
Property, Taxation Records ▊Free▊ Access to Allegheny County real estate database is free at
http://www2.county.allegheny.pa.us/realestate/Search.asp.

Armstrong County Prothonotary *Judgment, Tax Lien Records* www.co.armstrong.pa.us For online access see Register of Deeds.

Armstrong County Recorder *Real Estate, Deed, Marriage, Probate, Orphans Court Records* ▊Free & $$▊
Access is through a private company. For info, call Infocon at 814-472-6066 or www.infoconcountyaccess.com. Includes Orphan Court, Recorder of Deeds, Register of Wills images.

Beaver County Recorder *Real Estate, Deed, Mortgage Records* www.co.beaver.pa.us/Recorder/index.htm
▊Free▊ Access to the Recorder's database is free at www.co.beaver.pa.us/Recorder/disclaimer.htm. Deed index back to 1957, images to 1957.
Property, Taxation Records ▊Free▊ Access Assess office at www.co.beaver.pa.us/AssessmentPublic/.

Bedford County Prothonotary *Judgment, Tax Lien Records* For online access see Recorder of Deeds.

Bedford County Recorder *Real Estate, Deed, Probate, Marriage, Tax Claim Records*
www.bedford.net/regrec/home.html ▊Free & $$▊ Access is via a private company; call Infocon at 814-472-6066 or www.infoconcountyaccess.com. Includes Recorder of Deeds and Register of Wills images.

Berks County Prothonotary *Judgment, Lien, Civil Court Records*
www.co.berks.pa.us/berks/cwp/view.asp?a=1150&q=444559 ▊$$▊ Prothonotary offers internet access to info back to 1/1996. Fee is $300. For info, call 610-478-6967.

Berks County Recorder *Birth, Death, Marriage Records* www.berksrecofdeeds.com ▊Free▊ Access vital records from Register of Wills searchable indexes free at www.co.berks.pa.us/rwills/s/RegMain.htm and includes county and City of Reading; various dates.
Property, Taxation Records ▊Free▊ Access parcel records free at
http://ema.countyofberks.com/Parcel_Search/presentation/chameleon/search.asp.

Blair County Prothonotary *Judgment, Tax Lien, Civil Court Records* For online access see Recorder of Deeds.

Blair Recorder of Deeds *Real Estate, Deed, Will, Probate Records* www.blaircountyrecorder.com ▊$$▊ Access recorded index back to 1990 and images to 2003 by subscription to www.landex.com, 717-274-5890. Register of Will index goes back to 2000, images to 2005. Landex Remote and Landex Webstore (per piece) both available.
Property, Taxation Records ▊Free▊ A private company sells county tax claim property, view list free at www.xspand.com/investors/realestate_sale/index.aspx.

Bradford County Recorder *Real Estate, Deed, Mortgage, Will Records* www.bradfordcountypa.org
▊Free & $$▊ Access the index free at www.landex.com/webstore/jsp/cart/DocumentSearch.jsp. Full access to Recorder of Deeds and Wills and Orphans Court is by subscription at www.landex.com/remote/. Fee is $.10 per page view, $.50 per fax page. Recorder data goes back to 1971; images to 1970, also 1985-89. Wills and orphan court goes back to 1997.

Bucks County Prothonotary/Civil Div *Property, Tax Lien, Probate, Court, Will, Voter Registration Records* www.buckscounty.org/courts/ Free & $$ Access prothonotary records free at http://4.43.65.248/menu.asp back to 1980. Includes lending agency, Register of Wills, liens, sheriff sales, voter registration, civil and criminal courts as well as assessor and recorder of deeds records. For info on the fee system, contact Jack Morris 215-348-6579 or view details at website. Search civil cases directly at http://4.43.65.248/autoform.asp?app=cvr. Search family and domestic dockets free at http://4.43.65.248/autoform.asp?app=fcr.

Bucks County Recorder *Real Estate, Deed, Tax Lien, Judgment, Voter Registration Records* www.buckscounty.org/government/rowOfficers/RecorderofDeeds/index.aspx Free & $$ Access county records free at http://4.43.65.248/menu.asp back to 1980. Includes lending agency, Register of Wills, liens, sheriff sales, voter registration, courts, prothonotary as well as assessor and recorder of deeds records. For info on the fee system, contact Jack Morris at 215-348-6579 or visit the website.
Property, Taxation Records Free & $$ Access to parcel, sale, and property assessment data is free at http://4.43.65.248/autoform.asp?app=par. Access the index free at www.landex.com/webstore/jsp/cart/DocumentSearch.jsp. Full access to Recorder of Deeds and Wills and Orphans Court is by subscription at www.landex.com/remote/. Fee is $.10 per page view, $.50 per fax page.

Butler County Prothonotary *Judgment, Fed Lien, Divorce Records* www.co.butler.pa.us $$ Private company offers online access to most of the recorded records. Call Infocon at 814-472-6066, www.infoconcountyaccess.com.

Butler County Recorder *Real Estate, Deed, Marriage, Lien Probate, Orphans Court, Guardianship Records* www.co.butler.pa.us Free & $$ Access deeds records free at www.co.butler.pa.us/recorder/. Also, access marriage, probate, and prothonotary records via a private company; call Infocon at 814-472-6066, www.infoconcountyaccess.com. Images available. Also access probate court estate and guardianship records free at http://66.117.197.22/index.cfm?page=home. At bottom of webpage, click on the type of "lookup" you want.

Cambria County Prothonotary *Judgment, Lien, Civil Court, Divorce Records* www.co.cambria.pa.us/cambria/site/default.asp $$ Access prothonotary records via a private company. Subscription required. For info, call Infocon at 814-472-6066, www.infoconcountyaccess.com.

Cambria County Recorder *Marriage, Probate, Orphans Court, Will Records* www.co.cambria.pa.us/cambria/site/default.asp $$ Access county records via a private company. Subscription required; images available. For info, call Infocon at 814-472-6066, www.infoconcountyaccess.com.

Cameron County Recorder *Real Estate, Deed, Lien, Will Records* Free & $$ Access the index free at www.landex.com/webstore/jsp/cart/DocumentSearch.jsp. Full access to Recorder of Deeds and Wills and Orphans Court is by subscription at www.landex.com/remote/. Index and images go back to 8/2005.

Carbon County Prothonotary *Judgment, Lien, UCC, Probate, Will Records* www.carboncourts.com/prothy.htm Free Access to county prothonotary, Register of Wills, and Clerk of Courts remote public access dial-up database is free; 570-325-3288; instructions and registration at www.carboncourts.com/pubacc.htm.

Carbon County Recorder *Real Estate, Deed, Lien, Will Records* www.carboncounty.com/deeds.htm Free & $$ Access the index free at www.landex.com/webstore/jsp/cart/DocumentSearch.jsp. Full access to Recorder of Deeds and Wills and Orphans Court is by subscription at www.landex.com/remote/. Index goes back to 1988, images to 8/1994.
Property, Taxation Records Free Access assessor property data free at www.carboncounty.com/records.htm.

Centre County Prothonotary *Lien, Judgment Records* www.co.centre.pa.us/223.htm $$ Access Prothonotary data and more at http://epin.chesco.org; registration and fees required.

Centre County Recorder *Real Estate, Deed Records* www.co.centre.pa.us/133.asp $$ Access recorded data on the WEB IA subscription system; fee is $10.00 set-up plus $.06 per click or other per click plan. This replaces the old dial-up system. See http://webia.co.centre.pa.us/login.asp.
Property, Taxation Records $$ Assessment data on the WEB IA subscription system; registration and per page fees apply; see http://webia.co.centre.pa.us/login.asp.

Chester County Prothonotary *Lien, Court, Judgment Records* www.chesco.org/ $$ Full countywide records including court records requires a sign-up and credit card payment. Application fee is $50. with $10.00 per month minimum; no charge for no activity; $.10 each transaction beyond 100. Sign-up and logon at http://epin.chesco.org.

Chester County Recorder *Real Estate, Deed, Vital Statistic, Archive Records* http://dsf.chesco.org/recorder/site/default.asp Free & $$ Search Recorder of Deeds records free at http://rod.chesco.org/icris/splash.jsp. Also, full countywide records including court records requires a sign-up and credit card payment. Application fee is $50. with $10.00 per month minimum - no charge for no activity; $.10 each transaction beyond 100. Sign-up and/or logon at http://epin.chesco.org. Also, genealogical and older vital statistics are free at http://dsf.chesco.org/archives/site/default.asp.
Property, Taxation Records $$ Assessment data available by subscription at http://epin.chesco.org.

Clarion County Prothonotary *Judgment, Lien Records* **$$** For online access see Recorder of Deeds.

Clarion County Recorder *Real Estate, Deed, OCC/PC, Marriage, Voter Registration, Orphans Court,*
Probate, Tax Claim Records www.co.clarion.pa.us **$$** Access is through a private company. For info, call Infocon at 814-472-6066 or www.infoconcountyaccess.com. Includes images for Recorder, Register of Wills, and Orphans court.

Clearfield County Recorder *Real Estate, Deed, Mortgage, Probate, Orphans Court Records*
www.clearfieldco.org **Free & $$** Access the index free at www.landex.com/webstore/jsp/cart/DocumentSearch.jsp. Full access to Recorder of Deeds and Wills and Orphans Court is by subscription at www.landex.com/remote/. Fee is $.20 per minute, $1.00 per fax page. Recorder index goes back to 1986; images back to 1989. Wills and orphan court records go back to 1990.
Property, Taxation Records **Free** Assessors county tax sale list is updated weekly at www.clearfieldco.org/tax_sale_list.html.

Clinton County Prothonotary *Judgment, Tax Lien Records* www.clintoncountypa.com **$$**
Online access via a private company, see County Recorder of Deeds.

Clinton County Recorder *Real Estate, Deed, Probate, Orphan Court, Property, Treasurer, Tax Claim*
Records www.clintoncountypa.com/register_&_recorder.htm **$$** Access available via a private company. For info call Infocom at 814-472-6066 or www.infoconcountyaccess.com. Includes images for Recorder, Register of Wills, Orphans Court, prothonotary.
Property, Taxation Records **Free** Access to gis-mapping property and assessment data is free at www.clintoncountypa.com/giswelcome.htm. Also, access treasure's tax sale lists free at www.clintoncountypa.com/taxsale.htm.

Columbia County Recorder *Real Estate, Deed, Mortgage, UCC, Will Records*
www.columbiapa.org/reg_rec/index.html **Free & $$** Access the index free at www.landex.com/webstore/jsp/cart/DocumentSearch.jsp. Full access is via subscription at www.landex.com/remote/. Fee is $.20 per minute. Recorders index goes back to 1974; wills index back to 1995; UCCs to 1992; images go back to 1/1974; wills and UCCs to 10/1999.
Property, Taxation Records **Free** Access to gis-mapping property and assessment data is free at www.columbiapa.org/gis/disclaimer.html. Click on Search Database.

Cumberland County Prothonotary *Judgment, Lien, Civil Records* **Free** For online access see Cumberland
Recorder of Deeds or www.ccpa.net/cumberland/cwp/view.asp?a=1369&Q=461527. No name searching.

Cumberland County Recorder *Real Estate, Deed, Lien Records* www.ccpa.net **$$** Records access available
via a private company. For info call Infocon at 814-472-6066 or www.infoconcountyaccess.com. Includes images for Recorder of Deeds records. Access also available by subscription via www.landex.com/remote/.
Property, Taxation Records **Free** Access to the property assessment data is free at http://taxdb.ccpa.net/default.asp. No name searching. Access property data on the GIS-mapping site free at http://ccgis.ccpa.net/taxmapper/. Search delinquent tax index at http://taxdb.ccpa.net/delinquent/default.asp but no name searching. Tax Sale data at www.ccpa.net/index.asp?nid=2675.

Dauphin County Prothonotary *Real Estate, Deed, Mortgage, UCC Records* www.dauphinc.org/deeds/ **Free**
At www.dauphinc.org/deeds/ search document indexes and images in the Recorder of Deeds Office filed from 1979 to the present. Most documents are available for public inspection. UCCs go back to 10/1/93.

Dauphin County Recorder *Real Estate, Deed, Mortgage, Register of Wills Records* www.dauphinc.org/deeds
Free & $$ Access the register's land records database free at http://198.185.140.50/oncoreweb/Search.aspx. Access REgister of Wills and Orphan Ct docs free at www.landex.com/webstore/jsp/cart/DocumentSearch.jsp. Full access to Register of Wills and Orphans Court is by subscription at www.landex.com/remote/. Images go back 5/2006.
Property, Taxation Records **Free & $$** Access to county assessor property data is free at www.dauphinpropertyinfo.org/propertymax/rover30.asp. To search free, create a limited guest account. Full access fee is $50.00 per month.

Delaware County Prothonotary *Judgment, Civil Records* www.co.delaware.pa.us **Free**
Records available at http://www2.co.delaware.pa.us/pa/publicaccess.asp.

Delaware County Recorder *Real Estate, Deed, Judgment Records* http://www2.co.delaware.pa.us/pa/default.htm
Free Access to the public access system is free - temporarily - at http://w01.co.delaware.pa.us/pa/publicaccessRODFrame.asp. Records go back to 1982. No name searching. Also, search 1982 to 7/31/2001 deeds free at free at http://www2.co.delaware.pa.us/pa/PublicTerm.asp.
Property, Taxation Records **Free** Select #3 Real Estate and Assessment to access property tax data, 1982 to 7/31/2001 deeds, and delinquent taxes free at http://www2.co.delaware.pa.us/pa/PublicTerm.asp. Also search at http://w01.co.delaware.pa.us/pa/publicaccess.asp?real.x=71&real.y=50.

Erie County Recorder *Real Estate, Deed, Marriage, Probate, Orphan Court Records* www.eriecountygov.org
`$$` Recorder access is through a private company. Includes images, courts, and prothonotary; call Infocon at 814-472-6066 or www.infoconcountyaccess.com.
Property, Taxation Records `Free & $$` Access property records data free at www.eriecountygov.org/government/assessment/parcelsearch.aspx, no name searching. Also, full data for real estate professionals is available by subscription, click on "sign in" and follow the menu for details. Also, you may purchase judicial and/or sheriff sale property sale lists for $10.00 each, see www.eriecountygov.org/government/taxclaim/default.aspx.

Fayette County Prothonotary *Lien, Judgment Records* `$$` Access prothonotary index by subscription; call Infocon at 814-472-6066 or www.infoconcountyaccess.com.

Fayette County Recorder *Marriage, Will, Probate, Orphans Court Records* `$$` Search marriages, orphan court, and Register of Wills data from a private company; for info call Infocom at 814-472-6066 or www.infoconcountyaccess.com.
Property, Taxation Records `Free` Access to property assessments is free at www.fayetteproperty.org/assessor.

Franklin County Recorder *Real Estate, Deed, Probate Records* http://co.franklin.pa.us `$$`
Access is via a private company; call Infocon at 814-472-6066 or www.infoconcountyaccess.com.

Greene County Recorder *Real Estate, Deed, Mortgage Records*
www.co.greene.pa.us/secured/gc/depts/lo/rr/index.htm `$$` Access real estate deed records may be available by subscription at http://216.27.81.170/login.asp. Contact Recorder office for sign-up details.
Property, Taxation Records `Free & $$` Access Assessor property records by web subscription, see www.co.greene.pa.us/secured/gc/depts/cc/asses/prop-records.htm or call Pam at 724-852-5210. Fee is $700 per year or $200 per quarter; includes Property Record Card System. A free 30-day trial is offered.

Huntingdon County Prothonotary *Judgment, Tax Lien Records* `Free & $$` Access is through a private company. Includes courts and prothonotary; call Infocon at 814-472-6066 or www.infoconcountyaccess.com.

Huntingdon County Recorder *Real Estate, Deed, Marriage, Probate, Orphans Court Records*
http://huntingdoncounty.net/hunt_co/site/default.asp `$$` Access is via a private company; call Infocon at 814-472-6066 or www.infoconcountyaccess.com.

Indiana County Prothonotary *Civil, Judgment Records* www.countyofindiana.org `Free & $$` Access is through a private company. Includes courts and prothonotary; call Infocon at 814-472-6066 or www.infoconcountyaccess.com.

Indiana County Recorder *Real Estate, Deed Records* www.countyofindiana.org `Free & $$` Access is available by subscription at http://regrec.countyofindiana.org/countyweb/login.jsp?countyname=Indiana/ but you may login as Guest and search free.

Jefferson County Recorder *Real Estate, Deed, Lien, Marriage, Register of Wills Records* `$$`
Access recording index by subscription; call Infocon at 814-472-6066 or www.infoconcountyaccess.com.

Juniata County Recorder *Real Estate, Marriage, Probate, Orphans Court Records* `$$` Access is via a private company; call Infocon at 814-472-6066 or www.infoconcountyaccess.com. Includes Recorder of Deeds record images.

Lackawanna County Recorder *Real Estate, Deed, Will Records* www.lackawannacounty.org `Free & $$`
Access the index free at www.landex.com/webstore/jsp/cart/DocumentSearch.jsp. Full access to Recorder of Deeds and Wills and Orphans Court is by subscription at www.landex.com/remote/. Index and images go back to 8/1994.
Property, Taxation Records `Free` Access property data free at http://ao.lackawannacounty.org/agreed.php.

Lancaster County Prothonotary *Judgment, Civil Records* www.co.lancaster.pa.us/prothonotary `Free`
Access prothonotary court records free at www.co.lancaster.pa.us/scripts/bannerweb.dll. Civil index goes back to 7/1/1987; judgments back to 8/2/1993

Lancaster County Recorder *Real Estate, Deed, UCC, Probate, Death, Marriage Records*
www.lancasterdeeds.com/lanco_rod/site/default.asp `Free` Access to deeds, UCCs and other recordings is free after registration at http://icris.lancasterdeeds.com/icris/splash.jsp. Also, search probate, death and marriage records free at http://paperless.co.lancaster.pa.us/viewerportal/.
Property, Taxation Records `Free` Access assessor property data free at www.co.lancaster.pa.us/lanco/cwp/view.asp?a=565&q=537155. Access property data free on the GIS-mapping site at www.co.lancaster.pa.us/gis/site/default.asp?. Click on GIS-Property Search; choose Query to search by owner name. Sheriff sales list at www.co.lancaster.pa.us/sheriffsoffice/cwp/view.asp?a=3&q=582487.

Lawrence County Prothonotary *Judgment, Tax Lien Records* www.co.lawrence.pa.us `$$` Access is via Infocon, a private company; document images included; call Infocon at 814-472-6066 or www.infoconcountyaccess.com

Lawrence County Recorder *Real Estate, Deed, Marriage, Probate, Orphans Court Records*
www.co.lawrence.pa.us `$$` Access back to 12/2005 is via Infocon, a private company; document images included; call Infocon

at 814-472-6066 or www.infoconcountyaccess.com. Also, recorder data available by subscription at http://counties.recordfusion.com/countyweb/login.jsp?countyname=Lawrence; registration and fees required, contact Recorder of Deeds office for signup and details. Free trial available.

Property, Taxation Records **Free** Search assessments pdf pages by ward, borough or town at Access 2007 assessment values free at www.co.lawrence.pa.us/Preliminary_Assessment/Preliminary_Assessment.html. Search property records after free registration at www.lawrencecountyrecordspa.us/assessor/login.jsp?countyname=LawrenceAssessor or by registering at http://counties.recordfusion.com/assessor/login.jsp?countyname=LawrenceAssessor.

Lebanon County Recorder *Real Estate, Deed, Mortgage Records* www.lebcounty.org **Free & $$**
Access the index free at www.landex.com/webstore/jsp/cart/DocumentSearch.jsp. Full access to Recorder of Deeds official records is by subscription at www.landex.com/remote/. For info call OSS at 717-274-5890. Deed and mortgage index goes back to 1933; Misc index back to 1972; Deed images back to 1996; Mortgage images to 2000; Miscellaneous images go back to 2001.

Property, Taxation Records **Free & $$** Access property data by subscription at www.courthouseonline.com/MyProperty.asp. Sub fee $9.95 3-days, up to $275 per year. A free view available if you have control number and password from tax notice or are registered.

Lehigh County Prothonotary *Judgment, Lien, Court, County Grants Records* www.lccpa.org **Free & $$**
County's full-access internet pay system initial cost was $300.00 per year. For signup info, call the Fiscal Office at 610-782-3112. Also, at www.lehighcounty.org, the County Grants database is searched free; free registration required.

Lehigh County Recorder *Real Estate, Grantor/Grantee, Deed, Tax Lien, Game License, Civil, Marriage, Will, Judgment, Naturalization Records* www.lehighcounty.org **$$**
Access to the county's full-access internet pay system 1s $318.00 a year initial cost. Call Lehigh County Computer Svcs Dept at 610-782-3286 for signup or info. Also, subscribe to view naturalization, property tax, assessment, tax records for a fee at www.lehighcounty.org/public/public.cfm. Also, access grantor/grantee index by subscription at www.lehighcounty.org/Econ/econ_grants.cfm?doc=grant_login.cfm. Court records, marriages, and Register of Wills records online by subscription at www.lehighcounty.org/public/public.cfm?doc=ody_home.cfm.

Property, Taxation Records **Free** Access assessor property data free at www.lehighcounty.org/Assessment/Puba.cfm but no name searching. For deeper access, subscribe at www.lehighcounty.org/public/public.cfm. $300.00 yearly fee applies. Also, view tax sale data free at www.lehighcounty.org/Fiscal/taxsale.cfm. Also, view sheriff's tax sales lists free at www.lehighcounty.org/Fiscal/taxsale.cfm

Luzerne County Recorder *Real Estate, Deed, Mortgage, Register of Wills Records* www.luzernecounty.org **$$**
Access the index free at www.landex.com/webstore/jsp/cart/DocumentSearch.jsp. Full access is through a private company at www.landex.com/remote/. Fee is $.20 per minute. Index goes back to 1/1993; images back to 9/1983. Register of Will data is a separate subscription, also at Landex; Wills index and images go back to 8/2004.

Property, Taxation Records **Free & $$** Access property data at www.wbtimesleader.com/cgi-bin/authenticate.cgi. Access data by subscription at www.courthouseonline.com/MyProperty.asp. $9.95 3-day, up to $275 per year. Get free view with control number & password from tax notice-registration. Also, access property data by subscription at www.courthouseonline.com/MyProperty.asp. A free view available if you have control number and password from tax notice or are registered.

Lycoming County Recorder *Property, Taxation Records* **Free & $$** Access property data by subscription at www.courthouseonline.com/MyProperty.asp. Sub fee $9.95 3-days, up to $275 per year. A free view available if you have control number and password from tax notice or are registered.

McKean County Recorder *Real Estate, Deed, Lien, Mortgage Records* www.mckeancountypa.org **Free & $$**
Access the index free at www.landex.com/webstore/jsp/cart/DocumentSearch.jsp. Full access to Recorder of Deeds is by subscription at www.landex.com/remote/. Index goes back to 1973, images to 10/2002.

Mercer County Prothonotary *Judgment, Tax Lien Records* For online access see Recorder of Deeds.

Mercer County Recorder *Real Estate, Grantor/Grantee, Deed, Lien, Occ/PC, Tax Claim Records*
www.mcc.co.mercer.pa.us/ **Free & $$** Access to general records index back to 1972 is available at http://141.151.130.246/resolution/. Images go back to 7/15/2005. Also, access to index is via a private company; for info, call Infocon at 814-472-6066 or www.infoconcountyaccess.com. Search dog database at www.mcc.co.mercer.pa.us/DogOwnerSearch/default.htm but no name search.

Mifflin County Prothonotary *Judgment, Tax Lien Records*
www.co.mifflin.pa.us/mifflin/cwp/view.asp?a=657&Q=410994 **$$** Access is via a private company; call Infocon at 814-472-6066 or www.infoconcountyaccess.com.

Mifflin County Recorder *Real Estate, Deed, Probate, Orphans Court, Marriage, Tax Claim Records*
www.co.mifflin.pa.us/mifflin **$$** Access is via a private company; call Infocon at 814-472-6066 or www.infoconcountyaccess.com; recorder back to 1993, probate, orphans and marriages back to 2000; images soon to be available for Recorder records, indexes for others.

Property, Taxation Records **Free** Property data is free at http://gis.co.mifflin.pa.us/website/mifflincounty/viewer.htm?. Use the new free Web Mapping Parcel Application to name search for property data.

Monroe County Prothonotary *Judgment, Tax Lien, Marriage Records* **$$** Access is via a private company; call Infocon at 814-472-6066 or www.infoconcountyaccess.com.

Monroe County Recorder *Real Estate, Deed, Will, Mortgage, Map Records* **Free & $$**
Access the index free at www.landex.com/webstore/jsp/cart/DocumentSearch.jsp. Full access is through a private company at www.landex.com/remote/. Fee is $.20 per minute and $.50 per fax page. Land Index goes back to 1/1979; wills index back to 11/1836; images of land records go back to 1958, Will images to 1990. Map images are also available.

Montgomery County Prothonotary *Judgment, Lien Records* www.montcopa.org **Free & $$**
See Recorder of Deeds

Montgomery County Recorder *Real Estate, Deed, Mortgage, UCC, Lien, Estate, Judgment Records*
http://www2.montcopa.org/montco/site/default.asp **Free & $$** Recorder of Deeds records are at http://rodviewer.montcopa.org/countyweb/login.jsp?countyname=Montgomery. Login as Guest or subscribe. Records date back to 1990. Lending agency and prothonotary data on system.

Property, Taxation Records **Free** Search property records free at http://propertyrecords.montcopa.org/Main/home.aspx. Also, search parcels and court data at www.montcopa.org/prothy/PSIViewer/EntitySearch.aspx. Search Tax Claim history lookup free at www.montcopa.org/taxclaim/payment/HistoryLookup.asp. Also, a private company sells county tax claim property, view list free at www.xspand.com/investors/realestate_sale/index.aspx

Montour County Prothonotary *Judgment, Tax Lien Records* www.montourco.org/montour For online access see Recorder of Deeds.

Montour County Recorder *Real Estate, Deed, Probate, Marriage, Orphans Court, Will Records*
www.montourco.org/montour **Free & $$** Access to Register of Deeds data is by subscription from a private company, visit www.infoconcountyaccess.com. Also includes Prothonotary, Clerk of Courts. Will index 1850 to present is free at www.montour.org, click on Register & Recorder, then Will Index, or see www.montourco.org/montour/cwp/view.asp?a=770&Q=417826&montourNav=|8473|.

Northampton County Prothonotary *Judgment Records* www.northamptoncounty.org **Free**
Search court opinions free at http://library.nccpa.org/cgi-bin/om_isapi.dll?clientID=518 but records only 1991 to 2005.

Northampton County Recorder *Real Estate, Deed, Mortgage, Miscellaneous Records*
www.northamptoncounty.org/northampton/site/default.asp **Free & $$** Access the index free at www.landex.com/webstore/jsp/cart/DocumentSearch.jsp. Full access to recording records is via a private company at www.landex.com/remote/. Fee is $.20 per minute and $.50 per fax page. Deeds data goes back to 11/85; mortgages to 2/86; faxable images go back to 11/85.

Property, Taxation Records **Free** Access to assessor's property records data is free at www.ncpub.org/Main/Home.aspx.

Northumberland County Recorder *Real Estate, Deed, Mortgage, Probate, Will, Orphans Court Records*
Free & $$ Access the index free at www.landex.com/webstore/jsp/cart/DocumentSearch.jsp. Full access to Recorder of Deeds, Register of Wills and Orphans Court is by subscription at www.landex.com/remote/. Fee is $.22 per minute, $.50 per fax page. Land data and images go back to 1949; images to 1820; Wills back to 1999; Orphans to 1987.

Perry County Recorder *Real Estate, Deed, Will, Marrige Records* **$$** Access to Recorder of Deeds is by subscription at www.landex.com/remote/. Fee is $.22 per minute, $.50 per fax page. Recorder data goes back to 1973; images to 1820. Marriages and wills go back to 1900s. Also, access property data by subscription at www.courthouseonline.com/MyProperty.asp. Sub fee $9.95 3-days, up to $275 per year. A free view available if you have control number and password from tax notice or are registered.

Property, Taxation Records **Free** Access property data by subscription at www.courthouseonline.com/MyProperty.asp. Sub fee $9.95 3-days, up to $275 per year. A free view available if you have control number and password from tax notice or are registered.

Philadelphia County Prothonotary *Judgment, Lien Records* **Free** Assess to Prothonotary records is free at http://fjdweb2.phila.gov/fjd1/repl1/zk_fjd_public_qry_00.zp_main_idx.html. Also, includes judgments and liens on behalf of governmental entities.

Philadelphia County Recorder *Real Estate, Deed, UCC Records* http://philadox.phila.gov **$$**
Name search recorder data for a fee at http://philadox.phila.gov/; registration required; fee is $125.00 per month or $15.00 per hour or $750 per year or $60.00 per week. Images go back to 1976, index to 1957.

Property, Taxation Records **Free** Search property assessment data for free at http://brtweb.phila.gov/brt.apps/Search/SearchForm.aspx?url=search. No name searching. Also, search Board of Revision of Taxes records for free at http://brtweb.phila.gov/index.aspx. No name searching.

Pike County Recorder *Property, Taxation Records* `Free` Access parcel data free at www.pikegis.org/pike/viewer.htm.

Potter County Prothonotary *Judgment, Tax Lien Records* www.pottercountypa.net `$$`
Access is via a private company; call Infocon at 814-472-6066 or www.infoconcountyaccess.com.

Potter County Recorder *Real Estate, Deed, Probate, Marriage, Orphans Court Records* `$$`
Access is via a private company; call Infocon at 814-472-6066 or www.infoconcountyaccess.com.

Schuylkill County Prothonotary *Judgment, Marriage Records* www.co.schuylkill.pa.us `Free`
Search marriage dockets free at www.co.schuylkill.pa.us/info/Offices/Archives/MarriageDockets.csp. Also, judgments on civil court files at www.co.schuylkill.pa.us/info/Civil/Inquiry/Search.csp.

Schuylkill County Recorder *Property, Taxation Records* `Free` Access items for the sheriff sale free at www.co.schuylkill.pa.us/Offices/Sheriff/Sale.asp.

Snyder County Recorder *Real Estae, Deed, Lien, Will, Estate, Map Records* www.snydercounty.org
`Free & $$` Access the index free at www.landex.com/webstore/jsp/cart/DocumentSearch.jsp. Full access to Recorder of Deeds and Wills and Orphans Court is by subscription at www.landex.com/remote/. Index goes back to 2005, and images to 2005, Estates 1855 to 1977. Map images also available.

Somerset County Prothonotary *Lien, Judgment Records* www.co.somerset.pa.us `$$` See Recorder office for online access.

Somerset County Recorder *Real Estate, Deed, Lien, Mortgage, Map Records* www.co.somerset.pa.us
`Free & $$` Access property records by monthly subscription; $35.00 start-up fee plus $10.00 per month. For info or signup, call Cindy or John at 814-445-1536. Provide your email, company info and check. System to provide images and comparable sales. Also, access the index free at www.landex.com/webstore/jsp/cart/DocumentSearch.jsp. Full access through that private company by subscription at www.landex.com/remote/. Fee is $.20 per minute and $.50 per fax page. Map images also available. Landex recorders index and images go back to 1/1985. See also separate listing for prothonotary for other online access.
Property, Taxation Records `Free` Access property data free at www.co.somerset.pa.us/realpictsearch.asp. Property Sale records also available.

Sullivan County Recorder *Real Estate, Deed, Mortgage, Map Records* www.sullivancounty-pa.us `Free & $$`
Access the index free at www.landex.com/webstore/jsp/cart/DocumentSearch.jsp. Full access through that private company by subscription at www.landex.com/remote/. Fee is $.22 per minute and $.50 per fax page. Index and images go back to 6/2000. Map images are also available.

Susquehanna County Prothonotary *Judgment, Tax Lien Records* `$$` Access is via a private company; call Infocon at 814-472-6066 or www.infoconcountyaccess.com.

Susquehanna County Recorder *Real Estate, Deed, Lien, Mortgage, Will, Orphans Court Records*
www.susqco.com/subsites/gov/pages/govhome.htm `Free & $$` Access the index free at www.landex.com/webstore/jsp/cart/DocumentSearch.jsp. Full access to Recorder of Deeds, Register of Wills and Orphans Court is by subscription at www.landex.com/remote/. Fee is $.22 per minute, $.50 per fax page. Index goes back to 1972, images to 2000. Map images also available.
Property, Taxation Records `Free & $$` Access property data by subscription at www.courthouseonline.com/MyProperty.asp. Sub fee $9.95 3-days, up to $275 per year. A free view available if you have control number and password from tax notice or are registered.

Tioga County Recorder *Real Estate, Deed, Mortgage, Will Records* www.tiogacountypa.us/tioga/site/default.asp
`Free & $$` Access the index free at www.landex.com/webstore/jsp/cart/DocumentSearch.jsp. Full access to real estate and recorded data by subscription through a private company at www.landex.com/remote/. Fee is $.22 per minute and $.50 per fax page. Recorders data goes back to 1977; images and wills go back to 2/1999. Map images also available.
Property, Taxation Records `Free & $$` Access property data by subscription at www.courthouseonline.com/MyProperty.asp. Sub fee $9.95 3-days, up to $275 per year. A free view available if you have control number and password from tax notice or are registered. Sheriff sales lists also available free online - web URL too lengthy to show, so see sheriff pages at main website.

Union County Recorder *Real Estate, Deed, UCC Records* www.unionco.org `Free` Access to Register of Deeds land records is free at https://pa.uslandrecords.com/palr_new/PalrApp/index.jsp. Online records go back to 1/1982.
Property, Taxation Records `Free & $$` Access property data by subscription at www.courthouseonline.com/MyProperty.asp. Sub fee $9.95 3-days, up to $275 per year. A free view available if you have control number and password from tax notice or are registered.

Venango County Recorder *Property, Taxation Records* Free & $$ Access property data by subscription at www.courthouseonline.com/MyProperty.asp. Subscription fee $9.95 3-days, up to $275 per year. A free view available if you have control number and password from tax notice.

Washington County Prothonotary *Lien, Judgment, Divorce Records*
www.co.washington.pa.us/maindepartment.aspx?menuDept=28 Free & $$ With registration, username and password you may access court-related records at www.co.washington.pa.us/wccourtdocuments/code/login.asp.

Washington County Recorder *Real Estate, Property Tax, Treasurer, Deed, Mortgage, Map Records*
www.co.washington.pa.us Free & $$ Access the recorder index free at www.landex.com/webstore/jsp/cart/DocumentSearch.jsp. Full access to Recorder is by subscription at www.landex.com/remote/. Fee is $.22 per minute, $.50 per fax page. Index goes back to 1952, images to 1995. Map images are also available. Also, public record access available for a fee at Optical Storage Solutions Inc at 800-370-2836, option #4 to set-up account.
Property, Taxation Records Free Access treasurer real estate tax data free at www.co.washington.pa.us/wcmtp/tri.asp.

Wayne County Prothonotary *Property, Taxation Records* Free Access to public tax information for free go to www.co.wayne.pa.us/?pageid=19

Wayne County Recorder *Property, Taxation Records* Free Search assessor property data free after registering at http://taxpub.co.wayne.pa.us/Main.asp.

Westmoreland County Recorder *Real Estate, Deed, Tax Lien, Mortgage, UCC Records*
www.co.westmoreland.pa.us Free The Register's old fee-based system has been replaced by a free, searchable site at www.wcdeeds.us/dts/default.asp. Choose simple, advanced, or instrument search.
Property, Taxation Records Free & $$ Search property and tax parcel data free at http://westmorelandweb400.us:8088/EGSPublicAccess.htm. View data on the GIS-mapping site free at www.co.westmoreland.pa.us/gis/Login.aspx?S=1. Search free but $25 monthly minimum fee for full GIS services.

York County Recorder *Real Estate, Deed, Death, Vital, Registry Records* www.york-county.org/departments/deeds/deeds.htm Free & $$ Access to recorder land records is by subscription from Landex at www.landex.com/remote. Base fee is $.20 per minute, $.50 per fax page. Records go back to 1981; images to 1981. Map images also available. Search the death index prior to 1959 at www.york-county.org/cgi-bin/Affdeath.cgi. Search older vitals, registries, and assorted records from archives free at www.york-county.org/departments/archives/archavailable.htm.
Property, Taxation Records Free Online access to the assessor database is free through the GIS data at http://216.174.25.68/york. Also, search parcel numbers at www.york-county.org/departments/assessment/tx_asmnt.htm.

Other Pennsylvania Sites of Note:

Beaver County - Naturalization www.co.beaver.pa.us/Prothonotary/naturalization.htm
Use username NATURAL and password NATURAL.
Centre County - Domestic Relations Warrants - Child Support www.co.centre.pa.us/drs/default.asp
Chester County - Genealogy, Vital Statistics Archive http://dsf.chesco.org/archives/cwp/view.asp?a=3&Q=609990
Cumberland County - Cemetery www.rootsweb.ancestry.com/~usgenweb/pa/cumberland/cemet.htm This is an unofficial site.
Lancaster County - Inmates www.prison.co.lancaster.pa.us/lcprison/cwp/view.asp?a=705&q=526599
Lancaster County - Probate, Death, Marriage http://paperless.co.lancaster.pa.us/viewerportal/
Lancaster County - Termination List (Argument Report) www.co.lancaster.pa.us/lanco/LIB/lanco/pdfs/TermList2001.PDF
Prothonotary's list of court case termination list (argument report) for the previous year
Northampton County - Court Opinion, Judgment http://library.nccpa.org/
Searchable area of site is being re-structured, 5/2008
Philadelphia Area - Deaths www.legacy.com/philly/DeathNotices.asp This is the obituary page of the Philadelphia area.
Wayne County - Active Arrest Warrants www.co.wayne.pa.us/?pageid=42
Wayne County - Veteran Burial Records www.co.wayne.pa.us/?pageid=44.
York County - Inmates www.york-county.org/departments/prison/prison.htm

Rhode Island

Capital: Providence
         Providence County
Time Zone: EST
Population: 1,057,832
# of Counties: 5

Useful State Links

Website: www.ri.gov/
Governor: www.governor.state.ri.us
Attorney General: www.riag.ri.gov
State Archives: www.sec.state.ri.us/Archives/
State Statutes and Codes: www.rilin.state.ri.us/Statutes/
Legislative Bill Search: http://dirac.rilin.state.ri.us/BillStatus/webclass1.asp
Unclaimed Funds: www.treasury.ri.gov/unclaimedproperty/

Primary State Agencies

Sexual Offender Registry Free

Sex Offender Community Notification Unit, www.paroleboard.ri.gov/ Two name lists are presented at the web page for Level 2 and Level 3 offenders respectively.

Incarceration Records Free

Rhode Island Department of Corrections, Records, www.doc.ri.gov/index.php A free DOC search is available at www.doc.ri.gov/inmate_search/index.php.   Also,   search   free   on   a   private   company   site   at https://www.vinelink.com/vinelink/siteInfoAction.do?siteId=40900.

Corporation, LLC, LP, LLP, Fictitious Name Free

Secretary of State, Corporations Division, www.sec.state.ri.us/corps At the web, search filings for active and inactive Rhode Island and foreign business corporations, non-profit corporations, limited partnerships, limited liability companies, and limited liability partnerships. Weekly listings of new corporations are also available. There is no fee. *Other Options:* Various databases may be downloaded or purchased on CD. Call for pricing.

Uniform Commercial Code

UCC Section, Secretary of State, www.sec.state.ri.us/corps/ucc/ucc.html View debtor names in the Pubic Search Index at http://ucc.state.ri.us/psearch/. One may also search by file number or business organization. Rhode Island's UCC Public Search Index allows its users to search using both Standard Search Logic and Non-Standard Search Logic. *Other Options:* Bulk data can be purchased by request. Call for details.

Driver Records $$

Division of Motor Vehicles, Driving Record Clerk, Operator Control, www.dmv.ri.gov Driving records are available in two manners. From the home page above, anyone may request a record online, pay the $19.50 service fee with a credit card and the record will be mailed to the address shown on the DL. This record does not contain the driver's address or SSN. The driver name. DOB and license number must be submitted. Ongoing requesters who qualify to receive records with personal information may obtain a subscription account for interactive service. The same record fee applies. For more information about becoming a subscriber visit www.ri.gov/subscriber/.

Voter Registration Free

Secretary of State, Elections Division, www.sec.state.ri.us/elections A specific look-up is available online at www.sec.state.ri.us/vic/. The name, DOB and town is needed. The search shows voter preferences. *Other Options:* A database of all registered voters, only selected voters by town, is available for $25.00 per CD.

Occupational Licensing Boards

Acupuncturist .... www.health.state.ri.us/hsr/professions/index.php
Ambulatory Care Facility .... www.health.state.ri.us/hsr/professions/index.php
Asbestos Worker .... www.health.state.ri.us/hsr/professions/index.php
Assisted Living Facility.................... www.health.state.ri.us/hsr/professions/index.php
Athletic Trainer .... www.health.state.ri.us/hsr/professions/index.php
Auctioneer .... www.dbr.state.ri.us/divisions/commlicensing/auctioneer.php
Audiologist .... www.health.state.ri.us/hsr/professions/index.php
Automobile Body Shop .... www.dbr.state.ri.us/divisions/commlicensing/autobody.php
Automobile Glass Installer .... www.dbr.state.ri.us/divisions/commlicensing/autoglass.php
Automobile Wrecker .... www.dbr.state.ri.us/divisions/commlicensing/autowrecking.php
Barber Shop/Barber/Barber Instr'r .... www.health.state.ri.us/hsr/professions/index.php
Birth Center .... www.health.state.ri.us/hsr/professions/index.php
Blood Test Screener .... www.health.state.ri.us/hsr/professions/index.php
Business Filing/Annual Report.......... www.sec.state.ri.us/corps
Charter School .... www.ride.ri.gov
Chemical Dependency Profession'l... www.ribccdp.com/LISTS.html
Chiropractor...................................... www.health.state.ri.us/hsr/professions/index.php
Clinical Supervisor, Recognized........ www.ribccdp.com/LISTS.html
Contractor, Resid'l Building .... www.crb.state.ri.us/search.php
Contractor, Watch List .... www.crb.state.ri.us/watchlist.php
Controlled Substance Wholesaler...... https://healthri.mylicense.com/Verification/
Cosmetologist/Cosmetology Instr...... www.health.state.ri.us/hsr/professions/index.php
Counselor in Training........................ www.ribccdp.com/LISTS.html
CPA .... www.dbr.state.ri.us/divisions/accountancy/
Criminal Justice Professional .... www.ribccdp.com/LISTS.html
Day Care, Children .... www.dcyf.state.ri.us/day_care_provider.php
Dentist/or/Dental Hygienist.............. www.health.state.ri.us/hsr/professions/index.php
Dietitian/Nutritionist......................... www.health.state.ri.us/hsr/professions/index.php
Electrician... www.dlt.ri.gov/profregs/ElectricianMain.htm
Electrologist...................................... www.health.state.ri.us/hsr/professions/index.php
Embalmer .... www.health.state.ri.us/hsr/professions/index.php
Emergency Care Facility .... www.health.state.ri.us/hsr/professions/index.php
Emergency Med. Technician/Service www.health.state.ri.us/hsr/professions/index.php
Esthetician .... www.health.state.ri.us/hsr/professions/index.php
Funeral Director................................ www.health.state.ri.us/hsr/professions/index.php
Group Home .... www.health.state.ri.us/hsr/professions/index.php
Hairdresser/Hairdresser Instructor ..... www.health.state.ri.us/hsr/professions/index.php
Hazardous Waste Transporter............ www.dem.ri.gov/programs/benviron/waste/transpor/index.htm
Hearing Aid Dispenser .... www.health.state.ri.us/hsr/professions/index.php
Hoisting Engineer.............................. www.dlt.ri.gov/profregs/HoistMain.htm
Home Care Provider/Nursing Care.... www.health.state.ri.us/hsr/professions/index.php
Hospice Provider .... www.health.state.ri.us/hsr/professions/index.php
Hospital .... www.health.state.ri.us/hsr/professions/index.php
Hypodermic Dispenser .... https://healthri.mylicense.com/Verification/
Insurance Broker/Producer/Agent ..... www.dbr.ri.gov/divisions/insurance/licensed.php
Interpreter for the Deaf..................... www.health.state.ri.us/hsr/professions/index.php
Laboratory, Medical .... www.health.state.ri.us/hsr/professions/index.php
Lobbyist Registration .... www.sec.state.ri.us/resources_for/lobbyist.html
Manicurist... www.health.state.ri.us/hsr/professions/index.php
Manicurist Shop .... www.health.state.ri.us/hsr/professions/index.php
Marriage & Family Therapist .... www.health.state.ri.us/hsr/professions/index.php
Massage Therapist .... www.health.state.ri.us/hsr/professions/index.php
Medical Doctor................................. www.health.state.ri.us/hsr/professions/index.php
Medical Waste Transporter............... www.dem.ri.gov/programs/benviron/waste/transpor/index.htm

Mental Health Counselor .... www.health.state.ri.us/hsr/professions/index.php
Midwife .... www.health.state.ri.us/hsr/professions/index.php
Mobile Home Park .... www.dbr.state.ri.us/divisions/commlicensing/mobile.php
Mortgage Broker   ...   www.dbr.state.ri.us/documents/divisions/banking/program_operations/List_of_Licensees.pdf
Notary Public .... http://ucc.state.ri.us/notaries/notaries.htm#data
Nuclear Medicine Technologist .... www.health.state.ri.us/hsr/professions/index.php
Nurse-related Occupation .... www.health.state.ri.us/hsr/professions/index.php
Nursing Home Administrator .... www.health.state.ri.us/hsr/professions/index.php
Nursing Service .... www.health.state.ri.us/hsr/professions/index.php
Occupational Therapist .... www.health.state.ri.us/hsr/professions/index.php
Office Operatories (Medical) .... www.health.state.ri.us/hsr/professions/index.php
Open Meeting .... www.sec.state.ri.us/pubinfo/openmeetings
Optician .... www.health.state.ri.us/hsr/professions/index.php
Optometrist .... www.health.state.ri.us/hsr/professions/index.php
Osteopathic Physician .... www.docboard.org/ri/df/search.htm
Outpatient Rehabilitation .... www.health.state.ri.us/hsr/professions/index.php
Pharmacist/Pharmacy Technician ...... https://healthri.mylicense.com/Verification/
Pharmacy .... https://healthri.mylicense.com/Verification/
Phlebotomy Station .... www.health.state.ri.us/hsr/professions/index.php
Physical Therapist .... www.health.state.ri.us/hsr/professions/index.php
Physician/Physician Assistant .... www.health.state.ri.us/hsr/professions/index.php
Physicians Controlled Substance .... https://healthri.mylicense.com/Verification/
Podiatrist .... www.health.state.ri.us/hsr/professions/index.php
Prevention Specialist/Supvr./Adv'd ... www.ribccdp.com/LISTS.html
Prosthetist .... www.health.state.ri.us/hsr/professions/index.php
Psychologist .... www.health.state.ri.us/hsr/professions/index.php
Public Accountant-CPA/Firm .... www.dbr.state.ri.us/divisions/accountancy/
Radiation Therapist .... www.health.state.ri.us/hsr/professions/index.php
Radiographer .... www.health.state.ri.us/hsr/professions/index.php
Real Estate Agent/Sales .... www.dbr.state.ri.us/pdf_forms/RE-Real%20Estate%20Salespersons.pdf
Real Estate Appraiser .... www.dbr.state.ri.us/pdf_forms/RE-Real%20Estate%20Appraisers.pdf
Real Estate Broker .... www.dbr.state.ri.us/pdf_forms/RE-Real%20Estate%20Brokers.pdf
Residential Care Facility .... www.health.state.ri.us/hsr/professions/index.php
Respiratory Care Practitioner .... www.health.state.ri.us/hsr/professions/index.php
Roofer, Commercial .... www.crb.state.ri.us/search.php
Salvage Yard .... www.dbr.state.ri.us/divisions/commlicensing/autowrecking.php
Sanitarian .... www.health.state.ri.us/hsr/professions/index.php
School Principal/Superint't/Supvr ..... https://www.ricert.ride.ri.gov/RIDE/
Septic Transporter .... www.dem.ri.gov/programs/benviron/waste/transpor/index.htm
Social Worker .... www.health.state.ri.us/hsr/professions/index.php
Speech/Language Pathologist .... www.health.state.ri.us/hsr/professions/index.php
Student Assistance Counselor .... www.ribccdp.com/LISTS.html
Surgery Center, Freestanding .... www.health.state.ri.us/hsr/professions/index.php
Tanning Facility .... www.health.state.ri.us/hsr/professions/index.php
Tattoo Artist .... www.health.state.ri.us/hsr/professions/index.php
Teacher .... https://www.ricert.ride.ri.gov/RIDE/
Travel Agent/Agencies .... www.dbr.state.ri.us/divisions/commlicensing/travel.php
Veterinarian .... www.health.state.ri.us/hsr/professions/index.php
X-ray Facility & Portable .... www.health.state.ri.us/hsr/professions/index.php

State and Local Courts

State Court Structure: Rhode Island has five counties but only four Superior/District Court Locations— 2nd-Newport, 3rd-Kent, 4th-Washington, and 6th-Providence/Bristol Districts. Bristol and Providence counties are completely merged at the Providence location. Civil claims between $5000 and $10,000 may be filed in either Superior Court or District Court at the discretion of the filer. For questions regarding the Superior Courts, telephone 401-222-2622. For questions regarding the District Courts, telephone 401-458-5201. Probate is handled by the Town Clerk at the 39 cities and towns across Rhode Island, not at the courts.

Statewide Court Online Access: The Rhode Island Judiciary offers free access to an index of county criminal cases statewide at http://courtconnect.courts.state.ri.us. A word of caution, this website is provided as an informational service only and should not be relied upon as an official record of the court. Supreme Court and Appellate opinions are available from the judicial home page at www.courts.state.ri.us.

> ❖ **Statewide Access Offered For All Trial Courts – Read Above** ❖

Note: No individual Rhode Island courts offer online access.

Recorders, Assessors, and Other Sites of Note

Recording Office Organization: 5 counties and 39 towns, 39 recording offices. There is **no county recording** in this state. All recording is done at the city/town level. Be aware that three sites bear the same name as their respective counties. Therefore, the recordings within the counties of Bristol, Newport, and Providence can relate to property located in cities/towns other than the individual cities of Bristol, Newport, and Providence. The recording officers are the Town/City Clerks. The Town/City Clerk usually also serves as Recorder of Deeds. All federal and state tax liens on personal property and on real property are filed with the Recorder of Deeds.

Online Access Note: A private vendor has placed assessor records from a number of towns on the internet; visit www.visionappraisal.com/databases/ri/index.htm

Bristol County

Barrington Town *Property, Taxation Records* `Free` Access property data on a private site at www.appraisalresource.com/Search.aspx?town=Barrington.

Bristol Town *Property, Taxation Records* `Free` Access property data on a private site at www.clipboardinc.com/bristolsearchpage.html.

Warren Town *Property, Taxation Records* `Free` Access property and assessor data free on the private site at www.appraisalresource.com/Search.aspx?town=Warren. Tax bill data is available free at www.opaldata.net/ritaxbills/search.aspx?municipality=Warren&taxyear=2006. Also, plat records are available free at www.townofwarren-ri.gov/services/plats.htm. Requires registration, username and password.

Kent County

Coventry Town *Property, Taxation Records* `Free` Property data is listed on a private site at www.appraisalresource.com/Search.aspx?town=Coventry. Also, 2005 Assessment and property data available at www.town.coventry.ri.us/assess.htm.

East Greenwich Town *Property, Taxation Records* `Free` Access property data on a private site at www.appraisalresource.com/Search.aspx?town=East+Greenwich.

Warwick City *Property, Taxation Records* `Free` Access found at www.warwickri-assessor.org. Click on Property Search.

West Greenwich Town *Property, Taxation Records* `Free` Access property data free at www.crcpropertyinfo.com/crcdb/westgreenwich.htm.

West Warwick Town *Property, Taxation Records* `Free` Access property data free at http://westwarwick.univers-clt.com but no name searching. Also, access tax rolls and tax bills free at www.opaldata.net/ritaxbills/. Prior years available.

Newport County

Jamestown Town *Property, Taxation Records* `Free` Access property data on a private site at
www.appraisalresource.com/Search.aspx?town=Jamestown

Little Compton Town *Property, Taxation Records* `Free` Access assessor property data free at
http://data.visionappraisal.com/LittleComptonRI/DEFAULT.asp.

Middletown Town *Property, Taxation Records* `Free` Records on the town assessor database are online
at http://data.visionappraisal.com/MiddletownRI/. Free registration is required for full data.

Newport City *Property, Taxation Records* `Free` Access is via a private company at
http://data.visionappraisal.com/NewportRI/. Free registration is required for full data.

Portsmouth Town *Property, Taxation Records* `Free` Search town assessor database at
http://data.visionappraisal.com/PortsmouthRI/. Free registration for full data.

Tiverton Town *Property, Taxation Records* `Free` Access property data on a private site at
www.appraisalresource.com/Search.aspx?town=Tiverton. Also, access tax rolls and tax bills free at
www.opaldata.net/ritaxbills/search.aspx?municipality=Tiverton&taxyear=2005RP. Also search free at
www.crcpropertyinfo.com/crcdb/tiverton.htm.

Providence County

Burrillville Town *Property, Taxation Records* `Free` Access to property records is free at
www.opaldata.net/ritaxbills/search.aspx?municipality=Burrillville&taxyear=2005RP. Also, access property data free at
www.crcpropertyinfo.com/crcdb/burrillville.htm.

Central Falls City *Property, Taxation Records* `Free` Access to city property data is free at
http://data.visionappraisal.com/CentralFallsRI/. Does not require username & password, simply click on link. Also, search
property data free at www.appraisalresource.com/Search.aspx?town=Central+Falls.

Cranston City *Property, Taxation Records* `Free` Records on the city assessor database are online at
http://data.visionappraisal.com/CranstonRI/. Free registration is required for full data.

Cumberland Town *Property, Taxation Records* `Free` Access to property data is free at
www.opaldata.net/ritaxbills/search.aspx?municipality=Cumberland&taxyear=2006RP. Also, access property data free at
www.crcpropertyinfo.com/crcdb/cumberland.htm.

East Providence City *Property, Taxation Records* `Free` Access to Town property data is free at
http://data.visionappraisal.com/EastProvidenceRI/.

Foster Town *Property, Taxation Records* `Free` Access property data free at
www.crcpropertyinfo.com/crcdb/foster.htm.

Glocester Town *Property, Taxation Records* `Free` Access tax roll data free at
www.opaldata.net/ritaxbills/search.aspx?municipality=Glocester&taxyear=2007RP. Also, access property data free at
www.crcpropertyinfo.com/crcdb/glocester.htm.

Johnston Town *Property, Taxation Records* `Free` Access to Town property data is free at
http://data.visionappraisal.com/JohnstonRI/.

Lincoln Town *Property, Taxation Records* `Free` Property data free at
www.crcpropertyinfo.com/crcdb/lincoln.htm. Values here are the result of a proposed property tax revaluation recently
conducted for the Town.

North Providence Town *Property, Taxation Records* `Free` Access property data on a private site at
www.appraisalresource.com/Search.aspx?town=North+Providence.

North Smithfield Town *Property, Taxation Records* `Free` Access is via a private company at
http://data.visionappraisal.com/NorthsmithfieldRI/.

Pawtucket City *Real Estate, Deed Records* www.pawtucketri.com `Free` Access real estate data free at
http://72.248.180.6/alis/ww400r.pgm. Online indices go back to 1970.
Property, Taxation Records `Free` Search the assessor database free at http://pawtucket.ias-clt.com/.

Providence City *Property, Taxation Records* `Free` Property tax card data available free at
http://providence.ias-clt.com/parcel.list.php.

Scituate Town *Property, Taxation Records* `Free` Access to town property data is free at
www.crcpropertyinfo.com/crcdb/scituate.htm

Smithfield Town   *Property, Taxation Records*   `Free`   Access to town property data is free at http://data.visionappraisal.com/SmithfieldRI/. Tax Rolls and tax bills are also free online at www.opaldata.net/ritaxbills/search.aspx?municipality=Smithfield&taxyear=2007RP.

Woonsocket City   *Property, Taxation Records*   `Free`   Access assessor data free at http://data.visionappraisal.com/woonsocketRI/DEFAULT.asp.

Washington County

Charlestown Town   *Property, Taxation Records*   `Free`   Search town assessor database at http://data.visionappraisal.com/CharlestownRI/.

Exeter Town   *Property, Taxation Records*   `Free`   Access property data free at www.crcpropertyinfo.com/crcdb/exeter.htm. Access to real estate tax collection data is by subscription from a private company at www.opaldata.net/OnlineTax/.

Hopkinton Town   *Property, Taxation Records*   `Free`   Access to town property data is free at www.opaldata.net/ritaxbills/search.aspx?municipality=Hopkinton&taxyear=2007RP. Also, access property data free at www.crcpropertyinfo.com/crcdb/hopkinton.htm.

Narragansett Town   *Property, Taxation Records*   `Free`   Records on the town assessor database are online at http://data.visionappraisal.com/NarragansettRI/. Free registration is required for full data.

New Shoreham Town   *Property, Taxation Records*   `Free`   Access to Town property data is free at http://data.visionappraisal.com/NewShorehamRI/.

North Kingstown Town   *Property, Taxation Records*   `Free`   Access is via a private company at http://data.visionappraisal.com/NorthkingstownRI/. Free registration is required for full data.

Richmond Town   *Property, Taxation Records*   `Free`   Search town assessor database at http://data.visionappraisal.com/RichmondRI/.

South Kingstown Town   *Real Estate, Deed, Lien, Marriage, Death, Will, Mortgage, Judgment Records*   www.southkingstownri.com   `Free & $$`   Access town real estate data free at http://70.168.204.238/ALIS/WW400R.HTM. Land indexes and images go back to 5/2/2005; complete excluding maps. Land indexes only go back to 1980; More to be added. Registration required for full data.
Property, Taxation Records   `Free`   Access to the property values database is free at www.southkingstownri.com/code/propvalues_search.cfm. Also, some data available free or by sub at http://70.168.204.238/ALIS/WW400R.HTM under Assessor Document Group. Also, assess to Town property data is free at http://data.visionappraisal.com/SouthKingstownRI/. Does not require a username & password, simply click on link.

Westerly Town   *Property, Taxation Records*   `Free`   Access town property assessment data free at http://data.visionappraisal.com/WesterlyRI/. Also, assess 2006 tax rolls and tax bills free at www.opaldata.net/ritaxbills/search.aspx?municipality=Westerly&taxyear=2007RP.

South Carolina

Capital: Columbia
           Richland County
Time Zone: EST
Population: 4,407,709
# of Counties: 46

Useful State Links

Website: www.sc.gov
Governor: www.scgovernor.com
Attorney General: www.scattorneygeneral.org
State Archives: http://scdah.sc.gov/
State Statutes and Codes: www.scstatehouse.net/html-pages/research.html
Legislative Bill Search: www.scstatehouse.net/html-pages/legpage.html
Unclaimed Funds: http://treasurer.sc.gov/palm_payb_prog_uncla_prop/

Primary State Agencies

Criminal Records $$

South Carolina Law Enforcement Division (SLED), Criminal Records Section, www.sled.sc.gov/ SLED offers commercial access to criminal record history from 1960 forward on the website. Fees are $25.00 per screening or $8.00 if for a charitable organization. Credit card ordering accepted. Visit the website or call 803-896-7219 for details.

Sexual Offender Registry Free

Sex Offender Registry, c/o SLED, http://services.sled.sc.gov/sor/ Access is available from the website. Click on Sexual Offender Registry. Search by name or ZIP Code, county or city. Reports may also be obtained by school name (under the Report Generator).

Incarceration Records Free

Department of Corrections, Inmate Records Branch, www.doc.sc.gov The Inmate Search on the Internet is found at https://sword.doc.state.sc.us/incarceratedInmateSearch/index.jsp or click on Inmate search at the main website.

Corporation, LP, LLP, LLC, Trademarks/Servicemarks Free

Corporation Division, Capitol Complex, www.scsos.com This free web-based program is called the Online Business Filings, the search page is at www.scsos.com/corp_search.htm. The database provides access to basic filing information about any entity filed with the office. Registered agents' names and addresses, dates of business filings and types of filings are all available. The database is updated every 48 hours.

Uniform Commercial Code

UCC Division, Secretary of State, www.scsos.com/Uniform_Commercial_Code.htm Free access to index of records filed before 10/27/03 at www.scsos.com/uccsearch.htm. Search by debtor name or number. Information on filings after that date must be obtained by mail or email (SCUCC@INFOAVE.NET).

Driver License Information, Driver Records Free & $$

Department of Motor Vehicles, Driver Records Section, www.scdmvonline.com/DMVNew/default.aspx Commercial records are available from the portal https://dmvdhr.sc.gov/DriverHistoryRecords/Interactive/CDBLogin.aspx. Authorized businesses must establish an account through a formal approval and acceptance process. The fee is $7.25 per record and a $75.00 annual fee is required. Members have access to additional online services. For more information about setting up an account, call 803-737-2819 or email support@sc-egov.com. From www.scdmvonline.com/DMVNew/default.aspx one may obtain a summary of a driving record. The summary includes points history and current status. There is no fee. The DL, SSN and DOB are needed. SC drivers may purchase their own record after viewing; a certified copy is mailed for $6.00.

Voter Registration `Free`

State Election Commission, Records, www.scvotes.org/ Intended to check your own registration, free access is offered at www.scvotes.org/check_your_voter_registration. When checking information, you must provide the name, street name, county and date of birth exactly as registered. *Other Options:* Lists, labels, diskettes, and magnetic tapes are available with a variety of sort features. The minimum charge varies from $75 to $160 depending on the media.

Vital Records `$$`

South Carolina DHEC, Vital Records, www.scdhec.gov/administration/vr/ Order from state-designated vendor - www.vitalchek.com.

Occupational Licensing Boards

Accounting Practitioner-AP	https://verify.llronline.com/LicLookup/
Acupuncturist	www.llr.state.sc.us/POL/Medical/index.asp?file=licensure.htm
Airport Professional/Contact	www.scaeronautics.com/directorySearch.asp
Animal Health Technician	https://verify.llronline.com/LicLookup/
Architect/Archit'l Partnership/Corp	https://verify.llronline.com/LicLookup/
Attorney	www.scbar.org/member_resources/member_directory/
Auctioneer/Apprentice/Firm	https://verify.llronline.com/LicLookup/
Audiologist	https://verify.llronline.com/LicLookup/
Aviation Facility	www.scaeronautics.com/AirportSearch.asp
Barber-related Occupation	https://verify.llronline.com/LicLookup/
Bodywork Therapist	https://verify.llronline.com/LicLookup/
Building Inspector	https://verify.llronline.com/LicLookup/
Building Official	https://verify.llronline.com/LicLookup/
Burglar Alarm Contractor	https://verify.llronline.com/LicLookup/
Certified Public Accountant-CPA	https://verify.llronline.com/LicLookup/
Chiropractor	https://verify.llronline.com/LicLookup/
Contact Lens License	https://verify.llronline.com/LicLookup/
Contractor, General/Mech/Resid.	https://verify.llronline.com/LicLookup/
Cosmetology-related Occupation	https://verify.llronline.com/LicLookup/
Counselor, Professional	https://verify.llronline.com/LicLookup/
Dental Specialist/Technician	https://verify.llronline.com/LicLookup/
Dentist/or/Dental Hygienist	https://verify.llronline.com/LicLookup/
Embalmer	https://verify.llronline.com/LicLookup/
Engineer	https://verify.llronline.com/LicLookup/
Esthetician	https://verify.llronline.com/LicLookup/
Forester	https://verify.llronline.com/LicLookup/LookupMain.aspx
Funeral Director/Funeral Home	https://verify.llronline.com/LicLookup/
Geologist	https://verify.llronline.com/LicLookup/
Hair Care Master Specialist	https://verify.llronline.com/LicLookup/
Home Builder, Residential	https://verify.llronline.com/LicLookup/
Housing Inspector	https://verify.llronline.com/LicLookup/
Inspector, Bldg/Housing	https://verify.llronline.com/LicLookup/
Inspector, Mech./Elec./Plumb./Prov.	https://verify.llronline.com/LicLookup/
Lobbyist	www.scstatehouse.net/reports/ethrpt.htm
Lobbyist Principal	www.scstatehouse.net/reports/ethrpt.htm
Manicurist/ Manicure Assistant	https://verify.llronline.com/LicLookup/
Manufact'd Home-related Occupat'n	https://verify.llronline.com/LicLookup/
Marriage & Family Therapist	https://verify.llronline.com/LicLookup/
Massage Therapist	https://verify.llronline.com/LicLookup/
Medical Doctor	www.llr.state.sc.us/POL/Medical/index.asp?file=licensure.htm
Nail Technician	https://verify.llronline.com/LicLookup/
Nurses, RN / LPN	https://verify.llronline.com/LicLookup/
Nursing Home Administrator	https://verify.llronline.com/LicLookup/
Occupational Therapist/Assistant	https://verify.llronline.com/LicLookup/
Optician/Optician Apprentice	https://verify.llronline.com/LicLookup/
Optometrist	https://verify.llronline.com/LicLookup/

Osteopathic Physician.........................www.llr.state.sc.us/POL/Medical/index.asp?file=licensure.htm
Pharmacist/Pharmacy Technician......https://verify.llronline.com/LicLookup/
Pharmacy/Drug Outlet.......................https://verify.llronline.com/LicLookup/
Physical Therapist/Therapist Asst .....https://verify.llronline.com/LicLookup/
Physician Assistant............................www.llr.state.sc.us/POL/Medical/index.asp?file=licensure.htm
Pilot ....www.scaeronautics.com/AirportSearch.asp
Plans Examiner, Building..................https://verify.llronline.com/LicLookup/
Podiatrist...https://verify.llronline.com/LicLookup/
Produce Whlse Dealer.......................www.scda.state.sc.us/buyscproducts/wholesalers/wholesalers.htm
Psycho-Educational Specialist...........https://verify.llronline.com/LicLookup/
Psychologist......................................https://verify.llronline.com/LicLookup/
Public Accountant-PA ....https://verify.llronline.com/LicLookup/
Real Estate Appraiser ....http://verify.llronline.com/LicLookup/LookupMain.aspx
Residential Care, Community............https://verify.llronline.com/LicLookup/
Respiratory Care Practitioner ....www.llr.state.sc.us/POL/Medical/index.asp?file=licensure.htm
Shampoo Assistant ....https://verify.llronline.com/LicLookup/
Social Worker....................................https://verify.llronline.com/LicLookup/
Speech-Language Pathologist............https://verify.llronline.com/LicLookup/
Sprinkler Systems Contractor ....https://verify.llronline.com/LicLookup/
Surveyor, Land ....https://verify.llronline.com/LicLookup/
Veterinarian.......................................https://verify.llronline.com/LicLookup/
Wholesaler/Shipper (Food)...............www.scda.state.sc.us/buyscproducts/shippers/shippers.htm

State and Local Courts

State Court Structure: The 46 SC counties are divided among sixteen judicial circuits. Circuit Courts are the courts of general jurisdiction and consist of a Court of General Sessions (criminal) and a Court of Common Pleas (civil). A Family Court (juveniale cases) and Probate Court are found in each county. There are over a combined 300 different Magistrate and Municipal Courts (often referred to as "Summary Courts") that handle only handle misdemeanor cases involving a $500.00 fine and/or thirty days or less jail time.

Statewide Court Online Access: Appellate and Supreme Court opinions are available at www.sccourts.org. Also, some, not all, Circuit Court and Summary Courts records are available at www.sccourts.org/caseSearch/; counties on the state system are Anderson, Beaufort, Charleston, Cherokee, Clarendon, Dorchester, Edgefield, Florence, Georgetown, Greenville, Horry, Jasper, Lexington, Pickens, Richland, Spartanburg, Sumter, York, with more counties to be added or hotlinked. Some counties on the system also offer access to dockets – Beaufort, Jasper. Charleston is hot-linked but has its own online court records and dockets service, including judgments and traffic.

Anderson County

Circuit Court   www.judicial.state.sc.us/index.cfm   **Free**
Civil: Access Circuit Court records free at http://acpass.andersoncountysc.org/coc_main.htm. Includes Family Court records. Access more direct at www.andersoncountysc.org/web/scjdweb/publicindex/. *Criminal:* Access to criminal records is the same as civil.

Beaufort County

Circuit Court   **Free**
Civil: Access to public case index and court dockets for free go to www.beaufortcourt.org. *Criminal:* same.

Charleston County

Circuit Court   http://www3.charlestoncounty.org   **Free**
Civil: Access to civil records 1988 forward, also judgments and lis pendens are free at http://www3.charlestoncounty.org/connect. Online document images go back to 1/1/1999. Also accessible via www.sccourts.org/casesearch/. *Criminal:* Access to criminal records from 04/92 forward free at http://www3.charlestoncounty.org/connect. Search by name or case number. Also accessible via www.sccourts.org/casesearch/. Also, criminal records for a fee at www.sled.sc.gov/.

All Charleston Magistrate Court Locations   http://www3.charlestoncounty.org   **Free**
Civil: Access civil records from 1998 forward at http://www3.charlestoncounty.org/connect. *Criminal:* Access criminal and traffic records from 1993 forward free at http://www3.charlestoncounty.org/connect.

Cherokee County
Circuit Court   `Free`
Civil: Access court records online at http://publicindex.sccourts.org/cherokee/publicindex/. *Criminal:* same.

Clarendon County
Circuit Court   `Free`
Civil: Access court records free on state system at http://publicindex.sccourts.org/clarendon/publicindex/. *Criminal:* same.

Dorchester County
Circuit Court   www.dorchestercounty.net/   `Free`
Civil: Access court records free at www.dorchestercounty.net/scjdweb/publicindex/. *Criminal:* same.

Edgefield County
Circuit Court   `Free`
Civil: Access court records free at http://publicindex.sccourts.org/edgefield/publicindex/. *Criminal:* same.

Florence County
Circuit Court   www.florenceco.org   `Free`
Civil: Search judgments back to 1994 at http://web.florenceco.org/cgi-bin/coc/coc.cgi. Also accessible via www.sccourts.org/casesearch/. *Criminal:* Access criminal record from 1995 forward free at http://web.florenceco.org/cgi-bin/warrants/war.cgi. Also accessible via www.sccourts.org/casesearch/.

Georgetown County
Circuit Court   `Free`
Civil: Access court dockets free at http://secure.georgetowncountysc.org/courtdockets/. Also, access court records free at http://secure.georgetowncountysc.org/publicindex/. *Criminal:* same Also, to access public index search go to http://secure.georgetowncountysc.org/publicindex/.

Greenville County
Circuit Court   www.greenvillecounty.org   `Free`
Civil: Family Court and civil index at www.13th-judicial-circuit.org/disclaim.asp?County=23 *Criminal:* Access court records free at www.13th-judicial-circuit.org/disclaim.asp?County=23. Records go back to 1983.

Horry County
Circuit Court   `Free`
Civil: Access court records free at www.horrycounty.org/publicindex/. *Criminal:* same.

Jasper County
Circuit Court   www.jaspercourt.org/   `Free`
Civil: Access court records and dockets free at www.jaspercourt.org/. Access court records at www.jaspercourt.org/publicindex/. *Criminal:* same.

Lexington County
Circuit Court   www.lex-co.com/Departments/ClerkOfCourt/Index.html   `Free`
Civil: Search record index free at www.lex-co.com/applications/scjdweb/publicindex/. *Criminal:* Search the record index at www.lex-co.com/applications/scjdweb/publicindex/.

Pickens County
Circuit Court   www.co.pickens.sc.us   `Free`
Civil: Access court records free at www.13th-judicial-circuit.org/disclaim.asp?County=39. *Criminal:* same.

Liberty Magistrate Court   `Free`
Civil: Online access is same as criminal, see below. *Criminal:* Access to court records free at www.upstatepublicindex.org. Click on Pickens.

Richland County
Circuit Court   `Free`
Civil: Access court records free at http://www4.rcgov.us/publicindex/default.aspx. Limited court rosters online at www.richlandonline.com/departments/clerkofcourt/courtroster.asp; search by date. *Criminal:* Access court records free at http://www4.rcgov.us/publicindex/default.aspx. Access limited court rosters at www.richlandonline.com/departments/clerkofcourt/courtroster.asp; search by date.

Spartanburg County
Circuit Court   www.spartanburgcounty.org/govt/depts/coc/index.htm   `Free`
Civil: Access court records free at http://192.146.148.40/publicindex/. *Criminal:* same.

Sumter County

Circuit Court   www.sumtercountysc.org   **Free**

Civil: Civil record index is at www.sumtercountysc.org/publicindex/. Family court records online at the website. *Criminal:* Access criminal record index is at www.sumtercountysc.org/publicindex/.

York County

Circuit Court   www.yorkcountygov.com/   **Free**

Civil: Access court records free at www.yorkcountygov.com/judicial/scjdpublicindex/. *Criminal:* same.

Recorders, Assessors, and Other Sites of Note

Recording Office Organization: 46 counties, 46 recording offices. The recording officer is either the Register of Mesne Conveyances or Clerk of Court; this varies by county. All federal and state tax liens on personal property and on real property are filed with the Register of Mesne Conveyances or Clerk of Court.

Online Access Note: No statewide system, but a number of counties offer free record data via their websites.

Aiken County *Real Estate, Deed, Mortgage, Plat, Comparable Sale Records* www.aikencountysc.gov **Free &**
$$ Access to the county e-services are free at www.aikencountysc.gov/eGovDisclaimer1.cfm but not all modules allow name searching. For full data and name searching, registration and fees are required, $25 per month, $10 if county resident. Registration and password required for Property Cards and Comparable Sales. Also, access to property and deeds indexes and images is via a private company at www.titlesearcher.com. Fee/registration required. Deeds and index goes back to 1/1982; images back to 6/13/2005.
Property, Taxation Records **Free**   Search assessor property data free at http://cxap2.aikencountysc.gov/EGSV2Aiken/RPSearch.do but no name searching.

Anderson County *Real Estate, Deed, Sale, Marriage, Estate, Permit Records* www.andersoncountysc.org **Free**
Access to the county ACPASS super search site is free at http://acpass.andersoncountysc.org.
Property, Taxation Records **Free**   Search the Property Viewer free at http://gisserve.andersoncountysc.org/propertyviewer/ but no name searching. Access property tax and vehicle tax and other data free at http://acpass.andersoncountysc.org/welcome.shtml.

Beaufort County *Real Estate, Deed, Lien, Judgment Records* www.bcgov.net **Free & $$**   Access to the public records search database is free at www.bcgov.net/. A fuller records subscription service requiring registration, fees, and logon is under development.
Property, Taxation Records **Free**   Search assessor data free at www.bcgov.net/RealProperty/New_RealProp/Welcome.php.

Berkeley County *Real Estate, Deed, UCC, Lien, Plat, Property Sale Records* www.co.berkeley.sc.us **Free &**
$$ Access real estate data at http://server1.co.berkeley.sc.us/esrvmain.html. View comparable sales online. Also, search the clerks document database free at www.sclandrecords.com/sclr/controller. Also, access property records on a private site at www.landaccess.com and click on SC-Berkeley. Records go back to 1/2/1997.
Property, Taxation Records **Free**   Search assessor data free at http://server1.co.berkeley.sc.us/EGSBKLY/RPSearch.do. Search personal property and vehicle tax data free at http://server1.co.berkeley.sc.us/esrvmain.html

Calhoun County *Real Estate, Deed Records* **$$**   Access to property and deeds indexes and images is via a private company at www.titlesearcher.com. Fee/registration required. Images and indices go back to 8/2004.

Charleston County *Real Estate, Deed, Mortgage, Lien, UCC, Plat, Judgment, Marriage, Probate, Will/Estate,*
Business License Records www.charlestoncounty.org **Free**   Access RMC recording data free at
http://www2.charlestoncounty.org - land records go back to 2/1997. Search court judgments-
http://www3.charlestoncounty.org/connect?ref=MIE. Marriages-
http://www3.charlestoncounty.org/connect/LU_GROUP_2?ref=Marriage. Search probate, wills, guardianships free-
http://www3.charlestoncounty.org/connect/LU_GROUP_2?ref=Conserv. Business licenses-
http://www3.charlestoncounty.org/connect/LU_GROUP_3?s=b.
Property, Taxation Records **Free**   Access auditor & treasurer's tax system free at http://taxweb.charlestoncounty.org. Access the county's GIS mapping database of property records free at http://gisweb.charlestoncounty.org.

Colleton County *Property, Taxation Records* **Free**   Access property and vehicle tax data free at http://tax.colletoncounty.org/.

Darlington County *Property, Taxation Records* **Free**   Access property records free at www.darcosc.com/assessor/disclaimer.asp. Lookup tax records at www.darcosc.com/OnlineTaxes/.

Dorchester County *Real Estate, Deed Records* www.dorchestercounty.net **Free & $$**   Access to Register of Deeds real estate records is free at www.dorchestercounty.net/RMC/RMCMain.aspx. A subscription fee may apply in the future.

Property, Taxation Records `Free`   Search tax and property records free on the GIS-mapping site at http://gisweb.dorchestercounty.net/imap/.

Edgefield County   *Real Estate, Grantor/Grantee, Deed, Liens (2006), UCC Records*   www.edgefieldcounty.sc.gov
`Free & $$`   Access county land record index and images free at www.landaccess.com.
Property, Taxation Records `Free`   Access property assessor data free at www.edgefieldcountysc.com/search.aspx.

Fairfield County   *Property, Taxation Records*   `Free`   Search property/GIS data free at
www.emapsplus.com/SCFairfield/maps/.

Florence County   *Real Estate, Grantor/Grantee, Deed, Lien, Judgment Records*   http://web.florenceco.org   `Free`
Access recorder data free at http://web.florenceco.org/cgi-bin/coc/coc.cgi.
Property, Taxation Records `Free`   Access property tax records free at http://web.florenceco.org/cgi-bin/ta/tax-inq.cgi. Also, access vehicle tax records free at http://web.florenceco.org/cgi-bin/ta/vehinq.cgi.

Georgetown County   *Real Estate, Deed, UCC Records*   www.georgetowncountysc.org   `Free`   Access the
Register's database free at www.landaccess.com. Click on SC-Georgetown. Index goes back to 1/1977 for deeds, 7/1986 for mortgages, 1/1989 for UCC, 7/1989 for tax liens and 7/2002 for misc liens.
Property, Taxation Records `Free`   Access to property data on the GIS-mapping site is free at http://gismap.georgetowncountysc.org/viewer.htm. Click on the binoculars to get to the name search feature.

Greenville County   *Real Estate, Deed Records*   www.greenvillecounty.org   `Free`   Search the Register of Deeds
database free at www.greenvillecounty.org. Click on Register of Deeds Search. Index goes back to 1990, images to 2004.
Property, Taxation Records `Free`   Search the property tax and vehicles data at www.greenvillecounty.org/voTaxQry/wcmain.asp. Also, search real estate data at www.greenvillecounty.org/vrealpr24/clrealprop.asp. No name searching.

Greenwood County   *Real Estae, Grantor/Grantee, Deed, Mortgage, Lien, Judgment Records*
www.co.greenwood.sc.us   `Free`   Access to document search for free go to www.co.greenwood.sc.us/clerk.aspx or http://gis.greenwoodsc.gov/docsearch/default.aspx.
Property, Taxation Records `Free`   Search Property Tax, Personal Property, Tax Collector data free at www.greenwoodsc.gov/search.aspx.

Horry County   *Real Estate, Deed, Lien Records*   www.horrycounty.org/hcgPortal.asp   `Free`
Access the recorders database free at www.horrycounty.org/gateway/disclaimer/idx_rod.html.
Property, Taxation Records `Free`   Search the real property database free at www.horrycounty.org/gateway/disclaimer/idx_real.html.

Jasper County   *Real Estate, Grantor/Grantee, Deed, Mortgage, Lien, Judgment Records*   www.jaspercountysc.org
`Free & $$`   Access to recorders data is free via a private firm at http://counties.recordfusion.com/countyweb/login.jsp?countyname=Jasper. Liens and judgments go back to 2006. Logon as Guest to search free.

Kershaw County   *Property, Taxation Records*   `Free`   Access to property/vehicle tax for free go to
www.kershawcountysctax.com/

Lancaster County   *Real Estate, Deed Records*   www.lancastercountysc.net   `$$`   Access to property and deeds
indexes and images is via a private company at www.titlesearcher.com. Fee/registration required. Indices and images go back to 8/27/2002.
Property, Taxation Records `Free`   Access property data free at www.lancastercountysc.net/onlinetaxes/.

Laurens County   *Real Estate, Deed, Treasurer Records*   `$$`   Access to property and deeds indexes and images is via
a private company at www.titlesearcher.com. Fee/registration required. Deed records go back to 7/1991; indices back to 6/1/1996; images to 8/26/2006
Property, Taxation Records `Free`   Access property data free at www.laurenscountysctaxes.com.

Lexington County   *Real Estate, Deed, Lien, Mortgage, UCC Records*   www.lex-
co.com/Departments/RegisterOfDeeds/Index.html   `Free`   Access Register of Deeds records free at www.lex-co.com/Departments/RegisterOfDeeds/OnlineServices.html.
Property, Taxation Records `Free`   Access property and tax data free at http://maps.lex-co.com/PCSearch/tb001-pg.asp which includes sales, parcel, property cards, mobile homes, and auto tax.

Newberry County   *Property, Taxation Records*   `Free`   Access to assessor database is free at
www.newberrycounty.net/assessor/Index.html. Access to auditor's property data is free at www.newberrycounty.net/auditor/Index.html. Access to auditor and treasurer property tax data is free at www.newberrycountysctaxes.com/. Auditor data may also be free at http://71.226.156.248/vpn/auditor.htm.

Oconee County *Land, Deed, Mortgage, Plat Records* www.oconeesc.com `Free` Access recorder's index search
free at www.oconeesc.com/resolution/default.asp. Deeds go back to 1957; Plats and mortgages to 1992.

Property, Taxation Records `Free` Access county parcel data complete for free at www.oconeesc.com/GISDATA.html and click on pdf.

Orangeburg County *Property, Deed, Mortgage, UCC, Plat Records* www.orangeburgscrod.org `Free`
Access free deeds, mortgages and plat records back to 1989 at www.orangeburgscrod.org/welcome.asp.

Property, Taxation Records `Free` Access to county property tax records is free at
www.orangeburgcounty.org/Assessor/main.asp.

Pickens County *Real Estate, Deed, Lien, Mortgage, UCC, Plat Records* www.co.pickens.sc.us/regofdeeds/ `Free`
Access the recorders database back to 12/1986 free at http://67.32.48.38/oncoreweb/.

Property, Taxation Records `Free` Search property tax records at www.co.pickens.sc.us/onlinetaxes/. Also, search assessor property and sales records free at www.pickensassessor.org/

Richland County *Real Estate, Deed, Parcel, Marriage Records* www.richlandonline.com/ `Free` Search register
of deeds free at www.richlandonline.com/services/rodsearch.asp; no name searching. Also, search marriages free at www.richlandonline.com/services/onlineservices.asp.

Property, Taxation Records `Free` Search assessments at
www.richlandonline.com/services/assessorsearch/assessorsearch.asp; no name searching. Access to county property data is free at www.richlandmaps.com. Click on "Property Info" however, there is no name searching.

Spartanburg County *Real Estate, Deed, Lien, UCC, Plat, Charter Records* www.spartanburgcounty.org `Free`
Access recording data free at www.spartanburgcounty.org/rmsdmsclient/index.asp. Images being added daily.

Property, Taxation Records `Free` Access property tax data free at www.spartanburgcounty.org/asrinfo/index.aspx .

Sumter County *Real Estate, Deed Records* www.sumtercountysc.org `Free` Search county e-gov data free at
www.sumtercountysc.org/disclaim.htm.

Property, Taxation Records `Free` Search assessment data and property cards free at
www.sumtercountysc.org/EGSV2SMTR/PCSearch.do. Also, search county e-gov data free at www.sumtercountysc.org/disclaim.htm.

York County *Property, Taxation Records* `Free` Access to the county GIS and property data is free at
http://maps.yorkcountygov.com/gisonline/. Click on "GIS Online" and name search at the main map page.

Other South Carolina Sites of Note:

Charleston County - Business Licenses www3.charlestoncounty.org/connect/LU_GROUP_3?s=b
Cherokee County - Inmate, Most Wanted www.cherokeecountysheriff.net
Greenville County - Most Wanted, Missing Persons www.gcso.org
Pickens County - Most Wanted www.pickenscosheriff.org/most_wanted/most_wanted.htm
Richland County - Inmate, Lost Pets www.richlandonline.com/services/onlineservices.asp

South Dakota

Capital: Pierre
　　　　Hughes County

Time Zone: CST

South Dakota's eighteen western-most counties are MST:
They are: Bennett, Butte, Corson, Custer, Dewey,
Fall River, Haakon, Harding, Jackson, Lawrence,
Meade, Mellette, Pennington, Perkins, Shannon, Stanley, Todd, and Ziebach

Population: 796,214
# of Counties: 66

Useful State Links

Website: www.sd.gov
Governor: www.state.sd.us/governor/
Attorney General: www.state.sd.us/attorney
State Archives: www.sdhistory.org
State Statutes and Codes: http://legis.state.sd.us/statutes/index.aspx
Legislative Bill Search: http://legis.state.sd.us/sessions/2008/index.aspx
Bill Monitoring: http://legis.state.sd.us/mylrc/index.aspx
Unclaimed Funds:
　　　www.sdtreasurer.com/default.asp?page=unclaimed_property_page&section=search_claim

Primary State Agencies

Sexual Offender Registry `Free`

Division of Criminal Investigation, Identification Section - SOR Unit,　http://sor.sd.gov/disclaimer.asp?page=search&nav=2
Searching is available from the website.

Corporation, LP, LLP, LLC, Trademarks/Servicemarks `Free`

Corporation Division, Secretary of State,　www.sdsos.gov/corporations/　Search the Secretary of State Corporations Div. Database
free at　www.state.sd.us/applications/st02corplook/ASPX/ST32Main.aspx. Trademark searches may be requested via e-mail at
marianne.gabriel@state.sd.us.　*Other Options:* The corporate database may be purchased on CD for $1,000 with $500 monthly
updates.

Uniform Commercial Code, Federal Tax Liens

UCC Division, Secretary of State,　www.sdsos.gov/ucc　Dakota Fast File is the filing and searching service available at
www.sdsos.gov/busineservices/ucc.shtm. This is a commercial service that requires registration and a $120-360 fee per year. Certified
search also available.　*Other Options:* FTP downloads are available for purchase.

Birth Certificates `Free & $$`

South Dakota Department of Health, Vital Records,　http://doh.sd.gov/VitalRecords/order.aspx　Records may be ordered online at the
website via a state supported vendor. You can order recent (less than 100 years) birth records at the website, for a fee. You can search
free at http://apps.sd.gov/applications/PH14Over100BirthRec/index.asp for birth records over 100 years old.

Vital Records `$$`

South Dakota Department of Health, Vital Records,　http://doh.sd.gov/VitalRecords/order.aspx　Birth, death, and marriage records
may be ordered online at the website via a state supported vendor.

Driver Records ▓SS▓

Dept of Public Safety, Office of Driver Licensing, www.state.sd.us/dps/dl/ The system is open for batch requests 24 hours a day. There is a minimum of 250 requests daily. It generally takes 10 minutes to process a batch. The current fee is $4.00 per record and there are some start-up costs. For more information, call 605-773-6883. *Other Options:* Lists are available to the insurance industry.

Occupational Licensing Boards

Abstractor Company...........................www.state.sd.us/drr2/reg/abstracters/roster.htm
Ambulance Service............................www.state.sd.us/dps/ems/
Animal Remedy (medicine/drug) ......www.state.sd.us/doa/das/hp-af-ar.htm
Architect..www.state.sd.us/dol/boards/engineer/Roster/roster.htm
Athletic Trainer ....http://doh.sd.gov/boards/medicine/
Attorney..www.sdbar.net/
Auctioneer ....www.state.sd.us/drr2/reg/realestate/roster_licensees/roster.htm
Audiologist ....http://doh.sd.gov/boards/audiology/roster.aspx
Bail Bond Agent................................www.state.sd.us/drr2/reg/insurance/producers/bailbonds.xls
Bank www.state.sd.us/drr2/reg/bank/banktrust/banktrust.htm
Barber/Barber Shop ....www.state.sd.us/dol/boards/barber/roster.htm
Beauty Shop/Salon http://apps.sd.gov/applications/ld19cosmet/license.asp
Clinical Nurse Specialist ....https://ifmc.sd.gov/lookup.php
Cosmetology-related Occupation http://apps.sd.gov/applications/ld19cosmet/license.asp
Counselor ....http://dhs.sd.gov/brd/Counselor/roster.aspx
Crematory..http://doh.sd.gov/Boards/FuneralBoard/Roster.aspx
Dentist/Hygienist/Assistant ....www.sdboardofdentistry.com/
Driller, Oil and Gas Supervisor ....www.state.sd.us/denr/DES/Mining/Oil&Gas/NewPermit.htm
Embalmer ....http://doh.sd.gov/Boards/FuneralBoard/Roster.aspx
Engineer ....www.state.sd.us/dol/boards/engineer/Roster/roster.htm
Esthetician http://apps.sd.gov/applications/ld19cosmet/license.asp
Fertilizer ....www.state.sd.us/doa/das/hp-fert.htm
Funeral Director/Establishment ....http://doh.sd.gov/Boards/FuneralBoard/Roster.aspx
Gaming Manufacturer........................www.state.sd.us/drr2/reg/gaming/manufac.htm
Health Insurer ....www.state.sd.us/drr2/reg/insurance/consumer/major_med_carriers.html
Hearing Aid Dispenser ....http://doh.sd.gov/boards/audiology/roster.aspx
Home Inspector ....www.state.sd.us/drr2/reg/realestate/roster_licensees/roster.htm
Insurance Company www.state.sd.us/drr2/reg/insurance/consumer/index.html
Insurer of Health...............................www.state.sd.us/drr2/reg/insurance/consumer/major_med_carriers.html
Landscape Architect ....www.state.sd.us/dol/boards/engineer/Roster/roster.htm
Lobbyist...www.state.sd.us/applications/ST12ODRS/PublicLobbyistViewlist.asp?cmd=resetall
Manicurist/Nail Technician http://apps.sd.gov/applications/ld19cosmet/license.asp
Marriage & Family Therapist ....http://dhs.sd.gov/brd/Counselor/roster.aspx
Midwife Nurse...................................https://ifmc.sd.gov/lookup.php
Money Lender www.state.sd.us/drr2/reg/bank/licensees/moneylender.htm
Mortgage Broker/Lender www.state.sd.us/drr2/reg/bank/licensees/mortgagebrokers.htm
Nail Salon http://apps.sd.gov/applications/ld19cosmet/license.asp
Notary..www.state.sd.us/applications/ST12ODRS/aspx/frmNotaryViewlist.aspx?cmd=resetall
Nurse/or/Nurses' Aide.......................https://ifmc.sd.gov/lookup.php
Nurse Anesthetist...............................https://ifmc.sd.gov/lookup.php
Nursing Home Administrator ....http://doh.sd.gov/boards/nursingfacility/
Oil & Gas Driller Senior Geologist ...www.state.sd.us/denr/DES/Mining/Oil&Gas/NewPermit.htm
Optometrist..www.arbo.org/index.php?action=findanoptometrist
Osteopathic Physician........................http://doh.sd.gov/boards/medicine/
Pesticide Applicator/Dealer...............www.state.sd.us/doa/das/
Pet Health Insurer ....www.state.sd.us/drr2/reg/insurance/consumer/pet_companies.pdf
Petrol. Release Assessor/Remediator www.state.sd.us/dol/boards/engineer/Roster/roster.htm
Podiatrist...http://doh.sd.gov/boards/podiatry/
Property Manager ....www.state.sd.us/drr2/reg/realestate/roster_licensees/roster.htm

Psychologist...http://dhs.sd.gov/brd/Psychologist/roster.aspx
Public Accountant-CPA   www.state.sd.us/dol/boards/accountancy/Annual%20Registry%20NOVEMBER%202006.htm
Radiology (Dental) ....www.sdboardofdentistry.com/
Real Estate Agent/Seller/Broker/Firmwww.state.sd.us/drr2/reg/realestate/roster_licensees/roster.htm
Re-insurer, Accredited/Qualified.......www.state.sd.us/drr2/reg/insurance/Financial/AQReinsurers.pdf
Residential Rental Agent...................www.state.sd.us/drr2/reg/realestate/roster_licensees/roster.htm
Securities Agent/Broker/Dealer.........www.finra.org/InvestorInformation/InvestorProtection/p005882
Social Worker....................................http://dhs.sd.gov/brd/SocialWorker/roster.aspx
Storage Tank, Above/Below Ground. www.state.sd.us/denr/des/ground/tanks/register.htm
Surveyor, Land ....www.state.sd.us/dol/boards/engineer/Roster/roster.htm
Timeshare Project, Registered...........www.state.sd.us/drr2/reg/realestate/roster_licensees/roster.htm
Timeshare Real Estate ....www.state.sd.us/drr2/reg/realestate/roster_licensees/roster.htm
Trust Company www.state.sd.us/drr2/reg/bank/banktrust/banktrust.htm
Waste Water-related Occupation ....www.state.sd.us/denr/des/drinking/PDF/operator.pdf
Water Distributor..............................www.state.sd.us/denr/des/drinking/PDF/operator.pdf
Water Treatment Operator.................www.state.sd.us/denr/des/drinking/PDF/operator.pdf
Weapon, Concealed...........................www.sdsos.gov/adminservices/concealedpistolpermits.shtm

State and Local Courts

State Court Structure: The circuit courts are the general trial courts of the Unified Judicial System. These courts have original jurisdiction in all civil and criminal cases. They are the only court where a criminal felony case can be tried and determined as well as a civil case involving more than $10,000 in damages. Circuit courts also have jurisdiction over appeals from Magistrate Court decisions. Generally, Magistrate Courts assist the circuit courts in processing minor criminal cases and less serious civil actions.

There are 66 counties, but 64 courts. Cases for Buffalo County are handled at the Brule County Circuit Court. Cases for Shannon County are handled by the Fall River County Circuit Court.

Statewide Court Online Access: The Supreme Court calendar, opinions, rules and archived oral arguments may be searched from www.sdjudicial.com.

All active money judgments and inactive civil money judgments from 04/19/2004 forward are available from a web subscription service offered by this agency. The subscription cost is $250 monthly or $2500 annually. You may also access this system on a pay as you go basis where you deposit from a credit card and the system deducts from your balance. You can get more information on this system at https://apps.sd.gov/applications/judgmentquery/login.aspx. The money judgment system permits bulk downloading of information. However, the agreement with the agency disallows any resale of the data. This subscription system does not include probate or criminal information. For more details contact Ms. Jill Gusso at 605-773-8437.

> ❖ **Statewide Civil Access Offered For Most Counties – Read Above.** ❖

Note: No individual South Dakota courts offer online access.

Recorders, Assessors, and Other Sites of Note

Recording Office Organization: 66 counties, 66 recording offices. The recording officer is the Register of Deeds. Federal tax liens on personal property of businesses are filed with the Secretary of State. Other federal and state tax liens are filed with the county Register of Deeds. Most counties will perform tax lien searches.

Online Access Note: No statewide system, but a few counties offer free record data via their websites.

Brown County *Property, Taxation Records* **$$** Search assessor property data for a fee on the GIS system at http://beacon.schneidercorp.com/. Registration and username required.

Custer County *Property, Taxation Records* [SS] Search assessor property data for a fee on the GIS system at http://beacon.schneidercorp.com/. Registration and username required.

Fall River County *Property, Taxation Records* [SS] Search assessor property data for a fee on the GIS system at http://beacon.schneidercorp.com/. Registration and username required.

Harding County *Property, Taxation Records* [SS] Search assessor property data for a fee on the GIS system at http://beacon.schneidercorp.com/. Registration and username required.

McCook County *Property, Taxation Records* [SS] Access assessor property data for a fee on the GIS system at http://beacon.schneidercorp.com/ with registration and password.

Meade County *Property, Taxation Records* [SS] Search assessor property data for a fee on the GIS system at http://beacon.schneidercorp.com/ with registration and username required.

Minnehaha County *Property, Taxation Records* [Free] Access to the county property tax database is free at www.minnehahacounty.org/property_tax/Index.asp. No name searching at this time.

Moody County *Property, Taxation Records* [SS] Search assessor property data for a fee on the GIS system at http://beacon.schneidercorp.com/ with registration and username required.

Pennington County *Property, Taxation Records* [Free] Access to the county property tax database is free at www.co.pennington.sd.us/search/search.aspx.

Union County *Property, Taxation Records* [SS] Search assessor property data for a fee on the GIS system at http://beacon.schneidercorp.com/ with registration and username required.

Tennessee

Capital: Nashville
           Davidson County

Time Zone: CST

Tennessee's twenty-nine eastern-most counties are EST.
They are: Anderson, Blount, Bradley, Campbell, Carter, Claiborne, Cocke, Grainger, Greene, Hamilton, Hancock, Hawkins, Jefferson, Johnson, Knox, Loudon, McMinn, Meigs, Monroe, Morgan, Polk, Rhea, Roane, Scott, Sevier, Sullivan, Unicoi, Union, Washington.

Population: 6,156,719

# of Counties: 95

Useful State Links

Website: www.tennessee.gov/

Governor: www.tennesseeanytime.org/governor/Welcome.do

Attorney General: www.tn.gov/attorneygeneral/

State Archives: www.tennessee.gov/tsla/

State Statutes and Codes: www.tennessee.gov/sos/bluebook/index.htm

Legislative Bill Search: www.legislature.state.tn.us

Unclaimed Funds: www.tennesseeanytime.org/unclp/

Primary State Agencies

Criminal Records $$

Tennessee Bureau of Investigation, TN Open Records Information Srvs, www.tbi.state.tn.us Records may be requested online via email from the website, but this is not an interactive service. Records must still me manually searched and will it several days.

Sexual Offender Registry Free

Tennessee Bureau of Investigation, Sexual Offender Registry, www.ticic.state.tn.us Search sexual offenders at www.ticic.state.tn.us/sorinternet/sosearch.aspx by last name, city, county or ZIP Code. One may also search for missing children, and people placed on parole who reside in Tennessee. A map search is found at http://tnmap.state.tn.us/sor/map.aspx.

Incarceration Records Free

Tennessee Department of Corrections, Rachel Jackson Building, Ground Fl, www.state.tn.us/correction/ Extensive search capabilities are offered from the website at https://www.tennesseeanytime.org/foil/foil_index.jsp. *Other Options:* A CD-Rom is available with only public information from current offender database; nominal fee; contact the Planning & Research Division.

Corporation, LLC, LP, LLP, Fictitious Name, Assumed Name Free

TN Sec of State: Corporations, William R Snodgrass Tower, www.state.tn.us/sos/bus_svc/index.htm There is a free online search at www.tennesseeanytime.org/sosname/ for name availability and at www.tennesseeanytime.org/soscorp/ for business records. This gives online access to over 4,000,000 records relating to corporations, limited liability companies, limited partnerships and limited liability partnerships formed or registered in Tennessee. Also, search securities department enforcement actions at www.state.tn.us/commerce/securities/enfaction.html. *Other Options:* Some data can be purchased in bulk or list format. Call 615-532-9007 for more details.

Trademarks/Servicemarks, Trade Names Free

Secretary of State, Trademarks/Tradenames Division, www.state.tn.us/sos/bus_svc/trademarks.htm The Internet provides a record search of TN Trademarks, newest records are 3 days old. The search url is www.ja.state.tn.us/sos/iets2/ietm/PgTrademarkSearch.jsp. *Other Options:* The agency will provide a file update every three months for $1.00 per page. Requests must be in writing.

Uniform Commercial Code `Free`

TN Sec of State - UCC Records, William R Snodgrass Tower, www.state.tn.us/sos/ Free access to general, limited information at www.ja.state.tn.us/sos/iets3/ieuc/PgUCCSearch.jsp. Search by debtor name or file number. Images are not available.

Driver Records `$$`

Dept. of Safety, Financial Responsibility Section, Attn: Driving Records, www.tennessee.gov/safety/ Driving records are available to subscribers, signup at www.tennesseeanytime.org. There is a $75 registration fee. Records are available 24 hours daily on an interactive basis. Records are $7.00 each. Suggested only for ongoing users. Companies retrieving more than 500 records per month can use a "batch" process in which multiple license numbers can be searched and the results are returned in one file. Call 1-866-886-3468 for more information. Subscribers may also obtain a DL status check online for a fee of $1.25. *Other Options:* Bulk retrieval is available for high volume users. Purchase of the DL file is available for approved requesters. Call Information Systems at 615-251-5322.

Vehicle Ownership & Registration `$$`

Motor Vehicle Services, Taxpayer & Vehicle Services, www.tennessee.gov/revenue/ Online access is available for approved subscribers at www.tennesseeanytime.org/ivtr. This is the same subscription system used to pull driving records. The $75.00 annual fee includes 10 users. IVTR allows subscribers to retrieve vehicle, title, and registration information for vehicles registered in Tennessee. Search with license plate or VIN. The fee is $2.00 per search. All subscribers must be approved per DPPA.

Vital Records `Free & $$`

Tennessee Department of Health, Office of Vital Records, http://health.state.tn.us/vr/index.htm Records may be ordered from the website, but are returned by mail. See expedited services. The Cleveland (Tennessee) Public Library staff and volunteers have published the 1914-1925 death records of thirty-three counties at www.tennessee.gov/tsla/history/vital/death.htm. It should be noted that the records of children under two years of age have been omitted from this project.

Occupational Licensing Boards

Accounting Firm	http://licsrch.state.tn.us/
Alarm Contractor	http://licsrch.state.tn.us/
Animal Euthanasia Technician	http://health.state.tn.us/licensure/index.htm
Architect	http://licsrch.state.tn.us/
Athletic Trainer	http://health.state.tn.us/licensure/index.htm
Attorney	www.tbpr.org/Consumers/AttorneySearch/
Auctioneer/Auction Company	http://licsrch.state.tn.us/
Audiologist	http://health.state.tn.us/licensure/index.htm
Barber Shop/Barber School	http://licsrch.state.tn.us/
Barber/Barber Technician	http://licsrch.state.tn.us/
Boiler Operator	http://licsrch.state.tn.us/
Boxing/Racing Personnel	http://licsrch.state.tn.us/
Chiropractor/Chiropractic Assist.	http://health.state.tn.us/licensure/index.htm
Clinical Lab Technician/Personnel	http://health.state.tn.us/licensure/index.htm
Collection Agent/Manager	http://licsrch.state.tn.us/
Contractor	http://licsrch.state.tn.us/
Cosmetology-related Occupation	http://licsrch.state.tn.us/
Counselor, Alcohol & Drug Abuse	http://health.state.tn.us/licensure/index.htm
Counselor, Associate/Professional	http://health.state.tn.us/licensure/index.htm
Dental Hygienist	http://health.state.tn.us/licensure/index.htm
Dentist/Dental Assistant	http://health.state.tn.us/licensure/index.htm
Dietitian/Nutritionist	http://health.state.tn.us/licensure/index.htm
Electrologist/Instructor/School	http://health.state.tn.us/licensure/index.htm
Elevator Inspector	www.state.tn.us/labor-wfd/elevatorsinsp.html
Embalmer	http://licsrch.state.tn.us/
Emergency Med. Personnel/Dispatch	http://health.state.tn.us/licensure/index.htm
Emergency Medical Service	http://health.state.tn.us/licensure/index.htm
Engineer	http://licsrch.state.tn.us/
First Responder EMS	http://health.state.tn.us/licensure/index.htm
Funeral & Burial Director/Appren.	http://licsrch.state.tn.us/
Funeral & Burial Est./Cemetery	http://licsrch.state.tn.us/
Geologist	http://licsrch.state.tn.us/

Hearing Aid Dispenser .... http://health.state.tn.us/licensure/index.htm
Home Improvement .... http://licsrch.state.tn.us/
Insurance Agent/Firm .... http://licsrch.state.tn.us/
Interior Designer .... http://licsrch.state.tn.us/
Laboratory Personnel, Medical .... http://health.state.tn.us/licensure/index.htm
Landscape Architect/Architect Firm .. http://licsrch.state.tn.us/
Lobbyist .... www.state.tn.us/tref/lobbyists/lobbyists.htm
Manicurist .... http://licsrch.state.tn.us/
Marriage & Family Therapist .... http://health.state.tn.us/licensure/index.htm
Massage Therapist/Establishment ...... http://health.state.tn.us/licensure/index.htm
Medical Disciplinary Tracking .... http://health.state.tn.us/abuseregistry/index.html
Medical Doctor .... http://health.state.tn.us/licensure/index.htm
Midwife .... http://health.state.tn.us/licensure/index.htm
Motor Vehicle Dealer/Seller/Auction http://licsrch.state.tn.us/
Notary Public www.ja.state.tn.us/sos/iets1/ieny/PgIenySearch.jsp
Nurse-RN/LPN/or/ Nurses' Aide .... http://health.state.tn.us/licensure/index.htm
Nursing Home Administrator .... http://health.state.tn.us/licensure/index.htm
Occupational Therapist/Assistant ...... http://health.state.tn.us/licensure/index.htm
Optician, Dispensing .... http://health.state.tn.us/licensure/index.htm
Optometrist .... http://health.state.tn.us/licensure/index.htm
Orthopedic Physician Assistant .... http://health.state.tn.us/licensure/index.htm
Osteopathic Physician .... http://health.state.tn.us/licensure/index.htm
Pastoral Therapist, Clinical .... http://health.state.tn.us/licensure/index.htm
Personnel Leasing .... http://licsrch.state.tn.us/
Pharmacist/Pharmacy .... http://licsrch.state.tn.us/
Pharmacy Researcher .... http://licsrch.state.tn.us/
Physical Therapist/Assistant .... http://health.state.tn.us/licensure/index.htm
Physician Assistant .... http://health.state.tn.us/licensure/index.htm
Plumber/Plumbing Company .... http://licsrch.state.tn.us/
Podiatrist .... http://health.state.tn.us/licensure/index.htm
Polygraph Examiner .... http://licsrch.state.tn.us/
Private Investigator/Firm/Guard .... http://licsrch.state.tn.us/
Psychologist/ Psycholog'l Examiner . http://health.state.tn.us/licensure/index.htm
Public Accountant-CPA .... http://licsrch.state.tn.us/
Racetrack .... http://licsrch.state.tn.us/
Radiologic Assistant .... http://health.state.tn.us/licensure/index.htm
Real Estate Agent/Broker/Seller/Firm http://licsrch.state.tn.us/
Real Estate Appraiser .... http://licsrch.state.tn.us/
Refrigeration Installer/Contractor ...... http://licsrch.state.tn.us/
Respir'y Care Therapist/Tech./Asst ... http://health.state.tn.us/licensure/index.htm
School-related Profession www.k-12.state.tn.us/tcertinf/Search.asp
School Vocational Endorsement www.k-12.state.tn.us/tcertinf/Search.asp
Security Guard/Company .... http://licsrch.state.tn.us/
Security Trainer .... http://licsrch.state.tn.us/
Shampoo Technician .... http://licsrch.state.tn.us/
Social Worker, Master/Clinical .... http://health.state.tn.us/licensure/index.htm
Speech Pathologist .... http://health.state.tn.us/licensure/index.htm
Surveyor, Land .... http://licsrch.state.tn.us/
Teacher www.k-12.state.tn.us/tcertinf/Search.asp
Timeshare Agent .... http://licsrch.state.tn.us/
Veterinarian .... http://health.state.tn.us/licensure/index.htm
X-ray Operator/Technologist .... http://health.state.tn.us/licensure/index.htm

State and Local Courts

State Court Structure: Circuit Courts hear civil and criminal cases and appeals of decisions from City, Juvenile, Municipal and General Sessions courts. The jurisdiction of Circuit Courts often overlaps that of the Chancery Courts. Criminal cases are tried in Circuit Court except in districts with separate Criminal Courts established by the General Assembly. Criminal Courts relieve Circuit Courts in areas where they are justified by heavy caseloads. Criminal Courts exist in 13 of the State's 31 judicial districts. The Chancery Courts, in addition to handling probate, also hear certain types of equitable civil cases. Combining of Circuit Court and General Sessions Courts varies by county.

Statewide Court Online Access: Several counties offer online access to court records, but there is no statewide access system. Appellate Court opinions are found at www.tsc.state.tn.us/geninfo/Courts/AppellateCourts.htm.

Davidson County

20th District Criminal Court   http://ccc.nashville.gov   `Free`
Criminal: Access Davidson County Criminal Court database at ccc.nashville.gov.

Circuit Court   www.nashville.gov/circuit   `$$`
Civil: Access filed cases online on CaseLink at www.nashville.gov/circuit/caselink/; $20.00 per month fee required plus username, password. Email Caselink@Nashville.Gov for signup or add'l info. I .

General Sessions Court   www.nashville.gov/circuit/sessions   `Free`
Civil: Access filed cases online on CaseLink at www.nashville.gov/circuit/caselink/; $20.00 per month fee required, plus username and password. Email Caselink@Nashville.Gov for signup or add'l info. Intended to be free searching, soon.

Hamilton County

11th District Civil Court   www.hamiltontn.gov/courts   `Free`
Civil: Online access to current court dockets are free at www.hamiltontn.gov/courts/Default.aspx.

11th District General Sessions Court   www.hamiltontn.gov/courts/sessions/   `Free`
Civil: Online access to current (7 days) court dockets is free on the web. Search dispositions and calendars free at http://cjusgeneralsessions.hamiltontn.gov/appfolder/GS_Web_Calendar.aspx.

11th District Criminal Court   www.hamiltontn.gov/courts   `Free`
Criminal: Search court's disposition records and court dates free at http://cjuscriminal.hamiltontn.gov/AppFolder/CC_Web_Calendar.aspx and records go back to 1989. Also, online access to current court dockets is free at web page.

Chancery Court   www.hamiltontn.gov/courts/Default.aspx   `Free`
Civil: Chancery motions/dockets are online at www.hamiltontn.gov/courts/Default.aspx.

Shelby County

Circuit Court   www.circuitcourt.co.shelby.tn.us   `Free`
Civil: Search clerk's circuit court records for free at the website or at http://gs2.co.shelby.tn.us:7779/pls/crweb/ck_public_qry_main.cp_main_idx.

30th District Criminal Court   http://co4.shelbycountytn.gov/court_clerks/criminal_court/index.html   `Free`
Criminal: Search the criminal court records for free at http://jssi.co.shelby.tn.us/.

Chancery Court   http://chancerycourt.co.shelby.tn.us   `Free`
Civil: Search court records for free at http://gs2.co.shelby.tn.us:7779/pls/chweb/ck_public_qry_main.cp_main_idx.

General Sessions - Civil   http://generalsessionscourt.co.shelby.tn.us   `Free`
Civil: Search court records for free at http://gs2.co.shelby.tn.us:7779/pls/gnweb/ck_public_qry_main.cp_main_idx.

General Sessions - Criminal   http://generalsessionscourt.co.shelby.tn.us   `Free`
Criminal: Search criminal court records free at http://jssi.co.shelby.tn.us/.

Probate Court   http://www.shelbyprobate.com   `Free`   Probate court records and dockets are free at www.probatedata.co.shelby.tn.us/default2.htm. Search online by name or case number.

Sullivan County

Bristol General Sessions Court   www.bridgeweb.org/docketts.htm   `Free`

Civil: Access to dockets and rules is free at www.bridgeweb.org/docketts.htm. *Criminal:* Access to dockets and rules is free online at www.bridgeweb.org/docketts.htm.

White County

13th District Circuit & General Sessions Court   www.whiteccc.com/   **Free**
Court dockets available free at www.whiteccc.com/ but no historical data.

Recorders, Assessors, and Other Sites of Note

Recording Office Organization: 95 counties, 96 recording offices. The recording officer is the Register of Deeds. Sullivan County has two recording offices. All federal tax liens are filed with the county Register of Deeds. State tax liens are filed with the Secretary of State or the Register of Deeds.

Online Access Note: The State Comptroller of the Treasury Real Estate Assessment Database can be searched free at www.assessment.state.tn.us/. Select a county then search by name for real property information. Counties not on this system are Davidson, Hamilton, Knox, Shelby, and Unicoi.

Online access to a number of county' property and deeds indexes and images is available via a private company at www.titlesearcher.com or email support@TitleSearcher.com. Registration, login, and monthly $35 fee per county required, plus a one-time $20.00 set up fee. A $5 per day plan is also available.

Also, online access to a large group of county property, deeds, judgment, liens, and UCCs is available via a private company at www1.ustitlesearch.net/ or call 615-223-5420. Registration, login, and monthly $25 fee required, plus $50 set up fee. Use DEMO as your username to sample the system.

Also, www.tnrealestate.com offers free and fee services for real estate information from all Tennessee counties.

Anderson County   *Real Estate, Deed Records*   www.andersondeeds.com/   **Free**   Access property and deeds indexes/images at http://search.andersondeeds.com/menu.php. Also, see state introduction.

Bedford County   *Real Estate, Deed Records*   **$$**   Access property and deeds indexes/images at www.titlesearcher.com; fee/registration required. Also, see state introduction.

Bledsoe County   *Real Estate, Deed Records*   **$$**   Access property and deeds indexes/images at www.titlesearcher.com; fee/registration required. Also, see state introduction.

Bradley County   *Real Estate, Deed Records*   **$$**   Access property and deeds indexes/images at www.titlesearcher.com; fee/registration with software provider is required. Also, see state introduction.

Campbell County   *Real Estate, Deed Records*   **$$**   Access real estate records at www.ustitlesearch.net, registration/fee required, images go back to 6/2003. Also, see state introduction.

Cannon County   *Real Estate, Deed, Judgment, Lien, UCC Records*   **$$**   Access real estate records at www.ustitlesearch.net, registration/fee required; also see state introduction.

Carroll County   *Real Estate, Deed, Judgment, Lien, UCC Records*   **$$**   Access real estate indexes and images at www.ustitlesearch.net. Registration/monthly fee required. Also, see state introduction.

Carter County   *Real Estate, Deed Records*   www.carterdeeds.com   **$$**   Access property and deeds indexes/images at www.titlesearcher.com; fee/registration required. Also, see state introduction.

Cheatham County   *Real Estate, Deed, Judgment, Lien, UCC Records*   **$$**   Access real estate indexes/images at www.ustitlesearch.net; registration/monthly fee required. Also see state introduction.

Chester County   *Real Estate, Deed, Judgment, Lien, UCC Records*   **$$**   Access real estate indexes/images at www.ustitlesearch.net; registration/monthly fee required. Also see state introduction.

Claiborne County   *Real Estate, Deed Records*   **$$**   Access property and deeds indexes/images at www.titlesearcher.com; fee/registration required. Also, see state introduction.

Clay County   *Real Estate, Deed Records*   **$$**   Access property and deeds indexes/images at www.titlesearcher.com; fee/registration required. Also, see state introduction.

Cocke County   *Real Estate, Deed Records*   **$$**   Access property and deeds indexes/images at www.titlesearcher.com; fee/registration required. Also, see state introduction.

Coffee County   *Real Estate, Deed Records*   **$$**   Access property and deeds indexes/images at www.titlesearcher.com; fee/registration required. Also, see state introduction.

Crockett County *Real Estate, Deed, Judgment, Lien, UCC Records* `$$` Access real estate indexes/images at www.ustitlesearch.net; registration/monthly fee required. Also, see state introduction.

Cumberland County *Real Estate, Deed Records* `$$` Access property and deeds indexes/images at www.titlesearcher.com; fee/registration required. Also, see state introduction.
Property, Taxation Records `Free` Assessment data on state comptroller system is free at www.comptroller.state.tn.us/cpdivpa.htm

Davidson County *Real Estate, Deed, Judgment, Lien Records* www.nashville.gov/ROD/ `Free & $$` Property and mapping records on the Metro Planning Commission Nashville City database are free at http://www3.nashville.org/property/. Click on "text only search." Also, Register of Deeds offers access to recorded docs by subscription; monthly fees vary, a set-up fee is $25.00. For info, call 615-862-6790. Includes books A thru 3784.
Property, Taxation Records `Free` Search county assessments free at http://hobsvtxie01.nashville.org/default.asp.

Decatur County *Real Estate, Deed Records* `$$` Access property and deeds indexes/images at www.titlesearcher.com; fee/registration required. Also, see state introduction.

Dickson County *Real Estate, Deed, Judgment, Lien, UCC Records* `$$` Access real estate indexes/images at www.ustitlesearch.net, or a 2nd company at www.titlesearcher.com; registration/monthly fee required. Also see state introduction.

Dyer County *Real Estate, Deed, Judgment, Lien, UCC Records* www.co.dyer.tn.us `$$` Access real estate indexes/images at www.ustitlesearch.net; registration/monthly fee required. Also see state introduction.

Fayette County *Real Estate, Deed Records* `$$` Access property and deeds indexes/images at www.titlesearcher.com; fee/registration required. Also, see state introduction.

Fentress County *Real Estate, Deed Records* `$$` Access property and deeds indexes/images at www.titlesearcher.com; fee/registration required. Also, see state introduction.

Franklin County *Real Estate, Deed Records* `$$` Access property and deeds indexes/images at www.titlesearcher.com; fee/registration required. Also, see state introduction.

Gibson County *Real Estate, Deed, Judgment, Lien, UCC Records* `$$` Access real estate indexes/images at www.ustitlesearch.net; registration/monthly fee required. Also see state introduction.

Giles County *Real Estate, Deed Records* www.gilescounty-tn.us `$$` Access property and deeds indexes/images at www.titlesearcher.com; fee/registration required. Also, see state introduction.

Grainger County *Real Estate, Deed Records* `$$` Access property and deeds indexes/images at www.titlesearcher.com; fee/registration required. Also, see state introduction.

Greene County *Real Estate, Deed Records* `$$` Access property and deeds indexes/images at www.titlesearcher.com; fee/registration required. Also, see state introduction.

Grundy County *Real Estate, Deed, Judgment, Lien, UCC Records* `$$` Access property and deeds indexes/images at www.titlesearcher.com; fee/registration required. Also, see state introduction.

Hamblen County *Real Estate, Deed Records* `$$` Access property and deeds indexes/images at www.titlesearcher.com; fee/registration required. Also, see state introduction.

Hamilton County *Real Estate, Deed Records* www.hamiltontn.gov/register/ `$$` County Register of Deeds subscription service is $50 per month and $1.00 per fax page. Search by name, address, or book & page. For info, call 423-209-6560; or visit www.hamiltontn.gov/Register/. Credit cards accepted.
Property, Taxation Records `Free` Property assessor records are free at www.hamiltontn.gov/Assessor/. Search property taxes at www.hamiltontn.gov/trustee/default.aspx. Also, search City of Chattanooga property tax database at http://propertytax.chattanooga.gov.

Hancock County *Real Estate, Deed, Judgment, Lien, UCC Records* `$$` Access real estate indexes/images at www.ustitlesearch.net; registration/monthly fee required. Also see state introduction.

Hardeman County *Real Estate, Deed, Judgment, Lien, UCC Records* `$$` Access real estate indexes/images at www.ustitlesearch.net; registration/monthly fee required. Also see state introduction.

Hardin County *Real Estate, Deed, Judgment, Lien, UCC Records* `$$` Access real estate indexes/images at www.ustitlesearch.net; registration/monthly fee required. Also see state introduction.

Hawkins County *Real Estate, Deed Records* `$$` Access property and deeds indexes/images at www.titlesearcher.com; fee/registration required. Also, see state introduction.

Haywood County *Real Estate, Deed Records* SS Access real estate indexes/images at www.ustitlesearch.net; registration/monthly fee required. Also see state introduction.

Henderson County *Real Estate, Deed, Judgment, Lien, UCC Records* SS Access real estate indexes/images at www.ustitlesearch.net; registration/monthly fee required. Also see state introduction.

Henry County *Real Estate, Deed, Judgment, Lien, UCC Records* SS Access real estate indexes/images at www.ustitlesearch.net; registration/monthly fee required. Also see state introduction.

Hickman County *Real Estate, Deed Records* SS Access property and deeds indexes/images at www.titlesearcher.com; fee/registration required. Also, see state introduction.

Houston County *Real Estate, Deed, Judgment, Lien, UCC Records* Free & SS Access real estate indexes/images at www.ustitlesearch.net; registration/monthly fee required. Land records also available free at www.edoctecinc.com/. Also see state introduction.

Humphreys County *Real Estate, Deed Records* SS Access property and deeds indexes/images at www.titlesearcher.com; fee/registration required. Also, see state introduction.

Jackson County *Real Estate, Deed Records* SS Access property and deeds indexes/images at www.titlesearcher.com; fee/registration required. Also, see state introduction.

Jefferson County *Real Estate, Deed Records* www.jeffersoncountytn.gov SS Access property and deeds indexes/images at www.titlesearcher.com; fee/registration required. Also, see state introduction.

Johnson County *Real Estate, Deed Records* SS Access property and deeds indexes/images at www.titlesearcher.com; fee/registration required. Also, see state introduction.

Knox County *Real Estate, Deed Records* www.knoxcounty.org/register/ SS For online subscription for recorded document records call Ricky Deler at 865-215-3544.
Property, Taxation Records Free Search the property tax rolls for free at www.knoxcounty.org/trustee/tax_search/index.php. The GIS Dept offers a property map and details report at www.kgis.org/Portal/OnlineData/tabid/38/Default.aspx

Lake County *Real Estate, Deed, Judgment, Lien, UCC Records* SS Access real estate indexes/images at www.ustitlesearch.net; registration/monthly fee required. Also see state introduction.

Lauderdale County *Real Estate, Deed, Judgment, Lien, UCC Records* SS Access real estate indexes/images at www.ustitlesearch.net; registration/monthly fee required. Also see state introduction.

Lawrence County *Real Estate, Deed Records* www.co.lawrence.tn.us SS Access property and deeds indexes/images at www.titlesearcher.com; fee/registration required. Also see state introduction.

Lewis County *Real Estate, Deed, Judgment, Lien, UCC Records* SS Access real estate indexes/images at www.ustitlesearch.net; registration/monthly fee required. Also see state introduction.

Lincoln County *Real Estate, Deed Records* SS Access property and deeds indexes/images at www.titlesearcher.com; fee/registration required. Also, see state introduction.
Property, Taxation Records Free Assessment data on state comptroller system. Also, search property/GIS data free at www.emapsplus.com/TNLincoln/maps/.

Loudon County *Real Estate, Deed Records* SS Access property and deeds indexes/images at www.titlesearcher.com; fee/registration required. Also, see state introduction.

McMinn County *Real Estate, Deed, Judgment, Lien, UCC Records* SS Access real estate indexes/images back to 9/1999 at www.ustitlesearch.net; registration/monthly fee required. Also see state introduction.

McNairy County *Real Estate, Deed, Judgment, Lien, UCC Records* SS Access real estate indexes/images at www.ustitlesearch.net; registration/monthly fee required. Also see state introduction.

Macon County *Real Estate, Deed Records* www.maconcountytn.com/register_of_deeds.htm SS Access property and deeds indexes/images at www.titlesearcher.com; fee/registration required. Also, see state introduction.

Madison County *Real Estate, Deed Records* SS Access property and deeds indexes/images at www.titlesearcher.com; fee/registration required. Also, see state introduction.

Marion County *Real Estate, Deed Records* SS Access property and deeds indexes/images at www.titlesearcher.com; fee/registration required. Also, see state introduction.

Marshall County *Real Estate, Deed, Judgment, Lien, UCC Records* `$$` Access real estate indexes/images at www.ustitlesearch.net or a 2nd private company at www.titlesearcher.com; registration/monthly fee required. Also see state introduction.

Maury County *Real Estate, Deed Records* `$$` Access property and deeds indexes/images at www.titlesearcher.com; fee/registration required. Also, see state introduction.
Property, Taxation Records `Free` Assessment data on state comptroller system. Also, search property/GIS data free at www.emapsplus.com/TNMaury/maps/.

Meigs County *Real Estate, Deed Records* `$$` Access real estate indexes/images at www.ustitlesearch.net; registration/monthly fee required. Also see state introduction.

Monroe County *Real Estate, Deed Records* `$$` Access property and deeds indexes/images at www.titlesearcher.com; fee/registration required. Also, see state introduction.

Montgomery County *Real Estate, Deed, Judgment, Lien, UCC Records*
www.montgomerycountytn.org/county/register_of_deeds/register_of_deeds.htm `$$` Access real estate indexes/images at www.ustitlesearch.net; registration/monthly fee required. Also see state introduction.

Moore County *Real Estate, Deed Records* `$$` Access property and deeds indexes/images at www.titlesearcher.com; fee/registration required. Also, see state introduction.

Morgan County *Real Estate, Deed, Judgment, Lien, UCC Records* `$$` Access real estate indexes/images at www.ustitlesearch.net; registration/monthly fee required. Also see state introduction.

Obion County *Property, Taxation Records* `Free` Assessment data on state comptroller system is free at www.assessment.state.tn.us/.

Overton County *Real Estate, Deed Records* `$$` Access real estate indexes/images at www.ustitlesearch.net; registration/monthly fee required. Also see state introduction.

Perry County *Real Estate, Deed Records* `$$` Access property and deeds indexes/images at www.titlesearcher.com; fee/registration required. Also, see state introduction.

Polk County *Real Estate, Deed Records* `$$` Access property and deeds indexes/images at www.titlesearcher.com; fee/registration required. Also, see state introduction.

Putnam County *Real Estate, Deed, Judgment, Lien, UCC Records* `$$` Access real estate indexes/images at www.ustitlesearch.net; registration/monthly fee required.
Property, Taxation Records `Free` Assessment data on state comptroller system. Also, search property/GIS data free at www.emapsplus.com/TNputnam/maps/. Also see state introduction.

Rhea County *Real Estate, Deed Records* `$$` Access property and deeds indexes/images at www.titlesearcher.com; fee/registration required. Images go back to 5/28/03. Also, see state introduction.

Roane County *Real Estate, Deed Records* `$$` Access property and deeds indexes/images at www.titlesearcher.com; fee/registration required, images go back to 6/5/03. Also, see state introduction.

Robertson County *Real Estate, Deed, Judgment, Lien, UCC Records* `$$` Access real estate indexes/images at www.ustitlesearch.net; registration/monthly fee required. Also see state introduction.

Rutherford County *Real Estate, Deed, Judgment, Lien, UCC Records* `$$` Access real estate indexes/images at www.ustitlesearch.net; registration/monthly fee required. To subscribe call 615-223-1823. Also see state introduction.

Sequatchie County *Real Estate, Deed Records* `$$` Access property and deeds indexes/images at www.titlesearcher.com; fee/registration required. Also, see state introduction.

Sevier County *Real Estate, Deed Records* `$$` Access property and deeds indexes/images at www.titlesearcher.com; fee/registration required. Also, see state introduction.

Shelby County *Real Estate, Deed, Lien, Judgment Records* http://register.shelby.tn.us `Free & $$` Access the Register of Deeds database free at http://register.shelby.tn.us/index.php. Partial indexes and images go back to 1986; full to 12/2001. Also, access property and deeds indexes/images at www.titlesearcher.com; fee/registration required. Also see state introduction.

Smith County *Real Estate, Deed Records* `$$` Access property and deeds indexes/images at www.titlesearcher.com; fee/registration required. Also, see state introduction.

Stewart County *Real Estate, Deed, Judgment, Lien, UCC Records* `$$` Access real estate indexes/images at www.ustitlesearch.net; registration/monthly fee required. Also see state introduction.

Sumner County *Real Estate, Deed Records* www.deeds.sumnercounty.org `$$` Access real estate indexes/images back to 10/22/1989 at www.ustitlesearch.net; registration/monthly fee required. Also see state introduction.
Property, Taxation Records `Free` Assessment data on state comptroller system. Also, search property data free on the GIS site at http://tn.sumner.geopowered.com. At the map, click on "search for property" then name search.

Tipton County *Real Estate, Deed, Judgment, Lien, UCC Records* `$$` Access real estate indexes/images back to 10/22/1989 at www.ustitlesearch.net; registration/monthly fee required. Also see state introduction.

Trousdale County *Real Estate, Deed, Judgment, Lien, UCC Records* `$$` Access real estate indexes/images back to 10/22/1989 at www.ustitlesearch.net; registration/monthly fee required. Also see state introduction.
Property, Taxation Records `Free` Assessment data on state comptroller system is free at www.assessment.state.tn.us/.

Unicoi County *Real Estate, Deed Records* www.unicoicountytn.gov/ `$$` Access property and deeds indexes/images is via a private company at www.titlesearcher.com. Fee/registration required; images go back to 1/1997. Also see state introduction.
Property, Taxation Records `Free` Access to GIS/Mapping for free go to www.unicoicountytn.gov/index.php?option=com_content&task=view&id=33&Itemid=48.

Union County *Real Estate, Deed, Judgment Records* `$$` Access property and deeds indexes/images at www.titlesearcher.com; fee/registration required. Also, see state introduction.

Van Buren County *Real Estate, Deed Records* `$$` Access property and deeds indexes/images at www.titlesearcher.com; fee/registration required. Also, see state introduction.

Warren County *Real Estate, Deed, Judgment, Lien, UCC Records* `$$` Access real estate indexes/images at www.ustitlesearch.net; registration/monthly fee required. Also see state introduction.

Washington County *Real Estate, Deed, Judgment, Lien, UCC Records*
www.washingtoncountytn.com/?CONTEXT=art&cat=128&art=125&BISKIT=654779 `$$` Access property and deeds indexes/images at www.titlesearcher.com; fee/registration required. Also, see state introduction.

Wayne County *Real Estate, Deed Records* `$$` Access real estate indexes/images at www.ustitlesearch.net or at a 2nd company at www.titlesearcher.com; registration/monthly fee required. Also see state introduction.

Weakley County *Real Estate, Deed Records* `$$` Access property and deeds indexes/images at www.titlesearcher.com; fee/registration required. Also see state introduction.

White County *Real Estate, Deed Records* www.spartatn.com `$$` Access property and deeds indexes/images at www.titlesearcher.com; fee/registration required.

Williamson County *Real Estate, Deed Records* `$$` Access to the Professional Access database by subscription is a $50 per month fee. Info and sign-up at http://williamson-tn.org/co_gov/profacc.htm. Also, access property and deeds indexes/images back to 11/1992 at www.titlesearcher.com; fee/registration required. Also see state introduction.

Wilson County *Real Estate, Deed, Lien Records* www.wilsondeeds.com `$$` Access to the Register of Deeds database requires a $10 registration fee and $25.00 per month usage fee at www.wilsondeeds.com. Includes indices back to 1925; images back to 1992. Also, online access to property and deeds indexes and images is via a private company at www.titlesearcher.com. A per day only fee/registration required. Also see state introduction.

Texas

Capital: Austin
            Travis County

Time Zone: CST

> Texas' two most western ounties are in MST:
> They are El paso and Hudspeth.

Population: 23,904,380

# of Counties: 254

Useful State Links

Website: www.texasonline.com/portal/tol

Governor: www.governor.state.tx.us

Attorney General: www.oag.state.tx.us

State Archives: www.tsl.state.tx.us

State Statutes and Codes: www.legis.state.tx.us/

Legislative Bill Search and Monitoring: www.legis.state.tx.us/

Unclaimed Funds: https://txcpa.cpa.state.tx.us/up/Search.jsp

Primary State Agencies

Criminal Records $$

DPS - Access & Dissemination Bureau, Crime Records Service, https://records.txdps.state.tx.us/dps_web/Portal/index.aspx   The Texas Department of Public Safety offers two websites for accessing criminal records. One is for the public. The other is for eligible entities (authorized by law). Public requesters may use a credit card and establish an account to pre-purchase credits. The fee established by the Department (Sec. 411.135(b)) is $3.15 per request plus a $.57 handling fee. These checks are instantaneous and provide convictions and deferred adjudications only.

Sexual Offender Registry Free

Dept of Public Safety, Sex Offender Registration, https://records.txdps.state.tx.us/DPS_WEB/Sor/index.aspx Sex offender data is available at the web page. There is no charge for a sex offender search. Search by name or city/ZIP or by map.

Incarceration Records Free

Texas Department of Criminal Justice, Bureau of Classification and Records, www.tdcj.state.tx.us Name searching is available from this agency at http://168.51.178.33/webapp/TDCJ/index2.htm. You may also send an email search request to classify@tdcj.state.tx.us.

Corporation, LLC, LP, Fictitious Name, Trademarks/Servicemarks Free & $$

Secretary of State, Corporation Section, www.sos.state.tx.us There are several online methods available. Web access is available 24 hours daily. There is a $1.00 fee for each record searched. Filing procedures and forms are available from the website. Also, Corporate and other TX Sec of State data is available via SOSDirect on the Web; visit www.sos.state.tx.us/corp/sosda/index.shtml. Printing and certifying capabilities. Also, general corporation data available at no fee at http://ecpa.cpa.state.tx.us/coa/Index.html from the State Comptroller office. Also, search securities dept enforcement actions- www.ssb.state.tx.us/Enforcement/Recent_Enforcement_Actions.php. *Other Options:* The agency makes portions of its database available for purchase. Call 512-463-5589 for more information.

Uniform Commercial Code, Federal Tax Liens

UCC Section, Secretary of State, www.sos.state.tx.us/ucc/index.shtml UCC and other Texas Secretary of State data is available via SOSDirect on the Web at www.sos.state.tx.us/corp/sosda/index.shtml. UCC records are $1.00 per search, with printing $1.00 per page and certifying $10.00. General information and forms can also be found at the website. *Other Options:* This agency offers the database for sale, contact the Information Services Dept at 512-463-5609 for further details.

Sales Tax Registrations `Free`

Comptroller of Public Accounts, Sales Tax Permits, www.window.state.tx.us/taxinfo/sales/ This office makes general corporation information available at http://ecpa.cpa.state.tx.us/vendor/tpsearch1.html. There is no fee. Go to http://cpastar2.cpa.state.tx.us/index.html to search 25,000+ documents by index or collection, including case information. Send email requests, send to open.records@cpa.state.tx.us. *Other Options:* Sales tax registration lists are available to download as ftp files.

Workers' Compensation Records `Free`

Texas Department of Insurance - Worker's Comp, 7551 Metro Center Dr, #100, www.tdi.state.tx.us/wc/indexwc.html The website gives administrative decisions for cases back to 1991and also permits searching for employers with coverage.

Driver Records `$$`

Department of Public Safety, Driver Records Section, www.txdps.state.tx.us/administration/driver_licensing_control/dlindex.htm Access is limited to only high volume users who have a permissible use and sign an agreement. The fee is $6.50 for a three-year Type 2 record and $7.50 for a complete Type 3 record. Both batch and interactive modes are available. Call 512-424-5457 to receive a copy of the license agreement. The state also offers access to TX license holders to request their own record, at the web page. Fees vary from $4.50 to $22.00, depending on type of record and if certified. *Other Options:* Bulk data is available in electronic format for approved requesters. Weekly updates are available. The file does not include driver history data.

Vehicle Ownership & Registration `$$`

Department of Transportation, Vehicle Titles and Registration Division, www.txdot.gov/ Online access is available for pre-approved accounts by contract. A $200 deposit is required, there is a $23.00 charge per month and $.12 fee per inquiry. Look-ups are by VIN or plate number. Searching by name or owner is not permitted. For more information, contact Technology Support. *Other Options:* CD or FTP retrieval is offered for customized searches or the entire database to eligible organizations under signed contract. Weekly updates and batch inquiries are available. Database contains about 29,000,000 records.

GED Certificates `Free`

Texas Education Agency, GED Unit CC:350, www.tea.state.tx.us/ged/ The agency has a excellent verification search at www.tea.state.tx.us/ged/GEDsearch.html. Search by (SSN) or TEA assigned ID and DOB or by name (maiden) and DOB. Records go back to 1994. One may order a certificate to be sent to an employer.

Birth Certificates `$$`

Department of State Health Srvs, Bureau of Vital Statistics, www.dshs.state.tx.us/vs/default.shtm Records may be ordered online at www.dshs.state.tx.us/vs/default.shtm. *Other Options:* Birth Indexes from 1926-1995 are available on CD-Rom and microfiche.

Death Records `$$`

Department of State Health Srvs, Bureau of Vital Statistics, www.dshs.state.tx.us/vs/default.shtm Records may be ordered online at www.dshs.state.tx.us/vs/default.shtm. Death records from 1964 thru 1998 may be viewed at http://vitals.rootsweb.ancestry.com/tx/death/search.cgi. *Other Options:* Death Indexes from 1964-1998 are available on CD-Rom and microfiche.

Marriage Certificates `Free & $$`

Department of State Health Srvs, Bureau of Vital Statistics, www.dshs.state.tx.us/vs/default.shtm Records may be ordered online at www.dshs.state.tx.us/vs/default.shtm. The department provides marriage data commercially on CD-rom at www.dshs.state.tx.us/vs/marriagedivorce/mindex.shtm, or you may download each year of the marriage index for free, from 1966 to 2005. Also, marriage records for 1966 to 2006 are available through a private company website at www.genlookups.com/texas_marriages/.

Divorce Records `Free & $$`

Department of State Health Srvs, Bureau of Vital Statistics, www.dshs.state.tx.us/vs/default.shtm Records may be ordered online at www.dshs.state.tx.us/vs/default.shtm. The department provides divorce data commercially on CD-rom at www.dshs.state.tx.us/vs/marriagedivorce/dindex.shtm, or you may download each year of the divorce index for free, from 1968 to 2006. Also, a private company website at www.genlookups.com/texas_divorces/ offers records from 1968 to 2006.

Occupational Licensing Boards

Acupuncturist .... http://reg.tmb.state.tx.us/OnLineVerif/Phys_NoticeVerif.asp?
Air Condition'g/Refrigeration Contr.. www.license.state.tx.us/LicenseSearch/
Alarm Installer/Firm/Seller............... www.txdps.state.tx.us/psb/individual/individual_search.aspx
Alarm/Security Instructor .... www.txdps.state.tx.us/psb/individual/individual_search.aspx
Alcoholic Bev. Dist./Mfg./Retailer.... www.tabc.state.tx.us/pubinfo/rosters/default.htm
Alcoholic Beverage Permit................ www.tabc.state.tx.us/pubinfo/rosters/default.htm
Architect .... www.tbae.state.tx.us/PublicInfo/FindProfessional_Arch.shtml
Architectural Barrier.......................... www.license.state.tx.us/LicenseSearch/

Asbestos Related Occupation .... www.dshs.state.tx.us/asbestos/whocan.shtm#lists
Athletic Agent .... www.sos.state.tx.us/statdoc/index.shtml
Athletic Trainer .... www.dshs.state.tx.us/at/at_roster.shtm
Attorney... www.texasbar.com
Auctioneer .... www.license.state.tx.us/LicenseSearch/
Audiologist .... www.dshs.state.tx.us/plc/default.shtm
Audiology Assistant .... www.dshs.state.tx.us/plc/default.shtm
Automobile Club .... www.sos.state.tx.us/statdoc/index.shtml
Bank Agency, Foreign...................... www.banking.state.tx.us/supreglic_ent.asp
Bank, State Chartered....................... www.banking.state.tx.us/supreglic_ent.asp
Barber-related Occupation................. www.license.state.tx.us/LicenseSearch/
Beauty Shop/Salon .... www.license.state.tx.us/LicenseSearch/
Boiler Inspector/Installer .... www.license.state.tx.us/LicenseSearch/
Boxing/Combative Sports Event .... www.license.state.tx.us/LicenseSearch/
Business Opportunity Offering.......... www.sos.state.tx.us/statdoc/index.shtml
Career Counselor .... www.license.state.tx.us/LicenseSearch/
Chemical Dependency Counselor...... www.tcada.state.tx.us/licensure/pgSearch.shtml
Child Care Facility   ...   www.dfps.state.tx.us/Child_Care/Search_Texas_Child_Care/ppFacilitySearchDayCare.asp
Child Care Facility Admin. https://www.dfps.state.tx.us/Child_Care/Search_Texas_Child_Care/ppFacilityRegister.asp
Child Care Operation......................... https://www.dfps.state.tx.us/Child_Care/Search_Texas_Child_Care/
Child Support Agency, Private .... www.banking.state.tx.us/supreglic_ent.asp
Chiropractic Facility .... www.tbce.state.tx.us/disc_action_menu.html
Chiropractic Radiologic Technologistwww.tbce.state.tx.us/verify.html
Chiropractor..................................... www.tbce.state.tx.us/verify.html
Code Enforcement Officer................. www.dshs.state.tx.us/op/op_roster.shtm
Contact Lens Dispenser..................... www.dshs.state.tx.us/contactlens/cl_roster.shtm
Cosmetologist................................... www.license.state.tx.us/LicenseSearch/
Counselor, Professional..................... www.dshs.state.tx.us/counselor/lpc_rosters.shtm
Counselor, Professional Supervisor... www.dshs.state.tx.us/counselor/lpc_rosters.shtm
Courier Company .... www.txdps.state.tx.us/psb/individual/individual_search.aspx
Court Reporter/Firm .... www.crcb.state.tx.us/qry_Monthly_CSR-CRF_Web_List.html
CPA Individual/Firm/Sponsor .... www.tsbpa.state.tx.us/
Credit Service Organization .... www.sos.state.tx.us/statdoc/index.shtml
Currency Exchange .... www.banking.state.tx.us/supreglic_ent.asp
Day Care Center .... https://www.dfps.state.tx.us/Child_Care/Search_Texas_Child_Care/
Deaf Service Provider........................ www.dars.state.tx.us/dhhs/list.shtml
Dental Hygienist/ Dental Lab .... www.tsbde.state.tx.us/dbsearch/
Dentist .... www.tsbde.state.tx.us/dbsearch/
Dietitian.. www.dshs.state.tx.us/plc/default.shtm
ECA.. www.dshs.state.tx.us/emstraumasystems/NewCert.shtm
Elevator/Escalator............................. www.license.state.tx.us/LicenseSearch/
Emergency Medical Technician .... www.dshs.state.tx.us/emstraumasystems/NewCert.shtm
Engineer/Engineering Firm .... www.tbpe.state.tx.us/downloads.htm
Family Home Day Care   www.dfps.state.tx.us/Child_Care/Search_Texas_Child_Care/ppFacilitySearchDayCare.asp
Fire Alarm System Contractor........... www.tdi.state.tx.us/fire/fmli.html
Fire Extinguisher/Protection Contr.... www.tdi.state.tx.us/fire/fmli.html
Fire Inspector/Investigator................ https://www.tcfp.state.tx.us/standards/certification/certification_lookup.asp
Fire Suppression Specialist................ https://www.tcfp.state.tx.us/standards/certification/certification_lookup.asp
Firearm Instructor .... www.txdps.state.tx.us/psb/individual/individual_search.aspx
Firefighter... https://www.tcfp.state.tx.us/standards/certification/certification_lookup.asp
Fireworks Display .... www.tdi.state.tx.us/fire/fmli.html
Funeral Prepaid Permit Holder .... www.banking.state.tx.us/supreglic_ent.asp
Guard Dog Company......................... www.txdps.state.tx.us/psb/individual/individual_search.aspx
Health Spa .... www.sos.state.tx.us/statdoc/index.shtml
Hearing Instrument Dispenser/Fitter . www.dshs.state.tx.us/plc/default.shtm
Home Equity/2nd Mortgage Lender .. www.occc.state.tx.us/pages/searches.html
Independent Instructor....................... www.dshs.state.tx.us/massage/mt_rosters.shtm

Industrialized Housing.......................www.license.state.tx.us/LicenseSearch/
Insurance Adjuster............................www.texasonline.state.tx.us/NASApp/tdi/TdiARManager
Insurance Agency/Agent/Firm...........www.texasonline.state.tx.us/NASApp/tdi/TdiARManager
Interior Designer...............................www.tbae.state.tx.us/PublicInfo/FindProfessional_IntDes.shtml
Landscape Architect ....www.tbae.state.tx.us/PublicInfo/FindProfessional_LandArch.shtml
Loan Company ....www.occc.state.tx.us/pages/searches.html
Loan Officer www.sml.state.tx.us:8080/mblolookup/search.jsp
Lobbyist...www.ethics.state.tx.us/php/lobsearch.cfm
Manicurist/Manicurist Shop ....www.license.state.tx.us/LicenseSearch/
Marriage & Family Therapist ....www.dshs.state.tx.us/mft/mft_contact.shtm
Massage Therapy-related Occupat'n . www.dshs.state.tx.us/massage/mt_rosters.shtm
Medical Doctor/Physician ....http://reg.tmb.state.tx.us/OnLineVerif/Phys_NoticeVerif.asp?
Medical Physicist..............................www.dshs.state.tx.us/mp/mp_roster.shtm
Medical Specialty (Doctor)...............http://reg.tmb.state.tx.us/OnLineVerif/Phys_NoticeVerif.asp?
Money Service Business....................www.banking.state.tx.us/supreglic_ent.asp
Mortgage Banker/Broker...................www.sml.state.tx.us:8080/mblolookup/search.jsp
Motor Vehicle Sales Finance Firm ....www.occc.state.tx.us/pages/searches.html
Notary Public....................................https://direct.sos.state.tx.us/notaries/NotarySearch.asp
Nurse, RN/Advanced Practice ....https://www.bne.state.tx.us/olv/verification.html
Nurse, Vocational ....https://www.bne.state.tx.us/olv/verification.html
Occupational Therapist/Assistant ......www.ecptote.state.tx.us/license/verify_occupational_therapist.php
Occupation'l/Phys'l Therapy Facility www.ecptote.state.tx.us/license/verify_physical_therapist.php
Optician ....www.dshs.state.tx.us/optician/opt_roster.shtm
Optometrist.......................................www.tob.state.tx.us/tob%20verifications.htm
Orthotics & Prosthetics Facility.........www.dshs.state.tx.us/op/op_roster.shtm
Orthotist/Prosthetist.........................www.dshs.state.tx.us/op/op_rost.pdf
Paramedic ....www.dshs.state.tx.us/emstraumasystems/NewCert.shtm
Pawn Shop..www.occc.state.tx.us/pages/searches.html
Perfusionist......................................www.dshs.state.tx.us/perfusionist/pf_roster.shtm
Perpetual Care Cemetery ....www.banking.state.tx.us/supreglic_ent.asp
Personal Employment Service...........www.license.state.tx.us/LicenseSearch/
Pesticide Applicator/Dealer ....www.tda.state.tx.us/spcs/PIR/pir.htm
Pharmacist/Pharmacist Intern ....www.tsbp.state.tx.us/dbsearch/Default.htm
Pharmacy/Pharmacy Technician........www.tsbp.state.tx.us/dbsearch/Default.htm
Physical Therapist/Assistant..............www.ecptote.state.tx.us/license/verify_facility.php
Physician Assistant...........................http://reg.tmb.state.tx.us/OnLineVerif/Phys_NoticeVerif.asp?
Plumber Master/Journeyman ....www.tsbpe.state.tx.us/license_registration.asp
Podiatrist..www.foot.state.tx.us/verifications.htm
Political Action Committee List ....www.ethics.state.tx.us/dfs/paclists.htm
Political Contributor ....www.ethics.state.tx.us/php/cesearch.html
Polygraph School..............................www.tpeb.state.tx.us/schools.html
Private Business Letter of Authority . www.txdps.state.tx.us/psb/individual/individual_search.aspx
Private Investigator...........................www.txdps.state.tx.us/psb/individual/individual_search.aspx
Property Tax Consultant....................www.license.state.tx.us/LicenseSearch/
Psychological Associate ....www.tsbep.state.tx.us/roster_2007.html
Psychologist.....................................www.tsbep.state.tx.us/roster_2007.html
Public Accountant-CPA/CPA Firm ... www.tsbpa.state.tx.us/
Public Acc't't-CPA Educ'r/Sponsor .. www.tsbpa.state.tx.us/
Radiology Technician........................www.dshs.state.tx.us/mrt/mrt_roster.shtm
Real Estate Agent/Broker/Sales.........www.trec.state.tx.us
Real Estate Appraiser ....www.talcb.state.tx.us/appraisers/Appraiser_Search.asp
Real Estate Inspector ....www.trec.state.tx.us
Representative Office-foreign banks . www.banking.state.tx.us/supreglic_ent.asp
Respiratory Care Practitioner ....www.dshs.state.tx.us/respiratory/rc_roster.shtm
Sanitarian...www.dshs.state.tx.us/plc/default.shtm
Savings & Loan Association www.sml.state.tx.us:8080/mblolookup/search.jsp
Savings Bank....................................www.sml.state.tx.us:8080/mblolookup/search.jsp

School Psychology Specialist .... www.tsbep.state.tx.us/roster_2007.html
Security Agency, Private .... www.txdps.state.tx.us/psb/individual/individual_search.aspx
Security Agent/Service/Seller .... www.txdps.state.tx.us/psb/individual/individual_search.aspx
Service Contract Provider .... www.license.state.tx.us/LicenseSearch/
Shorthand Reporter .... www.crcb.state.tx.us/qry_Monthly_CSR-CRF_Web_List.html
Social Worker .... www.dshs.state.tx.us/socialwork/sw_rosters.shtm
Speech-Language Pathologist .... www.dshs.state.tx.us/plc/default.shtm
Staff Leasing .... www.license.state.tx.us/LicenseSearch/
Surveyor, Land http://txls.state.tx.us/sect03/rosters.html
Surveyor, Out-of-Texas http://txls.state.tx.us/sect03/rosters.html
Surveyor, State Land http://txls.state.tx.us/sect03/rosters.html
Talent Agency .... www.license.state.tx.us/LicenseSearch/
Tax Appraisal Professional .... www.txbtpe.state.tx.us
Teacher .... https://secure.sbec.state.tx.us/SBECONLINE/virtcert.asp
Temporary Common Worker .... www.license.state.tx.us/LicenseSearch/
Transportation Service Provider .... www.license.state.tx.us/LicenseSearch/
Trust Company .... www.banking.state.tx.us/supreglic_ent.asp
Underground Storage Tank Installer .. www.tceq.state.tx.us/comm_exec/cc/cc_db.html
Vehicle Protection Provider .... www.license.state.tx.us/LicenseSearch/
Veterans Organization Solicitation .... www.sos.state.tx.us/statdoc/index.shtml
Veterinarian .... www.tbvme.state.tx.us/verify.asp
Water Well & Pump Installer .... www.license.state.tx.us/LicenseSearch/
Weather Modification Service .... www.license.state.tx.us/LicenseSearch/

State and Local Courts

State Court Structure: Generally, Texas District Courts have general civil jurisdiction and exclusive felony jurisdiction, along with typical variations such as contested probate and divorce. There can be several districts in one courthouse.

The County Court structure consists of two forms of courts - "Constitutional" and "At Law." The Constitutional upper claim limit is $100,000 while the At Law upper limit is $10,000. For civil matters up to $10,000, we recommend searchers start at the Constitutional County Court as they, generally, offer a shorter waiting time for cases in urban areas. District Courts handle felonies. County Courts handle misdemeanors and general civil cases. In some counties the District Court or County Court handles evictions. In 69 counties, District Court and County Court are combined.

Probate is handled in Probate Court in the ten largest counties and in District Courts or County Courts At Law elsewhere. The County Clerk is responsible for the records in every county.

Statewide Court Online Access: A number of local county courts offer online access to their records but there is no statewide system of local level court records. Case records of the Supreme Court can be searched at www.supreme.courts.state.tx.us. Appellate Court case information is searchable free at the website of each Appellate Court, reached online from www.courts.state.tx.us/courts/coa.asp. Court of Criminal Appeals opinions are found at www.cca.courts.state.tx.us.

Angelina County

County Court   www.angelinacounty.net $$
Civil: Online access to dockets is through www.idocket.com; registration and password required. Civil cases from 11/30/96; probate from 1/31/95. *Criminal:* Online access to dockets is through www.idocket.com; registration and password required. Misdemeanor cases from 12/31/83.

Bailey County

District Court $$
Civil and criminal online access is through www.idocket.com; registration and password required. Records go back to 12/31/1995.

County Court $$
Online access is through www.idocket.com; registration and password required. Civil records go back to 12/31/1995 and 13/31/96 for probate and criminal.

Bandera County

District Court www.banderacounty.org/departments/district_clerk.htm `Free & $$`
Civil: Civil case information is free at www.idocket.com. Registration and password required. Free searching is limited. Records go back to 12/31/1990. *Criminal:* Felony record index access is through www.idocket.com; registration and password required; records go back to 12/31/1990.

County Court www.banderacounty.org/index.html `$$`
Civil: Online access to dockets is through www.idocket.com; registration and password required. Civil cases from 1/1994; probate from 1/1991. *Criminal:* Online access to dockets is through www.idocket.com; registration and password required. Misdemeanor cases from 1/1992.

Bee County

District Court www.co.bee.tx.us/ips/cms/districtcourt/ `Free & $$`
Civil: Online access is at www.idocket.com; registration and password required. A fee service; only one free name search per day. Records may go back to 12/31/1987. *Criminal:* Felony case record access at www.idocket.com; registration and password required. A fee service; only one free name search a day. Records may go back to 12/31/1994.

Bexar County

District Court - Central Records www.co.bexar.tx.us/dclerk `$$`
Civil: Access to the remote online system back to 1980 requires $100 setup fee, plus a $25 monthly fee, plus inquiry fees. Call BCIS for info at 210-335-0212. Also, search civil litigants free at www.co.bexar.tx.us/webapps/html/dklitinq01.asp. *Criminal:* same .

County Court - Criminal www.bexar.org/judges/html/countycourts.asp `$$`
Criminal: Access to the criminal online system requires $100 setup fee, plus a $25 monthly fee, plus inquiry fees. Call Roxanne Arellano at 210-335-0212 for more information.

Brazoria County

District Court www.brazoria-county.com/dclerk `Free`
Civil: Access civil record docket free at http://records.brazoria-county.com/. *Criminal:* Access criminal record docket free at http://records.brazoria-county.com; search of Sheriff bond and jail records also available.

County Court www.brazoria-county.com `Free`
Civil: Access civil record docket free at http://records.brazoria-county.com/. Also, access index and docs back to 1/1/1986 at www.idocket.com; registration and password required. This is a fee service; only one free name search per day. *Criminal:* Access criminal court and county inmate and bond records free at http://records.brazoria-county.com. Also, access index and docs back to 1/1/1986 at www.idocket.com; registration and password required. This is a fee service, unless only one name searched a day.

Probate Court http://www.brazoria-county.com `Free` Access probate records free at http://records.brazoria-county.com/.

Brazos County

District Court www.co.brazos.tx.us/courts `Free`
Civil: Civil case index and hearing index available at http://justiceweb.co.brazos.tx.us/judicialsearch/. *Criminal:* Criminal case index and hearing index available at http://justiceweb.co.brazos.tx.us/judicialsearch/.

County Court www.co.brazos.tx.us/courts/countyCourts.php
Current dockets available at web page.

Brooks County

District Court `Free & $$`
Civil: Civil case index and doc online at www.idocket.com. Free searching is limited. Records go back to 12/31/1993. *Criminal:* Criminal case index and docs online through www.idocket.com; registration and password required. Records go back to 12/31/1993.

County Court `Free & $$`
Criminal: Access misdemeanor case info back to 12/31/94 at www.idocket.com; registration and password required. This is a fee service; only one free name search per day.

Cameron County

District Court
Civil: Online access to cases is at www.idocket.com; registration and password required. A fee service; only one free name search per day. *Criminal:* Felony records access is at www.idocket.com; registration and password required. This is a fee service, unless only one name search a day. Records may go back to 12/31/1988.

County Court No. 1, 2 & 3 www.co.cameron.tx.us `Free & $$`
Civil: Access case records back to 12/01/93 including probate at www.idocket.com; registration and password required. A fee service; only one free name search per day. *Criminal:* same.

Chambers County

District Clerk   www.co.chambers.tx.us/offices/distclrk.html   `Free`
Search online for civil or criminal after registering free for login and password at www.chambersonline.net/districtclerk/.
County Court   www.co.chambers.tx.us   `Free`
Search online for civil or criminal after registering free for login and password at www.chambersonline.net/districtclerk/.

Cherokee County

County Court   `Free & $$`
Civil: Access cases back to 1988 at www.idocket.com; registration and password required. A fee service; only one free name search per day. *Criminal:* same.

Cochran County

District & County Court
Civil: Email address for search requests is cclerk@door.net. *Criminal:* same.

Collin County

District Clerk   www.co.collin.tx.us/district_courts/index.jsp   `Free`
Civil: Name and case look up is at www.co.collin.tx.us/rsp-bin/pbkr125.pgm. Search case schedules for free at www.co.collin.tx.us/ShowScheduleSearchServlet. There is also a commercial system- see county courts. Call Lisa Zoski at 972-548-4503 for subscription info. *Criminal:* Same.

County Court At Law   www.collincountytexas.gov   `Free`
Civil: Online access is free at www.co.collin.tx.us/ShowCaseLookupServlet?district_or_county_court=county. *Criminal:* Online access to misdemeanor records is the same as civil.

Comal County

District Court   www.co.comal.tx.us   `Free`
Civil: Online access county judicial records free at www.co.comal.tx.us/recordsearch.htm. Search by either party name. *Criminal:* Online access county criminal judicial records free at www.co.comal.tx.us/recordsearch.htm.

County Court at Law   www.comalcounty.net   `Free`
Civil: Online access county judicial records free at www.co.comal.tx.us/recordsearch.htm. Search by either party name. *Criminal:* Online access county criminal judicial records free at www.co.comal.tx.us/recordsearch.htm.

Crane County

District & County Court   www.co.crane.tx.us/ips/cms/districtcourt/   `Free`
Civil: Access to dockets is free at www.edoctecinc.com but may be a 2 wk to a month lag time. *Criminal:* Online access is same as civil, above.

Dallas County

District Court - Civil   www.dallascounty.org   `Free & $$`
Civil: Search civil judgment index at www.dallascounty.org/pars2/. No fee unless a record is viewed. Also, search district civil and family case index free at http://courts.dallascounty.org/. Cases go back to early 1960s.

District Court - Criminal   www.dallascounty.org   `Free`
Criminal: Name search free at www.dallascounty.org/pars2/#. Criminal index includes DOB.

County Court - Misdemeanor   www.dallascounty.org   `$$`
Criminal: The online Access System allows remote access at $1.00 per minute to this court and other court/public records. Dial-in access number is 900-263-INFO. Search by name or case number. Call the Public Access Admin at 214-653-7717 for more info and order $2.00 set-up CD-rom. Also, name search free at www.dallascounty.org/pars2/#. Criminal index includes DOB. There is no fee unless a record is viewed but most records viewed for free.

Criminal District Courts 1-5   www.dallascounty.org   `$$`
Criminal: The online Access System allows remote access at $1.00 per minute to this court and other court/public records. Dial-in access number is 900-263-INFO. Search by name or case number. Call the Public Access Admin at 214-653-7717 for more info and order $2.00 set-up CD-rom. Also, name search free at www.dallascounty.org/pars2/#. There is no fee unless a record is viewed but most records viewed for free.

County Court - Civil   www.dallascounty.org   `Free & $$`
Civil: Search civil judgment index at www.dallascounty.org/pars2/. No fee unless a record is viewed.

Probate Court #3   `Free & $$`   Search the probate civil judgment index at http://www.dallascounty.org/pars2/. There is no fee unless a record is viewed.

Denton County

District Court   http://dentoncounty.com/dept/main.asp?Dept=26   `Free`
Civil: Search civil records free at http://justice.dentoncounty.com. Search by name or cause number. *Criminal:* Criminal searches are free at http://justice.dentoncounty.com. Records go back to 1994 forward. Access also includes sheriff bond and jail records.

County Court   http://dentoncounty.com/deptall.asp   `Free`
Civil: Online access civil court records free at http://justice.dentoncounty.com/CivilSearch/civfrmd.htm. *Criminal:* Online access county criminal records free at http://justice.dentoncounty.com/CrimSearch/crimfrmd.htm. Jail, bond, and parole records are also available at http://justice.dentoncounty.com. Search for registered sex offenders by ZIP Code at http://sheriff.dentoncounty.com/sex_offenders/default.htm.

El Paso County

District Court   www.co.el-paso.tx.us/districtclerk   `Free`
Civil: Online access to civil court records is free at www.co.el-paso.tx.us/JIMSSearch/CivilRecordsearch.asp. Also, access index and images at www.idocket.com; registration and password required; online civil records go back to 12/31/1986. *Criminal:* Online access to criminal court active records is free at www.co.el-paso.tx.us/JIMSSearch/CriminalRecordsearch.asp   Also, online access index and images at www.idocket.com; registration and password required; online records go back to 12/31/1986.

County Court   www.co.el-paso.tx.us   `Free`
Civil: Online access to civil court records is free at www.co.el-paso.tx.us/JIMSSearch/CivilRecordsearch.asp. Also, search vital records and recordings. Also, access index and images at www.idocket.com; registration and password required. Civil records go back to 12/31/1986, probate to 12/31/1989. *Criminal:* Online access to misdemeanor criminal records is the same as civil at www.co.el-paso.tx.us/JIMSSearch/CriminalRecordsearch.asp and also at www.idocket.com with signup, see civil above.

Probate Court #1   `$$`   Access probate records through www.idocket.com; registration and password required. Records go back to 12/31/1986.

Erath County

District Court   www.co.erath.tx.us/ips/cms   `Free`
Civil: Access to District Clerk records requires registration, login and password; signup online at www.erathcountyonline.net/districtclerk/ *Criminal:* same.

County Court   `Free`
Civil: Access to County Court records requires registration, login and password; signup online at www.erathcountyonline.net/countyclerk/. *Criminal:* same.

Fort Bend County

District Court   www.co.fort-bend.tx.us   `Free`
Civil: Search for free at http://courtcn.co.fort-bend.tx.us/. Records go back to 9/2000; no DOBs. Also, search court records free at http://ccweb.co.fort-bend.tx.us/localization/menu.asp. *Criminal:* Criminal records are on the same system as civil records.

County Court   www.co.fort-bend.tx.us   `Free`
Civil: Online access to the civil records index free at www.co.fort-bend.tx.us/getSitePage.asp?sitePage=11895. The site includes probate records index online. Also search free at http://ccweb.co.fort-bend.tx.us/localization/menu.asp. *Criminal:* Online access to misdemeanor index is the same as civil.

Galveston County

District Court   www.co.galveston.tx.us/District_Courts/default.htm   `Free`
Civil: Online access to judge's daily calendars is free at the website. Civil cases under $100,000 are found at http://207.80.116.33/. *Criminal:* Online access to Judge's daily calendars is free at the website.

County Court   http://www2.co.galveston.tx.us/County_Clerk/   `Free`
Civil: Online access, including probate, is at http://207.80.116.33/. Records go back to 1995 generally. Access to the GCNET remote online service has been suspended. *Criminal:* Online access is at http://207.80.116.33/. Index search if free; records go back to 1995 generally.

Grayson County

District Court   www.co.grayson.tx.us   `Free`
Civil: Access to judicial records is free at http://24.117.89.66:3004/judsrch.asp. *Criminal:* same.

County Court   www.co.grayson.tx.us/courtsmain.htm   `Free`
Online access to civil, criminal and probate records free at http://24.117.89.66:3004/judsrch.asp.

Gregg County

District Court   www.co.gregg.tx.us/government/courts.asp   `Free`
Civil: Online access to county judicial records is free at www.co.gregg.tx.us/judsrch.htm. Search by name, cause number, status. *Criminal:* Same, also includes jail and bond search.

County Court   www.co.gregg.tx.us/government/commissionersCourt/county_judge.asp   `Free`
Civil: Online access to county judicial records is free at www.co.gregg.tx.us/judsrch.htm. Search by name, cause number, or status.
Criminal: Same. Jail and bond search also available.

Guadalupe County

District Court   www.co.guadalupe.tx.us   `Free`
Civil: Access to court records and hearings is available free at www.co.guadalupe.tx.us/judicialsearch/judsrch.asp. *Criminal:* Access to court records and hearings is available free at www.co.guadalupe.tx.us/judicialsearch/judsrch.asp. Search sheriff's jail and bond records also. Dockets go back to 12/31/1991.

County Court   www.co.guadalupe.tx.us   `Free`
Civil: Access to court records and hearings is available free at www.co.guadalupe.tx.us/judicialsearch/judsrch.asp. *Criminal:* Access to court records and hearings is available free at www.co.guadalupe.tx.us/judicialsearch/judsrch.asp. Also search sheriff's jail and bond records.

Hale County

County Court   `$$`
Civil: Online access is through www.idocket.com; registration and password required. *Criminal:* same.

Harris County

District Court   www.hcdistrictclerk.com/Home/Home.aspx   `Free`
Civil: First, an online case lookup service is free at http://legacy.hcdistrictclerk.com/CFTS/CaseLocationSearch.asp. Online records go back to 10/1989. Second, register for free-to-view e-docs service at https://e-docs.hcdistrictclerk.com/eDocs.Web/Login.aspx and pay $1 per page (credit cards accepted) for civil documents. Also, access to records is to qualified JIMs subscribers at www.jims.hctx.net. *Criminal:* Online criminal index case lookup is the same as civil. The e-docs service does not offer access to criminal records.

County Court   www.cclerk.hctx.net   `Free & $$`
Civil: Online access is free at www.cclerk.hctx.net. System includes civil data search and county civil settings inquiry and other county clerk functions. For further information, visit the website or call 713-755-6421. Also, civil case online access back to 12/31/1997 at www.idocket.com; registration and password required. A fee service; only one free name search a day.

Probate Court   `Free`   Probate dockets are available through the Harris County online system. Call 713-755-7815 for information. Dockets are available free at www.cclerk.hctx.net/coolice/default.asp?Category=ProbateCourt&Service=pc_inquiry. Records go back to 1837.

Hays County

District Court   www.co.hays.tx.us   `$$`
Civil: Online access is through www.idocket.com; registration and password required. Case records go back to 12/31/1986. *Criminal:* Online criminal access is through www.idocket.com; registration and password required. Case records go back to 12/31/1986.

County Court   www.co.hays.tx.us   `$$`
Civil: Online access is through www.idocket.com; registration and password required. Includes probate. Case records from 01/88. *Criminal:* Misdemeanor records online access is through www.idocket.com; registration and password required. Case records go back to 12/31/1987.

Hidalgo County

District Court   www.co.hidalgo.tx.us/dc/   `$$`
Civil: Online case access is through www.idocket.com; registration and password required. Records go back to 12/31/1986. *Criminal:* same.

County Court   www.hidalgo.tx.us.landata.com/   `$$`
Civil: Online case access is through www.idocket.com; registration and password required. Civil and probate records go back to 12/31/1986. *Criminal:* Misdemeanor case records access is through www.idocket.com; registration and password required. Records go back to 12/31/1991.

Hill County

District Court, Probate (County Court)   `Free & $$`
Civil: Online case access is through www.idocket.com. One search a day is free; subscription required for more. Records go back to 12/31/1990. *Criminal:* Criminal case access is through www.idocket.com; registration and password required. Records go back to 12/31/1990.

Hopkins County

District Court   `Free`
Civil: Search county court index free after registering for login and password at www.hopkinscountyonline.net/districtclerk/. *Criminal:* Online access to criminal is same as civil, see above.

County Court   www.hopkinscountytx.org/   **Free**
Civil: Search county court index free after registering for login and password at www.hopkinscountyonline.net/countyclerk/.
Criminal: Online access is the same as civil, see above.

Hutchinson County
District Court   **$$**
Civil: Online case access is available by subscription at www.idocket.com including civil (no probate) back to 1/1/1990. *Criminal:* Online case access is available by subscription at www.idocket.com including criminal back to 1/1/1989.

Jack County
County Court   **$$**
Civil: Online case access is available by subscription at www.idocket.com including civil and probate back to 1/2000. *Criminal:* Online misdemeanor case access is available by subscription at www.idocket.com including criminal back to 1/1999.

Jefferson County
District Court   www.co.jefferson.tx.us   **Free**
Civil: Online access to the civil records index at www.co.jefferson.tx.us/dclerk/civil_index/main.htm. Search by year by defendant or plaintiff by year 1985 to present. Also, you may name search at http://jeffersontxclerk.hartic.com/search.asp?cabinet=civil. Index goes back to 1995; images back to 12/1998. *Criminal:* Online access to criminal records index is at www.co.jefferson.tx.us/dclerk/criminal_index/main.htm. Search by name by year 1981 to present. Also, felony records are free at http://jeffersontxclerk.hartic.com/search.asp?cabinet=criminal. Add'l criminal records are being added.

County Court   www.co.jefferson.tx.us/cclerk/clerk.htm   **Free**
Civil: Search county clerk's civil index free at http://jeffersontxclerk.manatron.com. Index goes back to 1995; images back to 12/1998. $2.00 per page to obtain online docs. *Criminal:* Access to Class A&B and C Misdemeanor that are appealed indexes back to 1982 are free at http://jeffersontxclerk.manatron.com/. $1.00 per page to obtain online docs, $2.50 minimum. Add'l criminal records being added.

Johnson County
District Court   www.johnsoncountytx.org   **Free & $$**
Civil: Access index and images online at www.idocket.com; registration and password required. A fee service; only one free name search per day. Records go back to 11/10/1989. Images available. *Criminal:* same.

County Court   www.johnsoncountytx.org   **$$**
Civil: Access index and images online at http://idocket.com/homepage2.htm. Registration required. Civil records back to 12/31/85, probate to 12/31/88. *Criminal:* Access misdemeanor index and images online at http://idocket.com/homepage2.htm. Registration required. Records back to 12/31/88.

Kaufman County
District Court   **Free**
Civil: Access court records free at http://12.14.175.23/Login.aspx?ReturnUrl=/default.aspx and login as 'public' and password 'public.' *Criminal:* Access to criminal records online is same as civil.

County Court   www.kaufmancountyclerk.com/   **Free**
Civil: Access court records free at http://12.14.175.23/Login.aspx?ReturnUrl=/default.aspx and login as 'public' and password 'public.' *Criminal:* Access to criminal records online is same as civil.

Kerr County
District Court   www.co.kerr.tx.us/dclerk/districtclerk.html   **Free**
Civil: Search all court indexes also jail and bond indexes free at http://public.co.kerr.tx.us/CaseManagement/PublicAccess/default.aspx. *Criminal:* Online access is the same as civil.

County Court & County Court at Law   www.co.kerr.tx.us/   **Free**
Civil: For online access, see criminal section, below. *Criminal:* Search all court records also jail and bond records free at http://public.co.kerr.tx.us/CaseManagement/PublicAccess/default.aspx.

Kleberg County
District & County Court at Law   **Free & $$**
Civil: Online access is at www.idocket.com; registration and password required. A fee service, only one free name search per day. Records go back to 1/1992. *Criminal:* Online case access is at www.idocket.com; registration and password required. A fee service; only one free name search per day. Records go back to 12/31/1995.

County Court - Criminal   www.co.kleberg.tx.us/courtatlaw.html   **Free & $$**
Civil: Online access is at www.idocket.com; registration and password required. A fee service, only one free name search per day. Records go back to 1/1997. *Criminal:* Online case access at www.idocket.com; registration and password required. A fee service; only one free name search per day. Records go back to 1/1/1983.

Lamar County

District Court   www.co.lamar.tx.us   `Free`
Civil: Access to county judicial records is free at www.co.lamar.tx.us/. Search by either party name. *Criminal:* Access to county judicial records is free online at www.co.lamar.tx.us. Search by defendant name.

County Court   www.co.lamar.tx.us   `Free`
Civil: Access to county judicial records is free at http://68.89.102.225/. Search by either party name. *Criminal:* Access to county judicial records is free online at www.co.lamar.tx.us. Search by defendant name.

Llano County

District Clerk   http://dcourt.org   `Free`
Civil: Signup for email notifications of civil and criminal dockets at www.dcourt.org/_attys/dockets.htm. *Criminal:* same.

Lubbock County

County Courts   www.co.lubbock.tx.us/CCourt/c_courts.htm   `$$`
Criminal: Access criminal court data by subscription; for information call David Slayton, 806-775-1020.

Maverick County

District Court   `Free & $$`
Civil: Access cases online back to 11/1994 at www.idocket.com; registration and password required. A fee service; only one free name search per day. *Criminal:* Access felony cases back to 8/1/1995 at www.idocket.com; registration and password required. A fee service; only one free name search per day.

County Court   http://maverickcounty.org/365th/   `Free & $$`
Civil: Access cases online back to 1/2006 at www.idocket.com; registration and password required. A fee service; only one free name search per day. *Criminal:* Access misdemeanor cases back to 1/1999 at www.idocket.com; registration and password required. A fee service; only one free name search per day.

McCulloch County

District Court   `Free & $$`
Civil: Access civil cases at www.idocket.com. Free searching is limited. Records go back to 12/31/1995. *Criminal:* Access felony cases online through www.idocket.com; registration and password required. Records go back to 12/31/1995.

County Court   `$$`
Civil: Online case access is through www.idocket.com; registration and password required. Records go back to 12/31/1996; includes probate. *Criminal:* Online misdemeanor case access is through www.idocket.com; registration and password required. Records go back to 12/31/1996.

McLennan County

District Court   www.co.mclennan.tx.us   `$$`
Civil: Online index and image access is through http://idocket.com/homepage2.htm; registration, password and fees required. Records go back to 1/1955; no probate. *Criminal:* Online index and image access is through www.idocket.com; registration and password required. Felony records go back to 1/1981.

Midland County

District Court   www.co.midland.tx.us/DC/default.asp   `Free`
Civil: Online access to district Clerk database is at www.co.midland.tx.us/DC/Database/search.asp. Registration and password required; contact the clerk for access restrictions. *Criminal:* Same.

County Court   www.co.midland.tx.us/CC/default.asp   `Free`
Civil: Online access to the County Clerk database is free at www.co.midland.tx.us/CC/Database/default.asp. *Criminal:* Same.

Mitchell County

County Court   `Free`
Civil: Access to dockets is free at www.edoctecinc.com but may be a 2 wk to a month lag time. *Criminal:* Online access to criminal dockets is same as civil.

Montgomery County

County Court   www.co.montgomery.tx.us/cclerk/index.shtml   `Free`
Criminal: Search the county clerk's misdemeanor records free at www.co.montgomery.tx.us/cclerk/kiosk/criminalinquiry.asp. Access misdemeanor cases online at www.idocket.com; registration and password required. A fee service; only one free name search per day. Records go back to 12/31/1989.

Nacogdoches County

District Court   `$$`
Civil: Online case access is available by subscription at www.idocket.com including civil and family back to 12/31/1986. *Criminal:* Online case access is available by subscription at www.idocket.com; online records go back to 12/31/1986.

County Court   www.co.nacogdoches.tx.us $$
Civil: Online case access is available by subscription at www.idocket.com including civil and probate back to 12/31/1986. *Criminal:* Online case access is available by subscription at www.idocket.com; online records go back to 12/31/1986.

Navarro County
District Court   www.co.navarro.tx.us/ips/cms/districtcourt/   Free & $$
Civil: Online civil case access is through www.idocket.com. Free searching is limited. Records go back to 12/31/1990. *Criminal:* Online criminal case access is through www.idocket.com; registration and password required. Records go back to 12/31/1990.

Nueces County
District & County Court   www.co.nueces.tx.us/districtclerk   Free
Civil: Online access to civil District & County Court records are free at www.co.nueces.tx.us/districtclerk/. Click on Civil/Criminal Case Search, register, then search by name, company, or cause number. *Criminal:* Online access to criminal District & County Court records are free at www.co.nueces.tx.us/districtclerk/. Click on Civil/Criminal Case Search, register, then search by name, SID number, or cause number.

Oldham County
District & County Court $$
Civil: Online case access is through www.idocket.com; registration and password required. Records go back to 3/1998, probate to 2/1996. *Criminal:* Online case access is through www.idocket.com; registration and password required. Misdemeanor records go back to 1/1993, felony to 1/1992.

Panola County
District Court   Free
Civil: Access to civil records is free at www.panolacountyjudicial.com/. *Criminal:* Access to criminal records is free at www.panolacountyjudicial.com/.

Parker County
District Court   www.parkercountytx.com   Free
Civil: Access to court records is free at www.parkercountytx.com. Online civil records go back to 1/2003. Civil results include party names, case type, atty. *Criminal:* Access to criminal records and sheriff inmates and bonds search is free at www.parkercountytx.com. Online criminal records go back to 7/88. Online results include atty, offense, disposition.

County Court   www.parkercountytx.com   Free
Civil: Online access to civil is same as criminal, see below. *Criminal:* Online access is free at www.parkercountytx.com. Search the sheriff bond and jail lists here also.

Parmer County
District Court $$
Civil: Online case access is through www.idocket.com; registration and password required. Records go back to 12/31/1995. *Criminal:* same.

Potter County
District Court   www.co.potter.tx.us/districtclerk   Free & $$
Civil: Civil index and images back to 1988 online at www.idocket.com. Free case searching is limited. *Criminal:* Felony cases online at www.idocket.com. Free case searching is limited. Felonies go back to 1/1989.

County Court & County Courts at Law 1 & 2   www.co.potter.tx.us/countyclerk/index.html   Free & $$
Civil: Online case access is through www.idocket.com; registration and password required. Records go back to 9/1/1987, probate back to 1/1886. *Criminal:* Misdemeanor cases online at www.idocket.com. Free case searching is limited. Misdemeanors go back to 1/1991.

Randall County
District Courts   www.randallcounty.org
Civil: Civil case information at www.idocket.com. Free searching is limited. Records from 12/31/84. *Criminal:* Felony cases online at idocket at http://idocket.com/counties.htm. Is a fee service. Felony records go back to 1/1992.

County Court   www.randallcounty.org/cclerk/default.htm   Free & $$
Civil: Civil case information at www.idocket.com. Free searching is limited. Records go back to 1/2000; probate back to 9/11/1969. Direct email records requests to countyclerk@randallcounty.org. *Criminal:* Misdemeanor cases online at idocket at http://idocket.com/counties.htm. Is a fee service. Misd. records go back to 1/1985.

Refugio County
District Court   Free & $$
Civil: Access cases back to 1/1994 at www.idocket.com; registration and password required. A fee service; only one free name search per day. *Criminal:* same.

County Court   Free & $$
Civil: Access cases back to 1/1994 at www.idocket.com; registration and password required. A fee service; only one free name search per day. *Criminal:* same.

Rockwall County

District Court www.rockwallcountytexas.com Free
Civil: Online access is same as criminal, see below. *Criminal:* Online access is free at www.rockwallcountytexas.com/judicialsearch/. Search sheriff bond and jail lists too.

County Court at Law www.rockwallcountytexas.com Free
Civil: Online access is same as criminal, see below. *Criminal:* Online access is free at www.rockwallcountytexas.com/judicialsearch/. Search sheriff bond and jail lists too.

San Patricio County

District Court www.co.san-patricio.tx.us/ips/cms/districtcourt/districtClerk.html $$
Civil: Access civil cases online back to 11/1992 at www.idocket.com; registration and password required. *Criminal:* Online access to felony cases back to 1/1994 at www.idocket.com; registration and password required.

County Court www.co.san-patricio.tx.us $$
Civil: Access civil cases including probate online back to 1/1997 at www.idocket.com; registration and password required. *Criminal:* Online access to Misd. cases back to 1/1994 at www.idocket.com; registration and password required.

Shelby County

District Court Free
Civil: Access court records free at http://cc.co.shelby.tx.us/. *Criminal:* same.

County Court Free
Civil: Access court records free at http://cc.co.shelby.tx.us/. *Criminal:* same.

Smith County

District Court www.smith-county.com/ Free
Civil: Access court indexes and sheriff's jail and bond data free at http://judicial.smith-county.com/judsrch.asp. *Criminal:* Online access to criminal is same as civil above.

County Court at Law 1, 2, 3 www.smith-county.com/ Free
Civil: Access court and probate indexes and sheriff's jail and bond data free at http://judicial.smith-county.com/judsrch.asp. *Criminal:* Online access to criminal is same as civil above.

Starr County

District & County Court   Free & $$
Civil: Access index and images online at www.idocket.com; registration and password required. A fee service; only one free name search per day. Records go back to 1/1999. *Criminal:* Access felony index and images online at www.idocket.com; registration and password required. A fee service; only one free name search per day. Felony records go back to 1/2003.

County Court   Free
 Criminal: Online access is at www.idocket.com; registration and password required. A fee service; only one free name search per day. Records go back to 12/31/96.

Tarrant County

District Court www.tarrantcounty.com/ecourts/site/default.asp $$
Civil: Access to the remote online system requires $50 setup that includes software and a monthly fee of $35 per month with add'l month prepaid; for 1 to 5 users; fees increase with more users. Call 817-884-1345 for info and signup. Index records are available for free at http://cc.co.tarrant.tx.us/CivilCourts/ccl/default.asp. *Criminal:* Same.

County Court - Criminal www.tarrantcounty.com/ecourts/site/default.asp $$
 Criminal: Access to the remote online system requires $50 setup that includes software and a monthly fee of $35 per month with additional month prepaid to start. This is for 1 to 5 users. Fees increase with more users. The District Court records are on this system also. Call 817-884-3202 for more information.

Probate Court http://www.tarrantcounty.com/ecourts/site/default.asp Free Search probate records by name or case number at http://cc.co.tarrant.tx.us/CivilCourts/Probate/default.asp or http://cc.co.tarrant.tx.us/CivilCourts/Probate/default.asp?eprobatecourtsNav=|

Titus County

County Court   Free & $$
Civil: Access to court records is to be online at www.tituscountyonline.net/countyclerk/. Registration required. *Criminal:* Access to criminal court records is to be online, probably at www.tituscountyonline.net/countyclerk/. Registration required.

Tom Green County

District Court   www.co.tom-green.tx.us/distclrk/   Free
Civil: Online access to civil case records back to 1994 is online at http://justice.co.tom-green.tx.us. Search by name, case number. Also, online case access back to 4/4/1992 at www.idocket.com; registration and password required. *Criminal:* Online access to criminal case records back to 1994 at http://justice.co.tom-green.tx.us. Search by name, case number. Also, online felony case access back to 10/1/1991 at www.idocket.com; registration and password required.

County Court   http://justice.co.tom-green.tx.us   Free
Civil: Online access to civil records back to 1994 is free at http://justice.co.tom-green.tx.us. *Criminal:* Same. Website also includes sheriff's jail and bond records.

Travis County

County Court   www.co.travis.tx.us/   Free
Civil: Access to probate court records only is free at http://deed.co.travis.tx.us/search.aspx?cabinet=probate.

Trinity County

County Court $$
Civil: Online case access is through www.idocket.com; registration and password required. *Criminal:* same.

Upshur County

District Court   www.countyofupshur.com   Free
Civil: Access court records and hearings free at www.countyofupshur.com/judicialsearch/. *Criminal:* same.

County Court   www.countyofupshur.com/   Free
Civil: Access court records and hearings free at www.countyofupshur.com/judicialsearch/. *Criminal:* same.

Val Verde County

District Court   Free & $$
Civil: Access civil cases except probate at www.idocket.com; registration and password required. A fee service; only one free name search per day. Records go back to 12/31/89. *Criminal:* Access felonies at www.idocket.com; registration and password required. A fee service; only one free name search per day. Felonies go back to 12/31/93.

Victoria County

District Court   Free & $$
Civil: Online index and images at www.idocket.com; registration and password required. Records go back to 12/31/1993. Images available. *Criminal:* Access felony index and images at www.idocket.com; registration and password required. Records go back to 12/31/1993.

County Court   www.vctx.org $$
Civil: Online case access at www.idocket.com; registration and password required. Civil records go back to 12/31/1991; probate to 6/31//1991. *Criminal:* Access Misd. cases online at www.idocket.com; registration and password required. Records go back to 12/31/1989.

Washington County

District Court   Free & $$
Civil: Online case access at www.idocket.com. Dockets from 12/30/1988. One search a day is free; subscription required for more. *Criminal:* Access felony cases at www.idocket.com. Dockets from 12/30/1988. One search a day is free; subscription required for more.

County Court $$
Civil: Online case access at www.idocket.com; registration and password required. Civil records go back to 12/31/85; probate to 12/31/68. Subscription required. *Criminal:* Access Misd. cases at www.idocket.com; registration and password required. Misdemeanor records back to 12/31/1985.

Webb County

District Court   www.webbcountytx.gov $$
Civil: Online case access at www.idocket.com; registration and password required. Civil records (no probate) go back to 12/31/1988. *Criminal:* Online felony cases at www.idocket.com; registration and password required. Felonies go back to 12/31/1988.

Williamson County

County Court   www.wilcogov.org/   Free
Civil: Access to limited civil case records is free at http://judicialsearch.wilco.org. Also various court records available for free at https://deed.wilco.org/. JP Cout #1 records are free at www.edoctecinc.com but there may be a 2 week to 1 month lag time. *Criminal:* Access to a criminal case records from 1983 is free at http://judicialsearch.wilco.org. Sheriff bond and inmate data is also available. Also various court records available for free at https://deed.wilco.org/.

Wood County

District Court http://judicial.co.wood.tx.us `Free`
Civil: Search civil case index at http://judicial.co.wood.tx.us/CivilSearch/civfrmd.asp. *Criminal:* Search criminal case index at http://judicial.co.wood.tx.us/CrimSearch/crimfrmd.asp.

County Court www.co.wood.tx.us/ips/cms `Free`
Civil: Search all courts free at http://judicial.co.wood.tx.us/. *Criminal:* Search all courts and Sheriff bond and inmate lists free at http://judicial.co.wood.tx.us/.

Young County

District Court `Free & $$`
Civil: Access civil cases exceptprobate at www.idocket.com; registration and password required. A fee service; only one free name search per day. Civil cases go back to 3/1/1998. *Criminal:* Access felony cases at www.idocket.com; registration and password required. A fee service; only one free name search per day. Records go back to 3/1/1998.

Recorders, Assessors, and Other Sites of Note

Recording Office Organization: 254 counties, 254 recording offices. The recording officer is the County Clerk. Federal tax liens on personal property of businesses are filed with the Secretary of State. Other federal and all state tax liens are filed with the County Clerk.

Online Access Note: A search at the State Archives' TRAIL website at www2.tsl.state.tx.us/trail/index.jsp lets you locate information from over 180 Texas state agency web servers. A good place to link to county appraisal districts is http://appraisaldistrict.net/ where you can click through to many county appraisers, many with free searching.

Numerous counties offer online access to assessor and recorded document data via vendors summarized below.

www.txcountydata.com – offers assessor and property information records for many Texas counties on this TX site are available for no fee. At this site click on "County Search" then use the pull down menu in the county field to select the county to search. Generally, you can search any county account, owner name, address, or property ID number. A search allows you to access owner address, property address, legal description, taxing entities, exemptions, deed, account number, abstract/subdivision, neighborhood, valuation info, and more.

www.taxnetusa.com - offers appraisal district and property information records for a large number of Texas counties. They offer a free search as well as online subscriptions services using a sliding fee scale, or you may purchase bulk data as downloads. Visit the website or call 877-652-2707 for more information. To search free at the TaxNetUSA site, click on the "Coverage Area" and select a county.

www.titlex.com - offers recording office records in county grantor/grantee indices - including real estate, deeds, liens, judgments records and more - free for many Texas counties.

www.texaslandrecords.com - offers free land index searching at a group of 24 or more Texas counties, plus a deeper real estate subscription service for those counties which requires fees, registration, and password.

Anderson County *Real Estate, Grantor/Grantee, Deed, Judgment, Lien Records* www.co.anderson.tx.us/ `Free`
Access recorded records free at www.titlex.com; select Anderson county. Records range is 6/1972 to 12/2003.
Property, Taxation Records `Free & $$` Property tax inquiries can be made at www.co.anderson.tx.us/appraisal/PublicAccess/. Also at www.txcountydata.com/county.asp?County=001.

Angelina County *Real Estate, Grantor/Grantee, Deed, Lien, Vital Statistic, Judgment Records*
www.angelinacounty.net `Free` Search grantor/grantee index free at www.texaslandrecords.com. Registration and fees required for full data. Search probate records and judgment records back to 1996 at http://idocket.com/countycourt.htm. Also see note at beginning of section for add'l property data.
Property, Taxation Records `Free` Access appraisal district data free at www.angelinacad.org/Appraisal/PublicAccess/. Also, access assessment records at www.txcountydata.com.

Aransas County *Property, Taxation Records* `Free & $$` Access dated appraiser and property tax data at www.aransascad.org/Appraisal/PublicAccess/. Also, property tax inquiries can be made via www.txcountydata.com/selectCounty.asp. Other online access through private companies.

Archer County *Property, Taxation Records* `Free` Access property records free at www.taxnetusa.com/texas/archer/. For full info registration and password required; fee is $99 per year.

Atascosa County *Real Estate, Grantor/Grantee, Judgment, Deed, Lien Records* `Free` Access recording records free at www.titlex.com; select Atascosa County. Also, see note at beginning of section.
Property, Taxation Records `Free` Access appraisal data free at www.txcountydata.com/county.asp?County=007.

Austin County *Real Estate, Grantor/Grantee, Deed, Judgment, Lien Records* `Free` Access recording records free at www.titlex.com; select Austin county. Records range is 8/1997 to 9/2005. Also, see note at beginning of section for add'l property data.
Property, Taxation Records `Free` Search property tax records for free at www.austincad.org. Also, property tax inquiries can be made via www.txcountydata.com/selectCounty.asp.

Bailey County *Probate, Judgment Records* `Free` Search probate records and judgment records free at http://idocket.com/countycourt.htm.

Bandera County *Real Estate, Deed, Probate, Judgment Records* www.banderacounty.org `Free` Access to public record search is free at www.taxnetusa.com/publicrecords/. Also, See note at beginning of section. Also, to search probate records and judgment records go to http://idocket.com/countycourt.htm.
Property, Taxation Records `Free` Access to Appraisal District records is free at http://clientdb.trueautomation.com/clientdb/main.asp?id=61. Search Tax Collector data a www.banderacounty.org/departments/tax.htm Also, ccess property search is free at www.taxnetusa.com/publicrecords/.

Bastrop County *Real Estate, Grantor/Grantee, Deed, Judgment, Lien, UCC, Marriage Records* www.cc.co.bastrop.tx.us `Free` Access county clerk public access page for recorded documents free at www.cc.co.bastrop.tx.us. Also, access recording records free at www.titlex.com; select Bastrop county. Record range is 3/2001 to 8/31/2001.
Property, Taxation Records `Free` Access to tax office records is free at www.bastroptac.com/Appraisal/PublicAccess/. Also, property tax inquiries can be made via www.txcountydata.com/selectCounty.asp. Also, see note at beginning of section.

Bee County *Real Estate, Grantor/Grantee, Deed Records* `$$` Access Grantor/Grantee index by subscription at https://www.texaslandrecords.com/txlr/TxlrApp/index.jsp. Day or monthly pay plans.
Property, Taxation Records `Free` Access property records free at www.beecad.org/. Also, access delinquent sales list free at www.co.bee.tx.us/ips/cms/countyoffices/taxAssessorCollector.html.

Bexar County *Real Estate, Grantor/Grantee, Deed, Mortgage, Foreclosure, Marriage, UCC, Assumed Name, Probate Records* www.countyclerk.bexar.landata.com `Free & $$` Access to the County Clerk database is free after free registration at www.countyclerk.bexar.landata.com. Includes land records, deeds, UCCs, assumed names and foreclosure notices, and more. Probate is recently added. Images are to be added on a new subscription service.
Property, Taxation Records `Free` Access the county Central Appraisal District database free at www.bcad.org/clientdb/?cid=1.

Blanco County *Property, Taxation Records* `Free & $$` Access property data at www.txcountydata.com/county.asp?County=016. Other online access through private companies.

Bosque County *Property, Taxation Records* `Free & $$` Access property records at www.txcountydata.com/county.asp?County=018. Other online access through private companies.

Bowie County *Property, Taxation Records* `Free` Access to Appraisal District's Appraisal Roll data is free at www.bowiecad.org/Search.htm.

Brazoria County *Real Estate, Grantor/Grantee, Deed, Lien, Judgment Records* www.brazoria.tx.us.landata.com `Free` Access recording records free at www.titlex.com; select Brazoria county. Records range from 3/2001 to 4/2007. Also, see note at beginning of section for add'l property data.
Property, Taxation Records `Free` Access to the county Central Appraisal District database is free at www.brazoriacad.org. Click on "appraisal roll." Also, property tax inquiries can be made at www.txcountydata.com/selectCounty.asp.

Brazos County *Real Estate, Grantor/Grantee, Deed, Lien, Vital Statistic, Fictitious Name Records* `Free` Search grantor/grantee index free at www.texaslandrecords.com. Registration and fees required for full data.
Property, Taxation Records `Free` Access to County Appraisal District data is free at www.brazoscad.org/Appraisal/PublicAccess/. Also, property tax inquiries can be made via www.txcountydata.com/selectCounty.asp. Also, see notes at beginning of section.

Brooks County *Real Estate, Deed, Probate, Judgment Records* `Free & $$` Access recording office land data at www.etitlesearch.com; registration required, fee based on usage. Also, to search probate records and judgment records go to http://idocket.com/countycourt.htm

Brown County *Property, Taxation Records* `Free` Access to Appraisal District records is free at http://clientdb.trueautomation.com/clientdb/main.asp?id=30. Other online access through private companies.

Burleson County *Property, Taxation Records* `Free & $$` Access property tax records at www.txcountydata.com and click on Burleson. Also, property tax inquiries can be made at www.txcountydata.com/selectCounty.asp. Other online access through private companies.

Burnet County *Real Estate, Grantor/Grantee, Deed, Lien, Judgment Records*
www.burnetcountytexas.org/CountyClerk/tabid/127/Default.aspx `Free` Access recording records free at www.titlex.com; select Burnett county. Records range from 1/1998 to 11/2001. Also, see note at beginning of section.
Property, Taxation Records `Free & $$` Property tax inquiries can be made at www.txcountydata.com/selectCounty.asp. Also, see note at beginning of section. Or property records are at www.burnet-cad.org/.

Caldwell County *Property, Taxation Records* `Free` Access the county Appraisal District database now free at www.txcountydata.com. Also, see online notes in state summary at beginning of section.

Calhoun County *Real Estate, Grantor/Grantee, Deed, Judgment, Lien Records* `Free & $$` Access recording records free at www.titlex.com; select Calhoun county; login and password required. Records range up to 9/2003.
Property, Taxation Records `Free` Access Appraisal District records free at http://clientdb.trueautomation.com/clientdb/main.asp?id=24.

Callahan County *Property, Taxation Records* `Free` Find appraisal district data free at http://208.75.248.98/.

Cameron County *Real Estate, Grantor/Grantee, Deed, Lien Records*
www.co.cameron.tx.us/countyclerks/countyclerk.html `Free` Search grantor/grantee index free at www.texaslandrecords.com. Registration and fees required for full data. Also, access probate and judgment records free at http://idocket.com/countycourt.htm. Records go back to 1993. Also, see note at beginning of section for add'l property data.
Property, Taxation Records `Free` Access appraisal district property records free at www.cameroncad.org/ClientDB/PropertySearch.aspx?cid=1.

Camp County *Property, Taxation Records* `Free` Access property tax records free at www.campcad.org.

Cass County *Property, Taxation Records* `Free` Access to property records is free at www.casscad.org. Click on Search Our Data.

Chambers County *Real Estate, Deed Records* www.co.chambers.tx.us `Free` Access county clerk's real property records free after registering for a login name and password at www.chambersonline.net/realproperty/.
Property, Taxation Records `Free` Search the appraiser property tax database for free at www.chamberscad.org. Also, see note at beginning of section.

Cherokee County *Real Estate, Grantor/Grantee, Deed, Judgment, Lien, Birth, Death, Marriage, Probate Records* `Free` Access recording records free at www.titlex.com; select Cherokee county. Records range from 5/1973 to 2/2004. Also, see note at beginning of section. Also, search grantor/grantee index free at www.texaslandrecords.com. Registration and fees apply for full data. Also, to search probate records and judgment records go to http://idocket.com/countycourt.htm
Property, Taxation Records `Free` Search the Cherokee CAD database for free at http://clientdb.trueautomation.com/clientdb/main.asp?id=2.

Clay County *Property, Taxation Records* `Free` Access property tax records free at www.claycad.org/. Also, see note at beginning of section.

Coleman County *Property, Taxation Records* `Free & $$` Property tax inquiries can be made at www.txcountydata.com/county.asp?County=042`. Other access may be available through private companies.

Collin County *Real Estate, Deed, Lien, Judgment, Vital Statistic, Mortgage Records* www.co.collin.tx.us `Free` Access to the county clerk Deeds database is free at http://countyclerkrecords.co.collin.tx.us/webinquiry/. Also, see note at beginning of section for more property data.
Property, Taxation Records `Free` Search the Appraiser's property tax and business property database free at www.collincad.org/search.php. Also, search the tax assessor and collector look up free at www.co.collin.tx.us/tax_assessor/taxstmt_search.jsp.

Colorado County *Real Estate, Grantor/Grantee, Deed, Judgment, Lien Records* www.co.colorado.tx.us/ips/cms `Free` Access recording records free at www.titlex.com; select Colorado county. Records range is 5/1997 to 9/2001. For more land data, see note at beginning of section.
Property, Taxation Records `Free` For property search go to www.coloradocad.org/ and click on property search. Also, see note at beginning of section.

Comal County *Property, Taxation Records* `Free` Access property free at www.comalcad.org.

Comanche County *Property, Taxation Records* `Free` Access Appraisal District records free at www.txcountydata.com.

Crane County *Real Estate,Grantor/Grantee, Deed, Lien, Birth, Death, Marriage, Probate, Court Records* www.co.crane.tx.us `Free & $$` Search official records after choosing county at www.edoctecinc.com. If records are Unofficial, you search or copy them freely; if not Unofficial, a $1.00 per page fee applies. For details and signup, contact clerk or Jerry Anderson at 800-578-7746.

Dallas County *Real Estate, Deed, Lien, UCC, Voter Registration, Marriage, Assumed Name, Probate Records* www.dallascounty.org/applications/english/record-search/rec-search_intro.html `Free & $$` Search most records at www.dallascounty.org/pars2. Name search indices of deeds, marriages, assumed names, UCCs, probate, court records and real estate back to 1964 on the search page at www.realestate.countyclerk.dallascounty.org. Indices include DOB. Fee to view and print documents; credit cards accepted. Purchase per item, or subscribe for annual fee. Also, access County Voter Registration Records free at www.dalcoelections.org/voters.asp. Shows if registered and precinct.
Property, Taxation Records `Free` Access Central Appraisal District data free at www.dallascad.org/SearchOwner.aspx. Also search De Soto City and Glenn Heights tax office records free at www.texaspayments.com/057906/, and City of Garland taxes at www.texaspayments.com/057120/

Deaf Smith County *Property, Taxation Records* `Free` Access property and appriaser data free at http://clientdb.trueautomation.com/clientdb/main.asp.

Delta County *Property, Taxation Records* `Free` Access Appraisal District records free at http://clientdb.trueautomation.com/clientdb/main.asp?id=39.

Denton County *Real Estate, Grantor/Grantee, Deed, Lien, Death, Divorce, Marriage, Voter Registration Records* www.dentoncounty.com/dept/ccl.htm `Free & $$` Access county property database indices free for name/instrument searches; no fee for access, but to view and print images is $1.00 per page; see https://www.texaslandrecords.com/txlr/TxlrApp/index.jsp. With a full subscription search full indices and download images. Also, search voter registration rolls free at http://elections.dentoncounty.com/VRSearch/default.asp.
Property, Taxation Records `Free` Property tax inquiries can be made at www.dentoncad.com. Tax records are also online at http://taxweb.dentoncounty.com/tax/ but no name searching.

De Witt County *Property, Taxation Records* `Free` Access appraisal district property data free at www.dewittcad.org/ and click on Search our data. Also, access assessor tax payment data free at www.dewittcountyonline.net/tax/taxonline.jsp.

Ector County *Real Estate, Grantor/Grantee, Deed, Lien, Judgment, Marriage, Divorce Records* www.co.ector.tx.us `Free & $$` Search the grantor/grantee index free at www.texaslandrecords.com. Also has a subscription service with search/payment options for full document viewing.
Property, Taxation Records `Free` Search appraisal district property data and personal property free at www.ectorcad.org.

Ellis County *Property, Taxation Records* `Free` Search the property appraiser database for free at www.elliscad.org. Access to property tax information is at www.elliscountytax.com. Other online access through private companies.

El Paso County *Real Estate, Deed, Lien, Mortgage, Assumed Name, Vital Records, Judgment Records* www.epcounty.com `Free` Search official records including recordings, vital statistics and property free at www.epcounty.com/clerk/deedsearch.asp, also marriages at www.epcounty.com/clerk/marriagesearch.asp. Also, to search probate judgment records go to http://idocket.com/countycourt.htm. Search assumed names free at www.epcounty.com/clerk/assumed_search.asp. For county births, search www.epcounty.com/clerk/birthsearch.asp; deaths- www.epcounty.com/clerk/deaths.asp. Also, see note at beginning of section.
Property, Taxation Records `Free` Search property tax data free at www.elpasocad.org/search.htm. Also, see note at beginning of section. Search foreclosure notices by date free at www.epcounty.com/foreclosures/.

Erath County *Property, Taxation Records* `Free` Find appraisal district data free at http://208.75.248.98/. Also, search tax office records free at www.texaspayments.com/072000/. Also, see note at beginning of section.

Falls County *Property, Taxation Records* `Free` Access property data free at www.fallscad.org. Click on Search Our Data. Maps may also be available.

Fayette County *Real Estate, Grantor/Grantee, Deed, Lien, Judgment Records* www.co.fayette.tx.us `Free` Access recording records free at www.titlex.com; select Fayette County.
Property, Taxation Records `Free` Access assessor property records free at http://clientdb.trueautomation.com/clientdb/main.asp.

Floyd County *Property, Taxation Records* `Free` Find appraisal district data free at http://208.75.248.98/.

Fort Bend County *Real Estate, Grantor/Grantee, Deed, Lien, Judgment, UCC, Marriage, Death, Birth, Probate Records* www.co.fort-bend.tx.us `Free & $$` Recorded records can be searched for free at http://ccweb.co.fort-bend.tx.us/. Also, access recording records free at www.titlex.com; select Ft Bend county. Record range is 1/1974 to 11/2001. Search portal for county at http://ccweb.co.fort-bend.tx.us/localization/menu.asp. Also, search county probate and court records with subscription; for info, contact Diane Shepard at 281-341-8664. Also, see note at beginning of section.
Property, Taxation Records `Free` Access appraisal records free at www.fbcad.org/Appraisal/PublicAccess/. Also, property tax inquiries can be made free at www.txcountydata.com/selectCounty.asp.

Franklin County *Property, Taxation Records* `Free` Access to property data is free at www.franklincad.com. Click on Search Our Data. Also, see note at beginning of section.

Freestone County *Property, Taxation Records* `Free` Access to Appraiser's property data is free at www.freestonecad.org. Click on Search Our Data.

Gaines County *Property, Taxation Records* `Free` Access county parcel data free at www.gcad.org/Appraisal/PublicAccess/.

Galveston County *Real Estate, Grantor/Grantee, Deed, Lien, Judgment, UCC, Vital Statistic Records* www.co.galveston.tx.us/County_Clerk/ `Free` Several sources exist. Access the county online official records index free at http://207.80.116.33/. Also, a Grantor/Grantee index is at www.titlex.com; select Galveston County; records go back to 1/1965. Also, see note at beginning of section.
Property, Taxation Records `Free` Search Central Appraisal Dist. database free at www.galvestoncad.org/Appraisal/PublicAccess/. For info, call 409-766-5115.

Gillespie County *Property, Taxation Records* `Free` Access Appraiser property data free at http://propaccess.trueautomation.com/clientDB/?cid=52. Also, make Property tax inquiries at www.txcountydata.com/selectCounty.asp. Other online access through private companies.

Goliad County *Real Estate, Grantor/Grantee, Deed, Lien, Judgment Records* www.co.goliad.tx.us/ips/cms `Free` Access recording records free at www.titlex.com; select Goliad county. Records range is 1/1950 to 12/2003. Also, see note at beginning of section.

Grayson County *Real Estate, Grantor/Grantee, Deed, Mortgage, Lien, Death, Marriage, Judgment Records* www.co.grayson.tx.us/main.htm `Free & $$` Search grantor/grantee index free at www.texaslandrecords.com. Registration and fees required for full data. Access recording records free at www.titlex.com; select Grayson county.
Property, Taxation Records `Free` Search appraiser property data free at www.graysoncad.org. Search the Grayson CAD system for mortgage, and property data at http://clientdb.trueautomation.com/clientdb/main.asp?id=15.

Gregg County *Real Estate, Grantor/Grantee, Deed, Mortgage, Lien, Judgment, Vital Statistic, UCC Records* www.co.gregg.tx.us `Free & $$` Access to the County Clerk's Official Public Records database is free to view at www.co.gregg.tx.us/A2WebUI/. Fee to copy documents. Also, access recording records free at www.titlex.com; select Gregg county. Records range is 4/1977 to 5/2005. Also, see note at beginning of section.
Property, Taxation Records `Free` Search property tax records for free at www.co.gregg.tx.us/appraisal/publicaccess/. Also, property tax inquiries can be made at www.gcad.org/Appraisal/PublicAccess/.

Grimes County *Property, Taxation Records* `Free` Access property appraisal data free at http://67.76.234.90/Appraisal/PublicAccess/. Other online access through private companies.

Guadalupe County *Property, Taxation Records* `Free` Search appraisal roll, parcel tax data free at www.co.guadalupe.tx.us/Appraisal/PublicAccess/.

Hamilton County *Property, Taxation Records* `Free` Access property appraisal data free at www.txcountydata.com/county.asp?County=097.

Harris County *Real Estate, Grantor/Grantee, Lien, Judgment, Appraiser, Voter, UCC, Assumed Name, Vital Statistic, Probate Records* www.cclerk.hctx.net `Free` Access to Assumed Name records, UCC filings, vital statistic, and Real Property are at www.cclerk.hctx.net/coolice/default.asp?Category=RealProperty&Service=mastermenu. County Court Civil, marriage and informal marriage records also available. Also, access recording records free at www.titlex.com; select Harris county. Search voter registrations free at www.tax.co.harris.tx.us/voter/voter.asp. Also, search probate records and judgment records at http://idocket.com/countycourt.htm.
Property, Taxation Records `Free` Appraiser records are at www.hcad.org/Records. Search tax assessor data free at www.tax.co.harris.tx.us/dbsearch/dbsearch.asp. Also, search tax statements free at www.hctax.net/propertytax/current/currentsearch.asp

Harrison County *Property, Taxation Records* `Free` Find appraisal district data free at http://208.75.248.98/.

Hartley County *Property, Taxation Records* `Free` Find appraisal district data free at http://208.75.248.98/.

Haskell County *Property, Taxation Records* Free & $$ Property tax inquiries can be made at www.txcountydata.com/county.asp?County=104. Other online access through private companies.

Hays County *Real Estate, Grantor/Grantee, Deed, Line, Vital Statistic, Judgment, Probate Records*
www.co.hays.tx.us Free & $$ Search Grantor/Grantee index free at www.texaslandrecords.com. Registration and fees apply for full data. Access probate and judgment records back to 1997 free at http://idocket.com/countycourt.htm
Property, Taxation Records Free Access property appraiser dta free at www.hayscad.com/Appraisal/PublicAccess/default.aspx. Access tax collector property data free at http://66.90.254.60/appraisal/publicaccess/. Also, see notes at beginning of section for add'l property data.

Hemphill County *Property, Taxation Records* Free Access to county property data is free at www.hemphillcad.org. Site may be under construction.

Henderson County *Property, Taxation Records* Free Find appraisal district data free at http://208.75.248.98/. Add'l online access through private companies.

Hidalgo County *Real Estate, Grantor/Grantee, Deed, Judgment, Vital Statistic, Probate Records*
www.hidalgocountyclerk.us Free & $$ Search grantor/grantee index free at www.texaslandrecords.com. Registration and fees apply for full data. Access probate and judgment records back to 1986 free at http://idocket.com/countycourt.htm.
Property, Taxation Records Free Search appraiser property records free at www.hidalgoad.org/appraisal/publicaccess/. Also, see note at beginning of section for add'l property data.

Hill County *Probate, Judgment Records* Free Search probate court records and judgment records at http://idocket.com/countycourt.htm Also, see note at beginning of section.
Property, Taxation Records Free Access appraisal district property records free at www.hillcad.org/in/reportshome.php.

Hockley County *Property, Taxation Records* Free Access property records free at http://clientdb.trueautomation.com/clientdb/main.asp?id=50.

Hood County *Property, Taxation Records* Free Find appraisal district data free at http://208.75.248.98/. Add'l online access through private companies.

Hopkins County *Real Estate, Deed Records* www.hopkinscountytx.org Free Access real property records free after registering for login and password at www.hopkinscountyonline.net/realproperty/.
Property, Taxation Records Free Find appraisal district data free at http://208.75.248.98/.

Houston County *Real Estate, Deed, Official Records* www.co.houston.tx.us Free & $$ Search official records after choosing county at www.edoctecinc.com. If records are Unofficial, you search or copy them freely; if not Unofficial, a $1.00 per page fee applies. For details and signup, contact clerk or Jerry Anderson at 800-578-7746.
Property, Taxation Records Free Access to property tax records is free at www.houstoncad.org/.

Hunt County *Property, Taxation Records* Free Access property tax data and sheriff sales data free at www.hctax.info. Also, search tax information free at http://clientdb.trueautomation.com/clientdb/main.asp?id=68. Also see notes at beginning of section for add'l property data.

Hutchinson County *Property, Taxation Records* Free Access to property tax data is free at www.hutchinsoncad.org/.

Jackson County *Real Estate, Grantor/Grantee, Deed, Lien, Judgment Records* www.co.jackson.tx.us Free
Access recording records free at www.titlex.com; select Jackson county. Records range is 1/1993 to 9/2004. Also, see note at beginning of section. Also, property tax inquiries can be made at www.txcountydata.com/selectCounty.asp.
Property, Taxation Records Free Access appraiser property records free at www.jacksoncad.org/Appraisal/PublicAccess/. Also, property tax inquiries can be made at www.txcountydata.com/selectCounty.asp.

Jefferson County *Real Estate, Deed, Lien, Judgment, Marriage, UCC, Assumed Name Records*
www.co.jefferson.tx.us Free Access the recorder database free at http://jeffersontxclerk.manatron.com/. Recording index goes back to 1983; images to 1983. Marriages go back to 1995; UCCs to 7/2001. Also, see note at beginning of section.
Property, Taxation Records Free Access property tax records free at www.jcad.org/search/.

Jim Hogg County *Real Estate, Deed Records* $$ Access recording office land data at www.etitlesearch.com; registration required, fee based on usage.

Jim Wells County *Real Estate, Deed Records* $$ Access recording office land data at www.etitlesearch.com; registration required, fee based on usage.

Johnson County *Judgment, Probate Records* www.johnsoncountytx.org Free Search probate records and judgment records at http://idocket.com/countycourt.htm. Records go back to 1980s. Also, see note at beginning of section for add'l property data.

Property, Taxation Records Free Records from the County Appraiser are free at www.johnsoncountytaxoffice.org/accountSearch.asp or at Taxnet site at www.johnsoncad.com/search_appr.php.

Jones County *Property, Taxation Records* Free Access property tax records free at www.jonescad.org/Appraisal/PublicAccess/.

Kaufman County *Real Estate, Grantor/Grantee, Deed, Lien, Judgment, Marriage, Death, Divorce Records* www.kaufmancountyclerk.com Free & $$ Access recording records free at www.titlex.com; select Kaufman county. Records go back to 3/1/1969. Also, search grantor/grantee index free at https://www.texaslandrecords.com/txlr/controller; click on free search. Registration and fees or 1-day pass is required for full data. Also, see note at beginning of section.
Property, Taxation Records Free Search appraisal roll data free at www.kaufmancad.org and at http://clientdb.trueautomation.com/clientdb/main.asp?id=66.

Kendall County *Real Estate, Grantor/Grantee, Deed, Lien, Judgment Records* Free Access recording records free at www.titlex.com; select Kendall county. Also see note at beginning of section.
Property, Taxation Records Free Access property data free at http://clientdb.trueautomation.com/clientdb/main.asp?id=69.

Kerr County *Real Estate, Deed, Lien, Assumed Name, Marriage Records* www.co.kerr.tx.us/ Free & $$ Access to recorder land data by subscription at www.kerr.tx.us.landata.com. Registration and login required; $50.00 monthly fee. Also, search the old records system for deeds, assumed names, and marriage records free at www.edoctecinc.com/.
Property, Taxation Records Free Access appraiser's property records free at http://public.co.kerr.tx.us:8088/Appraisal/PublicAccess/. Also, see note at beginning of section.

Kimble County *Property, Taxation Records* Free Access appraiser's property data free at www.txcountydata.com/county.asp?County=134.

Kleberg County *Judgment, Property Records* www.co.kleberg.tx.us/ips/cms Free Search judgment records back to 1991 at http://idocket.com/countycourt.htm. County Clerk does not offter a searchable website at this time.
Property, Taxation Records Free Access to county appraisal rolls and property data is free at www.klebergcad.org/search_appr.php.

Knox County *Real Estate, Grantor/Grantee, Deed, Lien, Judgment Records* $$ Access recording records at www.titlex.com; select Knox county; login and password required.

Lamb County *Property, Taxation Records* Online access through private companies.

La Salle County *Property, Appraiser, Real Estate, Deed Records* www.co.la-salle.tx.us/ $$ Access recording office land data at www.etitlesearch.com; registration required, fee based on usage.

Lavaca County *Property, Taxation Records* Free Access appraiser's property data free at www.txcountydata.com/county.asp?County=143.

Lee County *Property, Taxation Records* Free Access Appraisal District records free at http://clientdb.trueautomation.com/clientdb/main.asp?id=9.

Liberty County *Property, Taxation Records* Free Access Appraisal District records free at http://clientdb.trueautomation.com/clientdb/main.asp?id=7. Online access through private companies.

Limestone County *Property, Taxation Records* Free Access appraiser's property data free at http://limestonecad.txcountydata.com/Appraisal/PublicAccess/. Also, see notes at beginning of section.

Lipscomb County *Property, Taxation Records* Free Find appraisal district data free at http://208.75.248.98/.

Llano County *Property, Taxation Records* Free Access appraiser's property data free at www.txcountydata.com/county.asp?County=150. Search tax office data free by selecting county at http://208.75.248.98/. Other online access through private companies.

Lubbock County *Property, Taxation Records* Free Search the property appraiser database for free at www.lubbockcad.org/Appraisal/PublicAccess/. Also, see note at beginning of section.

McCulloch County *Judgment, Court Records* www.co.mcculloch.tx.us/ips/cms Free Search judgment records at http://idocket.com/countycourt.htm.
Property, Taxation Records Free Search assessor properrty records free at www.taxnetusa.com/texas/mcculloch/. Subscription service also available.

McLennan County *Real Estate, Grantor/Grantee, Deed, Lien, Judgment, Property Tax Records* www.co.mclennan.tx.us/cclerk/index.html Free & $$ Access recording records free at www.titlex.com; select McLennan county. Records range from 1/1996 to 12/2002. Also, see note at beginning of section. Also, access land records at

http://etitlesearch.com. You can do a name search; choose from $50.00 monthly subscription or per-click account. Also, see note at beginning of section.
Property, Taxation Records **Free** Search real estate appraisal records at www.mclennancad.org or at http://propaccess.trueautomation.com/clientDB/?cid=20. Property Tax balance information free at https://actweb.acttax.com/act_webdev/mclennan/index.jsp.

Madison County *Real Estate, Grantor/Grantee, Deed, Lien, Judgment, Marriage, Divorce Records*
www.co.madison.tx.us/ips/cms **Free & $$** Search land records index free at www.texaslandrecords.com. Subscription and fees required for full records. Indexes back to 1974; images back to 1998.
Property, Taxation Records **Free** Access Appraisal District tax records free at www.txcountydata.com/county.asp?County=157.

Marion County *Real Estate, Grantor/Grantee, Deed, Lien, Judgment Records* **Free**
Access recording records free at www.titlex.com; select Marion county.
Property, Taxation Records **Free** Access property tax records free at www.marioncad.org.

Martin County *Property, Taxation Records* **Free** Access to property data is free at www.martincad.org/.

Matagorda County *Property, Taxation Records* **Free** Access to Appraisal District records is free at http://clientdb.trueautomation.com/clientdb/main.asp?id=25.

Maverick County *Property, Taxation Records* **Free** Visit www.maverickcad.org/searchaccounts.htm for the appraisal roll. Other online access through private companies.

Medina County *Real Estate, Deed, Lien Records* www.medina.tx.us.landata.com **Free & $$** Access to recorder's index is free at www.medina.tx.us.landata.com but there is a $4.00 fee per document image, or you may subscribe for $50.00 per month and pay $2.00 per document image. There is a $150.00 per doc processing fee. Visa/MC credit cards accepted online.

Midland County *Real Estate, Grantor/Grantee, Deed, Lien, Judgment, Divorce, Voter Registration Records*
www.co.midland.tx.us **Free & $$** Access recording records free at www.titlex.com; select Midland county. Also, search Grantor/Grantee and divorce index free at www.texaslandrecords.com or www.uslandrecords.com. Registration and fees required for full data. Also, access voter registration data free at www.co.midland.tx.us/Elections/VoterDatabase/input.asp.
Property, Taxation Records **Free** Access property tax data and delinquent taxes free at www.co.midland.tx.us/tax/Property/default.asp. Also, find appraisal district data free at http://208.75.248.98/. Also, search property data on the mapping page at www.midcad.org/Search/index.htm

Milam County *Real Estate, Grantor/Grantee, Deed, Lien, Judgment Records* **Free** Access recording records free at www.titlex.com; select Milam county. Records range is 5/2000 to 8/2001. Also, see note at beginning of section.
Property, Taxation Records **Free** Search appraisal district data free at www.txcountydata.com/county.asp?County=166. Also see note at beginning of section.

Mills County *Property, Taxation Records* **Free** Find appraisal district data free at http://208.75.248.98/.

Mitchell County *Land, Deed, Lien, Marriage, Death, Probate Records* **Free & $$** Search official records after choosing county at www.edoctecinc.com. If records are stamped Unofficial, you can copy them freely; Official, a $1.00 per page fee applies. For details and signup, contact Edoc Tec at 800-578-7746.
Property, Taxation Records **Free** Access to real property searches for free found at www.mitchellcad.org/

Montague County *Property, Taxation Records* **Free** Find appraisal district data free at http://208.75.248.98/.

Montgomery County *Real Estate, Grantor/Grantee, Deed, Lien, Judgment, Probate Records*
www.co.montgomery.tx.us **Free & $$** Access recording records free at www.titlex.com; select Montgomery county. Records go back to 1/1966. Similar index search may also be performed free at www.courthousedirect.com/IndexSearches.aspx. Registration and password required for full data. Also, to search probate records and judgment records go to http://idocket.com/countycourt.htm
Property, Taxation Records **Free** Access property appraiser data free at www.mcad-tx.org/html/records.html.

Moore County *Property, Taxation Records* **Free** Access to property data is free at www.moorecad.org.

Morris County *Property, Taxation Records* **Free** Find appraisal district data free at http://208.75.248.98/.

Nacogdoches County *Real Estate, Grantor/Grantee, Lien, Judgment, Deed, Death, Marriage, Court Records*
www.co.nacogdoches.tx.us **Free & $$** Access, view and search the Real Property grantor/grantee index free at https://www.texaslandrecords.com/txlr/TxlrApp/index.jsp. Monthly subscription is recommended; there is a pay as you go plan for $1 per document. Also, access court records at www.idocket.com. Fees involved.
Property, Taxation Records **Free** Access property tax data free at www.nacocad.org. Click on Search Our Data. Also, access to county Appraisal Roll from TaxNetUSA MAY be at www.taxnetusa.com/texas/nacogdoches/.

Navarro County *Judgment, Civil Records* www.co.navarro.tx.us/ips/cms `Free` Access civil and judgment records free at http://idocket.com/countycourt.htm. Also, see note at beginning of section for "Advanced" fee service.
Property, Taxation Records `Free` Find appraisal district data free at http://208.75.248.98/.

Newton County *Property, Taxation Records* `Free` Access Appraiser/property tax records free at www.newtoncad.org/Appraisal/PublicAccess/. Also, see note at beginning of section.

Nueces County *Real Estate, Grantor/Grantee, Deed, Judgment, Lien Records* www.co.nueces.tx.us `Free`
Access to county clerk recording records is free after registration at www.co.nueces.tx.us/countyclerk/records/; access is also free at www.titlex.com; select Nueces county. Also, see notes at beginning of section.
Property, Taxation Records `Free` Access County Appraiser records free at www.nuecescad.net/Appraisal/PublicAccess/. Also, see notes at beginning of section.

Orange County *Property, Taxation Records* `Free` Access to the county appraisal district records is free at www.orangecad.org or at the county site directly at www.orangecad.net/Appraisal/PublicAccess/.

Palo Pinto County *Property, Taxation Records* `Free` Access to property data is free at www.palopintocad.org. Click on Search Our Data.

Panola County *Real Estate, Grantor/Grantee, Deed, Lien, Judgment, Death, Marriage Records* `Free & $$`
Access recording records free at www.titlex.com; select Panola county. Also, search grantor/grantee index free at www.texaslandrecords.com. Registration and fees required for full access.

Parker County *Real Estate, Deed, Lien, Marriage, Birth, Death Records* www.co.parker.tx.us/ips/cms `Free & $$`
Access county clerk's index free after registration at www.parker.tx.us.landata.com/. Fees required for full data, $2.00 per doc.
Property, Taxation Records `Free` Find appraisal district data free at http://208.75.248.98/. Add'l online access through private companies.

Pecos County *Property, Taxation Records* `Free` Access to property data is free at www.pecoscad.org/. Click on Search Our Data.

Polk County *Real Estate, Deed, Lien Records* www.co.polk.tx.us `$$` Access to County Clerk's data is by subscription at www.co.polk.tx.us/ips/cms/countyoffices/countyClerk.html. Username and password required.

Potter County *Real Estate, Grantor/Grantee, Deed, Lien, Marriage, Divorce, Judgment, Probate Records*
`Free & $$` Access recording records free at www.titlex.com; select Potter county. Also, search grantor/grantee index free at www.texaslandrecords.com. Registration and fees required for full data. Also, to search probate records and judgment records go to http://idocket.com/countycourt.htm. Also, see note at beginning of section.
Property, Taxation Records `Free` Records on the Potter-Randall Appraisal District database are free at www.prad.org. Records periodically updated; for current tax info call Potter- 806-342-2600 or Randall- 806-665-6287.

Randall County *Real Estate, Deed, Lien, Deed, Marriage, Probate, Judgment Records* www.randallcounty.org
`Free` Access Real Estate records from 2000 forward free at http://ccopr.randallcounty.org/, click on Official Public Records and then OPR search, or marriages, or Comm Court for Commissioner's Court data. Also, criminal, probate and civil records found at www.idocket.com. Also, see notes at beginning of section for add'l property records.
Property, Taxation Records `Free` Randall County appraisal and personal property records are combined online with Potter County; see Potter County for access info or visit www.prad.org. Randall County sheriff sales records are combined online with Potter County; see Potter County for access info or visit www.prad.org.

Red River County *Property, Taxation Records* `Free` Access to county appraisal district records is free at www.redrivercad.org.

Refugio County *Property, Taxation Records* `Free` Access property data free at www.refugiocad.org. Click on Search Our Data.

Robertson County *Real Estate, Grantor/Grantee, Deed, Lien, Judgment Records* `Free & $$`
Access recording records free at www.titlex.com; select Robertson county. Also, access grantor/grantee index free at www.texaslandrecords.com but registration and fees required for full data.

Rockwall County *Real Estate, Grantor/Grantee, Deed, lien, Judgment, Vital Statistic Records*
www.rockwallcountytexas.com/ `Free & $$` Access grantor/grantee index free at www.texaslandrecords.com. Registration and fees required for full data.
Property, Taxation Records `Free` Access appraisal district property records free at www.rockwallcad.com. Also, access appraiser index free at http://clientdb.trueautomation.com/clientdb/main.asp?id=76.

Runnels County *Property, Taxation Records* `Free` Find appraisal district data free at http://208.75.248.98/.

Rusk County *Real Estate, Grantor/Grantee, Deed, Judgment, Lien Records* www.co.rusk.tx.us `Free & $$`
Access to grantor/grantee index free at www.texaslandrecords.com. Registration and fees required for full access. Also, see note at beginning of section. *Property, Taxation Records* `Free` Access property data free at www.ruskcad.org. Click on Search Our Data. Also see www.taxnetusa.com for property tax records.

San Jacinto County *Property, Taxation Records* Online access avilable through private companies.

San Patricio County *Property, Taxation Records* `Free` Search the Appraiser database for free at www.taxnetusa.com/texas/sanpatricio/. OR search via the county site, www.co.san-patricio.tx.us/ips/cms.

Scurry County *Real Estate, Grantor/Grantee, Deed, Lien, Vital Statistic, Judgment Records* `Free & $$`
Search index free at www.texaslandrecords.com. Fees and registration required for full data.

Shelby County *Real Estate, Deed, Lien, Judgment, UCC, Marriage, Court, Probate Records*
http://cc.co.shelby.tx.us/ `Free` Access the recorder's databases of records free at http://cc.co.shelby.tx.us/.
Property, Taxation Records `Free` Search appraisal district records free at www.txcountydata.com/county.asp?county=210.

Smith County *Real Estate, Grantor/Grantee, Deed, Lien, Judgment, Birth, Divorce, Marriage, Probate Records*
www.smith-county.com `Free & $$` Search grantor/grantee index free at www.texaslandrecords.com. Registration and fees required for full data access. Also, see note at beginning of section.
Property, Taxation Records `Free` Access to county appraisal district records is free at www.smithcountymapsite.org/smithgis/viewer.htm. Also, access property data on the GIS-mapping site free at www.smithcad.org/scadarc/viewer_temp.htm. Also, search business personal property free at www.smithcountymapsite.org/smithgis/ppmain.asp. Also, see note at beginning of section.

Somervell County *Property, Taxation Records* `Free` Access Appraisal District records free at http://clientdb.trueautomation.com/clientdb/main.asp?id=29 or via http://somervellcad.org. Other online access through private companies.

Starr County *Probate, Judgment Records* `Free` Probate and judgment records free at http://idocket.com/countycourt.htm

Stephens County *Property, Taxation Records* `Free` Find appraisal district data free at http://208.75.248.98/.

Tarrant County *Real Estate, Grantor/Grantee, Lien, Judgment, Deed, Assumed Name, Marriage, UCC Records*
www.tarrantcounty.com/eCountyClerk/site/default.asp `Free & $$` Search grantor/grantee index at http://ccanthem.co.tarrant.tx.us/search.aspx?cabinet=opr. Also, access a real estate and grantor/grantee index free at www.titlex.com where records range from 4/1997 to 11/2001 only; select Tarrant County. Also, search assumed names, marriages, courts, UCCs, Traffic at www.tarrantcounty.com/ecountyclerk/cwp/view.asp?A=735&Q=427570. Also see note at beginning of section.
Property, Taxation Records `Free` Access Appraisal District Property data free at www.tad.org/Datasearch/datasearch.htm. Access assessor's accounts search for tax data free at http://taxoffice.tarrantcounty.com/AccountSearch.asp. Access City of Grapevine and Coffeyville tax office free at www.texaspayments.com/validate.asp.

Taylor County *Real Estate, Grantor/Grantee, Deed, Vital Statistic Records* `Free & $$`
Access land records index free at www.texaslandrecords.com. Registration and fees required for full data. Also, see note at beginning of section for add'l property data.
Property, Taxation Records `Free` Access to the county Central Appraisal District database is free at www.taxnetusa.com/texas/taylor/ . Also, access Appraisal District records free at http://propaccess.trueautomation.com/clientdb/?cid=32. Also, search the treasurer's database of unclaimed property free at www.taylorcountytexas.org/unclaime.html.

Terry County *Property, Taxation Records* `Free` Tax roll information is available at www.terrycad.org/ .

Titus County *Real Estate, Deed, Lien, Court Records* `Free & $$` Access to county clerk records are free after registration at www.tituscountyonline.net/countyclerk/. *Property, Taxation Records* `Free` Access property and other tax data free at http://clientdb.trueautomation.com/clientdb/main.asp?id=71. Also, search the tax payments database free at www.tituscountyonline.net/tax/taxonline.jsp.

Tom Green County *Real Estate, Grantor/Grantee, Deed, Lien, Judgment, Marriage, Birth, Death, Fictitious Name Records* http://countyclerk.tomgreencountytx.gov `Free` Access official public records including vital stats and fictitious names free at http://countyclerk.tomgreencountytx.gov/. Also, access recording records free at www.titlex.com; select Tom Green County.
Property, Taxation Records `Free` Access appraisal district property data free at www.tomgreencad.com/.

Travis County *Real Estate, Grantor/Grantee, Deed, UCC, Marriage, Probate, Voter Registration Records*
www.co.travis.tx.us `Free` Access to recorders official records is free at http://deed.co.travis.tx.us/search.aspx?cabinet=opr. Images available back to 4/1999. Also, See note at beginning of section for add'l property records.

Property, Taxation Records `Free` Access the Central Appraisal District database free at www.traviscad.org/search.htm. Also search business personal property. Also, you may search on the county tax payment system at www.texasonline.state.tx.us/NASApp/rap/BaseRap.

Trinity County *Property, Taxation Records* `Free` Access property appraisal district data free at www.txcountydata.com/county.asp?County=228.

Tyler County *Property, Taxation Records* `Free` Access to the county appraisal district records is free at www.tylercad.org and also at www.txcountydata.com/county.asp?County=229

Upshur County *Real Estate, Grantor/Grantee, Deed, Lien, Judgment, Marriage, Birth, Death, Probate Records* www.countyofupshur.com `Free` Access County Clerks's OPR and other recorder records including civil and probate free at http://countyofupshur.com:8000/. Also, access recording records free at www.titlex.com; select Upshur county. Also, see note at beginning of section. *Property, Taxation Records* `Free` View property information free at www.trueautomation.com.

Upton County *Real Estate, Grantor/Grantee, Deed, Lien Records* www.co.upton.tx.us `Free & $$` Search grantor/grantee index free at www.texaslandrecords.com. Registration and fees required for fuller data, but images not available.

Uvalde County *Property, Taxation Records* `Free` Access to county appraisal district tax data may be available through www.uvaldecounty.com; search page may be temporarily down.

Val Verde County *Probate, Judgment Records* `Free` Search probate records and judgment records at http://idocket.com/countycourt.htm *Property, Taxation Records* `Free` Access Appraisal District records free at http://clientdb.trueautomation.com/clientdb/main.asp?id=42.

Van Zandt County *Real Estate, Grantor/Grantee, Deed, Judgment, Lien Records* www.vanzandtcounty.org `Free` Access recording records free at www.titlex.com; select Van Zandt county. Record range is 1/1971 to 9/2003. Also, see note at beginning of section.
Property, Taxation Records `Free` Search the county appraisal rolls for free at www.vanzandtcad.org; includes plat maps online. Also, find property data at www.myswdata.com/. Also, find appraisal district data free at http://208.75.248.98/.

Victoria County *Real Estate, Grantor/Grantee, Deed, Judgment, Lien, Probate Records* http://victoriacountytx.org/departments/county_clerk/cclerk.htm `Free` Access recording records free at www.titlex.com; select Victoria county. Records range is 1/1964 to 5/26/2005 only. Also, to search probate records and judgment records go to http://idocket.com/countycourt.htm. Also, see note at beginning of section
Property, Taxation Records `Free` Access to appraisal district records is free at www.victoriacad.org.

Walker County *Real Estate, Grantor/Grantee, Deed, Lien, Death, Divorce, Marriage Records* www.co.walker.tx.us `Free & $$` Search land records index free at www.texaslandrecords.com. Indexes from 1960-forward; images of the records back to 1/1/2003. Subscription required for full data.
Property, Taxation Records `Free` Access to county appraisal district records is free at http://clientdb.trueautomation.com/clientdb/main.asp?id=4.

Waller County *Property, Taxation Records* `Free`
Access appraiser property data free at www.txcountydata.com/county.asp?County=237.

Washington County *Real Estate, Grantor/Grantee, Deed, Judgment, Lien, Probate, Marriage, Birth, Death, Military Discharge Records* www.co.washington.tx.us/cclerk/index.html `Free & $$` Access recording records free at www.titlex.com; select Washington county. Records go back to 1/1965. Also, to search probate records and judgment records go to http://idocket.com/countycourt.htm. Also, see note at beginning of section. Also, search official records after choosing county at www.edoctecinc.com. If records are Unofficial, you search or copy them free; if not Unofficial, a $1.00 per page fee applies. For details and signup, contact clerk or Jerry Anderson at 800-578-7746.
Property, Taxation Records `Free` Access appraisal district property records free at www.washingtoncad.org:8008/Appraisal/PublicAccess/

Webb County *Real Estate, Deed, Probate, Judgment Records* www.webbcounty.com `Free & $$`
Access recording office land data at www.etitlesearch.com; registration required, fee based on usage. Also, to search probate records and judgment records go to http://idocket.com/countycourt.htm. Also, see note at beginning of section for add'l property data.
Property, Taxation Records `Free` Search the county Central Appraisal District database at www.webbcad.org/Propertysearch/propertysearch.html.

Wharton County *Real Estate, Grantor/Grantee, Deed, Lien, Judgment Records* `Free`
Access recording records free at www.titlex.com; select Wharton county. Records go up to 11/2003.
Property, Taxation Records `Free` Access appraisal district property data free at www.txcountydata.com/county.asp?County=241.

Wheeler County *Property, Taxation Records* `Free` Find tax office data free at http://208.75.248.98/.

Wichita County *Real Estate, Grantor/Grantee, Deed, Lien, Judgment, Marriage Records* `Free & $$`
Search grantor/grantee index free at www.texaslandrecords.com. Registration and fees required for full data. Some, not all, UCCs are available. Also, see note at beginning of section.
Property, Taxation Records `Free` Access to county appraisal district records is free at
http://clientdb.trueautomation.com/clientdb/main.asp?id=43. Also, see online notes in state summary at beginning of section.

Wilbarger County *Property, Taxation Records* `Free` Access to property data is free at
www.wilbargerappraisal.org/. Also, search the appraisal rolls for free at www.taxnetusa.com. Also see note at beginning of section.

Willacy County *Real Estate, Grantor/Grantee, Deed, Judgment, Lien Records* `Free` Access recording records free at www.titlex.com; select Willacy county. Record range is 8/1998 to 1/2004. Also, access land records back 20 years at www.landtitleusa.com.
Property, Taxation Records See note at beginning of section.

Williamson County *Real Estate, Grantor/Grantee, Deed, Lien, Judgment Records* www.wilco.org `Free`
Access recording records free at www.titlex.com; select Williamson county. Records go back to 5/1999.
Property, Taxation Records `Free` Access the appraiser database free at www.wcad.org. Also, access the monthly delinquent tax sale list at http://wcportals.wilco.org/tax%5Fassessor/. Also, see note at beginning of section.

Wilson County *Property, Taxation Records* See note at beginning of section.

Wise County *Real Estate, Grantor/Grantee, Deed, Lien, Mortgage, Divorce, Marriage Records* `Free & $$`
Search land records and vital records at www.texaslandrecords.com. Index search is free; subscription required for full data.
Property, Taxation Records `Free` Find appraisal district data free at http://208.75.248.98/. Also, search county property tax data free at www.taxnetusa.com/texas/wise/.

Wood County *Real Estate, Grantor/Grantee, Deed, Lien, Judgment Records* www.co.wood.tx.us `$$`
Access recording records at www.titlex.com; select Wood county. Registration and login required; purchase tokens in order to search.
Property, Taxation Records `Free` Search property tax records free at http://taxinfo.co.wood.tx.us/Appraisal/PublicAccess/.

Young County *Property, Taxation Records* `Free` Access to property data is free at www.youngcad.org. Click on Search Our Data.

Zapata County *Real Estate, Deed Records* `$$` Access recording office land data at www.etitlesearch.com; registration required, fee based on usage.
Property, Taxation Records `Free` Access to appraisal district records is free at
http://clientdb.trueautomation.com/clientdb/main.asp?id=28.

Other Texas Sites of Note:
Coryell County - Inmate, Sex Offender www.edoctecinc.com
Dallas County - Voter Registration www.dalcoelections.org/voters.asp Will show if registered and in what precinct.
Denton County - Jail Records, Sex Offenders, Most Wanted http://justice.dentoncounty.com
Denton County - Sex Offenders, Parolees, Jail & Bond http://sheriff.dentoncounty.com/main.asp?Dept=54&Link=515
Denton County - Voter Registration http://elections.dentoncounty.com/VRSearch/default.asp
El Paso County - Inmates www.co.el-paso.tx.us/JailSearch/fJailSearch.aspx
El Paso County - Sheriff's Warrants www.co.el-paso.tx.us/sheriff/information/FormDocs/Ops%20Due%20Diligence.pdf
Galveston County - Accident Reports, Most Wanted, Inmates www.co.galveston.tx.us/Sheriff/
Grayson County - Sex Offenders www.co.grayson.tx.us/Sheriff/SexOffenders/ShrfSex.htm This is offenders in the County lands only; it does not include cities such as Sherman.
Guadalupe County - Jail, Sheriff Bond, Judgment www.co.guadalupe.tx.us/judicialsearch/judsrch.asp
Harris County - Voter Registration www.tax.co.harris.tx.us/voter/voter.asp
Kerr County - Jail Inmate, Jail Bond http://public.co.kerr.tx.us/CaseManagement/PublicAccess/default.aspx
Lamar County - Sheriff Jail, Sheriff Bond http://68.89.102.225/
Midland County - Warrants www.co.midland.tx.us/Warrants/default.asp
Panola Copunty - Sheriff Bond, Inmate www.panolacountyjudicial.com/
Parker County - Inmates, Sheriff Bond www.parkercountytx.com
Randall County - Warrants www.randallcounty.org/sheriff/WARRANTS.HTM
Rockwall County - Sheriff Bond and Jail www.rockwallcountytexas.com/judicialsearch/
Tom Green County - Jail, Bond http://justice.co.tom-green.tx.us
Upshur County - Most Wanted www.countyofupshur.com/Most%20Wanted.htm
Upshur County - Sheriff Bond, Jail www.countyofupshur.com/judicialsearch/
Williamson County - Jail http://judicialsearch.wilco.org/SherSearch/jailfrmd.htm

Utah

Capital: Salt Lake City
          Salt Lake County
Time Zone: MST
Population: 2,645,330
# of Counties: 29

Useful State Links

Website: www.utah.gov
Governor: www.utah.gov/governor/
Attorney General: http://attorneygeneral.utah.gov
State Archives: www.archives.state.ut.us
State Statutes and Codes: http://le.utah.gov/Documents/code_const.htm
Legislative Bill Search: http://le.utah.gov/Documents/bills.htm
Bill Monitoring: http://le.utah.gov/asp/billtrack/track.asp
Unclaimed Funds: www.up.utah.gov/

Primary State Agencies

Sexual Offender Registry `Free`

Sex Offenders Registration Program, www.corrections.utah.gov The Registry may be searched from the web page. Records are searchable by name, ZIP Code, or name and ZIP Code. The information released includes photos, descriptions, addresses, vehicles, offenses, and targets. Also, requests nay be emailed to registry@utah.gov

Incarceration Records `Free`

Utah Department of Corrections, Records Bureau, www.cr.ex.state.ut.us No onilne access available through the state agency, however, a private company offers free search of inmates and offenders at https://www.vinelink.com/vinelink/siteInfoAction.do?siteId=45000 but it does not include county data from all counties. *Other Options:* Records are released in bulk on tape or CD. Call 801-545-5625 for details.

Corporation, LLC, LP, Fictitious Name, Trademarks/Servicemarks `Free & $$`

Commerce Department, Corporate Division, www.corporations.utah.gov/ A business entity/principle search service is available at www.utah.gov/services/business.html?type=citizen. Also search available names. Basic information (name, address, agent) is free. Detailed data is available for minimal fees, but registration is required. The website also offers an Unclaimed Property search page. Also, search securities professions database free at www.securities.utah.gov/search.html. *Other Options:* State allows e-mail access for orders of Certification of Existence at orders@br.state.ut.us.

Uniform Commercial Code `Free & $$`

Department of Commerce, UCC Division, http://corporations.utah.gov/ UCC uncertified records are available free online at https://secure.utah.gov/uccsearch/uccs. Search by debtor individual name or organization, or by filing number. Certified searches may also be ordered for $12.00 per search. To receive certified searches, you may be a registered user or use a credit card. The website gives details. Note for subscribers there is a $70 annual registration fee which includes 10 user logins. Email requests are accepted at orders@br.state.ut.us. *Other Options:* Records are available on CD-ROM. Suggest writing or faxing.

Vital Records `Free & $$`

Department of Health, Office of Vital Records & Statistics, http://health.utah.gov/vitalrecords/ Various indices are is found at http://historyresearch.utah.gov/indexes/index.html. Orders can be placed via a state designated vendor. Go to www.vitalchek.com. Fees are involved. *Other Options:* Search the state Cemetery and Burials database for free at http://history.utah.gov/apps/burials/execute/searchburials.

Driver Records 🔲 $$

Department of Public Safety, Driver License Division, Customer Service Section, http://driverlicense.utah.gov Driving records are available to eligible organizations through the eUtah. The system is available 24 hours daily. The fee per driving record is $9.00. There is an annual $75.00 subscription fee which includes access for 10 users. For more information, visit the website at www.utah.gov/registration/.

Vehicle, Vessel Ownership & Registration 🔲 $$

State Tax Commission, Motor Vehicle Records Section, http://dmv.utah.gov Motor Vehicle Dept. titles, liens, and registration searches are available at www.utah.gov/registration/. Registration and a $75.00 annual subscription fee is required plus $2.00 per record access. *Other Options:* Bulk requests are available for approved entities. Submit request in writing to Rick Kirkland.

Occupational Licensing Boards

Acupuncturist .... https://secure.utah.gov/llv/llv
ADRP/Arbitrator/Negotiator .... https://secure.utah.gov/llv/llv
Architect .... https://secure.utah.gov/llv/llv
Athletic Agent .... https://secure.utah.gov/llv/llv
Attorney.. www.utahbar.org/forms/members_directory_search.html
Bank .... www.dfi.utah.gov/Banks.htm
Bedding/Upholst'y Mfg/Whls/Dealer http://ag.utah.gov/licensing.html
Beekeeper.. http://ag.utah.gov/licensing.html
Brand Inspector .... http://ag.utah.gov/licensing.html
Building Inspector, Combo or Ltd..... https://secure.utah.gov/llv/llv
Burglar Alarm Firm/Agent/Temp...... https://secure.utah.gov/llv/llv
Check Cashier/Payday Lender........... www.dfi.utah.gov/ckcash.htm
Chiropractic Physician/or/Temp........ https://secure.utah.gov/llv/llv
Consumer Lender .... www.dfi.utah.gov/consumer.htm
Contractor-All .... https://secure.utah.gov/llv/llv
Control'd Substance Prec'r Dis/Prch .. https://secure.utah.gov/llv/llv
Cosmetologist/Barber .... https://secure.utah.gov/llv/llv
Cosmetology/Barber School/Instruct. https://secure.utah.gov/llv/llv
Counselor, Professional .... https://secure.utah.gov/llv/llv
Court Reporter, Shorthand/Voice ...... https://secure.utah.gov/llv/llv
CPA/Firm .... https://secure.utah.gov/llv/llv
Credit Union .... www.dfi.utah.gov/CreditUn.htm
Deception Detection Examin'r/Intern https://secure.utah.gov/llv/llv
Dental Hygienist/Local Anesthesia ... https://secure.utah.gov/llv/llv
Dentist/or/Dental Hygienist............... https://secure.utah.gov/llv/llv
Dietitian-Certified............................. https://secure.utah.gov/llv/llv
Egg & Poultry Inspector .... http://ag.utah.gov/licensing.html
Electric'n, Appren./Journey'n/Master https://secure.utah.gov/llv/llv
Electric'n, Resid'l/Journey'n/Master .. https://secure.utah.gov/llv/llv
Electrologist Instructor/School .... https://secure.utah.gov/llv/llv
Engineer, Structural Professional ...... https://secure.utah.gov/llv/llv
Engineer/Land Surveyor.................... https://secure.utah.gov/llv/llv
Enviro'l Health Scientist .... https://secure.utah.gov/llv/llv
Escrow Agent .... www.dfi.utah.gov/escrow.htm
Esthetician Master/Instructor/School. https://secure.utah.gov/llv/llv
Factory Built Housing Dealer............ https://secure.utah.gov/llv/llv
Feed.. http://ag.utah.gov/licensing.html
Food & Dairy Inspector.................... http://ag.utah.gov/licensing.html
Funeral Service Dir/Appren/Estab't .. https://secure.utah.gov/llv/llv
Genetic Counselor/Temp Counselor.. https://secure.utah.gov/llv/llv
Geologist .... https://secure.utah.gov/llv/llv
Grain & Seed..................................... http://ag.utah.gov/licensing.html
Health Facility Administrator/Temp.. https://secure.utah.gov/llv/llv
Hearing Instrument Specialist/Intern . https://secure.utah.gov/llv/llv

Holding Company .... www.dfi.utah.gov/HCSList.htm
Industrial Banks................................. www.dfi.utah.gov/industbk.htm
Insurance Agent.................................. https://secure.utah.gov/cas/search?page=index
Insurance Establishment .... https://secure.utah.gov/cas/search?page=index
Interpreter for the Deaf..................... www.aslterps.utah.gov/resources.php
Landscape Architect .... https://secure.utah.gov/llv/llv
Liquor License................................... http://javaweb.abc.state.ut.us/NASApp/orderweb/LLoginJsp.jsp
Liquor Store (Retail Liquor License). www.abc.utah.gov/license_permit/licensee_list.pdf
Lobbyist/Lobbyist Report.................. https://secure.utah.gov/lobbyist/lobbysearch
Marriage/Family Therapist .... https://secure.utah.gov/llv/llv
Massage Therapist/Apprentice .... https://secure.utah.gov/llv/llv
Meat Inspector .... http://ag.utah.gov/licensing.html
Mortgage Broker, Residential............ http://realestate.utah.gov/database/index.html
Mortgage Loan Service .... www.dfi.utah.gov/mortgage.htm
Nail Technician/Instructor/School ..... https://secure.utah.gov/llv/llv
Naturopath/ Naturopathic Physician .. https://secure.utah.gov/llv/llv
Nurse, LPN/RN/Practical .... https://secure.utah.gov/llv/llv
Nurse Midwife, Certified................... https://secure.utah.gov/llv/llv
Occupational Therapist/Assist. Temp https://secure.utah.gov/llv/llv
Optometrist/Cont'd Subst./Diagnostic https://secure.utah.gov/llv/llv
Osteo. Phys'n/Surg'n/Cont'd Subst..... https://secure.utah.gov/llv/llv
Pesticide Dealer/Applicator .... http://ag.utah.gov/licensing.html
Pharm. E -control'd substance license https://secure.utah.gov/llv/llv
Pharmac't/Intern/Tech./contr'd sub. ... https://secure.utah.gov/llv/llv
Pharmacy .... https://secure.utah.gov/llv/llv
Physical Therapist .... https://secure.utah.gov/llv/llv
Physician Assistant............................ https://secure.utah.gov/llv/llv
Physician/Surgeon, Cont'd Substance https://secure.utah.gov/llv/llv
Plumber Apprentice/Journeyman ...... https://secure.utah.gov/llv/llv
Podiatric Physic'n/Control'd Sub. ...... https://secure.utah.gov/llv/llv
Political Candidate............................. http://elections.utah.gov/candidates.html
Pre-Need Provider/Sales Agent .... https://secure.utah.gov/llv/llv
Probation Provider, Private................. https://secure.utah.gov/llv/llv
Psychologist/Resident/Temporary ..... https://secure.utah.gov/llv/llv
Radiology Technologist/or/Temp ...... https://secure.utah.gov/llv/llv
Real Estate Agent/Broker/Company .. http://realestate.utah.gov/database/index.html
Real Estate Appraiser .... http://realestate.utah.gov/database/index.html
Recreat'n'l Therapist/master/Spec'l'st https://secure.utah.gov/llv/llv
Respiratory Care Practitioner .... https://secure.utah.gov/llv/llv
Savings & Loan .... www.dfi.utah.gov/sls.htm
Security Company/Officer, Private.... https://secure.utah.gov/llv/llv
Social Worker-Certified/Clinical....... https://secure.utah.gov/llv/llv
Speech Pathologist/Audiologist......... https://secure.utah.gov/llv/llv
Substance Abuse Counselor/Temp .... https://secure.utah.gov/llv/llv
Third Party Payment Issuer .... www.dfi.utah.gov/montrans.htm
Title Lender .... www.dfi.utah.gov/titlelen.htm
Trust Company .... www.dfi.utah.gov/trslist.htm
Upholst'r/Upholstery Mfg/Whlse....... http://ag.utah.gov/licensing.html
Veterinarian/Vet Intern/cont'l sub...... https://secure.utah.gov/llv/llv
Weights & Measures .... http://ag.utah.gov/licensing.html
Wine Store.. www.alcbev.state.ut.us/Stores/wine_stores.html

State and Local Courts

State Court Structure: 41 District Courts are arranged in eight judicial districts. Branch courts in larger counties, such as Salt Lake, which were formerly Circuit Courts and now elevated to District Courts have full jurisdiction over felony as well as misdemeanor cases. Justice Courts are established by counties and municipalities and have the authority to deal with class B and C misdemeanors, violations of ordinances, small claims, and infractions committed within their territorial jurisdiction. The Justice Court shares jurisdiction with the Juvenile Court over minors 16 or 17 years old who are charged with certain traffic offenses– automobile homicide, alcohol or drug related traffic offenses, reckless driving, fleeing an officer, and driving on a suspended license are excepted. Those charges are handled through Juvenile Court.

Statewide Court Online Access: Case information from all Utah District Court locations is available online through Xchange; however, misdemeanor B's, C's, Infractions and Small Claims cases are often filed in limited jurisdiction courts and not available through this site. Fees include $25.00 registration and $30.00 per month which includes 200 searches. Each additional search is billed at $.10 per search. Information about XChange and the subscription agreement can be found at http://www.utcourts.gov/records.

One may search for Supreme Court or Appellate Courts opinions at the main website www.utcourts.gov.

> ❖ **Statewide Access Offered All Trial Courts – Read Above**
>
> **Below are Additional Sites** ❖

Salt Lake County

3rd District Court - Salt Lake Dept.   `$$`
Civil: Online access through Xchange, see www.utcourts.gov/records/. Also see state introduction. An automated court information line allows phone access to court dates, fine balances, and judgment/divorce decrees (case or citation number required) at 801-238-7830. *Criminal:* same.

Weber County

2nd District Court   `$$`
Civil: Online access through Xchange, see www.utcourts.gov/records/. Also see state introduction. Also, an automated court information line allows phone access to court dates, fine balances, and judgment/divorce decrees (case or citation number required) at 888-824-2678. *Criminal:* same.

Recorders, Assessors, and Other Sites of Note

Recording Office Organization: 29 counties, 29 recording offices. The recording officers are the County Recorder for real estate and the Clerk of District Court for state tax liens. All federal tax liens are filed with the County Recorder.

Online Access Note: A number of counties offer online access; some are fee-based.

Box Elder County   *Real Estate, Deed, Lien, Tax Roll, Plat Records*   www.boxeldercounty.org   `$$`   Access to county recordings data is available by subscription at www.boxeldercounty.org/opis.html. Monthly subscriptions and per doc payment plans available, contact Chad at 435-734-3301

Cache County   *Real Estate, Grantor/Grantee, Deed, Lien Records*   www.cachecounty.org/recorder/index.php   `$$`
Access to recording records is via subscription at www.landlight.com. Choose from 3 subscription plans; short free trial is offered. Grantor/Grantee Index goes back to 10/1980; Abstracts to 7/1984; images to 12/1992. Call 435-787-9003 for more info on access.
Property, Taxation Records   `$$`   A subscription service is available at www.landlight.com/ for assessor records.

Davis County   *Real Estate, Deed, Lien Records*   www.co.davis.ut.us   `$$`   Access to the recorder's land records database requires written registration and $15.00 per month fee plus $.10 per transaction. Records go back to 1981. For info and sign-up, contact Janet at 801-451-3347.
Property, Taxation Records   `Free`   Search property and tax data free at www.co.davis.ut.us/recorder/property_search/property_search.cfm.

Emery County *Plat, Real Estate Records* www.emerycounty.com `Free` Access plat map data by parcel ID number or location on county map free at www.emerycounty.com/recorder/needa_plat.htm

Kane County *Real Estate, Property, Lien Records* http://kane.utah.gov `Free` Access county property records free at http://eagleweb.kane.utah.gov/eaglesoftware/taxweb/search.jsp.
Property, Taxation Records `Free` Access property data free at http://eagleweb.kane.utah.gov/eaglesoftware/web/login.jsp but no name searching.

Rich County *Property, Taxation Records* `Free` Access current tax sale data at http://richcountyut.org/documents/delinquent_taxes.htm. Check main website for other record types to be added.

Salt Lake County *Real Estate, Deed, Lien, UCC, Judgment, Voter Registration Records*
http://slcorecorder.siredocs.com/rechome/main.aspx `Free & $$` Access to recording office records is by subscription; minimum $150 sign-up, $25.00 monthly, plus $.01 per screen view or image. Tax maps $1.00. Add'l info at http://recorder.slco.org or phone 801-468-3013 x2 for signup. Check an address on voter registration rolls free at https://secure.slco.org/cl/elections/index.cfm.
Property, Taxation Records `Free` Name search assessor records free at www.assessor.slco.org/cfml/Query/query2.cfm and also on the Truth-In-Tax Information website are free at www.slpropertyinfo.org but no name searching. Also, search parcel data at http://maps.slco.org/website/assessor/public_parcelviewer/viewer.htm but no name searching. Also, search property data free on the GIS-mapping site at www.assessor.slco.org/cfml/GIS.cfm but no name searching. Voter Registration at https://secure.slco.org/cl/elections/index.cfm Address required - no name searching.

Sevier County *Real Estate, Grantor/Grantee, Deed, Lien, Judgment, UCC Records* www.sevierutah.net
`Free & $$` Access to recorder's database index of data is available with free login at http://qdocs.sevierutah.net/recorder/web/login.jsp. No images available. *Property, Taxation Records* `Free & $$` Assessor data and sales included in recorder document search lookup with free login at http://qdocs.sevierutah.net/recorder/web/login.jsp.

Summit County *Real Estate, Deed, Mortgage, Lien, Judgment, UCC Records* www.co.summitcounty.org
`Free & $$` Access county doc search page free at http://property.summitcounty.org:8080/eaglesoftware/web/login.jsp?submit=Enter. For free search use username public and password public. *Property, Taxation Records* `Free & $$` Access property data free at http://property.summitcounty.org:8080/eaglesoftware/web/login.jsp?submit=Enter. For free search use username public and password public.

Tooele County *Property, Taxation Records* `Free` Access the property information database free at www.co.tooele.ut.us/taxinfo.html.

Uintah County *Real Estate, Lien, Judgment, UCC, Plat Records* www.co.uintah.ut.us `$$`
For a small subscription fee you can access public records at www.co.uintah.ut.us.
Property, Taxation Records `Free` Access assessor property data free at www.co.uintah.ut.us/recorder/ownerqueryform.php.

Utah County *Real Estate, Deed, Lien, Building Records* www.utahcountyonline.org `Free` Access to the land records database and also map searching is free at www.utahcountyonline.org/Dept/Record/LandRecordsandMaps/WebAccess.asp. Indexes go back to 1978; parcel indexes back to 1981. Document images go back to 1924. Building and GIS data is also online.
Property, Taxation Records `Free` Property and assessment data can be searched free at www.utahcountyonline.org/Dept/Record/LandRecordsandMaps/index.asp. Also, name search property data free at http://pbw.co.utah.ut.us/scripts/pbcgi70.exe/uc/u_functions/uof_namesearch. Delinquent tax list- http://pbw.co.utah.ut.us/scripts/pbcgi70.exe/ucl/u_functions/delinq_list.

Wasatch County *Real Estate, Grantor/Grantee, Deed, Marriage, Parcel Map Records*
www.co.wasatch.ut.us/d/recorder.html `Free` Access to a limited grantor/grantee index (entry#, book & page/date/KOI). Also, surveys & subdivisions www.co.wasatch.ut.us/SIRE/portal.aspx?sun=wasatch. Documents from 09/20/1993 to present are accessible. Grantor/Grantee data back to 5/20/2002.
Property, Taxation Records `Free` The county GIS Dept. plans to have "metadata" property information free at its GIS mapping site at in the future. All parcel maps by number are free at/www.co.wasatch.ut.us/plan/index.html.

Washington County *Property, Taxation Records* `Free` Search property data free via public login at http://eweb.washco.utah.gov/eaglesoftware/web/login.jsp?submit=Enter+Web+Search. Delinquent tax parcels at www.washco.state.ut.us/treasurer/delinquents.php. Access the treasurer's property tax data free at www.washco.utah.gov/treasurer/AccountQuery.php but no name searching. Search GIS free at http://maps.washco.utah.gov/imf/imf.jsp?site=washco_main and click on locate.

Weber County *Plats Records* http://www1.co.weber.ut.us/rs/recorder/index.php `Free`
Access recorder's dedicated plats data free at www.co.weber.ut.us/ded_plats.php
Property, Taxation Records `Free & $$` Property records on the County Parcel Search site are free at www.co.weber.ut.us/psearch/. Also, access Abstract Title Registrations for a monthly fee at www.co.weber.ut.us/abstract.php is being redeveloped in 2008. Multiple GIS-mapping aps avaialbe free at www.co.weber.ut.us/gis/?content=interactive.

Vermont

Capital: Montpelier
                 Washington County

Time Zone: EST

Population: 621,254

# of Counties: 14

Useful State Links

Website: http://vermont.gov/

Governor: http://governor.vermont.gov/

Attorney General: www.atg.state.vt.us

State Archives: http://vermont-archives.org

State Statutes and Codes: www.leg.state.vt.us/statutes/statutes2.htm

Legislative Bill Search: www.leg.state.vt.us/database/database2.cfm

Unclaimed Funds: www.vermonttreasurer.gov/unclaimed/

Primary State Agencies

Sexual Offender Registry `Free`

State Repository, Vermont Criminal Information Center, www.dps.state.vt.us/cjs/s_registry.htm The webpage gives access to the high-risk offenders only. The requestor must also acknowledge a statement which specifies the conditions under which the registry information is being released.

Incarceration Records `Free`

Vermont Department of Corrections, Inmate Information Request, www.doc.state.vt.us The website provides an Incarcerated Offender Locator to ascertain where an inmate is located. Click at the top of main page, or go directly to http://www1.doc.state.vt.us/offender/. The search results gives name, DOB, location and case worker. This is not designed to provide complete inmate records nor is it a database of all inmates past and present in the system.

Corporation, LLC, LLP, LP, Trade Name, Trademarks/Servicemarks `Free`

Secretary of State, Corporation Division, www.sec.state.vt.us Information on Corporate and trademark records can be accessed from the Internet for no fee. For the Corporation Name Finder, go to www.sec.state.vt.us/seek/database.htm#2. Many records, included corporation, UCC, trademark, trade name, and name look-ups are available. The Trade Name Finder is at www.sec.state.vt.us/seek/TRADSEEK.HTM. Also, search securities investment professionals free at www.bishca.info/php/BDIA/bdia01.htm. *Other Options:* There is an option on the Internet to download the entire corporation (and trade name) database.

Uniform Commercial Code `Free`

UCC Division, Secretary of State, www.sec.state.vt.us/tutor/dobiz/ucc/ucchome.htm UCC searches available free at www.sec.state.vt.us/seek/ucc_seek.htm. Search by debtor or business name. *Other Options:* The database may be downloaded from the web. The data file is in a self extracting, IBM compatible, generic dbf format. Also the last 30 days of images may be downloaded in a ZIP format.

Driver Records, Driver License Information `$$`

Department of Motor Vehicles, DI - Records Unit, www.aot.state.vt.us/dmv/dmvhp.htm Record access is available to approved requesters as a premium service from Vermont.gov. The fee is $13.00 per record; a $75.00 annual subscription fee is also required. Single inquiry and batch mode are both available. The system is open 24 hours a day, 7 days a week (except for file maintenance periods). Only the license number is needed when ordering, the system does not ask for the name and DOB. For more information about setting up an account, call Driver Improvement at 802-828-2061. To reach Vermont.gov visit www.vermont.gov or email vt_mvr@nicusa.gov. *Other Options:* This agency will sell its license file to approved requesters for non-commercial use, but customization is not available.

Vital Records Certificates [$$]

Reference & Research, Vital Records Section, www.bgs.state.vt.us/gsc/pubrec/referen/ The online Vital Records Request Service allows users to request certified copies of vital records including: birth, death, marriage, civil union, divorce, or dissolution. The fee is $10.00. Visit https://secure.vermont.gov/BGS/vitalrecords/. Use of a credit card is required.

Occupational Licensing Boards

Accounting Firm	www.sec.state.vt.us/seek/lrspseek.htm
Acupuncturist	www.sec.state.vt.us/seek/lrspseek.htm
Anesthesiologist Assistant	http://healthvermont.gov/hc/med_board/docfinder.aspx
Architect	www.sec.state.vt.us/seek/lrspseek.htm
Asbestos Contractor/Worker	http://healthvermont.gov/enviro/asbestos/documents/asbestos_list.pdf
Athletic Trainer	www.sec.state.vt.us/seek/lrspseek.htm
Attorney	www.vermontjudiciary.org/bbe/bbelibrary/publicattorneyinformation.htm
Auctioneer	www.sec.state.vt.us/seek/lrspseek.htm
Bank	www.bishca.state.vt.us/BankingDiv/banking_index.htm
Barber	www.sec.state.vt.us/seek/lrspseek.htm
Body Piercer	www.sec.state.vt.us/seek/lrspseek.htm
Boxing Professional	www.sec.state.vt.us/seek/lrspseek.htm
Chemical Suppression TQP Cert	www.dps.state.vt.us/fire/index.html
Chimney Sweep TQP Cert	www.dps.state.vt.us/fire/index.html
Chiropractor	www.sec.state.vt.us/seek/lrspseek.htm
Cosmetologist	www.sec.state.vt.us/seek/lrspseek.htm
Courier, Armed	www.sec.state.vt.us/seek/lrspseek.htm
Credit Union	www.bishca.state.vt.us/BankingDiv/banking_index.htm
Crematory	www.sec.state.vt.us/seek/lrspseek.htm
Dental Assistant/Dental Hygienist	www.sec.state.vt.us/seek/lrspseek.htm
Dentist	www.sec.state.vt.us/seek/lrspseek.htm
Dietitian	www.sec.state.vt.us/seek/lrspseek.htm
Electrician	www.dps.state.vt.us/fire/index.html
Electrologist	www.sec.state.vt.us/seek/lrspseek.htm
Elevator Inspector/Mechanic	www.dps.state.vt.us/fire/index.html
Embalmer	www.sec.state.vt.us/seek/lrspseek.htm
Engineer	www.sec.state.vt.us/seek/lrspseek.htm
Esthetician	www.sec.state.vt.us/seek/lrspseek.htm
Fire Alarm System Installer/Dealer	www.dps.state.vt.us/fire/index.html
Fire Sprinkler System Design/Install	www.dps.state.vt.us/fire/index.html
Funeral Director	www.sec.state.vt.us/seek/lrspseek.htm
Hearing Aid Dispenser	www.sec.state.vt.us/seek/lrspseek.htm
Lead Abatement Contractor/Worker	http://healthvermont.gov/enviro/asbestos/documents/lead_list.pdf
Lift Mechanic	www.dps.state.vt.us/fire/index.html
Liquor, Retail/Wholesale	www.state.vt.us/dlc/downloads.html#licensing
Lobbyist	http://vermont-elections.org/elections1/lobbyist.html
Lobbyist Employer/Firm	http://vermont-elections.org/elections1/lobbyist.html
LPG/Propane Installer	www.dps.state.vt.us/fire/index.html
Manicurist	www.sec.state.vt.us/seek/lrspseek.htm
Marriage & Family Therapist	www.sec.state.vt.us/seek/lrspseek.htm
Medical Doctor/Surgeon	http://healthvermont.gov/hc/med_board/docfinder.aspx
Mental Health Counselor, Clinical	www.sec.state.vt.us/seek/lrspseek.htm
Midwife, Licensed	www.sec.state.vt.us/seek/lrspseek.htm
Natural Gas System Installer	www.dps.state.vt.us/fire/index.html
Naturopathic Physician	www.sec.state.vt.us/seek/lrspseek.htm
Notary Public	http://vermont-archives.org/notary/notary.asp
Nurse/Nurse Practitioner/LNA	www.sec.state.vt.us/seek/lrspseek.htm
Nursing Home Administrator	www.sec.state.vt.us/seek/lrspseek.htm
Occupational Therapist	www.sec.state.vt.us/seek/lrspseek.htm

Oil Burning Equipment Installer .... www.dps.state.vt.us/fire/index.html
Optician .... www.sec.state.vt.us/seek/lrspseek.htm
Optometrist .... www.sec.state.vt.us/seek/lrspseek.htm
Osteopathic Physician .... www.sec.state.vt.us/seek/lrspseek.htm
Pesticide Applicator .... www.vermontagriculture.com/pest.htm
Pharmacist/Pharmacy .... www.sec.state.vt.us/seek/lrspseek.htm
Physical Therapist/Assistant .... www.sec.state.vt.us/seek/lrspseek.htm
Physician, Assistant .... http://healthvermont.gov/hc/med_board/docfinder.aspx
Plumber .... www.dps.state.vt.us/fire/licensing/plicenses.htm
Podiatrist .... http://healthvermont.gov/hc/med_board/docfinder.aspx
Private Investigator .... www.sec.state.vt.us/seek/lrspseek.htm
Psychoanalyst .... www.sec.state.vt.us/seek/lrspseek.htm
Psychologist/Psychotherapist .... www.sec.state.vt.us/seek/lrspseek.htm
Radiation Tech .... www.sec.state.vt.us/seek/lrspseek.htm
Real Estate Agent/Broker/Sales .... www.sec.state.vt.us/seek/lrspseek.htm
Real Estate Appraiser .... www.sec.state.vt.us/seek/lrspseek.htm
Respiratory Therapy .... www.sec.state.vt.us/seek/lrspseek.htm
Security Guard .... www.sec.state.vt.us/seek/lrspseek.htm
Social Worker .... www.sec.state.vt.us/seek/lrspseek.htm
Tattooist .... www.sec.state.vt.us/seek/lrspseek.htm
Teacher .... http://education.vermont.gov/new/html/licensing/disciplinary.html
Veterinarian .... www.sec.state.vt.us/seek/lrspseek.htm
Waste Water Treatm't Plant Oper'r ... www.anr.state.vt.us/dec/ww/opcert/WW_Operator_List.pdf

State and Local Courts

State Court Structure: The Superior Court hears predominantly civil, tort, real estate, and small claims cases. On rare occasion it hears criminal cases, but the District Court hears predominantly criminal cases. Specialty courts include Probate Courts Family Courts. In Vermont, the Judicial Bureau has jurisdiction over traffic, municipal ordinances, and Fish and Game violations, minors in possession, and hazing.

Statewide Court Online Access: Vermont Courts Online provides access to civil and small claim cases and court calendar information from 12 of the county Superior Courts. Access is not offered for Chittenden and Franklin. Go to https://secure.vermont.gov/vtcdas/user. Records are in real-time mode. There is a $12.50 activation fee plus a fee of $.50 per case for look-up after the 1st 5 cases.

Supreme Court opinions are available from the main website and are also maintained by the Vermont Department of Libraries at http://dol.state.vt.us.

Addison County
Bennington County
Caledonia County
Superior Court   Free & $$
Civil: Access civil and small claims case records by web subscription, $12.50 activation plus $.50 per page; registration info at https://secure.vermont.gov/vtcdas/user. Also, click on Calendars by Date and County to view calendars free.

Essex County
District & Superior Court   www.vermontjudiciary.org
Civil: Access case records by internet subscription, $12.50 activation plus $.50 per page; registration info at https://secure.vermont.gov/vtcdas/user. Also, click on Calendars by Date and County to view calendars free. *Criminal:* Click on Calendars by Date and County at https://secure.vermont.gov/vtcdas/user.

Grand Isle County
District & Superior Court   www.vermontjudiciary.org
Civil: Access case records by internet subscription, $12.50 activation plus $.50 per page; registration info at https://secure.vermont.gov/vtcdas/user. Also, click on Calendars by Date and County to view calendars free. *Criminal:* Click on Calendars by Date and County at https://secure.vermont.gov/vtcdas/user.

Lamoille County

Superior Court   Free & $$

Civil: Access civil and small claims case records by web subscription, $12.50 activation plus $.50 per page; registration info at https://secure.vermont.gov/vtcdas/user. Also, click on Calendars by Date and County to view calendars free.

Orange County

District & Superior Court   www.vermontjudiciary.org   Free & $$

Civil: Access case records by internet subscription, $12.50 activation plus $.50 per page; registration info at https://secure.vermont.gov/vtcdas/user. Also, click on Calendars by Date and County to view calendars free. *Criminal:* Click on Calendars by Date and County at https://secure.vermont.gov/vtcdas/user.

Orleans County
Rutland County
Washington County
Windham County
Windsor County

Superior Court   Free & $$

Civil: Access civil and small claims case records by web subscription, $12.50 activation plus $.50 per page; registration info at https://secure.vermont.gov/vtcdas/user. Also, click on Calendars by Date and County to view calendars free.

Recorders, Assessors, and Other Sites of Note

Recording Office Organization: Vermont has 14 counties and 246 towns/cities which have 246 recording offices. There is **no county recording** in this state. All recording is done at the city/town level. Many towns are so small that their mailing addresses are in different towns. 4 towns had the same names as cities - Barre, Newport, Rutland, and St. Albans. 11 cities or towns bear the same name as a Vermont county - Addison, Bennington, Chittenden, Essex, Franklin, Grand Isle, Orange, Rutland, Washington, Windham, and Windsor. All federal and state tax liens on personal property and on real property are filed with the Town/City Clerk in the lien/attachment book and indexed in real estate records.

Online Access Note: There is limited online access to county recorded documents, and a growing number of towns have contracted out online services, usually offering property assessment records or property cards.

Bennington Town   *Property, Taxation Records*   Free   Access to the Grand List search program is free at www.bennington.com/government/grandlist/index.html. No name searching at this time; site is under construction and data is incomplete.

Bridgewater Town   *Property, Taxation Records*   Free   Access assessor property data free at http://data.visionappraisal.com/BridgewaterCT/DEFAULT.asp.

Burlington City   *Property, Taxation Records*   Free   Access to city property tax data is free at http://ci.burlingtontelecom.com/assessor/search/.

Hartford Town   *Property, Taxation Records*   Free   Access assessor property data free at http://data.visionappraisal.com/hartfordvt/DEFAULT.asp.

Newport City   *Property, Taxation Records*   Free   Access to Newport City assessor data is free at http://data.visionappraisal.com/newportvt/.

Newport Town   *Property, Taxation Records*   Free   Search assessor records at http://data.visionappraisal.com/newportvt/.

Stratton Town   *Property, Taxation Records*   Free   Access assessor property data free at http://data.visionappraisal.com/strattonvt/search.asp

Wilmington Town   *Property, Taxation Records*   Free   The Grand List is available as a pdf in the Documents section of the main website www.wilmingtonvermont.us/.

Woodstock Town   *Property, Taxation Records*   Free   Access to the Lister's Grand Lists and Sales List is available free at www.townofwoodstock.org/listers/index.html.

Virginia

Capital: Richmond
                Richmond City County
Time Zone: EST
Population: 7,712,091
# of Counties: 95

Useful State Links

Website: http://www.virginia.gov/cmsportal3/
Governor: www.governor.virginia.gov
Attorney General: www.oag.state.va.us
State Archives: www.lva.lib.va.us
State Statutes and Codes: http://leg1.state.va.us/000/src.htm
Legislative Bill Search: http://leg1.state.va.us/051/bil.htm
Bill Monitoring: http://legis.state.va.us/SiteInformation/SubscriptionServices.htm
Unclaimed Funds: https://www.trs.virginia.gov/propertysearchdotnet/

Primary State Agencies

Criminal Records `$$`

Virginia State Police, CCRE, www.vsp.state.va.us Certain entities, including screening companies, are can apply for online access via the NCJI System. The system is ONLY available to IN-STATE accounts and allows you to submit requests faster. Fees are same as manual submission-$15.00 per record or $20.00 SOR record search. Username and password required. There is a minimum usage requirement of 10 requests per month. Turnaround time is 24-72 hours.

Sexual Offender Registry `Free`

Virginia State Police - Criminal records, Sex Offender and Crimes Against Minors Registry, http://sex-offender.vsp.virginia.gov/sor/index.htm Search by name, city, county or ZIP Code, or from a map at http://sex-offender.vsp.virginia.gov/sor/html/search.htm.

Incarceration Records `Free`

Virginia Department of Corrections, Records Unit, www.vadoc.state.va.us Visit http://www2.vipnet.org/cgi-bin/vadoc/doc.cgi for an Inmate Status/Locator to ascertain where an inmate is located. This is not designed to provide complete inmate records nor is it a database of all inmates past and present in the system. A DOC wanted/fugitives list is found at www.vadoc.virginia.gov/offenders/wanted/fugitive.shtm.

Corporation, LLC, LP, Fictitious Name, Business Trust Records `Free`

State Corporation Commission, Clerks Office, www.scc.virginia.gov/clk/bussrch.aspx An business entity search is at www.scc.virginia.gov/clk/bussrch.aspx. The Docket Search is available for the status of any case, public filings (by date or by company), the Commission's case calendar, and selected public documents associated with cases before the Commission. Visit http://docket.scc.virginia.gov:8080/vaprod/main.asp. Images of business entity documents are not currently available for electronic or online viewing, except for Corporate Annual Reports. Also, search securities companies, agents, and franchises registered with the state at www.scc.virginia.gov/srf/index.aspx. *Other Options:* The database is available for bulk purchase. Call for details.

Trademarks, Service Marks `Free`

State Corporation Commission, Virginia Securities Division, www.scc.virginia.gov/srf/bus/tmsm.aspx Searching Trademarks and Service Marks are available at www.scc.virginia.gov/srf/bus/tmsm.aspx.

Uniform Commercial Code, Federal Tax Liens `Free`

UCC Division, State Corporation Commission, www.scc.virginia.gov/clk/uccsrch.aspx Their system is called Clerk's Information System (CIS) and is available free at www.scc.virginia.gov/clk/uccsrch.aspx. Images of UCC filings and tax liens are not available for electronic or online viewing. Collateral information is not available in CIS but can be obtained if a search is ordered and the associated fee paid.

Driver Records $$

Department of Motor Vehicles, Customer Records Work Center, www.dmv.state.va.us Online service is provided by the Virginia Interactive. Online reports are provided via the Internet on an interactive basis 24 hours daily. There is a $95 annual administrative fee and records are $7.00 each. Go to www.virginiainteractive.org/cmsportal2/ for more information (search "online services") or call 804-786-4718. *Other Options:* The agency offers several monitoring programs for employers. Call 804-497-7155 for details.

Vehicle Ownership & Registration $$

Department of Motor Vehicles, Vehicle Records Work Center, www.dmv.state.va.us The online system, managed by the Virginia Interactive, open 24 hours daily. There is an annual $95.00 administration fee and records are $7.00 each. All accounts must be approved by both the DMV and Virginia Interactive. Call 804-786-4718 to request an information use agreement application. The URL is www.virginiainteractive.org/cmsportal2/ Also, a $12.00 vehicle verification search is for prospective vehicle buyers is available at https://www.dmv.virginia.gov/dmvnet/ppi/intro.asp. *Other Options:* Bulk release of vehicle or ownership information is not available except for statistical and vehicle recall purposes.

Vessel Ownership & Registration $$

Game & Inland Fisheries Dept, Boat Registration Dept, www.dgif.virginia.gov The VA boat registration database may be searched on the web at www.virginiainteractive.org/cmsportal2/. There are two options, one for commercial use, and for non-commercial use. Both require a subscription, which is $95.00 a year and record fees are incurred. Additional services are provided. *Other Options:* CDs with data can be sold to approved requesters.

Voter Registration Free

State Board of Elections, www.sbe.virginia.gov/cms/ One may verify registration status at www.sbe.virginia.gov/cms/Voter_Information/Index.html.

Occupational Licensing Boards

Acupuncturist .... http://www2.vipnet.org/dhp/cgi-bin/search_publicdb.cgi
Alcoholic Beverage Distributor .... www.abc.virginia.gov/licenseeSearch/jsp/controller.jsp
Architect .... www.dpor.virginia.gov/regulantlookup/selection_input.cfm
Asbestos-related Occupation .... www.dpor.virginia.gov/regulantlookup/selection_input.cfm
Athletic Trainer .... http://www2.vipnet.org/dhp/cgi-bin/search_publicdb.cgi
Attorney/Attorney Assoc .... www.vsb.org/attorney/attSearch.asp?S=D
Auctioneer/Auction Firm .... www.dpor.virginia.gov/regulantlookup/selection_input.cfm
Audiologist .... http://www2.vipnet.org/dhp/cgi-bin/search_publicdb.cgi
Bank .... www.scc.virginia.gov/bfi/index.aspx
Barber/Barber School/Business .... www.dpor.virginia.gov/regulantlookup/selection_input.cfm
Boxer .... www.dpor.virginia.gov/regulantlookup/selection_input.cfm
Boxing/Wresting Occupation .... www.dpor.virginia.gov/regulantlookup/selection_input.cfm
Carpenter .... www.dpor.virginia.gov/regulantlookup/selection_input.cfm
Cemetery Company/Seller .... www.dpor.virginia.gov/regulantlookup/selection_input.cfm
Check Casher .... www.scc.virginia.gov/bfi/index.aspx
Chiropractor .... http://www2.vipnet.org/dhp/cgi-bin/search_publicdb.cgi
Clinical Nurse Specialist .... http://www2.vipnet.org/dhp/cgi-bin/search_publicdb.cgi
Contractor .... www.dpor.virginia.gov/regulantlookup/selection_input.cfm
Cosmetic Procedure Certification ...... http://www2.vipnet.org/dhp/cgi-bin/search_publicdb.cgi
Cosmetologist/Cosmo School/Firm ... www.dpor.virginia.gov/regulantlookup/selection_input.cfm
Counselor, Professional .... http://www2.vipnet.org/dhp/cgi-bin/search_publicdb.cgi
Crematory .... http://www2.vipnet.org/dhp/cgi-bin/search_publicdb.cgi
Dental Hygienist .... http://www2.vipnet.org/dhp/cgi-bin/search_publicdb.cgi
Dentist .... http://www2.vipnet.org/dhp/cgi-bin/search_publicdb.cgi
Embalmer .... http://www2.vipnet.org/dhp/cgi-bin/search_publicdb.cgi
Engineer .... www.dpor.virginia.gov/regulantlookup/selection_input.cfm
Fair Housing .... www.dpor.virginia.gov/regulantlookup/selection_input.cfm
Funeral Director/Establ./Trainee .... http://www2.vipnet.org/dhp/cgi-bin/search_publicdb.cgi
Funeral Service Provider .... http://www2.vipnet.org/dhp/cgi-bin/search_publicdb.cgi
Gas Fitter .... www.dpor.virginia.gov/regulantlookup/selection_input.cfm
Geologist .... www.dpor.virginia.gov/regulantlookup/selection_input.cfm

Hair Braider..www.dpor.virginia.gov/regulantlookup/selection_input.cfm
Hearing Aid Specialist.......................www.dpor.virginia.gov/regulantlookup/selection_input.cfm
Home Inspector ....www.dpor.virginia.gov/regulantlookup/selection_input.cfm
Humane Society ....http://www2.vipnet.org/dhp/cgi-bin/search_publicdb.cgi
Interior Designer...............................www.dpor.virginia.gov/regulantlookup/selection_input.cfm
Investment Advisor/Advisor Agency www.scc.virginia.gov/srf/index.aspx
Landscape Architect ....www.dpor.virginia.gov/regulantlookup/selection_input.cfm
Lead-Related Occupation ....www.dpor.virginia.gov/regulantlookup/selection_input.cfm
Lobbyist...http://secure01.virginiainteractive.org/lobbyist/cgi-bin/search_lobbyist.cgi
Marriage & Family Therapist ....http://www2.vipnet.org/dhp/cgi-bin/search_publicdb.cgi
Massage Therapist ....http://www2.vipnet.org/dhp/cgi-bin/search_publicdb.cgi
Medical Doctor..................................http://www2.vipnet.org/dhp/cgi-bin/search_publicdb.cgi
Medical Equipment Supplier ....http://www2.vipnet.org/dhp/cgi-bin/search_publicdb.cgi
Medical Wholesaler/Mfg...................http://www2.vipnet.org/dhp/cgi-bin/search_publicdb.cgi
Money Transmitter ....www.scc.virginia.gov/bfi/index.aspx
Mortgage Lender/Broker ....www.scc.virginia.gov/bfi/index.aspx
Nail Technician ....www.dpor.virginia.gov/regulantlookup/selection_input.cfm
Nurse-LPN-RN-Nurses' Aide ....http://www2.vipnet.org/dhp/cgi-bin/search_publicdb.cgi
Nursing Home Admin'r/Preceptor.....http://www2.vipnet.org/dhp/cgi-bin/search_publicdb.cgi
Occupational Therapist......................http://www2.vipnet.org/dhp/cgi-bin/search_publicdb.cgi
Optician ....www.dpor.virginia.gov/regulantlookup/selection_input.cfm
Optometrist..http://www2.vipnet.org/dhp/cgi-bin/search_publicdb.cgi
Oral/Maxillofacial Surgeon ....http://www2.vipnet.org/dhp/cgi-bin/search_publicdb.cgi
Osteopathic Physician.......................http://www2.vipnet.org/dhp/cgi-bin/search_publicdb.cgi
Payday Lender...................................www.scc.virginia.gov/bfi/index.aspx
Pharmacist/Pharmacy ....http://www2.vipnet.org/dhp/cgi-bin/search_publicdb.cgi
Physical Therapist ....http://www2.vipnet.org/dhp/cgi-bin/search_publicdb.cgi
Physician/or/ Physician Assistant ......http://www2.vipnet.org/dhp/cgi-bin/search_publicdb.cgi
Pilot, Branch.....................................www.dpor.virginia.gov/regulantlookup/selection_input.cfm
Podiatrist...http://www2.vipnet.org/dhp/cgi-bin/search_publicdb.cgi
Polygraph Examiner ....www.dpor.virginia.gov/regulantlookup/selection_input.cfm
Prescriptive Authorization.................http://www2.vipnet.org/dhp/cgi-bin/search_publicdb.cgi
Property Association ....www.dpor.virginia.gov/regulantlookup/selection_input.cfm
Psychologist at School.......................http://www2.vipnet.org/dhp/cgi-bin/search_publicdb.cgi
Psychologist, Clinical/Applied ....http://www2.vipnet.org/dhp/cgi-bin/search_publicdb.cgi
Psychology School ....http://www2.vipnet.org/dhp/cgi-bin/search_publicdb.cgi
Radiologic Technologist-limited ....http://www2.vipnet.org/dhp/cgi-bin/search_publicdb.cgi
Real Estate Agent/Business/School ...www.dpor.virginia.gov/regulantlookup/selection_input.cfm
Real Estate Appraiser/Appra'r Firm ..www.dpor.virginia.gov/regulantlookup/selection_input.cfm
Rehabilitation Provider......................http://www2.vipnet.org/dhp/cgi-bin/search_publicdb.cgi
Respiratory Care Practitioner ....http://www2.vipnet.org/dhp/cgi-bin/search_publicdb.cgi
Savings Institution ....www.scc.virginia.gov/bfi/index.aspx
School Library Media Specialist........https://p1pe.doe.virginia.gov/tinfo/
School Principal/Superin./Counselor. https://p1pe.doe.virginia.gov/tinfo/
Securities Broker/Dealer/Agent.........www.scc.virginia.gov/srf/index.aspx
Social Worker, Clinical/Registered ...http://www2.vipnet.org/dhp/cgi-bin/search_publicdb.cgi
Soil Scientist.....................................www.dpor.virginia.gov/regulantlookup/selection_input.cfm
Speech Pathologist/Audiologist.........http://www2.vipnet.org/dhp/cgi-bin/search_publicdb.cgi
Substance Abuse Treatm't/Counsel'r. http://www2.vipnet.org/dhp/cgi-bin/search_publicdb.cgi
Surveyor, Land ....www.dpor.virginia.gov/regulantlookup/selection_input.cfm
Tattoo Artist/Body Piercing...............www.dpor.virginia.gov/regulantlookup/selection_input.cfm
Teacher..https://p1pe.doe.virginia.gov/tinfo/
Tradesman ....www.dpor.virginia.gov/regulantlookup/selection_input.cfm
University Limited Medical License .http://www2.vipnet.org/dhp/cgi-bin/search_publicdb.cgi
Veterinarian/Veterinary Technician ..http://www2.vipnet.org/dhp/cgi-bin/search_publicdb.cgi
Warehouser, Medical.........................http://www2.vipnet.org/dhp/cgi-bin/search_publicdb.cgi
Waste Managem't Facility Operator..www.dpor.virginia.gov/regulantlookup/selection_input.cfm

Waste Water Plant Operator .... www.dpor.virginia.gov/regulantlookup/selection_input.cfm
Wax Technician................................ www.dpor.virginia.gov/regulantlookup/selection_input.cfm
Wetlands Delineator .... www.dpor.virginia.gov/regulantlookup/selection_input.cfm
Wrestler .... www.dpor.virginia.gov/regulantlookup/selection_input.cfm

State and Local Courts

State Court Structure: The Circuit Courts in 31 districts are the courts of general jurisdiction. There are 132 District Courts of limited jurisdiction. Please note that a district can comprise a county or a city. The General District Court decides all criminal offenses involving ordinances laws, and by-laws of the county or city where it is located and all misdemeanors under state law. A misdemeanor is any charge that carries a penalty of no more than one year in jail or a fine of up to $2,500, or both.

Records of civil action from $4,500 to $15,000 can be at either the Circuit Court or District Court as either can have jurisdiction. It is necessary to check both record locations as there is no concurrent database nor index.

Statewide Court Online Access: There are 3 available systems. Each county must be searched separately. Cases from 132 General District Courts at www.courts.state.va.us/courts/gd.html may be searched free at http://epwsgdp1.courts.state.va.us/gdcourts/caseSearch.do?index=index. You can search records from over 120 Circuit courts at www.courts.state.va.us/courts/circuit.html. These 2 online systems usually include partial DOBs in criminal results, and civil results sometimes include addresses. Also, a dial-up access system known as LOPAS (Law Office & Public Access System) is available free with District and Circuit Ct records. Results include full name and address. Call Marguerite Steele, 804-786-6455 for LOPAS details. Also, the web page www.courts.state.va.us offers access to Supreme Court and Appellate opinions.

Accomack County

2nd Circuit Court   www.courts.state.va.us/courts/circuit.html   **Free**
Civil: Search free at www.courts.state.va.us/caseinfo/circuit.html. Also, remote online access to court case indexes via ILS (Int'l Land Systems) call 877-658-6018 to apply. *Criminal:* same.

2A General District Court   **Free**
Civil: Search free at http://epwsgdp1.courts.state.va.us/gdcourts/caseSearch.do?index=index. Results show name and sometimes address. Also search via LOPAS; call 804-786-5511 to apply. *Criminal:* Search free at http://epwsgdp1.courts.state.va.us/gdcourts/caseSearch.do?index=index. Results show DOB month and day, sex, race.

Albemarle County

16th Circuit & District Court   www.courts.state.va.us/courts/circuit.html   **Free**
Civil: Select and search Circuit Courts online at www.courts.state.va.us/caseinfo/circuit.html. Search District courts at http://epwsgdp1.courts.state.va.us/gdcourts/caseSearch.do?index=index. Results show name and sometimes address. Also search via LOPAS; call 804-786-5511 to apply. *Criminal:* Search Circuit Ct free at www.courts.state.va.us/caseinfo/circuit.html. Also, search District Ct only free at http://epwsgdp1.courts.state.va.us/gdcourts/caseSearch.do?index=index. Results show DOB month and day, sex, race. Remote online access to court case indexes via LOPAS; call 804-786-5511 to apply.

Alexandria City

18th General District Court   **Free**
Civil: Search free at http://epwsgdp1.courts.state.va.us/gdcourts/caseSearch.do?index=index. Results show name and sometimes address. *Criminal:* Search free at http://epwsgdp1.courts.state.va.us/gdcourts/caseSearch.do?index=index. Results show DOB month and day, sex, race.

Alleghany County

25th Circuit Court   **Free**
Civil: Search free at http://wasdmz1.courts.state.va.us/CJISWeb/circuit.html. *Criminal:* same.

25th General District Court   **Free**
Civil: Search free at http://epwsgdp1.courts.state.va.us/gdcourts/caseSearch.do?index=index. Results show name and sometimes address. Also search via LOPAS; call 804-786-5511 to apply. *Criminal:* Search free at http://epwsgdp1.courts.state.va.us/gdcourts/caseSearch.do?index=index. Results show DOB month and day, sex, race.

Amelia County

11th Circuit Court   **Free**
Search civil and criminal free at www.courts.state.va.us/caseinfo/circuit.html. Also search via LOPAS; call 804-786-5511 to apply.

11th General District Court   Free
Civil: Search free at http://epwsgdp1.courts.state.va.us/gdcourts/caseSearch.do?index=index. Results show name and sometimes address. Also search via LOPAS; call 804-786-5511 to apply. *Criminal:* Search free at http://epwsgdp1.courts.state.va.us/gdcourts/caseSearch.do?index=index. Results show DOB month and day, sex, race.

Amherst County
24th Circuit Court   www.courts.state.va.us/courts/circuit.html   Free
Civil: Access court records free at www.courts.state.va.us/caseinfo/circuit.html. Also, remote online access to court case indexes may also be via LOPAS; call 804-786-5511 to apply. *Criminal:* Access to criminal court records is same as civil, see above.

24th General District Court   Free
Civil: Search free at http://epwsgdp1.courts.state.va.us/gdcourts/caseSearch.do?index=index. Results show name and sometimes address. Also search via LOPAS; call 804-786-5511 to apply. *Criminal:* Search free at http://epwsgdp1.courts.state.va.us/gdcourts/caseSearch.do?index=index. Results show DOB month and day, sex, race.

Appomattox County
10th Circuit Court   www.courts.state.va.us/courts/circuit.html   Free
Search civil and criminal free at www.courts.state.va.us/caseinfo/circuit.html. Also search via LOPAS; call 804-786-5511 to apply.

10th General District Court   Free
Civil: Search free at http://epwsgdp1.courts.state.va.us/gdcourts/caseSearch.do?index=index. Results show name and sometimes address. Also search via LOPAS; call 804-786-5511 to apply. *Criminal:* Search free at http://epwsgdp1.courts.state.va.us/gdcourts/caseSearch.do?index=index. Results show DOB month and day, sex, race.

Arlington County
17th Circuit Court   www.courts.state.va.us/courts/circuit.html   Free
Civil: Online access free at www.courts.state.va.us/caseinfo/circuit.html. *Criminal:* Same.

17th General District Court   Free
Civil: Search free at http://epwsgdp1.courts.state.va.us/gdcourts/caseSearch.do?index=index. Results show name and sometimes address. Also search via LOPAS; call 804-786-5511 to apply. *Criminal:* Search free at http://epwsgdp1.courts.state.va.us/gdcourts/caseSearch.do?index=index. Results show DOB month and day, sex, race.

Augusta County
25th Circuit Court   www.courts.state.va.us/courts/circuit.html   Free
Civil: Online access free at www.courts.state.va.us/caseinfo/circuit.html. *Criminal:* Same.

25th General District Court   www.courts.state.va.us/courts/gd/Augusta/home.html   Free
Civil: Search online free at http://epwsgdp1.courts.state.va.us/gdcourts/caseSearch.do?index=index. Results show name and sometimes address. *Criminal:* Search free at http://epwsgdp1.courts.state.va.us/gdcourts/caseSearch.do?index=index. Results show DOB month and day, sex, race.

Bath County
25th General District Court   Free
Civil: Search free at http://epwsgdp1.courts.state.va.us/gdcourts/caseSearch.do?index=index. Results show name and sometimes address. Also search via LOPAS; call 804-786-5511 to apply. *Criminal:* Search free at http://epwsgdp1.courts.state.va.us/gdcourts/caseSearch.do?index=index. Results show DOB month and day, sex, race.

Bedford County
County Circuit Court   www.courts.state.va.us/courts/circuit.html   Free
Civil: Online access at www.courts.state.va.us/caseinfo/circuit.html. *Criminal:* Remote online access to court case indexes via LOPAS; call 804-786-5511 to apply.

24th General District Court   Free
Civil: Search free at http://epwsgdp1.courts.state.va.us/gdcourts/caseSearch.do?index=index. Results show name and sometimes address. Also search via LOPAS; call 804-786-5511 to apply. *Criminal:* Search free at http://epwsgdp1.courts.state.va.us/gdcourts/caseSearch.do?index=index. Results show DOB month and day, sex, race.

Bland County
27th Circuit Court   www.courts.state.va.us/courts/circuit.html   Free
Search civil and criminal free at www.courts.state.va.us/caseinfo/circuit.html. Also search via LOPAS; call 804-786-5511 to apply.

27th General District Court   www.bland.org/government/generaldistrictcourt.html   Free
Civil: Search free at http://epwsgdp1.courts.state.va.us/gdcourts/caseSearch.do?index=index. Results show name and sometimes address. Also search via LOPAS; call 804-786-5511 to apply. *Criminal:* Search free at http://epwsgdp1.courts.state.va.us/gdcourts/caseSearch.do?index=index. Results show DOB month and day, sex, race.

Botetourt County

25th Circuit Court   www.courts.state.va.us/courts/circuit/Botetourt/home.html   `Free`
Search civil and criminal free at www.courts.state.va.us/caseinfo/circuit.html. Also search via LOPAS; call 804-786-5511 to apply.

25th General District Court   `Free`
Civil: Search free at http://epwsgdp1.courts.state.va.us/gdcourts/caseSearch.do?index=index. Results show name and sometimes address. Also search via LOPAS; call 804-786-5511 to apply. *Criminal:* Search free at http://epwsgdp1.courts.state.va.us/gdcourts/caseSearch.do?index=index. Results show DOB month and day, sex, race.

Bristol City

28th Circuit Court   www.courts.state.va.us/courts/circuit.html   `Free`
Civil: Search index free at www.courts.state.va.us/caseinfo/circuit.html. Also search via LOPAS; call 804-786-5511 to apply.
Criminal: Online access to criminal records index is the same as civil.

28th General District Court   www.courts.state.va.us/courts/circuit/Bristol/home.html   `Free`
Civil: Search free at http://epwsgdp1.courts.state.va.us/gdcourts/caseSearch.do?index=index. Results show name and sometimes address. Also search via LOPAS; call 804-786-5511 to apply. *Criminal:* Search free at http://epwsgdp1.courts.state.va.us/gdcourts/caseSearch.do?index=index. Results show DOB month and day, sex, race.

Brunswick County

6th Circuit Court   www.courts.state.va.us/courts/circuit.html   `Free`
Civil: Search free at www.courts.state.va.us/caseinfo/circuit.html. Also search via LOPAS; call 804-786-5511 to apply. Also access record images via http://208.210.219.102/cgi-bin/p/rms.cgi; registration and password required. *Criminal:* Same.

6th General District Court   www.courts.state.va.us/courts/combined/Brunswick/home.html   `Free`
Civil: Search free at http://epwsgdp1.courts.state.va.us/gdcourts/caseSearch.do?index=index. Results show name and sometimes address. Also search via LOPAS; call 804-786-5511 to apply. *Criminal:* Search free at http://epwsgdp1.courts.state.va.us/gdcourts/caseSearch.do?index=index. Results show DOB month and day, sex, race.

Buchanan County

29th Circuit Court   www.courts.state.va.us/courts/circuit.html   `Free`
Civil: Search free at http://wasdmz1.courts.state.va.us/CJISWeb/MainMenu.do. Also, remote online access to court case indexes is via LOPAS; call 804-786-5511 to apply. *Criminal:* same.

29th General District Court   `Free`
Civil: Search free at http://epwsgdp1.courts.state.va.us/gdcourts/caseSearch.do?index=index. Results show name and sometimes address. Also search via LOPAS; call 804-786-5511 to apply. *Criminal:* Search free at http://epwsgdp1.courts.state.va.us/gdcourts/caseSearch.do?index=index. Results show DOB month and day, sex, race. Also search via LOPAS; call 804-786-5511 to apply.

Buckingham County

10th Circuit Court   www.courts.state.va.us/courts/circuit.html   `Free`
Civil: Remote online access to court case indexes is via LOPAS; call 804-786-5511 to apply. *Criminal:* Remote online access to court case indexes via LOPAS; call 804-786-5511 to apply.

Buckingham General District Court   `Free`
Civil: Search free at http://epwsgdp1.courts.state.va.us/gdcourts/caseSearch.do?index=index. Results show name and sometimes address. Also search via LOPAS; call 804-786-5511 to apply. *Criminal:* Search free at http://epwsgdp1.courts.state.va.us/gdcourts/caseSearch.do?index=index. Results show DOB month and day, sex, race.

Buena Vista City

25th Circuit & District Court   www.courts.state.va.us/courts/circuit.html   `Free`
Civil: Select and search Circuit Courts online at www.courts.state.va.us/caseinfo/circuit.html. Search District courts at http://epwsgdp1.courts.state.va.us/gdcourts/caseSearch.do?index=index. Results show name and sometimes address. Also search via LOPAS; call 804-786-5511 to apply. *Criminal:* Select and search Circuit Courts online at www.courts.state.va.us/caseinfo/circuit.html. Search district Ct free at http://epwsgdp1.courts.state.va.us/gdcourts/caseSearch.do?index=index. Results show DOB month and day, sex, race.

Campbell County

24th Circuit Court   www.courts.state.va.us/courts/circuit.html   `Free`
Civil: Remote online access to court case indexes is via LOPAS; call 804-786-5511 to apply. *Criminal:* Remote online access to court case indexes via LOPAS; call 804-786-5511 to apply.

24th General District Court   www.courts.state.va.us/courts/gd/Campbell/home.html   `Free`
Civil: Search free at http://epwsgdp1.courts.state.va.us/gdcourts/caseSearch.do?index=index. Results show name and sometimes address. Also search via LOPAS; call 804-786-5511 to apply. *Criminal:* Search free at http://epwsgdp1.courts.state.va.us/gdcourts/caseSearch.do?index=index. Results show DOB month and day, sex, race.

Caroline County
15th Circuit Court   www.courts.state.va.us/courts/circuit.html   `Free`
Civil: Access circuit court records free at http://wasdmz2.courts.state.va.us/CJISWeb/circuit.html and select Caroline. Also, remote online access to court case indexes is via LOPAS; call 804-786-5511 to apply. *Criminal:* Access circuit court records free at http://wasdmz2.courts.state.va.us/CJISWeb/circuit.html and select Caroline. Also, Remote online access to court case indexes via LOPAS; call 804-786-5511 to apply.

15th General District Court   `Free`
Civil: Search free at http://epwsgdp1.courts.state.va.us/gdcourts/caseSearch.do?index=index. Results show name and sometimes address. Also search via LOPAS; call 804-786-5511 to apply. *Criminal:* Search free at http://epwsgdp1.courts.state.va.us/gdcourts/caseSearch.do?index=index. Results show DOB month and day, sex, race.

Carroll County
27th Circuit Court   www.courts.state.va.us/courts/circuit.html   `Free`
Civil: Search free at www.courts.state.va.us/caseinfo/circuit.html. *Criminal:* Same.

Carroll Combined District Court   `Free`
Civil: Search free at http://epwsgdp1.courts.state.va.us/gdcourts/caseSearch.do?index=index. Results show name and sometimes address. Also search via LOPAS; call 804-786-5511 to apply. *Criminal:* Search free at http://epwsgdp1.courts.state.va.us/gdcourts/caseSearch.do?index=index. Results show DOB month and day, sex, race.

Charles City County
9th Circuit Court   www.courts.state.va.us/courts/circuit.html   `Free`
Search civil and criminal free at www.courts.state.va.us/caseinfo/circuit.html. Also search via LOPAS; call 804-786-5511 to apply.

9th General District Court   www.courts.state.va.us/courts/combined/Charles_City/home.html   `Free`
Civil: Search free at http://epwsgdp1.courts.state.va.us/gdcourts/caseSearch.do?index=index. Results show name and sometimes address. Also search via LOPAS; call 804-786-5511 to apply. *Criminal:* Search free at http://epwsgdp1.courts.state.va.us/gdcourts/caseSearch.do?index=index. Results show DOB month and day, sex, race.

Charlotte County
10th Circuit Court   www.courts.state.va.us/courts/circuit.html   `Free`
Civil: Search free at http://wasdmz2.courts.state.va.us/CJISWeb/MainMenu.do. Also, remote online access to court case indexes is via LOPAS; call 804-786-5511 to apply. *Criminal:* same.

Charlotte General District Court   www.courts.state.va.us/courts/gd/Charlotte/home.html   `Free`
Civil: Search free at http://epwsgdp1.courts.state.va.us/gdcourts/caseSearch.do?index=index. Results show name and sometimes address. Also search via LOPAS; call 804-786-5511 to apply. *Criminal:* Search free at http://epwsgdp1.courts.state.va.us/gdcourts/caseSearch.do?index=index. Results show DOB month and day, sex, race.

Charlottesville City
16th Circuit Court   www.courts.state.va.us/courts/circuit/Charlottesville/home.html   `Free`
Civil: Remote online access to court case indexes via LOPAS is not currently available; call 804-786-5511 for info. *Criminal:* same.

Charlottesville General District Court   www.courts.state.va.us/courts/gd/Charlottesville/home.html   `Free`
Civil: Search free at http://epwsgdp1.courts.state.va.us/gdcourts/caseSearch.do?index=index. Results show name and sometimes address. Also search via LOPAS; call 804-786-5511 to apply. *Criminal:* Search free at http://epwsgdp1.courts.state.va.us/gdcourts/caseSearch.do?index=index. Results show DOB month and day, sex, race.

Chesapeake County
1st Circuit Court   www.courts.state.va.us/courts/circuit.html   `Free`
Civil: Online access free at www.courts.state.va.us/caseinfo/circuit.html. *Criminal:* Same.

1st General District Court   `Free`
Civil: Search free at http://epwsgdp1.courts.state.va.us/gdcourts/caseSearch.do?index=index. Results show name and sometimes address. *Criminal:* Search free at http://epwsgdp1.courts.state.va.us/gdcourts/caseSearch.do?index=index. Results show DOB month and day, sex, race.

Chesterfield County
12th Circuit Court   www.co.chesterfield.va.us/JusticeAdministration/CircuitCourtClerk/clerhome.asp   `Free`
Civil: Search free at www.courts.state.va.us/caseinfo/circuit.html. Also, remote online access to court case indexes is via LOPAS; call 804-786-5511 to apply. *Criminal:* same.

12th General District Court   www.courts.state.va.us/courts/gd/Chesterfield/home.html   `Free`
Civil: Search free at http://epwsgdp1.courts.state.va.us/gdcourts/caseSearch.do?index=index. Results show name and sometimes address. Also search via LOPAS; call 804-786-5511 to apply. *Criminal:* Search free at http://epwsgdp1.courts.state.va.us/gdcourts/caseSearch.do?index=index. Results show DOB month and day, sex, race.

Clarke County

26th Circuit Court   www.courts.state.va.us/courts/circuit.html   `Free`
Civil: Remote online access to court case indexes is via LOPAS; call 804-786-5511 to apply. *Criminal:* Remote online access to court case indexes via LOPAS; call 804-786-5511 to apply.

General District Court   www.co.clarke.va.us   `Free`
Civil: Search free at http://epwsgdp1.courts.state.va.us/gdcourts/caseSearch.do?index=index. Results show name and sometimes address. Also search via LOPAS; call 804-786-5511 to apply. *Criminal:* Search free at http://epwsgdp1.courts.state.va.us/gdcourts/caseSearch.do?index=index. Results show DOB month and day, sex, race.

Clifton Forge City

25th General District Court   `Free`
Civil: Search free at http://epwsgdp1.courts.state.va.us/gdcourts/caseSearch.do?index=index. Results show name and sometimes address. Also search via LOPAS; call 804-786-5511 to apply. *Criminal:* Search free at http://epwsgdp1.courts.state.va.us/gdcourts/caseSearch.do?index=index. Results show DOB month and day, sex, race.

Colonial Heights City

12th Circuit Court   www.courts.state.va.us/courts/circuit.html   `Free`
Civil: Online access free at www.courts.state.va.us/caseinfo/circuit.html. *Criminal:* Same.

12th General District Court   `Free`
Civil: Search free at http://epwsgdp1.courts.state.va.us/gdcourts/caseSearch.do?index=index. Results show name and sometimes address. Also search via LOPAS; call 804-786-5511 to apply. *Criminal:* Search free at http://epwsgdp1.courts.state.va.us/gdcourts/caseSearch.do?index=index. Results show DOB month and day, sex, race.

Craig County

25th Circuit Court   www.courts.state.va.us/courts/circuit.html   `Free`
Civil: Remote online access to court case indexes is via LOPAS; call 804-786-5511 to apply. *Criminal:* Same.

25th General District Court   `Free`
Civil: Search free at http://epwsgdp1.courts.state.va.us/gdcourts/caseSearch.do?index=index. Results show name and sometimes address. Also search via LOPAS; call 804-786-5511 to apply. *Criminal:* Search free at http://epwsgdp1.courts.state.va.us/gdcourts/caseSearch.do?index=index. Results show DOB month and day, sex, race.

Culpeper County

16th Circuit Court   www.courts.state.va.us/courts/circuit/Culpeper/home.html   `Free`
Civil: Access civil record index at www.courts.state.va.us/caseinfo/circuit.html. There are no DOBs *Criminal:* Online access to criminal records is same as civil.

16th General District Court   `Free`
Civil: Search free at http://epwsgdp1.courts.state.va.us/gdcourts/caseSearch.do?index=index. Results show name and sometimes address. Also search via LOPAS; call 804-786-5511 to apply. *Criminal:* Search free at http://epwsgdp1.courts.state.va.us/gdcourts/caseSearch.do?index=index. Results show DOB month and day, sex, race.

Cumberland County

10th Circuit Court   www.courts.state.va.us/courts/circuit.html   `Free`
Civil: Search free at www.courts.state.va.us/caseinfo/circuit.html. Also search via LOPAS; call 804-786-5511 to apply. *Criminal:* Online access to criminal records is same as civil.

10th General District Court   `Free`
Civil: Search free at http://epwsgdp1.courts.state.va.us/gdcourts/caseSearch.do?index=index. Results show name and sometimes address *Criminal:* Same. Results show DOB month and day only.

Danville City

22nd Circuit Court   www.danville-va.gov/home.asp   `Free`
Online access free at www.courts.state.va.us/caseinfo/circuit.html. Also, search daily docket from the web page.

22nd General District Court   `Free`
Civil: Select and search District Courts at http://epwsgdp1.courts.state.va.us/gdcourts/caseSearch.do?index=index. Results show name and sometimes address. For information about the statewide online systems, see the state introduction. *Criminal:* Search free at http://epwsgdp1.courts.state.va.us/gdcourts/caseSearch.do?index=index. Results show DOB month and day, sex, race.

Dickenson County

29th Circuit Court   www.courts.state.va.us/courts/circuit.html   `Free`
Civil: Online access free at www.courts.state.va.us/caseinfo/circuit.html. *Criminal:* Same.

29th General District Court   `Free`
Civil: Search free at http://epwsgdp1.courts.state.va.us/gdcourts/caseSearch.do?index=index. Results show name and sometimes address. Also search via LOPAS; call 804-786-5511 to apply. *Criminal:* Search free at http://epwsgdp1.courts.state.va.us/gdcourts/caseSearch.do?index=index. Results show DOB month and day, sex, race.

Dinwiddie County
11th Circuit Court   www.courts.state.va.us/courts/circuit.html   `Free`
Civil: Select and search Circuit Courts online at www.courts.state.va.us/caseinfo/circuit.html. *Criminal:* Same.

11th General District Court   `Free`
Civil: Search free at http://epwsgdp1.courts.state.va.us/gdcourts/caseSearch.do?index=index. Results show name and sometimes address. Also search via LOPAS; call 804-786-5511 to apply. *Criminal:* Search free at http://epwsgdp1.courts.state.va.us/gdcourts/caseSearch.do?index=index. Results show DOB month and day, sex, race.

Emporia City
6th General District Court   `Free`
Civil: Search free at http://epwsgdp1.courts.state.va.us/gdcourts/caseSearch.do?index=index. Results show name and sometimes address. Also search via LOPAS; call 804-786-5511 to apply. *Criminal:* Search free at http://epwsgdp1.courts.state.va.us/gdcourts/caseSearch.do?index=index. Results show DOB month and day, sex, race.

Essex County
15th Circuit Court   www.courts.state.va.us/courts/circuit.html   `Free`
Civil: Remote online access to court case indexes is via LOPAS; call 804-786-5511 to apply. *Criminal:* Same.

15th General District Court   `Free`
Civil: Search free at http://epwsgdp1.courts.state.va.us/gdcourts/caseSearch.do?index=index. Results show name and sometimes address. Also search via LOPAS; call 804-786-5511 to apply. *Criminal:* Search free at http://epwsgdp1.courts.state.va.us/gdcourts/caseSearch.do?index=index. Results show DOB month and day, sex, race.

Fairfax County
19th Circuit Court   www.fairfaxcounty.gov/courts/circuit   `Free & $$`
Civil: Access to current court case indexes is via CPAN subscription; call 703-246-2366 or see www.fairfaxcounty.gov/courts/circuit/cpan.htm to apply. Fee is $25.00 per month per user. Also, Friday's Motion dockets are available free at www.fairfaxcounty.gov/courts/circuit/dockets/. *Criminal:* Online access to criminal same as civil, see above.

19th General District Court   www.fairfaxcounty.gov/courts/gendist   `Free`
Civil: Search free at http://epwsgdp1.courts.state.va.us/gdcourts/caseSearch.do?index=index. Results show name and sometimes address. *Criminal:* Search free at http://epwsgdp1.courts.state.va.us/gdcourts/caseSearch.do?index=index. Results show DOB month and day, sex, race.

Fairfax City
19th General District Court   www.courts.state.va.us/courts/gd/Fairfax_City/home.html   `Free`
Civil: Search free at http://epwsgdp1.courts.state.va.us/gdcourts/caseSearch.do?index=index. Results show name and sometimes address. *Criminal:* Search free at http://epwsgdp1.courts.state.va.us/gdcourts/caseSearch.do?index=index. Results show DOB month and day, sex, race.

Falls Church City
17th General District Courts Combined   www.fallschurchva.gov   `Free`
Civil: Search free at http://epwsgdp1.courts.state.va.us/gdcourts/caseSearch.do?index=index. Results show name and sometimes address. Also search via LOPAS; call 804-786-5511 to apply. *Criminal:* Search free at http://epwsgdp1.courts.state.va.us/gdcourts/caseSearch.do?index=index. Results show DOB month and day, sex, race.

Fauquier County
Circuit Court   www.fauquiercounty.gov/government/departments/circuitcourt   `Free`
Civil: Online access free at www.courts.state.va.us/caseinfo/circuit.html. *Criminal:* Same.

20th General District Court   `Free`
Civil: Search free at http://epwsgdp1.courts.state.va.us/gdcourts/caseSearch.do?index=index. Results show name and sometimes address. Also search via LOPAS; call 804-786-5511 to apply. *Criminal:* Search free at http://epwsgdp1.courts.state.va.us/gdcourts/caseSearch.do?index=index. Results show DOB month and day, sex, race.

Floyd County
27th Circuit Court   www.courts.state.va.us/courts/circuit.html   `Free`
Search civil and criminal free at www.courts.state.va.us/caseinfo/circuit.html. Also search via LOPAS; call 804-786-5511 to apply.

27th General District Court　　**Free**
Civil: Search free at http://epwsgdp1.courts.state.va.us/gdcourts/caseSearch.do?index=index. Results show name and sometimes address. Also, remote online access to court case indexes is via LOPAS; call 804-786-5511 to apply. *Criminal:* Search free at http://epwsgdp1.courts.state.va.us/gdcourts/caseSearch.do?index=index. Results show DOB month and day, sex, race.

Fluvanna County

16th Circuit Court　　www.courts.state.va.us/courts/circuit.html　　**Free**
Search civil and criminal free at www.courts.state.va.us/caseinfo/circuit.html. Also search via LOPAS; call 804-786-5511 to apply.

16th General District Court　　www.courts.state.va.us/courts/combined/Fluvanna/home.html　　**Free**
Civil: Search free at http://epwsgdp1.courts.state.va.us/gdcourts/caseSearch.do?index=index. Results show name and sometimes address. Also search via LOPAS; call 804-786-5511 to apply. *Criminal:* Search free at http://epwsgdp1.courts.state.va.us/gdcourts/caseSearch.do?index=index. Results show DOB month and day, sex, race.

Franklin County

22nd Judicial Circuit Court　　www.courts.state.va.us/courts/circuit/Franklin/home.html　　**Free & $$**
Civil: Select and search Circuit Courts online at www.courts.state.va.us/caseinfo/circuit.html. *Criminal:* Same.

22nd General District Court　　www.courts.state.va.us/courts/gd/Franklin_County/home.html　　**Free**
Civil: Search free at http://epwsgdp1.courts.state.va.us/gdcourts/caseSearch.do?index=index. Results show name and sometimes address. Also search via LOPAS; call 804-786-5511 to apply. *Criminal:* Search free at http://epwsgdp1.courts.state.va.us/gdcourts/caseSearch.do?index=index. Results show DOB month and day, sex, race.

Franklin City

5th Judicial General District Combined　　www.courts.state.va.us/courts/combined/Franklin_City/home.html　　**Free**
Civil: Search free at http://epwsgdp1.courts.state.va.us/gdcourts/caseSearch.do?index=index. Results show name and sometimes address. For info on the statewide online systems, see the state introduction. *Criminal:* Search free at http://epwsgdp1.courts.state.va.us/gdcourts/caseSearch.do?index=index. Results show DOB month and day, sex, race.

Frederick County

Circuit Court　　www.winfredclerk.com　　**Free**
Search civil and criminal free at www.courts.state.va.us/caseinfo/circuit.html. Also search via LOPAS; call 804-786-5511 to apply.

26th General District Court　　www.courts.state.va.us/courts/gd/Frederick~Winchester/home.html　　**Free**
Civil: Search free at http://epwsgdp1.courts.state.va.us/gdcourts/caseSearch.do?index=index. Results show name and sometimes address. Also search via LOPAS; call 804-786-5511 to apply. *Criminal:* Search free at http://epwsgdp1.courts.state.va.us/gdcourts/caseSearch.do?index=index. Results show DOB month and day, sex, race.

Fredericksburg City

15th Circuit Court　　www.courts.state.va.us/courts/circuit.html　　**Free**
Civil: Online access free at www.courts.state.va.us/. *Criminal:* Same.

15th General District Court　　www.courts.state.va.us　　**Free**
Civil: Search free at http://epwsgdp1.courts.state.va.us/gdcourts/caseSearch.do?index=index. Results show name and sometimes address. Also search via LOPAS; call 804-786-5511 to apply. *Criminal:* Search free at http://epwsgdp1.courts.state.va.us/gdcourts/caseSearch.do?index=index. Results show DOB month and day, sex, race.

Galax City

27th General District Court　　**Free**
Civil: Search free at http://epwsgdp1.courts.state.va.us/gdcourts/caseSearch.do?index=index. Results show name and sometimes address. Also search via LOPAS; call 804-786-5511 to apply. *Criminal:* Search free at http://epwsgdp1.courts.state.va.us/gdcourts/caseSearch.do?index=index. Results show DOB month and day, sex, race.

Giles County

27th Circuit Court　　www.courts.state.va.us/courts/circuit.html　　**Free**
Civil: Select and search Circuit Courts online at www.courts.state.va.us/caseinfo/circuit.html. *Criminal:* Same.

27th General District Court　　www.courts.state.va.us/courts/combined/Giles/home.html　　**Free**
Civil: Search free at http://epwsgdp1.courts.state.va.us/gdcourts/caseSearch.do?index=index. Results show name and sometimes address. Also search via LOPAS; call 804-786-5511 to apply. *Criminal:* Search free at http://epwsgdp1.courts.state.va.us/gdcourts/caseSearch.do?index=index. Results show DOB month and day, sex, race.

Gloucester County

9th Circuit Court　　www.gloucesterva.info　　**Free**
Civil: Online access free at www.courts.state.va.us/caseinfo/circuit.html. *Criminal:* same.

9th General District Court   **Free**
Civil: Search free at http://epwsgdp1.courts.state.va.us/gdcourts/caseSearch.do?index=index. Results show name and sometimes address. Also search via LOPAS; call 804-786-5511 to apply. *Criminal:* Search free at http://epwsgdp1.courts.state.va.us/gdcourts/caseSearch.do?index=index. Results show DOB month and day, sex, race.

Goochland County

16th Circuit Court   www.courts.state.va.us/courts/circuit.html   **Free**
Civil: Remote online access to court case indexes is via LOPAS; call 804-786-5511 to apply. *Criminal:* Remote online access to court case indexes via LOPAS; call 804-786-5511 to apply. Also, may be free online at http://208.210.219.132/vacircuit/select.jsp?court=.

General District Court   **Free**
Civil: Search free at http://epwsgdp1.courts.state.va.us/gdcourts/caseSearch.do?index=index. Results show name and sometimes address. Also search via LOPAS; call 804-786-5511 to apply. *Criminal:* Search free at http://epwsgdp1.courts.state.va.us/gdcourts/caseSearch.do?index=index. Results show DOB month and day, sex, race.

Grayson County

27th Circuit Court   www.courts.state.va.us/courts/circuit.html   **Free**
Civil: Select and search Circuit Courts online at www.courts.state.va.us/caseinfo/circuit.html. *Criminal:* Same.

27th General District Court   **Free**
Civil: Search free at http://epwsgdp1.courts.state.va.us/gdcourts/caseSearch.do?index=index. Results show name and sometimes address. Also search via LOPAS; call 804-786-5511 to apply. *Criminal:* Search free at http://epwsgdp1.courts.state.va.us/gdcourts/caseSearch.do?index=index. Results show DOB month and day, sex, race.

Greene County

16th Circuit Court   www.courts.state.va.us/courts/circuit.html   **Free**
Civil: Remote online access to court case indexes is via LOPAS; call 804-786-5511 to apply.

16th General District Court   **Free**
Civil: Search free at http://epwsgdp1.courts.state.va.us/gdcourts/caseSearch.do?index=index. Results show name and sometimes address. Also search via LOPAS; call 804-786-5511 to apply. *Criminal:* Search free at http://epwsgdp1.courts.state.va.us/gdcourts/caseSearch.do?index=index. Results show DOB month and day, sex, race.

Greensville County

6th Circuit Court   www.courts.state.va.us/courts/circuit.html   **Free**
Civil: Search free at www.courts.state.va.us/caseinfo/circuit.html. Also search via LOPAS; call 804-786-5511 to apply to this dial-up service. *Criminal:* Same.

Greenville/Emporia Combined Court   **Free**
Civil: Select and search District Courts at http://epwsgdp1.courts.state.va.us/gdcourts/caseSearch.do?index=index. Results show name only. *Criminal:* Search free at http://epwsgdp1.courts.state.va.us/gdcourts/caseSearch.do?index=index. Results show DOB month and day, sex, race.

Halifax County

10th Circuit Court   www.courts.state.va.us/courts/circuit.html   **Free**
Civil: Online access free at www.courts.state.va.us/caseinfo/circuit.html. *Criminal:* Online access free at http://208.210.219.132/vacircuit/select.jsp. For information about the statewide online systems, see the state introduction. Online access to criminal records same as civil, above.

10th General District Court   **Free**
Civil: Search free at http://epwsgdp1.courts.state.va.us/gdcourts/caseSearch.do?index=index. Results show name and sometimes address. Also search via LOPAS; call 804-786-5511 to apply. *Criminal:* Search free at http://epwsgdp1.courts.state.va.us/gdcourts/caseSearch.do?index=index. Results show DOB month and day, sex, race. Also, search on LOPAS; LOPAS shows the DOB.

Hampton City

8th Circuit Court   www.courts.state.va.us/courts/circuit.html   **Free**
Civil: Online access free at www.courts.state.va.us/caseinfo/circuit.html. *Criminal:* Same.

8th General District Court   www.courts.state.va.us   **Free**
Civil: Search free at http://epwsgdp1.courts.state.va.us/gdcourts/caseSearch.do?index=index. Results show name and sometimes address. Also search via LOPAS; call 804-786-5511 to apply. *Criminal:* Search free at http://epwsgdp1.courts.state.va.us/gdcourts/caseSearch.do?index=index. Results show DOB month and day, sex, race.

Hanover County

15th Circuit Court   www.co.hanover.va.us/circuitct/default.htm   **Free**
Civil: Access court cases from 2006 forward at www.courts.state.va.us/caseinfo/circuit.html Remote online access to court case indexes is via LOPAS; call 804-786-5511 to apply. *Criminal:* Same.

15th General District Court   `Free`
Civil: Search free at http://epwsgdp1.courts.state.va.us/gdcourts/caseSearch.do?index=index. Results show name and sometimes address. Also search via LOPAS; call 804-786-5511 to apply. *Criminal:* Search free at http://epwsgdp1.courts.state.va.us/gdcourts/caseSearch.do?index=index. Results show DOB month and day, sex, race.

Henrico County

14th Circuit Court   www.co.henrico.va.us/clerk/   `Free`
Civil: Remote online access to court case indexes is via LOPAS; call 804-786-5511 to apply. *Criminal:* Remote online access to court case indexes via LOPAS; call 804-786-5511 to apply.

14th General District Court   `Free`
Civil: Search free at http://epwsgdp1.courts.state.va.us/gdcourts/caseSearch.do?index=index. Results show name and sometimes address. Also search via LOPAS; call 804-786-5511 to apply. *Criminal:* Search free at http://epwsgdp1.courts.state.va.us/gdcourts/caseSearch.do?index=index. Results show DOB month and day, sex, race.

Henry County

Circuit Court   www.courts.state.va.us/courts/circuit/Henry/home.html   `Free`
Civil: Online access free at www.courts.state.va.us/caseinfo/circuit.html. *Criminal:* Online access to criminal records is same as civil.

21st General District Court   www.courts.state.va.us/courts/gd/Henry/home.html   `Free`
Civil: Search free at http://epwsgdp1.courts.state.va.us/gdcourts/caseSearch.do?index=index. Results show name and sometimes address. Also search via LOPAS; call 804-786-5511 to apply. *Criminal:* Search free at http://epwsgdp1.courts.state.va.us/gdcourts/caseSearch.do?index=index. Results show DOB month and day, sex, race.

Highland County

25th Circuit Court   www.courts.state.va.us/courts/circuit.html   `Free`
Civil: Remote online access to court case indexes is via LOPAS; call 804-786-5511 to apply. *Criminal:* Online access to criminal records is same as civil.

25th General District Court   `Free`
Civil: Search free at http://epwsgdp1.courts.state.va.us/gdcourts/caseSearch.do?index=index. Results show name and sometimes address. Also search via LOPAS; call 804-786-5511 to apply. *Criminal:* Search free at http://epwsgdp1.courts.state.va.us/gdcourts/caseSearch.do?index=index. Results show DOB month and day, sex, race.

Hopewell City

6th Circuit Court   www.courts.state.va.us/courts/circuit.html   `Free`
Search civil and criminal free at www.courts.state.va.us/caseinfo/circuit.html. Also search via LOPAS; call 804-786-5511 to apply.

Hopewell General District Court   www.courts.state.va.us/courts/combined/Hopewell/home.html   `Free`
Civil: Search free at http://epwsgdp1.courts.state.va.us/gdcourts/caseSearch.do?index=index. Results show name and sometimes address. Also search via LOPAS; call 804-786-5511 to apply. *Criminal:* Search free at http://epwsgdp1.courts.state.va.us/gdcourts/caseSearch.do?index=index. Results show DOB month and day, sex, race.

Isle of Wight County

5th Circuit Court   www.courts.state.va.us/courts/circuit.html   `Free`
Civil: Online access free at www.courts.state.va.us/caseinfo/circuit.html. *Criminal:* Online access to criminal records is same as civil.

5th General District Court   `Free`
Civil: Search free at http://epwsgdp1.courts.state.va.us/gdcourts/caseSearch.do?index=index. Results show name and sometimes address. Also search via LOPAS; call 804-786-5511 to apply. *Criminal:* Search free at http://epwsgdp1.courts.state.va.us/gdcourts/caseSearch.do?index=index. Results show DOB month and day, sex, race.

James City County

Williamsburg-James City Circuit Court   www.courts.state.va.us/courts/circuit.html   `Free`
Civil: Online access free at www.courts.state.va.us/caseinfo/circuit.html. *Criminal:* Same.

King and Queen County

9th Circuit Court   www.courts.state.va.us/courts/circuit.html   `Free`
Civil: Remote online access to court case indexes is via LOPAS, call 804-786-5511 to apply. *Criminal:* Remote online access to court case indexes via LOPAS, call 804-786-5511 to apply.

King & Queen General District Court   www.kingandqueenco.net/html/Govt/gendist.html   `Free`
Civil: Search free at http://epwsgdp1.courts.state.va.us/gdcourts/caseSearch.do?index=index. Results show name and sometimes address. Also search via LOPAS; call 804-786-5511 to apply. *Criminal:* Search free at http://epwsgdp1.courts.state.va.us/gdcourts/caseSearch.do?index=index. Results show DOB month and day, sex, race.

King George County

15th Circuit Court   www.courts.state.va.us/courts/circuit.html   **Free**
Civil: Online access free at www.courts.state.va.us/caseinfo/circuit.html. *Criminal:* Online access to criminal records is same as civil. Only month and day of birth shown in results.

15th General District Combined Court   **Free**
Civil: Online access is at http://epwsgdp1.courts.state.va.us/gdcourts/caseSearch.do?index=index. Results show name and sometimes address. *Criminal:* Search free at http://epwsgdp1.courts.state.va.us/gdcourts/caseSearch.do?index=index. Results show DOB month and day, sex, race.

King William County

9th Circuit Court   www.courts.state.va.us/courts/circuit.html   **Free**
Search civil and criminal free at www.courts.state.va.us/caseinfo/circuit.html. Also search via LOPAS; call 804-786-5511 to apply.

King William General District Court   **Free**
Civil: Search free at http://epwsgdp1.courts.state.va.us/gdcourts/caseSearch.do?index=index. Results show name and sometimes address. Also search via LOPAS; call 804-786-5511 to apply. *Criminal:* Search free at http://epwsgdp1.courts.state.va.us/gdcourts/caseSearch.do?index=index. Results show DOB month and day, sex, race.

Lancaster County

15th Circuit Court   www.courts.state.va.us/courts/circuit.html   **Free**
Search civil and criminal free at www.courts.state.va.us/caseinfo/circuit.html. Also search via LOPAS; call 804-786-5511 to apply.

15th General District Court   **Free**
Civil: Search free at http://epwsgdp1.courts.state.va.us/gdcourts/caseSearch.do?index=index. Results show name and sometimes address. Also search via LOPAS; call 804-786-5511 to apply. *Criminal:* Search free at http://epwsgdp1.courts.state.va.us/gdcourts/caseSearch.do?index=index. Results show DOB month and day, sex, race.

Lee County

30th Circuit Court   www.courts.state.va.us/courts/circuit/Lee/home.html   **Free**
Civil: Select and search Circuit Courts online at www.courts.state.va.us/caseinfo/circuit.html. *Criminal:* Same.

30th General District Court   **Free**
Civil: Search free at http://epwsgdp1.courts.state.va.us/gdcourts/caseSearch.do?index=index. Results show name and sometimes address. Also search via LOPAS; call 804-786-5511 to apply. *Criminal:* Search free at http://epwsgdp1.courts.state.va.us/gdcourts/caseSearch.do?index=index. Results show DOB month and day, sex, race.

Loudoun County

20th Circuit Court   www.loudoun.gov/clerk   **Free**
Civil: Access court records free at http://wasdmz1.courts.state.va.us/CJISWeb/circuit.html. Also, remote online access to court case indexes is via LOPAS; call 804-786-5511 to apply. Also, docket lists are free at www.loudoun.gov/Default.aspx?tabid=318&fmpath=/Dockets. *Criminal:* same Also, docket lists are online free at www.loudoun.gov/Default.aspx?tabid=318&fmpath=/Dockets.

20th General District Court   www.courts.state.va.us/courts/gd/Loudoun/home.html   **Free**
Civil: Search free at http://epwsgdp1.courts.state.va.us/gdcourts/caseSearch.do?index=index. Results show name and sometimes address. Also search via LOPAS; call 804-786-5511 to apply. *Criminal:* Search free at http://epwsgdp1.courts.state.va.us/gdcourts/caseSearch.do?index=index. Results show DOB month and day, sex, race.

Louisa County

16th Circuit Court   www.courts.state.va.us/courts/circuit.html   **Free**
Search civil and criminal free at www.courts.state.va.us/caseinfo/circuit.html. Also search via LOPAS; call 804-786-5511 to apply.

16th General District Court   **Free**
Civil: Search free at http://epwsgdp1.courts.state.va.us/gdcourts/caseSearch.do?index=index. Results show name and sometimes address. Also search via LOPAS; call 804-786-5511 to apply. *Criminal:* Search free at http://epwsgdp1.courts.state.va.us/gdcourts/caseSearch.do?index=index. Results show DOB month and day, sex, race.

Lunenburg County

10th Circuit Court   www.courts.state.va.us/courts/circuit.html   **Free**
Search civil and criminal free at www.courts.state.va.us/caseinfo/circuit.html. Also search via LOPAS; call 804-786-5511 to apply.

10th General District Court   **Free**
Civil: Search free at http://epwsgdp1.courts.state.va.us/gdcourts/caseSearch.do?index=index. Results show name and sometimes address. Also search via LOPAS; call 804-786-5511 to apply. *Criminal:* Search free at http://epwsgdp1.courts.state.va.us/gdcourts/caseSearch.do?index=index. Results show DOB month and day, sex, race.

Lynchburg City

24th Circuit Court   www.courts.state.va.us/courts/circuit.html   **Free**
Search civil and criminal free at www.courts.state.va.us/caseinfo/circuit.html. Also search via LOPAS; call 804-786-5511 to apply.

24th General District Court - Civil Division   **Free**
Civil: Search free at http://epwsgdp1.courts.state.va.us/gdcourts/caseSearch.do?index=index. Results show name and sometimes address. Also search via LOPAS; call 804-786-5511 to apply.

24th General District Court - Criminal Division   **Free**
Criminal: Search free at http://epwsgdp1.courts.state.va.us/gdcourts/caseSearch.do?index=index. Results show DOB month and day, sex, race.

Madison County

16th Circuit Court   www.courts.state.va.us/courts/circuit.html   **Free**
Civil: Select and search Combined Courts online at www.courts.state.va.us/caseinfo/circuit.html. *Criminal:* Same.

16th General District Court   **Free**
Civil: Search free at http://epwsgdp1.courts.state.va.us/gdcourts/caseSearch.do?index=index. Results show name and sometimes address. Also search via LOPAS; call 804-786-5511 to apply. *Criminal:* Search free at http://epwsgdp1.courts.state.va.us/gdcourts/caseSearch.do?index=index. Results show DOB month and day, sex, race.

Martinsville City

21st Circuit Court   www.ci.martinsville.va.us/circuitclerk   **Free**
Civil: Online access free at www.courts.state.va.us/caseinfo/circuit.html. Also, with subscription and password, access judgments at https://www.ci.martinsville.va.us/crms/. *Criminal:* Same.

21st General District Court   www.courts.state.va.us/courts/gd/Martinsville/home.html   **Free**
Civil: Search free at http://epwsgdp1.courts.state.va.us/gdcourts/caseSearch.do?index=index. Results show name and sometimes address. Also search via LOPAS; call 804-786-5511 to apply. *Criminal:* Search free at http://epwsgdp1.courts.state.va.us/gdcourts/caseSearch.do?index=index. Results show DOB month and day, sex, race.

Mathews County

9th General District Court   **Free**
Civil: Search free at http://epwsgdp1.courts.state.va.us/gdcourts/caseSearch.do?index=index. Results show name and sometimes address. Also search via LOPAS; call 804-786-5511 to apply. *Criminal:* Search free at http://epwsgdp1.courts.state.va.us/gdcourts/caseSearch.do?index=index. Results show DOB month and day, sex, race.

Mecklenburg County

10th Circuit Court   www.courts.state.va.us/courts/circuit.html   **Free**
Civil: Remote online access to court case indexes is via LOPAS; call 804-786-5511 to apply. *Criminal:* Remote online access to court case indexes via LOPAS; call 804-786-5511 to apply.

10th General District Court   www.courts.state.va.us/courts/gd/Mecklenburg/home.html   **Free**
Civil: Search free at http://epwsgdp1.courts.state.va.us/gdcourts/caseSearch.do?index=index. Results show name and sometimes address. Also search via LOPAS; call 804-786-5511 to apply. *Criminal:* Search free at http://epwsgdp1.courts.state.va.us/gdcourts/caseSearch.do?index=index. Results show DOB month and day, sex, race.

Middlesex County

9th Circuit Court   www.courts.state.va.us/courts/circuit.html   **Free**
Civil: Search free at www.courts.state.va.us/courts/circuit.html. Also, remote online access to court case indexes is via LOPAS; call 804-786-5511 to apply. *Criminal:* Search free at www.courts.state.va.us/courts/circuit.html..

9th General District Court   www.courts.state.va.us   **Free**
Civil: Search free at http://epwsgdp1.courts.state.va.us/gdcourts/caseSearch.do?index=index. Results include name and sometimes address. Also search via LOPAS; call 804-786-5511 to apply. *Criminal:* Search free at http://epwsgdp1.courts.state.va.us/gdcourts/caseSearch.do?index=index. Results show DOB month and day, sex, race.

Montgomery County

27th Circuit Court   www.courts.state.va.us/courts/circuit.html   **Free**
Civil: Online access free at www.courts.state.va.us/caseinfo/circuit.html. *Criminal:* Same.

27th General District Court   **Free**
Civil: Search free at http://epwsgdp1.courts.state.va.us/gdcourts/caseSearch.do?index=index. Results show name and sometimes address. Also search via LOPAS; call 804-786-5511 to apply. *Criminal:* Search free at http://epwsgdp1.courts.state.va.us/gdcourts/caseSearch.do?index=index. Results show DOB month and day, sex, race.

Nelson County

24th Circuit Court   www.courts.state.va.us/courts/circuit.html   `Free`
Civil: Online access free at www.courts.state.va.us/caseinfo/circuit.html. *Criminal:* Same.

24th General District Court   `Free`
Civil: Search free at http://epwsgdp1.courts.state.va.us/gdcourts/caseSearch.do?index=index. Results show name and sometimes address. Also search via LOPAS; call 804-786-5511 to apply. *Criminal:* Search free at http://epwsgdp1.courts.state.va.us/gdcourts/caseSearch.do?index=index. Results show DOB month and day, sex, race.

New Kent County

9th Circuit Court   www.courts.state.va.us/courts/circuit.html   `Free`
Civil: Online access free at www.courts.state.va.us/caseinfo/circuit.html. *Criminal:* Online access to criminal records is same as civil.

9th General District Court   `Free`
Civil: Search free at http://epwsgdp1.courts.state.va.us/gdcourts/caseSearch.do?index=index. Results show name and sometimes address. Also search via LOPAS; call 804-786-5511 to apply. *Criminal:* Search free at http://epwsgdp1.courts.state.va.us/gdcourts/caseSearch.do?index=index. Results show DOB month and day, sex, race.

Newport News City

7th Circuit Court   www.courts.state.va.us/courts/circuit/Newport_News/home.html   `Free`
Civil: Online access free at www.courts.state.va.us/caseinfo/circuit.html. *Criminal:* Same.

7th General District Court   `Free`
Civil: Search free at http://epwsgdp1.courts.state.va.us/gdcourts/caseSearch.do?index=index. Results show name and sometimes address. Also search via LOPAS; call 804-786-5511 to apply. *Criminal:* Search free at http://epwsgdp1.courts.state.va.us/gdcourts/caseSearch.do?index=index. Results show DOB month and day, sex, race.

Norfolk City

4th Circuit Court   www.courts.state.va.us/courts/circuit.html   `Free`
Civil: Online access free at www.courts.state.va.us/caseinfo/circuit.html. Also access record images via http://208.210.219.102/cgi-bin/p/rms.cgi; registration and password required. Also, the Clerk of Circuit court subscription online system contains judgment records, wills, marriages, recorded documents etc at www.norfolk.gov/Circuit_Court/remoteaccess.asp. Fee is $50 per month. Judgments, Wills, Marriages, etc back to 1993. *Criminal:* Online access to dockets is free at http://208.210.219.132/vacircuit/select.jsp. Also access record images via http://208.210.219.102/cgi-bin/p/rms.cgi; registration and password required.

4th General District Court   `Free`
Civil: Search free at http://epwsgdp1.courts.state.va.us/gdcourts/caseSearch.do?index=index. Results show name and sometimes address. Also search via LOPAS; call 804-786-5511 to apply. *Criminal:* Search free at http://epwsgdp1.courts.state.va.us/gdcourts/caseSearch.do?index=index. Results show DOB month and day, sex, race.

Northampton County

2nd Circuit Court   www.courts.state.va.us/courts/circuit.html   `Free`
Civil: Search free at www.courts.state.va.us/caseinfo/circuit.html. Also search via LOPAS; call 804-786-5511 to apply. Also, and annual subscription is available for $600.00 per year. *Criminal:* Online access to criminal index is same as civil.

Northampton General District Court   `Free`
Civil: Search free at http://epwsgdp1.courts.state.va.us/gdcourts/caseSearch.do?index=index. Results show name and sometimes address. Also search via LOPAS; call 804-786-5511 to apply. *Criminal:* Search free at http://epwsgdp1.courts.state.va.us/gdcourts/caseSearch.do?index=index. Results show DOB month and day, sex, race.

Northumberland County

15th Circuit Court   www.courts.state.va.us/courts/circuit.html   `Free`
Civil: Online access free at www.courts.state.va.us/caseinfo/circuit.html. *Criminal:* Same.

15th General District Court   `Free`
Civil: Search free at http://epwsgdp1.courts.state.va.us/gdcourts/caseSearch.do?index=index. Results show name and sometimes address. Also search via LOPAS; call 804-786-5511 to apply. *Criminal:* Search free at http://epwsgdp1.courts.state.va.us/gdcourts/caseSearch.do?index=index. Results show DOB month and day, sex, race.

Nottoway County

11th Circuit Court   www.courts.state.va.us/courts/circuit.html   `Free`
Search civil and criminal free at www.courts.state.va.us/caseinfo/circuit.html. Also search via LOPAS; call 804-786-5511 to apply.

11th General District Court   `Free`
Civil: Search free at http://epwsgdp1.courts.state.va.us/gdcourts/caseSearch.do?index=index. Results show name and sometimes address. Also search via LOPAS; call 804-786-5511 to apply. *Criminal:* Search free at http://epwsgdp1.courts.state.va.us/gdcourts/caseSearch.do?index=index. Results show DOB month and day, sex, race.

Orange County

16th Circuit Court   www.courts.state.va.us/courts/circuit.html   Free
Search civil and criminal free at www.courts.state.va.us/caseinfo/circuit.html. Also search via LOPAS; call 804-786-5511 to apply.

16th General District Court   Free
Civil: Search free at http://epwsgdp1.courts.state.va.us/gdcourts/caseSearch.do?index=index. Results show name and sometimes address. Also search via LOPAS; call 804-786-5511 to apply. *Criminal:* Search free at http://epwsgdp1.courts.state.va.us/gdcourts/caseSearch.do?index=index. Results show DOB month and day, sex, race.

Page County

26th Circuit Court   www.courts.state.va.us/courts/circuit.html   Free
Civil: Online access free at www.courts.state.va.us/caseinfo/circuit.html. *Criminal:* Same.

26th General District Court   www.co.page.va.us/   Free
Civil: Search free at http://epwsgdp1.courts.state.va.us/gdcourts/caseSearch.do?index=index. Results show name and sometimes address. Also search via LOPAS; call 804-786-5511 to apply. *Criminal:* Search free at http://epwsgdp1.courts.state.va.us/gdcourts/caseSearch.do?index=index. Results show DOB month and day, sex, race.

Patrick County

21st Circuit Court   www.courts.state.va.us/courts/circuit.html   Free
Civil: Search free at www.courts.state.va.us/caseinfo/circuit.html. *Criminal:* Same.

21st General District Court   www.courts.state.va.us/courts/gd/Patrick/home.html   Free
Civil: Search free at http://epwsgdp1.courts.state.va.us/gdcourts/caseSearch.do?index=index. Results show name and sometimes address. Also search via LOPAS; call 804-786-5511 to apply. *Criminal:* Search free at http://epwsgdp1.courts.state.va.us/gdcourts/caseSearch.do?index=index. Results show DOB month and day, sex, race.

Petersburg City

11th Circuit Court   www.courts.state.va.us/courts/circuit.html   Free
Civil: Online access free at www.courts.state.va.us/caseinfo/circuit.html. *Criminal:* Same.

11th General District Court   www.courts.state.va.us/courts/gd/Petersburg/home.html   Free
Civil: Search free at http://epwsgdp1.courts.state.va.us/gdcourts/caseSearch.do?index=index. Results show partial address. Also search via LOPAS; call 804-786-5511 to apply. *Criminal:* Search free at http://epwsgdp1.courts.state.va.us/gdcourts/caseSearch.do?index=index. Results show DOB month and day, sex, race.

Pittsylvania County

22nd Circuit Court   www.courts.state.va.us/courts/circuit.html   Free
Civil: Online access free at www.courts.state.va.us/caseinfo/circuit.html. If documents mailed, add $.50 per page if SASE not included. *Criminal:* Online access free at http://208.210.219.132/vacircuit/select.jsp. For information about the statewide online systems, see the state introduction.

22nd General District Court   www.courts.state.va.us/courts/gd/Pittsylvania/home.html   Free
Civil: Search free at http://epwsgdp1.courts.state.va.us/gdcourts/caseSearch.do?index=index. Results show name and sometimes address. Also search via LOPAS; call 804-786-5511 to apply. *Criminal:* Search free at http://epwsgdp1.courts.state.va.us/gdcourts/caseSearch.do?index=index. Results show DOB month and day, sex, race.

Portsmouth City

Circuit Court   www.courts.state.va.us/courts/circuit.html   Free
Civil: Online access free at www.courts.state.va.us/caseinfo/circuit.html. *Criminal:* Online access to criminal records is same as civil.

General District Court   Free
Civil: Search free at http://epwsgdp1.courts.state.va.us/gdcourts/caseSearch.do?index=index. Results show name and sometimes address. Also search via LOPAS; call 804-786-5511 to apply. *Criminal:* Search free at http://epwsgdp1.courts.state.va.us/gdcourts/caseSearch.do?index=index. Results show DOB month and day, sex, race.

Powhatan County

11th Circuit Court   www.courts.state.va.us/courts/circuit.html   Free
Civil: Remote online access to court case indexes is via LOPAS; call 804-786-5511 to apply. *Criminal:* Remote online access to court case indexes via LOPAS; call 804-786-5511 to apply.

11th General District Court   Free
Civil: Search free at http://epwsgdp1.courts.state.va.us/gdcourts/caseSearch.do?index=index. Results show name and sometimes address. Also search via LOPAS; call 804-786-5511 to apply. *Criminal:* Search free at http://epwsgdp1.courts.state.va.us/gdcourts/caseSearch.do?index=index. Results show DOB month and day, sex, race.

Prince Edward County
Circuit Court   www.courts.state.va.us/courts/circuit/Prince_Edward/home.html   `Free`
Civil: Online access free at www.courts.state.va.us/caseinfo/circuit.html. *Criminal:* Same.

General District Court   `Free`
Civil: Search free at http://epwsgdp1.courts.state.va.us/gdcourts/caseSearch.do?index=index. Results show name and sometimes address. Also search via LOPAS; call 804-786-5511 to apply. *Criminal:* Search free at http://epwsgdp1.courts.state.va.us/gdcourts/caseSearch.do?index=index. Results show DOB month and day, sex, race.

Prince George County
Circuit Court   www.courts.state.va.us/courts/circuit.html   `Free`
Search civil and criminal free at www.courts.state.va.us/caseinfo/circuit.html. Also search via LOPAS; call 804-786-5511 to apply.

6th General District Court   www.courts.state.va.us/courts/combined/Prince_George/home.html   `Free`
Civil: Search free at http://epwsgdp1.courts.state.va.us/gdcourts/caseSearch.do?index=index. Results show name and sometimes address. Also search via LOPAS; call 804-786-5511 to apply. *Criminal:* Search free at http://epwsgdp1.courts.state.va.us/gdcourts/caseSearch.do?index=index. Results show DOB month and day, sex, race.

Prince William County
31st Circuit Court   www.pwcgov.org/default.aspx?topic=040017   `Free`
Civil: Search records free at http://ccourt.pwcgov.org/ but popups must be enabled. *Criminal:* same.

31st General District Court   www.courts.state.va.us/courts/gd/Prince_William/home.html   `Free`
Civil: Search free at http://epwsgdp1.courts.state.va.us/gdcourts/caseSearch.do?index=index. Results show name and sometimes address. Also search via LOPAS; call 804-786-5511 to apply. *Criminal:* Search free at http://epwsgdp1.courts.state.va.us/gdcourts/caseSearch.do?index=index. Results show DOB month and day, sex, race.

Pulaski County
Circuit Court   www.pulaskicircuitcourt.com
Civil: Online access to court records is $300 annual fee http://records.pulaskicircuitcourt.com/icris/splash.jsp. Registration required; search by name, document type or number. Also, access is free at http://208.210.219.132/vacircuit/select.jsp. *Criminal:* Same.

27th General District Court   www.courts.state.va.us/courts/gd/Pulaski/home.html   `Free`
Civil: Search free at http://epwsgdp1.courts.state.va.us/gdcourts/caseSearch.do?index=index. Results show name and sometimes address. Also search via LOPAS; call 804-786-5511 to apply. *Criminal:* Search free at http://epwsgdp1.courts.state.va.us/gdcourts/caseSearch.do?index=index. Results show DOB month and day, sex, race.

Radford City
27th Circuit Court   www.courts.state.va.us/courts/circuit.html   `Free & $$`
Civil: Search free at www.courts.state.va.us/caseinfo/circuit.html. Also search via subscription service ILS; call 804-786-5511 to apply; $80 monthly fee. *Criminal:* Same.

27th General District Court   www.courts.state.va.us/courts/combined/Radford/home.html   `Free`
Civil: Search free at http://epwsgdp1.courts.state.va.us/gdcourts/caseSearch.do?index=index. Results show name and sometimes address. Also search via LOPAS; call 804-786-5511 to apply. *Criminal:* Search free at http://epwsgdp1.courts.state.va.us/gdcourts/caseSearch.do?index=index. Results show DOB month and day, sex, race.

Rappahannock County
20th Circuit Court   www.courts.state.va.us/courts/circuit.html   `Free`
Search civil and criminal free at www.courts.state.va.us/caseinfo/circuit.html. Also search via LOPAS; call 804-786-5511 to apply.
20th District Combined Court   `Free`
Civil: Search free at http://epwsgdp1.courts.state.va.us/gdcourts/caseSearch.do?index=index. Results show name and sometimes address. Also search via LOPAS; call 804-786-5511 to apply. *Criminal:* Search free at http://epwsgdp1.courts.state.va.us/gdcourts/caseSearch.do?index=index. Results show DOB month and day, sex, race.

Richmond County
15th Circuit Court   www.courts.state.va.us/courts/circuit.html   `Free`
Search civil and criminal free at www.courts.state.va.us/caseinfo/circuit.html. Also search via LOPAS; call 804-786-5511 to apply.
15th General District Court   `Free`
Civil: Search free at http://epwsgdp1.courts.state.va.us/gdcourts/caseSearch.do?index=index. Results show name and sometimes address. Also search via LOPAS; call 804-786-5511 to apply. *Criminal:* Search free at http://epwsgdp1.courts.state.va.us/gdcourts/caseSearch.do?index=index. Results show DOB month and day, sex, race.

Richmond City
13th Circuit Court - Division I   www.courts.state.va.us/courts/circuit/Richmond/home.html   `Free`
Civil: Online access free at www.courts.state.va.us/caseinfo/circuit.html. *Criminal:* Same.

13th General District Court - Civil Division **Free**
Civil: Search free at http://epwsgdp1.courts.state.va.us/gdcourts/caseSearch.do?index=index. Results show name and sometimes address. Also search via LOPAS; call 804-786-5511 to apply.

13th General District Court - Division II **Free**
Criminal: For information about the statewide online systems, see the state introduction. Select and search General District Courts at http://208.210.219.132/vadistrict/select.jsp.

Roanoke County

23rd Circuit Court www.roanokecountyva.gov **Free**
Civil: Online access free at www.courts.state.va.us/caseinfo/circuit.html. *Criminal:* Same.

23rd General District Court www.roanokecountyva.gov/ **Free**
Civil: Search free at http://epwsgdp1.courts.state.va.us/gdcourts/caseSearch.do?index=index. Results show name and sometimes address. Also search via LOPAS; call 804-786-5511 to apply. *Criminal:* Search free at http://epwsgdp1.courts.state.va.us/gdcourts/caseSearch.do?index=index. Results show DOB month and day, sex, race.

Roanoke City

23rd Circuit Court www.roanokecountyva.gov/Departments/CircuitCourtClerksOffice **Free**
Civil: Online access free at www.courts.state.va.us/caseinfo/circuit.html. *Criminal:* Same.

General District Court **Free**
Civil: Search free at http://epwsgdp1.courts.state.va.us/gdcourts/caseSearch.do?index=index. Results show name and sometimes address. *Criminal:* Search free at http://epwsgdp1.courts.state.va.us/gdcourts/caseSearch.do?index=index. Results show DOB month and day, sex, race.

Rockbridge County

25th Circuit Court www.courts.state.va.us/courts/circuit.html **Free**
Search civil and criminal free at www.courts.state.va.us/caseinfo/circuit.html. Also search via LOPAS; call 804-786-5511 to apply.

General District Court **Free**
Civil: Search free at http://epwsgdp1.courts.state.va.us/gdcourts/caseSearch.do?index=index. Results show name and sometimes address. Also search via LOPAS; call 804-786-5511 to apply. *Criminal:* Search free at http://epwsgdp1.courts.state.va.us/gdcourts/caseSearch.do?index=index. Results show DOB month and day, sex, race.

Rockingham County

26th Circuit Court www.courts.state.va.us/courts/circuit.html **Free**
Civil: Online access free at www.courts.state.va.us/caseinfo/circuit.html. *Criminal:* Same.

26th General District Court **Free**
Civil: Search free at http://epwsgdp1.courts.state.va.us/gdcourts/caseSearch.do?index=index. Results show name and sometimes address. Also search via LOPAS; call 804-786-5511 to apply. *Criminal:* Search free at http://epwsgdp1.courts.state.va.us/gdcourts/caseSearch.do?index=index. Results show DOB month and day, sex, race.

Russell County

29th Circuit Court www.courts.state.va.us/courts/circuit.html **Free**
Search civil and criminal free at www.courts.state.va.us/caseinfo/circuit.html. Also search via LOPAS; call 804-786-5511 to apply.

29th General District Court **Free**
Civil: Search free at http://epwsgdp1.courts.state.va.us/gdcourts/caseSearch.do?index=index. Results show name and sometimes address. Also search via LOPAS; call 804-786-5511 to apply. *Criminal:* Search free at http://epwsgdp1.courts.state.va.us/gdcourts/caseSearch.do?index=index. Results show DOB month and day, sex, race.

Salem City

23rd Circuit Court www.courts.state.va.us/courts/circuit.html **Free**
Search civil and criminal free at www.courts.state.va.us/caseinfo/circuit.html. Also search via LOPAS; call 804-786-5511 to apply.

23rd General District Court **Free**
Civil: Search free at http://epwsgdp1.courts.state.va.us/gdcourts/caseSearch.do?index=index. Results show name and sometimes address. Also search via LOPAS; call 804-786-5511 to apply. *Criminal:* Search free at http://epwsgdp1.courts.state.va.us/gdcourts/caseSearch.do?index=index. Results show DOB month and day, sex, race.

Scott County

Circuit Court www.courts.state.va.us/courts/circuit.html **Free**
Search civil and criminal free at www.courts.state.va.us/caseinfo/circuit.html. Also search via LOPAS; call 804-786-5511 to apply.

30th General District Court Free
Civil: Search free at http://epwsgdp1.courts.state.va.us/gdcourts/caseSearch.do?index=index. Results show name and sometimes address. Also search via LOPAS; call 804-786-5511 to apply. *Criminal:* Search free at http://epwsgdp1.courts.state.va.us/gdcourts/caseSearch.do?index=index. Results show DOB month and day, sex, race.

Shenandoah County
26th Circuit Court www.courts.state.va.us/courts/circuit.html Free
Search civil and criminal free at www.courts.state.va.us/caseinfo/circuit.html. Also search via LOPAS; call 804-786-5511 to apply.

26th General District Court Free
Civil: Search free at http://epwsgdp1.courts.state.va.us/gdcourts/caseSearch.do?index=index. Results show name and sometimes address. Also search via LOPAS; call 804-786-5511 to apply. *Criminal:* Search free at http://epwsgdp1.courts.state.va.us/gdcourts/caseSearch.do?index=index. Results show DOB month and day, sex, race.

Smyth County
28th Circuit Court www.courts.state.va.us/courts/circuit.html Free
Search civil and criminal free at www.courts.state.va.us/caseinfo/circuit.html. Also search via LOPAS; call 804-786-5511 to apply.

28th General District Court Free
Civil: Search free at http://epwsgdp1.courts.state.va.us/gdcourts/caseSearch.do?index=index. Results show name and sometimes address. Also search via LOPAS; call 804-786-5511 to apply. *Criminal:* Search free at http://epwsgdp1.courts.state.va.us/gdcourts/caseSearch.do?index=index. Results show DOB month and day, sex, race.

Southampton County
5th Circuit Court www.courts.state.va.us/courts/circuit.html Free
Search civil and criminal free at www.courts.state.va.us/caseinfo/circuit.html. Also search via LOPAS; call 804-786-5511 to apply.

5th General District Court Free
Civil: Search free at http://epwsgdp1.courts.state.va.us/gdcourts/caseSearch.do?index=index. Results show name and sometimes address. Also search via LOPAS; call 804-786-5511 to apply. *Criminal:* Search free at http://epwsgdp1.courts.state.va.us/gdcourts/caseSearch.do?index=index. Results show DOB month and day, sex, race.

Spotsylvania County
15th Circuit Court www.courts.state.va.us/courts/circuit.html Free
Civil: Search free at www.courts.state.va.us/caseinfo/circuit.html. Also search via LOPAS; call 804-786-5511 to apply. *Criminal:* Select and search Circuit Courts online at http://208.210.219.132/vacircuit/select.jsp. For information about the statewide online systems, see the state introduction.

15th General District Court Free
Civil: Search free at http://epwsgdp1.courts.state.va.us/gdcourts/caseSearch.do?index=index. Results show name and sometimes address. Also search via LOPAS; call 804-786-5511 to apply. *Criminal:* Search free at http://epwsgdp1.courts.state.va.us/gdcourts/caseSearch.do?index=index. Results show DOB month and day, sex, race.

Stafford County
15th Circuit Court www.co.stafford.va.us/Departments/Courts_&_Legal_Services/Index.shtml Free
Search civil and criminal free at www.courts.state.va.us/caseinfo/circuit.html. Also search via LOPAS; call 804-786-5511 to apply.

15th General District Court www.courts.state.va.us Free
Civil: Search free at http://epwsgdp1.courts.state.va.us/gdcourts/caseSearch.do?index=index. Results show name and sometimes address. Also search via LOPAS; call 804-786-5511 to apply. *Criminal:* Search free at http://epwsgdp1.courts.state.va.us/gdcourts/caseSearch.do?index=index. Results show DOB month and day, sex, race.

Staunton City
25th Circuit Court www.courts.state.va.us/courts/circuit.html Free
Search civil and criminal free at www.courts.state.va.us/caseinfo/circuit.html. Also search via LOPAS; call 804-786-5511 to apply.

Staunton General District Court Free
Civil: Search free at http://epwsgdp1.courts.state.va.us/gdcourts/caseSearch.do?index=index. Results show name and sometimes address. Records maintained 10 years. *Criminal:* Search free at http://epwsgdp1.courts.state.va.us/gdcourts/caseSearch.do?index=index. Results show DOB month and day, sex, race; records maintained 10 years.

Suffolk City
Suffolk Circuit Court www.courts.state.va.us/courts/circuit.html Free
Search civil and criminal free at www.courts.state.va.us/caseinfo/circuit.html. Also search via LOPAS; call 804-786-5511 to apply.

5th General District Court   `Free`
Civil: Search free at http://epwsgdp1.courts.state.va.us/gdcourts/caseSearch.do?index=index. Results show name and sometimes address. Also search via LOPAS; call 804-786-5511 to apply. *Criminal:* Search free at http://epwsgdp1.courts.state.va.us/gdcourts/caseSearch.do?index=index. Results show DOB month and day, sex, race.

Surry County

6th Circuit Court   www.courts.state.va.us/courts/circuit.html   `Free`
Civil: Remote online access to court case indexes is via LOPAS; call 804-786-5511 to apply. *Criminal:* Same.

6th General District Court   `Free`
Civil: Search free at http://epwsgdp1.courts.state.va.us/gdcourts/caseSearch.do?index=index. Results show name and sometimes address. Also search via LOPAS; call 804-786-5511 to apply. *Criminal:* Search free at http://epwsgdp1.courts.state.va.us/gdcourts/caseSearch.do?index=index. Results show DOB month and day, sex, race.

Sussex County

6th Circuit Court   www.courts.state.va.us/courts/circuit.html   `Free`
Civil: Access cases free at http://wasdmz2.courts.state.va.us/CJISWeb/circuit.html and select Sussex County Circuit. Also, Remote online access to court case indexes is via LOPAS; call 804-786-5511 to apply. *Criminal:* Same.

6th General District Court   `Free`
Civil: Search free at http://epwsgdp1.courts.state.va.us/gdcourts/caseSearch.do?index=index. Results show name and sometimes address. Also search via LOPAS; call 804-786-5511 to apply. *Criminal:* Search free at http://epwsgdp1.courts.state.va.us/gdcourts/caseSearch.do?index=index. Results show DOB month and day, sex, race.

Tazewell County

29th Circuit Court   www.courts.state.va.us/courts/circuit.html   `Free`
Civil: Access court records free at www.courts.state.va.us/caseinfo/circuit.html. *Criminal:* Same.

29th General District Court   `Free`
Civil: Search free at http://epwsgdp1.courts.state.va.us/gdcourts/caseSearch.do?index=index. Results show name and sometimes address. Also search via LOPAS; call 804-786-5511 to apply. *Criminal:* Search free at http://epwsgdp1.courts.state.va.us/gdcourts/caseSearch.do?index=index. Results show DOB month and day, sex, race.

Virginia Beach City

2nd Circuit Court   www.vbgov.com/courts   `Free`
Civil: Online access free at www.courts.state.va.us/caseinfo/circuit.html. *Criminal:* Same.

2nd General District Court   `Free`
Civil: Search free at http://epwsgdp1.courts.state.va.us/gdcourts/caseSearch.do?index=index. Results show name and sometimes address. Also search via LOPAS; call 804-786-5511 to apply. *Criminal:* Search free at http://epwsgdp1.courts.state.va.us/gdcourts/caseSearch.do?index=index. Results show DOB month and day, sex, race.

Warren County

Circuit Court   www.courts.state.va.us/courts/circuit/warren/home.html   `Free`
Civil: Online access free at http://wasdmz2.courts.state.va.us/CJISWeb/circuit.html. *Criminal:* Same.

26th General District Court   www.courts.state.va.us/courts/gd/Warren/home.html   `Free`
Civil: Search free at http://epwsgdp1.courts.state.va.us/gdcourts/caseSearch.do?index=index. Results show name and sometimes address. Also search via LOPAS; call 804-786-5511 to apply. *Criminal:* Search free at http://epwsgdp1.courts.state.va.us/gdcourts/caseSearch.do?index=index. Results show DOB month and day, sex, race.

Washington County

Circuit Court   www.courts.state.va.us/courts/circuit.html   `Free`
Civil: Search free at http://wasdmz1.courts.state.va.us/CJISWeb/circuit.html. Results show partial address. *Criminal:* Online access to criminal is same as civil, see above.

28th General District Court   `Free`
Civil: Search free at http://epwsgdp1.courts.state.va.us/gdcourts/caseSearch.do?index=index. Results show name and sometimes address. Also search via LOPAS; call 804-786-5511 to apply. *Criminal:* Search free at http://epwsgdp1.courts.state.va.us/gdcourts/caseSearch.do?index=index. Results show DOB month and day, sex, race.

Waynesboro City

25th Circuit Court   www.courts.state.va.us/courts/circuit.html   `Free`
Civil: Online access free at www.courts.state.va.us/caseinfo/circuit.html. *Criminal:* Same.

25th General District Court - Waynesboro   www.courts.state.va.us/courts/gd/Waynesboro/home.html   **Free**
Civil: Search court records free at http://epwsgdp1.courts.state.va.us/gdcourts/caseSearch.do?index=index. Results show name and sometimes address. *Criminal:* Search free at http://epwsgdp1.courts.state.va.us/gdcourts/caseSearch.do?index=index. Results show DOB month and day, sex, race.

Westmoreland County

15th Circuit Court   www.courts.state.va.us/courts/circuit.html   **Free**
Civil: Search free at http://wasdmz2.courts.state.va.us/CJISWeb/MainMenu.do. *Criminal:* same.

15th General District Court   **Free**
Civil: Search court records free at http://epwsgdp1.courts.state.va.us/gdcourts/caseSearch.do?index=index. Results show name and sometimes address. Also search via LOPAS; call 804-786-5511 to apply. *Criminal:* Search free at http://epwsgdp1.courts.state.va.us/gdcourts/caseSearch.do?index=index. Results show DOB month and day, sex, race.

Williamsburg-James City

County General District Court   **Free**
Civil: Search free at http://epwsgdp1.courts.state.va.us/gdcourts/caseSearch.do?index=index. Results show name and DOB month/day. Also search via LOPAS; call 804-786-5511 to apply. *Criminal:* Search free at http://epwsgdp1.courts.state.va.us/gdcourts/caseSearch.do?index=index. Results show DOB month and day, sex, race.

Winchester City

26th Circuit Court   www.winfredclerk.com   **Free**
Civil: Online access free at www.courts.state.va.us/caseinfo/circuit.html. *Criminal:* Same.

26th General District Court   **Free**
Civil: Search free at http://epwsgdp1.courts.state.va.us/gdcourts/caseSearch.do?index=index. Results show name and sometimes address. Also search via LOPAS; call 804-786-5511 to apply. *Criminal:* Search free at http://epwsgdp1.courts.state.va.us/gdcourts/caseSearch.do?index=index. Results show DOB month and day, sex, race.

Wise County

30th Circuit Court   www.wisecircuitcourt.com   **Free**
Civil: Online access free at www.courts.state.va.us/caseinfo/circuit.html. Also, court indexes and images are at www.courtbar.org. Registration and a fee is required. Records go back to June, 2000. *Criminal:* Same.

30th General District Court   **Free**
Civil: Search free at http://epwsgdp1.courts.state.va.us/gdcourts/caseSearch.do?index=index. Results show name and sometimes address. Also search via LOPAS; call 804-786-5511 to apply. *Criminal:* Search free at http://epwsgdp1.courts.state.va.us/gdcourts/caseSearch.do?index=index. Results show DOB month and day, sex, race.

Wythe County

27th Circuit Court   www.courts.state.va.us/courts/circuit.html   **Free & $$**
Civil: Remote online access to court case indexes is via LOPAS; call 804-786-5511 to apply. Also, access to court records is by subscription; $25.00 registration fee for username and password, also $25.00 per transaction fee. Contact the clerk office for signup. *Criminal:* Same.

Wythe General District Court   **Free**
Civil: Search free at http://epwsgdp1.courts.state.va.us/gdcourts/caseSearch.do?index=index. Results show name and sometimes address. Also search via LOPAS; call 804-786-5511 to apply. *Criminal:* Search free at http://epwsgdp1.courts.state.va.us/gdcourts/caseSearch.do?index=index. Results show DOB month and day, sex, race.

York County

9th Circuit Court   www.yorkcounty.gov/circuitcourt/   **Free**
Civil: Online access free at www.courts.state.va.us/caseinfo/circuit.html. *Criminal:* Same.

9th General District Court   www.yorkcounty.gov/districtcourt/   **Free**
Civil: Search free at http://epwsgdp1.courts.state.va.us/gdcourts/caseSearch.do?index=index. Results show name and sometimes address. Also search via LOPAS; call 804-786-5511 to apply. *Criminal:* Search free at http://epwsgdp1.courts.state.va.us/gdcourts/caseSearch.do?index=index. Results show DOB month and day, sex, race.

Recorders, Assessors, and Other Sites of Note

Recording Office Organization: 95 counties and 41 independent cities; 123 recording offices. The recording officer is the Clerk of Circuit Court. Sixteen independent cities share the Clerk of Circuit Court with the county – Bedford; Covington and Clifton Forge (Alleghany County); Emporia (Greenville County); Fairfax; Falls Church (Arlington or Fairfax County); Franklin (Southhampton County); Galax (Carroll County); Harrisonburg (Rockingham County); Lexington (Rockbridge County); Manassas and Manassas Park (Prince William County); Norton (Wise County); Poquoson (York County); South Boston (Halifax County); and Williamsburg (James City County).

Charles City and James City are counties, not cities. The City of Franklin is not in Franklin County. The City of Richmond is not in Richmond County. The City of Roanoke is not in Roanoke County.

Federal tax liens on personal property of businesses are filed with the State Corporation Commission. Other federal and all state tax liens are filed with the county Clerk of Circuit Court.

Online Access Note: A growing number of Virginia counties and cities provide free access to real estate related information via the Internet. A limited but growing private company network named VamaNet provides free residential, commercial, and vacant property data and tax records; visit www.vamanet.com/info/home.jsp

Virginia Counties (Virginia Cities listed as separate section after this County Section)

Accomack County *Real Estate, Grantor/Grantee, Deed, Mortgage, Lien, Judgment, Marriage, Will Records* www.co.accomack.va.us/index2.html **$$** Access recorder's index by subscription service ILS; call 877-658-6018 x2111 to apply; ask for Johnathan; $80 monthly fee ad credit cards accepted.
Property, Taxation Records **Free** Access parcel assessment value data free at http://accomack.mapsdirect.net/AdvancedSearch.aspx.

Albemarle County *Real Estate, Deed, Lien, Judgment, UCC Records* www.albemarle.org/index.asp **$$** Access to clerk's recorded index available by subscription; fee- $600 per year per user or $1200 for corporate 4-user sub. Does not include vital records. Land records go back to 1947. Contact clerk Shelby Marshall 434-972-4083.
Property, Taxation Records **Free** Search assessor data free at http://albemarlevapropertymax.governmaxa.com/propertymax/rover30.asp; search free by parcel, owner name, address, sales. Also, search parcel data on GIS-mapping site free at http://gisweb.albemarle.org/. Also, search zoning notices free at www.albemarle.org/upload/images/webapps/zoning/

Alleghany County *Property, Taxation Records* **Free** Access City of Covington property data free at www.vamanet.com/cgi-bin/MAPSRCHPGM?LOCAL=COV. Access Allegehany County data free at a sister website at www.vamanet.com/cgi-bin/MAPSRCHPGM?LOCAL=ALE.

Amelia County *Rel Estate, Deed Records* www.ameliacova.us/Clerk%20Circuit.htm **$$** Access real estate recording records by subscription only, contact Clerk of Circuit Court for information.
Property, Taxation Records **Free** Search for property card and assessment data free at www.ameliacountyrealestate.com/.

Amherst County *Property, Taxation Records* **$$** Access current assessment info and sales by VamaNet subscription at www.vamanet.com/cgi-bin/LOCS. Fee is $35 per month or $300 per year with discounts for multiple localities, regions.

Arlington County *Property, Taxation Records* **Free** Property records on the County assessor database are free at www.arlingtonva.us/Departments/RealEstate/reassessments/scripts/DREADefault.asp. Includes trade name search. Also, access Falls Church City property data free on the GIS-mapping site at http://property.fallschurchva.gov/public/ieprop.htm but no name searching.

Augusta County *Property, Taxation Records* **Free** Click on Augusta County to search property data for free at www.vamanet.com/cgi-bin/LOCS.

Bath County *Property, Taxation Records* **$$** Access current assessment info and sales by VamaNet subscription at www.vamanet.com/cgi-bin/LOCS. Fee is $35 per month or $300 per year with discounts for multiple localities, regions.

Bedford County *Property, Taxation Records* **Free** Real estate records on the Bedford County GIS site are free at www.co.bedford.va.us/Res/GIS/index.htm; however, no name searching at this time. Also access via www.onlinegis.net/VaBedford/. Click on Display Map then Search. property records on City of Bedford site are free at www.bedfordva.gov/taxf.shtml. Also, access City of Bedford property info on the GIS site free at http://bedfordgis.bedfordva.gov/bedfordcity/search.asp?skipopen=1.

Bland County *Property, Taxation Records* `$$` Access current assessment info and sales by VamaNet subscription at www.vamanet.com/cgi-bin/LOCS. Fee is $35 per month or $300 per year with discounts for multiple localities, regions.

Botetourt County *Property, Taxation Records* `Free` Access property data free at www.onlinegis.net/VaBotetourt/. Click on Display Map then Search, no name searching.

Brunswick County *Real Estate, Deed, Judgment, Will, Marriage Records* `$$` Access to Circuit Court Records Search System is by subscription at http://208.210.219.102/cgi-bin/p/rms.cgi. Includes images for other selected jurisdictions; $1200 per year, username and password required, signup with local Circuit Ct Clerk.

Buchanan County *Real Estate, Grantor/Grantee, Deed, Lien, Judgment, UCC, Marriage, Wills/Probate, Fictitious Name Records* www.courts.state.va.us/courts/circuit/Buchanan/home.html `$$` Access to the recorder's database is available by subscription, registration and password required; $75.00 per month. Contact clerk's office for signup and info. Data goes back to 8/2005 but new data being added back to 1991. Deeds index will go back to 1976.

Campbell County *Property, Taxation Records* `Free` Access county property data from Dept of Real Estate and Mapping free at http://campbellvapropertymax.governmaxa.com/propertymax/rover30.asp?. Also, search property by name on the county GIS-mapping site at http://gis.co.campbell.va.us/campbellims/gis.aspx. Login as guest; registration required for full data. Click on 'Find' to search.

Caroline County *Property, Taxation Records* `Free` Click on Caroline County to search property records for free at www.vamanet.com/cgi-bin/LOCS.

Carroll County *Real Estate, Deed, Judgment, UCC Records* www.chillsnet.org `$$` Access to Carroll county property data is a $25 monthly fee. Username and password required; signup through Clerk of Circuit Court, 276-730-3070. Land index and images go back to 1966; plats to 2002.
Property, Taxation Records `Free` Access Town of Hillsville property data on the gis-mapping site at http://arcims.webgis.net/va/Hillsville/default.asp .

Charles City County *Property, Taxation Records* `Free` View property cards free at www.charlescitycountyrealestate.com. Click on View Property Cards Online.

Chesterfield County *Property, Taxation Records* `Free` Search the real estate assessment data for free at www.co.chesterfield.va.us/ManagementServices/RealEstateAssessments/Rea_Search_Home.asp.

Clarke County *Real Estate, Grantor/Grantee, Deed, Judgment Records* www.clarkevacocc.org `$$` With username and password you may access recorder's land records at www.clarkevacocc.org. Includes deed book 153 back to 1984. Set up account online; fee is $25.00 per month.
Property, Taxation Records `Free` Click on Clarke County to search property data for free at http://mapsonline.net/clarkecounty/ but no name searching.

Culpeper County *Property, Taxation Records* `Free` Access property data free at www.onlinegis.net/VaCulpeper/. Click on Display Map, then Search; no name searching. Search Town of Culpeper data free at www.onlinegis.net/VACulpeper as well. Also, access current assessment info and sales by VamaNet subscription at www.vamanet.com/cgi-bin/LOCS. Fee is $35 per month or $300 per year with discounts for multiple localities, regions.

Cumberland County *Real Estate, Deed Records* www.cumberlandcounty.com `$$` County deed and land records available by subscription from private company at http://en.landsystems.com/index.php.

Dickenson County *Property, Taxation Records* `Free` Access to the Commissioner of Revenue tax data is free at www.smartmesh.net/Search.aspx.

Dinwiddie County *Property, Taxation Records* `$$` Access current assessment info and sales by subscription at www.vamanet.com/cgi-bin/LOCS. Fee is $35 per month or $300 per year with discounts for multiple localities, regions.

Essex County *Property, Taxation Records* `Free & $$` Search the treasurer's site free at www.essex-virginia.org/taxes.htm. Access county property cards free at https://county.essex-va.org/applications/txapps/PropCardsIndex.htm. RE taxes free at https://county.essex-va.org/applications/trapps/REIindex.htm. Also, access assessment info and sales by VamaNet subscription at www.vamanet.com/cgi-bin/LOCS. Fee- $35 per month or $300 per year with discounts for multiple localities.

Fairfax County *Real Estate, Deed Records* www.fairfaxcounty.gov/courts/circuit/ `Free` Hear about property descriptions, assessed values and sales prices. This Automated Information System operates Monday-Saturday 7AM-7PM at 703-222-6740. Fax-back service available.
Property, Taxation Records `Free` Records on the Dept. of Tax Administration RE Assessment database are free at http://icare.fairfaxcounty.gov/Search/GenericSearch.aspx?mode=ADDRESS. Also, the list of auction properties is free at www.fairfaxcounty.gov/dta/auction.htm. Also, search City Assessments for free at http://va-fairfax-assessment.governmax.com/propertymax/rover30.asp?sid=3817723E69D7454E9ED7F93D092E194C but no name searching.

Fauquier County *Real Estate, Deed Records* www.fauquiercounty.gov `$$` full real estate data may be available by subscription, $50.00 per month; call Commissioner of the Revenue at 540-347-8720.
Property, Taxation Records `Free` Search for property data and deed book info for free on the gis-mapping site at http://www2.undersys.com/fvawebnew/fauquier.html. Also, Search Town of Warrenton property index free at http://quicksearch.webgis.net/search.php?site=va_warrenton. Search property data free via the email response form at www.fauquiercounty.gov/government/departments/commrev/index.cfm?action=realestatetaxform.

Floyd County *Property, Taxation Records* `Free` Access the property assessment search page free at http://egov.mixnet.com/floyd_test/Search.asp.

Fluvanna County *Judgment Records* `Free` For free case information go to www.courts.state.va.us/caseinfo/home.html.
Property, Taxation Records `Free` Click on Fluvanna County to search property data for free at www.vamanet.com/cgi-bin/LOCS. Access property data free at www.onlinegis.net/VaFluvanna/. Click on Display Map then Search, no name searching.

Franklin County *Property, Taxation Records* `Free` Access property data free at http://arcims2.webgis.net/va/franklin/. Also, search delinquent tax data free at www.franklincountyva.org/taxes.htm. Also, access current assessment info and sales by VamaNet subscription at www.vamanet.com/cgi-bin/LOCS. Fee is $35 per month or $300 per year with discounts for multiple localities, regions.

Frederick County *Real Estate, Deed, Mortgage, Lien Records* www.winfredclerk.com `$$` Access to the County Records management System is by subscription; base fee is $500 per year for 3 users. Contact Debby Payne in the Circuit Court Clerk's office for info.
Property, Taxation Records `Free & $$` Access current assessment info and sales by VamaNet subscription at www.vamanet.com/cgi-bin/LOCS. Fee is $35 per month or $300 per year with discounts for multiple localities, regions. Also, access parcel data on the GIS-mapping site free at http://gis.co.frederick.va.us/ and click on Parcel Mapping Service.

Giles County *Real Estate, Deed Records* `$$` Acess land records and deeds on subscription service ILS; call 804-786-5511 to apply; $80 monthly fee.
Property, Taxation Records `Free` Click on Giles County to search for property records for free at www.vamanet.com/cgi-bin/LOCS. Search property info on the county GIS site for free at http://arcims2.webgis.net/giles/default.asp. To name search click on Quick Search.

Gloucester County *Judgment Records* www.gloucesterva.info/ `Free` Access to Law and Chancery judgments is free at www.courts.state.va.us/caseinfo/circuit.html.
Property, Taxation Records `Free` Click on Gloucester County to search property data for free at www.gloucesterva.info/coronlineapps/landbookdb/landbook1.asp

Goochland County *Property, Taxation Records* `Free` Click on Goochland County to search property data for free at www.vamanet.com/cgi-bin/LOCS.

Grayson County *Property, Taxation Records* `Free` Access the Real Estate Tax Search page free at www.graysoncountyva.com/graysonrealestatetax.asp. Also, access property data free at http://arcims2.webgis.net/va/grayson/.

Greene County *Real Estate, Deed, Judgement Records* www.gcva.us/dpts/cort/clerk.htm `$$` Access to recorded documents, deeds, judgments to be available July, 2008.
Property, Taxation Records `Free` Access real estate and parcel data free at www.onlinegis.net/VaGreene/. Click on Display Map then Search, no name searching. Also, search person property inquiry db free at http://71.0.81.15/applications/trapps/PPIindex.htm but not name searching. Access treasurer's real estate dtabase free at http://71.0.81.15/applications/trapps/REindex.htm but no name searching.

Greensville County *Property, Taxation Records* `$$` Access current assessment info and sales by subscription at www.vamanet.com/cgi-bin/LOCS. Fee is $35 per month or $300 per year with discounts for multiple localities, regions.

Hanover County *Property, Taxation Records* `Free` Access the parcel search function of the GIS site free at www.hanovercountygis.org/hanover/ but no name searching.

Henrico County *Real Estate, Deed Records* www.co.henrico.va.us/clerk/ `$$` County deed and land records available by subscription from private company at http://en.landsystems.com/index.php.

Isle of Wight County *Real Estate, Deed, Lien, Judgment, Will Records* www.co.isle-of-wight.va.us/ `$$` Access to recorder land records is by subscription; fee is $100 per month; online deed records go back to 1970, judgments to 1991. Contact Wanda Wills at 757-365-6233 for registration and info.
Property, Taxation Records `Free` Access the 2006 assessment database free at www.co.isle-of-wight.va.us/assessment.html but no name searching. Also, access property data via the GIS-mapping site free at www.spatialsys.com/isleofwight/ but no name searching. Also, click on Isle of Wight County to search for property records for free at www.vamanet.com/cgi-bin/MAPSRCHPGM?LOCAL=ISL.

James City County *Property, Taxation Records* `Free` Access assessment data free at http://property.jccegov.com/parcelviewer/. Search City of Williamsburg property assessor data free at http://williamsburggis.com/gis.aspx. Click on find to search. Search by name on tax payment website at https://first.jccegov.com/epayment/taxpayer.aspx.

King George County *Property, Taxation Records* `Free & $$` Access property data free at www.onlinegis.net/VaKingGeorge/. Click on Display Map then Search, no name searching. Also, access current assessment info and sales by VamaNet subscription at www.vamanet.com/cgi-bin/LOCS. Fee is $35 per month or $300 per year with discounts for multiple localities, regions.

Lancaster County *Real Estate, Deed, Judgment, Will, Marriage, Chancery Records* www.lancova.com `$$` Access to Circuit Court Records Search System is by subscription at http://208.210.219.102/cgi-bin/p/rms.cgi. Includes images for other selected jurisdictions; $1200 per year, username and password required, signup with local Circuit Ct Clerk. *Property, Taxation Records* `Free & $$` Access current assessment info and sales by VamaNet subscription at www.vamanet.com/cgi-bin/LOCS. Fee is $35 per month or $300 per year with discounts for multiple localities, regions. Also, access parcel data free on the GIS-mapping site free at www.lancova.com/GIS/map.asp.

Lee County *Real Estate, Deed, Lien, Judgment, Will, Marriage, UCC Records* `$$` Access to the recorder's database is available by subscription, registration and password required; $50 per month or $500 per year. Contact clerk's office for registration form. Deeds go back to 5/1972; judgments and wills to 8/1978, marriages to 1/1964, financing statements to 1/1995.

Loudoun County *Real Estate, Deed, Will, Estate, Judgment, Plat, UCC Records* www.loudoun.gov/clerk `$$` Access to recorders land records of deeds, wills, judgment, plats and UCCs is available by subscription, see Land Records in Quick Links at www.loudoun.gov/clerk/. Fee is $1300 per year; deeds go back to 1893, wills 1928, judgments 1985, UCCs 1996. *Property, Taxation Records* `Free` Search the property assessor data for free at http://inter1.loudoun.gov/webpdbs/. No name searching; search by address, number, or ID only. Access property data on the GIS-mapping site free at http://gisinter1.loudoun.gov/weblogis/agree.htm but no name searching.

Louisa County *Property, Taxation Records* `Free & $$` Search property and person property tax data for free at https://louweb.louisa.org/Applications/web/default.htm. Also, search property on the GIS-mapping site free at http://gis.timmons.com/louisaims/gis.aspx. Click on Search. Search assessment data free at http://louweb.louisa.org/assess/master_Q.asp, Also, access assessment info and sales by VamaNet subscription at www.vamanet.com/cgi-bin/LOCS. Fee- $35 per month or $300 per year; discounts for multiple localities, regions.

Madison County *Property, Taxation Records* `Free` Access property data free at www.onlinegis.net/VaMadison/. Click on Display Map then Search, no name searching. Also, access current assessment info and sales by VamaNet subscription at www.vamanet.com/cgi-bin/LOCS. Fee is $35 per month or $300 per year with discounts for multiple localities, regions.

Mecklenburg County *Property, Taxation Records* `Free` For access to land files free go to www.mecklenburgva.com/govt/meckcor.

Middlesex County *Property, Taxation Records* `$$` Access current assessment info and sales by subscription at www.vamanet.com/cgi-bin/LOCS. Fee is $35 per month or $300 per year with discounts for multiple localities, regions.

Montgomery County *Real Estate, Deed Records* `Free & $$` Land record access via subscription service ILS; call 804-786-5511 to apply; $80 monthly fee. *Property, Taxation Records* `Free` Search county property index free at http://quicksearch.webgis.net/search.php?site=va_montgomery. Also, access to the county Tax Parcel Information System database is free at www.montva.com/departments/plan/igis.php. Records on the Town of Blacksburg GIS site are free at http://arcims2.webgis.net/blacksburg/default.asp?. To name search, click on Quick Search.

New Kent County *Property, Taxation Records* `Free` Access to New Kent county assessor records is free at http://data.visionappraisal.com/NewKentCountyVA/. Register free for full data.

Northumberland County *Property, Taxation Records* `Free` Access Land Book data free at www.co.northumberland.va.us/NH-land-book.htm.

Nottoway County *Property, Taxation Records* `Free` Access property data free at http://arcims2.webgis.net/va/nottoway/.

Orange County *Property, Taxation Records* `Free` Access property data free at www.onlinegis.net/VaOrange/. Click on Display Map then Search, no name searching. Also search Town of Orange property free at www.onlinegis.net/VATOO. Click on Orange County to search for property records for free at www.vamanet.com/cgi-bin/LOCS.

Page County *Property, Taxation Records* `$$` Access current assessment info and sales by VamaNet subscription at www.vamanet.com/cgi-bin/LOCS. Fee is $35 per month or $300 per year with discounts for multiple localities, regions.

Patrick County *Property, Taxation Records* `Free` Access property data free at http://arcims.webgis.net/va/patrick/default.asp?pg=95. Map searching only, no name searching.

Pittsylvania County *Property, Taxation Records* `Free` Search parcel information free at http://www2.undersys.com/pvaweb/pittsylvania.html. Click on Search For Property to name search.

Powhatan County *Real Estate, Grantor/Grantee, Deed, Mortgage, Lien, Judgment, Marriage, Will Records* www.powhatanva.gov/ `$$` Access recorder's index by subscription service ILS; call 877-658-6018 x2111 to apply,, ask for Johnathan; $80 monthly fee ad credit cards accepted.
Property, Taxation Records `Free` Click on Powhatan County to search property data for free at www.vamanet.com/cgi-bin/LOCS. Also, search assessment and reassessment data free at www.powhatancountyrealestate.com/.

Prince William County *Real Estate, Deed, Lien, Mortgage, UCC, Plat, Judgment, Will, Fictitious Name, Marriage Records* www.pwcgov.org/default.aspx?topic=040017 `$$` Access to the clerk's exhaustive database is available by subscription; fee is $300 per quarter. Login in https://www3.pwcgov.org/panet/logon.asp. Most records go back to mid-1980's; deeds back to 1918.
Property, Taxation Records `Free` Records on the county Property Assessment Information database are free at http://www4.pwcgov.org/realestate/LandRover.asp but no name searching. Also, City of Manassas Park Commissioner of the Revenue's real estate assessment data is at http://data.visionappraisal.com/ManassasVA/. Free registration required to access full data.

Pulaski County *Property, Taxation Records* `Free` Access to the county GIS mapping info is free at http://arcims2.webgis.net/pulaski/default.asp. No name searching.

Rappahannock County *Property, Taxation Records* `$$` Access current assessment info and sales by VamaNet subscription at www.vamanet.com/cgi-bin/LOCS.jsp#rates. Fee is $35 per month or $300 per year with discounts for multiple localities, regions.

Richmond County *Real Estate, Deed, Lien Records* www.co.richmond.va.us `$$` Access recorders land data by subscription at https://csa.landsystems.com/LROnline/logon.aspx. Individual account- $80.00 per month; 5-user business account- $200 per month.
Property, Taxation Records `Free` Search county parcel data on the GIS-mapping site free at www.onlinegis.net/VaRichmond/.

Roanoke County *Property, Taxation Records* `Free` Access to GIS mapping and tax map for free go to www.roanokecountyva.gov/Departments/RealEstateValuation/Default.htm.

Rockbridge County *Property, Taxation Records* `Free` Access county records on the GIS-mapping site free at http://quicksearch.webgis.net/search.php?site=va_rockbridge. Also, access City of Lexington property data free at www.vamanet.com/cgi-bin/MAPSRCHPGM?LOCAL=LEX. Also, access county current assessment info and sales by subscription at www.vamanet.com/cgi-bin/LOCS. Fee is $35 per month or $300 per year with discounts for multiple localities, regions.

Rockingham County *Real Estate, Real Property Records* `$$` Access to real property by subscription at https://www.uslandrecords.com/uslr/UslrApp/index.jsp
Property, Taxation Records `Free` Access to real estate assessment records at http://rockingham.gisbrowser.com/home.cfm.

Russell County *Real Estate, Deed Records* `$$` County deed and land records available by subscription from private company at http://en.landsystems.com/index.php.
Property, Taxation Records `$$` Access current assessment info and sales by VamaNet subscription at www.vamanet.com/. Fee is $35 per month or $300 per year with discounts for multiple localities, regions.

Scott County *Lien, Judgment, UCC, Marriage, Probate, Fictitious Name Records* `$$` Access recorder's data by subscription; signup at clerk's office.
Property, Taxation Records `$$` Access current assessment info and sales by VamaNet subscription at www.vamanet.com/cgi-bin/LOCS.jsp#rates. Fee is $35 per month or $300 per year with discounts for multiple localities, regions.

Shenandoah County *Real Estate, Grantor/Grantor, Deed, Judgment, UCC, Marriage, Will/Probate Records* `$$` Recorded data available by subscription with images back to 1999 and earlier being added. Fee is $50.00 per month or $500.00 per year, contact Sarona Irvin 540-459-6153 in clerk's office.
Property, Taxation Records `Free & $$` Access current assessment info and sales by VamaNet subscription at www.vamanet.com/cgi-bin/LOCS.jsp#rates. Fee is $35 per month or $300 per year with discounts for multiple localities, regions. Also, access tax payment histories free at https://204.111.80.202/applications/trapps/index.htm. Also, access parcel data on the GIS-mapping site free at www.shenandoahgis.org/ and click on Find to name search.

Smyth County *Property, Taxation Records* `Free & $$` Access current assessment info and sales by VamaNet subscription at www.vamanet.com/cgi-bin/LOCS. Fee is $35 per month or $300 per year with discounts for multiple localities, regions. Also, search county property index free at http://quicksearch.webgis.net/search.php?site=va_smyth.

Southampton County *Property, Taxation Records* `Free` Click on Southampton County to search property data for free at www.vamanet.com/cgi-bin/LOCS. Also, only City of Franklin appraisal data is free at www.vamanet.com/cgi-bin/MAPSRCHPGM?LOCAL=FRA but this City site does not include county appraisal records. Also, county GIS tax map data is free at www.onlinegis.net/VaSouthampton/asp/controlVersion.asp. No name searching.

Spotsylvania County *Real Estate, Deed, Lien Records* `$$` Access the recorder's recording index and images by subscription; fee is $120.00 per month; contact Mary Ellen Garcia at 540-507-7605 at the clerk's office. Also, county deed and land records available by subscription from private company at http://en.landsystems.com/index.php.

Stafford County *Property, Taxation Records* `Free` Personal Property and RE Lookup free at http://taxpaid.stafford.va.us/. Also, access property data and interactive maps free at www.staffordcountygis.org/Website/StaffordInteractive/viewer.htm. Access properrty data free at http://staffordvapropertymax.governmaxa.com/propertymax/rover30.asp but no name searching.

Surry County *Real Estate, Deed, Judgment, Will, Marriage Records* `$$` Access to Circuit Court Records Search System is by subscription at http://208.210.219.102/cgi-bin/p/rms.cgi. Includes images for other selected jurisdictions; $1200 per year, username and password required, signup with local Circuit Ct Clerk.

Sussex County *Property, Taxation Records* `Free` Access to assessor property records is free at www.sussexcountyproperty.com.

Tazewell County *Property, Taxation Records* `Free` Click on Tazewell County to search property data for free at www.vamanet.com/cgi-bin/LOCS.

Warren County *Real Estate, Deed, Land, Lien, Will, UCC Records* www.warrencountyva.net/circuit_court.asp `Free & $$` Access the Clerk's data on the web for a fee; username and password required. For a fee username and password contact Jennifer Sims at 540-635-2435 or at jsims@courts.state.va.us. Images go back to 1994.
Property, Taxation Records `Free & $$` Access current assessment info and sales by VamaNet subscription at www.vamanet.com/cgi-bin/LOCS. Fee is $35 per month or $300 per year with discounts for multiple localities, regions. Also, search assessment data on the GIS-mapping site free at www.warrengis.org/default.aspx but no name searching. Also search treasurer data of real estate and personal property free at http://75.145.206.89/applications/trapps/index.htm.

Washington County *Property, Taxation Records* `$$` Access current assessment info and sales by subscription at www.vamanet.com/cgi-bin/LOCS. Fee is $35 per month or $300 per year with discounts for multiple localities, regions.

Westmoreland County *Property, Taxation Records* `Free` Access real estate tax payment database free at http://166.61.239.88/applications/trapps/REIindex.htm. Also, search property card records free at http://166.61.239.88/applications/txapps/PropCardsIndex.htm. Also, search utility payment records free at http://166.61.239.88/applications/trapps/UTIindex.htm.

Wise County *Real Estate, Deed, Lien, Probate, Marriage, UCC, Judgment, Permit Records* www.courtbar.org `$$` Access recording office records at www.courtbar.org/records.htm. For full access fee is $550 annually; see https://egov.mixnet.com/courts/ccwise2000/login.asp. This fee service includes index and images, court orders, land documents from 1970 and links to RE tax assessments, 50-year RE, tax maps, plat maps, delinquent taxes, permit images, probate, marriage, judgment liens for 20 years, and more. UCC-1 indices for past 5 years. Online records include City of Norton.
Property, Taxation Records `Free & $$` Property data is at http://egov.mixnet.com/wise/search.asp. Egov also offers a $440 per year subscription service. Also, search county parcel data free at http://quicksearch.webgis.net/search.php?site=va_wise.

Wythe County *Judgment Records* `$$` Access to court judgment records is by subscription; $25.00 registration fee for username and password, also $25.00 per transaction fee. Contact the clerk office (Brenda Atwell) for signup.
Property, Taxation Records `$$` Access current assessment info and sales by VamaNet subscription at www.vamanet.com/cgi-bin/LOCS. Fee is $35 per month or $300 per year with discounts for multiple localities, regions.

York County *Property, Taxation Records* `Free` Parcel records from the County GIS site are free at www.regis.state.va.us/york/pub/disclaimer.htm.

Virginia Cities - Administered As Counties

Alexandria City *Property, Taxation Records* `Free` Access to city real estate assessments is free at http://realestate.alexandriava.gov/ but no name searching. Search property free at the GIS-mapping site at http://gis.alexandriava.gov/parcelviewernet/viewer.htm but no name searching.

Bristol City *Property, Taxation Records* `$$` Access current assessment info and sales by VamaNet subscription at www.vamanet.com/cgi-bin/LOCS. Fee is $35 per month or $300 per year with discounts for multiple localities, regions.

Buena Vista City *Property, Taxation Records* `Free` Access city appraisal data free at www.vamanet.com/cgi-bin/MAPSRCHPGM?LOCAL=BUE.

Chesapeake City *Property, Taxation Records* `Free` Access to property appraiser data is free at www.chesva.com/realestate.html. No name searching at this time

Danville City *Property, Taxation Records* `Free` Access to Danville City assessor online records is free at www.danvillevaassessor.org. Also, see note at beginning of section for statewide land record access.

Falls Church City *Property, Taxation Records* `Free` Access city property data free on the GIS-mapping site at http://property.fallschurchva.gov/public/ieprop.htm but no name searching.

Fredericksburg City *Real Estate, Deed, Judgment, Will, Marriage Records* www.fredericksburgva.gov `$$` Access to Circuit Court Records Search System is by subscription at http://208.210.219.102/cgi-bin/p/rms.cgi. Includes images for other selected jurisdictions; $1200 per year, username and password required, signup with local Circuit Ct Clerk.
Property, Taxation Records `$$` Access current assessment info and sales by VamaNet subscription at www.vamanet.com/cgi-bin/LOCS. Fee is $35 per month or $300 per year with discounts for multiple localities, regions.

Hampton City *Judgment Records* www.hampton.gov `Free` Search for limited judgment records on the state court website at www.courts.state.va.us.
Property, Taxation Records `Free` Access the City Real Estate Information site free at http://198.252.241.11/realinfo/. No name searching. Search property transfer pdf lists free at www.hampton.gov/assessor/ see bottom of page and click on Real Estate Property Transfers now online. Search property data on the GIS-mapping site free at www.regis.state.va.us/hampton/public/property.htm but no name searching.

Hopewell City *Judgment Records* www.ci.hopewell.va.us `Free` Access to court records is free at www.courts.state.va.us/caseinfo/circuit.html.

Martinsville City *Real Estate, Deed, Judgment, Will, Marriage, Delinquent Tax Records*
www.ci.martinsville.va.us/Circuitclerk `$$` Access to Circuit clerk records is at www.ci.martinsville.va.us/Circuitclerk. Fee is $30.00 per month, or you may search at a rate of $1 per doc. For info, call office of Ashby Pritchett at 276-656-5106 or visit website.

Newport News City *Property, Taxation Records* `Free` Access to the City's "Real Estate on the Web" database is free at www.nngov.com/assessor/resources/reis. Search by address or parcel number; new "advanced search" may include name searching. Search for property data free on the gis-mapping site at http://gis.nngov.com/gis/(S(w0b4f145vfpgad45j0j40d45))/Default.aspx. No name searching. Use the black circle with the 'I' in it to show parcel data.

Norfolk City *Real Estate, Deed, Judgment, Will, Marriage Records* www.norfolk.gov/Circuit_Court/ccchome.asp `$$` Access Clerk of Circuit Court recording data by $50 per month subscription at www.norfolk.gov/Circuit_Court/remoteaccess.asp. Deeds and land records go back to 1988. Judgments, Wills, Marriages, etc, back to 1993. Also, access to Circuit Court Records Search System is by subscription at http://208.210.219.102/cgi-bin/p/rms.cgi. Includes images for other selected jurisdictions; $1200 per year, username and password required, signup with local Circuit Ct Clerk.
Property, Taxation Records `Free` Records on the City of Norfolk Real Estate Property Assessment database are free at www.norfolk.gov/RealEstate/search.asp.

Portsmouth City *Property, Taxation Records* `Free` Access to property records is free at www.portsmouthva.gov/assessor/data/realestatesearch.htm. No name searching. Access the treasurer's Real Estate Reeciveable Data free at www.portsmouthva.gov/treasurer/data/realestatereceivsearch.htm but not name searching. Also, search GIS-mapping site for parcel data free at www.portsmouthva.gov/website/parcel_flood/intro.htm. Use map tools to identify parcel data.

Radford City *Real Estate, Deed Records* `$$` Access to real estate recording docs to be available by subscription with Intern. Land Systems, call 877-658-6018 x205 for info.
Property, Taxation Records `$$` Access to City property info is at www.radford.va.us/inVizeDA/inVizeDA.aspx.

Richmond City *Property, Taxation Records* `Free` Search the city's Property & Real Estate Assessment data for free at www.ci.richmond.va.us/departments/gis/webmapper.aspx. If you click on Property Search, you cannot name search, but name searching available through the Webmapper. At the Webmapper page, click on "Advanced Search" then "Assessments" to name search.

Roanoke City *Property, Taxation Records* `Free` Access to property data is free on the City GIS website at http://gis.roanokeva.gov/text.htm.

Salem City *Property, Taxation Records* `$$` Access current assessment info and sales by VamaNet subscription at www.vamanet.com/cgi-bin/LOCS. Fee is $35 per month or $300 per year with discounts for multiple localities, regions.

Staunton City *Property, Taxation Records* `Free` Access property tax data on the City GIS site free at http://gis1.ci.staunton.va.us:8086/freeance/client/publicaccess1/index.html?appconfig=masterpublicaccess.

Suffolk City *Property, Taxation Records* `Free` Access property assessment data free at www.suffolk.va.us/realest/Search_Real_Estate_3.html but no name searching. Access parcel and property data free at GIS-mapping site at www.suffolk.va.us/gis/mapping.html but no name searching.

Virginia Beach City *Real Estate, Deed, Marriage, Judgment, UCC, Will, Estate, Business Name, Plat Records*
www.vbgov.com/ `Free & $$` Access the Clerk of Circuit Court database free at www.vblandrecords.com/index.aspx. The second method of access will be via a $100 per month Monthly Subscription using credit card. For credit card account, call 866-793-6505. Direct general questions to Emilie Inman at 757-385-8819. Also, browse document archives free at http://edocs.vbgov.com/weblink/
Property, Taxation Records `Free` Search the assessor database for free at http://va-virginiabeach-realestate.governmax.com/ but no name searching. Also, access Virginia Beach parcel and map records free at www.vbgov.com/e%2Dgov/emapping/.

Waynesboro City *Property, Taxation Records* `Free` Access to city property appraiser data is free at www.vamanet.com/cgi-bin/LOCS.

Winchester City *Real Estate, Deed, Mortgage, Lien Records* www.winfredclerk.com `$$` Access to the County Records management System is by subscription; base fee is $500 per year for 3 users. Contact Debby Payne in the Winchester County Circuit Court Clerk's office for info.
Property, Taxation Records `$$` Access current assessment info and sales by subscription at www.vamanet.com/cgi-bin/LOCS. Fee is $35 per month or $300 per year with discounts for multiple localities, regions. Also, access the surrounding Frederick County parcel data on the GIS-mapping site free at http://gis.co.frederick.va.us/ and click on Parcel Mapping Service.

Other Virginia Sites of Note:

Albemarle County - Zoning Notices www.albemarle.org/upload/images/webapps/zoning/ May be temporarily down.
City of Alexandria - Sheriff Crime Reports www.alexandriava.gov/police/crime_reports/reporter.php
City of Virginia Beach - Document Archives, Historical Deeds http://edocs.vbgov.com/weblink/
Pittsylvania County - Sheriff Wanted Lists www.pittsylvaniasheriff.org/wanted.asp
Sussex County - Ancient, Land Tax, Marriage, Will http://genealogyresources.org/index.html
Westmoreland County - Utility Payments http://166.61.239.88/applications/trapps/UTIindex.htm

Washington

Capital: Olympia
          Thurston County
Time Zone: PST
Population: 6,468,424
# of Counties: 39

Useful State Links

Website: http://access.wa.gov
Governor: www.governor.wa.gov
Attorney General: www.atg.wa.gov
State Archives: www.digitalarchives.wa.gov/default.aspx
State Statutes and Codes: www1.leg.wa.gov/LawsAndAgencyRules/
Legislative Bill Search: http://apps.leg.wa.gov/billinfo/
Bill Monitoring: https://leginfo.leg.wa.gov/user/login.aspx?ReturnUrl=%2fbilltracking%2fDefault.aspx
Unclaimed Funds: http://ucp.dor.wa.gov/

Primary State Agencies

Criminal Records $$

Washington State Patrol, Identification and Criminal History Section, www.wsp.wa.gov WSP offers access through a system called WATCH, which can be accessed from their website. The fee per search is $10.00. The exact DOB and exact spelling of the name are required. Credit cards are accepted online. To set up a WATCH account, call 360-705-5100 or email watch.help@wsp.wa.gov. WATCH stands for Washington Access To Criminal History. *Other Options:* See the State Court Administrator's office for information about their criminal records database (JIS-Link).

Sexual Offender Registry Free

Washington State Patrol, SOR, www.wsp.wa.gov In cooperation with the Washington Assoc. of Sheriffs and Police Chiefs, free online access to Level II and Level III sexual offenders is available at http://ml.waspc.org/.

Incarceration Records Free

Washington Department of Corrections, Office of the Secretary, www.doc.wa.gov No online searching provided; however, email requests can be directed to docpublicdisclosureunit@doc1.wa.gov. A private company provides access to the statewide SAVIN (victim notification) System but it excludes Pierce and King county jails; search free at https://www.vinelink.com/vinelink/siteInfoAction.do?siteId=48626. *Other Options:* Data is available by subscription for bulk users; for information, contact the Contracts Office at 360-725-8363.

Corporation, Trademarks/Servicemarks, LP, LLC Records Free

Secretary of State, Corporations Division, www.secstate.wa.gov/corps/ Free searching of corporation registrations is at www.secstate.wa.gov/corps/search.aspx. Information is updated daily. Also, search securities companies registered with the state and other financial institutions free at https://fortress.wa.gov/dfi/licenselu/dfi/licenseLU/default.aspx.

Trade Names Free & $$

Master License Service, Business & Professions Div, www.dol.wa.gov The web page give the ability to check trade name ability, assuming the business name listed is the trade name. *Other Options:* Records can be purchased on cartridges or 9 track tapes. Information includes date of registration, owner name, state ID numbers, and cancel date if cancelled. Call same number and ask for Jody Miller.

Uniform Commercial Code, Federal Tax Liens `Free & $$`

Department of Licensing, UCC Records, www.dol.wa.gov/business/UCC/ For online access, go to https://fortress.wa.gov/dol/ucc. There is no search fee for name search or by file number. Fee is $15.00 if copies are mailed. *Other Options:* The database may be purchased via FTP.

Sales Tax Registrations `Free`

Department of Revenue, Taxpayer Services, http://dor.wa.gov/ The agency provides a state business records database with free access on the Internet at http://dor.wa.gov/content/doingbusiness/registermybusiness/brd/. Lookups are by owner names, DBAs, and tax reporting numbers. Results show a myriad of data.

Viatl Records `Free & $$`

Department of Health, Center for Health Statistics, www.doh.wa.gov/EHSPHL/CHS/cert.htm Records may requested from www.Vitalchek.com, a state-endorsed vendor. *Other Options:* The Digital archives, launched in 2004, contains various periods for marriages, death, birth, military, naturalization, institution, and various historical records at www.digitalarchives.wa.gov/default.aspx.

Workers' Compensation Records `Free`

Labor and Industries, Public Records Unit, www.lni.wa.gov Claim information is accessible to authorized users at www.lni.wa.gov/orli/logon.asp. Claims inactive for 18+ months or crime victims claims are not in the Claim & Account Center.

Driver Records `Free & $$`

Department of Licensing, Driver Record Section, www.dol.wa.gov FTP retrieval is offered for high volume requesters, minimum of 2,000 requests per month. Requesters must be approved and sign a contract. Call Data Sales Management at 360-902-3851 Contract holders may also participate in a notification program (monitoring and notification of activity on a record), but strictly used for only insurance company needs. There is a secondary online check for status of a driver license, permit or ID card free at https://fortress.wa.gov/dol/ddl/dsd/.

Vehicle, Vessel Ownership & Registration `$$`

Department of Licensing, Public Disclosure Unit, www.dol.wa.gov/vehicleregistration/ This Internet Vehicle/Vessel Information Processing System is a commercial subscription service and all accounts must be pre-approved. A $25.00 deposit is required and there is a fee per hit. For more information, call 360-902-3760. *Other Options:* Large bulk lists cannot be released for any commercial purposes. Lists are released to non-profit entities and for statistical purposes. For more information, call 360-902-3760.

Voter Registration `Free`

Secretary of State, Office of Elections Division, www.secstate.wa.gov/elections/ A voter registration look-up link is found at http://wei.secstate.wa.gov/OSOS/VoterVault/Pages/MyVote.aspx - meant for voters to see and mainatin their own information. *Other Options:* Monthly CDs are available from the web for $30. A strong disclaimer states that the CD is restricted for use for political purposes only. Use of a credit card is required.

Occupational Licensing Boards

Acupuncturist	https://fortress.wa.gov/doh/providercredentialsearch/
Adult Family Home	www.aasa.dshs.wa.gov/Lookup/AFHRequestv2.asp
Animal Technician	https://fortress.wa.gov/doh/providercredentialsearch/
Announcer, Athletic Event/Ring	https://fortress.wa.gov/dol/dolprod/bpdLicenseQuery/
Applicator, Pesticide	http://agr.wa.gov/pestfert/LicensingEd/Search/default.aspx
Architect/Architectural Corp	https://fortress.wa.gov/dol/dolprod/bpdLicenseQuery/
Athlete, Professional/Inspector	https://fortress.wa.gov/dol/dolprod/bpdLicenseQuery/
Athletic-related Occupations	https://fortress.wa.gov/dol/dolprod/bpdLicenseQuery/
Attorney	http://pro.wsba.org/
Audiologist	https://fortress.wa.gov/doh/providercredentialsearch/
Bail Bond Agent/Agency	https://fortress.wa.gov/dol/dolprod/bpdLicenseQuery/
Bail Bond Recovery Agent	https://fortress.wa.gov/dol/dolprod/bpdLicenseQuery/
Bank	www.dfi.wa.gov/banks/commercial_banks.htm
Barber	https://fortress.wa.gov/dol/dolprod/bpdLicenseQuery/
Barber Instructor/School	https://fortress.wa.gov/dol/dolprod/bpdLicenseQuery/
Barber Shop/Mobile	https://fortress.wa.gov/dol/dolprod/bpdLicenseQuery/
Beauty Shop/Salon/Mobile	https://fortress.wa.gov/dol/dolprod/bpdLicenseQuery/
Boarding Home	www.aasa.dshs.wa.gov/Lookup/BHRequestv2.asp
Boiler Inspector	www.lni.wa.gov/TradesLicensing/Boilers/Inspectors/default.asp
Boxer	https://fortress.wa.gov/dol/dolprod/bpdLicenseQuery/
Bulk Hauler	www.dol.wa.gov/listoflicenses.html

Cemetery .... https://fortress.wa.gov/dol/dolprod/bpdLicenseQuery/
Cemetery Prearrangement Seller .... https://fortress.wa.gov/dol/dolprod/bpdLicenseQuery/
Certificate of Removal Registr'n .... https://fortress.wa.gov/dol/dolprod/bpdLicenseQuery/
Charitable Gift Annuity .... www.insurance.wa.gov/cgi-bin/PubInfoApps/CharitableGA.exe
Check Casher/Seller .... https://fortress.wa.gov/dfi/licquery/dfi/licquery/default.aspx
Child Care Facility/Provider.............. www.childcarenet.org/families/your-search/referral_form
Chiropractor...................................... https://fortress.wa.gov/doh/providercredentialsearch/
Collection Agency .... www.dol.wa.gov/listoflicenses.html
Consumer Loan Company .... https://fortress.wa.gov/dfi/licquery/dfi/licquery/default.aspx
Contractor, Construction/Firm/Gen'l. https://fortress.wa.gov/lni/bbip/
Contributor, Political .... http://web.pdc.wa.gov/public/campaign/default.aspx
Cosmetology-related Occupation ...... https://fortress.wa.gov/dol/dolprod/bpdLicenseQuery/
Counselor .... https://fortress.wa.gov/doh/providercredentialsearch/
Cremated Remains Dispositor .... https://fortress.wa.gov/dol/dolprod/bpdLicenseQuery/
Crematory.. https://fortress.wa.gov/dol/dolprod/bpdLicenseQuery/
Currency Exchange .... https://fortress.wa.gov/dfi/licquery/dfi/licquery/default.aspx
Dentist/ Dental Hygienist .... https://fortress.wa.gov/doh/providercredentialsearch/
Dietitian.. https://fortress.wa.gov/doh/providercredentialsearch/
Domestic Insurance Carrier .... https://fortress.wa.gov/oic/laa/LAAMain.aspx
Electrical Contractor/Administrator .. https://fortress.wa.gov/lni/bbip/
Electrician... https://fortress.wa.gov/lni/bbip/
Elevator Contractor/Mechanic........... https://fortress.wa.gov/lni/bbip/
Embalmer/Intern................................ https://fortress.wa.gov/dol/dolprod/bpdLicenseQuery/
Emergency Medical Technician .... https://fortress.wa.gov/doh/providercredentialsearch/
Employment Agency .... www.dol.wa.gov/listoflicenses.html
Employment Directory Service .... www.dol.wa.gov/listoflicenses.html
Engineer .... https://fortress.wa.gov/dol/dolprod/bpdLicenseQuery/
Engineering Geologist .... https://fortress.wa.gov/dol/dolprod/bpdLicenseQuery/
Engineering/Land Surveying Firm .... https://fortress.wa.gov/dol/dolprod/bpdLicenseQuery/
Escrow Company/Officers .... https://fortress.wa.gov/dfi/licquery/dfi/licquery/default.aspx
Esthetician/Esthetician Instructor ...... https://fortress.wa.gov/dol/dolprod/bpdLicenseQuery/
Esthetician/Salon/Mobile................... https://fortress.wa.gov/dol/dolprod/bpdLicenseQuery/
Feedlot... http://agr.wa.gov/FoodAnimal/Livestock/CertifiedFeedlots.htm
Fishing/Hunting License Dealer .... http://wdfw.wa.gov/lic/vendors/vendors.htm
Franchise .... https://fortress.wa.gov/dfi/licquery/dfi/licquery/default.aspx
Funeral Director/Intern/Establish't .... https://fortress.wa.gov/dol/dolprod/bpdLicenseQuery/
Funeral Prearrangement Contract ...... https://fortress.wa.gov/dol/dolprod/bpdLicenseQuery/
Gaming Operation .... www.wsgc.wa.gov/search/emp_lic_search.asp
Gaming-related Occupation............... www.wsgc.wa.gov/search/emp_lic_search.asp
Geologist .... https://fortress.wa.gov/dol/dolprod/bpdLicenseQuery/
Healthcare Service Company .... www.insurance.wa.gov/cgi-bin/PubInfoApps/CGIAuthComp.exe
Hearing Instrument Fitter/Dispenser . https://fortress.wa.gov/doh/providercredentialsearch/
HMO .... www.insurance.wa.gov/cgi-bin/PubInfoApps/CGIAuthComp.exe
Hydrogeologist .... https://fortress.wa.gov/dol/dolprod/bpdLicenseQuery/
Hypnotherapist .... https://fortress.wa.gov/doh/providercredentialsearch/
Insurance Agent/Broker..................... https://fortress.wa.gov/oic/laa/LAAMain.aspx
Insurance Company .... www.insurance.wa.gov/cgi-bin/PubInfoApps/CGIAuthComp.exe
Investment Advisors .... https://fortress.wa.gov/dfi/licquery/dfi/licquery/default.aspx
Kickboxer.. https://fortress.wa.gov/dol/dolprod/bpdLicenseQuery/
Land Surveyor/Surveyor-in-Training https://fortress.wa.gov/dol/dolprod/bpdLicenseQuery/
Landscape Architect .... https://fortress.wa.gov/dol/dolprod/bpdLicenseQuery/
Liquor Store...................................... www.liq.wa.gov/services/storesearch.asp
Livestock Market............................... http://agr.wa.gov/FoodAnimal/Livestock/PublicMarkets.htm
Lobbyist/Lobbyist Report.................. http://web.pdc.wa.gov/public/lobbyist/default.aspx
Manicure Salon/Mobile .... https://fortress.wa.gov/dol/dolprod/bpdLicenseQuery/
Manicurist/Manicurist Instructor .... https://fortress.wa.gov/dol/dolprod/bpdLicenseQuery/
Manufactured Home Dealer .... www.dol.wa.gov/listoflicenses.html

Marriage & Family Therapist	https://fortress.wa.gov/doh/providercredentialsearch/
Massage Therapist	https://fortress.wa.gov/doh/providercredentialsearch/
Medical Doctor	https://fortress.wa.gov/doh/providercredentialsearch/
Medical Gas Plumber	https://fortress.wa.gov/lni/bbip/
Mental Health Counselor	https://fortress.wa.gov/doh/providercredentialsearch/
Midwife	https://fortress.wa.gov/doh/providercredentialsearch/
Mobile Home/Travel Trailer Dealer	www.dol.wa.gov/listoflicenses.html
Money Transmitter	https://fortress.wa.gov/dfi/licquery/dfi/licquery/default.aspx
Mortgage Broker	https://fortress.wa.gov/dfi/licquery/dfi/licquery/default.aspx
Naturopathic Physician	https://fortress.wa.gov/doh/providercredentialsearch/
Nurse/Nursing Assistant	https://fortress.wa.gov/doh/providercredentialsearch/
Nursing Home	www.aasa.dshs.wa.gov/Professional/NFDir/directory.asp
Nursing Home Administrator	https://fortress.wa.gov/doh/providercredentialsearch/
Occupational Therapist	https://fortress.wa.gov/doh/providercredentialsearch/
Ocularist	https://fortress.wa.gov/doh/providercredentialsearch/
Optician	https://fortress.wa.gov/doh/providercredentialsearch/
Optometrist	https://fortress.wa.gov/doh/providercredentialsearch/
Osteopathic Physician	https://fortress.wa.gov/doh/providercredentialsearch/
Payday Lender	https://fortress.wa.gov/dfi/licquery/dfi/licquery/default.aspx
Pest Control-related Occupation	http://agr.wa.gov/PestFert/LicensingEd/Search/default.aspx
Pharmacist/ Pharmacy Technician	https://fortress.wa.gov/doh/providercredentialsearch/
Physical Therapist	https://fortress.wa.gov/doh/providercredentialsearch/
Physician Assistant	https://fortress.wa.gov/doh/providercredentialsearch/
Pilot, Marine, Commercial	www.pilotage.wa.gov/documents/Licensedpilots.PDF
Plumber	https://fortress.wa.gov/lni/bbip/
Podiatrist	https://fortress.wa.gov/doh/providercredentialsearch/
Political Candidate/Committee	http://web.pdc.wa.gov/Public/Searchdatabase/2007races.aspx
Private Investigative Agency/Trainer	https://fortress.wa.gov/dol/dolprod/bpdLicenseQuery/
Private Investigator, Armed/unarmed	https://fortress.wa.gov/dol/dolprod/bpdLicenseQuery/
Psychologist	https://fortress.wa.gov/doh/providercredentialsearch/
Public Accountant-CPA	www.cpaboard.wa.gov/LicenseeSearchApp/default.aspx
Purchasing Group (Insurance)	www.insurance.wa.gov/cgi-bin/PubInfoApps/CGIRiskPG.exe
Radiologic Technologist	https://fortress.wa.gov/doh/providercredentialsearch/
Real Estate Agent/Broker/Seller	www.dol.wa.gov/business/realestate/
Real Estate Appraiser	www.dol.wa.gov/listoflicenses.html
Real Estate LLC, LLP, Corp., etc.	www.dol.wa.gov/listoflicenses.html
Referee (Athletic)	https://fortress.wa.gov/dol/dolprod/bpdLicenseQuery/
Respiratory Therapist	https://fortress.wa.gov/doh/providercredentialsearch/
Risk Retention Group	www.insurance.wa.gov/cgi-bin/PubInfoApps/CGIRiskRG.exe
Savings & Loan/Savings Bank	www.dfi.wa.gov/banks/commercial_banks.htm
Scrap Processor	www.dol.wa.gov/listoflicenses.html
Securities Broker/Dealer/Seller	https://fortress.wa.gov/dfi/licquery/dfi/licquery/default.aspx
Security Guard, Private/Agency	https://fortress.wa.gov/dol/dolprod/bpdLicenseQuery/
Service Contract Provider (Ins)	www.insurance.wa.gov/cgi-bin/PubInfoApps/CGIServiceCP.exe
Sex Offender Treatment Provider	https://fortress.wa.gov/doh/providercredentialsearch/
Snowmobile Dealer	www.dol.wa.gov/listoflicenses.html
Social Worker	https://fortress.wa.gov/doh/providercredentialsearch/
Speech-Language Pathologist	https://fortress.wa.gov/doh/providercredentialsearch/
Structural Pest Inspector	http://agr.wa.gov/pestfert/LicensingEd/Search/default.aspx
Telephone Solicitor	www.dol.wa.gov/listoflicenses.html
Tow Truck Operator	www.dol.wa.gov/listoflicenses.html
Trust Company	www.dfi.wa.gov/banks/trusts.htm
Vehicle Dealer/Manufacturer	www.dol.wa.gov/listoflicenses.html
Vehicle for Hire	www.dol.wa.gov/listoflicenses.html
Vehicle Sales/Disposal/Transporter	www.dol.wa.gov/listoflicenses.html
Vessel Dealer	www.dol.wa.gov/listoflicenses.html
Veterinarian	https://fortress.wa.gov/doh/providercredentialsearch/

Veterinarian, Livestock .... http://agr.wa.gov/FoodAnimal/Livestock/CertifiedVeterinarians.htm
Veterinary Medical Clerk .... https://fortress.wa.gov/doh/providercredentialsearch/
Viatical Settlement Provider.............. www.insurance.wa.gov/cgi-bin/PubInfoApps/CGIViaticalSP.exe
Wastewater System Desig'r/Inspect. . https://fortress.wa.gov/dol/dolprod/bpdLicenseQuery/
Whitewater River Outfitter .... www.dol.wa.gov/listoflicenses.html
Wrecker .... www.dol.wa.gov/listoflicenses.html
Wrestler .... https://fortress.wa.gov/dol/dolprod/bpdLicenseQuery/
X-ray Technician .... https://fortress.wa.gov/doh/providercredentialsearch/

State and Local Courts

State Court Structure: Superior Court is the court of general jurisdiction, but District Courts have criminal jurisdiction over misdemeanors, gross misdemeanors, and criminal traffic cases. Many Municipal Courts combine their record keeping with a District Court housed in same building. All courts Pacific Standard Time.

Washington has a mandatory arbitration requirement for civil disputes for $35,000 or less. However, either party may request a trial in Superior Court if dissatisfied with the arbitrator's decision.

Statewide Court Online Access: The web offers free look-up of docket information at http://dw.courts.wa.gov/. Search by name or case number. This is an unofficial search. For more detailed case data, the AOC provides facilities that allow one to access information in the Judicial Information System's (JIS) statewide computer. This program of services is called JIS-Link. JIS-Link provides access to all counties and court levels. Case records include criminal, civil, domestic, probate, and judgments. Fees include a one-time $100.00 per site, a transaction fee of $.065. There is a $6.00 per month minimum. Call 360-753-3365 or visit www.courts.wa.gov/jislink. Supreme and Appellate opinions are at http://www.courts.wa.gov/opinions/. The page offers a notification service also.

❖ Statewide Access Offered All Trial Courts — Read Above.
Below are Additional Sites. ❖

Benton County

Superior Court   www.co.benton.wa.us/   `Free & $$`
Civil: Besides state searches, subscription access to court docs back to 3/2/1981 and indexes back to 4/1/1979 available at www.landlight.com. Demo subscription available. *Criminal:* Online access to criminal indexes is the same as civil.

Chelan County

Superior Court   www.co.chelan.wa.us/scc/scc_main.htm   `$$`
Civil: Besides state searches, subscription access to indexes back to 4/30/1984 available at www.landlight.com. Demo available. *Criminal:* Online access to criminal indexes is the same as civil.

Clark County

Superior Court   www.clark.wa.gov/courts/superior/index.html   `Free & $$`
Civil: Index online from JIS-Link; see www.courts.wa.gov/jislink/ (also, see state introduction for subscription service.). Also, search name index back to 1989 and calendars free at http://dw.courts.wa.gov/index.cfm. Also, daily dockets are at www.clark.wa.gov/courts/superior/docket.html. *Criminal:* Online access to criminal indexes is the same as civil.

District Court   www.clark.wa.gov/courts/district/index.html   `Free & $$`
Civil: Index online from JIS-Link; see www.courts.wa.gov/jislink/ (also, see state introduction for subscription service.). Also, search name index back to 1989 and calendars free at http://dw.courts.wa.gov/index.cfm. Also, daily dockets are at www.clark.wa.gov/courts/district/docket.html *Criminal:* Online access to criminal indexes is the same as civil. Also, daily dockets are at www.clark.wa.gov/courts/district/docket.html.

Franklin County

Superior Court   www.co.franklin.wa.us/clerk   `Free & $$`
Civil: Index online from JIS-Link; see www.courts.wa.gov/jislink/ (also, see state introduction for subscription service.). Also, search name index back to 1989 and calendars free at http://dw.courts.wa.gov/index.cfm. Also, search Superior court records fee at www.co.franklin.wa.us/clerk/search_frame.cfm. Direct email requests to civil court at mkillian@co.franklin.wa.us/clerk. *Criminal:*

Online access to criminal indexes is the same as civil. Also, criminal record index found at www.co.franklin.wa.us/clerk/search_frame.cfm.

Garfield County
Superior Court   Free & $$
You may direct email record requests to superiorcourt@co.garfield.wa.us.

King County
Superior Court   www.metrokc.gov/kcscc/   Free & $$
Civil: Index online from JIS-Link; see www.courts.wa.gov/jislink/ (also, see state introduction for subscription service.). Also, search civil, criminal and probate name indices back to 1989 and calendars free at http://dw.courts.wa.gov/index.cfm. Also, with registration, search county superior court civil, criminal and probate cases filed after 11/1/2004 at https://dja-ecreweb.metrokc.gov/ecronline. Fee of $.10 per page to view, print, or download documents. *Criminal:* Online access to criminal indexes is the same as civil.

Muckleshoot Tribal Court (NICS)   Free & $$
 riminal: Index online from JIS-Link; see www.courts.wa.gov/jislink/ (also, see state introduction for subscription service.). Also, search name index back to 1989 and calendars free at http://dw.courts.wa.gov/index.cfm. Direct email search requests to kelly.koon@muckleshoot.nsn.us.

Seattle Municipal Court   http://www.seattle.gov/courts/   Free   Search Seattle Muni Court records free at http://publicinformation.seattle.gov/cpi/smc.publicInformation.def.

Kitsap County
Superior Court   www.kitsapgov.com/clerk   Free & $$
Civil: Index online from JIS-Link; see www.courts.wa.gov/jislink/ (also, see state introduction for subscription service.). Also, search name index back to 1978 and calendars free at http://dw.courts.wa.gov/index.cfm. *Criminal:* Online access to criminal indexes is the same as civil. Also, subscription access to court docs back to 2/2/2000 and indexes back to 4/1/1978 available at www.landlight.com. Demo subscription available.

Recorders, Assessors, and Other Sites of Note

Recording Office Organization: 39 counties, 39 recording offices. The recording officer is the County Auditor. County records are usually combined in a Grantor/Grantee index. All federal tax liens are filed with the Department of Licensing. All state tax liens are filed with the County Auditor.

Charles City and James City are counties, not cities. The City of Franklin is not in Franklin County. The City of Richmond is not in Richmond County. The City of Roanoke is not in Roanoke County.

Federal tax liens on personal property of businesses are filed with the State Corporation Commission. Other federal and all state tax liens are filed with the county Clerk of Circuit Court.

Online Access Note: A growing number of counties offer access to assessor or real estate records.

Adams County   *Property, Taxation Records*   Free   Access to county property tax and sales records, and inmate records is free at http://adamswa.taxsifter.com/taxsifter/disclaimer.asp.

Asotin County   *Real Estate, Deed Records*   www.co.asotin.wa.us $$ Recording office land data to be available at a later date at www.etitlesearch.com; registration and fees required.

Benton County   *Real Estate, Grantor/Grantee, Deed, Parcel, Tax Roll, Court Records*   www.co.benton.wa.us
$$ Access to grantor/grantee index back to 1/2/1995, parcels back to 1/1997, recordings to 2/17/1985 and Superior court docs and tax rolls are available by subscription at www.landlight.com. Fees apply but you may get a Free Tax Roll Summary Report.
Property, Taxation Records   Free   Access to Benton County assessor data is free at http://bentonpropertymax.governmaxa.com/propertymax/rover30.asp. Search by parcel ID#, address or map; no name searching.

Chelan County   *Real Estate, Grantor/Grantee, Property, Marriage, Court Records*   www.co.chelan.wa.us
Free & $$ Access to the Auditor's iCRIS database is free at www.co.chelan.wa.us/ad/adr_help.htm. Images go back to 1974; marriage images to 1990. Also, subscription access to grantor/grantee index back to 8/26/90, parcels back to 1/1972, recordings to 4/6/1988 and Superior court docs available at www.landlight.com. Fees apply.
Property, Taxation Records   Free   Access tax rolls via www.landlight.com. Fees apply. With parcel number, get a free Tax Roll Summary Report. Also, access parcel data free on the GIS-mapping site at www.co.chelan.wa.us/bl/bl_mapoptix_disclaimer.htm Search historical plats and images free at www.co.chelan.wa.us/as/as_historicalimages_disclaimer.htm.

Clallam County *Property, Taxation Records* **Free** Access to assessor property data is free at
www.clallam.net/RealEstate/html/land_parcel_search.htm; search by address or property number only. Auditor property maps are also
downloadable at www.clallam.net/RealEstate/html/recorded_maps.htm. Auditor records will be online at a later date.

Clark County *Real Estate, Deed, Lien, Vital Statistic Records* www.co.clark.wa.us/ **Free**
Access County Auditor's database free at http://gis.clark.wa.gov/applications/gishome/auditor/index.cfm.
Property, Taxation Records **Free** Search maps online for property data at
http://gis.clark.wa.us/imf/imf.jsp?site=mapsonline. No name searching. Search property tax sales data free at
www.co.clark.wa.us/treasurer/salesinfo.html. Search treasurer property data free at www.co.clark.wa.us/treasurer/property/index.html
but no name search.

Cowlitz County *Real Estate, Grantor/Grantee, Deed, Lien, Vital Statistic, UCC, Judgment Records*
www.co.cowlitz.wa.us/auditor/ **Free** Access Auditor and recorded documents free at
www.co.cowlitz.wa.us/auditor/PublicSearch/index.asp. *Property, Taxation Records* **Free** Access Auditor property records
free at www.co.cowlitz.wa.us/auditor/PublicSearch/index.asp.

Douglas County *Property, Taxation Records* **Free** Access to the County Parcel Search including taxes, plats and
parcels is free at http://douglaswa.taxsifter.com/taxsifter/disclaimer.asp.

Ferry County *Property, Taxation Records* **Free** Access property data on the TaxSifter database free at
http://ferrywa.taxsifter.com/taxsifter/disclaimer.asp.

Franklin County *Property, Taxation Records* **Free** Search for assessor property data and sales data free at
http://franklinwa.taxsifter.com/taxsifter/disclaimer.asp. Also, search for property sales data.

Grant County *Property, Taxation Records* **Free** Access assessor data on the GIS-mapping site free at
http://gismapserver.co.grant.wa.us/ but no name searching.

Grays Harbor County *Judgment Records* www.co.grays-harbor.wa.us **Free** Access docket information for
judgments at www.co.grays-harbor.wa.us/info/clerk/docket/index.htm. *Property, Taxation Records* **Free**
Access to the county Parcel Database is free at http://bentonpropertymax.governmaxa.com/propertymax/rover30.asp. Search by parcel
ID#, address, legal description, but no name searching.

Island County *Property, Taxation Records* **Free** Access county property tax data free at
www.islandcounty.net/PublicInformation/Property/AccountSearch.aspx. No name searching.

Jefferson County *Real Estate, Grantor/Grantee, Deed, Vital Statistic, Lien, UCC, Permit Records*
http://icris.co.jefferson.wa.us **Free** Access the "Recorded Document Search" database at
www.co.jefferson.wa.us/_hidden/disclaimer.htm. Includes grantor/grantee index and records on the County Property (Tax Parcel)
Database Tool, also plats and survey images. Also, search for building permits but no name searching. Also, search iCRIS for
grantor/grantee, plats, etc, at http://icris.co.jefferson.wa.us/icris/splash.jsp.
Property, Taxation Records **Free** Search assessor data free at www.co.jefferson.wa.us/assessors/parcel/ParcelSearch.asp but
no names searching.

King County *Real Estate, Deed, Lien, Marriage, Judgment, Vital Statistic Records* www.kingcounty.gov/ **Free**
Access to the recorder's database is free at www.metrokc.gov/recelec/records or at http://146.129.54.93:8193/legalacceptance.asp?.
Property, Taxation Records **Free** Access property records on Developmental and Environmental Resources database free at
www.metrokc.gov/ddes/gis/parcel. After the disclaimer page, search by parcel number, address, street intersection, or map.

Kitsap County *Real Estate, Grantor/Grantee, Deed, Lien, Vital Statistic, Judgment Records*
www.kitsapgov.com/aud/default.htm **Free & $$** Search property data free on the land information system site at
http://kcwaimg.co.kitsap.wa.us/recorder/web/. Click on Public Login. Fee to print official documents. Also, subscription access to
grantor/grantee index, parcels back to 8/26/1990, recordings back to 4/6/1988 and Superior court docs and tax rolls are
available at www.landlight.com. Fees apply but you may get a Free Tax Roll Summary Report.
Property, Taxation Records **Free & $$** Search property and tax data free on the land information system site at
http://kcwppub3.co.kitsap.wa.us/ParcelSearch/. No name searching. Fee to print official documents.

Kittitas County *Property, Taxation Records* **Free** Access property data free at
www.co.kittitas.wa.us/taxsifterpublic/disclaimer.asp but no name searching.

Klickitat County *Property, Taxation Records* **Free** Access GIS-mapping site free at
http://kcgis2004.klickitatcounty.org/website/kcmap/viewer.htm but no name searching.

Lewis County *Property, Taxation Records* **Free** Access property data free on the PATS system at
https://fortress.wa.gov/lewisco/home/ click on PATS. No name searching.

Mason County *Property, Taxation Records* **Free** Access to Assessor data is free at www.co.mason.wa.us/disclaimer.php and at www.co.mason.wa.us/astr/index.php. Access parcel data free on the GIS-mapping site at www.co.mason.wa.us/gis/index.php but not name searching.

Okanogan County *Property, Taxation Records* **Free** Access to county assessment data is free at http://okanoganwa.taxsifter.com/taxsifter/t-parcelsearch.asp.

Pacific County *Property, Taxation Records* **Free** Access County Auditor property data free on the TaxSifter system at http://pacificwa.taxsifter.com/taxsifter/T-Parcelsearch.asp. Foreclosures are posted on the website in August.

Pend Oreille County *Property, Taxation Records* **Free** Access property records free at http://66.45.209.110/pend-propertysearch/index.jsp but no name searching.

Pierce County *Real Estate, Deed, Lien, Vital Statistic, Judgment, Assumed Name, Marriage Records* www.piercecountywa.org/auditor **Free** Search index back to 1984 and images back to 3/1998 on the auditor's recording database for free at http://hartweb.piercecountywa.org/search.asp?cabinet=opr. Marriage records at http://hartweb.piercecountywa.org/search.asp?cabinet=oprmarriage. *Property, Taxation Records* **Free** Property records on County Assessor-Treasurer database are free at www.co.pierce.wa.us/CFApps/atr/epip/search.cfm or www.co.pierce.wa.us/abtus/ourorg/at/at.htm.

San Juan County *Real Estate, Deed, Lien Records* www.sanjuanco.com/ **Free** Access to the auditor database of real estate recording records is free at http://sjc-imaging.rockisland.com/SJCdocSearch/?. Images go back to 1997; index goes back to 1/1984. *Property, Taxation Records* **Free** Access to assessor property records is free at www.gartrellgroup.net/sjcparcelsearch/. No name searching.

Skagit County *Real Estate, Grantor/Grantee, Deed, Lien, Marriage, Permit Records* www.skagitcounty.net/Common/asp/default.asp?d=Home&c=General&P=main.htm **Free** Access auditor's recorded documents as well as permits free at www.skagitcounty.net; click on Record Searches. *Property, Taxation Records* **Free** Search assessor data free at www.skagitcounty.net Click-Record Searches; no name search.

Snohomish County *Real Estate, Deed, Lien, Marriage Records* http://www1.co.snohomish.wa.us/Departments/Auditor/ **Free** Access to the Auditor's office database back to 1997 is free at http://198.238.192.100/localization/menu.asp. Search on the recorded documents or marriage icons. *Property, Taxation Records* **Free** Search the assessor property data for free at http://web5.co.snohomish.wa.us/propsys/asr-tr-propinq/ but no name searching.

Spokane County *Property, Taxation Records* **Free** Search the County Parcel Locator database for free at www.spokanecounty.org/pubpadal/. No name searching. You may search sales by parcel number free at www.spokanecounty.org/pubpadal/SalesSearch.aspx.

Stevens County *Property, Taxation Records* **Free** Access assessor property data free at http://209.173.246.99/screalprop/index.php but no name searching.

Thurston County *Real Estate, Deed Records* www.co.thurston.wa.us/auditor **Free & $$** Access the Auditor Recording data at www.co.thurston.wa.us/auditor. Click on Public Record Index Available Online. Guests may log in using the "Public Log In" button. *Property, Taxation Records* **Free** Assessor and property data on Thurston GeoData database is free at www.geodata.org/parcelsrch.asp. No name searching.

Wahkiakum County *Property, Taxation Records* **Free** Access the yearly property sales list for free at www.co.wahkiakum.wa.us/depts/assessor/index.htm. Click on List name at bottom of page. Print out of current sales available free at www.co.wahkiakum.wa.us/depts/assessor/pdf/SalesThruApr2008.pdf.

Walla Walla County *Property, Taxation Records* **Free** Access to the TaxSifter parcel search and sales is free at http://wallawallawa.taxsifter.com/taxsifter/disclaimer.asp.

Whatcom County *Voter Registration Records* www.co.whatcom.wa.us/auditor **Free** Acquire voter registration lists for political purposes only; info and request form at www.co.whatcom.wa.us/auditor/election_division/labels_lists/index.jsp. *Property, Taxation Records* **Free** Search the assessor parcel database information system free at www.co.whatcom.wa.us/cgibin/db2www/assessor/search/RPSearch.ndt/disclaimer.

Yakima County *Property, Taxation Records* **Free** Assessor and property data on County Assessor database are free at www.co.yakima.wa.us/assessor/propinfo/asr_info.asp. No name searching. Access to the treasurer parcel database is free at www.co.yakima.wa.us/treasurer/database/taxes.asp. No name searching. Search City of Grandview business licenses at www.grandview.wa.us/Web%20Page/City%20Hall/BusinessLicenseListings.htm.

West Virginia

Capital: Charleston
            Kanawha County
Time Zone: EST
Population: 1,812,035
# of Counties: 55

Useful State Links

Website: www.wv.gov
Governor: www.wvgov.org
Attorney General: www.wvago.gov/
State Archives: www.wvculture.org/history/wvsamenu.html
State Statutes and Codes: www.legis.state.wv.us/WVCODE/Code.cfm
Legislative Bill Search: www.legis.state.wv.us/Bill_Status/bill_status.cfm
Bill Monitoring: www.legis.state.wv.us/billstatus_personalized/persbills_login.cfm
Unclaimed Funds: www.wvsto.com/Unclaimed+Property/DefaultUP.htm

Primary State Agencies

Sexual Offender Registry `Free`

State Police Headquarters, Sexual Offender Registry, www.wvstatepolice.com/sexoff/ Online searching is available from website, search by county or name, or by most wanted. Email questions to registry@wvsp.state.wv.us. You can also search the offender database to determine if a specific email address or username used on the internet belongs to a registered sex offender and has been reported.

Incarceration Records `Free`

West Virginia Division of Corrections, Records Room, www.wvdoc.com/wvdoc/ This agency offers a free search from www.wvdoc.com/wvdoc/OffenderSearch/tabid/117/Default.aspx

Corporation, LLC, LP, LLP, Trademarks/Servicemarks `Free`

SOS - Business Organizations Division, 1900 Kanawha Blvd E, www.wvsos.com Corporation and business types records on the Secretary of State Business Organization Information System are available free online at www.wvsos.com/wvcorporations/. Search by organization name. Certified copies may be ordered online at https://www.wvsos.com/ecomm/main.htm or via email to business@wvsos.com. *Other Options:* Bulk sale of records is available in CD or DVD format, retrievable in CSV, Access or XML. Monthly or weekly updates are offered. Call for further details.

Uniform Commercial Code `Free & $$`

SOS-UCC Division, Bldg 1, Suite 157-K, www.wvsos.com/ucc/main.htm There is a free service to search, and the website also gives the ability to order copies. Search the database free at www.wvsos.com/UccSearch/index-noecomm.aspx to determine if a specific individual/organization has active, expired or terminated liens filed. Results give UCC number, secured party, debtor and status. Online record requesters can be invoiced via email, an account must be set-up first. *Other Options:* Bulk sale of records is available in CD or DVD format, retrievable in CSV, Access or XML. Monthly or weekly updates are offered. Call for further details.

Driver License Information, Driver Records `$$`

Division of Motor Vehicles, 1800 Kanawha Blvd, www.wvdot.com/6_motorists/dmv/6G_DMV.HTM Online access is available 24 hours a day. Batch requesters receive return transmission about 3 AM. Users must access through AAMVAnet. A contract is required and accounts must pre-pay. Fee is $5.00 per record. For more information, call 304-558-3915. *Other Options:* This agency will sell its DL file to commercial vendors, but records cannot be re-sold.

Voter Registration `Free`

Sec of State - Election Division, Bldg 1 #157-K, www.wvsos.com/elections/main.htm Search to see if someone is registered at www.wvvotes.com/voters/am-i-registered.php. *Other Options:* Lists are available for political purposes for approx $.015 per name. A complete statewide list is approx. $6,800 ($.005 per name plus $1,000). Turnaround time is generally 48 hours. Call for further information.

Occupational Licensing Boards

Aesthetician	www.wvdhhr.org/bph/wvbc/licensees.cfm
Architect	http://wvbrdarch.org/roster/lic/searchdb.asp
Asbestos Clearance Air Monitor	www.wvdhhr.org/rtia/allair.cfm
Asbestos Contractor	www.wvdhhr.org/rtia/allcon.cfm
Asbestos Inspector	www.wvdhhr.org/rtia/allinsp.cfm
Asbestos Laboratory	www.wvdhhr.org/rtia/licensing.asp
Asbestos Project Designer/Planner	www.wvdhhr.org/rtia/alldesign.cfm
Asbestos Supervisor	www.wvdhhr.org/rtia/allsup.cfm
Asbestos Worker	www.wvdhhr.org/rtia/allwork.cfm
Athlete Agent	www.wvsos.com/licensing/LicenseeSearch.asp
Athletic Trainer	http://wvde.state.wv.us/certification/
Attorney	www.wvbar.org/barinfo/mdirectory/
Authorized Company	www.wvpebd.org/authorized_co.htm
Barber	www.wvdhhr.org/bph/wvbc/licensees.cfm
Barber/Beauty Culture School	www.wvdhhr.org/bph/wvbc/licensees.cfm
Contractor, General	http://wvlabor.org/contractsearch.cfm
Cosmetologist	www.wvdhhr.org/bph/wvbc/licensees.cfm
Educational Audiologist	http://wvde.state.wv.us/certification/
Embalmer	www.wvfuneralboard.com/licenseesearch.htm
Engineer	www.wvpebd.org/professional_eng.htm
Forester	www.wvlicensingboards.com/foresters/roster.cfm
Forestry Technician	www.wvlicensingboards.com/foresters/roster.cfm
Funeral Director; Funeral Home	www.wvfuneralboard.com/licenseesearch.htm
Insurance Agency	www.wvinsurance.gov/agency%5Fdetail/
Insurance Agent	www.wvinsurance.gov/agent%5Fdetail/
Insurance Company	www.wvinsurance.gov/company%5Fdetail/
Lobbyist/or/ Lobbying Employer	www.wvethicscommission.org/lobby.htm
Manicurist	www.wvdhhr.org/bph/wvbc/licensees.cfm
Medical Corporation	www.wvdhhr.org/wvbom/licensesearch.asp
Medical Doctor	www.wvdhhr.org/wvbom/licensesearch.asp
Medical License, Special Volunteer	www.wvdhhr.org/wvbom/licensesearch.asp
Medical Professional LLC/Firm	www.wvdhhr.org/wvbom/licensesearch.asp
Milk Shipper	www.wvdhhr.org/phs/milk/records.asp
Minister License	www.wvsos.com/licensing/LicenseeSearch.asp
Notary Public	www.wvsos.com/notary/search/index.aspx
Nurse-LPN	https://www.wva.state.wv.us/wvrnboard/lookup.aspx
Occupation'l Therap't/Asst/Practit'n'r	http://wvbot.org/dharris/members.pdf
Optometrist	www.wvbo.org/verify-license.php
Osteopathic Physician/Phys'c'n Asst	www.wvbdosteo.org/DirectoriesComplaintForm/tabid/757/Default.aspx
Pesticide Applicat'n Busi. (RPAB)	www.kellysolutions.com/WV/RPAB/index.htm
Pesticide Applicator	www.kellysolutions.com/WV/Applicators/index.htm
Pesticide Applicator-Business	www.kellysolutions.com/WV/Business/index.htm
Pesticide Dealer, Restricted Use	www.kellysolutions.com/WV/Dealers/index.htm
Pesticide Registration	www.kellysolutions.com/WV/pesticideindex.htm
Pharmacist	www.state.wv.us/pharmacy/index.cfm
Physician Assistant	www.wvdhhr.org/wvbom/licensesearch.asp
Podiatrist	www.wvdhhr.org/wvbom/licensesearch.asp
Private Detective/Firms	www.wvsos.com/licensing/LicenseeSearch.asp

Public Accountant-CPA .... www.wvboacc.org/Verify_A_Licensee.htm
Radiologic Technologist..................... www.wvrtboard.org/LICENSESEARCH/tabid/358/Default.aspx
Rafting Outfitter, Whitewater www.wvexplorer.com/Recreation/Whitewater%20Rafting/guidesoutfitters.asp
Real Estate Appraiser (Nat'l) .... www.asc.gov/content/category1/appr_by_state.asp
Real Estate Appraiser (WV list) .... www.wvappraiserboard.org/roster.pdf
Retired Engineer .... www.wvpebd.org/retired_eng_search.htm
School Nurse/Psychologist/Counsel .. http://wvde.state.wv.us/certification/
School Principal/Superintendent .... http://wvde.state.wv.us/certification/
Security Guard................................... www.wvsos.com/licensing/LicenseeSearch.asp
Speech/Language Pathologist............ http://wvde.state.wv.us/certification/
Supervisor of Instruction .... http://wvde.state.wv.us/certification/
Teacher .... http://wvde.state.wv.us/certification/status/
Veterinarian .... www.wvlicensingboards.com/vetmed/licensed.cfm
Water Bottler www.wvdhhr.org/phs/bottledwater/records2.asp
Water Brands, Bottled www.wvdhhr.org/phs/bottledwater/records3.asp

State and Local Courts

State Court Structure: The trial courts of general jurisdiction are the Circuit Courts which handle civil cases at law over $300 or more or in equity, felonies and misdemeanor and appeals from the Family Courts. The Magistrate Courts, which are akin to small claims courts, issue arrest and search warrants, hear misdemeanor cases, conduct preliminary examinations in felony cases, and hear civil cases with $5,000 or less in dispute. Magistrates also issue emergency protective orders in cases involving domestic violence.

The Circuit Courts hear appeals of Magistrate Court cases. Probate is handled by the Circuit Court. The highest court is the Supreme Court of Appeals of West Virginia.

Statewide Court Online Access: 18 circuit courts have accessible records at www.swcg-inc.com/products/circuit_express.html. $125 set-up fee plus a $38.00 or $120 monthly fee plan. Call 800-795-8593. Records are from 02/1997. Supreme Court of Appeals Opinions and Calendar are available at www.state.wv.us/wvsca.

The following courts provide online access to civil and criminal via www.swcg-inc.com/products/circuit_express.html, see note above.

- **Calhoun County**
- **Doddridge County**
- **Fayette County**
- **Grant County**
- **Hancock County**
- **Kanawha County**
- **Logan County**
- **Marshall County**
- **Mason County**
- **McDowell County**
- **Mercer County**
- **Mineral County**
- **Nicholas County**
- **Ohio County**
- **Putnam County**
- **Roane County**
- **Wetzel County**
- **Wyoming County**

Recorders, Assessors, and Other Sites of Note

Recording Office Organization: 55 counties, 55 recording offices. The recording officer is the County Clerk. All federal and state tax liens are filed with the County Clerk.

Online Access Note: There is no statewide system open to public, but a growing number of counties offer online access. A private company offers subscription access to land book assessment information statewide at http://digitalcourthouse.com.

Berkeley County *Property, Taxation Records* `Free` Access property tax data free at www.softwaresystems.com/ssi/taxinquiry/. Also, access property data free at www.onlinegis.net/WvBerkeley/. Click on Display Map then Search, no name searching. Access sheriff tax sale data free at http://208.253.88.4:8003/.

Boone County *Property, Taxation Records* `Free` Access property tax data free at www.softwaresystems.com/ssi/taxinquiry/.

Cabell County *Property, Taxation Records* `Free` Access property tax data free at www.softwaresystems.com/ssi/taxinquiry/.

Greenbrier County *Property, Taxation Records* `Free` Access property tax data free at www.softwaresystems.com/ssi/taxinquiry/.

Hampshire County *Property, Taxation Records* `Free` Access to property data is free on the mapping site at www.co.hampshire.wv.us/hampshire/public/property.htm. Scroll down the map page to access search fields.

Hardy County *Real Estate, Grantor/Grantee, Deed, Mortgage Records* www.hardycounty.com `Free & $$`
Access recorded index free at www.onlinecountyrecords.com. Username Id and Password is hardywv, all small letters. Index goes back to 1/1993.

Jefferson County *Property, Taxation Records* `Free` Access property tax data free at www.softwaresystems.com/ssi/taxinquiry/.

Kanawha County *Property, Taxation Records* `Free` Access property tax data free at www.softwaresystems.com/ssi/taxinquiry/.

Monongalia County *Property, Taxation Records* `Free` Access the County Parcel Search database free at www.assessor.org/parcelweb. Search by a wide variety of criteria including owner name and address. Access property tax data free at www.softwaresystems.com/ssi/taxinquiry/.

Nicholas County *Property, Taxation Records* `Free` Access property tax data free at www.softwaresystems.com/ssi/taxinquiry/.

Putnam County *Property, Taxation Records* `Free` Access property tax data free at www.softwaresystems.com/ssi/taxinquiry/.

Randolph County *Property, Taxation Records* `$$` Search County Assessor information at www.randolphcountyassessor.com/portal/ (requires username and password to login).

Summers County *Property, Taxation Records* `Free` Access the tax inquiry database free at http://129.71.205.119/.

Wayne County *Real Estate, Deed, Lien, Marriage, Birth, Death, Will, UCC Records* www.waynecountywv.us
`Free` Access recorded document index back to 4/1/1991 free at www.waynecountywv.us/WEBInquiry/.
Property, Taxation Records `Free` Access property tax data free at www.waynecountywv.us/WEBTax/.

Wood County *Real Estate, Deed, Will, Death, Birth, Marriage, Lien Records*
www.woodcountywv.com/countyclerk/index.html `Free` Access is by dial-up modem; visit www.woodcountywv.com/countyclerk/modem.htm for instructions for free connection. Records go back to 7/1/1988. Click on 'document imaging' to download.
Property, Taxation Records `Free` Access assessment data free at www.woodcountywv.com/webcama/. Access property data on the GIS-mapping site free at www.onlinegis.net/WvWood/. Click on Display Map then Search; no name searching. Also, search the tax inquiry site free at www.woodcountywv.com/webtax/.

Wisconsin

Capital: Madison
　　　　 Dane County
Time Zone: CST
Population: 5,601,640
# of Counties: 72

Useful State Links

Website: www.wisconsin.gov
Governor: www.wisgov.state.wi.us
Attorney General: www.doj.state.wi.us/ag/
State Archives: www.wisconsinhistory.org/libraryarchives/
State Statutes and Codes: www.legis.state.wi.us/rsb/stats.html
Legislative Bill Search: www.legis.state.wi.us
Bill Monitoring: http://notify.legis.state.wi.us/(sqsdjq45dnqby045cvkinq45)/Home.aspx
Unclaimed Funds: www.ost.state.wi.us/home/UCPWeb/ucpsearch.aspx

Primary State Agencies

Criminal Records $$

Wisconsin Department of Justice, Crime Information Bureau, Record Check Unit, www.doj.state.wi.us/dles/cib/crimback.asp The agency offers Internet access at http://wi-recordcheck.org. An account with PIN is required or a credit card can be used. Records must be "picked up" at the website within 10 days. They are not returned by mail. Fee is $13 per request, $2.00 if a non-profit, and $10.00 if a government agency. Only daycare centers and other caregivers can receive immediate online response but pay an additional $2.50 per record. Email questions to wi-recordcheck-account@doj.state.wi.us. *Other Options:* There is a free Internet service for access to the state's Circuit Courts' records, except for Portage county. Visit http://wcca.wicourts.gov/index.xsl.

Sexual Offender Registry　Free

Department of Corrections, Sex Offender Registry Program, http://offender.doc.state.wi.us/public/ Search for offenders at the web by either name or by location.

Corporation, LP, LLC, LLP　Free & $$

Division of Corporate & Consumer Services, Corporation Record Requests, www.wdfi.org Selected elements of the database ("CRIS" Corporate Registration System) are available online on the department's website at www.wdfi.org/apps/CorpSearch/Search.aspx?. A Certificate of Status can be ordered online for $10.00 at https://www.wdfi.org/apps/ccs/directions.asp. To place orders for status, copy work, or ID Reports go to https://www.wdfi.org/apps/oos/. Also, search securities companies and investment advisors free at www.wdfi.org/fi/securities/licensing/licensee_lists/default.asp. *Other Options:* Some data is released in database format and is available electronically via email or on CD.

Trademarks/Servicemarks, Trade Names　Free

Secretary of State, Tradenames/Trademarks Division, www.sos.state.wi.us/trademark.htm Search by trademark description or corporate name from the web page. *Other Options:* Bulk access is offered - requests are handled on an individual basis.

Uniform Commercial Code, Federal & State Tax Liens　Free & $$

Department of Financial Institutions, CCS/UCC, www.wdfi.org/ucc/ There is free Internet access for most records. Some records may require a $1.00 fee. You may do a free debtor name search at www.wdfi.org/ucc/search/. Instant filings are available immediately. The search will include federal tax liens. *Other Options:* Bulk Index data is available on CD. The initial subscription is $3,000, monthly updates are $250.00. Images are available on CD for $200.00 per month.

Driver Records `Free & $$`

Division of Motor Vehicles, Driver Records, www.dot.wisconsin.gov/drivers/index.htm Interactive services is available for approved requesters. Records are provided as an image in PDF format for $5.00 per record. The program is called PARS. Call Citations and withdrawals Section at 608-266-0928 for more information. PARS participants can also participate in an employer notification program. Employers can enroll CDL drivers and will be notified when activity occurs on the employees record. The fee is also $5.00 per record when accessed. Also, a free status check of a DL is at www.dot.wisconsin.gov/drivers/online.htm. Must submit either DL, SSN, and DOB, or submit full name and DOB.

Vital Records `$$`

Bureau of Health Information and Policy, Vital Records, www.dhfs.wisconsin.gov/vitalrecords/ Records may be ordered online via www.vitalchek.com, a state approved vendor.

Occupational Licensing Boards

Accounting Firm	http://drl.wi.gov/lookupjump.htm
Acupuncturist	http://drl.wi.gov/drl/drllookup/LicenseLookupServlet?page=lookup_health
Adjustment Service Company	www.wdfi.org/fi/lfs/licensee_lists
Aesthetics Establishm't/School	http://drl.wi.gov/lookupjump.htm
Aesthetics Instructor	http://drl.wi.gov/lookupjump.htm
Appraiser, General/Residential	http://drl.wi.gov/lookupjump.htm
Architect	http://drl.wi.gov/lookupjump.htm
Architectural Corporation	http://drl.wi.gov/lookupjump.htm
Art Therapist	http://drl.wi.gov/drl/drllookup/LicenseLookupServlet?page=lookup_health
Attorney	www.wisbar.org/AM/Template.cfm?Section=Lawyer_Directory
Auction Company	http://drl.wi.gov/lookupjump.htm
Auctioneer	http://drl.wi.gov/lookupjump.htm
Audiologist	http://drl.wi.gov/drl/drllookup/LicenseLookupServlet?page=lookup_health
Bank	www.wdfi.org/fi/savings_institutions/licensee_lists/
Barber-related Occupation	http://drl.wi.gov/lookupjump.htm
Boiler Repairer	http://apps.commerce.state.wi.us/SB_Credential/SB_CredentialApp
Boxer	http://drl.wi.gov/lookupjump.htm
Boxing Club, Amateur/Prof.	http://drl.wi.gov/lookupjump.htm
Boxing Show	http://drl.wi.gov/lookupjump.htm
Building Inspector	http://apps.commerce.state.wi.us/SB_Credential/SB_CredentialApp
Cemetery Authority/Warehouse	http://drl.wi.gov/lookupjump.htm
Cemetery Pre-Need Seller/Sales	http://drl.wi.gov/lookupjump.htm
Charitable Organization	http://drl.wi.gov/lookupjump.htm
Check Seller	www.wdfi.org/fi/lfs/licensee_lists
Chiropractor	http://drl.wi.gov/drl/drllookup/LicenseLookupServlet?page=lookup_health
Collection Agency	www.wdfi.org/fi/lfs/licensee_lists
Cosmetology-related Occupation	http://drl.wi.gov/lookupjump.htm
Counselor, Professional	http://drl.wi.gov/drl/drllookup/LicenseLookupServlet?page=lookup_health
Credit Service Organization	www.wdfi.org/fi/cu/chartered_lists/default.asp
Credit Union	www.wdfi.org/fi/cu/chartered_lists/default.asp
Currency Exchange	www.wdfi.org/fi/lfs/licensee_lists
Dance Therapist	http://drl.wi.gov/drl/drllookup/LicenseLookupServlet?page=lookup_health
Debt Collector	www.wdfi.org/fi/lfs/licensee_lists
Dentist/or/Dental Hygienist	http://drl.wi.gov/drl/drllookup/LicenseLookupServlet?page=lookup_health
Designer, Engineering Systems	http://drl.wi.gov/lookupjump.htm
Dietitian	http://drl.wi.gov/drl/drllookup/LicenseLookupServlet?page=lookup_health
Drug Distributor/Mfg	http://drl.wi.gov/lookupjump.htm
Electrical Inspector	http://apps.commerce.state.wi.us/SB_Credential/SB_CredentialApp
Electrician	http://apps.commerce.state.wi.us/SB_Credential/SB_CredentialApp
Electrologist/Electrology Instructor	http://drl.wi.gov/lookupjump.htm
Electrology Establishment/School	http://drl.wi.gov/lookupjump.htm
Employee Benefits Plan Administ'r	https://ociaccess.oci.wi.gov/ProducerInfo/PrdIndividual.oci
Engineer/Engineer in Training/Corp	http://drl.wi.gov/lookupjump.htm

Firearms Permit .... http://drl.wi.gov/lookupjump.htm
Fireworks Manufacturer .... http://apps.commerce.state.wi.us/SB_Credential/SB_CredentialApp
Fund Raiser, Professional/Counsel .... http://drl.wi.gov/lookupjump.htm
Funeral Director/Director Apprentice http://drl.wi.gov/lookupjump.htm
Funeral Establishment .... http://drl.wi.gov/lookupjump.htm
Funeral Pre-Need Seller..................... http://drl.wi.gov/lookupjump.htm
Geologist/ Geology Firm .... http://drl.wi.gov/lookupjump.htm
Hearing Instrument Specialist........... http://drl.wi.gov/drl/drllookup/LicenseLookupServlet?page=lookup_health
HMO .... https://ociaccess.oci.wi.gov/CmpInfo/CmpInfo.oci
Home Inspector .... http://drl.wi.gov/lookupjump.htm
HVAC Contractor............................... http://apps.commerce.state.wi.us/SB_Credential/SB_CredentialApp
Hydrologist/ Hydrology Firm .... http://drl.wi.gov/lookupjump.htm
Insurance Company/Intermediary...... https://ociaccess.oci.wi.gov/ProducerInfo/PrdIndividual.oci
Insurance Premium Financier .... www.wdfi.org/fi/lfs/licensee_lists
Insurance Producer .... https://ociaccess.oci.wi.gov/ProducerInfo/PrdFirm.oci
Interior Designer................................ http://drl.wi.gov/lookupjump.htm
Investment Advisor/Advisor Rep ...... www.wdfi.org/fi/securities/licensing/licensee_lists/default.asp
Land Surveyor .... http://drl.wi.gov/lookupjump.htm
Landscape Architect .... http://drl.wi.gov/lookupjump.htm
Loan Company .... www.wdfi.org/fi/lfs/licensee_lists
Loan Solicitor/Originator .... www.wdfi.org/fi/lfs/licensee_lists/default.asp
Lobbying Organization, Principal...... http://ethics.state.wi.us/Scripts/2003Session/OELMenu.asp
Lobbyist... http://ethics.state.wi.us/Scripts/2003Session/LobbyistsMenu.asp
Manicurist Establ./Specialty School .. http://drl.wi.gov/lookupjump.htm
Manicurist/Manicurist Instructor .... http://drl.wi.gov/lookupjump.htm
Marriage & Family Therapist .... http://drl.wi.gov/drl/drllookup/LicenseLookupServlet?page=lookup_health
Massage Therapist/Bodyworker .... http://drl.wi.gov/drl/drllookup/LicenseLookupServlet?page=lookup_health
Medical Doctor/Surgeon.................... http://drl.wi.gov/drl/drllookup/LicenseLookupServlet?page=lookup_health
Midwife Nurse.................................... http://drl.wi.gov/drl/drllookup/LicenseLookupServlet?page=lookup_health
Mobile Home & RV Dealer............... www.wdfi.org/fi/lfs/licensee_lists
Mortgage Banker/Broker .... www.wdfi.org/fi/lfs/licensee_lists/default.asp
Motor Club .... https://ociaccess.oci.wi.gov/CmpInfo/CmpInfo.oci
Motorcycle Dealer .... www.wdfi.org/fi/lfs/licensee_lists
Music Therapist.................................. http://drl.wi.gov/drl/drllookup/LicenseLookupServlet?page=lookup_health
Nurse-RN/LPN.................................... http://drl.wi.gov/drl/drllookup/LicenseLookupServlet?page=lookup_health
Nursing Home Administrator .... http://drl.wi.gov/lookupjump.htm
Occupational Therapist/Assistant ...... http://drl.wi.gov/drl/drllookup/LicenseLookupServlet?page=lookup_health
Optometrist.. http://drl.wi.gov/drl/drllookup/LicenseLookupServlet?page=lookup_health
Osteopathic Physician........................ http://drl.wi.gov/drl/drllookup/LicenseLookupServlet?page=lookup_health
Payday Lender..................................... www.wdfi.org/fi/lfs/licensee_lists
Pesticide Applicator........................... www.kellysolutions.com/WI/Applicators/index.asp
Pesticide Applicator Business............ www.kellysolutions.com/WI/Business/searchbyCity.asp
Pesticide Dealer.................................. www.kellysolutions.com/WI/Dealers/searchbyCity.asp
Pesticide Manufacturer/Labeler......... www.kellysolutions.com/wi/pesticideindex.asp
Pharmacy/Pharmacist .... http://drl.wi.gov/drl/drllookup/LicenseLookupServlet?page=lookup_health
Physical Therapist .... http://drl.wi.gov/drl/drllookup/LicenseLookupServlet?page=lookup_health
Physician Assistant............................ http://drl.wi.gov/drl/drllookup/LicenseLookupServlet?page=lookup_health
Plumber .... http://apps.commerce.state.wi.us/SB_Credential/SB_CredentialApp
Podiatrist.. http://drl.wi.gov/drl/drllookup/LicenseLookupServlet?page=lookup_health
Private Detective/or/Detective Agcy . http://drl.wi.gov/lookupjump.htm
Psychologist.. http://drl.wi.gov/drl/drllookup/LicenseLookupServlet?page=lookup_health
Public Accountant .... http://drl.wi.gov/lookupjump.htm
Rate Service Org................................. https://ociaccess.oci.wi.gov/CmpInfo/CmpInfo.oci
Real Estate Agent/Broker/Seller/Firm http://drl.wi.gov/lookupjump.htm
Real Estate Appraiser .... http://drl.wi.gov/lookupjump.htm
Respiratory Care Practitioner .... http://drl.wi.gov/drl/drllookup/LicenseLookupServlet?page=lookup_health
Risk Purchasing Group...................... https://ociaccess.oci.wi.gov/CmpInfo/CmpInfo.oci

Sales Finance/Loan Company .... www.wdfi.org/fi/lfs/licensee_lists
Savings & Loan Financer .... www.wdfi.org/fi/lfs/licensee_lists
Savings Institution .... www.wdfi.org/fi/savings_institutions/licensee_lists/
School Librarian/Media Specialist https://www2.dpi.wi.gov/lic-tll/home.do
School Psychology Private Practice .. http://drl.wi.gov/drl/drllookup/LicenseLookupServlet?page=lookup_health
Securities Broker/Dealer/Agent .... www.wdfi.org/fi/securities/licensing/licensee_lists/default.asp
Security Guard .... http://drl.wi.gov/lookupjump.htm
Social Worker .... http://drl.wi.gov/drl/drllookup/LicenseLookupServlet?page=lookup_health
Soil Science Firm/Soil Scientist .... http://drl.wi.gov/lookupjump.htm
Soil Tester .... http://apps.commerce.state.wi.us/SB_Credential/SB_CredentialApp
Speech Pathologist/Audiologist .... http://drl.wi.gov/drl/drllookup/LicenseLookupServlet?page=lookup_health
Teacher https://www2.dpi.wi.gov/lic-tll/home.do
Timeshare Salesperson .... http://drl.wi.gov/lookupjump.htm
Veterinarian/Veterinary Technician .. http://drl.wi.gov/drl/drllookup/LicenseLookupServlet?page=lookup_health
Viatical Settlement Broker .... https://ociaccess.oci.wi.gov/ProducerInfo/PrdIndividual.oci
Welder .... http://apps.commerce.state.wi.us/SB_Credential/SB_CredentialApp

State and Local Courts

State Court Structure: The Circuit Court is the court of general jurisdiction. The majority of Municipal Court cases involve traffic and ordinance matters, Probate filing is a function of the Circuit Court, however each county has a Register in Probate who maintains and manages the probate records, guardianship, and mental health records. Probate records are available online at the http://wicourts.gov web page. Most Registers in Probate are putting pre-1950 records on microfilm and destroying the hard copies. This is done as "time and workloads permit," so microfilm archiving is not uniform across the state.

Statewide Court Online Access: Wisconsin Circuit Court Access (WCCA) allows users to view Circuit Court case information on the Wisconsin court system website at http://wcca.wicourts.gov. Data is available from all counties (except only probate records are available from Portage). Searches can be conducted statewide or county-by-county. WCCA provides detailed information about circuit cases and for civil cases, the program displays judgment and judgment party information. WCCA also offers the ability to generate reports. Due to statutory requirements, WCCA users will not be able to view restricted cases. There are probate records for all counties. Appellate Courts and Supreme Court opinions are available from http://wicourts.gov.

> ### ❖ Statewide Access Offered All Trial Courts — Read Above.
> ### Below are Additional Sites. ❖

Milwaukee County

Circuit Court - Criminal Division   www.county.milwaukee.gov/display/router.asp?docid=10507   **Free**
Criminal: Access criminal index free at http://wcca.wicourts.gov/index.xsl. Also, although not from this court, criminal case records on Milwaukee Municipal Court Case Information System database are free at www.court.ci.mil.wi.us/. Search by Case Number, by Citation Number, or by Name.

Ozaukee County

Circuit Court   www.co.ozaukee.wi.us/ClerkCourts/default.htm   **Free**
Civil: Civil court records free online at http://wcca.wicourts.gov/index.xsl. Access is also with the use of county "Remote Access". This data is for inquiries only and includes civil, family, and traffic courts. For info, contact the Technology Resources Dept. at 262-284-8309. *Criminal:* Access criminal index free at http://wcca.wicourts.gov/index.xsl.

Portage County

Circuit Court (Branches 1, 2 & 3)   www.co.portage.wi.us/   **$$**
Civil: Internet access is upon approval. Request in writing to Data Processing Dept, 1462 Strong Ave, Stevens Point 54481. Explain purpose of record requests. *Criminal:* same.

Recorders, Assessors, and Other Sites of Note

Recording Office Organization: 72 counties, 72 recording offices. The recording officers are the Register of Deeds for real estate and Clerk of Court for state tax liens. County Clerks hold marriage records and state tax liens. Federal tax liens on personal property of businesses are filed with the Secretary of State. Only federal tax liens on real estate are filed with the county Register of Deeds. State tax liens are filed with the Clerk of Court, and at the State Treasurer at the State Department of Revenue.

Online Access Note: A number of cities and a few counties offer online access to assessor and property records. The Wisconsin Register of Deeds Association website at www.wrdaonline.org/RealEstateRecords offers helpful guidance to which counties are online.

Adams County *Real Estate, Deed, Lien Records* `Free`
Access Register of Deeds data free at www.adamscountylandrecords.com but no name searching.
Property, Taxation Records `Free` Access assessor parcel data free at www.adamscountylandrecords.com but no name searching.

Ashland County *Real Estate, Grantor/Grantee, Deed, Birth, Death, Marriage, Records* www.co.ashland.wi.us
`$$` Access records for a fee at https://mylocalgov.com/wrdaashlandcountywi/wrdaexplanation.asp. You must be able to print, sign and fax the receipt screen to the County. Current law requires a physical signature. Also, search grantor/grantee for free at http://co.ashland.wi.gov/
Property, Taxation Records `Free` Search property records free at www.ashlandcogiws.com/AshlandCoWi/txt_default.htm

Barron County *Real Estate, Deed, Lien Records* www.co.barron.wi.us `$$` Recording office data by subscription on either the Laredo system using subscription and fees or the Tapestry System using credit card, http://tapestry.fidlar.com; $3.99 search; $.50 per image. Index and images go back to 1/1999.
Property, Taxation Records `$$` Access to county property records is at www.co.barron.wi.us/treasurer_taxdata.htm. Registration, $300.00 annual fee, username, password required; call Yvonne at the county treasurer's office, 715-537-6280.

Brown County *Real Estate, Deed, Lien Records* www.co.brown.wi.us/register_of_deeds/ Recording office data by subscription on either the Laredo system using subscription and fees or the Tapestry System using credit card, www.landrecords.net; $5.95 search; $.50 per image. Index goes back to 1986; images to 5/1/1996.
Property, Taxation Records `Free` Land records without name searching is at www.co.brown.wi.us/treasurer/landrecordssearch/entryform.asp. Also, land records can be downloaded from an ftp site; contact the Land Information office at 920-448-6295 to register and user information. Also, search for property data free on the GIS-mapping site at www.gis.co.brown.wi.us/website/basemap/viewer.htm. Also, search for property data free at www.co.brown.wi.us/planning_and_land_services/land_information_office/

Buffalo County *Property, Taxation Records* `Free` Access to county land records is free at www.gcssoftware.com/applications/search/index.asp?County=Buffalo.

Burnett County *Property, Taxation Records* `Free & $$` Access to limited county property and assessment records is free at www.burnettcounty.org/. No name searching. For full data, an online subscription service is $100 per year.

Calumet County *Property, Taxation Records* `Free` Access to assessor property tax data is free at http://calum400.co.calumet.wi.us/nsccalo/nsclndrec. .

Chippewa County *Real Estate, Deed, Judgment Records*
www.co.chippewa.wi.us/Departments/RegisterDeeds/index.htm `Free & $$` Search Register of Deeds data at https://landshark.co.chippewa.wi.us/eddie/, index search is free, but fees apply for images and copies, $2.00 1st page, $1.00 2nd page. Credit cards accepted. Also, access to real estate records for free www.co.chippewa.wi.us/Departments/RegisterDeeds/index.htm
Property, Taxation Records `Free` Search property assessment database free at http://cctax.co.chippewa.wi.us/CCTax/Taxrtr?.

Clark County *Real Estate, Deed, Delinquent Property Records* www.co.clark.wi.us `$$`
Real estate recording, property data, and delinquent tax info is available by subscription, see https://secure.propertymanagementportal.com/pmp/wi/clark/default.aspx. Fee is $25 per month and $1.20 per transaction.
Property, Taxation Records `Free` Search for assessor/property tax data on the county GIS-mapping site at www.co.clark.wi.us/Website/ClarkIMS/viewer.htm. Search by PIN or address.

Columbia County *Real Estate, Deed, GIS-mapping, Parcel Records* www.co.columbia.wi.us/ColumbiaCounty/
`$$` Access recording office data by subscription on either the Laredo system using subscription and fees or the Tapestry System using credit card, http://tapestry.fidlar.com; $3.99 search; $.50 per image. Index goes back to 11/1987; images back to 1/1998.

Property, Taxation Records `Free` Access the county tax parcel system free at
http://lrs.co.columbia.wi.us/lrsweb/search.aspx. Also, search property info free on the GIS-mapping site at
http://lrs.co.columbia.wi.us/website/ColumbiaCo/ColumbiaCo.asp.

Crawford County *Real Estate, Deed, Judgment Records* www.crawfordcountywi.org `Free & $$`
Search Register of Deeds data at https://landshark.crawfordcountywi.org/LandShark/login.jsp, index search is free, but fees apply for
images and copies, $2.00 1st page, $1.00 2nd page. Credit cards accepted.

Dane County *Real Estate, Deed, Lien Records* www.co.dane.wi.us/regdeeds/rdhome.htm `$$` A fee-based system is
at www.co.dane.wi.us/regdeeds/laredotapestry/accesstorealestate.htm. Also, access recording office land data at
www.etitlesearch.com; registration required, fee based on usage. Also, access recording office data by subscription or using credit
card at http://tapestry.fidlar.com. Index goes back to 8/1978, images to 1992.

Property, Taxation Records `Free` City of Madison tax assessor data is at www.ci.madison.wi.us/assessor/property.html.
Search Sun Prairie property at http://db.sun-prairie.com/property/ and its deathlist at http://db.sun-prairie.com/deathlist/. Also, search
property info for Cross Plains, Mazomanie, Black Earth villages at www.wendorffassessing.com/municipalities.htm. Also, register to
use assessor/land record services at www.co.dane.wi.us and select "AccessDane" from the bottom of this home page.

Door County *Real Estate, Deed, Lien Records* `$$` Access to land records images is by internet subscription or on
CD-rom. Subscription or CD is $300 monthly; call Register of Deeds 920-746-2270 for info and signup.

Douglas County *Real Estate, Grantor/Grantee, Deed, Lien Records* www.douglascountywi.org `Free & $$`
Access to the county Landshark system is at http://rdlandshark.douglascountywi.org/LandShark/login.jsp. Free registration is required.

Property, Taxation Records `Free` Access county land and property tax records free at
www.gcssoftware.com/douglas/Search.aspx but no name searching.

Dunn County *Real Estate, Deed, Lien Records* `$$` Recording office data by subscription on either the Laredo
system using subscription and fees or the Tapestry System using credit card, http://tapestry.fidlar.com; $3.99 search; $.50 per image.
Index and images go back to 12/1998.

Eau Claire County *Real Estate, Deed, Lien Records* www.co.eau-claire.wi.us `$$` Recording office data by
subscription on either the Laredo system using subscription and fees or the Tapestry System using credit card,
http://tapestry.fidlar.com; $3.99 search; $.50 per image. Index and images go back to 3/1994.

Florence County *Property, Taxation Records* `Free` Access property search free at http://rmgis.ruekert-
mielke.com/florenceco/GISWebPortal.asp.

Fond du Lac County *Property, Taxation Records* `Free` Access to parcel data is free through the GIS-mapping
site at http://gis.fdlco.wi.gov/Website/FondduLacIMS/viewer.htm. No name searching.

Forest County *Property, Taxation Records* `Free` Access to county property and assessor data free is at
www.gcssoftware.com/applications/search/index.asp?County=Forest.

Grant County *Property, Taxation Records* `$$` Access to county property and assessor data is at
www.gcssoftware.com/Products/WebSearch.aspx and click on Grant County. Registration, $200.00 annual fee, username, and
password required; call John at the Tax Lister office, 608-723-2666.

Green County *Property, Taxation Records* `Free` Access to parcel data is free on the GIS-mapping site at
http://gis.msa-ps.com/greencounty/publicviewer/startup.htm.

Green Lake County *Property, Taxation Records* `Free` Search GIS-mapping site for property data free at
http://gis.co.green-lake.wi.us/website/GIS_Viewer_limit/viewer.htm but no name searching.

Iron County *Real Estate, Grantor/Grantee, Deed Records* www.ironcountywi.org `$$` Access to land records is
available at http://records.ironcountywi.org/LandShark/login.jsp registration is required. Fees to search. Records go back to 1994.

Jefferson County *Real Estate, Grantor/Grantee, Deed, Lien Records* www.co.jefferson.wi.us `Free & $$`
Access parcel data free at http://lrs.co.jefferson.wi.us/jclrs/LIO/LIO_Search but no name searching. To order full records online using
your credit card, see http://lrs.co.jefferson.wi.us/. Call 920-674-7254 for info, fees, and signup. Land records data is available by
subscription on JCLRP; fee is $40 per month paid quarterly.

Property, Taxation Records `Free` Search assessment records free at http://lrs.co.jefferson.wi.us/jclrs/LIO/LIO_Search but
no name searching. Also, search property data on the GIS-mapping site at http://lrs.co.jefferson.wi.us/jcgis/main.do but no name
searching.

Juneau County *Real Estate, Deed, Mortgage Records* www.co.juneau.wi.gov `$$` The ROD offers subscription,
escrow and credit card services for Real Estate. Documents go back to 05/11/1999 at https://landshark.co.juneau.wi.us/LandShark

Property, Taxation Records `Free & $$` Search the GIS-mapping site for property and assessment data free at
http://gis.co.juneau.wi.us/pvweb22/index.htm. Click on free account login, then click "Search Data" but no name searching. Also a
subscription service for complete property data. To search land sales by town, click on Land Sales at www.co.juneau.wi.gov.

Kenosha County *Real Estate, Deed, Lien Records* www.co.kenosha.wi.us `Free & $$` Access to land records is available at https://landshark.co.kenosha.wi.us/LandShark/login.jsp registration is required. Fees to search. Records go back to 1994.
Property, Taxation Records `Free` Search the Kenosha City Assessor's property database for free at www.kenosha.org/departments/assessor/search.html or the county at www.co.kenosha.wi.us/apps/propinq/propinq_policy.phtml. No name searching at either site. Access real estate records free at www.co.kenosha.wi.us/ and select under Property, Mapping & Environment. Also access parcel data free on the GIS-mapping site free at http://kcmapping.co.kenosha.wi.us/mapping_public/.

Kewaunee County *Real Estate, Grantor/Grantee, Deed Records* www.kewauneeco.org `$$` Access to the Register of Deeds CherryLAN Indexing and Imaging System is available for a monthly subscription fee of $300. Escrow subscription with an initial $100 deposit are also available. Index begins 2/1992.
Property, Taxation Records `Free & $$` Search land/tax records free at www.gcssoftware.com/applications/search/index.asp?County=Kewaunee. Also, search parcel maps and property tax data free on the GIS mapping site at www.kewauneeco.org. Subscription required for full data.

La Crosse County *Land, Deed, Property Owner, Lien Records* www.co.la-crosse.wi.us/Departments/departments.htm `$$` Recording office data by subscription on either the Laredo system using subscription and fees or the Tapestry System using credit card, http://tapestry.fidlar.com; $3.99 search; $.50 per image. Index and images go back to 6/1992. **Property, Taxation Records** `Free` Search for property owner and land data for free at www.co.la-crosse.wi.us/landrecordsportal/default.aspx.

Lafayette County *Real Estate, Deed, Lien Records* `$$` Recording office data by subscription on either the Laredo system using subscription and fees or the Tapestry System using credit card, http://tapestry.fidlar.com; $3.99 search; $.50 per image. Index and images go back to 1/1995.

Langlade County *Birth, Death Records* www.co.langlade.wi.us `Free` Access county birth index free at www.co.langlade.wi.us/Births/; search death index free at www.co.langlade.wi.us/Deaths/.
Property, Taxation Records `Free` Access property data free at www.langladecogiws.com/ no name searching.

Manitowoc County *Real Estate, Deed Records* www.manitowoc-county.com `$$` Access to Register of Deeds recorded land records system requires username and password at http://rod.manitowoc-county.com/landweb.dll; contact Register of Deeds office for sign-up.
Property, Taxation Records `Free` Access tax records free at http://manitowoc-county.com/taxquery/main.htm but no name searching. Search on GIS-map site at http://webmap.manitowoc-county.com/website/pasystem/. Foreclosures- www.manitowoc-county.com/ftp/treasurer/Reference/Foreclosed.htm. Manitowoc City Assessor database free at http://assessor.manitowoc.org/CityAssessor/a1.aspx?. No name searching. Access Two Rivers assessor data free at http://tworivers.patriotproperties.com/default.asp.

Marathon County *Property, Taxation Records* `Free & $$` See county property records is free at www.co.marathon.wi.us/online/apps/lrs/index.asp. No name searching. Access by subscription is also available for full data. Also, access GIS parcel/property data free at http://gismaps.co.marathon.wi.us/gisweb/ccdcc_pub/ccdcc.asp. No name searching.

Marinette County *Real Estate, Deed Records* www.marinettecounty.com `Free & $$` Access to real estate index at http://landshark.marinettecounty.com/LandShark/login.jsp. Requires account. Search index free but $2.00 fee (plus $1.00 each add'l.) to view document. Registration and escrow account required.

Milwaukee County *Real Estate, Grantor/Grantee, Deed, Lien, Parcel Records* www.milwaukee.gov `$$` Recording office data by subscription on either the Laredo system using subscription. and fees or the Tapestry System using credit card, http://tapestry.fidlar.com. Grantor index goes back to 2/1998; Grantor to 1/1991; images back to 1/2/1990; tracts to 2/1998. $3.99 search; $.50 per image at www.landrecords.net.
Property, Taxation Records `Free` Assessment data & sales data on Milwaukee City (not county) database at www.city.milwaukee.gov/DataampDataSearches673.htm. Search City of Cudahy assessor data at http://exch02.ci.cudahy.wi.us/Scripts/GVSWeb.dll/Search, search Wauwatosa property at www.wauwatosa.net/display/wspTosaAssessmentTemplate.asp. Franklin- at http://taxassessment.franklinwi.gov/assessmentsearch.cfm. Glendale- http://ts.glendale-wi.org; West Allis- www.ci.west-allis.wi.us/property_search/psearch.aspx.

Monroe County *Property, Taxation Records* `Free` Access assessment data on the GIS-mapping site free at www.monroecogiws.com/MonroeCoWi/. Click on Go To Tax and Assessment Data.

Oconto County *Parcel, Grantor/Grantee, Real Estate, Lien Records* www.co.oconto.wi.us `$$` Access to Registrar of Deeds available by subscription or escrow account at https://landshark.co.oconto.wi.us/LandShark. You may also purchase a document with a credit card.
Property, Taxation Records `Free` Access to the county SOLO tax parcel search is free or by subscription at http://solo.co.oconto.wi.us/ocontoco/. The free service does not include name searching. Subscription fee for full data is $300 per calendar year. Phone 920-834-6800 for more info. Also, access to Registrar of Deeds available by subscription or escrow account at https://landshark.co.oconto.wi.us/LandShark/login.jsp. You may also purchase a document with a credit card.

Oneida County *Property, Taxation Records* `Free` Access to property tax data is available free at http://octax.co.oneida.wi.us/ONCTax/Taxrtr. Also, search land records by name on the GIS mapping site at http://ocgis.co.oneida.wi.us/oneida/index.htm.

Outagamie County *Real Estate, Deed, Judgment Records* www.co.outagamie.wi.us `Free & $$` Access to deeds, real estate taxes and maps for free go to www.co.outagamie.wi.us/. Click on deeds/real estate taxes/maps (GIS). Also, access recorded documents data at https://landshark.co.outagamie.wi.us/LandShark/login.jsp. Registration and fees required for full data. *Property, Taxation Records* `Free & $$` Search assessor data free at www.co.outagamie.wi.us/OutagamieCoWi/txt_default.htm, no name searching. Sub required for full data. Access parcel data on the GIS-mapping site at www.co.outagamie.wi.us/OutagamieCoWi/txt_default.htm but no name searching. Also, access a variety of property records at www.co.outagamie.wi.us/planning/Maps_main.htm.

Ozaukee County *Real Estate, Grantor/Grantee, Deed Records* www.co.ozaukee.wi.us `$$` Access is by "Remote Access" requiring dial-up modem. This data is for inquiries only. Software is supplied by the county. First month is free, then $50.00 per month subscription. For info, contact the Technology Resources Dept. at 262-284-8309. Also, recording data by subscription on either the Laredo system (subscription & fees) or Tapestry System (use credit card) at http://tapestry.fidlar.com; $3.99 search; $.50 per image. Index goes back to 12/11/1972; images to 9/15/1984.

Pepin County *Property, Taxation Records* `Free` Access maps, land records and tax data free at www.co.pepin.wi.us.

Pierce County *Real Estate, Deed, Lien Records* www.co.pierce.wi.us/Register%20of%20Deeds/Register_Deeds_Main.htm `$$` Access recording office data by subscription on either the Laredo system using subscription and fees or the Tapestry System using credit card, http://tapestry.fidlar.com; $3.99 search; $.50 per image. Visit www.co.pierce.wi.us/Register%20of%20Deeds/Register_Deeds_Main.html for more Tapestry info. Index and images go back to 1998. *Property, Taxation Records* `Free` Access to county property data is free at www.co.pierce.wi.us/Land%20Information%20Disclaimer.html. Click on Property Data Search.

Polk County *Property, Taxation Records* `Free` Access assessor and GIS-mapping records free at http://216.56.44.70/default.htm and click on Parcel Search.

Portage County *Real Estate, Deed Records* www.co.portage.wi.us `Free & $$` Access to county records is free at https://landshark.co.portage.wi.us. Registration required; searching is free; fee for copies of images. Property tax data does not include Stevens Point City. *Property, Taxation Records* `Free` Search the county tax application database free at http://pctax.co.portage.wi.us/PCTax/Taxrtr?action=taxdefault but no name seraching. Property data on the GIS mapping site free at http://gisinfo.co.portage.wi.us/website/portagepa/viewer.htm. click on Search but no name searching.

Racine County *Real Estate, Deed Records* www.racineco.com `$$` Real estate record access is via a dial-up system; email or call the Racine County Register of Deeds Office, 262-636-3208, or see www.racineco.com/registerofdeeds/. *Property, Taxation Records* `Free` Tax inquiry should be available free at www.racineco.com/rodtax/.

Richland County *Real Estate, Grantor/Grantee, Deed Records* www.rclrs.net/rod/default.asp `Free & $$` Search recorded land index for free at www.rclrs.net/cds/rod/search.aspx but fees apply to print images. Records go back to 7/30/1993. *Property, Taxation Records* `Free` Access parcel data free from the Land Information office at www.rclrs.net/cds/parcel/. Also, access property data free at http://gis.msa-ps.com/MAPS/WI/Counties/Richland/Publicviewer/viewer.htm but no name searching.

Rock County *Real Estate, Deed, Lien Records* www.co.rock.wi.us/Dept/RegisterDeeds/ROD.htm `$$` Real estate record access available via a dial-up system; email or call the Rock County Register of Deeds Office, 608-757-5650. Also, access recording office data by subscription on either the Laredo system (subscription & fees) or Tapestry System (use credit card) at http://tapestry.fidlar.com; $3.99 search; $.50 per image. Index goes back to 8/1986; images back to 1989. *Property, Taxation Records* `Free` Access the City of Janesville Assessor database free at www.ci.janesville.wi.us/Scripts2/gvsweb.dll/search. No name searching.

Rusk County *Property, Taxation Records* `Free` Access assessor land data free at www.ruskcogiws.com/RuskCoWi/

St. Croix County *Real Estate, Deed, Lien Records* www.co.saint-croix.wi.us `$$` Recording office data by subscription on either the Laredo system using subscription and fees or Tapestry System using credit card, http://tapestry.fidlar.com; $3.99 search; $.50 per image. Index goes back to 1/1997; images to 11/1974; Liens back to 1990.

Sauk County *Real Estate, Deed Records* www.co.sauk.wi.us/dept/regodeed/index.html `Free & $$` Access to recorder's land records is available free or by subscription for full-time access at http://landshark.co.sauk.wi.us/. Registration required; setup account thru Recorder office. Occasional users search free, but view documents for $2 first page, $1 add'l. *Property, Taxation Records* `Free` Search Village of Spring Green property data free at www.wendorffassessing.com/Spring_Green_options.htm. No name searching. Also, search Village of Plain property data at www.wendorffassessing.com/Plain_options.htm.

Sawyer County *Real Estate, Deed, Lien, Subdivision, Condo, Plat, Survey Map Records*
http://sawyercountygov.org `Free & $$` Recording office data by subscription on either the Laredo system using subscription and fees or the Tapestry System using credit card, http://tapestry.fidlar.com; $3.99 search; $.50 per image. Index and images go back to 5/1992.

Shawano County *Property, Taxation Records* `Free` Access parcel data free at http://gis.co.shawano.wi.us/portal/ but no name searching.

Sheboygan County *Real Estate, Deed, Lien Records* www.co.sheboygan.wi.us/html/d_regdeeds.html `$$`
Recording office data by subscription on either the Laredo system using subscription and fees or the Tapestry System using credit card, http://tapestry.fidlar.com; $3.99 search; $.50 per image. Index and images go back to 1/1992; tract data to 7/18/1996.
Property, Taxation Records `Free` Lookup parcel and property tax data free at
www.co.sheboygan.wi.us/landinformation/portal_public.aspx but no name searching. Also, lookup parcel, property tax, and GIS mapping and surveys free at www.co.sheboygan.wi.us/landinformation/portal_public.aspx but no name searching.

Taylor County *Real Estate, Deed, Lien, Mortgage Records* www.co.taylor.wi.us/departments/rod/rod.html `$$`
Access county land records back to 1/1998 with subscription to Landshark at https://landshark.co.taylor.wi.us/LandShark/about.jsp. Index search is free; images are $2.00 1st page, $1.00 each add'l.
Property, Taxation Records `Free` Search property and tax data free at http://taylorwi.mapping-online.com/TaylorCoWi/default.htm and click on Search button at righthand top.

Trempealeau County *Property, Taxation Records* `Free` Access to the county assessor's database is free at www.tremplocounty.com/Search/Search.asp.

Vilas County *Property, Taxation Records* `Free` Access property data free by municipality name at http://webtax.co.vilas.wi.us/taxrec1.php but no name searching.

Walworth County *Real Estate, Grantor/Grantee, Deed Records* www.co.walworth.wi.us `Free`
Search the Register of Deeds index for free on the county e-government public search page at www.co.walworth.wi.us. Click on "Public Records." Online records go back to 1976. *Property, Taxation Records* `Free` Search the treasurer's tax roll list under "Tax Roll Documents" at www.co.walworth.wi.us. Search parcel and land data free on the gis-mapping site at www.co.walworth.wi.us/Information%20Systems/LID%20Website/divpageims.htm but no name searching.

Washington County *Real Estate, Deed Records* www.co.washington.wi.us/washington/contacts.jsp `$$`
Access to Landshark for real estate records available for a fee at
www.co.washington.wi.us/departments.iml?mdl=departments.mdl&ID=REG.

Waukesha County *Real Estate, Deed, Lien, Marriage, UCC Records*
www.waukeshacounty.gov/page.aspx?SetupMetaId=10568&id=9690 `Free` Access the recording database free at http://dwprd.waukeshacounty.gov/applications/production/ROD_TRACT_DOCUMENTS/.
Property, Taxation Records `Free` Search assessor property data at www.ci.waukesha.wi.us/Parcel/DataInquiry1.jsp. Search county tax listings at http://dwprd.waukeshacounty.gov/applications/production/ROD_TAX_LISTING/ but no name searching at either site. Waukesha City assessor database or sales lists free at www.ci.waukesha.wi.us/Assessor/propertySalesInformation.html. Personal property at www.ci.waukesha.wi.us/Assessor/Documents/ppAssessmentRoll.txt. Wauwatosa at www.wauwatosa.net/display/wspTosaAssessmentTemplate.asp.

Waupaca County *Real Estate, Deed Records* www.co.waupaca.wi.us `$$` Access to the Register of Deeds data requires subscription, username and password. Monthly fee is $450.00. For info, call 715-258-6250. Records go back to 1982; monthly or daily subscriptions available. *Property, Taxation Records* `Free & $$` Access land information office data free at http://public1.co.waupaca.wi.us/CountyMap_Public/. A fee and registration is required for name searching; no free name searching.

Waushara County *Property, Taxation Records* `Free` Search property data free on the county land information system at www.co.waushara.wi.us/Website/WausharaPA/viewer.htm.

Winnebago County *Real Estate, Deed, Lien Records* www.co.winnebago.wi.us `$$` Recording office data by subscription on either the Laredo system using subscription and fees or the Tapestry System using credit card, http://tapestry.fidlar.com; $3.99 search; $.50 per image. Index goes back to 11/1995; images to 1985.
Property, Taxation Records `Free` Property records on the City of Oshkosh assessor database are free at http://bids.ci.oshkosh.wi.us/Care/ProcessSearch.asp?cmd=NewSearch. Also, City of Neenah property data is at http://www3.ci.neenah.wi.us/WebInquiry/ but no name searching. Also, access the City of Menasha Tax Roll Information database free at www.cityofmenasha-wi.gov/content/departments/finance/(3)tax_roll_information.php.

Wood County *Real Estate, Deed, Lien Records* www.co.wood.wi.us `$$` Recording office data by subscription on either the Laredo system using subscription and fees or the Tapestry System using credit card, http://tapestry.fidlar.com; $3.99 search; $.50 per image. Index goes back to 1979; images to 8/1999.

Wyoming

Capital: Cheyene
           Laramie County
Time Zone: MST
Population: 522,830
# of Counties: 23

Useful State Links

Website: http://wyoming.gov/
Governor: http://governor.wy.gov/
Attorney General: http://attorneygeneral.state.wy.us
State Archives: http://wyoarchives.state.wy.us/index.htm
State Statutes and Codes: http://legisweb.state.wy.us/titles/statutes.htm
Legislative Bill Search: http://legisweb.state.wy.us/sessions/legsess.htm
Unclaimed Funds: http://treasurer.state.wy.us/uphome.asp

Primary State Agencies

Sexual Offender Registry  Free

Division of Criminal Investigation, ATTN: WSOR, http://wysors.dci.wyo.gov/sor/home.htm Use this web address. Search is by last name, street name, city, county or ZIP. Data includes name including AKA, physical address, date and place of birth, date and place of conviction, crime for which convicted, photograph and physical description.

Corporation, LLC, LP, Fictitious Name, Trademarks/Servicemarks Free

Business Division, Attn: Records, http://soswy.state.wy.us/corporat/corporat.htm Information is available through the Internet site listed above. You can search by corporate name or even download the whole file. Also, they have several pages of excellent searching tips. Also, search the Secretary of State securities department enforcement actions/opinions free at http://soswy.state.wy.us/securiti/enforce.htm.

Uniform Commercial Code, Federal Tax Liens $$

Secretary of State, UCC Division - Records, http://soswy.state.wy.us/uniform/uniform.htm The online filing system permits unlimited record searching. There is a $150 annual fee, with no additional fees charged for searches. Subscribers are entitled to do filings at a 50% discount. Visit the webpage. *Other Options:* Lists of filings on CD or diskette are available for purchase. Download the database for $2,000 per year.

Driver License Information, Driver Records $$

Wyoming Department of Transportation, Driver Services, www.dot.state.wy.us This method is available using FTP and RJE technology. Only approved vendors and permissible users are supported. Write or call Marianne Zivkovich at the above address for details. *Other Options:* The entire driver license file may be purchased for $2,500.

Vital Records $$

Wyoming Department of Health, Vital Records Services, www.health.wyo.gov/rfhd/vital_records/index.html Order from an approved vendor At www.vitalcheck.com. Extra fees involved.

Occupational Licensing Boards

Attorney..www.wyomingbar.org/directory/index.html
Bank ....http://audit.state.wy.us/banking/banking/bankingregulatedentities.htm
Check Casher...http://audit.state.wy.us/banking/uccc/uccclicensees.htm

Child Care Licensee .... http://dfswapps.state.wy.us/DFSDivEC/General/Contacts.asp
Collection Agency .... http://audit.state.wy.us/banking/cab/cablicensees.htm
Controlled Substance Registrants ...... http://pharmacyboard.state.wy.us/search.asp
Engineer .... http://engineersandsurveyors.state.wy.us/roster/rosterSearch.aspx
Feed/Fertilizer .... www.kellysolutions.com/wy/
Funeral Pre-Need Agent .... http://insurance.state.wy.us/search/search.asp
Geologist .... http://wbpg.wy.gov/roster_search.asp
Guide, Outdoor .... http://mt.gov/dli/bsd/license/bsd_boards/out_board/board_page.asp
Insurance Claims Adjuster .... http://insurance.state.wy.us/search/search.asp
Insurance Consult/Prod./Rep .... http://insurance.state.wy.us/search/search.asp
Lender, Supervised .... http://audit.state.wy.us/banking/uccc/uccclicensees.htm
Lobbyist .... http://soswy.state.wy.us/election/lob-list.htm
Medical Doctor/Psychiatrist .... http://wyomedboard.state.wy.us/roster.asp
Motor Club Agent .... http://insurance.state.wy.us/search/search.asp
Nurse/Nursing Assistant .... http://nursing.state.wy.us/Main.asp?MainMode=3
Nurse-LPN .... http://nursing.state.wy.us/Main.asp?MainMode=3
Occupational Therapist .... http://ot.state.wy.us/search.aspx
Optometrist .... www.arbo.org/index.php?action=findanoptometrist
Outfitter .... http://mt.gov/dli/bsd/license/bsd_boards/out_board/board_page.asp
Pawnbroker .... http://audit.state.wy.us/banking/uccc/uccclicensees.htm
Pharmacist/Pharmacy Technician ...... http://pharmacyboard.state.wy.us/search.asp
Physician Assistant .... http://wyomedboard.state.wy.us/PARoster.asp
Prescrip/n Drugs/Substance Mfg/Sell http://pharmacyboard.state.wy.us/search.asp
Psychologist .... http://plboards.state.wy.us/psychology/
Public Accountant-CPA .... http://cpaboard.state.wy.us/database.aspx
Real Estate Agent .... www.arello.com/
Reinsurance Intermediary .... http://insurance.state.wy.us/search/search.asp
Rental Car Agents .... http://insurance.state.wy.us/search/search.asp
Rent-to-own Company .... http://audit.state.wy.us/banking/uccc/uccclicensees.htm
Retail Pharmacies (Resi/Non-Resi) ... http://pharmacyboard.state.wy.us/search.asp
Risk Retention .... http://insurance.state.wy.us/search/search.asp
Sales Finance Company .... http://audit.state.wy.us/banking/uccc/uccclicensees.htm
Savings & Loan Association .... http://audit.state.wy.us/banking/banking/bankingregulatedentities.htm
Surplus Line Broker, Resident .... http://insurance.state.wy.us/search/search.asp
Surveyor, Land .... http://engineersandsurveyors.state.wy.us/roster/rosterSearch.aspx
Third Party Administrator .... http://insurance.state.wy.us/search/search.asp
Travel & Baggage Agent .... http://insurance.state.wy.us/search/search.asp
Trust Company .... http://audit.state.wy.us/banking/banking/bankingregulatedentities.htm

State and Local Courts

State Court Structure: Each county has a District Court of "higher jurisdiction" and a Circuit Court of limited jurisdiction. Effective January 1, 2003 all Justice Courts became Circuit Courts and follow Circuit Court rules.

Circuit Courts handle civil claims up to $7,000 and small claims to $5,000. The District Courts take cases over the applicable limit in each county. Three counties have two Circuit Courts each: Fremont, Park, and Sweetwater. Cases may be filed in either of the two court offices in those counties, and records requests are referred between the two courts. Municipal courts operate in all incorporated cities and towns; their jurisdiction covers all ordinance violations and has no civil jurisdiction. The Municipal Court judge may assess penalties of up to $750 and/or six months in jail.

Probate is handled by the District Court.

Statewide Court Online Access: There are no known Wyoming courts open online to the public; Wyoming's statewide case management system is for internal use only. Planning is underway for a new case management system that will ultimately allow public access. Supreme Court opinions are listed by date at www.courts.state.wy.us/Opinions.aspx.

Recorders, Assessors, and Other Sites of Note

Recording Office Organization: 23 counties, 23 recording offices. The recording officer is the County Clerk. Federal tax liens on personal property of businesses are filed with the Secretary of State. Other federal and all state tax liens are filed with the County Clerk.

Online Access Note: A growing number of counties offer online access to various property records and databases of recorded documents.

Albany County *Property, Taxation Records* `Free` Search the county assessor database free at http://assessor.co.albany.wy.us. Click on Search.

Campbell County *Property, Taxation Records* `Free` Search property records free at www.ccgov.net/assessor/online/property/index.rsp

Laramie County *Property, Taxation Records* `Free` Search property data free at http://arcims.laramiecounty.com/ but no name searching.

Lincoln County *Real Estate, Deed, Coroner, Plat Records* www.lcwy.org `Free` Access to land records is free at www.lcwy.org/weblink7/Browse.aspx. Click on Land Documents and search by year then book number. Coroner and plats are in separate folders.
Property, Taxation Records `Free` Plat records available free at www.lcwy.org/weblink7/Browse.aspx

Natrona County *Property, Taxation Records* `Free` Access to GIS/maps free go to www.natronacounty-wy.gov/?load=GIS/GISHome.

Sheridan County *Property, Taxation Records* `Free` Access county property tax records free at http://webtax.csa-inc.net/sheridanwy/. Also, a GIS-mapping site provides parcel data free at www.sheridancounty.com/info/gis/overview.php.

Sublette County *Property, Taxation Records* `Free` Access property data and GIS-mapping free at www.sublettewyo.com/gis/index.html.

Teton County *Real Estate, Deed, Lien Records* http://www2.tetonwyo.org/clerk/ `Free` Access to the Clerk's database of scanned images is free at http://www2.tetonwyo.org/clerk/query/. Search for complete documents back to 7/1996; partial documents back to 4/1991.
Property, Taxation Records `Free` Download assessor property data lists free at www.tetonwyo.org/assessor/nav/100084.asp

Chapter 6

Searching Federal Court Records

Searching records at the federal court system can be one of the easiest or one of the most frustrating experiences that public record searchers may encounter. Although the federal court system offers advanced electronic search capabilities, at times it is practically impossible to properly identify a subject when searching civil or criminal records. Before reviewing searching procedures, a brief overview is in order.

Federal Court Structure

At the federal level, all cases involve federal or U.S. constitutional law or interstate commerce. The federal court system includes three levels of courts, plus several specialty courts.

United States District Courts

The United States District Courts are the courts of general jurisdiction, or trial courts. There are 89 districts in the 50 states, which are listed with their divisions in Title 28 of the U.S. Code, Sections 81-144. District courts also exist in Puerto Rico, the U.S. Virgin Islands, the District of Columbia, Guam, and the Northern Mariana Islands. In total there are 94 U.S. district courts in 500 court locations. Some states, such as Colorado, are composed of a single judicial district. Others, such as California, are composed of multiple judicial districts – Central, Eastern, Northern, and Southern.

The task of locating the right court is seemingly simplified by the nature of the federal system—

- All court locations are based upon the plaintiff's county of domicile.
- All civil and criminal cases go to the U.S. District Courts.
- All bankruptcy cases go to the U.S. Bankruptcy Courts.

Bankruptcy Courts are separate units of the district courts and have exclusive jurisdiction over bankruptcy cases. States with more than one court are divided further into judicial districts — e.g., the State of New York consists of four judicial districts: the Northern, Southern, Eastern, and Western. Further, many judicial districts contain more than one court location, usually called a division.

The bankruptcy courts generally use the same hearing locations as the district courts. If court locations differ, the usual variance is to have fewer bankruptcy court locations.

A plaintiff or defendant may have cases in any of the 500 court locations, so it is really not all that simple to find them.

United States Court of Appeals

The United States Court of Appeals consists of thirteen appellate courts that hear appeals of verdicts from the district and bankruptcy courts. Courts of Appeals are designated as follows:

- The Federal Circuit Court of Appeals hears appeals from the U.S. Claims Court and the U.S. Court of International Trade. It is located in Washington, DC.

- The District of Columbia Circuit Court of Appeals hears appeals from the district courts in Washington, DC as well as from the Tax Court.

- Eleven geographic Courts of Appeals — each of these appeal courts covers a designated number of states and territories.[1]

Supreme Court of the United States

The Supreme Court of the United States is the court of last resort in the United States. The Supreme Court is located in Washington, DC, where it hears appeals from the United States Courts of Appeals and from the highest courts of each state.

Other Federal Courts of Note

There are three significant special/separate courts created to hear cases or appeals for certain areas of litigation that demand special expertise. These courts are the U.S. Tax Court, the Court of International Trade, and the U.S. Court of Federal Claims. A profile of each of these courts is located at the end of this chapter.

How Federal Trial Court Cases are Organized

Indexing and Case Numbering

When a case is filed with a federal court, a case number is assigned. District courts index by defendant and plaintiff as well as by case number. Bankruptcy courts usually index by debtor and case number. Therefore, when you search by name you will first receive a listing of all cases where the name appears, both as plaintiff and defendant.

To view case records you will need to know or find the applicable case number.

Case numbering procedures are not consistent throughout the federal court system. One judicial district may assign numbers by district while another may assign numbers by location (division) within that judicial district or by judge within the division. Remember that case numbers appearing in legal text citations may not be adequate for searching unless they appear in the proper form for the particular court.

Docket Sheet

As in state court systems, information from cover sheets and from documents filed as a case goes forward is recorded on the docket sheet, which then contains the case history from initial filing to its current status. While docket sheets differ somewhat in format, the basic information contained on a docket sheet is consistent from court to court. As noted previously in the state court chapter, all docket sheets contain—

- Name of court, including location (division) and the judge assigned;

---

[1] The profiles at the end of the chapter list the circuit numbers (1 through 11) and location of the Court of Appeals for each state.

- Case number and case name;

- Names of all plaintiffs and defendants/debtors;

- Names and addresses of attorneys for the plaintiff or debtor;

- Nature and cause (e.g., U.S. civil statute) of action;

- Listing of documents filed in the case, including the date, docket entry number, and a short description (e.g., 12-2-92, #1, Complaint).

All basic civil case information entered onto docket sheets and into computerized systems like the Case Management/Electronic Case Filings (CM/ECF) starts with standard form JS-44, the Civil Cover Sheet, or the equivalent.

Assignment of Cases and Computerization

At one time, cases were assigned within a district based on the county of origination. Although this is still true in most states, computerized tracking of dockets has led to a more flexible approach to case assignment. For example in Minnesota and Connecticut, rather than blindly assigning all cases from a county to one judge, their districts use random numbers and other methods to logically balance caseloads among their judges.

This trend may appear to confuse the case search process. Actually, finding cases has become significantly easier with the wide availability of the U.S. Party/Case Index and PACER.[2] Also helpful is when on-site terminals in each court location contain the same database of district-wide information.

Electronic Access to Federal Court Records

Numerous programs have been developed for electronic access to federal court records. Over the years, the Administrative Office of the United States Courts in Washington, DC has developed a number of innovative public access programs—

- The U.S. Party/Case Index

- PACER

- Case Management/Electronic Case Files (CM/ECF)

- VCIS (via the telephone)

Search the U.S. Party/Case Index

The U.S. Party/Case Index, actually part of PACER, is a national locator index for U.S. District, Bankruptcy, and Appellate courts. By using the U.S. Party/Case Index searchers may conduct nearly nationwide search to determine whether or not a party is involved in federal litigation.

If you find there is a case in existence involving a particular subject, then you need to visit the PACER or CM/ECF site for the particular jurisdiction where the case is located. The *Case Number* field in the output will be a direct link to the full case information on the court's

---

[2] PACER - **P**ublic **A**ccess to **C**ourt **E**lectronic **R**ecords - is explained on pages to follow.

computers, whether the court is running the Internet version of PACER or the newer PACER on the CM/ECF system.

You may access the U.S. Party/Case Index via the Internet at http://pacer.uspci.uscourts.gov. Subscribers to PACER automatically have access to the U.S. Party/Case Index. Subscribers may use their existing PACER login and password.

The U.S. Party/Case Index allows searches 1) by party name or Social Security Number in the bankruptcy index, 2) party name or nature of suit in the civil index, 3) defendant name in the criminal index, and 4) party name in the appellate index. The information provided by the search result will include the party name, the court where the case is filed, the case number and the filing date.

To find the date ranges for the cases in a particular court, choose the option "Date Ranges" at the main menu. This option provides how far back the search will go and the date the U.S. Party/Case Index was last updated for each court.

To retrieve more information on a particular case found while searching the U.S. Party/Case Index, access the PACER system for the jurisdiction where the case resides as indicated by the court abbreviation. Usually the Case Number will be a link to the case summary information at that court's PACER site.

At press time, there were a number of courts not participating in the U.S. Party Case Index. Non-participating Appellate Courts include the Second, Fifth, Seventh, and Eleventh Circuits. Non-participating District Courts include the Indiana Southern District, New Mexico District, and the U.S. Virgin Islands District.

PACER

PACER, the acronym for **P**ublic **A**ccess to **E**lectronic **C**ourt **R**ecords, provides docket information online for open and some closed case information at **all U.S. Bankruptcy Courts** and **most U.S. District Courts**. Cases for the U.S. Court of Federal Claims are also available.

A key point to consider is that each court maintains its own database with case information and decides what to make available on PACER. Also, several courts provide case information on Internet sites without support of the PACER Service Center.

PACER sign-up and technical support is handled at the PACER Service Center in San Antonio, Texas; phone 800-676-6856. A single sign-up is good for all courts; however, some individual courts may require further registration procedures. Many judicial districts offer to send a PACER Primer that has been customized for that district. The primer contains a summary of how to access PACER, how to select cases, how to read case numbers and docket sheets, some searching tips, who to call for problem resolution, and district specific program variations.

You may search by case number, party name, SSN, or tax identification number in the U.S. Bankruptcy Courts. You may search by case number, party name, or filing date range in the U.S. District Courts. You may search by case number or party name in the U.S. Courts of Appeals.

PACER provides the following information

- A listing of all parties and participants including judges, attorneys, trustees

- A compilation of case related information such as cause of action, nature of suit, dollar demand
- A chronology of dates of case events entered in the case record
- A claims registry
- A listing of new cases each day in the bankruptcy courts
- Appellate court opinions
- Judgments or case status
- Types of case documents filed for certain districts.

PACER Problems

There are two inherent problems when searching PACER records—

1. How far back records are kept
2. Lack of identifiers

Since each court determines how records will be indexed and when records will be purged, this can leave a searcher guessing how a name is spelled or abbreviated, and how much information about closed cases a search will uncover. The bottom line is that a PACER search may not come close to matching a full seven-year search of the federal court records available by written request from the court itself or through a local document retrieval company.

Another problem is the lack of identifiers. Most federal courts do not show the full DOB on records available to the public. Some courts show no DOB at all. Thus, if the name searched for is common and the search results show two or more hits, each individual case file may need to be reviewed to determine if the case belongs to the subject in mind.

An excellent FAQ on PACER is at http://pacer.psc.uscourts.gov/faq.html.

Miscellaneous Online Systems

RACER is a comparable system to PACER. A few courts still maintain and offer access through RACER. Over the years some courts have developed their own legacy online systems. In addition to RACER, Idaho's Bankruptcy and District Courts have other searching options available on their websites. Likewise, the Southern District Court of New York offers CourtWeb, which provides information to the public on selected recent rulings of those judges who have elected to make information available in electronic form.

Case Management/Electronic Case Files (CM/ECF)

CM/ECF is the relatively new case management system for the Federal Judiciary for all bankruptcy, district, and appellate courts, replacing the aging electronic docketing and case management systems. CM/ECF allows courts to accept filings and provide access to filed documents over the Internet. Attorneys may use CM/ECF to file documents and manage official documents related to a case. Case Management/Electronic Case Files case information is available to the public. Searchers access CM/ECF via PACER.

For details, visit http://pacer.psc.uscourts.gov/cmecf/index.html.

It is important to note that when you search ECF, you may be searching ONLY cases that have been filed electronically. Since a case may not have been filed electronically through CM/ECF, you must still conduct a search using PACER to determine if a case exists.

Most individual courts offer tutorials on how to use CM/ECF for their district. Functioning as a search mechanism, CM/ECF attaches to the relevant docket entries and to PDF versions of related documents filed with or issued by the court. A user may access PDF attachments through a hyperlink that appears with the docket entry.

Because PACER and CM/ECF database systems are maintained within each court, each jurisdiction will have a different URL or modem number. Accessing and querying information from PACER and CM/ECF is comparable; however the format and content of information provided may differ slightly.

Other Search Methods

Voice Case Information System (VCIS)

Another access system is **VCIS** – Voice Case Information System. At one time, nearly all of the U.S. Bankruptcy Court judicial districts provided **VCIS**, a means of accessing information regarding OPEN bankruptcy cases by merely using a touch-tone telephone. The advantage? There is no charge. Individual names are entered last name first with as much of the first name as you wish to include. For example, Joe B. Cool could be entered as COOLJ or COOLJOE. Do not enter the middle initial. Business names are entered as they are written, without blanks.

VCIS, like the RACER System, is being replaced by newer technology. Each bankruptcy court that still offers VCIS access is shown in the court profiles section at the end of this chapter.

VCIS should only be used to locate information about open cases. Do not attempt to use VCIS as a substitute for a PACER search.

Searching Records by Mail and In Person

There are certain pre-set standards for federal courts that most all courts follow. The search fee is $26 per item. 'A search' is one party name or case number. The court copy fee is $.50 per page. Certification fee is $9 per document, double for exemplification, if available. If you request documents by mail, it is best to always enclose a stamped self-addressed envelope unless a court indicates otherwise. Most courts accept fax requests or will suggest a copying/search vendor. Before releasing records, assume that the court will require prepayment, as most do.

More Federal Courts Searching Hints

- Check the assigned counties of jurisdiction for each court within a state. Usually accessible from the web, this is a good starting point for determining where case records may be found.

- Searchers need to be sure that the court's case index includes all cases open or closed for that particular period, especially important if using CM/ECF. Be aware that some courts purge older, closed paper case files after a period of time, making a search there incomplete after the purge date. Purge times vary from court to court and state to state. **Some courts purge within a few months of a case closing.**

- Often, court personnel are very knowledgeable open cases, but are sometimes fuzzy in answering questions about how far back case records go on PACER, and whether closed cases have been purged. If you are looking for cases older than a year or two, there is no substitute for paying for a real, on-site search performed by court personnel or by a local document retriever. An accurate on-site search can be performed if the court allows full access to its indexes, and most do through public access terminals in their offices.

- Most federal courts no longer provide the date of birth or the Social Security Number on search results. However, a handful will provide the last four digits of the SSN, or they may provide the birth month and year of birth, but not the day. **The court summary pages at the end of this chapter show which districts provide personnel identifiers for record searchers.**

- Some courts may be more willing than others to give out information by telephone. This is because most courts now have fully computerized indexes that clerks can access while on the phone.

What If the Record Search Results Do Not Include Identifiers?

Approximately 5 percent of the criminal records in the U.S. are records of federal offenses. A well-known concern of the employment screening industry is the fact it is next to impossible for employers to verify that a new hire does not have a federal criminal record.

This is a struggle and a tough problem to solve, especially if a searcher is dealing with a common name. Here are several ideas for trying to ferret out a false-positive:

View Case Files

If possible, review the documents found in the case files for any hints of identification. At some district courts, clerks will look at paper case file records, if any, to determine if other identification exists that can match the requester's identifiers.

Incarceration Records

Searching prison records is sometimes an excellent alternative means for identity verification. Search the Bureau of Prisons at /www.bop.gov/.

News Media

Some record searchers have been successful in confirming an identity by using news media sources such as newspapers and web news media. Even blogs may help.

Federal Records Centers and the National Archives

After a federal case is closed, the documents are held by the federal courts location for a predetermined number of years. This can be as little as six months, or, rarely, until the court reaches its capacity to store files. The closed cases are then sent to and stored at a designated Federal Records Center (FRC). After 20 to 30 years, the records are then transferred from the FRC to the regional archives offices. All of these offices are administered by the National Archives and Records Administration (NARA).

Each court has its own transfer cycle and determines access procedures to its case records even after they have been sent to the FRC.

When case records are sent to an FRC, the boxes of records are assigned accession, location, and box numbers. These numbers, which are called *case locator information*, must be obtained from the originating court and are necessary to retrieve documents from the FRC. Some courts will provide case locator information over the telephone, but other courts may require a written request. In certain judicial districts this information is now available on PACER.

The Federal Records Center location for each state is shown below.

Federal Record Center Locater Table

State	Circuit	Appeals Court	Federal Records Center
AK	9	San Francisco, CA	Anchorage (Some records are in temporary storage in Seattle)
AL	11	Atlanta, GA	Atlanta
AR	8	St. Louis, MO	Fort Worth
AZ	9	San Francisco, CA	Los Angeles
CA	9	San Francisco, CA	Los Angeles (Central & Southern CA) San Francisco (Eastern & Northern CA)
CO	10	Denver, CO	Denver
CT	2	New York, NY	Boston
DC		Washington, DC	Washington, DC
DE	3	Philadelphia, PA	Philadelphia
FL	11	Atlanta, GA	Atlanta
GA	11	Atlanta, GA	Atlanta
GU	9	San Francisco, CA	San Francisco
HI	9	San Francisco, CA	San Francisco
IA	8	St. Louis, MO	Kansas City, MO
ID	9	San Francisco, CA	Seattle
IL	7	Chicago, IL	Chicago
IN	7	Chicago, IL	Chicago
KS	10	Denver, CO	Kansas City, MO
KY	6	Cincinnati, OH	Atlanta
LA	5	New Orleans, LA	Fort Worth
MA	1	Boston, MA	Boston
MD	4	Richmond, VA	Philadelphia
ME	1	Boston, MA	Boston
MI	6	Cincinnati, OH	Chicago
MN	8	St. Louis, MO	Chicago
MO	8	St. Louis, MO	Kansas City, MO
MS	5	New Orleans, LA	Atlanta
MT	9	San Francisco, CA	Denver
NC	4	Richmond, VA	Atlanta

State	Circuit	Appeals Court	Federal Records Center
ND	8	St. Louis, MO	Denver
NE	8	St. Louis, MO	Kansas City, MO
NH	1	Boston, MA	Boston
NJ	3	Philadelphia, PA	New York
NM	10	Denver, CO	Denver
NV	9	San Francisco, CA	Los Angeles (Clark County, NV) San Francisco (Other NV counties)
NY	2	New York, NY	New York
OH	6	Cincinnati, OH	Chicago (Dayton has some bankruptcy)
OK	10	Denver, CO	Fort Worth
OR	9	San Francisco, CA	Seattle
PA	3	Philadelphia, PA	Philadelphia
PR	1	Boston, MA	New York
RI	1	Boston, MA	Boston
SC	4	Richmond, VA	Atlanta
SD	8	St. Louis, MO	Denver
TN	6	Cincinnati, OH	Atlanta
TX	5	New Orleans, LA	Fort Worth
UT	10	Denver, CO	Denver
VA	4	Richmond, VA	Philadelphia
VI	3	Philadelphia, PA	New York
VT	2	New York, NY	Boston
WA	9	San Francisco, CA	Seattle
WI	7	Chicago, IL	Chicago
WV	4	Richmond, VA	Philadelphia
WY	10	Denver, CO	Denver

Identifiers and Case Files for U.S. District and U.S. Bankruptcy Court Locations

Listed in order by state are brief summaries for U.S. District Courts, and U.S. Bankruptcy Courts. Summaries include the district's website URL, the district's VCIS phone numbers if available, what personal identifiers appear on search results if any, and duration before closed case files are shipped to the Federal Records Center for archiving. Also shown are the division locations within the district. In most cases, a court's website reveals if specific counties are under its jurisdiction.

Alabama Middle District- US District Court www.almd.uscourts.gov
Search results do not include DOB or SSN. **Divisions-** Dothan, Montgomery, Opelika.

Alabama Middle District- US Bankruptcy Court www.almb.uscourts.gov
VCIS: 334-954-3868. Search results include SSN. Case files sent to archives 3 years after closed. **Location-** Montgomery.

Alabama Northern District- US District Court www.alnd.uscourts.gov
Search results do not include SSN or DOB. Case files sent to archives 18 months after closed. **Divisions-** Birmingham, Gadsden, Huntsville, Jasper.

Alabama Northern District- US Bankruptcy Court www.alnb.uscourts.gov
VCIS: 877-466-0795, 205-254-7337. Search results include last 4 SSN digits. Paper case files sent to archives 1 years after closed; cases kept electronically indefinitely. **Divisions-** Anniston, Birmingham, Decatur, Tuscaloosa.

Alabama Southern District- US District Court www.als.uscourts.gov
Search results do not include SSN, DOB. **Divisions-** Mobile (South), Selma (North).

North Southern District- US Bankruptcy Court www.alsb.uscourts.gov
VCIS: 251-441-5637. Search results include SSN. **Location-** Mobile.

Alaska- US District Court www.akd.uscourts.gov
VCIS: 907-222-6940. Search results do not include SSN or DOB. Tried case files sent to Anchorage Records Center. If the case did not go to trial, file sent to Seattle Records Center. **Divisions-** Anchorage, Fairbanks, Juneau, Ketchikan, Nome.

Alaska- US Bankruptcy Court www.akb.uscourts.gov
VCIS: 888-878-3110, 907-271-2658. Search results do not include DOB; SSN only before 12/04. If a case was tried, file sent to Anchorage Records Center. If the case did not go to trial, file sent to Seattle Records Center. Case records sent to a Center 3 months after case closed. **Location-** Anchorage.

Arizona- US District Court www.azd.uscourts.gov
Search results do not include SSN or DOB. Case files sent to archives 5 years after closed. **Divisions-** Phoenix, Prescott, Tucson.

Arizona- US Bankruptcy Court www.azb.uscourts.gov
VCIS: 602-682-4001. Search results include last 4 SSN digits. Closed case files kept 6 months; electronic files kept indefinitely. **Divisions-** Phoenix, Tucson, Yuma.

Arkansas Eastern District- US District Court www.are.uscourts.gov
Search results do not include SSN or DOB. Case files sent to archives 4 years after closed. **Divisions-** Batesville, Helena, Jonesboro, Little Rock, Pine Bluff.

Arkansas Eastern District- US Bankruptcy Court www.areb.uscourts.gov
VCIS: 800-891-6741, 501-918-5555. Search: Index includes last 4 SSN digits and any other identifiers remaining on document. Case files sent to archives 6 month to a year after closed. **Location-** Little Rock.

Arkansas Western District- US District Court www.arwd.uscourts.gov
Search results do not include SSN or DOB. Closed cases sent to archives after 5 years. **Divisions-** El Dorado, Fayetteville, Fort Smith, Hot Springs, Texarkana.

Arkansas Western District- US Bankruptcy Court www.arb.uscourts.gov
VCIS: 800-891-6741, 501-918-5555. Search results include last 4 SSN digits. All paper files have been sent to archives. **Location -** Fayetteville.

California Central District- US District Court www.cacd.uscourts.gov
Search results do not include SSN or DOB. Case files sent to archives 2-3 years after closed. **Divisions-** Los Angeles (Western), Riverside (Eastern), Santa Ana (Southern).

California Central District- US Bankruptcy Court www.cacb.uscourts.gov
VCIS: 866-522-6053, 213-894-4111. Search results include last 4 SSN digits. Case files sent to archives 1 year after closed. **Divisions-** Los Angeles, Riverside (East), San Fernando Valley, Santa Ana, Santa Barbara (Northern).

California Eastern District- US District Court www.caed.uscourts.gov
Search results do not include SSN or DOB. Case files sent to archives at varying intervals, usually as time permits. **Divisions-** Fresno, Sacramento.

California Eastern District- US Bankruptcy Court www.caeb.uscourts.gov
Search results include last 4 SSN digits. All cases before 3/99 sent to archives. **Divisions-** Fresno, Modesto, Sacramento.

California Northern District- US District Court www.cand.uscourts.gov
Search results do not include SSN or DOB, but office can confirm or deny. Case files sent to archives 6 months after closed. **Divisions-** Oakland, San Francisco, San Jose.

California Northern District- US Bankruptcy Court www.canb.uscourts.gov
> VCIS: 888-457-0604, 415-705-3160. Search results include last 4 SSN digits. Case files sent to archives up to 1 year after closed. **Divisions-** Oakland, San Francisco, San Jose, Santa Rosa.

California Southern District- US District Court www.casd.uscourts.gov
> Search results do not include SSN or DOB. When local space becomes unavailable, closed cases are transferred to archives. **Location** - San Diego.

California Southern District- US Bankruptcy Court www.casb.uscourts.gov
> VCIS: 619-557-6521. Search results include last 4 SSN digits. Case files sent to archives 6 months after closed. **Location-** San Diego.

Colorado- US District Court www.co.uscourts.gov
> Search results do not include SSN or DOB. Closed records sent to archives at irregular intervals. **Location-** Denver.

Colorado- US Bankruptcy Court www.cob.uscourts.gov
> VCIS: 720-904-7419. Search results do not include SSN or DOB. Docket sheet includes last 4 digits of SSN. Closed electronic cases not purged. **Location-** Denver.

Connecticut- US District Court www.ctd.uscourts.gov
> Search results do not include SSN or DOB. **Divisions-** Bridgeport, Hartford, New Haven.

Connecticut- US Bankruptcy Court www.ctb.uscourts.gov
> VCIS: 800-800-5113. Search results include last 4 SSN digits, also address. Case files sent to archives 1 year after closed. **Divisions-** Bridgeport, Hartford, New Haven.

Delaware- US District Court www.ded.uscourts.gov
> Search results do not include SSN or DOB. Closed cases are not sent to the archives for a minimum of 6 months. **Location-** Wilmington.

Delaware- US Bankruptcy Court www.deb.uscourts.gov
> VCIS: 302-252-2560. Search results include last 4 SSN digits. Case files sent to archives when court has collected 150 records boxes. **Location-** Wilmington.

District of Columbia- US District Court www.dcd.uscourts.gov
> Search: Criminal search results include DOB; civil returns name only. Case files sent to archives 5 years after closed.

District of Columbia- US Bankruptcy Court www.dcb.uscourts.gov
> VCIS: 202-208-1365. Search results include last 4 SSN digits. Case files sent to archives 1 year after closed.

Florida Middle District- US District Court www.flmd.uscourts.gov
> Search results do not include SSN or DOB. Case files sent to archives 3 years after closed. **Divisions-** Fort Myers, Jacksonville, Ocala, Orlando, Tampa.

Florida Middle District- US Bankruptcy Court www.flmb.uscourts.gov
> VCIS: 866-879-1286, 904-301-6490. Search results include last 4 SSN digits. No specific time when closed records sent to Atlanta Records Center. **Divisions-** Jacksonville, Orlando, Tampa.

Florida Northern District- US District Court www.flnd.uscourts.gov
> Search results do not include SSN or DOB. Closed cases sent to archives depending on case type. **Divisions-** Gainesville, Panama City, Pensacola, Tallahassee.

Florida Northern District- US Bankruptcy Court www.flnb.uscourts.gov
> VCIS: 850-435-8477. Search results include last 4 SSN digits. All case files are electronicly stored. **Divisions-** Pensacola, Tallahassee.

Florida Southern District- US District Court www.flsd.uscourts.gov
> Search: Recent cases do not include SSN or DOB. Case files sent to archives 5 years after closed, then sent to Atlanta Records Center. **Divisions-** Fort Lauderdale, Fort Pierce, Key West, Miami, West Palm Beach.

Florida Southern District- US Bankruptcy Court www.flsb.uscourts.gov
VCIS: 800-473-0226, 305-536-5979. Search results do not include SSN or DOB. Case files sent to archives 6 months after closed. **Divisions-** Fort Lauderdale, Miami, West Palm Beach.

Georgia Middle District- US District Court www.gamd.uscourts.gov
Search results do not include SSN or DOB. Case files sent to archives 2 years after closed. **Divisions-** Albany/Americus, Athens, Columbus, Macon, Thomasville, Valdosta.

Georgia Middle District- US Bankruptcy Court www.gamb.uscourts.gov
VCIS: 800-211-3015, 912-752-8183. Search results do not include SSN or DOB. **Divisions-** Columbus (West), Macon (East).

Georgia Northern District- US District Court www.gand.uscourts.gov
Search results include last 4 SSN digits. **Divisions-** Atlanta, Gainesville, Newnan, Rome.

Georgia Northern District- US Bankruptcy Court www.ganb.uscourts.gov
VCIS: 800-510-8284, 404-730-2866. Search results include last 4 SSN digits. Paper case files archived 6 months after closing; electronic files maintained indefinitely. **Divisions-** Atlanta, Gainesville, Newnan, Rome.

Georgia Southern District- US District Court www.gasd.uscourts.gov
Search results do not include SSN or DOB. **Divisions-** Augusta, Brunswick, Savannah.

Georgia Southern District- US Bankruptcy Court www.gas.uscourts.gov
Search results include last 4 SSN digits. **Divisions-** Augusta, Savannah.

Guam- US District and Bankruptcy Court www.gud.uscourts.gov
Search results include last 4 SSN digits only. All closed case records maintained here.

Hawaii- US District Court www.hid.uscourts.gov
Search results do not include SSN or DOB. Case files sent to archives 1 year after closed.

Hawaii- US Bankruptcy Court www.hib.uscourts.gov
VCIS: 808-522-8122. Search results include last 4 SSN digits.

Idaho- US District Court www.id.uscourts.gov
Search results do not include SSN or DOB. **Divisions-** Boise, Coeur d' Alene, Moscow, Pocatello.

Idaho- US Bankruptcy Court www.id.uscourts.gov
VCIS: 208-334-9386. Search results include last 4 SSN digits and address. **Divisions-** Boise, Coeur d' Alene, Moscow - Northern, Pocatello.

Illinois Central District- US District Court www.ilcd.uscourts.gov
Search results do not include SSN or DOB; court will confirm if identifiers provided in request. Case files sent to archives 5-7 years after closed. **Divisions-** Peoria, Rock Island, Springfield, Urbana.

Illinois Central District- US Bankruptcy Court www.ilcb.uscourts.gov
VCIS: 800-827-9005, 217-431-4820. Search results do not include SSN or DOB. No paper files available. **Divisions-** Danville, Peoria, Springfield.

Illinois Northern District- US District Court www.ilnd.uscourts.gov
Search results do not include SSN or DOB. Case files sent to archives 1-5 years after closed. **Divisions-** Chicago (Eastern), Rockford (Western).

Illinois Northern District- US Bankruptcy Court www.ilnb.uscourts.gov
VCIS: 888-232-6814, 312-408-5089. Search results include last 4 SSN digits. **Divisions-** Chicago (Eastern), Rockford.

Illinois Southern District- US District Court www.ilsd.uscourts.gov
Search results do not include SSN or DOB. Case files sent to archives as deemed necessary. **Divisions-** Benton, East St Louis.

Illinois Southern District- US Bankruptcy Court www.ilsb.uscourts.gov
VCIS: 800-726-5622, 618-482-9365. Search results do not include SSN or DOB. **Divisions-** Benton, East St Louis.

Indiana Northern District- US District Court www.innd.uscourts.gov/fortwayne.shtml
Search results do not include SSN or DOB. **Divisions-** Fort Wayne, Hammond, Lafayette, South Bend.

Indiana Northern District- US Bankruptcy Court www.innb.uscourts.gov
VCIS: 800-755-8393, 574-968-2275. Search results do not include full SSN. Paper files sent to archives 2 years after closed. **Divisions-** Fort Wayne, Hammond, Hammond at Lafayette, South Bend.

Indiana Southern District- US District Court www.insd.uscourts.gov
Search results include SSN or DOB year for criminal cases; civil includes only last 4 SSN digits. **Divisions-** Evansville, Indianapolis, New Albany, Terre Haute.

Indiana Southern District- US Bankruptcy Court www.insb.uscourts.gov
VCIS: 800-335-8003, 317-229-3888. Search results include last 4 SSN digits. Paper case files sent to archives as cases are closed. Electronic cases maintained indefinitely. **Divisions-** Evansville, Indianapolis, New Albany, Terre Haute.

Iowa Northern District- US District Court www.iand.uscourts.gov
Search results do not include SSN or DOB or any personal identifiers. **Divisions-** Cedar Rapids (Eastern), Sioux City (Western).

Iowa Northern District- US Bankruptcy Court www.ianb.uscourts.gov
VCIS: 800-249-9859, 319-286-2282. Search results include name and address only. **Divisions-** Cedar Rapids (Eastern), Sioux City (Western).

Iowa Southern District- US District Court www.iasd.uscourts.gov
Search results do not include SSN or DOB. Case files are all electronic; never purged. **Divisions-** Council Bluffs (Western), Davenport (Eastern), Des Moines (Central).

Iowa Southern District- US Bankruptcy Court www.iasb.uscourts.gov
VCIS: 888-219-5534, 515-284-6427. Search results include dba, fka (alias) **Location-** Des Moines.

Kansas- US District Court www.ksd.uscourts.gov
Search results do not include SSN or DOB. Case files sent to archives 12 months after closed. **Divisions-** Kansas City, Topeka, Wichita.

Kansas- US Bankruptcy Court www.ksb.uscourts.gov
VCIS: 800-827-9028, 316-269-6668. Search results include last 4 SSN digits. Case files sent to archives every 6 months. **Divisions-** Kansas City, Topeka, Wichita.

Kentucky Eastern District- US District Court www.kyed.uscourts.gov
Search results do not include SSN or DOB. Case files sent to archives 5 years after closed. **Divisions-** Ashland, Covington, Frankfort, Lexington, London, Pikeville.

Kentucky Eastern District- US Bankruptcy Court www.kyeb.uscourts.gov
VCIS: 800-998-2650, 859-233-2650. Search results include last 4 SSN digits only. **Location-** Lexington.

Kentucky Western District- US District Court www.kywd.uscourts.gov
Search results do not include SSN or DOB. **Divisions-** Bowling Green, Louisville, Owensboro, Paducah.

Kentucky Western District- US Bankruptcy Court www.kywb.uscourts.gov
VCIS: 800-263-9385, 502-627-5660. Search results include last 4 SSN digits only. **Location-** Louisville.

Louisiana Eastern District- US District Court www.laed.uscourts.gov
Search results do not include SSN or DOB. Case files sent to archives 6 months after closed. **Location-** New Orleans.

Louisiana Eastern District- US Bankruptcy Court www.laeb.uscourts.gov
VCIS: 504-589-7879. Search results do not include SSN or DOB. **Location-** New Orleans.

Louisiana Middle District- US District Court www.lamd.uscourts.gov
Search results do not include SSN or DOB but pre-2003 crim recs may have DOBs. Case files sent to archives 1 year after closed. **Location-** Baton Rouge.

Louisiana Middle District- US Bankruptcy Court www.lamb.uscourts.gov
VCIS: 225-382-2175. Search results include last 4 SSN digits and address. Almost all closed paper files have been sent to archives. **Location-** Baton Rouge.

Louisiana Western District- US District Court www.lawd.uscourts.gov
Search results do not include SSN or DOB. Cases files now all electronic; never purged. **Divisions-** Alexandria, Lafayette, Lake Charles, Monroe, Shreveport.

Louisiana Western District- US Bankruptcy Court www.lawb.uscourts.gov
VCIS: 800-326-4026, 318-676-4234. Search results include last 4 SSN digits only. Case files sent to archives 5 years after closed. **Divisions-** Alexandria, Lafayette-Opelousas, Lake Charles, Monroe, Shreveport.

Maine- US District Court www.med.uscourts.gov
Search results include partial DOB; no SSN. There is no set date when closed case files sent to archives. **Divisions-** Bangor, Portland.

Maine- US Bankruptcy Court www.meb.uscourts.gov
VCIS: 800-650-7253, 207-780-3755. Search results include last 4 SSN digits only. Case files sent to archives 2 years after closed. **Divisions-** Bangor, Portland.

Maryland Northern District- US District Court www.mdd.uscourts.gov
Search results do not include SSN or DOB. Case files sent to archives 3 years after closed. **Location-** Baltimore.

Maryland Northern District- US Bankruptcy Court www.mdb.uscourts.gov
VCIS: 800-829-0145, 410-962-0733. Search results include name and address only. Case files sent to archives 6 months after closed. **Location-** Baltimore.

Maryland Southern District- US District Court www.mdd.uscourts.gov
Search results do not include SSN or DOB. Case files sent to archives 3 years after closed. **Location-** Greenbelt.

Maryland Southern District- US Bankruptcy Court www.mdb.uscourts.gov
VCIS: 800-829-0145, 410-962-0733. Search results include SSN. Case files sent to archives 6 months after closed. **Location-** Greenbelt.

Massachusetts- US District Court www.mad.uscourts.gov
Search results do not include SSN or DOB. Criminal case files sent to archives 4 years after closed; 3 years for civil. **Divisions-** Boston, Springfield, Worcester.

Massachusetts- US Bankruptcy Court www.mab.uscourts.gov
VCIS: 888-201-3572, 617-565-6025. Search results include SSN last 4 digits only, partial address. Case files sent to archives 6 months after closed. **Divisions-** Boston, Worcester.

Michigan Eastern District- US District Court www.mied.uscourts.gov
Search results do not include SSN or DOB. Closed cases are kept electronically; paper files sent to archives. **Divisions-** Ann Arbor, Bay City, Detroit, Flint.

Michigan Eastern District- US Bankruptcy Court www.mieb.uscourts.gov
VCIS: 877-422-3066. Search results include last 4 SSN digits. Case files sent to archives 2 years after closed. **Divisions-** Bay City, Detroit, Flint.

Michigan Western District- US District Court www.miwd.uscourts.gov
Search results do not include SSN or DOB. Closed electronic cases not purged. **Divisions-** Grand Rapids, Kalamazoo, Lansing, Marquette-Northern.

Michigan Western District- US Bankruptcy Court www.miwb.uscourts.gov
VCIS: 866-729-9098, 616-456-2075. Search results include last 4 SSN digits. Case files sent to archives 1 year after closed. **Divisions-** Grand Rapids, Marquette-Northern.

Minnesota- US District Court www.mnd.uscourts.gov
Search results do not include SSN or DOB. **Divisions-** Duluth, Minneapolis, St Paul.

Minnesota- US Bankruptcy Court www.mnb.uscourts.gov
VCIS: 800-959-9002. Search results include last 4 SSN digits. **Divisions-** Duluth, Fergus Falls, Minneapolis, St Paul.

Mississippi Northern District- US District Court www.msnd.uscourts.gov
> Search results do not include SSN or DOB. Civil cases sent to archives 5 years after disposition; 10 years for criminal. **Divisions-** Aberdeen-Eastern, Delta, Greenville, Oxford-Northern.

Mississippi Northern District- US Bankruptcy Court www.msnb.uscourts.gov
> VCIS: 800-392-8653, 662-369-8147. Search results include last 4 SSN digits. **Location-** Aberdeen.

Mississippi Southern District- US District Court www.mssd.uscourts.gov
> Search results do not include SSN or DOB. **Divisions-** Eastern, Hattiesburg, Jackson, Southern, Western.

Mississippi Southern District- US Bankruptcy Court www.mssb.uscourts.gov
> VCIS: 800-601-8859, 601-965-6106. Search results include last 4 SSN digits only; court can also verify using address. **Divisions-** Biloxi, Jackson.

Missouri Eastern District- US District Court www.moed.uscourts.gov
> Search results do not include SSN or DOB, but they may verify over phone. Case files sent to archives 4 years after closed. **Divisions-** Cape Girardeau, St Louis.

Missouri Eastern District- US Bankruptcy Court www.moeb.uscourts.gov
> VCIS: 888-223-6431, 314-244-4999. Search results include last 4 SSN digits, address. Case files sent to archives 4-5 years after closed. **Location-** St Louis.

Missouri Western District- US District Court www.mow.uscourts.gov
> Search results do not include SSN or DOB. Case files sent to archives as deemed necessary. **Divisions-** Jefferson City - Central, Joplin - Southwestern, Kansas City - Western, Springfield-Southern, St Joseph.

Missouri Western District- US Bankruptcy Court www.mow.uscourts.gov
> VCIS: 888-205-2527, 816-512-5110. Search results include last 4 SSN digits. **Location-** Kansas City - Western.

Montana- US District Court www.mtd.uscourts.gov
> Search results do not include SSN or DOB. Case files sent to archives 4-5 years after closed. **Divisions-** Billings, Butte, Great Falls, Helena, Missoula.

Montana- US Bankruptcy Court www.mtb.uscourts.gov
> VCIS: 888-879-0071, 406-782-1060. Search results include last 4 SSN digits. **Location-** Butte.

Nebraska- US District Court www.ned.uscourts.gov
> Search results do not include SSN or DOB or gender; Pre-2004 cases may provide some identifiers. Case files sent to archives approx. 1 year after closed. **Divisions-** Lincoln, North Platte, Omaha.

Nebraska- US Bankruptcy Court www.neb.uscourts.gov
> VCIS: 800-829-0112, 402-221-3757. Search results include last 4 SSN digits, address. Case files sent to archives 6 months after closed. **Divisions-** Lincoln, North Platte, Omaha.

Nevada- US District Court www.nvd.uscourts.gov
> Search results do not include SSN or DOB. **Divisions-** Las Vegas, Reno.

Nevada- US Bankruptcy Court www.nvb.uscourts.gov
> VCIS: 800-294-6920, 702-388-6708. Search results include last 4 SSN digits. All cases stored electronically and kept indefinitely. **Divisions-** Las Vegas, Reno.

New Hampshire- US District Court www.nhd.uscourts.gov
> Search results do not include SSN or DOB. Paper case files sent to archives 1 years after closed; electronic maintained indefinitely **Location-** Concord.

New Hampshire- US Bankruptcy Court www.nhb.uscourts.gov
> VCIS: 800-851-8954, 603-222-2626. Search results include last 4 SSN digits. Case files sent to archives 1 year after closed. **Location-** Manchester.

New Jersey- US District Court www.njd.uscourts.gov
> Search: Court will examine identifiers for possible match. Closed case files sent to archives irregularly. **Divisions-** Camden, Newark, Trenton.

New Jersey- US Bankruptcy Court www.njb.uscourts.gov
VCIS: 877-239-2547, 973-645-6044. Search results include last 4 SSN digits. **Divisions-** Camden, Newark, Trenton.

New Mexico- US District Court www.nmcourt.fed.us/web/DCDOCS/dcindex.html
Search results do not include SSN or DOB on civil; older criminal cases may include last 4 SSN digits. Case files sent to archives 6 months after closed. **Location-** Albuquerque.

New Mexico- US Bankruptcy Court www.nmcourt.fed.us/web/BCDOCS/bcindex.html
VCIS: 888-435-7822, 505-348-2444. Search results include last 4 SSN digits. Case files sent to archives 5 years after closed. **Location-** Albuquerque.

New York Eastern District- US District Court www.nyed.uscourts.gov
Search results do not include SSN or DOB after 2003 **Divisions-** Brooklyn, Central Islip.

New York Eastern District- US Bankruptcy Court www.nyeb.uscourts.gov
VCIS: 800-252-2537, 718-852-5726. Search results do not include SSN or DOB; pre-2003 closed cases may include SSN. Paper closed case files sent to archives 1 year after closed; computer records never purged. **Divisions-** Brooklyn, Central Islip.

New York Northern District- US District Court www.nynd.uscourts.gov
Search results include last 4 SSN digits, also birth year. Results do not include SSN or DOB if case after 2003. Case files sent to archives 1 year after closed. **Divisions-** Albany, Binghamton, Syracuse, Utica.

New York Northern District- US Bankruptcy Court www.nynb.uscourts.gov
VCIS: 800-206-1952. Search results may include SSN. **Divisions-** Albany, Syracuse, Utica.

New York Southern District- US District Court www.nysd.uscourts.gov
Search results do not include SSN or DOB, though DOB may appear on records prior to 2004. Case files sent to archives 5 years after closed (due to construction, closed cases were recently purged.) **Divisions-** New York City, White Plains.

New York Southern District- US Bankruptcy Court www.nysb.uscourts.gov
VCIS: 212-668-2772. Search results include last 4 SSN digits. Case files sent to archives approx. 2 years after closed. **Divisions-** New York, Poughkeepsie, White Plains.

New York Western District- US District Court www.nywd.uscourts.gov
Search results do not include SSN or DOB. Closed electronic cases are not purged. **Divisions-** Buffalo, Rochester.

New York Western District- US Bankruptcy Court www.nywb.uscourts.gov
VCIS: 800-776-9578, 716-551-5311. Search results include last 4 SSN digits. Closed electronic cases not purged. **Divisions-** Buffalo, Rochester.

North Carolina Eastern District- US District Court www.nced.uscourts.gov
Search results do not include SSN or DOB. Civil records retained 2 years. All criminal records after 1979 forwarded to Raleigh. **Divisions-** Eastern, Northern, Southern, Western.

North Carolina Eastern District- US Bankruptcy Court www.nceb.uscourts.gov
VCIS: 888-847-9138, 919-856-4618. Search results include last 4 SSN digits. **Divisions-** Raleigh, Wilson.

North Carolina Middle District- US District Court www.ncmd.uscourts.gov
Search results do not include SSN or DOB, only case numbers and cases found. Closed electronic cases not purged. **Divisions-** Greensboro.

North Carolina Middle District- US Bankruptcy Court www.ncmb.uscourts.gov
VCIS: 888-319-0455, 336-338-4057. Search results include full name and attorney. **Divisions-** Greensboro, Winston-Salem.

North Carolina Western District- US District Court www.ncwd.uscourts.gov
Search results do not include SSN or DOB. Closed cases sent to archives after 5 years. **Divisions-** Asheville, Bryson City, Charlotte, Statesville.

North Carolina Western District- US Bankruptcy Court www.ncwb.uscourts.gov
VCIS: 800-324-5614, 704-350-7509. Search results do not include SSN or DOB. Case files sent to archives upon closing. Cases after 1/1997 are scanned and not retired. **Location-** Charlotte.

North Dakota- US District Court www.ndd.uscourts.gov
Search results do not include SSN or DOB. Records posted after 11/2005 are retained indefinitely. **Divisions-** Bismarck-Southwestern, Fargo-Southeastern, Grand Forks-Northeastern, Minot-Northwestern.

North Dakota- US Bankruptcy Court www.ndb.uscourts.gov
VCIS: 701-297-7166. Search results include last 4 SSN digits. **Location-** Fargo.

Ohio Northern District- US District Court www.ohnd.uscourts.gov
Search results include full name and case number only. Case files sent to archives 5 years after closed. **Divisions-** Akron, Cleveland, Toledo, Youngstown.

Ohio Northern District- US Bankruptcy Court www.ohnb.uscourts.gov
VCIS: 800-898-6899. Search results include SSN. Prior to 1995, closed cases sent to Chicago Records Center; case records now sent to Dayton Records Center every few years. **Divisions-** Akron, Canton, Cleveland, Toledo, Youngstown.

Ohio Southern District- US District Court www.ohsd.uscourts.gov
Search results do not include SSN or DOB. Closed cases sent to archives after 5 years. **Divisions-** Cincinnati, Columbus, Dayton.

Ohio Southern District- US Bankruptcy Court www.ohsb.uscourts.gov
VCIS: 800-726-1004, 937-225-2544. Search results include last 4 SSN digits. Case files sent to archives 6 months after closed. **Divisions-** Cincinnati, Columbus, Dayton.

Oklahoma Eastern District- US District Court www.oked.uscourts.gov
Search results do not include SSN or DOB. Case files sent to archives 3-5 years after closed. **Location-** Muskogee.

Oklahoma Eastern District- US Bankruptcy Court www.okeb.uscourts.gov
VCIS: 877-377-1221, 918-756-8617. Search results include last 4 SSN digits. Closed cases prior to 1998 sent to archives; electronic case held indefinitely. **Divisions-** Okmulgee.

Oklahoma Northern District- US District Court www.oknd.uscourts.gov
Search results do not include SSN or DOB. Case files sent to archives 1 year after closed. **Location-** Tulsa.

Oklahoma Northern District- US Bankruptcy Court www.oknb.uscourts.gov
VCIS: 888-501-6977, 918-699-4001. Search results include last 4 SSN digits only. Closed electronic cases not purged. **Location-** Tulsa.

Oklahoma Western District- US District Court www.okwd.uscourts.gov
Search results do not include SSN or DOB. Closed civil case files sent to archives 5 years after closed, 7 for criminal. **Location-** Oklahoma City.

Oklahoma Western District- US Bankruptcy Court www.okwb.uscourts.gov
VCIS: 800-872-1348, 405-231-4768. Search results include all or partial SSN. Closed cases prior to 1996 have been sent to the archives; newer files available electronically. **Location-** Oklahoma City.

Oregon- US District Court www.ord.uscourts.gov
Search results do not include SSN or DOB. The Documentation index may have DOBs on judgments. Case files sent to archives 3-5 years after closed. **Divisions-** Eugene, Medford, Portland.

Oregon- US Bankruptcy Court www.orb.uscourts.gov
VCIS: 800-726-2227, 503-326-2249. Search results include last 4 SSN digits or DOB; debtor may have chosen to release full SSN. Case files sent to archives irregularly after at least 6 months. **Location-** Eugene, Portland.

Pennsylvania Eastern District- US District Court www.paed.uscourts.gov
Search results do not include SSN or DOB. Closed electronic cases not purged. **Divisions-** Allentown/Reading, Philadelphia.

Pennsylvania Eastern District- US Bankruptcy Court www.paeb.uscourts.gov
VCIS: 215-597-2244. Search results do not include SSN or DOB. Cases sent to archives as early as 6 months after closed. **Divisions-** Philadelphia, Reading.

Pennsylvania Middle District- US District Court www.pamd.uscourts.gov
Search results do not include SSN or DOB. Closed electronic cases not purged. **Divisions-** Harrisburg, Scranton, Williamsport.

Pennsylvania Middle District- US Bankruptcy Court www.pamb.uscourts.gov
VCIS: 877-440-2699. Search results include last 4 SSN digits. Case files sent to archives 6 months after closed. **Divisions-** Harrisburg, Wilkes-Barre.

Pennsylvania Western District- US District Court www.pawd.uscourts.gov
Search results do not include SSN or DOB. Closed electronic cases not purged. **Divisions-** Erie, Johnstown, Pittsburgh.

Pennsylvania Western District- US Bankruptcy Court www.pawb.uscourts.gov
VCIS: 412-355-3210, 866-299-8515. Search results include last 4 SSN digits. Closed cases are sent to archives as storage space fills. **Divisions-** Erie, Pittsburgh.

Puerto Rico- US District Court www.prd.uscourts.gov
Search results do not include SSN or DOB, but judgments may have SSN. Case files sent to archives 1 year after closed.

Puerto Rico- US Bankruptcy Court www.prb.uscourts.gov
Search results include SSN. Cases shipped to Missouri Records Center 3 months after closed.

Rhode Island- US District Court www.rid.uscourts.gov
Search results do not include SSN or DOB. Case files maintained at court 25 years after closed.

Rhode Island- US Bankruptcy Court www.rib.uscourts.gov
VCIS: 800-843-2841, 401-626-3076. Search results include last 4 SSN digits. All closed files on paper have been sent to the archives.

South Carolina- US District Court www.scd.uscourts.gov
Search results do not include SSN or DOB. **Divisions-** Anderson, Beaufort, Charleston, Columbia, Florence, Greenville, Greenwood, Spartanburg.

South Carolina- US Bankruptcy Court www.scb.uscourts.gov
VCIS: 800-669-8767, 803-765-5211. Search results include last 4 SSN digits. Closed case files sent to archives irregularly. **Location-** Columbia.

South Dakota- US District Court www.sdd.uscourts.gov
Search results do not include SSN or DOB. Case files sent to archives 6 months after closed. **Divisions-** Aberdeen, Pierre, Sioux Falls, Western Div - Rapid City.

South Dakota- US Bankruptcy Court www.sdb.uscourts.gov
VCIS: 800-768-6218, 605-357-2422. Search results include partial SSN. Case files are all electronic; never purged. **Divisions-** Pierre, Sioux Falls.

Tennessee Eastern District- US District Court www.tned.uscourts.gov
Search results do not include SSN or DOB. Closed electronic cases not purged. **Divisions-** Chattanooga, Greeneville, Knoxville, Winchester.

Tennessee Eastern District- US Bankruptcy Court www.tneb.uscourts.gov
VCIS: 800-767-1512. Search results include last 4 SSN digits only. Closed records sent to archives 2-3 years after closing. **Divisions-** Northeastern, Northern, Southern.

Tennessee Middle District- US District Court www.tnmd.uscourts.gov
Search results do not include SSN or DOB. Case files sent to archives 1 year after closed. **Divisions-** Columbia, Cookeville, Nashville.

Tennessee Middle District- US Bankruptcy Court http://www2.tnmb.uscourts.gov
VCIS: 615-736-5584 x4. Search results include last 4 SSN digits. Closed case files sent to archives at variable intervals. **Location-** Nashville.

Tennessee Western District- US District Court www.tnwd.uscourts.gov
Search results do not include SSN or DOB. **Location-** Jackson, Memphis.

Tennessee Western District- US Bankruptcy Court www.tnwb.uscourts.gov
VCIS: 888-381-4961, 901-328-3509. Search results include last 4 SSN digits only. Case files sent to archives 3-6 months after closed. **Divisions-** Jackson/Eastern, Memphis/Western.

Texas Eastern District- US District Court www.txed.uscourts.gov
Search results do not include SSN or DOB. Case files sent to archives 1 year after closed. **Divisions-** Beaumont, Lufkin, Marshall, Sherman, Texarkana, Tyler.

Texas Eastern District- US Bankruptcy Court www.txeb.uscourts.gov
VCIS: 800-466-1694, 903-590-3251. Search results do not include SSN or DOB; you may call and they may verify. Case files sent to archives 1 year after closed. **Divisions-** Beaumont, Marshall, Plano, Texarkana, Tyler.

Texas Northern District- US District Court www.txnd.uscourts.gov
Search results do not include SSN or DOB. Closed case files sent to archives yearly. **Divisions-** Abilene, Amarillo, Dallas, Fort Worth, Lubbock, San Angelo, Wichita Falls.

Texas Northern District- US Bankruptcy Court www.txnb.uscourts.gov
VCIS: 800-886-9008, 214-753-2128. Search results include last 4 SSN digits, address and name. Case files sent to archives 6 months after closed. **Divisions-** Amarillo, Dallas, Fort Worth, Lubbock, Wichita Falls.

Texas Southern District- US District Court www.txs.uscourts.gov
Search results do not include SSN or DOB. Case files sent to archives 6 months after closed. **Divisions-** Brownsville, Corpus Christi, Galveston, Houston, Laredo, McAllen, Victoria.

Texas Southern District- US Bankruptcy Court www.txsd.uscourts.gov
VCIS: 800-745-4459, 713-250-5049. Search results include last 4 SSN digits only. Case files sent to archives 6 months after closed. **Divisions-** Corpus Christi, Houston.

Texas Western District- US District Court www.txwd.uscourts.gov
Search results do not include SSN or DOB. Case files kept a minimum 2 years before sending to archives. **Divisions-** Austin, Del Rio, El Paso, Midland, Pecos, San Antonio, Waco.

Texas Western District- US Bankruptcy Court www.txwb.uscourts.gov
VCIS: 888-436-7477, 210-472-4023. Search results do not include SSN or DOB; clerk will verify if your SSN is correct. Case files sent to archives 6-8 months after closed. **Divisions-** Austin, El Paso, Midland/Odessa, San Antonio, Waco.

Utah- US District Court www.utd.uscourts.gov
Search results do not include SSN or DOB; will include case number and date of sentencing. Case files sent to archives 3-4 years after closed.

Utah- US Bankruptcy Court www.utb.uscourts.gov
VCIS: 800-733-6740, 801-524-3107. Search results include last 4 SSN digits only.

Vermont- US District Court www.vtd.uscourts.gov
Search results do not include SSN or DOB. Closed electronic cases not purged. **Divisions-** Burlington, Rutland.

Vermont- US Bankruptcy Court www.vtb.uscourts.gov
VCIS: 800-260-9956, 802-776-2007. Search results include last 4 SSN digits and possibly address. Closed electronic cases not purged. **Location-** Rutland.

Virginia Eastern District- US District Court www.vaed.uscourts.gov
Search results do not include SSN or DOB. Closed electronic cases not purged. **Divisions-** Alexandria, Newport News, Norfolk, Richmond.

Virginia Eastern District- US Bankruptcy Court www.vaeb.uscourts.gov
VCIS: 800-326-5879. Search results include last 4 SSN digits. Closed electronic cases not purged. **Divisions-** Alexandria, Newport News, Norfolk, Richmond.

Virginia Western District- US District Court www.vawd.uscourts.gov
Search results may include last 4 SSN digits. Case files sent to archives 1 year after closed.
Divisions- Abingdon, Big Stone Gap, Charlottesville, Danville, Harrisonburg, Lynchburg, Roanoke.

Virginia Western District- US Bankruptcy Court www.vawb.uscourts.gov
Search results include last 4 SSN digits. Paper case files sent to archives 2 years after closed. Electronic cases maintained indefinitely. **Divisions-** Harrisonburg, Lynchburg, Roanoke.

Washington Eastern District- US District Court www.waed.uscourts.gov
Search results do not include SSN or DOB. Case files sent to archives 6 months after closed. **Divisions-** Spokane, Yakima.

Washington Eastern District- US Bankruptcy Court www.waeb.uscourts.gov
VCIS: 509-353-2404. Search results do not include SSN or DOB. **Location-** Spokane.

Washington Western District- US District Court www.wawd.uscourts.gov
Search: Most results do not include SSN or DOB. Case files sent to archives 2-3 years after closed. **Divisions-** Seattle, Tacoma.

Washington Western District- US Bankruptcy Court www.wawb.uscourts.gov
VCIS: 888-409-4662, 206-370-5285. Search results include last 4 SSN digits. Closed paper files sent to archives; electronic cases maintained indefinitely. **Divisions-** Seattle, Tacoma.

West Virginia Northern District- US District Court www.wvnd.uscourts.gov
Search results do not include SSN or DOB. Civil cases sent to archives every 5 years; every 10 years for criminal. **Divisions-** Clarksburg, Elkins, Martinsburg, Wheeling.

West Virginia Northern District- US Bankruptcy Court www.wvnb.uscourts.gov
VCIS: 800-809-3028, 304-233-7318. Search results include last 4 SSN digits. Case files sent to archives 2 years after closed. **Location-** Wheeling.

West Virginia Southern District- US District Court www.wvsd.uscourts.gov
Search results do not include SSN or DOB. Paper case files sent to archives as deemed necessary. **Divisions-** Beckley, Bluefield, Charleston, Huntington, Parkersburg.

West Virginia Southern District- US Bankruptcy Court www.wvsd.uscourts.gov
VCIS: 304-347-5680. Search results include last 4 SSN digits. Closed electronic cases not purged. **Location-** Charleston.

Wisconsin Eastern District- US District Court www.wied.uscourts.gov
Search results include last 4 SSN digits, also birth year. Case files sent to archives 3 years after closed. **Location-** Milwaukee.

Wisconsin Eastern District- US Bankruptcy Court www.wieb.uscourts.gov
VCIS: 877-781-7277, 414-297-3582. Search results include full SSN. Case files sent to archives once 100-150 boxes are filled. **Location-** Milwaukee.

Wisconsin Western District- US District Court www.wiwd.uscourts.gov
Search results do not include SSN or DOB. Closed electronic cases not purged. **Location-** Madison.

Wisconsin Western District- US Bankruptcy Court www.wiw.uscourts.gov/bankruptcy
VCIS: 800-743-8247, 608-264-5035. Search results include last 4 SSN digits. **Divisions-** Eau Claire, Madison.

Wyoming- US District Court www.wyd.uscourts.gov
Search results do not include SSN or DOB. Case files sent to archives when the right number of boxes filled. **Location-** Cheyenne.

Wyoming- US Bankruptcy Court www.wyb.uscourts.gov
VCIS: 888-804-5537, 307-433-2238. Search results include last 4 SSN digits only. Case files sent to archives 1 year after closed. **Location-** Cheyenne.

Other Federal Courts

U.S. Court of Federal Claims

The Court of Federal Claims is authorized to hear primarily money claims in regard to federal statutes, executive regulations, the Constitution, or contracts, expressed- or implied-in-fact, with the United States. Approximately a quarter of the cases involve complex factual and statutory construction issues in tax law. About a third of the cases involve government contracts. Cases involving environmental and natural resource issues make up about 10 percent of the caseload. Another significant category of cases involve civilian and military pay questions. In addition, the Court hears intellectual property, Indian Tribe, and various statutory claims against the United States by individuals, domestic and foreign corporations, states and localities, Indian Tribes and Nations, and foreign nationals and governments.

Direct questions to the U.S. Court of Federal Claims, Attention: Clerks Office, 717 Madison Place, NW, Washington, DC 20005, or call 202-357-6400.

www.uscfc.uscourts.gov and www.uscfc.uscourts.gov/opinions.htm

U.S. Tax Court

The jurisdiction of the U.S. Tax Court includes the authority to hear tax disputes concerning notices of deficiency, notices of transferee liability, certain types of declaratory judgment, readjustment and adjustment of partnership items, review of the failure to abate interest, administrative costs, worker classification, relief from joint and several liability on a joint return, and review of certain collection actions. For a less formal and speedier disposition in certain tax disputes involving $50,000 or less, taxpayers may choose to have the case conducted under the Court's simplified small tax case procedure. However, these decisions may not be appealed.

Docket information is available for cases filed on or after May 1, 1986. Call Docket Information at 202-521-4650. For case records, call Records and Reproduction at 202-521-4688.

Direct questions to United States Tax Court, 400 Second Street, NW, Washington, DC 20217. The main number is 202-521-0700. Dockets and opinions also may be searched on the web at www.ustaxcourt.gov.

U.S. Court of International Trade

The U.S. Court of International Trade oversees disputes within the international trade community including individuals, foreign and domestic manufacturers, consumer groups, trade associations, labor unions, concerned citizens, and other nations.

The geographical jurisdiction of the United States Court of International Trade extends throughout the U.S. The court does hear cases anywhere in the nation and is also authorized to hold hearings in foreign countries.

Appeals from final decisions of the court may be taken to the United States Court of Appeals for the Federal Circuit and, ultimately, to the Supreme Court of the United States.

The Court provides online access to opinions and judgments. From 1999-2006, the Court published only the slip opinions online. Since January 1, 2007, the online postings contain both the slip opinion and judgment in each case. Registered users of the CM/ECF system have the ability to open a case as of October 11, 2006.

The Court's Administrative Office is located at One Federal Plaza, New York, NY 10278-0001, or call 212-264-2800. www.cit.uscourts.gov

Chapter 7

Public Record Database Vendors

Before you sign up with every interesting online vendor that catches your eye, you need to narrow your search to the type of vendor suitable for your needs. Selecting the right record vendor for your particular search or case is important.

Types of Public Record Vendors

There are six definable and distinct main categories of public record professionals: distributors, gateways, search firms, local document retrievers, verification or screening firms and private investigation firms. Knowledge of how each these vendor categories operates and how they work with clients is invaluable.

Distributors (Proprietary Database Vendors)

Distributors, generally, are automated public record dealers who combine public sources of bulk data and/or online access to develop their own in-house database products. Also known as Primary Distributors, they collect or buy public record information from government repositories and reformat the information in useful ways for clients. They may also purchase or license records from other information vendors, like the phone companies. In the past distributors purchased the "credit header" information from the credit bureaus, but this is no longer a standard practice. In the U.S. there are at least 300 public record vendors in this category that collect and warehouse information to some degree. This does not include marketing list companies.

By nature, most of these entities are either vertical (multiple types of info collected on a local or regional basis) or horizontal (dedicated single purpose type of info collected on regional or national basis). An example of a vertical distributor is Record Information Services (www.public-record.com). This Illinois-based company offers online access to a number of different public records (real estate, recorded documents, bankruptcies, vital records, etc.) from many Illinois counties. An example of a horizontal distributor is Aristotle (www.aristotle.com). Aristotle purchases voter registration records nationwide and sells customized lists to political candidates and political parties.

Some distributors are both vertical and horizontal in nature. An example is ChoicePoint (www.choicepoint.com), a company with multiple divisions that offers access to many and varied nationwide databases for a wide variety of clients.

As mentioned, when a database vendor sells data, the vendor is bound by the same disclosure laws attached to the original government repository. Access restrictions can range from zero for recorded documents, level three sexual predators, etc. to severe for voter registration, criminal court case records, etc.

Gateways

Gateways are companies that provide their clients with an automated electronic access to 1) multiple proprietary database vendors or 2) government agencies online systems. Gateways are similar to distributors except gateways do not warehouse records – they merely provide a sophisticated method to access existing databases. Gateways provide "one-stop shopping" for multiple geographic areas and/or categories of information. Gateways are the companies that are most evident on the Internet, advertising access to records for many different purposes.

Many states have outsourced some of their record access services and other business services such as license registrations to gateways. For example, the National Information Consortium (www.nicusa.com) has over 20 individual state affiliates. To view one, visit www.nebraska.gov and click on "Become a Subscriber." Keep in mind, the state's data still resides with the state. The NIC affiliate offers a gateway of access to the records.

Companies can be both Primary Distributors and Gateways. For example, a number of online database companies are both primary distributors of corporate information and also gateways to real estate information from other primary distributors.

Search Firms

Search firms are companies that furnish individual clients public record search and document retrieval services using online services and/or through a network of specialists, including their own employees or correspondents (see Retrievers below). Search firms may rely on other vendors such as distributors, gateways and/or networks of retrievers (see below), or they may go direct to the government agency. Search firms combine online proficiency with document retrieval expertise. Search firms may focus either on one geographic region – like New England – or on one specific type of public record information – like criminal records. Many search firms have been started by private investigators with a savvy knowledge of vendors and online expertise. There are literally hundreds of search firms in the U.S.

Search firms are very prominent on the web, which is not to say they are necessarily good. Many of the web vendors are working to sell to the general consumer market. The prices these web search firms charge for their services can be very high.

Record Retrievers

A vendor somewhat similar to a search firm is known as a Local Document Retriever or simply, a Record Retriever. Retrievers are hands-on researchers for hire who visit government agencies in-person. Their clients request name searches or document retrieval services usually for legal compliance (e.g., incorporations), hiring, lending, real estate (e.g., abstracting) or for litigation purposes. Retrievers do not usually review or interpret the results or issue reports in the sense that investigators do, but rather return the results of searches along with document copies. Retrievers tend to be localized, but there are companies that offer a national network of retrievers and/or correspondents. Since the retriever or their personnel go directly to the agency to look up information, they may be relied upon for their strong knowledge on record searching in a local area.

Record retrieving is not necessarily a profession. Many other vocations offer record retrieval services including private investigators, process servers, genealogists, and paralegals. There are approximately 4,000 active local document retrievers in the U.S.

The 775+ members of the Public Record Retriever Network (PRRN) are listed by state and counties served at www.brbpub.com/PRRN. This organization has set industry standards for the retrieval of public record documents. Members operate under a Code of Professional Conduct. Using one of these record retrievers is an excellent way to quickly access records in jurisdictions where clerks do not perform record searching or are not within driving distance.

Verification Firms (Pre-employment Screeners, Tenant Screeners, MVR Vendors)

Verification firms provide services to employers and businesses when the subject has given consent for the verification. In this category are pre-employment screening firms and tenant screening firms (both governed by the Fair Credit Reporting Act - FCRA) and motor vehicle record vendors (governed by the Drivers Privacy Protection Act – DPPA). Since verification firms usually only perform their services for clients who have specifically received consent from the subjects, they do not warehouse or collect data to be resold. The service provided by a pre-employment screening company is often called a background screen or a background report. Their service should not be confused with an investigation as provided by private investigators (see below) or with search firms with an Internet presence. There are at least 2,000 pre-employment screening firms in the U.S., not counting the many private investigators that may also offer the service when asked to do so. The National Association of Professional Background Screeners is an excellent trade association that actively promotes best practices and industry standards. Visit www.napbs.com.

After the FCRA was passed, many PIs ceased doing employment screening.

Private Investigation Firms

Private investigators use public records as tools rather than as ends in themselves. Depending on the purpose, investigators use public records in order to create an overall, comprehensive "picture" of an individual or company. The investigator interprets the information gathered in order to identify further investigation tracks. They summarize their results in a report compiled from all the sources used. An investigator may be licensed and may perform the types of services traditionally thought of as detective work, such as surveillance. In many instances, a private investigator doing an investigation does not have the consent of the subject.

Many investigators also act as search firms or record retrievers and provide search results to other investigators. As mentioned, some investigators offer pre-employment screening per the FCRA (and some not per the FCRA).

Other Vendors of Note

There are several other types of firms worthy of mention that occasionally utilize public records. The Association of Independent Information Professionals (AIIP), at www.aiip.org, has over 700 experienced professional information specialist members from 21 countries. They refer to themselves as Information Brokers (IBs). They gather information intended to help their clients make informed business decisions. Their work is usually done on a custom basis with each project being unique. IBs are extremely knowledgeable in online research of full text databases and most specialize in a particular subject area such as patent searching or competitive intelligence.

A similar organization is the Society of Competitive Intelligence Professionals (SCIP), see www.scip.org. Per their web "…SCIP provides education and networking opportunities for business professionals working in the rapidly growing field of competitive intelligence (the legal and ethical collection and analysis of information regarding the capabilities, vulnerabilities, and intentions of business competitors)."

> **Author TIP❖** Also, see Chapter 1 starting on page 7 for information about other vendor types, such as web links lists.

Which Type of Vendor is Right for You?

With all the variations of vendors and the categories of information, the obvious question is "How do I find the right vendor to go to for the public record information I need?" Before you start calling every interesting online vendor that catches your eye, you need to narrow your search to the type of vendor for your needs. To do this, ask yourself the following questions—

What is the Frequency of Usage?

If you have ongoing, recurring requests for a particular type of information, it is probably best to choose a different vendor then one you use infrequently. Setting up an account with a primary distributor such as LEXIS or Westlaw will give you an inexpensive per search fee, but the monthly minimum requirements will be prohibitive to the casual requester who would be better off using a vendor who accesses that distributor.

What is the Complexity of the Search?

The importance of hiring a vendor who understands and can interpret the information in the final format increases with the complexity of the search. Pulling a corporation record in Maryland is not difficult, but doing an online criminal record search in Maryland, when only a portion of the felony records are online, is not so easy.

Thus, part of the answer to determining which vendor or type of vendor to use is to become conversant with what is and is not available from government agencies. Without knowing what is available and what restrictions apply, you cannot guide the search process effectively. Once you are comfortable knowing the kinds of information available in the public record, you are in a position to find the best method to access needed information.

What are the Geographic Boundaries of the Search?

A search of local records close to you may require little assistance, but a search of records nationally or in a state 2,000 miles away will require seeking a vendor who covers that area. Many national primary distributors and gateways combine various local and state databases into one large comprehensive system available for searching. However, if your record searching is narrowed by a region or locality, then an online source that specializes in a specific geographic region (like Superior Information Services in NJ) may be an alternative. Keep in mind that many national firms allow you to order a search online, even though results cannot be delivered immediately; some hands-on local searching is required.

Of course, you may want to use the government agency online system, if available, for the kind of information you need.

10 Questions to Ask a Public Record Vendor

(Or a Vendor Who Uses Online Sources)

The following discussion focuses specifically on automated sources of information because many valuable types of public records have been entered into a computer and, therefore, require a computer search to obtain reliable results. The original version of the text to follow was written by Mr. Leroy Cook. Mr. Cook is the founder and Director of ION and The Investigators Anywhere Resource Line (800-338-3463, http://ioninc.com). Mr. Cook has graciously allowed us to edit the article and reprint it for our readers.

1. Where does the vendor get the information?

You may feel awkward asking a vendor where he or she obtained the information you are purchasing. The fake Rolex watch is a reminder that even buying physical things based on looks alone — without knowing where they come from — has risks.

Reliable information vendors will provide verification material such as the name of the database or service accessed, when it was last updated, and how complete it is.

It is important that you know the gathering process in order to better judge the reliability of the information being purchased. There are certain investigative sources that a vendor will not be willing to disclose to you. However, that type of source should not be confused with the information that is being sold item by item. Information technology has changed so rapidly that some information vendors may still confuse "items of information" with "investigative reports." Items of information sold as units are not investigative reports.

The professional reputation of an information vendor is a guarantee of sorts. Still, because information as a commodity is so new, there is little in the way of an implied warranty of fitness.

2. How long does it take for the new information or changes to get into the system?

Any answer except a clear, concise date and time or the vendor's personal knowledge of an ongoing system's methods of maintaining information currency is a reason to look elsewhere. In view of question #1, this question might seem repetitive, but it really is a different issue. Microfiche or a database of records may have been updated last week at a courthouse or a DMV, but the department's computer section may also be working with a three-month backlog. In this case, a critical incident occurring one month ago would not show up in the information updated last week. The importance of timeliness is a variable to be determined by you, but to be truly informed you need to know how "fresh" the information is. Ideally, the mechanism by which you purchase items of information should include an update or statement of accuracy — as a part of the reply — without having to ask.

3. What are the searchable fields? Which fields are mandatory?

If your knowledge of "fields" and "records" is limited to the places where cattle graze and those flat discs that play music, you could have a problem telling a good database from a bad one. An MVR vendor, for example, should be able to tell you that a subject's middle initial is critical when pulling an Arizona driving record. You don't have to become a programmer to use a computer and you need not know a database management language to benefit from databases, but it is very helpful to understand how databases are constructed and (at the least) what fields, records, and indexing procedures are used.

As a general rule, the computerized, public-record information world is not standardized from county to county or from state to state. In the same way, there is little standardization within or between information vendors. Look at the system documentation from the vendor. The manual should include this sort of information.

4. How much latitude is there for error (misspellings or inappropriate punctuation) in a data request?

If the vendor's requirements for search data appear to be concise and meticulous, then you're probably on the right track to selecting a good vendor. Some vendor computer systems will tell (or "flag") an operator when they make a mistake such as omitting important punctuation or using an unnecessary comma. Other systems allow you to make inquiries by whatever means or in whatever format you like — and then tell you the requested information has not been found. When data is not found, the desired information may actually be there but the computer didn't understand the question because of the way it was asked. It is easy to misinterpret "no record found" as "there is no record." Of course the meanings of these two phrases are quite different.

5. What method is used to place the information in the repository and what error control or edit process is used?

In some databases, information may be scanned in or may be entered by a single operator as it is received. In others, information may be entered twice to allow the computer to catch input errors by searching for non-duplicate entries. You don't have to know everything about all the options, but the vendor selling information in quantity should.

6. How many different databases or sources does the vendor access and how often?

The chance of obtaining an accurate search of a database increases with the frequency of access and the vendor's/searcher's level of knowledge. If he or she only makes inquiries once a month — and the results are important — you may need to find someone who sells data at higher volume. The point here is that it is better to find someone who specializes in the type of information you are seeking than it is to utilize a vendor who can get the information, but actually specializes in another type of data or is inexperienced.

7. Does the price include assistance in interpreting the data received?

A report that includes coding and ambiguous abbreviations may look impressive in your file, but may not be too meaningful. For all reports, except those you deal with regularly, interpretation assistance can be very important. Some information vendors offer searches for information they really don't know much about and access data through sources that they only use occasionally. Professional pride sometimes prohibits them from disclosing their limitations — until you ask the right questions.

8. Do vendors "keep track" of requesters and the information they seek (usage records)?

This may not seem like a serious concern when you are requesting information you agree legally entitled to; however, there is a possibility that your usage records could be made available to a competitor.

Most probably, the information itself is already being (or will be) sold to someone else, but you may not necessarily want everyone to know what you are requesting and how often. If the vendor keeps records of who-asks-what, the confidentiality of that information should be addressed in your agreement with the vendor.

9. Will the subject of the inquiry be notified of the request?

If your inquiry is sub rosa or if the subject's discovery of the search could lead to embarrassment, double check! There are laws that mandate the notification of subjects when certain types of inquiries are made into their files. If notification is required, the way it is accomplished could be critical.

10. Is the turnaround time and cost of the search made clear at the outset?

You should be crystal clear about what you expect and need; the vendor should be succinct when conveying exactly what will be provided and how much it will cost. Failure to address these issues can lead to disputes, delays and hard feelings.

These are excellent questions and concepts to keep in mind when searching for the right public record vendor to meet your needs.

Presentation of Database and Gateway Vendors

Why These Vendors Appear in the Book

Obviously, there are many more public record vendors than the 160+ firms appearing in this book. The reason these particular companies were chosen is because they provide either a Proprietary Database or offer a non-intervention Gateway.

There are plenty of excellent record vendors not listed in this book who most likely use these companies or government agencies as their primary source. We call these companies "Search Firms." For information about 1500 vendors of all categories, go to www.brbpub.com/pubrecsites_ven.asp.

Record Information Categories

This index consists of 13 Information Categories. The vendors are listed alphabetically within each category. Each listing includes geographic coverage area and the vendor's web address. Note that CD = Canada and Intl = International.

The information categories are listed below.

Bankruptcy	SEC/Other Financial
Corporate/Trade Name Data	Trademarks
Criminal Information	Uniform Commercial Code
Driver and/or Vehicle	Vessels
Licenses/Registrations/Permits	Vital Records
Litigation/Judgments/Tax Liens	Voter Registration
Real Estate/Assessor	

Bankruptcy

Bankruptcy Vendor	Website	Region
Accurint	www.accurint.com	US
Accu-Source Inc	www.accu-source.com	AK, AR, AZ, CA, CO, FL, GA, HI, IA, ID, IL, IN, KS, KY, LA, MN, MO, NC, ND, NE, NM, NV, OK, OH, OR, SC, SD, TN, TX, UT, WA, WI, WY
Acxiom Risk Mitigation	www.acxiom.com	US
Banko	www.banko.com	US
CCH Washington Service Bureau	www.wsb.com	US
CSC	https://www.incspot.com/public/index.html	US
ChoicePoint Inc.	www.choicepoint.com	US
Diligenz Inc	www.diligenz.com	US
Dun & Bradstreet	www.dnb.com/us/	US
Experian Online	www.experian.com	US
IQ Data Systems	www.iqdata.com	US
KnowX	www.knowx.com	US
LEXISNEXIS CourtLink	www.lexisnexis.com/courtlink/online/	US
Merlin Information Services	www.merlindata.com	US
Motznik Information Services	www.motznik.com	AK
OPENonline	www.openonline.com	US
Record Information Services Inc	www.public-record.com	IL
UCC Direct Services	www.uccdirectservices.com	US
US SEARCH.com	www.ussearch.com/consumer/index.jsp	US
Virtual Docket LLC	www.virtualdocket.com	DE

Corporate/Trade Name Data

Corporate/ Trade Name Vendor	Website	Region
Accurint	www.accurint.com	US
Accutrend Data Corporation	www.accutrend.com	US
Acxiom Risk Mitigation	www.acxiom.com	US
Alacra	www.alacra.com	US, Intl
Attorneys Title Insurance Fund	www.thefund.com/portal/	FL
Background Information Services Inc.	www.bisi.com	CO
Better Business Bureau	www.bbb.org	US
CSC	https://www.incspot.com/public/index.html	US
ChoicePoint Inc.	www.choicepoint.com	US
Derwent Information - Thomson Search Svcs	http://scientific.thomsonreuters.com/searchservices/	US
Dialog (Thomson)	www.dialog.com	US
Diligenz Inc	www.diligenz.com	US
Dun & Bradstreet	www.dnb.com/us/	US
Experian Online	www.experian.com	US
GuideStar	www.guidestar.org	US
Hoovers Inc	www.hoovers.com/free/	US

Corporate/ Trade Name Vendor	Website	Region
Household Drivers Reports Inc (HDR Inc)	www.hdr.com	TX
Idealogic	www.idealogic.com	CD
IQ Data Systems	www.iqdata.com	AK,CO,CT,FL,IN,IA,ME,MD,MA,MI,MN,MS,MO,MT,NE,NH,NC,ND,OH,OK,SC,SD,TN,UT,VA,DC,WV,WI
IRB - International Research Bureau	www.irb-online.com	US
KnowX	www.knowx.com	US
Kompass USA Inc	www.kompass-intl.com	US, Intl
LEXISNEXIS	www.lexisnexis.com	US
LocatePlus.com Inc	https://www.locateplus.com/welcome.asp	AL,AK,AZ,AR,CA,CO,CT,FL,GA,ID,IA,KS,KY,LA,ME,MD,MA,MI,MN,MS,MO,NE,NV,NM,NY,NC,ND,OH,OK,OR,PA,RI,SC,SD,TN,VT,VA,WA,WI,WY
Merlin Information Services	www.merlindata.com	CA, US
Motznik Information Services	www.motznik.com	AK
OPENonline	www.openonline.com	US
Oso Grande Technologies Inc	www.osogrande.com	NM
Pallorium Inc	www.pallorium.com	US, PR
Residentialdatabase.com	www.residentialdatabase.com	FL, US
SEAFAX Inc	www.seafax.com	US
Thomson Compumark	http://compumark.thomson.com/do/pid/1	US
UCC Direct Services	www.uccdirectservices.com	US
US SEARCH.com	www.ussearch.com/consumer/index.jsp	US
USADATA	www.usadata.com	US

Criminal Information

Criminal Data Vendor	Website	Region
Acxiom Risk Mitigation	www.acxiom.com	CO
Appriss Inc/VineLink	www.appriss.com/VINE.html	AR, AZ, CA, FL, GA, ID, IL, KY, LA, MA, MD, MN, MO, MT, NC, NE, OR, RI, TX, VA, WI, WV
Background Information Services Inc.	www.bisi.com	CO
backgroundchecks.com	https://www.backgroundchecks.com/	US
ChoicePoint Inc.	www.choicepoint.com	US
Circuit Court Express	www.swcg-inc.com/products/circuit_express.html	WV
CoCourts.com	https://www.cocourts.com	CO
Court PC of Connecticut	http://courtpcofct.com	CT
Criminal Information Services Inc	www.criminalinfo.com	US
Data-Trac.com, USCrimsearch.com	www.data-trac.com	NY, US
DCS Information Systems	www.dcsinfosys.com/	TX,US
Doxpop	https://www.doxpop.com/prod/	IN
Household Drivers Reports Inc (HDR	www.hdr.com	TX

Criminal Data Vendor	Website	Region
Inc)		
iDocket.com	www.idocket.com	TX
Infolynx Systems	www.dynalynx.net	OH
IQ Data Systems	www.iqdata.com	AL,AK,AZ,CA,CO,CT,DC,DE,FL,GA,HI,IA,IN,IL,KS,KY,MD,MA,MI,MN,MO,MT,NV,NH,NJ,NM,NC,OH,OR,PA,PR,RI,SC,TN,TX,UT,VA,VT,WA,WV,WI
IRB - International Research Bureau	www.irb-online.com	US
Judici	www.judici.com	IL
KnowX	www.knowx.com	US
LEXISNEXIS	www.lexisnexis.com	US
Merlin Information Services	www.merlindata.com	US
Merlin Information Services	www.merlindata.com	CA
Motznik Information Services	www.motznik.com	AK
National Background Data	https://www.nationalbackgrounddata.com	US
National Public Information Corp	https://www.npiconline.com/login.asp	FL
OPENonline	www.openonline.com	OH,IN,MI
OPENonline	www.openonline.com	AZ, AR, CT, FL, GA, ID, IL, IN, KY, ME, MI, MN, MS, MO, NE, NJ, NY, NC, OH, OK, OR, SC, TN, TX, UT, WA
Rapidcourt.com - NC	www.rapidcourt.com/	US, NC, CT, TN, TX
Tracers Information Specialists Inc	www.tracersinfo.com	40 States
TransUnion Vantage Data	www.vantagedatasolutions.com	AL,AZ,CA,CO,CT,DC,DE,FL,GA,IA,ID,IL,IN,KS,KY,LA,MD,ME,MI,MN,MS,MT,NC,ND,NE,NH,NJ,NM,NY,OK,SC,TN,TX,UT,VA,WA,WI,WV,WY
US SEARCH.com	www.ussearch.com/consumer/index.jsp	US
USIS Commercial Services	www.usis.com/commercialservices/default.htm	US
Virtual Docket LLC	www.virtualdocket.com	DE
WestLaw CourtExpress.com (D.C.)	http://courtexpress.westlaw.com	AR,AZ,CA,CT,DC,DE,FL,GA,IL,KS,LA,MA,MD,MI,MO,MS,NC,NJ,NV,NY,OH,OK,PA,RI,SC.TN,TX,UT,VA,WA,WI
XPOFACT	www.xpofact.com	MN

Driver and/or Vehicle

Motor Vehicle Vendor	Website	Region
Accurint	www.accurint.com	FL
Acxiom Risk Mitigation	www.acxiom.com	40 States
American Business Information	www.infousa.com	US
American Driving Records	www.mvrs.com	US
AutoDataDirect, Inc	www.add123.com	FL
CARFAX	www.carfaxonline.com	US
ChoicePoint Inc.	www.choicepoint.com	US
Datalink Services Inc	www.imvrs.com	CA

Motor Vehicle Vendor	Website	Region
DCS Information Systems	www.dcsinfosys.com/	TX
Experian Online	www.experian.com	US
Explore Information Services	https://www.exploredata.com/publish/default.htm	AL, AZ, CA, CO, CT, DE, FL, ID, IA, KS, KY, MA, MD, ME, MI, MN, MO, MT, NE, NH, NV, NY, OH, OR, SC, TN, TX, UT, WI, WV, WY
First InfoSource	https://secure.firstinfosource.com	MO
Household Drivers Reports Inc (HDR Inc)	www.hdr.com	TX
iiX (Insurance Information Exchange)	www.iix.com	US
IRB - International Research Bureau	www.irb-online.com	US
LocatePlus.com Inc	https://www.locateplus.com/welcome.asp	AL,AR,NE,UT,MS,ME,NH,VT,MA,CT,OH, WV,MD, FL,TN,KY,IN,MI,WI,LA,MO,IA,MN,TX,CO, WY,ID,AZ,OR
Logan Registration Service Inc	www.loganreg.com	CA, US
MDR/Minnesota Driving Records	www.mdrecords.us	MN
Motznik Information Services	www.motznik.com	AK
National Public Information Corp	https://www.npiconline.com/login.asp	AL, AR, FL, IL, IN, MS, NJ, NY, NC TN
OPENonline	www.openonline.com	US
Oso Grande Technologies Inc	www.osogrande.com	NM
Pallorium Inc	www.pallorium.com	US
Records Research Inc	www.recordsresearch.com	CA,US
Samba MVRSearch	www.samba.biz/mvrsearch.html	AK,AL,AR,AZ,CA,CO,CT,DC,FL,GA,HI,IA,ID,IL,IN,KS,KY, LA,MA,MD,ME,MI,MN,MO,MS,MT,NC,ND,NE,NJ,NM,NV,NY, OH,OK,OR,PA,RI,SC,SD,TN,TX,UT,VA,VT,WI, WV
Softech International Inc	www.softechinternational.com	US
USIS Commercial Services	www.usis.com/commercialservices/default.htm	US
Westlaw Public Records	www.westlaw.com	AK, AL, CO, CT, DC, DE, FL, IA, ID, IL, KY, LA, MA, MD, ME, MI, MN, MO, MS, MT, ND, NE, NH, NM, NY, OH, SC, TN, UT, WI, WV, WY

Licenses/Registrations/Permits

Licenses/Registrations/Permits	Website	Region
Accutrend Data Corporation	www.accutrend.com	US
Acxiom Risk Mitigation	www.acxiom.com	FL, ID, IA, LA, MN, MS, MO, NV, NC, OR, TX, UT, WI, WY
ChoicePoint Inc.	www.choicepoint.com	US
E-Merges.com	www.e-merges.com	AK,AR,CT,DE,FL,GA,KS,MS,MO,NV,NJ,NC,ND,OH,SC,UT,VA,WA
IQ Data Systems	www.iqdata.com	CA
KnowX	www.knowx.com	US

Licenses/Registrations/Permits	Website	Region
LEXISNEXIS	www.lexisnexis.com	CA, CT, FL, GE, IL, MA,MI,NE,NJ,NC,OG,PA,TX,VA,WI
Merlin Information Services	www.merlindata.com	US
Motznik Information Services	www.motznik.com	AK
Record Information Services Inc	www.public-record.com	IL
Thomson Compumark	http://compumark.thomson.com/do/pid/1	US
Westlaw Public Records	www.westlaw.com	AZ, CA, CO, CT, FL, GA, IL, IN, LA, MA, MD, MI, NJ, OH, PA, SC, TN, TX, VA, WI

Litigation/Judgments/Tax Liens

Litigation/Judgment/Tax Liens	Website	Region
Accurint	www.accurint.com	US
Acxiom Risk Mitigation	www.acxiom.com	CO
Attorneys Title Insurance Fund	www.thefund.com/portal/	FL
Banko	www.banko.com	US
CSC	https://www.incspot.com/public/index.html	US
ChoicePoint Inc.	www.choicepoint.com	US
Circuit Court Express	www.swcg-inc.com/products/circuit_express.html	WV
CoCourts.com	https://www.cocourts.com	CO
Court PC of Connecticut	http://courtpcofct.com	CT
CourthouseData	www.courthousedata.com	AR
CourthouseDirect.com	http://courthousedirect.com/courth/	AZ, CA, FL, HI, IL, NY, OK, PA, TX, UT, WA
Diligenz Inc	www.diligenz.com	US
Doxpop	https://www.doxpop.com/prod/	IN
Dun & Bradstreet	www.dnb.com/us/	US
iDocket.com	www.idocket.com	TX
Infocon Corporation	www.infoconcorporation.com	PA
IQ Data Systems	www.iqdata.com	US
IRB - International Research Bureau	www.irb-online.com	US
Judici	www.judici.com	IL
KnowX	www.knowx.com	US
LEXISNEXIS CourtLink	www.lexisnexis.com/courtlink/online	US
LocatePlus.com Inc	https://www.locateplus.com/welcome.asp	AK,AZ,AR,CA,CO,DC,FL,HI,ID,IL,IN,IA,KS,KY,LA,MN,MS,MO,NE,NV,NM,NC,ND,OH,OK,OR,SD,TN,TX,UT,VA,WA,WI,WY
Merlin Information Services	www.merlindata.com	US
Motznik Information Services	www.motznik.com	AK
MyFloridaCounty.com	www.myfloridacounty.com	FL
National Service Information	www.nsii.net	IN, OH, KY, MI
OPENonline	www.openonline.com	US
Property Data Center Inc	www.mypdc.com	CO

Litigation/Judgment/Tax Liens	Website	Region
Public Data Corporation	www.pdcny.com	NY
Rapidcourt.com - NC Recordsonline.com	www.rapidcourt.com/	NC
TitleSearcher.com	www.titlesearcher.com	TN
TransUnion Vantage Data	www.vantagedatasolutions.com	AK,AR,CA,CO,CT,DE,DC,FL,ID,IL,IN,IA, KY,KS,LA,MA,MI,MD,MN,MS,MT,NE,NV, NJ, M,NC,ND,NY,OH,OK,OP,PA,SD,TN, TX, UT,VA,WA,WI
UCC Direct Services	www.uccdirectservices.com	US
Virtual Docket LLC	www.virtualdocket.com	DE
WestLaw CourtExpress.com (D.C.)	http://courtexpress.westlaw.com	AZ,CA,CT,FL,IA,MO,VA
Westlaw Public Records	www.westlaw.com	US

Real Estate/Assessor

Real Estate/Assessor Record Vendors	Website	Region
Accurint	www.accurint.com	US
AccuriZ.com	www.AccuriZ.com	NY, NJ, MD, MA
Acxiom Risk Mitigation	www.acxiom.com	US
American Business Information	www.infousa.com	US
ARCountyData.com - Apprentice Information Systems	www.arcountydata.com	AR
Attorneys Title Insurance Fund	www.thefund.com/portal/	FL
ChoicePoint Inc.	www.choicepoint.com	US
Courthouse Retrieval System Inc	www.crsdata.net/home/	AL, NC, TN
CourthouseData	www.courthousedata.com	AR
CourthouseDirect.com	http://courthousedirect.com/courth/	AZ, CA, FL, HI, IL, NY, OK, PA, TX, UT, WA
DataQuick	www.dataquick.com	US
DCS Information Systems	www.dcsinfosys.com/	TX,US
DigitalCourthouse	http://digitalcourthouse.com/search.asp	WV
eTitleSearch	www.etitlesearch.com	AR, IA, IL, MO, OK
Experian Online	www.experian.com	US
First American Corporation, The	www.firstam.com/	US
First American Real Estate Solutions	www.facorelogic.com/global/index.jsp	US
Foreclosure Freesearch.com	www.foreclosurefreesearch.com	US
Infocon Corporation	www.infoconcorporation.com	PA
IQ Data Systems	www.iqdata.com	US
KnowX	www.knowx.com	US
LEXISNEXIS	www.lexisnexis.com	US
LocatePlus.com Inc	https://www.locateplus.com/welcome.asp	US
Merlin Information Services	www.merlindata.com	CA
Metro Market Trends Inc	www.mmtinfo.com	FL, AL
Motznik Information Services	www.motznik.com	AK
MyFloridaCounty.com	www.myfloridacounty.com	FL

Real Estate/Assessor Record Vendors	Website	Region
National Public Information Corp	https://www.npiconline.com/login.asp	FL
NETR Real Estate Research and Information	www.netronline.com	US
OPENonline	www.openonline.com	US
Pallorium Inc	www.pallorium.com	US
Plat System Services Inc	www.platsystems.com	MN
Property Data Center Inc	www.mypdc.com	CO
Property Info	www.propertyinfo.com	US
Public Data Corporation	www.pdcny.com	NY
real-info.com	www.real-info.com	US
Record Information Services Inc	www.public-record.com	IL
SKLD Information Services LLC	www.skld.com	CO
Tapestry	https://tapestry.fidlar.com	IL, IN, KS, MI, MN, WI
TitleSearcher.com	www.titlesearcher.com	TN
TitleX.com	www.titlex.com	TX
tnrealestate.com	www.tnrealestate.com	TN
UCC Direct Services	www.uccdirectservices.com	US
US SEARCH.com	www.ussearch.com/consumer/index.jsp	US
US Title Search Network	www1.ustitlesearch.net/	TN - 32 Counties
USADATA	www.usadata.com	US
Vision Appraisal Technology	www.visionappraisal.com	CT, ME, MA, NH, RI
Westlaw Public Records	www.westlaw.com	US

SEC/Other Financial

SEC/Financial Records Vendor	Website	Region
Alacra	www.alacra.com	US, CD, Intl
American Business Information	www.infousa.com	US
CCH Washington Service Bureau	www.wsb.com	US
CSC	https://www.incspot.com/public/index.html	US
CountryWatch Inc	www.countrywatch.com	Intl
Dialog (Thomson)	www.dialog.com	US
Dun & Bradstreet	www.dnb.com/us/	US
Global Securities Information, Inc	www.gsionline.com	DC
Hoovers Inc	www.hoovers.com/free/	US

Trademarks

Trademark Records Vendor	Website	Region
CSC	https://www.incspot.com/public/index.html	US
Dialog (Thomson)	www.dialog.com	US
Dun & Bradstreet	www.dnb.com/us/	US
Idealogic	www.idealogic.com	CD

Trademark Records Vendor	Website	Region
MicroPatent USA	www.micropat.com/static/index.htm	US, Intl

Uniform Commercial Code

UCC Records Vendor	Website	Region
Accurint	www.accurint.com	US
Background Information Services Inc. Colorado	www.bisi.com	CO
Capitol Lien Records & Research Inc	www.capitollien.com	WI,US
CSC	https://www.incspot.com/public/index.html	US
ChoicePoint Inc.	www.choicepoint.com	US
CourthouseData	www.courthousedata.com	AR
Diligenz Inc	www.diligenz.com	US
Dun & Bradstreet	www.dnb.com/us/	US
Experian Online	www.experian.com	US
IQ Data Systems	www.iqdata.com	CA
KnowX	www.knowx.com	US
LEXISNEXIS	www.lexisnexis.com	US
LocatePlus.com Inc	https://www.locateplus.com/welcome.asp	AK,AZ,CA,CO,CT,FL,GA,ID,IL,IA,KS,KY, MD,ME,MN,MS,MO,NE,NV,NM,ND,OH,OR, PA,SC,SD,TX,WA,WI
Merlin Information Services	www.merlindata.com	US
Motznik Information Services	www.motznik.com	AK
National Service Information	www.nsii.net	IN, OH, KY, MI
OPENonline	www.openonline.com	US
Public Data Corporation	www.pdcny.com	NY
UCC Direct Services	www.uccdirectservices.com	US
West Group - Thomson West	http://west.thomson.com/home.aspx?	US

Vessels

Vessel Record Vendor	Website	Region
AutoDataDirect, Inc	www.add123.com	FL
E-Merges.com	www.e-merges.com	US
First InfoSource	https://secure.firstinfosource.com	MO
KnowX	www.knowx.com	US
LEXISNEXIS	www.lexisnexis.com	AL, AZ, AR, CO,CT,FL,GE,IA,ME,MD, MA,MS, MO, MN,MT,NE,NV,NH, NC,ND, OH,OR,SC,UT,VA,WV,WI
LocatePlus.com Inc	https://www.locateplus.com/welcome.asp	US
Merlin Information Services	www.merlindata.com	US
Motznik Information Services	www.motznik.com	AK, US
National Marine Fisheries Service	www.st.nmfs.noaa.gov/st1/commercial/index.html	US

Vessel Record Vendor	Website	Region
OPENonline	www.openonline.com	US
Pallorium Inc	www.pallorium.com	US
UCC Direct Services	www.uccdirectservices.com	US
US SEARCH.com	www.ussearch.com/consumer/index.jsp	US
Westlaw Public Records	www.westlaw.com	US

Vital Records

Vital Records Companies	Website	Region
Acxiom Risk Mitigation	www.acxiom.com	US
Ameridex Information Systems	www.ameridex.com	US
Ancestry	www.ancestry.com	US, Intl
Cambridge Statistical Research Associates	www.csrainc.com	US
DCS Information Systems	www.dcsinfosys.com/	TX
Household Drivers Reports Inc (HDR Inc)	www.hdr.com	TX
Infocon Corporation	www.infoconcorporation.com	PA
IQ Data Systems	www.iqdata.com	CA,CO,FL,KY,ME,NV,TX
Merlin Information Services	www.merlindata.com	US
MyFloridaCounty.com	www.myfloridacounty.com	FL
Vital Records Information	http://vitalrec.com	US
VitalChek Network	www.vitalchek.com	US

Voter Registration

Voter Registration Records Companies	Website	Region
Accu-Source Inc	www.accu-source.com	TX
Acxiom Risk Mitigation	www.acxiom.com	AK, AR, CO, DE, GA, KS, MI, NV, OH, OK, TX, UT
ARISTOTLE International	www.aristotle.com/	US
E-Merges.com	www.e-merges.com	US
Merlin Information Services	www.merlindata.com	US
Motznik Information Services	www.motznik.com	AK
Pallorium Inc	www.pallorium.com	US

Latest Due Diligence Titles from
Facts on Demand Press

The Public Record Research Tips Book

The Public Record Research Tips Book provides "Insider Information" for searching for public records at thousands of government public record agencies and web pages. This resource provides the tips and practical knowledge to guide you to the right source and help you become an ultra-efficient searcher.

Michael Sankey • 1-889150-50-9 • 336 pages • $19.95

Business Background Investigations

Business Background Investigations provides the blueprint to perform proper due diligence and discover competitive intelligence when examining the backgrounds of businesses and the principals who run them. "Hetherington's methods" can be immediately integrated into an investigative operation – resulting in tremendous savings of time, effort, and money.

Cynthia Hetherington • 1-889150-49-5 • 288 pages • $21.95

The Criminal Records Manual 3rd Ed.

The Criminal Records Manual is for anyone who uses criminal records when making business or hiring decisions. Analyze the compliance issues connected to complicated federal and state laws that employers, financial institutions, attorneys, corporate security centers, private investigators and others must abide by when obtaining and using criminal records.

Henry & Hinton • 1-889150-54-1 • 420 pages • $24.95

The Safe Hiring Manual

The Safe Hiring Manual goes far beyond the typical hiring handbook. The Manual details how to exercise due diligence throughout the hiring process, significantly increasing an employer's chance of avoiding the financial and legal nightmares of even one bad hiring decision.

Lester S. Rosen, Esq. • 1-889150-44-4 • 512 • $24.95

Available at your favorite bookstore.

Facts on Demand Press • 1-800-929-3811 • www.brbpub.com

Quick Find...

~ Use this handy index to find starting pages for these topics of interest ~

Meet the Authors

Cynthia Hetherington has more than 16 years of experience in research, investigations and corporate intelligence. A Managing Director for Aon Consulting's Corporate Investigative and Security Services Practice, she most recently was the principal of Hetherington Information Services, LLC, a competitive intelligence research firm.

Cynthia applies her expertise in investigative knowledge and information systems to provide clients with strategic insight into research and complex investigations. During her career, she has assisted a vast number of clients with Internet investigations related to employee theft and intellectual property loss. Cynthia has applies her research skills while conducting online and database research to uncover well-hidden relations between fraudulent associates, their assets and secrets. She often oversees international investigations for Fortune 500 companies and other organizations in the Middle East, Europe and Asia.

A widely-published author, Cynthia is the former publisher of *Data2know.com: Internet & Online Intelligence Newsletter* and has co-authored articles on computer forensics, Internet investigations and other security-focused monographs. She also is a nationally known speaker and is well recognized for providing corporate security officials, military intelligence units, and federal, state and local agencies with training on online intelligence practices.

Cynthia holds graduate degrees from New Jersey Institute of Technology Master of Information Systems Management) and Rutgers University (Master of Library Science). She sits on the boards for the Economic Crime Committee of ASIS International, United States Professional Investigator Association, Institute of Corporate Forensic Professionals, New Jersey Institute of Technology, Information Technology Program, and is current President to the New Jersey Association of Licensed Private Investigators, as well as Past President to the Alpha Lambda Honor Society.

To contact Ms. Hetherington, please email her at ch@data2know.com.

Michael Sankey is founder and CEO of BRB Publications, Inc. and Co-Director of the Public Record Retriever Network, the nation's largest membership organization of professionals in the public record industry. Michael has more than 25 years of experience in research and public record access. He has authored or edited over 75 publications.

In the 1980s, he was president and CEO of Rapid Info Services, one of the nation's leading suppliers of electronic processed driving records to the insurance industry. Rapid Info was the first vendor to offer online access of driving records to their clientele.

Michael was part of the steering committee that founded the National Association of Professional Background Screeners (NAPBS), a professional trade association for the screening industry. He was also elected to the first Board of Directors in 2004 and served two years.

He is regarded as a leading industry expert in public records, criminal record access, state DMV policies and procedures, as well as knowing who's who in the commercial arena of public information vendors. Michael, who resides in Tempe Arizona with his wife Lynn and 2 children, is a graduate of Arizona State University and enjoys thoroughbred horse racing and baseball.

To contact Michael, please email him at msankey@brbpub.com or call 480-829-7475.